HANDBOOK OF FORENSIC PSYCHOLOGY

HANDBOOK OF FORENSIC PSYCHOLOGY

RESOURCE FOR MENTAL HEALTH AND LEGAL PROFESSIONALS

Edited by

WILLIAM T. O'DONOHUE
UNIVERSITY OF NEVADA, RENO

ERIC R. LEVENSKY
UNIVERSITY OF NEVADA, RENO

ELSEVIER
ACADEMIC
PRESS

AMSTERDAM • BOSTON • HEIDELBERG • LONDON
NEW YORK • OXFORD • PARIS • SAN DIEGO
SAN FRANCISCO • SINGAPORE • SYDNEY • TOKYO

Academic Press is an imprint of Elsevier

Elsevier Academic Press
525 B Street, Suite 1900, San Diego, California 92101-4495, USA
84 Theobald's Road, London WC1X 8RR, UK

This book is printed on acid-free paper.

Copyright 2004, Elsevier, Inc. All rights reserved.

No part of this publication may be reproduced or transmitted in any form or by any means, electronic or mechanical, including photocopy, recording, or any information storage and retrieval system, without permission in writing from the publisher.

Permissions may be sought directly from Elsevier's Science & Technology Rights Department in Oxford, UK: phone: (+44) 1865 843830, fax: (+44) 1865 853333, e-mail: permissions@elsevier.com.uk. You may also complete your request on-line via the Elsevier Science homepage (http://elsevier.com), by selecting "Customer Support" and then "Obtaining Permissions."

Library of Congress Cataloging-in-Publication Data
Application submitted

British Library Cataloguing in Publication Data
A catalogue record for this book is available from the British Library

ISBN: 0-12-524196-8

For all information on all Academic Press publications
visit our website at www.academicpress.com

Printed in the United States of America
03 04 05 06 07 08 9 8 7 6 5 4 3 2 1

To the most principled person I know,
my wife, Jane Fisher.
—W. T. O.

To my grandfather, Dr. Maurice J. Rotkow,
who has always been an unyielding
source of support, a wonderful friend,
and an admirable role model.
—E. R. L.

Contents

Contributors   xxi
Preface   xxv

Part I Basic Issues

Chapter 1 Psychology and the Law
M. Gino Brogdon, Sr., Jann H. Adams, and Ritu Bahri

Psychiatrist/Psychologist–Patient Privilege   4
Expert Testimony   9
Involuntary Civil Commitment   14
Criminal Commitment   17
Duality and Sexual Relationships with Clients   19
Memory Enhancement Techniques: Repressed Memories   20
Internet Psychotherapy   23
References   24

Chapter 2 An Introduction to Psychology for Attorneys
William T. O'Donohue, Kendra Beitz, and Eric R. Levensky

Psychology as a Science   28
Some General Considerations: Why Isn't Psychology as Progressive as Physics?   31
Getting the Most from Psychology   38
Conclusions   44
References   44

Chapter 3 Ethical Issues in Forensic Psychology
Michael Lavin

Fundamentals of Moral Philosophy   46
Pedophilia as a Forensic Example   51
Lessons   58
References   60

Chapter 4 Forensic Report Writing
Jeffrey E. Hecker and R. Jamie Scoular

Unique Features of Forensic Reports   64
The Forensic Report   66
Forensic Report Writing: General Guidelines   76
References   80

Part II Assessment

Chapter 5 Assessment of Dangerousness and Criminal Responsibility
Lynne Eccleston and Tony Ward

Overview   86
Criminal Responsibility   87
Clinical versus Actuarial Assessment   89
Dangerousness Research   90
Methodological Limitations   92
Static versus Dynamic Predictors of Dangerousness   94
Risk Assessment: The Clinical Interview   95
Future Directions   97
References   97

Chapter 6 Issues in the Assessment, Communication, and Management of Risk for Violence
Rebecca J. Dempster

- Violence Risk Assessment   104
- Risk Communication   116
- Risk Management   119
- Conclusions   123
- References   124

Chapter 7 Forensic and Ethical Issues in the Assessment and Treatment of the Suicidal Patient
Kirk Strosahl

- Goals of this Chapter   131
- The Anatomy of a Wrongful Death Lawsuit: From Adverse Event to the Courtroom   132
- Key Tenets of a Wrongful Death Claim   136
- Characteristic Claims in a Wrongful Death Suit   137
- The Search for the Elusive "Standard of Care"   140
- Suicide and Malpractice: A Study in Legal Paradox   141
- The Problematic Interface of Ethics and Risk Management   144
- Reducing the Risk of Lawsuit: Suggestions for Organizations and Clinical Practitioners   149
- Risk Management after the Index Suicide   152
- Conclusion   154
- References   154

Chapter 8 Assessing Intent and Criminal Responsibility
Ronald Roesch, Jodi Viljoen, and Irene Hui

- Legal Standards   157
- Assessing Mental Disorders   160
- Specialized Scales for Criminal Responsibility Assessments   165

CONCLUSION 169
REFERENCES 170

CHAPTER 9 ASSESSING ADJUDICATIVE COMPETENCY: USING LEGAL AND EMPIRICAL PRINCIPLES TO INFORM PRACTICE
JENNIFER SKEEM, STEPHEN L. GOLDING, AND PAULA EMKE-FRANCIS

CONCEPTUALIZING ADJUDICATIVE COMPETENCY 176
OPERATIONALIZING AND ASSESSING ADJUDICATIVE COMPETENCY 189
IMPROVING COMPETENCY ASSESSMENT PRACTICES 201
CONCLUSION 205
REFERENCES 205

CHAPTER 10 ASSESSING MENTAL COMPETENCY IN THE ELDERLY
CRAIG YURY, RUTH A. GENTRY, HILLARY LEROUX, JEFFREY A. BUCHANAN, AND JANE E. FISHER

MENTAL COMPETENCE 213
CONCLUSION 228
REFERENCES 228

CHAPTER 11 CHILD CUSTODY EVALUATIONS
APRIL R. BRADLEY

CURRENT STATUTES 234
ETHICAL GUIDELINES 234
PROCEDURES 235
COLLATERAL INFORMATION AND RECORD REVIEW 239
INTEGRATING TEST RESULTS AND INTERPRETING THE DATA 240
ADDITIONAL ISSUES 240
CONCLUSION 241
REFERENCES 242

Chapter 12 Forensic Interviewing and Assessment Issues with Children
Matthew Fanetti and Richard Boles

Children as Witnesses in Court   246
Trends in the Empirical Research into Children's Event Memory   249
Perspectives Prior to Evidence Gathering   256
Standardized Assessment Procedures   258
Conclusion   262
References   263

Chapter 13 Evaluation of Psychological Damages
Alix M. McLearen, Christina A. Pietz, and Robert L. Denney

Tort Law   267
Case Law   269
Types of Injury   271
Professional Issues   273
Approach to Evaluation: Multiple Data Source Model   275
Psychological Testing   278
Evaluation for Intellectual and Neuropsychological Impairment   282
Model Application   289
Future Directions   291
Conclusion   293
Acknowledgments   293
References   294

Chapter 14 Detecting Malingering in Forensic Neuropsychological Evaluations in Litigants with Mild Traumatic Brain Injury
Kyle E. Ferguson

What Is Malingering?   303
Conclusion   311
References   311

CHAPTER 15 THE FORENSIC ASSESSMENT OF SUBSTANCE ABUSE
ELIZABETH V. GIFFORD, BARBARA S. KOHLENBERG, MELISSA M. PIASECKI, AND EMILY J. WEBBER

SUBSTANCE USE AND CRIMINAL BEHAVIOR   316
LEGAL ISSUES AND SUBSTANCE ABUSE   319
ASSSESSMENT   323
SUBSTANCE ABUSE TREATMENT   332
ASSESSMENT FOR TREATMENT PLACEMENT AND PLANNING   335
CONCLUSION   337
REFERENCES   338

CHAPTER 16 ASSESSMENT OF POST-TRAUMATIC STRESS DISORDER
KIMBERLI TREADWELL AND EDNA FOA

DIAGNOSIS OF PTSD   347
PREVALENCE   349
GOALS FOR ASSESSMENT   350
METHODS OF ASSESSMENT   351
CONCLUSION   362
REFERENCES   362

PART III MENTAL DISORDERS AND FORENSIC PSYCHOLOGY

CHAPTER 17 CONDUCT DISORDERS AND IMPULSE CONTROL IN CHILDREN
STEVEN G. LITTLE, K. ANGELEQUE AKIN-LITTLE, AND UTA H. MOCNIAK

CONDUCT DISORDER   370
ATTENTION DEFICIT HYPERACTIVITY DISORDER   380
CONCLUSION   388
REFERENCES   388

CHAPTER 18 WHAT EVERY FORENSIC PSYCHOLOGIST SHOULD KNOW ABOUT PSYCHOPATHIC PERSONALITY
ELLISON M. CALE AND SCOTT O. LILIENFELD

CONCEPTUALIZATIONS OF PSYCHOPATHY 396
PSYCHOPATHY'S RELATIONS TO ASPD AND CRIME 397
PSYCHOPATHY IN VARIOUS FORENSIC POPULATIONS 398
PSYCHOPATHY: ASSESSMENT ISSUES 400
PSYCHOPATHY AND DISSIMULATION 408
PSYCHOPATHY: CONCURRENT AND PREDICTIVE RELATIONS WITH
   CRIMINAL BEHAVIOR 410
THE PROGNOSIS OF PSYCHOPATHIC CRIMINALS 415
CONCLUSION: TEN TAKE-HOME MESSAGES FOR FORENSIC PSYCHOLOGISTS 418
REFERENCES 420

CHAPTER 19 SEXUAL DEVIANCE AND FORENSIC PSYCHOLOGY: A PRIMER
TAMARA PENIX SBRAGA

SEXUAL DEVIANCE: A SOCIALLY DRIVEN PROBLEM 430
FORENSIC PSYCHOLOGY AND SEXUAL DEVIANCE: WHERE THE TWAIN MEET 434
FORENSIC ATTENTION: THE BIG SIX 435
TRENDS IN THE MANAGEMENT OF SEXUAL DEVIATES 456
CONCLUSION 458
REFERENCES 460

CHAPTER 20 DISORDERS OF IMPULSE CONTROL
STEPHEN J. HUCKER

IMPULSIVITY AND PERSONALITY DISORDERS 471
IMPULSIVITY AND CEREBRAL DAMAGE 472
IMPULSIVITY AND SUBSTANCE ABUSE 472
IMPULSIVITY AND MAJOR MENTAL DISORDERS 472
IMPULSIVITY AND CHILDHOOD PSYCHIATRIC DISORDERS 472

SPECIFIC DISORDERS OF IMPULSE CONTROL   473
IMPULSE CONTROL DISORDER, NOT OTHERWISE SPECIFIED   480
REPETITIVE SELF-MUTILATION   481
COMPULSIVE SHOPPING   481
CONCLUSION   482
REFERENCES   483

CHAPTER 21 DEVELOPMENTAL DISABILITIES AND MENTAL RETARDATION
W. LARRY WILLIAMS, PATRICK M. GHEZZI, AND ERIC BURKHOLDER

THE NATURE OF DEVELOPMENTAL DISABILITIES AND MENTAL RETARDATION   489
A BRIEF HISTORY   490
DEVELOPMENTAL DISABILITIES, MENTAL RETARDATION, AND THE LAW   493
FREQUENT QUESTIONS AND ANSWERS   496
COMPETENCE ASSESSMENTS OF PEOPLE WITH DEVELOPMENTAL DISABILITIES   499
TREATMENT AND SERVICE ASSESSMENTS   504
CONCLUSION   505
REFERENCES   506

PART IV SPECIAL TOPICS

CHAPTER 22 ISSUES IN EYEWITNESS TESTIMONY
SIMONA GHETTI, JENNIFER M. SCHAAF, JIANJIAN QIN, AND GAIL S. GOODMAN

BASIC MEMORY PROCESSES   514
STRESS AND EYEWITNESS ACCURACY   519
EYEWITNESS IDENTIFICATION   522
THE RELATION BETWEEN ACCURACY AND CONFIDENCE   526
INTERVIEWING TECHNIQUES   531
THE CHILD WITNESS   533
EMERGING RESEARCH THEMES   539

CONCLUSION 542
REFERENCES 543

CHAPTER 23 IN SEARCH OF RECOVERED MEMORIES
AMY C. TSAI, SARAH K. MORSBACH, AND ELIZABETH F. LOFTUS

LEGAL HISTORY OF REPRESSION 556
SCIENTIFIC EVIDENCE FOR REPRESSION 561
SUGGESTIONS FOR PRACTICE 569
FUTURE DIRECTIONS 574
REFERENCES 574

CHAPTER 24 A *DAUBERT* TESTING OF HYPNOTICALLY REFRESHED TESTIMONY IN THE CRIMINAL COURTS
EARL F. MARTIN

THE COMMON-LAW APPROACH TO HYPNOTICALLY REFRESHED TESTIMONY 580
THE *DAUBERT* TEST FOR SCIENTIFIC RELIABILITY 585
HYPNOTICALLY REFRESHED TESTIMONY AND THE *DAUBERT* TEST 587
CONCLUSION 597
ACKNOWLEDGMENTS 598
REFERENCES 598

CHAPTER 25 A CRITICAL ANALYSIS OF THE POLYGRAPH
ERIN M. OKSOL AND WILLIAM T. O'DONOHUE

POLYGRAPH TEST PROCEDURES 602
EXAMINING THE EVIDENCE 604
A LOOK AT THE POLYGRAPH: THE METHODS 613
THE ETHICS OF USE OF THE POLYGRAPH: TRANSGRESSIONS AND CONCERNS 627
CONCLUSION 630
REFERENCES 631

Chapter 26 NONVERBAL DETECTION OF DECEPTION IN FORENSIC CONTEXTS
Mark Frank and Paul Ekman

What Is a Lie?   635
What Happens When Someone Lies?   637
How Good Are We at Spotting Lies?   644
How the Legal Process Affects Catching Lies Through Behavioral Clues   646
Conclusion   649
References   650

Chapter 27 FORENSIC ISSUES IN SEXUAL HARASSMENT
Claudia Avina, Adrian H. Bowers, and William T. O'Donohue

What Is Sexual Harassment?   655
How Frequently Does Sexual Harassment Occur?   658
Who Are the Targets of Sexual Harassment?   659
What Are the Psychological Effects on Victims of Sexual Harassment?   660
When Does Sexual Harassment Occur?   661
The Sexual Harassment Investigation   662
Sexual Harassment Treatment   675
Future Directions   677
References   679

Chapter 28 LEGAL ISSUES IN CHILD ABUSE AND NEGLECT
Sandra T. Azar and Nina Olsen

The Weighing of Children's Needs: New Assessment Roles for Mental Health Professionals   685
An Overview of the Legal Process   686
Conclusion   703
Acknowledgment   704
References   704

Chapter 29 Partner Violence: Assessment, Prediction, and Intervention
Eric R. Levensky and Alan E. Fruzzetti

Definition of Partner Violence   714
Prevalence, Course, and Consequences of Male-to-Female Partner Violence   714
Assessment of Past Partner Violence   715
Predicting Future Partner Violence   721
Interventions in Partner Violence Cases   728
Conclusion   734
References   735

Chapter 30 Elder Abuse: Guidelines for Treatment
Deborah Henderson, Duane Varble, and Jeffrey A. Buchanan

Theoretical Explanations for Elder Abuse   744
Risk Factors Associated with Elder Abuse   746
Barriers to Identifying Elder Abuse   751
Guidelines for the Treatment of Elder Abuse   751
Conclusions and Future Directions   762
References   763

Chapter 31 Involuntary Commitment
Bradley R. Johnson

The History of Involuntary Commitment   768
The Legal Basis of Civil Commitment   770
Involuntary Commitment Procedures   770
Civil Commitment of Sexual Offenders   776
Conclusion: Ethical Issues   778
References   779

CHAPTER 32 JURORS CAN BE SELECTED: NONINFORMATION, MISINFORMATION, AND THEIR STRATEGIC USES FOR JURY SELECTION
DEBORAH DAVIS AND WILLIAM C. FOLLETTE

SCIENCE AND NONSCIENCE IN JURY SELECTION   782
USES OF SCIENTIFIC JURY RESEARCH   782
EVALUATION/SELECTION OF THE JURY POOL   783
DIAGNOSTIC PROFILING: IDENTIFYING (UN)DESIRABLE JURORS   786
GETTING THE JURORS YOU WANT: THE DIPP METHOD   791
CONCLUSION   801
REFERENCES   801

CHAPTER 33 ISSUES OF ETHNICITY IN FORENSIC PSYCHOLOGY: A MODEL FOR HISPANICS IN THE UNITED STATES
MARTHA B. MAHAFFEY

COMPETENCE   808
SOURCES OF BIAS IN THE LEGAL SYSTEM   810
CULTURALLY COMPETENT FORENSIC ASSESSMENT   813
PSYCHOLOGICAL TESTING   821
FORENSIC SPECIFIC MEASUREMENT   830
CONCLUSIONS AND DIRECTIONS FOR FUTURE RESEARCH   837
REFERENCES   838

CHAPTER 34 PSYCHOLOGY IN A SECURE SETTING
KIRK A. BRUNSWIG AND ROBERT W. PARHAM

ENVIRONMENTAL ASPECTS OF CORRECTIONAL AND SECURE SETTINGS   852
PSYCHOLOGIST ROLES IN CORRECTIONAL AND SECURE SETTINGS   854
ETHICAL ISSUES IN THE CORRECTIONAL AND SECURE SETTINGS   862
RESEARCH IN CORRECTIONAL AND SECURE SETTINGS   864

CONCLUSION 867
REFERENCES 868

CHAPTER 35 EVALUATION OF YOUTH IN THE JUVENILE JUSTICE SYSTEM
RANDY OTTO AND RANDY BORUM

BRIEF HISTORY OF THE JUVENILE JUSTICE SYSTEM 873
CLINICAL ISSUES RELEVANT TO JUVENILE FORENSIC EVALUATION 875
PSYCHOLEGAL QUESTIONS INVOLVING YOUTH IN THE JUVENILE JUSTICE SYSTEM 883
CONCLUSION 891
REFERENCES 891

CHAPTER 36 THE ROAD TO PERDITION: EXTREME INFLUENCE TACTICS IN THE INTERROGATION ROOM
DEBORAH DAVIS AND WILLIAM T. O'DONOHUE

FORKS IN THE ROAD: VARIETIES OF CONFESSION 900
THE ROAD TO PERDITION: COMMON INTERROGATION PRACTICES 901
SIMPLE ESCAPE: PHYSICAL AND EMOTIONAL STRESS AS IMPETUS TO CONFESSION 917
ALPHA AND OMEGA: TWO BASIC APPROACHES TO PERSUASIVE INFLUENCE 920
THE ROLE OF PERSONALITY VARIABLES AND PSYCHOPATHOLOGY 963
THE CONSEQUENCES OF FALSE CONFESSION 967
THE ROLE OF THE EXPERT WITNESS 980
REFERENCES 981

CHAPTER 37 WHAT'S GOOD FOR THE GOOSE COOKS THE GANDER: INCONSISTENCIES BETWEEN THE LAW AND PSYCHOLOGY OF VOLUNTARY INTOXICATION AND SEXUAL ASSAULT
DEBORAH DAVIS AND ELIZABETH F. LOFTUS

DOES ALCOHOL USE ENHANCE SEXUAL MOTIVATION/AROUSAL? 1000
DO MEN AND WOMEN BELIEVE ALCOHOL INCREASES INTEREST IN VOLUNTARY SEXUAL ACTIVITY? 1003
DOES ALCOHOL USE ACTUALLY PROMOTE VOLUNTARY SEXUAL ACTIVITY? 1008

ARE MEN AND WOMEN AWARE OF THE LINK BETWEEN INTOXICATION AND
  VICTIMIZATION? 1009
DOES WOMEN'S ALCOHOL CONSUMPTION DEPEND UPON SEXUAL INTENTIONS? 1012
IMPLICATIONS FOR THE LEGAL SYSTEM 1015
CONCLUSIONS 1020
REFERENCES 1022

INDEX 1033

CONTRIBUTORS

Numbers in parentheses indicate the pages on which the author's contributions begin.

Jann Adams (3) Department of Psychology, Morehouse College, Atlanta, Georgia 30314

K. Angeleque Akin-Little (369) Department of Educational and School Psychology, University of the Pacific, Stockton, California 95211

Claudia Avina (655) Department of Psychology, University of Nevada, Reno, Reno, Nevada 89557

Sandra T. Azar (685) Department of Psychology, The Pennsylvania State University, University Park, Pennsylvania 16802

Ritu Bahri (3) Superior Court of Fulton County, Atlanta, Georgia 30303

Kendra Beitz (27) Department of Psychology, University of Nevada, Reno, Reno Nevada 89557

Richard Boles (245) University of Kansas, Lawrence, Kansas 66045

Randy Borum (873) Department of Mental Health Law and Policy, Florida Mental Health Institute, University of South Florida, Tampa, Florida 33612

Adrian H. Bowers (655) Department of Psychology, University of Nevada, Reno, Reno Nevada 89557

April R. Bradley (233) Department of Psychology, University of North Dakota, Grand Forks, ND 58202

M. Gino Brogdon (3) Superior Court of Fulton County, Atlanta, Georgia 30303

Kirk A. Brunswig (851) Department of Psychology, University of Nevada, Reno, Reno Nevada 89557

Jeffrey A. Buchanan (213, 743) Minneapolis VA Medical Center (116B), Minneapolis, Minnesota 55417

Eric Burkeholder (489) Department of Psychology, University of Nevada, Reno, Reno Nevada 89557

Ellison M. Cale (395) South Carolina Department of Juvenile Justice, Columbia, South Carolina 29209

Deborah Davis (781, 897, 997) Department of Psychology, University of Nevada, Reno, Reno, Nevada 89557

Rebecca J. Dempster (103) Law and Mental Health Program, Centre for Addiction and Mental Health, Toronto, Ontario M5T 1R8, Canada

Robert L. Denney (267) Forest Institute of Professional Psychology, United States Medical Center for Federal Prisoners, Springfield, Missouri 65807

Łynne Eccleston (85) Department of Criminology, University of Melbourne, Victoria 3010, Australia

Paul Ekman (635) Department of Psychology, University of California, San Francisco, San Francisco, California 94143

Paula Emke-Francis (175) Department of Psychology, University of Nevada, Las Vegas, Las Vegas, Nevada 89154

Matthew Fanetti (245) Department of Psychology, Southwest Missouri State University, Springfield, MO 65804

Kyle Ferguson (301) Department of Psychology, University of Nevada, Reno, Reno, Nevada 89557

Jane E. Fisher (213) Psychological Service Center, University of Nevada, Reno, Reno, Nevada 89557

Edna Foa (347) Center for the Treatment and Study of Anxiety, University of Pennsylvania, Philadelphia, Pennsylvania 19104

William C. Follette (781) Department of Psychology, University of Nevada, Reno, Reno Nevada 89557

Mark G. Frank (635) Department of Communication, Rutgers University, New Brunswick, New Jersey 08091

Alan E. Fruzzetti (713) Department of Psychology, University of Nevada, Reno, Reno, Nevada 89557

Ruth A. Gentry (213) Psychological Service Center, University of Nevada, Reno, Reno, Nevada 89557

Simona Ghetti (513) Research Institute on Judicial Systems, National Research Council (IRSIG-CNR), Bologna, Italy

Patrick M. Ghezzi (489) Department of Psychology, University of Nevada, Reno, Reno, Nevada 89557

Elizabeth V. Gifford (315) Veterans Affairs and Stanford University Medical Centers, Palo Alto, California 94025

Stephen L. Golding (175) Department of Psychology, University of Utah, Salt Lake City, Utah 84112

Gail S. Goodman (513) Department of Psychology, University of California, Davis, Davis, California 95616

Jeffrey E. Hecker (63) Department of Psychology, University of Maine, Orono, Maine 04469

Deborah Henderson (743) Department of Psychology, University of Nevada, Reno, Reno, Nevada 89557

Stephen J. Hucker (471) Department of Psychiatry and Behavioural Neuroscience, McMaster University, Hamilton, Ontario L8N 3Z5, Canada

Irene Hui (157) Simon Fraser University, Burnaby, British Columbia V5A 1S6, Canada

Bradley R. Johnson (767) Private Practice, Tucson, Arizona 85704

Barbara S. Kohlenberg (315) Department of Psychiatry and Behavioral Sciences, University of Nevada School of Medicine, Reno, Nevada 89557

Michael Lavin (45) Private Practice, and Baltimore-Washington Institute for Psychoanalysis, Washington, District of Columbia 20036

Hilary LeRoux (213) Psychological Service Center, University of Nevada, Reno, Reno, Nevada 89557

Eric R. Levensky (27, 713) Department of Psychology, University of Nevada, Reno, Reno Nevada 89557

Scott O. Lilienfeld (395) Department of Psychology, Emory University, Atlanta, Georgia 30322

Steven G. Little (369) Department of Educational and School Psychology, University of the Pacific, Stockton, California 95211

Elizabeth F. Loftus (555, 997) Department of Psychology and Social Behavior, University of California, Irvine, Irvine, California 92697

Martha B. Mahaffey (807) Private Practice, Reno, Nevada 89502

Earl F. Martin (579) Department of Academic Affairs and Law Department, Texas Wesleyan University School of Law, Ft. Worth, Texas 76102.

Alix McLearen (267) Federal Correctional Complex (FCC) Coleman, Coleman, Florida, 33521

Uta H. Mocniak (369) Department of Psychology, Hofstra University, Hempstead, New York, 11549

Sarah Morsbach (555) University of South Carolina, Columbia, South Carolina 29208

William T. O'Donohue (27, 601, 655, 897) Department of Psychology, University of Nevada, Reno, Reno, Nevada 89557

Erin M. Oksol (601) Department of Psychology, University of Nevada, Reno, Reno, Nevada 89557

Nina Olsen (685) Frances L. Hiatt School of Psychology, Clark University, Worcester, Massachusetts 01610

Randy Otto (873) Department of Mental Health Law and Policy, Florida Mental Health Institute, University of South Florida, Tampa, Florida 33612

Robert W. Parham (851) Washington School of Professional Psychology, Argosy University, Seattle, Steilacoom, Washington 98388

Melissa M. Piasecki (315) Department of Psychiatry and Behavioral Sciences, University of Nevada School of Medicine, Reno, Nevada 89557

Christina A. Pietz (267) Forest Institute of Professional Psychology, United States Medical Center for Federal Prisoners, Springfield, Missouri 65807

Jianjian Qin (513) Department of Psychology, California State University, Sacramento, Sacramento, California 95819

Ronald Roesch (157) Mental Health, Law, and Policy Institute, Simon Fraser University, Burnaby, British Columbia V5A 1S6, Canada

Tamara Penix Sbraga (429) Department of Psychology, Central Michigan University, Mt. Pleasant, Michigan 48859

Jennifer M. Schaaf (513) Frank Porter Graham Child Development Institute, University of North Carolina, Chapel Hill, North Carolina 27599

R. Jamie Scoular (63) Department of Psychology, University of Maine, Orono, Maine 04469

Jennifer Skeem (175) Department of Psychology, University of Nevada, Las Vegas, Las Vegas, Nevada 89154

Kirk Strosahl (129) Mountainview Consulting Group, Inc., Moxee, Washington 98936

Kimberli Treadwell (347) Department of Psychology, University of Connecticut, Waterbury, Connecticut 06710

Amy C. Tsai (555) University of Washington, Seattle, Washington 98125

Duane Varble (743) Department of Psychology, University of Nevada, Reno, Reno, Nevada 89509

Jodi L. Viljoen (157) Simon Fraser University, Burnaby, British Columbia V5A 1S6, Canada

Tony Ward (85) School of Psychology, Victoria University of Wellington, Wellington, New Zealand

Emily J. Webber (315) Division of Criminal Justice, University of Cincinnati, Cincinnati, Ohio 45221

W. Larry Williams (489) Department of Psychology, University of Nevada, Reno, Reno, Nevada 89557

Craig A. Yury (213) Psychological Service Center, University of Nevada, Reno, Reno, Nevada 89557

Preface

The field of forensic psychology has grown rapidly in recent years. Increasingly, psychologists and other mental health professionals are being called upon to provide expertise in a wide variety of legal proceedings. This expertise often evolves presenting relevant findings from the psychological literature, conducting assessments of some dimension of psychological functioning, making conclusions about past behavior and predictions about future behavior, providing recommendations of interventions, and in some cases providing treatment. The core reason for the involvement of the psychologist in the courtroom is that the law concerns human behavior and psychologists have some expertise in this area.

A primary purpose of this volume is to provide psychologists and other mental health practitioners with a source of current, practical, and empirically based information they can use to guide their work in forensic settings. A second purpose is to provide legal professionals with a reference to enable them to be better consumers of information and services provided by mental health professionals. An additional purpose is to show the gaps in knowledge and thus the future research agenda. Contributors to this volume were chosen because of their scholarly and clinical expertise in the specific areas that are most often relevant to the science and practice of forensic psychology.

This volume is organized into four sections: Basic Issues, Assessment, Mental Disorders and Forensic Psychology, and Special Topics. The Basic Issues section is intended to orient mental health professionals to the practice of law and orient legal professionals to the science, practice, abilities, and limitations of psychology. An important competency for any mental health professional working in forensic settings is having, at a minimum, a basic understanding of the law and legal processes and procedures. In Chapter 1, M. Gino Brogdon, Jann H. Adams, and Ritu Bahri provide a legal overview for mental health professionals. It is also important that attorneys who call upon psychology and its practitioners become critical consumers of the methodology, information, tools, and services provided. William O'Donohue, Kendra Beitz, and Eric Levensky discuss in Chapter 2 the strengths and limitations of the science and practice of psychology, and they provide specific recommendations for how legal professionals can get the most from the field.

Many mental health professionals find the current ethical standards for the practice of psychology difficult to apply in forensic settings. In Chapter 3, Michael Lavin discusses moral and ethical issues in forensic psychology and argues that current American Psychological Association ethical codes and guidelines are not adequate for guiding clinicians in many difficult forensic cases. Lavin presents a set of alternate guidelines and uses sexual offender cases as an example of their utility (see also O'Donohue and Ferguson [2003] for further limitations of the Ethical Code).

In Chapter 4, Jeffrey Hecker and R. Jamie Scoular discuss the writing of forensic reports, which often have unique features and require unique skill sets (as compared with other psychological reports). The authors present specific guidelines for completing each section of the forensic report, including identifying information and the referral question, informed consent, basis of assessment, psychological history, clinical findings, clinical impressions, and recommendations. The authors also present several more general guidelines for effective forensic report writing.

Competent, comprehensive, and clinically responsible assessment is often a crucial component of the practice of forensic psychology. The Assessment section provides an overview of methods, tools, and issues relevant to the assessment of forensic populations.

The assessment, prediction, and management of dangerousness are often at issue in the practice of forensic psychology and can have very important implications. Therefore three chapters have been devoted to this general area. In Chapter 5, Lynne Eccleston and Tony Ward provide an overview of legal standards for addressing dangerousness and criminal responsibility. These authors also review and evaluate the literature on the assessment of dangerousness, including the use of clinical versus actuarial assessment methods and static versus dynamic variables in risk assessment. Finally, the authors present a set of guidelines for conducing an effective clinical interview to determine risk of dangerousness. In Chapter 6, Rebecca Dempster reviews the literature on the assessment, communication, and management of risk for violence and emphasizes the important interrelationships between each of these. Specifically, Demptster discusses (1) advancements and limitations in methods for predicting violence, (2) methods and considerations for effective and responsible communication of risk assessment findings to others, and (3) strategies for reducing identified risk and preventing future violence. As Kirk Strosahl points out in Chapter 7, the assessment and treatment of suicidal individuals presents many difficult clinical and legal challenges. Of particular concern to many clinicians in the management of suicidal patients is effectively balancing responsible client care on the one hand and avoiding malpractice litigation on the other. In his chapter, Strosahl discusses the "anatomy" of wrongful death lawsuits and presents a set of strategies for managing the suicidal patient in a way that is both ethical and reduces the likelihood malpractice litigation should a patient actually commit suicide.

Forensic psychologists are also at times called upon to speak to an individual's criminal intent at the time of a crime and competency to stand trial for that crime. In Chapter 8, Ronald Roesch, Jodi Viljoen, and Irene Hui provide legally informed and empirically based guidelines for assessing intent and criminal responsibility. These guidelines address the areas of determining "mental disease or defect" and ability to understand, appreciate, and/or control criminal behavior at the time of the crime as well as whether a mental disorder is causal in the crime. The authors review assessment tools commonly used for conducting evaluations of criminal responsibility and discuss the challenges to conducting these evaluations.

The assessment of an individual's competency can be a challenging and complex undertaking. In Chapter 9, Jennifer Skeem, Stephen Golding, and Paula Emke-Francis address the assessment of adjudicative competency. These authors discuss current conceptualizations of the construct of competency, review tools and methods for assessing this construct, describe common challenges in assessing competency, and provide a number of empirically based recommendations for practice. The assessment of mental competency in the elderly in particular is often at issue in court proceedings. In Chapter 10, Craig Yury, Ruth Gentry, Hillary LeRoux, Jeffrey Buchanan, and Jane Fisher discuss definitions of competence and evaluate their advantages and limitations. The authors also review the diseases/disorders and the consequences of the normal aging process that can affect mental competence, and they present specific recommendations for the assessment process and review commonly used assessment methods.

The forensic evaluation of children can have its own unique challenges and considerations. April Bradley reviews standards of practice in conducting child custody evaluations in Chapter 11. She discusses typical state laws on child custody, ethical guidelines, data collection methods, and available assessment instruments. Bradley also discusses the relative utility of the available assessment methods and tools as well as the interpretation of collected data. Currently very few psychometrically sound instruments exist relevant to this legal question. Additionally, she provides specific guidelines for conducting child custody evaluations and providing results and recommendations. In Chapter 12, Matthew Fanetti and Richard Boles discuss conducting assessments with children in child sexual abuse cases. These authors discuss special considerations in interviewing children, including issues regarding children's memories and reporting of past events as well as interviewer predispositions and behaviors that can facilitate and hinder valid and reliable reporting from children. Recommendations are made for maximizing the validity and reliability of assessments with children regarding sexual abuse. This is a critical area because children's testimony is often the most important prosecution evidence. If this testimony was biased because of problematic interviews, then innocent individuals can be falsely imprisoned and children can be given a false victim identity.

Increasingly, forensic evaluations are being called for in civil litigation cases to determine the extent of psychological damages incurred. In Chapter 13, Alix McLearen, Christina Pietz and Robert Denney examine the legal standards for defining psychological damages and negligence. Often tort litigation is concerned not only with physical damages but also with emotional and psychological damages. The issues involved often include an accurate and comprehensive assessment of the client's past, present, and future functioning as well as a causal model for what influenced problems in these areas. Additionally, the authors present a general framework for conducting evaluations of psychological damages, and describe and evaluate specific tools and methods for identifying and differentiating actual psychological injury and malingering.

The issue of malingering can be of particular concern in neuropsychological evaluations. Kyle Ferguson discusses in Chapter 14 the issue of detecting malingering in litigants with mild traumatic brain injury (MTBI). Unlike severe and moderate injuries, in which deficits are often clearly evident (e.g., ataxic gate), determining the extent of impairment with MTBI poses unique challenges. Individuals with MTBI often report cognitive impairment despite the fact that neuroimaging tests come up negative and neurological signs are not present. Thus, neuropsychological test findings are usually the only objective evidence of impairment. This chapter provides guidelines for detecting probable malingering in cases where litigants stand to gain economically from having deficits (i.e., psychological damages) or avoid legal responsibility during criminal prosecution.

Substance abuse is involved in many forensic cases, and the assessment of substance abuse can have an impact on the outcomes of the cases. "Driving under the influence," or DUI, for example, is responsible for many traffic fatalities, and a majority of these offenders have had prior legal involvement. Substance abuse can also be a risk factor for criminal behavior and hence an important risk factor for relapse. Elizabeth Gifford, Barbara Kohlenberg, Melissa Piasecki, and Emily Webber provide an overview in Chapter 15 of the assessment and treatment of substance abuse in forensic settings. Specifically, these authors discuss the interaction between substance abuse and criminal behavior, examine legal guidelines and precedents, describe and evaluate assessment tools and methods, and review the literature on substance abuse treatment.

Post-Traumatic Stress Disorder (PTSD) is implicated in many criminal and civil court cases. Many of the more serious criminal acts can result in trauma and thus result in the problems associated with PTSD. There are also issues if PTSD can impair decision making and thus reduce criminal responsibility—for example, in the so-called battered wife syndrome. In Chapter 16, Kimberli Treadwell and Edna Foa discuss the nature and prevalence of PTSD as well as the assessment goals for this disorder. The authors spend the majority of the chapter describing assessment methods and reviewing and critically evaluating a wide variety of psychometrically sound assessment measures of PTSD, including structured diagnostic interviews, structured clinical interviews, and self-report measures.

The assessment and treatment of mental disorders is often a complex challenge in forensic psychology. The Mental Disorders and Forensic Psychology section of this volume is intended to provide guidelines for working effectively with these populations. The presence of mental disorders can be relevant for predicting future behavior, such as relapses, and is also relevant in determining sentencing. In Chapter 17, Steven Little, Angeleque Akin-Little, and Uta Mocniak provide an overview of conduct disorder and attention deficit hyperactivity disorder. Specifically, for each of these disorders the authors discuss diagnostic criteria, prevalence, risk factors, developmental progression, assessment issues, intervention and treatments, and forensic considerations. Effective identification and management of psychopathic individuals is often an important yet challenging task for clinicians working in forensic settings. In Chapter 18, Ellison Cale and Scott Lilienfeld review the literature on psychopathic personality. The review includes conceptualizations of psychopathic personality and its relationship to antisocial personality disorder and a number of criminal behaviors, psychopathology in various forensic populations, assessment methods, tools, and issues in psychopathology. The authors also discuss issues of particular concern in working with psychopathic individuals, such as malingering and impression management, prognoses, treatment options and outcomes, institutional misbehavior, and recidivism.

One of the more heinous set of crimes is sexual assault, from the rape of adult to the molestation of a child. In Chapter 19, Tamara Penix Sbraga provides an overview of the etiology, course, epidemiology, assessment, and treatment of a number of forms of sexual misbehavior that are most often the subject of forensic cases: voyeurism, exhibitionism, frotteurism, sexual sadism, rape, and pedophilia. Sbraga also discusses challenges unique to working with this population in the criminal justice system as well as issues of risk assessment, imprisonment, and civil incarceration.

Much of criminal behavior can be considered to be problematic impulse control. In Chapter 20, Stephen Hucker addresses disorders of impulse control. Hucker first discusses the relationship between impulsivity and a number of psychological disorders such as personality disorders, substance abuse, affective disorders, and childhood psychiatric disorders. He then reviews the specific disorders of impulse control, including pathological gambling, trichotillomania, pyromania, intermittent explosive disorder, kleptomania, repetitive self-mutilation, and compulsive shopping. Hucker discusses issues of diagnostic criteria, etiology, and treatment for each of these disorders. Mental retardation is a mental disorder that impairs cognition and thus is relevant forensically to such issues as criminal intent. Chapter 21, authored by W. Larry Williams, Patrick Ghezzi, and Eric Burkeholder, reviews the historical development, prevalence, and diagnostic criteria for developmental disabilities (DD) and mental retardation (MD). The authors also discuss assessment and treatment methods for DD and MD as well as issues of competency, rights, and social issues.

The Special Topics section of this text was included to address a variety of specific issues, methods, populations, and controversies encountered in forensic settings. Eyewitness testimony can be crucial and highly influential in court cases and has been a controversial form of evidence. In Chapter 22, Simona Ghetti, Jennifer Schaaf, Jianjian Qin, and Gail Goodman discuss a number of important issues related to eyewitness testimony. These include a discussion of basic memory processes, eyewitness accuracy, eyewitness identification, interviewing techniques, and children's eyewitness memory. The authors also include a section on emerging research topics in the area of eyewitness testimony.

The issues of repressed and recovered memories of past events, such as childhood sexual abuse, has received widespread attention. Additionally, the validity and existence of repressed and recovered memories has been extremely controversial and can have important forensic implications. Amy Tsai, Sarah Morsbach, and Elizabeth Loftus review in Chapter 23 the key research and clinical issues in repressed memories. Issues discussed include the legal history of repressed memories, scientific evidence for repression, and suggestions for research practice.

The use of hypnosis in criminal investigations has increased significantly. The primary focus of Chapter 24 is an examination of the validity and reliability of hypnotically refreshed testimony in criminal courts. In this chapter, Earl Martin discusses legal precedents regarding standards with relevance to psychological testing and hypnotically refreshed memories, and he evaluates the extent to which research in this area can support the use of hypnotically refreshed testimony in criminal cases.

Polygraph testing is widely used to detect deception in criminal investigations, yet its reliability, validity, and ethicality continue to be controversial. Chapter 25, authored by Erin Oksol and William O'Donohue, provides a critical analysis of the polygraph. In this chapter, the authors review and evaluate polygraph test procedures and the empirical evidence of the validity and reliability of various polygraph methods, and they discuss ethical and clinical issues in the use of the polygraph. The authors conclude that there is little scientific evidence to support the appropriate widespread use of this assessment device.

Correctly determining the veracity of individuals' self-reports is crucial in conducting effective forensic evaluations. In Chapter 26, Mark Frank and Paul Ekman discuss the nonverbal detection of lying in forensic contexts. The authors discuss the nature of a lie, behavioral indicators that an individual may be lying, mental health and legal professionals' ability to detect lying, and the effects of the legal process on the successful detection of lying.

Sexual harassment has become an increasingly important social problem and is frequently at issue in legal proceedings. In Chapter 27, Claudia Avina, Adrian Bowers, and William O'Donohue illustrate important forensic issues related to sexual harassment, including legal and psychological definitions, epidemiological data, characteristics of victims and perpetrators, and common psychological effects of sexual harassment. Lastly, the authors discuss the assessment and investigation of sexual harassment allegations and the treatment of sexual harassment victims and perpetrators.

Psychologists have an array of special duties in certain cases involving children. Chapter 28 addresses three specific areas often relevant to forensic child abuse and neglect cases: mandated reporting, risk assessment, and evaluation of parental fitness. Sandra Azar and Nina Olsen review the research literature and standards of practice in each of these areas and make specific practice recommendations.

In recent years, the number of partner abuse cases in the nation's courts has increased significantly, and there has been a corresponding increase in the frequency of requests for mental health clinicians to provide evaluations and recommendations in these cases. In Chapter 29, Eric Levensky and Alan Fruzzetti discuss (1) the known prevalence and typical course and consequences of partner violence, (2) assessment of past partner violence, (3) prediction of future partner violence, and (4) intervention options and empirical outcomes in partner violence cases.

With the aging of the American population has come a corresponding increase of forensic issues with the elderly. In Chapter 30, Deborah Henderson, Duane Varble, and Jeffery Buchanan discuss issues relevant to elder abuse cases. These authors first review a variety of theoretical explanations and empirically derived risk factors for elder abuse, then present specific guidelines for the identification, assessment, and intervention of elder abuse.

The issue of involuntary commitment presents significant challenges because it relies on difficult prediction tasks and because recommendations in this area can have many adverse consequences. Bradley Johnson discusses in Chapter 31 the issues relevant in making recommendations on civil commitment. Johnson addresses the history of involuntary commitment in the United States, the legal basis and procedures for commitment, relevant case law, the criteria for involuntary commitment, and ethical issues in this area.

For obvious reasons, the selection of a jury can have significant impact on the outcome of a trial. However, many lawyers have great difficulty identifying favorable jury members and successfully selecting them. Rather, many lawyers focus only on identifying and deselecting unfavorable potential jurors. In Chapter 32, Deborah Davis and William Follette review the literature on jury selection and present a set of recommendations for identifying and selecting favorable jury members.

Hispanics are a fast-growing population segment in the United States, and many special considerations and issues must be taken into account in working with Hispanic individuals in forensic settings. In Chapter 33, Martha Mahaffey discusses issues of competency in working with Hispanic individuals, sources of bias specific to Hispanics in the legal system, and culturally competent forensic assessment and psychological testing.

Many forensic psychologists work in secure settings. In Chapter 34, Kirk Brunswig and Robert Parham describe the practice of psychology in secure settings, such as jails, prisons, mental health hospitals, secure forensic units, and civil commitment facilities. The authors discuss environmental aspects of these settings, the various roles of psychologists working in correctional and secure settings, and ethical issues pertaining to these settings.

There are a number of important special considerations in evaluating juveniles in the legal system. In Chapter 35, Randy Otto and Randy Borum provide a brief history of the juvenile justice system, then review three central clinical issues relevant to juvenile forensic evaluations: (1) psychosocial maturity and developmental status, (2) risk for future offending or violence, and (3) the nature and extent of antisocial behavior and character. The authors conclude with a discussion of the areas to which each of these three central issues are most frequently applied, including transfer, competency, criminal intent and responsibility, and dispositional evaluations.

In Chapter 36, Deborah Davis and William O'Donohue discuss the paradoxical phenomenon of false confessions. There have been several high-profile cases in which individuals have falsely claimed in police interrogations that they have committed serious crimes such as murders and rape and then have had to serve long prison terms. Davis and O'Donohue discuss factors present in both the interrogation process and the individual under interrogation that may lead to false confessions. One critical set of factors is mental disorders. This set of factors is particularly worrisome because these impairments can lead to further harm to individuals after they have falsely confessed (e.g., false imprisonment).

Current rape laws in many states specify that intercourse with a woman who is intoxicated is to be considered rape, regardless of other indications of consent. In Chapter 37, Deborah Davis and Elizabeth Loftus examine the argument that the psychology of voluntary intoxication and sexual consent does not support the law that intoxicated alleged victims should be presumed unable to consent/raped.

We as editors owe a number of debts to others who have contributed much to the formation of this book. First, we would like to thank the chapter authors for all their hard work and scholarship. We would like to thank our editor at Academic Press, Barbara Makinster, whose invaluable assistance greatly contributed to the success of this book. We would also like to thank people who have assisted in the preparation of this book: Sara Ashby, Nanci Fowler, and Elizabeth Yeater. We would especially like to thank the production manager for this book, Aaron Downey at Matrix Productions. Mr. Downey's incredible professionalism, patience, sense of humor, and tireless commitment to this project made our jobs a true pleasure and contributed greatly to making the book what it is today. Finally, we would like to thank our families for their support and encouragement. William O'Donohue would like to thank Jane Fisher, Katie O'Donohue, and Anna O'Donohue. Eric Levensky would like to thank Elizabeth Yeater, Elayne Levensky, Mark Levensky, Amy Anderson, John Anderson, Timothy Anderson, and Maurice Rotkow.

PART I

BASIC ISSUES

CHAPTER 1

PSYCHOLOGY AND THE LAW

M. GINO BROGDON, SR.
SUPERIOR COURT OF FULTON COUNTY, ATLANTA, GEORGIA

JANN H. ADAMS
MOREHOUSE COLLEGE

RITU BAHRI
SUPERIOR COURT OF FULTON COUNTY, ATLANTA, GEORGIA

Every profession is governed by internally created and self-imposed guidelines, rules, and principles. These professions also function under a legal umbrella consisting of numerous laws either enacted by Congress or state legislatures or resulting from an evolutionary process from case law. A professional's failure to conduct his or her work in accordance with legally accepted principles can result in exposure to significant criminal and civil liability upon a showing of misfeasance or, in certain circumstances, nonfeasance. Practice in mental health is no exception to this rule. Thus, it is imperative that mental health professionals[1] have a full and working understanding of the laws and legal principles that govern and materially affect the manner and substance of delivery of mental health services to the public.

This chapter will include a discussion of the primary legal issues facing mental health professionals. The paramount concern of most such professionals is the extent of the legal boundaries and exceptions to the psychiatrist/psychologist–patient privilege. An exception to the privilege, the duty to warn third parties of immediate, threatened danger, will be discussed in depth since breach of the duty exposes the mental health professional to civil liability, possibly resulting in significant monetary damages. The practice of many mental health professionals

---

[1] The term *mental health professional* refers collectively to psychologists, psychiatrists, and psychotherapists.

may require them to testify in court regarding the mental health of their patient. Accordingly, this chapter sets forth the role of a mental health professional in the courtroom in providing expert testimony and the legal standards and parameters applicable thereto. In addition, the mental state of certain patients may inevitably subject them to involuntary civil commitment or criminal commitment. The legal standards used in the determination of the propriety and parameters of involuntary civil commitment and criminal commitment are discussed in detail. This chapter also deals with the difficult topic of the strictly prohibited practice of duality and engaging in sexual relationships with patients and the legal implications thereto. Finally, it will address the recent legal issues regarding the phenomenon of memory enhancement techniques in the area of repressed memories and Internet psychotherapy.

PSYCHIATRIST/PSYCHOLOGIST–PATIENT PRIVILEGE

Historically, the psychiatrist-patient privilege or the psychologist-patient privilege was excluded from those privileges recognized at common law.[2] Although privileges were generally disfavored in common law because they hindered the truth-seeking goal of the judicial system, evidentiary privileges such as the attorney-client privilege and the spousal privilege were initially established and shaped primarily based on public policy concerns (Nielsen, 1997). For example, the attorney-client privilege was recognized under common law to encourage the truthful and complete communication between attorneys and their clients in the interest of the broader public interest of effective administration of justice (*Upjohn Co. v. United States*, 1981). The spousal privilege was developed to further the public interest in marital harmony (*Trammel v. United States*, 1980).

Today, with a greater understanding of the substantive and legal complexities of the psychotherapy relationship, courts and state legislatures have extended necessary and appropriate protection to the relationship between the mental health practitioner and her patient. Currently all 50 states and the District of Columbia recognize and, to some extent, provide protection through legislation to the psychotherapist-patient relationship (*Trammel v. United States*, 1980, p. 1129). Although all states agree on the existence of the privilege, many differ on its impact, reach, and scope (Klein, 1997). Eleven states treat the psychiatrist-patient privilege in a similar way to the attorney-client privilege: Alabama, Arizona, Georgia, Idaho, Kansas, Montana, New Jersey, New York, Pennsylvania, Ohio, and Washington. In these states the psychiatrist-patient privilege protects generally all communications between the therapist and patient given or received for the purpose of professional treatment and advice. Five states recognize the privilege without specifically limiting or defining any conditions thereto: Kentucky, Minnesota,

---

[2] *Common law* refers to that body of law formulated from judgments and decrees of courts as opposed to law formulated by the legislature (*Black's Law Dictionary*, 1968, pp. 345–346).

Mississippi, Missouri, and South Dakota. Five states recognize the privilege with some limitations: Colorado (limiting the privilege to information gained while the patient is in therapy); New Hampshire; North Carolina (limiting the privilege in cases of child abuse and where disclosure is necessary for a proper administration of justice); Utah; and Virginia (limiting the privilege only to civil actions and allowing for the exercise of the court's discretion). Twenty-one states have established several exceptions to the privilege: Alaska, Arkansas, California, Connecticut, Delaware, District of Columbia, Florida, Hawaii, Indiana, Maine, Maryland, Massachusetts, Michigan, North Dakota, New Mexico, Oklahoma, Oregon, Rhode Island, Wisconsin, Wyoming, and Illinois. Four states recognize the privilege for only psychiatrists, and not for psychologists, social workers, or psychotherapists: South Carolina, Tennessee, Vermont, and West Virginia. Four states recognize the psychiatrist-patient privilege under statutes setting forth privileges for physicians or mental health professionals in general: Iowa, Louisiana, Nebraska, and Nevada. Finally, Texas protects all communications between patients and people licensed or certified by the state of Texas in the diagnosis, evaluation, or treatment of any mental or emotional disorder or people involved in the treatment or examination of drug abusers (Klein, 1997).

Generally, few states limit the protection to only those communications between patients and their psychiatrist or psychologist (Klein, 1997). Most states, however, do extend the privilege to include physicians and non-M.D./Ph.D. psychotherapists (Klein, 1997). For example, Arizona extends the privilege to all communications between patients and behavioral health professionals (Klein, 1997). Utah's statutory scheme goes so far as to extend protection to all confidential communications made to marriage and family therapists, professional counselors, advanced practice registered nurses designated as psychiatric mental health nurse specialists, and clinical or certified social workers (Klein, 1997).

Prior to 1996, the existence of the psychiatrist-patient privilege depended in large part on the jurisdiction before which the case was pending. As discussed earlier, all 50 states and the District of Columbia recognize some form of the privilege with varying limitations thereon. However, federal circuit courts were divided on its existence at the federal level. In 1996, the U.S. Supreme Court addressed the issue of the existence of the psychiatrist-patient privilege at the federal level. The Supreme Court concluded that the Federal Rules of Evidence protected communications not only between the patient and licensed psychologists and psychiatrists, but also with licensed social workers in the course of psychotherapy (*Jaffee v. Raymond*, 1996). The Court reasoned that exceptions to the general rule disfavoring privileges is justified by a "public good transcending the normally predominant principle of utilizing all rational means for ascertaining truth" (*Jaffee v. Raymond*, 1996). The Court analogized the psychiatrist-patient privilege to the attorney-client and spousal privileges and held that it similarly is "rooted in the imperative need for confidence and trust" (*Jaffee v. Raymond*, 1996). Significantly, the Court noted that in order for a psychotherapist to render effective treatment, the patient must be able to make truthful and complete disclosure of facts, emotions, memories and fears "in an atmosphere of confidence and trust" (*Jaffee v. Raymond*, 1996). Effective mental treatment depends in large part on communications of a confidential nature, disclosure of which could cause the patient great embarrassment or disgrace and result in a chilling effect on candor and full disclosure required in an effective therapeutic relationship (*Jaffee v. Raymond*, 1996). Therefore, a psychotherapist must be able to assure patients that communications will indeed have a cloak of confidentiality in the legal arena. Additionally, because all 50 states and the District of Columbia have enacted some form of the psychiatrist-patient privilege, federal courts' refusal to recognize the privilege would render the states' privilege laws effectively meaningless if patients were aware that the privilege may not be honored in federal courts (*Jaffee v. Raymond*, 1996). In extending the privilege to licensed social workers in the course of psychotherapy, the Court recognized that modern-day social workers provide significant mental health treatment, often to clients who have limited financial resources and who could not otherwise afford counseling or therapy by a psychiatrist or psychologist (*Jaffee v. Raymond*, 1996, at 1931).

In establishing the existence of the psychotherapist-patient privilege in federal courts, the Supreme Court specifically declined to define the full contours of the newly established privilege and directed that the same be developed on a case-by-case basis (*Jaffee v. Raymond*, 1996, at 1932). Thus the parameters of the privilege continue to be defined by state law. The Supreme Court did recognize that the privilege would yield to disclosure in certain circumstances, such as where the patient communicates a serious threat of harm to himself and/or others that can be averted only through disclosure (*Jaffee v. Raymond*, 1996, at 1932). The Court hereby recognized the paramount importance for public safety over the confidential nature of the therapy relationship.

Because the privilege differs significantly from state to state and because the Supreme Court declined to clearly define the scope of the same, mental health professionals are encouraged to refer to the state law applicable to their practice to confirm the limits on the privilege relating to their communications with their patients.[3] Mental health practitioners have an ethical responsibility to maintain a general awareness of the legal parameters of the confidentiality of communications with their clients and to advise their clients of the same. The confidential nature of doctor-patient communications is far from being a modern concept and has been historically recognized, notably in the Hippocratic Oath (Nielsen, 1997). Significantly, professional codes define and guide a mental health professional's obligation with respect to the confidential nature of communications with their patients. Though professional codes of ethics vary from state to state, each has two common provisions imposing an ethical duty to maintain confidentiality in

---

[3] Because the various state jurisdictions differ significantly on the scope of the psychiatrist-patient relationship and because there exists no clear definition of the same under federal law, the definition and examination of this relationship requires a detailed and comprehensive analysis beyond the scope of this chapter.

certain circumstances and to inform the patient of the limits of the same (Poulin, 1998). For example, the American Psychiatric Association imposes upon a psychiatrist the duty to advise the patient of the "connotations of waiving the privilege" and to inform the patient as to communications occurring outside the protected parameters (Poulin, 1998). Psychologists and social workers have similar obligations to advise the patient as to the limitations on confidentiality (Poulin, 1998).

Exceptions to the Privilege

Exceptions to the psychotherapist-patient privilege have been established for circumstances where the need for the information far outweighs the public interest encouraging confidentiality (Klein, 1995). In recognizing the privilege, the U.S. Supreme Court explicitly recognized that circumstances exist that would require the privilege to give way to disclosure (*Jaffee v. Raymond*, 1996, at 18, n. 19). Commonly referred to as the *dangerous patient exception*, a situation in which the patient communicates threats of violence against another during therapy, the mental health professional has a duty to warn the potential victim of the threatened harm (*Jaffee v. Raymond*, 1996). In addition, all 50 states refuse to recognize the privilege in circumstances arising out of threats of or revelation of past incidents of child abuse (*Jaffee v. Raymond*, 1996). Here, all states impose a statutory duty to report instances of child abuse (Klein, 1995).

Where the patient makes his or her mental condition an element of a claim or defense in such a way that his or her mental condition is put at issue in litigation, some states hold that the patient has waived the privilege (Klein, 1995). Additionally, where the communications occurred as a result of court-ordered psychological examination, the results are not privileged (Klein, 1995). Finally, the privilege is not recognized in commitment proceedings resulting from a psychotherapist's determination during the course of treatment that the patient requires hospitalization (Klein, 1995).

Because psychotherapists' duty to warn third parties has given rise to their significant exposure to civil liability, the following subsection provides greater analysis of the duty and means for discharging the same.

Duty to Warn

Common law imposed liability upon persons only for their acts, or misfeasance, as opposed to their failure to act, or nonfeasance, regardless of whether harm ensued from the inaction (Freedman, 1998). Accordingly, common law did not recognize a duty to control the conduct of another or to protect third parties in circumstances where their safety was threatened by the conduct of another (Freedman, 1998). Over the years, several exceptions were carved to this general rule based on the existence of some special relationship. Examples of such exceptions include the innkeeper-guest relationship, the employer-employee relationship, and the business establishment–customer relationship (Freedman, 1998). Here the law created a duty of reasonable care toward the person with whom a special relationship existed to take action when the party knew or had reason to know of a threatened danger to that person (Freedman, 1998). This duty of reasonable care was extended to cover the duty to control the conduct of a third party where a special relationship existed between the third party and the actor based on the rationale that the actor had custody or control of another and knew or should have known of the threatened harm (Freedman, 1998).

One such special relationship is that of the psychiatrist or psychologist with his or her patient. The psychiatrist's or psychologist's duty of reasonable care to protect third parties from threatened harm posed by a patient was first recognized by the California Supreme Court in 1976. The Court held that "[w]hen a therapist determines, or pursuant to the standards of his profession should determine, that his patient presents a serious danger of violence to another, he incurs an obligation to use reasonable care to protect the intended victim against such danger" (*Tarasoff v. Regents of the University of California*, 1976, at 340). The duty to protect does not require that the therapist render perfect performance, but only that reasonable degree of skill, knowledge, and care ordinarily possessed and exercised by members of the same profession under similar circumstances. Thus, where a moment's reflection would reveal the potential victim's identity, the therapist's duty to protect exists. The therapist may discharge this duty to protect in several ways, including warning the potential victim or others who are likely to communicate the danger to the potential victim, notifying the police, or undertaking other steps reasonably necessary depending on the circumstances. In formulating the duty to protect, the Court balanced conflicting public policy concerns: the important public interest in the treatment of mental illnesses, the protection of patients' privacy and the confidential nature of psychiatrist/psychologist–patient communications, and the important public interest in protecting against threatened violence. In striking a balance between such concerns, the Court concluded that protection of members of the public from threatened violence far outweighed the psychiatrist-patient privilege: "the protective privilege ends where the public peril begins" (*Tarasoff v. Regents of the University of California*, 1976, at 346). The rationale for creating this duty of care is that the therapist's superior knowledge of the threatened danger and his or her opportunity to intervene to protect the third party may be the most effective, if not the only, means of preventing violent acts (Goldstein & Katz, 1962).

Since the California Supreme Court's decision in 1976, the majority of the states, through case law and/or legislative action, now recognize therapists' duty of reasonable care to protect third parties but differ as to its scope (Harris, 1999). Most states, having adopted this duty of care, do agree that the psychiatrist should be responsible for warning and/or protecting only specific, identifiable victims (Harris, 1999). Six states have enacted a statutory exception to the psychiatrist-patient privilege for the prevention of harm to a third party: Connecticut, Rhode Island, South Carolina, Tennessee, West Virginia, and Wyoming (Harris,

1999). Six states analogize the privilege with the attorney-client privilege, which excludes from protected communications those respecting proposed infractions of the law: Alabama, Arizona, Kansas, Montana, New York, and Washington (Harris, 1999). Oregon has not established a statutory exception to the psychiatrist-patient privilege and further has refused to recognize an implied exception (*Oregon v. Miller*, 1985). Three states follow the California Supreme Court's decision and impose a common law duty upon a psychotherapist to warn readily identifiable potential victims of the threatened violence: Michigan, New Jersey, and Vermont (Gammon & Hulston, 1995). Connecticut and Delaware impose a duty to warn identifiable *classes* of potential victims (Gammon & Hulston, 1995). Ohio and Georgia have extended the California Supreme Court's holding to include a duty to protect and/or control the patient (Gammon & Hulston, 1995). Florida courts rejected the existence of such duty on grounds that the psychotherapist-patient relationship is insufficient to support the duty (Gammon & Hulston, 1995). Subsequently, the Florida legislature enacted legislation allowing a psychiatrist to disclose those confidential communications necessary to warn potential victims or others who are likely to apprise the potential victims of the threatened danger (Gammon & Hulston, 1995).

Very few states have addressed the dangerous patient exception as an evidentiary issue—that is, whether the psychotherapist can be compelled to testify about confidential communications with a patient in a subsequent criminal proceeding against that patient (Harris, 1999). California and Oregon, the only states that have addressed this issue, have reached opposite conclusions (Harris, 1999). Thus far, California is the lone state that, having applied its statutory exception to the psychiatrist-patient privilege, compelled a psychotherapist's testimony on confidential communications in criminal proceedings against the patient instituted subsequent to the commission of the crime (Harris, 1999).

Predicting Dangerousness

Predicting the dangerousness of a patient is an inherently difficult task because of the psychotherapist's inability to objectively verify this factor (Posin, 1988). In discharging the duty to warn, a psychotherapist should take into account the clinical diagnosis of the patient; the circumstances surrounding the communication of the threat; the circumstances prompting the patient's desire to do violent acts; the patient's relationship to the potential victim; the patient's ability and opportunity to act on the threat; any history of past violence; and the patient's response to treatment (Posin, 1988).

EXPERT TESTIMONY

Often, psychiatrists, psychologists, and other mental health professionals may find themselves, either voluntarily or pursuant to court-ordered subpoena, in the courtroom testifying in front of a judge and/or a jury regarding the mental state of their patient. The courtroom is a foreign arena for most mental health professionals. Accordingly, preparation for their testimony is the key to successfully apprising the judge and/or the jury of their opinion regarding the mental condition of the subject patient. To adequately prepare for their testimony, mental health professionals must understand the legal parameters for the admissibility of their testimony.

Generally, under both the federal and Georgia evidentiary rules, witnesses must testify on matters within their personal knowledge and are prohibited from stating opinions, unless based on their own personal observations (*Atlantic Line Coast Railway v. Smith*, 1963; Federal Rules of Evidence 701, 702). An exception is made for the testimony of expert witnesses. An expert witness is one who through education, training, or experience has peculiar knowledge regarding some matter of scientific, technical, or other specialized knowledge to which his or her testimony relates (*Tifton Brick and Block Co. v.* Meadow, 1955). Expert witnesses may express opinions on facts, principles, or rules involved in the science in which they are educated so long as the subject matter is outside the scope of the ordinary layperson's knowledge and experience (*Jones v. State*, 1974). The testimony must be helpful to the jury; where the expert opinion testimony is within the scope of the ordinary layman's knowledge and experience, it is usually inadmissible (*Jones v. State*, 1974). Expert opinions may be based on facts personally observed or on facts proved by other witnesses (OCGA 24-9-67).

However, experts cannot base their opinions on the opinions of other witnesses or other experts, thereby acting as mere conduits to the opinions of others (*Hyles v. Cockrill*, 1983). Expert opinions are never binding on the jury and the jury is authorized to disregard the same in reaching its verdict (*American Mutual Liability Insurance Co. v. King*, 1953). The testimony of an expert witness carries no more weight under the law than that of other witnesses (*Longshore v. State*, 1978).

Before the opinion testimony of an expert is admissible in evidence, the party offering the witness must first establish the witness's qualification to the satisfaction of the court (*Dimambro North End Association v. Williams*, 1983). The knowledge of an expert witness may be derived from books alone, experience alone, or the combination of both (*Owen v. Bair*, 1975). There is no requirement that the witness have received formal training as a prerequisite to being qualified as an expert (*Brown v. State*, 1980).

Admissibility of Scientific Evidence

> Just when a scientific principle or discovery crosses the line between the experimental and demonstrable stages is difficult to define. Somewhere in this twilight zone the evidential force of the principle must be recognized, and though courts will go a long way in admitting expert testimony deduced from a

well-recognized scientific principle discovery, the thing from which the deduction is made must be sufficiently established to have gained general acceptance in the particular field in which it belongs. (*Frye v. United States*, 1923)

This now famous passage sets forth the test commonly referred to as the *Frye test* or the *general acceptance test* for the federal courts' determination of the admissibility of novel scientific evidence. The *Frye* test was the prevailing standard for 70 years after its formulation. Over the years, a sharp division had arisen among circuits regarding the proper standard for the admission of expert testimony. In 1993, the U.S. Supreme Court granted certiorari in the case of *Daubert v. Merrell Dow Pharmaceuticals, Inc.* to put to rest the division. In reaching its decision, the Supreme Court held that the adoption of the Federal Rules of Evidence, around 50 years subsequent to the *Frye* decision, had superseded the *Frye* test (*Daubert v. Merrell Dow Pharmaceuticals*, 1993).

In setting forth the appropriate standard for determining the admissibility of expert testimony, the Court relied on Rule 702, which provides that "[i]f scientific, technical, or other specialized knowledge will assist the trier of fact to understand the evidence or to determine a fact in issue, a witness qualified as an expert by knowledge, skill, experience, training, or education may testify thereto in the form of an opinion or otherwise." Rule 702 establishes a relevance standard for the admission of expert testimony where such testimony is helpful to the jury and balances between helpfulness of such testimony and the possibility that it will be misunderstood, misapplied, or will lead to confusion (Johnson, 1994). The *Daubert* Court held that Rule 702 does not set forth "general acceptance" as an absolute prerequisite to the admissibility of expert testimony (*Daubert v. Merrell Dow Pharmaceuticals*, 1993, at 2794). The Court further reasoned that the "rigid 'general acceptance' requirement would be at odds with the 'liberal thrust' of the Federal Rules and their general approach of relaxing the traditional barriers to opinion testimony" (*Daubert v. Merrell Dow Pharmaceuticals*, 1993, citing *Beech Aircraft Corporation v. Rainey*, 1988).

The rejection of the *Frye* test as the appropriate standard for determining admissibility did not vitiate the trial court's responsibility to screen expert testimony prior to its introduction into evidence. The Supreme Court held that Rule 702 obligated the trial court to maintain some gatekeeping role to ensure that all scientific testimony or evidence be both relevant and reliable (*Daubert v. Merrell Dow Pharmaceuticals*, 1993). In connection with the gatekeeping role, the trial judge must first determine, pursuant to Rule 104(a)[4], whether the expert is proposing to testify to (1) scientific knowledge that (2) will assist the jury to understand or determine a fact in issue (*Daubert v. Merrell Dow Pharmaceuticals*, 1993). This two-part test requires the trial court to make a preliminary assessment of whether the reasoning or methodology underlying the testimony is scientifically

---

[4] Rule 104(a) provides that "[p]reliminary questions concerning the qualification of a person to be a witness, the existence of a privilege, or the admissibility of evidence shall be determined by the court. . . ."

valid and whether that reasoning or methodology can be properly applied to the facts in issue. In making this determination, there are four nonexclusive, flexible factors that trial courts should consider:

1. Whether the technique or theory can be or has been tested—that is, whether the expert's theory can be challenged in an objective sense as opposed to it simply being a subjective or conclusory theory that is not amenable to assessment for reliability.
2. Whether the theory or technique has been subjected to peer review and publication. As for publication, which is an element of peer review, it is not necessarily correlative to reliability because innovative, well-grounded theories may not have been published. But as for peer review, allowing the scientific community to have an opportunity to scrutinize the theory is a component of good science because it increases the chances of detection of flaws in methodology.
3. Whether potential rate of error is known.
4. Whether the theory is generally accepted in the scientific community (*Daubert v. Merrell Dow Pharmaceuticals*, 1993).

In making its determination, the trial court must focus solely on principles and methodology, not on the conclusions that they generate (*Daubert v. Merrell Dow Pharmaceuticals*, 1993). Additionally, an expert witness may base his or her opinion or inference on inadmissible hearsay only if the facts or data are of the type reasonably relied upon by experts in the field in forming opinions or inferences on the subject (*Daubert v. Merrell Dow Pharmaceuticals*, 1993). With respect to shaky but admissible evidence, cross-examination, presentation of contrary evidence, and a jury charge on the burden of proof sufficiently address such concerns (*Daubert v. Merrell Dow Pharmaceuticals*, 1993).

Additional criteria have been developed by courts applying *Daubert* as factors relevant for courts in implementing their gatekeeping function. These factors include:

1. Whether experts are proposing to testify about matters growing naturally and directly out of research they have conducted independent of the litigation, or whether they have developed their opinions for the purpose of rendering testimony (*Daubert v. Merrell Dow Pharmaceuticals*, 1993).
2. Whether the expert has unjustifiably extrapolated from an accepted premise to a groundless conclusion (*General Electric Co. v. Joiner*, 1997).
3. Whether the expert has sufficiently accounted for obvious alternative explanations (*Claar v. Burlington N.R.R.*, 1994).
4. Whether in rendering an opinion the expert has adhered to the same standards of intellectual rigor that are demanded in his or her professional work (*Kumho Tire Co., Ltd. v. Carmichael*, 1999).

Although *Daubert* limited its discussion to the scientific context, it noted that Rule 702 is not limited in similar nature and also applies to technical or other specialized skill. In 1999, the U.S. Supreme Court resolved the uncertainty among district courts about whether the *Daubert* analysis applies to expert testimony, which is characterized as based on technical or other specialized knowledge. In *Kumho Tire Company, Ltd. v. Carmichael*, the Supreme Court held that *Daubert's* gatekeeping obligation, requiring a determination of both relevance and reliability, applies broadly to the admissibility of all expert testimony. Although *Kumho* clarifies the applicability of *Daubert*, it does not set forth a higher standard of admissibility than that which existed under *Daubert*.

Application of *Daubert* in State Courts

Because the *Daubert* decision is based on the interpretation of the Federal Rules of Evidence, its analysis and two-part test is binding only in the determination of admissibility of expert testimony in federal courts. The majority of states have statutorily adopted Rule 702 (Kessler & Koritzinsky, 1996) and apply *Daubert* as highly persuasive authority (John, 1994, citing Imwinkelried, 1993). Other states, including Georgia, which have not expressly adopted Rule 702, have looked to *Daubert* in analyzing and/or establishing their own standards governing admissibility of expert testimony (see, e.g., *Orkin Exterminating Company, Inc., vs. Carder et al.*, 1994; *Jordan v. Georgia Power Company*, 1995; *Norfolk Southern Railway Company v. Baker*, 1999). In Georgia, for example, "[t]he opinions of experts on any question of science, skill, trade or like questions shall always be admissible; and such opinions may be given on the facts as proved by other witnesses" (OCGA 24-9-67). "Provided an expert witness is properly qualified in the field in which he offers testimony, and the facts relied upon are within the bounds of the evidence, whether there is sufficient knowledge upon which to base an opinion or whether it is based upon hearsay goes to the weight and credibility of the testimony, not its admissibility" (*Orkin Exterminating Company, Inc., v. Carder et al.*, 1994). Challenges to the conclusions drawn by an expert from testimony and evidence are a matter for the jury's determination and do not affect the admissibility of the expert testimony (*Orkin Exterminating Company, Inc., v. Carder et al.*, 1994).

In 1982, the Georgia Supreme Court set forth in *Harper v. State* the standard for admissibility for expert testimony regarding scientific procedures or techniques: "With respect to a particular scientific procedure or technique, the trial court makes a determination 'whether the procedure or technique in question has reached a scientific stage of verifiable certainty,' based upon evidence, expert testimony, treatises, or the rationale of cases in other jurisdictions." In making its determination, the trial court relies on the evidence available to it and cannot simply calculate the consensus in the scientific community. In reaching the standard for admissibility, the Georgia Supreme Court expressly rejected the *Frye* test of general acceptance in the scientific community as an inappropriate rule of "counting heads" in the scientific community (*Harper v. State*, 1982). The *Harper* standard for admissibility is limited to expert testimony relating to scientific principles (*Cromartie v. State*, 1999). The question of what type of evidence constitutes scientific evidence subject to the *Harper* standard of admissibility has not been directly decided by Georgia courts. The types of expert testimony to which the *Harper* standard has been applied includes the existence of a possible genetic basis for violent and impulsive behavior in certain individuals (*Mobley v. State*, 1995); the phenomenon of sleep talking (*Godfrey v. State*, 1988); penile plethysmograph test designed to measure changes in the circumference of the subject's penis to determine physiological changes in blood flow (*Gentry v. State*, 1994); and the "child sexual abuse accommodation syndrome" (*Rolader v. State*, 1991).

Analysis

All expert testimony is subject to the federal courts' gatekeeping function in ensuring that all expert testimony received in evidence is both relevant and reliable. Experts in all fields of scientific, technical, and other specialized knowledge and skill expecting to testify in federal courts and in state jurisdictions that have adopted Rule 702 can count on challenges to their testimony based on challenges to the principles and methodology applied. Of course, the safest way of ensuring that the testimony will be admissible is to base the opinion on methodology customarily employed by an expert in the field. However, reliance on methodology customarily used is not always possible depending on the nature of the case. Accordingly, in analyzing the issues regarding which he or she is requested to render an opinion, the expert should focus on the factual basis for his or her opinion; the objective, verifiable methodology employed in reaching a conclusion; the sources or data reviewed and relied upon and whether the same is customarily relied upon by other experts in the field; the bases for any assumptions; the link between the accepted premise and the conclusion (i.e., eliminating the danger of misapplication of the accepted premise); and consideration and exclusion of other potential causes for the injury or damages (*Diviero v. Uniroyal Tire Co.*, 1996). It is important to note that expert testimony will be found to be particularly suspect where it appears that the expert reached a conclusion first and then sought to gather supporting material (*Claar v. Burlington N.R.R.*, 1994). Here, the expert appears to be a "hired gun" forcing a fit between a conclusion beneficial to the proponent of the testimony and the specific facts of the case.

INVOLUNTARY CIVIL COMMITMENT

Involuntary civil commitment is the process by which persons who have been determined to be a danger to themselves or others are hospitalized against their will, even in the absence of the commission of a criminal act. Civil commitment differs from criminal commitment in that the former contemplates a threat of harm in the future, whereas the latter governs confinement for criminal acts already committed. The authority to involuntarily commit dangerous persons derives from the state's police power and *parens patriae*, that is, the state's sovereign power of guardianship over persons under disability, such as minors and insane and incompetent persons (Freedman, 1988; *Black's Law Dictionary*, 1968, p. 264). The state's police power authorizes it to enact laws to protect the health, welfare, and safety of the general community. The state's status as *parens patriae* empowers it to act on behalf of and in the best interest of persons who lack the capacity to do the same. All 50 states and the District of Columbia provide for laws by which an individual may be civilly committed against his or her will in a mental institution based on some showing that the individual is suffering from a mental disorder. Involuntary civil commitment is one of the means by which a psychotherapist may discharge his or her duty to exercise reasonable care to protect third parties against threatened violence confidentially communicated by a patient. The threshold procedural requirements for securing involuntary civil commitment vary greatly from state to state, and practitioners are encouraged to refer to the local law applicable to their practice for the specific procedures and requirements.[5] However, the consensus among the states generally limits involuntary commitment to those persons suffering from mental disorders who are diagnosed to be dangerous to themselves or others.

Rights of Mental Patients

Involuntary civil commitment has been criticized as constituting a violation of a person's constitutional right to liberty and right to the due process of law. Concern over mental health patients' rights has resulted in both legislative and judicial action responding to concerns relating to patients' right to minimum standards for environmental conditions in mental health institutions, right to treatment, and right to refuse treatment. The most notable legislative action took place in 1980, when the U.S. Congress passed the Mental Health Systems Act, which included provisions such as minimization of restrictions on patients, access to medical records, reasonable explanation of treatment, and right to refuse treatment (Sue, Sue, & Sue, 2000). Judicial action has taken the form of recognition and enforcement of patients' constitutional rights to treatment and to refuse treatment, topics that are discussed in the following sections.

Right to Treatment

The concept of the *right to treatment* provides that persons who have been involuntarily committed have a right to mental health therapy to improve their mental

---

[5] Because the various state jurisdictions differ significantly on the threshold procedural requirements for securing proper involuntary civil commitment, the examination of the same requires a detailed and comprehensive analysis beyond the scope of this chapter.

condition so that, where possible, they may return to their normal lives. The right-to-treatment concept also recognizes that a person cannot be the subject of involuntary civil commitment without some parameters on the general conditions of mental health institutions. In three landmark decisions, *Rouse v. Cameron*, *Wyatt v. Stickney*, and *O'Connor v. Donaldson*, the courts recognized the right to treatment and established additional policy concerns. In *Rouse v. Cameron*, the court held that the right to treatment is a constitutional right and that the state's failure to provide the same cannot be justified by a lack of resources. *Wyatt v. Stickney* went one step further and held that not only does a patient have a constitutional right to treatment, but the mental health institution must conform to a specified minimum level of appropriate living conditions and mental health treatment. The court held that the purpose of involuntary civil commitment is not custodial care or punishment, but treatment, and denial of the same constitutes a violation of the patient's constitutional right to liberty. In addition, the court held that the practice of requiring patients to engage in physical labor to maintain the condition of the institution was unconstitutional and could only be offered on a voluntary basis with financial compensation for the same. In *O'Connor v. Donaldson*, the U.S. Supreme Court held that nondangerous persons who are capable of caring for themselves outside the mental institution or who have family or friends willing to assist in their care cannot be confined against their will. The Supreme Court held that mental illness alone, without a showing of a threat of danger to self or others, cannot justify confinement in violation of a person's constitutional right to liberty. Furthermore, the mere fact that the state can ensure a higher living standard in an institution versus the community at large is insufficient to justify involuntary confinement.

Right to Refuse Treatment

Like the right-to-treatment concept, the concept of a patient's *right to refuse treatment* is based on a person's constitutional rights to liberty and due process (*Rennie v. Klein*, 1981). Courts have held that a patient who has not been involuntarily committed has a right to refuse the administration of drugs against his or her will (*Rennie v. Klein*, 1981). The state cannot circumvent patients' right to due process by seizing their persons and administering drugs without their consent. Involuntary civil commitment has been recognized as a "massive curtailment of liberty." Patients who have been involuntarily committed have a constitutional right to liberty that guarantees their right to refuse antipsychotic drugs having long-term or permanent disabling side effects. The right to be free from treatment by antipsychotic drugs may be limited only by a less intrusive infringement that does not exceed that required by needed care or by legitimate administrative concerns. A person's right to liberty may be diminished by involuntary confinement only to that extent necessary to prevent the person from being a danger to himself or to others. Additionally, the confinement cannot be more restrictive than necessary and cannot continue upon termination of the mental condition (*Rennie v. Klein*, 1981).

CRIMINAL COMMITMENT

Criminal commitment is the imprisonment of mentally impaired individuals who have either pled guilty to or have been found guilty by a jury of one or more criminal offenses. Generally, two significant issues arise with respect to the offender's mental health in the criminal commitment process: (1) the offender's competency to stand trial; and (2) defenses to criminal responsibility based on mental state of the offender at the time of the act.

Competency to Stand Trial

Based on constitutional law and common law principles, the cardinal rule has been that an incompetent person cannot be required to stand trial and be convicted in a criminal proceeding (Dunlap, 1997). The concept of *competency to stand trial* deals not with the defendant's mental state at the time the crime was committed, but with the mental state during the time after arrest and before and during trial. Where the psychiatric evaluation concludes that the defendant does not possess a "sufficient present ability" to consult with a lawyer with a "reasonable degree of rational understanding" and, further, that the defendant does not possess "a rational as well as factual understanding of the proceedings against [him or her]", the defendant is considered legally incompetent to stand trial (Dunlap, 1997, citing *Dusky v. United States*, 1960). Essentially, the psychiatric evaluation is aimed at determining whether a defendant is able to understand the nature of the proceedings against him or her and is able to assist in his or her defense. Although the psychiatrist's role in the issue of a defendant's competency to stand trial is generally implicated prior to the commencement of trial, the U.S. Supreme Court has held that the courts have a continuing obligation to make an inquiry into the defendant's competence where, during a criminal trial, sufficient doubt exists as to the same based on the presence of one or more of the following factors bearing on the defendant's competence: (1) evidence of irrational behavior, (2) conduct during trial, and (3) prior testimony regarding competence (Dunlap, 1997, citing *Drope v. Missouri*, 1974). Where a defendant is determined to be incompetent to stand trial, criminal proceedings are stayed pending mental health treatment and restoration to the legal level necessary for competency to stand trial (Winick, 1985).

In addition, a criminal defendant must be competent when confronted with the issues of whether to plead guilty to the criminal charges and whether to waive right to counsel. The standard for determining competence to plead guilty and waive right to counsel is identical to the standard for determining competence to stand trial. However, because a criminal defendant's waiver of rights must be knowing and voluntary, the criminal defendant must be shown to have more than just the ability to understand the proceeding and must actually understand the significance and consequences of a decision and must reach the same free of coercion.

Defendant's Mental State during the Commission of the Crime

The Insanity Defense

The defense of *insanity* is based on the premise that those who are mentally disturbed or insane cannot be held criminally responsible for their acts because they lack the requisite intent to complete the elements of a crime (Robitscher & Haynes, 1982). Several legal standards have been established to assess the defendant's sanity to be held criminally accountable for his or her acts: (1) the *M'Naghten* rule, (2) the irresistible impulse test, (3) the *Durham* standard, and (4) the Model Penal Code test (Sue, Sue, & Sue, 2000). The definition of the legal standards for determining the defendant's sanity at the time the crime was committed is important because it provides guidance and relevant parameters to the psychiatrist's substantive evaluation of the defendant. The *M'Naghten* rule, commonly referred to as the *right-wrong test*, provides that defendants who, because of a mental impairment, are unable to understand the nature or quality of their conduct (i.e., did not know what they were doing at the time they committed the crime) or are unable to comprehend right from wrong cannot be held criminally responsible for their acts. The *irresistible impulse test* provides that a defendant must be acquitted where, because of a mental impairment, he or she lacked the will power to control his or her acts. The *Durham* test, also known as the *products test*, requires a determination of whether the criminal act was the product of a mental disease or defect. Finally, the Model Penal Code, established by the American Law Institute, set forth the standard for determining insanity as follows: A person is not responsible for his or her criminal acts if, at the time of the acts and as a result of a mental disease or defect, he or she lacked substantial capacity to appreciate the criminality of this conduct or to conform this conduct to lawful parameters (Sue, Sue, & Sue, 2000).

Diminished Capacity

The doctrine of *diminished capacity* is a modification of the insanity defense and was established to deal with cases wherein the defendant's mental impairment at the time of the criminal act did not rise to the level of legal insanity (Robitscher & Haynes, 1982). Diminished capacity differs from the previously defined legal standards for determining insanity because it deals with the question not of *whether* the defendant should be held criminally responsible for his or her acts, but *to what degree* he or she should be held responsible. The defense of diminished capacity enables the defendant to get a conviction for a lesser offense or to get a reduced penalty for the crime.

Guilty But Mentally Ill

The plea of *guilty but mentally ill* is the result of legislative modifications of the insanity defense designed to ensure that the convicted offender is institutionalized and given treatment for the abnormal mental condition (Robitscher & Haynes, 1982). States having adopted the plea aim to hold criminals accountable for their acts while providing the necessary treatment for their abnormal mental condition. The plea does not entitle the defendant to a reduced penalty or to a conviction for a lesser offense but simply makes certain that the mentally impaired defendant receives the appropriate treatment for the illness. In some respects, the guilty but mentally ill plea is similar to the defense of diminished capacity, with the distinguishing factor being that the latter does not envision mental health treatment for the abnormal offender.

Psychiatrists and other mental health professionals are encouraged to refer to the law applicable to their practice to confirm the applicable legal standard in assessing the defendant's sanity to be held criminally responsible for his acts.

Duality and Sexual Relationships with Clients

Considered one of the most egregious violations of ethical standards, the issue of personal and sexual relationships between patients and their psychotherapists has recently been receiving increasing and widespread attention (Sue, Sue, & Sue, 2000). Complaints regarding therapists' sexual misconduct with their patients have increased significantly in recent years. The American Psychological Association, recognizing that engaging in a sexual relationship with patients is a serious obstacle to the patient's treatment and recovery, has stated flatly: "Psychologists do not engage in sexual intimacies with current patients or clients." An obvious adverse impact on the patient results from the therapist's exploitation of the patient's vulnerability and the inequity in mental and emotional powers between the therapist and the patient. Personal involvement with patients is further condemned because of the therapist's inability to remain objective during the patient's treatment and recovery.

A nationwide survey conducted in 1977 indicated that sexual intimacy is most prevalent between a female patient and a male therapist (Sue, Sue, & Sue, 2000). Of the 5.5 percent of male therapists and 0.6 percent of female therapists who had previously engaged in sexual relations with patients, 80 percent were likely to be repeat offenders. From the 500 male and 500 female respondents to the survey, 70 percent of the male therapists and 88 percent of the female therapists agreed that sexual intimacy with patients is detrimental to the patient. On the other hand, in a survey of 559 patients who had previously had sexual involvement with their therapists, 90 percent reported adverse emotional consequences resulting from the same. The Committee on Women in Psychology of the American Psychological Association issued a statement that clients can never be deemed to have consented to sexual relationships with their therapists and that such conduct on the part of therapists should never be excused.

Therapists who have engaged in improper sexual relationships with their patients are generally held accountable on two levels: (1) in civil suits filed by their patient alleging professional malpractice; and (2) in the applicable state agency or licensing board empowered to conduct reviews of ethical complaints (Sue, Sue, &

Sue, 2000). Malpractice actions require proof upon a preponderance of the evidence of the following elements: (1) the existence of a professional relationship whereby the therapist agrees to render treatment for the mental health of the patient; (2) breach of a duty of care owed by the therapist to the patient; (3) injury or damage to the patient; and (4) a causal connection between the breach of duty and the resultant injury or damage. Very often, civil suits for malpractice yield successful monetary recoveries because very seldom do courts deem the vulnerable, emotionally unstable patient to have consented to the sexual relationship.

MEMORY ENHANCEMENT TECHNIQUES: REPRESSED MEMORIES

Gaining widespread attention in the mid-1980s, the concept of recovered repressed memories initially went generally unchallenged and was understood to be an accurate and truthful recount of past events (Leo, 1997). Many recounts related to child molestation and sexual abuse, alien abductions, and bizarre satanic rituals including infant sacrifices (Parnell, 1996). To respond to the significant number of such recovered repressed memory reports, a majority of states enacted statutes allowing suits to be filed within a certain time period after the alleged victim of abuse *remembers* the events, as opposed to a certain period after the occurrence of the event, resulting in a near-unlimited statute of limitations (Leo, 1997). A statute of limitations sets forth a specific time within which a suit shall be brought after the right accrued. Because victims' confrontation of their alleged abusers by the filing of lawsuits is advocated by recovered memory therapists as an effective path toward recovery, around one in every 16 cases of recovered repressed memories results in a lawsuit (Leo, 1997).

However, experience proves that memory enhancement techniques have the potential of causing, and do actually cause, false memories of abuse that patients are convinced to be true (Leo, 1997). Some studies indicate that implanting false memories of disturbing events is a relatively easy task (Parnell, 1996). A large number of individuals who initially recounted, through recovered repressed memories, events related to childhood sexual abuse have subsequently realized them to be false and have retracted their claims (Parnell, 1996). The American Medical Association (AMA) has issued warnings against the use of memory enhancement techniques such as guided visualization, sodium amytal ("truth serum"), and hypnosis as being "fraught with problems of potential misapplication" (Parnell, 1996). Upon direction by the AMA, the Council on Scientific Affairs investigated issues concerning memory enhancement techniques and commented upon the potential for their misapplication, recommending that the uncertain authenticity of recovered repressed memories necessitates verification and corroboration. Additionally, in 1993 the Board of Trustees of the American Psychiatric Association issued a statement asserting that because many adults had reported false recovered memories of childhood sexual abuse, corroboration of such recounts is necessary and that, absent the same, the accuracy and validity of such recovered repressed memories could not be determined (Parnell, 1996).

Legal Liability of Therapists

As a result of implantation of false memories of childhood abuse, many retractors and, where state law permits, third parties wrongly accused of child molestation have filed lawsuits against therapists for implantation of false memories of childhood sexual abuse (Parnell, 1996). Where state law permits, third-party actions have been lodged against the therapist, most commonly setting forth causes of action in negligent and/or intentional infliction of emotional distress and malpractice.

Infliction of Emotional Distress

In negligent infliction of emotional distress claims generally, a purely emotional injury is not compensable in the absence of some physical impact upon the plaintiff (Whitesell, 1996–97). In recent years, California and Colorado have dispensed with the necessity of alleging and proving a physical injury based on the rationale that the physical injury requirement is an outdated concept in cases where the plaintiff establishes a causal connection between the foreseeable emotional suffering by a foreseeable plaintiff (Whitesell, 1996–97, citing *Molien v. Kaiser Foundation Hospitals*, 1980, and *Montoya v. Bebensee*, 1988). *Intentional infliction of emotional distress* is defined as the intentional or reckless infliction, by extreme and outrageous conduct, of severe emotional or mental distress. A cause of action for intentional infliction of emotional distress allows monetary recovery for damages resulting from purely emotional injuries because it does not require the existence of any bodily harm. The federal court for the eastern district of Pennsylvania held that in certain circumstances therapists owe an independent duty to the parents of a minor patient to refrain from intentionally inflicting emotional suffering upon the parents (Whitesell, 1996–97, citing *Tuman v. Genesis*, 1997). Colorado has upheld the viability of a parent's claim for intentional infliction of emotion distress where the therapist's actions were not undertaken in good faith and amounted to outrageous conduct (Whitesell, 1996–97, citing *Montoya v. Bebensee*, 1988). Additionally, a federal court sitting in Illinois upheld a third-party action against a therapist for intentional infliction of emotional distress resulting from implantation of false memories of child sexual abuse, asserting that a jury should decide whether the therapist's actions amounted to extreme and outrageous conduct (*Lindgren v. Moore*, 1995).

Malpractice

Generally, courts have been reluctant to allow third-party malpractice actions against health-care professionals on grounds that no duty of care is owed to persons other than the patient (Leo, 1997). In recent years, however, more courts have been willing to hold health-care professionals liable for the foreseeable consequences of their negligent acts on third parties. For example, some courts have held that a health-care professional owes a duty to warn identifiable third parties of contagious diseases. Additionally, health-care professionals may be liable to third parties for failing to advice their patients of a prescribed drug's side effects that result in impaired driving ability (Leo, 1997).

The elements of a malpractice claim are (1) a duty of care to conform to the applicable standard of care to protect against unreasonable harm, (2) breach of the duty of care by failing to conform to the applicable standard of care, (3) causal connection between the breach and the resulting harm, and (4) damages (Whitesell, 1996–97). In medical malpractice cases, the professional must have that minimum-level knowledge, skill, and care ordinarily possessed and employed by members of the profession, generally. A bad result is not necessarily tantamount to malpractice where the conduct under complaint is in compliance with good or customary practice.

Whether to allow third-party actions for malpractice in misdiagnosing child sexual abuse has been based primarily on public policy concerns. Very few states have addressed the issue and are divided on the existence of a duty of care to the accused third parties. New York and Pennsylvania have recognized that certain mental health professionals owe a duty of care to an alleged sexual abuser for negligently misdiagnosing sexual abuse (Casperson, 1998). Colorado, California, Texas, and Illinois have applied statutory immunity for a professional's report to appropriate authorities of child sexual abuse. Texas has additionally held that a mental health professional owes no duty of care to the parent. Arkansas addressed the issue in 1975 and held that no cause of action existed because no physician-patient relationship existed where the child was treated on behalf of the mother. Finally, Connecticut held that a psychiatrist owed no duty of care to the third party for misdiagnosing child abuse (Casperson, 1998).

Courts that have allowed third-party actions against therapists for implantation of false memories of childhood sexual abuse have focused primarily on the concept of foreseeability and have held that harm to the wrongly accused abuser resulting from the misdiagnosis (in many cases, the patient's parent) is undoubtedly foreseeable (Whitesell, 1996–97). The courts have held that the risk and severity of injury is too significant in light of the emotional, economic, and reputational harm of an innocent family member. Often the family is torn apart, with the innocent parent not only losing contact with loved ones, but also being convicted on criminal charges and serving jail time. The innocent family member, unable to cope with the emotional distress resulting from the wrongful accusation of such a horrendous crime, often ends up committing suicide. The severity of consequences on the patient as well as the alleged abuser resulting from accusations of this nature demand that the therapist approach treatment carefully and in a nonnegligent manner. The courts have further reasoned that the threat of third-party actions against therapists for misdiagnosis has a deterrent effect that motivates therapists to properly examine and test recovered repressed memories to minimize false accusations. On the other hand, courts finding against the existence of a duty of care have held that the risk of injury to a wrongfully accused parent is far outweighed by the social utility of mental health professionals' ability to exercise their independent professional judgment in diagnosing child abuse without the fear of having suits filed against them by the alleged abusers (Whitesell, 1996–97). Because of the social utility in reporting child abuse, all states have enacted statutes making it mandatory for health-care professionals to report all incidents of child abuse and granting limited immunity from civil suits for the same (Casperson, 1998).

Expert Testimony and Recovered Repressed Memories

In states that have enacted favorable laws relating to statute of limitations allowing lawsuits to be filed against the abuser based on recovered repressed memories long after the alleged violation, expert testimony may be required on the theory of repressed memory to help the jury in understanding the concept. As set forth earlier, federal courts and the majority of state courts, having adopted *Daubert*, must perform a gatekeeping function in determining the admissibility of such expert testimony. Among the factors set forth by *Daubert* in determining admissibility, the courts must consider the known potential rate of error of the theory, whether the theory has attained general acceptance in the scientific community, whether the theory can be or has been objectively tested, and whether the theory has been subjected to peer review and publication. However, research on repressed memory has failed to yield any empirical support for the same (Leo, 1997). Furthermore, the scientific community is very much divided on the validity of the concept and the legitimacy and accuracy of recovered repressed memories. Undoubtedly, these concerns will have a negative impact on the admissibility of expert testimony to support a suit prompted by recovered repressed memories.

INTERNET PSYCHOTHERAPY

The increased popularity of the Internet has affected almost every facet of a person's day-to-day life. Every business and profession has benefited to some extent from riding the information superhighway. The mental health profession has made significant advances in making mental health therapy more readily available via the Internet. Internet psychotherapy differs from radio or television psychotherapy or from newspaper advice columns because it enables a one-on-one, individualized, longer-term treatment plan. Though it is highly unlikely that Internet psychotherapy will replace the traditional forms of mental health treatment, it is becoming increasingly popular because it facilitates a cost-effective, geographically unlimited, and temporally unimposing means of obtaining mental health therapy (Pergament, 1998). Persons with busy schedules or persons living in small communities who do not have ready access to a psychotherapist can benefit from the ready access to mental health treatment via the Internet.

Additionally, persons with certain phobias, such as agoraphobia, can maintain a regular treatment plan from the comfort of their home.

Because the legal issues surrounding Internet psychotherapy are generally unexplored by the courts or the legislatures, raising practitioners' general awareness of the key legal implications arising from the rendering of mental health care via the Internet is of paramount concern. Internet psychotherapy has virtually no geographic limitations. Accordingly, the primary concern for mental health professionals is the determination of the applicable law governing their practice. Is it sufficient for mental health professionals to maintain a license to practice in their state of residence or must they additionally obtain a license to practice in every state in which their various Internet patients reside? California has addressed this question and requires psychotherapists rendering professional services to California residents via Internet to be licensed in the state of California (California Board of Behavioral Services, 2003). Additionally, legal principles relating to their practice will vary largely depending on the applicable state and/or federal laws. For instance, the duty to warn, which exposes mental health professionals to significant civil liability, transforms depending on the law of the applicable state. Accordingly, must mental health professionals govern their practice in accordance with the legal principles of the state of their residence or on a case-by-case basis depending on their patients' state of residence? In rendering professional services via the Internet, the mental health professional must always be mindful of rendering services within the bounds of the law by first ascertaining the law applicable to the same.

REFERENCES

Airone, T. J. (1995, Summer). Hedonic damages and the admissibility of expert testimony in Connecticut after *Daubert v. Merrell Dow Pharmaceuticals, Inc. Quarterly Law Review*, *15*, 235, n. 77.
American Mutual Liability Insurance Co. v. King, 88 Ga. App. 176, 76 S.E.2d 81 (1953).
Atlantic Coast Line Railway v. Smith, 107 Ga. App. 384, 130 S.E.2d 355 (1963).
Beech Aircraft Corp. v. Rainey, 488 U.S. 153, 169, 109 S.Ct. 439, 450 (1988).
Brown v. State, 245 Ga. 588, 266 S.E.2d 198 (1980).
California Board of Behavioral Services. (2003, January 24). Notice to California consumers regarding psychotherapy on the Internet. http://www.bbs.ca.gov/comp-5.htm.
Casperson, D. (1998). False accusations of childhood sexual abuse: Who should pay the price? *UMKC Law Review*, *67*, 387, 388, n. 6.
Claar v. Burlington N.R.R., 29 F.3d 499 (9th Cir. 1994).
Cromartie v. State, 270 Ga. 780, 1999 Ga. Lexis 262 (1999).
Daubert v. Merrell Dow Pharmaceuticals, Inc., 113 S.Ct. 2786, 509 U.S. 579 (1993).
Dimambro Northend Association v. Williams, 169 Ga. App. 219, 312 S.E.2d 386 (1983).
Drope v. Missouri, 420 U.S. 162 (1974).

Dunlap, J. A. (1997). What's competence got to do with it: The right not to be acquitted by reason of insanity. *Oklahoma Law Review, 50,* 495, 499.

Dusky v. United States, 362 U.S. 402 (1960).

Freedman, F. A. (1988). The psychiatrist's dilemma: Protect the public or safeguard individual liberty? *University of Puget Sound Law Review, 11,* 255, 258.

Frye v. United States, 54 App. D.C. 46, 47, 293 F. 1013, 1014 (1923).

Gammon, T. E., & Hulston, J. K. (1995). The duty of mental health care providers to restrain their patients or warn third parties. *Missouri Law Review, 60,* 749, 751.

General Electric Co. v. Joiner, 118 S.Ct. 512, 519 (1997).

Gentry v. State of Georgia, 213 Ga. App. 24, 443 S.E.2d 667 (1994).

Godfrey v. State of Georgia, 258 Ga. 28, 365 S.E.2d 93 (1988).

Godinez v. Moran, 509 U.S. 389 (1992).

Goldstein, A. S., & Katz, J. (1962). Psychiatrist-patient privilege: The GAP proposal and the Connecticut statute, *Connecticut B.J. 36,* 175.

Harper v. State of Georgia, 249 Ga. 519, 525(1), 292 S.E.2d 389 (1982).

Harris, G. C. (1999). The dangerous patient exception to the psychotherapist-patient privilege: The *Tarasoff* duty and the Jaffee footnote. *Washington Law Review, 74,* 33, 47.

Hyles v. Cockrill, 169 Ga. App. 132, 312 S.E.2d 124 (1983).

Imwinkelried, E. J. (1993). The *Daubert* decision: Frye is dead, long live the Federal Rules of Evidence. *Trial,* 64.

Jaffee v. Redmond, 116 S. Ct. 1923 (1996).

Johnson, K. C. (1994). Exiting the Twilight Zone: Changes in the standard for the admissibility of scientific evidence in Georgia. *Georgia State University Law Review, 10,* 401.

Jones v. State of Georgia, 232 Ga. 762, 208 S.E.2d 850 (1974).

Jordan v. Georgia Power Company, 219 Ga. App. 690, 466 S.E.2d 601 (1995).

Kessler, J. F., & Koritzinsky, A. R. (1996, Summer). Guide your expert through the thicket. *Sum Fam. Advoc. 19,* 29.

Klein, J. S. (1995). "I'm your therapist, you can tell me anything": The Supreme Court confirms the psychotherapist-patient privilege in *Jaffee v. Redmond. Depaul Law Review 47,* 701, 720–721 nn. 166–172.

Kumho Tire Company, Ltd. v. Carmichael, 119 S.Ct. 1167, 1176 (1999).

Lamkin, A. D. (1995). Recent development: Evidentiary privileges: Should psychotherapist-patient privilege be recognized? *American Journal of Trial Advocacy, 18,* 721, 723–725.

Leo, R. A. (1997). The social and legal construction of repressed memory. *Law and Social Inquiry, 22,* 653, 666.

Lindgren v. Moore, 907 F. Supp. 1183 (N.D.Ill. 1995).

Longshore v. State of Georgia, 242 Ga. 689, 251 S.E.2d 280 (1978).

Mobley v. State of Georgia, 265 Ga. 292, 455 S.E.2d 61 (1995).

Molien v. Kaiser Foundation Hospitals, 616 P.2d 813 (Cal. 1980).

Montoya v. Bebensee, 761 P.2d 285 (Colo. Ct. App. 1988).

Nielsen, W. J. (1997). Privileged communications: The psychotherapist-patient privilege as adopted in the federal courts includes not only all communications to licensed psychiatrists and psychologists, but also all communications to licensed social workers in the course of psychotherapy—*Jaffee v. Redmond. Seton Hall Law Review, 27,* 1123–1126.

Norfolk Southern Railway Company v. Baker, 237 Ga. App. 292, 514 S.E.2d 448 (1999).
O'Connor v. Donaldson, 422 U.S. 563 (1975).
Oregon v. Miller, 709 P.2d 225 (1985).
Orkin Exterminating Company, Inc., v. Carder et al., 215 Ga. App. 587, 452 S.E.2d 159 (1994).
Owen v. Bair, 137 Ga. App. 30, 223 S.E.2d 8 (1975).
Parnell, C. S. (1996). Trial report: Third party suits against therapists for implanting false memory of childhood molestation. *American Jury Trials*, *57*, 313, § 7.
Pergament, D. (1998). Internet psychotherapy: Current status and future regulation. *Health Matrix*, *8*, 233, 237–238.
Posin, M. L. (1988). Psychotherapist's liability for failure to protect third person. *American Jurist*, *2*.
Poulin, A. B. (1998). The psychotherapist-patient privilege after *Jaffee v. Redmond*: Where do we go from here? *Washington University Law Quarterly*, *76*, 1341, 1348.
Rennie v. Klein, 653 F.2d 836 (3rd Cir. N.J. 1981).
Robitscher, J., & Haynes, A. K. (1982). In defense of the insanity defense. *Emory Law Journal*, *31*, 9–60.
Rolader v. State of Georgia, 202 Ga. App. 134, 413 S.E.2d 752 (1991).
Rouse v. Cameron, 373 F.2d 451 (1967).
Sue, D., Sue, D. W., & Sue, S. (2000). *Understanding Abnormal Behavior* (6th ed.) (p. 567). Boston: Houghton Mifflin.
Tarasoff v. Regents of the University of California, 551 P.2d 324 (1976).
Tifton Brick & Block Co. v. Meadow, 92 Ga. App. 328, 88 S.E.2d 569 (1955).
Trammel v. United States, 445 U.S. 40, 53 (1980).
Tuman v. Genesis, 894 F. Supp. 183 (E.D.Pa. 1995).
Upjohn Co. v. United States, 449 U.S. 383, 389 (1981).
Whitesell, J. M. (1996–97). Ridicule or recourse: Parents falsely accused of past sexual abuse fight back. *Journal of Law and Health*, *11*, 303, 321.
Winick, B. J. (1985). Restructuring competency to stand trial. *UCLA Law Review*, *32*, 921, 924.
Wyatt v. Stickney, 325 F. Supp. 781 (M.D. Ala. 1971).

CHAPTER 2

AN INTRODUCTION TO PSYCHOLOGY FOR ATTORNEYS

WILLIAM T. O'DONOHUE, KENDRA BEITZ, AND ERIC R. LEVENSKY
UNIVERSITY OF NEVADA, RENO

It is the thesis of this chapter that when an attorney comes into contact with a psychologist, or even considers this possibility, he or she needs to properly understand the nature of psychology, even the "best" psychology (evidence/theory based), in order to have an optimal interaction or collaboration. Psychology has unique limitations as well as unique contributions. Some attorneys may have expectations of psychologists that are too high. For example, attorneys may liken psychologists to physicists or engineers who use universal laws found in the natural sciences, and therefore assume that psychologists can make point predictions or opine with certainty or near certainty about some state of affairs. Others may think that psychology is only an art, a matter of mere taste and opinion with no empirical basis, and that therefore psychologists are substantively useless (except maybe for purposes of obfuscation) because there is no knowledge in their field. We argue that both of these positions are wrong and that the value of psychology lies somewhere in the middle: It is a science and an art, and the best psychologists can provide expertise that can be helpful in legal contexts. However, we also argue that psychology has a different status than some other sciences such as physics and chemistry and that one must properly understand the status of psychology in order to understand what are acceptable scientific conclusions and opinions versus what might be considered "junk science."

PSYCHOLOGY AS A SCIENCE

In order to understand psychology as a science, it is important to review several basic points about science. Philosophers of science have suggested that there are three kinds of scientific statements: descriptive, predictive, and explanatory. Psychological phenomena do lend themselves to description, prediction, and explanation, but in ways that are somewhat different from the phenomena studied by the natural sciences.

1. *Descriptive statements.* Take, for example, the statement: "This substance is pure iron and it has a mass of 1 kg." Or, in psychology: "This person is clinically depressed and currently reports no thoughts of suicide." These statements use general categories such as "matter," "elements," and "iron" and even use general verbs to discuss how these entities can legitimately relate to one another (e.g., "engage in electron transfer"). In the natural sciences, many of these categories and processes are settled issues. Controversy is only left at the cutting edge (e.g., Do quarks exist? Is cold fusion possible?). In psychology, however, there is much more debate about these basic matters (Kuhn, 1972). Psychologists can often be placed in schools or, in Kuhn's less flattering terms, "preparadigmatic factions." Psychologists can mention entities such as "id," "self-actualization," and "mands" that other psychologists from other schools think either don't exist or are problematic terms to describe some actual phenomenon. Psychologists can also describe processes that other psychologists think either do not happen or are poor descriptors of what is actually happening (e.g., "countertransference," "altering in a multiple personality disorder," or "recovering a repressed memory"). Some philosophers of science have argued that scientists agree on pragmatic grounds on what kinds of entities there are and what kinds of processes there are. That is, whatever entities and processes result in the most order (e.g., accuracy at prediction) are taken to be the existents. The controversies in psychology, however, do not point out that there is no truth of the matter. We will discuss this issue more fully in the sections that follow.

2. *Predictive statements.* These are claims about either the future or the past (more technically, postdiction): This iron will rust (oxidize) if exposed to sufficient oxygen. Or, in psychology: "If this client cooperates with cognitive behavior therapy, he or she has a significantly increased chance of having depression remit within 16 weeks." Predictive statements depend upon a law—that is, a scientific regularity. Scientific laws are generally thought to be of two main types: *universal laws*—laws that stipulate that "All x without exception" ("All copper

conducts electricity") or *probabilistic laws* ("The probability of snow in Reno is greater in December than in June"). Probabilistic laws do not state an impossibility (e.g., in some particular year it may snow in June and not in December), but by either understanding other laws affecting the phenomenon or simply having accurate frequency records, probabilistic laws do make an accurate, substantive claim—that is, they reduce uncertainty.

3. *Explanatory statements.* These statements attempt to subsume some set of events under scientific laws. In other words, explanatory statements provide the reasons that events occurred the way they did. For example, the reason this object fell to the earth with this impact is that momentum is calculated by mass times velocity. The mass of the object is y and its terminal velocity was 18 meters/second, given that it fell from a height of 2 meters and the gravitation constant is 9 meters/sec^2. In psychology, there are few to no universal laws (see later). However, using probabilistic laws, psychologists can say: "If a child's tantrum behavior is ignored, then after an extinction burst there is a high probability (though not a certainty) that this behavior will decrease in frequency." Although there is some controversy in the philosophy of science about the nature of explanation, the most prevalent view is the *covering law model* of explanation in which events are explained by being subsumed under a more general law. Thus, our remarks in the preceding section about laws are also relevant here.

Before we discuss the issues relevant to forensic psychology for making accurate and useful statements in each of these categories, we would like to make a few general remarks about some of the logical and substantive issues involved in each of these kinds of statements.

The Scientific Method and Error Elimination

The philosopher of science Karl Popper and the psychologist and philosopher Donald Campbell have suggested that science begins with *fallibilism*—the notion that our current beliefs, despite the fact that they are "ours" and despite all the attractions that they hold for us, may still be wrong. (Fallibilism also applies to the previously stated belief; see Bartley [1984] for his comprehensive critical rationalism.) It is our thesis that psychologists who are in the tradition of science can add information to forensic settings by accurately depicting the strengths and weaknesses of various theories, interventions, claims, and the like as well as by accurately summarizing the scientific evidence that has attempted to find error with these.

When we are engaged in forensic practice, we can make the following kinds of errors:

1. *False descriptive statements:* A psychologist can claim, for example, that a client never thought of suicide in the preceding week when in fact she thought of it four times.

2. *False causal statements:* A psychologist can believe that a client's erectile dysfunction is caused by performance anxiety when in fact it is caused by a neurological problem.
3. *False ontic statements:* A psychologist can believe that things exist when in fact they do not. A psychologist can believe that there is something like an inner child when there is not.
4. *False relational claims:* A psychologist can believe that therapy X produces more change than therapy Y when this is not the case.
5. *False predictions:* A psychologist can believe that therapy X in certain situations will result in the greatest change for a client when it does not.
6. *False professional ethical claims:* A psychologist can believe that it is ethically permissible to have a certain kind of extratherapeutic relationship with a client when it is actually ethically impermissible.

Next, one must realize that *all professional forensic behavior is based upon knowledge claims*. That is, when a psychologist recommends that his or her client take test T to measure his depression, this act is based on a knowledge claim, to wit, that in this situation test T is the most accurate, cost-efficient manner for this client's depression to be measured. Furthermore, this act is based on the knowledge claim that the psychologist knows that it is a priority to measure the client's depression in this situation.

Psychological research employs scientific methodology, which is directly concerned with error and ways of eliminating error. A vigorous scientific attitude involves a desire to detect error in one's beliefs and to attempt to replace these beliefs with ones of greater accuracy. An assumption of psychometric assessment, for example, is that all measurement contains error. Statistical inference is concerned with errors or falsely rejecting the null hypotheses. Experimentation is concerned with valid (not invalid) causal inference. This is as it should be: We need to be worried that our confirmation biases and other heuristic errors may be influencing us to believe something we ought not to believe. Competent forensic practice involves utilizing those assessment strategies, interventions, and other techniques that have been shown to contain the least error.

The decision regarding what epistemic methods we should use has been made for us. Our profession, through its training model and through its ethical code, has explicitly stated that the way we seek to gain knowledge is through science. This is a wise decision because the application of science to problems has caused a historically unprecedented growth of knowledge. The problem is not that our profession is committed to a problematic epistemology. The problem is that too many psychologists' commitment to this epistemology has been too superficial, sporadic, and rhetorical. We conjecture that this may be due (beyond the seven deadly sins) to the failure to see the intimate connection among science, rationality, and the problem solving involved in life itself.

Next, we must realize that *epistemic errors in forensic clinical practice can cause serious harm*. When we make an untrue descriptive claim about a client, for example, we can mislead authorities attempting to make an important decision relevant to the individual or to others. We may miss something that actually required treatment and thus prolong the client's suffering. On the other hand, overdiagnosis can stigmatize clients and cause them and others to have negative and untrue beliefs about themselves. Practicing therapies that we erroneously believe cause change, when they do not, wastes everyone's resources. Treating a client with therapy X when therapy Y is more effective needlessly prolongs the client's suffering or the suffering of others if the client should reoffend and results in an inefficient expenditure of resources. Economists state that all activities have opportunity costs: engaging in one activity has the cost of forcing the actor to forgo engaging in another. All ineffective therapies have opportunity costs because they displace the opportunity to engage in other, more productive options. A fallibilist epistemology, by contrast, suggests that we should accept the fact that our beliefs may contain error. Such a stance allows us to seek to minimize error by exposing our beliefs to criticism and revising accordingly.

SOME GENERAL CONSIDERATIONS: WHY ISN'T PSYCHOLOGY AS PROGRESSIVE AS PHYSICS?

Building on the points just made, this section discusses how phenomena studied by the social sciences differ from phenomena studied by the natural sciences. Several scholars have argued that because of these differences progress made in the field of psychology has been slower as compared to fields such as physics.

Psychology Often Addresses Complex Urgent Problems

One reason given for the slow progress of psychology is the complexity of the phenomena that psychologists study. Kuhn (1972), for example, has stated:

> The insulation of the scientific community from society permits the individual scientist to concentrate his attention upon problems that he has good reason to believe he will be able to solve. Unlike the engineer, and many doctors, and most theologians, the scientist need not choose problems because they urgently need solution and without regard for the tools available to solve them. In this respect, also, the contrast between natural scientists and many social scientists proves instructive. The latter often tend, as the former almost never do, to defend their choice of a research problem—e.g., the effects of racial discrimination or the causes of the business cycle—chiefly in terms of the social importance of achieving a solution. Which group would one then expect to solve problems at a more rapid rate? (p. 164)

Essentially, social scientists, including psychologists, tend to target problems that are of social importance, even if the technology is not available to do so. For example, racial discrimination is an extremely complex yet important social problem that cannot be isolated in a scientific laboratory in ways that the phenomena of the natural sciences can be. Therefore, problems studied by the social sciences are much more difficult to solve. Thus, one practical heuristic for the attorney may be to understand how complex a question he or she is posing to the psychologist. Some questions are less complex because they are impacted by fewer variables and psychologists have made more scientific progress in these areas. For example, how should a profoundly gifted 7-year-old child's educational curriculum be modified? Other questions are much more complex: Will this convicted psychopathic sex offender rape again, i.e. in the next forty years? To state the obvious, psychologists can address the less complex questions more definitely than the more complex ones.

Psychology Is a Big Tent

Another reason that psychology may be less progressive than the natural sciences is that the discipline subsumes many branches. Kuhn (personal communication, 1989, April) also remarked:

> Psychology is probably too much of a catchall field to generalize about. I've not reason to suppose that the same answers would be forthcoming if the same questions were addressed, say, to learning theory, clinical psychology, perceptual psychology, and intelligence testing. What the answers would be if the field were appropriately subdivided, I'm not the one to say. You have to know the fields from the inside to do that.

Attorneys need to understand that very few psychologists consider themselves (general) psychologists. Rather, psychologists see themselves as specialists or even subspecialists in some more specific area of psychology, including clinical psychology, educational psychology, industrial/organizational psychology, developmental psychology, social psychology, perceptual psychology, learning psychology, neuropsychology, psychophysiology, cognitive psychology, personality psychology, cultural psychology, geropsychology, community psychology, and forensic psychology, to name some of the major conventional subdivisions.

Even within these speciality areas, however, there is another level of complexity and further subspecialties. Within developmental psychology, for example, psychologists can further specialize in infant or adolescent development. Within clinical psychology, psychologists can further specialize in anxiety disorders or even in research methodology. Thus, the attorney should understand what specialties are involved in the case being considered. It may also be that multiple specialty areas are relevant. In custody decisions, for example, clinical psychologists can opine about the presence or absence of relevant mental disorders; developmental psychologists can opine about normal developmental processes that may be affected by these disorders.

Other Key Differences

In 1978, one of the most renowned scholars in clinical psychology, Paul Meehl, wrote an important paper in which he tried to explain the slow progress made by psychology. We will discuss here the relevance of some of his points for forensic psychology. In doing so, it is our hope that an attorney will better understand the nature of psychology, including its potential contributions and its weaknesses.

Response-class and Situation-taxonomy Problems

A *response class* is composed of behaviors that impact the environment in a similar way, are influenced by the same types of antecedent stimuli, or are affected similarly by the same contingencies (Haynes & O'Brien, 2000). For instance, tantrums, baby talk, and feigning illness are all behavioral responses that may be in the same class because they all function to obtain attention, all occur in the absence of attention (i.e., being ignored), and all are reinforced when parents provide attention as the behaviors are exhibited. It should be noted that humans are behaving constantly and we, as scientists, classify behaviors in terms of antecedent stimuli and responses. A tantrum can also be classified as a stimulus for which the response is attention paid to the child. The point is that stimuli and responses do not "exist" in a true sense; rather, they only exist in the descriptions of scientists, designed to be successful for predictive and explanatory purposes.

Scientists are further faced with the challenge of how to classify stimuli and responses into meaningful units. For example, a response might be as simple as an eye blink or as complex as robbing a bank, an act that is composed of smaller responses. Similarly, a stimulus can be as simple as a telephone ring or as complex as seeing an unsupervised child in a park. Meehl (1978) states that the response class problem "involves the well-known difficulties of slicing up raw behavioral flux into meaningful intervals identified by causally relevant attributes on the response side" and the situation-taxonomy problem concerns the same issue on the stimulus side (p. 808). When psychologists attempt to organize and understand human social behavior, the stimuli and responses of interest typically are not as simple as telephone rings and eye blinks. Because of the richness and complexity of human behavior, identifying and partitioning meaningful, more complex stimulus and response units are much more difficult to accomplish.

Polygenic Heredity

Because human behavior is multiply determined, causal inferences about such behaviors are difficult to make. As noted by Meehl (1978), with the exception of some conditions that are transmitted in a Mendelizing manner "most of the attributes studied by soft-field psychologists are influenced by polygenic systems" (p. 809). Further, genes are rarely the sole determiners of complex behavioral repertoires (Skinner, 1974). Many contemporary theories of human behavior, such as the diathesis-stress model and the Biosocial Theory (Linehan, 1993), posit that genetic endowment predisposes individuals to certain conditions, such as depression or schizophrenia, but that whether or not the condition is manifest depends on environmental stressors (i.e., frustration, pressure, conflicts, etc.). That is, an individual who is genetically predisposed to developing depression might only exhibit symptoms of depression when undergoing a certain kind of divorce or involved in interpersonal conflicts at work. The task of identifying the cause of a patient's behavior, when considering biological and environmental determinants, is extremely complicated. For example, it is unrealistic to assume that a sex offender perpetrates against a child because of factor X and therefore, when controlling for factor X, we can estimate the likelihood of recidivism. Instead, it is assumed that a confluence of factors contribute to criminal behavior and to human behavior in general.

The Idiographic Problem

The *nomothetic approach* to psychology attempts to identify attributes of populations and develop models of human behavior that are generalizable to the average person (Haynes & O'Brien, 2000; Meier, 1994). Idiographic theorists are interested in individual differences and how these characteristics form the unique personality of an individual (Allport, 1937). Meehl (1978) emphasizes that in soft disciplines, such as psychology, using nomothetic approaches to characterize human behavior is much more difficult than when making generalizations about phenomena studied in the physical and biological sciences (p. 809). Natural sciences lend themselves to covering laws, such as Newton's inverse square law of gravitational attraction. In psychology, there are few such covering laws, and those that are established are arguably not dissimilar to laws employed by the natural sciences. The types of phenomena studied in the natural sciences can be reduced to natural, categorical kinds, such as the periodic table of elements. "Natural kinds" refers to classes in which one thing is representative of all things of that particular class: For instance, one hydrogen atom is likely to be representative of all other hydrogen atoms.

In clinical psychology, it is not the case that one depressed client is representative of all depressed clients. However, we attempt to classify human behavior by natural kinds using nomothetic approaches. A primary example of this is the *Diagnostic and Statistical Manual of Mental Disorders*, fourth edition (DSM-IV) diagnostic system, which groups psychological disorders according to topographical distinctions. The problem is that psychology, like other social sciences, is faced with what may be important idiosyncrasies. Phenomena affiliated with the natural sciences, such as atoms, are only individuated in terms of time and place; atom X is the same as atom Y, with the exception of temporal and spatial differences. Humans are individuated by much more: Characteristics are radically diverse, as are contextual settings and the complex interactions of these. All of these differences are important to the study of human behavior. Despite our efforts, we have not yet precisely reduced human behavior or characteristics into distinct and natural categories. When attempting to do so, we may compromise the human individuality that is central to the study of clinical phenomena.

Unknown Critical Events

Humans are such that their lives and personalities can be highly influenced by a myriad of events, some very distant in time and others they may not even be aware of. Meehl states: "They are sometimes observable events that, however, were not in fact observed and recorded, such as the precise tone of the voice and facial expression that a patient's father had when he was reacting to an off-color joke that the patient innocently told at the dinner table at age 7" (p. 810). Because these very important histories are not available to us and because these histories are so complex and are processed in ways that may be obscure, understanding the causal structure of a particular patient's behavior becomes complex.

Nuisance Variables

Meehl (1978) describes nuisance variables as those that are systematic and sizably influence other variables, but whose degree of influence is difficult to ascertain (p. 810). An example is socioeconomic status (SES), where it may be difficult to disentangle genetic and environmental contributors to intelligence (Meehl, 1978). Also, the causal directionality of nuisance variables is often difficult to determine. For instance, is SES a cause of intellectual functioning, is SES caused by intellectual functioning, or is this a bidirectional process? Another way to describe this phenomenon is in terms of moderating factors. A *moderator variable* is one that can influence the strength and/or direction of the relation between two or more variables (Baron & Kenny, 1986). For example, the effectiveness of treatment for depression can be "moderated" by other variables, such as therapeutic alliance, gender, and age as well as possibly other factors that are more idiosyncratic to the patient or the therapist. In psychology, we can speculate about and sometimes measure the direction of causal influence of these types of variables, but precise conclusions are not always possible (Meehl, 1978). As discussed, individual differences in human behavior further compound this problem because nuisance or moderator variables do not necessarily impact other psychological variables in a "lawlike" fashion, at least as compared with the universal laws of natural sciences.

Feedback Loops

Part of the complexity of human behavior is that it affects the social and physical environment in ways that, in turn, affect behavior in the future. A wife's depression may result in a positive feedback loop by causing her husband's affect to become more negative; this, in turn, may result in the wife becoming further depressed. One of the difficulties of predicting and controlling human behavior is that humans are constantly engaging in complex social interactions in which we affect and are affected by others.

Random Walks

Events may occur in the lives of humans that are impossible or difficult to predict (such as winning the lottery, being mugged, and the like) that affect human development. Meehl (1978) suggests that we largely evolve through the process known as a "random walk" or a "chance affair": "Luck is one of the most important contributors to individual differences in human suffering, satisfaction, illness, achievement, and so forth, an embarrassingly 'obvious' point that social scientists readily forget" (p. 811). Thus it can be said that the individual wins the lottery because of "good luck," whereas the inverse is true for the individual who is mugged. Humans no doubt engage in behaviors that increase the probability of encountering certain consequences (i.e., buying a lottery ticket or walking alone in a dark alley), but because of the complex nature of human behavior and the environments in which we live, social scientists are not likely to be able to predict the probability of a single forthcoming event or some events at all.

Sheer Number of Variables

All behavior occurs in a context, which affects how humans respond to given stimuli. The social sciences are concerned with how the influence of many different genetic, historical, and situation variables all contribute to human behavior. In attempting to determine a person's child abuse potential, for example, the answer depends on the psychologist's ability to identify and measure many of these variables. A 5-year-old has already experienced billions of stimuli and emitted billions of responses, all of which can be seen as variables influencing other sets of variables. What biological vulnerabilities (e.g., emotional reactivity), historical variables (e.g., being a former victim of child abuse), antecedent stimuli (e.g., misbehavior of children), physiological states (e.g., intoxication or illness), reinforcement/punishment contingencies (e.g., experienced or understood legal ramifications of child abuse), and the like are present; what are the interactions among these variables; and with what accuracy can we measure them? Meehl (1978) notes: "The variables, although large in number, are each nuisance variables that carry a significant amount of weight, interact with each other, and contribute to idiographic development via the divergent causality mode" (p. 812). Hence, these variables are important to the causal system, but, because of the in sheer number, complicate the process of making causal inferences and predictions about human behavior.

Cultural Factors

Meehl (1978) suggests that cultural factors and subsequent causal influences by these factors are not fully understood. The difficulty in understanding cultural factors is that culture can often be a proxy variable. A proxy variable is used as a substitute for some other theoretically relevant variable; however, it not only reflects the factor of interest, but other factors as well (Judd & Kenny, 1981). For example, if it is assumed that differing value systems of different cultural groups might affect teen pregnancy rates, cultural identity can be assessed and evaluated as a moderator variable. The problem, however, is that in assessing cultural identity one might also be inadvertently assessing socioeconomic status. Therefore, it might be erroneous to conclude that cultural identity, broadly defined, is a contributing factor to teen pregnancy. This is why controlling for a factor such as culture in the social sciences is not synonymous with controlling for a factor such as temperature in the natural sciences. Nonetheless, Meehl (1978) notes that understanding factors like culture, and all that is subsumed by culture, is crucial and important to reconstructing the history of an individual (p. 812). (See Rice and O'Donohue [2002] for other issues related to culture.)

Open Concepts

Open concepts are concepts that are not clearly defined by necessary and sufficient conditions or by operational definitions. Their boundaries are somewhat open and fuzzy. Most, if not all, constructs in psychology are open constructs. Meehl (1978) sees this openness due to three factors: "(a) openness arising from the indefinite extensibility of our provisional list of operational indicators of the construct; (b) openness associated with each indicator singly, because of the empirical fact that indicators are only probabilistically, rather than nomologically, linked to the inferred theoretical construct; and (c) openness due to the fact that most of our theoretical entities are introduced by an implicit or contextual definition" (p. 815). Thus, the construct of depression is open. The DSM may have diagnostic criteria but openness is introduced by (1) variability in the construal of these individual criteria (e.g., what constitutes "hypersomnia"?); (2) variability in the "Chinese menu" approach, to which criteria need to be satisfied in order to merit the diagnosis; and (3) variability in whether the DSM definition is regarded as canonical, or whether other definitions are used. Problems arise with open concepts in classifying human behavior because the less clearly defined psychological phenomena are, the more likely there is room for disagreement. For example, studies have demonstrated low interobserver agreement for DSM diagnoses of personality disorders (Perry, 1992).

Intentionality, Purpose, and Meaning

Meehl (1978) points out that human beings think, plan, and intend and these factors complicate description and prediction. The first complication is the fact that thinking, planning, and intending can be covert acts knowable only to the actor. Second, there is a social psychology literature suggesting that because human beings engage in self-deception, even if they want to be accurate reporters on their intentions they may not be. Third, this suggests that predictions cannot be made without this sort of information. Humans do not just react to external stimulus conditions but process these stimuli in light of their intentions and plans. This effect can make prediction more difficult.

Uniquely Human Properties

Meehl (1978) states that "only man speculates about nonpractical, theoretical matters; only man worships; only man systematically goes about seeking revenge, years later, for an injury done to him; only man carries on discussions about how to make decisions" (p. 816). These unique human properties do not allow animal models to be studied; generally they are complex behaviors that are difficult to subsume under scientific laws.

Ethical Constraints on Research

Research in the social sciences, much more so than in the natural sciences, is ethically constrained. Essentially, some questions can never be definitively answered because the research that would need to be conducted to answer these questions would potentially endanger human subjects. Examples include randomly assigning children in custody or foster care placements to caregivers of low- and high-risk abuse potential groups to determine whether or not a measure of abuse potential actually predicts abuse. Or, while conducting a longitudinal study, subjecting people to various experimental environments to determine the process by which psychological disorders emerge. Because of the immorality involved in both of these examples, along with countless other conceivable yet unethical studies, psychology is somewhat limited in its ability to make causal inferences about, and predictions of, human behavior.

GETTING THE MOST FROM PSYCHOLOGY

Despite the limitations in the science and practice of psychology just described, the field does have much to offer to the practice of law. The "best" psychology is based on empirical findings from research that follows the scientific method as implemented in psychology. As such, psychology can and does provide useful information, tools, and services in a variety of relevant areas, including assessment and description of psychological functioning and characteristics, explanations for human behaviors, predictions of future behavior, and treatments and interventions. (Psychology's contributions in these areas are described throughout the chapters in this volume.) However, it is critical that attorneys who call upon psychology and its practitioners become critical consumers of the methodology, information, tools, and services provided. The purpose of this section is to provide lawyers with some basic knowledge that will aid them in getting the best (and leaving the rest) from psychology's large tent. This discussion is fairly general in nature because of the space constraints of this chapter and because these issues are discussed in greater detail elsewhere in this volume.

Psychological Assessment

A very common function that psychologists serve in forensic cases is the assessment of psychological characteristics and functioning. Assessment can cover depression, substance abuse, competency, criminal intent, dangerousness, parental fitness, and intelligence, to name a few areas. Literally thousands of assessment tools and methods have been created to measure hundreds of psychological constructs. However, the quality of these tools varies widely.

Standards for psychological test construction, validation, and usage are in place to minimize the various types of errors (i.e., false statements, predictions, and claims) discussed in an earlier section. For example, the American Psychological Association (APA, 1985) has specified specific standards for educational and psychological testing. The APA testing standards relevant to the practice of forensic psychology, and appropriate to discuss given the scope of this chapter, are as follows: (1) tests should have empirically established validity and reliability, (2) testing norms should be available, (3) a comprehensive administration manual should be included, and (4) specific guidelines concerning test usage should be explicated and followed. These standards can be used to determine the quality of an assessment measure and are described in Table 2.1. It is recommended that lawyers inquire about the extent to which tests and measures that are to be used in cases meet these standards. This can be accomplished through consulting with the test administrator, or by consulting sources such as the *Mental Measurement Yearbook* (1941), an annual review of available tests.

Explanations for Behavior

Psychologists in forensic settings are also frequently called upon to address questions of why individuals behave as they do, such as: Why is this individual aggressive, depressed, drug abusing, or stealing cars? A number of theories have been developed and tested to answer questions regarding the etiology of behaviors. Such theories are generally considered valid to the extent that they have been shown to be falsifiable, testable, able to accurately predict the behavior of interest, and useful in guiding practice. Additionally, a theory of human behavior is considered to be valid to the extent that it has been researched extensively and its fundamental tenets have been supported empirically. Several psychological theories of human behavior that have met these criteria are listed here:

- *Biological theory*: Holds that much of human behavior is governed by biological processes within the individual.
- *Behavioral theory*: Holds that behavior is acquired and maintained through learning (e.g., *operant conditioning*, where behavior is a function of rewards and punishers, and *classical conditioning*, where behavior is a function of learned associations).
- *Social Learning theory*: Holds that behavior is acquired through observation and modeling and is maintained though reinforcement and punishment.
- *Cognitive theory*: Holds that much of human behavior is governed by the individual's thought processes.
- *Biopsychosocial theory*: Holds that behavior is influenced by biological, psychological, and social factors.

Every psychologist comes to the forensic consultation with a theoretical stance, implicit or explicit, empirically based or not. In consuming explanatory information from psychologists regarding human behavior, lawyers must be aware of both the theoretical model on which the information is based as well as the empirical basis of the theory.

TABLE 2.1
Selected American Psychological Association Standards for Educational and Psychological Testing

Type of Standard	Required or Recommended	Description
Validity	required	The validity of the test must be established empirically. The validity of a test refers to the extent to which an inference from a test is "appropriate and meaningful." The validity of a test can be established in a number of ways (see below).
Construct related	recommended	The extent to which a test assesses the theoretical construct (e.g., psychological characteristic) of interest. Often assessed through measuring convergent and discriminant validity.
Content related	recommended	The extent to which the content of a test item reflects the construct intended for measure.
Criterion related	recommended	The extent to which a test score correlates with a criterion of interest—e.g., the extent to which a measure of dangerousness correlates with future violent behavior.
Differential prediction	recommended	The extent to which a test yields different scores or predictions for the same domain among groups that are distinct with regard to that domain—e.g., predicts less academic achievement for developmentally disabled children than for normal children.
Reliability	required	The reliability of a test must be established empirically. The reliability of a test refers to the extent to which the test scores are "consistent, dependable, or repeatable." Good reliability indicates that a test is free of errors of measurement. Test reliability can also be established in several ways (see below).
Test-retest	recommended	The extent to which a test yields the same score when readministered to the same individuals.
Internal consistency	recommended	The consistency or homogeneity of responding to items within a test scale. To the extent that responses are similar across items within a scale, internal consistency will be high. Types of measures of internal consistency include coefficient alpha and split half reliability.
Norms	recommended	The summarization of average test scores for specified populations or groups.
Administration Guide	required	Provides detailed instructions on test usage, administration, scoring, and interpretation.
Test usage		General standards for test use.
Revalidation of test when modifications are made	required	When a test user makes substantial changes in the test format, mode of administration, instructions, language, or content, he or she must revalidate the new version or provide a rationale for why this is not necessary
Validation for new testing purposes	required	When a test is used for a purpose for which it has not been empirically validated, the user must provide evidence of the test's validity for the new purpose—e.g., when a test that has only been validated to measure depression is used to assess suicide risk.
Following specified testing procedures	required	Test administrators must closely follow the testing procedures specified by the test publisher. These include instructions for usage, administration, scoring, and interpretation of results.

Adapted from American Psychological Association (1985).

Predicting Future Behavior

Psychologists working in forensic settings are often concerned with predicting an individual's future behavior (e.g., violence, criminal behavior, treatment outcomes, etc.). Although a number of factors have been identified in the literature as predictors of relevant behaviors and a number of assessment instruments have been developed for predicting these behaviors, the *accurate* prediction of the occurrence or nonoccurrence of future behaviors, as discussed previously in this chapter, is a difficult and often elusive task (see Chapters 5 and 6 of this volume for additional discussions on this issue). Psychologists can often only make general statements about risks for future behaviors.

Consequently, when statements of risk are made, they often have both poor sensitivity and poor specificity. That is, current assessment methods do not accurately and reliably identify who *will* engage in a specific behavior in the future (sensitivity) while also accurately and reliably identifying who *will not* engage in that behavior (specificity). Because any forensic practice is prone to making various types of errors, it is important that a method of predicting many future behaviors (for example, violence) has both sensitivity and specificity because we do not want to falsely identify dangerous individuals as nondangerous, and similarly we do not want to falsely identify nondangerous individuals as dangerous.

The accuracy and limitations of any predictive assessment tool that has been recommended or used by a psychologist should be noted and accounted for. Because of the limitations in currently available behavior prediction methods, we must be careful in how we use these methods and must be careful not to make strong conclusions based on them.

Treatments and Interventions

There are many different types of treatment or intervention recommendations a psychologist can make, and lawyers can also be good consumers of these recommendations. The question of what treatment is best for any particular individual is a difficult one, but several recommendations can be made for evaluating the effectiveness of treatments in general. Chambless and her workgroup (Chambless et al., 1998) have developed a set of standards for identifying *well-established* and *probably efficacious* psychological treatments. These standards are outlined in Table 2.2. The workgroup also identified current treatments that meet each of these standards. The identified treatments are listed in Figure 2.1.

General Recommendations

Some general considerations in critical and educated consumption of psychological information are worth noting. These considerations generally have to do with the quality and rigor of the scientific research that forms the basis of the information. Although determining the quality of the scientific basis of psychological

TABLE 2.2
Criteria for Well-Established and Probably Efficacious Treatments

Well-Established Treatments:

I. At least two good between-group design experiments demonstrating efficacy in one or more of the following ways:
   A. Superior (statistically significantly so) to a pill or psychological placebo, or to other treatment.
   B. Equivalent to an already established treatment in experiments with adequate sample sizes.

or

II. A large series of single-case design experiments ($n > 9$) demonstrating efficacy. These experiments must have:
   A. Used good experimental design.
   B. Compared the intervention to another treatment in IA.

Further criteria for both I and II:
III. Experiments must be conducted with treatment manuals.
IV. Characteristics of samples must be clearly specified.
V. Effects must be demonstrated by at least two different investigators or investigating teams.

Probably Efficacious Treatments:

I. Two experiments showing the treatment is superior (statistically significantly so) to waiting list control group.

or

II. One or more experiments meeting the Well-Established Treatment Criteria IA or IB, III, and IV above but not V.

or

III. A small series of single-case design experiments ($n \geq 3$) otherwise meeting the Well-Established Treatment Criteria.

Reprinted from Chambless, Baker, Baucum, Beutler, Calhoun, Crits-Christoph, et al. (1998). Used by permission of the publisher.

claims is often a complex and involved task, a lawyer can take steps to make this determination. Namely, he or she can find answers to the following questions:

1. Was the journal that published the report of the study *peer reviewed*?
2. Have the results of the study been replicated by other researchers?
3. Are the results of the study, and the interpretation of these results, generally consider valid by others (e.g., not refuted in other papers)?
4. Is the information, assessment instrument, or treatment widely used in the field?

Answers of *yes* to these questions would suggest that the scientific basis of the information is likely to be sound.

WELL-ESTABLISHED TREATMENTS
Anxiety and Stress:
Cognitive behavior therapy for panic disorder with and without agoraphobia
Cognitive behavior therapy for generalized anxiety disorder
Exposure treatment for agoraphobia
Exposure/guided mastery for specific phobia
Exposure and response prevention for obsessive-compulsive disorder (OCD)
Stress Inoculation Training for coping with stressors
Depression:
Behavior therapy for depression
Cognitive therapy for depression
Interpersonal therapy for depression
Health Problems:
Behavior therapy for headache
Cognitive-behavior therapy for bulimia
Multicomponent cognitive-behavior therapy for pain associated with rheumatic disease
Multicomponent cognitive-behavior therapy with relapse prevention for smoking cessation
Problems of Childhood:
Behavior modification for enuresis
Parent training programs for children with oppositional behavior
Marital Discord:
Behavioral marital therapy

PROBABLY EFFICACIOUS TREATMENTS
Anxiety:
Applied relaxation for panic disorder
Applied relaxation for generalized anxiety disorder
Cognitive behavior therapy for social phobia
Cognitive therapy for OCD
Couples communication training adjunctive to exposure for agoraphobia
EMDR (Eye Movement Desensitization and Reprocessing) for civilian Post-traumatic Stress Disorder (PTSD)
Exposure treatment for PTSD
Exposure treatment for social phobia
Stress Inoculation Training for PTSD
Relapse prevention program for OCD
Systematic desensitization for animal phobia
Systematic desensitization for public speaking anxiety
Systematic desensitization for social anxiety
Chemical Abuse and Dependence:
Behavior therapy for cocaine abuse
Brief dynamic therapy for opiate dependence
Cognitive-behavioral relapse prevention therapy for cocaine dependence
Cognitive therapy for opiate dependence
Cognitive-behavior therapy for benzodiazepine withdrawal in panic disorder patients
Community Reinforcement Approach for alcohol dependence
Cue exposure adjunctive to inpatient treatment for alcohol dependence
Project CALM for mixed alcohol abuse and dependence (behavioral marital therapy plus disulfiram)
Social skills training adjunctive to inpatient treatment for alcohol dependence
Depression:
Brief dynamic therapy
Cognitive therapy for geriatric patients
Reminiscence therapy for geriatric patients
Self-control therapy
Social problem-solving therapy
Health Problems:
Behavior therapy for childhood obesity
Cognitive-behavior therapy for binge-eating disorder
Cognitive-behavior therapy adjunctive to physical therapy for chronic pain
Cognitive-behavior therapy for chronic low back pain
EMG biofeedback for chronic pain
Hypnosis as an adjunct to cognitive-behavior therapy for obesity
Interpersonal therapy for binge-eating disorder
Interpersonal therapy for bulimia
Multicomponent cognitive therapy for irritable bowel syndrome
Multicomponent cognitive-behavior therapy for pain of sickle cell disease
Multicomponent operant-behavioral therapy for chronic pain
Scheduled, reduced smoking adjunctive to multicomponent behavior therapy for smoking cessation
Thermal biofeedback for Raynaud's syndrome
Thermal biofeedback plus autogenic relaxation training for migraine
Marital Discord:
Emotionally focused couples therapy for moderately distressed couples
Insight-oriented marital therapy
Problems of Childhood:
Behavior modification of encopresis
Cognitive-behavior therapy for anxious children (separation anxiety and avoidant disorders)
Exposure for simple phobia
Family anxiety management training for anxiety disorders
Sexual Dysfunction
Hurlbert's combined treatment approach for female hypoactive sexual desire
Masters & Johnson's sex therapy for female orgasmic dysfunction
Zimmer's combined sex and marital therapy for female hypoactive sexual desire
Other:
Behavior modification for sex offenders
Dialectical behavior therapy for borderline personality disorder
Family intervention for schizophrenia
Habit reversal and control techniques
Social skills training for improving social adjustment of schizophrenic patients
Supported employment for severely mentally ill clients

Adapted from Chambless, Baker, Baucum, Beutler, Calhoun, Crits-Christoph, et al. (1998). Used by permission of the publisher.

FIGURE 2.1 Examples of Well-Established and Probably Efficacious Treatments

CONCLUSIONS

Psychology has a different status than the natural sciences and may, for the reasons we have described here, always have a distinct status. This does not mean that it cannot make contributions to eliminating uncertainty and increasing the accuracy of descriptive, predictive, and explanatory statements. Scientific psychology looks for the errors in theories, measurements, interventions, predictions, and explanations. Conjectures that seemed reasonable (at least to someone) can be tested and found to be in error. Thus, legal professionals can learn from psychologists which possibilities have what kinds of errors and which possibilities seem to best survive empirical and conceptual criticism.

REFERENCES

Allport, G. W. (1937). *Personality: A psychological interpretation.* New York: Holt.
American Psychological Association (1985). *Standards for educational and psychological testing.* Washington, DC: Author.
Baron, R. M., & Kenny, D. A. (1986). The moderator-mediator variable distinction in social psychological research: Conceptual, strategic and statistical considerations. *Journal of Personality and Social Psychology, 51,* 1173–1182.
Bartly, W. W. (1984). *The retreat to commitment.* La Salle, IL: Open Court.
Chambless, D. L., Baker, M., Baucum, D. H., Beutler, L. E., & Calhoun, K. S. Crits-Christoph, et al. (1998). Update on empirically validated therapies, II. *The Clinical Psychologist, 51* (1), 3–16.
Haynes, S. N., & O'Brien, W. H. (2000). *Principles and practice of behavioral assessment.* New York: Kluwer Academic/Plenum Publishers.
Judd, C. M., & Kenny, D. A. (1981). *Estimating the effects of social interventions.* New York: Cambridge University Press.
Kantor, J. R. (1962). *The logic of modern science.* Chicago: Principia Press.
Kuhn, T. S. (1970). *The structure of scientific revolutions* (2nd ed.). Chicago: University of Chicago Press.
Linehan, M. M. (1993). *Cognitive-behavioral treatment of borderline personality disorder.* New York: Guilford Press.
Meehl, P. E. (1978). Theoretical risks and tabular asterisks: Sir Karl, Sir Ronald, and the slow progress of soft psychology. *Journal of Consulting and Clinical Psychology, 46* (4), 806–834.
Meier, S. T. (1994). Consistency of measurement across and within individuals. *The Chronic Crisis in Psychological Measurement and Assessment* (pp. 35–69). San Diego: Academic Press.
Perry, J. C. (1992). Problems and considerations in the valid assessment of personality disorders. *American Journal of Psychiatry, 149* (12), 1645–1653.
Rice, N. & O'Donohue, W. (2002). Cultural sensitivity: A critical examination. *New Ideas in Psychology, 20* (1), 35–48.
Skinner, B. F. (1974). *About behaviorism.* New York: Random House.
The Mental Measurements Yearbook (1941–). Highland Park, NJ: Buros Institute.

CHAPTER 3

ETHICAL ISSUES IN FORENSIC PSYCHOLOGY

MICHAEL LAVIN

PRIVATE PRACTICE
WASHINGTON, DC
CANDIDATE, BALTIMORE-WASHINGTON INSTITUTE FOR PSYCHOANALYSIS

If moral philosophy has a practical purpose, it is to answer the question "How should I live?" This is not the kind of question that can be answered by any code of professional ethics. For one thing, codes of professional ethics have a narrower scope than the how-should-I-live question has. The American Psychological Association's Code of Ethics (2002) has a structure that is typical of professional codes. It begins with a hortatory section delineating principles described as aspirational. If psychologists fail to satisfy one of the Code's aspirational principles, they need fear no disciplinary action for their failure. But the code also contains "standards" that are proclaimed to bind all members of the American Psychological Association (APA). When APA member psychologists fail to comply with a Code standard, they run the risk of facing disciplinary action by the APA if they are found out. In the view of the APA, disobedience to standards is unethical behavior.

Persons wondering why APA members have a duty to abide by its Code learn that compliance with the APA Code is a condition of APA membership. If one wonders why one shouldn't join with a wink, the APA Code cannot settle that question without begging it. That question concerns whether, for example, I should live by a Code I have publicly acknowledged. If some psychologists think it obvious that I should, they are almost certainly assuming that the APA's Code is morally defensible, or at least has no provisions so obnoxious that a person is not morally obliged to ignore them. If somebody objects that nobody should swear allegiance to a public organization whose code is objectionable to him, that objection assumes one cannot be justified in belonging to an organization that has a morally indefensible position as part of its regulative principles. Is it the homosexuals, for example, who are *necessarily* in the wrong when they serve as soldiers in the United States Army while engaging on the sly in same-sex sex?

The interesting questions about how to live have less to do with what a professional code says than with what careful moral reasoning reveals about what one ought to do. Probably, at least in the hard cases, an ethics code counts as but one element in serious thinking about how one should live. In this chapter, I intend to explore a few moral problems in forensic psychology. From my perspective as a working clinician, neither the APA's Code nor its guidelines for forensic psychologists (Committee on Ethical Guidelines for Forensic Psychologists, 1991) is of much use when thinking about the hardest issues in forensic psychology. I want to amplify an approach to thinking well about moral issues that I hope will take readers beyond the Code or APA Guidelines.

FUNDAMENTALS OF MORAL PHILOSOPHY

Systematic moral philosophy has a rich tradition in the occident that runs at least as far back as Plato's Socratic dialogues. The Greeks divided reasoned inquiry into two kinds. When persons engage in theoretical reasoning, they seek to establish what is true. When they engage in practical reasoning, they seek to determine what they *ought* to do. Practical principles help answer questions about what a person ought, relative to certain circumstances, to do. Practical reasoning, as the Greeks understood it, did not have to be moral in the sense that persons today would think of the term. Rather, practical reasoning was a form of means-ends reasoning. If you want beer and you believe there is beer in your icebox, you ought to go to your icebox. Moral answers to the how-should-I-live question normally set limits on the desires I ought to allow myself to have or whose satisfaction I ought to pursue. Even egoists, who believe they ought to do what has the best consequences for themselves, grant that certain desires—for example, a desire to engage in sex whenever they have the urge—must be constrained (Parfit, 1984). A person who never constrains his sexual appetites is almost certain to have a bad life. For better or worse, moral philosophy is in the desire-evaluation business. So the type of inquiry that moral inquiry is emerges. It is a practical inquiry, since it is aimed at telling a person what he should do. But it is also comprehensive. Practical reasoning about how to live refuses to proceed from our desires and habits as we find them. It also deals with what kind of human being I should try to become (Williams, 1985, 1993). So one of the ways moral philosophy seeks to help people decide what to do is by forcing them to ask themselves what sorts of desires need constraining if their lives are to go morally well.

As a species of practical reasoning, moral inquiry insists on reasons. If I am disgusted at the sight of body piercings, I need offer no reason for my disgust. I don't have to *justify* myself. If women with pierced tongues do not disgust my wife, however, but I say they ought to, I do have to offer reasons. Moral judgments, unlike expression of mere personal tastes, require reasons (Hare, 1952). And moral reasons are of a special kind. They are *impartial*. If, for example, I get her to feel disgusted by describing genital piercing while giving her an emetic, that is not a moral reason. Moral reasons are special by virtue of justifying a moral judgment without reference to the particular circumstances of a person, even a common circumstance like a horror of genital damage. A moral justification of the judgment that body piercing is wrong might proceed by getting the concession that self-mutilation is wrong, then arguing that body piercing is a species of self-mutilation. Alternatively, one might justify the moral judgment by showing how it follows from other moral principles, whatever these may be.

It is impractical to consider here all viable approaches to moral theory. One great divide exists that does sort moral theories into two broad groups. There are consequentialist theories, with utilitarianism being the most famous (Williams, 1972; Brandt, 1979). *Consequentialist theories* hold that the rightness or wrongness of an action depends solely on the goodness or badness of its consequences. Consequentialist theories instruct moral agents to act so as to make the consequences of their action as good as possible. Disagreement arises over what counts as a good consequence. It is the job of a theory of value to identify what good consequences are. Typically, these theories identify some things that are valued for their own sake and others that are valued because they are instrumental to getting something that is valued for its own sake.

Nonconsequentialist theories hold that what a moral agent ought to do does not depend solely on the goodness or badness of an act's consequences (Donagan, 1977). Although consequences may well matter, they are not decisive in determining how one should live. Often people take this position because they wish to place constraints on what a person may do to maximize good outcomes. So many psychologists believe that they should keep the confidences of their patients, even though breaching some confidences is likely to lead to better outcomes overall. Two nonconsequentialist approaches to moral theory are Kantianism and casuistry. In fact, I favor casuistry as a moral method. Casuists, following method of the courts, try to keep their principles narrow. The idea is avoid premature embrace of principles that prove untenable when they confront unanticipated circumstances. Casuists tend to favor citing moral principles that are widely accepted in seeking to settle moral disputes. No claim is made, as it is by some consequentialists, that if an action achieves the best consequences possible, its rightness is a settled matter.

Despite the genuine differences that separate moral theories, they often can agree on subsidiary moral principles or, more vaguely, on value. In bioethics, for example, ethicists tend to accept four values: autonomy, beneficence, nonmaleficence, and justice (Beauchamp & Childress, 1994). Although individuals having a moral disagreement may disagree about how to weigh principles of autonomy, beneficence, nonmaleficence, and justice, there is an overwhelming presumption that they have some weight. So if somebody can be shown that an action furthers liberty interests (as legalizing drugs would do), valuing autonomy gives him reason for favoring legalization—even if he concludes that, all things considered, it is not obligatory to favor it. Likewise, since permanently prohibiting competent adult patients and psychologists from dating lessens their liberty, autonomy gives everybody reason to favor eliminating this prohibition—even if, all things considered, the harm of permitting this liberty is too grave to allow it, as the APA Code asserts.

Although consequentialists and nonconsequentialist moral theory disagree about what justifies or makes autonomy, beneficence, nonmaleficence, and justice important in moral thinking—or even what autonomy, beneficence, nonmaleficence, and justice are, as casuists tend to stress—there is enough agreement to reach reasonable conclusions about many moral issues. For many moral arguments, it is enough to agree that hospitalizing a man against his will limits his liberty, that certain medicines benefit certain patients, that causing a research subject to suffer for the benefit of somebody else is acting malevolently toward him, even if it might be counterbalanced by benefits obtained by the research for other people. Most of what I write in this chapter about specific cases does not rely on an understanding of moral concepts any deeper than I have just illustrated.

If psychologists began to think like philosophers about the APA's Code of Ethics in any of its incarnations (American Psychological Association, 1953, 1959, 1963, 1968, 1977, 1979, 1981, 1990, 1992, 2002), they would likely find themselves puzzled about its provisions for at least two reasons. First, why are these the principles and standards that govern psychological practice rather than other principles and standards? Second, why are some standards that are legally and ethically redundant included while other matters of moral importance receive no mention or no direct mention at all? For example, the APA Code requires that psychologists obtain the informed consent of their patients. But the requirement of clinicians to obtain informed consent from research subjects and patients is a settled matter of law. Psychologists would have that legal duty even if the Code did not require them to obtain it. And why, for example, does the Code have no prohibition against deliberately misleading a patient or, assuming the Code was right to skip a prohibition against lying to patients, do research subjects receive more protection against deceptive practices than patients do? And why, to take a more comic omission, does the Code contain a prohibition against sexual intimacies with patients, but not a prohibition against killing them? I am not saying that there are not good reasons for what the framers of the Code included and excluded from it. A profession's history does matter. Psychologists do have sex with more patients than they kill. What is opaque in the case of the APA Code, as opposed to the Decalogue, is the justifications for its wording, inclusions, and exclusions.

To make matters worse, I doubt the Code does much moral work in any case. I propose to look briefly at one friend of the Code to see what moral or ethical work it does.

Koocher and Keith-Spiegel's *Ethics in Psychology*, second edition (1998) has been among the influential works in ethics for psychologists. It has been in print since its publication in 1985. Its authors offer a nine step decision-making process that advises psychologists to proceed as follows.

1. Determine the matter is an ethical one.
2. Consult the guidelines already available that might apply to a specific identification and possible mechanism of resolution.
3. Consider, as best as possible, all sources that might influence the kind of decision you will make.
4. Locate a trusted colleague with whom you can consult.
5. Evaluate the rights, responsibilities, and vulnerability of all affected parties.
6. Generate alternative decisions.
7. Enumerate the consequences of making each decision.
8. Make the decision.
9. Implement the decision. (pp. 12–15)

Koocher and Keith-Spiegel are rather vague about how to accomplish step 5. They do not provide much guidance in how to "make the decision among alternatives," which is the alleged purpose of these nine steps. They claim to identify nine ethical principles and cite a hodge-podge of sources as their precedents. The sources include bioethicists (Beauchamp and Childress) who hold different moral theories; a philosophy professor at the University of Michigan (the late William Frankena, 1973), but not material drawn from the most recent version of his text; two Harvard developmental psychologists who are in profound disagreement on moral development (Kohlberg, 1981, and Gilligan, 1982); a business ethicist whose work was published by his own institute (Josephson, 1991); an educator who wrote on ethics; and a philosophy don who obtained a reputation as a translator of Aristotle and as a champion of ethical intuitionism of the most hide-bound variety. From this group, Koocher and Keith-Siegel claim to identify nine core ethical principles.

1. Doing no harm
2. Respecting autonomy
3. Benefiting others
4. Being just
5. Being faithful
6. According dignity
7. Treating others with caring and compassion
8. Pursuing excellence
9. Accepting accountability

They do not explain why the list ends at nine, other than perhaps the notion that that is all their parade of authorities offered them. But Koocher and Keith-Spiegel do not bother much with either their decision procedures, the code, or their own principles in analyzing cases. Take a typical Koocher and Keith-Spiegel (1978) vignette and its analysis:

> On termination of 9 years of psychotherapy, Mattie Stringalong, Ph.D., suggested that she and Lenny Endure "keep in touch." They exchanged intimate cards and letters, spoke on the phone almost every week, and occasionally met for lunch. After 20 months, Dr. Stringalong informed Endure that their relationship could become intimate soon if he were interested. They eventually married. Endure asked for divorce a year later, also complaining to a state licensing board that Dr. Stringalong had been "laying in wait" for him so that she could get her hands on his substantial family fortune. (p. 220)

The Koocher and Keith-Spiegel analysis is as follows:

> The sexual activity occurred in the "correct time frame" [i.e., after the two-year cool-off period required by Standard 4.07 governing sexual intimacies with former clients], but the therapist kept an uninterrupted relationship afloat. Even if Dr. Stringalong were not guilty of plotting to gain financially, her active perpetuation of an emotionally charged relationship was unethical. (p. 220)

That is it. That is the analysis. The code has no substantive role. The nine steps are not used. Instead, the perpetuation of the relationship is cited as decisive. Perhaps an analysis would reveal that it is. Unfortunately, the reasoning for the conclusion is so skeletal that one suspects, especially given the atmosphere in which psychologists work, that they could have proclaimed the wrongness of Dr. Stringalong's behavior without any analysis.

Readers will have to take my assurance that this example is typical of Koocher and Keith-Spiegel's case analyses in their book. And it does nothing to meet objections by Dawes (1994) that both the APA Code and Koocher and Keith-Spiegel's support of it are grounded in a morally indefensible paternalism. Koocher and Keith-Spiegel deny they are paternalists on the grounds that "psychotherapists have an exceptional responsibility to respect the rights of all clients and to advance their well-being as professional consultants or advisors in partnership with them." They add that this "stance should be enabling in every respect, not paternalistic" (p. 79). Despite the denial, the view is paternalistic. A patient has no "right" to enter into a romantic relationship with another adult because it is contrary to his well-being. He may think he wishes to enter into this relationship, but Koocher and Keith-Spiegel, along with the APA Code, deny it. Perhaps they are right, but this is paternalistic, even if it does enable clients. Again, notice that neither the Code nor an application of the decision-making procedure recommended by Koocher and Keith-Spiegel is applied to determine whether anybody has good reason to accept this feature of the Code.

Why does a code-driven ethics prove so irrelevant to aiding psychologists in understanding how they should practice as psychologists, let alone as forensic psychologists? Even when friends of the Ethics Code, as I have shown, take to handling cases, they make scant use of the Code. What is worse is that codes invite psychologists to forget to look long and hard at controversial areas of practice. For example, the APA has gone on record that it is wrong, not just misguided, to seek to change a person's sexual orientation. Long before the APA built that conclusion into its Code, serious moral thinking had challenged the idea of viewing same-sex sex as sick or wrong. A morally driven political movement began that succeeded in having homosexuality removed from the American Psychiatric Association's diagnostic manual. Before that time, however, some psychologists did offer views on whether, for example, it was safe to let homosexuals hold security clearances, teach children, or be held responsible for violating anti-sodomy laws. This view of homosexuality caused great pain. It resulted, to take but one instance, in the genius Allen Turing's being forced to take anti-hormonal drugs for his allegedly diseased desire to have sex with other men. Turing, deprived of much that was dear to him, killed himself. The codes operative at the time would have held that Turing got "ethical" care. The APA is now on record as holding that that kind of treatment is now wrong, but notice that only moral thinking outside the Code could have motivated this conclusion. It is this kind of thinking that I hope to illustrate.

PEDOPHILIA AS A FORENSIC EXAMPLE

Perhaps no dimension of being human raises more problems than sexuality. Consensual sexual activity between adults, whether it involves heterosexual or same-sex activity, has ceased to be a major concern. Instead, much current concern focuses on sexual activity between adults of different status and even more intensely, adults and minors. Sexual relations between faculty and students and between bosses and employees are often challenged on the ground that they only appear consensual. There is hot controversy on this topic. About the activities of pedophiles there is no serious controversy. When sexual activity occurs between a prepubescent child and an adult, it is unequivocally against the law and is viewed as a moral outrage by the overwhelming majority of the public. In addition to the penalties imposed for sexual contact between children and adults, many states impose registration requirements on released sex offenders and sometimes require them to receive sex-offender treatment as well. I propose to look at the issue of sex-offender treatment to illustrate a problem area that forensic psychologists should be submitting to intense moral evaluation.

Sex-offender treatment is different from ordinary therapy in a number of ways. How well sex-offender treatment works, if at all, is a matter of controversy. Nevertheless, a number of common practices have marked sex-offender treatment. These practices have had the effect of giving what I shall argue is morally indefensible privileging of one form of sex-offender treatment.

Five features mark the delivery of treatment to persons with histories of sexual offending. These features, it should be noted, are unusual in ordinary therapies: relative transparency, mixed allegiance, external motivation, therapeutic coercion and sanctions, and nonnegotiable goals. Let me consider each in turn:

1. *Relative transparency.* Sex-offender therapy is relatively transparent, whereas psychodynamic therapy tends to be cloaked. Ordinary patients assume that what they tell their therapist will remain confidential. Patients in sex-offender treatment routinely experience the gaze of others into their therapies. At the individual level, parole officers may review treatment notes, discuss progress in therapy, or discuss the patient's case with the treating clinician. Clinicians make it plain that their discovery of new or old crimes will result in reports to authorities. These reports may lead to the patient's arrest.
2. *Mixed allegiance.* In ordinary therapy, the patient's good is the therapist's primary concern. Although therapists may believe their patients often engage in behavior harmful to the well-being of others, in ordinary therapy the protection of others is an exceptional, rather than a routine, consideration. Instead, the therapist and patient confine themselves to working on the patient's issues. The persons a patient is or may be harming are left to watch out for themselves. Sex-offender treatment places, at least in theory, safety of the public from sex crimes and the detection of past sex crimes above the patient's well-being.
3. *External motivation.* As painful as therapy may be, the ordinary patient has chosen to engage in it. Sex offenders are typically court ordered to therapy and normally end therapy as soon as they are no longer compelled to be in it.
4. *Therapeutic coercion and sanctions.* Ordinary patients, like sex-offending patients, are encouraged to be as disclosing about themselves as they can be, but their resistance to doing so carries fewer penalties than it does for sex-offending patients. A patient in sex-offender treatment who is not cooperating runs a real risk of being threatened with a variety of sanctions, including revocation of parole. Resistance is far more likely to be bulldozed with threats than to be viewed as an interesting clinical phenomenon in its own right, and one that perhaps is worth interpreting.
5. *Nonnegotiable treatment goals.* In ordinary therapy, psychologists tend to avoid taking a moral stance on what a good outcome is. Psychologists assist patients in achieving change. They may or may not agree about the desirability of what a patient is seeking to achieve. In addition to taking a moral stance against sexual molestation, psychologists of a cognitive-behavioral orientation come perilously close to believing that nobody seeks sex with anybody other than a consenting adult unless he has cognitive distortions or thinking errors. (If only it were so.) Their moral engagement also means that they routinely enjoin certain behaviors that they deem to be high risk.

In at least these five ways sex-offender is different than ordinary therapy, especially psychodynamic therapy. To the extent that these are required elements of sex-offender treatment, they block ordinary therapeutic process as psychodynamic psychologists are likely to understand it.

Consider attempting to do psychoanalytic therapy under these constraints. In the psychoanalytic situation, there is a patient-analyst dyad. The patient is expected to say whatever he can without censorship. The analyst seeks to assist the patient by offering interpretations. Activities like giving advice, seeking clarifications, or confronting the patient are not what best characterize what the analyst does, even though it is a virtual certainty that some advising, clarifying, and confronting will take place (Eissler, 1953). The favored therapeutic intervention is interpretation. In the psychoanalytic context, confronting is not what some people have come to mean by the term, however. In psychoanalytic therapy, confronting tends to center on drawing attention to the patient's inconsistencies and incongruencies in the patient's behavior. For example, the analyst might invite a patient to say more about why he is grinning in describing the day of his arrest or why, since he has said he cares nothing about money, he is flushed and complaining about paying for his treatment.

Classical psychoanalysis's emphasis on interpretation and related insights will strike many people as unsuitable for treating persons with histories of sexual offending. The goal of sex-offender treatment should be to stop sexual offending rather than understanding why somebody does it. The therapist, the objection continues, must be active and goal directed. These are features of cognitive-behavioral treatments. Hence cognitive-behavioral treatments of sexual offending routinely involve exercises designed to enable patients to identify their risk situations, triggers, and offense cycles as well as specific cognitive and behavioral strategies for coping with these.

But analytic technique has two further aspects that put it in opposition to the cognitive-behavioral sex-offender treatment: abstinence and neutrality (Greenson, 1967). Abstinence requires the analyst to avoid seeking to supply a patient's needs for such supports as praise and blame. Buying food for a group session would be a clear example of being nonabstinent towards patients, but so would telling a patient that you are worried about him or praising him for his handling of a risk situation. Neutrality in analytic therapy would be in direct conflict with the cognitive-behavioral technique of openly taking sides against an undesired, in this case criminal, behavior.

The demands of analytic therapy thus make it unsuitable for patients without the ego strength to tolerate the pressure of a method requiring patients to engage in uncensored free association to a neutral, abstinent, interpreting therapist. Hence there are modifications of analytic technique designed for patients unable to tolerate the method of the standard model. These modifications are sometimes called *parameters*. In the case of borderline patients, for example, Clarkin, Yeoman, and Kernberg (1999) have suggested a number of modifications that are designed to handle some of the behaviors many patients with borderline pathology use to devastate their therapy. A patient might be required to contract not to engage in suicidal behavior or to quit a job, since these acts would endanger the therapy. Nevertheless, it is a hallmark of psychoanalytic therapies to minimize or eliminate explicit advice giving and other supportive measures when feasible. This is an important difference between psychoanalytic and cognitive-behavioral therapy. Cognitive-behavioral therapy does not, as a matter of principle, view telling persons how to live to be a temporary expedient that would ideally be absent from therapy. Supportive and directive techniques suffuse standard sex-offender treatment. Anybody doubting this fact can consult Marshall, Fernandez, Hudson, and Ward's (1998) sourcebook on sex-offender treatment programs.

My own hypothesis is that the frequent departures of sex-offender treatment from ordinary therapeutic practices is a possible reason sex-offender treatment has had so much less success in demonstrating treatment effects, even for favored cognitive-behavioral therapy, than ordinary therapy. For psychoanalytic treatment meets all of the characteristics of what I called ordinary therapy. It is conducted in secrecy rather than transparency. The therapist's allegiance is to the patient, not some other parties. The patient has chosen the therapist and comes to therapy because he has chosen and continues to choose to do so. Wise money will despair of seeing improvement in the efficacy and effectiveness of sex-offender treatment until psychologists return to conducting it more like ordinary therapy, including ordinary therapy's emphasis on the welfare of the patient and on patient privacy. There is reason, however, to be optimistic about the fashioning of efficacious psychoanalytically inspired therapies for sexual offenders, if it again becomes possible to treat persons with histories of sexual offending the way that ordinary patients are treated. In fact, one interesting conjecture is that the well-known dodo effect, indicating equivalent therapeutic power for all well-designed therapies, is often thought a possible consequence of common factors. That is, the active ingredients of therapies are the same across the board. If that proves to be so, it may well explain why sex-offender therapies that deviate from ordinary therapy apparently do not work: They have excluded active ingredients. But I am only guessing.

Relative transparency and mixed allegiance are especially key issues here. I can easily understand why persons believe it is horrendous to suggest laws mandating reports of past molestation may need rethinking. They may, for example, argue that stopping the molestation of children is more important than protecting the confidences of a sex-offending patient. It is this same desire to protect that has fostered the relative transparency (mandated reporting) and mixed agency (the child's welfare take precedence over the patient's) that characterizes sex-offender treatment.

I contend the benefit to protecting the public from a policy of relative transparency and mixed allegiance is illusory. Whether psychologists have a mandated reporting requirement or not, some persons in therapy will reoffend. The key question is not whether there will be reoffense under either regime, but whether a system of mandated reporting results in more persons molested than fewer. My own strong suspicion is that mandated reporting does not serve its intended protective purpose. The actual answer, though, is still a matter of controversy. But defenders of transparency may object that psychologists have a duty to inform authorities of past or present molestations, for it is monstrous for psychologists to stand by when they know the identity of a child being molested and not report it. To observe confidentiality is to be complicit in a dangerous man's crimes against children.

There is much to think about here, but would anybody find it credible that a requirement that psychologists report infidelities to partners would enhance patients' candor about their sexual behavior? If, as seems likely, mandatory reporting makes persons committing sexual offenses readier to lie about it, thoughtful critics of transparency have reason to conclude that mandatory reporting requirements, though helpful to some children, harm more children than they help. If a patient tells his therapist he is still molesting when he is, she is in a better position to get him to stop than if he lies to her. This argument has a consequentialist structure but is available to nonconsequentialists as well, provided it does not violate other moral commitments of those theories. Further, within the framework of familiar principles, the argument can be viewed as an application of the principles of nonmaleficence and beneficence. I am claiming that on balance a policy of respecting confidentiality does more to minimize harms to parties and further benefits to them than a policy of transparency.

Obviously no one example or one study of one embodiment of current trends in sex-offender treatment can show that current practices are misguided or that ethical guidelines favoring current "best practices" are mistaken. Nevertheless, there are reasons to be skeptical that use or refinement of cognitive-behavioral therapies for sex-offender treatment deserves to be ethically favored. Cognitive-behavioral therapy has become, as the Association for the Treatment of Sexual Abusers' ethical guidelines make clear, the favored approach for handling men with histories of sexual offending. If cognitive-behavioral therapies had a big treatment effect, one would expect that completion of a cognitive-behavioral treatment program would lower the actuarial risk of relapse into reoffending in the same way that improvements in chemotherapy have improved the mortality rates for Hodgkin's disease. Prior treatment does not reduce actuarial risk calculation on standard actuarial risk assessment instruments (Doren, 2002).

But other conceptual problems pervade cognitive-behavioral approaches to sex-offender treatment. First, cognitive-behavioral therapy routinely posits a central role for cognitions that "permit" sex offenses to take place. Although certain kinds of thinking undoubtedly do sometimes permit the commission of sexual offenses, theoreticians and clinicians ought to have doubts about assuming that this is the routine causal pathway to a sexual offense. Suppose you ask what cognitions permit a man to have sex with a 30-year-old consenting partner. Now ask what cognitions permit a man to have sex with an 8-year-old or a 15-year-old assenting partner? Is it anything other than an unestablished hypothesis that enabling cognitive chains are typically, let alone invariably, significant causal pathways to sex with any partner? Instead, wishes, fantasies, unconscious processes, sexual orientation, situational factors, and a rich array of unknown or unattended to factors likely cause legal or illegal behavior.

Cognitive-behavioral therapy's stress on enabling cognitions would likely be less popular if we looked at a wider range of behavior. Take just one more example of what premature notions of causality do to understanding a problem. Consider speeding on highways. I do it. Most drivers do. Do speeding drivers *typically*, let alone invariably, have cognitive distortions that permit their speeding? If I speed from time to time, does it follow that I have a cycle? When you think of it, it is a fairly moralistic view of a problem to insist that enabling cognitions are a crucial element in its generation. In regard to illegal sexual behavior, it is a moralism rooted, I conjecture, in adult heterosexual biases about what a person must tell himself *not* to engage in heterosexual adult relations. The more one meditates on heterosexual adult behavior rather than sexual behavior alien to one's own personal experience, the less plausible these claims about enabling cognitions are likely to seem. If this is so, it is wrong to insist on giving primacy to one approach. Further, respecting the autonomy of psychologists would seem to favor permitting the use of alternative therapies, since it is not known that cognitive-behavioral therapy causes less harm (a nonmaleficent consideration) or produces greater benefits (a beneficent consideration).

In considering the alleged benefits of mandatory reporting requirements, psychologists treating men with histories of sexual offending should recall that when Abel, Becker, Mittelman, Cunningham-Rathner, Rouleau, and Murphy (1987) obtained certificates of confidentiality reducing the fear of being prosecuted for reporting current or past sex crimes, they discovered their subjects reported vastly more sexually proscribed behavior than they did without the certificates. Protection from future prosecution has been demonstrated to be an effective device for loosening tongues, as any lawyer could have told you before Abel and colleagues got to work. The implications of this finding for therapy are serious indeed. Suppose we imagine a therapy in which, say, a therapist will report any infidelities or rank fantasies to the patient's spouse. Anybody's best guess is that most psychologists would tell you that therapy this transparent would imperil, if not make impossible, any serious work aimed at changing sexual behavior in all but the most shameless patients. But this level of transparency is, as I have repeatedly observed, pervasive in sex-offender work. In an effort to protect potential victims, a body of laws has evolved that mandates psychologists to notify legal authorities of any credible report of certain kinds of sexual offenses. Under these circumstances it is perhaps unsurprising that therapy has yet to show itself effective or, as in California's Sex Offender Treatment Evaluation Program (SOTEP), show a cognitive-behavioral therapy to lead to higher rates of recidivism than no treatment (Marques and Day, 1998, May). Again, consideration of what is known suggests that the favoritism extended to cognitive-behavioral treatments is unwarranted.

Given what I am contending about cognitive-behavioral therapies receiving favored status in sex-offender treatment, it is worth taking a moment to challenge a positive spin of its treatment effect that recently appeared in *Sexual Abuse* (Hanson et al., 2002). In particular, it seemed to me this Hanson meta-analysis was unwarrantedly optimistic in its characterization of the effectiveness of treatment of persons with sexual offense histories. Many therapists labor under an illusion that their treatment is more effective than it is and that cognitive-behavioral therapy, if anything is, is effective. The Hanson meta-analysis is the kind of evidence offered in support of the effectiveness of sex-offender treatment. In it, the authors identified 43 studies that met their criteria for inclusion in their meta-analysis. Of these 43 studies, only four were randomized. The largest randomized study was that of Marques (1999) on California's Sex Offender Treatment Evaluation Program (SOTEP), with 190 offenders in the treatment group and 225 offenders in the control group. The intervention group received a form of cognitive-behavioral therapy. No difference was observed in the control and treatment group, and 16 percent of them recidivated. If anything, the reported odds ratio shows the treatment group at slightly greater odds of recidivating than the control group (odds ratio = 1.06). The recidivism for any offense was also greater in the treatment group compared to the controls (odds ratio = 1.30). This outcome is scarcely encouraging.

Before continuing, a reminder may be in order about odds ratios. An odds ratio tells us how to compare two groups. The fact that the odds ratio that was greater in the treatment group is 1.30 means this in practice: For every 100 recidivists in the control group, we predict there will be 130 recidivists in the treatment group. If the odds ratio is 1, there is no difference between recidivism in the two groups.

Yet another randomized study included in the Hanson meta-analysis had 148 subjects in the treatment group and 83 subjects in the control group. The untreated group again did substantially better than the treatment group. The odds ratio was 1.96, meaning, of course, that there would be 196 recidivists in the treatment group for every 100 recidivists in the control. The treatment group, however, did reoffend for any offense at a lower rate than the controls. Borduin, Henggeler, Blaske, and Stein (1990) and Robinson (1995) also each did randomized studies, though it is not clear that Robinson's was a true randomized study, as Hanson and colleagues note. Each of these papers reported good treatment effect sizes, though in the case of Borduin the sample size was smallish, having only 24 in the control group and 24 in the treatment group. Further, Borduin's sample is of adolescent sex offenders, not adults. Robinson had a good effect size for all recidivism, but no report is made of the effect size for sexual offending. It is hard to see that a meta-analysis of the randomized studies is going to prove encouraging.

The problem here appears to be a familiar one. Freedman, Pisani, and Purves (1998) identify it in their superb third edition *Statistics*. They used papers on portacaval shunts to make their point. They reported on 51 studies of the shunt. There were 32 uncontrolled studies of the shunt, and 75 percent of these reported positive results. There were an additional 15 studies with nonrandomized control; of these studies, two-thirds were markedly positive about the shunt. There were four randomized studies. None of these were markedly positive, and three of the four showed no benefit from the shunt. The shunt ultimately proved to be an unbeneficial procedure. Notice that the inclusion of the uncontrolled studies in a meta-analysis of the shunt would have pumped the number of cases and lead to a meta-analytic verdict of the kind Hanson and colleagues are reporting. It seems to me that a close reading should make one very cautious about embracing this popular conclusion about the effectiveness of cognitive-behavioral sex-offender treatment.

Hanson and colleagues (2002) do at one point seem close to conceding the complaint I am raising when they write:

> There is only one random assignment study examining a current sex offender specific treatment (Sex Offender Evaluation and Treatment Project SOTEP; Marques, 1999), which, so far, has not found a positive effect of treatment. Rather than limit the entire sex offender treatment debate to the strengths and weaknesses of the SOTEP study, the Collaborative Project considered research studies using methods other than random assignment. (p. 186)

To my own way of thinking, the SOTEP result, when combined with such phenomena as the failure of completed sex-offender treatment to lower risk level in current actuarial assessments, calls for more pessimism than is being shown by Hanson and colleagues. I view the refusal to limit the field to debate about the SOTEP study as akin to arguing that debate about the portacaval shunt should not be limited to the randomized studies that found it valueless but should include all the nonrandomized studies by fans of the shunt who found it valuable. Finally, I detect again a level of leniency in the evaluation of cognitive-behavioral treatments that is not extended to other treatments. My reading of Hanson and colleagues is that it would be wise to widen our therapeutic stance to include a wider range of therapy. After all, the best bet is that sex-offender treatment would show the celebrated dodo effect, if all were allowed to compete for prizes (i.e., if all treatments applied would be equally effective).

LESSONS

Why do I think any of this matters morally? First, I think the field is in a rut and that progress is not likely going to be made unless there is greater openness to a variety of approaches other than cognitive-behavioral therapy. Even within the cognitive-behavioral camp, the stress on risk reduction as the central target in therapy has been challenged by Tony Ward's promising Good Lives approach (Ward, Laws, & Hudson, 2003).

The widespread belief that what we do works has had baleful effects. Let me mention two. First, if psychologists believe they have treatments that work for a disorder, they are less likely to be willing to push for randomized tests of its efficacy and effectiveness. It is on all moral accounts suspect to deprive an afflicted person of a beneficial intervention. Second, if everybody admits we do not yet know what works, it is far easier to see the need for randomized trials. Furthermore, if psychologists believe they already have treatments that work, they are presumably more likely to believe that psychologists providing treatment to sex offenders should be certified, lest untrained psychologists be tempted to use "unproven" methods on persons with histories of sexual offending. This has happened in several states—West Virginia, Virginia, Colorado, and Washington for example. An interesting experiment indeed would be to compare the outcomes of psychologists with extensive experience treating persons with histories of sexual offending with the outcomes of therapist with extensive experience treating other problems, if both were randomly assigned caseloads of sexually offending patients.

I have offered a specimen of the kind of moral reasoning that forensic psychologists need to be engaging in. Although the Code has its role in the moral thinking of psychologists, it must not become a blinding light. Too often codes keep their adherents from noticing vast unexplored areas of moral concern. I have offered sex-offender treatment as an example. I have argued in a casuistical manner to the conclusion that the conventional thinking about what constitutes proper treatment of persons with histories of sexual offending has a number of undesirable consequences. I reached a number of harsh conclusions about the conventional wisdom regarding sex-offender treatment. What has the conventional wisdom done? Here is a partial list of explicit and implied conclusions. It has made psychologists and other therapists tolerant of routine waivers of patient-therapist confidentiality. It has encouraged the intrusion of third parties into the patient-therapist dyad. It has resulted in unjustified favoring of one approach to sex-offender treatment. It has created a double standard in regard to treatment evaluation, with a favored treatment being held to a lower standard than proposed alternatives. It has increased the willingness of psychologists to advise their patients. It has led to having hypotheses about the genesis of deviant or any sexual behavior treated as facts. And it has fostered a heterosexism about sexuality, or so say I.

My arguments offered are not intended to be conclusive. Instead, they initiate what I would hope will be a dialogue on new directions for sex-offender treatment. I have hinted that consequentialist and nonconsequentialist views can be marshaled to support my conclusions. I have also given explicit guidance about the support some of these conclusions get from moral principles like nonmaleficence, beneficence, and autonomy. It is an implied theme that ordinary therapy better respects what we value for its own sake than current practice in the treatment of persons with sexual offense histories. Although I have not said that I value not harming others, helping others, leaving people at liberty, and doing justice, I do value these principles. If others value them as mere instruments to other states that are valuable in themselves, I still believe my arguments have force. It is unlikely that beneficence, nonmaleficence, autonomy, and justice do not routinely serve as instrumental goods to states we value for their own sake. If I am right, then in the area of sex-offender treatment, at a minimum, a psychologist who asks, "How should I live?" must answer "Differently than I now do."

REFERENCES

Abel, G. G., Becker, J. V., Mittelman, M. S., Cunningham-Rathner, J., Rouleau, J. L., & Murphy, W. D. (1987). Self-reported crimes of nonincarcerated parahiliacs. *Journal of Interpersonal Violence*, *2(6)*, 3–25.

American Psychological Association. (1953). *Ethical standards of psychologists*. Washington, DC: Author.

American Psychological Association. (1959). Ethical standards of psychologists. *American Psychologist*, *14*, 279–282.

American Psychological Association. (1963). Ethical standards of psychologists. *American Psychologist*, *18*, 56–60.

American Psychological Association. (1968). Ethical standards of psychologists. *American Psychologist*, *23*, 357–361.

American Psychological Association. (1977, March). Ethical standards of psychologists. *APA Monitor*, 22–23.

American Psychological Association. (1979). *Ethical standards of psychologists*. Washington, DC: Author.

American Psychological Association. (1981). Ethical principles of psychologists. *American Psychologist*, *36*, 633–638.

American Psychological Association. (1990). Ethical principles of psychologists (Amended June 2, 1989). *American Psychologist*, *45*, 390–395.

American Psychological Association. (1992). Ethical principles of psychologists. *American Psychologist*, *47*, 1597–1611.

American Psychological Association. (2002). Ethical principles of psychologists. *American Psychologist*, *57*, 1060–1063.

Beauchamp, T. L., & Childress, J. F. (1994). *Principles of biomedical ethics* (4th ed.). New York: Oxford University Press.

Bibring, E. (1954). Psychoanalysis and the dynamic psychotherapies. *Journal of the American Psychoanalytic Association*, *2*, 745–770.

Borduin, C. M., Henggeler, S. W., Blaske, D. M., & Stein, R. J. (1990). Multisystemic treatment of adolescent sexual offenders. *International Journal of Offender Therapy and Comparative Criminology*, *34*, 105–113.

Brandt, R. B. (1979). *A theory of the right and the good*. Oxford: Clarendon Press.

Clarkin, J. F., Yeoman, F. E., & Kernberg, O. F. (1999). *Psychotherapy for borderline personality*. New York: John Wiley and Sons.

Committee on Ethical Guidelines for Forensic Psychologists. (1991). Specialty guidelines for forensic psychologists. *Law and Human Behavior*, *15*, 655–665.

Dawes, R. (1994). *House of cards*. New York: Free Press.

Donagan, A. (1977). *The theory of morality*. Chicago: University of Chicago. Press.

Doren, D. (2002). *Evaluating sex offenders*. Thousand Oaks, CA: Sage.

Eissler, K. R. (1953). The effect of the structure of the ego on psychoanalytic technique. *Journal of the American Psychoanalytic Association*, *1*, 104–143.

Frankena, W. K. (1973). *Ethics*. Englewood Cliffs, NJ: Prentice-Hall.

Freedman, D., Pisani, R., & Purves, R. (1998). *Statistics* (3rd ed.). New York: W. W. Norton.

Gilligan, C. (1982). *In a different voice*. Cambridge, MA: Harvard University Press.

Greenson, R. (1967). *The technique and practice of psychoanalysis*. Madison, CT: International University Press.

Hanson, R. K., Gordon, A., Harris, A. J. R., Marques, J. K., Murphy, W., Quinsey, V. L., & Seto, M. C. (2002). First report of the collaborative outcome data project on the effectiveness of psychological treatment for sex offenders. *Sexual Abuse, 14*, 169–194.

Hare, R. M. (1952). *The language of morals*. London: Oxford University Press.

Josephson, M. (1991). *Ethical values and decision making in business*. Marina Del Rey, CA: Josephson Institute for Ethics.

Kohlberg, L. (1981). *The philosophy of moral development*. San Francisco: Harper & Row.

Koocher, G. P., & Keith-Spiegel, P. (1998). *Ethics in psychology: Professional standards and cases* (2nd ed.). New York: Oxford University Press.

Marques, J. K. (1999). How to answer the question, "Does sex offender treatment work?" *Journal of Interpersonal Violence, 14 (4)*, 437–451.

Marques, J. K., & Day, D. M. (1998, May). *Sex offender treatment evaluation project*. Sacramento, CA: California Department of Mental Health.

Marshall, W. L., Fernandez, Y. M., Hudson, S. M., & Ward, T. (1998). *Sourcebook of treatment programs for sexual offenders*. New York: Plenum Press.

Parfit, D. (1984). *Reasons and persons*. New York: Oxford University Press.

Robinson, D. (1995). *The impact of cognitive skills training on post-release recidivism among Canadian federal offenders* (No. R-41). Ottawa, ON: Correctional Service Canada, Correctional Research and Development.

Ward, T., Laws, R. D., & Hudson, S. M. (2003). *Sexual deviance*. Thousand Oaks, CA: Sage.

Williams, B. (1972). *Morality*. New York: Harper & Row.

Williams, B. (1985). *Ethics and the limits of philosophy*. Cambridge, MA: Harvard University Press.

Williams, B. (1993). *Shame and necessity*. Berkeley: University of California Press.

CHAPTER 4

FORENSIC REPORT WRITING

JEFFREY E. HECKER AND R. JAMIE SCOULAR
UNIVERSITY OF MAINE

Report writing is an essential activity for most mental health professionals. In clinical settings, psychologists write intake reports, reports of psychological evaluations, progress reports, and reports justifying the need for third-party reimbursement for therapy. The necessity of documentation has become increasingly clear in our ever-more litigious society (Wiger, 1999). Consequently, most mental health professionals develop some degree of competence in report writing through training and professional experiences. When they find themselves in the legal arena, however, psychologists, psychiatrists, and social workers often discover that their report-writing skills and knowledge are not adequate for the task at hand. Forensic settings differ from therapeutic settings in many important ways (Greenburg & Shuman, 1999). The courtroom is foreign territory for many mental health professionals, and success in this new territory requires reexamining some basic skills, including report writing.

When mental health professionals get involved in legal issues, it is usually because they have specialized knowledge that can assist the judge or jury in deciding a legal issue. Psychologists have been recognized as experts in matters involving mental health issues since as early as 1962 (Blau, 1984). As expert witnesses, mental health professionals have as their primary goal to use specialized knowledge to educate the courts about matters that are not well understood by the general public. The expert is expected to give an opinion that will help the judge or jury to understand evidence before them and to reach a determination on a psycholegal issue (Melton, Petrila, Poythress, & Slobogin, 1997). In writing a report for the courts, psychologists must not only provide their opinion, they must also describe for the courts the basis of that opinion.

Written reports serve several essential functions (Melton et al., 1997). First, the report is a record of the professional activity that has taken place. It includes a description of the purpose, setting, and circumstances of the evaluation; the sources of information used; the findings; the professional's opinion; and the limitations of the data upon which the findings were based. Second, the process of writing the report requires the professional to organize and evaluate data. Impressions that are formed during the face-to-face interview with a client may be reevaluated in the face of collateral information. When a thoughtful approach to report writing is taken, the clinician looks not only for evidence that is consistent with his or her initial hypotheses but also for information that may disprove early opinions. In a way, report writing is a rehearsal for testimony. The process of thinking through and articulating one's logic at the keyboard, where one has the opportunity to try out arguments that can be reworked or withdrawn with the click of a few keys, helps one to be a more effective advocate for one's opinions on the witness stand. There are many instances in which mental health professionals do not have the opportunity to testify. In these cases, the written report is the only means by which the expert's opinion is made available to the court. Third, written reports can allow the courts to reach a legal disposition without a hearing. A high-quality report can help both sides in a legal disagreement reach some conclusions without having to take the matter to trial. Depending upon the nature of the case, a well-written psychological report may be the key impetus to an out-of-court settlement or plea bargain agreement (Melton et al., 1997).

UNIQUE FEATURES OF FORENSIC REPORTS

Forensic reports can be distinguished from other types of psychological reports in several ways. Perhaps most obviously, the audience for a forensic report is different than the audience for most other reports written by mental health professionals. For the most part, forensic reports are written for legal professionals—attorneys and judges—and other non–mental health professionals. Therefore, forensic reports cannot contain clinical jargon or esoteric terminology. The professional needs to convey his or her ideas so that they can be understood by an intelligent reader who does not share the same professional background as the writer.

Given the purpose of forensic evaluations, the report must address the psycholegal issues relevant to the case. Often the issues that must be addressed are spelled out in relevant state or federal law. For example, in an evaluation of a defendant's competence to stand trial, the forensic report should discuss the defendant's appreciation of the charges, his or her understanding of the trial process, and ability to collaborate with counsel. Custody evaluations should discuss the best interest of the child. And in an evaluation of an adolescent being considered for prosecution in adult court, the report needs to discuss the maturity of the youth. Although our point that evaluations for specific legal purposes must address the relevant psycholegal issues may seem obvious, studies examining reports produced by practitioners have found that relevant psycholegal issues were not addressed in a surprising number of cases (Nicholson & Norwood, 2000).

Though it is important that forensic reports address psycholegal issues, it is equally important that forensic examiners not take over the role of the court by pronouncing on the ultimate legal issue. Generally, the ultimate legal issue refers to the legal question that the courts have been asked to address: Is the defendant competent to stand trial? Should a defendant be found not guilty of a crime because he could not appreciate the wrongfulness of his criminal behavior? Should a parent's parental rights be terminated? Most forensic experts agree that it is not appropriate for mental health professionals to give opinions about ultimate legal issues (Allnut & Chaplow, 2000; Grisso, 1998; Melton et al., 1997; Ziskin & Faust, 1988). Forensic evaluators "provide an adequate description of the individual's mental state as it pertains to the relevant [psycholegal] issue, the judge or jury will be able to draw its own inference on the ultimate issue" (Allnut & Chaplow, 2000, p. 986). Clearly, there are times when the distinction between the psycholegal issue and the ultimate legal issue is blurry at best. Nonetheless, most scholarly commentators agree that the onus of responsibility is on the mental health professional to keep the distinction clear in his or her mind and to communicate findings appropriately. Using the examples just cited, the distinction between psycholegal and ultimate issues may be clearer now. A psychologist may conclude that a defendant's limited intellectual ability impairs his ability to appreciate the legal charges that have been brought against him (psycholegal issue). The court then decides whether or not he is competent to stand trial (ultimate legal issue). Similarly, a psychiatrist could conclude that at the time a defendant immersed her child's hands in boiling water she was markedly delusional as a result of untreated schizophrenia and could not appreciate the wrongfulness of her behavior (psycholegal issue). It would be up to the judge (or jury) to decide if she is not guilty by reason of insanity. Finally, although a mental health professional may testify that a man who is alcohol dependent will likely neglect his child (psycholegal issue), it is up to the judge to determine whether or not his parental rights should be terminated (ultimate legal issue).

Although there is near-unanimous agreement about the ultimate-issue question among scholars of psychology and the law, many practitioners have not gotten the word. Borum and Grisso (1996) found that about 50 percent of the experienced forensic psychologists and psychiatrists they surveyed reported that it was "essential" that forensic evaluators offer an opinion about trial competence. Only 10 percent thought it was "contraindicated." Regarding the ultimate issue in criminal responsibility cases, fewer experienced clinicians thought it was essential that the report offer an opinion about the ultimate legal issue and about 20 percent thought it was not appropriate (Borum & Grisso, 1996).

Before we move on to discuss the content of forensic reports, one additional distinguishing feature of the forensic report bears mentioning. As they are writing a forensic report, mental health professionals need to be mindful that their report may need to be defended. Ideally, of course, any psychologist, psychiatrist, or social worker should be able and willing to defend an opinion as expressed in their reports. But the fact is, they are not asked to do so with much frequency outside the forensic setting. In the legal setting, in contrast, mental health professionals should expect that their reports will undergo careful scrutiny—often by individuals who are looking for weaknesses in their data and logic. Adjusting to the adversarial nature of forensic work can be very difficult for mental health professionals (Melton et al., 1997). To ignore this important characteristic of forensic psychology is to court humiliation and, worse yet, the charge of incompetence. In reviewing one's forensic reports, it is useful to put oneself in the role of the attorney whose case will be weakened by this testimony. What is unclear in the report? What is open to misinterpretation? What can be defended, and how? What cannot?

THE FORENSIC REPORT

The content and structure of forensic reports may vary according to the referral question, the preference of the referring agent, and the professional's style, but several core features should appear in most forensic reports (Barnum, 2000; Borum & Grisso, 1996; Melton et al., 1997). These features include information that identifies the person or persons evaluated; description of the referral questions; basis of assessment including a list of all data sources; informed-consent information (e.g., what the defendant was told about the evaluation); relevant psychosocial history; clinical findings, including mental status examination and psychological testing; impressions and opinions of the examiner; and recommendations. Although these features are not unique to forensic reports, there are both ethical and practical considerations specific to forensic assessment that substantially shape the content of each section. In the following section of this chapter we provide a generic outline for forensic reports and discuss the characteristics of each section that merits special consideration in forensic reports.

Identifying Information and Referral Question

Before an evaluation, the practitioner is given a referral. Generally, there is some indication as to what kinds of information the referent hopes to ascertain from the evaluation. The evaluator needs to carefully consider the referral question and determine its clarity (Melton et al., 1997). Given a clearly stated referral question that falls within the bounds of the practitioner's competence, the evaluation can proceed. When the referral question is ambiguous or not available, the practitioner should consult with the referent. This step allows for the evaluator to work with the referent to structure concrete, clinically addressable referral questions. It is up to the forensic examiner to educate the referent about the specific kinds of questions that scientifically oriented mental health professionals can answer, discuss possible limitations in the evaluator's competence in addressing the restructured referral questions, and make clear the evaluator's stance on the ultimate legal question. As we have seen, there is a disparity between what forensic scholars recommend regarding the ultimate legal issue and what many practitioners do. It is in the best interest of all involved for the forensic examiner to let the referent know whether, or to what degree, the examiner will offer an opinion about the ultimate issue. The final step prior to beginning the evaluation is to accept or deny the referral. This decision would, of course, depend upon a variety of factors—most importantly the professional's competence to address the referral question.

The referral question section of a forensic report contains information about the referent, the agreed upon referral question(s), and the immediate circumstances leading to the referral (Melton et al., 1997; Gould, 1998; Sattler, 1998). Referent information should include name, position, and affiliation. The referral question(s), as mentioned, should be scientifically addressable, specific, and pertinent to the legal issue. Finally, in writing about the circumstances leading to the referral, it is helpful to include behaviors or symptoms linked to the legal issue. This subsection may include information gleaned from official court documents, arrest records, victim statements, client interview, or other collateral sources (Gould, 1998). All information included in the referral section must be objective and pertinent to the referral.

In practice, mental health professionals appear to follow at least one of these guidelines fairly consistently. A summary of six studies that examined the content of criminal forensic reports across five states (Nicholson & Norwood, 2000) found that only a small percentage of reports (from 1–4%) failed to mention the legal issue that triggered the referral. Although practitioners mention the legal issue leading to referral, they do not consistently address the issue in their reports. McGarry (1965, cited in Melton et al., 1997) examined 106 trial competence evaluations performed in Massachusetts and found that none "spoke to the issue of the defendant's competency to stand trial" (p. 525).

Informed Consent

The Informed Consent section of the forensic report serves to document that the evaluator has notified the examinee of all pertinent issues prior to the evaluation and that the client both understands and agrees to the conditions of the assessment.

Of the many contextual differences between therapeutic and forensic settings, one is the evaluator's approach to the examinee. The examiner is not conducting therapy and thus should not rely on standard therapeutic approaches. Therapeutic alliance relies on support, acceptance, and empathy (Greenberg & Shuman, 1999). Theoretically, these factors contribute to disclosure and personal growth (Rogers, 1957). The goal of forensic evaluation is not personal growth; rather, the forensic evaluator is working to answer the referral questions. Within this context, the evaluator's relationship with the client is neutral, objective, and detached (Greenberg & Shuman, 1999). Although it is not necessary to leave all therapeutic skills out of forensic evaluation, deliberate use of empathy may be construed as coercing the examinee into admittance of unintended material (Shuman, 1993).

Many characteristics of forensic evaluation should be discussed with examinees before commencing the evaluation. Primarily, the client must be informed of the limitations of confidentiality. The examinee should understand that he or she is not the *client*. Rather, the referent is the client and is therefore privy to any findings that are relevant to the referral question. Maintenance of report confidentiality is at the discretion of the referent and not under the evaluator's sole control. A second issue to cover is the purpose of the evaluation. Generally, this discourse discloses referent information (e.g., name, agency, etc.) and the referral questions the evaluator has been asked to address. Along with a discussion of purpose, it is necessary to include a summary of possible risks and benefits associated with participation. Most risks to participants can be traced to the limited confidentiality of forensic reports and can include implicating oneself or third parties in unreported crimes, exposing personal information to the community, or contributing to more restrictive legal consequences. In cases where the findings may be used by the courts to make decisions that would have negative ramifications for the examinee (e.g., termination of parental rights, longer incarceration, denial of parole), the examinee needs to understand this. Possible benefits of cooperating with a forensic evaluation might include increased access to mental health care and avoidance of legal proceedings. The procedures to be used in the psychological evaluation (e.g., interviews, collateral information, standardized assessments) also need to be explained to forensic clients. Finally, the evaluator should describe the probable contents of the report. As the examiner has not yet completed the evaluation, report contents can be described generally. For example, it is acceptable to state that the report will contain objective information gathered from interviews and tests, impressions about mental health and psychological functioning pertinent to the referral questions, and recommendations for mental health treatment.

For evaluations where the client is under the age of consent, both the juvenile and the legal guardian should be included in any informed-consent discussions. The juvenile's verbal or written assent to proceed should usually be sought and documented.

Once again, in the area of documentation of informed consent, we find a disparity between the recommendations of forensic scholars and the behavior of many practicing examiners. Nicholson and Norwood (2000) identified three studies that looked at whether or not forensic reports included descriptions of the consent process. Two studies of forensic practitioners in Florida found that only about 30 percent of forensic reports contained documentation of the examiner's notification to the defendant (e.g., limits of confidentiality and purpose of evaluation). The third study examined 362 forensic reports produced in Oklahoma and found that notification of informed consent was left out of 95 percent of them. It is important to note that these data do not speak to whether informed consent issues were discussed prior to the evaluation or whether the client gave consent, but only to the lack of documentation.

Basis of Assessment

The Basis of Assessment section of the written report contains a wide array of information and can be thought of as a catalogue of the methods and procedures used by the forensic examiner to complete the evaluation (Gould, 1998). This catalogue should contain date(s) and nature (e.g., interviewing, testing, etc.) of client contact; collateral sources of information (e.g., interviews or assessments with third parties, or other written material such as medical, academic, health, or psychological records); and psychological or forensic assessment tools used. This information should be presented in the order listed, with all contacts in chronological order.

Although the Basis of Assessment section appears straightforward, there are two important issues that must be considered. The first stems from the adversarial nature of the forensic context. Evaluators and examinees may develop a positive working relationship, but the results of forensic evaluations can be detrimental to the examinee's legal position (Greenberg & Shuman, 1999). This adversarial context pressures many examinees to limit or distort the kinds of information they provide. Specifically, there may be reasons for forensic examinees to feign incompetence, deny responsibility for criminal actions, malinger, or generally present only the best possible qualities as an attempt to influence legal outcomes. This adversarial nature of forensic work highlights the need for multi-source, multimethod assessment (Azar, Lauretti, & Loding, 1998; Emiley, 2002; Gould, 1998). The success of this approach to assessment is dependent upon the examiners' interviewing skills, ability to choose relevant assessment instruments, and ability to gain access to a cross section of collateral information. This model allows the examiner to analyze patterns of convergence or divergence of information for the purpose of obtaining a more valid client profile.

Because multimethod forensic assessments frequently include psychological tests, forensic evaluators must be exceptionally careful in choosing assessment instruments. Knowledge of the psychometric properties of tests should be a prerequisite for their use in any setting. The forensic context, however, demands increased attention to these psychometric issues. In 1993, a Supreme Court decision in response to *Daubert v. Merrell Dow Pharmaceuticals, Inc*. provided legal standards for admissibility of expert testimony in legal proceedings (Dixon & Gill, 2002). The resulting *Daubert Standard* speaks indirectly to the kinds of psychological instruments that are acceptable as the basis for expert testimony. To meet the Daubert standard, a psychological test must be peer reviewed; generally accepted; constructed upon the methods and procedures of science; and possess known error rates (Dixon & Gill, 2002). Psychologists called to testify in court should be prepared to discuss several of the following issues: the test's underlying theory of science; peer review status; psychological community acceptance; and psychometric properties (e.g., reliability, validity, base rate estimates, and falsifiability) (Gould, 1998).

The Basis of Assessment section of forensic reports is where documentation of the multiple methods used in the assessment takes place. Survey studies find that clinical interviews and, to a slightly lesser extent, mental status examinations appear in nearly all forensic evaluations (Nicholson & Norwood, 2000). There is considerably more variability in the frequency with which psychological tests are used in forensic assessments. Nicholson and Norwood reported that survey studies find that from 9 percent to 69 percent of mental health professionals report using psychological tests routinely in their forensic work. The range of test use can be accounted for partially by expected professional training differences (e.g., psychologist versus psychiatrist). However, many forensic reports written by psychologists did not include psychological testing.

Great variability has also been found in the type of collateral information cited in forensic reports. Collateral sources cited in reports spanned from the frequently used review of records (e.g., arrest reports, prior mental health, etc.) to the less frequently used third-party interviews (e.g., relatives, jail personnel, etc.). Surprisingly, interviews with relatives were almost never used (Nicholson & Norwood, 2000). Perhaps most troubling, in some studies greater than 50 percent of the forensic reports did not include any description of the methods or procedures used to acquire information.

As discussed previously, exclusion of information does not indicate that some part of the evaluation did not take place. For example, a clinician may have spoken to a corrections office about the examinee, but this was not documented in the report. Our practice is to gain information from all relevant sources (e.g., collateral reports, third-party interviews, and psychological testing) within the scope of the referral questions. Although it can be laborious, we document every source of collateral information individually in the report.

Psychosocial History

The primary purpose of the Psychosocial History section is to summarize historical information about the examinee that is relevant to the referral question (Melton et al., 1997). Although this may sound straightforward, it is not always so. Forensic questions are highly variable and cannot be addressed in a stereotyped manner (Allnutt & Chaplow, 2000; Melton et al., 1997; Sattler, 1998). The examiner must consider the kind of evaluation to be performed (e.g., risk, child custody, mental harm, trial competence, etc.) and the specific referral question(s) involved. Whereas an evaluation of mental injury for the purpose of compensation suggests special attention to psychiatric and developmental history (Allnutt

& Chaplow, 2000), trial competency evaluations usually include only limited historical information (Melton et al., 1997). The type of evaluation, however, may be trumped by the referral questions. Referral questions always determine the ultimate scope of the evaluation. Thus the examiner may search for information beyond that which is suggested by the type of evaluation alone.

We suggest a multistep model to determine the contents of the Psychosocial History section. First, the examiner should have an adequate understanding of the kinds of information that are important in assessing the average client. Generally, clinicians seek data regarding developmental history; family information; interpersonal functioning; academic, occupational, medical, criminal, and psychiatric history; and information about the context of the referral. With this in mind, the examiner must consider the type of evaluation to be performed and the associated referral question. From the general assessment model, the forensic evaluator will choose only certain areas to investigate. As described previously, the type of evaluation might suggest a limited psychosocial history while the referral question pulls for more information. In this case, the examiner always follows the referral question. Once the examiner has chosen the critical areas of assessment and completed the evaluation, the next step is to delete information that is potentially damaging to the client or is not directly relevant to the referral question (Sattler, 1998). Forensic reports can become public records. And, although an examinee does consent to the evaluation, he or she does not waive all rights to privacy. If historical information is sensitive and not relevant to the clinician's formulation, it should not be included in the report.

The Psychosocial History section lays some of the groundwork for the professional's clinical impressions described later in the report. A well-written forensic report is structured so that the reader can follow the clinician's logic. The case formulation (or clinical impression) will likely be more acceptable when supported by a logical chain of relevant information. After reviewing the forensic report, the consumer should have no trouble connecting information included in the report with the evaluator's conclusions.

A conceptual issue that should be considered by examiners prior to writing this section is related to the context of the forensic evaluation. In contrast to therapy, forensic assessment is often guided by external (e.g., referral question) rather than collaborative or patient-guided goals (Greenberg & Shuman, 1997). In this context, there are many reasons for the forensic examinee to distort personal history information. Often the most critical information is left out or altered. This is not to imply that therapy clients never distort, but rather that the forensic examinees may have more conscious motivation for distortion than others. Considering this fact, the forensic examiner may wish to include a disclaimer statement in this section (Gould, 1998). The disclaimer should include a clear indication of the source(s) of information (e.g., client interview, self-report, collateral interviews) and that there is no attempt to present the data as factual or supported by evidence (Gould, 1998). When the psychosocial history is based primarily upon the examinee's self-report, we typically begin this section of the report with a statement such as "The following history is based upon my interview with Mr. X unless otherwise indicated." In addition to the disclaimer, subheadings can be used in the psychosocial history section clarifying the source of information (e.g., *Interview with Mr. X*).

Research investigating the Psychosocial History section of forensic reports is limited. Available information stems from surveys of forensic examiners who demonstrated competency in criminal evaluations. For example, Borum and Grisso (1996) reported that most practitioners felt that psychiatric history and current psychotropic medication use were essential in adjudicative competence evaluations. For evaluation of criminal responsibility, the essentials included those listed for adjudicative competence along with information from past mental health records, substance abuse information, and police reports (Borum & Grisso, 1996). Clearly, the Psychosocial History section of forensic reports is highly variable and, perhaps, underresearched.

Clinical Findings

The Clinical Findings section functions to summarize objective information the examiner has gathered through interviews, psychological tests, and collateral records. This section presents both factual information and descriptive material based on clinical observation (Melton et al., 1997). This section can be divided into subheadings for clarity of information.

Mental Status

The Mental Status section is based on an examination that can be conducted formally or informally over the course of the interview process. Regardless of how the examiner conducts the mental status examination, there are standard components that should be addressed. In general, the examiner should note the client's appearance, manner, approach to the assessment, orientation, alertness, thought processes, unusual thought content, affect, and mood. There are many excellent sources for detailed information about conducting and writing up mental status exams.

Behavioral Observations

The Behavioral Observations section is meant to describe the evaluator's observations of the examinee over the course of evaluation. Some observations are, of course, relevant to the mental status examination and would be presented in that section. The purposes of this section are threefold. First, the type of observations listed in this section help the reader to understand what the evaluator considers to be *important* behavior. Next, behavioral observations lend objectivity to the report because they provide information about the types of behavior tied to specific clinical impressions. Last, the behavioral descriptions may be tied directly to recommendations regarding treatment (Sattler, 1998).

Some things to keep in mind when describing behavior observations in a report include the following: First, the examiner has only a *sample* of behavior and that sample is usually from an unusual setting (i.e., the evaluation). External validity of observations is, of course, improved if the evaluator can observe the examinee in multiple settings. This is often not possible. Therefore, clinicians should avoid descriptors that imply stable characteristics. Second, following from the previous point, statements included in this section should describe rather than interpret behavior. Clinicians should use concrete descriptors of what they saw, heard, or smelled. Finally, relevance should guide decision making about what to include in this section. There is no need to report information not relevant to the referral question.

Psychological Testing

As discussed earlier, psychological tests chosen for a forensic evaluation should conform to the Daubert standard and address issues related to the referral question(s). Assuming that the examiner has chosen appropriate measures, the next task is to report test results in the Psychological Testing section in a manner that is useful to the reader. Educating the consumer about the properties of the chosen psychological measures serves a dual purpose. First, a brief description of test characteristics (i.e., method, purpose) provides the reader with information necessary to place the test results in their proper context. Second, disclosure of the limitations of psychological testing improves the examiner's credibility (Melton et al., 1997). To ensure that the reader is properly prepared to understand the various test results, the examiner should describe the manner in which the test was administered (e.g., self-report, report by other, etc.); the areas the test is meant to assess (e.g., behavior problems, intellectual functioning, etc.); the meaning of the scores; and possible interpretive limitations. It can be useful to note some of the universal concerns about testing. For example, it might be explained that the test results are merely probabilistic in nature because they reflect the similarity, or lack thereof, of the examinee to a normative sample. In some circumstances it may be important to educate the reader that test results, by themselves, are not confirmatory or diagnostic. Rather, the results are best viewed as hypotheses to be compared and combined with information gained over the whole evaluation (Gould, 1998). A final suggestion is to remain firmly objective. For example, when describing test results, provide margins of error when applicable and use qualifying words (e.g., "Mr. X is *likely* to react to stress by withdrawing from others").

Clinical Impressions

The Clinical Impressions section is where the examiner offers conclusions and clinical judgments about the examinee relevant to the referral question(s). Whereas previous sections required only objective data, the content of this section reflects the clinician's impressions of how the findings relate to the psycholegal questions (Allnutt & Chaplaw, 2000). As in any psychological report, the examiner must integrate all pertinent data and organize the findings so as to show a logical progression from data to inference (Melton et al., 1997).

Considering the legal context, the examiner must give special attention to several conceptual and practical issues. Conceptually, the impressions provided are based on data gathered from multiple sources of varied validity. Thus all opinion should be couched in terms that demonstrate the clinician's trust in the data (Gould, 1998). In addition, the language used in this section should reinforce the notion that the impressions are not evidence of causality, but rather "educated guesses" based on data (Sattler, 1998). A final conceptual issue involves the ultimate legal question. As described earlier, it is generally agreed that mental health professionals do not address the ultimate question. Considering this, the examiner should offer opinion relevant only to the referral questions. In cases where the line is blurred between ultimate and referral questions, the examiner should help restructure the questions before performing the evaluation.

Beyond the conceptual issues, an awareness of the practical guidelines will help structure this section. Primarily, the examiner must keep in mind that the goal of this section is to address the psycholegal questions. As such, the section can be organized to allow the consumer to follow the examiner's logic. A general outline to follow would be to discuss the presence of psychopathology; summarize the phenomenological characteristics of the pathology; explain the impact of the pathology on behavior; then describe how the pathology and associated behaviors apply to the psycholegal issue (Allnutt & Chaplaw, 2000). A second guideline informs the use of data. The examiner must present data that supports as well as contrasts the primary formulation. The inclusion of data supportive of clinical impressions allows the consumer access to the examiner's logic. Reporting data that diverge from the predominant impression demonstrates the objectivity of the examiner and promotes overall credibility (Melton et al., 1997).

Clinical formulations should follow from the data. But often in forensic work the data may be inconsistent. In criminal work, for example, offenders and victims often provide dramatically different accounts of the same event. Collateral sources may report information about an examinee that he or she emphatically denies to be true. In some instances, forensic examiners may need to offer alternative formulations in the same report. In these cases, the examiner has discovered contradictory information and has no means by which to judge the relative validity of the information. Assuming one set of findings to be true leads to one clinical formulation, whereas assuming the contradictory information to be true leads to a very different formulation. As an example, we have been asked to evaluate men who have been convicted of sexual offenses. In these referrals, the key question is evaluating the risk the individual presents for future offending. One approach to risk assessment is to compare the characteristics of the alleged offender to those of convicted sexual offenders who have committed additional offenses (e.g., Quinsey, Harris, Rice, & Cormier, 1998). But this approach is only defensible if the examinee has in fact committed an offense. In cases where there have been allegations of sexual offending but no conviction and denial on the part of the alleged offender, we discuss risk twice in the Clinical Impressions section. First, we discuss risk assuming the offense has occurred. Second, we discuss risk assuming that there was no offense.

Risk assessment, as an issue for forensic report writers, deserves special attention. Controversy over when, and if, mental health professionals should discuss risk stems from early findings that suggested that there was no scientific basis for risk prediction (see Grisso & Applebaum, 1992). The implication of these findings was that mental health professionals who performed risk assessments were operating unethically. Since that time, the acceptance of risk assessment has widened appreciably because both risk assessment technology and the standards for language to communicate risk have improved (Grann & Pallvik, 2002; Grisso & Applebaum, 1999). Practitioners who get involved in risk assessment need to become familiar with instruments and protocols designed specifically for risk assessment. As with any assessment technology, mental health professionals need to familiarize themselves with the instruments' psychometric properties. Before applying a risk assessment strategy with an examinee, the professional needs to be confident that it is appropriate to compare the examinee to the sample upon which the assessment instrument was developed. Clinicians should, of course, be familiar with the base rates of the behaviors of interest. This is crucial in understanding the risk of false-positive and false-negative predictions. A final consideration is the meaning of risk. Perhaps the most important advice we can offer is that risk is not a dichotomous (e.g., "yes" or "no") variable. Rather, risk should be viewed on a continuum on which certain examinee and/or contextual characteristics increase or decrease the chances that the target behavior will appear in the future.

When conducting and describing risk assessments, mental health professionals should (1) clearly identify the risk behavior, (2) use multiple sources to gather risk data, (3) indicate data sources that support their risk estimate, (4) list the factors known to increase or decrease risk, and (5) reinforce the continuous nature of risk with the proper descriptive language (e.g., "increased risk" versus "risk is present") (Towl & Crighton, 1996). In reporting results of a risk assessment, clinicians should avoid general statements about the risk presented by the examinee (Grisso, 1998). Rather, the factors associated with increased and decreased level of risk should be discussed. In addition, the time frame for the risk assessment should be specified (e.g., within the next year).

The Clinical Impressions section of a forensic report is probably the section that receives the most attention from consumers. Ideally, this section incorporates pertinent information from all previous sections and delivers the clinician's opinions regarding the referral questions. Consequently, it may be the only section of the report read by some attorneys and judges.

Studies that have examined psychological reports produced by forensic practitioners in the field suggest that may clinicians fall short of the standard suggested by experts. Many forensic examiners routinely offer pronouncements on the ultimate legal issue in the summary sections of their reports (Nicholson &

Norwood, 2000). Failure to articulate the relationships between test results and the clinical impressions is common, as is omission of diagnostic information pertinent to the case formulation (Nicholson & Norwood, 2000).

Recommendations

After the examiner has completed the evaluation and integrated all pertinent findings, the next task is to suggest appropriate means by which to address examinee weaknesses or dysfunction. Recommendations should be practical and realistic (Sattler, 1998). To develop appropriate recommendations, the clinician must consider the resources of the client and his or her support network, the accessibility to treatment services, and the possible stresses associated with each recommendation. Sometimes over the course of an assessment questions arise that demand additional evaluation time or fall outside the practitioner's competence. When this occurs, the examiner should feel comfortable recommending further assessment or referring the client to an outside evaluator (e.g., a neuropsychologist) (Sattler, 1998). Above all else, the evaluator should offer suggestions that will most benefit the examinee with issues relevant to the psycholegal question.

FORENSIC REPORT WRITING: GENERAL GUIDELINES

We conclude this chapter with seven guidelines for effective forensic report writing. The guidelines are:

1. *Advocate for the data—not the case.*
2. *Organize the report—data first, then conclusions.*
3. *Minimize clinical jargon.*
4. *Write concisely.*
5. *Cite sources.*
6. *Be detailed enough—but not too much.*
7. *Get feedback.*

Advocate for the Data—Not the Case

Mental health professionals can find themselves drawn into the adversarial nature of forensic work. Particularly when they are hired by one side in a legal dispute, the temptation to want to win for their side can be strong. We caution clinicians to be mindful of this temptation and encourage them to remain neutral with respect to the ultimate legal decisions in cases in which they become involved. However, remaining neutral should not be interpreted to mean remaining passive. In contrast, clinicians should be strong advocates for their findings and their conclusions (Melton et al., 1997). In fact, all the remaining guidelines are suggested as ways to help clinicians be more effective advocates for their data. Clear communication in a forensic report is essential if one is to be an effective advocate for one's findings and conclusions.

There are some cases in which the goals of advocating for one's findings and winning the legal dispute go hand in hand. However, there are others in which one's success at promoting one's findings may be undermined if one simultaneously tries to win the case. The credibility of the data can be legitimately questioned when the mental health professional is obviously motivated to win the case. In contrast, one's credibility is generally enhanced if one is seen as an advocate for one's findings, including their strengths and limitations.

Organize the Report—Data First, Then Conclusions

The analogy of a forensic report to a scientific journal article is a useful one. The introduction to an article sets the stage for the study, providing enough background information so that the reader knows what led up to the study and what the researcher hopes to find. Similarly, the beginning of a forensic report provides the background for the evaluation—why the examinee was referred to the clinician and what questions was he or she asked to address. The Basis of Assessment component of a report is like the Methods section of a research article; it describes how the data were collected. The Results section of a research article describes what was found. In a forensic report, the findings are summarized in the Psychosocial History, Mental Status, Behavioral Observations, and Psychlogical Testing sections. Finally, one's Clinical Impressions and Recommendations sections are analogous to the Discussion section of an article. Here the findings are interpreted, the questions described in the introduction to the report are addressed, and recommendations about future directions are made.

In forensic reports the descriptive findings are separated from clinical inferences (Melton et al., 1997). In a way, the clinician is building the case for his or her impressions and recommendations throughout the report. In reading a journal article, the reader should not be surprised by the points the author makes in the Discussion section; the conclusions should follow from the Methods and Results sections. Similarly, the reader of a forensic report should not be surprised by the clinician's clinical impressions and recommendations. They should follow from the questions asked and the data collected. One writing tip that may help clinicians to be clear about what is fact and what is opinion is the use of verb tense. Generally, observations and clinical data should be described in the past tense. Clinical impressions should be written in the present tense (Allnut & Caplow, 2000).

Minimize Clinical Jargon

There is universal agreement among experts on forensic report writing that the use of clinical jargon should be kept to a minimum (e.g., Allnut & Chaplow, 2000; Grisso, 1998; Melton et al., 1997; Sattler, 1998). For mental health professionals who have trained and functioned in clinical settings, clinical jargon is their natural language. Psychiatrists learn to say that patients are "oriented times three" very early in their training. Psychologists refer to "characterological disturbance" in their reports, and social workers may describe a client as having "control issues." These phrases, rightly or wrongly, usually yield no more than knowing head nods from other mental health professionals. However, attorneys and judges have not gone to the same schools and do not speak the same language. Petrella and Poythress (1979; cited in Melton et al., 1997) surveyed judges and lawyers and found that they tended to label as "unclear" such words and phrases as "affect," "neologisms," "delusional ideation," "personality deficit," and "flat affect."

Whenever possible, mental health professionals should use common expressions to describe their findings. This may not always be possible; in fact, at times it may be important to use technical language to demonstrate that the mental health professional is conversant in the language of his or her profession (Melton et al., 1997). The general rule of thumb is that whenever clinicians use technical terms, these terms should be accompanied by a brief explanation of their meaning. For example, if a client is described as having "blunted affect," a brief description such as "he demonstrated no emotion" should be added.

Write Concisely

In his essay "Politics and the English Language," George Orwell (1946) recommended: "If it is possible to cut a word out, always cut it out." Forensic report writers would be well served to follow Orwell's sage advice. Wordy sentences, useless repetition, and abstract word choices should be avoided in forensic reports. The goal is to convey one's findings and conclusions as succinctly as possible. One common way in which mental health professionals are often unnecessarily wordy is when they use trite phases ("as of this writing") when a simpler word or phrase ("currently") would do (Sattler, 1998).

Cite Sources

Forensic assessments tend to be based upon multiple sources of information. In addition to the interview with the examinee, historical information may be gathered from collateral interviews and police or institutional records. It is important that clinicians make clear the source of the data described in the report. Phrases such as "according to the arrest report," "Mr. X's wife reported," and "according to the discharge summary from X hospital" provide documentation of information sources (Sattler, 1998).

Citing sources of information is another means for clinicians to distinguish the findings of the evaluation from the clinician's own impressions and conclusions. For example, the statement "Mr. Y abuses alcohol" is appropriate for the Clinical Impressions section, whereas the statements "Mr. Y reported that he drinks 6 to 12 beers every evening" and "Mr. Y's mother described him as an alcoholic" would be more appropriate earlier in the report.

Be Detailed Enough—But Not Too Much

Our review of the literature did not reveal a consensus among forensic experts about the length or detail of psychological reports. It is clear that page-number guidelines would not be useful. A myriad of factors, such as the purpose of the evaluation, the amount of collateral information available, and the need for psychological testing, impact report length. Rather than setting arbitrary page limits, what should guide decision making about the length and detail of forensic reports is the relevance of information to the referral question. Background information and psychological test findings should be detailed enough to provide the foundation for the clinical impressions and conclusions that follow. A forensic report should be as detailed and comprehensive as it needs to be and no more. Melton and colleagues (1997) suggest "examiners should confine themselves to inquiries legitimately raised by the referral source and should restrict the substance of their reports accordingly" (p. 524).

Sources of extraneous information included in some forensic reports include unnecessarily detailed description of personal history, highly technical and detailed accounts of test findings, and inclusion of collateral information of questionable relevance (e.g., old mental health records or medical information). In wading through a psychological report, it should not be the reader's job to separate the wheat from the chaff.

Judges and attorneys are busy people. Presented with a lengthy forensic report, they may be tempted to skip to the Conclusions section or, worse yet, leave the report unread. In the editing process, clinicians should ask themselves questions such as the following to help decide what information needs to be included and what can be deleted: How will this information help the reader to understand the client? Does the report contain potentially harmful information? If so, is this information necessary to address the referral question and to support my conclusions? Does the reader really need to know this information? Clinicians should not feel obligated to include information simply because they have it. "No matter how interesting or true it is, information that does not contribute to an understanding of the interviewee and the referral question is irrelevant" (Sattler, 1998, p. 239).

Get Feedback

Forensic report writing can be a lonely process, more so even than other forms of professional writing. Journal articles pass through colleagues, journal editors, and reviewers, undergoing revisions at each stage before presentation to their intended audience. Book authors need to respond to the criticisms of editors, reviewers, and copy editors before they see their work in print. The forensic report, on the other hand, typically goes from one's head to one's computer to the reader without review or input from another person. This is unfortunate because all forms of writing tend to benefit from feedback and revision.

Ethical and legal mandates to maintain confidentiality limit opportunities for feedback and collaboration on forensic reports. However, mental health professionals' hands are not completely tied by the need to maintain confidentiality. There are at least three ways to elicit professional feedback about forensic reports. First, clinicians can be their own editors. Whenever possible, write a report and leave it alone for a few days, then review it with a critical eye. Keep in mind the guidelines we have suggested in this chapter in reviewing the work. Second, solicit the help of a colleague. The miracle of word processing has made deleting identifying information in professional reports much easier than it once was. Share a report with a colleague and ask for constructive feedback. Better yet, form an ongoing relationship with a colleague in which you review and critique each other's written work. Third, go to the consumers. Seek feedback from the judges, attorneys, or other professionals who routinely use your work. What did they find helpful about your reports? What seemed superfluous? Was there language that was unclear? Were there things they hoped to get out of your reports that were not there? Some attorneys and judges may want things you cannot provide (e.g., pronouncement on the ultimate legal issue), but by asking for their feedback you open the door for a dialogue about what mental health professionals can and cannot do in forensic evaluations.

REFERENCES

Allnutt, S. H., & Chaplow, D. (2000). General principles of forensic report writing. *Australian and New Zealand Journal of Psychiatry, 34*, 980–987.

Applebaum, P. S. (1997). The parable of the forensic psychiatrist: Ethics and the problem of doing harm. *International Journal of Psychiatry and the Law, 25*, 233–247.

Azar, S. T., Lauretti, A. F., & Loding, B. V. (1998). The evaluation of parental fitness in termination of parental rights cases: A functional-contextual perspective. *Clinical Child and Family Psychology Review, 1*, 77–100.

Barnum, R. (2000). Competence to stand trial. In T. Grisso & R. G. Schwartz (Eds.), *Youth on trial: A developmental perspective on juvenile justice*. Chicago: University of Chicago Press.

Blau, T. (1984). *The psychologist as expert witness*. New York: Wiley-Interscience.

Borum, R., & Grisso, T. (1996). Establishing standards for criminal forensic reports: An empirical analysis. *Bulletin of the American Academy of Psychiatry and Law, 24*, 297–317.

Dixon, L., & Gill, B. (2002). Changes in the standards for admitting expert evidence in federal civil cases since the Daubert decision. *Psychology, Public Policy, and Law, 8*(3), 251–308.

Emiley, S. F. (2002). Forensic psychological evaluations: Back to basics. *The Forensic Examiner, 6*, 31–40.

Gould, J. W. (1998). *Conducting scientifically crafted child custody evaluations.* Thousand Oaks, CA: Sage.

Grann, M., & Pallvik, A. (2002). An empirical investigation of written risk communication in forensic psychiatric evaluations. *Psychology, Crime, & Law, 8,* 113–130.

Greenberg, S. A., & Shuman, D. W. (1997). Irreconcilable conflict between therapeutic and forensic roles. In D. N. Bersoff (Ed.), *Ethical conflicts in psychology* (2nd ed.). Washington, DC: American Psychological Association.

Grisso, T. (1998). *Forensic evaluation of juveniles.* Sarasota, FL: Professional Resource Press.

Grisso, T., & Applebaum, P. S. (1999). Is it unethical to offer predictions of future violence? In D. N. Bersoff (Ed.), *Ethical conflicts in psychology* (2nd ed.). Washington, DC: American Psychological Association.

Melton, G. B., Petrila, J., Poythress, N. G., & Slobogin, C. (1997). *Psychological evaluations for the courts: A handbook for mental health professionals and lawyers* (2nd ed.). New York: Guilford Press.

Nicholson, R. A., & Norwood, S. (2000). The quality of forensic psychological assessments, reports, and testimony: Acknowledging the gap between promise and practice. *Law and Human Behavior, 24* (1), 9–44.

Orwell, G. (1946). Politics and the English language. *Horizon.* (Electronic Version) Retrieved February 14, 2003
from http://eserver.org/theory/politics-and-english-lang.txt.

Quinsey, V. L., Harris, G. T., Rice, M. E., & Cormier, C. A. (1998). *Violent offenders: Appraising and managing risk.* Washington, DC: American Psychological Association.

Rogers, C. (1957). The necessary and sufficient conditions of therapeutic personality change. *Journal of Consulting Psychology, 21,* 95–103.

Sattler, J. M. (1998). *Clinical and forensic interviewing of children and families: Guidelines for the mental health, education, pediatric, and child maltreatment fields.* San Diego: Jerome M. Sattler.

Shuman, D. W. (1993). The use of empathy in forensic examinations. *Ethics and Behavior, 3,* 289–302.

Towl, G. J., & Crighton, D. A. (1996). *The handbook of psychology for forensic practitioners.* New York: Routledge.

Wiger, D. E. (1999). *The psychotherapy documentation primer.* New York: Wiley.

Ziskin, J., & Faust, D. (1988). *Coping with psychiatric and psychological testimony, Vols. 1–3* (4th ed.). Marina Del Ray, CA: Law and Psychology Press.

PART II

ASSESSMENT

CHAPTER 5

ASSESSMENT OF DANGEROUSNESS AND CRIMINAL RESPONSIBILITY

LYNNE ECCLESTON
UNIVERSITY OF MELBOURNE, AUSTRALIA

TONY WARD
VICTORIA UNIVERSITY OF WELLINGTON, NEW ZEALAND

Dangerousness is universally associated with acts of violence and harm towards others. Dangerousness is a complex construct: It implies characteristics within an individual that interact with external environmental factors that manifest as violent acts, but more subtle forms of harm to others such as poisoning or stalking can also be defined as dangerous (Mason, 1999). Violence denotes overt acts that cause excessive physical harm to victims but can include coerced violence committed by pedophiles and rapists. A violent criminal act is a legally defined behavior that is targeted towards a victim, ranging from aggravated burglary, aggravated assault, and forcible rape to manslaughter, murder, and sadistic rape/murder (Feldman, 1993). The relationship between violence and the mental status of offenders has become an important clinical and social issue. Some violent crimes are considered to be so heinous, particularly those involving sadistic practices, that the sanity of the perpetrator, and his or her degree of criminal responsibility, is closely scrutinized. Relatedly, the treatment, management, and release from institutional or correctional settings of dangerous individuals who exhibit mental disorder and/or criminal behavior are sensitive issues and generate societal concern (Poythress, 1999).

In this chapter we provide an overview of the legal standards for dangerousness and criminal responsibility. Next we briefly consider the debate on clinical versus actuarial assessments of dangerousness and risk and provide a synopsis of the current research on dangerousness and the methodological limitations of this research. This is followed by a discussion of the use of static versus dynamic variables in risk assessment and guidelines for addressing specific content areas in the clinical interview risk assessment process.

OVERVIEW

Since the 1970s, legal standards for dangerousness assessment by clinicians have emerged from two benchmark cases. In *O'Connor v. Donaldson* (1975) dangerousness was seen as the critical justification for civil commitment to impose involuntary treatment and provide a standard of care for dangerous individuals. The Donaldson case held that an individual with mental illness had a "right to liberty" and that he or she could not be confined to a psychiatric institution, even for the express purpose of treating the illness, unless deemed likely to harm himself or herself or others if released. Emphasis was placed on the fact that the individual must be *proved* to be dangerous before being deprived of freedom. Legal guidelines concerning the duty to warn or protect a potential victim of imminent dangerousness, albeit breaching client-therapist confidentiality, emerged from *Tarasoff v. Regents of the University of California* (1976). Following a second hearing of the case the court held that a clinician had a duty to protect and warn an intended victim about potential danger or to take other steps that included notifying the police of potential dangerousness (McMahon, 1992). This case created a duty for mental health professionals to protect third parties against threats of potential violence elicited during risk assessments with clients. *Tarasoff* implied that clinicians must be able to adequately assess the potential for violence in their clients.

Mental health professionals in forensic settings are increasingly called upon to assess the probability of dangerous behavior, or level of risk, that certain individuals pose to the community. Short-term risk assessment of imminent dangerousness to others also has implications for the containment and management of violent offenders within forensic settings. Clinicians' assessments of violent offenders' future dangerousness and potential short- and long-term risk to the community are sought by judicial decision makers in considering sentences and bail and parole applications (Melton, Petrila, Poythress, & Slobogin, 1997). Similarly, risk assessment informs decisions regarding hospital commitment orders placed on mentally disordered offenders and hospital discharge of individuals acquitted not guilty by reason of insanity (NGRI) (Quinsey, Coleman, Jones, & Altrows, 1997; Poythress, 1999; Rice, 1997). Discharge decisions are particularly susceptible to political and societal pressure to protect the rights and needs of mentally disordered individuals without applying disproportionate social control, balanced against threats to community safety (Poythress, 1999).

To protect the offender and the community from premature release of a dangerous individual, mental health professionals are guided in their clinical judgment by specific legal rules (Poythress, 1999). Judgment is based on the stability of symptoms and perceived compliance with community-based treatment. Clinical decisions regarding the level of risk while under community supervision is based on the individual's potential risk of dangerousness. The level of supervision required is weighed against protective factors such as whether the individual has cooperated with supervision and has supportive social networks (Melton et al., 1997; Poythress, 1999; Quinsey, Harris, Rice, & Cormier, 1998; Zamble & Quinsey, 1997).

Controversy exists concerning the predictive accuracy of dangerousness assessments and the ethical implications of releasing potentially violent offenders into the community. Moreover, studies have found that clinical prediction was not significantly associated with recidivism and was reported to be only marginally better than chance, except in the prediction of nonviolent reoffending (Dawes, Faust, & Meehl, 1989; Hall, 1988; Mossman, 1994). Attempts to accurately predict dangerousness based on measures used to evaluate percent correctly classified that focus on sensitivity and specificity (Baldessarini, Finkelstein, & Arana, 1983), and differentiate between false negatives (releasing dangerous individuals) and false positives (confining nondangerous individuals), present ethical and judgmental dilemmas to clinicians. Community safety is threatened particularly if an individual is incorrectly assessed as low risk and released prematurely to commit further acts of dangerousness. Conversely, an individual may be incorrectly assessed as dangerous and subsequently be deprived of his or her freedom, which raises ethical questions concerning excessive containment (Linburn, 1998; Litwack & Schlesinger, 1999; Mulvey & Lidz, 1995). Developers of risk assessment instruments must aim to correctly identify high-risk dangerous individuals while simultaneously minimizing the number of incorrectly identified dangerous individuals (false positives).

CRIMINAL RESPONSIBILITY

Criminal responsibility within the law pertains to the criteria necessary to determine criminal liability (Morse, 1999). Attributions of criminal responsibility are based on the assumption that the offender has violated societal norms; thus, individuals who are deemed incompetent to uphold these norms are exonerated from criminal responsibility. An accused is considered criminally responsible if it can be proved beyond a reasonable doubt (that is, culpability for the criminal act reflects a high degree of certainty) that the accused's behavior matched the essential criteria of the crime in question (Berman & Coccaro, 1998; Morse, 1999). Criminal responsibility requires that two elements be present in the commission of a criminal act before guilt can be established: *actus reus*, the act of committing the offence, and *mens rea*, a corresponding mental state or intent to commit the criminal act. Both *actus reus* and *mens rea* must be established beyond a reasonable doubt to establish *prima facie* guilt (Clark, 1999; Felthous, 1999; Melton et al., 1997).

The determination of intent, *mens rea*, is a central concept in criminal proceedings. In cases of murder, for example, the intentional act of killing another individual will satisfy the conduct component to meet the criteria (intentional body movement)—that is, the defendant must have acted with the intent to commit murder—but it is only the additional mental state of the defendant that determines *mens rea* (Morse, 1999). Diminished responsibility concerning the wrongfulness of the act, an inability to control behavior because of mental disease or illness, can be used in the courtroom to eliminate the defendant's culpability with consequences for sentencing and punishment (Felthous, 1999). If deficits in judgment or cognition caused by mental disorder can be proved at the time of the offense, then a defendant may not be found guilty due to an absence of *mens rea*. In defense trials an individual's mental state may be cited as an extenuating circumstance and a plea of insanity may be entered (Clark, 1999; Golding, Skeem, Roesch, & Zapf, 1999).

The insanity defense (NGRI) is based on the notion that the criminal behavior of the defendant results from an underlying mental disorder that diminishes the person's level of responsibility for his or her actions. The same behavior exhibited by an offender without a mental disorder is perceived to be caused by criminogenic needs, which renders the person criminally responsible for his or her actions (Monahan & Steadman, 1994). Historically, the influential insanity trial of Daniel M'Naghten in 1843, and his controversial acquittal, led to the "M'Naghten test" of insanity that is currently used, albeit in modified form (Melton et al., 1997). M'Naghten, who was charged with the murder of the British prime minister's private secretary, claimed that he was suffering from complex paranoid and persecutory delusions. The defense argued that M'Naghten had been unable to resist his delusions and had subsequently lost control. The "M'Naghten rules" were introduced in response to the controversial acquittal and became the accepted rule in Great Britain and the United States. The key points were: (1) every man is presumed sane until proved otherwise; and (2) it must be proved that at the time of committing the act, the accused was laboring under a defect of reason, caused by mental disease, so as to not know the nature of the act or that he was doing wrong (Feldman, 1993; Melton et al., 1997).

Criticism of the M'Naghten rules was extensive, especially by the medical community, and the rules were first modified in the early 1960s by the American Law Institute (ALI) to address the "knowledge of wrongfulness" test. The amendments were designed to make it easier to demonstrate a lack of criminal responsibility by (1) acquitting an individual who lacked the capacity to appreciate the extent of the criminality of his or her behavior, and (2) adding to the cognitive emphasis on the M'Naghten rules by introducing a volitional element (Feldman, 1993). The amended rules were employed by half the states in the United States and were later reformed in the 1980s following the Hinckley trial for the attempted assassination of President Reagan (Grisso, 1996). The jury accepted the defense claim that Hinckley was motivated to impress an actress he admired (Jodie Foster) and decided there was reasonable doubt as to his sanity (Feldman, 1993).

Following the cases of M'Naghten and *O'Connor v. McDonald*, a distinction has been made within the law as to what constitutes mental disorder. The specific rules under *McDonald*, for example, exclude evidence of an anxiety disorder or personality disorder since such a diagnosis does not meet the criteria for "abnormal condition of the mind which substantially affects mental or emotional processes and substantially impairs behavior controls" (Slovenko, 1999). Jurisdictions within the United States that adhere to the ALI's test of criminal responsibility exclude "psychopathy" or antisocial personality disorder from "mental disease or defect." Thus, a "psychopath is not insane within the meaning of the law" (Slovenko, 1999).

There is a dearth of sound psychometric measures of criminal responsibility. The two most popular instruments, the *Mental State Examination* (Slobogin, Melton, & Showalter, 1984) and the *Rogers Criminal Responsibility Assessment Scale* (Rogers, 1984), are both useful instruments.

CLINICAL VERSUS ACTUARIAL ASSESSMENT

Evidence has accumulated since the 1980s for the superiority of actuarial methods over clinical judgment alone in predicting dangerousness and violent recidivism (Borum, 1996; Borum, Otto, & Golding, 1993; Dawes et al., 1989; Holland, Holt, Levi, & Beckett, 1983; Mossman, 1994; Quinsey & Maguire, 1986). Risk factors identified by actuarial measures tend to fall within four broad domains: (1) dispositional factors such as psychopathic or antisocial personality characteristics, cognitive variables, and demographic data; (2) historical factors such as adverse developmental history, prior history of crime and violence, prior hospitalization, and poor treatment compliance; (3) contextual antecedents to violence such as criminogenic needs, deviant social networks, and lack of positive social supports; and (4) clinical factors such as diagnosis, poor level of functioning, and substance abuse (Borum, 1996). The fact that actuarial methods are based exclusively on empirically established relationships between the variables and the criterion suggests they may function as more valid predictors of risk of dangerousness compared to clinical judgment. Multivariate techniques such as logistic regression, discriminant function analysis, and survival analysis are typically utilized to produce prediction models of statistical probability (Convit, Jaeger, Lin, Klassen, & O'Connor, 1989).

Increasingly, clinicians are making dangerousness and risk assessment decisions using a combination of actuarial assessment tools, guided clinical interviewing, and assisted actuarial approaches. Recently, advanced risk assessment technology has been introduced to define guidelines for clinical assessment. Clinical judgment can thus be enhanced when clinicians use actuarial information to aid them in the decision-making process. Moreover, clinical judgments in the form of structured behavioral rating scales can assist in the construction of actuarial risk assessment and prediction instruments (Quinsey et al., 1998). This "structuring discretion" approach to clinical decision making ensures clinical judgment is anchored by utilizing an actuarial estimate of risk of future dangerousness (Gottfredson, Wilkins, & Hoffman, 1978). The use of standardized assessment instruments in guided clinical assessment can improve the reliability and validity of risk assessment (Borum, 1996).

DANGEROUSNESS RESEARCH

The prediction of general and violent recidivism of offenders released from correctional facilities has been extensively researched and well documented. Canadian researchers have dominated actuarial prediction of violent recidivism with additional studies in America and Great Britain (for reviews, see Andrew & Bonta, 1994; Blackburn, 1993, Monahan, 1981; Quinsey et al., 1998). Much of the Canadian research has focused on psychiatric patients in forensic institutions and/or antisocial behavior among insanity acquittees discharged from hospitals, whereas other investigators have studied either recidivism among adult prisoners released from prison or juvenile offenders (Quinsey et al., 1998). The general consensus from the literature suggests that for forensic patients and prisoners the most common predictors of violent recidivism include gender (male); youthfulness; past criminal and violent behavior; number of previous offenses; age at first arrest; criminal versatility (variety of offending); low educational attainment; alcohol/drug abuse; and childhood variables, such as a history of conduct disorder and physical abuse.

Mental Disorder

Several studies have reported that dangerousness in the form of interpersonal violence increases when psychotic symptomatology is present (Cirincione, Steadman, Clark-Robbins, & Monahan, 1992, Monahan, 1992; Nestor, Haycock, Doiron, Kelly, & Kelly, 1995; Rice & Harris, 1992; Swanson, Borum, Swartz, & Monahan, 1996). Some offenders also attribute their criminal behavior to symptomatology rather than contextual factors. For example, Taylor (1985) studied a group of psychotic male prisoners who reported active psychotic symptoms at the time of committing a criminal offense. These prisoners attributed their criminal behavior directly to their psychotic symptoms or blamed their behavior on auditory hallucinations. Studies of prisoners have shown the prevalence of psychiatric diagnosis to be higher than anticipated, including schizophrenia, major depression, bipolar disorder, organic brain syndrome, substance abuse/dependence, and antisocial personality disorder (Steadman, Fabisiak, Dvoskin, & Holohean, 1987).

The relationship among diagnosis, crime, and violence in psychiatric patients is, however, ambiguous. Early research reported that a diagnosis of personality disorder was related to higher recidivism rates in mentally disordered offenders (Quinsey, Pruesse, & Fernley, 1975). Other researchers posited that psychotic patients, especially those with a diagnosis of paranoid schizophrenia, were more dangerous on release (Bieber, Pasewark, Bosten, & Steadman, 1988; Krakowski, Volavka, & Brizer, 1986, cited in Rice & Harris, 1992). Severely violent offenders were found to have more delusional beliefs about specific targets and paranoid ideas about significant others being replaced by imposters (Nestor et al., 1995). Conversely, other studies suggest that a diagnosis of schizophrenia does not increase the risk of violent reoffending and has been found to predict lower risk for future dangerousness than violent offenders without schizophrenia (Harris, Rice, & Quinsey, 1993; Teplin, Abram, & McClelland, 1994). A recent meta-analysis (Bonta, Law, & Hanson, 1998) reported that the best predictors of violent recidivism across all groups of offenders were criminal history, antisocial personality or psychopathy, early antisocial behavior, and alcohol abuse. The presence of psychotic symptoms or schizophrenia at the time of the index offense or hospital admission was negatively related to risk. It may be difficult to separate the confounding impact of psychiatric diagnosis in predicting criminal behavior since past criminal offenses have proved to be the best single predictor of future criminal acts. One weakness of the Bonta et al. review is that the number of studies it surveyed containing both violent and mentally ill offenders was relatively small. However, despite the mixed research finding, we agree with Douglas and Webster (1999) that there does appear to be a significant relationship between major mental disorder and violence, although the exact strength of this relationship is still open to dispute.

Psychopathy

Psychopathy has traditionally been defined as a cluster of affective, interpersonal, and behavioral characteristics (Cleckley, 1976; Hare, 1998). Typically a psychopath exhibits glibness and superficial charm; lack of empathy, guilt, and remorse; egocentricity; selfishness, deceitful, and manipulative behavior; impulsive and irresponsible behavior; and a lack of interpersonal attachments (Hare & Hart, 1993). Hare (1998) makes a distinction between psychopathy and antisocial personality disorder (ASPD). He argues that the *DSM-IV* criteria for diagnosis relies on specific violations of social and legal norms as well as identifiable and persistent antisocial personality characteristics, but that these individuals are not necessarily psychopathic. In addition to impulsive and explosive forms of violence, psychopaths also engage in more predatory, dispassionate, remorseless, and instrumental violence than antisocial individuals.

Hare (1998) argues that within the criminal justice system psychopathy should be used as a clinical construct, particularly when decisions surrounding risk assessment and prediction of dangerousness and violent recidivism are made.

Researchers have reported that the relationship between psychopathy and violent crime is considerable. Psychopathy scores have been reported to predict violent behavior in high-risk samples of correctional inmates. High scorers on measures of psychopathy ("psychopaths") have also been reported to commit a disproportionately greater number of general and violent crimes than other criminals (Hall, 1988; Heilbrun, 1979; Quinsey & Maguire, 1986, Serin, 1996). Presence of these personality characteristics suggests individuals may exhibit greater antisocial and violent behavior. Harris, Rice, and Cormier (1991) reported the violent recidivism rate of high-scoring offenders on the Psychopathy Checklist Revised (PCL-R) to be four times greater than scores of "nonpsychopaths." Other researchers have reported a relationship among such personality characteristics as feelings of alienation, lack of social closeness, risk-taking behavior, health risk behaviors, and crime (Caspi, Begg, Dickson, Harrington, Langley, Moffitt, & Silva, 1997; Kreuger, Schmutte, Caspi, Moffitt, Campbell, & Silva, 1994).

Substance Use

Studies have generally revealed a positive relationship between criminal behavior and abuse of alcohol and other drugs (Awad & Saunders, 1991; Chick, 1998; Dawkins, 1997; Richards, 1996; Spunt, Goldstein, Brownstein, & Fendrich, 1994; Villeneuve & Quinsey, 1995). In particular, violent crimes and offenses against other people were more likely to be committed by individuals who abused alcohol and "hard" drugs such as heroin, cocaine, marijuana, and amphetamines (Anglin & Speckhart, 1988; Dawkins, 1997; Wieczorek, Welte, & Abel, 1990). The nexus between alcohol/drug use and psychiatric diagnosis has been found to escalate an offender's propensity towards violence. A Melbourne study (Wallace, Mullen, Burgess, Palmer, Ruschena, & Browne, 1998) reported that male offenders with personality disorders were almost sixteen times more likely to commit violent offenses when there was a comorbidity of substance abuse. These findings support earlier research suggesting that a dual diagnosis increased the likelihood of contact with the criminal justice system (Rice & Harris, 1995a; Swanson, 1994). Swanson (1994) found that 27 percent of offenders had a major psychiatric diagnosis combined with alcohol or drug dependence, compared with 13 percent of offenders who presented with a mental health diagnosis alone. Additionally, offenders with dual diagnoses were three times more likely than offenders with a single diagnosis to be in contact with the criminal justice system.

METHODOLOGICAL LIMITATIONS

Although several risk factors for future dangerous behavior have been identified, researchers' conclusions have been tentative and contradictory, with varying degrees of prediction accuracy (Bonta & Hanson, 1995; Gendrau, Little, &

Goggin, 1996; Mulvey & Lidz, 1995; Prentky, Lee, Knight, & Cerce, 1997; Quinsey, Rice, & Harris, 1995; Rice, 1997; Rice & Harris, 1995b; Villeneuve & Quinsey, 1995).

Although actuarial measures have identified some common predictors of future dangerousness, studies have varied in their methodology and the research is fragmented. Some studies have obtained information directly from correctional patient-prisoner records that may be incomplete or prone to clerical error, which threatens the reliability and validity of the research. Differences in methodology also occur in: the length and consistency of the follow-up period; the study sample, such as the demographic characteristics of the sample; the criterion for recidivism, such as how it is defined (arrest for a crime, conviction); the source of criterion information (multiple or single record source); the operationalization and measurement of recidivism (self-reported reoffending, arrests, charges, or conviction); and the kind of outcome criminal activity assessed (Hall & Proctor, 1987; Quinsey et al., 1998). It is feasible that such variation in definitions of recidivism may result in significant fluctuations in dangerousness predictions.

One intrinsic difficulty in accurately predicting risk and dangerousness in violent offenders has been the problem of low base rates for violent offenses. For example, if 5 percent of violent offenders committed another violent offense, you would be correct 95 percent of the time if you predicted that none of these individuals would reoffend (Quinsey et al., 1998). Violent sexual offenses in particular are relatively rare events, although acts of rape occur frequently compared to acts of child molestation (Doren, 1998). Difficulties arise in attempting to predict relatively rare events since the possibility of predicting an offense when none occurs is high, leading to false-positive errors (offenders wrongly classified as dangerous). In fact, as the base rate of an offense approaches zero, the chance of accurate prediction is very high by simply predicting that the offense will not occur, regardless of any risk factors that may be present and potentially ignored.

Evidence has accumulated, however, during the last decade from Quinsey and his colleagues that the base rates of violent recidivism are high enough among certain groups of offenders to suggest that assessment of potential dangerousness in individuals is attainable (Quinsey et al., 1995; Rice & Harris, 1995b). Quinsey et al. (1998) reported that efficient predictors of violent recidivism can be detected with an optimal base rate of .50. They contend that researchers have underestimated base rates of violent behavior in the past by using "rap sheet" information rather than obtaining descriptions of the behavior from witnesses such as police or prison officers (p. 42). Offenders with extensive histories of violent offenses, psychopathic individuals, and prisoners-patients who consistently refused parole or release are more likely to display high base rates of violence. Interestingly, in 1978 Monahan posited that contextual factors should be considered in determining base rates of violent offenses. He argued that in emergency commitment decisions and bail decisions, base rates would be higher and more accurate since the context of the violent behavior to be predicted was more immediate temporally and situationally.

STATIC VERSUS DYNAMIC PREDICTORS OF DANGEROUSNESS

Risk factors for dangerous behavior can be categorized into static (fixed) and dynamic (changeable) variables. *Static risk factors* are defined by past events such as a history of childhood maladjustment, having criminal biological parents, offense history, or previous substance abuse. Historical static predictors may indicate an offender's deviant developmental trajectory and propensity to violence and have a role to play in determining criminal misconduct (Hanson, 1998; Quinsey et al., 1998). *Dynamic risk factors* of dangerousness reflect the contextual, situational, and temporal criminogenic needs of the offender prior to an offense (Andrews & Bonta, 1994; Quinsey et al., 1998). Typically, dynamic risk factors include difficulties offenders experience in interpersonal relationships, the presence or absence of social support networks, difficulties in finding (and keeping) legal employment, money problems, substance abuse, criminogenic needs (the antecedents of offending), and continued contact with peers with criminal attitudes and behaviors.

Static variables that consistently predict violent recidivism have been reliably identified by researchers during the past decade, notably criminal history and background variables (for a review, see Quinsey et al., 1998). Static variables, however, are severely limited since the predictors of dangerousness and violent recidivism identified in the literature rely almost exclusively on measures defined by past events such as age, having criminal biological parents, offense history, or previous substance abuse. These predictors are subject to slow and incremental change, if any, such as an increase in the offense rate (Zamble & Quinsey, 1997). Moreover, the predictive accuracy of static variables used in studies of dangerousness and violence is relatively small, and no variable has proved to be an adequate predictor to justify its use in isolation. Historical static variables, however, are still important in determining criminal misconduct and for understanding the origins of violent behavior in an offender and for their already proven predictive capability.

Since models of dangerousness and risk prediction that use static predictors typically account for only 20 to 30 percent of the variance in dangerous reoffending, controversy has surrounded the efficacy of using static predictors alone to predict dangerousness in violent offenders. Static prediction models fail to identify contextual factors that may be intrinsically more important in precipitating dangerousness and violent recidivism. Dynamic factors that reflect the contextual, situational, and temporal criminogenic needs of a potentially dangerous offender need to be incorporated into assessments of dangerousness. Dynamic factors such as substance abuse, level of community support, presence or absence of social support networks, or opportunity for crime may prove to be more influential antecedent variables in elevating dangerousness and increasing an offender's chance of violent reoffending (Monahan, 1981).

Improving prediction models by incorporating dynamic variables may be particularly important for predicting dangerousness and violence in the short term. Because of their very nature, continuously varying acute dynamic variables such as an offender's mood or cognitive state may be far more relevant to short-term rather than long-term prediction of dangerousness (Hanson & Harris, 2000). Zamble and Quinsey (1997) reported that two-thirds of offenders participating in a study on criminal recidivism had been rearrested within six months of their previous release. The majority of these offenders had a history of both violent and nonviolent convictions and had been released from medium and minimum-security prisons. In an attempt to understand the determinants and events occurring before and during recidivism, they examined several dynamic variables that were potentially changeable. These factors included relatively stable behavioral patterns of offenders that could be subject to change such as coping style, antisocial attitudes and values, and criminal socialization. In addition, more transitory dynamic variables were measured, including current emotional experiences, thoughts, and perceptions.

Assessment Tools

Attempts to improve the reliability and validity of risk judgments have relied on standardized assessment instruments to predict dangerousness and risk of violence. The following scales are particularly useful: *Statistical Information on Recidivism* (Cormier, 1997; Rice & Harris, 1995b); *Level of Service Inventory Revised* (Andrews & Bonta, 1995; Rice & Harris, 1997); *Psychopathy Checklist Revised* (Hare; 1991); and the *Violence Risk Appraisal Guide* (Harris, Rice, & Quinsey, 1993; Quinsey et al., 1998).

RISK ASSESSMENT: THE CLINICAL INTERVIEW

A pervasive theme concerning issues of risk assessment is the extent to which scientific knowledge may inform and improve clinicians' risk assessment practices (Towl & Crighton, 1996). Monahan (1981) proposed that clinicians can improve their risk assessment practices by becoming familiar with basic concepts in risk assessment, such as predictor and criterion variables, true and false positives and negatives, decision rules, and base rates, in addition to the latest findings of key risk assessment research. Low base rates for homicide, for example, can result in high false positives. In practice it may mean that clinicians may overpredict the risk of homicidal reoffending and dangerousness unless they familiarize themselves with current research. Clinicians need to understand not only the base rates and the specific target behavior, but importantly they should also be aware of the impact of high and low base rates on predictions of risk (Towl & Crighton, 1996).

When clinicians are conducting risk assessments of dangerousness, they are making assumptions about criminogenic needs in relation to violence and making assumptions about the psychology of criminal conduct. In assessing dangerousness, Towl and Crighton (1996) emphasize examining in detail the individual's personality and worldview, the situations in which he or she is more (or less) likely to offend in, and, crucially, how the individual's disposition and the relevant situations may interact. They suggest the following strategies to help clinicians in their risk assessments:

1. When examining statistical data, try to ensure that the characteristics of the population used are similar to the client's.
2. Note the temporal parameters used in studies and how they match the time frame used in the risk assessment. It is good practice to use the same time frame for risk assessment alluded to in the research studies—for example, two years.
3. Explore and examine fully the client's perspective on his or her violence. Individuals vary in their violent behavior, and there are many different reasons for individuals becoming violent—for example, his or her motivations. A full assessment of the individual's perspective on his or her violence is imperative not only in helping to inform the risk assessment process but also in terms of future reoffending.
4. Examine the offender's pattern of offending, personality, and behavioral propensities in the context of his or her social situation to gain an understanding of the key factors that impact on future dangerousness. For example, a behavioral factor, which may increase the risk of dangerousness, might be the individual's planning to put himself/herself in situations that would give him/her greater access to potential victims.
5. Aim at getting as full an understanding as possible of how an offender views himself or herself in relation to others as a critical component of any risk assessment process.
6. Use psychometric tests as needed to aid risk assessments. These can be particularly useful to help structure the specific aspects of the individual's profile that may be of concern. Some psychometric tests are also helpful as tools to help measure the efficacy of clinicians' subsequent interventions aimed at reducing the risk of specific reoffending.
7. Have a clear understanding of the individual's strengths and deficits in social skills. A number of these skills may directly impact upon the risk of dangerousness.
8. Get a detailed understanding of the recency, severity, and frequency of specified violent acts, often corroborated by relevant documentation from other family members or significant others and professionals.
9. When piecing together the individual's violent history, attempt to make a judgment about whether or not the degree and frequency of violent acts is increasing. Open-ended questions such as "What is the most violent thing that you have ever done?" can be helpful.

FUTURE DIRECTIONS

It would appear from a great deal of the research on dangerousness that the relationship between mental disorder and violent behavior is complex and may be confounded by a dual *DSM-IV* diagnosis of substance abuse and/or a diagnosis of personality disorder. Although schizophrenia is found at a higher rate among prisoners than in the general population, drug and alcohol abuse are reported to be the most common mental health problems, with rates of between 50 and 80 percent. Moreover, depressive disorders are relatively common, and although some may be induced by the stress of imprisonment, others may have occurred prior to incarceration (Wallace et al., 1998).

Monahan (quoted in Edwards, 1986, p. 10) suggested with the second generation of risk prediction that "the research would indicate that clinicians are [now] better than chance, but worse than perfection" at predicting dangerous and violent behavior. Clinicians are now able to use the information from improved actuarial methods of risk assessment, which include reduced rates of false positives (individuals predicted to commit dangerous acts who do not) and false negatives (individuals predicted not to behave dangerously who do) to assist them in risk assessments. It is important to stress, however, that clinical judgment and risk assessment decision making should be based on a combination of information gleaned from the clinical interview, collateral documentation from records and reliable informants, and current research and assessment tools. Clinicians well practiced in the scientific method increase their chances of accurate risk assessment, particularly in assessments of imminent dangerousness (such as in the emergency room) when it may be impossible to access actuarial risk assessment tools.

REFERENCES

Andrews, D. A., & Bonta, J. (1994). *The psychology of criminal conduct.* Cincinnati: Anderson.

Andrews, D. A., & Bonta, J. (1995). *The level of service inventory—Revised.* Toronto: Multi-Health Systems.

Anglin, M., & Speckart, G. (1988). Narcotics use and crime: A multisample, multimethod analysis. *Criminology, 26,* 197–233.

Awad, G. A., & Saunders, E. B. (1991). Male adolescent sexual assaulters: Clinical observations. *Journal of Interpersonal Violence, Vol. 6,* 446–460.

Baldessarini, R. J., Finkelstein, S., & Arana, G. W. (1983). The predictive power of diagnostic tests and the effect of prevalence of illness. *Archives of General Psychiatry, 40,* 569–573.

Berman, M. E., & Coccaro, E. F. (1998). Neurobiologic correlates of violence: Relevance to criminal responsibility. *Behavioral Sciences and the Law, 16,* 303–318.

Bieber, S., Pasewark, R., Bosten, K., & Steadman, H. (1988). Predicting criminal recidivism of insanity acquittees. *International Journal of Law and Psychiatry, 11,* 105–112.

Blackburn, R. (1993). *The psychology of criminal conduct: Theory, research and practice.* Chichester, UK: Wiley.

Bonta, J., & Hanson, R. K. (1995). *Violent recidivism of men released from prison.* Paper presented at the 103rd Annual Convention of the American Psychological Association at New York, August 11, 1995.

Bonta, J., Law, M., & Hanson, R. K. (1998). The prediction of criminal and violent recidivism among mentally disordered offenders: A meta-analysis. *Psychological Bulletin, 123*, 123–142.

Borum, R. (1996). Improving the clinical practice of violence risk assessment: Technology, guidelines and training. *American Psychologist, 51*, 945–956.

Borum, R., Otto, R., & Golding, S. (1993). Improving clinical judgment and decision making in forensic evaluation. *Journal of Psychiatry and Law, 21*, 35–76.

Caspi, A., Begg, D., Dickson, J., Harrington, H., Langley, J., Moffitt, T. E., & Silva, P. A. (1997). Personality differences predict health-risk behaviors in young adulthood: Evidence from a longitudinal study. *Journal of Personality and Social Psychology, 73*, 1052–1063.

Chick, J. (1998). Treatment of alcoholic violent offenders: Ethics and efficacy. *Alcohol and Alcoholism, 33*, 20–25.

Cirincione, C., Steadman, H. J., Clark-Robbins, P., & Monahan, J. (1992). Schizophrenia as a contingent risk factor for criminal violence. *International Journal of Law and Psychiatry, 15*, 347–358.

Clark, C. R. (1999). Specific intent and diminished capacity. In A. K. Hess & I. B. Weiner (Eds.), *The handbook of forensic psychology.* New York: John Wiley & Sons.

Cleckley, H. M. (1976). *The mask of sanity* (5th ed.). St. Louis: Mosby.

Convit, A., Jaeger, J., Lin, S. P., Meisner, M., & Volavka, J. (1988). Predicting assaultiveness in psychiatric inpatients: A pilot study. *Hospital and Community Psychiatry, 39*, 429–434.

Cormier, R. B. (1997). Yes, SIR: A stable risk prediction tool. *Forum, 9(1)*, 1–6.

Dawes, R., Faust, D., & Meehl, P. (1989). Clinical versus actuarial judgment. *Science, 243*, 1668–1674.

Dawkins, M. P. (1997). Drug use and violent crime among adolescents. *Adolescence, 32*, 395–405.

Diagnostic and Statistical Manual of Mental Disorders (4th ed.) (1994). Washington, DC: American Psychiatric Association.

Doren, D. M. (1998). Recidivism base rates, predictions of sex offender recidivism, and the "Sexual Predator" Commitment Laws. *Behavioral Sciences and the Law, 16*, 97–114.

Douglas, K. S., & Webster, C. D. (1999). Predicting violence in mentally and personality disordered individuals. In R. Roesch, S. D. Hart, & J. R. P. Ogloff (Eds.), *Psychology and law: The state of the discipline* (pp. 175–239). New York: Kluwer Academic Plenum Publishers.

Edwards, S. S. M. (1986). The real risks of violence behind closed doors. *New Law Journal, 136*, 1191–1193.

Feldman, P. (1993). *The psychology of crime.* Cambridge: Cambridge University Press.

Felthous, A. R. (1999). Introduction to mental illness and criminal responsibility. *Behavioral Sciences and the Law, 17*, 143–146.

Gendreau, P., Little, T., & Goggin, C. (1996). A meta-analysis of the predictors of adult offender recidivism: What works! *Criminology, 34*, 575–607.

Golding, S. L., Skeem, J. L., Roesch, R., & Zapf, P. A. (1999). The assessment of criminal responsibility: Current controversies. In A. K. Hess & I. B. Weiner (Eds.), *The handbook of forensic psychology*. New York: John Wiley & Sons.

Gottfredson, D. M., Wilkins, L. T., & Hoffman, P. B. (1978). *Guidelines for parole and sentencing: A policy control method*. Toronto: Lexington Books.

Grisso, T. (1996). Pretrial clinical evaluations in criminal cases: Past trends and future directions. *Criminal Justice and Behavior, 23*, 90–106.

Hall, G. C. N. (1988). Criminal behavior as a function of clinical and actuarial variables in a sexual offender population. *Journal of Consulting and Clinical Psychology, 56*, 773–775.

Hall, G. C. N., & Proctor, W. C. (1987). Criminological predictors of recidivism in a sexual offender population. *Journal of Consulting and Clinical Psychology, 55*, 111–112.

Hanson, R. K. (1998). What do we know about sex offender risk assessment? *Psychology, Public Policy and Law, 4*, 50–72.

Hanson, R., & Harris, A. (2000). *The Sex Offender Need Assessment Rating (SONAR): A method for measuring change in risk levels*. Available at: www.sgc.gc.ca/epub/Corr/e200001b/e200001b.htm.

Hare, R. D. (1991). *The revised psychopathy checklist*. Toronto: Multi-Health Systems.

Hare, R. D. (1998). The Hare PCL-R: Some issues concerning its use and misuse. *Legal and Criminological Psychology, 3*, 99–119.

Hare, R. D., & Hart, S. D. (1993). Psychopathy, mental disorder and crime. In S. Hodgins (Ed.), *Mental disorder and crime*. London: Sage.

Harris, G. T., Rice, M. E., & Cormier, C. A. (1991). Psychopathy and violent recidivism. *Law and Human Behavior, 15*, 625–636.

Harris, G. T., Rice, M. E., & Quinsey, V. L. (1993). Violent recidivism of mentally disordered offenders: The development of a statistical prediction instrument. *Criminal Justice and Behavior, 20*, 315–335.

Harris, G. T., Rice, M. E., & Quinsey, V. L. (1994). Psychopathy as a Taxon: Evidence that psychopaths are a discrete class. *Journal of Consulting and Clinical Psychology, 62*, 387–397.

Heilbrun, A. B. (1979). Psychopathy and violent crime. *Journal of Consulting and Clinical Psychology, 47*, 509–516.

Holland, T. R., Holt, N., Levi, M., & Beckett, G. E. (1983). Comparison and combination of clinical and statistical predictions of recidivism among adult offenders. *Journal of Applied Psychology, 68*, 203–211.

Kreuger, R. F., Schmutte, P. S., Caspi, A., Moffitt, T. E., Campbell, K., & Silva, P. A. (1994). Personality traits are linked to crime among men and women: Evidence from a birth cohort. *Journal of Abnormal Psychology, 103*, 328–338.

Linburn, G. E. (1998). Donaldson revisited: Is dangerousness a constitutional requirement for civil commitment? *Journal of the American Academy of Psychiatry and Law, 26*, 343–351.

Litwack, T. R., & Schlesinger, L. B. (1999). Dangerousness risk assessment: Research, legal and clinical considerations. In A. K. Hess, & I. B. Weiner (Eds.), *The handbook of forensic psychology* (2nd ed.). New York: John Wiley.

Mason, T. (1999). The psychiatic "Supermax"? Long-term, high-security psychiatric services. *International Journal of Law and Psychiatry, 22*, 155–166.

McMahon, M. (1992). Dangerousness, confidentiality, and the duty to protect. *Australian Psychologist, 27*, 12–16.

Melton, G. B., Petrila, J., Poythress, N. G., & Slobogin, C. (1997). *Psychological evaluation for the courts: A handbook for mental health professionals and lawyers* (2nd ed.). New York: Guilford Press.

Monahan, J. (1978). Prediction research and the emergency commitment of dangerous mentally ill persons: A reconsideration. *American Journal of Psychiatry, 135,* 198–201.

Monahan, J. (1981). *Predicting violent behavior: An assessment of clinical techniques.* Beverly Hills, CA: Sage.

Monahan, J. (1992). Mental disorder and violent behavior. *American Psychologist, 47,* 511–521.

Monahan, J. (1996). Violence prediction: The past twenty and the next twenty years. *Criminal Justice and Behavior, 23,* 107–120.

Monahan, J., & Steadman, H. (1996). *Violence and mental disorder.* Chicago: University of Chicago Press.

Morse, S. J. (1999). Craziness and criminal responsibility. *Behavioral Sciences and the Law, 17,* 147–164.

Mossman, D. (1994). Assessing predictions of violence: Being accurate about accuracy. *Journal of Consulting and Clinical Psychology, 62,* 783–792.

Mulvey, E. P., & Lidz, C. W. (1995). Conditional prediction: A model for research on dangerousness to others in a new era. *International Journal of Law and Psychiatry, 18,* 129–143.

Nestor, P. G., Haycock, J., Doiron, S., Kelly, J., & Kelly, D. (1995). Lethal violence and psychosis: A clinical profile. *Bulletin of the American Academy of Psychiatry and Law, 23,* 331–339.

O'Connor v. Donaldson, 422 U. S. 563 (1975).

Poythress, N. G. (1999). Prediction of dangerousness and release decision making. In V. B. Van Hasselt & M. Hersen (Eds.), *Handbook of psychological approaches with violent offenders: Contemporary strategies and issues.* New York: Plenum.

Prentky, R. A., Lee, A. F. S., Knight, R. A., & Cerce, D. (1997). Recidivism rates among child molesters and rapists: A methodological analysis. *Law and Human Behavior, 21,* 635–659.

Quinsey, V. L., Coleman, G., Jones, B., & Altrows, I. F. (1997). Proximal antecedents of eloping and reoffending among supervised mentally disordered offenders. *Journal of Interpersonal Violence, 12,* 794–813.

Quinsey, V. L., Harris, G. T., Rice, M. E., & Cormier, C. A. (1998). *Violent offenders: Appraising and managing risk.* Washington: American Psychological Association.

Quinsey, V. L., & Maguire, A. (1986). Maximum security psychiatric patients: Actuarial and clinical prediction of dangerousness. *Journal of Interpersonal Violence, 1,* 143–171.

Quinsey, V. L., Pruesse, M., & Fernley, R. (1975). Oak Ridge patients: Prerelease characteristics and postrelease adjustment. *Journal of Psychiatry and the Law, 3,* 63–77.

Quinsey, V. L., Rice, M. E., & Harris, G. T. (1995). Actuarial prediction of sexual recidivism. *Journal of Interpersonal Violence, 10,* 85–105.

Rice, M. E. (1997). Violent offender research and implications for the criminal justice system. *American Psychologist, 52,* 414–423.

Rice, M. E., & Harris, G. T. (1992). A comparison of criminal recidivism among schizophrenia and nonschizopohrenic offenders. *International Journal of Law and Psychiatry, 15,* 397–408.

Rice, M. E., & Harris, G. T. (1995a). Psychopathy, schizophrenia, alcohol abuse, and violent recidivism. *International Journal of Law and Psychiatry, 18*, 333–342.

Rice, M. E., & Harris, G. T. (1995b). Violent recidivism: Assessing predictive validity. *Journal of Consulting and Clinical Psychology, 63*, 737–748.

Rice, M. E., & Harris, G. T. (1997). The treatment of mentally disordered offenders. *Psychology, Public Policy, and Law, 3*, 126–183.

Richards, I. (1996). Psychiatric disorder among adolescents in custody. *Australian and New Zealand Journal of Psychiatry, 30*, 788–793.

Rogers, R. (1984). *Rogers Criminal Responsibility Assessment Scales.* Odessa, FL: Psychological Assessment Resources.

Serin, R. C. (1996). Violent recidivism in criminal psychopaths. *Law and Human Behavior, 20*, 207–217.

Slobogin, C., Melton, G. B., & Showalter, C. R. (1984). The feasibility of a brief evaluation of mental state at the time of the offense. *Law and Human Behavior, 8*, 305–321.

Slovenko, R. (1988). The therapist's duty to warn or protect third persons. *The Journal of Psychiatry and Law*, Spring, 139–209.

Spunt, B., Goldstein, P., Brownstein, H., & Fendrich, M. (1994). Alcohol and homicide: Interviews with prison inmates. *Journal of Drug Issues, 24*, 143–163.

Steadman, H. J., Monahan, J., Robbins, P. C., Appelbaum, P., Grisso, T., Klassen, D,, Mulvey, E. P., & Roth, L. (1993). From dangerousness to risk assessment: Implications for appropriate research strategies. In S. Hodgins (Ed.), *Mental disorder and crime.* Newbury Park, CA: Sage.

Swanson, J. W. (1994). Mental disorder, substance abuse, and community violence: An epidemiological approach. In J. Monahan & H. J. Steadman (Eds.), *Violence and mental disorder: Developments in risk assessment.* Chicago: University of Chicago Press.

Swanson, J. W., Borum, R., Swartz, M. S., & Monahan, J. (1996). Psychotic symptoms and disorders and the risk of violent behavior in the community. *Criminal Behavior and Mental Health, 6*, 309–329.

Tarasoff v. Regents of the University of California, Sup. 131 Cal. Rptr. 14 (1976).

Taylor, P. J. (1985). Motives for offending among violent and psychotic men. *British Journal of Psychiatry, 147*, 491–498.

Teplin, L. A., Abram, K. M., & McClelland, G. M. (1994). Does psychiatric disorder predict violent crime among released jail detainees? *American Psychologist, 49*, 335–342.

Towl, G. J., & Crighton, D. A. (1996). *The handbook of psychology for forensic practitioners.* London: Routledge.

Villeneuve, D. B., & Quinsey, V. L. (1995). Predictors of general and violent recidivism among mentally disordered inmates. *Criminal Justice and Behavior, 22*, 397–410.

Wallace, C., Mullen, P., Burgess, P., Palmer, S., Ruschena, D., & Browne, C. (1998). Serious criminal offending and mental disorder. *British Journal of Psychiatry, 172*, 477–484.

Wieczorek, W., Welte, J., & Abel, E. (1990). Alcohol, drugs and murder: A study of convicted homicide offenders. *Journal of Criminal Justice, 18*, 217–227.

Zamble, E., & Quinsey, V. L. (1997). *The criminal recidivism process.* Cambridge: Cambridge University Press.

CHAPTER 6

ISSUES IN THE ASSESSMENT, COMMUNICATION, AND MANAGEMENT OF RISK FOR VIOLENCE

REBECCA J. DEMPSTER

CENTRE FOR ADDICTION AND MENTAL HEALTH
TORONTO, ONTARIO, CANADA

Mental health professionals are regularly called upon to make assessments of patients' risk of harm to other individuals. The demand for violence risk assessment is on the rise (Douglas & Webster, 1999), and occurs in a variety of contexts. Demands for violence risk assessment are often explicit in the context of sentencing hearings, dangerous offender and sexual predator hearings, applications for raise to adult court for young offenders, bail hearings, civil commitment proceedings, conditional release hearings, and insanity defense disposition hearings (Heilbrun, Ogloff, & Picarello, 1999). At other times, the need for an assessment of violence risk is implicit, as in child protection statutes that require consideration of whether a child is at risk of harm from a certain individual or individuals. Douglas and Webster (1999) attributed the increased call for violence risk assessment—or, as they termed it, the rise in risk—to a number of factors, including the deinstitutionalization movement, public outcry over highly publicized violent crimes committed by mentally ill individuals, society's fear of the mentally ill as violent, as well as changes in both case law and statutes regarding the detention and confinement of potentially violent mentally ill individuals.

Early articles on dangerousness suggested that clinicians possessed no special ability to predict violent behavior and performed at chance or below chance levels of accuracy (e.g., Mulvey & Lidz, 1985). Nonetheless, clinicians continued to be charged with the task of assessing and managing dangerousness. The rise of risk has only added to the pressure on clinicians in this regard. Risk prediction and risk management have become unavoidable requirements of clinical practice, made so by court rulings (e.g., *Barefoot v. Estelle*, *Tarasoff v. Regents of the University of California*), social pressures, and ethical codes (Mulvey & Lidz, 1985). Once considered the domain of clinicians working in forensic settings, the Tarasoff case has brought violence risk assessment into the realm of the general practitioner. Nonforensic and forensic clinicians alike must possess some ability to assess their clients' propensity for imminent violence and take action where necessary. As Mulvey and Lidz (1985) noted, given that clinicians cannot avoid the task, many in the field have advocated an "ameliorationist" position, calling for improvements in violence risk assessment as opposed to an outright abandonment of the task.

This chapter concerns itself with the unavoidable task of assessing, communicating, and managing risk. Of the three areas covered in this chapter, risk assessment has received the bulk of attention by researchers. Risk communication is an oft overlooked but extremely important component of the violence risk assessment process. Variations in how risk information is communicated (e.g., probability statements versus categorical statements) have a significant impact on how risk is construed, both by the evaluators and the consumers of violence risk assessments. Much like risk communication, management of risk has received far less attention in the empirical literature than has the assessment of risk. However, risk management is increasingly being recognized as an essential component of violence risk assessment. Although the chapter is divided into three sections devoted to each of these topics, it is important to underscore the interrelatedness of assessment, communication, and management. Many authors subsume risk communication and risk management under the general heading of risk assessment, and with just cause, as both can be construed as steps in the process of a violence risk assessment. For the purposes of the present chapter, however, issues in risk communication and risk management are reviewed separately from issues in assessment.

VIOLENCE RISK ASSESSMENT

Understanding the violence risk literature and competently conducting a risk assessment require comprehension of what risk means.

Defining Risk

The *Oxford Encyclopedic English Dictionary* defines risk as "(1) a chance or possibility of danger, loss, injury, or other adverse consequences (*a health risk; a risk of fire*). (2) a person or thing causing a risk or regarded in relation to risk (*is a poor risk*)" (emphasis in the original). In relation to predicting violence, Hart (2000) defined risk as a hazard that, by definition, is not known and thus only can be predicted with uncertainty. Carson's (1997) definition of risk involves consideration of both possible harm and possible benefits. Risk is dynamic, that is, it changes across time and across situations.

Although most studies of risk focus on the likelihood of an event, many have argued that risk incorporates more than the *probability* of an event (Douglas, Cox, & Webster, 1999; Halstead, 1997; Hart, 2000; Monahan & Steadman, 1996). Additional components of risk include the *nature* of the event (the manner in which the person will be violent, e.g., sexual violence versus spousal violence), *severity* of the event (ranging from no or minor physical injury to multiple deaths), *imminence* (the time frame in which the person will be violent, e.g., imminent violence versus violence ten years after release), *frequency* (how often will this person be violent, e.g., isolated acts of violence versus chronic, persistent violence), and *context* (the circumstances and victim or victims). These components of risk are gradually being incorporated into research and clinical practice of violence risk assessment. For instance, the development of specialized instruments for spousal assault (e.g., Spousal Assault Risk Assessment Guide; Kropp, Hart, Webster, & Eaves, 1998) and sexual offending (e.g., Rapid Risk Assessment for Sex Offense Recidivism; Hanson, 1997) have increased our understanding of the nature of risk. As well, the use of survival analyses has incorporated the notion of imminence into violence risk studies.

Defining Risk Assessment

Hart (1998) provided the following definition of violence risk assessment: "*the process of evaluating individuals to (1) characterize the likelihood they will commit acts of violence and (2) develop interventions to manage or reduce that likelihood*" (p. 122; emphasis in the original). Most research on violence risk assessment has examined the accuracy of static, one-time risk assessments. More recently, however, researchers and clinicians have come to view violence risk assessment as a process rather than a static or "one-off" event (Davison, 1997; Hart, 1998; Kaliski, 1997; Litwack, Kirschner, & Wack, 1993). Davison underscored the argument that risk itself is dynamic—that is, the risk for violence posed by an individual is not a static, unchanging entity. As such, risk assessment should not be a "one-off" deal; it must be flexible and involve ongoing assessment and monitoring of a person's risk and response to intervention.

Although the terms are often used interchangeably, violence risk assessment is distinct from both the assessment of dangerousness and the prediction of violence. Dangerousness can be conceptualized as a trait or characteristic of the person. Prediction of violence, on the other hand, implies prediction of a specific behavior, not of a personality characteristic. The term *dangerousness* is a vague, ill-defined construct (Mulvey & Lidz, 1985). Although seldom explicitly defined, it has been construed dichotomously, that is, to mean that people are either dangerous or not dangerous (Towl & Crighton, 1997). Prediction, on the other hand, can be viewed in two ways. Towl and Crighton distinguish between prediction of an event and prediction as the act of estimating a probability of that event. As they noted, most of the empirical literature on risk has focused on the first type of prediction. They argued that the second definition, the act of estimating likelihood, more properly defines the task of risk assessment. Thus, risk assessment is not a prediction per se but rather a probability estimate. Risk assessment involves not only an estimate of the risk posed but also a decision about what to do about that risk—in other words, risk management. Prediction does not (Towl & Crighton, 1997).

One approach that clearly advocates viewing risk assessment as a process is that of Davison (1997). She outlines a multistage model of violence risk assessment in which the first stage is recognizing the need for a violence risk assessment. In practice, this stage may come in the form of an explicit referral or may arise from events or characteristics of the person that alert the clinician of the need, such as a client's disclosing violent fantasies. The second stage involves determining the exact question or reason for referral. The task of the assessor is not typically to answer a single question (e.g., Will this person be violent at some point in the future?), but more typically to address issues such as the nature of the risk posed, the degree of confidence one can hold in the assessment, and the time period for which the assessment is valid. The third stage involves consideration of the legality and ethicality of conducting a violence risk assessment for the particular individual in the particular circumstances, including consideration of the assessor's qualifications to conduct such an assessment. Fourth, according to Davison, assessors must collect information germane to the question of risk. At this stage, the assessor must consider whether the available information is sufficiently complete to permit a thorough risk assessment.

Accuracy of Violence Risk Assessment

In 1985, Mulvey and Lidz agreed with Monahan's (1981) conclusion that clinicians have been "vastly overrated as predictors of violence" (Monahan, 1981, p. 1). The so-called first generation of risk assessment research, conducted in the 1970s and early 1980s, called into question the ability of clinicians to predict violence. Results from these studies indicated that clinicians do not have any ability or only some modest ability to predict violence. More recently, however, there has been an improvement in the accuracy of violence risk assessment to the extent that it is generally recognized that clinicians have some modest ability to predict violent behavior (Borum, 1996). The second generation of risk research, beginning in the mid-1980s, was characterized by short-term predictions, a focus on situational variables, and special populations (Heilbrun, Ogloff, & Picarello, 1999). Even greater improvements in the accuracy of violence predictions were seen in the third generation of violence risk research. Generally, the focus has moved from a question of whether future violence can be predicted to how this aim is best achieved (Monahan, 1996).

Improvements in the accuracy of violence risk assessment have been attributed to a number of factors. Austin (2000) outlined a few: "making shorter term predictions, stating predictions in probabilistic rather than dichotomous terms, specifying more exactly the population addressed, using broader outcome measures (i.e., verbal and behavioral aggression as well as violence), and measuring a variety of psychological predictor variables" (p. 195). Borum (1996) attributed improvements in the accuracy of violence risk assessment to advances in research methodology.

A reexamination of first-generation studies on dangerousness provides an alternate explanation for the improvements in accuracy currently described in the risk literature, namely that clinicians were not nearly so inaccurate as had been traditionally believed. Litwack and his colleagues (1994; Litwack et al., 1993) outlined several methodological flaws in dangerousness and violence prediction studies that they argued preclude drawing strong conclusions about the ability of clinicians in this area. These arguments will be reviewed in the section on clinical decision making. Regardless, however, of the explanation for improved accuracy, it is generally recognized that mental health professionals possess specialized knowledge in the area of violence risk assessment that allows them to make reasonably accurate assessments of individuals' risk for future violent behavior.

Approaches to Decision Making

In conducting an assessment of risk for violence, the assessor is being asked to make a decision, or multiple decisions: What is the likelihood of violence, what type of violence, how often, how severe, in what context and to whom? A currently debated topic in the violence risk literature concerns the best approach to decision making. Three main approaches are reviewed here: actuarial decision making (including the iterative classification tree approach used in the MacArthur Violence Risk Assessment Study), clinical decision making, and structured clinical judgment. Empirical research comparing these approaches is also reviewed.

Prediction versus Measurement

Before discussing approaches to decision making, it is important to differentiate between prediction and measurement (Buchanan, 1999; Sawyer, 1966). *Prediction* is a form of decision making; it refers to ways of combining data in order to make a decision or assessment. It is distinct from *measurement*, which refers to the way in which data are collected. Sawyer differentiated prediction from measurement as follows: "Prediction concerns itself mainly with different methods of combining already collected data" (1966). As he noted, data can be collected in three ways: clinically, mechanically, or by a combination of clinical and mechanical means. Similarly, data can be combined in two ways: clinically or mechanically. Sawyer argued that although much more attention had been paid to the integration of data (i.e., prediction), prediction cannot be assessed independently from measurement. The accuracy of any assessment depends on both the modes of collecting data and the modes of combining data, on both measurement and prediction.

Violence risk assessments can and do involve various permutations of measurement and prediction. For example, clinical data can be combined using explicit rules to form an actuarial prediction. An instrument is denoted as actuarial or clinical on the basis of the way risk factors are combined, and not on the basis of the kinds of risk factors included or the way in which the information was gathered. Thus, clinical prediction refers to a clinical approach to combining data, and not to prediction that is based on clinical variables. Similarly, actuarial prediction refers to an actuarial method of combining data, and not to prediction based on variables collected without clinical judgment.

Actuarial Prediction

The defining characteristic of *actuarial* (also called mechanical, statistical, formalistic, algorithmic) decision making is the reliance on a set of fixed and explicit decision criteria. In actuarial prediction, no expert judgment is involved in the decision process. Data are combined according to fixed and explicit rules, which are clear, preset, and applied consistently and uniformly across cases. Sawyer (1966) defined actuarial prediction as "any set of rules whose application is objective, whatever mixture of experience and intuition their derivation involves" (p. 180). Similarly, he wrote, "data collection is mechanical if rules can be prescribed so that no clinical judgment need be involved in the procedure" (p. 181). Actuarial, as it has come to be defined in the violence risk literature, refers to a mathematical method of combining data, although, as Buchanan (1999) noted, this is not the definition used in other areas and would likely not be recognized by an actuary. Examples of actuarial violence risk assessment measures include the Violence Risk Appraisal Guide (Quinsey, Harris, Rice, & Cormier, 1998), the Rapid Risk Assessment for Sex Offender Recidivism (Hanson, 1997), and the Sex Offender Risk Appraisal Guide (Quinsey et al., 1998). All of these instruments have fixed and explicit rules for combining data.

The main advantage of actuarial decision making as compared to clinical prediction is that of increased reliability and validity. Actuarially based violence predictions have been shown consistently to have higher interrater reliability than have clinical judgments of risk. Further, the accuracy of actuarial instruments has also surpassed that observed with clinical judgments, leading Quinsey and colleagues (1998) to conclude: "Whether clinical adjustment can ever improve the predictive accuracy of actuarial prediction schemes seems doubtful" (p. 65). Grove, Zald, Lebow, Snitz, and Nelson (2000) conducted a meta-analysis of decision making across studies of human health and behavior, including several studies of the prediction of violence and criminal behavior. Their findings confirmed the earlier writings of Meehl (1954; 1996) arguing for the superiority of actuarial predictions over clinical predictions. Using a modest definition of superiority (i.e., more than 10% increase in accuracy), they found actuarial prediction superior to clinical prediction in 33 to 47 percent of the 136 studies included. Grove and colleagues' conclusions reiterated the arguments of many before them: Humans are inherently susceptible to errors in judgment, and this susceptibility to error inevitably means that objective approaches to decision making will always outperform subjectively made decisions. Their argument was buttressed by their finding that clinicians did not fare better when given more information and that clinical predictions were actually substantially worse than actuarial predictions when clinicians had access to a clinical interview. Interestingly, Grove and colleagues (2000) did find that clinical prediction was often as good, and in a small number of cases (6–16%) was superior, to actuarial decision making. They concluded: "The ball is in the clinicians' court . . . to show that clinicians' predictions are more beneficial to clients in terms of cost-weighted errors, overall costs of decision-making, or both" (p. 26).

Actuarial predictions, however, are not without limitations (Dolan & Doyle, 2000; Hart, 1998). Hart (1998) outlined a number of these. Specifically, he noted that actuarial violence risk instruments tend to ignore individual variations in risk, overfocus on relatively static factors, fail to prioritize clinically relevant variables, and minimize the role of professional judgment. Actuarial decision making has also been criticized because of the reliance on group data. Actuarial instruments are typically constructed from research on groups; the difficulty in using them thus lies in the fact that clinicians are faced with an individual, not a group, and are left struggling with the question of whether this individual is the same as those included in group analyses (Grubin, 1997; Taylor & Meux, 1997).

Actuarial instruments, by virtue of their explicitness, also restrict the risk factors that can be considered (Taylor, 1997). Relying solely on the factors included in an actuarial instrument may lead clinicians to fail to explore other relevant risk factors. Given that no instrument can include every factor that may be relevant in any given case, this strategy results in some factors potentially being overlooked. This becomes particularly problematic in the event of case-specific factors, such as an individual's stated intent to commit a violent offense. If "intent to harm" were not included on an actuarial instrument, a clinician using actuarial decision making would not use this information to assess the risk posed by this individual.

Iterative Classification Tree Method

A variation on the unilinear approach used in most actuarial instruments has been to adopt a *classification tree* method (Monahan et al., 2000; Steadman et al., 2000). The classification tree approach is a form of actuarial decision making that takes into account both interactions between, and contingencies among, risk factors for violence. Thus, it explicitly recognizes that there are multiple pathways to violent behavior. In doing so, the classification tree approach allows many different combinations of risk factors in producing a final risk rating of low or high risk. The risk factors considered and the questions asked in a classification tree risk assessment will be dependent on the risk factors already deemed present and the answers already provided.

Results from a number of studies using the ITC instrument developed by the MacArthur Violence Risk Assessment Study research team are promising (Monahan et al., 2000, Steadman et al., 2000). In an effort to make the instrument applicable to actual practice, they restricted the risk factors included in the instrument to those that are readily available in everyday clinical practice (e.g., easily obtainable, routinely available in clinical records.) Using this approach, they developed an ITC model with an AUC of .80 with violent outcome. The focus was on relative, not absolute, risk; groups of participants were designated as low risk when they had a rate of violence that was less than half of the base rate of total sample, and as high risk when they had a rate of violence that was more than twice the base rate in the total sample.

Clinical Prediction

In *clinical* decision making (also referred to as *unstructured* or *impressionistic*), the decision maker combines available data using "informal, subjective methods" (Grove et al., 2000, p. 19). Clinical prediction leaves discretion entirely to the assessor or evaluator, and is thus based on personal, clinical judgment. No structure is imposed on either the evaluation or the decision; that is, there are no rules regarding what data to consider, and how it should be combined. Buchanan (1999) noted that clinical prediction has sometimes been defined by exclusion—that is, everything that is not actuarial is considered clinical.

Advocates of clinical prediction argue that the strength of clinical prediction lies in the freedom it allows assessors to consider any information they deem relevant (Dolan & Doyle, 2000; Hart, 1998, Litwack, 1994). The lack of explicit rules allows clinical predictions to be comprehensive in terms of the data included in the decision. Additionally, clinical predictions are narrative in approach; they consider each individual to constitute a unique case. Clinical predictions apply to the individual in question; that is, they speak to absolute risk as opposed to relative risk. Finally, clinical predictions are often more relevant to risk management than are predictions made via actuarial approaches.

Clinical decision making has been heavily criticized, however. Because clinical predictions are not restricted by explicit rules, the judgment of the assessor determines what information is to be included and how this information is to be combined. Not only does this reduce interrater reliability, it leaves ample room for errors in human judgment to diminish the validity of the assessment. To quote Grove and colleagues (2000) in their recent meta-analysis: "These include ignoring base rates, assigning non-optimal weights to cues, failure to take into account regression toward the mean, and failure to properly assess covariation" (2000, p. 25). Research has consistently shown clinical judgment to be less consistent and less accurate than actuarial approaches to decision making (Boer et al., 1997; Grove et al., 2000; Quinsey et al., 1998). Clinicians are prone to overestimating the likelihood of violence, leading to a high rate of false-positive errors (i.e., deeming as dangerous an individual who ultimately does not violently recidivate).

Further, the lack of explicit decision criteria results in a lack of specificity in the decision-making process (Dolan & Doyle, 2000). Consequently, the rationale behind a clinical decision and the factors that entered into it are often unknown or at least not explicitly stated.

As mentioned previously, proponents of clinical approaches to decision making have reexamined the first-generation research on the assessment of dangerousness and argued the conclusions drawn from those studies—namely, that clinicians were inaccurate assessors—are not supported by the data (Davison, 1997; Litwack, 1994, Litwack et al., 1993). Litwack outlined four methodological flaws in existing research that limit the conclusions that can be drawn: (1) many studies do not involve individual assessments by a representative group of mental health professionals; (2) many studies included mentally ill persons who were only marginally dangerous; (3) most studies do not account for undetected violence in the community; and (4) outcome often was measured only after intervention had occurred (e.g., after hospitalization and/or treatment that may have significantly modified the basis for the original assessment of dangerousness).

Towl and Crighton (1997) have noted that time-limited risk assessment is typically more accurate than is long-term assessment and yet most studies evaluating the accuracy of clinical predictions have focused on accuracy over the long term, thereby failing to take into account intervening factors. One of the most important intervening factors that has been overlooked is the tendency of clinicians to act upon their assessments. The impact of interventions may obfuscate distinctions between inaccurate predictions and successful management of correct predictions. In many first-generation violence risk studies, participants were assessed as dangerous several years prior to their release into the community. Despite the intervening years between the assessment and the opportunity for violence, these studies are often cited as proof of clinicians' inability to accurately predict violence. An alternative explanation, and that favored by Litwack, is that clinicians were not unskilled in predicting violence but were actually skilled in managing risk.

Litwack (1994) also argued that a decision to release an individual from custody or confinement does not mean that this person has been clinically assessed as low risk, but rather may be based on a balancing of the risk posed by the individual and the issues of civil liberties inherent in his or her continued confinement. Mulvey and Lidz (1985) pointed out that many studies purporting to investigate accuracy of dangerousness were really examining decisions about the need for commitment. Further, Litwack called into question the meaning of a false positive. As he noted, the term *dangerousness*, like *risk*, incorporates more than likelihood. He noted that clinical concern regarding a patient's risk for violence might stem from the potential for very serious acts of violence, as opposed to a very high likelihood of violence. An individual may be assessed as dangerous on the basis of the severity of the risk as opposed to the likelihood. Most research on violence risk assessment has evaluated the accuracy of assessments of the likelihood of risk and ignored components such as severity; thus clinicians' accuracy in this regard remains untested. An additional problem with early dangerousness research is the view taken of dangerousness as a trait when it is in fact complex behavior influenced by both individual and situational factors (Mulvey & Lidz, 1985).

In addition, problems with measurement of the outcome (e.g., violence) may give the appearance of low accuracy where it does not exist. That is, individuals who are false positives in violence risk studies may have committed violence without being detected, or charged, or convicted. This concern was echoed by Buchanan (1997), who outlined the difficulties inherent in measuring violence, dangerousness, and other antisocial behavior. By virtue of the event of interest, researchers have to rely on proxy variables that occur after the fact such as arrest, reconvictions, or rehospitalizations. Doing so necessarily introduces error into the research. Buchanan observed that the rates of crime found in victimization studies differed by over 10 percent, depending on the company used to conduct the survey. Interestingly, he found that the process of attrition from a victim's report of a crime to conviction differed between mentally ill and nonmentally ill individuals. Offenses committed by mentally ill offenders were more likely to be reported to police; 28 percent of offenders with schizophrenia turned themselves in, compared with only 1 percent overall (Robertson, 1988, as cited in Buchanan, 1997). Offenders with schizophrenia were also much more likely to be caught at the scene of a crime. However, once the offense has come to the attention of police, those offenses committed by mentally ill individuals showed a higher rate of attrition, presumably because they are more likely to be diverted from the criminal justice system into mental health facilities. Mental illness may thus increase the chances of detection while decreasing the chances of prosecution (Buchanan, 1997). Thus, studies using reconviction or rearrest rates could find a very different effect for mentally ill offenders than studies using self-report.

There exists some empirical support for the argument that clinical predictions are not as inaccurate as once thought. Mossman (1994) reanalyzed the data from 44 published studies on violence risk assessment using Receiver Operator Characteristic (ROC) analyses. He argued that the poor performance of violence predictions found in early studies was the result of reliance on inappropriate statistics. He proposed the use of ROC analyses because ROC is not affected by base rates or by preferences for avoiding one type of prediction error over another. Using this type of analysis, Mossman illustrated that clinical assessments of risk were significantly better than chance. Although he cautioned that no simple conclusion could be drawn about clinical predictions, Mossman's findings showed higher predictive accuracy for actuarial over clinical methods for predictions over the long term, and no difference for predictions over the short-term.

Recognition of clinicians' ability to predict violence at levels significantly greater than chance should not, however, be construed as evidence that clinical prediction is the most accurate or most efficient approach to violence risk assessment. Litwack has concluded that there has yet to be, and possibly never will be, a study of the accuracy of predictions of a truly representative sample. This is because those individuals who most clearly pose a serious risk of violence are never released from confinement.

Structured Clinical Judgment

A third type of decision making has emerged in violence risk assessment. *Structured clinical judgment* (also referred to as *clinical practice parameters* and *aide mémoire*) combines empirical findings on risk factors with professional clinical judgment (Dolan & Doyle, 2000; Douglas et al., 1999). Structured clinical risk assessments are based on professional guidelines that detail the relevant risk factors to be considered and the best method of using clinical judgment to evaluate these risk factors in making decisions about risk. In terms of professional discretion, structured clinical guidelines fall somewhere between actuarial and unstructured clinical predictions. Like clinical judgment, some discretion is afforded the assessor: There is little structure imposed on the process of decision making, the weights for each factor are not specified, and there is no explicit method provided for combining the data (Hart, 2000). On the other hand, as with actuarial judgment, the factors to be considered are explicit. Unlike unstructured clinical judgment, structured clinical judgment is systematic and data driven (Douglas et al., 1999). The HCR-20 (Webster, Douglas, Eaves, & Hart, 1997), the Spousal Assault Risk Assessment Guide (Kropp et al., 1998), and the Sexual Violence Risk–20 (Boer, Hart, Kropp, & Webster, 1997) are examples of structured clinical guidelines in the area of violence risk assessment.

The advantages of structured clinical judgment and the use of professional guidelines to inform clinical decision making include the flexibility afforded the assessor and the ease with which the guidelines can be adapted to new cases and contexts (Hart, 2000). They are also ideographic—that is, they speak to the risk of the individual being assessed and not to the group to which the individual belongs. These types of guidelines also provide information to guide risk management decisions. However, as with unstructured clinical judgment, the lack of explicit rules for decision making in structured clinical judgment leaves room for human error. Douglas and colleagues (1999) argued in favor of structured clinical judgment on the grounds that it can be used to avoid some of the problems associated with actuarial measures (e.g., the "broken leg case," lack of generalizability) and some of the difficulties associated with unstructured clinical judgment (e.g., low reliability).

Preliminary research on structured clinical judgment supports this approach as a reliable and valid method of violence risk assessment. Kropp and Hart (2000) studied the reliability and validity of structured clinical judgments made using the Spousal Assault Risk Assessment Guide (SARA) in six samples of adult male offenders. The SARA (Kropp et al., 1994, 1995, 1998) is a set of professional guidelines developed for the assessment of risk for spousal violence. In their study, correctional, mental health, and research staff made ratings on each of the individual SARA items as well as summary risk ratings—that is, judgments of the offenders' risk for recidivistic spousal assault as low, moderate, or high. They found high interrater reliability at the item level and moderate interrater reliability at the summary risk rating level. They also found significant differences between recidivists and nonrecidivists with respect to the summary risk ratings. Perhaps most important, their multivariate analyses (hierarchical logistic regression) showed that summary risk ratings significantly differentiated between recidivist and nonrecidivist offenders even when controlling for treatment suitability, time at risk, and continuous (actuarial) scores on the SARA. That is, structured clinical judgments made using the SARA guidelines outperformed judgments of risk made by simply summing the scores.

Similarly, Dempster (1998) found support for structured clinical judgments of sexual violence risk. In her study of adult male sexual offenders, she compared the performance of a number of risk assessment instruments, including the Sexual Violence Risk–20 (SVR-20; Boer et al., 1998). The SVR-20, like the SARA, is a set of professional guidelines that includes 20 items relevant to sexual violence recidivism. Summary ratings of risk made using the SVR-20 were found to be moderately associated with sexual offense recidivism. Additionally, structured clinical judgments of risk added incremental validity to actuarial ratings of risk made using the Sexual Offender Risk Appraisal Guide (SORAG; Quinsey et al., 1998) and the Rapid Risk Assessment for Sexual Offense Recidivism (RRASOR; Hanson, 1997).

Static versus Dynamic Predictors

Violence risk assessment research to date has focused on *static* (also referred to as *unchangeable*, *historical*, *fixed*) risk factors almost to the exclusion of *dynamic* (also referred to as *changeable* or *variable*) factors. Many have noted the need for inclusion of dynamic risk factors if any headway is to be made in the area of risk management (Lindqvist & Skipworth, 2000; Zamble & Quinsey, 1991). Static risk factors appear particularly important in the prediction of reoffending over the long term (e.g., Hanson & Bussiere, 1998); however, management of risk requires a consideration of risk in the short term, including a consideration of proximal risk factors. Grubin (1997) noted that dynamic risk factors are much more difficult to measure than are static factors. Dynamic risk factors may be relevant as proximal factors relating to violent or sexual reoffending, and thus are unlikely to be picked up on in traditional risk assessment studies in which the independent variables are measured prior to release. Variable risk factors may also be more idiosyncratic, that is, apply only to specific individuals and thus not be picked up on in a controlled trial, particularly in a study of an actuarial instrument. Douglas and Webster (1999) included a third category of risk markers: future adjustment and risk management factors. They define this category to include factors that are "future and situationally oriented, and deal with projections of circumstances that may aggravate or, conversely, mitigate, violence risk" (p. 197).

Kraemer and colleagues (1997) argued for the need to adopt a common language across risk assessment researchers with respect to static and dynamic risk factors. They suggested the following terms: *Fixed markers* are those risk factors that do not change. Examples include age at first violence (HCR-20 item H2; Webster et al., 1997) and elementary school maladjustment (VRAG item 2; Quinsey et al., 1998). A *variable risk factor*, as defined by Kraemer and colleagues (1997), is a risk factor that changes either spontaneously or through intervention. Examples include lack of insight (HCR-20 item C1; Webster et al., 1997) or negative attitude toward intervention (SVR-20 item 20; Boer et al., 1997). Kraemer and colleagues further divided variable risk markers into two types: causal risk factors and variable markers. A *causal risk factor* is a variable risk factor that can be manipulated or responds to intervention and also changes the risk of the outcome. Andrews and Bonta (1994) have referred to these as criminogenic factors. A *variable marker* is a variable risk factor that cannot be changed through intervention or manipulation (even though it may change spontaneously) or, if it can be manipulated, does not relate to changes in the outcome risk. Hanson and Harris (2000) further divided dynamic (i.e., variable) risk markers into *acute* and *stable*. They denoted those risk factors that are expected to remain unchanged for months or years as stable (e.g., substance abuse) whereas acute dynamic factors included those factors that change rapidly over the course of days, hours, and in some cases, minutes (e.g., intoxication from substances). They argued that acute risk factors relate to the timing of offending but are not particularly useful in terms of long-term prediction of the likelihood of reoffending. Nonetheless, consideration of acute risk factors may have particular import for supervision and management of individuals at risk for violence.

Although risk assessment research has focused predominately on historical risk factors, dynamic risk factors do play an important role in the assessment of future offending. Several studies have shown that dynamic risk factors are predictive of future offending (Dempster & Hart, 2002; Gendreau, Little, & Goggin, 1996; Hanson & Harris, 2000). Gendreau and colleagues (1996) conducted a meta-analysis of 131 studies on the prediction of criminal offending and found that dynamic predictors such as antisocial companions and criminogenic needs were among the most robust of predictors. Overall, they found that dynamic risk factors performed at least as well as static risk factors in predicting future criminal behavior.

In their study of the dynamic predictors of sex offense recidivism, Hanson and Harris (2000) collected data on dynamic predictors six months and one month prior to recidivistic offenses, and at equivalent time periods for the nonrecidivists. Data collection included both interviews with the parole supervisors (conducted after the recidivistic offenses) and review of the contemporaneous notes made by parole supervisors. They followed the performance of federally sentenced sexual offenders on conditional release in the community, including 208 recidivists and 201 nonrecidivists matched on offense history, victim type, and jurisdiction. They found that many of the stable dynamic risk factors were also predictive as acute (i.e., proximal) dynamic factors. In short, the recidivists' functioning as measured by items such as negative mood, drug use, appearance, and cooperation with supervision deteriorated across the course of supervision, whereas the behavior of nonrecidivists tended to improve on these same variables. For example, both any substance use (stable dynamic risk factor) and an increase in substance use (acute dynamic risk factor) were associated with recidivism. In addition, factors that have not been shown to be predictive in long-term prediction were significant predictors when considered as acute dynamic risk factors. Their findings suggested that sex offenders were most at risk for sexual reoffending when they are sexually preoccupied, have access to victims, lack insight into the risk for reoffending they present, and have an increase in dysphoric and angry moods.

The importance of dynamic predictors of violence was also investigated by Dempster and Hart (2002) in a study that compared the relative utility of static and dynamic risk factors in discriminating between recidivist and nonrecidivist sexual offenders. Risk factors from the Sexual Violence Risk—20 (SVR-20; Boer et al., 1997) were categorized as fixed (static) or variable (dynamic) markers; the fixed risk markers were further divided into offense history and psychosocial factors. Consistent with previous research, the findings indicated that offense history factors were highly predictive of both general and sexual violent recidivism. In addition, the variable (i.e., dynamic) psychosocial factors (e.g., relationship problems) improved on the predictions made using static factors alone, particularly in the case of sexually violent recidivism.

Risk Communication

Risk communication refers to the process of imparting the findings of a violence risk assessment to a legal or clinical decision maker. Risk communication, heretofore overshadowed by assessment issues, is increasingly being recognized as an important topic in its own right. "Understanding how best to communicate assessments of risk is as important to mental health law as improving the validity of those assessments themselves" (Monahan & Steadman, 1996, p. 937). There exists some debate as to how risk ought to be communicated. At present, there are no generally accepted standards regarding the communication of violence risk assessment findings (Slovic et al., 2000). Undoubtedly, communication of risk assessment findings depends, in part, on the context of the risk assessment. Nonetheless, there are components of risk communication that apply across the context of the referral. Schopp (1996) outlined the requisite characteristics for communication of risk that would apply regardless of the setting: "An ideal system for communicating assessments of risk would provide clear, precise, and complete information regarding those assessments in a form that would be fully accessible to the parties who must make decisions and take action on the basis of those assessments. It would communicate this information in a manner that would reflect and facilitate the appropriate allocation and discharge of responsibility among the participants in light of their competence and authority" (p. 939).

The debate over how risk for violence should be communicated has focused on different forms of risk statements. Slovic and Monahan (1995) noted that terms such as "dangerousness, likelihood, prediction, risk, and probability" have been used interchangeably in the violence risk assessment literature. Yet research on risk perception and decision theory suggest that these terms are not simply synonymous and further that subtleties of each may have some impact on the assessments made by clinicians and the interpretations made by consumers of the assessment. Probabilistic statements offer risk information in the form of a probability statistic—for example, this individual has a .42 likelihood of violently reoffending or 42 percent of individuals scoring in the same range as this individual violently reoffended after release. Risk ratings, on the other hand, provide information about violence risk in the form of a categorical rating—for example, this individual presents a high risk of violent reoffending. There is also a distinction between absolute and relative risk where *absolute risk* refers to an individual's absolute likelihood of violence and *relative risk* involves a comparison of an individual's risk for violence compared to other individuals from the same population.

In a study of the actual practice of forensic clinicians, Heilbrun and colleagues (1999) found that, with one exception, the 55 clinicians who participated in their study did not use numerical probabilities in communicating risk assessment findings. A number of reasons were cited against the use of probability statements, including: (1) "I don't know how to go from base rates to single cases"; (2) "the state of the research literature doesn't justify using specific numbers"; (3) "I don't know the (research, scales, procedures) that would let me do it differently"; (4) "numbers can be misinterpreted more easily"; and (5) "I don't want to be held accountable for being that precise."

Monahan and Steadman (1996) used the foundation of knowledge in weather prediction and communication to suggest ways to improve the communication of violence risk assessment. They drew an analogy between meteorology and the forecasting of rare and severe weather-related events on one hand and mental health law and the forecasting of rare and severe violence-related events on the other. As Monahan and Steadman noted, the National Weather Service (NWS) utilizes a categorical system of communication for rare events (e.g., hurricanes) and a probabilistic system of communication for common events (e.g., precipitation). In the case of severe weather events, the NWS provides prescriptive statements regarding the need for additional information (analogous to monitoring risk for violence) or action (analogous to risk management).

Monahan and Steadman noted that the NWS decision to adopt categorical risk communication has been criticized. Specifically, advocates of probabilistic risk communication have argued that categorical statements provide less information and are less precise than are probabilistic statements, and they also have unclear cutoffs. Further, they argue that use of categorical approaches awards decision-making power to the assessor, who may not be equipped or trained in the ability to make decisions of this kind. It also opens up the communication to be influenced by the values of the decision maker (e.g., the cost of false positives versus false negatives). These criticisms notwithstanding, the NWS has continued to use categorical risk communication for rare and severe events. Their decision to do so, according to Monahan and Steadman, resulted in part from concerns that probability statements are misconstrued by the general public. More specifically, research has shown that laypersons overvalue or undervalue relatively small probabilities and tend to view them in a relative rather than an absolute sense.

In considering the application of categorical risk communication to mental health law (e.g., violence risk communication), Monahan and Steadman had a number of observations. First, they indicated that categorical risk communication need not be restricted to three categories. Second, they indicated that risk communication that includes recommendations for risk management (monitoring and/or intervention) needs to be tied to the specific context. Finally, Monahan and Steadman noted that categorical risk communication could be combined with probabilistic statements about risk in a single risk communication.

Slovic and Monahan (1995) studied the impact of the structure of response scales on ratings of dangerousness, probability of violence, and the need for confinement. They provided vignettes about mental patients to laypersons and forensic clinicians, asking them to make ratings of the mental patient's dangerousness and probability of violence as well as the need for coercion to administer treatment. They varied the scales used to estimate probability to include 11 categories ranging from 0 to 100 in 10 percent increments for one group of participants to a scale that included five small probabilities (less than 1 chance in 1000, 1 chance in 1000, 1%, 2%, and 5%) and grouped probabilities over 40 percent in one category. Although there was a strong association between probability ratings and dangerousness ratings, Slovic and Monahan found that the probability scale used had a significant impact on judgments of risk by both laypersons and forensic clinicians. Specifically, when forensic clinicians were provided a probability scale with more categories at the lower end of the scale, they rated more cases as less than .10 probability of violence. Conversely, variation in the probability scale had no impact on their ratings of dangerousness. Slovic and Monahan concluded that judges used the probability scale as a rank order, meaningless in an absolute sense but meaningful in a relative sense.

These findings were replicated in a second study by Slovic, Monahan, and MacGregor (2000). In this study, they also looked at the impact of providing instructions on the meaning of probabilities and the impact of the use of frequencies as opposed to probabilities. The effect of the response scale did not diminish with the use of frequencies. Further, Slovic and colleagues found differences between probability scales and frequency scales, with probability scales leading to higher likelihood ratings than did the use of frequency scales. These differences affected the recommendations made about the need for close supervision and hospitalization. These effects were found even when judges were provided instructions on making probability estimates and were not negated by the experience level of the clinicians.

Although limited by the dearth of research on risk communication, Heilbrun, Dvoskin, Hart, and McNiel (2000) offered preliminary guidelines for the practice of risk communication: (1) Plain language should be used and technical jargon avoided. (2) The purpose of the task should be clearly stated, including the nature of the decision and whether intervention may follow. (3) A clear description of procedures used should be provided. (4) Results should be described in terms of their consistency with other sources and the reasons for inconsistencies should be clarified. (5) The report should summarize data that form the basis for opinions and recommendations. As well, the context assumed should be described. In addition, the report should use language describing the nature of the harm; risk factors and protective factors; and the risk level expressed in categorical, probabilistic, or conditional terms. (6) The time period over which the assessment is valid should be specified. (7) Predictions should be grounded in actuarial data whenever available. (8) Management recommendations should specify dynamic risk factors and relevant interventions, including the likely effectiveness of the intervention. (9) Recommendations should distinguish components of risk (e.g., imminence, probability, nature, frequency, severity). (10) Cautionary and explanatory language should be used in written reports. (11) In answering the question "Will he be violent?" assessors can refer to and paraphrase the relevant language in the report, indicate that it would be misleading to answer that question with a yes or no, and describe the factors on which the answer depends. (12) In answering the question "Is he dangerous?" assessors can refer to and paraphrase the relevant language; reply, "It depends" or ignore the term "dangerous" and describe the risk of the target behavior; and/or ask for clarification on the meaning of "dangerous" (adapted from Heilbrun et al., 2000, pp. 102–103). In conclusion, they state: "Mental health professionals must report risk assessment findings in ways that are accurate, precise, relevant and well grounded in observable behavior, history, actuarial data and good common sense" (p. 103).

RISK MANAGEMENT

Risk management refers to the "process whereby decisions are made to accept a known or assessed risk and/or the implementation of actions to reduce the consequences or probability of occurrence" (Halstead, 1997, p. 218). Although risk management has received far less attention than risk assessment, the importance of risk management has been noted by many (Grann, Belfrage, & Tengström, 2000; Grubin, 1997; Lindqvist & Skipworth, 2000; Taylor, 1997). Lindqvist and Skipworth (2000) argued that more research needs to be focused on "whether or not, to what extent and when forensic psychiatric rehabilitation alters the individual's level of risk" (p. 320). The ultimate goal of risk management is the prevention of harm to the patient or offender and to others (Taylor & Meux, 1997).

Risk management should be differentiated from forensic treatment. Forensic treatment, as defined by Heilbrun and Griffin (1999), involves mental health interventions such as diagnostic assessment, psychopharmacology, therapy, case management, and psychoeducational and skills-based therapy.

Forensic treatment is subsumed under the rubric of risk management. However, risk management includes other strategies. Interventions with respect to violence risk management can be construed widely to include such disparate strategies as incarceration, commitment at a psychiatric facility, psychological or pharmacological treatment, or supervision and monitoring. Risk management may also include periodic reassessment or taking no action at all.

Mulvey and Lidz (1985) noted that violence prediction studies often lack relevance to risk management since predictions do not instruct as to appropriate interventions. Much of the prediction literature focuses on factors that are not amenable to change (i.e., static factors), and thus this literature provides little in the way of instruction for risk managers (Zamble & Quinsey, 1991). The focus on risk management concomitant with risk assessment necessarily generates a different focus. Heilbrun (1997), in differentiating two models of risk assessment, prediction versus management, noted that a prediction model is necessarily concerned with accuracy whereas a management model is more focused on the reduction of risk. Quinsey and Walker (1992) stated that risk management could be improved by combining knowledge from three areas: prediction of violence, approaches to decision making, and treatment outcome and program evaluation. "Regrettably, however, there remains a yawning chasm between the bulk of the empirical prediction literature and practical violent offender release policies" (p. 248). As they noted, most of the risk factors that have been the subject of study in violence risk research have been static, fixed factors. However, those responsible for monitoring and intervening with offenders require information about predictors that can change and thus the bulk of risk assessment literature is of limited use to them. They recommended study of the antecedents of recidivism, such as those dynamic factors, either conditions of the offender or environmental events, that precede recidivism.

Risk management must focus on those risk factors that can be changed (e.g., variable) and, when changed, lead to a decrease in risk (Lindqvist & Skipworth, 2000). Proper assessment must include not only factors within the individual but also a consideration of factors external to the individual that are relevant to risk management, such as the availability and quality of forensic rehabilitation services. Lindqvist and Skipworth noted a number of factors in the rehabilitative environment important to producing a good outcome with mentally ill patients, including shared values and goals across the components of the rehabilitative system, reasonable continuity in care providers, early initiation of the rehabilitation process, strong alliance with family members, consideration of the social network and peers, a focus on development of insight into the purpose and process of rehabilitation, and, finally, consideration of patients' plans and perceptions of the future. Risk management must also balance the rights of the offender or patient and the need for treatment with the protection of the public (Heilbrun & Griffin, 1999). More specifically, the restrictiveness and intrusiveness of a risk management strategy must be balanced against consideration of the rights of the individual. A review of the efficacy of treatment programs is beyond the scope of this chapter. However, a brief review of various risk management strategies follows. This section is divided by the form of management, beginning with a review of interventions involving supervision and monitoring strategies, followed by a review of forensic treatment interventions.

Supervision and Monitoring

Incapacitation

Unarguably, the most restrictive and intrusive risk management strategy involves the principle of incapacitation through incarceration or other confinement. This strategy is applied within both the criminal justice and mental health systems to correctional offenders, forensic psychiatric patients, and civil psychiatric patients. As Kaliski (1997) noted, most patients spend far more time in hospital than they do under community care, thus hospitalization should be viewed as part of risk management.

Community Supervision

The vast majority of correctional inmates and forensic and civil psychiatric patients return to the community (Zamble & Quinsey, 1991). Quinsey and Walker (1992) have stated that the issues involved in managing risk in these populations are virtually identical. Although community supervision often involves other interventions, such as medication maintenance or psychotherapy, it can be viewed as a risk management strategy in its own right. Conditional release typically includes requirements for reporting/supervision; other requirements can be added. Among correctional parolees, these typically involve restrictions against the use of drugs or alcohol and orders to keep the peace. In most jurisdictions, the intensity, and thereby the intrusiveness, of community supervision can be varied in accordance with the rights of the individual and concerns about public safety. Offender behavior on supervision is presumably highly related to the behavior and skills of the supervising officer (Hanson & Harris, 2000). However, there is little empirical literature on the effectiveness of supervision in the prevention of recidivism, and what does is exist is limited by methodological problems (Zamble & Quinsey, 1991). Generally, the impact of parole supervision seems to be limited to the supervisory period and seems to be not particularly large in terms of effect size (Gottfredson, Mitchell-Herzfeld, & Flanagan, 1982). Regular and thorough monitoring of dynamic risk factors combined with appropriate and timely interventions could lead to a decrease in recidivism among supervised offenders.

Forensic treatment Interventions

Outpatient Commitment

There is often little in the way of services provided to patients once discharged from hospital, and much of it focuses on monitoring behavior, establishing a residence, and improving compliance with medication (Kaliski, 1997). An exception to this, however, is involuntary outpatient commitment statutes that mandate more intense case management and clinical supervision. The strength of community treatment lies in the fact that the intervention occurs in the setting in which the behavior of concern (i.e., violence) occurs (Quinsey & Walker, 1992). Involuntary outpatient commitment involves the ongoing provision of psychiatric services in the community. According to Swanson (2000), outpatient commitment interventions were designed to target individuals who require care and support in the community and yet are reluctant to involve themselves in community-based treatment. They noted that traditional approaches to preventing violence are not effective among severely mentally ill individuals; high-risk patients are often non-compliant with medication or fail to keep appointments.

Some authors have raised concerns about the monitoring of mentally ill offenders through legislation such as involuntary outpatient commitment (Kaliski, 1997). One such concern is that the targeting of high-risk mentally ill individuals will reduce the availability and quality of community services for people with mental illness who are assessed as lower risk (Munro & Rumgay, 2000). Good outcome is often defined as preventing readmission or violent behavior; much less focus is placed on improving overall functioning or quality of life for the severely mentally ill (Kaliski, 1997).

Swanson and colleagues (2000) studied the impact of involuntary outpatient commitment on violent recidivism among individuals with severe mental illness released from a psychiatric hospital. Excepting individuals with a history of serious assault involving weapons or physical injury, participants in their study were randomly assigned to the control group (no outpatient commitment) or the experimental group (outpatient commitment). Individuals with a history of serious assault (i.e., high-risk individuals) were placed in the experimental group for legal and ethical reasons. Individuals in the experimental group were initially placed on outpatient commitment (OPC) for a period not exceeding 90 days. Renewals of the OPC order could be made for up to 180 days. Both the control and experimental groups received case management and outpatient treatment. Individuals who remained on outpatient commitment for six months or longer had lower rates of violent behavior in the community than those who did not receive outpatient commitment services, even when the investigators controlled for the baseline history of violence. The lowest rate of violent behavior was associated with extended outpatient commitment that included regular outpatient services, adherence to prescribed medications, and no substance misuse. Findings showed that extended (greater than six months) outpatient commitment orders combined with regular use (i.e., three or more visits per month) of outpatient services reduced rates of violent behavior; shorter periods of OPC did not produce these results.

These results are particularly promising given that the experimental group included those individuals with histories of serious assault in the past, thereby constituting a higher-risk group than the control group. Swanson and colleagues (2000) speculated that increasing medication compliance and decreasing substance abuse may be the mechanisms by which OPC exact a decrease in community violence by severely mentally ill individuals. Based on their findings, they suggested that users of OPC systems should be prepared to monitor clients for extended periods and make available adequate services to address medication compliance and substance abuse as well as social services and other problems commonly faced by individuals suffering from severe mental illness.

CONCLUSIONS

It is generally recognized in the violence risk literature that predictions of violence can be made with a sufficiently high degree of accuracy to justify continued study and refinement of the technique. However, Borum (1996) and others (Douglas, Cox, & Webster, 1999; Heilbrun et al., 1999) have argued that the advances in second- and third-generation studies of violence risk assessment have not been incorporated by mental health practitioners into everyday clinical practice. The failure of the scientist-practitioner model in the area of violence risk assessment was underscored by Webster and colleagues (1997) in their decisive statement: "The greatest challenge in what remains of the 1990s is to integrate the almost separate worlds of research on the prediction of violence and the clinical practice of assessment. At present the two domains scarcely intersect" (p. 1).

Implications for Research

The interest in violence risk assessment has produced a large body of knowledge about the factors that are related to risk and the relative accuracy of approaches to decision making. It may be worthwhile to focus future efforts on investigating additional components of risk (e.g., nature, severity, imminence). As well, Douglas and Webster (1999) argued for consideration of new research methodologies, and efforts to improve measures and statistical approaches to studying violence risk assessment.

With respect to approaches to decision making, the promise of structured clinical judgment remains almost untested. Although Douglas and Webster (1999) advocated for the use of structured clinical judgment as the most optimal method of combining risk assessment data, a considerable amount of research is required before this approach can be adopted wholeheartedly. Preliminary findings (Dempster, 1998; Kropp & Hart, 2000) are encouraging, and point to the need for further research on this topic.

Clearly, risk communication and risk management remain understudied areas. In reviewing the sparse literature on risk communication, Heilbrun and colleagues (2000) noted the need for research on normative issues, such as the ways in which risk assessors actually communicate their findings in practice and the perception of risk communication by consumers of risk assessments. Additionally, Heilbrun and colleagues argued for research on the manner in which risk ought to be communicated, focusing on both risk assessors and risk consumers. Research on risk management will need to focus on the applicability of interventions to specific criminogenic factors, the impact of risk management strategies on violent behavior and other quality of life issues, and the ways in which information about an individual's response to risk management can be incorporated into reassessments of the individual's risk for violence.

Implications for Clinicians

Borum (1996) outlined three areas in which clinicians could better incorporate findings from the violence risk literature: risk assessment technology, the development of clinical practice guidelines for violence risk assessment and management, and the development of training programs and other educational initiatives. He noted that practitioners have often failed to keep abreast of developments in the field, and in the case of violence risk assessment, may have failed to incorporate findings about the accuracy of actuarial methods versus clinical judgment. Borum argued that the state of the discipline of violence risk assessment has advanced to the point that would allow for the development of practice guidelines. Douglas and colleagues (1999) argued for "empirically validated violence risk assessment" in which practice must be influenced by science and vice versa.

Other areas of importance include a familiarity with the literature, as limited as it may be, on the communication and management of risk. As knowledge in these domains increases, clinicians will need to incorporate findings into their everyday practice. The practice guidelines for risk communication outlined by Heilbrun and colleague (1999) and described earlier in this chapter will provide an excellent starting position for clinicians practicing in this area.

REFERENCES

Andrews, D. A., & Bonta, J. (1994). *The psychology of criminal conduct.* Cincinnati, OH: Anderson.

Austin, W. G. (2000). A forensic psychology model of risk assessment for child custody relocation law. *Family and Conciliation Courts Review*, *38*, 192–207.

Barefoot v. Estelle, 463 U.S. 880 (1983).

Boer, D. P., Hart, S. D., Kropp, P. R., & Webster, C. (1997). *Manual for the Sexual Violence Risk—20: Professional guidelines for assessing risk for sexual violence.* Vancouver: British Columbia Institute Against Family Violence.

Borum, R. (1996). Improving the clinical practice of violence risk assessment. *American Psychologist*, *51*, 945–956.

Buchanan, A. (1997). Assessing risk: Limits to the measurement of the target behaviours. *International Review of Psychiatry*, *9*, 195–200.

Buchanan, A. (1999). Risk and dangerousness. *Psychological Medicine*, *29*, 465–473.

Carson, D. (1997). Good enough risk taking. *International Review of Psychiatry*, *9*, 303–308.

Davison, S. (1997). Risk assessment and management—a busy practitioner's perspective. *International Review of Psychiatry, 9*, 201–206.

Dempster, R. J. (1998). *Predicting sexually violent recidivism: A comparison of risk assessment instruments.* Unpublished master's thesis. Simon Fraser University, Vancouver, BC.

Dempster, R. J., & Hart, S. D. (2002). The relative utility of dynamic and historical risk factors in predicting recidivism among sexual offenders. *Sexual Abuse: A Journal of Research and Treatment, 14*, 121–138.

Dolan, M., & Doyle, M. (2000). Violence risk prediction: Clinical and actuarial measures and the role of the Psychopathy Checklist. *British Journal of Psychiatry, 177*, 303–311.

Douglas, K. S., Cox, D. N., & Webster, C. D. (1999). Violence risk assessment: Science and practice. *Legal and Criminological Psychology, 4*, 149–184.

Douglas, K. S., & Webster, C. D. (1999). Predicting violence in mentally and personality disordered individuals. In R. Roesch, S. D. Hart, & J. R. P. Ogloff (Eds.), *Psychology and law: The state of the discipline* (pp. 176–239). New York: Kluwer Academic.

Gendreau, P., Little, T., & Goggin, C. (1996). A meta-analysis of the predictors of adult offender recidivism: What works! *Criminology, 34*, 575–605.

Gottfredson, M. R., Mitchell-Herzfeld, S. D., & Flanagan, T. J. (1982). Another look at the effectiveness of parole supervision. *Journal of Research in Crime and Delinquency, 19*, 277–232.

Grann, M., Belfrage, J., & Tengström, A. (2000). Actuarial assessment of risk for violence: Predictive validity of the VRAG and the historical part of the HCR-20. *Criminal Justice and Behavior, 27*, 97–114.

Grove, W. M., Zald, D. H., Lebow, B. S., Snitz, B. E., & Nelson, C. (2000). Clinical versus mechanical prediction: A meta-analysis. *Psychological Assessment, 12*, 19–30.

Grubin, D. (1997). Inferring predictors of risk: Sex offenders. *International Review of Psychiatry, 9*, 225–231.

Halstead, S. (1997). Risk assessment and management in psychiatric practice: Inferring predictors of risk. A view from learning disability. *International Review of Psychiatry, 9*, 217–224.

Hanson, R. K. (1997). *The development of a brief actuarial scale for sexual offense recidivism.* (User report 97-04). Ottawa: Department of the Solicitor General of Canada.

Hanson, R. K., & Bussiere, M. T. (1998). Predictors of sexual recidivism: A meta analysis. *Journal of Consulting and Clinical Psychology, 66*, 348–362.

Hanson, R. K., & Harris, A. J. R. (2000). Where should we intervene? Dynamic predictors of sexual offence recidivism. *Criminal Justice and Behavior, 27*, 6–35.

Hart, S. D. (1998). Psychopathy and risk for violence. In D. Cooke, A. E. Forth, & R. D. Hare (Eds.), *Psychopathy: Theory, research, and implications for society* (pp. 355–375). Dordrecht, The Netherlands: Kluwer.

Hart, S. D. (2000, November). The promise and peril of sex offender risk assessment. In R. Laws (Chair), *Structured professional guidelines for assessing risk in sexual offenders.* Symposium presented at the Annual Conference of the Association for the Treatment of Sexual Abusers, San Diego, California.

Heilbrun, K. (1997). Prediction versus management models relevant to risk assessment: The importance of legal decision-making context. *Law and Human Behavior, 21*, 347–359.

Heilbrun, K., Dvoskin, J., Hart, S., & McNiel, D. (1999). Violence risk communication: Implications for research, policy, and practice. *Health, Risk, & Society*, *1*, 91–106.

Heilbrun, K., & Griffin, P. (1999). Forensic treatment: A review of programs and research. In R. Roesch, S. D. Hart, & J. R. P. Ogloff (Eds.) *Psychology and law: The state of discipline.* Perspectives in law and psychology, Vol. 10, pp. 241–274. New York: Kluwer Academic/Plenum Publishers.

Heilbrun, K., Ogloff, J. R. P., & Picarello, K. (1999). Dangerous offender statutes in the United States and Canada. *International Journal of Law and Psychiatry*, *22*, 393–415.

Kaliski, S. Z. (1997). Risk management during the transition from hospital to community care. *International Review of Psychiatry*, *9*, 249–256.

Kraemer, H. C., Kazdin, A. E., Offord, D. R., Kessler, R. C., Jensen, P. S., & Kupfer, D. J. (1997). Coming to terms with the terms of risk. *Archives of General Psychiatry*, *54*, 337–343.

Kropp, P. R., & Hart, S. D. (2000). The Spousal Assault Risk Assessment (SARA) Guide: Reliability and validity in adult male offenders. *Law and Human Behavior*, *24*, 101–118.

Kropp, P. R., Hart, S. D., Webster, C. D., & Eaves, D. (1994). *Manual for the Spousal Assault Risk Assessment Guide.* Vancouver: British Columbia Institute on Family Violence.

Kropp, P. R., Hart, S. D., Webster, C. D., & Eaves, D. (1995). *Manual for the Spousal Assault Risk Assessment Guide* (2nd ed). Vancouver: British Columbia Institute on Family Violence.

Kropp, P. R., Hart, S. D., Webster, C. D., & Eaves, D. (1998). *Spousal Assault Risk Assessment: User's guide.* Toronto: Multi-Health Systems.

Lindqvist, P., & Skipworth, J. (2000). Evidence-based rehabilitation in forensic psychiatry. *British Journal of Psychiatry*, *176*, 320–323.

Litwack, T. R. (1994). Assessments of dangerousness: Legal, research, and clinical developments. *Administration and Policy in Mental Health*, *21*, 361–377.

Litwack, T. R., Kirschner, S. M., & Wack, R. (1993). The accuracy of predictions of violence to others. *Psychiatric Quarterly*, *64*, 245–273.

Meehl, P. E. (1996). *Clinical versus statistical prediction: A theoretical analysis and a review of the literature.* Northvale, NJ: Jason Arsonson. (Original work published in 1954.)

Monahan, J. (1981). *The clinical prediction of violent behavior.* Rockville, MD: National Institute of Mental Health.

Monahan, J. (1996). Violence prediction: The last 20 years and the next 20 years. *Criminal Justice and Behavior*, *23*, 107–120.

Monahan, J., & Steadman, H. J. (1996). Violent storms and violent people: How meteorology can inform risk communication in mental health law. *American Psychologist*, *51*, 931–938.

Monahan, J., Steadman, H. J., Appelbaum, P. S., Robbins, P. C., Mulvey, E. P., Silver, E., Roth, L. H., & Grisso, T. (2000). Developing a clinically useful actuarial tool for assessing violence risk. *British Journal of Psychiatry*, *176*, 312–319.

Mossman, D. (1994). Assessing predictions of violence: Being accurate about accuracy. *Journal of Consulting and Clinical Psychology*, *62*, 783–792.

Mulvey, E. P., & Lidz, C. W. (1985). A critical analysis of dangerousness research in a new legal environment. *Law and Human Behavior*, *9*, 209–219.

Munro, E., & Rumgay, J. (2000). Role of risk assessment in reducing homicides by people with mental illness. *British Journal of Psychiatry*, *176*, 116–120.

Quinsey, V. L., Harris, G. T., Rice, M. E., & Cormier, C. A. (1998). *Violent offenders: Appraising and managing risk*. Washington, DC: American Psychological Association.

Quinsey, V. L., Lalumiere, M. L., Rice, M. E., & Harris, G. T. (1995). Predicting sexual offenses. In J. C. Campbell (Ed.), *Assessing dangerousness: Violence by sexual offenders, batterers, and child abusers* (pp. 114–137). Thousand Oaks, CA: Sage.

Quinsey, V. L, Rice, M. E., & Harris, G. T. (1995). Actuarial prediction of sexual recidivism. *Journal of Interpersonal Violence, 10*, 85–105.

Quinsey, V. L., & Walker, W. D. (1992). Dealing with dangerousness: Community risk management strategies with violent offenders. In R. D. Peters, R. J. McMahon, & V. L. Quinsey (Eds.), *Aggression and violence throughout the life span* (pp. 244–262). London: Sage.

Sawyer, J. (1966). Measurement *and* prediction, clinical *and* statistical. *Psychological Bulletin, 66*, 178–200.

Schopp, R. F. (1996). Communicating risk assessments: Accuracy, efficacy, and responsibility. *American Psychologist, 51*, 939–944.

Slovic, P., & Monahan, J. (1995). Probability, danger, and coercion: A study of risk perception and decision-making in mental health law. *Law and Human Behavior, 19*, 49–65.

Slovic, P., Monahan, J., & MacGregor, D. (2000). Violence risk assessment and risk communication: The effects of using actual cases, providing instruction, and employing probability versus frequency formats. *Law and Human Behavior, 24*, 271–296.

Steadman, H. J., Silver, E., Monahan, J., Appelbaum, P. S., Robbins, P. C., Mulvey, E. P., Grisso, T., Roth, L. H., & Banks, S. (2000). A classification tree approach to the development of actuarial violence risk assessment tools. *Law and Human Behavior, 24*, 83–100.

Swanson, J. W., Swartz, M. S., Borum, R., Hiday, V. A., Wagner, H. R., & Burns, B. J. (2000). Involuntary out-patient commitment and reduction of violent behavior in persons with severe mental illness. *British Journal of Psychiatry, 176*, 324–331.

Tarasoff v. Regents of the University of California, 551 P.2d 334 (Cal. 1976).

Taylor, C., & Meux, C. (1997). Individual cases: the risk, the challenge. *International Review of Psychiatry, 9*, 289–302.

Taylor, P. J. (1997). Mental disorder and risk of violence. *International Review of Psychiatry, 9*, 157–161.

Towl, G. J., & Crighton, D. A. (1997). Risk assessment with offenders. *International Review of Psychiatry, 9*, 187–193.

Webster, C. D., Douglas, K. S., Eaves, D., & Hart, S. D. (1997). *HCR-20: Assessing Risk for Violence (Version 2)*. Vancouver: Mental Health, Law, and Policy Institute, Simon Fraser University.

Zamble, E., & Quinsey, V. L. (1991). *Dynamic and behavioral antecedents to recidivism: A retrospective analysis.* (User report R-17). Ottawa: Correctional Service of Canada.

CHAPTER 7

FORENSIC AND ETHICAL ISSUES IN THE ASSESSMENT AND TREATMENT OF THE SUICIDAL PATIENT

KIRK STROSAHL

MOUNTAINVIEW CONSULTING GROUP
MOXEE, WASHINGTON

The assessment and treatment of a suicidal patient is not only a formidable clinical challenge, but also presents the behavioral health clinician with significant legal and risk management issues. Approximately 10 to 20 percent of mental health outpatients and 30 to 40 percent of inpatients present for care with a clinically significant suicidal behavior (Chiles & Strosahl, 1995). The pervasiveness of suicidal behavior is better illustrated by the 1997 National Youth Risk Survey, which showed that approximately 1 in 5 youths under age 18 had experienced serious suicidal ideation and an additional 7 percent had made a suicide attempt. These results show a striking similarity to similar studies in adult populations, the only difference being that adults have a much higher lifetime prevalence of serious suicidal ideation and suicide attempts (Strosahl, Linehan, & Chiles, 1984).

To make matters more complicated, suicidal behavior is not a single entity but rather is a continuum of behaviors that can vary in frequency, duration, and intensity. The most common behavior seen in clinical settings is suicidal ideation, or the act of thinking about killing oneself. Suicidal ideation can range from very brief, fleeting thoughts of suicide to highly specific thinking that occurs for prolonged periods of time on a daily basis. Some patients experiencing suicidal ideation will verbalize these thoughts to significant others; others will mention their struggles to no one. Behavioral health providers also treat a large number of patients who have made one or more suicide attempts in which a pervasive clinical and legal issue is the potential for a repeat suicide attempt or a completed suicide. Although the odds of any one suicidal patient dying from suicide are microscopic, most therapists believe that the primary goal of treatment is to prevent a suicide.

The maturation of the mental health field has had enormous benefits for patients who previously had little or no access to behavioral health care. However, this transformation from cottage industry to service industry has been accompanied by an increased risk of malpractice litigation. Clinicians who in the early part of their careers practiced with relative immunity from malpractice claims now find themselves compelled to review the legal and risk management implications of their clinical decision making on a daily basis. Malpractice insurance is now a prerequisite for any practitioner who wishes to provide behavioral health services. Larger institutions such as psychiatric hospitals or mental health centers have risk management departments staffed with attorneys who specialize both in interpreting the risk associated with clinical services and in devising protocols to minimize the civil and criminal risks associated with such services. When an adverse event such as a patient suicide occurs, not only is the clinician left to cope with the anguish of losing a patient, but the odds are also much greater that he or she also may have to answer to a plaintiff's attorney, a judge, and a jury.

In response to the increasingly litigious nature of the health care environment, many texts and journal articles have been introduced to articulate both clinical and legal standards for medically and nonmedically trained providers (Bongar, 1991; Bongar, Berman, et al., 1998; Jobes & Berman, 1993; Klespies et al., 1999; Robertson, 1998). As Klespies and associates note, a defining feature of legal standards is that they are derived from failed clinical care and the outcome of subsequent malpractice litigation. However useful they are for risk management purposes, standards developed in this fashion do not inform clinicians of clinically effective strategies in the treatment of suicidal patients.

Practicing clinicians know all too well how legal and risk management issues can interfere with the ethical requirement to provide high-quality mental health care. When they are working with suicidal patients, the fear of litigation can directly contribute to the destruction of the therapeutic alliance, counterproductive confrontations, and client- and therapist-assisted dropouts from therapy (Rudd, Joiner, Jobes, & King, 1999). Many legally required interventions have questionable clinical effectiveness, with the result being that behavioral health providers consciously or unconsciously engage in treatment practices that provide legal protection but limited clinical benefits. For example, repetitiously suicidal patients, many of whom engage in high-risk self-destructive and self-injurious behavior on nearly a daily basis, are the bane of every clinician's existence. Their high-risk behavior places behavioral health providers under the continual threat of adverse legal consequences to the extent that treatment may devolve into a poorly disguised exercise in risk management. This dilemma highlights another problematic question in the era of malpractice litigation: How does one navigate the legal risks associated with providing care while adhering to the ethical responsibility to deliver the right kind of care?

GOALS OF THIS CHAPTER

While many texts and articles describe legal standards of care for suicidal patients, much less is written for clinicians about the central processes of malpractice litigation. In essence, clinicians are given legal standards of care in a vacuum, and this custom tends to result in rather mindless rule following. To help address this void in the literature, this chapter will examine the process of wrongful death litigation from the trenches. The author has worked as an expert witness in the area of suicide malpractice lawsuits for nearly twenty years. This work has involved comprehensive analyses of wrongful death malpractice claims as well as expert testimony in both depositions and civil trials. In addition, the author has provided case-specific risk reviews for insurance companies that provide liability coverage for both institutions and individual practitioners.

Most mental health clinicians have scant contact with civil law until they are sued for malpractice or are a party to a lawsuit for other reasons. This results in a basic lack of understanding of how a lawsuit is conducted, how civil negligence is determined in a wrongful death suit, and how to minimize (but never eliminate) the risk of a malpractice claim. Consequently, the mental health field is overrun with myths about the way lawsuits function. For example, few behavioral health providers know how "standard of care" is defined in a lawsuit or how negligence is determined. Even fewer can apply clinical practices that reduce the likelihood of a lawsuit in treating a suicidal patient. Paradoxically, many providers actually engage in what they believe to be risk management practices, but that actually expose them to additional risk! If behavioral health providers develop a more common-sense understanding of how the legal system really works, the relationship between clinical and legal standards of care will become much more apparent. This knowledge ultimately will help behavioral health providers engage in more effective and more ethical interventions with suicidal patients.

To achieve the objective of providing a helpful forensic framework for the practitioner in the field, this chapter will first address the "anatomy" of a lawsuit. Specifically, we will examine how wrongful death lawsuits are initiated, what legal standards are used to define and determine negligence, and what aspects of clinical practice with suicidal patients are the subject of malpractice claims. As a part of this process, two central paradoxes in civil litigation related to wrongful death will be examined: the predictability and preventability of death by suicide. To effectively navigate the legal issues in working with suicidal patients, clinicians need to have a solid grasp of the interface of ethical and legal considerations. Guidelines for managing the interface of ethical and legal requirements will be discussed, as well as a set of practical strategies for reducing the risk of a malpractice lawsuit in the event of a patient suicide.

The Anatomy of a Wrongful Death Lawsuit: From Adverse Event to the Courtroom

Most practitioners do not realize that there is a considerable time lag from the time of an adverse event such as a patient suicide to the filing of a negligence claim. In this author's experience, a delay of two to four years is not at all unusual. Typically, in the case of a suicide, the survivors may be too griefstricken to pursue litigation for months or even years. At a content level, they may even be ambivalent about filing a lawsuit. It generally takes a long time for a plaintiff to decide to become a plaintiff.

The time lag between a patient suicide and the filing of a negligence claim has many practical implications. First, most clinicians will have moved on from the adverse event until they receive the notice that a claim has been filed. They may not remember many of the specifics of the case, nor the immediate circumstances that prevailed at the time of the patient's death. For this reason, the clinician will have to rely extensively on written documents such as intake reports, progress notes, medication summaries, and discharge summaries. This emphasis means the quality of these documents and the content they contain is critical to a defense against a lawsuit.

Second, the time lag between the occurrence of a tragic event such as a patient suicide and the decision to file a lawsuit suggests that there may be opportunities to intervene with the survivors of suicide in a way that may short-circuit their decision to seek civil remedies. At the psychological level, a lawsuit is a systematic attempt to prove that someone else other than the survivor is to blame for a patient's suicide. Working through the sense of guilt and responsibility is a key theme in clinical work with survivors of suicide, and if this process goes awry the decision to file a lawsuit may be the result. This author's experience suggests that many civil negligence lawsuits are induced by the reactions of the providers and institutions involved. For example, one psychiatric hospital was sued as a direct result of billing a suicide survivor for the psychiatric inpatient treatment of a spouse who committed suicide in the inpatient unit.

Third, most clinicians are thunderstruck when a patient commits suicide and it may take many months to resolve feelings of guilt and failure resulting from the conviction that somehow they failed to deliver appropriate care. By definition, if that care had been delivered, the patient would not be dead. Being drawn back into a review of one's professional competence after putting these issues to rest can be a traumatic experience. Once this Pandora's box is reopened, the providers involved see the lawsuit as a chance to be vindicated—only to be bitterly disappointed when their insurance company reaches an out-of-court settlement.

Finally, it is important to realize that the Anglo-American legal system is anything but a system of "justice." The ability to procure effective legal representation, the characteristics of the presiding judge, and the composition of the jury as well as the sympathy factor are all important elements of a legal proceeding. Much like behavioral health itself, the majority of the outcome in lawsuits is determined by nonspecific factors. Juries in particular are highly variable in their application of the law. As the O. J. Simpson trial suggests, anything can happen once the jury is out.

The Malpractice Claim

Normally, the plaintiff's attorney within a local or regional jurisdiction files a negligent death claim. The claim has to establish a set of facts about the process of care that transpired before the suicide. Then the claim will attempt to demonstrate how the actions of one or more providers were negligent. The typical claim is usually chronologically organized, starting with the first providers and services delivered that are alleged to be part of the "causal chain." Then the claim will list each allegation of negligence on a provider-by-provider and event-by-event basis. Finally, there will be a request that the court award the plaintiff monetary damages. Normally, monetary damages are awarded separately for the loss of the decedent's likely lifetime earnings and for the survivors' pain, suffering, and the loss of companionship. It is important to understand that the case itself will be fought not only on the negligence claim, but also on the amounts of lost earnings capacity and the actual pain and suffering of the survivors.

In most lawsuits, the most common strategy is to create a laundry list of negligent acts, a simple study in probability theory that is widely employed by plaintiffs' attorneys. The more negligent actions are alleged, the greater the likelihood that the judge or jury will agree with at least one allegation. This strategy is somewhat analogous to the "big lie" approach used in Nazi Germany; the more numerous and outrageous the claims, the more likely it is that a jury will conclude that some malfeasance had to occur to generate that many complaints. A similar litigation philosophy is used to name defendants. Normally, a plaintiff's attorney will name several defendants, both at the agency and at the individual provider level. The more defendants are named, the greater the likelihood that at least one will be found guilty of a negligent action. On a practical level, naming more defendants activates more liability insurance policies, which increases the pool of funds that can be drawn from in case a settlement is reached. In a typical suicide negligence lawsuit, there may be multiple defense attorneys involved, each with a separate charge from a different insurance company to defend the interests of their defendant.

Once an insurance company (1) is notified that a patient suicide has occurred, and/or (2) is involved as an insurer for a provider who has been sued, a very specific process is initiated that most providers do not understand. If the patient has committed suicide but no lawsuit has been filed, the insurance company will immediately conduct its own internal review of the specifics of the case with the aim of quantifying the risk of a successful malpractice suit. Normally, this internal review is not subject to subpoena. After this review is completed, the insurance company will identify an adverse event loss figure. This is the amount of money the company estimates it could spend in attorneys' fees, travel expenses, and expert witness fees as well as the likely award to the plaintiff if the jury believes that a negligent death has occurred. This figure is supposed to be a closely held secret, but a skillful plaintiff's attorney can generally determine what the loss reserve is based upon responses received during settlement discussions.

The vast majority of lawsuits never make it to trial because most insurance companies believe it is in their best interests to reach an out-of-court settlement. Some behavioral health providers are shocked to discover that their liability insurance policy has a provision that requires them to participate in a reasonable settlement as determined by the insurance company. Failure to do so may cause the insurance company to refuse to pay subsequent attorneys' fees or a malpractice award. If this sounds like big business at work, it is. The civil litigation industry is a multibillion-dollar enterprise involving the transfer of great sums of money between the legal and insurance communities. Unfortunately, an out-of-court settlement is viewed by most state licensing authorities and behavioral health credentialing systems as a successfully prosecuted action against the licensed provider: Without ever admitting guilt, the provider is viewed as guilty. Before agreeing to a settlement in a wrongful death suit, defendants should make sure they understand all of the licensing and credentialing implications of agreeing to a settlement.

The Process of Discovery

Discovery is a general term used to describe the process of fact finding that eventually leads to one of three outcomes: (1) an out-of-court settlement is reached; (2) the judge delivers a summary judgment that effectively decides the lawsuit, usually for the defendant; and (3) the judge orders the case to go to trial. There are two major components to the process of discovery, which are important to understand.

The *interrogatories* are a process designed to make sure that all records, tests, personal diaries, and any other documents that may have any potential bearing on the case are available to all parties. These documents are instrumental in helping the court determine whether negligence occurred and how to adjudicate the subsequent financial award. Interrogatories are bidirectional in nature; either side in a lawsuit can make rather extensive requests for this type of information. Practitioners involved in a lawsuit can expect to produce all pertinent patient care records, including such items as "shadow records," original session notes, correspondence with other practitioners, phone records, and billing records, to name a few.

An important part of the interrogatory process is the production of expert witness reports, which evaluate whether the defendants involved in a case met or did not meet the standard of care. Normally, both sides will hire expert witnesses to review all data pertinent to the case and then render a set of opinions about whether negligence was involved. In an amazing twist of fate, the experts for the plaintiff will nearly always describe the defendant's care as negligent, while the defense experts will maintain that the defendant's care was well within the standard of care.

Although every state has a legal definition of how the standard of care will be defined, the job of the expert witness is to convince the jury of what the standard of care actually is. For this reason, an expert witness will normally be a provider of the same discipline with some acknowledged expertise with suicidal patients. Often, this expertise will be established by producing a record of publications, presentations, or trainings in the area of suicidal behavior. Functionally, two types of experts are involved. One is an expert witness in the subject area that the case may revolve around (in this case, suicidal behavior), even if the expert's discipline is different than the defendant's. The second type of expert is a *treating expert*, usually a provider of the same discipline who can testify on the standard of care for that discipline. This type of expert may have no special expertise in the arena of suicidal behavior but will be used to establish what would be expected from a competently trained provider of the same discipline. Nearly every suicide lawsuit will utilize both types of expert witnesses.

The other major component of the discovery process is the taking of *depositions*. The overall goal of the deposition process is to provide each side with a complete information set. In effect, each side is attempting to "discover" in advance what a witness is going to say on the stand. A deposition is a court-ordered process that involves obtaining information about the case from various witnesses under oath. Usually, depositions will be taken from all plaintiffs and defendants, expert witnesses, family members and friends of the decedent, forensic economists, and any other person that may have information bearing on the facts of the case. Testimony given in a deposition can and will be used in the trial portion of the lawsuit. There is much jockeying in this phase of the lawsuit as the respective parties attempt to establish an edge over their opponent. The outcome of depositions often directly influences the outcome of the settlement discussions that are always going on behind the scenes.

For the defendant in a suicide lawsuit, the deposition can be a harrowing experience. The plaintiff's attorney will not only dig relentlessly for information, but will attempt to get the defendant to provide conflicting answers to questions, to second-guess his or her clinical care, and, in the best case, to admit under oath to one or more of the negligence claims made in the original legal claim. In a later section, we will discuss strategies not only for surviving the deposition, but for actually promoting the chances of a favorable out-of-court settlement or even a "defendant's verdict" from the jury. The deposition is an adversarial process, meaning that attorneys for the deposed witness will be busy lodging their objections to certain kinds of questions or interview tactics. In some cases, attorneys may instruct their clients not to answer a question until the presiding judge has had the opportunity to rule on a particular legal point. As depositions are being collected, the presiding judge will often be issuing rulings around certain key legal points that are coming up during the process. Collectively, the interrogatories and deposition process can generate boxes of paperwork that allow each party to have a complete and thorough understanding of all the information that could be presented at trial.

The Civil Trial

Assuming that the presiding judge has not issued a summary judgment to dismiss the case, the trial phase begins with the selection of a jury. The composition of a jury is just as important in a civil suit as it is in a criminal proceeding. Attorneys will take a good deal of time interviewing prospective jurors in an attempt to qualify or disqualify them. This is also the attorney's opportunity to form a positive relationship with each juror, who may later sway other jurors over to a more favorable verdict. In many respects, however traumatic the trial phase is for the defendant, it is really an anticlimax. Because of the usual intensity of the discovery process, very little new information is presented at a trial. Each side will attempt to highlight the facts and opinions that support their point of view.

The major difference between a civil and criminal trial involves the standard of evidence required to deliver a verdict. Civil law uses a standard called a *preponderance of evidence*. This standard requires that the majority of the evidence suggest that negligence did or did not occur, and the "preponderance" could be as small as 51 to 49 percent. In contrast, criminal proceedings use the standard of *beyond a reasonable doubt*, which means that in returning a guilty verdict, there should be no significant reason for believing a defendant is not guilty. The civil standard for returning a verdict is so much more lenient than the criminal standard that it was possible for O. J. Simpson to be acquitted of murder in criminal court, then found guilty of wrongful death in the subsequent civil proceeding.

In many states, juries are required to allocate responsibility for an outcome between the plaintiff and defendant. For example, the jury may conclude that the plaintiff was 70 percent responsible for committing suicide and the defendant contributed 30 percent to the outcome. The allocation then determines how much of the award amount is the responsibility of the defendant and the plaintiff. Typically, juries are more bimodal in these allocations. In other words, they are likely to award 90 percent to the plaintiff or 95 percent to the defendant rather than "splitting the pie." This common outcome arises from the fact that any allocation to the defendant represents an award to the plaintiff, whereas the opposite relationship does not hold.

KEY TENETS OF A WRONGFUL DEATH CLAIM

Now that process of civil litigation has been described, it will be useful to look at how negligence is defined in legal terms. Although state laws vary in the definition of negligence, they are much more alike than different.

Malpractice is defined as a pattern of negligent or willful misconduct on the part of the behavioral health provider. The burden of proof is on the plaintiff to provide a preponderance of evidence that the negligence was the result of a lack of knowledge, skill, or care that would ordinarily be exercised by a similarly trained provider under similar circumstances. Further, the plaintiff must prove that the defendant's lack of knowledge, skill, or care was the proximate cause of the death that otherwise would not have occurred.

There are several assumptions contained in this rather standard definition of malpractice. First, there is a commonly accepted standard of knowledge, skill, or care that should be exercised by any competently trained provider. Second, negligent actions can be errors of omission or commission. *Errors of omission* are actions that should have been taken but were not. *Errors of commission* are inappropriate or badly misguided actions. Third, there is the concept of a pattern of negligence or willful misconduct. This means that negligence is very hard to prove based upon a single error. It is a *pattern of negligence* or errors that leads to the determination of negligence. Fourth, *willful misconduct* implies that the provider deliberately engaged in negligent or substandard care, perhaps for sexual reasons. Willful misconduct is generally less likely to be the claim in a wrongful death suit unless financial or personal motives are suspected. Perhaps most important, the concept of *proximal cause* means that a direct and uninterrupted link exists between the last in the pattern of negligent acts and the resulting death. For example, if the defendant can prove that the decedent was badly intoxicated and lacked any capacity for judgment just prior to a suicide, intoxication would become the proximal cause of the suicide and malpractice may be harder to prove.

Collectively, in lay terms, *negligence* involves providing either grossly substandard assessment and treatment and/or not providing needed assessment and treatment when the provider could have, and should have, known that these actions would result in the patient's demise. Further, had the provider engaged in the appropriate actions, the suicide would have been prevented. As should be obvious, a key component of the definition of negligence is the assumption that the provider can predict that a suicide is going to occur and can deliver treatments or interventions that are known to prevent suicide. With respect to the prediction and prevention of suicide, this is a highly problematic assumption.

CHARACTERISTIC CLAIMS IN A WRONGFUL DEATH SUIT

Keeping in mind that negligence can involve both inappropriate and omitted clinical actions, it will be useful to examine the kinds of claims that are made in a negligent death suit. In truth, a wrongful death lawsuit is an exercise in "20–20" hindsight. In the hypothetical world of law, there are an endless number of levels of analysis, leading to a type of infinite regress. It is impossible, however, for a competently trained provider to engage in every single action that is cited in a negligent death suit. For example, in one lawsuit, the provider had done a competent job of assessing suicidal risk and formed a "no suicide contract" with a severely depressed patient along with an aggressive schedule of therapy sessions. The patient subsequently killed himself before the next regularly scheduled session two days later. The legal challenge did not focus on the legitimacy of a "no suicide contract" per se, but rather challenged the mental competency of the patient to follow through with such an agreement, given the severity of the patient's depression.

In any domain of negligence, the plaintiff's attorney will attempt to portray the provider as possessing inadequate skill or knowledge and thus rendering substandard care. Consequently, a general strategy is to first identify what books and/or treatises the provider has read about suicidal behavior and then to use those treatises to show that the provider failed to follow the recommended clinical strategies. Further, an attempt will be made to show that the provider has not made a reasonable effort to seek continuing education in the area of suicidal behavior.

The goal in describing typical negligence claims is not to elucidate legal standards of care, but rather to give readers a sense of the incredibly broad range of complaints that are routinely incorporated into negligence lawsuits. As noted previously, it is rare to encounter a malpractice lawsuit that does not entail multiple claims of negligence.

Inappropriate or Inadequate Assessment

In almost every case, the plaintiff will try to prove that the practitioner made an incomplete or inappropriate assessment of the patient's suicidal risk and failed to properly judge other clinical factors that might contribute to suicidal potential. An *incomplete* assessment is an error of omission. An *inaccurate* assessment is simply drawing a badly misguided conclusion about the level of suicidal risk. With regard to the assessment of suicidal risk, typical problem areas are the alleged failure to assess the remote or immediate history of suicidal behavior, to properly evaluate current suicidal potential, or to corroborate information obtained from the patient with significant others. If the provider has documented a suicide risk assessment, the plaintiff will claim that the provider drew the wrong conclusion based upon the omission of other contributing factors in the clinical decision-making process. Contributing factors might involve not asking about current drug or alcohol abuse or failing to adequately diagnose depression or some other life circumstance known to dramatically increase emotional distress and suicidal tendencies.

Failure to Hospitalize or Treat Aggressively

The most common claim in this arena is that the patient should have been hospitalized rather than treated as an outpatient. If the patient was treated as an inpatient and then released, the claim will be that the patient required additional inpatient care and should not have been released. If outpatient care is part of the suit, the claim will be that session frequency was insufficient to constitute a meaningful response to the patient's level of suicidality. When a suicidal patient has canceled an outpatient treatment session, the claim will be that the provider should have seen this as a sign of increased suicidal risk. This will occur even in cases where the ostensible reason is actually evidence of a positive treatment response (i.e., the patient has returned to work and needs to reschedule the therapy appointment).

Failure to Refer for Consultation

Most often, this claim involves a nonmedically trained provider's decision to treat a suicidal patient without the use of a medicine that might be indicated. Another claim is that the provider should have sought a psychiatric consultation to determine if the patient should be hospitalized. If a referral to another provider is made, a common claim is that not enough information was shared between the providers, leading to the second provider's underestimating the patient's real suicide risk. Another claim is the failure of two providers to communicate on a predictable basis, leading to a lack of shared knowledge of an emerging risk factor. In inpatient suicide cases, the most typical complaint is that various hospital staff failed to communicate essential information in shift change briefings or that one or more staff had access to patient information that was not effectively communicated to shift supervisors and other hospital staff.

Failure to Reassess Suicidality

Many suicides occur well into the treatment process rather than right after the initial visit. The typical claim here is that the provider(s) did not reassess the patient's suicide risk and establish a revised treatment protocol at every visit. Another common claim is that the provider failed to involve family members and other informants to provide additional information about the patient's suicidality over time.

Failure to Follow Patient Protection Protocols

This claim is most common in hospital-based suicides. A typical claim is that the "suicide precautions" level was not intensive enough, given the patient's degree of risk, or that the required line-of-sight observation of the patient did not occur according to hospital policies. If the patient was placed on suicidal precautions, then moved to normal status, the challenge will be that the decision to go to normal status was inappropriate. In nearly every hospital suicide case, there is a claim that the hospital has failed to provide adequate continuing education to all staff in the assessment and treatment of suicidality.

Failure of Facility Safeguards

The most common complaints involve the inadequacy of suicide protections in the design of inpatient units. For example, a floor plan that leaves the nurse station out of the line of sight of the restraint and seclusion room might be cited as the cause of a patient's suicide while in seclusion. Another lawsuit will claim that the failure to install breakaway showerheads in patient rooms is the cause of a death by hanging from a showerhead. Yet another negligence claim might focus on the security of window locks after a patient has picked the lock and jumped.

THE SEARCH FOR THE ELUSIVE "STANDARD OF CARE"

A key element in the outcome of a malpractice suit is how the "standard of care" will be defined for the jury. This is the linchpin for determining whether the defendant is guilty of negligent practice. *In most states, the standard of care is legally defined as the care that would have been exercised in similar circumstances by a similarly trained provider in the community at the time the alleged negligent action occurred.* It is important to realize that the crux of the contested nature of a lawsuit is that both sides will try to establish a different standard of care. The defendant's legal team will portray the defendant's care in the most positive possible light; the plaintiff will try to do the opposite. Ultimately, the jury will create a consensus definition of what the standard of care was at the time of the adverse event.

This definition of standard of care has several important implications. First, the adequacy or inadequacy of professional care is established with reference to a provider of the same discipline. If a psychologist is sued, the standard of care is defined by what a similarly trained psychologist would do under similar circumstances. This means that different standards will be used for determining negligence, depending upon the discipline of the provider. Social workers, psychologists, marriage and family counselors, and psychiatrists are each held to a unique standard of care. In lawsuits where more than one provider is named, the jury may be asked to form opinions about several distinct standards of care. Second, the "standard of care" is a hypothetical concept that is developed on a case-by-case basis. A text on standards of care for the suicidal patient may be produced as an authoritative source but in and of itself cannot conclusively establish the standard. Generally, expert witnesses produced by the defendant and plaintiff will have the greatest influence in helping the jury derive a standard of care. A third implication is that the standard of care can vary from locality to locality. A provider in a distant and remote rural community may not have access to a psychiatric facility, and the general practice in that community may be to deliver care that does not require the use of a psychiatric facility. Finally, the standard of care may vary according to the date of the adverse event. Generally, a defendant cannot be held accountable for delivering a type of care that was not generally available in the community at the time of the suicide. A new and more effective treatment may have appeared after the adverse event, but negligence cannot be determined with respect to a clinical practice that was not common at the time of the event.

The typical text on legal standards of care will attempt to present recommendations that may reduce the likelihood of malpractice litigation. Following such standards, however, is not a panacea. There is always the potential that a patient will commit suicide, a lawsuit will be prosecuted, and the plaintiff will be successful in convincing the jury that a heretofore ignored practice issue is actually a practice standard. This is why legal standards are an additive and often jumbled set of clinical concepts. Juries from state to state and city to city may disagree about what constitutes a standard.

In clinical practice with the suicidal patient, it is safer to follow more general standards. The following definition provides the type of guidance that would generalize to almost any mental health setting and would place any provider in good stead in a standard of care dispute: *The standard of care requires the mental health provider to collect enough relevant information during the initial and return appointments to estimate the patient's mental status, establish relevant mental health diagnoses, properly understand the patient's current functioning, and finally, to use this information to arrive at an assessment of the patient's relative risk for self-harm. The provider must use this information to determine if it is clinically appropriate and safe to continue treatment in the outpatient setting. If the patient is a minor, the provider's duty is to collect information from both the patient and parents/guardians, to accumulate a reasonable history, to compare the minor and parent's point of view, and to corroborate important information.*

SUICIDE AND MALPRACTICE: A STUDY IN LEGAL PARADOX

Previous sections have described the process of wrongful death litigation and defined the key legal elements that underpin a determination of negligence. Unfortunately, the climate of malpractice litigation has simply swallowed up the scientific literature on the prediction and prevention of suicide. There are some basic legal requirements to establish negligence that, when examined in the light of science, cannot be sustained.

The Prediction of Suicide

As noted earlier, a chief tenet of malpractice claims is that the provider could have, or should have, known that the suicide was going to occur. This assumption raises the general question of whether it is possible to predict suicide with any accuracy whatsoever. Suicidal behavior is extremely common in the general population, yet the overwhelming majority of suicidal behavior is nonfatal. This state of affairs results in what is referred to as a "base rate" problem; specifically, it is virtually impossible to predict a very rare event such as a patient suicide. In addition to cross-sectional studies that have suggested serious problems with conventional suicide risk indicators (i.e., Murphy, 1984; Strosahl, Chiles, & Linehan, 1992; Strosahl, Linehan, & Chiles, 1984), two large prospective clinical trials have examined the clinical accuracy of suicide risk indicators within high-risk clinical populations (Goldstein, Black, Nasrallah, & Winokur, 1991; Pokorney, 1983). Both of these latter studies used various suicide risk indicators that have been developed over the last 20 years to classify psychiatric inpatients as either high or low suicide risks. These patients were then followed prospectively over a follow-up period of several years to determine the frequency of suicide and the predictive accuracy of cumulative risk indicators. Both studies reported remarkably similar results: 98 percent of the patients assigned the highest levels of suicide risk never completed suicide. In the more recent prospective study (Goldstein et al., 1991), a very sobering finding was observed: All 43 suicides occurred in the group of patients categorized as showing low suicide risk.

Currently there is no scientific reason to believe that a therapist can accurately predict which suicidal patient will commit suicide. Conversely, therapists will be remarkably accurate (99%) if they predict that a given client will not commit suicide. This fact is tacitly acknowledged by nearly every well-respected clinical suicidologist. In an unfortunate departure from the principles of evidence-based care, many will proceed to articulate standards of assessment and treatment that imply that suicides can be predicted. The rationale for continuing to promote this clinical myth is that it keeps the clinical focus on high-risk behavior that might otherwise be ignored by the provider. This double message has even been codified in some widely cited texts and articles on treatment of the suicidal patient (e.g., Bongar, 1991; Jobes & Berman, 1993). In addition to seriously misleading practitioners about what is possible in clinical practice, these "standard of care" treatises are used by plaintiffs' attorneys to support their legal claims. It is important to clarify this issue once and for all: *There is no current scientific evidence to suggest that any competent mental health provider has the ability to accurately predict a patient suicide within a clinically relevant time frame.* The therapist should not be legally required to do what the science says cannot be done. The fool's errand and its potentially destructive effects on the therapy process should not be supported by the clinical or scientific community.

The Prevention of Suicide

Assuming for the sake of argument that suicide could be predicted in a clinically relevant time frame, there is still another issue related to establishing negligence. Specifically, it must be shown that the provider could have and should have taken actions that are known to prevent suicide. What evidence is there to suggest that suicide can be prevented through outpatient and/or inpatient interventions?

Several scientifically sound studies have examined the efficacy of inpatient hospitalization for suicidal patients. None has found a benefit in terms of reduced suicide rates, but some studies have suggested that there is an increased risk of suicide following hospitalization (for a review, see Chiles & Strosahl, 1995). The hospital is often cast as a "safe haven" for the suicidal patient. The structure of the inpatient milieu and the availability of various close observation and seclusion protocols are generally believed to have a preventive impact on suicidal behavior. Unfortunately, as many as 5 percent of all suicides occur in psychiatric inpatient units (Chiles & Strosahl, 1995). Next to the county jail, the psychiatric hospital is the most dangerous setting on the face of the earth in terms of suicide risk.

What explains these pervasively disappointing findings? First, many studies have shown that being hospitalized produces a social labeling effect. The patient learns to believe that he or she is different, abnormal, or out of control. For many suicidal patients, this is exactly what they fear and seek to have disconfirmed in therapy. Thus, for chronically suicidal patients, hospitalization may actually reinforce suicidal behavior. Being admitted to the hospital following a suicide attempt, however, also allows the patient to escape what is often a tumultuous, unsupportive environment. The behavior itself has a powerful impact on the behavior of friends and family, not to mention therapists. In many ways, being put in the hospital becomes a primary problem-solving strategy that works well in the short run but has disastrous consequences in the long run.

Second, many studies have looked at the course of treatment for hospitalized suicidal patients. The results suggest that these patients are not well liked by hospital staff, and they tend to receive the least intensive and least preferred forms of treatment. Instead of participating in a positive therapeutic milieu, suicidal patients tend to have interactions marked by hostility, mistrust, and confrontation. Not surprisingly, the AMA (Against Medical Advice) discharge rate for suicidal patients is close to 50 percent, roughly the same dropout rate that occurs in outpatient therapy (cf. Chiles & Strosahl, 1995).

The evidence on the efficacy of outpatient treatments is similarly discouraging. There are no studies that show that outpatient psychotherapy prevents suicide. With the advent of evidence-based treatments for depression, panic, and other common mental disorders that are associated with increased suicide risk, the expected reduction in the rate of suicides in these conditions has not materialized. A similarly disappointing picture emerges from the pharmacotherapy literature. Sophisticated antipsychotics and antidepressant medications have been available for 35 years. Drug companies advertise, without a scientific basis, that the advantage of these new agents is that they can prevent suicidal deaths. Patients with schizophrenia who had no hope of having their symptoms managed can now live in and be productive members of the community. Yet, the suicide rates among patients with various forms of schizophrenia have not changed in the last 35 years. Further, the suicide rate in depressed patients has been quite consistent over the same number of years.

There is some promising evidence on the effectiveness of time-limited cognitive-behavioral therapy for patients with suicide ideation. However, there are very few positive findings for a reduction in suicide attempts, a behavior with a much more proximal relationship to suicidal death. Long-term cognitive-behavioral treatment may have some impact on the incidence and medical severity of suicide attempts for chronically suicidal patients. However, it bears repeating that suicides and suicide attempts may originate in different and only mildly overlapping populations. Suicide attempting is far more prevalent than suicide, and the behavior may be shaped and maintained by different processes. Further, no study has shown that outpatient treatment eliminates suicide attempting, regardless of the population studied. Since only one suicide attempt is needed to result in death, the clinical significance of a rate and/or severity reduction is unclear.

At this point, a scientific review of the effectiveness of treatments for suicidal patients leads to the following conclusion: *There is no convincing scientific or clinical evidence that either inpatient hospitalization or outpatient treatment is capable of preventing a patient suicide. In terms of treatment modality, there is no scientific evidence that drug treatments and psychosocial treatments, alone or in combination, prevent patient suicides.*

At this point, we are left to contemplate the following dilemma. When the very definition of negligence hinges on the provider's ability to predict and prevent a suicide, how can the legal community sustain the argument that a patient suicide is the result of negligent actions? In all but the most blatant cases (i.e., the provider loads the gun, gives it to the patient, and encourages the patient to pull the trigger), the existing science simply does not support the key tenets that define negligence. Even in blatant cases, the more likely result is criminal prosecution, as was the case with Jack Kevorkian.

THE PROBLEMATIC INTERFACE OF ETHICS AND RISK MANAGEMENT

The threat of litigation is an increasing concern for all members of the health care professions. Mental health providers have been subjected to an increasing number of lawsuits related to negligent care. The fear of being sued is so pervasive that many therapists freeze up when confronted with high-risk behavior, such as that exhibited by an acutely suicidal patient. Most therapists are taught that suicidal deaths can be predicted and prevented despite the lack of scientific support for these notions. Therapists thus believe that their job is to assess suicidality and try to prevent that which cannot be prevented. If an adverse outcome occurs, the therapist learns that a lawsuit may be filed, an agency review will occur, and sanctions may be imposed. Faced with this impossible task and the fears it generates, the therapist engages in self-protective treatment strategies such as prematurely hospitalizing the patient, dumping the patient into the civil commitment system, transferring the patient to another provider, and so forth. Often, therapists will cite their ethical requirement to prevent suicide at any cost as justification for engaging in such self-protective actions. At its extreme, some therapists insist they will hospitalize any patient who engages in any type of suicidal behavior, primarily to regulate their sense of legal exposure. Other therapists hide behind civil commitment statutes or agency risk management protocols by claiming that they are "forced" to comply with the demands of those regulations. In the contemporary clinical community, suicidal patients are much more likely to be treated using risk management interventions than by clinical interventions. This regrettable state of affairs is largely the result of myths and misconceptions that feed the legal fears of providers while underemphasizing their ethical obligations to their patients. This section will attempt to develop an ethical framework for managing legal standards while maintaining a central focus on what is best for the client.

Ethical principles are designed to provide clinicians with underlying values/principles that provide a framework for analysis and decision making. It is surprising how few mental health professionals have been exposed to courses that examine ethics in general and their discipline-specific ethical principles in particular. Ethics have their roots in philosophy and religion and in contemporary times are codified in many state licensing laws. Consequently, most contemporary ethical standards try to prescribe what is believed to be "good medicine" on the one hand and what is to be avoided on the other. The prescriptive (do this) and proscriptive (don't do that) quality of ethical standards signals that they represent contemporary social mores. As a result, there is nothing about any particular ethical principle that represents a universal "truth." Ethics can never be scientifically or logically derived. Rather, they are shaped, reinforced, and maintained in much the same way as other socially inculcated values, beliefs, and attitudes.

Understanding this quality of ethical systems is important for the clinician, because many ethical issues in clinical practice can be attributed to overarching social influences that are silently transformed into seemingly unassailable core beliefs. The beliefs and attitudes are transferred to the individual through the process of language acquisition and basic acculturation. The very processes we rely on to understand the application of ethics in practice (i.e., language and thought) are the same vehicles through which the beliefs underpinning ethics are transmitted in the first place. In a figurative sense, we are both the tree (the individual responding to acculturated notions of what is right) and the forest (participants in a highly complicated maze of social rules, leading to ethical imperatives that may be internally inconsistent). Many basic ethical principles reflect our socially learned responses to behaviors that touch upon the basic social fabric and/or species survival issues. These rule-governed reactions are imprinted so early in our development and are so resistant to self-evaluation (and awareness!) that they can become problematic, especially if they involve issues that also surface in clinical practice.

For example, almost everyone, including mental health providers, has an immediate negative response to the idea of a person committing suicide. This reaction is seldom based in a logical approach to the question of suicide. Rather, it is basic social programming at work. We are taught to believe that suicide is bad, and there are severe verbal and behavioral consequences if we engage in the behavior without sufficient justification. The genesis of this socially ingrained reaction no doubt relates both to the preservation of the species and to the need to exercise social control over blatantly nonconforming forms of individual behavior. Imagine a society where otherwise healthy individual members were free to terminate their lives without fear of social censure, family disgrace, or other negative consequences. This type of permissiveness would be a basic threat to the biological and social welfare of the community. On the other hand, the interests of the community tend to be expressed in primitive ways that do not do justice to the nuances of individual circumstance. These basic social mandates can and do collide with the interests of the individual client. When this conflict of interest occurs, the social order (largely embodied in the rule of law) will normally enforce its interests to the detriment of the individual member. However, as thinking and feeling beings, it is hard for us to ignore the individual who is paying the price for the social good. The clinician ordinarily participates in these moments through the impact of a healing relationship with a single client and is at the same time conditioned to respond in a way that conforms to social rules.

Many clinical suicidologists maintain that it is the duty of every therapist to prevent a patient from committing suicide (cf. Bongar, Maris, Berman, & Litman, 1998; Joiner, Walker, Rudd, & Jobes, 1999). As we have seen, this is easier said than done. Further, the extent to which this "requirement" supersedes any of our many ethical obligations to attend to the client's best interests is completely unclear. Some providers argue that the duty to preserve life legitimizes any number of actions, however invasive they might be (i.e., breaching confidentiality, involuntary hospitalization). At the level of clinical practice, this black-and-white ethical stance grossly oversimplifies the complexities of any one patient's life circumstance. People do not engage in suicidal behavior out of the blue. They generally feel a deep sense of pain and suffering that is experienced as intolerable, inescapable, and never ending (Chiles & Strosahl, 1995). This is not to suggest that legal and ethical standards must necessarily conflict. Rather, it is to point out that the application of ethics in clinical practice is not a simple matter, and with the growing influence of legal fears the clinician may not easily differentiate what is ethically indicated from what is legally indicated. As Szasz (1986) points out, if clinicians do not maintain awareness of these divergent influences, they can end up enforcing the interests of the society to the detriment of the individual. The interpretation and application of ethics in these circumstances is an entirely subjective exercise, even when colleagues are called upon to provide guidance. Ultimately, ethics are not played out in the lofty seat of philosophers, priests, or ethicists. Instead, they are applied in the trenches, where the analytical picture is cloudy, human suffering is great, and the clinician must respond as much from the gut as from the head.

For these reasons, ethical principles are a work in progress that must be put to the test of workability. *Workability* means that whenever an ethical dilemma is encountered, the goal is to do the right thing for the client, regardless of what the legal precedents call for. This is the basic paradox in applying ethics to clinical work with the suicidal patient. We must learn to be aware of our legal responsibilities without becoming trapped in them. Does the legal requirement provide useful guidance, or does it cause a client to be damaged even though the "correct" risk management procedures have been followed? Who is being protected in this situation—the client, the therapist, or the interests of society? Is the law being applied to hide what amounts to a negative moral and/or emotional response toward the client? What should be done when the law and professional ethics suggest conflicting courses of action? Each of these questions will surface again and again in the clinical treatment of the suicidal patient.

Ethical Requirements in the Treatment of Suicidal Patients

Every therapist must be aware of and mitigate the negative effects of moral and affective responses to actual or potential suicidal behavior that may arise during the course of therapy. In both Eastern and Western theological and philosophical writings, the topic of suicide has elicited a range of philosophical, religious, and moral perspectives, ranging from the reification of suicide to complete moral and religious condemnation. Each clinician has a belief system that is located somewhere along this acceptance-rejection continuum. If we are to be of benefit to our suicidal clients, we must accept the fact that we each engage in personal evaluations and moral judgments about suicidal behavior. Attempting to deny the existence of or suppress awareness of these reactions has far more destructive potential than simply owning our reactions for what they are. Legal standards of care are most likely to be abused or misused precisely in instances where a clinician is unwilling to come to grips with his or her personal reactions to a client's suicidal behavior.

Ethically speaking, it is the responsibility of the therapist to make sure that moral and/or religious beliefs do not cloud the process of selecting and implementing treatment strategies that are in the client's best interests. In one instance, the therapist may believe that suicide is an individual choice that should not be restricted by legal sanctions. In another, the therapist may believe that by contemplating suicide, the client has sinned against God. Both stances can produce destructive effects if they are allowed to intermix with therapy in an uncontrolled fashion. The more permissive therapist may not work as hard to find alternatives to suicide as a way to solve the client's problems or may subtly grant the client permission to complete the act. The anti-suicide therapist may engage in blaming, moral lecturing, confrontation, and threats of incarceration in a state hospital.

The solution to this dilemma is simple in concept, hard in practice. The therapist must attend to the client's beliefs, moral evaluations, and perspectives on suicide; work to create more alternative solutions for the client; and not confuse personal beliefs with those of the client. These goals can best be accomplished by following some specific guidelines.

First, therapists should regularly inventory their moral position on the issue of suicide. Morals, like many belief systems, can and do change with maturation and specific life experiences. It is critical to periodically check in with one's moral beliefs in order to detect any drift from previous self-assessments.

Second, the therapist must determine whether his or her moral stance precludes being able to treat suicidal clients. There is no shame in concluding that one's reactions to a particular clinical problem makes it very difficult or impossible to work effectively with patients who present with that problem. It is better to acknowledge this problem up front than to engage in ineffective or even destructive treatment. When in doubt, it is often useful to share these reactions with a colleague who may be able to provide some much-needed perspective.

Third, the therapist should communicate directly and nondefensively with the client about the issue of suicide. This is tantamount to educating the client about the therapist's approach to treating suicidal behavior with the goal of reaching informed consent. The goal of this interchange is a mutual exchange of beliefs about suicidal behavior. This exchange should include a discussion of the types of treatment available, the risks and benefits of each, and an attempt to engage the client in the process of treatment planning. In essence, this ethical requirement amounts to seeking the client's informed consent to treatment.

Fourth, the therapist must make it clear to the client what he or she is prepared to do if the client engages in suicidal behavior or presents with suicidal risk. This includes discussing the conditions in which the therapist may call for emergency medical care, seek to have the patient hospitalized, or be willing to receive crisis phone calls from the client.

Fifth, the therapist must make it clear that the job of therapy is to help people find the best solutions possible to life's difficulties. The therapist should clearly communicate hope that the patient will not commit suicide so that therapy will have a chance to identify other solutions. What should not be communicated is that the patient is mentally ill or morally bankrupt for contemplating suicide. Rather, the therapist should acknowledge that suicide is a form of problem-solving behavior and that other less costly solutions may be available. The therapist's job is to work with the client to discover alternative solutions, weigh their costs and benefits, and pick a life-enhancing course of action.

A second set of ethical issues involves treatment of the patient with repetitious suicidal ideation and attempts. Whereas therapists typically have a rather philosophical stance on suicide, they tend to have a much more visceral reaction to chronic suicidal behavior. When working with a repetitiously suicidal patient, the therapist must be aware of, but not controlled by, legal fears. Chronically suicidal patients often engage in persistent high-risk suicidal and self-destructive behavior and tend to elicit pronounced legal fears in providers. For example, the chronic patient may be repeatedly hospitalized for legal and risk management purposes when the scientific and clinical evidence suggests that this treatment will have limited or no clinical benefit for the patient. Therapists need to be reminded that, agency risk management guidelines and/or state statutes notwithstanding, there is an ethical requirement only to use treatments with established efficacy. Further, mental health providers are obligated to protect their patients from the application of potentially harmful treatments by other systems and/or providers. The best remedy in the case of chronically suicidal patients is to be completely familiar with treatments that have been shown to work with these conditions.

Reducing the Risk of Lawsuit: Suggestions for Organizations and Clinical Practitioners

Every practicing clinician needs to understand that the risk of a lawsuit goes hand in hand with being a human services professional. There is no "silver bullet" for preventing lawsuits, just as there is no magic solution for the problem of suicide. Whereas the number of things that can go wrong in clinical treatment of the suicidal patient are too numerous to mention, the best medicine for protecting oneself from, and preparing oneself for, a negligence lawsuit is fairly direct. The following guidelines are not derived from the precedents set in civil lawsuits, but rather reflect the contributions of clinical common sense, scientific inquiry, and ethically sound practice.

Conduct a Competent Clinical Assessment and Document the Plan

Good clinical practice involves conducting a reasonably thorough initial assessment of the patient's suicidal behavior. Even if the goal is not to predict a suicide, it is always useful to conduct at least a cursory suicidal behaviors assessment. This will usually include a review of past suicidal behavior, recent suicidal ideation or behavior leading up to the patient's seeking therapy, and a review of the patient's beliefs about the efficacy of suicide as a problem-solving strategy. This can be done in a way that is direct, matter of fact, and not terribly time consuming. It is reassuring to patients struggling with suicidal thinking or behavior to see a therapist approaching these behaviors in a nonalarming, straightforward way. Without writing a novel, it is important to document in the patient's chart what the suicidal behaviors assessment reveals and how this will be addressed (or not addressed) in the treatment plan. If the decision is to continue with outpatient treatment or to involve family members in some way, make sure this plan is written in the chart. Mental health providers get paid to make clinical decisions based upon their professional judgment. The legal risk of being found guilty of malpractice is much less likely when a clinical decision is clearly made and documented, even if the outcome is adverse. The most common problem encountered in the courtroom is an incomplete documentation of what assessment data were collected, the clinical decision that was made, and the resulting treatment plan. Remember this legal mantra: *If it isn't written in the patient care note, it didn't happen.*

Seek Informed Consent

It is always useful to seek informed consent at the first contact and document what was discussed with the patient in terms of treatment options, risks and benefits, agreed-upon protocols for addressing suicidal emergencies, and the patient's choices regarding selection of various treatment alternatives. This does not have to be an onerous process, but it helps to offset any notion that the client and/or significant others were not allowed to participate in the treatment planning process. In a fairly high percentage of negligent death lawsuits, the plaintiffs will claim that the patient and significant others were not fully informed about the various treatment options available, nor were they educated about the risks and benefits of each option. Inpatient hospitalization, in particular, is the subject of such claims. Documentation of the treatment alternatives discussed and what was agreed to by the patient and/or significant others is a very good countermeasure for the pervasive problem of selective recall once a lawsuit has been filed.

Reassess Suicidal Behavior over Time

If a patient enters therapy with suicidal behavior as a presenting problem, or develops suicidality over the course of treatment, it is important to periodically reassess the patient's suicidal behavior at each session. Again, this does not have to be a time-consuming, nerve-wracking risk management exercise, but just an open, matter-of-fact attempt to collect data about the patient's status since the last session. If there is a change in the patient's status, note the change and any clinical decisions that are made. It is important to remember that the appearance or reappearance of suicidality is not an automatic indication that the treatment is not working. In other words, if the impression is that the patient is working in therapy, then the treatment plan may not need to be revised. If the treatment plan is revised (i.e., some additional sessions are scheduled), note the revision in the chart. Remember that the chart note will often be the best method for recalling what care was given, and why, if a legal challenge is made.

Document Peer Review and Professional Consultations

If a suicidal patient is staffed in an interdisciplinary team meeting, document that fact and any core feedback that might be important to the treatment plan. Even when an interdisciplinary group agrees wholeheartedly with a treatment plan, this should be noted, however briefly, in the chart. The standard of care does not require a therapist to seek peer review or second opinions, but when they occur and are noted in the chart, it creates the impression that the provider was practicing cautiously and deliberately. When a patient is referred to another provider for a second evaluation, note the rationale for making the referral and include either the second provider's consultation note or a summary of the feedback. While seeking consultation can be a bonus in terms of impression management in a lawsuit, it can be a minus if it appears that the provider did not integrate the second opinion into the treatment process. Again, proper documentation provides the "ounce of medicine" that is needed.

Make Evidence-Based Decisions

In developing a treatment plan, clinicians will often find it helpful to throw in a sentence or two about how the scientific evidence supports the treatment that is being delivered. For example, if the decision is to treat the suicidal patient on an outpatient basis, the provider might note that the evidence suggests that the best outcomes are likely to be achieved using that modality instead of an inpatient one. Providers who show a commitment to delivering treatments that are supported by science generally impress members of a jury. Expert witnesses generally try to impress jurors with the same type of tactic, so it is a positive strategy to behave like an expert in documenting evidence-based care treatment rationales.

Don't Be Fooled by Suicide Prevention Measures

It is worth repeating one more time: No interventions have been shown to prevent or reduce the risk of suicide. This includes the traditional crisis intervention model that is routinely recommended by experts and incorporated in risk management protocols. Paradoxically, suicide prevention strategies such as "no suicide" contracts can actually lull the provider into thinking that the level of suicide risk has been substantially reduced when in fact it hasn't. This may decrease the likelihood that the provider will maintain the proper level of vigilance around increasing suicide risk. This author has been involved in several cases where patient suicides occurred shortly after the "successful" implementation of classic suicide prevention strategies. If the decision is made to use such interventions, they should always be regarded as interim and time-limited strategies. Just because a no-suicide contract was obtained at the first session does not mean it is still in force at the second session. Some lawsuits have focused on the fact that a suicide-prevention strategy is initiated, but then is not reviewed and reaffirmed at each subsequent contact. Generally, such interventions should be documented at each session, if they are going to be used at all. Again, prevention measures are not "treatment," but they may be part of an integrated treatment plan.

Reduce Policy and Procedure Driven Services

One of the paradoxes of civil negligence lawsuits is that a provider/agency can be found negligent simply for failing to follow agency policies and procedures, even if those policies incorporate clinically useless strategies for treating the suicidal patient. A provider can dramatically exceed the typical standard of care but be found guilty of negligence for violating agency policies and procedures. This is the danger of codifying too many risk management strategies into practice standards. These policies become the de facto standard of care in relation to a claim of negligence. The plaintiff will claim that the policies constitute a separate standard of care that can be applied to any clinical employee covered by the policy. Generally, it is advisable to keep the number of required clinical interventions to the bare minimum. Instead, craft risk management policies and procedures so that they are evidence based and emphasize the singular role of clinical judgment in determining specific interventions. For example, an agency policy that requires inpatient hospitalization for a patient who refuses to sign a no-suicide contract is simply an invitation to disaster. It is better to describe a range of factors that may or may not contribute to a clinical decision to hospitalize a patient.

Risk Management after the Index Suicide

On hearing of the suicidal death of a patient, most mental health providers enter into a state of emotional shock and disbelief. In the vast majority of the cases, the suicide is an unexpected event. Even though the client had difficulties, the magnitude of the act seems to far outstrip the problems that were being confronted. In the midst of this turmoil, it is important to remember that the behavior of the providers involved, as well as risk management policies, can have an significant impact on the likelihood of a subsequent lawsuit. In addition to immediately notifying the liability insurance carrier of the adverse event (allowing them the opportunity to do a risk management appraisal of the case), the providers involved should also try to follow certain guidelines.

Make a Proactive Contact with the Survivors

The days, weeks, months, and often years after the suicide of a loved one is an unenviable time for the survivors of a suicide. Most suicides have a trajectory that sweeps family members, siblings, and spouses up in an unstable interpersonal process that ultimately ends with the suicidal death. Often, the patient is in conflict with others; a divorce or separation may be imminent. In other cases, the patient has struggled with alcohol or drug abuse, or the degree of psychological distress present has resulted in isolative behavior. After the suicide, the survivors are left to deal not only with a sudden unanticipated death, but a self-inflicted one as well. Recalling the fact that it is the survivors who invariably file the wrongful death lawsuits, one must conclude that there is a strong association between the outcome of grieving a suicidal death and the likelihood of filing a lawsuit.

It is simply a humane and ethical act to make contact with the immediate survivors of the deceased patient and to invite them to participate in some form of grief counseling. Either the therapist of record or another provider may conduct counseling, but the recommendation is to try to connect the survivors and the therapist of record. An attempt should be made to have the survivors enter into a longer episode of counseling, such as in a local "survivors of suicide" group. If an agency is involved, the agency should make every effort to allow the survivors immediate access to all records pertinent to the patient's care. Any effort to sequester records from survivors will automatically generate suspicion that the provider or agency is hiding something. The survivors should be relieved of all financial responsibility for clinical services predating the suicide attempt.

This outreach response should be immediate, unequivocal, and nondefensive. Such responses tend to engender sympathy from the survivors, who realize that the providers involved with the patient are also in a state of shock and grief. Survivors often feel stigmatized and isolated from friends and other social supports in the community. The natural tendency among mental health providers is to engage in similar avoidance strategies, including refusing to meet with surviving family members or discussing the case with colleagues. When isolation is allowed to fester, survivors tend to engage in a pernicious cycle of self-directed anger, guilt, and blame. Eventually, some survivors will project this anger and blame externally, and a lawsuit may be a direct psychological manifestation of this process. The author's impression over the years is that reaching out to the survivors has positive effects, both clinically and as a basic risk management strategy.

Never Alter the Clinical Record after the Fact

If a patient commits suicide, providers should avoid the temptation to alter existing chart notes (often to specifically mention that they had assessed the patient's suicidal risk in the last session) or to add new chart notes containing retrospective analyses. In a state of shock, some providers begin their process of soul searching by analyzing the process of care in the patient's chart. This may include comments about what the provider thinks he or she missed or reflects upon clinical strategies the provider should have used. In some circumstances, these notes have actually incriminated other providers who may have had a role in the treatment of the patient. In general, it is important to be very cautious about what goes in the patient's chart after the suicide. These chart notes are very difficult to explain in court and they may not only discredit the patient's primary provider, but provide ammunition for incriminating other providers as well.

Never Second-Guess a Decision

Once an adverse event like suicide has occurred, it is always easy to imagine what could have been done differently in the course of clinical care. This is, in fact, the trump card of the plaintiff's attorney. Again and again, the attorney will return to the question of what the provider should have done differently. This, of course, is the layperson's definition of negligent care, and it is a very powerful tool used to influence jurors. The more the defendant acknowledges that different assessment or treatment strategies would have produced a better outcome, the more the stage is set for a determination of negligence. Here it is important to remember again that there is no evidence that suicide can be predicted in the individual case and that there is no evidence that any selected intervention has been shown to prevent a suicide. Thus, the selection of any different set of assessment or treatment strategies would not improve the likelihood that the suicide would have been prevented. Here it is critical that the provider reaffirms the proper relationship between time frame and event. Specifically, given the information that was available at the time and the provider's clinical experience and training, it is highly likely that the provider would draw the same conclusions and recommend the same treatment plan. If done nondefensively, this type of response convinces jurors that the provider reached clinical decisions that, given the information at hand, were clearly within the standard of care.

CONCLUSION

This chapter has provided a view of the civil negligence process as it applies to the assessment and treatment of the suicidal patient. This is a complicated area laden with harmful myths and misconceptions. The result has been much more "heat than light" about what constitutes clinically effective and ethically appropriate management of the suicidal patient. As Mark Twain once remarked, "The ethics of legality are the ethics of a scoundrel." Clinicians need to remember that doing the legally defensible thing with suicidal patients is not the same as doing the right thing. By understanding our limitations with respect to the prediction and prevention of suicide, clinicians can be relieved of the responsibility to work miracles. Although a lawsuit is possible regardless of the clinical actions taken by a mental health provider, experience suggests that the safest course is to place the needs of the suicidal patient first and foremost. In the vast majority of cases, providing this type of superior treatment is the best possible protection.

REFERENCES

Bongar, B. (1991). *The suicidal patient: Clinical and legal standards of care*. Washington DC: American Psychological Association.

Bongar, B., Berman, A., Maris, R., Silverman, M., Harris, E., & Packman, W. (Eds.) (1998). *Risk management with suicidal patients*. New York: Guilford Press.

Bongar, B., Maris, R., Berman, A., & Litman, R. (1998). Outpatient standards of care and the suicidal patient. In B. Bongar, A. Berman, R. Maris, M. Silverman, E. Harris, & W. Packman (Eds.), *Risk management with suicidal patients*. New York: Guilford Press.

Chiles, J., & Strosahl, K. (1995). *The suicidal patient: Principles of assessment, treatment and case management*. Washington DC: American Psychiatric Press.

Goldstein, R., Black, D., Nasrallah, A., & Winokur, G. (1991). The prediction of suicide: Sensitivity, specificity and predictive value of a multivariate model applied to suicide among 1906 patients with affective disorders. *Archives of General Psychiatry, 48*, 418–422.

Jobes, D., & Berman, A. (1993). Suicide and malpractice liability: Assessing and revising policies, procedures and practice in outpatient settings. *Professional Psychology: Research and Practice, 24*, 91–99.

Klespies, P., Deleppo, J., Gallagher, P., & Niles, B. (1999). Managing suicidal emergencies: Recommendations for the practitioner. *Professional Psychology: Research and Practice, 30*, 454–463.

Murphy, G. (1984). The prediction of suicide: Why is it difficult? *American Journal of Psychotherapy*, *38*, 341–349.
Pokorney, A. (1983). Prediction of suicide in psychiatric patients: Report of a prospective study. *Archives of General Psychiatry*, *40*, 249–257.
Robertson, J. (1998). *Psychiatric malpractice: Liability of mental health professionals.* New York: John Wiley.
Rudd, M., Joiner, T., Jobes, D., & King, C. (1999). The outpatient treatment of suicidality: An integration of science and the recognition of its limitations. *Professional Psychology: Research and Practice*, *30*, 437–446.
Strosahl, K., Chiles, J., & Linehan, M. (1992). Prediction of suicide intent in hospitalized parasuicides: Depression, hopelessness and reasons for living. *Comprehensive Psychiatry*, *33*, 356–363.
Strosahl, K., Linehan, M., & Chiles, J. (1984). Will the real social desirability please stand up? Hopelessness, depression, social desirability and the prediction of suicidal behavior. *Journal of Consulting and Clinical Psychology*, *52*, 449–457.
Szasz, T. (1986). The case against suicide prevention. *American Psychologist*, *41*, 806–812.

CHAPTER 8

ASSESSING INTENT AND CRIMINAL RESPONSIBILITY

RONALD ROESCH, JODI L. VILJOEN, AND IRENE HUI
SIMON FRASER UNIVERSITY

Criminal responsibility evaluations can be extremely challenging for evaluators. One unique and complicated feature is that they require a *retrospective* evaluation of a defendant's mental state at the time of the alleged offense. Adding to this, the relevant legal standards for criminal responsibility change over time and vary from state to state. Defendants can be uncooperative or dishonest (Melton, Petrila, Poythress, & Slobogin, 1997), and these evaluations often occur within highly charged atmospheres, characterized by considerable public skepticism. The purpose of this chapter is to provide clinicians who conduct criminal responsibility evaluations with a framework that is legally informed and empirically guided.

In assessing criminal responsibility, evaluators must answer three primary questions. First, at the time of the crime, did the defendant have a "mental disease or defect," as defined by the law? Second, at the time of the crime, did the defendant demonstrate impairment in his or her abilities to understand, appreciate, and/or control his or her criminal behavior? Finally, if the answer is yes to both of the previous questions, is there evidence that the cognitive and/or volitional impairment was *caused* by the mental disorder? In the following sections, we discuss approaches to evaluating each of these three questions.

LEGAL STANDARDS

The underlying principle establishing the need for an insanity defense is that individuals who commit crime for irrational reasons or because they were unable to control their behavior should not be convicted and punished. Such individuals may be considered in need of treatment in a forensic facility rather than confinement in a prison. That said, the history of the insanity defense is characterized by controversy and misperceptions about whether and how it should be used.

Although there were early forms of provisions in the law for determining that an individual lacked the capacity to be held responsible for a criminal act, it was not until the case of Daniel M'Naghten (*Regina v. M'Naghten*, 1843) that a more explicit standard for criminal responsibility was established. M'Naghten was acquitted by reason of insanity of the murder of an assistant to the prime minister of England. The murder of the assistant was a mistake, as M'Naghten believed he was shooting the prime minister. The basis of the insanity defense in this case was M'Naghten's delusional belief that the prime minister was plotting against him. Thus, this case established that mental illness could be used as a defense but made it clear that a causal link between the mental illness and the criminal act must be established.

Although there are various forms and refinements of the M'Naghten standard (for a review, see Rogers & Shuman, 2000), this provision forms the basis of modern-day statutes in most states, although various refinements have been made. In *Durham v. United States* (1954), Judge David Bazelon established that the act must be a product of mental disease or defect, and he gave mental health professionals a greater role in assessing criminal responsibility. Many thought that this ruling gave mental health professionals too much influence (see Golding, 1992; Shapiro, 1991), and Bazelon himself later admonished psychiatrists and psychologists for using conclusory labels and not providing the courts with the foundation for their opinion (Bazelon, 1982). In 1972, in the case of *United States v. Brawner*, the District of Columbia Court of Appeals replaced the Durham standard with the one proposed by the American Law Institute. This standard created a broader standard that included both volitional and cognitive elements. The ALI standard, as set out in Section 4.01 of the Model Penal Code, is as follows:

1. A person is not responsible for criminal conduct if at the time of such conduct as a result of mental disease or defect he lacks substantial capacity either to appreciate the criminality (wrongfulness) of his conduct or to conform his conduct to the requirements of law.
2. As used in this Article, the terms "mental disease of defect" do not include an abnormality manifested only by repeated criminal or otherwise anti-social conduct. (ALI, 1962, §4.01)

Point 2 was intended to rule out psychopathy or antisocial personality disorder as a basis for an insanity defense. In 1984, the Insanity Defense Reform Act (IDRA) eliminated the volitional prong of the ALI standard, with the result that the IDRA is not much different than the M'Naghten standard.

There is considerable variability in the standards used by each state. Clinicians should consult their state statute to determine the applicable standard and practice in their jurisdiction. Giorgi-Guarnieri and colleagues (2002), who prepared the American Academy of Psychiatry and Law practice guidelines for insanity evaluations, include an appendix listing the relevant source of law and the standard used by each state.

The public often views the insanity defense skeptically, believing that it is used too frequently and that defendants successfully raising the defense get off easily (Hans, 1986). In fact, the insanity defense is raised quite rarely, and when it is raised, it is rarely successful (for a review, see Melton et al., 1997). In terms of disposition, the reality is that while length of confinement does vary, those charged with more serious crimes tend to be detained for longer periods than those charged with lesser offenses (Ogloff, Schweighofer, Turnbull, & Whittemore, 1992), and overall most insanity acquittees spend considerable time in an institution. Despite these realities, there have been many movements to abolish the insanity defense, especially in the aftermath of the Hinckley decision (Finkel, 1988; Simon & Aaronson, 1988), and, indeed, some states have eliminated it. Other states have introduced what is referred to as the Guilty But Mentally Ill (GBMI) verdict. The GBMI verdict differs from the insanity defense in that defendants are held criminally responsible for their acts (i.e., found guilty), but if the defendant is considered to be mentally ill, sentencing could take that into account by providing opportunity for mental health treatment. Many view this as a compromise verdict for a jury (see Perlin, 1989), and the reality is that GBMI offenders are no more likely than mentally disordered offenders to receive treatment in prison, since there is no guarantee that treatment will be provided (Golding & Roesch, 1987; Simon & Aaronson, 1988).

Diminished capacity is also an option in some states. This defense allows the use of mental health issues as a mitigating factor that hinders a defendant's ability to form a specific intent. For example, it could be argued that a defendant was incapable of possessing the mental state required to commit a murder, in that the defendant was incapable of intending to cause death and therefore must have at most caused such a death recklessly. A successful plea in murder trial would reduce the charge to manslaughter. The diminished capacity also allows for the possibility of other factors that might affect intent, including intoxication, and more liberal interpretations might even allow the introduction of personality characteristics (see Melton et al., 1997, and Shapiro, 1991, for more detailed discussion).

Varying standards defining criminal responsibility may not actually make a difference in trial outcome. Ogloff (1991) asked mock jurors to watch a videotaped murder trial. Jury instructions were varied by insanity standard and burden of proof. Results revealed that jurors do not make distinctions between standards or burden of proof (see also Finkel & Handel, 1989, and Roberts, Sargent, & Chan, 1993, who found similar results in a study of ALI and other instruction variations). Finkel (1995) commented that jurors' "intuitive constructs of 'sane' and 'insane' remained powerfully determinative" (p. 290).

Assessing Mental Disorders

As described in the *Diagnostic and Statistical Manual of Mental Disorders* (*DSM-IV-TR*; American Psychiatric Association, 2000), clinical definitions of mental disorder do not always equate to legal definitions. Instead, as Slovenko (1995) describes, "Whether we label a cluster of characteristics 'mental illness' or exclude certain categories rests on policy decisions" (p. 177). The appropriateness of various disorders in forming the basis of an insanity defense has been widely discussed and heavily debated. The purpose of this section is to provide clinicians with an understanding of disorders that are currently considered relevant to criminal responsibility.[1]

Legal Criteria

Psychotic disorders are widely accepted as a basis for an insanity defense. Salekin and Rogers (2001), in their review of the literature, found that an average of 67 percent of insanity acquittees are diagnosed with any type of psychotic disorder, and 54 percent with schizophrenia. Given that schizophrenia is associated with broad cognitive impairment across a variety of domains (Heinrichs & Zakzanis, 1998), delusional thinking (for a review, see Golding, Skeem, Roesch, & Zapf, 1999), as well as volitional impairments such as impulsivity and disorganized behavior (Baxter, 1997), these high rates are not surprising. Importantly, however, most individuals with psychoses are found criminally responsible (Ogloff, Roberts, & Roesch, 1993).

Mental retardation, organic disorders, and affective disorders are also relatively common among insanity defense cases, reflecting approximately 5, 7, and 10 percent, respectively (Salekin & Rogers, 2001). In the past several decades, increasing attention has been paid to postpartum depression as a possible basis for an insanity defense, particularly in infanticide cases. In 1989, Rosenberg noted that over 18 cases in the United States had involved the use of postpartum depression or psychosis defenses in infanticide cases. In about half of these cases, it was successful.

Another disorder that has generated interest is Post-Traumatic Stress Disorder (PTSD). Since 1980, a growing number of defendants have used PTSD as either a basis of an insanity defense or as a mitigating factor in sentencing. Sparr, Reaves, and Atkinson (1987) argue that PTSD may reduce criminal liability through its behavioral correlates such as sensation seeking, guilt and self-punishment, substance abuse, and dissociative state. However, Sparr and Atkinson (1986) conclude that an insanity defense is rarely appropriate and perhaps only in the case of severe dissociative symptoms. Within the legal system, battered women's syndrome has been considered a form of Post-Traumatic Stress

---

[1] Epilepsy and sleep disorders have been used as the basis for reduced culpability. However, since they typically fall under an automatism defense rather than an insanity defense, they are not discussed here.

Disorder rather than a separate disorder (Giorgi-Guarnieri et al., 2002). In general, it is rarely used as a basis for an insanity defense. Instead, it has been more commonly introduced as evidence of self-defense.

There is a clear reluctance to use personality disorders as a basis of an insanity defense, particularly antisocial personality disorders (American Bar Association, 1989; American Psychiatric Association, 1983). Most times, personality disorders would not lead to the impairments in rationality, cognition, and volition that are required for a successful insanity defense (Rudnick & Levy, 1994). Nevertheless, Salekin and Rogers (2001) note that 20 percent of insanity acquittees meet criteria for personality disorder as a primary diagnosis, and 10 percent meet criteria for an antisocial personality disorder.

Although substance use may be introduced as evidence of diminished capacity or as a mitigating factor in sentencing,[2] North American courts have generally not accepted substance use as a basis for an insanity defense (American Bar Association, 1989; Marlowe et al., 1999). This is because it is presumed that the act of substance use is in itself voluntary, and individuals are generally aware of the negative effects of substance use (Marlowe et al., 1999).

In certain instances, however, substance use has been recognized as a basis for an insanity defense (Marlowe et al., 1999; Watterson, 1991). First, it is recognized in cases in which sustained use has resulted in another more permanent disorder, such as delirium tremens or toxic psychosis. Second, it may be recognized in cases involving involuntary intoxication. The most common prototypes of this scenario are when an individual is coerced or tricked into substance use, such as when someone drugs his or her drink. Finally, it may be recognized in cases of "pathological intoxication," such as when an individual experiences a very potent or unusual reaction to a drug that he or she was unable to foresee.

Dissociative identity disorder, previously known as multiple personality disorder, is a controversial diagnosis that has been particularly challenging and confusing to the courts. Over the past several decades, the incidence in which insanity defenses have been raised on the basis of dissociative disorders has increased (Owens, 1997). Reflecting the confusing nature of these claims, the courts have adopted a number of conflicting approaches in these cases (Giorgi-Guarnieri et al., 2002; Owens, 1997). The most common approach, the Alter Approach, has been to judge the culpability of the personality that was in control of the behavior at the time of the offense (Owens, 1997). Within this model, a defendant could be found Not Guilty by Reason of Insanity (NGRI) if the alter personality who was in control of the behavior at the time of the crime did not meet the legal requirements for culpability. Within the Host Approach, in contrast, a defendant would be found NGRI if the host personality was not aware of the criminal act or was unable to prevent it.

---

[2] It has also been introduced as an aggravating factor in sentencing (Marlowe, Lambert, & Thompson, 1999; Watterson, 1991).

The central feature of impulse control disorders, such as intermittent explosive disorders, pyromania, kleptomania, and pathological gambling, is a failure to resist impulses to carry out an act that is harmful to oneself or others. Based solely on this definition, impulse control disorders appear to be an ideal foundation for an insanity defense. However, Blaszcayski and Silove (1996) note that at least in the case of pathological gambling, the disorder is unlikely to cause impairments in cognition and volition that are severe enough to warrant an insanity defense. Moreover, in general, there is skepticism about the use of impulse control disorders as a basis for an insanity defense, with some states explicitly excluding it (Giorgi-Guanieri et al., 2002).

Assessment Instruments

From this review, it is apparent that considerable uncertainty remains regarding the viability of certain disorders as bases of insanity defenses. Certain disorders, such as antisocial personality disorder, paraphilias, and voluntary intoxication, have generally been excluded from consideration (Giorgi-Guarnieri, 2002; Slovenko, 1995). Other disorders, such as dissociative disorders and impulse control disorders, have been broached with suspicion. At the same time, however, courts have shown considerable openness to hearing testimony on various disorders. As our diagnostic nomenclature has evolved, such as with the introduction of PTSD as a diagnosis, so too have legal definitions.

In light of this dynamic context, it is important for clinicians to complete a broad and comprehensive psychodiagnostic assessment, preferably as soon after the offense as possible. While current mental state may provide inferences about mental state at the time of the offense, this relationship is probabilistic at best (Ogloff et al., 1993).

As emphasized in the Specialty Guidelines for Forensic Psychologists (Committee on Ethical Guidelines for Forensic Psychologists, 1991), forensic psychologists should use multiple sources of data. In a survey of forensic psychologists and psychiatrists, respondents generally agreed that it was important to obtain police reports; mental health, employment, and school records; and collateral information from family, friends, co-workers, and eyewitnesses (Borum & Grisso, 1996). Also, over 60 percent of respondents rated psychological testing as essential or recommended. In practice, however, test use in criminal responsibility evaluations appears to be considerably lower than what these aspirational estimates would suggest (Heilbrun & Collins, 1995).

The test that is perhaps most commonly used in forensic evaluations is the Minnesota Multiphasic Personality Inventory-2 (MMPI-2; Borum & Grisso, 1995; Heilbrun & Collins, 1995). The MMPI-2 may be an appropriate psychodiagnostic instrument in criminal responsibility evaluations, given that a large body of literature supports its psychometric properties, including research based on forensic samples (Ben-Porath & Graham, 1995). If required to testify, a clinician may find it useful to review the set of potential courtroom questions on the MMPI-2 that Pope, Butcher, and Seelan (2000) have prepared.

In comparison to the MMPI-2, the Personality Assessment Inventory (PAI; Morey, 1991) is a relatively new self-report instrument. Already, however, it has generated considerable research. A number of studies have found support for its reliability and validity in forensic samples (e.g., Rogers, Ustad, & Salekin, 1998). Given its attention to antisocial personality disorders and aggression, this test may be particularly valuable in forensic settings (Douglas, Hart, & Kropp, 2001).

Recently, considerable debate has arisen regarding the use of the Millon Clinical Multiaxial Inventory-III in forensic settings (MCMI-III; Millon, Davis, & Millon, 1997). While some commentators argue that it does not meet admissibility standards for testimony under the *Daubert* rule (Rogers, Salekin, & Sewell, 2000), others assert its reliability and validity are adequate (Dyer & McCann, 2000).

In addition to these self-report measures of psychopathology and personality, a number of diagnostic interviews exist. One of the most common of these is the Structured Clinical Interview for the DSM-IV (SCID; First, Spitzer, Gibbon, & Williams, 1994). Rogers (2001), however, convincingly argues that the Schedule for Affective Disorders and Schizophrenia (SADS) is preferable to the SCID because it provides more sensitive ratings of the severity of symptoms, facilitates retrospective evaluation, has shown high reliability, and has been used specifically in research on criminal responsibility.

As noted, cognitive and neuropsychological disorders frequently serve as a basis for a finding of Not Guilty by Reason of Insanity (NGRI). Therefore, it is often appropriate to assess intelligence and other cognitive features in addition to Axis I mental disorders. The Wechsler Adult Intelligence Scale–Third Edition (WAIS-III; Wechsler, 1997) is commonly used in forensic settings (Borum & Grisso, 1996). Although this instrument is clearly supported by a large body of literature (Hess, 2001), it takes considerable time to administer. Clinicians may, at times, choose to use screening instruments such as the Kaufman Brief Intelligence Test (K-BIT; Kaufman & Kaufman, 1990). If a neuropsychological disorder is suspected, it is important that the evaluator has expertise in this area or is able to consult with someone who does.

It is important to note that the instruments discussed here may not be appropriate for all defendants being evaluated for criminal responsibility. Currently, for instance, there appears to be increasing interest in criminal responsibility of juvenile offenders (Scott, 2000). With this population, the use of developmentally appropriate instruments, such as the Minnesota Multiphasic Personality Inventory-A (MMPI-A), is clearly a necessity. Also, some instruments may not be appropriate for ethnic minorities, particularly in cases where English is not a first language. Evaluators should carefully consider cultural appropriateness when choosing instruments. For well-known instruments such as the MMPI-2, various translations are available.

Malingering and Minimization

In order to facilitate the validity of an assessment, it is argued that psychologists have an ethical responsibility to always assess for response biases (Franzen, Iverson, & McCracken, 1990). This is perhaps especially true in criminal forensic evaluations, in which malingering is a common if not constant concern. Importantly, it is also possible that insanity defendants may not wish to be found NGRI and may minimize or deny psychopathology. Consistent with this, Grossman and Wasyliw (1988) found that in a sample of criminal responsibility evaluations 22 to 39 percent of defendants showed evidence of minimizing psychopathology. NGRI defenses may not be attractive to defendants because it will lead to stigma and possibly longer periods of incarceration than being found guilty (Silver, 1995). Also, patients lacking in insight tend to deny that they even have a mental disorder and are less likely to want to raise an insanity defense (Neumann, Walker, & Weinstein, 1996). In approximately 35 percent of U.S. jurisdictions, however, the insanity defense may be imposed on a defendant against his or her wishes (Miller et al., 1996).

Many common self-report measures, such as the MMPI-2, contain scales that measure exaggeration of psychopathology, minimization of psychopathology, and inconsistent responding. In general, considerable evidence has accumulated in support of the MMPI-2's ability to detect feigning. Rogers, Sewell, and Salekin (1994), in a meta-analysis of malingering on the MMPI-2, found support for the use of the Infrequency Scale (F), the Infrequency minus Correction Scale ($F - K$), and the Obvious minus Subtle Scales ($O - S$). The Infrequency Psychopathology Scale ($F_{(p)}$) has also been shown to be effective (Arbisi & Ben-Porath, 1998). Studies have, however, varied in their conclusions on which MMPI-2 scale is the most effective (Lewis, Simcox, & Berry, 2002).

On the PAI, Roger's Discriminant Function index has been shown to be particularly effective in detecting feigning (Bagby, Nicholson, & Bacchiochi, 2002). On the Rorschach, feigners have been distinguished by the use of dramatic content in responses (Ganellen, Wasyliw, & Haywood, 1996). Rogers (1997) notes that malingerers apply several strategies on the SADS, including contradictory symptoms, symptom combinations, and indiscriminant symptom endorsement. On the WAIS-III, reliability of digit span has been proved to be an effective tool for detecting deception in forensic settings (Duncan & Ausborn, 2002).

In addition to measures of response bias that are built in to common tests, a number of specialized malingering instruments have been developed. Of these, the Structured Interview of Reported Symptoms (SIRS; Rogers, Bagby, & Dickens, 1992) is the "most extensively validated objective approach to the identification of feigned psychological symptoms" (Lewis et al., 2002, p. 171). This instrument has been shown to be effective in detecting feigning of a variety of disorders, including schizophrenia, mood disorders, and PTSD (Rogers, Kropp, & Bagby, 1992).

For malingering cognitive impairments, such as memory deficits, a number of specialized instruments exist. Symptom validity testing (e.g., Validity Indicator

Profile), in which examinees must choose between two or more alternatives, has been shown to be effective (Frederick & Crosby, 2000). Within this approach, performance that is sufficiently below chance is interpreted as evidence of malingering. Despite promising research findings, these types of specialized malingering assessment instruments are used relatively infrequently in criminal responsibility evaluations (Borum & Grisso, 1996).

Clinically, one of the most commonly suggested practices in detecting malingering is to look for consistencies of patterns of results across measures. Clinicians also should be careful to consider all possible interpretations on scales indicative of malingering. For example, on the MMPI-2, F could be elevated as a result of feigning, careless responding, random responding, cultural factors, or severe psychological distress (Pope et al., 2000). On the SIRS, Pollock (1996) found that high scores might also reflect acquiescent responding.

SPECIALIZED SCALES FOR CRIMINAL RESPONSIBILITY ASSESSMENTS

Two specialized scales were developed in the 1980s to standardize and facilitate insanity evaluations: the Rogers Criminal Responsibility Assessment Scales (R-CRAS) and the Mental State at the Time of the Offense Screening Evaluation (MSE).

Rogers Criminal Responsibility Assessment Scales (R-CRAS)

The Rogers Criminal Responsibility Assessment Scales (R-CRAS; Rogers, 1984) was the first standardized measure of criminal responsibility, and is currently the only instrument of this type. In Borum and Grisso's (1995) survey of forensic psychologists and psychiatrists, 66 percent of psychologists and 91 percent of psychiatrists reported that they rarely or never use forensic instruments in criminal responsibility evaluations. Of the forensic instruments mentioned by respondents, the R-CRAS was most common, with 41 percent of psychologists and 10 percent of psychiatrists indicating that they had used it in criminal responsibility evaluations.

Although the R-CRAS is focused on assessing the ALI standard, Rogers notes that it may be applicable to the *M'Naghten* standard as well (Rogers & Shuman, 2000). The R-CRAS serves as a guide for the evaluator to ensure that key issues are evaluated, and is scored on the basis of interview and testing of a defendant. The R-CRAS is divided into two parts: Part I, which addresses the severity of psychological impairments that are relevant to the insanity evaluation, comprises 30 items that are rated on a 5- or 6-point ordinal scale, with 0 = *no information*, 1 = *not present*, 2 = *clinically insignificant*; a score of 3 to 6 indicates the degree of severity of clinically relevant symptoms (Rogers & Shuman, 2000). The R-CRAS items are grouped into the following five areas: Patient's

Reliability (e.g., reliability of patient's self report under voluntary control), Organicity (e.g., presence of brain damage or disease), Psychopathology (e.g., anxiety), Cognitive Control (e.g., planning and preparation), and Behavioral Control (e.g., responsible social behavior). The clinician then uses the ratings to make the judgments covered in the relevant decision model, which could be the ALI standard for the determination of criminal responsibility, or *M'Naghten* or GBMI standard. The judgment or conclusion about criminal responsibility, though based on the item scores, is not based on cutoff scores.

Several studies by Rogers and his colleagues have examined the interrater reliability of evaluators, which was evaluated by independent evaluators conducting separate interviews, often several weeks apart (Rogers & Shuman, 2000). Interrater reliabilities averaged .58, with kappa coefficients ranging from .49 to 1.00. As well, there is a high concordance rate of 88 percent between evaluators using the R-CRAS and court decisions (see Rogers & Shuman, 2000, for a summary). Normative data on several samples of actual cases are also available. Interestingly, factor analysis of the R-CRAS items results in three factors that do not mirror the five scales just noted. The three factors are bizarre behavior, high activity, and high anxiety (see Borum, 2003).

Criticisms of the R-CRAS have centered on the use of an ordinal rather than an interval scale and the limitations inherent in quantifying the relationship between a particular symptom and the criminal act (Melton et al., 1997). Rogers and Shuman (2000) counter that nearly all clinical assessment is ordinal and that the R-CRAS has demonstrated superior reliability and validity compared to the Mental Status Exam, which will be reviewed later in this chapter. Perhaps the clear value of the R-CRAS is that it, as Golding (1992) concluded, serves "the heuristic value of (a) highlighting the aspects of the defendant's psychological state that are relevant, (b) describing a purported relationship to control and judgment capacities, and (c) organizing data about the empirical relationships between disorder and capacities in various states and situations" (p. 236).

Mental State at the Time of the Offense Screening Evaluation (MSE)

The Mental State at the Time of the Offense Screening Evaluation (MSE) is a semistructured interview technique that was developed as an outpatient screening device to screen out defendants who clearly did not have "significant mental abnormality" (i.e., any legally relevant disorders in *DSM-III*) during the time of the offense (Slobogin, Melton, & Showalter, 1984). The use of screening would allow cases in which mental disorder is not an issue to be evaluated in a short period of time, thus resulting in both economic and time savings as well as minimizing the detention of pretrial defendants. Melton and colleagues (1997) also proposed the use of MSE "to detect the obviously insane individual for whom a more comprehensive evaluation is unnecessary" (p. 235).

The MSE comprises three parts. Part I: Historical Information assesses defendants' premorbid psychological and cognitive functioning. Part II: Offense

Information gathers information of the offense from both the defendant and some external sources (e.g., attorney's notes). Part III: Present Mental Status Examination examines current mental status.

There have been no studies of the reliability of the MSE. Validity was evaluated in a study by Slogobin and colleagues (1984), who trained 24 mental health professionals to use the MSE and then asked them to assess 36 cases. They were given only the description of the charge and the preliminary hearing transcript prior to their assessment and their decisions were compared with the decision made by the inpatient forensic evaluation team, which included one psychiatrist, one psychologist, and one social worker. Overall, there was a satisfactory agreement (72.2 percent, or 26 of 36 cases) between trainees and the evaluation team. There was 44.4 percent agreement (16 of 36 cases) on the screen-out cases. Using the decisions made by the evaluation team as the criterion, the decisions made by the trainees were found to have 0 percent false negative rate (screened out the defendants who were "screened in" by the evaluation team) and 27.7 percent (10 cases) false positive rate ("screened in" defendants who were screened out by the evaluation team). Compared with the evaluation team's decisions, the trainees' decisions showed less agreement with the court's verdict. Of the 10 defendants for whom the evaluation team suspected some "significant mental abnormality," one was convicted, seven had their charges nolle prossed, and two were found insane. On the other hand, of the 20 defendants whom the trainees suspected had some "significant mental abnormality," six were convicted as charged, four were convicted of a lesser charge, six had charges nolle prossed, and two were found insane.

The limitations of the MSE have been debated (see Poythress, Melton, Petrila, & Slobogin, 2000; Rogers & Shuman, 2000). Given the lack of reliability research and only limited validity data, the MSE should perhaps be most appropriately viewed as a guide for evaluators to ensure that relevant areas are reviewed. Indeed, evaluators can include the MSE and the R-CRAS in a comprehensive evaluation that would include multiple sources of data (e.g., psychological tests, third-party information, defendant's interview, police report).

Assessing the Link between Mental Disorder and Legal Abilities

To be found NGRI, it is not enough that a defendant has a mental disorder and impaired understanding, appreciation, and/or control of the criminal behavior. The mental disorder must cause these cognitive or volitional impairments. This causal question is clearly a difficult question to answer. Nevertheless, most psychologists appear to consider a discussion of the relationship between psychopathology and legal capacities an essential feature of criminal responsibility reports (Borum & Grisso, 1995).

As Borum (2003) comments, neither the R-CRAS nor the MSE provide much guidance in assessing this link between a defendant's mental disorder and his or her alleged offense. However, several other sources of information may be useful. First, a growing body of research has investigated the link between mental disorders and crime, particularly violent crime.[3] Paranoia and command hallucinations (Link, Monahan, Stueve, & Cullen, 1999; McNiel, Eisner, & Binder, 2000), substance abuse (Bushman, 1993; Rajartnam, Redman, & Lenne, 2000), and neuropsychological impairments (Moffitt, 1993; Raine, 2002) have been shown to be associated with violence.

This research may be relevant in hypothesizing mechanisms between a defendant's mental disorder and an offense. Importantly, however, the role of this type of research in criminal responsibility evaluations is relatively limited. It is difficult to generalize from this group aggregate data to an individual case, and while these studies provide evidence of correlation, causation cannot be implied. Finally, these studies have generally not investigated the particular functional legal abilities relevant to NGRI, particularly cognitive and volitional capacity.

A second source of data in proposing a link between mental disorder and cognitive and volitional impairments is through a detailed review of the circumstances of the crime, particularly the sequence of events, evidence of planning, and possible motivations. Was the crime planned prior to the onset of the mental symptoms? Was it carried out in a coherent, careful way? Does the defendant have any motives, such as revenge, which might factor prominently in the criminal behavior? If the crime was planned prior to symptom onset, was carefully carried out, and appears heavily motivated by factors other than mental illness, it may be less likely that it was caused by the mental disorder. Here, collaborative data from numerous sources, in addition to the defendant's self report, are especially important.

In order to assist evaluators in answering this question on the link between mental disorders and criminal responsibility, additional research on causal links proposed by clinicians and those that are accepted by the court would be valuable (Borum, 2003). However, it is important to note that clinicians need not provide definitive links but rather descriptive information and hypotheses that the courts can use to guide their decision (Hoge & Grisso, 1992).

In suggesting these causal hypotheses, Ogloff and colleagues (1993) recommend that clinicians strive to provide possibilities without offering conclusions on the ultimate legal issue (i.e., whether or not a defendant is NGRI). Various positions have been taken on whether psychologists should address the ultimate legal issues (see Borum, 2003). Overall, the prevailing opinion appears to be that clinicians should avoid offering ultimate opinions in NGRI evaluations (American Bar Association, 1989; American Psychiatric Association, 1983; Ogloff et al., 1993).

Common Criticisms and Challenges

Forensic evaluations, particularly criminal responsibility evaluations, have been the target of great criticism, and concern has been expressed that these evalua-

---

[3] Most defendants evaluated for NGRI defenses and insanity acquittees are charged with violent offenses (Cirincione, Steadman, & McGreevy, 1995).

tions have fallen short of their promise (Nicholson & Norwood, 2000). Despite the criticisms, there is evidence that these evaluations have improved and promise that they have the potential to further improve. In this section, the common criticisms and challenges are outlined, and possibilities for avoiding and rectifying these potential pitfalls are suggested.

One common criticism is that evaluators have a tendency to ignore the functional legal abilities relevant to these evaluations and to incorrectly reformulate legal concepts as mental health concepts. Rogers, Turner, Helfied, and Dickens (1988) surveyed forensic psychiatrists and psychologists and found their understanding of the legal standards for the insanity defense to be very poor.

Also, Heilbrun and Collins (1995) found that these functional legal abilities were not routinely addressed in a sample of community-based criminal responsibility evaluations. In particular, 41 percent of reports commented on the defendant's understanding of his or her behavior at the time of the alleged crime, 27 percent on the defendant's understanding of the consequences of the crime, and 29 percent on the defendant's appreciation of the wrongfulness of his or her behavior. Forensic assessment instruments, such as the R-CRAS, may orient clinicians to the appropriate legal issues. Also, clinicians should make a particular point of becoming familiar with legal standards in their jurisdictions, especially as these standards have historically undergone frequent revision.

Another contentious issue is whether mental health professionals are able to diagnose mental disorders reliably (Faust & Ziskin, 1988). Over time, there is evidence that the ability of mental health professionals to diagnose mental illness reliably has improved with the delineation of explicit operational definitions of mental disorder (Nathan & Langenbucher, 1999). However, as noted, in criminal responsibility evaluations a retrospective assessment is required. As described earlier, the SADS may be particularly useful in making the retrospective assessments required in criminal responsibility evaluations (Rogers, 2001).

Adding to this, these evaluations occur within a highly charged, adversarial setting. In this context, psychologists may feel pulled by the party they are hired by to obtain findings that support this party's position (Otto, 1989). It might help to reduce this pressure by communicating results to the lawyer they are employed by in advance of writing a report (Borum, 2003). Lawyers can then decide whether they wish to have a report. Also, there is considerable apprehension that defendants undergoing criminal responsibility evaluations malinger mental disorders. Given this climate, it is recommended that response biases routinely be evaluated in some form.

CONCLUSION

Criminal responsibility evaluations are extremely challenging because of the pressures of the adversarial setting in which they occur, the climate of distrust toward insanity pleas, the retrospective nature of the assessments, and the constantly changing legal standards. The consequences at stake for defendants are enormous. Also, in comparison with other types of forensic evaluations such as competency evaluations, there has been less research in this area and fewer developments in forensic assessment instruments (Borum, 2003). Within this context, it is important for clinicians to be aware of potential limitations in their evaluations, explicitly acknowledge these limitations, and strive to provide high-quality evaluations that meet ethical, empirical, and legal standards.

REFERENCES

American Bar Association (1989). *ABA criminal justice mental health standards*. Washington, DC: Author.

American Law Institute (1962). *Model Penal Code* §4.01. Philadelphia: Author.

American Psychiatric Association (2000). *Diagnostic and statistical manual of mental disorder–Text revision* (4th ed.). Washington, DC: Author.

American Psychiatric Association, Insanity Defense Work Group (1983). American Psychiatric Association statement on the insanity defense. *American Journal of Psychiatry, 140*, 681–688.

Arbisi, P. A., & Ben-Porath, Y. S. (1998). The ability of Minnesota Multiphasic Personality Inventory-2 scales to detect fake-bad responses in psychiatric inpatients. *Psychological Assessment, 10*, 221–228.

Bagby, R. M., Nicholson, R. A., & Bacchiochi, J. R. (2002). The predictive capacity of the MMPI-2 and PAI validity scales and indexes to detect coached and uncoached feigning. *Journal of Personality Assessment, 78*, 69–86.

Baxter, R. (1997). Violence in schizophrenia and the syndrome of disorganization: *Criminal Behaviour and Mental Health, 7*, 131–139.

Bazelon, D. L. (1982). Veils, values and social responsibility. *American Psychologist, 36*, 633–638.

Ben-Porath, Y. S., & Graham, J. R. (1995). Scientific bases of forensic applications of the MMPI-2. In Y. S. Ben-Porath & J. R. Graham (Eds.), *Forensic applications of the MMPI-2* (pp. 1–17). Thousand Oaks, CA: Sage.

Blaszczynski, A., & Silove, D. (1996). Pathological gambling: Forensic issues. *Australian and New Zealand Journal of Psychiatry, 30*, 358–369.

Borum, R. (2003). Not guilty by reason of insanity. In T. Grisso (Ed.), *Evaluating competencies* (2nd ed.). New York: Kluwer/Plenum.

Borum, R., & Grisso, T. (1995). Psychological test use in criminal forensic evaluations. *Professional Psychology: Research and Practice, 26*, 465–473.

Borum, R., & Grisso, T. (1996). Establishing standards for criminal forensic reports: An empirical analysis. *Bulletin of the American Academy of Psychiatry and the Law, 24*, 297–317.

Bushman, B. J. (1993). Human aggression while under the influence of alcohol and other drugs: An integrative research review. *Current Directions in Psychological Science, 2*, 148–152.

Circincione, C., Steadman, H. J., & McGreevy, M. A. (1995). Rates of insanity acquittals and the factors associated with successful insanity pleas. *Bulletin of the American Academy of Psychiatry & the Law, 23*, 399–409.

Committee on Ethical Guidelines for Forensic Psychologists (1991). Specialty guidelines for forensic psychologists. *Law and Human Behavior, 15*, 655–665.

Douglas, K. S., Hart, S. D., & Kropp, P. R. (2001). Validity of the Personality Assessment Inventory for forensic assessments. *International Journal of Offender Therapy and Comparative Criminology, 45*, 183–197.

Duncan, S. A., & Ausborn, D. L. (2002). The use of reliable digits to detect malingering in a criminal forensic pretrial populations. *Assessment, 9*, 56–61.

Durham v. United States, 214 F.2d 862 (D.C. Cir. 1954).

Dyer, F. J., & McCann, J. T. (2000). The Millon clinical inventories: Research critical of their forensic application and Daubert criteria. *Law and Human Behavior, 24*, 487–497.

Faust, D., & Ziskin, J. (1988). The expert witness in psychology and psychiatry. *Science, 241*, 31–35.

Finkel, N. J. (1988). *Insanity on trial*. New York: Plenum.

Finkel, N. J. (1995). *Commonsense justice: Jurors's notions of the law*. Cambridge, MA: Harvard University Press.

Finkel, N. J., & Handel, S. F. (1989). How jurors construe "insanity." *Law and Human Behavior, 13*, 41–59.

First, M. D., Spitzer, R. L., Gibbon, M., & Williams, J. B. (1994). *Structural clinical interview for Axis I DSM-IV disorders: Patient edition* (SCID-I/P, Version 2.0). Biometrics Research Department, New York State Psychiatric Institute.

Franzen, M. D., Iverson, G. L., & McCracken, L. M. (1990). The detection of malingering in neuropsychological assessment. *Neuropsychology Review, 1*, 247–279.

Frederick, R. I., & Crosby, R. D. (2000). Development and validation of the Validity Indicator Profile. *Law and Human Behavior, 24*, 59–82.

Ganellen, R. J., Wasyliw, O. E., & Haywood, T. W. (1996). Can psychosis be malingered on the Rorschach? An empirical study. *Journal of Personality Assessment, 66*, 65–80.

Giorgi-Guarnieri, D., Janofsky, J., Keram, E., Lawsky, S., Merideth, P., Mossman, D., et al. (2002). AAPL practice guideline for forensic psychiatric evaluations of defendants raising the insanity defense. *Journal of the American Academy of Psychiatry and the Law, 30*, S3–S40.

Golding, S. L. (1992). The adjudication of criminal responsibility: A review of theory and research. In D. Kagehiro & W. Laufer (Eds.), *Handbook of psychology and law*. New York: Springer-Verlag.

Golding, S. L., & Roesch, R. (1987). The assessment of criminal responsibility: A historical approach to a current controversy. In I. B. Weiner & A. K. Hess (Eds.), *Handbook of forensic psychology* (2nd ed.) (pp. 395–436). New York: Wiley.

Golding, S. L., Skeem, J. L., Roesch, R., & Zapf, P. A. (1999). The assessment of criminal responsibility: Current controversies. In I. B. Weiner & A. K. Hess (Eds.), *Handbook of forensic psychology* (2nd ed.) (pp. 379–408). New York: Wiley.

Grossman, L. S., & Wasyliw, O. E. (1988). A psychometric study of stereotypes: Assessment of malingering in a criminal forensic group. *Journal of Personality Assessment, 52*, 549–563.

Hans, V. P. (1986). An analysis of public attitudes toward the insanity defense. *Criminology, 4*, 393–415.

Heilbrun, K., & Collins, S. (1995). Evaluations of trial competency and mental state at time of offense: Report characteristics. *Professional Psychology: Research and Practice, 26*, 61–67.

Heinrichs, R. W., & Zakzanis, K. K. (1998). Neurocognitive deficit in schizophrenia: A quantitative review of the evidence. *Neuropsychology, 12,* 426–445.

Hess, A. K. (2001). Review of the WAIS-III. In B. S. Plake & J. C. Impara (Eds.), *The fourteenth mental measurements yearbook.* (pp. 1332–1336). Lincoln, NE: Buros Institute of Mental Measurement.

Hoge, S. K., & Grisso, T. (1992). Accuracy and expert testimony. *Bulletin of the American Academy of Psychiatry and the Law, 20,* 67–76.

Kaufman, A., & Kaufman, N. (1990). *Kaufman brief intelligence test.* Circle Pines, MN: American Guidance Service.

Lewis, J. L., Simcox, A. M., & Berry, D. T. R. (2002). Screening for feigned psychiatric symptoms in a forensic sample by using the MMPI-2 and the Structured Inventory of Malingered Symptomatology. *Psychological Assessment, 14,* 170–176.

Link, B. G., Monahan, J., Stueve, A., & Cullen, F. T. (1999). Real in their consequences: A sociological approach to understanding the association between psychotic symptoms and violence. *American Sociological Review, 64,* 316–332.

Marlowe, D. B., Lambert, J. B., & Thompson, R. G. (1999). Voluntary intoxication and criminal responsibility. *Behavioral Sciences and the Law, 17,* 195–217.

McNiel, D., Eisner, J. P., & Binder, R. L. (2000). The relationship between command hallucinations and violence. *Psychiatric Services, 51,* 1288–1292.

Melton, G. B., Petrila, J., Poythress, N. G., & Slogobin, C. (1997). *Psychological evaluations for the courts: A handbook for mental health professionals and lawyers* (2nd ed.). New York: Guilford.

Miller, R. D., Olin, J., Johnson, D., Doidge, J., Iverson, D., & Fantone, E. (1996). Forcing the insanity defense on unwilling defendants: Best interests and the dignity of the law. *Journal of Psychiatry and Law, 24,* 487–509.

Millon, T., Davis, R., & Millon, C. (1997). *Millon Clinical Multiaxial Inventory-III* (2nd ed.). Minneapolis: National Computer Systems.

Moffitt, T. E. (1993). Adolescence-limited and life-course-persistent antisocial behavior: A developmental taxonomy. *Psychological Review, 100,* 674–701.

Morey, L. C. (1991). *Personality Assessment Inventory: Professional manual.* Tampa, FL: Psychological Assessment Resources.

Nathan, P. E., & Langenbucher, J. W. (1999). Psychopathology: Description and classification. *Annual Review of Psychology, 50,* 79–107.

Neumann, C. S., Walker, E. F., & Weinstein, J. (1996). Psychotic patients' awareness of mental illness: Implications for legal defense proceedings. *Journal of Psychiatry and Law, 24,* 421–442.

Nicholson, R. A., & Norwood, S. (2000). The quality of forensic psychological assessments, reports, and testimony: Acknowledging the gap between promise and practice. *Law and Human Behavior, 24,* 9–44.

Ogloff, J. R. P. (1991). A comparison of insanity defense standards on juror decision making. *Law and Human Behavior, 15,* 509–531.

Ogloff, J. R. P., Roberts, C. F., & Roesch, R. (1993). The insanity defense: Legal standards and clinical assessment. *Applied and Preventative Psychology, 2,* 163–178.

Ogloff, J. R. P., Schweighofer, A., Turnbull, S., & Whittemore, K. (1992). How much do we really know? A review of the empirical research on the insanity defense. In J. R. P. Ogloff (Ed.), *Law and psychology: The broadening of the discipline.* (pp. 171–210). Durham, NC: Carolina Academic Press.

Otto, R. K. (1989). Bias and expert testimony of mental health professionals in adversarial proceedings: A preliminary investigation. *Behavioral Sciences and the Law, 7,* 267–273.

Owens, S. M. (1997). Criminal responsibility and multiple personality defendants. *Mental and Physical Disability Law Reporter, 21,* 133–143.

Perlin, M. L. (1989). *Mental disability law: Civil and criminal.* Charlottesville, VA: The Mitchie Company.

Pollock, P. H. (1996). A cautionary note on the determination of malingering in offenders. *Psychology, Crime and Law, 3,* 97–110.

Pope, K. S., Butcher, J. N., & Seelen, J. (2000). *The MMPI, MMPI-2 & MMPI-A in court: A practical guide for expert witnesses and attorneys* (2nd ed.). Washington, DC: American Psychological Association.

Poythress, N., Melton, G. B., Petrila, J., & Slobogin, C. (2000). Commentary on "The Mental State at the Time of the Offense Measure." *Journal of the American Academy of Psychiatry & the Law, 28,* 29–32.

Raine, A. (2002). Biosocial studies of antisocial and violent behavior in children and adults: A review. *Journal of Abnormal Child Psychology, 30,* 311–326.

Rajaratnam, S. M. W., Redman, J. R., & Lenne, M. G. (2002). Intoxication and criminal behavior. *Psychiatry, Psychology and Law, 7,* 59–69.

Regina v. M'Naghten, 10 Cl. and F. 200, 8 Eng.Rep. 718 (1843).

Roberts, C. F., Sargent, E. L., & Chan, A. S. (1993). Verdict selection processes in insanity cases: Juror construals and the effects of guilty but mentally ill instructions. *Law and Human Behavior, 17,* 261–275.

Rogers, R. (1984). *Rogers criminal responsibility assessment scales (R-CRAS) and test manual.* Odessa, FL: Psychological Assessment Resources.

Rogers, R. (1997). *Clinical assessment of malingering and deception* (2nd ed.). New York: Guilford Press.

Rogers, R. (2001). *Handbook of diagnostic and structured interviewing.* New York: Guilford Press.

Rogers, R., Bagby, R. M., & Dickens, S. E. (1992). *SIRS Structured Interview of Reported Symptoms: A professional manual.* Odessa, FL: Psychological Assessment Resources.

Rogers, R., Kropp, P. R., & Bagby, R. M. (1992). Faking specific disorders: A study of the Structured Interview of Reported Symptoms (SIRS). *Journal of Clinical Psychology, 48,* 643–648.

Rogers, R., Salekin, R. T., & Sewell, K. W. (2000). The MCMI-III and the Daubert standard: Separating rhetoric from reality. *Law and Human Behavior, 24,* 501–506.

Rogers, R., Sewell, K. W., & Salekin, R. T. (1994). A meta-analysis of malingering on the MMPI-2. *Assessment, 1,* 227–237.

Rogers, R., & Shuman, D. W. (2000). *Conducting insanity evaluations.* New York: Guilford Press.

Rogers, R., Turner, R. E., Helfied, R., & Dickens, S. (1988). Forensic psychiatrists' and psychologists' understanding of insanity: Misguided expertise? *Canadian Journal of Psychiatry, 33,* 691–695.

Rogers, R., Ustad, K. L., & Salekin, R. T. (1998). Convergent validity of the Personality Assessment Inventory: A study of emergency referrals in a correctional setting. *Assessment, 5,* 3–12.

Rosenberg, B. E. (1989). Postpartum psychosis as a defense to infant murder. *Touro Law Review*, *7*, 287–308.

Rudnick, A., & Levy, A. (1994). Personality disorders and criminal responsibility: A second opinion. *International Journal of Law and Psychiatry*, *17*, 409–420.

Salekin, R. T., & Rogers, R. (2001). Treating patients found not guilty by reason of insanity. In J. B. Ashford, B. D. Sales, & W. H. Reid (Eds.), *Treating adult and juvenile offenders with special needs* (pp. 171–195). Washington, DC: American Psychological Association.

Scott, E. S. (2000). Criminal responsibility in adolescence: Lessons from developmental psychology. In T. Grisso & R. G. Schwartz (Eds.), *Youth on trial: A developmental perspective on juvenile justice* (pp. 291–324). Chicago, IL: University of Chicago Press.

Shapiro, D. L. (1991). *Forensic psychological assessment: An integrative approach.* Boston: Allyn & Bacon.

Silver, E. (1995). Punishment or treatment? Comparing the lengths of confinement of successful and unsuccessful insanity defendants. *Law and Human Behavior*, *19*, 375–388.

Simon, R. J., & Aaronson, D. E. (1988). *The insanity defense: A critical assessment of law and policy in the post-Hinckley era.* New York: Praeger.

Slobogin, C., Melton, G. B., & Showalter, C. R. (1984). The feasibility of a brief evaluation of mental state at the time of the offense. *Law and Human Behavior*, *8*, 305–320.

Slovenko, R. (1995). *Psychiatry and criminal culpability.* New York: Wiley.

Sparr, L. F., & Atkinson, R. M. (1986). Post-traumatic stress disorder as an insanity defense: Medicolegal quicksand. *American Journal of Psychiatry*, *143*, 608–613.

Sparr, L. F., Reaves, M. E., & Atkinson, R. M. (1987). Military combat, post-traumatic stress disorder, and criminal behavior in Vietnam veterans. *Bulletin of the American Academy of Psychiatry and the Law*, *15*, 141–162.

United States v. Brawner, 471 F.2d 969 (D.C. Cir. 1972).

Watterson, R. T. (1991). Just say no to the charges against you: Alcohol intoxication, mental capacity, and criminal responsibility. *Bulletin of the American Academy of Psychiatry and the Law*, *19*, 277–290.

Wechsler, D. (1997). *Wechsler Adult Intelligence Scale–Third edition.* San Antonio, TX: Psychological Corporation.

CHAPTER 9

ASSESSING ADJUDICATIVE COMPETENCY: USING LEGAL AND EMPIRICAL PRINCIPLES TO INFORM PRACTICE

JENNIFER SKEEM
UNIVERSITY OF NEVADA, LAS VEGAS

STEPHEN L. GOLDING
UNIVERSITY OF UTAH

PAULA EMKE-FRANCIS
UNIVERSITY OF NEVADA, LAS VEGAS

A simplified form of competency to stand trial was recognized as early as the thirteenth century. Trial procedure of the day required that a defendant enter a plea, and when that person could or did not, the issue[1] was whether the defendant was "mute by malice" as opposed to "mute by visitation by God" (Roesch & Golding, 1980, p. 2). As sociopolitical conceptions of justice and scientific understanding of mental disorder matured, so did conceptualizations of competency. By the eighteenth century, Hale, in his *Pleas of the Crown*, articulated the essential principle of competency: "If it appear that [a defendant] is mad, the judge, in his

---

[1] The competency assessment technique of the day, *peine forte et dure*, involved piling rocks upon the defendant's chest until a sound was uttered.

discretion, may discharge the jury of him, and remit him to gaol [jail], to be tried after the recovery of his understanding" (quoted in Silten and Tullis, 1977, p. 1053). During that period the trial of an incompetent defendant was viewed as an unjust adversarial contest, "in which the defendant, like a small boy being beaten by a bully, is unable to dodge or return the blows" (*Frith's Case*, 1790). In 1899, these principles were drawn into American case law when the conviction of a defendant was reversed on the basis that his epilepsy at trial and inability to provide information to counsel should have been considered and investigated (*Youtsey v. United States*, 1899).

The modern constitutional standard for competency to stand trial was established in *Dusky v. United States* (1960). In this case, the U.S. Supreme Court ruled that it was a fundamental violation of fairness and due process to proceed against a defendant who, by virtue of mental or physical impairment, did not possess "sufficient present ability to consult with his lawyer with a reasonable degree of rational understanding" or "a rational as well as factual understanding of the proceedings against him" (at 402). Years later, the Court added that a defendant must also possess an ability to "assist in preparing his defense" (*Drope v. Missouri*, 1972, at 171). Competency to stand trial, now commonly referred to as *adjudicative competency* (Golding & Roesch, 1988; Bonnie, 1992), refers to a jurisprudential construct and an accompanying set of procedures that allows for the postponement of criminal proceedings for individuals who are unable to take part in their own defense because of "mental disease or defect."[2]

The evaluation of adjudicative competence is arguably the single most significant mental health inquiry pursued in criminal law (Nicholson & Kugler, 1991), in part because "more defendants are evaluated for competency and more financial resources are expended for their evaluation, adjudication, and treatment than for any other class of forensic activities" (Golding, 1992, p. 77). Thus, legal and mental health professionals who work at the interface between psychology and criminal law are likely to encounter issues related to adjudicative competency. This chapter is designed to familiarize these professionals with (1) modern conceptualizations of the competency construct and relevant legal procedures, (2) forensic assessment instruments specifically designed to operationalize adjudicative competency, and (3) basic recommendations for practice based on available research.

CONCEPTUALIZING ADJUDICATIVE COMPETENCY

Basic Nomological Aspects of Adjudicative Competency

Competency is a different construct than psychopathology or intelligence. The mere presence of some level of psychological disturbance or disability (e.g.

---

[2] The common wording in most statutes.

psychosis or mental retardation), is only a threshold issue that must be established in order to "get one's foot in the incompetency door" (Bonnie, 1992; Golding & Roesch, 1988; Grisso, Appelbaum, Mulvey, & Fletcher, 1995; Skeem, Golding, Cohn, & Berg, 1998). At the heart of the competency construct lies the *linkage* between such disturbance or disability and impairment in the abilities necessary to understand legal proceedings and participate in one's defense (Skeem & Golding, 1998).

Adjudicative competency is also an *open construct* that cannot be reduced to a fixed set of psycholegal abilities. The constitutional standard for competency, based on *Dusky* and *Drope*, may be understood as requiring that defendants be able "(1) to consult with defense counsel, (2) to otherwise assist with their defense, and (3) to have both a rational and factual understanding of the proceedings" (American Bar Association, 1989, p. 170). Given the vagueness of this standard, a few legislatures and courts have added lists of specific psycholegal abilities (e.g., appreciation of charges, capacity to disclose pertinent facts to counsel, reasoned choice of legal options) that decision makers must consider in addition to the basic standard (e.g., Florida Rules of Criminal Procedure [FRCP], 2002; Utah Annotated Code, 2002; *Wieter v. Settle*, 1961). Nevertheless, most statutes merely restate the *Dusky* standard without elaboration (Zapf, 2002), and virtually all statutes include language that conveys competency as an open construct (e.g., "and any other factors deemed relevant"; FRCP, 2002, §3.211). This is consistent with the U.S. Supreme Court's observation that "[t]here are, of course, no fixed or immutable signs which invariably indicate the need for further inquiry to determine fitness to proceed; the question is often a difficult one in which a wide range of manifestations and subtle nuances are implicated" (*Drope v. Missouri*, 1972, at 180).

Thus, the psycholegal abilities for adjudicative competency vary, depending on such contextual demands of the case as the complexity of charges, types of evidence available to counsel without the defendant's report, probable length of proceedings, qualities of the defense attorney, and likely defense strategy (see Grisso, 1988). When mental illness is linked with a psycholegal deficit, the essential question is whether that deficit "in *this* defendant, facing *these charges, in light of existing* evidence, anticipating the substantial effort of a *particular* attorney with a *relationship of known characteristics* results in a defendant being unable to rationally assist the attorney or to comprehend the nature of the proceedings and their likely outcome" (Golding & Roesch, 1988, p. 79).

Given its open nature, the construct of adjudicative competency also embraces "other competencies" such as competency to plead guilty, to waive counsel and proceed *pro se*, and to confess, depending upon the case context. Until 1993, the issue of whether the constitutional standard for these "other competencies," which involve the waiver of constitutional rights, was higher or different than the standard for competency to proceed (or stand trial) was an issue of debate in the legal and mental health literature. Some scholars (e.g., Bonnie, 1992; Roesch & Golding, 1980) had made a useful distinction between "foundational" abilities thought minimally necessary to proceed (e.g., basic understanding of the charges and adversary system; ability to disclose relevant information to counsel) and higher-order "decisional" capacities (e.g., to grasp legal alternatives and rationally choose among optional courses of action) required in more demanding case contexts that might involve waiving basic constitutional rights.

In *Godinez v. Moran* (1993), the U.S. Supreme Court held that the *standard* by which the various competency contexts (i.e., competency to plead guilty, to waive counsel, to stand trial with the assistance of counsel) are assessed can constitutionally be the same, though individual states may adopt higher or different standards for different contexts, if they wish.[3] Thus, although jurisdictions are permitted to adopt specific standards or "tests" comprised of different psycholegal abilities for different adjudicative competency contexts, there is no constitutional basis that requires them to do so. We return to this issue of "other competencies" after outlining basic procedural aspects of adjudicative competency.

Procedural Aspects of Adjudicative Competency

There are three uniform procedural stages associated with adjudicative competency: (1) raising the issue of competency, (2) evaluating competency, and (3) if the defendant is found incompetent, providing treatment and evaluating progress toward competency. Procedural protections and ethical standards of practice govern each stage of this process.

Raising the Issue

Because conviction of an incompetent defendant violates due process, all officers of court (e.g., the judge, prosecution, and defense) are obligated to raise the issue whenever there is a "bona fide" doubt[4] as to a defendant's competency (*Pate v. Robinson*, 1966). The issue may be raised at any time during proceedings, from indictment to sentencing. A *Pate* motion for an evaluation of competency can be denied only "if frivolous... not in good faith, or does not set forth the grounds for believing that the accused may be incompetent" (*United States v. Bradshaw*, 1982, at 712). Although states may place the burden of proof on the defendant (*Medina v. California*, 1992), defendants are required to prove incompetency only by a preponderance of the evidence (*Cooper v. Oklahoma*, 1996).

Despite the requirement of a bona fide doubt as to the defendant's competency, the issue may often be raised for other reasons. For example, the issue may

---

[3] "While psychiatrists and scholars may find it useful to classify the various kinds and degrees of competence, *and while States are free to adopt competency standards that are more elaborate than the Dusky formulation*, the Due Process Clause does not impose these additional requirements" (*Godinez* at 2682, emphasis added).

[4] "Bona fide" doubt does not mean a "constructive doubt" based upon presence of psychosis or prior mental health history, but rather a present substantial doubt based upon linkage to competency to proceed.

be raised when there is a "scintilla of evidence of psychiatric impairment" (Peszke, 1980, p. 132), rather than any substantial doubt about competence per se. Similarly, the issue may be raised as a legal tactic to delay trial, to help establish a defense, or as a means of discovery by the prosecution (e.g., Roesch & Golding, 1979). Examiners who evaluate competency should attempt to ascertain why the issue was raised (Grisso, 1986) and should be aware of inappropriate motivations for raising the issue to avoid inadvertently participating in strategic schemes (Melton, Petrila, Poythress, & Slobogin, 1987).

Evaluating and Adjudicating Competency

Once the court grants a motion for examination of a defendant's competency, one or more examiners evaluate the defendant and submit a written report to the court. The courts have long realized that this competency evaluation process risks jeopardizing defendants' right against self-incrimination, given that the process of examining psycholegal abilities inevitably involves possible confessions, admissions of fact, and statements that may contradict trial testimony. To protect against this risk, protections of the defendant's Fifth Amendment rights have been established. In all jurisdictions, information obtained during a court ordered competency evaluation may not be used by the prosecution at the guilt or sentencing phases of the trial unless the defendant is deemed to have placed his mental state into evidence (e.g., by raising an insanity defense).

Moreover, in light of the jurisprudential complexity and constitutional considerations involved in this issue (*Estelle v. Smith*, 1981), defense counsel must be notified of a competency evaluation and examiners must provide defendants with some form of "forensic warning" on the limited confidentiality associated with the competency evaluation (Committee on Ethical Guidelines for Forensic Psychologists, 1991). Discussing the complex limitations of privilege in this context is difficult with defendants with overt psychosis, extreme depression or mania, or developmental disabilities. With these types of defendants, this is best approached not as a fixed warning or signed statement, but as a clinical process (e.g., a cycle of assessing understanding, providing information, eliciting and responding to questions, and reassessing understanding; see Stiles, Poythress, Hall, Falkenbach, & Williams, 2001). Similarly, when interviewing defendants facing severe penalties, care must be taken to discuss the potential implications of their (perhaps natural) tendencies to shade the truth, whether by exaggeration or minimization, both at trial and at sentencing.[5]

In addition to these safeguards, experts must be mindful of these issues when writing their report to the court. This report is *the* tangible product of the evaluation process. Typically, the court will rely solely on such reports to adjudicate

---

[5] For example, a capital murder defendant, later found competent, may well exaggerate the nature of the physical and sexual abuse he was subjected to as a child. At the death penalty phase, when he presents mitigating evidence, the prosecution may introduce his distortions to impeach him or his experts.

competency, with rates of examiner-judge agreement typically exceeding 90 percent (e.g., Hart & Hare, 1992; Reich & Tookey, 1986; Williams & Miller, 1981). Because hearings are relatively rarely held, examiners' reports will often be the only basis for judicial decisions about competency. To permit the court to make informed decisions, examiners must clearly explicate the data and reasoning that underlie each of their conclusions. This concern, however, must be balanced against the risk of violating rights against self-incrimination. Generally, examiners should omit statements made by the defendant about novel facts related to the alleged crime unless these facts are absolutely essential for substantiating an opinion related to competency.

Treating and Reevaluating Incompetent Defendants

In most jurisdictions, the vast majority of defendants who are evaluated for adjudicative competency are deemed competent to proceed (approximately 70%; Nicholson & Kugler, 1991). Those found incompetent are usually committed to the public mental health system for treatment focused on attaining competency and returning the defendant to court.

For some defendants (e.g., those with irreversible brain damage, severe developmental disabilities, or treatment-resistant psychoses), competency is unlikely to be restored. Such defendants cannot be indefinitely institutionalized as incompetent. The U.S. Supreme Court has ruled that a defendant committed on the basis of incompetency "cannot be held more than the reasonable period of time necessary to determine whether there is a substantial probability that he will attain that capacity in the foreseeable future" (*Jackson v. Indiana*, 1972, p. 738). Thus, committed defendants typically are reexamined on a regular basis to determine whether competency (1) has been attained, (2) is likely to be attained with continued treatment, or (3) is unlikely to be attained in the foreseeable future. The courts typically rely upon examiners' reports to determine the probability that a defendant will regain competency. When a defendant is deemed "unrestorable," the commitment based on incompetency must terminate. In this case, the charges are dismissed, often with the provision that prosecution may reinstate charges if the defendant ever attains competency, and civil commitment procedures are initiated.

In *Jackson*, the Court required that the nature of the commitment bear "some reasonable relationship to the purpose for which the individual [was] committed" (p. 738). However, the majority of forensic facilities treat incompetent patients no differently than other patients (Siegel & Elwork, 1990). Several group treatment and psychoeducational approaches that specifically focus on adjudicative incompetency have been developed (Davis, 1985; Nelson, 1989; Pendleton, 1980). Some of these approaches culminate in the defendant's participation in a mock trial. Preliminary evidence suggests that such approaches are effective. Specifically, Siegel and Elwork (1990) found that traditional treatment supplemented with competency-tailored strategies was significantly more effective in restoring competency than traditional treatment alone.

Because solely treating the underlying mental disorder is not what constitutional law mandates, we recommend that clinicians who work in relevant forensic settings augment "treatment as usual" with individual and group strategies that specifically target the defendant's functional deficits and lack of legal knowledge (Elwork, 1992). Ideally, the treatment targets will be deficits that formed the basis for finding the defendant incompetent. As noted earlier, adjudicative competency may embrace a broad range of competencies. Thus, clinicians must be prepared to address a range of deficits that extend beyond those that pertain narrowly to trial competency (e.g., behaving appropriately in the courtroom; understanding where courtroom personnel sit and what their function is). Unfortunately, the field's understanding of effective methods for restoring adjudicative competency is in its infancy and has recently had a slow rate of growth (see Mumley, Grisso, & Tillbrook, 2003; Otto & Heilbrun, 2002). Future collaborations among researchers and practitioners may advance the field toward relatively systematic approaches for treating incompetency.

Treatment Refusal in the Competency Restoration Context

Legal Developments

Currently, psychotropic medication appears to be the dominant mode for treating incompetent defendants. For a number of reasons, defendants may wish to refuse psychotropic medication. The legal principles that govern when defendants may refuse medication are evolving. This began with *Washington v. Harper* (1990), where the U.S. Supreme Court ruled that individuals who have been lawfully convicted retain certain constitutional rights including "a significant interest in avoiding unwanted administration of antipsychotic drugs" (p. 211). Nevertheless, an inmate may be involuntarily treated if he "is dangerous to himself or others and the treatment is in the inmate's medical interest" (*Washington v. Harper*, at 227). In *Riggins v. Nevada* (1992), the Court extended its analysis to pretrial detainees.

Based on complaints of hearing voices and insomnia, Riggins was treated with Dilantin and high doses of Mellaril. Despite conflicting expert reports, he was found competent to stand trial while medicated. Two months later, defense counsel asked that Riggins's medication be suspended, arguing that continued administration infringed upon his freedom and that the drugs' effect on his mental state and demeanor during trial would deny him due process. Riggins also asserted that he had a right to show jurors his "true mental state" at trial to support a defense of insanity. In response, the State argued that medication was needed to maintain Riggins's competency. The trial court denied Riggins's motion. Riggins continued to receive strong doses of Mellaril each day through the completion of his trial several months later. At trial, Riggins presented an insanity defense and testified on his own behalf. He was found guilty of capital murder and sentenced to death.

Ultimately, Riggins appealed his case to the U.S. Supreme Court, arguing that the medication had interfered with his ability to assist his counsel and had affected his mental state, appearance, and demeanor at trial, thereby prejudically affecting the jury's interpretation of the evidence and his testimony. The Supreme Court reversed Riggins's conviction, observing that

> once Riggins moved to terminate administration of antipsychotic medication, the State became obligated to establish the need for Mellaril and the medical appropriateness of the drug. Although we have not had occasion to develop substantive standards for judging forced administration of such drugs in the trial or pretrial settings, Nevada certainly would have satisfied due process if the prosecution had demonstrated . . . that treatment with antipsychotic medication was medically appropriate and, considering less intrusive alternatives, essential for the sake of Riggins' own safety or the safety of others.[6] . . . Similarly, the State might have been able to justify medically appropriate, involuntary treatment with the drug by establishing that it could not obtain an adjudication of Riggins' guilt or innocence by using less intrusive means. . . . Because the record contains no finding that might support a conclusion that administration of antipsychotic medication was necessary to accomplish an essential state policy, however, we have no basis for saying that the substantial probability of trial prejudice in this case was justified. (pp. 136–137)

Thus, the Court held that due process may be violated if, absent a compelling state interest, a defendant is forced to stand trial while on antipsychotic drugs that may negatively affect his demeanor and ability to participate in proceedings. An important subtext of *Riggins*, however, is found in Justice Kennedy's concurring opinion, which he wrote to express the view

> that the Due Process Clause prohibits prosecuting officials from administering involuntary doses of antipsychotic medicines for purposes of rendering the accused competent for trial absent an *extraordinary* showing, and to express doubt that the showing can be made, given our present understanding of the properties of these drugs. . . . When the State commands medication during the pretrial and trial phases of the case for the avowed purpose of changing the defendant's behavior, the concerns are much the same as if it were alleged that the prosecution had manipulated material evidence . . . elementary protections against state intrusion require the State in every case to make a showing that there is no significant risk that the medication will impair or alter in any material way the defendant's capacity or willingness to react to the testimony at trial or to assist his counsel. Based on my understanding of the medical literature, I have substantial reservations that the State can make that showing. (pp. 140–142)

Justice Kennedy will soon have an opportunity to examine whether or not the state can make that showing, given that the U.S. Supreme Court recently granted *certiorari* in the case of *Sell v. United States* (2002). The American

---

[6]Thus, applying *Harper* in the context of pretrial detainees.

Psychiatric Association has filed an amicus brief to argue that Justice Kennedy's "substantial reservations" have been addressed by the new atypical antipsychotics.[7] Sell was evaluated for competency after being charged with Medicaid fraud, and subsequently with conspiring and attempting to kill a witness against him and an FBI agent. The trial court found him incompetent, based on deficits associated with a persecutory delusional disorder. The institution charged with Sell's restoration attempted to treat him with psychotropic medication. Sell asserted his right to refuse treatment, presenting evidence that, assuming he had a delusional disorder, it was unlikely to respond to psychotropic medication. Although the Eighth Circuit Court found that Sell was not dangerous to himself or others and hence could not be forcibly medicated under a strict *Harper* rationale, the court articulated a multipronged test for resolving the issue. Specifically, the court ruled that Sell could be forcibly medicated if the State showed (1) a compelling interest in bringing the case to trial that outweighed the defendant's liberty interest,[8] (2) that there was no less intrusive alternative means to bring the defendant to trial, and (3) that the treatment was "medically appropriate," i.e., likely to restore competency, with greater anticipated beneficial than adverse effects, and in the defendant's best *medical* interests. Applying that standard, the Court approved involuntarily medicating Sell. Sell appealed.

Practice Implications

As is evident from Justice Kennedy's concurring opinion in *Riggins*, when a defendant is restored to competency by medication, he or she may be disadvantaged at trial in the sense that:

1. The defendant may need to take the witness stand but may appear very constrained, emotionally withdrawn, and without affect or remorse, leading the trier of fact to an adverse inference about the credibility of other testimony that he was insane or otherwise psychologically disturbed at the time of the alleged offense (this was precisely the underlying issue in *Riggins* that was not directly addressed by the majority).
2. The psychotropic medications may produce adverse effects that alter consciousness, degree of awareness, and emotionality such that the defendant is cognitively confused and less involved in the trial proceed-

---

[7] It will be interesting to watch the briefs in *Sell* to see if a balanced and scientifically defensible analysis of the strength and weaknesses of atypical antipsychotics is placed before the Court.

[8] Interestingly, the American Bar Association, in their Criminal Justice Mental Health Standards, comes down on the side of the State's interests: "A person determined to be incompetent to stand trial and detained or committed for treatment or habilitation or ordered to appear for outpatient treatment or habilitation should have no right to refuse ordinary and reasonable treatment or habilitation designed to effect competence. However, a defendant should have the right to refuse any treatment or habilitation which may impair the defendant's ability to prepare a defense to the charge, which is experimental or which has an unreasonable risk of serious, hazardous or irreversible side effects" (1989, §7–4.10).

ings, thereby reducing the effectiveness of his assistance of trial counsel (so-called iatrogenic incompetency).
3. The psychotropic medications may alter the defendant's mental state such that he or she will appear distinctly different to court-appointed insanity defense examiners who may not have assessed the defendant prior to competency restoration (altering material evidence).

In light of these concerns, examiners should consider the following guidelines in a competency evaluation or restoration cases where treatment refusal is, or may be, an issue. First, assess the defendant's prior response to treatment in an effort to predict the nature of clinical change that is likely with treatment, including its beneficial and adverse effects. Second, assess the defendant's history of refusing medication, including the bases for that refusal (see Grisso & Appelbaum, 1998a, 1998b). "Treatment refusal" is a longitudinal process that reflects not only a defendant's psychopathology, but also his or her subjective reactions to prior treatments, prior relationships with treating personnel, experience with adverse effects, and information or misinformation about medication. Even the process of determining this information in a collaborative atmosphere may have positive effects on a developing "treatment refusal" situation.[9] Third, assess treatment needs, including (a) whether the defendant may be over- or under-medicated, and (b) the extent to which continued treatment is necessary to maintain competency (an issue particularly relevant during moves between jail and hospital settings). If the court should ultimately conclude that the defendant is competent only when medicated, this decision should be based upon an evaluation that addresses the issues outlined above and whether or not the side effects manifested in *this defendant*[10] are likely to compromise fundamental fairness. Fourth, inform the trier of fact of medication effects. Assuming that a "*Riggins* defendant" proceeds to trial,[11] the judge and jury should be provided with a report or testimony about the effects of involuntarily administered medication on the defendant's demeanor and behavior.[12] Finally, if relevant, consider attempting to

---

[9] For an excellent discussion of treatment refusal, reasons for refusal, and the research and clinical literatures, see Appelbaum (1994).

[10] From a professional mental health perspective, one of the problems with many court decisions in this area is a presumption of generality of adverse effects in all individuals, based upon data that they occur in some individuals. Given the great variability of individual differences, a person-specific analysis seems warranted.

[11] That is, assuming that the result of a *Riggins* hearing is that the State prevails, or that the defendant agrees to trial while medicated and the hearing judge determines that fundamental fairness will not be compromised.

[12] All courts that have considered the issue agree that expert testimony is the *minimum* required. *Riggins* can be read as questioning whether this is sufficient: "We also are persuaded that allowing Riggins to present expert evidence about the effect of Mellaril on his demeanor did nothing to cure the possibility that the substance of his own testimony, his interaction with counsel, or his comprehension at trial were compromised . . ." (at 1816). Similarly, as noted in *Lawrence v. Georgia* (1995), "Although a defendant is not entitled to have the jury view him or her in an unaltered, undrugged state in those instances where the requirements of Riggins are met, we hold henceforth that a defen-

preserve evidence of a defendant's pre-medication mental state, particularly if the defendant intends to raise a mental state defense.[13]

"Other Competencies" Embraced by Adjudicative Competency

As noted earlier, based on the *Godinez* case, adjudicative competency may embrace such "other competencies" as competency to proceed *pro se*, to plead guilty, and to confess. In this section, we analyze *Godinez* and its practical implications for assessing these "other competencies."

Competency to proceed pro se and to plead guilty[14]

For a variety of reasons, some defendants wish to represent themselves or plead guilty. Since the right to counsel and the right to trial are fundamental constitutional rights, a waiver of them must be "knowing and intelligent." To assess this ability, one must conduct an inquiry into whether the waiver was "made with full awareness of both the nature of the right being abandoned and the consequences of the decision to abandon it" (*Godinez v. Moran*, 1993, p. 2682; *Johnson v. Zerbst*, 1938; *Boykin v. Alabama*, 1969).

---

dant, who is under medication that may affect his demeanor, is entitled, upon the motion of defense counsel, to have the jury informed by the court at the beginning of the trial and in the charge to the jury that the defendant is under the influence of medication, that the defendant's behavior in their presence is conditioned by the medication, and that the insanity asserted as defendant's defense is to be evaluated as of the time alleged criminal acts were committed" (at 452).

[13] Many insanity pleaders are found unfit for trial and are treated, primarily with psychotropic medication, until their (predominantly) psychotic symptomatology remits. Golding, Eaves, & Kowaz (1989) have shown that considerable change occurs during this time period. It is therefore extremely likely that a defendant who pleads not guilty by reason of insanity comes to trial disadvantaged if his premedication mental state is not preserved. An extensive "sanity" evaluation is unlikely to have taken place, and no relatively neutral record of his or her pretreatment behavioral or perceptual, cognitive, affective and judgmental capacities at the time of the offense will exist. The defendant may have changed dramatically by the time of the "insanity" evaluation, and, medicated or not, if the defendant was in a disturbed state at the time and in a different state later, he or she will have difficulty recalling or describing the relevant mental state during a subsequent interview. Finally, the defendant, many months later, has a difficult time convincing a judge or jury of his or her mental state, especially given the strong societal suspicion of malingering and the defendant's current presentation (if fit, he or she is likely to appear in court looking like anyone else; there will be no overt symptoms of agitation, psychotic anxiety, behaving as if hallucinating, etc). Moreover, as Justice Kennedy observed, the jury may draw erroneous conclusions about remorse and other mental state attributes because of the defendant's (medication induced) reduced affect. In light of these considerations, while it may not be practical in all competency evaluations, examiners should consider adopting a policy of videotaping examinations when the underlying charges are especially serious. It is difficult to conduct a proper "mental status at the time of offense" when a defendant is currently psychotic, and most often a retrospective evaluation is employed (see, generally, Simon & Shuman, 2002). Nevertheless, an attempt should be made to videotape as much of a detailed record of the defendant's pretreatment mental state and the mental state at the time of the offense as possible (Golding & Roesch, 1987).

[14] An infrequent, but extremely complicated, variant is when a defendant wishes to proceed *pro se* in order to prevent the introduction of a mental state defense. This is addressed in the section on competency to waive an insanity defense.

In *Faretta v. California* (1975), the U.S. Supreme Court held that a defendant had a right to waive counsel as long as the waiver was "literate, competent, and understanding" and the defendant was "voluntarily exercising his informed free will" (at 836). The wiseness of the defendant's decision is not the issue.[15] Trial courts have had a difficult time dealing with potentially incompetent defendants who seek to waive their right to counsel. While extremely disorganized and psychotic defendants are relatively easy cases, those with highly organized religious or paranoid delusions, suicidal ideation, or extremely idiosyncratic social, personal, or political belief systems are not. Whether the standard for competence is higher or different in the *pro se* context, the courts and forensic examiners have a difficult time pragmatically, as well as scientifically, distinguishing between delusionally influenced incompetent decision making and idiosyncratically inspired (foolish) decisions (see Golding, Skeem, Roesch, & Zapf, 1999). This is a fertile ground for politically expedient inconsistencies and the influence of the evaluator's own personal belief systems. Simply put, there are too many possibilities for abuse.

The case of *Goode v. Florida* (1978) illustrates this point. Goode had a long history of treatment refractory psychosis, sexual assault, and murder and had been committed several times. Facing capital murder charges, Goode this time asserted his right to waive counsel in order to prevent his counsel from offering a mental state defense. While there was little doubt that Goode was mentally ill, there was considerable debate as to whether his volunteering for execution was a "rational" decision. Nevertheless, Goode was permitted to volunteer for execution.

This interpretation of *Faretta* is most troublesome. Goode is not atypical in viewing his situation and his disorder as hopeless and therefore wishing to die. What would the result have been if, absent the murders, Goode had sought approval from the courts for passive suicide because he had grown tired and dispirited after battling severe mental disorder until the age of 27? Clearly, all courts would have refused to cooperate and would have committed him as mentally ill, dangerous to self, and incompetent to refuse treatment. Is it jurisprudentially consistent to reach a different result solely on the basis that he committed murder (while arguably insane) and wished to assert his *Faretta* right to represent himself and thereby block any attempt to adjudicate his case short of a death sentence?

This case also raises the essential practical issue with respect to competency to proceed *pro se* or to plead guilty. The issue is not whether a higher or different standard than *Dusky* applies, but rather *whether or not a full inquiry is made into a defendant's decisional capacities* and his or her ability to make a "reasoned

---

[15] Justice Blackmun, in his dissent, characterized the majority's position as one conferring a constitutional right to make a fool of himself upon the defendant.

choice" given a mental disorder. The key element is the nature and quality of the defendant's cognitive functioning and decisional abilities.[16]

In the *Godinez* case, when Moran's competence was evaluated the examination focused solely upon his capacity to stand trial *with the assistance of counsel*. While one examiner stated that Moran "may be inclined to exert less effort towards his own defense" (at 8) and another characterized Moran as "very depressed," both found him competent. When Moran appeared at trial three months later, seeking to discharge his public defender, waive his right to counsel, and plead guilty to all three charges of capital murder, the trial judge relied upon the prior competency evaluations and a rather perfunctory colloquy to accept his waiver and guilty plea. At his sentencing hearing, Moran presented no defense, no witnesses, and no mitigating evidence. He, like Goode, volunteered for execution.

These details are offered to highlight the fact that the U.S. Supreme Court never addressed the practical issue in *Godinez*. Regardless of whether the *standard* of competence varies across contexts, how can an evaluation in one context generalize to another? Clearly, Moran's mental state, like the change in context, may have changed. If so, a new inquiry into competency would be constitutionally required under *Pate*. Arguably, the central flaw in *Godinez* is the assumption that competency assessed in a particular context and time frame generalizes across contexts. Although other courts have accepted *Godinez* that the standard for competence is invariant across contexts, they have been less accepting of this central flaw. For example, in *Miles v. Stainer* (1997), the Ninth Circuit Court of Appeals overturned the conviction of a defendant who had been adjudicated competent and then later pled guilty. The court ruled that the lower court should have conducted another evaluation, specific to the context in which Miles pled guilty. Miles's level of competency had been fluctuating as a function of his compliance with medication, and he had been on medication when initially evaluated and off medication when he pled guilty.

One way that forensic examiners can ensure that their evaluations in one context will not be misapplied to some other context is to directly address the issue in their reports. Thus, such language as the following should be considered: "At the time of this report, the defendant has a good relationship with his attorney and his capacity to engage in rational choice of trial strategies, with the assistance of counsel, was unaffected by his mental disorder. Should the context of his case change, I would need to reevaluate this defendant in order to render a reliable and current opinion as to his competency."

Competency to Confess

In some contexts, adjudicative competency may embrace the defendant's competency to confess. The broad parameters of the relationship among competency,

---

[16] This can best be accomplished by adopting *both* an "articulated standard" approach in statutory regulation and by conducting "articulated interviews," as exemplified by the IFI-R.

mental illness, and the admissibility of a defendant's confession are reasonably clear. First, in *Colorado v. Connelly* (1986), the Supreme Court established that the interrogation in which the defendant alleges involuntariness,[17] on any grounds, must be custodial in nature.[18] Second, prior to any custodial interrogation, a defendant must be appraised of his or her rights under *Miranda v. Arizona* (1966). Third, since those rights are constitutional in nature, any waiver of those rights must be made in a voluntary, knowing, and intelligent manner (see earlier). Competency to confess becomes an issue when there is a nexus between a defendant's mental disorder or disability and his ability to waive *Miranda* rights, voluntarily, knowingly, and intelligently.

In the custodial interrogation context, the "voluntariness" criterion is judged by examining the "totality of the circumstances" (*Fare v. Michael C.*, 1976) as they bear on whether the decision to waive the rights is "knowing and intelligent" and "is a product of a free and deliberate choice rather than intimidation, coercion or deception" (*Moran v. Burbine*, 1986, at 421). Thus, under *Connelly*, although external coercion and custody are a necessary predicate for suppressing a confession on the grounds of voluntariness, a confession deemed "uncoerced" may still be suppressed on grounds that it was not made knowingly or intelligently (*State v. Clemens*, 2001).

Since a large number of cases are "solved" by confession, it is common for competency examinations to involve some inquiry into a defendant's competency to waive his or her *Miranda* rights. It should be acknowledged that a complete evaluation of this issue requires specialized training, knowledge, and experience. Nevertheless, if evidence against a defendant involves his or her confession, a competency examiner should be sufficiently trained to screen the issue, and make a specialty referral if appropriate.

This screening inquiry may be conceptualized within the framework of a defendant's capacity to disclose to counsel pertinent facts, events, and states of mind (Golding, 1993). Specifically, it involves an evaluation of the defendant's ability to provide an account of police behavior at the time of apprehension and interrogation, the defendant's comprehension of the nature of the *Miranda* warning, the circumstances surrounding the interrogation, and the defendant's "confession behavior" (i.e., the nature of the statement, the influence of mental disorder on the nature of the statement, the defendant's suggestibility, and its effect on compliance with interrogation pressures). Police accounts of their behav-

---

[17] Justices Stevens, Brennan, and Marshall, in strongly worded dissents, challenged the legal as well as moral logic of the majority's view that since Connelly was not in "police custody," there need be no further inquiry into voluntariness ["Coercive police activity is a necessary predicate to finding that a confession is not 'voluntary'" (at 167)]. Fundamentally, they argued that a confession could not be considered voluntary unless the decision to do so was the product of a free and deliberate choice rather than the product of psychotic delusions and command hallucinations.

[18] Hence, since Connelly was not in police "custody" at the time of his statement to them, his confession statement could not be suppressed on involuntariness grounds. Connelly's incompetence to proceed was established later, but that pertained to other issues.

ior and the statements of defendants during custodial interrogation may be at variance with the defendant's memory or independent evidence. A defendant's ability to recognize potential distortion in the testimony of police officers, especially where interrogation interviews are not recorded, can be essential to the defense.

Excellent guidance and methods can be found in the instruments developed by Grisso (1986; 1998). These are designed to assess the capacities of defendants (both adult and juvenile) to waive their *Miranda* rights in a meaningful fashion. Grisso's work is a substantial contribution because these instruments provide a specific means to assess the cognitive aspects of comprehension of *Miranda* rights and intelligence is too global a construct to be useful.

Evaluation of the circumstances surrounding an interrogation is a complex task involving specialized knowledge of police interrogation techniques (Inbau, Reid, & Buckley, 1986; Kassin, 1997; Leo, 1996), an analysis of the relationship between crime scene evidence and a defendant's statements, an analysis of the structure of the interrogator's and the defendant's language (see Shuy, 1998), and an evaluation of a defendant's susceptibility to influence and coercion (see Gudjonsson, 1992; Gudjonsson & Sigurdsson, 1999). False confessions, once thought to be a puzzling rarity, are anything but rare, as demonstrated by the Innocence Project (see www.innocenceproject.org/docs/Master_List_False_Confessions.html; see also Kassin, 1997; Rattner, 1988; Huff, Rattner, & Sagarin, 1996).

OPERATIONALIZING AND ASSESSING ADJUDICATIVE COMPETENCY

Over the past three decades, various professional groups have developed specialized instruments to improve the legal and clinical rigor of assessments of adjudicative competency. A small subgroup of these instruments (Golding, 1993; Poythress et al., 1999) assess key aspects of "other competencies" noted earlier, whereas most instruments focus on more traditional notions of trial competency. At the heart of each of these instruments lies an assessment of a particular set of functional competency abilities. A comprehensive list of such abilities, organized into 11 broad domains and 31 subdomains, is provided in Table 9.1, which will organize our discussion in this section of promising competency assessment tools for adults (see chap. 35 of this text for juveniles). Notably, virtually all research on adjudicative competency has been conducted with male defendants. Given that the rate of felony convictions for females is growing at a rate more than twice that of males (Greenfeld & Snell, 1999), future research must address concerns about the generalizability of research findings and competency assessment measures to this population (see Poythress et al., 1998; Redding, 1997; Riley, 1998).

We recommend that examiners carefully choose a competency assessment tool to include routinely in their evaluations. We do so for two reasons. First, these

TABLE 9.1
Adjudicative Competency Domains and Subdomains

Domain	Subdomain
1. Capacity to comprehend and appreciate the charges or allegations	a. Factual knowledge of the charges (ability to report charge label) b. Understanding of the behaviors to which the charges refer c. Comprehension of the police version of events
2. Capacity to disclose to counsel pertinent facts, events, and states of mind	a. Ability to provide a reasonable account of one's behavior around the time of the alleged offense b. Ability to provide information about one's state of mind around the time of the alleged offense c. Ability to provide an account of the behavior of relevant others around the time of the alleged offense d. Ability to provide an account of police behavior e. Comprehension of the *Miranda* warning f. Confession behavior (influence of mental disorder, suggestibility, and so forth on confession)
3. Capacity to comprehend and appreciate the range and nature of potential penalties that may be imposed in the proceedings	a. Knowledge of penalties that could be imposed (e.g., knowledge of the relevant sentence label associated with the charge, such as "5 to life") b. Comprehension of the seriousness of charges and potential sentences
4. Basic knowledge of legal strategies and options	a. Understanding of the meaning of alternative pleas (e.g., guilty and mentally ill) b. Knowledge of the plea bargaining process
5. Capacity to engage in reasoned choice of legal strategies and options	a. Capacity to comprehend legal advice b. Capacity to participate in planning a defense strategy c. Plausible appraisal of likely outcome (e.g., likely disposition for one's own case) d. Comprehension of the implications of a guilty plea or plea bargain (i.e., the rights waived on entering a plea of guilty) e. Comprehension of the implications of proceeding *pro se* (e.g., the rights waived and the ramifications of waiver) f. Capacity to make a reasoned choice about defense options (e.g., trial strategy, guilty plea, proceeding *pro se*, pleading insanity) without distortion attributable to mental illness (an ability to rationally apply knowledge to one's own case)
6. Capacity to understand the adversary nature of the proceedings	a. Understanding of the roles of courtroom personnel (i.e., judge, jury, prosecutor) b. Understanding of courtroom procedure (the basic sequence of trial events)
7. Capacity to manifest appropriate courtroom behavior	a. Appreciation of appropriate courtroom behavior b. Capacity to manage one's emotions and behavior in the courtroom
8. Capacity to participate in trial	a. Capacity to track events as they unfold (not attributable to the effects of medication) b. Capacity to challenge witnesses (i.e., recognize distortions in witness testimony)
9. Capacity to testify relevantly	
10. Relationship with counsel	a. Recognition that counsel is an ally b. Appreciation of the attorney-client privilege c. Confidence in and trust in one's counsel d. Confidence in attorneys in general e. Particular relationship variables that may interfere with the specific attorney-client relationship (i.e., attorney skill in working with the client; problematic socioeconomic or demographic differences between counsel and client)
11. Medication effects on CST[a]	a. Capacity to track proceedings given sedation level on current medication b. Potentially detrimental effects of medication on the defendant's courtroom demeanor

[a] CST = competency to stand trial.

tools have been shown to improve the reliability (and perhaps validity) of competency evaluations (see Nicholson & Kugler, 1991; Poythress & Stock, 1980; Roesch & Golding, 1980; Skeem et al., 1998). This finding is not surprising, given that researchers and clinicians have long used tools that structure the data collection and decisional process to improve the reliability and validity of psychiatric diagnoses (see Luria & Guziec, 1981). Second, despite the advantage of competency assessment tools, examiners rarely use them. In fact, extant research indicates that examiners tend to rely on traditional clinical measures of personality and intelligence (e.g., the MMPI-2) much more often than competency assessment tools that directly target the legal question at issue (Grisso, 1987; Heilbrun & Collins, 1995; Skeem et al., 1998). For these reasons, we provide a relatively detailed review of tools associated with three alternative approaches to competency assessment: screening tools, structured and semistructured interviews, and normed tests.

Screening Tools

Given that most defendants are found competent, screening tests have been developed to identify clearly competent defendants and eliminate them from this costly process. These tools may be used in evaluation systems to "screen in" potentially incompetent defendants for further assessment. We review two of the most thoroughly researched and frequently used screening tools here.[19]

Competency Screening Test

The Competency Screening Test (CST: Lipsitt, Lelos, & McGarry, 1971) is a 22-item sentence completion task that addresses the defendant's perceptions of counsel and aspects of the trial that might induce emotional reactions (Grisso, 1986). Repsonses are scored on a three-point scale, with total scores of 20 and higher considered indicative of competency. Administration time is 25 minutes or less (see Nicholson, 1988; Shatin, 1979).

The CST has acceptable interscorer reliability and internal consistency, and it significantly predicts examiner opinions and judicial determinations of competency (Lipsitt et al., 1971; Nottingham & Mattson, 1981; Randolph, Hicks, & Mason, 1981; Schreiber, Roesch, & Golding, 1987), with rates of agreement ranging from 72 to 84 percent (Nicholson, Briggs, & Robertson, 1988). Most classification errors are false positives, with rates as high as 53 percent (Ustad et al., 1996; see also Grisso, 1986; Schreiber et al., 1987). This troubling tendency to label many competent defendants as incompetent may be based in part on the CST's scoring criteria, which discriminate against defendants who express doubt in judicial fairness or disagreement with attorney advice (Brakel, 1974; Roesch &

---

[19] Others include the Metropolitan Toronto Forensic Service Fitness Questionnaire (Nussbaum, Mamak, Tremblay, Wright, & Callaghan, 1998), Computer-Assisted Determination of Competency to Proceed (Barnard et al., 1991, 1992), or Mosley Forensic Competency Scale (Mosley, Thyer, & Larrison, 2001). Although some of these tools are promising, they currently are best viewed as research instruments rather than clinical assessment tools.

Golding, 1987). Arguably, the criteria require defendants to respond in the way the court system should be rather than the way in which it often is.

There is little or no support for the construct validity of the CST. Because the CST has an unclear factor structure (Bagby, Nicholson, Rogers, & Nussbaum, 1992; Nicholson et al., 1988; see also Roesch & Golding, 1980), the nature of the deficits assessed and their consistency with the construct of adjudicative competency are uncertain. Moreover, the measure bears little relation to more comprehensive measures of adjudicative competency (Schreiber et al., 1987). For these reasons, the CST is best viewed as a brief tool for identifying areas for further inquiry in a subsequent, full evaluation. Given its limited predictive utility and poor operationalization of the competency construct, it should not be used alone.

Georgia Court Competency Test

The Georgia Court Competency Test (GCCT; Wildman et al., 1978) is a 17-item screening test that includes a courtroom picture that defendants use to discuss the location and function of courtroom participants (Nicholson, Robertson, Johnson, & Jenson, 1988). A "Mississippi" revision is available (GCCT-MSH; Johnson & Mullett, 1987), as is a malingering scale that may (if validated) prove to be a valuable addition (Gothard, Viglione, Meloy, & Sherman, 1995). Administration time is 10–15 minutes.

The GCCT (Wildman et al., 1978) and GCCT-MSH possess acceptable interrater reliability and internal consistency (Nicholson et al., 1988), and reasonable rates (75–81%) of predictive utility for staff competency decisions (Nicholson et al., 1988; Wildman et al., 1978; Wildman et al., 1990). Notably, Nicholson et al. (1988) found that the GCCT-MSH was more likely to correctly predict staff's competency decisions than the CST. Nevertheless, like the CST, the GCCT and GCCT-MSH obtain high rates of false positives, with reported estimates as high as 68 percent (Nicholson et al., 1988).

The GCCT and GCCT-MSH also have questionable construct validity. Although some investigators have found a two-factor (Wildman et al., 1978) or three-factor (Bagby et al., 1992; Nicholson et al., 1988, Bagby et al., 1992) structure for these measures, others have been unable to replicate these findings (Rogers et al., 1996; Ustad et al., 1996). Moreover, the three factors that several investigators have identified (general legal knowledge, courtroom layout, and specific legal knowledge) provide poor coverage of the competency construct, emphasizing factual knowledge to the exclusion of decisional capacities and the ability to consult with counsel (Bagby et al., 1992). For these reasons, the GCCT-MSH, like the CST, is best conceptualized as a checklist to note possible competency deficits for further assessment in a more thorough review (Rogers et al., 2001).

Structured and Semistructured Interviews

Assessment of adjudicative competency may simply begin with one of these interviews, which have been a staple in competency assessment for the past thirty years.

These interviews delineate areas of inquiry for trained examiners, including potential probe questions and scoring criteria for capturing various competency deficits. Because semistructured interview formats simulate attorney-client consultations, they provide direct examination of defendants' relational abilities that may affect their ability to assist counsel. In this section, we review three well-researched interviews and note a fourth newcomer to the field.

Competency to Stand Trial Assessment Instrument

The Competency to Stand Trial Assessment Instrument (CAI; Laboratory of Community Psychiatry [LCP], 1973) was designed as a companion tool for the CST. This semistructured interview covers 13 competency domains that are meant to assess (1) the ability to cooperate with counsel, (2) understanding of the nature and object of the proceedings, and (3) understanding of the consequences of the proceedings (LCP, 1973). Based on interview data, trained examiners rate each domain on a five-point scale. Each domain is intended to be interpreted and integrated into a final opinion; scores are not summed, nor are norms available.

The scoring criteria and coverage of the CAI have been subjects of criticism. The scoring criteria are vague and must be extrapolated from case examples. Moreover, because the criteria assume that a defendant is effectively represented by a competent attorney in a fair court system (Brakel, 1974; Lipsitt et al., 1974), they may be somewhat biased against cynical defendants (Grisso, 1986). Of greater concern is the CAI's limited coverage of the competency construct. For example, such key competency domains as the defendant's capacity for reasoned choice and understanding of the implications of a guilty plea are not represented (see Table 9.1). The CAI also fails to cover psychopathology, which must be linked with any competency deficits in order to support a finding of incompetency (Schreiber, Roesch, & Golding, 1987), and contextual factors of the trial (Grisso, 1986).

Although the CAI possesses acceptable interrater reliability (LCP, 1973; Roesch & Golding, 1980), a meta-analysis suggests that it is only moderately predictive of independent examiners' opinions on competency ($r = -.52$; Nicholson & Kugler, 1991). Also, based on a sample of 120 defendants, Schreiber, Roesch, and Golding (1987) found that classifications of competency based on the CAI agreed with independent court rulings in 82 percent of cases, and with the consensus opinion of a "blue ribbon panel" of forensic experts in 78 percent of cases. The CAI found a greater proportion of defendants incompetent than the expert panel, suggesting that the measure may be prone to false positives in "gray area" cases where defendants are neither clearly competent nor incompetent.

Aside from moderate associations found between the CAI and other measures of competency (Schreiber et al., 1987), there are concerns about its coverage and construct validity. If used, it should be to help structure an assessment of psycholegal deficits and supplemented with an assessment of symptomatology and consideration of the case context. Its use cannot be recommended in "gray area" or challenging cases.

Interdisciplinary Fitness Interview

The Interdisciplinary Fitness Interview (IFI; Golding & Roesch, 1983) was developed in part to refine prior instruments like the CAI by adding psychopathological and trial-contextual substance to the legal content. The revised IFI (IFI-R; Golding, 1993) elaborated the original IFI concepts and methods. Although designed to be administered jointly by an examiner and attorney, the IFI may be administered by an examiner alone. This semistructured interview assesses current psychopathology with respect to six relevant symptoms (rated as present/absent) and psycholegal abilities with respect to four overarching competency domains (the capacity to appreciate charges and disclose pertinent facts; courtroom demeanor and capacity to understand the adversarial nature of proceedings; quality of relationship with attorney; and appreciation of, and reasoned choice with respect to, legal options and consequences). Each domain is composed of three to five functional abilities that are rated on a three-point scale for degree of incapacity. The evaluator also rates each domain and symptom on a three-point scale for its relevance to the competency decision in the defendant's particular case and then considers the likely demands of the defendant's case. The interview procedure is designed as an idiographic measurement of competency, and hence no summed scores or normed data are provided.

Two aspects of the IFI's scoring criteria have been criticized. First, Melton and colleagues (1987) have argued against the notion of rating the importance of each deficit in determining a defendant's competency. They reason that because importance ratings are a function not only of competency deficits and trial demands, but also of moral judgment regarding how much deficiency produces injustice in trying a defendant, evaluators may overstep their bounds in providing these ratings. Nevertheless, courts may find it useful to understand what weights an expert places on certain data in reaching their opinions. Grisso (1987) has also criticized the lack of standard scoring criteria for each IFI item, although a comprehensive scoring manual is available.

The IFI possesses acceptable interrater reliability at both the item (kappa = .40–.91) and overall judgment levels (kappa = .93; Golding, Roesch, & Schreiber, 1984; see also Schreiber et al., 1987). Although the IFI has strong predictive utility for examiner opinions and judicial determinations of competency (Nicholson & Kugler, 1991; Schreiber et al., 1987), its ability to predict the consensus opinion of a "blue ribbon panel" of forensic experts is more impressive. Schreiber and colleagues (1987) found that IFI classifications were in agreement with those of this panel in 90 percent of cases. This finding arguably provides some support for the construct validity of the IFI, as does its moderate correlation with other competency assessment tools (Schreiber et al., 1987).

Despite the promising results of this relatively sophisticated study, little recent research has been conducted on the IFI. As discussed later, further research on the psychometric properties and comparative validity of the IFI-R may be particularly helpful in advancing the field. Nevertheless, available data support the view that the IFI is one of the most comprehensive and "tightly conceptualized of the structured competency assessment guides" (Melton et al., 1987, p. 84). As such, it may prove a useful tool to examiners.

Fitness Interview Test

The Fitness Interview Test (FIT; Roesch, Webster, & Eaves, 1984) was developed to assess the Canadian conceptualization of fitness to stand trial, which at the time closely resembled the *Dusky* standard (McDonald, Nussbaum, & Bagby, 1991). This structured interview addresses legal understanding (24 items) and relevant psychiatric impairment (11 items) to arrive at a general opinion (1 item). Each item is rated on a five-point scale for degree of incapacity.

Based on a sample of 255 pretrial defendants in Canada, McDonald, Nussbaum, and Bagby (1991) found that the FIT possessed good interrater reliability and internal consistency. In fact, correlations among FIT legal items (average $r = .72$) were high enough to suggest that the measure oversampled a single aspect of fitness, perhaps "basic legal knowledge," given the FIT's strong association with the GCCT ($r = -.71$). Although the FIT was in good agreement with independent judgments of "fitness or unfit" (kappa = .73), agreement was more limited when these independent judgments were classified as "fit," "questionable," and "unfit" (kappa = .49).

Following a revision of the Canadian criteria for fitness (C.C.C., S. 2, 1991; *Regina v. Taylor*, 1992), Roesch, Zapf, Eaves, and Webster (1998) extensively revised the FIT to address these new criteria. Unlike the FIT, the FIT-R addresses only abilities to (1) understand the nature and object of the proceedings, (2) understand the possible consequences of the proceedings, and (3) confer with counsel and assist in a defense. Following a 30-minute structured interview designed to assess these abilities, the evaluator rates whether the defendant can perform each of these three general competency abilities, determines whether the accused has a mental disorder, and arrives at an overall decision on competency.

Preliminary evidence supports the use of the FIT-R as a screening device. Specifically, based on a select sample of 57 pretrial defendants in Canada, Zapf and Roesch (1997) found that FIT-R classifications often (86%) agreed with independent hospital staff decisions. All disagreements were false positives, the rate of which (14%) was substantially lower than that often found with other screening tools (e.g., CST, GCCT). As the authors note, it is preferable for a screening tool to make false positive rather than false negative errors, given that the latter risks allowing an unfit defendant to proceed.

Additional research suggests that use of the FIT-R should be restricted to Canada. Unlike the criteria for fitness applied in the United States, the more "narrow" Canadian criteria do not require defendants to possess a rational understanding of the proceedings or a capacity for making reasoned choices among legal options (see Roesch, Hart, & Zapf, 1996). To determine whether operationalizations of adjudicative competency in Canada differed from those in the United States, Zapf and Roesch (2001) administered the FIT-R and MacArthur

Competency Assessment Tool–Criminal Adjudication (MacCAT-CA; Poythress et al., 1999) to 100 pretrial defendants in Canada. The two measures manifested modest agreement (kappa = .53) in their overall classifications of defendants as competent or incompetent. However, as expected, given differences in Canadian and United States law, a larger proportion of defendants were deemed unfit to stand trial based on the MacCAT (48%) than the FIT-R (32%). This suggests that the FIT-R may be overly conservative in deeming defendants incompetent when applying U.S. conceptualizations of adjudicative competency, which include rationality.

In summary, although more research with larger samples is needed, the FIT-R appears to be a promising screening tool for Canadian settings. Notably, however, its reliability and construct validity have yet to be established.

Evaluation of Competency to Stand Trial

Rogers recently developed the Evaluation of Competency to Stand Trial (ECST; see Rogers et al., 2001) to (1) assess more explicitly than extant measures the three prongs of the *Dusky* standard, and (2) create a standardized format for assessing feigned incompetency. The ECST includes four multi-item scales: Consult-with-Counsel, Factual Understanding, Rational Understanding, and Atypical Presentation (i.e., potential malingering).

After exploring the ECST's reliability in two unpublished studies of small samples, several items were deleted to create the revised ECST (ECST-R; Rogers et al., 2001). The ECST-R has acceptable rates of interrater reliability ($r = .97–1.0$) and internal consistency ($\alpha \geq .72$), according to recent studies with larger samples. A study of 149 defendants suggests that the ECST-R has a two-factor structure: (a) factual understanding, and (b) rational understanding and ability to consult with counsel (Rogers et al., 2001). The items that loaded most strongly on the latter factor reference the impact of psychotic symptoms on competency abilities and may provide too narrow a view of rational understanding and ability to consult. Moreover, this structure is inconsistent with the three-pronged version of the *Dusky* criteria that the measure was designed to assess. Thus, although the ECST-R is a promising tool, the data currently are too preliminary to support a recommendation for its clinical use.

Standardized, Normed Assessment Tool

Until recently, structuring interviews was viewed as the chief means for increasing the reliability and validity of competency assessment. Indeed, most tools are semistructured interviews that produce basic scores based on subjective ratings. Long ago, Grisso (1988; see also Grisso, 1992) called for a dramatically different approach to competency assessment. He argued for the creation of a competency assessment tool with such traditional psychometric properties as standardized administration, criterion-based scoring, and normative data. Moving the practice of competency assessment under the umbrella of traditional psychological testing would involve a shift from an idiographic (case-based) to a nomothetic (group-based) framework. As explained later, this move has important and controversial implications.

The MacArthur Research Network on Mental Health and the Law responded to Grisso's call by developing the MacArthur Competency Assessment Tool–Criminal Adjudication (MacCAT-CA; Hoge, Bonnie, Poythress, & Monahan, 1999; Poythress et al., 1999).[20] After the MacArthur Structured Assessment of the Competencies of Criminal Defendants (MacSAC-CD; Hoge, Poythress, et al., 1997), was pilot tested, refined, and field tested (Bonnie et al., 1997; Hoge, Bonnie, et al., 1997; Otto et al., 1998), the results were used to develop the streamlined MacCAT-CA. The MacCAT-CA was designed to assess three lower-order constructs (*understanding*, *reasoning*, and *appreciation*), and two higher-order constructs (*foundational competency/competency to assist counsel*, and *decisional competency*, see Bonnie, 1992) believed to comprise adjudicative competency.

These three lower-order constructs organize the MacCAT-CA's 22 items into three sections. The examiner begins by reading a hypothetical vignette to the defendant about a character who is charged with assault. This vignette grounds the first two sections (16 items). The first section assesses the defendant's ability to *understand* information about the legal system and the process. For each item, the defendant is asked a question related to the vignette and is awarded two points (items are rated 0, 1, 2) if he or she demonstrates full understanding. If the defendant earns less than two points, the examiner discloses the answer and asks the defendant to repeat the disclosure in his or her own words to assess separately the defendant's capacity to understand and his or her actual or preexisting understanding. The second section (8 items) assesses the defendant's ability to *reason*, or ability to (1) consider two pieces of factual information and identify the most important or legally relevant piece of information that the character in the vignette should disclose to his lawyer, and (2) weigh and evaluate the character's legal options.

The final section (6 items) assesses the defendant's ability to appreciate his or her own legal circumstances and situation. This section departs from the hypothetical vignette format to explore the defendant's beliefs and perceptions about his or her personal role as a defendant and how he or she will be treated during the course of adjudication. These items are scored on the basis of the reasons that the defendant provides for his or her judgment and whether they are plausible or implausible (i.e., grounded in reality or based on delusional beliefs). Administration of the MacCAT-CA requires approximately 25–55 minutes (Otto et al., 1998) and produces criterion-based scores that may be compared with normative data on 729 defendants who (1) have been adjudicated incompetent to stand trial, (2)

---

[20] The Competency Assessment Screening Test–Mental Retardation (CAST–MR; Everington & Luckasson, 1992) is also an exceptionally promising tool but is designed specifically for defendants with developmental disabilities, a topic addressed elsewhere in this book (see chap. 11).

are receiving mental health treatment in jail, or (3) are not receiving mental health treatment in jail.

The MacCAT-CA has been the subject of two main criticisms. First, Rogers et al. (2001) have argued that the measure fails to assess a defendant's ability to consult with counsel. Instead, they argue, the MacCAT assesses reasoning abilities that relate only peripherally to the defendant's ability to communicate and consult effectively with his or her attorney (i.e., the ability to identify relevant hypothetical information and to make decisions about plea bargaining). Second, and more critically, the nomothetic approach that underlies the MacCAT-CA has been criticized as inappropriate to the inherently idiographic nature of adjudicative competency (see Roesch, Hart, & Zapf, 1996; Veiel & Coles, 1999; Zapf, Skeem, & Golding, 2003). The nomothetic approach assumes that competency is a personal trait or ability that is relatively stable across situations. Because the construct of competency is context dependent, involving the functioning of a person within the demands of a particular legal situation (Golding & Roesch, 1988), it may not be amenable to this approach. Moreover, the nomothetic approach tends to assume that the trait or ability of interest is additive or dimensional. In contrast, the construct of competency involves "facets of competency [that] are singly necessary and jointly sufficient" (Roesch et al., 1996) for defining competency. Stated otherwise, adjudicative competency is a conjunctive concept that requires the presence of several potentially unrelated capacities (Cole & Pos, 1985). Depending on contextual characteristics of the case (e.g., consideration of "competency for what?" Rogers & Mitchell, 1991), a deficit in even one area may be sufficient for a finding of incompetency. With a nomothetic approach, such a deficit may result in only a slightly lower score on a particular dimensional scale. Again, adjudicative competency is an "open" construct that cannot be reduced to an inflexible list of requisite abilities or limited set of measurement rules (Zapf et al., 2003).

Despite these concerns, it is clear that the MacCAT-CA's structure and systematization are associated with relatively strong psychometric properties. These properties were examined based on the normative sample of 729 felony defendants (Otto et al., 1998; see also Rogers, Grandjean, et al., 2001). In this sample, the three scales of the MacCAT-CA demonstrated acceptable levels of internal consistency ($\alpha \geq .81$) and interrater reliability (intraclass $R \geq .75$). With respect to predictive utility, study participants who were competent, incompetent, and questionably competent obtained significantly different MacCAT-CA scores (Otto et al., 1998). Similarly, the three MacCAT-CA scales were moderately predictive of examiners' global ratings of competency ($r = .36-.49$). As noted earlier, Zapf and Roesch (1998) found relatively good levels of agreement between the FIT and MacCAT-CA, providing independent support for the scale's convergent validity.

Otto and colleagues (1998) report that support for the construct validity of the MacCAT-CA was "found in the pattern of correlations between the MacCAT-CA measures and select clinical variables" (p. 439). The MacCAT-CA scales were moderately positively (average $r = .29$) associated with a measure of intelligence, and moderately negatively associated ($r = -.29$) with a measure of psychopathology. In contrast with Otto and colleagues' (1998) assertion that these relationships support the construct validity of the MacCAT-CA, Zapf and colleagues (2003) have argued that incompetency should not be confounded with psychopathology or retardation. The MacCAT-CA's strength of relation to intelligence and psychopathology is similar to that of its relation to clinical ratings of competency, which raises issues about its discriminant validity.

The construct validity of the MacCAT-CA has not been supported by confirmatory factor analyses conducted with the original normative sample (Zapf et al., 2003) nor with exploratory factor analyses conducted with an independent sample of 149 mentally disordered offenders (Rogers et al., 2001). For example, Zapf and colleagues (2003) found that neither the three-factor model in which the scale is organized (understanding, reasoning, and appreciation) nor the two-factor model consistent with Bonnie's theory (competency to assist counsel; decisional competency) fit the normative data well. Their findings are consistent with those of Rogers and colleagues (2001), who found that the items based on the hypothetical vignette tended to form one factor, whereas those based on the defendant's personal case loaded on another. Thus, the factor structure appears more a function of method variance (or the cognitive functions tapped by a particular method) than theoretical coherence.

In short, the MacCAT-CA generally appears to represent a sound normative approach to assessing adjudicative competency. The measure is unique in its attempt to assess systematically reasoning and decision-making capacities relevant to competency. The MacCAT-CA's primary weakness lies in the fact that, however appealing norms may be, in the end such scores still need to be linked to individual and contextualized factors, as is acknowledged in the test manual. Examiners who use the MacCAT-CA must heed its creators' advice that the tool cannot be the sole basis for a competency assessment and is not intended as a "test" of competency (Poythress et al., 1999). Given the issues raised earlier, it is clear that the MacCAT-CA must be accompanied by case-specific inquiries about a defendant's psycholegal abilities and consideration of his or her unique case context. Moreover, the MacCAT-CA must also be accompanied by a careful assessment of psychopathology, given that it does not include scales for assessing symptoms.

Advancing Assessment Technology

This review of contemporary normative, interview-based, and screening tools for assessing adjudicative competency suggests that there have been substantial technological advances in the field over recent years. Nevertheless, it is clear that issues remain to be resolved in future research. First, many of these measures have been criticized for their insufficient coverage of the competency construct. Most screening tools (CST, GCCT) and some interview tools (CAI, FIT-R) appear to assess only basic factual knowledge or "foundational" competency. Fewer tools (MacCAT-CA, ECST-R, and IFI-R) also appear to assess the rational knowledge and decisional capacities deemed crucial to conceptualizations of adjudicative competency in the United States. The ability of any of these tools (but perhaps particularly the MacCAT-CA) to operationalize defendants' ability to consult with counsel has yet to be established. Notably, only the IFI-R appears to assess directly relevant "other competencies" that may be embraced by adjudicative competency. Ideally, these measures' coverage of the competency construct will be better defined and, if necessary, improved via future research. These investigations should move beyond factor analytic studies and "eyeball analyses" of content to comparisons of scores on various measures with independent expert ratings of the basic *Dusky* facets and relevant aspects of "other competencies."

Second, extant data do not speak to the issue of whether normative or interview-based tools for assessing adjudicative competency are more reliable and valid. As we are reminded by Roesch and colleagues (1996), "any improvement with respect to internal validity and statistical conclusion validity that stem from increased structure and systematization are achieved at the expense of reduced external and construct validity" (p. 110). Nevertheless, because normative and interview-based tools have not been subjected to a comparative trial, the extent to which the former possess relatively greater reliability and internal validity, and the latter possess greater external and construct validity is an open empirical question. The nature of this comparative trial should be responsive to two issues that have plagued past research on competency assessment tools.

First, although these leading approaches to assessing adjudicative competency differ in their theoretical structures, in practice they may lead to the same professional conclusion in all but the most difficult cases. Thus, the comparison will be strongest if conducted with "gray area" or challenging cases. As noted earlier, the vast majority of defendants who are referred for competency evaluations are deemed competent to stand trial. An additional proportion of defendants may be clearly "incompetent." Thus, the best test of the discriminative power of these tools occurs in cases in which defendants are neither clearly competent nor incompetent (perhaps those who would score in the "questionable" range on a competency screening tool). Second, the criterion for assessing the predictive utility of the measures must be chosen carefully. In past research, researchers have relied heavily on judicial or staff findings as a criterion representing "true" competency status. Since judges typically accept the conclusory opinion of an evaluator, defining judicial agreement as a criterion for accurate assessment is tautological. Similarly, if some staff evaluators conduct unstructured or unsystematic competency assessments, their findings may represent an inappropriate basis for assessing validity. This "criterion problem" (Golding & Roesch, 1988) in assessing the predictive validity of competency determinations may be remedied, as it has in the past (Schreiber et al., 1987) by using the consensus competency judgments of a blue-ribbon panel of forensic and legal experts as the criterion. Close examination of the reasons for disagreement among competing instruments, mirroring the best principles of cross-examination, may be a valuable method for exploring the relative construct validity of semistructured and norm-based assessment tools.

As such research accumulates, it will further inform practitioners' choice of a competency assessment tool. As noted earlier, we strongly recommend that such tools be used to increase the reliability of the data collection and decision-making process. However, even in the unlikely event that a "perfect" test for assessing competency was identified, the availability of that tool would not ensure high quality competency assessment practices. In the final section of this chapter, we provide general recommendations for completing and communicating evaluations of adjudicative competency that meet contemporary professional and ethical standards of practice.

IMPROVING COMPETENCY ASSESSMENT PRACTICES

Over the past decade, a growing number of studies have focused on the practice of competency assessment by systematically analyzing examiners' evaluations and reports (Heilbrun & Collins, 1995; Heilbrun, Rosenfeld, Warren, & Collins, 1994; LaFortune & Nicholson, 1995; Robbins, Waters, & Herbert, 1997; Skeem et al., 1998). Theses studies consistently indicate that even now, "the level of practice falls far short of professional aspirations for the field" (Nicholson & Norwood, 2000, p. 9). In this concluding section, we summarize five recommendations for improving evaluations of competency to stand trial, based on common problems identified in these investigations (see also Skeem & Golding, 1998). Because the standards of accountability for forensic evaluation are higher than those for traditional clinical assessment (American Psychological Association, 1992; Committee on Ethical Guidelines for Forensic Psychologists, 1991; Grisso, 1988), we encourage examiners to apply these recommendations.

Use the Right Tools

First, we recommend that examiners use the right tools. The right tools are those that directly target the relevant psycholegal issue, that is, competency to stand trial. Examiners would do well to use one of the promising competency assessment tools reviewed above to structure their assessments. Use of these tools, with clear recognition of their necessary limitations, is likely to enhance the reliability and quality of the competency assessment. Nevertheless, examiners rarely use them (e.g., Skeem et al., 1998).

In contrast, as noted previously, examiners use traditional clinical instruments relatively often (e.g., Heilbrun & Collins, 1995; Skeem et al., 1998). Historically, examiners have been criticized for relying on such tools and failing to explain their relationship to the defendants' competence (Eizenstadt, 1968;

Elwork, 1984; Grisso, 1986, 1987). Because psychological constructs like personality and intelligence do not translate neatly into adjudicative competency, examiners would be better served by using specialized competency assessment tools than traditional clinical ones. Measures of clinical constructs that may relate to the legal issue of the defendant's competency may be used when *relevant* and necessary (see Heilbrun, 1992).

Get the Right Information

Second, we recommend that examiners supplement their use of a promising competency assessment tool with additional information obtained both within and outside the interview. In the interview, the examiner must make inquiries about competency domains that are relevant to the particular case (see Table 9.1) but may not be covered well by the competency assessment tool applied. Moreover, when competency deficits are identified through the use of the tool or interview, careful inquiries must be made to determine whether the deficit is based on a symptom of mental illness or disability. Again, the central issue with respect to adjudicative competency is the link between psycholegal deficits and psychopathology.

Clearly, information obtained within the interview should be supplemented with third-party sources of information. In practice, examiners rarely secure such information (Heilbrun & Collins, 1995; Heilbrun et al., 1994; Skeem et al., 1998). As observed by Grisso (1988), an "examiner will be at a considerable disadvantage in evaluating the defendant's competency . . . if the examiner does not know the basic facts of the case" (p. 41). The basic facts of the case are obtained by contacting key players (e.g., defense counsel) and obtaining necessary records (e.g., police, mental health). For example, defense counsel is a vital source of information for determining the *Pate* issue, the nature of the attorney-client relationship, and the contextual characteristics and likely demands of the defendant's case. Mental health records are crucial sources of information for assessing exaggeration or minimization of symptoms. The police report on the alleged offense forms the backbone of the information necessary to make an informed assessment of the defendant's capacity to disclose relevant information to counsel and appraisal of the charges and potential penalties (Golding, 1993). For these reasons, we strongly recommend that third-party sources of information be routinely consulted in conducting competency assessments. Examiners must make specific and, if necessary, repeated efforts to obtain as much information as is reasonably possible when completing the evaluation.

Take Context Seriously

Third, in determining what competency inquiries to add to the interview and how to weigh any competency deficits, examiners should take the context of the case seriously. As discussed at the opening of this chapter, adjudicative competency is, at its core, an open-textured, context-dependent construct. Thus, when attempting to assess whether a defendant is competent, an examiner must ask him or herself, "Competent for what?" (Rogers & Mitchell, 1991). Apparently, examiners rarely consider the likely demands of the defendant's case in assessing competency. For example, despite the fact that the vast majority of criminal cases (over 90%) are resolved via plea bargain, we have found that examiners rarely (12%) address a defendant's understanding of the implications of a guilty plea (Skeem et al., 1998).

Generally, examiners tend to emphasize minimal competence abilities to the exclusion of higher-order, decisional capacities that lie at the heart of the "rational" language of the *Dusky* standard (Nicholson et al., 1995; Skeem et al., 1998). Given that all defendants must choose their basic legal strategy, and most must be capable of competently waiving the rights involved in pleading guilty, examiners should routinely assess a defendant's capacity for reasoned choice among relevant legal options. Although it is infinitely easier merely to assess such basic abilities as whether the defendant knows the name of his or her charge, there are compelling reasons for also ensuring that the defendant's reasoning with respect to his or her legal choices is clear (for guidance, see Skeem and Golding, 1998).

To address the issue of "Competent for what?" examiners must weigh any identified psycholegal deficits against the likely demands of the case, considering such factors as the severity of the charges, any fundamental constitutional rights that may be waived (e.g., right to counsel, to a jury trial, against self-incrimination), and the qualities of the defense attorney. Unfortunately, extant research suggests that examiners rarely (12%) or never (0%) assess the congruence between a defendant's abilities and his or her case context (Skeem et al., 1998; Robbins et al., 1998, respectively). We recommend that examiners routinely conceptualize and assess adjudicative competency as a context-textured construct.

As mentioned earlier, we also recommend that examiners clearly specify the limits of generalizability associated with their competency assessments in their reports to the court (see "Competency to proceed *pro se* and plead guilty"). The decisions that defendants will actually face are difficult to predict. Defendants may change their mind about their case (as in *Godinez*), or the case situation itself may change. Because competency for one purpose (e.g., pleading guilty) is unlikely to generalize to another (e.g., proceeding *pro se*), it is important to clearly communicate which domains were and were not actually assessed (Grisso et al., 1995; Whittemore, Ogloff, & Roesch, 1997).

Test and Substantiate Your Conclusions

Fourth, during the evaluation process and while you are writing the evaluation report, carefully test your conclusions and substantiate them with clear data and reasoning. As noted by Skeem and Golding (1998):

The trier of fact determines the weight to be assigned to an examiner's opinion by evaluating the strength and persuasiveness of the expert's analysis of the data. When examiners fail to specify the reasoning underlying their conclusions, they preempt the trier of fact from arriving at an independent and informed opinion and thereby usurp the judicial decision making role. Thus, it is essential that examiners specifically communicate their process of data interpretation to the courts. Moreover, psychologists have an ethical obligation to substantiate their conclusions in forensic reports by carefully documenting their factual bases. (p. 362, citations omitted)

Nevertheless, extant data suggest that examiners rarely substantiate their conclusions about a defendant's competency deficits (Robbins et al., 1997; Skeem et al., 1998). Most notably, examiners rarely address the heart of the competency doctrine by describing *how* a particular competency deficit is related to symptoms of psychopathology or intellectual impairment. Because competency deficits based on malingering, ignorance, or transient states (e.g., fatigue, noncompliance) are not sufficient bases for incompetence, they must be ruled out. It is not enough that psychopathology and competency deficits merely coexist, given that even defendants with mental disorders can and do exhibit competency deficits based on factors other than psychopathology. In short, an examiner must demonstrate that a deficit is caused by mental illness or disability.

Obtain Specialized Forensic Training

Fifth, we recommend that examiners obtain specialized didactic training and expert supervision in conducting assessments of adjudicative competency. Any expertise attained must be maintained by keeping abreast of new legal and technological developments in the field. Most problems that have been identified with competency evaluations may be attributable to a lack of formal specialized training. Examiners who rely upon their basic skills for assessing psychopathology and attempt to generalize these skills to competency assessment are likely to fall short across key dimensions. Their evaluations may resemble minimally modified standard clinical assessments. As concluded by Skeem and Golding (1998): "Given their lack of familiarity with the competence construct, these examiners apparently focused primarily upon assessing psychopathology. If psychopathology was present concomitantly with even minimal psycholegal impairment, they often deemed the defendant incompetent *without* describing the link between the psychopathology and psycholegal impairment and *without* considering the context of the case" (p. 365, citations omitted).

Informally reading articles or attending two- to three-day workshops is unlikely to be sufficient for improving the quality of competency evaluations (see Skeem et al., 1998). Comprehensive workshops accompanied by supervised evaluation are likely to be substantially more effective (Melton et al., 1985), if comprehensive predoctoral or postdoctoral training is not an option.

Conclusion

In this chapter, we have analyzed conceptualizations of adjudicative competency, alternative measures of the competency construct, and common problems in assessing competency in practice. Future research needs to examine the comparative strengths and weaknesses of the most robust and clinically useful measures. To date, only one comparative study has been published. Regardless of the availability of several good measures, the quality of typical forensic practice leaves much to be desired. We have attempted to propose practice guidelines that will assist both novice and experienced examiners. Two relatively recent developments hold promise for narrowing the gap between professional standards and practice in competency assessment. First, several states are developing (a) more stringent requirements for certifying clinicians as forensic examiners, and (b) systems for monitoring report quality through such mechanisms as peer review (see Appelbaum, 1992; Farkas et al., 1997). Second, with the recent creation of a specialty of forensic psychology, systems for credentialing and training are likely to become more systematized (see Otto & Heilbrun, 2002). With the institution of such measures, the quality of forensic assessments and reports would improve to a much greater extent over the next two decades than they have in the past.

References

American Bar Association (1989). *Criminal justice mental health standards.* Buffalo, NY: Author.
American Psychological Association (1992). Ethical principles of psychologists and code of conduct. *American Psychologist, 47,* 1597–1611.
Appelbaum, P. (1992). Forensic psychiatry: The need for self-regulation. *Bulletin of the American Academy of Psychiatry and Law, 20,* 153–162.
Appelbaum, P. (1994). *Almost a revolution: Mental health law and the limits of change.* New York: Oxford.
Bagby, R. M., Nicholson, R. A., Rogers, R., & Nussbaum, D. (1992). Domains of Competency to Stand Trial. *Law and Human Behavior, 16 (5),* 491–507.
Barnard, G., Nicholson, R. A., Hankins, G. C., Raisani, K. K., et al. (1992). Itemmetric and scale analysis of a new Computer-Assisted Competency Assessment Instrument (CADCOMP). *Behavioral Sciences and the Law, 10 (3),* 419–435.
Barnard, G. W., Thomson, J. W., Freeman, W. C., Robbins, L., et al. (1991). Competency to Stand Trial: Description and initial evaluation of a new computer assessment tool (CADCOMP). *Bulletin of the American Academy of Psychiatry and the Law, 19 (4),* 367–381.
Bennet, G. (1985). A guided tour through selected ABA standards relating to incompetence to stand trial. *Georgetown Law Review, 53,* 375–413.
Bonnie, R. J. (1992). The competence of criminal defendants: A theoretical reformulation. *Behavioral Sciences and the Law, 10,* 291–316.
Bonnie, R. J., Hoge, S. K., Monahan, J., Eisenberg, M., & Feucht-Haviar, T. (1997). The MacArthur Adjudicative Competency Study: A comparison of criteria for

assessing the competence of criminal defendants. *Journal of the American Academy of Psychiatry and the Law, 25 (3)*, 249–259.

Boykin v. Alabama, 359 U.S. 238 (1969).

Brakel, S. (1974). Presumption, bias, and incompetency in the criminal process. *Wisconsin Law Review*, 1105–1130.

Cole, E. M., & Pos, R. (1985). Assessment of fitness to stand trial: The need for a profile rather than a scale. *Psychological Reports, 57 (3, Pt.2)*, 1051–1054.

Colorado v. Connelly, 479 U.S. 157 (1986).

Committee on Ethical Guidelines for Forensic Psychologists (1991). Specialty guidelines for forensic psychologists. *Law and Human Behavior, 15*, 655–665.

Cooper v. Oklahoma, 116 S. Ct. 1373 (1996).

Criminal Code of Canada, R.S.C., c.C-46, as am. (1985).

Cruise, K. R., & Rogers, R. (1998). An Analysis of Competency to Stand Trial: An integration of case law and clinical knowledge. *Behavioral Sciences and the Law, 16*, 35–50.

Davis, D. L. (1985). Treatment planning for the patient who is incompetent to stand trial. *Hospital and Community Psychiatry, 36 (3)*, 268–271.

Drope v. Missouri, 420 U. S. 162 (1975).

Dusky v. United States, 362 U.S. 402 (1960).

Eizenstadt, S. (1968). Mental competency to stand trial. *Harvard Civil Rights–Civil Liberties Law Review, 4*, 379–403.

Elwork, A. (1984). Psychological assessments, diagnosis and testimony: A new beginning. *Law and Human Behavior, 8*, 197–203.

Elwork, A. (1992). Psycholegal treatment and intervention: The next challenge. *Law and Human Behavior, 16 (2)*, 175–183.

Estelle v. Smith, 451 U.S. 454 (1981).

Everington, C. T., & Luckasson, R. (1992). *Competence Assessment to Stand Trial for Defendants with Mental Retardation (CAST-MR)*. Worthington, OH: IDS Publishing.

Fare v. Michael C., 442 U.S. 707 (1976).

Faretta v. California, 422 U.S. 806 (1975).

Farkas, G., DeLeon, P., & Newman, R. (1997). Sanity examiner certification: An evolving national agenda. *Professional Psychology: Research & Practice, 28*, 73–76.

Florida Rules of Criminal Procedure §3.211 (2002).

Frith's Case, 22 Howes' State Trials 307, 318 (1790).

Godinez v. Moran, 113 S.Ct. 2680 (1993).

Golding, S. L. (1992). Studies of incompetent defendants: Research and social policy implications. *Forensic Reports, 5*, 77–83.

Golding, S. L. (1993). *Interdisciplinary Fitness Interview–Revised: A training manual.* Unpublished monograph from State of Utah Division of Mental Health.

Golding, S. L., Eaves, D., & Kowaz, A. (1989). The assessment, treatment and community outcome of insanity acquittees. *International Journal of Law and Psychiatry, 12*, 149–179.

Golding, S. L., & Roesch, R. (1983). The Interdisciplinary Fitness Interview. *Newsletter of the Division of Psychology and Law, 4*, 8–10.

Golding, S. L., & Roesch, R. (1987). The assessment of criminal responsibility: A historical approach to a current controversy. In I. B. Weiner & A. K. Hess (Eds.), *Handbook of forensic psychology* (pp. 395–436). New York: Wiley.

Golding, S. L., & Roesch, R. (1988). Competency for adjudication: An international analysis. In D. Weisstub (Ed.), *Law and mental health: International perspectives, Vol. 4* (pp. 73–109). New York: Pergamon.

Golding, S. L., Roesch, R., & Schreiber, J. (1984). Assessment and conceptualization of competency to stand trial: Preliminary data on the Interdisciplinary Fitness Interview. *Law and Human Behavior, 8 (3–4)*, 321–334.

Golding, S. L., Skeem, J. L., Roesch, R., & Zapf, P. A. (1999). The assessment of criminal responsibilty: Current controversies. In A. K. Hess & I. B. Weiner (Eds.), *The handbook of forensic psychology* (2nd ed.) (pp. 327–349). New York: Wiley.

Goode v. Florida, 365 So. 2d 381 (Sup. Ct. Florida, 1978), cert den 99 S. Ct. 2419.

Gothard, S., Viglione, D. J., Meloy, J. R., & Sherman, M. (1995). Detection of malingering in competency to stand trial evaluations. *Law and Human Behavior, 19 (5)*, 493–505.

Greenfeld, L. A., & Snell, R. L. (1999). *Bureau of Justice Statistics Special Reports: Women offenders.* Washington, DC: US Department of Justice.

Grisso, T. (1986). *Evaluating competencies* (see especially, Waiver of rights to silence and legal counsel, pp. 11–155). New York: Plenum.

Grisso, T. (1987). The economic and scientific future of forensic psychological assessment. *American Psychologist, 42*, 831–839.

Grisso, T. (1988). *Competency to stand trial evaluations: A manual for practice.* Sarasota, FL: Professional Resource Exchange.

Grisso, T. (1992). Five-year research update (1986–1990): Evaluations for competence to stand trial. *Behavioral Sciences & the Law, 10 (3)*, 353–369.

Grisso, T. (1998). *Instruments for assessing understanding and appreciation of Miranda rights.* Sarasota, FL: Professional Resource Press.

Grisso, T., & Appelbaum, P. S. (1998a). *Assessing competence to consent to treatment: A guide for physicians and other health professionals.* London: Oxford University Press.

Grisso, T., & Appelbaum, P. S. (1998b). *MacArthur Competence Assessment Tool for Treatment (MacCAT-T).* Sarasota, FL: Professional Resource Press.

Grisso, T., Appelbaum, P., Mulvey, E., & Fletcher, K. (1995). The MacArthur treatment competence study II: Measures of abilities related to competence to consent to treatment. *Law & Human Behavior, 19*, 127–148.

Gudjonsson, G. H. (1992). *The psychology of interrogations, confessions and testimony.* Chichester, UK: Wiley.

Gudjonsson, G. H., & Sigurdsson, J. F. (1999). The Gudjonsson Confession Questionnaire–Revised (GCQ–R): Factor structure and its relationship with personality. *Personality and Individual Differences, 27 (5)*, 953–968.

Hart, S., & Hare, R. (1992). Predicting fitness for trial: The relative power of demographic, criminal and clinical variables. *Forensic Reports, 5*, 53–54.

Heilbrun, K. (1992). The role of psychological testing in forensic assessment. *Law & Human Behavior, 16*, 257–272.

Heilbrun, K., & Collins, S. (1995). Evaluations of trial competency and mental state at time of offense: Report characteristics. *Professional Psychology: Research and Practice, 26*, 61–67.

Heilbrun, K., Rosenfeld, B., Warren, J., & Collins, S. (1994). The use of third-party information in forensic assessments: A two-state comparison. *Bulletin of the American Academy of Psychiatry and the Law, 22 (4)*, 551–560.

Hoge, S. K., Bonnie, R. J., Poythress, N., & Monahan, J. (1999). *The MacArthur Competence Assessment Tool–Criminal adjudication.* Odessa, FL: Psychological Assessment Resources.

Hoge, S. K., Bonnie R. J., Poythress, N., Monahan, J., Einsenberg, M., Feucht-Haviar, T. (1997). The MacArthur adjudicative competency study: Development and validation of a research instrument. *Law and Human Behavior, 21 (2),* 483–489.

Hoge, S. K., Poythress, N., Bonnie, R. J., Monahan, J., Einsenberg, M., & Feucht-Haviar, T. (1997). The MacArthur adjudicative competency study: Diagnosis, psychopathology, and competence related abilities. *Behavioral Sciences and the Law, 15 (3),* 329–345.

Huff, C., Rattner, A., & Sagarin, E. (1996). *Convicted but innocent: Wrongful conviction and public policy.* Thousand Oaks, CA: Sage.

Inbau, F., Reid, J., & Buckley, J. (1986). *Criminal interrogation and confessions* (3rd ed.). Baltimore, MD: Williams and Wilkins.

Jackson v. Indiana, 402 U.S. 715 (1972).

Johnson, W. G., & Mullet, N. (1987). Georgia Court Competency Test–R. In M. Herson & A. S. Bellack (Eds.), *Dictionary of behavioral assessment techniques* (p. 234). Elmsford, NY: Pergamon.

Johnson v. Zerbst, 304 U.S. 458 (1938).

Kassin, S. M. (1997). The psychology of confession evidence. *American Psychologist, 52 (3),* 221–233.

Laboratory of Community Psychiatry. (1973). *Competency to stand trial and mental illness.* (DHEW Publication No. ADM77–103). Rockville, MD: Department of Health, Education and Welfare.

Lafortune, K. A., & Nicholson, R. A. (1995). How adequate are Oklahoma's mental health evaluations for determining competency in criminal proceedings? The bench and the bar respond. *Journal of Psychiatry and Law, 23 (2),* 231–262.

Lawrence v. Georgia, 265 Ga. 310; 454 S.E.2d 446 (1995).

Leo, R. A. (1996). Inside the interrogation room. *Journal of Criminal Law and Criminology, 86 (2),* 266–303.

Lipsitt, P. D., Lelos, D., & McGarry, A. L. (1971). Competency for trial: A screening instrument. *American Journal of Psychiatry, 128 (1),* 105–109.

Luria, R., & Guziec, R. (1981). Comparative description of the SADS and PSE. *Schizophrenia Bulletin, 7 (2),* 248–257.

McDonald, D. A., Nussbaum, D. S., & Bagby, R. M. (1991). Reliabilty, validity, and utility of the Fitness Interview Test. *Canadian Journal of Psychiatry, 36,* 480–484.

Medina v. California, 112 S. Ct. 2572 (1992).

Melton, G., Petrila, J., Poythress, N., & Slobogin, C. (1987). *Psychological evaluations for the courts: A handbook for mental health professionals and lawyers.* New York: Guilford Press.

Melton, G. B., Weithorn, L. A., & Slobogin, C. (1985). *Community mental health centers and the courts: An evaluation of community-based forensic services.* Lincoln: University Nebraska Press.

Miles v. Stainer, 108 F. 3d 1109 (Ninth Cir. 1997).

Miranda v. Arizona, 394 U.S. 436 (1966).

Moran v. Burbine, 475 U.S. 412 (1986).

Mosley, D., Thyer, B. A., & Larrison, C. (2001). Development and preliminary validation of the Mosley Forensic Competency Scale. *Journal of Human Behavior in the Social Environment, 4 (1),* 41–48.

Mumley, D., Grisso, T., & Tillbrook, C. (2003). Five-year research update, 1996–2000: Evaluations for competence to stand trial. *Behavioral Sciences and the Law, 21,* 329–350.

Nelson, K. T. (1989). The patient-litigant's knowledge of the law: Importance in treatment to restore sanity and in competency proceedings. *American Journal of Forensic Psychology, 7 (3),* 29–41.

Nicholson, R. A., Briggs, S. R., & Robertson, H. C. (1988). Instruments for assessing competency to stand trial: How do they work? *Professional Psychology: Research and Practice, 19 (4),* 383–394.

Nicholson, R. A., & Kugler, K. E. (1991). Competent and incompetent defendants: A quantitative review of comparative research. *Psychological Bulletin, 109,* 355–370.

Nicholson, R., LaFortune, K., Norwood, S., & Roach, R. (1995). Pretrial competency evaluations in Oklahoma: Report characteristics and consumer satisfaction. Paper presented at the American Psychological Association's 103rd Annual Convention, New York, August 1995.

Nicholson, R. A., & Norwood, S. (2000). The quality of forensic psychological assessments, reports, and testimony: Acknowledging the gap between promise and practice. *Law and Human Behavior, 24 (1),* 9–44.

Nicholson, R. A., Robertson, H. C., Johnson, W. G., & Jensen, G. (1988). A comparison of instruments for assessing competency to stand trial. *Law and Human Behavior, 12 (1),* 313–321.

Nottingham, E. J., & Mattson, R. E. (1981). A Validation Study of the Competency Screening Test. *Law and Human Behavior, 5 (4),* 329–335.

Nussbaum, D., Mamak, M., Tremblay, H., Wright, P., & Callaghan, J. (1998). The METFORS Fitness Questionnaire (MFQ): A self-report measure for screening competency to stand trial. *American Journal of Forensic Psychology, 16 (3),* 41–65.

Otto, R. K., & Heilbrun, K. (2002) The practice of forensic psychology: A look toward the future in light of the past. *American Psychologist, 57 (1),* 5–18.

Otto, R. K., Poythress, N. G., Nicholson, R. A., Edens, J. F., Monahan, J., Bonnie, R. J., et al. (1998). Psychometric properties of the MacArthur Competence Assessment Tool–Criminal Adjudication (MacCAT-CA). *Psychological Assessment, 10,* 435–443.

Pate v. Robinson 383 U.S. 375 (1966).

Pendleton, L. (1980). Treatment of persons found incompetent to stand trial. *American Journal of Psychiatry, 137 (9),* 1098–1100.

Peszke, M. (1980). Competency to stand trial: An abridgment of due process. *Hospital and Community Psychiatry, 31,* 132–133.

Poythress, N. G., Hoge, S. K., Bonnie, R. J., Monahan, J., Eisenberg, M., & Feucht-Haviar, T. (1998). The competence-related abilities of women criminal defendants. *Journal of the American Academy of Psychiatry and the Law, 26 (2),* 215–222.

Poythress, N., Nicholson, R., Otto, R. K., Edens, J. F., Bonnie, R. J., Monahan, J., et al. (1999). *The MacArthur Competence Assessment Tool–Criminal Adjudication: Professional manual.* Odessa, FL: Psychological Assessment Resources.

Poythress, N., & Stock, N. (1980). Competency to stand trial: A historical review and some new data. *Journal of Psychiatry and Law, 8,* 131–146.

Randolph, J. J., Hicks, T., & Mason, D. (1981). The Competency Screening Test: A replication and extension. *Criminal Justice and Behavior, 8 (4),* 471–481.

Rattner, A. (1988). Convicted but innocent: Wrongful conviction and the criminal justice system. *Law and Human Behavior, 12,* 283.

Redding, R. E. (1997). Depression in jailed women defendants and its relationship to their adjudicative competence. *Journal of the American Academy of Psychiatry and the Law, 25 (1)*, 105–119.

Regina v. Taylor, 77 C.C.C. (3d) 551 (Ont. C.A. 1992).

Reich, J., & Tookey, L. (1986). Disagreements between court and psychiatrist on competency to stand trial. *Psychiatry Journal of Clinical, 47*, 616–623.

Riggins v. Nevada, 504 U.S. 127, 112 S.Ct. 1810 (1992).

Riley, S. E. (1998). Competency to stand trial adjudication: A comparison of female and male defendants. *Journal of the American Academy of Psychiatry and the Law, 26 (2)*, 223–240.

Robbins, E., Waters, J., & Herbert, P. (1997). Competency to stand trial evaluations: A study of actual practice in two states. *Journal of the American Academy of Psychiatry and the Law, 25*, 469–483.

Roesch, R., & Golding, S. L. (1979). The treatment and disposition of defendants found incompetent to stand trial: A review and a proposal. *International Journal of Law and Psychiatry, 2*, 349–370.

Roesch, R., & Golding, S. (1980). *Competency to stand trial.* Urbana-Champaign: University of Illinois Press.

Roesch, R., & Golding, S. L. (1987). Defining and assessing competency to stand trial. In I. B. Weiner & A. K. Hess (Eds.), *Handbook of forensic psychology* (pp. 378–394). Oxford: Wiley.

Roesch, R., Hart, S. D., & Zapf, P. A. (1996). Conceptualizing and assessing competency to stand trial: Implication and applications of the MacArthur Treatment Competence Model. *Psychology, Public Policy, & Law, 2 (1)*, 96–113.

Roesch, R., Webster, C. D., & Eaves, D. (1984). *The Fitness Interview Test: A method for assessing fitness to stand trial.* Toronto: University of Toronto Centre of Criminology.

Roesch, R., Zapf, P. A., Eaves, D., & Webster, C. D. (1998). *The Fitness Interview Test* (rev. ed.). Burnaby, BC: Mental Health, Law, & Policy Institute, Simon Fraser University.

Rogers, R., Grandjean, N., Tillbrook, C. E., Vitacco, M. J., & Sewell, K. W. (2001). Recent interview-based measures of competency to stand trial: A critical review augmented with research data. *Behavioral Sciences and the Law, 19*, 503–518.

Rogers, R., & Mitchell, C. N. (1991). *Mental health experts and the criminal courts.* Scarborough, ON: Thomson Professional Publishing Canada.

Rogers, R., Ustad, K. L., Sewell, K. W., & Reinhart, V. (1996). Dimensions of incompetency: A factor analytic study of the Georgia Court Competency Test. *Behavioral Sciences and the Law, 14*, 323–330.

Schreiber, J., Roesch, R., & Golding, S. (1987). An evaluation of procedures for assessing competency to stand trial. *Bulletin of the American Academy of Psychiatry and Law, 15*, 187–203.

Sell v. United States, 01–1862, (Eighth Circuit Court of Appeals, March 7, 2002).

Shatin, L. (1979). Brief form of the Competency Screening Tool for mental competence to stand trial. *Journal of Clinical Psychology, 35 (2)*, 464–467.

Shuy, R. (1998). *The language of confession, interrogation, and deception.* Thousand Oaks, CA: Sage.

Siegel, A. M., & Elwork, A. (1990). Treating incompetence to stand trial. *Law and Human Behavior, 14 (1)*, 57–65.

Silten, P. R., & Tullis, R. (1977). Mental competency in criminal proceedings. *Hastings Law Journal, 28*, 1053–1074.

Simon, R., & Shuman, D. (Eds.). (2002). *Retrospective assessment of mental states in litigation.* Washington, DC: American Psychiatric Publishing.

Skeem, J., & Golding, S.L. (1998). Community examiners' evaluations of competence to stand trial: Common problems and suggestions for improvement. *Professional Psychology: Research and Practice, 29*, 357–367.

Skeem, J. L., Golding, S. L., Cohn, N. B., & Berge, G. (1998). Logic and reliability of evaluations of competence to stand trial. *Law and Human Behavior, 22*, 519–547.

State v. Clemens, 2001 Ohio 3212 (Ct. App. Ohio, 7th District, March 23, 2001).

Stiles, P., Poythress, N., Hall, A., Falkenbach, D., & Williams, R. (2001). Improving understanding of research consent disclosures among persons with mental illness. *Psychiatric Services, 52*, 780–785.

United States v. Bradshaw, 690 F. 2d 704, 712 (9th Cir. 1982).

Ustad, K. L., Rogers, R., Sewell, K. W., & Guarnaccia, C. A. (1996). Restoration of competency to stand trial: Assessment with the Georgia Court Competency Test and the Competency Screening Test. *Law and Human Behavior, 20 (2)*, 131–145.

Utah Code Annotated §77-15-5 *et seq.* (2002).

Veiel, H. O. F., & Coles, E. M. (1999). Measuring unfitness to stand trial: Psychological analysis of a legal issue. *Canadian Journal of Psychiatry, 44*, 356–361.

Washington v. Harper, 494 U.S. 210, 211 (1990).

Whittemore, K. E., Ogloff, J. R. P., & Roesch, R. (1997). An investigation of competence to participate in legal proceedings in Canada. *Canadian Journal of Psychiatry, 42*, 869–875.

Wieter v. Settle, 193 F.Supp. 318 (1961), W. D. Mo.

Wildman, R. W., Batchelor, E. S., Thompson, L., Nelson, F. R., Moore, J. T., Patterson, M. E., et al. (1978). *The Georgia Court Competency Test: An attempt to develop a rapid, quantitative measure of fitness for trial.* Unpublished manuscript, Forensic Services Division, Central State Hospital, Milledgeville, GA.

Wildman, R. W., White, P. A., & Brandenburg, C. E. (1990). The Georgia Court Competency Test: The base rate problem. *Perceptual & Motor Skills, 70*, 1055–1058.

Williams, W., & Miller, K. (1981). The processing and disposition of incompetent mentally ill offenders. *Law and Human Behavior, 5*, 245–261.

Youtsey v. United States, 97 F. 937 (6th Cir. 1899).

Zapf, P. A. (2002). A comparison of competency statutes. Unpublished manuscript.

Zapf, P. A., & Roesch, R. (1997). Assessing fitness to stand trial: A comparison of institution-based evaluations and a brief screening interview. *Canadian Journal of Community Mental Health, 16 (1)*, 53–66.

Zapf, P. A., & Roesch, R. (2001). A comparison of the MacCAT-CA and the FIT for making determinations of competency to stand trial. *International Journal of Law and Psychiatry, 24*, 81–92.

Zapf, P. A., Skeem, J. L., & Golding, S. L. (2003). A critical empirical analysis of the factor structure of the MacArthur Competence Assessment Tool–Criminal Adjudication. Unpublished manuscript under review.

CHAPTER 10

ASSESSING MENTAL COMPETENCY IN THE ELDERLY

CRAIG YURY, RUTH A. GENTRY, HILLARY LEROUX, AND JANE E. FISHER

UNIVERSITY OF NEVADA, RENO

JEFFREY A. BUCHANAN

MINNEAPOLIS VA MEDICAL CENTER

MENTAL COMPETENCE

Psychologists' role in the determination of a client's mental competence is among the most extraordinary they play in society. Professional judgments about a client's mental competence have direct and profound consequences for the client's self-determination and autonomy. When a court must judge whether a defendant can stand trial, a physician requests information regarding whether a patient is competent to refuse treatment, or a family member attempts to gain guardianship over a cognitively impaired elderly person, reliance on psychologists' judgments in these circumstances can have a beneficial or devastating effect on the trajectory of their clients' lives. With this caveat in mind we approach the topic of psychologists' role in the assessment of mental competence.

This chapter will first examine various definitions of competence and evaluate their advantages and limitations. Following this review, an overview of diseases/disorders and the consequences of the normal aging process that can affect mental competence is presented in order to provide a context in which questions of competence emerge and to forge a pathway for conceptualizing the assessment process. We then present specific recommendations for the assessment process and review commonly used assessment methods. Finally, the chapter concludes with a discussion of ethical issues in research and health care with cognitively impaired persons.

Defining Competence

In attempting to establish a definition of *competence*, it is important to identify the context in which questions about mental competence are being raised. Gutheil and Appelbaum (2000) divide competence into two types: (1) competence to make decisions, and (2) competence to perform an act. Unfortunately, clear operational definitions of competence based on these distinctions have not emerged in the literature. Legal professionals, medical professionals, and psychologists employ unique definitions of competence that are specific to certain populations, settings, circumstances, and the like. With this in mind, we review decisional and performance-based forms of competence as they are applied in different circumstances and in making guardianship decisions.

Decision Making

Five basic questions have been identified in the literature as key in the determination of decisional competencies including the abilities to consent to treatment and to care for self and/or property: (1) Can the individual make and express choices about his or her life? (2) Are the outcomes of these choices reasonable? (3) Are the choices based on rational reasons? (4) Is the individual capable of understanding the personal implications of choices? (5) Does the individual understand the implications of choices about his or her life? (Appelbaum & Gutheil, 1991; Kapp, 1992; Smyer, Schaie, & Kapp, 1996). The relevance of these questions for the determination of competence depends upon the domain of functioning that is raising concern.

Legal definitions of competency have a critical role in assessing suspects' ability to waive any of their legal rights. Federal courts in the United States require that defendants have a basic understanding of interrogation rights as opposed to an appreciation of the consequences of waiving these rights (*Colorado v. Connelly*, 1986). *Dusky v. the United States* (1960) established the American standard for competency to stand trial. It requires that a defendant have "sufficient present ability to consult with his lawyer with a reasonable degree of rational understanding—and whether he has a rational as well as factual understanding of the proceedings against him." Thus, a defendant does not have to demonstrate any ability to reason or appreciate consequences of his or her decision to waive interrogation rights but must have some appreciation and understanding of court proceeding to stand trial.

The criterion of possessing a basic understanding of one's legal rights implies that an individual is able to make a decision that will be most beneficial to him or her. From these definitions it is clear that an individual who may not be able to make a wise decision regarding his or her legal rights can still meet the criteria for competency. Furthermore, diagnosed mental illness is not a requisite for a determination of incompetence to waive interrogation rights. Courts consider criteria such as previous legal experience or education in making these determinations (Oberlander & Goldstein, 2001).

Within the medical domain, physicians are regularly confronted with the decision to respect or override a patient's decision to refuse life-preserving treatment. This decision is influenced by the physician's perception of the patient's ability to enact autonomy. The definition of *autonomy* has as its basis the ability to be a "good ruler" over oneself and includes: (1) the ability to adopt values, principles, and goals; (2) the ability to understand a situation; (3) the ability to make choices that reflect one's commitments; and (4) the ability to act on the choice(s) (Capozzi & Rhodes, 2002).

The medical perspective of competence adopts broader criteria than the legal perspective. Although both perspectives place an emphasis on an individual's ability to understand the facts and to invoke rational thinking or reasoning of the relevant facts, the medical perspective differs from the legal perspective in that it places a greater emphasis on the ability to logically tie values to facts, to reach a conclusion, and to adhere to the conclusion. The absence of a focus on an understanding of consequences has been characterized as a major shortcoming of the legal perspective.

Functional Abilities

The definition of competence to perform functional acts is focused on specific rather than a global determination of an individual's competence or incompetence to participate in decision making (see Smyer & Qualls, 1996, for an expanded discussion of this issue). This definition emphasizes the individual's functional abilities within a specific and current context. Questions regarding functional abilities emerge when there are safety concerns regarding an elderly person with a cognitive or physical disability. In this type of case the degree of congruence between an individual's functional abilities and the demands of the environment is pertinent for making judgement about an individual's safety or danger to self.

Willis (1996) offers a definition of functional abilities that focuses on what a person understands, believes, or can do. Within an assessment process based on this definition, each ability is evaluated in relation to a specific competency question. Judgments about the successful execution of a specific skill are not judged based on any specific topography, duration, or other type of quantitative measure. Instead, the definition is aimed at how well the skill serves the individual. Assessment of specific abilities (management of finances, self-care, etc.) informs a determination of the "least restrictive alternative" in order to provide support in only those domains for which competence is determined to be impaired.

Functional abilities are typically divided into two types: activities of daily living (ADLs) and instrumental activities of daily living (IADLs). ADLs include self-care activities such as feeding, toileting, bathing, and basic mobility. IADLs involve more complex tasks that require both physical and cognitive abilities, such as managing medications, shopping, managing finances, using transportation and the telephone, the use of household appliances, and meal preparation and nutrition.

Varying definitions of competence can have profound consequences for intervention. Assessment models that are based on skill performance assess an individual's ability to fulfill the function presented to him or her. Assuming that society values an individual's autonomy, a psychologist's approach to assessment is ethical to the extent that it produces outcomes that maximize the client's opportunities to exercise autonomy. Within the function-based model, the inability to perform a specific skill as operationalized or in a fashion that resembles how the majority performs the skill does not necessarily result in a negative judgment regarding the individual's mental competence. Unfortunately, the functional approach is not easily applied to the assessment of complex decision making. It is difficult to operationalize and hence reliably assess an individual's comprehension of the implications or consequences of a decision and alternative options.

Guardianship

Guardianship refers to the appointment, by a court, of a third party to assume decision making and handle the affairs of an individual whom the court has found to be "incompetent" or "incapacitated" (Hommel, 1996). Most courts require the filing of a medical report documenting the individual's disability. The report typically describes the nature of the disability, the individual's physical and mental condition, and the degree of impairment and limitations on decision-making ability (Fitten, 1999). Definitions of competence for the purpose of granting guardianship vary from state to state. In addition, definitions and assessment of competence vary depending on the reason guardianship is being sought. For instance, guardianship over financial affairs involves an assessment of decision-making competence, whereas guardianship of self-care issues involves an assessment of skill performance.

In the area of competence to make decisions, some states take a medicalized approach that requires that one or more types of disorders or conditions be present that render the individual disabled. The American Bar Association found that 34 states include "mental illness" among the specified disabilities, 15 include "mental retardation" or "developmental disability," 31 refer to chronic use of drugs or chronic intoxication, 15 include "advanced age," and 34 employ general terms such as "mental deficiency," "mental disability," or "in need of treatment" (Anderer, 1990). The Uniform Guardianship and Protective Proceeding Act (1997) defines an incompetent individual as "any person who is impaired by reason of mental illness, mental deficiency, physical illness or disability, chronic use of drugs, chronic intoxication, or other cause (except minority) to the extent of lacing sufficient understanding or capacity to make or communicate responsible decisions." Medicalized definitions such as this assume that there is an underlying disease or disorder that impairs the individual's ability to comprehend decisions. These definitions do not parse out the various domains of competency but instead result in a general, all-encompassing determination. The global nature of this approach precludes the assessment of functioning in areas in which the individual may still be competent to make decisions, thus increasing the risk of unnecessarily limiting an individual's autonomy.

As described earlier, physicians have been observed to overrule an individual's decision regarding treatment if the physician has sufficient reason to doubt that the individual understands the treatment options or their potential outcomes. Consistent with this practice, the Uniform Health Care Decisions Act (1993) states: "'Capacity' means an individual's ability to understand the significant benefits, risks, and alternatives to proposed health care, and to make and communicate a health-care decision." This definition is consistent with the previously described criteria in that it includes a clear understanding of the relevant facts or options and an appreciation of the potential outcomes.

Self-Care

Definitions of competency to care for self are typically based on a functional approach. Although many states utilize this approach, most emphasize the importance of the individual's not endangering him or herself. Alaska and Oregon, for example, focus on the ability to take care of the "essential requirements for the individual's physical health or safety." Some states, such as Minnesota, extend this criterion by specifying the essential requirements of proper self-care, including meeting personal needs for medical care, nutrition, clothing, shelter, or safety.

Physical Health and Mental Competency

Certain physiological, cognitive, and behavioral changes are considered to be part of the normal process of aging. Knowledge of healthy age-associated changes can inform the interpretation of findings of a competency evaluation and the determination of whether any observed deficits exceed what is expected given a client's age. The following sections will provide a brief overview of normal age-associated changes in cognitive abilities and changes associated with high-prevalence medical conditions in order to establish a context in which questions of competency tend to emerge. The degree to which these changes may impact decisions regarding competency will also be discussed.

Physiological Changes

Normal aging results in several structural brain changes, including brain atrophy, a decline in brain weight, and an enlargement of the ventricles (Vinters, 2001). Estimates indicate that there is an average lifetime loss of 7 to 10 percent of brain weight, with loss accelerating to a rate of 2–3 percent per year after the age of 65 (Vinters, 2001; Powers, 2000). Tissue loss is prominent in the cerebral cortex, where shrinkage in gyri (i.e., convolutions of the brain) and widening of sulci (i.e., grooves between gyri) are observed (Martin & Rubin, 1997). Brain areas showing more pronounced atrophy include the frontal and temporal lobes (Powers, 2000).

Subcortical areas such as the hippocampus, basal ganglia, and thalamus are also affected (Powers, 2000).

Age-associated neuronal changes have also been observed. For example, it appears as if normal aging is associated with both the death of neurons as well as the shrinkage of larger neurons that begins around age 60 (Martin & Rubin, 1997; Powers, 2000). Synaptic density also declines with age, particularly in the hippocampus (Haug & Eggers, 1991). Atrophy is also observed in the dendrites of aging neurons such that dendritic spines are lost and eventually dendritic shafts are lost (Powers, 2000).

Changes in Intellectual Functioning

Studies examining changes in intellectual functioning associated with age have produced several consistent findings. First, age-associated declines tend to occur on tasks that require speed. Second, longitudinal studies indicate that general intellectual functioning does not begin to decline until after age 60 and marked decline does not begin until age 80 (Schaie, 1996). Third, declines associated with aging tend to be more pronounced under conditions that are stressful or novel. Overall, Zarit and Zarit (1998) conclude, "At a functional level, the changes associated with aging probably do not affect performance of familiar activities" (p. 20).

Changes in Memory

Research has shown that certain changes in memory are consistently associated with nonpathological aging. Regarding short-term memory, one of the most robust findings is that older adults perform at lower levels than younger adults on tasks that involve working memory (i.e., tasks that require an individual to simultaneously store and process information) (Backman, Small, & Wahlin, 2001). Age difficulties are particularly pronounced when tasks are more complex, when a large amount of information is presented, and when the information must be manipulated (Salthouse & Babcock, 1991).

Long-term memory, semantic memory (i.e., recall of word, meaning, and grammar), and procedural memory (i.e., recall of motor learning) have generally been found to be unaffected by age (Zarit & Zarit, 1998). However, age-associated declines in episodic memory (i.e., the ability to remember a specific event) have been documented indicating poorer performance on tasks involving recall of information (Backman, Small, & Wahlin, 2001). When cognitive supports are provided (e.g., cued recall or recognition), age-associated differences tend to diminish. Declines in episodic memory tend to start in early adulthood and occur gradually over the lifespan (Backman, Small, & Wahlin, 2001).

Consistent findings regarding memory and aging also indicate that performance decrements occur when stimuli are presented at high rates, when distractions are present, and when the period allowed for recall is brief (Zarit & Zarit, 1998, p. 24). Although these age-associated declines can affect daily functioning, compensatory strategies such as writing down information, using mnemonics, or allowing more time to learn new material can be very useful and appear to limit the degree to which age-associated memory changes affect competency.

Specific Disorders Associated with Mental Competence

Dementia. Dementia is an umbrella term that refers to an acquired syndrome characterized by progressive decline in several areas of intellectual functioning that affects one's social or occupational functioning (Reichman, 2000). Prevalence estimates of dementia depend largely on the specific cause of dementia and vary widely depending on the criteria used to define the particular disorder. However, prevalence rates for dementia in those ages 65 and older generally range between 6 and 10 percent (Hendrie, 1997). The risk of dementia is clearly age associated (Bachman et al., 1993; Evans, 1996; Hendrie, 1997). In general, for most forms of dementia, onset before age 65 is rare. For those ages 65–70, prevalence estimates are approximately 1–2 percent, whereas for those ages 85 and older, prevalence estimates are between 25 percent and 30 percent (Albert & Drachman, 2000; Hendrie, 1997).

It has been estimated that 50 different conditions may cause dementia (Cummings, 1987). Although some conditions are reversible (e.g., vitamin B12 deficiencies, metabolic disturbance, normal pressure hydrocephalus), the most prevalent forms are currently irreversible (i.e., Alzheimer's disease and vascular dementia).

Alzheimer's Disease. Alzheimer's disease (AD) is the most common cause of degenerative dementia, accounting for up to 65 percent of all cases of dementia (Evans et al., 1989). The risk for developing AD increases with age, with prevalence rates increasing with each decade of life (Miller & Gustavson, 2000). It is estimated that up to 10 percent of individuals over the age of 65 suffer from AD (Evans et al., 1989).

AD is a progressive degenerative brain disorder that is associated with several changes in brain chemistry and brain pathology. Amyloid plaques and neurofibrillary tangles are two of the primary features of AD. Amyloid plaques are accumulations of degenerative nerve endings and other materials located near synapses, and neurofibrillary tangles are twisted strands of protein inside neurons (Zarit & Zarit, 1998, p. 40). Deficits in the neurotransmitter acetylcholine are also observed in persons with AD (Perry et al., 1978). Neuroimaging studies have found general cerebral atrophy in persons with AD (Miller & Gustavson, 2000) with the temporal and parietal lobes, anterior frontal cortex, and hippocampus most affected (Cummings & Benson, 1992).

The cognitive impairments observed in the early stages of AD can vary considerably but are generally characterized by deficits in memory and at least one other domain of cognitive functioning. Memory and learning deficits are often the first symptoms observed. Immediate (i.e., primary) and recent (i.e., secondary) memory for verbal and visual material is often impaired early in the disease process (Zec, 1993). In addition, individuals with AD will often not respond well to cueing or prompting except in the very early stages, a finding that may differentiate AD from normal aging. Deficits in new learning are also common (Miller & Gustavson, 2000).

Besides memory, several other changes in cognition are associated with AD, including declines in language abilities (aphasia), anomia (impaired naming), and diminished verbal fluency (Zec, 1993). Visuospatial deficits tend to develop early in the course of AD, impairing the individual's ability to draw or manipulate objects (Miller & Gustavson, 2000). Changes in executive functioning or higher-order cognitive abilities such as judgment, problem solving, and abstract thinking are also affected by AD. Impaired executive functioning may manifest itself in many ways. For example, the individual may have difficulties making decisions regarding his or her care or carrying out complex tasks related to care that require planning (e.g., managing medication or finances). Declines in abstract reasoning and a general psychomotor slowing are also common in the early stages of AD (Zec, 1993).

Clearly, many of the cognitive declines associated with AD can seriously impact an elderly person's risk of having his or her competence questioned. However, it should be noted that individuals in the early stages of AD may still have the capacity to comprehend and express well-informed preferences (Kane, Ouslander, & Abrass, 1999). Competence should not be assumed to be necessarily impaired when someone is diagnosed with AD but instead should be empirically evaluated.

Vascular Dementia. *Vascular dementia* involves cognitive impairment caused by a variety of vascular conditions including numerous small strokes (i.e., blood vessels in the brain are blocked, resulting in reduced blood flow and death of surrounding tissue) or brain hemorrhages (Zarit & Zarit, 1998, p. 47). Prevalence rates of vascular dementia range between 12 and 20 percent (Kase, 1991) and account for anywhere between 4.5 and 39 percent of all cases of dementia (Reichman, 1994). This large discrepancy in estimates is caused by a lack of consensus regarding the definition of vascular dementia (Metter & Wilson, 1993).

Vascular dementia differs from AD in several ways. The onset of vascular dementia is often earlier than that of AD, although it is rare before the age of 50 (Zarit & Zarit, 1998, p. 47). Also, the course of cognitive impairment tends to be characterized by stepwise progression in which periods of stability are followed by periods of progressive deterioration.

Cognitive deficits associated with vascular dementia vary according to the areas of the brain affected. Impairment often occurs in memory, abstract thinking, and language (Zarit & Zarit, 1998, p. 48). The most frequent type of vascular dementia, multiinfarct dementia, may affect language abilities, such as naming, verbal fluency, word recognition, and shorter, simpler verbalizations (McPhearson & Cummings, 1997). Memory impairments in persons with multiinfarct dementia tend to be indistinguishable from those associated with AD (McPhearson & Cummings, 1997).

Unfortunately, few generalizations can be made about how vascular dementia affects abilities related to competence. Changes in memory and language may be expected, but changes in more complex cognitive abilities that are more likely related to issues regarding competence—such as the abilities to logically tie values to facts, to reach a conclusion, and to adhere to the conclusion—may or may not be present. Therefore, individuals suffering from vascular dementia must be evaluated carefully and thoroughly, particularly in the early stages of the disease process.

Parkinson's Disease. *Parkinson's disease* (PD) is characterized by loss of neurons in the substantia nigra that produce the neurotransmitter dopamine, resulting in dopamine deficiencies. Prevalence rates range from 31 to 341 per 100,000 in community-based samples (Troster, Fields, & Koller, 2000). The primary symptoms of PD are motor symptoms such as resting tremor, increased muscle tone (rigidity), and difficulty initiating voluntary movement (Bondi & Troster, 1997).

Changes in cognitive functioning are also present in persons with PD. Mild and circumscribed cognitive declines and a general slowing of thought processes are characteristic of the disease in the earlier stages. Changes in executive functioning (e.g., planning, reasoning, cognitive flexibility), memory, and visuoperceptual functioning are most common in the earlier stages of the disease (Bondi & Troster, 1997).

Dementia is rare in the earlier stages of PD but is more likely to occur as the disease progresses. Estimates of the prevalence of dementia in PD vary widely, but the most accepted figures range from 20 to 40 percent (Bondi & Troster, 1997). Dementia in PD is characterized by declines in several domains of cognitive functioning. Deficits in memory and new learning tend to be less pronounced as those observed in AD. Deficits in recall are common, but recognition memory tends to be preserved and patients benefit from cueing (Troster, Fields, & Koller, 2000). Language impairments include poor performance on tests of verbal fluency and visual confrontation naming (Troster, Fields, & Koller, 2000).

It appears as if cognitive deficits characteristic of early PD are generally not severe enough to affect abilities related to competence. As the disease progresses, however, signs of dementia should be monitored closely since many of the cognitive deficits observed in AD may occur in PD patients.

Brain Injury. *Traumatic brain injury* (TBI) is relatively common in elderly individuals. Although rates are highest among young adult males, after the age of 65 rates of TBI increase sharply (Krause, et al., 1984). Falls and pedestrian accidents appear to account for most cases of TBI in elderly individuals (Naugle, 1990).

Elderly individuals are at a greater risk for many negative outcomes following a TBI. For instance, after controlling for severity of TBI, older adults have poorer overall outcomes, have longer hospital stays, are more likely to be discharged to a nursing home, and have an increased risk of death following a TBI (Fields, Cisewski, & Coffey, 2000). Furthermore, advancing age predicts poorer outcome on certain indices of pre-injury functioning such as return to work, ability to perform activities of daily living, and general disability (Fields, 1997). Severity of initial injury appears to be the most important factor in predicting postinjury outcomes (Fields, Cisewski, & Coffey, 2000).

Changes in cognitive functioning following TBI depend on the severity, type, and location of the injury. Although it is difficult to predict which cognitive abilities will be compromised and the degree to which the individual will recover, studies have indicated that general cognitive impairment is common following TBI in elderly individuals, producing deficits in language (e.g., visual naming, verbal fluency), memory tasks (e.g., verbal learning), and executive functioning (e.g., card sorting) (Goldstein et al., 1994). This pattern of cognitive deficit is also found in younger adults who suffer a TBI, although several studies have found poorer outcomes in older adults even when controlling for initial severity of TBI. Older adults are less likely to return to pre-injury levels of cognitive functioning and may have a course of recovery that is slower when compared to that of younger adults (e.g., difficulties with slowed information processing) (see Fields, Cisewski, & Coffey, 2000, for a review).

Assessment of Competence

Most definitions of competence include multiple criteria and refer to a condition that is causing mental impairment (Moye, 1999; Smyer & Qualls, 1999; Willis, 1996). The goal of assessment is to accurately describe the functional abilities of the individual, determine if the individual is able to meet the demands of the environment, and ultimately provide a recommendation that addresses any discrepancy between the person's functional abilities and the demands of the environment while maximizing the person's autonomy. For instance, if the individual cannot provide self-care, then institutionalization may be required; if the individual only requires assistance with financial decision making and IADLs, however, then guardianship will be granted for only those activities.

There is a consensus in the literature regarding specific cognitive abilities that should be assessed as part of any competency evaluation. These include (1) orientation, (2) recent and remote memory, (3) intellectual capacity (i.e., reasoning and the ability to understand abstract ideas), (4) attention, and (5) judgment (Kapp, 1996). Mathematical abilities should be assessed when an individual's ability to manage his or her finances is questioned. As described earlier, these cognitive abilities can be affected by the normal process of aging as well as by a variety of age-associated conditions.

Clarifying the Assessment Question

Four aspects of decisional capacity tend to drive the development of assessment questions: ability to understand diagnostic and treatment-related information; ability to appreciate the significance of this information; ability to reason about the risks and benefits of treatment alternatives; and ability to evidence a choice (Moye, 1999). A problem in one of these areas may lead to a determination of incompetence.

In assessing the various domains of functioning, specific questions that typically emerge in a competency evaluation that then drive the selection of assessment methods include (1) Can the individual make and express choices about his or her life? (2) Are the outcomes of these choices reasonable? (3) Are the choices based on rational reasons? (4) Is the individual capable of understanding the personal implications of choices? and (5) Does the individual understand the implications of choices about his or her life? The underlying abilities associated with these questions are described in further detail in the following paragraphs.

Understanding diagnostic and treatment-related information involves the abilities to remember and comprehend newly presented words and phrases as well as the ability to describe in one's own words what a health-care provider is communicating regarding medical treatment and treatment risks (Marson, Ingram, Cody, & Harrell, 1995; Moye, 1999; Grisso & Appelbaum, 1998a; Gutheil & Appelbaum, 2000).

Appreciating a situation and its consequences, especially concerning illness and probable consequences of various treatments, involves both cognitive and affective components. Typical items used to assess this domain include: "Do you believe you need some kind of treatment" or "Please explain to me what you really believe is wrong with your health now" (Marson et al., 1995; Moye, 1999; Grisso & Appelbaum, 1998a; Gutheil & Appelbaum, 2000).

Reasoning involves rational manipulation of information, that is, the ability to take relevant information about treatment and engage in a logical process of weighting treatment options (Marson et al., 1995; Moye, 1999; Grisso & Appelbaum, 1998a; Gutheil & Appelbaum, 2000). This ability involves a comparison of alternative consequences, arriving at a treatment decision by integrating, analyzing, and manipulating information that may affect everyday life.

The ability to *express a choice* is the final decisional aspect assessed in the determination of competency (Marson et al., 1995; Moye, 1999; Grisso & Appelbaum, 1998a; Gutheil & Appelbaum, 2000). Once understanding, appreciation, and reasoning have been performed, the relevant question is whether the individual can then communicate his or her wishes to others.

Methods of Assessment

Several methods of assessment have been employed in the determination of competence. Although there are significant variations in the specific measures used, most assessments involve a thorough medical history review, the administration of the Mini-Mental Status Examination (Folstein, Folstein, & McHugh, 1975), and the administration of a battery of tests designed to assess specific ADL and IADL skills and higher cognitive domains of functioning, including general cognitive ability, attention and concentration, memory, language, conceptualization or abstraction and problem solving, and executive motor skills (constructional or visual-spatial skills, executive, and motor) (Mattis, 1990; Smyer & Qualls, 1999).

Comprehensive Batteries. The Multidimensional Functional Assessment of Older Adults is designed to assess competency using a multicomponent approach (Fillenbaum, 1988). This assessment battery utilizes the OARS Multidimensional Functional Assessment Questionnaire (OMFAQ) and a questionnaire administered in an interview format to examine functioning in specific areas relevant to competence. The first part of the questionnaire assesses five different areas: (1) social; (2) economic; (3) mental health; (4) physical health; and (5) activities of daily living. The second part of the questionnaire focuses on assessment of service utilization and the impact of service use on functional state. Responses to the questions on this assessment can be provided by an informed observer or by the individual being evaluated (Lawton, 1988).

Validity and reliability of the OMFAQ have been evaluated by comparing the responses to questions against normative samples of individuals living independently in the community, attending adult daycare, and residents within institutions (Fillenbaum, 1988). These samples allow an assessor to adequately compare daily functioning based on living arrangement and perceived level of functioning. Based on these data, level of impairment and effect on competency can be determined. The OMFAQ is a multidimensional functional assessment that has been shown to provide criterion valid information regarding functioning for clients in a variety of settings and in several domains.

The MacArthur Competence Assessment Tool for Treatment (MacCAT-T) (Grisso & Appelbaum, 1998a) is designed to assess functional abilities related to competency in individuals. The MacCAT-T was originally used to assess competency in individuals diagnosed with schizophrenia, major depression, and medical problems found in hospital and legal settings (Grisso & Appelbaum, 1995; Hoge et al., 1997) but was recently adapted and validated to assess competency to consent to research participation and medical treatment (Grisso & Appelbaum, 1998b; Grisso, Appelbaum, & Hill-Fotouchi, 1997; Kim et al., 2001; Moye, 1999). The MacCAT-T is a structured interview that is designed to assess specific physical and psychiatric symptoms, functional abilities, treatment options, and life circumstances (Grisso & Appelbaum, 1998a).

Additional measures are often used in combination with instruments described above in order to examine specific domains of functioning. For example, instruments such as the Comprehensive Assessment and Referral Evaluation (CARE), a structured interview that assesses limitations in ADLs and IADLs (Lawton, 1988) or the Self-Evaluation of Life Function Scale (SELF) and the Community Competence Scale have been used to supplement the assessment of functional abilities (Kbauss, 1990; Lawton, 1988). In addition, a variety of instruments designed to assess specific cognitive functions associated with mental competence (e.g., memory, executive functioning, verbal reasoning) may be employed in the assessment process when the presenting problem indicates that more detailed examination is warranted.

Ethical Issues

When a psychologist's work is used in the decision regarding whether a client is mentally competent, there is a direct impact on the client's civil liberties. It should not be assumed that, even with the most noble of intentions, the behavior of the psychologist can have only a beneficial effect on the client's welfare. Individuals with diminished mental capacities are vulnerable to harm by virtue of the nature of the deficits in their repertoires. Unfortunately, within the current state of the field the interpretation of psychological assessment results is an inherently subjective process and test results are not always unambiguous. These characteristics of psychological assessment coupled with the gravity of the potential impact of psychologists' judgments on the lives of vulnerable persons speak to the need for guidelines that can facilitate the psychologist's ability to make decisions that do no harm and preserve the rights of others to self-determination. Here we discuss ethical issues relevant to providing services to persons when mental competence has been empirically determined to be compromised or when it is questioned.

The National Commission for the Protection of Human Participants (NCPHS) has been instrumental in the development of the currently accepted regulations for ensuring the rights of research participants. From 1974 to 1978, the NCPHS published reports that established the significant ethical problems in human research and developed the basic guidelines for the use of human participants (Cassell, 1988). The issue of respect is the most fundamental principle promoted in documents published by NCPHS. The NCPHS *Belmont Report* describes that the principle of respect assumes that all persons are entitled to the basic right of ethical or "respectful" treatment and have the right to determine for themselves whether or not the treatment being conducted will grant them the respect they feel they deserve. The requirement of informed consent in research stems from the principle of respect (Cassel, 1988).

Informed Consent

Obtaining informed consent for health-care or research participation is intended to safeguard the autonomy of the individual and to ensure that the individual understands the implications of his or her decision to participate. Informed consent requires three conditions: (1) disclosure of information relevant to the proposed project; (2) freedom of choice in a noncoercive setting; and (3) the competency of the patient to make an informed decision for his or her own self about participation (Stanley, Stanley, Guido, & Garvin, 1988). Though the informed consent procedure is seemingly straightforward, a host of practical problems can emerge when researchers attempt to implement it. This is evidenced by numerous studies that have found that the typical procedures used in seeking informed consent leave the participant uninformed. In addition, a review of the literature on research with psychiatrically impaired participants and cognitively impaired older adults shows that many participants do not understand the research process or the information provided to them in seeking their consent to participate (DeRenzo, 1994; High, 1993; Stanley, Stanley, Guido, & Garvin, 1988; Tymchuk, Ouslander, & Rader, 1986). These findings indicate that providing pertinent information related to a medical procedure or research study does not guarantee comprehension of the information.

There currently is a lack of consensus in research ethics concerning whether cognitively impaired older adults and people experiencing psychiatric problems require protection beyond what is necessary for the general population. One argument is that individuals experiencing cognitive or psychiatric impairment should have the same rights, and hence participate in the same consent process, as those who are deemed competent. The opposing viewpoint is that psychiatric illnesses and cognitive impairment involve inherent complications that directly affect the competency of the individual to make important decisions, limiting true consent in research (Candilis, 2001). Therefore, the competency of an individual to consent is an imperative issue because for consent to be legally effective the participant first must be competent to consent, give consent voluntarily, and be able to comprehend the risks involved (Berkowitz, 1978).

The requirement that research participation be voluntary is another important aspect of the informed consent procedure. In the case of elderly persons with cognitive disorders, the threat to voluntary participation involves the concern that they are more likely to give consent because of their diminished cognitive functioning and may consequently may be more susceptible to unintentional coercion from family members or health-care providers (Kapp, 1992). Thus, it is the duty of the researcher to address any coercion, intentional or unintentional, that might affect the individual's right to voluntarily consent.

Competency in regards to informed consent refers to the participant's actual mental and decisional capacity to agree to the research procedure. The first and most fundamental challenge in conducting a true informed consent procedure lies in deciding if the person is competent to give informed consent. Mental incompetence is a legal judgment made officially by a judge on the individual's behalf (Kapp, 1992). Thus, a person not declared incompetent is assumed to be competent in the legal sense even when his or her behavior is suggestive of impairment.

Decisional competence for informed consent involves an individual's ability to perform a set of four basic functions: communication, understanding, appreciation, and manipulation (Artnak, 1997). The following questions are relevant to the decisional competence required for informed consent: (1) Do potential participants truly comprehend all of the information given to them regarding the study? and (2) Are they capable of communicating their decision to the researchers? The participant's decisional competence at the time consent is requested should not be assumed. It is the duty of the researcher and participating parties to carefully consider the potential participant's decisional competence before initiating any informed consent procedure and to terminate the recruitment process when decisional competence is problematic.

The complexity of the informed consent process is compounded by the fact that mental capacity can fluctuate over time (Artnak, 1997). For example, persons with neurodegenerative disorders such as Alzheimer's disease or vascular dementia might be able to provide informed consent and to communicate their decision to participate early in the disease process, but at some point they will lose this capacity as the disease progresses. Assessment of a research participant's decisional competence requires continued monitoring from the researcher to ensure that the individual understands all procedures throughout his or her participation in research.

In working with participants with cognitive impairment, researchers may find it useful to employ a set of standards known as *negotiated consent* when attempting to adhere to the principles underlying informed consent (Moody, 1988). Negotiated consent has as its foundation the ideal of *normative ethics*, which strives for the identification of what ought to be appreciated in terms of the quality of life for the individual (Fisher & Yury, 2003). In other words, who is most concerned with the individual's quality of life in terms of their receiving ethical treatment? The standard of negotiated consent involves participation not only by the patient or a third-party member, but by all related parties in the life of the patient. Negotiated consent is more heuristic in style than informed consent. It has been argued that consideration by and consensus among interested parties of the participant produces the most ethical rationale for the outcome at hand (Moody, 1988). The negotiated consent process encourages all related parties involved with the participant to consult, discuss, clarify differences, and come to a consensus about what is best for the impaired person. Although this alternative to the standard informed consent procedure has been utilized with persons with cognitive or psychiatric disabilities, it is not without difficulty because it requires the researcher to identify persons appropriately interested in the participant's interests.

Confidentiality

Researchers and health-care providers have the ethical duty to hold in confidence the private information entrusted to them by their patients. Confidentiality in research is protected by restricting access to the participant's information to only those for whom it is necessary for the proper conduct of the research. Within medical research, the context of the relationship between the patient and the health-care provider is the basis for the principle of confidentiality. Federal law mandates that consent must be attained from the patient whose medical information is being used for research purposes and before this information can be revealed to family members (Gutheil & Appelbaum, 2000).

Ethical issues associated with maintaining confidentiality frequently emerge in health care and research with cognitively impaired participants. The principle of confidentiality is only presumptively applicable and not an absolute obligation and thus can place providers in difficult ethical situations in addressing the medical or psychiatric problems of impaired persons. For instance, an investigator may discover medical or personal information about a participant that has significant implications for treatment, yet disclosure may be slowed by the requirement of confidentiality (Cassel, 1988). Alternatively, it may be suspected that an elderly research participant has been abused or neglected.

There are several situations when confidentiality can be breached: (1) when a participant waives the right to confidentiality; (2) when the rights of innocent third-party members are at stake; and (3) when the health-care provider is mandated by law to reveal the existence of problems related to the conditions of a patient (Kapp, 1992). The last situation is important when the health-care provider is confronted with suspected violence or elder abuse. The reporting of unethical conditions, as in the case of elder abuse, may be mandated under the state's law (depending on the state) to protect individuals who are unable, for whatever reason, to care for their own needs.

Conclusion

Competence lacks an agreed upon definition, yet deciding which definition to use is the cornerstone of any competency issue. It is important to distinguish between abilities to perform skills versus decision making. A successful working approach maximizes an individual's autonomy whenever there is a question regarding competency to perform a skill. Decision making, on the other hand, must utilize a definition that encompasses both an understanding of relevant facts and an appreciation of the consequence of the decision. The most pertinent aspect of any definition is that it focuses on maximizing an individual's opportunities to express his or her autonomy.

References

Albert, M. S. (1988). Assessment of cognitive dysfunction. In M. S. Albert, & M. B. Moss (Eds.), *Geriatric neuropsychology*. New York: Guilford Press.

Albert, M. S., & Drachman, D. A. (2000). Alzheimer's disease: What is it, how many people have it, and why do we need to know? *Neurology, 55*, 166–168.

Anderer, S. (1990). *Determining competency in guardianship proceedings*. Washington, DC: American Bar Association.

Appelbaum, P. S., & Gutheil, T. G. (1991). *Clinical handbook of psychiatry and the law*. Baltimore, MD: Williams & Wilkins.

Artnak, K. (1997). Informed consent in the elderly: Assessing decisional capacity. *Seminars in Perioperative Nursing, 6*, 59–64.

Bachman, D. L., Wolf, P. A., Linn, R. T., Knofel, J. E., Cobb, J. L., Belanger, A. J., et al. (1993). Incidence of dementia and probable Alzheimer's disease in a general population: The Framingham study. *Neurology, 43*, 515–519.

Backman, L., Small, B. J., & Wahlin, A. (2001). Aging and memory: Cognitive and biological perspectives. In J. E. Birren, & K. W. Schaie (Eds.), *Handbook of the psychology of aging* (5th ed.) (pp. 349–377). San Diego: Academic Press.

Barresi, C. M., & McConnell, D. J. (1987). Adult day care participation among impaired elderly. *Lifestyles. Special Issue: Family & Economic Issues: Diversity in the Lifestyles of Older People*, *8* (3–4), 82(212)–94(224).

Berkowitz, S. (1978). Informed consent, research, and the elderly. *The Gerontologist*, *18*, 237–243.

Bondi, M. W., & Troster, A. I. (1997). Parkinson's disease: Neurobehavioral consequences of basal ganglia dysfunction. In P. D. Nussbaum (Ed.), *Handbook of neuropsychology and aging* (pp. 216–245). New York: Plenum.

Candilis, P. (2001). Advancing the ethics of research. *Psychiatric Annals*, *31*, 119–124.

Capozzi, J. D., & Rhodes, R. (2002). Assessing a patient's capacity to refuse treatment. *The Journal of Bone and Joint Surgery*, *84A* (4), 691–693.

Cassel, C. (1988). Ethical issues in the conduct of research in long term care. *The Gerontologist*, *28*, 90–96.

Colorado v. Connely, 107 S. Ct. 515 (1986).

Cummings, J. L. (1987). Dementia syndromes: Neurobehavioral and neuropsychiatric features. *Journal of Clinical Psychiatry*, *48* (5, Suppl.), 3–8.

Cummings, J. L., & Benson, D. F. (1992). *Dementia: A clinical approach* (2nd ed.). Stoneham, MA: Butterworth-Heinemann.

Dawson, D., Hendershot, G., & Fulton, J. (1987, June 10). *Functional limitations of individuals age 65 years and over*. National Center for Health Statistics. Advance Data, Vital and Health Statistics, No. 133, Hyattsville, MD: U.S. Public Health Service.

DeRenzo, E. (1994). The ethics of involving psychiatrically impaired persons in research. *IRB: A review of human subjects research*, *16*, 7–11.

Dusky v. United States, 362 U.S. 402 (1960).

Evans, D. A. (1996). Descriptive epidemiology of Alzheimer's disease. In Z. S. Khachaturian, & T. S. Radebaugh (Eds.), *Alzheimer's disease: Cause(s), diagnosis, treatment, and care* (pp. 51–62). Boca Raton: CRC Press.

Evans, D. A., Funkenstein, H., Albert, M. S., Scherr, P. A., Cook, N. R., Chown, M. J., et al. (1989). Prevalence of Alzheimer's disease in a community population of older persons. *Journal of American Medical Association*, *262*, 2551–2556.

Fields, R. B. (1997). Geriatric head injury. In P. D. Nussbaum (Ed.), *Handbook of neuropsychology and aging* (pp. 280–297). New York: Plenum.

Fields, R. B., Cisewski, D., & Coffey, C. E. (2000). Traumatic brain injury. In J. L. Cummings & E. C. Coffey (Eds.), *Textbook of geriatric neuropsychiatry* (2nd ed.) (pp. 621–654). Washington: American Psychiatric Press.

Fillenbaum, C. G. (1988). *Multidimensional Functional Assessment of Individuals: The Duke older Americans resources and services procedures*. Hillsdale, NJ: Lawrence Erlbaum Associates.

Fisher, J. E., & Yury, C. A. (2003). Issues in the ethical treatment of older adults. In W. T. O'Donohue of K. E. Ferguson (eds.), *Handbook of professional ethics for psychologists*. Thousand Oaks, CA: Sage.

Fitten, L. J. (1999). Frontal lobe dysfunction and patient decision making about treatment and participation in research. In B. L. Miller & J. L. Cummings (Eds.), *The human frontal lobes: Functions and disorders*. New York: Guilford Press.

Fletcher, J., Dommel, W., & Cowell, D. (1985). Consent to research with impaired subjects. *IRB: A review of human subjects research, 7*, 1–6.

Folstein, M. F., Folstein, S. E., & McHugh, P. R. (1975). "Mini-Mental State," a practical guide for grading cognitive state of patients for the clinician. *Journal of Psychiatric Research, 12*, 189–198.

Goldstein, F. C., Levin, H. S., Presley, R. M., Searcy, J., Colohan, A. R. T., Eisenberg, H. M., et al. (1994). Neurobehavioral consequences of closed head injury in older adults. *Journal of Neurology, Neurosurgery, and Psychiatry, 57*, 961–966.

Grisso, T., & Appelbaum, P. S. (1995). The MacArthur treatment competence study. III: Abilities of patients to consent to psychiatric and medical treatments. *Law and Human Behavior, 19* (2), 149–174.

Grisso, T., & Appelbaum, P. S. (1998a). *Assessing competence to consent to treatment: A guide for physicians and other health professionals*, New York: Oxford University Press.

Grisso, T., & Appelbaum, P. S. (1998b). *MacArthur Competence Assessment Tool for Treatment (MacCAT-T)*. Sarasota, FL: Professional Resource Press.

Grisso, T., Appelbaum, P. S., & Hill-Fotouchi, C. (1997). The MacCAT-T: A clinical tool to assess patients' capacities to make treatment decisions. *Psychiatric Services, 48*, 1415–1419.

Gutheil, T. G., & Appelbaum, P. S. (2000). *Clinical handbook of psychiatry and the law*. Philadelphia, PA: Lippincott Williams & Wilkins.

Haug, H., & Eggers, R. (1991). Morphometry of the human cortex cerebri and corpus striatum during aging. *Neurobiology of Aging, 12*, 336–338.

Hendrie, H. C. (1997). Epidemiology of Alzheimer's disease. *Geriatrics, 52*, S4–S8.

High, D. (1993). Advancing research with Alzheimer disease subjects: Investigator's perceptions and ethical issues. *Alzheimer Disease and Associated Disorders, 7*, 165–178.

Hoge, S. K., Poythress, N., Bonnie, R. J., Monahan, J., Eisenberg, M., & Feucht-Haviar, T. (1997). The MacArthur adjudicative competence study: Diagnosis, psychopathology, and competence-related abilities. *Behavioural Sciences and the Law, 15*, 329–345.

Hommel, P. A. (1996). Guardianship reform in the 1980s: A decade of substantive and procedural change. In M. Smyer, K. W. Schaie, & M. B. Kapp (Eds.), *Older adults' decision-making and the law* (pp. 225–253). New York: Springer.

Kane, R. J., Ouslander, J. G., & Abrass, I. B. (1999). *Essentials of clinical geriatrics* (4th ed.). New York: McGraw-Hill.

Kapp, M. (1992). *Geriatrics and the law*. New York: Springer.

Kapp, M. (1996). Alternatives to guardianship: Enhanced autonomy for diminished capacity. In M. Smyer, K. W. Schaie, & M. B. Kapp (Eds.), *Older adults' decision-making and the law* (pp. 182–201). New York: Springer.

Kase, C. S. (1991). Epidemiology of multi-infarct dementia. *Alzheimer's Disease and Associated Disorders, 5*, 71–76.

Kbauss, I. K. (1990). Guardianship and competency: A gerontological perspective. *Forensic Reports, 3*, 81–89.

Kim, S. Y. H., Caine, E. D., Currier, G. W., Leibovici, A., & Ryan, J. M. (2001). Assessing the competence of persons with Alzheimer's Disease in providing informed consent for participation in research. *The American Journal of Psychiatry, 158*, 712–717.

Kovar, M. G., & LaCroix, A. Z. (1987). Ability to perform work-related activities. *National Center for Health Statistics. Advance Data, Vital and Health Statistics, No. 136*, Hyattsville, MD: U.S. Public Health Service.

Krause, J. F., Black, M. A., Hessol, N., Ley, P., Rokaw, W., Sullivan, C., et al. (1984). The incidence of acute brain injury and serious impairment in a defined population. *American Journal of Epidemiology*, *119*, 186–201.

Lawton, M. P. (1988). Scales to measure competence in everyday activities. *Psychopharmacology Bulletin*, *24* (4), 609–614.

Marson, D. C., Ingram, K. K., Cody, H. A., & Harrell, L. E. (1995). Assessing the competency of patients with Alzheimer's Disease under different legal standards. *Archives of Neurology*, *52*, 949–954.

Martin, D. C., & Rubin, F. H. (1997). Anatomy and physiology of the aging human brain. In P. D. Nussbaum (Ed.), *Handbook of neuropsychology and aging* (pp. 32–43). New York: Plenum.

Mattis, S. (1990). Neuropsychological assessment of competency in the elderly. *Forensic Reports*, *3* (1), 107–114.

McPhearson, S. E., & Cummings, J. L. (1997). Vascular dementia: Clinical assessment, neuropsychological features, and treatment. In P. D. Nussbaum (Ed.), *Handbook of neuropsychology and aging* (pp. 177–188). New York: Plenum.

Metter, E. J., & Wilson, R. S. (1993). Vascular dementias. In R. W. Parks, R. F. Zec, & R. S. Wilson (Eds.), *Neuropsychology of Alzheimer's disease and other dementias* (pp. 416–437). New York: Oxford University Press.

Miller, B. L., & Gustavson, A. (2000). Alzheimer's disease and frontotemporal dementia. In J. L. Cummings & E. C. Coffey (Eds.), *Textbook of geriatric neuropsychiatry* (2nd ed.) (pp. 511–530). Washington: American Psychiatric Press.

Moody, H. (1988). From informed consent to negotiated consent. *The Gerontologist*, *28*, 64–70.

Moye, J. (1999). Assessment of competency and decision making capacity. In P. A. Lichtenberg (Ed.), *Handbook of assessment in clinical gerontology*. New York: Wiley.

Naugle, R. I. (1990). Epidemiology of traumatic brain injury in adults. In E. D. Bigler (Ed.), *Traumatic brain injury* (pp. 69–103). Austin, TX: Pro-Ed.

Oberlander, L. B., & Goldstein, N. E. (2001). A review and update on the practice of evaluating Miranda comprehension. *Behavioural Sciences and the Law*, *19*, 453–471.

Pepper, S. C. (1942). *World hypotheses*. Berkeley, CA: University of California Press.

Perry, E. K., Tomlinson, B. E., Blessed, G., Gergmann, K., Gibson, P. H., & Perry, R. H. (1978). Correlation of cholinergic abnormalities with senile plaques and mental test scores in senile dementia. *British Medical Journal*, *2*, 1457–1459.

Powers, R. E. (2000). Neurobiology of aging. In J. L. Cummings & E. C. Coffey (Eds.), *Textbook of geriatric neuropsychiatry* (2nd ed.) (pp. 33–80). Washington, DC: America Psychiatric Press.

Rankin, E. D. (1990). Caregiver stress and the elderly: A familial perspective. *Journal of Gerontological Social Work*, *15* (1–2), 57–73.

Reichman, W. E. (1994). Nondegenerative dementing disorders. In C. E. Coffey, & J. L. Cummings (Eds.), *The American Psychiatric Press textbook of geriatric neuropsychiatry* (pp. 369–388). Washington, DC: American Psychiatric Press.

Reichman, W. E. (2000). Nondegenerative dementing disorders. In J. L. Cummings & E. C. Coffey (Eds.), *Textbook of geriatric neuropsychiatry* (2nd ed.) (pp. 491–510). Washington, DC: American Psychiatric Press.

Rogers, W. A., & Fisk, A. D. (2001). Understanding the role of attention in cognitive aging research. In J. E. Birren & K. W. Schaie (Eds.), *Handbook of the psychology of aging* (5th ed.) (pp. 241–266). San Diego: Academic Press.

Salthouse, T. A., & Babcock, R. L. (1991). Decomposing adult age differences in working memory. *Developmental Psychology, 27*, 763–776.

Schaie, K. W. (1996). *Intellectual development in adulthood: The Seattle longitudinal study.* Cambridge: Cambridge University Press.

Silver, M. (2002). Reflections on determining competency. *Bioethics, 16* (5), 455–468.

Smyer, M. A., Schaie, K. W., & Kapp, M. B. (1996). *Older adults' decision-making and the law.* New York: Springer.

Smyer, M. A., & Qualls, S. H. (1999). *Aging and mental health.* Cambridge, MA: Blackwell.

Stanley, B., Stanley, M., Guido, J., & Garvin, L. (1988). The functional competency of elderly at risk. *The Gerontologist, 28*, 53–58.

Troster, A. I., Fields, J. A., & Koller, W. C. (2000). Parkinson's disease and parkinsonism. In J. L. Cummings & E. C. Coffey (Eds.), *Textbook of geriatric neuropsychiatry* (2nd ed.) (pp. 559–600). Washington DC: American Psychiatric Press.

Tymchuk, A., Ouslander, J., & Rader, N. (1986). Informing the elderly: A comparison of four methods. *Journal of American Geriatric Society, 34*, 818–822.

Uniform Guardianship and Protective Proceedings Act (1997). *National conference of commissioners on uniform state laws.* Sacramento, California.

Uniform Health-Care Decisions Act (1993). *National conference of commissioners on uniform state laws.* Charleston, South Carolina.

Vinters, H. V. (2001). Aging and the human nervous system. In J. E. Birren & K. W. Schaie (Eds.), *Handbook of the psychology of aging* (5th ed.) (pp. 135–160). San Diego: Academic Press.

Whetten, D. A., & Cameron, K. S. (1993). *Developing management skills: Managing conflict.* New York: HarperCollins.

Willis, S. L. (1996). Assessing everyday competence in the cognitively challenged elderly. In M. Symer, K. W. Schaie, & M. B. Kapp (Eds.), *Older adults' decision-making and the law.* New York: Springer.

Zarit, S. H., & Zarit, J. M. (1998). *Mental disorders in older adults.* New York: Guilford Press.

Zec, R. F. (1993). Neuropsychological functioning in Alzheimer's disease. In R. W. Parks, R. F. Zec, & R. S. Wilson (Eds.), *Neuropsychology of Alzheimer's disease and other dementias* (pp. 3–80). New York: Oxford University Press.

CHAPTER 11

CHILD CUSTODY EVALUATIONS

APRIL R. BRADLEY
UNIVERSITY OF NORTH DAKOTA

The Centers for Disease Control and Prevention (2000) report that the divorce rate in the Uniteds States has more than doubled from 2.0 divorces per 1,000 in 1940 to 4.1 divorces per 1,000 in 2000. A significant proportion of these divorces involve children. Divorce and its impact on children have been greatly researched in the past 20 years. Wallerstein (1985) describes the immediate effects of divorce on children to be loneliness, vulnerability, powerlessness, and fear of abandonment. Howell, Portes, and Brown (1997) report poorer academic performance following divorce. Others indicate hostility, antisocial behavior, aggressiveness, and depression to be correlates of divorce (Howell et al., 1997; Portes et al., 1992; Sorenson & Goldman, 1990). Because of the potential negative impact of divorce on the child's functioning, child custody evaluations are conducted to determine the placement (or visitation schedule) that is most likely to promote the psychological health of the child.

Ash and Guyer (1986) found that expert recommendations from mental health professionals were used as bargaining chips in 71 percent of their sample, indicating a substantial use of expert recommendations in divorce settings. Because of the increase in the number of divorces involving children and the demand for mental health professionals to aid in the custody process, child custody evaluations have become an important part of forensic psychology.

This chapter will outline several issues relevant to child custody evaluations, including state laws, ethical guidelines, data collection, tests used, and interpretation of results. Recommendations for conducting child custody evaluations are provided.

Current Statutes

Most states in the United States have legislated a Best Interests of the Child (BIC) standard through which placement decisions are made. However, specific statutes governing what variables are attended to in order to assess the best interests of the child vary from state to state. Therefore, it is important for the custody evaluator to understand the specific statutes of his or her state (Grisso, 1990). Without this knowledge, the evaluator may assess legally irrelevant dimensions (as in the case of *Palmore v. Sidoti*), wasting time and resources of the parents and courts.

Hall, Pulver, and Cooley (1996) conducted a survey of statutes or codes regarding the Best Interests of the Child standard and found little consistency across states. For example, Nevada has five factors that the courts must consider: (1) the child's wishes, (2) any history of abuse, (3) the parents' wishes, (4) each parents' ability to share the child with the other parent, and (5) the environment that best promotes the development of physical, mental, and spiritual faculties. Arkansas maintains statutes that include: (1) considering the child's wishes, (2) parental fitness to care for the child, (3) ability of the parent to share love, affection, and contact with the child, and (4) parental attachment. These differ from statutes in California, which consider the willingness of the parents to maintain the child in an environment consistent with the child's cultural background (Hall, Pulver, & Cooley, 1996). Furthermore, some states, including California, have legislated a preference for joint custody or a preference for custody to be given to the primary caretaker, or the one who spends the most time with the child (Mason, 1994).

Varying statutes are problematic for the mental health professional because it may be unclear which variables should be emphasized or more heavily weighted in making a custody recommendation. Any mental health professional who conducts custody evaluations must make him- or herself knowledgeable of these laws. In addition, it is helpful if the evaluator requests that the court (or person requesting evaluation) provide specific questions that are to be answered through the custody evaluation process.

Ethical Guidelines

It is important that the custody evaluator know and understand the ethical guidelines for conducting child custody evaluations. Currently, the American Psychological Association (APA) and the Association of Family and Conciliation Courts (AFCC) have published guidelines for conducting child custody evaluations. The APA's Guidelines for Child Custody Evaluations in Divorce Proceedings (1994) state that the purpose of the evaluation is to assess the best psychological interests of the child and that the focus of the evaluation should be parenting capacity and psychological and developmental needs of the child. The APA states that the evaluator should use multiple methods of data collection and neither overinterpret nor inappropriately interpret the data. These guidelines are in addition to guidelines set for forensic evaluators in general (APA, 1996).

The AFCC's Model Standards of Practice for Child Custody Evaluations (1995) are more specific than the APA guidelines. The AFCC guidelines state that child custody evaluations should identify the developmental needs of the child; identify strengths and needs of other family members; identify positive and negative family interactions; identify a plan for custody and access that meets the best interests of the child; and provide the court, parents, and attorneys with a written report outlining these recommendations. The guidelines further state that a custody evaluator should be familiar with the statutes and case law governing child custody. The AFCC also recommends that the custody evaluator use multiple methods of data collection and that the methods of data collection (e.g., objective tests, structured interviews) should be used equally with adult parties. Evaluators are advised to be aware of the limits of testing and to outline these limits in their report. The AFCC recommends that the evaluator assess the following dimensions: parent-child relationship, relationship between the parents, parenting ability, psychological health of the parent, psychological health of the child, and domestic violence patterns.

Procedures

Many different psychological assessment procedures have been recommended by mental health professionals as relevant to custody decisions. Hysjulien, Wood, and Benjamin (1994) discuss the use of the Minnesota Multiphasic Personality Inventory–2 (MMPI-2; Graham, Watts, & Timbrook, 1991), Child Abuse Potential Inventory (Milner, 1989), Achenbach Child Behavior Checklist (McConaughy & Achenbach, 1996), FACES III (Edmon, Cole, & Howard, 1990), and the Parent Attachment Structured Interview (Roll, Lockwood, & Roll, 1981) for use in custody evaluations. Other recommended tests include the Child Perception of Parent and Parent Awareness Skills Survey (Bricklin, 1995), and the Parental Discipline Techniques Self Report Instrument (Gardner, 1997). Lyons (1993) discusses the use of art psychotherapy and its subsequent interpretation in custody evaluations. Freedman et al. (1993) provide an in-depth discussion of the clinical assessment of countertransference problems in custody evaluations, and Jackson and Donovan (1990) discuss looking for defense mechanisms such as projection and denial in the clinical interview as indicators of a detrimental environment.

All of these different recommendations can become overwhelming for the custody evaluator. In addition, what is recommended in the literature and what occurs in practice are often different. To assess this situation, Keilin and Bloom (1986) conducted a survey study including 82 psychologists, psychiatrists, and master's-level practitioners nationally. Results indicated that nearly 100 percent of these mental health professionals conducted interviews with both parents and children. Seventy-five percent used psychological tests with both the parents and the child(ren). Sixty-eight percent observed parent-child interactions. The MMPI was used by 88 percent and projectives (e.g. Rorschach, Thematic Apperception Test [TAT]) were used by 67 percent of the responders. Eighty-five percent also used intelligence tests. On average, practitioners reported that they spent 18.8 hours (direct and indirect time) per family conducting an assessment. The three most commonly used instruments for adults were the MMPI, Rorschach, and TAT. The three most common tests used with children were the Weschler Intelligence Scale for Children, Child's Apperception Test (CAT), and projective drawings.

Ackerman and Ackerman (1997) replicated the Keilin and Bloom (1986) study with a national sample of 201 psychologists. The results indicated that the average length of time spent on a custody evaluation increased 7.6 hours to a total of 26.4 hours. The average fee per assessment was $2,646, triple the amount in the Keilin and Bloom study. Over 90 percent of those surveyed indicated that they used psychological tests with either the parent or child, also an increase. The MMPI-2 was used by 92 percent of the respondents and the Rorschach was used by 48 percent. Forty-three percent of the respondents used intelligence tests (e.g., Weschler Adult Intelligence Scale–III, Weschler Intelligence Scale for Children–III).

Quinnell and Bow (2001) conducted a survey of 279 master's or doctoral level psychologists who perform child custody evaluations. Results indicated that professionals rank the importance of psychological testing after clinical interviews with the parent and child and parent-child observations. Only 30 percent of respondents used intelligence tests with parents and children, indicating a decline in their use. The MMPI-2 continued to be used by most examiners, and the use of the Millon Clinical Multiaxial Inventory (MCMI III) has increased (52%). The Rorschach continues to be used at about the same rate as previous studies (44%), and the CAT continues to be used with children at about the same rate (35%). The use of the MMPI-A and Millon Adolescent Clinical Inventory (MACI) has doubled (43% and 21%, respectively). The use of parent inventories has increased sevenfold. Their survey results indicate that 44 percent of respondents use the Parent-Child Relationship Inventory, 41 percent use the Parenting Stress Index, and 21 percent use the Child Abuse Potential Inventory.

These survey studies indicate some shifts in current professional practice. First, there is a marked increase in the use of self-report measures relevant to the child custody setting, such as parenting skills and parent satisfaction. Second, traditional use of intelligence testing has declined. Third, the use of tests designed specifically for child custody evaluations has increased.

Ackerman (1995) states that custody evaluations should provide an assessment of history, intelligence, achievement, and personality and recommends that custody evaluators use clinical interviews of both parents and all children, objective psychological tests, and observations of the parent and child. Gould (2000) provides a recommended method for conducting child custody evaluations that follows the guidelines set forth by the AFCC's (1995) Model Standards of Practice for Child Custody Evaluations. He states that a child custody evaluation should include five different sources of information, including a structured interview, self-report data, standardized psychological tests, collateral interview data and record review, and direct observation. These methods allow the examiner to obtain information from multiple resources, increasing the reliability and validity of the data and subsequent inferences made from that data.

The use of so many different psychological tests may confuse the basic reason for giving them. For example, it is not clear why intelligence tests are given to parents and children. Most important in choosing the type of information to be collected, and the method by which to collect the information, is to have a sound reason (based on the existing scientific literature) for collecting that information. Whatever instrument evaluators choose in conducting a custody evaluation, they should use a standard battery to reduce variance (Gould, 1999).

Clinical Interviews

Clinical interviews should be conducted with both caregivers and with each child separately. Because it is important that the same information is gathered from each parent, structured interviews are preferred over nonstructured interviews. The information gathered from these interviews should be relevant to the specific question being asked and to the legally relevant criteria (e.g., ability to parent, attachment, etc.). Ackerman (1995) provides a structured interview to be given to parents.

Psychological Tests

Psychological tests provide information about the individual as well as comparative information, such as family cohesion, and should have an empirical basis (Gould, 1999). Gould (1999) states, "The work product that results from the systematic gathering of data, its analysis, and its interpretation is a scientific work product and should be expected to meet at least minimal evidentiary standards of scientific admissibility" (p. 160). Gould (1999) lists several reasons supporting the use of psychological tests in child custody evaluations. These include objective means of gathering information, an assessment of the person's response style, and confirmation or disconfirmation of information gathered during the interview, among others.

The following tests are commonly used in child custody evaluations. However, it is important to note that not all of the tests commonly used have been validated for the custody context. The evaluator must make inferences from this data to the relevant context, and this should be noted explicitly in the report. (For a more in-depth discussion of conceptual and empirical issues in child custody evaluations, see O'Donohue & Bradley, 2000.)

MMPI

For personality assessment, Ackerman (1995) recommends the use of the MMPI-2 and MMPI. As stated earlier, the MMPI and MMPI-2 are the most commonly used psychological tests in child custody evaluations. However, it should be noted that the MMPI-2 was constructed for use with clinical populations and may have unknown predictive validity with regard to making custody or parenting predictions (Grisso, 1990). Siegel (1996) cautions mental health professionals on the use of the MMPI-2 in the custody setting because the parent profiles are often invalid (clinically elevated L and K scales), indicating an overly defensive or positive response style. Otto and Collins (1995) recommend the use of the MMPI-2 to assess the parents' emotional functioning but caution the mental health professional on making inferences from this data to how it affects the children, as there is no current research to substantiate such claims.

Projective Tests

As stated earlier, the Rorschach and TAT are the most commonly used projective techniques during custody evaluations. However, projective tests may have questionable validity and reliability with any population for any question (Wood, Nezworski, & Stejskal, 1996). Inferences made based on responses to projective tests should be made with caution, and the lack of empirical support for these inferences should be made explicit in the report.

Intelligence and Achievement Tests

Ackerman (1995) recommends using the Weschler Adult Intelligence Scale or Stanford Binet Intelligence Test with adults, and the Weschler Intelligence Scale for Children, or the Kaufman Assessment Battery for Children to assess intelligence and the Wide Range Achievement Test to assess academic achievement. However, it is unclear what relevant data intelligence testing provides (in the absence of significant cognitive impairment), and it is time consuming for both the evaluator and examinee. This may be why the Quinnell and Bow (2001) survey indicate a decline in their use.

Other Measures

There are many self-report measures available to child custody evaluators. These cover parenting skills, attachment, parent satisfaction, emotional well-being, and ability to cooperate with the other parent, among others. These measures may help the examiner quantify data gathered from the examinee.

Quinnell and Bow (2001) found an increase in the use of other tests to measure constructs relevant to the custody context. These included the Child Behavior Checklist (used by 31% of the sample), Conner's Parent Rating Scale (used by 26% of the sample), Parent Stress Index (used by 41% of the sample), Child Abuse Potential Inventory (21% of sample), and the Parent Child Relationship Inventory (44% of the sample). Bricklin's scales, such as the Bricklin Perceptual Scale and Parent Awareness Skills Survey, were used by 28 percent and

21 percent of the sample, respectively. Other tests that are being used include assessment batteries designed specifically for the child custody context, such as the Ackerman-Schoendorg Scales for Parent Evaluation of Custody (ASPECT), Bricklin's ACCESS, and the Uniform Child Custody Evaluation System. Although these newer measures provide information more directly applicable to the child custody context, evaluators should be aware that less well-known self-report measures often lack empirical validity.

Direct Observation

Several authors recommend that custody evaluators conduct direct parent-child observations (preferably in multiple settings) (Ackerman, 1995; Gould, 1999). In fact, conducting such observations is listed in the APA guidelines (1994). APA guidelines state that during parent-child observations clinicians should evaluate the quality of the child's interactions with the parent, communication patterns, behaviors, and the quality of the interactions between caregivers. Although this seems like a common-sense activity, it is more complicated than most evaluators realize. For example, what are the behavioral correlates of "good" parent-child interactions? What communication patterns are harmful to the psychological growth of the child?

Threats to valid inference from direct observations include reactivity, unreliable coding systems, insufficient samples of observed behavior, and problematic data compilation and analysis. Reactivity is a serious concern in parent-child observations, especially when observations are conducted in the office. Both the child and parent are likely to feel uncomfortable and behave in unnatural ways. In addition, this may place caretakers who currently have visitation at a disadvantage. Parent-child observations should be conducted in multiple settings and long enough for the examinees to habituate to the presence of an observer. However, this is often unfeasible because of limited resources. Just as psychological tests should be standardized, data gathered from parent-child observations should have a reliable coding system. The constructs (and their relevance to custody) should be stated explicitly, and the behavioral correlates of these constructs should be outlined. Without this level of standardization, the evaluator is not likely to gather reliable and valid information. Finally, the evaluator should state how he or she compiled the data from these observations to form an inference.

COLLATERAL INFORMATION AND RECORD REVIEW

The AFCC guidelines (1995) recommend that the custody evaluator obtain collateral information when appropriate. In forensic assessments, such as child custody evaluations, establishing historical truth is important. Gould (1999) states, "a competent child custody evaluation includes verification of the accuracy of each party's story against other information sources" (p. 161). Gould

(1999) recommends obtaining collateral data, such as interviews with new spouses, and a review of relevant records, such as the child's school records, or psychotherapy reports. It is important for the evaluator to obtain appropriate consents from the participants of the evaluation and to obtain equivalent collaborative information from each participant.

INTEGRATING TEST RESULTS AND INTERPRETING THE DATA

Conducting a structured interview, administering psychological tests, obtaining self-report data and collateral information, and reviewing records is the easy part of the child custody evaluation. The difficult part is interpreting and reporting the data. Cases in which one parent is clearly unable to safely care for a child are less common than those in which there are two relatively competent parents with different strengths and weaknesses. The difficulty becomes how to weight each test score. An important rule to follow is to report and weigh more heavily the data that are relevant to the best interests of the child. Gould and Stahl (2000) state that a child custody report should include only the results of psychological testing that are relevant to the evaluation (i.e., parenting, etc.). Negative personality traits or irrelevant diagnoses should not be included in the report. In addition, the evaluator should avoid including negative comments made by one parent against the other unless outside collaborative information is available.

ADDITIONAL ISSUES

There are many potential problems with tests used during the child custody evaluation. These include validity and reliability problems, cultural biases, impression management, and the evaluator's own values or biases. As stated earlier, most psychological tests currently used in child custody evaluations have not been empirically validated for this setting. Evaluators must remain aware of this fact throughout the assessment process. In addition, custody evaluations are normally conducted during a very stressful and unusual time in the parents' and children's lives. The APA's Standards for Educational and Psychological Testing (1985) state that "a test taker's score should not be accepted as a reflection of a lack of ability with respect to the characteristic being tested for without consideration of alternate explanations for the test taker's inability to perform on that test at that time" (p. 43). The question is whether the stress and the atypical situation presented by a divorce and the custody dispute constitutes a reasonable "alternative explanation" that must be taken into account when interpreting a test score. For example, if a parent is depressed (e.g., a spouse has left the marriage and financial stressors are building), can the custody evaluator make inferences about the parent's ability to parent in two months, when he or she may no longer be depressed?

The problem of the unusual timing of custody evaluations is also possible in intelligence testing. For example, severe stressors, such as the dissolution of a marriage and/or moving, may cause decreases in ability to concentrate. This may lower performance on standard intelligence tests. Can the custody evaluator make inferences from this test to the parent's normal functioning? These issues of interpretation must be resolved by the evaluator on a case-by-case basis. However, it is crucial that the evaluator be explicitly aware of these concerns when making interpretations.

Another basic methodological problem in custody evaluations concerns impression management of participants. Beaber (1982) states that most parents during a custody evaluation will tend to present themselves in a positive light while presenting only negative or predominantly negative information about their spouse. Some parents may exaggerate their spouse's faults and their own positive attributes. Children may state preferences of one parent over another because of coaching or fear of hurting someone's feelings. The practitioner must be aware that the data presented by parents and child(ren) may not be entirely accurate. Ash and Guyer (1991) conducted a study that included 196 families referred for court ordered custody evaluations. Both the mother and father were given the Achenbach Child Behavior Checklist. Results indicated that "in custody cases, custodial (possessory) parents rated the children as less disturbed than did non-custodial parents" (p. 836). There is presently no system for accurately distinguishing among lies, exaggerations, and the truth.

Custody evaluators must also remain aware of potential cultural biases in the interview and testing process. Several authors have discussed cultural biases with standard intelligence tests, and some research indicates the need for separate MMPI norms for Latino populations. The cultural background of the parents and children must be taken into account throughout the assessment process. Because much of a child custody evaluation is based on the evaluator's professional opinion, one must be aware of his or her own biases and values. This is of particular importance when evaluating people from cultures and socioeconomic levels other than the evaluator's.

Conclusion

This chapter has outlined some of the issues that the evaluator should be aware of prior to conducting child custody evaluations. These include a basic knowledge of relevant statutes and case law from his or her state, the ethical guidelines for conducting custody evaluations, and the empirical basis of psychological tests used during the evaluation. Child custody evaluations should be conducted in an ethical manner, using the existing scientific knowledge base. In addition, potential problems in the custody evaluation (e.g., cultural bias, test validity) should be made explicit in the final report.

REFERENCES

Ackerman, M. J. (1995). *Clinician's guide to child custody evaluations*. New York: Wiley.

Ackerman, M. J., & Ackerman, M. C. (1997). Custody evaluation practices: A survey of experienced professionals (Revised). *Professional Psychology, Research and Practice, 28* (2), 137–145.

American Psychological Association (1985). *Standards for educational and psychological testing*. Washington, DC: American Psychological Association.

American Psychological Association (1994). APA guidelines for child custody evaluations in divorce proceedings. *American Psychologist, 49* (7), 677–680.

Ash, P., & Guyer, M. J. (1991). Biased reporting by parents undergoing child custody evaluations. *Journal of the American Academy of Child and Adolescent Psychiatry, 30* (5), 835–838.

Association of Family and Conciliation Courts (1995). *Model standards of practice for child custody evaluation*. Madison, WI: Author.

Beaber, R. J. (1982). Custody quagmire: Some psycholegal dilemmas. *The Journal of Psychiatry and Law, 10* (3), 309–326.

Bricklin, B. (1995). *The custody evaluation handbook*. New York: Brunner/Mazel.

Centers for Disease Control and Prevention (2000). *National Center for Health Statistics*. Atlanta: U.S. Department of Health and Human Services.

Edmon, S., Cole, D. A., & Howard, G. S. (1990). Convergent and discriminant validity of FACES-III: Family adaptability and cohesion. *Family Process, 29*, 95–103.

Gardner, R. A. (1997). An instrument for objectively comparing parental disciplinary capacity in child custody disputes. *Journal of Divorce and Remarriage, 27* (3/4), 1–15.

Gould, J. W. (1999). Scientifically crafted child custody evaluations, Part two: A paradigm for forensic evaluation of child custody determination. *Family and Conciliation Courts Review, 37* (2), 159–178.

Gould, J. W., & Stahl, P. M. (2000). The art and science of child custody evaluations: Integrating clinical and forensic mental health models. *Family and Conciliation Courts Review, 38* (3), 392–414.

Graham, J. R., Watts, D., & Timbrook, R. E. (1991). Detecting fake-good and fake-bad MMPI-2 profiles. *Journal of Personality Assessment, 57* (20), 264–277.

Grisso, T. (1990). Evolving guidelines for divorce/custody evaluations. *Family and Conciliation Courts Review, 28* (1), 35–41.

Hall, A. S., Pulver, C. A., & Cooley, M. J. (1996). Psychology of best interests standard: Fifty state statutes and their theoretical antecedents. *The American Journal of Family Therapy, 24* (2), 171–180.

Howell, S. H., Portes, P. R., & Brown, J. H. (1997). Gender and age differences in child adjustment to parental separation. *Journal of Divorce and Remarriage, 27* (3/4), 141–158.

Hysjulien, C., Wood, B., & Benjamin, G. A. H. (1994). Child custody evaluations: A review of methods used in litigation and alternative dispute resolution. *Family and Conciliation Courts Review, 32* (4), 466–489.

Jackson, B. L., & Donovan, R. L. (1990, Spring). Psychological assessment in child custody cases. *TACD Journal*, 47–54.

Keilin, W. G., & Bloom, L. J. (1986). Child custody evaluation practices: A survey of experienced professionals. *Professional Psychology Research and Practice, 1* (4), 338–346.

Lyons, S. J. (1993). Art psychotherapy evaluations of children in custody disputes. *The Arts in Psychotherapy, 20*, 153–159.

Mason, M. A. (1994). *From father's property to children's rights: The history of child custody in the United States*. New York: Columbia University Press.

McConaughy, S. H., & Achenbach, T. M. (1996). Contributions of a child interview to multimethod assessment of children with EBD and LD. *School Psychology Review, 25* (1), 24–39.

Milner, J. (1989). Applications of the Child Abuse Potential Inventory. *Journal of Clinical Psychology, 45* (3), 450–454.

O'Donohue, W., & Bradley, A. R. (1999). Conceptual and empirical issues in child custody evaluations. *Clinical Psychology: Science and Practice, 6* (3), 310–322.

Otto, R. K., & Collins, R. P. (1995). Use of the MMPI-2/MMPI-A in child custody evaluations. In Y. S. Ben-Porath, J. R. Graham, G. C. N. Hall, & M. S. Zaragoza (Eds.), *Forensic applications of the MMPI-2* (pp. 222–252). Thousand Oaks, CA: Sage.

Portes, P. R., Howell, S. C., Brown, J. H., Eichenberger, S., & Mas, C. A. (1992). Family functions and children's postdivorce adjustment. *American Journal of Orthopsychiatry, 62* (4), 613–617.

Quinnell, F. A., & Bow, J. N. (2001). Psychological tests used in child custody evaluations. *Behavioral Science and the Law, 19*, 491–501.

Roll, S., Lockwood, J., & Roll, E. (1981). *Preliminary manual: Parent Attachment Structured Interview*. Albuquerque, NM: Author.

Siegel, J. C. (1996). Traditional MMPI-2 validity indicators and initial presentation in custody evaluations. *American Journal of Forensic Psychology, 14* (3), 55–63.

Sorensen, E. D., & Goldman, J. (1990). Custody determinations and child development: A review of the current literature. *Journal of Divorce, 13* (4), 53–67.

Wallerstein, J. S. (1985). The overburdened child: Some long-term consequences of divorce. *Social Work, 30* (2), 116–123.

Wood, J. M., Nezworski, M. T., & Stejskal, W. J. (1996). The comprehensive system for the Rorschach: A critical examination. *Psychological Science, 7* (1), 3–10.

CHAPTER 12

FORENSIC INTERVIEWING AND ASSESSMENT ISSUES WITH CHILDREN

MATTHEW FANETTI
SOUTHWEST MISSOURI STATE UNIVERSITY

RICHARD BOLES
UNIVERSITY OF KANSAS

In Florida during the 1980s, a district attorney, Janet Reno, oversaw the prosecution of several individuals who were alleged to have committed sexual abuse. A relatively recent *Frontline* episode (Frontline, 1998) looked at the failings, perils, and outcomes of that series of investigations. Reportedly, these included strong preconceived notions of guilt, problematic interviewing procedures, and alterations to case construction by law enforcement that seemed to have more effect on convincing juries than on clarifying truth. Similar but even more dramatic disasters occurred in the McMartin case (Garven, Wood, Malpass, & Shaw, 1998), the Edenton, North Carolina, case (Ceci & Bruck, 1995), and the Kelly Michaels case (Rosenthal, 1995), all of which have been heavily reported in various media and scientific publications. These cases represent the core of the dilemma in sexual abuse assessments: How do you balance the need to protect children with the need to treat defendants fairly and discover the truth?

The decade of the 1980s found the field of assessment unprepared for an increasing number of claims of sexual abuse. During that decade there was a rise in reports of sexual abuse that has been estimated to be near 2000 percent (Salter, 1992). Although this number is large and has dramatic impact, it requires thought for interpretation. In fact, Salter posited that the magnitude of the increase could be accounted for in several ways. First, the number of actual cases of sexual abuse might have increased and they had been, and are being, accurately measured.

Second, this trend might occur in situations where sexual abuse was relatively unseen and through some mechanism people become aware of abuse and report it. In this case, the measurement of the incidence and prevalence of sexual abuse becomes more accurate and false negatives decrease. Once again, however, this relies somewhat on a notion that the assessment of child sexual abuse is currently done accurately. Finally, the number of reports of sexual abuse had increased dramatically, but there was a less dramatic, or nonexistent, increase in actual cases of sexual abuse. In other words, there may have been no real change in incidence or prevalence, but rather an increase in false positives. For example, a public perception of an increase in real cases may have led to bias in an uncertain and malleable assessment process, thereby resulting in more reports, "cases," or convictions.

Although the first and second explanations rely on the assumption that the assessment process in cases of alleged sexual abuse is accurate, the third explanation relies on the notion that there is enough uncertainty or variability in the forensic interview process with children to make room for the introduction of bias and flawed conclusions. Without data to demonstrate the reliability or validity of the current state of the child sexual abuse (CSA) assessment field, it is difficult to determine which explanation, or which combination of explanations, is the more likely. However, a growing and stable literature base hints that there is a potential for the introduction of bias in such interviews (e.g., Bruck & Ceci, 1997; Ceci, Leichtman, & Bruck, 1995; Goodman, Sharma, Thomas, & Considine, 1995). Furthermore, if psychology is to be viewed as a science, it should be skeptical of its own measurement tools. This said, the most logical first place to look for an explanation for Salter's dark findings is in the psychometric properties of the assessment, or measurement, process.

The goal of this chapter is to briefly examine the CSA assessment process as well as methods for generating new assessment techniques that can be evaluated psychometrically. In order to accomplish this goal, the chapter will examine some relevant data related to childhood memory for events. Though this will not be a comprehensive literature review (e.g., Bruck, & Ceci, 1999; Ceci & Bruck, 1992, Eisen, Goodman, Davis, & Qin, 1999; Fundudis, 1997), we will describe the main points of interest for any clinician or scientist interested in forensic interviews of children.

CHILDREN AS WITNESSES IN COURT

Children can be called to provide their testimony in several types of judicial proceedings. These may include, but are not limited to, child sexual or physical abuse cases, custody hearings, or even as witnesses to nonabuse crimes committed by others. Whereas the evidence accumulating in the empirical literature may have seen a greater focus on cases of child sexual abuse, it is logical that the processes at work with CSA testimony should be similar to those at play in other types of interviews.

Children are occasionally called on to provide their testimony in judicial proceedings because of a lack of other physical evidence (Poole & Lamb, 1998). One of these instances, child sexual abuse, is often a secretive and witnessless crime. The nature of the social stigma and the legal ramifications for engaging in the behavior may induce a perpetrator to maintain secrecy and to avoid confessions. Additionally, in sexual abuse cases there may be a relative lack of physical evidence. Some cases do not involve any physical evidence at all (Poole & Lamb, 1998; Salter, 1992). In those cases with physical evidence, only a portion contain identifying physical evidence. *Identifying physical evidence* is that which contains some means of identifying the perpetrator (e.g., semen, blood, fingerprints, videotapes, photos, etc.). Therefore, the child's testimony may begin to increase in importance as the lack of corroborating evidence becomes pronounced. When the judicial system is called to render a judgment regarding a case, the evidence utilized should be as well understood as possible.

The ramifications of incorrect judgments in these cases can be harsh or can open the door for further abuse. The incorrect acquittal of a sexual child abuser puts children at further risk for abuse. In contrast, the incorrect conviction of an innocent individual effectively ends the context of that person's life as it had been known. Although it is not within the scope of this paper to review them all, the legal penalties for child sexual abuse are often severe, including long-term incarceration, permanent requirements to notify communities of the convict's record, removal from support networks, and a child's potential loss of a parent. When decisions are accurate, this may be the appropriate action. However, the possibility of incorrect decisions leaves open an important area for clinical scientists to address. As a field, we should work to gather as much information as possible about children's memory and our techniques for assessing it to ensure that they are as accurate as possible and that our tools and techniques have no iatrogenic or harmful effect, including decreasing child event recall accuracy. At present, we have some information about children's memory abilities, but no information about the effects of our current assessment techniques, including their helpful or harmful qualities.

Psychometric Evaluation and Forensic Interviews of Children

One of the most important components of test or measurement construction is psychometric evaluation. This involves the analysis of the stability and accuracy of the measurement tool. Any measurement tool should be able to accomplish two main goals. The first is to measure the same phenomenon twice yielding the same conclusion. This is called *reliability*. Anastasi (1988) states that "reliability is the consistency of scores obtained by the same person when retested with the identical test or with an equivalent form of the test" (p. 27). Sattler (1992) states that reliability implies that test results should be reproducible and stable (p. 25). If we are interested in measuring the length of a wall, we certainly will want to use a ruler that yields the same data twice in a row. However, reliability is especially difficult to establish when we are measuring human recall. After all, humans can recall target events as well as previous discussions of target events. So two interviews yielding the same or differing information may produce data correlated with the target event and/or correlated with *discussions* of the target event, two different and sometimes contradictory collections of information. In addition, lack of reliability can be the result of inherent instability of the measurement tool (i.e., it is a poor measure), the inherent instability of the target phenomenon (i.e., the malleability or mobility of the target), or the lack of adherence to the measurement tool. In the absence of any psychometric data, which is the case with most or all forensic interviews of children, the first step should be to determine whether the interviews (i.e., measurement tools) are administered with any consistency (e.g., do interviewers adhere to the interview procedures?).

In order to assess the reliability of the information produced by an interview process, we must be assured that the same process is used in the same way twice. This is called *administration adherence*. To do this, we must have procedures with enough specificity of administration to decide whether interviewers are following protocol. When general rules are utilized but their implementation is left to the user with some degree of flexibility, we must assume that some will implement the rule in one fashion, and others will choose a different method. This differing method of rule implementation can have implications for differential effectiveness, utility, or even harmfulness. Unfortunately, the field of child sexual abuse assessment does not currently contain assessments with enough specificity to ensure that some very good rules are implemented effectively or consistently. While there are many excellent guidelines (Aldridge & Wood, 1998; Boury et al., 1999; Ceci & Bruck, 1993), these are often left up to the interviewer to implement. Only interviews with structure can provide this specificity. Only after we can adequately measure adherence can the field begin to adequately address problems with the malleability or mobility of the target phenomenon (which is not a true problem with, e.g., instrument reliability), or with the tool's ability to accurately measure the target (i.e., validity), which is discussed next.

Reliability does not imply validity. In contrast, if two interviews yield contradictory information, it may be difficult to determine whether the data has become more or less accurate (i.e., valid). Anastasi (1988) defines validity as "the degree to which the test actually measures what it purports to measure" (p. 28). Sattler (1992) agrees and adds to this definition "the appropriateness with which inferences can be made on the basis of the test results" (p. 30). Validity is the step that seems to be almost spellbinding to the forensic assessment field. Law enforcement agencies, child protective agencies, and the judicial system as well as others all seek assessment strategies that yield "valid" information. After all, few want the guilty to go free and the innocent to go to prison. However, we must be willing to do the hard work of adherence measurement and reliability measurement before we can make any statements about validity.

We suggest that those who offer guidelines for conducting interviews also engage in critical examinations of the user's ability to effectively and consistently administer these tests. This seems a straightforward task for developers: simply determine the ability of users to use the product.

TRENDS IN THE EMPIRICAL RESEARCH INTO CHILDREN'S EVENT MEMORY

Ideally, the goal of the perfect witness is to report experienced events in the most accurate manner possible. However, there has been a notion that individuals are not always completely accurate when attempting to recall experienced events (Bruck, Ceci, & Francoeur, 1999; Loftus, 1979); thus, the number of security cameras placed, usually unflatteringly, has increased in most convenience stores and other public venues. If individuals were able to retrieve memories with no errors of omission (i.e., correct details left out of recall) or errors of commission (i.e., incorrect details added to recall), then there would be less need for such devices. This seems to be understood generally by the population. However, since individuals do have event memory and it is not perfect, their accuracy must be somewhere between 0 and 100 percent. Are all individuals endowed with the same accuracy? Is each individual equally accurate in every context? What are the factors that decrease or increase accuracy? The judicial system struggles with these very questions. How much can we trust a witness's ability to recall events in a given situation? Adults regularly provide event recall–based testimony in courtroom or judicial settings, even though very notable research has been conducted that demonstrates that memory can be a dynamic (rather than static) process and might therefore be subject to bias and error (e.g., Loftus, 1979). However, the testimony of children is more often openly controversial. Possibly the main reason for the controversy is differences in opinion about the ability of children to remember accurately or to provide accurate testimony (McGough, 1994; Goodman & Schaaf, 1997).

Opinions about children's ability to serve as witnesses can include, but are not limited to the following: (1) "children's memory is too unreliable," (2) "children lie frequently," (3) "children never lie about X," (4) "children's memory is just as reliable as adults'," or (5) "children can remember accurately under some conditions." Although any of these statements may be true, logic and empirical data can be used to address them. First, it is common knowledge that adults lie occasionally, even in court. Nevertheless, their testimony is still sought and taken into consideration. In addition, there is no evidence that children lie at a greater or lesser rate than adults in such settings, and there is no data to support the notion that children don't lie, or lie constantly, when providing event recall. In concession, a lack of data does not illustrate the nonexistence of the trend. However, social scientists need to illustrate the trend before making such a claim. Specifically, if a factual argument is to be made regarding children's behavior, it must be support by some data; otherwise it is a logical, intuitive, or opinion-based argument. With regard to children's ability to recall events, there is a substantial and growing empirical database that addresses that very issue. The next section of this chapter will briefly investigate studies of children's event recall. We will provide a description of some classic and some newer studies but do not intend to provide a comprehensive review of the entire literature base. Other notable authors (Bruck & Ceci, 1999; Ceci & Bruck, 1993; Fivush, 1998) have completed excellent reviews and review updates that better serve that purpose.

Several studies have demonstrated that children's accuracy in recalling experienced events can be affected by the type of questioning used to elicit their report. In fact, specific trends in children's accuracy began to emerge in the 1980s and early 1990s (for a review, see Ceci & Bruck, 1993) and continued through the last decade (Bruck & Ceci, 1999). The next portion of this chapter will briefly examine the findings of empirical studies that provide useful information about the effects of different types of questioning on the reported recall of children.

Recall accuracy is routinely measured via errors of omission and errors of commission. A report filled only with errors of omission will contain details that are factually accurate but will be incomplete. A report filled only with errors of commission will contain all the details of an event but will also contain details that did not occur. For example, if a child is grossly terrified of the interview process and does not speak, we can assume that he or she will not provide any false details (i.e., errors of commission). However, that child will provide no true details, either, and can be seen as filled with errors of omission. In contrast, if the interviewed child becomes highly motivated to continue providing details and runs out of recalled data, he or she may begin to provide nonrecalled data. In this case, while the child may have hit all of the correct details (i.e., no errors of omission), he or she may have made an abundance of errors of commission. It is important to understand these concepts and their implications for false positives and false negatives. Specifically and in pure form, *omission errors* may increase the likelihood of missing abuse events that actually happened and *commission errors* may increase the likelihood of charges of abuse that did not happen.

One of the strongest trends reported in the extant literature is that, in free recall, younger children tend to engage in more omission errors than older children, who engage in more omission errors than adults (Ceci & Bruck, 1993; Bruck & Ceci, 1999; Hutcheson, Baxter, Telfer, & Warden, 1995; Peterson & Bell, 1996). Stated differently, completeness increases as age increases. However, the same literature also illustrates that children, once again in free recall, engage in the similar proportions of commission errors as do adults. Humans may have the same *relative* accuracy across the age continuum. Nevertheless, in a legal context, errors of omission are troubling. Details are the stuff of which court cases are made. If children provide fewer details in free recall, interviewers may be asked to help fill in the holes, or omissions. They may find themselves in a position where they are asked to balance the need for cueing to elicit recall with the need to cue properly and carefully to prevent contamination. This can be an extraordinarily difficult task and may lead to the potential introduction of techniques that may decrease the accuracy of children in measures of errors of commission and perhaps omission.

Effects of Preconceived Interviewer Perspective

When individuals begin the interview process with a child, the presence of a set of interviewer beliefs about the alleged event may affect the accuracy of the child's reported recollection. This list may manifest itself through the types of questions utilized in the interview process. A good example of this process is a study by Petit and colleagues (1990, cited in Ceci & Bruck, 1995). In this study, children were exposed to an enacted scenario and then interviewed. All interviewers were given accounts of the story regarding the child they were interviewing. However, some interviewers were given accurate accounts and other were given inaccurate accounts. All were warned about leading questions. Results indicated that interviewers who were given inaccurate accounts resorted to using four to five times more misleading questions (which they probably believed were accurately leading) than those who were given accurate accounts. Furthermore, the children interviewed by misinformed interviewers assented to 41 percent of the misleading questions asked and thus were markedly less accurate.

This study is important for two main reasons. First, it suggests a pattern that may exist in forensic interviews of children conducted by perhaps well-intentioned professionals who have preconceived notions about an alleged event or else perceive themselves as "child advocates" whose duty is to end abuse. The pattern may be the initial use of nonleading techniques until the resulting report is different than expected. The interviewer may then use less ideal techniques, thus bringing the child's report into harmony with his or her own beliefs.

The second reason that this study is important is that it highlights the need for a more controlled approach to interviewing children. A strong hypothesis might be that if the interviewers were asked to use a structured interview, they would not have been able to initiate the use of misleading or problematic questions. Thus, the resulting reports may have seemed less accurate to the misinformed interviewers but would actually have been more accurate. Several studies have also investigated the effects of overtly stated beliefs on child report accuracy. Specifically, can inaccurate but directly stated beliefs or overtly stated accounts of events affect a child's reported recollection of the event, or are children able to resist incorporating such overt perspectives?

A study that highlights the problems of overt interviewer beliefs was conducted by Leichtman and Ceci (1995). Preschool children enrolled in a daycare center were told that a visitor who had not yet arrived, Sam Stone, was clumsy and always broke things that weren't his. When "Sam" came to visit, he did not touch or break anything. On the next day the children saw a soiled stuffed bear and a torn book. Even though no child had seen "Sam" do anything, when asked, 25 percent hinted that he might have had a part in the problem. Over the next ten weeks they were asked misleading questions by the first interviewer such as, "I wonder if Sam Stone got the teddy bear dirty on purpose or by accident?" On the tenth week, a second (seemingly independent) interviewer asked what had happened. Seventy-two percent of the children overtly accused Sam of having ruined the toys, and 45 percent reported remembering having seen Sam do it.

Another study (Thompson et al., 1997), sought to determine whether reported memory for observed events could be changed by suggestions made by an authoritative adult. Groups of 5–6-year-old children observed a janitor named Chester. One group saw a working janitor who was cleaning a doll, a second group saw a playing janitor who was behaving mildly abusively with the doll. Shortly thereafter, the children were questioned by Chester's "boss." This interviewer was assertive but not aggressive. The children were asked what Chester had been doing, using three interview characteristics: an interview asserting that Chester must have been playing, an interview asserting that Chester must have been working, and an interview making no assertions. Children reported accurate details in either the no-assertion interview or the interview that made the assertion in line with their observations. However, those children who were interviewed with assertions contrary to their observations quickly altered their report to match the assertion of the interviewer. In fact, 75 percent reported observations consistent with the interviewer's statements but inconsistent with their own observations.

These classic studies highlight the perhaps intuitive notion that children may be susceptible to the stated or unstated beliefs of interviewers in an unstructured format. They indicate that children may give credence to the interviewer's perspective regarding event details and suspect attributes. This trend may be related to perceived credibility, the child's beliefs that adults have access to better information, or the notion that children are compliant conversational partners.

Effects of Question Wording and Style

Children's reported recall might also be affected by more subtle, language-based processes. Dale and colleagues (1978) demonstrated that children's accuracy can be altered by changing function words within a question. Function words are those which are not related directly to a detail, but are used to tied the sentence together. However, words may also provide information about the interviewer's beliefs. Children were asked to view each of four short films. Ten minutes after the last film, children were asked to answer eight questions regarding the films. When children were asked about events that *were* actually in the film, the form of the question had no differential impact. However, when the questions were asked about events that *were not* in the film, the form of the question had a significant impact. For example, if they were asked about a bridge that was in the film, it made no statistically significant difference whether the question was worded as "Did you see a (the) bridge?" or "Didn't you see a (the) bridge?" Children were 73–90 percent likely to answer correctly in either case. However, when asked about a car (that was not in the film) the children were likely to answer affirmatively to questions such as "Did you see the car?" and negatively to questions such as "Didn't you see the car?" In fact, when asked about an absent event, 56 percent responded affirmatively to questions such as *"Did you see the . . . ?"* and 33 percent responded affirmatively to questions such as *"Did you see a . . . ?"* The 33 percent false-positive rate when the question was asked with the word *a* is not notably different than expected. However, the 56 percent false-positive rate when the question was asked with the word *the* is significantly different than expected. This outcome raises the possibility that children's accuracy can be affected by wording that seems to be very subtle. However, an objective perusal may indicate that the questions have different suggestions *about the interviewer's beliefs*. These findings are important because they indicate how relatively small semantic differences in questions can generate different responses in preschool children even after a relatively short distraction period.

Brigham & Bothwell (1986) conducted a study of the event memory of students (fourth graders, eighth graders, and eleventh graders) who witnessed an enacted burglary. They were then asked to recall the event by either an authority figure or by a nonauthority figure (both adults but with more or less formal dress). Questions were designed to elicit information about the criminal's height, weight, age, and the like. Some questions were designed to contain a mildly leading word, while others were designed to be free of the suggestion (e.g., "How *tall* was he?" vs. "What was his height?"). Students were also asked to pick out the criminal from a photo lineup.

In the photo lineup, the fourth grade children were less accurate (accuracy = .68) than the eighth grade children (accuracy = .93), who did not differ significantly from the eleventh grade children (accuracy = .88). According to the authors (data were not presented in the table as indicated by the text, which minimized evaluation opportunity), children were likely to report correct identifying information when asked nonleading questions but were likely to report incorrect identifying information in the direction of the suggestion when asked leading questions (e.g., "How tall was he?" resulted in greater estimates of height than did "What was his height?"). However, the authors suggest that this effect was more pronounced for younger children than for the older children. The authors state that the results also suggest the "authority" of the interviewer who was asking the leading questions had no differential effect on the child's report. Upon closer examination, however, this variable may not have been manipulated to an extent that there was a significant difference in the perceived credibility of the questioner by the children.

Repeated Questions/Repeated Interviews

Laumann and Elliot (1992) conducted a study that investigated this factor. A group of 6-year-olds were asked to view a class film and then answer some questions about it. Immediately thereafter, the first interviewer was replaced by a second interviewer who asked both identical and similar questions. Results suggested that children were more likely to change their answers to questions when the same question was asked a second time (50%) than when different questions (semantically and syntactically) were asked about the same information (22%).

Mosten (1987) also conducted an experiment in which 6-year-old, 8-year-old, and 10-year-old children were asked several sets of questions about a school program they viewed. Some questions were complemented by a repetition of that question later in the interview, and some were complemented by a similar (but not identical) question later in the interview. In both tests, the child was more likely to correctly answer the first question and then change his or her response to the second question. This change was usually to an "I don't know" response but sometimes to an incorrect response (46% changed responses to the repeated question).

These results suggest that asking repeated questions can result in a child's change of response from a correct response to an incorrect response. What is not clear in these studies is the nature of the role of interpersonal variables in this process. The child may perceive the repetition as a mechanism by which the interviewer is revealing that the interviewer thinks the initial answer was not correct. The child's comfort in providing an "I don't know" response may be a variable that produces differential results (i.e., don't know vs. incorrect detail). What is clearer is that children are better able to provide accurate responses when questions are not repeated verbatim, or almost verbatim.

Sexually Anatomically Detailed Dolls as Memory Cues

The use of retrieval cues in the forensic interview of children is a debated topic. One occasionally used nonverbal cue is the sexually anatomically detailed (SAD) doll. These dolls are not only used as memory cues, they are sometimes also used as measurement devices (e.g., children who touch and are interested in the genitalia of the dolls are more likely to have been abused).

There are currently no scientifically sound studies that suggest that SAD dolls can be used with any reliability or that they offer a valid measurement/assessment strategy. In contrast, there are studies on the rates of sexual play with these dolls in *normative* populations of children (i.e., children who are thought never to have been sexually abused) that will be discussed later. Boat and Everson (1988) compiled demographic and observational data on a sample of 209 children ranging in age from 2 to 5 years old. The children in the sample composed a group that was ethnically and racially diverse as well as diverse across socioeconomic status. They were exposed to an interview that mimicked an investigatory interview (without leading questions) designed to assess the child's level of understanding of and terminology for basic external anatomy. After the interview, children were observed while playing with the dolls and each videotaped play session was then rated by observers trained to identify six classes of sexual play: clear oral, suggestive oral, clear anal, suggestive anal, clear genital, and suggestive genital. The study suggested that rates of normative sexual play were relatively high, ranging from a low of 22 percent for 5-year-olds to 87 percent for the 2-year-olds.

Jampole and Weber (1987) studied the responses of sexually abused and nonabused children who were 3 to 8 years old. Ten children from each group were selected for whom sexual abuse was either ruled out or had been forensically demonstrated. The children were interviewed in a room with two adults. One adult interacted with the child, while the other recorded the child's play behavior with SAD dolls that were ethnically matched to the child. Results indicated that whereas 90 percent of the children in the abused group placed the dolls in clearly sexual positions/activities, only 20 percent of the nonabused group did so. In this study, the rate of sexual play by the nonabused group is fairly high. Use of this behavior as an indicator of sexual abuse may lead to false positives at an unacceptably high rate.

Saywitz and colleagues (1991) conducted a study designed to assess children's ability to accurately report their experience of a physical examination that did or did not involve genital touch. They selected seventy-two 5- and 7-year-old girls to participate in the study. Half of the children experienced a routine physical examination that involved anal and genital components. The other half of the subjects experienced a medical scoliosis examination that did not involve anal or genital touch. The children's memory was later assessed using free recall of the event (with and without SAD dolls), and direct misleading and direct nonmisleading questions.

Results suggested that, in free recall, children were less likely to report genital and anal touch (22% without the SAD doll, 17% with the SAD doll), than in the direct question condition (86%). The only errors of commission occurred from direct, misleading questions asked of the subjects in the nongenital condition. Only three children made these errors and, when asked further details, were able to provide none. There was a significant age-based trend for errors of omission: Younger children made more errors of omission than did older children. The mean proportion of omission errors for the 5-year-old group was .22 at one week and .26 at one month, while that for the 7-year-old group was .14 at one week and .19 at one month. Overall, the results suggest that while use of the dolls did not result in errors of commission, they did not provide incremental utility, and most children did not report the genital touch until asked directly about the event. The authors suggest that their results support the notion that children are relatively resistant to misleading questions about genital touch in a medical examination. However, there are some problems with this conclusion. The wording of questions suggests that they were affirmative (e.g., "Did he touch you here?"). Previous work reviewed earlier (Dale et al., 1978) has indicated that this question type is much less suggestive than a question such as, "Didn't he touch you here?" The latter question implied some expectation on the part of the interviewer, which may in fact be the active variable.

McIver and colleagues (1989) studied the responses of 60 children. Ten of these children were victims, or thought to be victims, of sexual abuse (not well substantiated), and the other 50 were considered nonabused. The children's responses to the presentation of the SAD dolls were recorded and rated for sexual content. The rate of sexual/aggressive comment/play for the abused group was 62 percent, while the rate of sexual/aggressive comment/play for the nonabused group was 50 percent. These findings are difficult to interpret. The behavioral target was sexual and/or aggressive play. This is not an adequate distinction because the authors do not discuss why they believe that sexual play and aggressive play should indicate the same etiology, and a lack of differentiation allows few conclusions to be drawn. Additionally, the lack of substantial verification of sexual abuse for the children in that group leaves open the possibility that some children in that group may not have been sexually abused.

PERSPECTIVES PRIOR TO EVIDENCE GATHERING

In preparing to interview children, interviewers may proceed with distinct ideological and applied perspectives. There may be a disparity between the role we believe we should take or verbally gravitate toward and the role we adopt in practice. For example, it is probably safe to suggest that few interviewers would disagree with the statement, "The job of the interviewer is to identify the truth." However, some interviewers may start the process with a notion that the truth is already understood. Thus, the perspective they have actually adopted might be stated as, "The role of the interviewer is to *reveal* the truth to the judicial system." There may be truth seeking in the interview, but it may be relegated to molecular details of abuse rather than molar validity of the claim. The role of the interviewer can become one of advocacy rather than discovery. One viewpoint this author (Fanetti) has heard on a number of occasions is, "You cannot advocate for a perpetrator and for a [CSA] victim at the same time." While this may be true, the notion that an interviewer, or interview evaluator, is advocating for any one party reveals the preexisting mindset or perspective. When truth is sought, the identity of the beneficiary should be irrelevant. If it is not irrelevant, advocacy rather than truth seeking may begin to emerge.

Howard Garb (1998) has edited an excellent collection on the ways in which decision making can theoretically be influenced and inaccurate when it is not guided by clear evidence. Clear evidence is that which requires neither inference nor inferential causal links. For example, a videotape of a child sexual abuse act requires no inference of CSA, whereas the presence of specific "symptoms" of child sexual abuse requires the inference that these are accurate indicators and that, if they exist, CSA occurred. The introduction of inference in decision making can be a point at which bias is also introduced. Bias can take the form of base-rate errors and representativeness heuristic errors (Meehl, 1986), confirmatory bias errors (Ceci, Crossman, Gilstrap, & Scullin, 1998), availability heuristic errors (Garb, 1998; Read, 1995; Stalans, 1994), and primacy effects (Ambady & Rosenthal, 1992).

Base-rate errors are related to the representativeness heuristic. When the assumption is made that a phenomenon has become "epidemic," the decision maker may overestimate the likelihood that a specific case with presenting "symptoms" is in fact a member of the epidemic. In other words, if interviewers believe that children are being sexually victimized at an extraordinarily high rate, they are more likely to believe that vague symptom clusters are causally related to the experience of CSA than to another explanation. This assumption may set an *a priori* notion about the disposition of a case. In a somewhat related fashion, primacy effects and the availability heuristic may account for some *a priori* disposition predictions that are not statistically accurate. The explanations that occur first to an interviewer may be the explanations that are given the most credence. In a context that was designed to investigate CSA, it is understandable that this might be among the first hypothesized explanations of a given symptom cluster, even if the cluster is statistically unable to indicate causal factors. These preconceived notions then may influence the assessment process itself.

Confirmation bias refers to the process by which interviewers may attend more closely to information that supports their hypothesis than to information that does not support their hypothesis. Even though hypothesis testing is theoretically designed to posit then test rival hypotheses, confirmatory hypotheses that are done in an unstructured manner may begin to take a more prominent role and exculpatory hypotheses may begin to disappear. Therefore, the opportunities for exculpatory information to emerge may become reduced in frequency. To be useful and informative, the hypothesis-testing approach should investigate all rival hypotheses, even those that are exculpatory.

Availability heuristic errors (Garb, 1998; Read, 1995; Stalans, 1994) occur when decisions are influenced by the memory of associated events or objects. For example, after viewing a news show related to the terrors of child sexual abuse, an observer may be more likely to believe that a given set of symptoms represents a case of child sexual abuse. Conversely, after viewing a news show related to the horrors of zealous prosecution, an observer may be more likely to believe that an investigation represents a miscarriage of justice.

Primacy effects (Ambady & Rosenthal, 1992) are errors made by attending heavily on information that is presented early in consideration while not attending as heavily to disconfirmatory information occurring later. For example, when cases arrive at appropriate law enforcement or child protective agencies, the bearer may have already formed a strong argument for the possibility of sexual abuse, including a list of positive indicators used to foster the concern. This preconclusion may be incorporated by the investigator, forming a kind of preconceived notion or early-conceived notion of guilt or innocence.

The processes by which investigations may become biased are not a direct indictment of current interviewing strategies, but of human nature itself. We are not suggesting that current interviewing strategies involve any malicious components, just that an understanding of the ways in which we can be biased should be utilized in future interview methods. In an unstructured assessment procedure, it may be exceedingly difficult to resist these sources of bias and to demonstrate that they had no effect on the data produced. Therefore, the more beneficial avenue for assessment may be the pursuit of structured methodologies. Structured methods allow for a closer control of the assessment process and for a greater opportunity for psychometric evaluation.

STANDARDIZED ASSESSMENT PROCEDURES

One somewhat-structured assessment strategy is *statement validity assessment*, often based on a hypothesis that true recollections differ qualitatively from untrue recollections, or that children making true allegations differ from children making false allegations. Examples of this type of assessment include approaches such as the Polygraph and Statement Validity Analysis (SVA; Raskin & Esplin, 1991; Yuille, 1989). In its most common form, SVA is constructed of three components, an interview guideline designed to elicit a child's verbal report, a criterion-based content analysis (CBCA) of the report, and a form of contextual check to make inferences regarding validity. In essence, this type of assessment attempts to draw conclusions about whether an abuse event occurred or did not occur based on the characteristics of the child report and reporting style (e.g., amount of detail), under the aforementioned assumption that there are qualitative, reliable, and valid markers of actual statement validity. The product of this type of assessment generally is a conclusion about the truth or falsity of the allegation. However, there is no sound evidence that SVA is able to accurately distinguish true allegations from false allegations. In fact, in the absence of definitive evidence (e.g., videotape) the accuracy of a claim cannot be known, only inferred. In the judicial system, inference may be better left to the true decision-making body (e.g., judge or jury). The interview may be a tool to better inform that body regarding the child's recall as well as the potential influences to its accuracy.

Attempting to estimate the truth of a sexual abuse allegation based on one or a set of qualities of the child's verbal report is currently problematic. For example, if one criterion is that true reports are more complete than false reports, increased detail does not necessarily indicate increased validity. Also, it is not possible to accurately determine how much to increase the validity estimate as a function of a specific level of detail. The amount of detail provided by a child might be influenced by a number of factors that are unrelated to whether the child actually experienced the event (for a review, see Ceci & Bruck, 1993, or O'Donohue & Fanetti, 1996). Given a specific state of reality (i.e., abuse that did or did not occur), the completeness of the report might be altered by varying any one of a number of factors, or any combination. Therefore a true report of abuse might be *lacking in detail* because of issues such as inadequate interview rapport, fear of threats by others, and the like, whereas a false report of abuse might be *rich in detail* because of issues such as numerous previous interviews, problematic reinforcement in the interview, and so on (Brigham & Bothwell, 1986; Ceci & Leichtman, 1992; Thompson, Clarke-Stewart, & Lepore, 1997; Dale, Loftus, & Rathburn, 1978; Fivush & Hamond, 1989; Garven et al., 1998). Determining how these intra-interview factors *affect valid inference* is then a daunting, if not impossible task.

Additionally, although we can establish the *existence* of a potential influence, there is no empirical evidence that we can accurately determine the *effect* of that influence. To do so would be to argue counterfactually what the child would have said if x had or had not happened. However, the empirical literature can provide data on some influences that have the *potential* to affect a child's report. Also, professional agreement can establish a wider set of factors that might be expected to do the same. Drawing from these two sources, a list can be created that enumerates the influences that either need to be controlled in an interview or assessed by the interviewer, for the purpose of understanding the processes that may or may not be active and potentially affecting the child's report. We have attempted to compile such a list in Table 12.1. These are influences supported either logically or empirically that can be critiqued for completeness or relevance. They are divided into (1) influences within the social context of the interview itself

TABLE 12.1
Potential Source of Bias

Factors related to social processes within the interview
1. The child, because of rapport problems, may not have been comfortable and therefore may not have answered in a full, accurate manner.
2. There were leading questions.
3. The child's verbalizations were at times disconfirmed.
4. The interviewer inappropriately reinforced certain types of answers.
5. There were repetitive and perhaps coercive questions.
6. Aspects of the child's total response (e.g., body posture, facial expression) gave a different interpretation to the child's answer.
7. The interviewer encouraged the child to speculate about important details, after the child indicated that he/she was not sure about an answer or did not have the information.
8. The interviewer referenced the fact that other individuals (e.g., peers) had been interviewed regarding the interview topic and/or indicated what the other individuals' responses were.
9. The interviewer focused or redirected the child toward information about a specific detail or individual.
10. The interviewer utilized an appropriate mnemonic device to improve the child's report.

Factors related to child-based phenomenon
11. The child's report has been contaminated by some outside source (previous experience with another professional), e.g., retroactive interference from some other interviews.
12. The child did not understand his/her role in the interview or the purpose of the interview and therefore his/her answers may have been distorted.
13. The child had experienced some sort of externally derived threatening experience that may have served to distort answers (e.g., fear of threats to self, loved-ones, or property).
14. Child did not understand what it means to tell the truth.
15. Child did not know the importance of stating the truth.
16. Child did not know that he/she could say, "I don't know" when the child did not know.
17. The child answered in a certain way in an attempt to please an authority figure.
18. The child did not feel as though he/she had a choice in type of response.

that the interviewer can control, or (2) influences that exist outside that context but that can nevertheless be assessed by the interviewer. Even with such explication, a clear understanding of the presence or absence of these influences does not prevent the ultimate decision (e.g., guilt or innocence, abuse or no abuse) from being subjective.

If children can be accurate under some circumstances and inaccurate under other circumstances, and if interviewer beliefs, stated or not, can have impact on the accuracy of a child's report generated in unstructured formats, how can interviews be constructed to minimize these influences, or can they be? We believe interviews can be constructed to minimize threats to accuracy. In fact, it is possible and even likely that many excellent interviews are completed regularly. However, it is currently difficult or even impossible to *demonstrate* that one interview method is used the same way twice, not to mention whether one approach is more sound than another. This stated, administering or evaluating interviews becomes an interview-by-interview task rather than a methodology-based task.

One important step in this field of child sexual abuse assessment may be the development of structured interviewing protocols. A structured interview can be evaluated for content, questioning style, inclusiveness, or any other content-related issue (Wells et al., 1997). In other words, experts from different perspectives can contribute to development by having a say in the manner in which issues are assessed. The implementation of a hypothesis-testing approach (see O'Donohue & Fanetti, 1996) simplifies this process even further. In essence, each reasonable potential influence on a child's memory can be either controlled or assessed. The net result is the child's report produced in a cleanly controlled interview, accompanied by statements about external influences that can be "ruled out" or "not ruled out." The field can have a clear say on the items being assessed in addition to how they are assessed.

The structured approach also makes possible *psychometric evaluation*. This type of evaluation must be done if the results of an interview are ever to be used as the foundation for legal proceeding. In their absence, questions about the reliability or validity can only really be answered with an intellectual shoulder shrug. The same can be said for the manner in which "final product" interviews are critiqued. Occasionally second, "independent" professionals are asked to judge the quality of a completed interview. As yet, there are no standards for such meta-evaluations. If information can be collected from the field about what things should and should not be done in a forensic interview of children, structured approaches can be devised for both interviewing and critiquing interviews already done. Structured interviews and protocols have several very distinct advantages: (1) They have a specified protocol that facilitates adherence measurements and thus reliability estimates, and (2) they are completely open and available for critiques of both approach and application of approach. The author (Fanetti) has currently engaged in the initial studies designed to implement empirical literature from the child memory and child interviewing fields to build a structured interview (i.e, the Sexual Abuse Structured Interview for Children or SASIC) and a structured interview evaluation protocol (i.e., the Protocol for Evaluating Forensic Interviews of Children or PEFIC). These will be briefly described next, not as an example of the best techniques, but as an example of an *approach* to assessment construction that facilitates both psychometric evaluation and assessment refinement. The actual utility and psychometric properties of the instruments will be easily revealed in other contexts by psychometric evaluation and peer review.

The Sexual Abuse Structured Interview for Children (SASIC)

In order to develop a sound interview assessment device, an epistemologically valid framework must be used to guide the development. The framework proposed consists of two major components: (1) an hypothesis-testing approach to ruling out or ruling in the presence of possible biasing behaviors in an interview, and (2) a large, although not exclusive, reliance on children's information processing to derive the specific alternative hypotheses regarding the interview behavior.

Children's information processing comes into play at two distinct levels in this model. The child will bring into the interview session some set of cognitive processes that serve to produce responses to the interviewers' questions (i.e., "memories" of the event, memories of subsequent events related to the original event in some manner). Additionally, the child will incorporate this new experience (i.e., the interview experience) into their "memories" of events that are related to the original event. The tasks of a skilled interviewer are (1) to evaluate whether the child has experienced other events that may affect his or her ability or willingness to recall information about the original event (e.g., previous interviews, parental coaching, police coaching, etc.), (2) to evaluate hypotheses regarding other factors that may have biased the child's recall, and (3) not to engage in behavior within the interview that may negatively influence the child's ability to recall accurate information.

We have utilized the list of potential biasing influences (Table 12.1) that need to be evaluated in order to narrow the set of plausible interpretations of interview content. The set was developed by first using an information-processing model of event recall to enumerate a set of possible biasing factors, then evaluating the set using current cognitive research on the effect of specific behaviors or events as well as preliminary expert consultation. The first working set is designed to facilitate an information-processing, hypothesis-testing approach (Hawkins, 1979) and includes biases that may occur in an interview with a child, biases that may be introduced by the social-interactive nature of the interview as well as from other confounds that have appeared in the literature.

The SASIC contains a predetermined set of questions with a predetermined decision tree. The order and manner in which certain areas are addressed and assessed are controlled to minimize the possibility of improper administration. However, a complete lack of flexibility in areas filled with idiosyncratic events is not desirable. Therefore, the SASIC also includes areas of less structured assessment that can be utilized only when the provided structure does not adequately deal with a highly idiosyncratic response.

An NIMH research grant was awarded (Fanetti, 1997) to determine the feasibility of a structured approach to child forensic assessment. If such an interview is not administrable, it is not useful, no matter how inclusive or empirically derived. Results from the first pilot study suggest that interviewers with low-level training were able to administer the SASIC in a controlled setting with adherence levels near .90. Adherence was measured by subtracting divergences from the structured decision tree from total decision points and dividing this number by the total number of decision points. A mean values across subjects was computed. Although this adherence level is promising for a prototype interview, it is not acceptable for forensic purposes and Phase II funding is currently being designed to address this problem. The route chosen to address the adherence problem is a computer-assisted interview. In effect, such an interview will include a programmed decision tree that frees the interviewer from the task of hunting for and implementing obscure and complicated branches of a large tree. The interviewer will then be able to focus exclusively on recording responses and reading questions. In this case, adherence will no longer be an issue. Feedback can be focused primarily on the construction of questions, decision trees, and interview hierarchy.

Not all evaluation is completed during the interview itself. The PEFIC (Fanetti & O'Donohue, 2003) is a post hoc interview evaluation tool (i.e., meta-evaluation) that utilizes a basic behavioral identification task, based on the organizing empirical and logical structure of the SASIC. In essence, raters are trained to identify the presence of specific behaviors that are related to potential sources of bias. Several issues are involved in such an undertaking. First, there must be some agreement on the types of potential sources of bias that need to be controlled or assessed. Next, there must be some agreement on the definition of each hypothesized-biasing factor. For example, most would probably agree that "leading questions" are not the best interviewing technique and should be eliminated, or that their presence in an interview weakens the interview. However, there may be less agreement than expected on the behaviors that define a leading question. The reliability of such a determination relies on some explication and standardization of the definition. This is true for each potential source of bias. However, even after such agreement is reached, it is still necessary to determine the degree to which raters can reliably identify examples of the problem behavior.

CONCLUSION

If the field can come to reasonable agreement on the things that need to be controlled or assessed and how they are behaviorally defined, and if these can then be reliably identified in context, the procedure for such evaluations becomes clear. The net result of such an identification task would not be related to the accuracy of the child's report—a fruitless task—but rather to the presence or absence of the most obvious and empirically derived sources of bias or contamination. In other words, the product would be related more to the quality of the interview than to the child's accuracy. After all, though we might be able to say that a leading question was present, we will not be able to say that the child was inaccurate because of it. This decision is thus left with the proper authority, the judicial system.

We do, however, offer a challenge to the empirical community: Improve upon our approach, utilize our approach more effectively than we have, or develop another approach that will provide consistency and measurability in the child forensic assessment field. We are in desperate need of assessment that is open to true psychometric evaluation.

REFERENCES

Aldridge, M., & Wood, J. (1998). *Interviewing children: A guide for child care and forensic practitioners.* New York: Wiley.

Ambady, N., & Rosenthal, R. (1992). Thin slices of expressive behavior as predictors of interpersonal consequences: A meta-analysis. *Psychological Bulletin, 111,* 256–274.

Anastasi, A. (1988). *Psychological testing* (6th ed.). New York: Macmillan.

Boat, B., & Everson, M. (1988). Interviewing young children with anatomical dolls. *Child Welfare, 67,* 337–352.

Boury, W., Broderick, R., Flagor, R., Kelly, D. M., Ervin, D. L., & Butler, J. (1999). *A child interviewer's guidebook.* Thousand Oaks, CA: Sage.

Brigham, J., & Bothwell, R. (1986). Accuracy of children's eyewitness identifications in a field setting. *Basic and Applied Social Psychology, 7* (4), 295–306.

Bruck, M., & Ceci, S. J. (1997). The suggestibility of young children. *Current Directions in Psychologica Science, 6,* 75–79.

Bruck, M., & Ceci, S. J. (1999). The suggestibility of children's memory. *Annual Review of Psychology, 50,* 419–439.

Bruck, M., Ceci, S. J., & Francoeur, E. (1999). The accuracy of mothers' memories of conversations with their preschool children. *Journal of Experimental Psychology: Applied, 5,* 89–106.

Ceci, S. J., & Bruck, M. (1993). Suggestibility of the child witness: A historical review and synthesis. *Psychological Bulletin, 113,* 403–439.

Ceci, S. J., & Bruck, M. (1995). *Jeopardy in the courtroom: A scientific analysis of children's testimony.* Washington, DC: American Psychological Association.

Ceci, S. J., Crossman, A. M., Gilstrap, L. L., & Scullin, M. H. (1998). Social and cognitive factors in children's testimony, in C. P. Thompson, D. J. Herrmann, et al. (Eds.), *Eyewitness memory: Theoretical and applied perspectives* (pp. 15–30). Mahwah, NJ: Lawrence Erlbaum.

Ceci, S. J., Leichtman, M. D., & Bruck, M. (1995). The suggestibility of children's eyewitness reports: Methodological issues. In F. E. Weinert, W. Schneider, et al. (Eds.), *Memory performance and competencies: Issues in growth and development* (pp. 323–347). Mahwah, NJ: Lawrence Erlbaum.

Dale, P., Loftus, E., & Rathburn, L. (1978). The influence of the form of the question on the eyewitness testimony of preschool children. *Journal of Psycholinguistic Research*, *7* (4), 269–277.

Eisen, M. L., Goodman, G. S., Davis, S. L., & Qin, J. (1999). Individual differences in maltreated children's memory and suggestibility. In L. M. Williams, V. L. Banyard, et al. (Eds.). *Trauma and Memory* (pp. 31–46). Thousand Oaks, CA: Sage.

Fanetti, M. (1997). *A Structured Interview for Assessing Child Sexual Abuse, Phase One, SBIR research grant*. National Institutes of Mental Health, #1R43MM57194-01.

Fanetti, M., & O'Donohue, W. (2003). A protocol for evaluating forensic interviews of children. Manuscript in preparation.

Fivush, R. (1998). Children's recollections of traumatic and nontraumatic events. *Development and Psychopathology*, *10*, 699–716.

Fivush, R., & Hamond, N. (1989). Time and again: Effects of repetition and retention interval on 2 year olds' event recall. *Journal of Experimental Child Psychology*, *47* (2), 259–273.

Frontline (1998). The child terror. Episode 1707, October 27, 1998, PBS.

Fundudis, T. (1997). Young children's memory: How good is it? How much do we know about it? *Child Psychology and Psychiatry Review*, *2*, 150–158.

Garb, H. (1998). *Study the clinician*. Washington, DC: APA.

Garven, S., Wood, J. M., Malpass, R. S., & Shaw, J. S. III (1998). More than suggestion: The effect of interviewing techniques from the McMartin Preschool Case. *Journal of Applied Psychology*, *83*, 347–359.

Goodman, G. S., & Schaaf, J. M. (1997). Over a decade of research on children's eyewitness testimony: What have we learned? Where do we go from here? *Applied Cognitive Psychology*, *11*, 5–20.

Goodman, G. S., Sharma, A., Thomas, S. F., & Considine, M. G. (1995). Mother knows best: Effects of relationship status and interviewer bias on children's memory. *Journal of Experimental Child Psychology*, *60*, 195–228.

Hawkins, R. P. (1979). The functions of assessment: Implications for selection and development of devices for assessing repertoires in clinical, educational, and other settings. *Journal of Applied Behavior Analysis*, *12*, 501–516.

Hutcheson, G. D., Baxter, J. S., Telfer, K., & Warden, D. (1995). Child witness statement quality: Question type and errors of omission. *Law and Human Behavior*, *19*, 631–648.

Jampole, L., & Weber, M. (1987). An assessment of the behavior of sexually abused and non-sexually abused children with anatomically correct dolls. *Child Abuse and Neglect*, *11*, 187–192.

Laumann, L., & Elliot, R. (1992). Reporting what you have seen: Effects associated with age and mode of questioning on eyewitness reports. *Perceptual and Motor Skills*, *75* (3), 799–818.

Leichtman, M. D., & Ceci, S. J. (1995). The effects of stereotypes and suggestions on preschoolers' reports. *Developmental Psychology*, *31*, 568–578.

Loftus, E. F. (1979). *Eyewitness testimony*. Cambridge, MA: Harvard University Press.

Loftus, E. F. (2000). Suggestion, imagination, and the transformation of reality. In A. A. Stone, J. S. Turkkan, et al. (Eds.), *The science of self-report: Implications for research and practice* (pp. 201–210). Mahwah, NJ: Lawrence Erlbaum.

McGough, L. S. (1994). *Child witnesses: Fragile voices in the American legal system*. New Haven, CT: Yale University Press.

McIver, W., Wakefield, H., and Underwager, R. (1989). Behavior of abused and non-abused children in interviews with anatomically correct dolls. *Issues in Child Abuse Accusations*, *1*, 39–48.

Meehl, P. E. (1986). Diagnostic taxa as open concepts: Metatheoretical and statistical questions about reliability and construct validity in the grand strategy of nosological revision. In T. Millon & G. Klerman (Eds.), *Contemporary directions in psychopathology* (pp. 215–231). New York: Guilford.

Mosten, S. (1987). The suggestibility of children in interview studies. *First Language*, *7*, 67–78.

O'Donohue, W., & Fanetti, M. (1996). Assessing the occurrence of child sexual abuse: An information processing, hypothesis testing approach. *Aggression and Violent Behavior*, *1* (3), 269–281.

Peterson, C., & Bell, M. (1996). Children's memory for traumatic injury. *Child Development*, *67*, 3045–3070.

Poole, D. A., & Lamb, M. E. (1998). *Investigative interviews of children: A guide for helping professionals*. Washington, DC: American Psychological Association.

Raskin, D., & Esplin, P. (1991). Statement validity assessment: Interview procedures and content analysis of children's statements of sexual abuse. *Behavioral Assessment*, *13* (3), 265–291.

Read, J. (1995). The availability heuristic in person identification: The sometimes misleading consequences of enhanced contextual information. *Applied Cognitive Psychology*, *2*, 91–121.

Rosenthal, R. (1995). State of New Jersey v. Margeret Kelly Michaels: An overview. *Psychology, Public-Policy, and Law*, *2*, 246–271.

Salter, A. (1992). Epidemiology of child sexual abuse. In W. O'Donohue & J. Geer (Eds.), *The sexual abuse of children: research and practice, vol. 1.* Hillsdale, NJ: Lawrence Erlbaum.

Sattler, J. (1992). *Assessment of children, 3rd ed.* San Diego: J. M. Sattler.

Saywitz, K., Goodman, G., Nicholas, E., & Moan, S. (1991). Children's memories of a physical examination involving genital touch: Implications for reports of child sexual abuse. *Journal of Consulting and Clinical Psychology*, *59* (5), 682–691.

Stalans, L. (1994). Citizens' crime stereotypes, biased recall, and punishment preferences in abstract cases: The educative role of interpersonal sources. *Law and Human Behavior*, *17* (4), 451–470.

Thompson, W. C., Clarke-Stewart, K. A., & Lepore, S. J. (1997). What did the janitor do? Suggestive interviewing and the accuracy of children's accounts. *Law and Human Behavior*, *21* (4), 405–426.

Wells, R., McCann, J., Adams, J., Voris, J., & Dahl, B. (1997). A validational study of the Structured Interview of Symptoms Associated with Sexual Abuse (SASA) using three samples of sexually abused, allegedly abused, and non-abused boys. *Child Abuse and Neglect*, *21*, 1159–1167.

Yuille, J. (1989). The systematic assessment of children's testimony. *Canadian Psychology*, *29* (3), 247–262.

CHAPTER 13

EVALUATION OF PSYCHOLOGICAL DAMAGES

ALIX M. MCLEAREN
FEDERAL CORRECTIONAL COMPLEX (FCC) COLEMAN
COLEMAN, FLORIDA

CHRISTINA A. PIETZ AND ROBERT L. DENNEY
FOREST INSTITUTE OF PROFESSIONAL PSYCHOLOGY
SPRINGFIELD, MISSOURI

Forensic evaluations are often construed as criminal matters, but mental health professionals actually play a large role in civil litigation as well. In most jurisdictions, an injured individual (the plaintiff) is allowed to seek monetary damages for the harm caused by a responsible party (the defendant). Although the harm can be either physical or emotional, this chapter focuses only on issues pertaining to psychological damages. Persons seeking legal redress in personal injury suits often require psychological evaluation to demonstrate the nature and extent of their injuries. This chapter will review relevant standards defining psychological damages and negligence. Additionally, readers will be provided with a framework for conceptualizing psychological evaluations of emotional distress and related states. Finally, specific procedures will be delineated to detect both real injury and feigned suffering in civil litigants.

TORT LAW

In the process of seeking damages, a claimant or plaintiff alleges that harm was caused by another party. There are specific requirements that must be met for an act to be considered the cause of distress, and for its perpetrator to be held accountable. Known as a tort, this behavior is a wrongful act that causes harm to an individual. According to *Black's Law Dictionary*, a tort is defined as "A private or civil wrong or injury, including action for bad faith breach of contract, for which the court will provide a remedy in the form of an action for damages. . . . A violation of a duty imposed by general law or otherwise upon all persons occupying the relation to each other which is involved in a given transaction." Additionally, as implied in the American Law Institute's definition, torts can result from one of several acts: intentional behavior, negligent behavior, and strict liability in which harm was not preventable. The various behaviors that can comprise a tort are discussed in more detail later in this chapter.

For a plaintiff to receive compensation, the tort claim must be proven in the courtroom. In proving the tort, the filing party must meet four criteria, often referred to as the *4 Ds*: duty, dereliction, direct causation, and damages. Of course, the initial step in the sequence is that an act or omission thereof occurs. Once this happens, the plaintiff must demonstrate that a duty was owed by the defendant. There are certain principles that govern relationships between individuals, and these principles comprise the duty. For example, an individual offering a service may have a duty to perform that service as promised, to provide treatment, or to prevent harm (i.e, a physician has a duty to treat patients in accordance with professional standards).

Second, it must be established that the defendant was derelict in performing these duties. This charge could range from failure to perform the act to malpractice of some sort. As stated previously, dereliction can occur through intent or negligence or can be imposed as a strict liability. Intentional acts are the products of deliberate or considered conduct, while negligence is more nebulous. Typically, the standard for negligence is the *reasonable-person test*. Basically, this principle attempts to assess whether a reasonable person would have engaged in the same behavior (or lack thereof) as the defendant. Most often, the defendant is judged by community standards. Negligence is behavior that falls below the standard established by law for protecting the plaintiff against unreasonable risk of harm. Using the reasonable-person test, the question becomes: Would a reasonable person have acted similarly as the defendant in the same circumstances? Intentional acts are those in which the defendant meant for the outcome to occur.

Once these basic criteria have been established, it must be shown that there is a link between the event and the damage. In other words, the dereliction must cause the injury, commonly known as *proximate cause*. In essence, an act is described as the proximate cause of an injury if it was the logical predecessor to the harm incurred. The reasonable-person test is the standard to determine whether one event is the proximate cause of another. In other words, could one reasonably predict the act would cause the harm? Various states define proximate cause differently, and the reader is referred to individual jurisdiction guidelines (Daller, 2000).

The fourth criterion in proving a tort is determined by rigid legal standards that are governed by case law. The harm must be shown to involve a legally protected right or interest for which the plaintiff can seek to recover damages suffered. There are many instances wherein an individual may believe an injury has occurred, but the harm is not compensable unless the law defines it as such. Protection from property loss, for example, is typically more easily defined as a legal right than prevention of emotional distress, which some jurisdictions view as tantamount to "sour grapes" or hurt feelings.

As is the case for most civil issues, the standard of proof is a preponderance of the evidence. Some legal scholars have attempted to quantify this standard by assigning a numerical value to this concept, that is, more than 50 percent. In essence, the plaintiff is attempting to convince the jury that the damages occurred and were due to the act more likely than not.

As will be demonstrated in more detail later in this chapter, the evaluator could be involved in assessments pertaining to any of these four areas. However, the examiner typically is asked to address only damages and proximate cause. Most commonly, the clinician will be asked to detail whether or not damages exist as well as to explain several parameters associated with the damage. For example, if damages exist, what is the extent of those damages? What is the impact of those damages on daily functioning? What are the treatment needs to restore premorbid, or at least optimal functioning? Lastly, the expert is likely to be asked to provide an opinion on whether or not the current damages are due to the actions or inactions of the defendant. Consequently, clinicians performing civil forensic work must understand the concept of proximate cause as it is outlined in that specific jurisdiction (Daller, 2000).

CASE LAW

The standards just referenced by which tort claims are evaluated have evolved over time, and the current trend is fairly liberal in favor of the plaintiff. Personal injury law has emerged within the evolution of tort law. Knowledge of these standards may be enhanced through discussion of the cases that led to their development. An understanding of relevant case law is imperative in the formulation of clinical opinions on psychological injury. Although many salient cases have been decided in state court, the rules of law they established are often referred to by other jurisdictions.

Throughout history, there has been skepticism over the idea of rewarding persons for emotional damages, as their quality is often intangible. Until recently, psychological injury still implied physical contact or, at the least, physical proximity. Regardless, the United States has compensated its citizens for psychological wrongs for nearly a century.

The first instance in which a plaintiff was successful in suing for mental suffering without physical injury occurred in 1928 (*Christy Brothers Circus v. Turnage*, 1928). In this case, a business owner treated his employees to an afternoon at the Christy Brothers Circus. During a performance by circus animals, the plaintiff was the victim of "humiliation, embarrassment, and mental suffering" when a horse evacuated the contents of his bowels in the plaintiff's lap. The trial court awarded the plaintiff $500 in damages, and the decision was affirmed by the Georgia Court of Appeals. In ruling, the court stated, "Damages for mental suffering, humiliation, or embarrassment resulting from a physical injury maybe be recovered where the injured party exercised ordinary care in avoiding such an injury" (*Christy Brothers Circus v. Turnage*, 1928). Further, the court opined actual physical hurt was not required, but psychological damages required contact with the body of the injured party. This concept is sometimes referred to as the *impact rule*.

At the time of this ruling, mental injury was deemed compensable without actual physical injury, yet the differentiation between emotional and physical damage was not clarified. In the minds of many, claims of emotional suffering remained tenuous, whereas damages incurred from physical injury were easy to see and thus easy to reward monetarily. In *Carter v. General Motors* (1961), the Michigan Supreme Court ruled that the Workmen's Compensation Act required financial reparation for emotional disability, regardless of whether the injury was the result of physical damage or "mental shock." Furthermore, the court found that emotional and physical injury should not be treated differently in deciding tort claims. Finally, this case established that mental health injuries were compensable when touch was not involved. In other words, stress alone provides an adequate basis for a disability suit. This ruling, however, pertained only to disability law or workmen's compensation claims.

After the initial finding that emotional injury was tortious conduct eligible for remuneration, courts began to see an influx of such claims. The determination of emotional damage was difficult, but as discussed, cases such as *Christy Brothers Circus v. Turnage* established that actual physical damage was not necessary provided physical contact was sustained. Other states later determined that even physical touch was not a necessary element of emotional torts. The question then became one of determining what comprised legitimate distance from the plaintiff in psychological damage torts. The common legal standard for psychological damage became the *zone of danger*. Although this concept is still relied on in some jurisdictions, it has been overturned in others.

In 1968, the California Supreme Court did away with the "touch doctrine" in favor of the zone of danger (*Dillon v. Legg*, 1968). On September 27, 1964, Margorie Dillon was with her two children when one of the children ran out in the street and was hit and killed by a car driven by David Legg while she and the other child watched. She brought suit against Legg on behalf of herself and her surviving daughter, claiming she experienced emotional distress as a result of witnessing her daughter's death. The defendant maintained the woman's case was invalid on its face, in that she was not "in the zone of danger and fearing for her own life." The court sided with the plaintiff, citing earlier cases expanding emotional suffering to include those in which physical contact was not present. However, the court went further than those decisions, finding not only that physical trauma was not essential, but that fear of physical harm was also not necessary. The Court established three criteria to clarify and expand the zone of danger concept: (1) the plaintiff is located in close proximity to the scene of the accident, (2) the emotional shock resulted from "a direct emotional impact upon plaintiff from the sensory and contemporaneous observance of the accident," and (3) the plaintiff and the victim are closely related.

This issue was reexamined by the state of California in 1980, when a husband successfully sued a physician who incorrectly diagnosed his wife with the sexually acquired disease, syphilis (*Molien v. Kaiser Foundation Hospital*, 1980). This diagnosis led to marital discord and eventual divorce. Aside from the emotional suffering of believing the diagnosis, the plaintiff alleged additional psychological damages incurred by his wife's questioning his fidelity and initiating divorce proceedings. The court was asked to determine whether Molien's emotional distress was compensable since it occurred via negligence to another person and no physical injury was sustained by any of the parties involved. In this case, no physical contact occurred and there was no direct observation of the event, yet the court recognized a right to compensation when subjected to emotional distress. The court held that the requirement of physical injury was not justifiable and suggested such a mandate encouraged exaggeration or fabrication of physical symptoms to prove legitimate emotional distress. Attempting to differentiate physical and psychological injury was considered unnecessary and potentially confusing. This finding occurred in state court and thus is not binding for all jurisdictions.

Recently, the issue of compensating mental injury when physical contact did not occur was argued before the Supreme Court (*Norfolk and Western Railway Company v. Freeman Ayers et al.*, 2002). In the original case, the plaintiff sued for emotional damages relating to tortious conduct that allegedly created the fear of developing cancer. Although a ruling has not yet been issued, federal guidelines on compensable psychological damages are likely to follow. The astute reader is urged to remain abreast of developments in this area.

TYPES OF INJURY

As many as three types of injury resulting in psychological damage are compensable under tort law in various jurisdictions. The preceding sections have alluded to these distinctions. Further, it has been discussed that even though these distinctions exist, they serve little practical purpose in modern times because courts have begun to recognize each as equally worthy of attention. However, the informed practitioner should be aware of laws and standards particular to the jurisdiction of practice, as some areas are more or less likely to consider various emotional distress claims. The following section elaborates on types of injuries that may be compensable in various regions.

As noted, the earliest claims of emotional injury in American courts resulted from *physical injuries leading to psychological damages*. Certainly, such claims are easiest for outsiders to comprehend and for plaintiffs to prove since there is some noticeable physical damage to the claimant. Furthermore, common reasoning holds that observable physical impact legitimizes mental injury claims stemming from the incident (Melton, Petrila, Poythress, & Slobogin, 1997). For example, an individual may acquire a fear of automobiles that limits travel after sustaining severe injury in a vehicular accident or may suffer from a diagnosable mental disease, such as Acute Stress Disorder, following an assault (crime) or accident (negligence). All could become the subjects of tort cases. Additionally, neurological trauma often causes neuropsychological deficits in such areas as attention, concentration, learning, memory, abstract reasoning, concept formation, planning, organization, mental flexibility, sensory-perceptual abnormalities, and motor weakness, slowness, or incoordination. Often these deficits can have a deleterious affect on a person's ability to sustain employment and, to a considerable extent, life enjoyment. It is not uncommon for a person who experiences a significant traumatic brain injury to have notable personality changes as well. All of these changes can have serious implications for the plaintiff's life, particularly, employment, family support, and family relations. Such issues need assessment by a competent and thorough clinical neuropsychologist.

Although ultimately not compensable psychological damage, the converse of such damages deserves brief mention. *Psychological injuries leading to physical damages* can also become issues under tort law. Typically, these cases involve plaintiff's suffering heart-related damage as the result of some mental stressor. For example, an employee who is consistently overworked could experience myocardial infarction as a result of prolonged mental strain. In this context, the psychologist may be called upon to address whether or not the mental stressor actually existed and to what extent it may have contributed to the propensity to develop the physical difficulty.

Perhaps the most disputed type of emotional suffering case is that in which a plaintiff asserts *strict psychological damages*. As noted, such claims have been allowed only in the past few decades, and may continue to be limited in a minority of jurisdictions. Clearly, injuries in cases of this nature are much more difficult to define and are more likely to require evaluation by a mental health professional. Consider the previous example of an employee suffering prolonged stress because of working conditions. Under this category, no actual physical injury is required; instead, the plaintiff must show that the stress has occurred or that the job environment has somehow directly caused emotional suffering. In worker's compensation cases, for example, parties bringing suit are required to demonstrate that a set percentage of the suffering experienced is caused by the working conditions (California Statute 3208.3, 1995).

A final area comprising compensable psychological damages is cases in which an individual experiences *exacerbation of a preexisting mental condition*. Perhaps a subsection of the mental injury leading to psychological damages taxon, cases of this type may be the most difficult to prove, and establishment of premorbid functioning is essential. An individual with schizophrenia, for instance, could claim exacerbation of mental disorder if symptoms were under control prior to negligence on the part of others. Again, there must be present some type of measurable damages as a result. Understanding the type of injury is important for the evaluator since differing standards of proof or causation may apply.

At times, claims do not fall clearly into one of these categories, or plaintiffs are seeking both physical and psychological damages resulting from a more complex incident. For example, recent trends suggest the courts will see an increase in cases relating to lost enjoyment of life (LEL). Persons suing under LEL standards are seeking compensation for "limitations on the person's life created by the injury" (*Thompson v. National Railroad Passenger Corp.*, 1980, p. 824). Such a claim would likely occur in addition to a claim of damages resulting in physical or psychological damages. Poser, Bornstein, and McGorty (2003) found that mock jurors gave larger awards when given instructions allowing for a separate LEL award as part of the juror's charge.

PROFESSIONAL ISSUES

Both attorneys and mental health professionals must be aware of various professional standards and mandates that govern the civil litigation and evaluation process. Some case law has been discussed earlier in this chapter. Though somewhat disparate, we include the remaining topics together, since their use constitutes ethical practice.

Before accepting a referral, the clinician should ensure that he or she has the necessary competence and is qualified to perform the evaluation. As noted, some states have legal standards or administrative standards that the clinician is bound to follow in completing such an evaluation. In addition, the Speciality Guidelines for Forensic Psychologists provide "specific guidance to forensic psychologists in monitoring their professional conduct when acting in assistance to courts, parties to legal proceedings, correctional and forensic mental health facilities, and legislative agencies" (Committee on Ethical Guidelines for Forensic Psychologists, 1991, p. 655). Both the American Psychological Association's (APA; 2002) ethical guidelines and the Forensic Speciality Guidelines note that psychologists engaging in forensic work should have sufficient competence to practice. Forensic psychologists "have an obligation to provide services in a manner consistent with the highest standards of their profession." As such, forensic psychologists are expected to possess a specialized knowledge base and expertise. Likewise, forensic psychologists completing evaluations of psychological damage are expected to have specialized knowledge and competency. The APA outlines general principles for ensuring ethical practice. We cannot stress enough the importance of ethical practice and adherence to relevant guidelines in forensic settings, given their nature.

Although general forensic ethical and professional issues are reviewed elsewhere in this volume, we quickly highlight the most relevant to psychological damage evaluations here. Some very basic differences exist between the psychologist acting as therapist and the psychologist acting in a forensic capacity. For example, unlike treatment relationships, contact is initiated by the attorney. Thus, the client for the examiner is the retaining attorney, not the patient. The Speciality Guidelines for Forensic Psychologists make it clear that the forensic psychologist's role is "as expert to the court, whose task it is to assist the trier of fact" to understand the psychological aspects of the evidence and legal issues before the court (p. 665). Issues such as role clarification and confidentiality must be addressed before beginning any forensic evaluation.

Aside from general professional standards, an understanding of statutes pertaining to all civil topics is helpful in the preparation of reports for the courts. It is imperative that the clinician is aware of rules specific to the jurisdiction from which the case stems. Occasionally, the forensic psychologist may render an opinion that is not helpful to the retaining counsel. It behooves the forensic psychologist to know whether or not the psychological report, and the information upon which it is based, is considered attorney-client work product. Thus, the clinician is responsible for knowing if the state he or she is practicing in follows the *United States v. Alvarez* (1975) or *Edney v. Smith* (1976) decision. In *United States v. Alvarez*, a third circuit decision, the court ruled that the defendant's communication to an examining psychiatrist or psychologist is protected by the attorney-client privilege following the work product rule. Specifically, "If the defendant does not call the expert to the stand, the same privilege applies with respect to communications from the defendant as applies to communications to the attorney himself.... It is now almost universally accepted in this country that the scope of the attorney-client privilege, at least in criminal cases, embraces those agents whose services are required by the attorney in order that they may properly prepare his client's case." In contrast, in the *Edney v. Smith* (1976) decision, the New York Court of Appeals held that where a defense of insanity is asserted and the defendant offers evidence tending to show insanity, then a complete waiver of the doctor/attorney-patient privilege is effected and the government can call this witness. Thus, in civil cases, once the patient's emotional condition is placed in litigation, the privilege is waived.

Another professional issue concerns evaluations across jurisdictions when the practitioner is not licensed in a given region. Typically, clinicians obtain licenses to practice where they reside. Because psychological damage evaluations often require experts working in specialized areas, it is fairly common for experts to travel to their clients, especially those who are hospitalized, incarcerated, or otherwise immobile (Reid, 2000). As Dower, Gragnola, and Finnochio (1998) assert, laws governing mental health practices vary considerably across the country. The reason such standards and associated licensing boards exist is twofold: to protect citizens from incompetent practitioners and to identify those who meet practice standards (Association of State and Provincial Psychology Boards, 2001). Tucillo, DeFillipis, Denney, and Dsurney (2002) note that most American jurisdictions (over 70%) allow for the out-of-area clinician to conduct time-limited practice in the region. However, the onus is on the professional to access and follow the laws and standards of the particular jurisdiction. This lack of consistency across state lines invites unintentional malpractice, suggesting the need for a uniform model of standards on this issue (Tucillo et al., 2002).

Although this review of ethical practice standards is brief, we refer readers to other chapters in this book for greater detail. Additionally, we strongly recommend that practitioners obtain intensive supervision for initial forensic work. Before beginning any type of practice, local standards and laws for practice should be thoroughly understood.

Approach to Evaluation: Multiple Data Source Model

Once practitioners have updated themselves on relevant tort law issues and professional standards, forensic work can begin. Mental health professionals may be involved in personal injury cases as either treatment providers or evaluators. Although psychotherapy practitioners could potentially be called to testify regarding premorbid or postincident functioning, they should limit their opinions to issues of diagnosis, treatment progress, and prognosis, specifically the impact on daily functioning and quality of life issues. They should refrain from providing expert opinions on the ultimate issue, that is, whether or not the damages were caused by actions of the defendant. The Forensic Speciality Guidelines clearly delineate the importance of avoiding dual roles.

An evaluation of psychological damage is, in many ways, similar to an evaluation of mental state at the time of the offense. The difficulty is that the clinician must assess not only current abilities, but future strengths and weaknesses. In many cases, the financial award is determined by the future losses resulting from the injury. Consider an individual who has been harmed on the job, limiting mobility. Though not entirely disabled, this individual may no longer be able to complete activities or duties as he or she once did. Thus, the expert will be expected to predict the extent of the future impairments as well as to link those future weaknesses to the event in question. As has been shown repeatedly, one of psychology's greatest shortcomings is in the accurate prediction of future behavior. Professionals may also be asked the impact a given mental disorder has on future earning capacity. Thus, clinicians are faced with the issue of how to measure the degree or permanence of a mental disability, and this can be very difficult to quantify.

To encourage uniformity in these evaluations, the American Medical Association has provided a guide for their completion, titled Guides to the Evaluation of Permanent Impairment. According to a survey conducted in 1990, 36 states require by statute or administrative policy that these guidelines be followed when completing worker compensation evaluations (Spaulding, 1990). Although thorough assessment and documentation should be part of any psychological endeavor, it is essential that the evaluating clinician obtain the maximum amount of information in civil cases. Research shows that the base rate of significant symptom exaggeration in civil litigation cases regarding neuropsychological issues approximates 40 percent (Larrabee, in press), and about 50 percent of the variance in neuropsychological test results is accounted for by examinee effort (Green, Rohling, Lees-Haley, & Allen, 2001). In light of this information, we suggest the use of an *a priori* model of conducting evaluations of psychological damages that ensures complete coverage of relevant data. Specifically, we recommend an adaptation of the Multiple Data Source Model (MDSM; Denney & Wynkoop, 2000; Mrad, 1996).

The MDSM (Figure 13.1) was initially developed to guide examiners through the process of evaluating criminal responsibility and/or insanity, but it can easily be modified to assist in civil litigation cases. As its name implies, the model requires the forensic clinician to obtain and analyze multiple data sources in formulating an opinion regarding current and future impairments caused by

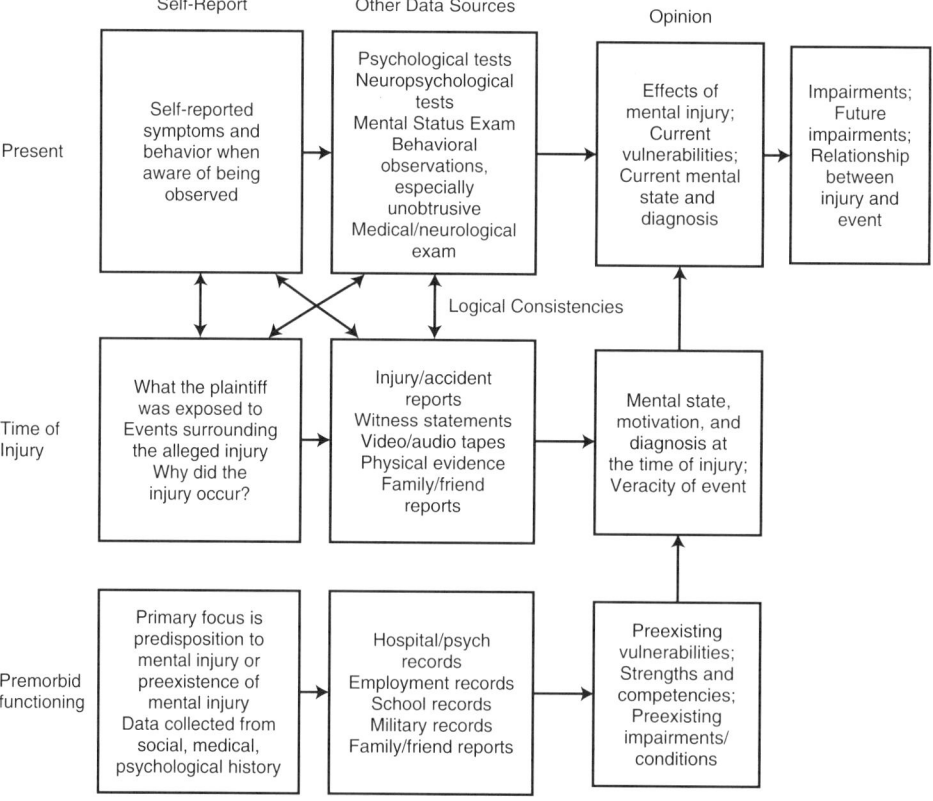

FIGURE 13.1 Multiple Data Source Model

the act in question. The goal is to assess the continuity or discontinuity in psychological functioning and incident veracity across time via consistencies or inconsistencies between times and data sources. For example, an evaluator could be asked to answer the question of whether a plaintiff's psychological impairments existed prior to the injury. Although on the surface this question may seem simple, it is considerably more challenging to establish premorbid functioning in persons for whom no psychological records are available. Furthermore, the clinician may be assessing whether the incident was the proximate cause of an injury or the exacerbation of some preexisting condition. The goal, obviously, is to establish consistency between past mental status and present mental status. By establishing this consistency, the clinician can establish a context in which to place the psychological injury and its potential impact on current functioning at a particular point in time.

Because the work of a forensic psychologist could be subjected to the scrutiny of the criminal justice system, the Forensic Speciality Guidelines note that the forensic psychologist conducts clinical work at a standard higher than that of general clinical practice. He or she is expected to document and be prepared to make available all work and supporting documents. Specifically, when forensic psychologists are aware that their professional services could be used in a judicial process, "they incur a special responsibility to provide the best documentation possible under the circumstances." The MDSM provides an exhaustive foundation for completing these evaluations by assessing the patient's functioning over three points in time. In addition, the evaluator gathers information from the patient as well as outside sources creating a robust evaluation. Information obtained from the patient and corroborative sources is then combined to render an opinion about current mental state and deficits in contrast to functioning prior to the injury. A connection must be made between any current deficits and the injury itself. The evaluator uses these sources to formulate an ultimate opinion. As Figure 13.1 depicts, an opinion of the present functioning is drawn from several sources including self-report, external corroborative sources (family), and evaluative corroborating sources (test data). This information is both objective and subjective. For example, tests used should provide norm-referenced data and can include both medical and psychological evaluation findings. Additionally, this information can be obtained through observations of the evaluee when this individual is unaware that such observations are being conducted. Subjective information refers to that provided by the examinee when he or she is aware evaluation is occurring and may thus be motivated to provide self-serving data. The examiner should always be aware of potential malingering; therefore, measures to assess the intention of the patient (to perform well or perform poorly) and effort (high to low) must comprise some portion of the assessment (Frederick, 1997; Rogers, 1997). Methods of evaluating response style and validity will be discussed in more detail later in this chapter.

Aside from information obtained by direct examination of the plaintiff, corroborative information is requisite for a thorough evaluation. This third-party data can be gleaned from interviews of family members, associates, and employers. Record review (educational, military, etc.) is also an important component of the evaluation. A thorough record review can help identify past diagnoses and level of functioning. However, it is imperative that the examiner cautiously consider this information. It can be tough to disagree with diagnoses or other clinical findings compiled over a long time period. Still, consistency between past diagnoses and current presentation is necessary. It is possible that records originated from self-report information and are the result of falsification or exaggeration. The MDSM forces the examiner to review multiple sources and carefully consider them all.

An opinion on the effects of the mental injury and relationship between injury and event is derived from self-report and corroborative data (investigative records, witness statements, family, and employer) and should be consistent with present and historical conditions. Obviously, the examiner should consider the fluctuating nature and natural course of the impairment in question. However, the identified illness should be consistent with the current presentation and history.

Once the clinician has obtained subjective and objective information addressing the premorbid functioning, present functioning, and veracity of the event, the examiner can render an opinion on the ultimate issue, that is, current impairments and future impairments. Foremost, there must be a direct connection between the injury and the event, and the examiner must provide evidence of this relationship. Additionally, care should be taken to ensure that the injury, as well as hypothesized effects of the injury, makes sense when *all* available evidence is considered.

To summarize, this model stresses the importance of logical consistency between information sources (presentation, history, and behavior) and the nature of the suspected injury and its impact. It also highlights the importance of eliminating malingering as a contributing factor when inconsistencies arise.

PSYCHOLOGICAL TESTING

Although the American Medical Association has provided a guide for completing these evaluations, there is no general agreement on the set of psychological tests to be used for personal injury examinations. Unlike competency evaluations, there is no psychological test designed specifically to address the particular legal question posed by psychological injury examinations. In other words, the examiner is tasked with responding to questions about preexisting conditions, proximately caused damage, the effects of mental injury, and the relationship between injury and event without an instrument designed specifically for this purpose. Most examiners completing psychological injury evaluations use the standard battery of psychological tests along with malingering instruments (Greenberg, 2003). There is little difference between the use of psychological testing to identify psychological damages and that of psychological test use in general clinical practice, with three notable exceptions: test selection based on psychometric soundness and empirical data, thoughtful and thorough documentation, and systematic evaluation of effort. It is important to select tests that have good psychometric properties and empirical basis. Reviewing all psychological tests in use today is outside the scope of this chapter. Rather, we will discuss test selection principles and those tests commonly used for important areas of psychological functioning.

Test selection, administration, and interpretation in the forensic context should occur based on an acceptable standard of care. Under most circumstances, test use requires sound empirical support (Heilbrun, 1992). Tests used as an aspect of the overall evaluation should meet admissibility standards for whatever jurisdiction in which the evaluation occurs. Until 1993, admissibility of scientific evidence was based on the *Frye v. United States* (1923) rule throughout the United States. This criteria allowed admission of procedures and scientific constructs that were considered generally accepted within the respective scientific community. In 1993, the U.S. Supreme Court reviewed that admissibility standard in light of the Federal Rules of Evidence, (particularly Rule 702) and found the "general acceptance test" lacking (*Daubert v. Merrell Dow*, 1993). The Court recommended that the trial judge perform a gatekeeping role in determining whether or not methods used in deriving the evidence were scientifically valid. Four factors were outlined to assist judges in this endeavor: (1) Has the method been subjected to hypothesis testing? (2) Has it been subjected to peer review and publication? (3) Does it have a known or potential error rate? and (4) Is there widespread acceptance in the scientific community? Although these factors allow more flexibility in evaluating the merits of scientific evidence, they also require more scrutiny. As a result, it is even more imperative that forensic practitioners consider well what measures they use.

Given these broad guidelines, test usage varies considerably by examiner. Boccaccini and Brodsky (1999) found the most commonly used psychological instruments in forensic assessments were the MMPI-1 or -2, WAIS-R or III, Millon Clinical Multiaxial Inventory II or III, Rorschach, Beck Depression Inventory, Trauma Stress Inventory, and Symptoms Checklist–90–Revised. However, these authors also noted that no two examiners completing psychological injury examinations used the same battery of psychological tests. Given the numerous tests available and variability of test preference, Heilbrun (1992) suggested these seven general principles for test selection, administration, and interpretation:

Selection
1. *The test is commercially available and adequately documented in two sources. First, it is accompanied by a manual describing its development, psychometric properties, and procedure for administration. Second, it is listed and reviewed in* Mental Measurements Yearbook *or some other readily available source.*

2. *Reliability should be considered. The use of tests with a reliability coefficient of less than .80 is not advisable. The use of less reliable tests would require an explicit justification by the psychologist.*
3. *The test should be relevant to the legal issue, or to a psychological construct underlying the legal issue. Whenever possible, this relevance should be supported by the availability of validation research published in refereed journals.*

Administration

4. *Standard administration should be used, with testing conditions as close as possible to the quiet, distraction-free ideal.*

Interpretation

5. *Applicability to this population and for this purpose should guide both test selection and interpretation. The results of a test (distinct from behavior observed during testing) should not be applied toward a purpose for which the test was not developed (e.g., inferring psychopathology from the results of an intelligence test). Population and situation specificity should guide interpretation. The closer the fit between a given individual and the population and situation of those in the validation research, the more confidence can be expressed in the applicability of the results.*
6. *Objective tests and actuarial data combination are preferable when there are appropriate outcome data and a "formula" exists.*
7. *Response style should be explicitly assessed using approaches sensitive to distortion, and the results of psychological testing interpreted within the context of the individual's response style. When response style appears to be malingering, defensive, or irrelevant rather than honest/reliable, the results of psychological testing may need to be discounted or even ignored and other data sources emphasized to a greater degree.*

Heilbrun's principles should be viewed as guiding principles rather than absolutes. There are exceptions to each of these points, but the principles make it clear that test selection, administration, and interpretation must be based upon a reasonable and rational process of considered thought, grounded on empirical support. Nowhere are these principles more relevant than in selection and use of projective testing techniques.

Although projective testing techniques have enjoyed a long and robust history, their use in personal injury assessments appears to be declining (Boccaccini & Brodsky, 1999; Lees-Haley, 1992). Lees-Haley, Smith, Williams, and Dunn (1996) reported that among neuropsychologists using tests in forensic evaluations, the use of the Rorschach decreased from previous years. They identified actual test use based upon the report's author having been named as an expert in litigation. Results were identified from 100 experts from 20 states and the province of Ontario, Canada, from reports dating from 1987 to 1994. In this group of neuropsychologists, 14 percent of the evaluations included the Rorschach, 12 percent included Human Figure Drawing, House-Tree-Person, or Draw-A-Person tests, and 6 percent included the Thematic Apperception Test (TAT). A caveat here is that these results only relate to neuropsychology practitioners. Boccaccini and Brodsky (1999) present data from a recent survey sent out to APA Division 41 (American Psychology-Law Society) and Division 12 (Clinical Psychology) members. Four hundred randomly selected psychologists were sent the survey and 140 (35%) responded. Of that 140, 80 had done emotional injury evaluations (10,500 lifetime estimates, 1,371 over the past year). Twenty-eight percent indicated they used the Rorschach, and only 3 percent indicated they used the TAT. Use of other projectives were apparently not reported with any significant frequency since the report only listed the eleven tests that were used by five or more practitioners. Though these results have limited generalizability because of low survey return rates, they suggest that the Rorschach is the only projective test with substantial use in emotional injury cases. Additionally, it has been suggested that the Rorschach is the only projective test that meets the psychometric standards of ethical practice (Parker, 1983).

Evaluation for Psychological and Psychiatric Disorders

The most commonly used tests for the assessment of general psychological functioning and psychiatric disorder include the Minnesota Multiphasic Personality Inventory–2, Millon Clinical Multiaxial Inventory (2nd and 3rd editions), Rorschach, Beck Depression Inventory, Symptom Checklist–90–Revised, and Personality Assessment Inventory (Boccaccini & Brodsky, 1999). The benefit of using the MMPI-2, MCMI, and PAI is the fact they include scales of test-taker response style. In this regard, it is less easy to exaggerate or minimize distress on these measures than the BDI, SCL-90, and Rorschach. Because these measures are widely known clinical instruments, they will not be reviewed in detail here.

Evaluation for Post-traumatic Stress

Guidelines have been presented for the evaluation of post-trauma stress conditions (Simon, 1995a), to which the interested reader is referred for more detail. Within this work, Simon (1995b) outlined five questions each evaluator should answer when conducting forensic evaluations addressing possible Post-Traumatic Stress Disorder (PTSD): (1) Does the alleged PTSD claim actually meet specific clinical criteria for this disorder? (2) Is the traumatic stressor that is alleged to have caused the PTSD of sufficient severity to produce this disorder? (3) What is the pre-incident psychiatric history of the claimant? (4) Is the diagnosis of PTSD based solely on the subjective reporting of symptoms by the claimant? and (5) What is the claimant's actual level of functional psychiatric impairment? These questions are essential aspects of a thorough evaluation of post-trauma stress, but there are a number of psychological tests specifically designed to assist in the assessment of post-trauma stress as well. We will present three tools designed to address post-trauma stress: the Impact Event Scale (IES), the Trauma Symptom Inventory (TSI), and the Detailed Assessment of Post-traumatic Stress (DAPS). As with measures of general psychological/psychiatric functioning, it is optimal in forensic settings to use instruments that have imbedded validity measures. In this regard the TSI and DAPS have a clear edge over the IES.

The Impact Event Scale (Horowitz, Wilner, & Alvarez, 1979) is a self-report inventory designed to assess the essential aspects of stress disorders. It assesses two aspects of traumatic stress, intrusions and avoidance. It does not assess physiological arousal, so it is not diagnostic by itself. In a review of the test, Joseph (2000) concluded it was a useful instrument clinically. As a self-report inventory, it is vulnerable to symptom exaggeration and it contains no specific validity scales within it. Lees-Haley (1990) demonstrated that post-traumatic symptoms are easy to simulate on this measure. More recently, McGuire (2002) compared litigating post-trauma patients with undergraduates simulating post-trauma difficulties. There was little difference in performance between groups, and results were consistent with previous findings that the IES is vulnerable to simulation.

The Trauma Symptom Inventory (Briere, 1995) is a 100-item inventory designed to evaluate acute and chronic symptoms of post-trauma stress. It contains 10 clinical scales under the three broad categories of trauma, self, and dysphoria. The publisher indicates it takes twenty minutes to administer and is appropriate for ages 18 and older. There is also a TSI-A version that omits the Sexual Concerns scale, the Dysfunctional Sexual Behavior scale, and two critical items with sexual content. Both of these inventories have three validity scales (Response Level, Atypical Response, and Inconsistent Response) to assist in identifying those individuals who are attempting to minimize or exaggerate their symptoms.

The Detailed Assessment of Post-traumatic Stress (Briere, 2001) is similar to the TSI but less broad in its range of symptom assessment. It is a 104-item, self-administered inventory designed to assist in the specific task of diagnosing Post-Traumatic Stress and Acute Stress Disorders. The instrument evaluates all three PTSD symptom clusters (Reexperiencing, Avoidance, and Hyperarousal) as well as three related concepts (Trauma-Specific Dissociation, Suicidality, and Substance Abuse). It includes two validity scales, Positive Bias and Negative Bias, to assist in identifying overexaggeration and excessive denial, respectively. Like the TSI, it is used for adults, 18 years and older. It takes from 35 to 50 minutes to administer and score.

EVALUATION FOR INTELLECTUAL AND NEUROPSYCHOLOGICAL IMPAIRMENT

A number of evaluation instruments are available to measure impairment.

Neuropsychological Evaluation

There has been ongoing debate between methods regarding neuropsychological practitioners who use flexible and process approaches and those who use fixed battery approaches (Lezak, 1995; Russell, 1998). Although both have their respective merits (Bauer, 2000; Russell, 2000a), recent literature has highlighted the issue of differential scientific admissibility of neuropsychological evidence gained through either fixed or flexible assessment strategies. Reed (1996) interpreted a Washington State Court's determination in *Chapple v. Ganger* (1994) as not favorable toward the flexible approach under *Daubert* (1993). A similar issue arose in a California case under the general acceptance standard, and the flexible approach was found admissible despite voiced criticisms (McKinzey & Ziegler, 1999). The review of Lees-Haley and colleagues (1996) suggests the use of both the fixed battery and flexible approach are widespread and acceptable as a standard of care.

Another issue of debate involves neuropsychological corrections based on age and education. Heaton, Grant, and Matthews (1991) and Russell and Starkey (1993) have published demographically corrective norms and software programs for expanded versions of the Halstead-Reitan Battery (see Russell, 2000b, for an interesting comparison). Although many neuropsychological tests have incorporated such corrections for years, the issue of using them with the Halstead-Reitan Battery has been debated on methodological (Axelrod & Goldman, 1996; Fastenau & Adams, 1996; Fastenau, 1998; Heaten, Matthews, Grant, & Avitable, 1996; Morgan & Caccappolo-van Vliet, 2001) and theoretical grounds (Reitan & Wolfson, 1995; Vanderploeg, Axelrod, Sherer, Scott, & Adams, 1997). Jarvis and Barth (1994) strongly suggest the corrections improve diagnostic accuracy, but an empirical basis for the conclusion is not presented. It appears to us, given the literature thus far, that neuropsychologists using demographic corrections make up a substantially large group of neuropsychological practitioners today.

Estimating Premorbid Level of Intellectual Functioning

Identifying premorbid level of intellectual functioning is an extremely important consideration. In order to identify loss of function, the plaintiff's premorbid level of functioning must be demonstrated. It is not possible to review this entire area in detail in this chapter, but the interested reader is referred to Franzen, Burgess, and Smith-Seemiller (1997) and Schinka and Vanderploeg (2000). Some of the most common methods of determining premorbid intellectual functioning will be discussed briefly here. The best method to determine premorbid functioning is past testing, but the luxury of having such testing available is a rarity. Several statistical methods have been developed over the years to help with this problem. Barona, Reynolds, and Chastain (1984) designed a system of determination using the demographic variables of sex, race, education, age, region, residence (urban vs. rural), and occupation. Many other authors have evaluated the effectiveness of using demographic variables in regression equations with some success. Another option is to use a *best performance method* by using the highest level of cognitive ability the subject demonstrated on postmorbid testing as an indicator of general functioning, but this method has not fared well because it leads to gross overestimations of prior functioning (Schinka & Vanderploeg, 2000). There has been considerable activity in developing reading tests as measures of premorbid function based on the premise that previously learned reading skill is rather resistant to loss (with the exception of clear aphasia). This finding has been noted particularly for atypical words. In this regard the National Adult Reading Test was developed (NART; Nelson, 1982). The NART has 50 atypical words that the patient reads aloud. The resulting score is placed in a regression formula to achieve estimated premorbid IQ. As the test was developed and standardized with British samples, it was revised in the United States by Schwartz and Saffran (as cited in Schinka and Vanderploeg, 2000) and called the AMNART. A third version was developed by Blair and Spreen (1989), called the NART-R, or the North American Adult Reading Test. Follow-up attempts to improve predictive accuracy have included adding demographic variables to NART regression formulas. Combined demographic and reading formulas have been generally successful (Schinka & Vanderploeg, 2000). The Wide Range Achievement Test–Revised reading score has also been used to determine premorbid intellectual functioning (Weins, Bryan, & Crossen, 1993). Vanderploeg, Schinka, & Axelrod (1996) devised three regression equations based on WAIS-R Information, Vocabulary, and Picture Completion subtests, termed the BEST-3. Krull, Scott, and Scherer (1995) developed a regression equation based on WAIS-R Vocabulary and Picture Completion subtests and demographic variables. This strategy has been termed the Oklahoma Pre-morbid Intelligence Estimate (OPIE).

The most recent entry to this line of research is the Wechsler Test of Adult Reading (WTAR; 2001). This test is based on the same premise as the NART but was developed in conjunction with the WAIS-III and WMS-III. There is a possibility that WTAR scores could accurately project past learning and memory functioning, based on the test's development alongside the WMS-III. This possibility has less theoretical basis than prediction of intellectual functioning, however. Future research will likely need to demonstrate this claim. The WTAR enhances predictive capability by also including demographic variables in the scoring, and the clinician is able to choose among WTAR prediction, demographic prediction, and WTAR/demographic predictions. Because of its unique development as a partner test to the WAIS-III, the WTAR is theoretically the best instrument for determining premorbid level of intellectual functioning available today.

Ecological Validity of Neuropsychological Test Results

In the forensic arena, particularly tort matters, the neuropsychologist is expected to provide opinions not only on nature and cause of any injury, but also on likely future functioning. In cases of severe traumatic brain injury, the cost of nursing home care, in-home nursing, or extensive supportive therapies is readily identifiable. In this regard, attorneys often incorporate certified life planners who identify the financial cost of future treatment and project this cost over the plaintiff's expected lifetime. When the injury is less severe, however, the neuropsychologist is often expected to draw conclusions from the test data regarding impact of neurocognitive deficits on daily functioning in such real-world areas as independent living, occupational success, and academic capabilities. The ability of neuropsychological tests to provide this information is termed *ecological validity*. Test results are often used to determine potential future functioning, but the fact of the matter is that most neuropsychological tests were not designed to perform this function (Sbordone, 1996). Most neuropsychological tests are performed in a laboratory setting where extraneous noise is kept to a minimum. Real-world function rarely includes a well-controlled, quiet environment. It is not uncommon for subtle neurocognitive difficulties to reveal themselves only when the subject is forced to function in noisy and busy environments.

In addition, by their very nature neuropsychological tests do not measure initiation and functioning aside from evaluator imposed structure. In this regard, neuropsychological tests may not reveal executive function deficits in the areas of planning, organization, initiation, and social competence (Sbordone & Guilmette, 1999). Competent neuropsychologists are aware of these potential limitations of neuropsychological testing and strive to include collateral information from family members, work supervisors, and others who are aware of the subject's functioning in a more real-world setting. Using a multiple data source evaluative model, as we have outlined here, helps address these potential limitations in testing, particularly when the evaluator realizes that occasionally corroborative informants have unknown biases or agendas as well (Denney & Wynkoop, 2000). Using a wide variety of assessment strategies, including corroborative interviewing, makes it more likely that predictions of future real-world functioning will be accurate enough to assist the trier of fact (Sbordone & Guillmette, 1999).

Malingering

The base rate for malingering varies across studies, but individuals in forensic settings clearly have greater incentive to feign psychopathology (Rogers, 1997). In fact, the DSM-IV-TR specifies that the medicolegal context itself should raise the suspicion of malingering. Research has found considerable variation in the rate of malingering, even within the civil forensic arena. Authors have estimated base rates of malingering brain injury in personal injury cases to range from 2 to even 64 percent (Gouvier, Hayes, and Smiroldo, 1998; Heaton, Smith, Lehman, & Vogt, 1978; Schretlen, 1988). Larrabee (in press) reviewed malingering studies that reported base rates of malingering in forensic settings and found an overall base rate of 40 percent. In their meta-analytic review, Binder and Rohling (1996) found that the presence of financial incentives had a moderate effect size on level of impairment. In fact, there was greater disability among those with financial incentives even though they had less severe injuries. Also important to realize is the impact of effort on neuropsychological test scores. Green and colleagues (2001) demonstrated that effort appeared to change neuropsychological test scores more than severe brain injury.

Although it is logical to conclude that effort plays a significant role in test performance, it is also important to realize the potential significant attorney influence in personal injury cases (Lees-Haley, 1997). Wetter and Corrigan (1995) surveyed attorneys and law students and found 63 percent felt they should provide clients with information about psychological test validity measures prior to such evaluations. A case of confirmed attorney-client coaching was identified by Youngjohn (1995). In this case, the attorney researched Dr. Youngjohn's publications and used that information to teach the plaintiff how to circumvent the malingering detection strategies prior to his evaluation. The court, upon learning this information, instructed the attorney to discontinue such behavior, but no sanction was brought against him. Evaluators need to be aware of such potential systematic bias in their evaluations. Taking together the significant potential financial gain, potential client coaching, and substantial base rates for malingering, mental injury evaluations must include thorough assessment of response style and symptom validity. Rogers (1997) concluded that the "assessment of response styles continues to be an essential component of clinical assessment" and that "psychologists and other mental health professionals must employ the same degree of thoroughness in the assessment of malingering and defensiveness as they would in establishment of any diagnosis" (p. 396). The evaluator who fails to assess malingering in a systematic manner during forensic evaluations performs an incomplete evaluation and potentially could be considered incompetent (Shapiro, 1999; Denney & Wynkoop, 2000).

Increased attention from the courts, in addition to ever-evolving standards of practice, necessitates evaluation of malingering in all forensic settings. Comparing self-report to third-party data can reveal inconsistencies arising from symptom exaggeration and falsification as well as more general clinical findings of poor insight and lack of awareness. Direct, extended observation of the plaintiff is sometimes the only way to identify symptom exaggeration and feigning (Lezak, 1995; Denney, 1999). Symptoms that remit when the plaintiff is unaware of observation provide the single most convincing piece of evidence suggesting malingering. The MDSM provides the clinician a cogent framework within which to properly address malingering.

Symptom exaggeration can occur in intellectual, neurocognitive, learning and memory, and emotional/psychiatric areas. Often, domains are exaggerated together or in combinations. We will discuss the most common techniques used today to identify symptom exaggeration and poor effort based on type of difficulty presented.

Neurocognitive Malingering Assessment Techniques

There are many techniques for identifying poor effort and symptom exaggeration. We will briefly review several commonly used strategies and report recent research regarding the known sensitivity and specificity rates for each. Many of the following strategies are free-standing tests to be mixed in with other traditional psychological testing. Others are atypical pattern performances within standard tests.

The Rey 15-Item Memory Test (Rey, 1958) is the most widely known of Rey's malingering tests. It is a simple memory procedure that takes little time to complete and has received a great deal of research attention. Frederick (2002) reviewed the procedure and found sensitivity rates to vary from 40 to 89 percent depending on the cutoff, with the specificity generally placing in the mid to upper nineties. There appeared to be a difference in test performance between civil litigants and criminal defendants. Boone, Salazar, Lu, Warner-Chacon, and Razani (2002) reviewed the test and found sensitivities to range from 7 to 72 percent for volunteer simulators and 5 percent to 72 percent for clinical samples of patients in litigation and those suspected of malingering. Vallabhajosula and van Gorp (2001) suggest the procedure would not meet *Daubert* admissibility standards because of low sensitivity, but Frederick (2002) suggests it is a reasonable procedure to use as long as it is not used in isolation.

The Portland Digit Recognition Test (Binder, 1990; Binder & Willis, 1991) is a forced-choice, two-alternative digit recognition test patterned after the Hiscock Digit Memory Test (Hiscock & Hiscock, 1989) and incorporating three trials of what appear to be increasingly difficult stimuli. The entire test requires about 40 minutes to administer, although an abbreviated form has been developed for individuals who appear to be performing well (Binder, 1993). Binder (2002) recently reviewed the procedure and noted sensitivity rates to vary between 39 to 77 percent depending on the type of subject, whereas specificity rates held constant at 100 percent. The benefit of using such forced-choice, two-alternative tests as the PDRT is the fact that occasionally subjects will perform below chance and, in effect, demonstrate the very ability they are trying to claim they do not have (Denney, 1999). The Victoria Symptom Validity Test (Slick, Hopp, Strauss, & Thompson, 1997; see Thompson, 2002, for a review) and Computerized Assessment of Response Bias (CARB; Allen, Conder, Green, & Cox, 1997; see Allen, Iverson, & Green, 2002, for a recent review) are similar strategies, but they use computer administration. The great benefit of the CARB is the fact that it includes norm references that allow the examiner to compare the subject's performance to known neurological, amnestic, and severe brain injury patients. Often, this comparison by itself provides substantial indication of poor subject effort.

The Validity Indicator Profile (VIP; Frederick, 1997) is unique because it uses performance curve analysis and establishes a fourfold classification system of performance, including valid, invalid–careless, invalid–irrelevant, and invalid–malingering (Frederick, Crosby, & Wynkoop, 2000). The VIP has nonverbal and verbal components, both of which are based on the combination of two-alternative, forced-choice testing and progressive item difficulty. In a recent review, Frederick (in press) reported sensitivity/specificity rates of 73.5/85.7 for the nonverbal subtest and 67.3/83.1 for the verbal subtest during cross-validation. Frederick suggested these rates were underestimates of test performance because of criterion group contamination. The VIP is a major breakthrough in attempting to understand the nature of malingering as more than simply a dichotomous occurrence.

The Test of Memory Malingering (TOMM; Tombaugh, 1996) is also a two-alternative, forced-choice test of memory, but it uses line drawings rather than digits. In a recent review, Tombaugh (2002) reported 84 percent and 88 percent detection rates for simulators with a 100 percent specificity rate using the recommended cutoff of 45 correct. A follow-up study using TBI patients in litigation resulted in 77 percent correct classification rate. Specificity dropped to only 90 percent when including severely impaired neurological patients. It is extremely unlikely that the TOMM would incorrectly classify a mild to moderate brain injury patient as malingering.

The Word Memory Test (WMT; Green, Allen, & Astner, 1996) is unique in the area of malingering tests in being a forced-choice, two-alternative procedure that also includes legitimate memory assessment for words and word pairs. It is available as a computer-administered test that automatically calculates z-score comparisons to a variety of normal and neurologically impaired groups. Although the test initially met with a cool review (Wynkoop & Denney, 2001) because of difficult computer software and lack of peer-reviewed, published research, it has now become a widely researched tool with a strong empirical basis (Hartman, 2002). In a recent review, Green, Lees-Haley, and Allen (2002) note the WMT demonstrates overall sensitivity rates of about 97 percent and specificity rates of 100 percent for simulation studies. It appears that, with the current research literature available, the WMT is the most effective freestanding malingering detection strategy available.

A host of other exaggeration indices are incorporated within widely used neuropsychological measures. These strategies are beneficial because they take little additional time to administer and the connection between poor performance on the validity scale and poor performance on the genuine test is clear. These strategies are likely less specific to malingering because they incorporate aspects of tests sensitive to genuine brain injury. Vallabhajosula and van Gorp (2001) point out the ideal in malingering detection is to have measures sensitive to feigning but not genuine impairment. Nevertheless, the trend of designing exaggeration detection methods within already established neuropsychological measures appears to be a reasonable pursuit. Examples of such malingering detection strategies based on established clinical measures include the Warrington Recognition Memory test (see Millis, in press, for a review), atypical pattern analysis on the Wechsler Scales, Weschler Memory Scale–Revised, and Halstead-Reitan Battery (see Mittenberg, Aquila-Puentes, Patton, Canyock, & Heilbronner, 2002, for a review of each), Reliable Digit Span (Greiffenstein, Baker, & Gola, 1994), Rarely Missed Index of the Wechsler Memory Scale-III (Killgore & DellaPietra, 2000), California Verbal Learning Test (Millis, Putnam, Adams, & Ricker, 1992), Wisconsin Card Sorting Test (see Greve, Bianchini, Mathias, Houston, & Crouch, 2002, for comparison of various methods), Finger Tapping (Larrabee, in press), Category Test (see Sweet & King, 2003, for a review), and test-retest changes on the Halstead-Reitan Battery (see Reitan & Wolfson, 2002, for a review). Lastly, the Lees-Haley Fake Bad Scale (Lees-Haley, English,

& Glenn, 1992) within the MMPI-2 has been found to be a sensitive indicator of somatic malingering apart from the standard MMPI-2 validity measures (Larrabee, 1998).

Regarding general psychological functioning and psychiatric symptom exaggeration, many commonly used tests have embedded validity scales (e.g., MMPI-2, MCMI-II & III, PAI). Less commonly known is the Infrequency-Psychopathology Scale, F(p), within the MMPI-2. This scale has been shown effective in identifying exaggerated psychosis (Arbisi & Ben-Porath, 1998). The Structured Interview of Reported Symptoms (Rogers, Bagby, & Dickens, 1992) is an excellent structured interview to identify feigned psychosis, and the Miller Forensic Assessment of Symptoms Test (Miller, 2001) has been demonstrated to be an effective screening tool that takes less time to administer than the SIRS. Given these instruments, the astute forensic evaluator should be able to find exaggeration detection methods to fit nearly any personal injury evaluation.

MODEL APPLICATION

In writing this chapter, we strove to provide both requisite historical information and useful practice-oriented information. Thus far, we have reviewed components of both areas. We now attempt to draw these two concepts together through the use of a case example. In doing so, we hope to make the model tangible enough that an informed practitioner can begin to apply it. The text presents a case description, including possible records to be used and information provided by the plaintiff and others. Figure 13.2 shows how the clinician moves along three separate trajectories (Present, Premorbid functioning, and Time of injury) to arrive at the ultimate opinion.

In our example, we present the case of an adult male, Mr. Neller, claiming loss of neurocognitive function resulting from a head injury received in a motor vehicle accident. Mr. Neller, a married father of two, was evaluated over a period of several days in the office of a private practitioner at the request of a personal injury attorney. According to the subject, while waiting at a stop sign in his vehicle, his car was hit by another vehicle moving at a speed of 40 miles per hour. Because he was wearing a seatbelt, he was pinned in the car when the front end collapsed, and his head was lacerated by shattering glass. He reported being unconscious immediately following the crash, awakening shortly after arrival of the paramedics, with no memory subsequent to impact. He said he recalled hearing the crunching of metal as the car hit him. During the initial interview, the claimant indicated he had always been bright, performing well in school, and eventually becoming an accountant. He described himself as "quick-witted." In describing his functioning after the accident, he stated he suffered from memory impairments and that he had forgotten some basic information from his past, including the faces of his parents and the meanings of certain words. He also indicated difficulty learning new information and reported he was no longer capable

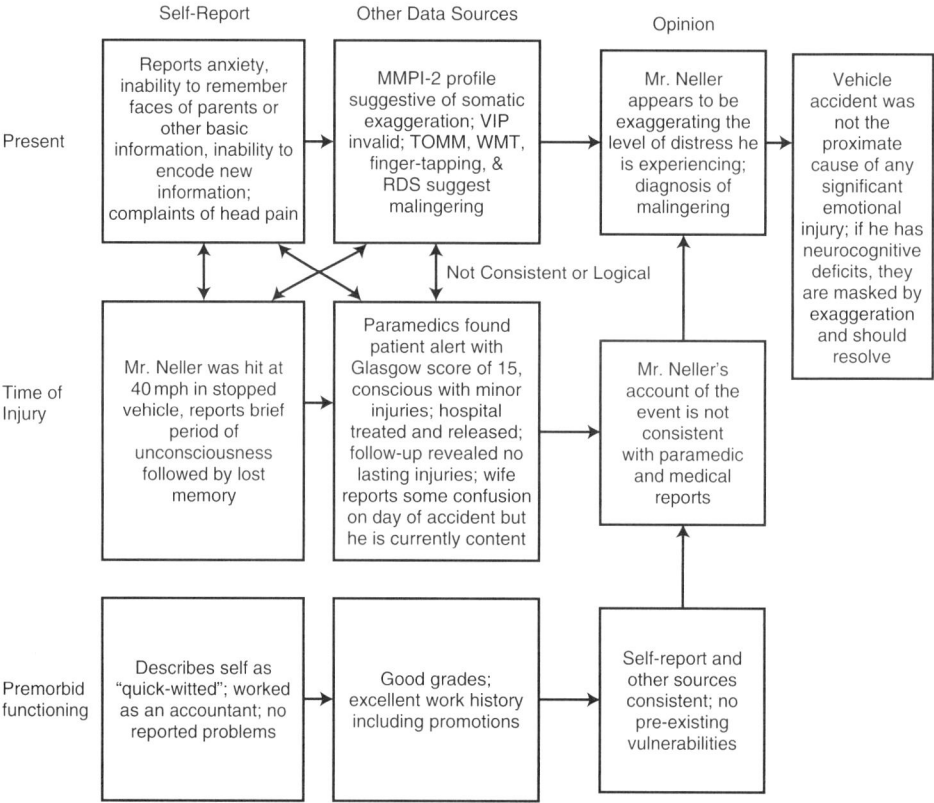

FIGURE 13.2 Case Example

of conducting complex calculations. Consequently, he did not believe he could return to his work as an accountant. He described the experience of anxiety when asked to discuss the accident.

Mr. Neller signed release of information forms, and records were collected from the treating hospital, his family physician, police, and his employer. College transcripts were also obtained. Family members and his employer were interviewed. Hospital records included the report of the senior paramedic, who reported that upon arriving at the scene of the accident, he found that Mr. Neller was not unconscious; he was alert, and oriented, with a Glasgow Coma Score of 15. The emergency room physician treated the victim for whiplash, fractured ribs, and a sprained left ankle. There was also bruising, but no swelling, on his face and temple. CT scan of the head revealed no abnormalities. He was seen for follow-up regarding his ribs and ankle. Although he had not seen his family physician since the accident, records were obtained indicating a history of hypertension, controlled with propranolol SR. His work evaluations were consistently positive, and he had been promoted twice within his company. Transcripts showed a 3.6 GPA. Mr. Neller had one previous arrest for marijuana possession.

An interview with Mrs. Neller revealed some changes in behavior since the accident, although the deficits were not to the extent alleged by the plaintiff. Specifically, he did seem slightly confused the day he returned from the hospital. She noted he used to awaken early in the day, but now sleeps later. He did not seem interested in returning to work. She reported that he appeared to be enjoying his time at home, and that he spent a good deal of time playing strategy games on the computer. He also liked woodworking and had constructed several items in his backyard workshop. She reported that he complained to her about being forgetful, although she noticed no change. His employer was also interviewed. He had seen Mr. Neller several times socially since the accident, and they had occasionally discussed various work accounts. The two were good friends and often golfed together.

As part of a comprehensive assessment battery, Mr. Neller completed the WAIS-III, MMPI-2, VIP, WMT, and the Halstead-Reitan Battery (HRB). Observations during testing were that he did not express frustration at failed tasks, frequently attempted to engage the examiner in conversation regarding the status of his case, and often complained that his head hurt. Using demographic corrections for the HRB, the following test performances were in the impaired range: Finger Tapping–bilaterally; Finger-Tip Number Writing–bilaterally; Finger Recognition–bilaterally; and Tactual Performance Test–Total Time, Memory, and Localization. On the WAIS-III, he obtained Full-Scale, Verbal, and Performance IQ scores of 99, 102, and 96, respectively. The verbal subtest of the VIP was considered valid and the nonverbal invalid-careless. Of the malingering indices on the WMT, Mr. Neller achieved more than one score suggestive of dissimulation, and he performed eight standard deviations below the severely traumatically brain damaged comparison group. His combined Finger Tapping score was 60, suggesting poor effort. His Reliable Digit Span (taken from the WAIS-III) was six and suggested poor effort. The Mittenberg WAIS-III discriminant function was within normal limits. The MMPI-2 profile was valid and not suggestive of overwhelming clinical distress. Nevertheless, he achieved significant elevations on scales 1, 3, and 7. Lees-Haley FBS was 27 and suggestive of somatic exaggeration.

Given the nature of the accident, lack of documented altered consciousness, absence of CT abnormalities, collateral reports, and performance on psychological and neuropsychological measures, Mr. Neller's current presentation was not consistent with genuine mild traumatic brain injury. Although it was not possible to completely rule out the possibility of very mild neurocognitive difficulties, his overexaggeration of deficits on testing made identifying his current strengths and weaknesses impossible.

FUTURE DIRECTIONS

Psychologists provide a great benefit to society by applying empirically derived knowledge and methodologically sound procedures to evaluate psychological difficulties after traumatic events. Nonetheless, there remain several areas that require additional clarification through research.

We must improve the ecological validity of our testing procedures. Over the years, psychology has developed a great number of strategies to assess psychological function, but the ability of these measures to predict real-world functioning is somewhat less satisfying. It appears that a multisource model will have better accuracy in predicting future return to work (Sbordone & Guillmette, 1999). It is likely that a combination of test results and demographic characteristics will prove the best predictors of future vocational functioning. Actuarial models need to be developed and validated to assist in this effort.

We must develop a better understanding of base rates for typical symptom complaints associated with various psychological conditions. It is easy to consider psychological complaints as resulting from traumatic events in retrospect, but there appears to be a difficulty with misattribution. Such a difficulty was demonstrated with the Post-Concussion Syndrome (Lees-Haley, Fox, & Courtney, 2001). The authors found that orthopedic controls reported similar levels of classic post-concussive symptoms as those of subjects with a recent history of mild traumatic brain injury. This research demonstrates the need to have appropriate controls in clinical research and to better understand the base rate of that symptom cluster in the nonimpaired, and certainly vocationally functional, population.

We as mental health professionals also need to refine our methods of predicting premorbid functioning in areas other than intellectual ability. The WTAR appears to be a major step forward in determining premorbid intellectual functioning. Additional research needs to occur with the WTAR, particularly in the area of premorbid learning and memory prediction. It may be helpful to develop other methods of determining premorbid levels of neurocognitive function that could be integrated in an actuarial model of function that includes consideration of demographic variables.

All intellectual, achievement, and neuropsychological measures need improved validation with normative groups screened for poor effort. Recent research indicates that effort plays a significant role in neuropsychological assessment of litigants (Green, Rohling, & Lees-Haley, 2001), but it is not clear how great a contribution effort makes in nonlitigating populations. In this regard, the standardization studies used to develop most of our psychological tests, certainly neuropsychological tests, did not include measures of participant effort. It is very possible that our norms are adulterated with performances from individuals not applying themselves appropriately. Inclusion of such subjects in our normative and standardization studies likely affects the accuracy of the overall procedures, but the nature and extent of this effect is unclear.

Finally, there remains the ongoing task of identifying sensitivity and specificity rates for various malingering detection strategies for differing forensic and clinical populations. Relatedly, base rates of symptom exaggeration need better clarification for differing forensic and clinical populations as well. New effort identification strategies must be developed in an ongoing basis as the public learns

Conclusion

Throughout this chapter, we have emphasized that assessing for psychological damages is only slightly different from conducting traditional forensic evaluations, such as competency and responsibility evaluations. Basically, the examiner is asked to determine if a specific incident has impacted a person's functioning and to identify the associated level of damage or impairment. The key difference is the importance of differentiating between pre- and postinjury functioning. Rather than simply focusing on an evaluee's functioning at a given point in time (i.e., *mens rea*), the clinician is expected to identify and contrast premorbid and postinjury/current functioning. In essence, the evaluator is charged with completing two separate examinations. The former entails addressing premorbid functioning, whereas the latter involves an examination of postinjury/current functioning. The clinician must then weave together these separate evaluations and present them in such a way that they become meaningful for the jurors, who must ultimately decide whether damages occurred and if so, how they should be compensated.

Additionally, because the defendant may be expected to compensate the plaintiff for damages, these evaluations have the added dynamic of financial gain or loss for the parties involved. This fact presents a number of issues for clinicians. Foremost, it becomes very important to act ethically and resist temptation to offer opinions for sale. Further, the examiner may be asked the difficult question of what impact a given mental disorder has on future earning capacity. Thus, clinicians are faced with how to measure the degree or permanence of a mental disability, and this can be a very challenging issue to quantify or agree upon.

It is our opinion that these evaluations should be conducted by well-trained, ethical clinicians. As noted, the Speciality Guidelines remind us that forensic examiners are expected to adhere to the highest standards of the profession. This is particularly true in conducting evaluations of damages because of the monetary involvement. Assuming these criteria are met, we assert the MDSM as the most direct avenue to comprehensive, ethical assessment of psychological damages.

Acknowledgments

The authors would like to thank David Mrad, Ph.D., and Chris Renfrow for their assistance in the preparation of this chapter.

REFERENCES

Allen, L. M., Conder, R. L., Green, P., & Cox, D. R. (1997). *CARB '97: Manual for the Computerized Assessment of Response Bias*. Durham, NC: CogniSyst.

Allen, L. M., Iverson, G. L., & Green, P. (2002). Computerized Assessment of Response Bias in forensic neuropsychology. *Journal of Forensic Neuropsychology, 3*, 205–225.

American Psychological Association. (1992). Ethical principles of psychologists and code of conduct. *American Psychologist, 47*, 1597–1611.

Arbisi, P. A., & Ben-Porath, Y. S. (1998). The ability of Minnesota Multiphasic Personality Inventory–2 validity scales to detect fake-bad responses in psychiatric inpatients. *Psychological Assessment, 10*, 221–228.

Association of State and Provincial Psychology Boards. (2001). *Licensure requirements in general*. Retrieved December 20, 2001, from www.asppb.org/reqs.htm.

Axelrod, B. N., & Goldman, R. S. (1996). Use of demographic corrections in neuropsychological interpretation: How standard are standard scores? *Clinical Neuropsychologist, 10*, 159–162.

Barona, A., Reynolds, C. R., & Chastain, R. (1984). A demographically based index of premorbid intelligence for the WAIS-R. *Journal of Consulting and Clinical Psychology, 52*, 885–887.

Bauer, R. M. (2000). The flexible battery approach to neuropsychological assessment. In R. D. Vanderploeg (Ed.), *Clinician's guide to neuropsychological assessment* (2nd ed.) (pp. 419–448). Mahwah, NJ: Lawrence Erlbaum.

Binder, L. M. (1990). Malingering following minor head trauma. *Clinical Neuropsychologist, 4*, 25–36.

Binder, L. M. (1993). An abbreviated form of the Portland Digit Recognition Test. *Clinical Neuropsychologist, 7*, 104–107.

Binder, L. M. (2002). The Portland Digit Recognition Test: A review of validation data and clinical use. *Journal of Forensic Neuropsychology, 2*, 27–41.

Binder, L. M., & Rohling, M. L. (1996). Money matters: Meta-analytic review of the effects of financial incentives on recovery after closed-head injury. *American Journal of Psychiatry, 153*, 7–10.

Binder, L. M., & Willis, S. C. (1992). Assessment of motivation after financially compensable minor head trauma. *Psychological Assessment, 3*, 141–147.

Blair, J. R., & Spreen, O. (1989). Predicting premorbid IQ: A revision of the National Adult Reading Test. *Clinical Neuropsychologist, 3*, 129–136.

Boccaccini, M. T., & Brodsky, S. L. (1999). Diagnostic test usage by forensic psychologists in emotional injury cases. *Professional Psychology: Research and Practice, 30 (3)*, 253–259.

Boone, K. B., Salazar, X., Lu, P., Warner-Chacon, K., & Razani, J. (2002). The Rey 15-item Recognition Trial: A technique to enhance sensitivity of the Rey 15-item Memorization Test. *Journal of Clinical and Experimental Neuropsychology, 24*, 561–573.

Briere, J. B. (1995). *Trauma Symptom Inventory*. Lutz, FL: Psychological Assessment Resources.

Briere, J. B. (2001). *Detailed Assessment of Post-traumatic Stress*. Lutz, FL: Psychological Assessment Resources.

California Statute, Section 3208(a)(b) (1995).

Carter v. General Motors, 106 NW.2d 105 (MI Sup. Ct. 1961).

Chapple v. Ganger, 851 F. Supp. 1481 (E.D. Wash. 1994).

Christy Brothers Circus v. Turnage, 144 S.E. 680 (App. Ct. Ga. 1928).
Committee on Ethical Guidelines for Forensic Psychologists. (1991). Specialty guidelines for forensic psychologists, *Law and Human Behavior, 15,* 655–665.
Daller, M. F. (2000). *Tort law desk reference: A fifty state compendium.* New York: Aspen Law and Business.
Daubert v. Merrell Dow Pharmaceuticals, Inc., 509 US 579 (U.S. Sup., 1993).
Denney, R. (1999). A brief Symptom Validity Testing procedure for Logical Memory of the Wechsler Memory Scale–Revised which can demonstrate verbal memory in the face of claimed disability. *Journal of Forensic Neuropsychology, 1,* 5–26.
Denney, R., & Wynkoop, T. F. (2000). Clinical neuropsychology in the criminal forensic setting. *Journal of Head Trauma Rehabilitation, 15,* 804–828.
Dillon v. Legg, 441 P.2d 912 (Cal. Sup. Ct.1968).
Dower, C. M., Gragnola, C. M., & Finocchio, L. J. (1998). Changing nature of physician licensure: Implications for medical education in California. *Western Journal of Medicine, 168,* 422–427.
Edney v. Smith, 425 F. Supp. 1038 (EDNY 1976).
Fastenau, P. S. (1998). Validity of Regression-Based Norms: An empirical test of the Comprehensive Norms with older adults. *Journal of Clinical and Experimental Neuropsychology, 20,* 906–916.
Fastenau, P. S., & Adams, K. M. (1996). Heaton, Grant, and Matthews' Comprehensive Norms: An overzealous attempt. *Journal of Clinical and Experimental Neuropsychology, 18,* 444–448.
Franzen, M. D., Burgess, E. J., & Smith-Seemiller, L. (1997). Methods of estimating premorbid functioning. *Archives of Clinical Neuropsychology, 12,* 711–738.
Frederick, R. I. (1997). *Validity Indicator Profile Manual.* Minneapolis, MN: National Computer Systems.
Frederick, R. I. (2002). A review of Rey's strategies for detecting malingered neuropsychological impairment. *Journal of Forensic Neuropsychology, 2,* 1–25.
Frederick, R. I., Crosby, R., & Wynkoop, T. F. (2000). Performance curve classification of invalid responding on the Validity Indicator Profile. *Archives of Clinical Neuropsychology, 15,* 281–300.
Frye v. United States, 293 F. 1013 (D.C. Cir 1923).
Gouvier, W. D., Hayes, J. S., Smiroldo, B. B. (1998). The significance of base rates, test sensitivity, test specificity, and subject's knowledge of symptoms in assessing TBI sequelae and malingering. In C.R. Reynolds (Ed.), *Detection of malingering during head injury litigation* (pp. 55–79). New York: Plenum.
Green, P., Allen, L. M., & Astner, K. (1996). *The Word Memory Test.* Durham, NC: CogniSyst.
Green, P., Lees-Haley, P. R., & Allen, L. M. (2002). The Word Memory Test and the validity of neuropsychological test scores. *Journal of Forensic Neuropsychology, 2,* 97–124.
Green, P., Rohling, M. L., Lees-Haley, P. R., Allen, L. M. (2001). Effort has a greater effect on test scores than severe brain injury in compensation claimants. *Brain Injury, 15,* 1045–1060.
Greenberg, S. A. (2003). Personal injury examinations in torts for emotional distress (pp. 233–257). In I. B. Weiner (Series Ed.) & A. M. Goldstein (Vol. Ed.), *Handbook of psychology, Vol. 11: Forensic psychology.* Hoboken, NJ: Wiley.
Greiffenstein, M. F., Baker, W. J., & Gola, T. (1994). Validation of malingered amnesia measures with a large clinical sample. *Psychological Assessment, 6,* 218–224.

Greve, K. W., Bianchini, K. J., Mathias, C. W., Houston, R. J., & Crouch, J. A. (2002). Detecting malingered performance with the Wisconsin Card Sorting Test: A preliminary investigation in traumatic brain injury. *Clinical Neuropsychologist, 16,* 179–191.

Hartman, D. E. (2002). The unexamined lie is a lie worth fibbing: Neuropsychological malingering and the Word Memory Test. *Archives of Clinical Neuropsychology, 17,* 709–714.

Heaton, R. K., Grant, I., & Matthews, C. G. (1991). *Comprehensive norms for an expanded Halstead-Reitan Battery: Demographic corrections, research findings, and clinical applications.* Odessa, FL: Psychological Assessment Resources.

Heaton, R. K., Matthews, C. G., Grant, I., & Avitable, N. (1996). Demographic corrections with comprehensive norms: An overzealous attempt or a good start? *Journal of Clinical and Experimental Neuropsychology, 18,* 449–458.

Heaton R. K., Smith, H. H., Lehman, R. A. W., and Vogt, A. T. (1978). Prospects for faking believable deficits on psychological testing. *Journal of Consulting and Clinical Psychology, 46,* 892–900.

Heilbrun, K. (1992). The role of psychological testing in forensic assessment. *Law and Human Behavior, 16,* 257–272.

Hiscock, M., & Hiscock, C. K. (1989). Refining the forced-choice method of the detection of malingering. *Journal of Clinical and Experimental Neuropsychology, 11,* 967–974.

Horowitz, M., Wilner, N., & Alvarez, W. (1979). Impact of Event Scale: A measure of subjective distress. *Psychosomatic Medicine, 41,* 209–218.

Jarvis, P. E., & Barth, J. T. (1994). *The Halstead-Reitan Neuropsychological Battery: A guide to interpretation and clinical applications.* Odessa, FL: Psychological Assessment Resources.

Joseph, S. (2000). Psychometric evaluation of Horowitz's Impact of Event Scale: A review. *Journal of Traumatic Stress, 13,* 101–113.

Killgore, W. D., & DellaPietra, L. (2000). Using the WMS-III to detect malingering: Empirical validation of the Rarely Missed Index (RMI). *Journal of Clinical and Experimental Neuropsychology, 22,* 761–771.

Krull, K. R., Scott, J. G., & Scherer, M. (1995). Estimation of premorbid intelligence from combined performance and demographic variables. *Clinical Neuropsychologist, 9,* 83–88.

Larrabee, G. J. (1998). Somatic malingering on the MMPI and MMPI-2 in litigating subjects. *Clinical Neuropsychologist, 12,* 179–188.

Larrabee, G. J. (in press). Detection of malingering using neuropsychologically atypical performance patterns on standard neuropsychological tests. *Clinical Neuropsychologist.*

Lees-Haley, P. R. (1990). Malingering mental disorder on the Impact of Event Scale: Toxic exposure and cancerphobia. *Journal of Traumatic Stress, 3,* 313–321.

Lees-Haley, P. R. (1992). Psychodiagnostic test usage by forensic psychologists. *American Journal of Forensic Psychology, 10 (1),* 25–30.

Lees-Haley, P. R. (1997). Attorneys influence expert evidence in forensic psychological and neuropsychological cases. *Assessment 4,* 321–324.

Lees-Haley, P. R., English, L. T., & Glenn, W. J. (1991). A fake bad scale on the MMPI-2 for personal injury claimants. *Psychological Reports, 68,* 203–210.

Lees-Haley, P. R., Fox, D. D., & Courtney, J. C. (2001). A comparison of complaints by mild brain injury claimants and other claimants describing subjective experiences immediately following their injury. *Archives of Clinical Neuropsychology, 16,* 689–695.

Lees-Haley, P. R., Smith, H. H., Williams, C. W., & Dunn, J. T. (1996). Forensic neuropsychological test usage: An empirical survey. *Archives of Clinical Neuropsychology, 11*, 45–51.

Lezak, M. D. (1995). *Neuropsychological assessment.* (3nd ed.). New York: Oxford University Press.

McGuire, B. E. (2002). Malingered post-traumatic stress symptoms on the Impact of Event Scale. *Legal and Criminological Psychology, 7*, 165–171.

McKinzey, R. K., & Zeigler, T. G. (1999). Challenging a flexible neuropsychological battery under Kelly/Frye: A case study. *Behavioral Sciences and the Law, 17 (4)*, 543–551.

Melton, G. B., Petrila, J., Poythress, N. G., & Slobogin, C. (1997). *Psychological evaluations for the courts: A handbook for mental health professionals and lawyers* (2nd ed.) New York: Guilford.

Miller, H. A. (2001). *Miller-Forensic Assessment of Symptoms Test (M-FAST): Professional Manual.* Odessa, FL: Psychological Assessment Resources.

Millis, S. R. (2002). Warrington's Recognition Memory Test in the detection of response bias. *Journal of Forensic Neuropsychology, 2*, 147–166.

Millis, S. R., Putnam, S. H., Adams, K. M., & Ricker, J. H. (1992). The California Verbal Learning Test in the detection of incomplete effort in neuropsychological evaluation. *Psychological Assessment, 7*, 463–471.

Mittenberg, W., Aguila-Puentes, G., Patton, C., Canyock, E. M., & Heilbronner, R. (in press). Neuropsychological profiling of symptom exaggeration and malingering. *Journal of Forensic Neuropsychology.*

Molien v. Kaiser Foundation Hospital, 27 Cal 3d 916 (1980).

Morgan, J. E., & Caccappolo-van Vliet, E. (2001). Advanced years and low education: The case *against* the Comprehensive Norms. *Journal of Forensic Neuropsychology, 2*, 53–69.

Mrad, D. (1996). *Criminal responsibility evaluations.* Paper presented at Issues in Forensic Assessment symposium, Federal Bureau of Prisons, September, Atlanta, GA.

Nelson, H. E. (1982). *National Adult Reading Test (NART): Test manual.* Windsor, UK: NFER-Nelson.

Norfolk & Western Railway Company v. Freeman Ayers et. al., 27 S. Ct. 57; L. Ed. 2d (2002).

Parker, K. C. H. (1983). A meta-analysis of the reliability and validity of the Rorschach. *Journal of Personality Assessment, 42*, 227–231.

Poser, S., Bornstein, B. H., & McGorty, E. K. (2003). Measuring damages for lost enjoyment of life: The view from the bench and the jury box. *Law and Human Behavior, 27*, 53–68.

Reed, J. E. (1996). Fixed vs. flexible neuropsychological test batteries under the Daubert standard for the admissibility of scientific evidence. *Behavioral Sciences and the Law, 14*, 315–322.

Rey, A. (1958). *L'examen clinique en psychologie* [The psychological examination]. Paris: Presses Universitaires de France.

Reid, W. H. (2000). Licensure requirements for out-of-state forensic examinations. *Journal of the American Academy of Psychiatry and the Law, 28*, 433–437.

Reitan, R. M., & Wolfson, D. (1995). Influence of age and education on neuropsychological test results. *The Clinical Neuropsychologist, 9*, 151–158.

Reitan, R. M., & Wolfson, D. (2002). Detection of malingering and invalid test results using the Halstead-Reitan Battery. *Journal of Forensic Neuropsychology, 3*, 275–314.

Rogers, R. (1997). Current status of clinical methods. In R. Rogers (Ed.), *Clinical assessment of malingering and deception* (pp. 373–397). New York: Guilford Press.

Rogers, R., Bagby, R. M., & Dickens, S. E. (1992). *The SIRS Test Manual*. Odessa, FL: Psychological Assessment Resources.

Russell, E. W. (1998). In defense of the Halstead Reitan Battery: A critique of Lezak's review. *Archives of Clinical Neuropsychology, 13*, 365–381.

Russell, E. W. (2000a). The cognitive-metric, fixed batter approach to neuropsychological assessment. In R. D. Vanderploeg (Ed.), *Clinician's guide to neuropsychological assessment* (2nd ed.) (pp. 449–481). Mahwah, NJ: Lawrence Erlbaum.

Russell, E. W. (2000b). The application of computerized scoring programs to neuropsychological assessment. In R. D. Vanderploeg (Ed.) *Clinician's guide to neuropsychological assessment* (2nd ed.) (pp. 483–515). Mahwah, NJ: Lawrence Erlbaum.

Russell, E. W., & Starkey, R. I. (1993). *Halstead, Russell Neuropsychological Evaluation System* [Manual and computer program]. Los Angeles: Western Psychological Services.

Sbordone, R. J. (1996). Ecological validity: Some critical issues for the neuropsychologist. In R. J. Sbordone & C. J. Long (Eds.), *The ecological validity of neuropsychological testing* (pp. 15–41). Orlando, FL: GR/St. Lucie Press.

Sbordone, R. J., & Guillmette, T. J. (1999). Ecological validity: Prediction of everyday and vocational functioning from neuropsychological test data. In J. J. Sweet (Ed.), *Forensic neuropsychology: Fundamentals and practice* (pp. 227–254). Lisse, the Netherlands: Swets & Zeitlinger.

Schinka, J. A., & Vanderploeg, R. D. (2000). Estimating premorbid level of functioning. In R. D. Vanderploeg (Ed.), *Clinician's guide to neuropsychological assessment* (pp. 39–67). Mahwah, NJ: Lawrence Erlbaum.

Schretlen, D. J. (1988). The use of psychological tests to identify malingered symptoms of mental disorder. *Clinical Psychology Review, 8*, 451–476.

Shapiro, D. L. (1999). *Criminal responsibility evaluations: A manual for practice*. Sarasota, FL: Professional Resource Press.

Simon, R. I. (Ed.) (1995a). *Post-traumatic Stress Disorder in litigation: Guidelines for forensic assessment*. Washington, DC: Georgetown University.

Simon, R. I. (1995b). Toward the development of guidelines in the forensic psychiatric examination of post-traumatic stress disorder claimants. In R. I. Simon (Ed.), *Post-traumatic Stress Disorder in litigation: Guidelines for forensic assessment* (pp. 31–84). Washington, DC: Georgetown University.

Slick, D., Hopp, G., Strauss, E., & Thompson, G. B. (1997). *Victoria Symptom Validity Test version 1.0 Professional Manual*. Odessa, FL: Psychological Assessment Resources.

Spaulding, W. J. (1990). A look at the AMA Guides to the Evaluation Impairment: Problems in workers' compensation claims involving mental disability. *Behavioral Sciences and the Law, 8*, 361–369.

Sweet, J. J., & King, J. H. (2002). Category Test validity indicators: Overview and practice recommendations. *Journal of Forensic Neuropsychology, 3*, 241–274.

Thompson v. National Railroad Passenger Corp., 621 F.2d 814 (6th Cir. 1980). Applying Tennessee law.

Thompson, G. B. (2002). The Victoria Symptom Validity Test: An enhanced test of symptom validity. *Journal of Forensic Neuropsychology, 2*, 43–67.

Tombaugh, T. N. (1996). *The Test of Memory Malingering (TOMM)*. Toronto, Canada: Multi-Health Systems.

Tombaugh, T. N. (2002). The Test of Memory Malingering (TOMM) in forensic psychology. *Journal of Forensic Neuropsychology, 2*, 69–96.

Tucillo, J. A., Defilippis, N. A., Denney, R. L., & Dsurney, J. (2002). Licensure requirements for interjurisdictional forensic evaluations. *Professional Psychology: Research and Practice, 33 (4)*, 377–383.

United States v. Alvarez, 519 F2d 1036 (3rd Cir 1995).

Vallabhajosula, B., & van Gorp, W. (2001). Post-Daubert admissibility of scientific evidence on malingering of cognitive deficits. *Journal of the American Academy of Psychiatry and the Law, 29*, 207–215.

Vanderploeg, R. D., Axelrod, B. N., Sherer, M., Scott, J., & Adams, R. L. (1997). The importance of demographic adjustments on neuropsychological test performance: A response to Reitan and Wolfson (1995). *The Clinical Neuropsychologist, 11*, 210–217.

Vanderploeg, R. D., Schinka, J. A., & Axelrod, B. N. (1996). Estimation of WAIS-R premorbid intelligence: Current ability and demographic data used in a best-performance fashion. *Psychological Assessment, 80*, 404–411.

Wechsler Test of Adult Reading (2001). San Antonio, TX: The Psychological Corp.

Weins, A. N., Bryan, J. E., & Crossen, J. R. (1993). Estimating WAIS-R FIQ from national adult reading test-revised in normal subjects. *Clinical Neuropsychologist, 7*, 70–84.

Wetter, M. W., & Corrigan, S. K. (1995). Providing information to clients about psychological tests: A survey of attorneys' and law students' attitudes. *Professional Psychology: Research and Practice, 26*, 474–477.

Wrightsman, L. S., Nietzel, M. T., & Fortune, W. H. (1998). *Psychology and the legal system* (4th ed). Pacific Grove, CA: Brooks/Cole.

Wynkoop. T. F., & Denney, R. L. (2001). Test reviews: Computerized Assessment of Response Bias (CARB), Word Memory Test (WMT), and Memory Complaints Inventory (MCI). *Journal of Forensic Neuropsychology, 2*, 71–77.

Youngjohn, J. R. (1995) Confirmed attorney coaching prior to neuropsychological evaluation. *Assessment 2*, 279–283.

CHAPTER 14

DETECTING MALINGERING IN FORENSIC NEUROPSYCHOLOGICAL EVALUATIONS IN LITIGANTS WITH MILD TRAUMATIC BRAIN INJURY

KYLE E. FERGUSON

UNIVERSITY OF NEVADA, RENO

As many as 1.5 million Americans sustain traumatic brain injuries (TBI) every year (Centers for Disease Control and Prevention, 1999). Of these, approximately 80 percent are categorized as mild injuries (Sohlberg & Mateer, 2001). Mild traumatic brain injury (MTBI) is defined as *traumatically induced physiological disruption of brain function manifested by at least one of the following*:

1. Loss of consciousness
2. Loss of memory for events immediately before or after the accident
3. Change in mental state at the time of the accident (e.g., feeling dazed, disoriented, or confused)
4. Focal neurological deficit(s) that may or may not be transient but where the severity of the injury does not exceed the following:
    a. loss of consciousness of approximately 30 minutes or less
    b. after 30 minutes, an initial Glasgow Coma Scale (GCS) of 13–15
    c. post-traumatic amnesia (PTA) not greater than 24 hours (Mild Traumatic Brain Injury Committee of Head Injury Special Interest Group of the American Congress of Rehabilitation Medicine, 1993, pp. 86–87)

Unlike severe and moderate injuries, in which deficits are usually more obvious as evidenced by dysarthria (slurred speech), hemiplegia (paralysis to one side of the body), ataxia (awkward volitional movements), and the like, determining the extent of impairment with MTBI poses unique challenges. In the case of MTBI, survivors often suffer from subtle, higher-cerebral impairment characterized by problems with executive functioning (e.g., planning, organization, and abstract reasoning), mental fatigue, and personality disturbances (e.g., impulsivity and mood instability), to name only a few (Prigatano, 1999). Colloquially, practitioners often refer to such cases as the "walking wounded" because at first blush they appear relatively "normal" (i.e., not head injured) when compared to moderate or severe cases. By and large, individuals suffering from MTBI can complete many routine tasks without too much difficulty, much like how they were functioning premorbidly, before their accidents. It is only after they have tested their cognitive limits that impairment is suspected. Interestingly, in spite of these higher cognitive deficits, neuroimaging tests often come up negative and neurological signs are seldom present (Inman & Berry, 2002; Smith et al., 1995). Accordingly, neuropsychological test findings are usually the only objective evidence of impairment.

Given that TBI is most often caused by motor vehicle accidents (MVA), falls, and violence, many neuropsychological evaluations potentially have forensic implications (Centers for Disease Control and Prevention, 1999). This is especially the case where it is found that the client is not at fault (i.e., proximate cause) for his or her injury (Youngjohn, Lees-Haley, & Binder, 1999). The purpose of neuropsychological evaluations, therefore, is to establish the extent of damage caused by the injury to assist the court in determining the amount of monetary compensation the victim ought to receive (i.e., apportionment of damages; Léon-Jimenez, 1998, p. 124; see Chapter 13 in this volume for an in-depth discussion on how such damages are assessed). In criminal proceedings, neuropsychological evaluations also are used to determine criminal responsibility and competence to stand trial. In either case, whenever litigation is concerned the neuropsychologist will invariably be asked: "How confident are you that these results were not faked?" And the follow-up question to that, "What tests did you employ and/or what criteria did you use to rule out malingering?" (McKinzey, 1997). As we will shortly see, malingering is simply the faking or embellishment of symptoms so as to appear more impaired than one actually is for purposes of secondary gain (e.g., worker's compensation).

Although one might predict that patients with more marked brain injuries would be more likely to pursue apportionment of damages, since damage would extend above and beyond higher cerebral deficits, there is evidence to suggest otherwise. In a recent meta-analytic review, for example, patients with milder injuries, as determined by post-traumatic neurological data, are much more likely to seek out monetary compensation (Binder & Rohling, 1996, p. 9). Binder and Rohling's analysis also revealed that individuals with MTBI are more likely to be affected by monetary incentives as regards disability and symptom presentation when compared to other individuals with moderate or severe injuries. Specifically, all other things being equal, those individuals involved in litigation versus those who are not tend to present with greater overall impairment.

Given these findings, one might expect a high base rate for malingering and symptom exaggeration with MTBI litigants. And, indeed, this seems to be the case. Caution is in order, however. As we shall soon see, these data remain speculative. In a recent survey of the American Board of Clinical Neuropsychology, for example, probable malingering was suspected in 39 percent of cases involving MTBI (Mittenberg, Patton, Canyock, & Condit, 2002; cf. Binder et al., 1993, and Frederick et al., 1994). These estimates were derived from 33,531 cases involving personal injury, disability, criminal, and medical matters. Malingering was suspected because of inconsistent test patterns, scores that fell below empirical cutoffs on forced-choice tests, and implausible self-reported symptoms, among other criteria. Of course, as is the case in most studies of malingering, these are estimates, not actual rates. Malingerers are reluctant to admit to this, even when confronted with evidence, as they would be confessing to having committed a fraudulent act (e.g., insurance fraud; Babin & Gross, 2002; Brandt, 1992).

This chapter addresses the issue of detecting malingering in neuropsychological evaluations in litigants with MTBI. The first part of the chapter provides a definition of malingering followed by a brief discussion of how it is differentially diagnosed from psychological disturbances that mimic these patterns. The reader should note that even though malingering is included in the *Diagnostic and Statistical Manual of Mental Disorders–IV* (*DSM-IV*; American Psychiatric Association, APA, 1994), it is not a disorder per se. Malingering falls under the rubric of "additional conditions" as a V-Code (APA, 1994, p. 675ff.). Moreover, to complicate matters further, malingering is not an "all-or-nothing phenomenon"; rather it takes place "on several levels" (Hebben & Milberg, 2002, p. 173). The second part of the chapter describes these levels, and the third part provides guidelines for detecting probable malingering.

WHAT IS MALINGERING?

Malingering is the deliberate fabrication or exaggeration of symptoms and/or deficits for the purposes of secondary gain (Rogers & Vitacco, 2002). Secondary gain from a legal standpoint might include, though is not limited to, monetary compensation for personal injury, worker's compensation, and avoiding culpability in criminal cases (not guilty by reason of insanity verdict because of a "condition known to create brain insult"; Hall & Poirier, 2001, p. 137; Puente & Gillespie, 1991). Over and above "willful production of poor performance on psychological and neuropsychological tests," Iverson and Binder (2000) also suggest other areas of probable exaggeration, including "pain, stiffness, dizziness, depression, memory disturbance, poor concentration, and personality change . . . blindness or visual loss, numbness, grossly restricted mobility or range of motion, or severe amnesia" (p. 830). Thus, patterns of malingering not only differ by degrees but also in kind.

Differential Diagnostic Process

Before arriving at the conclusion that a client is malingering, alternative explanations must first be entertained during the evaluative process (Iverson & Binder, 2000). The most likely alternative explanations are Factitious Disorder and the Somatoform Disorders.

Malingering is not be confused with Factitious Disorder. Malingering suggests an external incentive, whereas in Factitious Disorder external incentives are not at issue (APA, 1994, p. 683). Patients who are diagnosed with Factitious Disorder are said to *volitionally* produce symptoms as a means of assuming the "sick" or "invalid role" (Hebben & Milberg, 2002, p. 174). Simply, if the client stands to gain economically from having deficits or avoids legal responsibility, Factitious Disorder is ruled out. Before ruling in malingering, however, the forensic psychologist also needs to rule out Somatoform Disorders.

Somatoform Disorders are characterized by "the presence of physical symptoms that suggest a general medical condition," although there "is no diagnosable general medical condition to fully account for the physical symptoms" (APA, 1994, p. 445). Most important, Somatoform Disorders differ from malingering and Factitious Disorder in that the physical symptoms are not considered intentional. Unfortunately, the *DSM-IV* provides little guidance in the way of making the distinction between intentional and unintentional symptomology. Three subtypes of Somatoform Disorders are particularly relevant to differential diagnosis: Somatization Disorder, Undifferentiated Somatoform Disorder, and Conversion Disorder.

The most important feature of Somatization Disorder is "a pattern of recurring, multiple, clinically significant somatic complaints" (APA, 1994, p. 446). By being clinically significant, the somatic complaints must result in some form of medical treatment. In describing their symptoms, individuals with Somatization Disorder often lack specific factual information. Laboratory findings generally fail to support their subjective complaints. These complaints must have begun before the age of 30 and have been present for several years. In fact, the diagnostic criteria are usually met before the age of 25. Additional criteria include the presence of at least four pain symptoms (e.g., abdomen), two gastrointestinal symptoms (e.g., nausea), one sexual symptom (e.g., erectile dysfunction), and one pseudoneurological symptom (e.g., conversion symptoms such as double vision).

The most important feature of Undifferentiated Somatoform Disorder is "one or more physical complaints that persist for 6 months or longer" (APA, 1994, p. 450). Chronic fatigue, loss of appetite, or gastrointestinal or genitourinary symptoms are the most common complaints. Again, as with Somatization Disorder, medical test results fail to corroborate the symptoms. Or, should there be a preexisting medical condition, the extent of disability is in excess of what one would expect in light of diagnostic findings.

The most important feature of Conversion Disorder is "the presence of symptoms or deficits affecting voluntary motor or sensory function that suggest neurological or other general medical condition" (APA, 1994, p. 452). Motor symptoms include impaired coordination, paralysis or partial paralysis, aphonia (i.e., loss of voice), and difficulty swallowing, among others. Sensory symptoms include diplopia (i.e., double vision), blindness, deafness, and hallucinations (not on account of psychosis). In extreme cases individuals might also suffer from seizures or convulsions (APA, 1994, p. 452). Last, motoric and/or sensory dysfunction are believed to be involuntary, the likes of which are not "fully" corroborated by a general medical condition. After ruling out Factitious Disorder and Somatoform Disorders, malingering might very well account for discrepancies in performance.

General Malingering Levels or Patterns

Malingering is not an all-or-nothing phenomenon. It varies along a continuum, ranging from an obvious to a subtle clinical presentation. Since the inception of the Internet, with scores of websites (largely maintained by legal practices) providing information about the nuances of MTBI and its medicolegal implications, clients are becoming increasingly sophisticated in the presentation of neurocognitive deficits. Observe, too, that clients also have become more sophisticated psychometrically because of the Internet and coaching on the part of their legal representatives. In a recent study, for example, roughly half of the attorneys or law students sampled believed that clients should be told particulars regarding psychological tests as well as be informed about validity indices on such measures (Wetter & Corrigan, 1995). The direct effect of warning malingerers about the presence of symptom validity assessment techniques is less exaggerated, more believable feigned deficits (Youngjohn, Lees-Haley, & Binder, 1999). Thus, within the last decade malingering has become much harder to detect as "faked" symptoms better emulate genuine symptoms.

With all this in mind, let us examine the four major patterns of malingering (Hebben & Milberg, 2002, p. 174). The first pattern suggests symptom exaggeration. For example, on the Wechsler Memory Scale–Third Edition (WMS-III), clients (with bona fide memory problems) might elect to withhold certain details on the Logical Memory (II) and Visual Reproduction (II) delayed recall subtests, despite remembering these. By recalling the gist of the stories or drawing the basic gestalt of the figures even while intentionally leaving out details, clients embellish the severity of extant memory deficits while performing well enough so as not to raise suspicion.

Impairment is also exaggerated by artificially inflating premorbid cognitive/intellectual status in one's retrospective report. As a case in point, comparable deficits as indicated by the Wechsler Adult Intelligence Scales (WAIS-III) have different implications if the individual was an A student throughout most of his or her life rather than D student (suggesting more impairment in the former). Interestingly, as is the case with symptom exaggeration more generally, within the adversarial context litigants are more likely to embellish premorbid functioning in their retrospective reports. Namely, they will grossly overinflate their GPA (Greiffenstein, Baker, & Johnson-Greene, 2002). Given that clients are often unreliable self-reporters, neuropsychologists must obtain this information from actual educational records whenever possible.

The second pattern of malingering is maintaining symptoms after they have been resolved. For example, after sustaining a severe enough blow to the head (though with very mild disruption of neurological function), many individuals experience postconcussion symptoms such as problems with attention and concentration, headache, double vision, and memory difficulties, to name only a few (Evans, 1992). However, over time these problems should resolve themselves. In fact, 70 percent of individuals with MTBI show no symptoms after three to six months (Kraus & Nourjah, 1998). And at one year post-injury, only 8–12 percent still report symptoms (Sohlberg & Mateer, 2001). In other words, approximately 90 percent of those individuals with suspected MTBI will be symptom free after one year.

The third pattern of malingering involves the presence of symptoms or deficits that resulted from an earlier brain injury or disability even though the client maintains that these are attributable to the event in question (e.g., car accident). Preexisting learning disabilities, for example, affect performance on neuropsychological tests. In some cases of malingering, clients might deny a history of learning disability, since this would in all likelihood weaken their case. Obviously, the preexisting learning disability would to some extent account for deficient performance shown on academic achievement tests, attention, and abstract reasoning indices, to name only a few.

Similarly, in addition to exploring whether the client has a preexisting learning disability, the forensic psychologist should also assess for substance abuse and prior psychiatric history, since either of these factors might impact cognitive functioning. Most important, comorbid substance and/or psychiatric condition(s) are related to significant complications during the recovery process, an increased likelihood of repeat injuries, and overall poorer neurocognitive prognosis (Corrigan, 1995; Mooney & Speed, 2001). Regarding previous brain injuries, neurodiagnostics (e.g., magnetic resonance imaging or MRI) should illuminate residua if these were significant (e.g., appearing as multiple infarcts).

Accordingly, a critical first step in forensic neuropsychological evaluation is to obtain all relevant information regarding the client's premorbid functional status including educational, psychological, and substance abuse history (Spreen & Strauss, 1998). It is strongly recommended that clinicians obtain a release of all pertinent educational and psychological records as soon as possible. This information will undoubtedly influence what tests are selected, and these tests are critical in case conceptualization.

The fourth pattern of malingering entails an out-and-out fabrication of symptoms or deficits. For example, the Wisconsin Card Sorting Test (WCST), a test of executive functions (e.g., planning and reasoning), is sensitive to impairment in moderate or more severe cases of TBI (Lezak, 1995). Such individuals are expected to perseverate and make more perseverative errors relative to non-brain-injured individuals. Conversely, individuals with MTBI are to a large extent expected to manifest "normal" performance while differing markedly with respect to difficulties maintaining set (Mateer, 1992). Should an individual with probable MTBI make an excessive amount of perseverative responses, he or she is very likely fabricating symptoms (see Greve et al., 2002, for a recent discussion of detecting malingering using the WCST).

General Guidelines in Detecting Malingering

As a rule, malingering is particularly suspect when a combination of two or more of the following features are present: (1) the client is referred by an attorney; (2) there are marked discrepancies in test data; (3) the client extends little effort or is not cooperative throughout the evaluation; (4) the client has been or meets the criteria for Antisocial Personality Disorder (APA, 2000, pp. 309–310).

Regarding item 2, marked discrepancies in test data, the psychologist should look for intertest inconsistency, inconsistency between obtained and expected scores, and between-evaluation inconsistencies (Iverson & Binder, 2000). *Intertest inconsistency* is differential performance on measures purported to measure the same cognitive ability. An obvious example would be performing well on the Paced Auditory Serial Addition Test (PASAT) and performing in the moderately impaired or severely impaired range on Trail-Making, since both of these tests require sustained attention. *Inconsistency between obtained and expected scores* has to do with the nature of the client's injury and what one might anticipate given the injury (i.e., normatively speaking). For example, a person with MTBI should have no difficulty copying the Rey Complex Figure or completing the Categories Test of the Halstead-Reitan Neuropsychological Battery with no more than a handful of perseverative errors. *Between-evaluation inconsistencies* relates to marked performance discrepancies across multiple neuropsychological evaluations. An obvious example would be an initial performance suggesting mild memory impairment and a subsequent performance on similar or identical tests suggesting severe memory problems. Barring undetected neurological complications (e.g., increased intracranial pressure resulting from untreated hydrocephalus), one does not predict the worsening of symptoms with MTBI; quite the contrary. The most probable course for MTBI is the alleviation of symptoms after about six months. Other qualitative signs of malingering, pertaining to test-taking behavior more specifically, are as follows: (1) higher recall scores versus recognition scores on memory items; (2) failing easy items while passing more difficult ones (e.g., doing better on digits backward than digits forward); (3) near misses;

(4) disproportionately high "I don't know" responses (Tombaugh, 1996, as cited in Hebben & Milberg, 2002, p. 179).

Whereas overall test-taking patterns might indicate malingering, examiners also have the option of employing tests that are designed to evoke malingering from clients. These tests have a "low true difficulty level, but a high face difficulty level," the purpose of which is to entice malingerers to perform poorly all the while allowing motivated examinees to perform reasonably well in spite of their deficits (Inman & Berry, 2002, p. 3). In assessing the relative merits of using one instrument over another, consider the following criteria proffered by Hartman (2002). Does (is) the instrument:

- Measure willingness to exert basic effort, and is it insensitive to the cognitive dysfunction being assessed (sensitivity and specificity)?
- Appear to the patient to be a realistic measure of the cognitive modality under study (face validity)?
- Measure abilities that are likely to be exaggerated?
- Based on validation studies that include normals, patient populations, and individuals who are suspected and/or verified malingerers in actual forensic or disability assessment conditions?
- Difficult to fake or coach?
- Relatively easy to administer?
- Supported by continuing research? (p. 710)

Before implementing specific malingering tests, examiners should briefly survey the literature to determine what tests would be most appropriate given the client, his or her litigation status, and initial presenting complaints. They should also be wary of those tests whose empirical bases overly rely on simulation studies. Simulation studies typically employ university students who are asked to feign neurocognitive impairment. A university student who participates for extra credit and a malingerer who stands to lose thousands of dollars in a personal injury case are governed by two very different sets of contingencies (Rogers, 1997). Tests largely based on simulation studies are suspect and are not defensible upon cross-examination. Most important, examiners should never rely on just one measure of malingering, since deficient performance on any one measure might be related to a bona fide cognitive deficit, albeit rarely. Or perhaps poor performance is related to a misdiagnosed psychiatric disorder. Examiners should consider employing several tests of malingering, interspersed throughout the standard battery of tests, and look for patterns of malingering across these, as well as on other neuropsychological and personality tests (e.g., Lees-Haley's MMPI-2 Fake Bad Scale; Greiffenstein et al., 2002).

Let us turn next to several malingering tests commonly employed in forensic neuropsychological evaluations. This list is not intended to be exhaustive; its purpose is to briefly acquaint the reader with tests of malingering that are relatively easy to administer.

Detecting Malingering Using Specific Tests of Malingering: Four Examples

In every medicolegal context where the base rate of malingering is expectedly high, the clinician should disperse tests that are sensitive to motivation, effort, and compliance throughout the standard battery of tests (Hebben & Milberg, 2002). As such, forced-choice tests are often used as a means of assessing the client's effort and overall compliance within the assessment proper. According to Pankratz & Binder (1997),

> Forced-choice testing is comprised of two elements: (1) A specific ability is assessed by a large number of items presented in a multiple-choice format; and (2) a person's performance is compared to the likelihood of success based on chance alone. . . . All widely used forced-choice tests have two multiple-choice alternatives; therefore, the probability of purely guessing . . . the correct response is 50 percent. Scores significantly lower than chance performance suggest that sensory cues must have been perceived, but the patient chose not to report the correct answer. . . . The compelling conclusion is that the patient who scores below probabilities is deliberately motivated to perform poorly. (p. 228)

Hiscock and Hiscock (1989) created a forced-choice test, called the Digit Recognition Test (DRT), designed to assess motivation to perform on tests of recent memory. The DRT is composed of three different sets of stimuli, each of which contains 72 cards. Within each set, one-third of the cards contain a single five-digit target number; one-third of the set consists of the target numbers along with distracter items, that is, the choice cards (i.e., the target and one other five-digit number per card); one-third are blanks inserted between the target cards and choice cards. Before being shown the cards, examinees are told that they will be given a test of memory. They will then be shown the target stimuli for 5 seconds each. After every target stimulus, a blank card is presented for 5 seconds and immediately thereafter the choice card is presented. The client is then asked to point to the target stimulus given the distracter; the next target card is drawn, and so on. After the first set is completed, delays between the target and choice card are increased by 5 seconds for the second set (i.e., 10-second delay) and 10 seconds for the third (i.e., 15-second delay). Examinees are informed that the task becomes increasingly difficult as they advance through the cards.

Ideally, malingerers should score below chance, or 50 percent. However, this does not seem to be the case. Prigatano and Amin (1993) and Prigatano and colleagues (1997) found that suspected malingerers performed above chance (i.e., a mean of 74 percent in the former study and approximately 85 percent in the latter). Moreover, they showed progressive decline across the three sets. By contrast, "brain dysfunctional" subjects and normal controls performed at around 95 percent and did not show this pattern of progressive decline.

Another forced-choice test is the Test of Memory Malingering (TOMM; Tombaugh, 1996). The TOMM is a clinical test designed to detect malingering of memory impairments. It consists of two learning trials. On each trial pictures of

50 everyday objects are administered one at a time, followed by a forced-choice recognition task, composed of 50 two-choice recognition panels (Rees et al., 1998). Subjects are then asked to point to the picture that was previously shown. The TOMM also has an optional delayed forced-choice recognition task, where only the 50 two-choice recognition panels are administered. Given that this test is largely insensitive to neurological impairment, even gross impairment, nonmalingerers should score above 90 percent across trials (Tombaugh, 1997).

One of the major problems that mitigate against forced-choice tests is that after attorney coaching these measures rapidly lose their sensitivity to exaggeration (Green, Iverson, & Allen, 1999). Accordingly, other more open-ended tests for malingering should also be considered for inclusion in the clinician's repertoire, given that many attorneys are expected to coach their clients about validity and psychometric issues in general. Two largely open-ended malingering tests are the Rey 15-Item Visual Memory Test and Word Memory Test (WMT; Lezak, 1995).

The Rey 15-Item Visual Memory Test was developed in 1964 as a method of assessing the validity of memory complaints (Rey, 1964). The instructions emphasize that there are 15 "unique" items to recall when in actuality these items naturally fall into one of five groups (uppercase and lowercase letters, numbers and roman numerals, and three shapes). Subjects are then shown the 15 items arranged in three columns of five rows and are given 10 seconds to memorize the items. After the 10 seconds are up, the examiner removes the cards and the examinee is asked to recall as many of the items as possible on a blank sheet of paper.

Although the instructions suggest that the task is difficult, in reality it is not. In fact, only the most "severely brain damaged or retarded persons" do not fare well on this measure (Lezak, 1983, p. 618). Most individuals are expected to "recall at least three of the five character sets, or 9 items" (Lezak, 1983, p. 619). Examiners should suspect malingering if the client scores below seven items (Lee et al., 1992). Moreover, confabulations, reversals, or improper placement of numbers and letters also raise suspicion of a malingering pattern (Hebben & Milberg, 2002, pp. 123–124).

The Word Memory Test (WMT), a computer-based instrument, is designed to measure verbal memory and biased responding (e.g., suboptimal effort or the feigning of symptoms; Green, Allen, & Astner, 2000). As with the paired-associates learning task of the WMS-III test, clients learn a list of paired associates. Half of these pairs, a total of 20, bear a close semantic resemblance and as such are easily learned. The other half of the word pairs are unrelated. An immediate recognition subtest follows in which clients have to select each of the original 40 words from pairs that now include distracter items; 30 minutes later, without warning, clients are given a similar delayed recognition subtest.

The WMT is also composed of a multiple-choice cued recall task and a paired-associates recall task, both of which are administered after the 30-minute delayed recognition subtest. Among other metrics, a malingering pattern is suspected when clients score below 82 percent on the delayed recognition task (i.e.,

6 standard deviations below the mean, or 95.4 percent; Green, Iverson, & Allen, 1999, p. 814).

Conclusion

Given that many neuropsychological evaluations of MTBI have forensic implications and the fact that as a group MTBI survivors are particularly litigious, the issue of malingering cannot be ignored by clinicians who practice in clinical neuropsychology. There are simply too many incentives to feign or embellish symptoms in the adversarial context. When psychologists are not oriented to malingering, they fail to recognize it when it is present (see the classic study by Heaton et al., 1978, or the study by Faust, Hart, & Guilmette, 1988, often cited by attorneys upon cross-examining reports of suspected malingering). By contrast, when examiners are oriented to malingering, they are much more likely to detect it (Pankratz & Binder, 1997). This is especially the case when malingering is more obvious (Trueblood & Binder, 1997). Above all, although no set of guidelines or specific tests are foolproof in detecting malingering patterns, clinicians with a thorough understanding of neurological functioning and a familiarity with what to expect, given demographics, the nature of the injury, and the like, are in a much more favorable position to parse out highly motivated from suboptimal performance shown in litigants with MTBI.

References

American Psychiatric Association. (1994). *Diagnostic and statistical manual of mental disorders* (4th ed.). Washington, DC: Author.

American Psychiatric Association. (2000). *Quick reference to the diagnostic criteria from DSM-IV-TR*. Washington, DC: Author.

Babin, P. R., & Gross, P. (2002). When symptoms don't add up: Conversion and malingering in rehabilitation settings. *Journal of Rehabilitation, 68,* 4–13.

Binder, L. M., & Rohling, M. L. (1996). Money matters: A meta-analytic review of the effects of financial incentives on recovery after closed-head injury. *American Journal of Psychiatry, 153,* 7–10.

Binder, L. M., Villanueva, M. R., Howieson, D., & Moore, R. T. (1993). The Rey AVLT Recognition Memory Task measures motivational impairment after mild head trauma. *Archives of Clinical Neuropsychology, 8,* 137–147.

Brandt, J. (1992). Detecting amnesia's imposters. In L. R. Squire & N. Butters (Eds.), *Neuropsychology of memory* (2nd ed.) (pp. 156–165). New York: Guilford Press.

Centers for Disease Control and Prevention. (1999). *Traumatic brain injury in the United States: A report to Congress.* Washington, DC: Author. Retrieved April 22, 2003, from http://www.cdc.gov/ncipc/pub-res/tbi_congress/TBI_in_the_US.PDF

Corrigan, J. D. (1995). Substance abuse as a mediating factor in outcome for traumatic brain injury. *Archives of Physical Medicine and Rehabilitation, 76,* 302–309.

Evans, R. W. (1992). The postconcussion syndrome and the sequelae of mild head injury. *Neurologic Clinics, 10,* 815–847.

Faust, D., Hart, K., & Guilmette, T. J. (1988). Pediatric malingering: The capacity of children to fake believable deficits on neuropsychological testing. *Journal of Consulting and Clinical Psychology, 56,* 578–582.

Frederick, R. I., Sarfaty, S. D., Johnston, D., & Powel, J. (1994). Validation of a detector of response bias on a forced-choice test of nonverbal ability. *Neuropsychology, 8,* 118–125.

Green, P., Allen, L. M., & Astner, K. (2000). *Word Memory Test.* Durham, NC: CogniSyst.

Green, P., Iverson, G. L., & Allen, L. (1999). Detecting malingering in head injury litigation with the Word Memory Test. *Brain Injury, 13,* 813–819.

Greiffenstein, M. F., Baker, W. J., Gola, T., Donders, J., & Miller, L. (2002). The Fake Bad Scale in atypical and severe closed head injury litigants. *Journal of Clinical Psychology, 58,* 1591–1600.

Greiffenstein, M. F., Baker, W. J., & Johnson-Greene, D. (2002). Actual versus self-reported achievement of litigating postconcussion and severe closed head injury claimants. *Psychological Assessment, 14,* 202–208.

Greve, K. W., Bianchini, K. J., Mathias, C. W., Houston, R. J., & Crouch, J. A. (2002). Detecting malingered performance with the Wisconsin Card Sorting Test: A preliminary investigation in traumatic brain injury. *Clinical Neuropsychologist, 16,* 179–191.

Hall, H. V., & Poirier, J. G. (2001). *Detecting malingering and deception: Forensic distortion analysis* (2nd ed.). New York: CRC Press.

Hartman, D. E. (2002). The unexamined lie is a lie worth fibbing: Neuropsychological malingering and the Word Memory Test. *Archives of Clinical Neuropsychology, 17,* 709–714.

Heaton, R. K., Smith, H. H., Lehman, R. A. W., & Vogt, A. T. (1978). Prospects for faking believable deficits on neuropsychological testing. *Journal of Consulting and Clinical Psychology, 46,* 892–900.

Hebben, N., & Milberg, W. (2002). *Essentials of neuropsychological assessment.* Hoboken, NJ: Wiley.

Hiscock, M., & Hiscock, D. (1989). Refining the forced-choice method for the detection of malingering. *Journal of Clinical and Experimental Neuropsychology, 11,* 967–974.

Inman, T. H., & Berry, D. T. R. (2002). Cross-validation of indicators of malingering: A comparison of nine neurological tests, four tests of malingering, and behavioral observations. *Archives of Clinical Neuropsychology, 17,* 1–23.

Iverson, G. L., & Binder, L. M. (2000). Detecting exaggeration and malingering in neuropsychological assessment. *Journal of Head Trauma Rehabilitation, 15,* 829–858.

Kraus, J. F., & Nourjah, P. (1998). The epidemiology of mild uncomplicated head injury. *Trauma, 28,* 1637–1643.

Lee, G., Loring, D., & Martin, R. (1992). Rey's 15-item visual memory test for the detection of malingering: Normative observations on patients with neurological disorders. *Psychological Assessment, 4,* 43–46.

Lees-Haley, P. R., Williams, C. W., & English, L. T. (1996). Response bias in self-reported history of plaintiffs compared with nonlitigating patients. *Psychological Reports, 79,* 811–818.

Léon-Jimenez, F. (1998). Ethical and legal issues in brain injury rehabilitation. *NeuroRehabilitation, 11*, 119–127.

Lezak, M. D. (1983). *Neuropsychological assessment*. New York: Oxford University Press.

Lezak, M. D. (1995). *Neuropsychological assessment* (3rd ed.). New York: Oxford University Press.

Mateer, C. A. (1992). Systems of care for post-concussive syndrome. In L. J. Horn & N. D. Zasler (Eds.), *Rehabilitation of post-concussive disorders: State of the art reviews* (pp. 143–155). Philadelphia: Henley & Belfus.

McKinzey, R. K. (1997). The cross-examination of neuropsychologists: Countering the claim of brain damage. *Prosecutor's Brief, 19* (2), 13–20.

Mild Traumatic Brain Injury Committee of the Head Injury Interdisciplinary Special Interest Group of the American Congress of Rehabilitation Medicine. (1993). Definition of mild traumatic brain injury. *Journal of Head Trauma Rehabilitation, 8*, 86–87.

Mittenberg, W., Patton, C., Canyock, E. M., & Condit, D. C. (2002). Base rates of malingering and symptom exaggeration. *Journal of Clinical and Experimental Neuropsychology, 24*, 1094–1102.

Mooney, G., & Speed, J. (2001). The association between mild traumatic brain injury and psychiatric conditions. *Brain Injury, 15*, 865–877.

Pankratz, L., & Binder, L. M. (1997). Malingering on intellectual and neuropsychological measures. In R. Rogers (Ed.), *Clinical assessment of malingering and deception* (2nd ed.) (pp. 223–236). New York: Guilford Press.

Prigatano, G. P. (1999). *Principles of neuropsychological rehabilitation*. Oxford: Oxford University Press.

Prigatano, G. P., & Amin, K. (1993). Digit Memory Test: Unequivocal cerebral dysfunction and suspected malingering. *Journal of Clinical and Experimental Neuropsychology, 15*, 537–546.

Prigatano, G. P., Smason, I., Lamb, D. G., & Bortz, J. J. (1997). Suspected malingering and the Digit Memory Test: A replication and extension. *Archives of Clinical Neuropsychology, 12*, 609–619.

Puente, A. E., & Gillespie, J. B. Jr. (1991). Worker's compensation and clinical neuropsychological assessment. In D. Dywan, R. D. Kaplan, & Pirozzolo, F. J. (Eds.), *Neuropsychology and the law* (pp. 39–63). New York: Springer-Verlag.

Rees, L. M., Tombaugh, T. N., Gansler, D. A., & Moczynski, N. P. (1998). Five validation experiments of the Test of Memory Malingering (TOMM). *Psychological Assessment, 10*, 10–20.

Rey, A. (1964). *L'examen clinique en psychologie*. Paris: Presses Universitaires de France.

Rogers, R. (Ed.). (1997). *Clinical assessment of malingering and deception* (2nd ed.). New York: Guilford Press.

Rogers, R., & Vitacco, M. J. (2002). Forensic assessment of malingering and related response styles. In B. Van Dorsten (Ed.), *Forensic psychology: From classroom to courtroom* (pp. 83–104). New York: Kluwer Academic.

Smith, D. H., Meaney, D. F., Lenkinski, R. E., Alsop, D. C., Grossman, R., Kimura, H., et al. (1995). New magnetic resonance imaging techniques for the evaluation of traumatic brain injury. *Journal of Neurotrauma, 12*, 573–577.

Sohlberg, M. M., & Mateer, C. A. (2001). *Cognitive rehabilitation: An integrative neuropsychological approach*. New York: Guilford Press.

Spreen, O., & Strauss, E. (1998). *A compendium of neuropsychological tests* (2nd ed.). New York: Oxford University Press.

Tombaugh, T. N. (1996). *Test of Memory Malingering*. New York: Multi-Health Systems.

Tombaugh, T. N. (1997). The Test of Memory Malingering (TOMM): Normative data from cognitively intact and cognitively impaired individuals. *Psychological Assessment, 9*, 260–268.

Trueblood, W., & Binder, L. M. (1997). Psychologists' accuracy in identifying neuropsychological test protocols of clinical malingerers. *Archives of Clinical Neuropsychology, 12*, 13–27.

Wetter, M. W., & Corrigan, S. K. (1995). Providing information to clients about psychological tests: A survey of attorneys' and law students' attitudes. *Professional Psychology: Research and Practice, 26*, 474–477.

Youngjohn, J. R., Lees-Haley, P. R., & Binder, L. M. (1999). Comment: Warning malingerers produces more sophisticated malingering. *Archives of Clinical Neuropsychology, 14*, 511–515.

CHAPTER 15

THE FORENSIC ASSESSMENT OF SUBSTANCE ABUSE

ELIZABETH V. GIFFORD
VETERANS AFFAIRS AND STANFORD UNIVERSITY MEDICAL CENTERS

BARBARA S. KOHLENBERG AND MELISSA M. PIASECKI
UNIVERSITY OF NEVADA, RENO

EMILY J. WEBBER
UNIVERSITY OF CINCINNATI

Forensic assessments of substance abuse have tremendous potential impact. Conclusions from forensic assessments contribute to decisions regarding guilt or innocence, affect sentencing, and/or influence the kind of treatment or rehabilitation offered to individual offenders. Given the responsibility attached to this level of influence, psychiatrists, psychologists, lawyers, and other professionals must attend to the quality of the data used to inform their recommendations.

Historically, the roots of psychological assessment lie in examining individual differences via psychological testing. However, *assessment* is a broad term reflecting the fact that there are many methods for evaluating individuals. Psychometric testing is one way, but behavioral observation, biochemical confirmation, and various interviewing strategies are also legitimate and necessary means of evaluating individual problems (Goldstein & Hersen, 1990). These alternatives to traditional testing are particularly important in forensic evaluations of substance abuse.

A chapter on the forensic assessment of substance abuse is necessarily broad in scope. This chapter is a brief overview of a large and complex area, one that may serve to orient interested readers and direct them to further sources. In the sections that follow, we first review the interaction between criminal behavior and substance use. We then discuss legal guidelines and precedents in the courts. We provide an overview of assessment tests, tools, and techniques that can be applied to evaluate substance use. Last, we briefly discuss the literature on the treatment of individuals with a substance use disorder.

Substance Use and Criminal Behavior

The interaction between substance use and criminal activity is substantial. As Marlowe, Lambert, and Thompson (1999) observe, "the shared variance between substance abuse and crime is so high that, from a purely statistical standpoint, there may even be little justification for treating them as wholly distinct phenomena." Historically, the substance abusing offender's behavior was considered a subset of sociopathy. As recently as 1952, when the first iteration of current diagnostic categories appeared, the *Diagnostic and Statistics Manual, First Edition* (*DSM-I*, American Psychiatric Association, 1952), alcoholism and drug dependence were identified as subsets of sociopathic personality disturbance. All those diagnosed in this manner were considered a threat to society (Nathan, 1991).

Today it is widely acknowledged that the relationship between substance use and criminal behavior is far more complex than the *DSM-I* suggested (as might be predicted from the risks involved in inferring causal relationships between correlated variables). However, there is unequivocal support for the strong association between substance use and criminal behavior (e.g. Anglin, 1992; Kermani & Castaneda, 1996). For example, perpetrators of violent crimes are intoxicated more often than perpetrators of nonviolent crimes (Murdoch, Piho, & Ross, 1990).

From a legal perspective, there are two general issues in the relationship between criminal behavior and substance use: (1) the possession, sale, and use of illegal drugs as criminal behavior; and (2) antisocial behavior resulting from the effect of drugs. This chapter is concerned with the second issue. Criminal behavior related to substance use varies significantly between drugs of abuse. Some specific substances are discussed here, reviewed in order of their association with crimes of violence.

Marijuana

The majority of arrests for the offense of drug abuse violations are for possession of marijuana (FBI, 1997). Marijuana is the most commonly used illicit drug in the United States, with reports of up to 68.5 million Americans trying marijuana at least once in their lifetime (SAMSHA, 1998). Approximately 10 million Americans use marijuana in an average month (Office of Applied Studies, 1995). However, the National Commission on Marijuana and Drug Abuse reviewed the literature and concluded, "there is no systematic empirical evidence ... to support the thesis that the use of marijuana either inevitably or generally causes, leads to or precipitates criminal, violent aggressive or delinquent behavior of sexual or nonsexual nature" (1972, p. 470). According to Grinspoon and Bakalar, "only the most unsophisticated continue to believe that cannabis leads to violence and crime. Indeed, instead of inciting criminal behavior, cannabis may tend to suppress it" (1997, pp. 201–212). Marijuana use predicts the use of more serious drugs only if it begins early. This is also true of alcohol: The age of first use of drugs predicts later drug involvement (Robins, 1984).

Heroin

The most heavily used illegal narcotic in America is heroin. Recently two factors have caused an increase in heroin use: the greater availability of extremely pure heroin, which can be smoked, and an increase in the use of heroin by individuals of middle- and upper-class socioeconomic status (Meyer, 1992). Heroin is strongly associated with money-producing crime. More than 95 percent of opiate-dependent persons, during an 11-year at-risk interval, reported committing crimes (Lamb, Greenlick, & McCarty, 1998). For example, Inciardi (1986) found that 573 narcotics users were responsible for approximately 6,000 robberies, 25,000 instances of shoplifting, 6,700 burglaries, and 46,000 other crimes of larceny and fraud. However, research indicates that heroin addicts do not, as a general rule, participate in crimes of violence such as rape, homicide, or assault (National Institute on Drug Abuse, 1978).

Cocaine

The most common form of cocaine use in the United States is smoking or "freebasing" crack cocaine (so called because it makes a crackling sound when smoked; Abadinsky, 1993). Most crack users appear to be polysubstance abusers and have an extensive history of prior drug use, drug selling, and nondrug income-generating criminality (Golub & Johnson, 1997). The Panel on the Understanding and Control of Violent Behavior evaluated the literature and found "there is no evidence to support the claim that snorting or injecting cocaine stimulates violent behavior. However, research is urgently needed on the behavioral effects of smoking cocaine in crack form, which affects the brain more directly" (Roth, 1996, p. 6). Although a stimulant, cocaine is far less commonly associated with toxic psychosis than amphetamines (see the following section).

Amphetamines

The effects of amphetamines on aggressive behavior are complex and poorly understood (see King & Ellinwood, 1997, for a review). It is clear, however, that amphetamines used in chronically large doses can produce or precipitate *toxic psychosis*. This psychotic condition is characterized by paranoid ideation accompanied by ideas of reference and "an extremely well-formed delusional structure" (King & Ellinwood, 1997). It is possible that these delusions, "when coupled with the loss of insight, the exhaustion produced by a binge, or the co-administration of sedatives, and the hyperreactivity to stimuli can produce a confused, panicky, fugue-like state that can result in sudden acts of violence" (King & Ellinwood, 1997, p. 215). Generally, these symptoms dissipate as the drug is metabolized and excreted, although the individual is susceptible for future episodes with ongoing amphetamine use.

Phencyclidine

A pharmaceutical company first developed phencyclidine, or PCP, as a general anesthetic. However, it was removed from the market after studies indicated that up to half of patients developed severe reactions, including agitation and hallucinations (Zukin, Sloboda, & Javitt, 1997). PCP is associated with "behavioral disinhibition, which can be coupled with severe anxiety, panic, rage, and aggression . . . the disruption of sensory input by PCP causes unpredictable, exaggerated, distorted, or violent reactions to environmental stimuli" (Zukin, Sloboda, & Javitt, 1997, p. 243). In two studies, PCP was prevalent among arrestee populations (Wish, 1986). However, the majority of the arrests were related to income-generating crimes rather than violent offenses. Many PCP users are polysubstance abusers who engage in a variety of antisocial behavior prior to their PCP usage.

Alcohol

Although the physiological effects of amphetamines and PCP appear to contribute to aggressive behavior under certain conditions, alcohol is the only drug that is strongly and consistently associated with violent criminal activity. According to the National Institute on Alcohol Abuse and Alcoholism (NIAAA), "in both animal and human studies, alcohol more than any other drug, has been linked with a high incidence of violence and aggression" (1990, p. 92). If one includes deaths as a result of driving under the influence, alcohol is responsible for more deaths and violence than all other drugs combined. Approximately 25,000 individuals are killed each year in traffic accidents in which a driver was under the influence of alcohol.

More direct indices of violent crime are also highly associated with alcohol. According to Pernanen (1986), 50 percent of the violent crimes in North America involve alcohol. Large epidemiological studies conducted in Finland set the numbers between 60 and 70 percent. Byles (1978), interviewing men and women in family court, found that violence was more than twice as likely to occur in families with alcohol problems. The causal pathways for the relationship between alcohol and violence are widely debated. However, most researchers agree that disinhibition, physiological effects, and social cognitive determinants of behavior all play a role (see Collins, 1986).

Substance Use among Arrestees

Although the nature of the relationship between crime and substance use is complex, it is clear that substance use is epidemic among those arrested for criminal activity. When researchers systematically screen arrestees, a very high number test positive for the use of drugs. In a 1998 multisite study of adults, 60 percent of individuals tested positive for drugs at the time of intake into the criminal justice system (National Institute of Justice, 1998b). The Arrestees Drug Abuse Monitoring program (ADAM) routinely tested adult and juvenile offenders in 35 cities. This program reported two thirds of adults testing positive for at least one drug, with marijuana the most common drug in adult men in most cities. More than one half of the juvenile arrestees tested positive for one or more drugs (National Institute of Justice, 1998b). Thirty-three percent of adults incarcerated in state facilities and 22 percent in federal facilities state they were under the influence of a drug at the time of their offense (Bureau of Justice Statistics, 1999). Lightfoot and Hodgins (1988), using interview surveys and screening instruments, report that 47 percent of the offenders interviewed reported alcohol abuse or dependence, and that 63.5 percent reported substance abuse or dependence. Yarvis (1994) focused on those found guilty of murder (both with and without co-morbid psychiatric diagnoses), and found that over half were using a substance at the time of the crime. Not surprisingly, many of the people arrested for drug or alcohol related crimes not only were using at the time of arrest but also met criteria for substance use disorder. In its 1994 public policy statement relating to substance use and the criminal justice system, the American Society of Addiction Medicine (ASAM) noted that in the state of Nevada 75 percent of inmates who have drug related crimes are alcohol or drug dependent (ASAM, 1994).

Prior drug use by offenders is reported by a 1995 national survey of probationers. Almost 70 percent of adults on probation reported past drug use, and 32 percent stated they were using within a month of their offense (Bureau of Justice Statistics, 1998). Of those in treatment for substance use problems, a growing percentage has criminal justice ties. In 1982 a NIDA report found that 27 percent of the men in substance use treatment were on probation, parole, or mandatory release (National Institute on Drug Abuse, 1982).

In spite of the overwhelming confirmation of substance use among arrestees, it is important to note that substance use disorders can be overdiagnosed in offenders. For example, overestimation of substance use disorders is found among those who receive DUI arrests but have no other alcohol-related problems. This population appears to be a different group than those who have both DUI arrests and other alcohol-related problems, though both groups may be described as alcohol abusers (Hasin, Paykin, Endicott, & Grant, 1999).

LEGAL ISSUES AND SUBSTANCE ABUSE

Alcohol and other drugs have been addressed in innumerable cases in both civil and criminal law. Two landmark cases underlie current legal thinking on criminal responsibility and alcoholism and drug addiction. In the first, California police officers examined a suspect's arms, found needle tracks and scar tissue, acquired a confession that the suspect had previously used heroin, and charged the suspect with being an addict. In *Robinson v. California* (1962), the Supreme Court ruled this California statute unconstitutional. The judge noted that "a state law which imprisons a person thus afflicted as a criminal, even though he has never touched any narcotic drug within the State or been guilty of any irregular behavior there, inflicts a cruel and unusual punishment in violation of the Fourteenth Amendment" (p. 667).

The second case found that while status as an addict is not punishable, the behavior of an addict is not exempt from punishment. In *Powell v. Texas,* Powell had been found guilty of public intoxication and fined twenty dollars. In spite of Powell's attorney's arguments following *Robinson v. California*, Justice Thurgood Marshall of the Supreme Court stated that the case did not come under the *Robinson* ruling, because Powell was not convicted for his status as an alcoholic but rather for his behavior of being intoxicated in public on a particular occasion (see Meyer, 1992). The court thus established the precedent that although addicts could not be convicted of crimes based on the presence of addiction, they were nonetheless responsible for any criminal behavior occurring under the use of chemical intoxicants.

Criminal Responsibility

Simply stated, the use of alcohol or drugs does not excuse a person from civil or criminal liability (Meyer, 1992). Voluntary intoxication at the time of a crime does not decrease criminal responsibility for an offense occurring during the intoxication. However, jurisdictions vary regarding the admissibility and application of evidence related to intoxication. Approximately one-quarter of U.S. jurisdictions bar any evidence whatsoever of voluntary intoxication, and most jurisdictions limit the extent that a defendant can use intoxication in his or her defense.

However, definitions of criminal behavior require the voluntary commission of a bad act or harmful omission (*actus reus*), in combination with a bad intent or state of mind (*mens rea*). Although intoxication cannot be a defense for recklessness, it can be applied to crimes of "general intent" and/or crimes of "specific intent" in certain jurisdictions (general and specific intent involve, respectively, any deliberate offense, or specific deliberation preceding an offense; Marlowe et al., 1999). The presentation of evidence of intoxication and other mental conditions to assert a defendant's lack of intent or *mens rea* is permitted by the common law doctrine. However, forensic experts stress that the establishment of lack of intent is often quite difficult to accomplish in practice (see LaFave & Scott, 1986, for a review).

The insanity defense does not in general apply for crimes occurring in an intoxicated state, as courts do not consider the cognitive impairment resulting from voluntary intoxication to be "a mental disease or defect" (Kermani & Castaneda, 1996). However, in some jurisdictions a defendant can claim "settled insanity" resulting from substance use. Settled insanity is an identified psychiatric syndrome (such as dementia) that results from chronic substance use. To qualify, the symptoms must predate and continue beyond the offense (Marlowe et al., 1999). For example, in *People v. Kelly* an 18-year-old girl had been using drugs excessively for several years. The police found her wandering around an airport under the use of drugs and turned her over to the custody of her parents. The girl then stabbed her mother with a number of kitchen knives. The California Supreme Court found that the defendant's continued ingestion of drugs for two months prior had triggered a legitimate psychosis, which was still ongoing at the time of appeal. In a contrasting case, a young man under the influence of LSD killed a stranger during an argument at a party. The defendant was reportedly naïve about the effects of these drugs and claimed total amnesia about the shooting. He entered an insanity plea based on his drug-induced condition but was found sane. Legal experts attribute the jury's decision to the fact that the defendant was no longer psychotic at the time of the trial (see Brooks, 1974).

A final legal distinction in the consideration of substance use is "involuntary intoxication," when an individual becomes intoxicated not of his or her own will but as a result of force or trickery. This term can also apply to individuals who have an unexpected reaction to prescription medications. Involuntary intoxication is rarely a successful defense because defendants are usually unable to prove a lack of voluntary behavior (Watterson, 1991; Marlowe et al., 1999). However, when it can be shown that a person was "tricked" into using a substance, the person responsible for the "trick" may be held legally responsible for the act (Meyer, 1992).

Court Intervention

In cases where substance abuse is present, the court may order various conditions, including substance abuse or mental health treatment, depending upon the individual case (Brennan, 1992). Court intervention is a critical interface between mental health and criminal justice systems. Folk wisdom to the contrary, research has shown that court interventions can produce positive outcomes for the criminal justice client in substance abuse treatment (Hubbard, Collins, Rachal, & Cavanaugh, 1998). Those clients under legal coercion tend to stay in treatment for a longer period of time and have outcomes equal to or better than those not under similar legal pressure (Stitzer & McCaul, 1987; National Institute on Drug Abuse, 1999). For example, Mark (1988) found that minority group members who were mandated to treatment were significantly more likely to complete the treatment than those who were not. Court intervention may also facilitate entry of offenders into treatment systems earlier than would otherwise occur. According to Brennan (1992), many defendants who come before the court do in fact need treatment services, but are not motivated to seek out treatment on their own. Indeed, caseworkers generally describe defendants as compliant with court orders.

There are many possible points of intervention within the criminal justice process, although these vary between states. According to the Center for Substance Abuse Treatment (CSAT), assessment and treatment may occur upon arrest, in jail, or on release from jail at a pretrial hearing, at a presentencing hearing (where in certain states offenders may be placed in a diversion program; see later), at trial or sentencing as part of a probation agreement, in prison or corrections, and/or during parole (USDHHS, 1999a).

A recent development for nonviolent drug offenders is the establishment of drug diversion courts. The focus of these courts is to keep nonviolent drug offenders out of overcrowded prisons and in treatment programs where the court monitors participation in treatment. According to Brown (1997), drug diversion courts have three primary characteristics:

> First, they treat offenders with illicit drug abuse problems differently from traditional courts by focusing on treatment rather than punishment. Second, clients who successfully complete a drug court treatment program will likely have their current charges dismissed or mitigated in some other way. Finally, the courts use "*judicial* authority (rather than a probation officer's) to directly supervise and support the . . . [client's] performance in treatment and rehabilitation programs." (p.93)

Factors Affecting Pleas and Sentences

Where treatment systems are integrated with the criminal justice system, as in the case of diversion programs, then prosecutors can plea bargain. For example, prosecutors can avoid charging arrestees who agree to comply with treatment (a type of plea bargain known as *charge bargain*). Prosecutors can also charge and then make treatment a condition of probation. There may also be intermediary sanctions lying between imprisonment and probation that incorporate more intensive supervision, such as drug testing and treatment in the community (West Publishing Co., 1989). Again, the available alternatives vary between states.

There is minimal research on the factors affecting offender pleas. In the lower courts, pleas of not guilty are rare but are more likely to result from more serious cases (Brickey & Miller, 1975). Albonetti (1990) reports that in felony courts, recidivists and those facing longer terms are less likely to plead guilty. More research has been done on factors affecting sentencing. Offense severity and prior arrests are known to increase sentence harshness for felons (e.g. Myers, 1987; Spohn, 1990). Some researchers have found that misdemeanor sentences appear related to offense severity (e.g. Lange & Greene, 1990; Meeker, Jesilow, & Aranda, 1992). However, for misdemeanants both offense and sentence severity tend to be low.

Many states require judges to follow legislatively prescribed sentencing guidelines. Under the current Revised Federal Sentencing Guidelines, a federal judge may not reduce sentencing (exercise a "downward departure from the legislated guidelines") on the basis of voluntary intoxication (Burglass, 1997, p. 817). However, in some federal jurisdictions addiction has been accepted as evidence of diminished capacity and therefore may be used as a basis for reduced sentences.

Driving under the Influence

There have been more arrests for drunk driving than for any other offense, including larceny (Maguire & Pastore, 1994), and drunk driving has been called "the crime most frequently committed by a noncriminal" (Joye, 1986). The state of Illinois' Department of Alcohol and Substance Abuse is an example of the efforts to improve integration of assessment and treatment in the courts. In Illinois, the DUI defendant is assessed by a licensed agency "to determine if an alcohol or other drug abuse problem exists and the extent of such a problem" (Brennan, 1992). The assessments are then made available to the court at the time the disposition is entered. The department monitors both assessment and education/treatment programs that provide service to DUI offenders.

Biochemical assessment obviously plays a primary role in the processing of DUI offenders. For example, Scoles, Fine, and Steer (1986) report that of 132 offenders with a positive blood alcohol level (BAL) at the time of evaluation, 75 (56.8%) were diagnosed with an alcoholism disorder by a licensed psychiatrist experienced in treating alcoholics. One study found a significant relationship between the presence of a positive BAL at the time of the presentencing evaluation and the receipt of an alcoholism disorder diagnosis as well as higher BALs at the time of the arrest. Even though the majority of offenders had wisely not shown up intoxicated for their interviews, the practice of using breath analyzer tests on the day of pretrial evaluation identified a number of offenders whose drinking behaviors needed to be evaluated more intensively.

In order to decrease DUI recidivism, it is becoming increasingly clear to the courts that the DUI offender needs either treatment or education, or both, as well as casework intervention. With this realization comes the demand for more productive assessment and treatment programs for the DUI offender.

ASSESSMENT

Assessment plays a significant role in the criminal justice system. Forensic data and expert testimony are often sought on questions regarding whether the accused was using substances at the time of the crime, whether the accused can be said to be substance dependent, and whether the substance use is likely to be treatable. Arguments may be made that substance use and/or dependence should or should not be a mitigating factor when guilt is considered. Further, once guilt is determined arguments may be made that an individual is likely or unlikely to benefit from treatment or rehabilitation. As is evident from these questions, in legal settings the assessment of substance use frequently results in immediate, significant, decision making. The general goals of substance use assessment in forensic settings can be described as assessment for the purpose of general screening (the presence or absence of substance use), more involved assessments that allow for diagnosis and/or an estimate of the severity of any diagnosed problem, instruments that lead to ideas for treatment and relapse prevention, and more comprehensive batteries that consider functioning across life domains (cf. USDHHS, 1999a). In forensic settings, assessments also provide information relevant to maintaining the safety of the community. Behavioral observation, laboratory tests, collateral informants, neurological examinations, and self-report measures (including interviews) are the most common assessment categories (Nathan, 1991).

Behavioral Observation and Collateral Informants

When a person is acting clearly under the influence, it is likely that further biochemical assessment will corroborate substance use. There is, however, a danger of false negatives in behavioral observation, as the very tolerance that defines substance dependence can also mask behavioral signs of use. In addition, Langenbucher and Nathan (1983) caution that it is actually quite difficult to detect intoxication in people we do not know well, despite the widespread belief that it is easy to do so.

Under these conditions, collecting observations from collateral informants, or individuals who know the offender, can be useful. In Best Estimate procedures, collateral reports from family members and medical reports have been shown to increase diagnostic sensitivity (Kosten, Anton & Rounsaville, 1992). In addition, if a significant person in an offender's life reports a pattern of substance use, their report can serve as an initial screen prompting more thorough assessments.

Laboratory Assessments

Laboratory tests can detect substances in blood, saliva, sweat, hair, and urine. These tests can be useful for screening and confirming drug and alcohol use and can corroborate self-report and behavioral observation.

Toxicology labs use a variety of methods to test samples of body fluids or hair. Thin layer chromatography and enzyme-multiplied immunoassay technique are widely used as "first screens" because they are relatively inexpensive. However, these techniques are also less sensitive and more likely to result in false negatives (where substance was present but not detected) and false positives (where a substance was reported but was not present). Gas chromatography–mass spectrometry is a highly reliable method. Because it is more expensive, it is commonly used to verify positive results and therefore limit the number of false positives (Rosse, Giese, Deutsch, & Morihisa, 1989; Vereby & Buchan, 1997). Over the last 20 years, analytical instrumentation has improved to the point of detecting picogram quantities of drugs in urine, saliva, and sweat using mass spectrometry (Kidwell, Holland, & Athanaselis, 1998).

There are a number of decision points in selecting among laboratory assessments. Screens for illicit drugs can be ordered as "panels" that automatically screen for a number of drugs relevant to the area (typically THC, cocaine, methamphetamine, benzodiazepines, opioids, and barbiturates.) Drug screens can also be ordered for a single substance, which is usually less costly than a panel screen.

In testing for use of illicit substances, one may focus on recent use or on use over longer periods of time. In general, testing in a forensic context is most concerned with recent use and with the ability to reserve part of the specimen for retesting, and therefore focuses on the analysis of blood or urine.

Blood alcohol levels are always quantitative, because it is both legally and clinically relevant to know an individual's current blood alcohol content (or BAC; see DUI section, earlier). Usually, the BAC is reported in milligrams of alcohol per deciliter of blood (mg/dl). Each alcoholic beverage (ounce of whiskey, 12 ounces of beer, glass of wine) will raise blood alcohol 15–25 mg/dl, reaching peak levels 30 minutes to three hours after the drink. Women sometimes have higher blood levels because of relatively increased absorption. Blood alcohol levels will have varied effects because of individual differences in tolerance to alcohol's effects. A BAC of 150 mg/dl in a person who does not appear to be grossly intoxicated suggests a high tolerance for alcohol from chronic heavy use. Above 300 mg/dl, some nontolerant individuals will fall into an alcohol coma whereas others may appear only somewhat intoxicated (Wallach, 1986).

Breath and saliva tests for alcohol use are faster and easier than BACs but do not preserve a sample that can be retested later. Breath analyzers, which may at times underestimate the BAC, require the cooperation of the subject to give a good effort as they blow through a mouthpiece. Recent alcohol or tobacco use can decrease the validity of the reading (Sobell, Toneatto, & Sobell, 1994). Saliva tests require subjects to place a strip of plastic in their mouths for 10 seconds in order to saturate a small reagent pad. After two minutes, color changes indicate alcohol levels in ranges from 0.02 to 0.30 percent (e.g., Alco-screen saliva test, Alcopro drug, and alcohol screening products).

Drug screens are usually reported qualitatively—the drug is either detected or not. In some circumstances, such as clinical research, quantitative analyses are available (Tennant, 1990). Although drug screening is most often intended to detect very recent use, some screens are able to detect metabolites of drugs after the original compound has been cleared from the system. The timeline for parent compound and metabolite clearance varies with individuals' use patterns (chronic use of a drug such as marijuana can lead to detectable levels of metabolites in the urine for 30 days after the last use), the specific metabolites assessed for by the test, and sensitivity of methods used by a particular laboratory. Laboratories provide guidelines that indicate the timeline for detecting different substances for their lab.

Saliva testing is available for alcohol, marijuana, cocaine, PCP, and other substances. Tests of saliva, like blood tests, reflect circulating levels and current intoxication. This is in contrast to urine tests, which cannot distinguish between current and very recent use (Sobell et al., 1994). A major disadvantage of saliva tests in forensic work is the lack of ability to preserve a specimen for independent retest (Kidwell et al., 1998). Sweat is used in testing less often than saliva, partly because it is more difficult to obtain a sample. Samples can be obtained by occlusive wrapping or gloves or by an absorbent patch. The use of "wipes," which collect a sample from a single wipe of the skin, is an emerging technology that may prove useful if it becomes possible to distinguish between drug exposure and drug use (Kidwell et al., 1998).

Chain of custody procedures in forensic samples is critical. All samples must be well marked and logged in and out as they are transferred from the site of collection to the site of analysis. Also important is appropriate monitoring of urine screens, which includes direct observation of the collection of the sample and checking temperature and specific gravity to avoid false positives. Blood samples are more labor intensive and costly than urine but have a much lower chance of tampering at the time of collection.

Recently, onsite urine testing has become reliable and inexpensive. Small kits that test for a panel or a single substance are available and provide qualitative information in a few minutes after the sample is obtained (e.g., EZ Screen kits by Alcopro drug and alcohol screening products). Kits should have a "control" component to indicate that the reagents are active and to confirm any positive findings. Similar to other convenient tests such as saliva and breath tests, onsite kits do not provide a reserve of the sample for later retesting, which is a disadvantage for use in forensic settings.

At times, long-term assessment of drug or alcohol use is relevant. Hair testing can target heroin, cocaine, amphetamines, barbiturates, and benzodiazepines and can give information about drug use in the previous months to years. More recent use is generally not detectable until the hair shaft grows beyond the surface of the skin, after one to two weeks (Spiehler, 2000).

Neuropsychological Testing

In legal settings, a thorough battery of neuropsychological tests by a neuropsychologist or other expert is often critical to establishing the presence of diminished capacity. For forensic purposes, testing should be extensive and highly specific, beyond the traditional batteries such as the Luria-Nebraska or the Halstead-Reitan (Kane, 1991). Thorough expert testing is particularly important for those clients with chronic histories of abuse, those with learning disabilities or similar conditions, and those who have histories of prior central nervous system insult such as head trauma. In addition, experts recommend that, "when working with a neuropsychologist, always ask that he or she assess temporal sequencing, as this is the higher cortical function that enables the discrimination of cause and effect" (Burglass, 1997, p. 814).

Self-Report

All other assessments for substance use, whether they consist of an unstructured interview, a structured interview, or paper and pencil/computerized questions, are considered self-reports. Under certain conditions, it has been widely concluded that substance abusers' self-reports are reasonably accurate (see Sobell, Toneatto, & Sobell, 1994). Reasonable accuracy is more likely if the client is interviewed in a clinical or research setting, is alcohol and drug free, and is given assurances of confidentiality (Sobell et al., 1994). For the arrestee, self-report is less reliable for obvious reasons. Some arrestees may be under the impression that use of or intoxication with a substance might decrease criminal responsibility and thus they may actually overreport drug or alcohol use. Conversely, an offender may fear incurring additional charges for illegal substance use and thus may deny or minimize use (Carroll, 1995).

The timing of assessments also plays a role in assessment in the criminal justice system. The delays between arrest, conviction, assignment to prison and/or treatment, and release can render certain assessments meaningless. For example, a urine drug screen taken days after an offense would yield little useful information about drug use at the time of the offense. Similarly, a more thorough self-report screen such as the Alcohol Severity Index may minimize the severity of the offender's problem if it is administered after being in a controlled environment with no opportunities for use. In assessing for relapse triggers, which is an important part of many treatment programs, the problem of retrospective accounts may be relevant if the offender is questioned a significant period of time after he or she has left his natural environment. Generally speaking, in-depth screening is probably most useful when done early in the offender's entry into the criminal justice system.

Self-Report Screening Instruments

A variety of screening instruments is available. We will survey some of them here.

Brief Screening Instruments

These instruments are used to quickly and easily identify the potential presence of a substance use problem. In general, the face validity of brief screening instruments is both their strength and weakness; that is, the questions are obvious, clear, and direct, so persons who choose to hide their substance use can easily do so. The brief screening instruments reviewed here are used only as initial screens. These instruments do not have utility for treatment planning, nor do they address the comprehensive manifestation of the disorder. Most do not have impressive psychometrics (i.e., reliability and validity), and are used primarily for pragmatic purposes. We will briefly review several of the most commonly used brief screening tools.

Alcohol Use Disorders Identification Test (AUDIT; Babor, de la Fuente, Saunders, & Grant, 1992). This 10-item scale, which takes about 2 minutes to administer, focuses on identifying problem drinkers with an emphasis on related health hazards. The items focus on consumption patterns, dependence symptoms, and the extent to which alcohol use has interfered with life activities. These categories were selected to match the definitions of alcohol dependence and alcohol use provided in the *International Classification of Diseases—10th edition* (ICD-10, World Health Organization, 1992). Although originally designed for general medical settings, Allen and Columbus (1995) suggest that the AUDIT is appropriate for prison populations, and the World Health Organization endorses this position (Babor, de la Fuente, Saunders, & Grant, 1992). This test is available in English, Japanese, Spanish, Norwegian, and Romanian and has good cross-cultural validity.

The CAGE (Mayfield, McCloud, & Hall, 1974). This four-question instrument ("*c*ut down," "*a*nnoyed," "*g*uilt," and "*e*ye-opener") is very brief to administer, generally taking less than one minute. Inciardi (1994) suggests that two yes answers will correctly identify 74 percent of the alcoholics and will accurately eliminate 96 percent of the nonalcoholics. Inciardi (1994) further suggests that this test is easy to modify for use with drugs as well. This test is strictly a screen, with the items giving no information about the context of use, and thus is not useful for treatment planning (see Allen, Eckardt, & Wallen, 1998, for a discussion of screening for alcoholism.

The Michigan Alcoholism Screening Test (MAST; Selzer, 1971). This test was developed as a 25-question screen and can be administered in less than 7 minutes. It functions similarly to the CAGE, in that it appears to discriminate alcoholics from nonalcoholics when there is no motivation to hide substance use. In psychiatric settings, the MAST has been shown to have relatively high (78%) agreement with psychiatrists' opinions (Moore, 1972), though sensitivity estimates are higher than specificity estimates, and validity estimates appear to be higher in samples with a greater proportion of women and in samples that exhibited higher base rates of alcohol-use disorder (Teitelbaum & Mullen, 2000). Internal consistency and test-retest reliability are good (see USDHHS, 1999a, for a review). A short version of the test is also available.

Intermediate Screening Instruments

Substance Abuse Subtle Screening Inventory (SASSI; Miller, 1985). This measure was developed in order to minimize some of the face validity issues that plague brief screening instruments. This instrument is used frequently in alcohol treatment agencies (Myerholtz & Rosenberg, 1997). Allen and Columbus (1995) argue that the SASSI effectively discriminates early stage substance abuse in those who may be in denial.

The SASSI-2 (Miller, 1994) consists of 62 true-false items. Myerholtz and Rosenberg (1997) studied the psychometric properties of this instrument using a population of DUI offenders and found that the instrument correlates moderately with the CAGE, the MacAndrew Scale, and the Michigan Alcoholism Screening Test. Myerholtz and Rosenberg (1997) found the instrument to be face valid; that is, if subjects were instructed to "fake good" or to "fake bad," they were able to do so. See Myerholtz and Rosenberg (1997) for a discussion of the psychometric properties of this instrument.

Comprehensive Substance Use Assessment Instruments

The following two assessments were developed and validated in research settings and as a result have considerable established reliability and validity. Both are interviews designed to capture a comprehensive picture of an individual's substance involvement history. The interviews are time consuming to administer and require training, but their psychometric properties and breadth of information are creditable.

Addiction Severity Index (ASI; McLellan, Luborskey, Woody, & Obrien, 1980). The ASI is a standardized structured interview widely used in substance use assessment. The ASI assesses both alcohol and drug use. It is also a broad assessment tool designed to assess life areas that can precipitate substance use and/or show the impact of substance use. This 40–60-minute inventory results in a separate score in each of the following areas: medical; employment/financial; drug/alcohol use; legal/criminal justice involvement; family/social; and psychological/psychiatric. Computer scoring is required, and the scores obtained reflect both current and previous functioning across the six life domains. While the information gathered using this instrument is often entered and scored on a computer, the authors of the fifth edition oppose computer based test administration, due to the importance of subjective clinical ratings (McLellan, Kushner, Metzger, & Peters, 1992). Test-retest reliability (average values between .83 and .89) is good, and interrater reliability is also good, with average concordance of .89. In addition, it has recently been shown that the ASI's internal consistency and validity hold up accurately in actual clinical settings (Leonhard et al., 2000). This instrument has also been used with incarcerated populations (Allen & Columbus, 1995; Breteler, Van Den Hurk, Schippers, & Meerkerk, 1996).

Time Line Follow Back (TLFB; Sobell et al., 1980). The Time Line Follow Back procedure developed by Mark and Linda Sobell and colleagues is an interview designed to aid accurate self-reports of drinking behavior over the previous twelve months. The interviewer follows a specified hierarchy of questions designed to facilitate recall. For example, the clinician uses a calendar to help the client identify "anchor points," which are distinctive events both common (such as holidays) and unique to the individual. The longest period of high levels of drug consumption during the previous year is noted. The second longest period can then similarly be defined. Other identifiable patterns that occurred over certain times are identified, such as not drinking or using drugs until the weekends (Sobell et al., 1980).

This method has been found to be quite reliable when compared with collateral reports (e.g., reports of total drinking days correlated .91 in one study; O'Farrell et al., 1984). Extending this method to drug-abusing patients has also resulted in self-reports that have high test-retest reliability, high convergent and discriminant validity with other measures, high agreement with collateral informant's reports of patients drug use, and high agreement with results from urine screens (Fals-Stewart, O'Farrel, Freitas, McFarlin & Rutigliano, 2000).

Traditional Comprehensive Screening Measures Also Used to Assess Substance Use

Many measures of substance use are based on the *Diagnostic and Statistical Manual of Mental Disorders* (*DSM-III-R*; *DSM-IV*, American Psychiatric Association, 1987; 1994), or the *International Classification of Diseases* (ICD-10, World Health Organization, 1992). A selection of these instruments, listed here, has certain characteristics in common: All are generally time consuming to administer, have been normed on psychiatric populations, and assess a broad spectrum of psychiatric and psychological problems as well as substance use. These instruments are time consuming (administration commonly takes over an hour) and require administration by a trained psychologist or psychiatrist. Thus, they may be more useful when substance use and other co-morbid conditions are being assessed together. However, it is argued that some have high reliability, particularly the Structured Clinical Interview for DSM-IV (SCID; First, Spitzer, Gibbon, & Williams, 1995), and that this reliability warrants more frequent use. In addition, some argue that their comprehensive nature increases their treatment utility (e.g., Gastfriend, Baker, Najavits, & Reif, 1998). These measures include the Psychiatric Research Interview for Substance and Mental Disorders (PRISM; Spitzer & Williams, 1987); the Structured Clinical Interview for DSM-IV (SCID; First, Spitzer, Gibbon, & Williams, 1995); the Diagnostic Interview Schedule (DIS; Robbins, Cottler, & Keating, 1989); the Minnesota Multiphasic Personality Inventory and the MacAndrew subscale (MMPI; MacAndrew, 1965); and the Millon Clinical Multiaxial Inventory (MCMI; Millon, 1983). There are precedents for using instruments such as the MCMI in forensic settings (see Breteler, Van Den Hurk, Schippers, & Meerkerk, 1996).

The Unstructured Substance Use Clinical Interview

The most commonly employed method of assessment used in alcohol treatment agencies to diagnose substance use disorders is the clinical interview (Myerholtz & Rosenberg, 1997). Unfortunately, the unreliability of unstructured clinical interviews may limit the accuracy and impartiality of assessments. The interviewing mental health professional uses the criteria for substance abuse, dependence, intoxication, and withdrawal in the *DSM-IV*. Clinicians may apply these criteria to data obtained from a detailed interview with an individual as well as a review of medical records, laboratory values, and, in some cases, interviews with others such as friends or family members. A physical examination may be part of the assessment as well.

The *DSM-IV* describes guidelines for diagnosis of substance use disorders in terms of clinical signs and symptoms (APA, 1994). The diagnosis of abuse of a substance is based on information that reveals "a maladaptive pattern of substance use manifested by recurrent and significant adverse consequences" (APA, 1994, p. 182). Negative consequences may involve neglect of obligations (at work or with family), substance-related legal problems, social or interpersonal problems, or using a substance in a potentially dangerous situation (such as driving under the influence).

Substance dependence is diagnosed when three or more of the following are found to be true for an individual: tolerance to a substance (using increased amounts for effect), a withdrawal syndrome (or use of another substance to avoid withdrawal symptoms), the quantity and duration of substance use that exceeds the individual's intent, inability to decrease use of the substance, or a great amount of time spent in the pursuit or use of the substance. In addition, the individual may have reduced important social or occupational activities because of substance use or continued to use a substance despite known health problems related to the substance (APA, 1994, p. 181). Dependence can be described as with or without physiologic dependence. For individuals who use substances compulsively but do not have evidence of tolerance or withdrawal, their substance use disorder can be described as without physiologic dependence (APA, 1994, p. 179).

Substance intoxication is usually diagnosed by characteristic signs and symptoms and a positive history of use or laboratory screen for the substance. Intoxication is by definition reversible and is associated with maladaptive behavioral and mental status changes. The *DSM-IV* details the substance-specific syndromes associated with intoxication according to the different substance classes (APA, 1994, pp. 183–264).

Substance withdrawal is a physiologic and psychological syndrome that occurs when an individual stops or decreases use of a substance. Withdrawal syndromes are similar to intoxication states in that they are substance specific and in some cases (especially withdrawal from sedative type drugs) can represent a medical emergency. The *DSM-IV* describes the signs and symptoms of substance withdrawal for each drug category (APA, 1994, pp. 184–266).

Structured Interviews

Structured interviews based on *DSM* criteria are also available. Such measures currently focus on assessing a broad spectrum of psychiatric and psychological disorders, as well as substance use. These measures include the Structured Clinical Interview for DSM-IV (SCID; First et al., 1995) and the Diagnostic Interview Schedule (DIS; Robins, Helzer, Croughan, & Ratcliff, 1981). As noted, in comparison with unstructured clinical interviews, the SCID is a more reliable assessment instrument, and is recommended on this basis. In addition, the comprehensive nature of the structured clinical interviews may provide important information for treatment matching and treatment planning.

Assessing Readiness to Change

Assessment strategies focused on readiness to change (RTC) attempt to measure how motivated a person is to change problematic behaviors. The construct of RTC is increasingly popular, primarily because of its predictive value in substance treatment outcomes. RTC in substance abuse citations (found in PsycLit and MEDLINE) have increased by 520 percent from 1986 to 1995 (Carey, Purnine, Maisto, & Carey, 1999). The RTC construct is based on the stages of change model proposed by Prochaska, Di Clemente, and Norcross (1992). Twelve measures are currently used to assess readiness to change substance abuse, although none have been normed on offenders. In addition, limited psychometric evidence is available for any of the existing measures. For a review of these measures, see Carey and colleagues (1999).

SUBSTANCE ABUSE TREATMENT

Substance abuse treatment programs historically provided both detoxification and/or rehabilitation. Although often necessary for medical and psychological stabilization, detoxification does not in itself constitute effective treatment. In fact, in both alcohol and heroin abuse, detoxification-only treatments are "associated with relapse rates so high that they have little bearing on the natural history of the disorder" (Vaillant, 1995).

As stated by McLellan and McKay (1998), the primary purposes of rehabilitative treatment for alcohol and drug addiction are:

1. To prevent return to active substance use that would require detoxification/stabilization.
2. To assist the patient in developing control over urges to use alcohol and/or drugs (usually through attaining and sustaining total abstinence from all drugs and alcohol).
3. To help the patient to attain (or attain for the first time) improved personal health and social function, as both a secondary part of the rehabilitation function and because these improvements in lifestyle are important for maintaining sustained control over substance use. (p. 328)

Several treatment factors are related to positive treatment outcomes. These include length of treatment (longer treatments are correlated with higher success rates), participation in a twelve-step community program (this is particularly well documented with alcohol abuse), and the relationship with the therapist or counselor who provides the treatment (e.g., counseling in general tends to improve outcomes, and certain counselors or treatment providers have much better client outcomes than others).

Twelve-Step Programs

Twelve-step programs are described as self-help or mutual-help programs, not as formal treatment (McCrady, 1998). Nonetheless, Alcoholics Anonymous is highly valued by the medical community, more so than some of the empirically supported treatments reviewed later (Roche, Parle, Stubbs, Hall, & Sanders, 1995). Indeed, twelve-step programs define "treatment" in many forensic settings. Perhaps for this reason there has been an increase in the use of AA among more severely alcohol dependent men who are experiencing more social consequences from their addiction, perhaps because of more mandatory referrals to treatment that stem often from the legal system (McCrady, 1998). Speiglman (1994) notes that in four counties in California the vast majority of offenders mandated to parole or to probation-defined treatment were required to attend AA, typically two to three meetings per week. Correlational data suggest that continued AA involvement predicts better abstinence rates than non-AA involvement, and research focused on understanding the change processes encompassed within AA programs is currently being conducted (see McCrady, 1998, for a review).

Empirically Supported Psychotherapies

The research literature paints a somewhat cautious view on substance abuse psychosocial treatment outcomes. At their best, treatment outcome rates remain fair, particularly when considered in light of retention problems. DeRubeis and Crits-Christoph (1998), using Chambless and Hollon's categories of efficacious and specific, efficacious, and possibly efficacious treatments (Chambless & Hollon, 1998), placed several treatments for substance dependence into the possibly efficacious category. According to their reading of the research literature, social skills training for alcohol dependence, cue exposure, and "urge coping skills" for alcohol dependence are possibly efficacious treatments. DeRubeis and Crits-Christoph (1998) also list supportive-expressive therapy for opiate dependence, relapse prevention for cocaine dependence, and behavior therapy (reinforcement) for opiate dependence as possibly efficacious.

The Community Reinforcement Approach (CRA) for treating alcohol problems, an approach that focuses on the role that environmental contingencies play in encouraging or discouraging drinking or drug-related behavior, has also proven to be efficacious and cost-effective alcohol treatment (Smith & Meyers, 2000). This categorization is based on a meta-analytic review of cost-effective alcohol treatments (Holder, Longabaugh, Miller, & Rubonis, 1991).

Project Match (Project MATCH Research Group, 1997), in a multisite, randomized controlled trial (with 1726 participants), compared twelve-step facilitation (a structured treatment facilitating participation in twelve-step groups and meaningful interaction with twelve-step principles), cognitive behavioral therapy, and motivational enhancement therapy as treatments for problem drinkers. None of the three therapies performed significantly better than the others at one year post treatment. All showed modest effects. Subsequent critiques have called into question the methodology of the study (Marlatt, 1999). Reanalysis of the MATCH data has suggested that the therapeutic alliance was the best predictor of treatment retention and good outcome (Connors, Carroll, DiClemente, Longabaugh, & Donovan, 1997).

Dimeff and Marlatt (1998) reviewed the empirical support for relapse prevention as a treatment strategy and concluded that relapse prevention does not "inoculate" against relapse. They argue, however, that harmful consequences of addictive behavior can be reduced based on treatment sensitive to the relapse prevention model.

Medications

Medications for substance abuse are the focus of a great deal of research by the National Institutes of Health. Currently, agonist medications such as methadone and levo-alpha-acetyl methadol (LAAM, a longer acting form of methadone) are the most empirically supported treatments for opiate addiction, when combined with counseling (Strain et al., 1993).

Antagonist and abuse blocking agents are also used in opiate dependence. The FDA has approved naltrexone, an orally administered opiate antagonist that binds competitively to opiate receptors, for use in opiate addiction treatment. Disulfiram (Antabuse®) is widely used in the treatment of alcoholism. Both of these antagonists effectively block the cognitive and behavioral effects of substances. They can produce immediate withdrawal symptoms in actively using patients, with potentially serious effects. Both treatments are generally used post detoxification, and in earlier phases of treatment, as part of a broader treatment program incorporating behavioral counseling.

Treatment and Rehabilitation within the Legal System

The legal system primarily attempts to influence outcomes by providing controlled environments and regulating treatment and substance use after release. The goal of these interventions is the reduction of recidivism.

Drug courts capitalize on the opportunity to provide treatment to substance users as they enter the criminal justice system. Features of drug courts include a specialized "team" of legal professionals who work to divert substance users from prison into treatment. Brumbaugh (1994) reports outcomes from the Miami Drug Court program, which in 1989 was a prototype for drug courts in other states. Of the 4,296 felony drug possession arrestees, most (90%) accepted the offer of a drug court program. Rearrest rates decreased dramatically (to 7% or less) for the year following participation. Out of the 4,296, 1,043 failed to comply with the program. The authors note that the individuals were first- or second-time offenders for cocaine possession and the success rates would be much less if multiple repeat offenders were studied.

An important factor in the success of a drug court is cooperation and education among the legal professionals. In the Miami court, a treatment program counselor sat at the judge's bench and was able to provide information about each defendant at the initial appearance and reappearances. The treatment program counselor was also able to work closely with the prosecutor, defense attorney, and probation officer for a "seamless" program (Brumbaugh, 1994).

Treatment can also occur during incarceration, with in-house programs offered to inmates. However, as Mahon (1997) notes, "drug treatment is the exception rather than the rule in prisons and jails" (p. 456). Many of the programs offered in prisons do not follow a comprehensive treatment model, lack standards for delivery of treatment programs, and fail to gather outcome data (Leukefeld & Tims, 1992). This is particularly unfortunate since there are existing models of prison-based effective programs with evidence supporting treatment outcomes. Two such models are prison-based therapeutic communities such as Stay'N Out, and jail-based methadone programs such as the Key Extended Entry Program (KEEP) (see Mahon, 1997, for a discussion). Studies of drug-free detention programs show that certain populations are most likely to benefit: those inmates who remain in treatment for 9–12 months, are in an older age group, and have a shorter criminal history sustain better long-term outcomes (Lipton, 1994).

ASSESSMENT FOR TREATMENT PLACEMENT AND PLANNING

Effective treatment placement and planning requires an individualized and multidimensional approach to both assessment and treatment. CSAT endorses a widely accepted biopsychosocial perspective (Donovan, 1988), incorporating medical, psychological, and social factors. Proponents argue that a model that describes the broadest possible approach to etiology encourages more accurate assessments of clinical severity.

The American Society of Addiction Medicine has published six dimensions along which to define biopsychosocial severity: (1) acute intoxication and/or withdrawal potential, (2) biomedical conditions and complications, (3) emotional/behavioral conditions and complications, (4) treatment acceptance/resistance, (5) relapse potential, and (6) recovery/living environment (see Mee-Lee, Shulman, & Gartner, 1996). Unfortunately, there is not widespread agreement on the best methods for assessing severity along these dimensions, nor for applying these assessments to treatment decisions.

Assessing Relevant Domains

As described by McLelland and McKay (1998), above, a primary goal of substance abuse treatment involves helping clients improve their personal health and social functioning. Such factors play a key role in treatment outcome and maintenance of treatment gains. For example, necessary psychosocial interventions may include marital or family therapy, social skills training, stress or anxiety management, psychotropic medication, treatment of co-morbid psychiatric disorders, and/or cognitive rehabilitation (Moreland, Fowler, & Honaker, 1994). Likewise, necessary primary health interventions may include screening and referral for infectious disease.

In certain populations so-called wraparound or survival services may be necessary, including drug-free housing, medical screening and referral, parenting classes, and employment counseling. Patients who are assigned to such "enhanced care" services show 20–40 percent improvement over patients assigned to standard outpatient programs (McLellan & McKay, 1998), perhaps because such services reduce barriers to treatment.

Currently, CSAT has launched an effort to encourage the development of Uniform Patient Placement Criteria (UPPC). It is hoped that this effort will result in guidelines that reduce unwarranted variability and encourage more accurate assessment and more effective placement decisions (USDHHS, 1999a). CSAT recommends that the following elements be included in a comprehensive substance abuse assessment: (1) a medical examination; (2) an alcohol and other drug use history; (3) a psychosocial evaluation; (4) a psychiatric evaluation (where warranted); (5) a review of socioeconomic factors; and (6) a review of eligibility for public health, welfare, employment, and educational assistance programs. Although a discussion of these areas exceeds the scope of this chapter, the concerned practitioner is advised to consider the broader context in selecting appropriate assessment and treatment strategies.

Stepped-Care Models of Treatment

Hayes, Nelson, and Jarrett (1987) argue that the value of assessment lies in its treatment utility. More recently, Moreland, Fowler, and Honaker (1994) argue that given the economic climate, Hayes and colleagues' (1987) assessment utility criteria should be applied to stepped-care models of treatment. Assessment in a stepped-care model is directed toward assigning substance users to the "least expensive appropriate level of care" (Moreland et al., 1994, p. 585). For example, those with low alcohol dependence and high social stability (e.g., married and employed) may not require a formal intervention or may only require outpatient group psychotherapy. Those with these characteristics in combination with depression may have better outcomes when assigned to outpatient individual psychotherapy. Finney and Moos (1998) also recommend that residential options be retained for "those with few social resources and/or a living environment that is a serious impediment to recovery" (p. 350). Inpatient treatment options would then be retained for those with serious medical/psychiatric conditions.

The American Society of Addiction Medicine (ASAM, 1996) has proposed a set of criteria for matching patients to four general levels of care: hospital, non-hospital inpatient, day treatment, and outpatient. However, these criteria have been described as more accurately a description of *intensity* of service provided

(USDHHS, 1999a). The Institute of Medicine (IOM; 1990) defines four levels of care designed to more accurately represent the full continuum of treatment options: inpatient, residential, intermediate, and outpatient. The American Psychiatric Association has published a guideline for the treatment of alcohol, cocaine, and opioids that describes the conditions under which these various levels are appropriate (APA, 2000).

It is important to note that numerous studies have demonstrated that inpatient care is no more efficacious than intensive outpatient treatment (McLellan & McKay, 1998). In fact, for individuals with less severe dependence, outcomes may be worse in more intensive treatment (see Miller & Hester, 1986). Stepped-care models should be designed to identify those who will benefit from more intensive, expensive, and intrusive treatments.

CONCLUSION

The assessment of substance use in forensic settings is a complex undertaking. In general, the goals of any assessment guide its course. In forensic assessments of substance use, the concern lies with generating accurate descriptions of an individual so that informed rehabilitative and legal decisions may occur. The selection of instruments will differ depending on the information to be gathered, and the information to be gathered will differ depending on the perceived role of the assessor. Additionally, in any given assessment the goals of the mental health and forensic fields may vary. For example, mental health treatment typically measures abstinence and change in other major life areas. Outcomes in the justice system are more specifically focused on recidivism related to ongoing criminal behavior. These two outcomes may be correlated and yet are not equivalent. In areas where domains intersect, such as the intersection between the legal and the mental health domains, the clarification of goals is a necessary prerequisite to the assessment process.

As the field stands there is sufficient science on assessment and treatment to base many decisions on the best empirical evidence. Indeed, professional ethics requires that assessment and treatment decisions be so informed. Nonetheless, there remain reasons for caution. If assessment is defined as evaluation linked to treatment aimed at behavior change, there are gaps in knowledge about all the features of this chain: the treatment utility of assessment, the integration of treatment into the criminal justice system, patient placement criteria for matching clients to efficacious treatments, and the role of treatment in reducing recidivism.

Progress in the area of assessment and treatment of substance use in the forensic setting is limited by several factors. First, substance use is a problem that cuts across many different populations, and studies addressing assessment and treatment that are specific to forensic populations are limited. It is also unclear whether findings based on nonoffending populations generalize to the forensic setting. Most important, there are no empirically supported theoretical models that clarify the complex relationship between substance use and criminal behavior, and thus research aimed at refining effective assessment and treatment linkages does not proceed in a parsimonious manner. Given the impact that the statements of mental health professionals can have on the lives of human beings in forensic settings, the field must continue to improve the strength and utility of the knowledge base that guides these conclusions.

ACKNOWLEDGMENT

Supported by NCI grant RO3CA84813, NIDA grant RO1DA13106, and by the Department of Veterans Affairs Health Research and Development Service and Mental Health Strategic Healthcare Group.

REFERENCES

Abadinsky, H. (1993). *Drug abuse* (2nd ed.). Chicago: Nelson-Hall.
Albonetti, C. A. (1989). Race and the probability of pleading guilty. *Journal of Quantitative Criminology, 6*, 315–334.
Allen, J. P., & Columbus, M. (Eds.). (1985). *Assessing alcohol problems: A guide for clinicians and researchers*. Bethesda, MD: NIAAA.
Allen, J. P., Eckardt, M. S., & Wallen, J. (1998). Screening for alcoholism: Techniques and issues, *Public Health Rep, 103*, 586–592.
Anglin, M. D. (1992). Alcohol and criminality. In E. M. Pattison & E. Kaufman (Eds.), *Encyclopedic handbook of alcoholism* (pp. 383–394). New York: Gardner Press.
American Psychiatric Association. (1952). *Diagnostic and statistical manual of mental disorders* (1st ed.). Washington, DC: Author.
American Psychiatric Association. (1987). *Diagnostic and statistical manual of mental disorders* (3rd ed., rev.). Washington, DC: Author.
American Psychiatric Association (1994). *Diagnostic and statistical manual of mental disorders* (4th ed., rev.). Washington, DC: Author.
American Psychiatric Association (2000, June 11). *Practice Guideline for the Treatment of Patients with Substance Use Disorders Alcohol, Cocaine, Opioids*. American Psychiatric Association Clinical Resources [Online]. Available: www.psych.org/clin_res/prac_guide.cfm.
ASAM Board of Directors. (1994). Public policy statement on persons with alcohol and other drug (AOD) problems in the criminal justice system. *Experimental Therapeutics in Addiction Medicine*, 234–236.
Babor, T. F., de la Fuente, J. R., Saunders, J., & Grant, M. (1992). *The Alcohol Use Disorders Identification Test: Guidelines for use in primary health care*. Geneva: World Health Organization.
Babor, T. F., Steinberg, K., Anton, R., & Del Boca, F. (2000). Talk is cheap: Measuring drinking outcomes in clinical trials. *Journal of Studies on Alcohol, 61*, 55–63.
Brennan, T. P. (1992). The ideal meets the real with the D.U.I. offender. *Federal Probation, 56*, 40–47.

Breteler, M. H. M., Van Den Hurk, A. A., Schippers, G. M., & Meerkerk, G. J. (1996). Enrollment in a drug-free detention program: The prediction of successful behavior changes of drug-using inmates. *Addictive Behaviors*, *21*, 665–669.

Brooks, A. D. (1974). *Law, psychiatry and the mental health system*. Boston: Little, Brown.

Brown, J. R. (1997). Drug diversion courts: Are they needed and will they succeed in breaking the cycle of drug-related crime? *New England Journal on Criminal and Civil Confinement*, *23*, 63–99.

Brumbaugh, A. G. (1994). *Why drug courts work* [Online]. Available: www.silcom.com/alexb/drugcrts.htm

Bureau of Justice Statistics. (1998). *Substance abuse and treatment of adults on probation, 1995*. Washington, DC: U.S. Department of Justice.

Bureau of Justice Statistics. (1999). *Substance abuse and treatment, state and federal prisoners, 1997*. Washington, DC: U.S. Department of Justice.

Burglass, M. E. (1997). Forensics, In J. H. Lowinson, P. Ruiz, R. B. Millman, & J. G. Langrod (Eds.), *Substance abuse: A comprehensive textbook* (3rd ed.) (pp. 812–822). Baltimore, MD: Williams & Wilkins.

Byles, J. A. (1978), Violence, alcohol problems and other problems in disintegrating families. *Journal of Studies on Alcohol*, *39*, 551–553.

Carey, K. B., Purnine, D. M., Maisto, S. A., & Carey, M. P. (1999). Accessing readiness to change substance abuse: A critical review of the instruments. *Clinical Psychology: Science and Practice*, *6*, 245–266.

Carroll, K. M. (1992). Methodological issues and problems in the assessment of substance use. *Psychological Assessment, 7,* 349–358.

Chambless, D. L., & Hollon, S. D. (1998). Defining empirically supported therapies. *Journal of Consulting and Clinical Psychology*, *61*, 248–260.

Collins, J. J. (1986). The relationship of problem drinking to individual offending sequences. In A. Blumstein, J. Cohen, J. A. Roth, & C. A. Visher (Eds.), *Criminal careers and "career criminals."* Vol. 2. Washington, DC: National Academy Press.

Connors, G. J., Carroll, K. M., DiClemente, C. C., Longabaugh, R., & Donovan, D. M. (1997). The therapeutic alliance and its relationship to alcoholism treatment participation and outcomes. *Journal of Consulting and Clinical Psychology*, *65* (4), 588–598.

Cronbach, L. J. (1960). *Essentials of psychological testing* (2nd ed.). New York: Harper & Brothers.

DeRubeis, R. J., & Crits-Christoph, P. (1998). Empirically supported individual and group psychological treatments for adult mental disorders. *Journal of Consulting and Clinical Psychology*, *66*, 37–52.

Dimeff, L. A., & Marlatt, G. A. (1998). Preventing relapse and maintaining change in addictive behaviors. *Clinical Psychology, Research and Practice*, 513–525.

Donovan, D. M. (1988). Assessment of addictive behaviors: Implications of an emerging biopsychosocial model. In D. M. Donovan & G. A. Marlatt (Eds.), *Assessment of addictive behavior*. New York: Guilford Press.

Fals-Stewart, W., O'Farrel, T. J., Freitas, T. T., McFarlin, S. K., & Rutigliano, P. (2000). The timeline followback reports of psychoactive substance use by drug-abusing patients: Psychometric properties. *Journal of Consulting and Clinical Psychology*, *68*, 134–144.

Federal Bureau of Investigation. (1997). *Uniform Crime Reports 1996*. Washington, DC: U.S. Government Printing Office.

Finney, J. W., & Moos, R. H. (1998). What works in treatment: Effect of setting, duration and amount. In A. W. Graham & T. K. Schultz (Eds.), *Principles of addiction medicine* (2nd ed.) (pp. 345–352). Chevy Chase, MD: American Society of Addiction Medicine.

First, M. G., Spitzer, R. L., Gibbon M., & Williams, J. B. W. (1995). *Structured clinical interview for DSM-IV—Patient version (SCID-I/P, version 2.0)*. New York: Biometrics Department, New York State Psychiatric Institute.

Fromme, K. (1999). Randomized clinical trials and alternatives to evaluating treatment efficacy. *The Behavior Therapist, 22*, 120–122.

Gastfriend, G. R., Baker, S., Najavits, L. M., & Reif, S. (1998). Assessment instruments. In A. W. Graham & T. K. Schultz (Eds.), *Principles of addiction medicine* (2nd ed.) (pp. 273–278). Chevy Chase, MD: American Society of Addiction Medicine.

Gatewood, R., & Perloff, R. (1990). Testing and industrial application. In G. Goldstein & M. Hersen (Eds.), *Handbook of psychological assessment* (2nd ed.) (pp. 486–501). New York: Pergamon Press.

Goldstein, P. (1985). The drug/violence nexus: A tripartite conceptual framework. *Journal of Drug Issues, 15*, 493–501.

Goldstein, G., & Hersen, M. (1990). Historical perspectives. In G. Goldstein & M. Hersen (Eds.), *Handbook of psychological assessment* (2nd ed.) (pp. 3–20). New York: Pergamon Press.

Golub, A. L., & Johnson, B. D. (1997, July). *Crack's decline: Some surprises across U.S. cities*. NIJ Research in Brief. Washington, DC: U.S. Department of Justice.

Grinspoon, L., & Bakalar, J. B. (1997). Marijuana. In J. H. Lowinson, P. Ruiz, R. B. Millman, & J. G. Langrod (Eds.), *Substance abuse: A comprehensive textbook* (3rd ed.) (pp. 199–206). Baltimore, MD: Williams & Wilkins.

Hammersley, R., Forsyth, A., Morrison, V., & Davies, J. B. (1989). The relationship between crime and opioid use. *British Journal of Addiction, 84*, 1029–1043.

Hasin, D., Paykin, A., Endicott, J., & Grant, B. (1999). The validity of DSM-IV alcohol abuse: Drunk drivers vs. all others. *Journal of Studies on Alcohol, 61*, 746–755.

Hayes, S. C., Nelson, R. O., & Jarrett, R. B. (1987). The treatment utility of assessment: A functional approach to evaluating assessment quality. *American Psychologist, 42*, 963–974.

Holder, H., Longabaugh, R., Miller, W., & Rubonis, A. (1991). The cost effectiveness of treatment for alcoholism: A first approximation. *Journal of Studies on Alcohol, 52*, 517–540.

Hubbard, R. L., Collins, J. J., Rachal, J. V., & Cavanaugh, E. R. (1998). The criminal justice client in drug abuse treatment. In C. G. Leukefeld & F. M. Tims (Eds.), *Compulsory treatment of drug abuse: Research and clinical practice* (NIDA Research Monograph 86). Washington, DC: U.S. Government Printing Office.

Inciardi, J. A. (1986). *The war on drugs: Heroin, cocaine, crime and public policy*. Palo Alto, CA: Mayfield.

Inciardi, J. A. (1994). *Screening and assessment for alcohol and other drug use among adults in the criminal justice system*. Rockville, MD: Center for Substance Abuse Treatment.

Institute of Medicine (1990). *Broadening the base of treatment for alcohol problems*. Washington, DC: National Academy Press.

Ito, T. A., Miller, N., & Pollock, V. E. (1996). Alcohol and aggression: A meta-analysis on the moderating effects of inhibitory cues, triggering events, and self-focused attention. *Psychological Bulletin, 120*, 60–82.

Kane, R. L. (1991). Standardized and flexible batteries in neuropsychology: An assessment update. *Neuropsychological Review*, *2*, 281–339.

Kermani, E. J., & Castaneda, R. (1996). Psychoactive substance use in forensic psychiatry. *American Journal of Drug and Alcohol Abuse*, *22* (1), 1–27.

Kessler, R. C., Sonnega, A., Bromet, E., Hughes, M., & Nelson, C. B. (1995). Post-traumatic stress disorder in the National Comorbidity Survey. *Archives of General Psychiatry*, *52*, 1048–1060.

Kidwell, D. A., Holland, J. C., & Athanaselis, S. (1998). Testing for drugs of abuse in saliva and sweat. *Journal of Chromatography B*, *7* (13), 111–135.

King, G. R., & Ellinwood, E. H. Jr. (1997). Amphetamines and other stimulants. In J. H. Lowinson, P. Ruiz, R. B. Millman, & J. G. Langrod (Eds.), *Substance abuse: A comprehensive textbook* (3rd ed.) (pp. 207–223). Baltimore, MD: Williams & Wilkins.

Kosten, T. A., Anton, S. F., & Rounsaville, B. J. (1992). Ascertaining psychiatric diagnosis with the family history method in a substance abuse population. *Journal of Psychiatric Research*, *26*, 135–147.

LaFave, W. R., & Scott, A. W. (1986). *Substantive criminal law.* St. Paul, MN: West.

Lamb, S., Greenlick, M., & McCarty, D. (1998). *Bridging the gap between practice and research*. Washington, DC: National Academy Press.

Lange, T., & Greene, E. (1990). The judges sentence DUI offenders: An experimental study. *The Journal of Drug and Alcohol Abuse*, *16*, 125–133.

Langenbucher, J. W., & Nathan, P. E. (1983). Psychology, public policy, and the evidence for alcohol intoxication. *American Psychologist*, *38*, 1070–1077.

Leonhard, C., Mulvey, K., Gastfriend, D. R., & Shwartz, M. (2000). The Addiction Severity Index: A field study of internal consistency and validity. *Journal of Substance Abuse*, *18*, 129–135.

Leukefeld, C. G., & Tims, F. M. (1992). *The challenge of drug abuse treatment in prisons and jails*. National Institute on Drug Abuse research monograph no. 118. Washington, DC: U.S. Government Printing Office.

Lightfoot, L. O., & Hodgins, D. (1988). A survey of alcohol and drug problems in incarcerated offenders. *International Journal of the Addictions*, *23*, 687–706.

Lipton, D. S. (1994). The correctional opportunity: Pathways to drug abuse treatment for offenders. *Journal of Drug Issues*, *24 (2)*, 331–348.

MacAndrew, C. (1965). The differentiation of male alcoholic outpatients from nonalcoholic psychiatric outpatients by means of the MMPI. *Quarterly Journal of Studies on Alcohol*, *26*, 238–246.

Mahon, N. (1997). Treatment in prisons and jails. In J. H. Lowinson, P. Ruiz, R. B. Millman, & J. G. Langrod (Eds.), *Substance abuse: A comprehensive textbook* (3rd ed.) (pp. 455–458). Baltimore, MD: Williams & Wilkins.

Mark, F. O. (1988). Does coercion work? The role of referral source in motivating alcoholics in treatment. *Alcoholism Treatment Quarterly*, *5*, 5–22.

Marlatt, G. A. (1999). From hindsight to foresight: A commentary on Project MATCH. In J. Tucker, D. Donovan, & A. Marlatt (Eds.), *Changing addictive behavior: Bridging clinical and public health strategies* (pp. 45–66). New York: Guilford Press.

Marlowe, D. B., Lambert, J. B., & Thompson, R. G. (1999). Voluntary intoxication and criminal responsibility. *Behavioral Sciences and the Law*, *17*, 195–217.

Mayfield, D., McLeod, G., & Hall, P. (1974). The CAGE questionnaire: Validation of a new alcoholism screening instrument. *American Journal of Psychiatry*, *130*, 1121–1123.

McCrady, B. S. (1998). Recent research in twelve-step programs. In A. Graham & T. Schultz (Eds.), *Principles of addiction medicine* (pp. 707–717). Chevy Chase, MD: American Society of Addiction Medicine.

McLellan, A. T., Kushner, H., Metzger, D., & Peters, R. (1992). The fifth edition of the Addiction Severity Index. *Journal of Substance Abuse Treatment, 9*, 199–213.

McLellan, A. T., Luborskey, L., Woody, G. E., & O'Brien, C. P. (1980). An improved diagnostic instrument for substance abuse patients: The Addiction Severity Index. *Journal of Nervous and Mental Diseases, 168*, 26–33.

McLellan, A. T., & McKay, J. R. (1998). Components of successful treatment programs: Lessons from the research literature. In A. W. Graham & T. K. Schultz (Eds.), *Principles of addiction medicine* (2nd ed.) (pp. 327–344). Chevy Chase, MD: American Society of Addiction Medicine.

Meeker, J. W., Jesilow, P., & Aranda, J. (1992). Bias in sentencing: A preliminary analysis of community service sentences. *Behavioral Sciences and the Law, 10*, 197–206.

Mee-Lee, D., Shulman, G., & Gartner, L. (1996). *Patient placement criteria for the treatment of substance-related disorders, second edition (PPC-2)*. Chevy Chase, MD: American Society of Addiction Medicine.

Meyer, R. G. (1992). *Abnormal behavior and the criminal justice system*. New York: Lexington Books.

Miller, G. A. (1985). *The Substance Abuse Subtle Screening Inventory (SASSI): Manual*. Bloomington, IN: Spencer Evening World.

Miller, G. A. (1994). *The Substance Abuse Subtle Screening Inventory manual: Adult SASSI-2 manual supplement*. Spencer, IN: Spencer Evening World.

Miller, W. R., & Hester, R. K. (1986). Inpatient alcoholism treatment: Who benefits? *American Psychologist, 41*, 794–805.

Miller, W. R., Brown, J. M., Simpson, T. L., Handmaker, N. S., Bien, T. H., Luckie, L. F., Montgomery, H. A., Hester, R. K., & Tonigan, J. S. (1995). What works: A methodological analysis of the alcohol treatment outcome literature. In R. K. Hester & W. R. Miller (Eds.), *Treating addictive behaviors: Processes of change* (pp. 121–174). New York: Plenum Press.

Millon, T. (1983). *Millon Clinical Multiaxial Inventory manual*. Minneapolis, MN: National Computer Systems.

Moore, R. A. (1972). The diagnosis of alcoholism in a psychiatric hospital: A trial of the Michigan Alcoholism Screening Test (MAST). *American Journal of Psychiatry, 128*, 115–119.

Moreland, K. L., Fowler, R. D., & Honaker, L. M. (1994). Future directions in the use of psychological assessment for treatment planning and outcome assessment: Predictions and recommendations. In M. E. Maruish (Ed.). *The use of psychological testing for treatment planning and outcome assessment.* (p. 581–602). Hillsdale, NJ: Lawrence Erlbaum.

Mueser, K. T., Bellack, A. S., & Blanchard, J. J. (1992). Comorbidity of schizophrenia and substance abuse: Implications for treatment. *Journal of Consulting and Clinical Psychology, 60*, 845–856.

Murdoch, D., Piho, R. O., & Ross, D. (1990). Alcohol and crimes of violence: Present issues. *International Journal of the Addictions, 25*, 1065–1081.

Myerholtz, L. E., & Rosenberg, H. (1997). Screening DUI offenders for alcohol problems: Psychometric assessment of the Substance Abuse Subtle Screening Inventory. *Psychology of Addictive Behaviors, 11*, 155–165.

Myers, M. (1987). Economic inequality and discrimination in sentencing. *Social Forces, 65* (3), 376.

Nathan, P. E. (1991). Substance use disorders in the DSM-IV. *Journal of Abnormal Psychology, 100*, 356–361.

Nathan, P. E. (1996). Assessing substance abusers. In L. L. Murphy & J. C. Impara (Eds.), *Assessment of substance abuse* (pp. xvii–xxix). Lincoln, NE: University of Nebraska Press.

National Commission on Marihuana and Drug Abuse (1972). *Marihuana: A signal of misunderstanding.* Appendix, Vol. 1. Washington, DC: U.S. Government Printing Office.

National Institute on Alcohol Abuse and Alcoholism (1997). *Alcohol, violence and aggression.* October Alcohol Alert. Rockville, MD: U.S. Government Printing Office.

National Institute on Drug Abuse (1978). Drug abuse and crime. In L. D. Savitz and N. Johnson (Eds.), *Crime in society.* New York: Wiley.

National Institute on Drug Abuse. (1982). *Data from the Client Oriented Data acquisition process (CODAP).* Rockville, MD: NIDA.

National Institute on Drug Abuse (1999). Principles of drug addiction treatment: A research-based guide. Washington, DC: U.S. Government Printing Office.

National Institute of Justice (1998a). *Drug use forecasting. Special report.* Washington, DC: Author.

National Institute of Justice (1998b). *1998 Annual Report on marijuana use among arrestees, Arrestees Drug Abuse Monitoring (ADAM).* Washington, DC: Author.

O'Farrell, T. J., Cutter, H., Bayog, R. D., Deutch, G., & Fortgang, J. (1984). Correspondence between one-year retrospective reports of pre-treatment drinking by alcoholics and their wives. *Behavioral Assessment, 6*, 263–274.

Office of Applied Studies. (1995). *Preliminary estimates from the 1993 National Household Survey on Drug Abuse.* Rockville, MD: Substance Abuse and Mental Health Services Administration.

Pernanen, K. (1986). Theoretical aspects of the relationship between alcohol use and crime. In J. J. Collins (Ed.), *Drinking and crime* (pp. 1–69). New York: Guilford Press.

Prochaska, J. O., DiClemente, C. C., & Norcross, J. C. (1992). In search of how people change: Applications to the addictive behaviors. *American Psychologist, 47*, 1102–1114.

Project MATCH Research Group. (1997). Matching alcoholism treatment to client heterogeneity: Project MATCH post-treatment drinking outcomes. *Journal of Studies on Alcohol, 58*, 7–29.

Robbins, L., Cottler, L., & Keating, S. (1989). *The NIMH diagnostic interview schedule. Version III, revised (DIS-III-R).* Rockville, MD: National Institute on Mental Health.

Robins, L. N. (1984). The natural history of adolescent drug use. *American Journal of Public Health, 74*, 656–657.

Robins, N. L., Helzer, J. E., Croughan, H., & Ratcliff, K. S. (1981). National Institute of Mental Health Diagnostic Interview Schedule: Its history, characteristics, and validity. *Archives of General Psychiatry, 38*, 381–389.

Robinson, v. California. 370 U.S. 660 (1962).

Roche, A. M., Parle, M. D., Stubbs, J. M., Hall, W., & Saunders, J. B. (1995). Management and treatment efficacy of drug and alcohol problems: What do doctors believe? *Addiction, 90*, 1357–1366.

Rosse, R. B., Giese, A. A., Deutsch, S. I., & Morihisa, J. M. (1989). *Laboratory diagnostic testing in psychiatry*. Washington, DC: American Psychiatric Press.

Roth, J. A. (1996). *Psychoactive substances and violence.* Washington, DC: U.S. Department of Justice.

Scholttenfeld, R. S. (1989). Involuntary treatment of substance use disorders—Impediments to success. *Psychiatry, 52*, 164–176.

Scoles, P. E., Fine, E. W., & Steer, R. A. (1986). DUI offenders presenting with positive blood alcohol levels at presentencing evaluation. *Journal of Studies on Alcohol, 47*, 500–502.

Selzer, M. L. (1971). The Michigan Alcoholism Screening Test: The quest for a new diagnostic instrument. *American Journal of Psychiatry, 127*, 1653–1658.

Smith, J .E., & Meyers, R. J. (2000). CRA: The community reinforcement approach for treating alcohol problems. In M. Dougher (Ed.), *Clinical behavior analysis* (pp. 207–230). Reno: Context Press.

Smith, S., & Newman, J. P. (1990). Alcohol and drug abuse-dependence disorders in psychopathic and nonpsychopathic criminal offenders. *Journal of Abnormal Psychology, 99*, 430–439.

Sobell, L. C., Maisto, S. A., Sobell, M. B., Cooper, A. M., Cooper, T. C., & Sanders, B. (1980). Developing a prototype for evaluating alcohol treatment effectiveness. In L. C. Sobell, M. B. Sobell, & E. Ward (Eds.), *Evaluating alcohol and drug abuse treatment effectiveness: Recent advances* (pp. 129–150). New York: Pergamon Press.

Sobell, L. C., Toneatto, T., & Sobell, M. B. (1994). Behavioral assessment and treatment planning for alcohol, tobacco and other drug problems: Current status with an emphasis on clinical applications. *Behavioral Therapy, 25*, 533–580.

Speiglman, R. (1994). Mandated AA attendance for recidivist drinking drivers: Ideology, organization, and California criminal justice practices. *Addiction, 89*, 859–868.

Spiehler, V. (2000). Hair analysis by immunological methods from the beginning to 2000. *Forensic Science International, 107*, 249–259.

Spitzer, R., & Williams, J. (1987). *Structured clinical interview for DSM-III-R. Biometrics Research Department*. New York: New York State Psychiatric Institute.

Spohn, C. (1990). The sentencing decisions of Black and White judges: Expected and unexpected similarities. *Law and Society Review, 24*, 1197–1216.

Stitzer, M. L., & McCaul, M. E. (1987). Criminal justice interventions with drug and alcohol abusers. In E. K. Morris & C. J. Braukmann (Eds.), *Behavioral approaches to crime and delinquency: A handbook of application, research, and concepts*. New York: Plenum.

Strain, E. C., Stitzer, M. L., Liebson, I. A., & Bigelow, G. E. (1993). Methadone dose and treatment outcome. *Drug and Alcohol Dependence, 33*, 105–117.

Substance Abuse and Mental Health Services Administration (SAMHSA) (1998). *National Household Survey on Drug Abuse*. Maryland: Public Health Service.

Swanson, J. W., Holzer, C. E., Ganju, V. K., & Jono, R. T. (1990). Violence and psychiatric disorder in the community: Evidence from the Epidemiologic Catchment Area surveys. *Hospital and Community Psychiatry, 41*, 761–770.

Teitelbaum, L., & Mullen, B. (2000). The validity of the MAST in psychiatric settings: A meta-analytic integration. *Journal of Studies on Alcohol, 61*, 254–261.

Tennant, F. (1990). Quantitative urine levels of abusable drugs for clinical purposes. *Clinical Laboratory Medicine, 10* (2), 301–309.

U.S. Department of Health and Human Services. Center for Substance Abuse Treatment (1999a). *Screening and assessment for alcohol and other drug abuse among adults in the criminal justice system*. Treatment Improvement Protocol series, no. 7. Rockville, Maryland: Public Health Service.

U.S. Department of Health and Human Services. Center for Substance Abuse Treatment (1999b). *The role and current status of patient placement criteria in the treatment of substance use disorders*. Treatment Improvement Protocol series, no. 13. Rockville, Maryland: Public Health Service.

Vaillant, G. E. (1995). *The natural history of alcoholism revisited*. Cambridge, MA: Harvard University Press.

Vereby, K. G., & Buchan, B. J. (1997). Diagnostic laboratory. In J. H. Lowinson, P. Ruiz, R. B. Millman, & J. G. Langrod (Eds.), *Substance abuse: A comprehensive textbook* (3rd ed.) (pp. 369–376). Baltimore, MD: Williams & Wilkins.

Wallach, J. (1986). *Interpretation of diagnostic tests: A synopsis of laboratory medicine*. Boston/Toronto: Little Brown.

Watterson, R. T. (1991). Just say no to the charges against you: Alcohol intoxication, mental capacity and criminal responsibility. *Bulletin of the American Academy of Psychiatry and the Law, 19* (3), 277–290.

West Publishing Company. (1989). *The American criminal justice process: Selected rules, statutes, and guidelines*. Saint Paul, MN: West.

Wish, E. D. (1986). PCP and crime: Just another illicit drug? In D. H. Clouet (Ed.), *Phencyclidine: An update*. Rockville, MD: National Institute on Drug Abuse.

World Health Organization (1992). *International classification of diseases* (10th ed.). Geneva: Author.

Yarvis, R. M. (1994). Patterns of substance abuse and intoxication among murderers. *Bulletin of the American Academy of Psychiatry and the Law, 22*, 133–144.

Zukin, S. R., Sloboda, Z., & Javitt, D. C. (1997). Phencyclidine (PCP). In J. H. Lowinson, P. Ruiz, R. B. Millman, & J. G. Langrod (Eds.), *Substance abuse: A comprehensive textbook* (3rd ed.) (pp. 238–246). Baltimore, MD: Williams & Wilkins.

CHAPTER 16

ASSESSMENT OF POST-TRAUMATIC STRESS DISORDER

KIMBERLI TREADWELL
UNIVERSITY OF CONNECTICUT

EDNA FOA
UNIVERSITY OF PENNSYLVANIA

Post-Traumatic Stress Disorder (PTSD) affects from 9 to 15 percent of the general population (Breslau, Davis, Andreski, & Peterson, 1991; Davidson, Hughes, Blazer, & George, 1991), and almost 50 percent of women who have been raped (Rothbaum et al., 1992). Although human reactions to trauma have been described for more than a century under various labels, persistent post-traumatic symptoms were introduced into the psychiatric lexicon in 1980 with the third edition of the *Diagnostic and Statistical Manual of Mental Disorders* (*DSM-III*; American Psychiatric Association, 1980) and have been slightly modified for the current edition of this manual (*DSM-IV*). Once established, PTSD symptoms are usually persistent and debilitating.

As with any psychological disorder, assessment is an integral and ongoing process in the context of treatment. In this chapter we outline goals and the purpose of accurate assessment of PTSD. Next, we discuss methods of assessment and review the measures with established psychometric data to support their use. Finally, we note several common problems in assessment of PTSD and related concerns.

DIAGNOSIS OF PTSD

PTSD requires the presence of a traumatic event in which an individual directly experiences or witnesses an event that involves actual or threatened death or serious injury, or threat to one's own or another person's physical integrity. The traumatic event must also engender a reaction in the individual that involves intense fear, horror, or helplessness. These two aspects of the traumatic event, the characteristics of the event itself and the person's perceptions of the threat, must be present for a diagnosis of PTSD. These criteria are subsumed under Criterion A in the *DSM-IV*.

PTSD symptoms, as defined in the *DSM-IV* (APA, 1994), are divided into three clusters: reexperiencing (Criterion B), avoidance (Criterion C), and arousal (Criterion D) symptoms. These clusters were based on clinical observation of traumatized victims rather than on empirical research. The reexperiencing cluster includes symptoms such as intrusive, distressing thoughts related to the traumatic event, nightmares or distressing dreams about the trauma, flashbacks, and intense psychological or physiological arousal when exposed to cues that resemble the trauma. A person must exhibit one or more of these reexperiencing symptoms to warrant a PTSD diagnosis.

Persistent avoidance of stimuli associated with the event form the second symptom cluster. These symptoms are manifested as avoidance of thoughts and feelings associated with the trauma; avoidance of activities, situations, or people that remind the victim of the trauma; an inability to recall important aspects of the trauma; diminished interest in leisure activities; feelings of detachment from other people; a restricted range of emotion; and a sense of foreshortened future (e.g., the person may not expect to live as long a life because of the event). At least three of these symptoms must be evident to reach diagnostic criteria for PTSD.

The third symptom cluster involves symptoms of hyperarousal that became evident after the traumatic event. Examples of these symptoms include difficulty falling or staying asleep, feeling irritable or prone to angry outbursts, difficulty concentrating, hypervigilance, and an exaggerated startle response. At least two symptoms from this category are necessary for diagnosis.

Two final criteria must be satisfied to qualify for a diagnosis of PTSD. The fifth criterion, E, requires that the symptoms have endured for greater than one month. The final Criterion F states that the symptoms must impact one's general functioning. Areas that might be impeded include work performance, relationships with others, schoolwork, and social functioning.

Two subtypes are used to describe the symptom course of PTSD. The first subtype, *acute*, signifies that the post-trauma reactions occurred within six months of the traumatic event but have not endured longer than six months. The second subtype, *chronic* or *delayed*, denotes reactions that developed at least six months after the trauma or have endured for greater than six months.

Initially the three symptom clusters of PTSD were determined by clinical observation of trauma victims. Recently, empirical validation of these clusters has provided some empirical support for the distinction among categories. Foa and colleagues investigated the 17 symptoms that comprise the three clusters in a statistical analysis called factor analysis (Foa, Riggs, & Gershuny, 1995). The factor analysis produced three clusters, called factors, as well, but these factors did not entirely overlap with the clinical clusters defined in *DSM-IV*. An important distinction that emerged was a difference in categorizing the second *DSM* cluster, which combined avoidance symptoms (e.g., efforts to avoid thoughts and feelings associated with the trauma) and numbing symptoms (e.g., feeling of detachment from others). When examined statistically, numbing and avoidance symptoms belonged to different factors. Another study supports the separate importance of numbing symptoms in PTSD. Solomon and colleagues also used factor analysis to analyze PTSD symptoms in Israeli soldiers one year after combat (Solomon, Mikulincer, & Benbenishty, 1989). A psychic numbing factor emerged as more prominent that any other symptom cluster. The numbing factor included symptoms such as detachment from others, numbing of responses, and mental escape. Both studies point to the prominent position of dissociation in post-trauma sequelae.

These results also support the conclusion that numbing and effortful avoidance may represent different aspects of PTSD symptomatology. Irritability and anger symptoms belonged to the numbing factor, even though they are assigned to the third cluster, the arousal category, in *DSM-IV*. This finding suggests that angry arousal and anxious arousal may be somewhat different. Riggs and colleagues suggested that anger inhibits feelings of anxiety in assault victims and, like numbing symptoms, may serve to protect the victim from anxiety when efforts to avoid fail (Riggs, Rothbaum, & Foa, 1995).

Interestingly, numbing symptoms better distinguished victims with PTSD from those without PTSD than the remaining symptom categories (Foa et al., 1995). Very few of the victims without PTSD reported numbing symptoms, although many reported symptoms of intrusion, arousal, and effortful avoidance that did not meet full diagnostic criteria. Thus, the presence of numbing symptoms better differentiated victims with and without PTSD. This was an interesting finding because, according to the *DSM-IV*, a victim can receive a diagnosis of PTSD without having any numbing symptoms.

Consistent with the diagnosis of PTSD, criminal victimization produces a variety of disturbances, including anxiety, depression, intrusive thoughts and images of the assault, and sleep disturbance such as nightmares and insomnia (Frank & Stewart, 1984; Kilpatrick & Veronen, 1984; Kilpatrick, Veronen, & Resick, 1979). Rape victims report intrusive thoughts and images of the rape that they actively try to avoid (Kilpatrick & Veronen, 1984). They also report more sleep disturbances (Ellis, Atkeson, & Calhoun, 1981) and more difficulty concentrating (Nadelson, Notman, Zackson, & Gornick, 1982) than nonvictimized individuals. Thus, the postassault psychopathology of rape victims can best be characterized as PTSD.

PREVALENCE

After a major trauma, the vast majority of people will experience psychological disturbance, but most will recover over time. It is therefore important to distinguish between a normal reaction to trauma and a chronic pathological reaction. In a prospective study of female victims of rape and other crime, 94 percent of victims met the symptom criteria for PTSD at an assessment within two weeks of the assault (Rothbaum, Foa, Riggs, Murdock, & Walsh, 1992). Duration criteria for PTSD were not yet met. One month following the assault, 65 percent of victims continued to meet the criteria for PTSD; this figure decreased to 46 percent three months postassault. At the final assessment, nine months after the assault, 47 percent of the women fulfilled criteria for PTSD. In this study, women who did not meet criteria for PTSD after three months showed steady improvement over time, whereas those women whose PTSD persisted did not show much improvement after three months elapsed. Thus, nearly all victims of rape appeared to meet symptom criteria immediately following their assault, but just less than half continued to meet criteria for this disorder three months later. The course of PTSD for victims of nonsexual criminal assault (e.g., aggravated assault, robbery) was similar to that found for rape victims. Initially, 71 percent of women and 50 percent of men met symptomatic criteria, but not duration, for PTSD; these figures decreased to 21 percent of women, and none of the men, three months postassault (Riggs, Rothbaum, & Foa, 1995). Thus, a majority of crime victims reported many PTSD symptoms initially, but the incidence of PTSD decreased over time. Although these patterns are the same, it is important to note that the rape victims were more likely to develop PTSD initially and to maintain it over time. Evidence from other populations of trauma victims, such as firefighters (McFarlane, 1988a, 1988b), indicate that the reactions of rape and assault victims are not unique to these types of trauma. A similar symptom course was noted in firefighters surviving major disasters.

GOALS FOR ASSESSMENT

One of the major goals of assessment is to determine the extent of PTSD symptoms to evaluate whether a diagnosis of PTSD is warranted. Common problems associated with trauma, such as depression, ritualized behaviors, and substance use, must also be evaluated. Once diagnostic status is formulated, the prioritization of the presenting concerns will aid in choosing the treatment direction. For instance, if a person presents with full-blown PTSD as well as alcohol abuse, she may initially require treatment for the substance abuse prior to addressing concerns related to the reexperiencing of the traumatic event. Similarly, if a person presents with comorbid depression that limits his daily functioning, or he is suicidal, these problems should be addressed first and controlled prior to addressing assault-related symptoms.

Another goal of assessment is to provide an accurate baseline of functioning. The severity of the person's presenting problems, prior to intervention, must be ascertained and measured in an objective fashion to be used as a comparison against which gains in treatment can be compared. Even if the person does not fully respond to a treatment intervention, the post-treatment level of symptoms can be compared to the baseline level, and gains can be highlighted to encourage the person to continue to work on trauma-related symptoms and/or interpret any residual low-severity symptoms within the context of the gains made since the initiation of treatment.

This baseline assessment of initial symptom severity can also be used to provide an ongoing, accurate record of the response during the intervention. We perform ongoing assessment throughout treatment to provide a record of the patient's progress to date, and to clarify what treatment components or experiences were most helpful. An objective measure is more accurate than relying on the person's appraisal of his or her status, such as, "I think I'm doing much better." Instead, a reliable record of symptoms is recommended to provide an ongoing record of the response. This record can be used to highlight gains as well as to outline remaining problems to be worked on. We take these measurements to provide a quick and objective means to establish the patient's "PTSD temperature." It is useful to administer assessment at least at pre-, mid-, and post-treatment. This information can then be used to evaluate functioning over a long period of time once treatment is completed.

A final goal of assessment is to provide education about typical trauma reactions to the patient. We have found this tool invaluable to educate our clients about PTSD, its common symptoms, and the rationale for why they are experiencing these symptoms. Understanding that their reexperiencing, for example, goes along with PTSD, is commonly experienced, and is not a sign that they can't "control their minds" helps to validate their reexperience and normalize their reactions. Given the common reactions of feeling isolated and incompetent to deal with stress, it is often helpful to know that these symptoms are accounted for by PTSD, that this is a normal response shared by other survivors, and is to be expected. Frequently, patients do not connect their symptoms, such as jumpiness, hypervigilance, and sleep disturbance, to the assault when it is clear from a professional's view that the symptoms are a result of the assault. Linking these problems to the assault helps patients to be more aware that their reactions are typical and therefore predictable of surviving the assault—that this is a part of the syndrome labeled PTSD. This labeling helps patients to label their internal events more accurately rather than misattributing them to personal incompetence or failure.

METHODS OF ASSESSMENT

There are multiple methods of assessment, each with advantages and disadvantages. We discuss three main types: self-monitoring, clinical interviews, and standardized measures.

Self-Monitoring

Self-monitoring involves asking the patient to record the occurrence of a target behavior (e.g., each and every occurrence of a flashback). Other methods of self-monitoring include keeping a count of the occurrence of a target behavior within specified time parameters (e.g., the presence of flashbacks between 12 and 2 o'clock) or by making duration ratings (e.g., the length of each flashback). Often, this self-monitoring involves indicating on a form the number of occurrences of the target behavior as well as other relevant information, such as the date, time, situation, cognitions, and anxiety level. Anxiety level may be recorded on a common scale, the subjective units of discomfort (SUDS) scale, rated from 0–100, where 0 indicates no anxiety or discomfort and 100 indicates panic-level anxiety or discomfort.

The date and time are important elements to include in self-monitoring to elucidate the patterns of problems—for example, higher-risk times for strong reactions. The situation (e.g., activity, location) is also important in determining relevant factors to the discomfort or possible triggers, say, of flashbacks. A patient may report that it scares him to drive a car; however, what actually scares him may be driving alone at night on country roads. He may not be bothered by driving his car to the local supermarket during the day or while accompanied. The patient's thoughts surrounding the occurrence of a target behavior are also important and should be recorded. These thoughts can be examined in therapy for possible dysfunctional interpretations of the world that can be altered with cognitive restructuring. Common thoughts associated with PTSD include safety concerns, embarrassment, guilt, trust, and other issues.

In using self-monitoring with a patient, the clinician must explain the rationale, identify specific target behaviors, and emphasize accuracy. Accuracy is vital to ensure that the self-monitoring information reflects both the rate and severity of the problem as well as to establish baseline rates and ongoing treatment response. Without accuracy, treatment effects cannot be determined and the patient will not be aware of progress or regress. Self-monitoring can also have therapeutic effects, which should be discussed with the patient. A portion of the assessment and treatment sessions should be used to examine self-monitoring to ascertain compliance and the extent of symptoms.

An advantage of self-monitoring is that it collects information about symptoms as they occur and thus is more accurate in recording. In addition, it increases a patient's awareness of the target behaviors and situations that are problematic, thus teaching the patient to think of symptoms in contextual terms. A disadvantage of this technique is that self-monitoring initially can have a reactive quality to it and may not reflect an accurate baseline. In other words, when a person begins to monitor his or her behavior, it often changes in the desired direction based on the mere fact that the person is recording it, thus influencing the baseline rates. Overall, as an ongoing measure during treatment, self-monitoring is a valuable tool.

Clinical Interviews

A sensitive *clinical interview* is also a valuable method of assessing PTSD and related symptoms. Information collected during an interview should include trauma-specific reactions as well as an evaluation of the patient's social support network, other past traumatic experiences, coping behaviors, legal actions, ongoing contact with the assailant, use of alcohol and illicit drugs, psychiatric history, and general psychosocial adjustment. Past trauma history is especially important to ascertain because these experiences may influence the reactions to the current trauma of focus. The greater the amount of information collected, the more assistance the clinician can provide in therapy. Furthermore, while discussing ways in which a patient's life has changed as a result of the assault, you may discover avoidance patterns that will be important to address in treatment.

An advantage of clinical interviewing is that the clinician begins to establish rapport with the patient as they begin together to overcome assault-related symptoms. A second advantage of the clinical interview is that it allows greater flexibility in responding to information gathered and conducting ongoing assessment. A major disadvantage is that clinical interviews are often unstructured, with the result that important information may be missed if the interviewer does not query certain areas or the patient does not volunteer the information. A talkative or distressed patient may also sidetrack the interview into areas that are not as relevant for treatment planning or using a large proportion of time in one specific area. The use of structured clinical interviews, such as the Assault Information and History Interview developed at our clinic, increases the likelihood of a thorough interview and may overcome some disadvantages (Foa & Rothbaum, 1998). Even so, a clinical interview should not be the only tool in assessment and should be part of an assessment package that includes objective ratings of symptoms and their severity.

Standardized Measures

A standardized measure involves specific questions to obtain responses, whether by self-report or by clinician inquiry, that are objectively asked and can be psychometrically evaluated. Standardized measures permit the reliable and valid measurement of symptom severity and change. Disadvantages of this method include the retrospective nature of reporting symptoms and dependence on the patient's self-report. Currently, no common standardized measure of PTSD exists. A critical review of standardized measures with published psychometric data follows and is divided into the categories of structured diagnostic interviews, structured clinical interviews, and self-report measures.

Structured Diagnostic Interviews

Several structured diagnostic interviews have been developed with PTSD modules as comprehensive diagnostic assessment tools, and are reviewed here. The advantage of such a method includes a sensitive interview by a trained clinician as in a clinical interview with the addition of structured questions to ascertain specific diagnoses. This format can be subjected to psychometric evaluation. The disadvantages of structured diagnostic interviews include the necessity of a skilled, trained interviewer and the length of time to administer the full interview.

Structured Clinical Interview for DSM-III-R *(SCID).* The SCID is the most widely used and thoroughly researched diagnostic interview (Spitzer, Williams, Gibbon, & First, 1990). A PTSD module is provided that begins with a history of psychosocial stressors. It then proceeds to establish the presence or absence of each of the 17 items in the *DSM-III-R* constituting Criteria B, C, and D. Duration of symptoms (Criterion E), interference with daily functioning, and date of onset are also assessed. The SCID has been widely used, usually as a screening instrument. Current and lifetime diagnosis can be established. Items are scored as absent, subthreshold, or present. The SCID requires special training and a clinical background to administer and takes about 1–2 hours to complete. It has demonstrated overall high interrater reliability and strongly correlates with measures of PTSD. Further specific evaluation of the PTSD module is necessary.

Diagnostic Interview Schedule (DIS). The DIS provides a PTSD module (Robins, Helzer, Croughan, & Ratcliff, 1981; Robins, Helzer, Croughan, Williams, & Spitzer, 1981). In 440 cases, the DIS-PTSD demonstrated a sensitivity of only .22, a specificity of .98, and kappa of .26 (Helzer, Robins, & McEvoy, 1987). The diagnostic sensitivity of the DIS has been questioned when used in community samples, and those studies that utilized this measure suggested the use of additional psychometric evaluation in these community populations (Keane & Penk, 1988; Kulka et al., 1990). For instance, the PTSD module from the DIS did not compare favorably to the SCID in community surveys. Thus, further evaluation of its psychometric properties is necessary.

Anxiety Disorders Interview Schedule–Revised (ADIS-R). The ADIS-R was developed to provide an in-depth assessment of the class of anxiety disorders, including the later addition of PTSD (DiNardo & Barlow, 1988). If Criterion A is not met, the ADIS-R does not question any remaining symptoms. Diagnostic agreement has been fair to good, with kappa coefficients reported to be .86 (Blanchard, Gerardi, Kolb, & Barlow, 1986) and .55 (DiNardo et al., 1993). However, no reliability or further psychometric evaluation was reported. Thus, the ADIS-R may not be the best choice when focusing on PTSD.

Structured Clinical Interviews

Structured clinical interviews offer the same advantage of clinical interviews with the addition of structured questions. They offer the advantage of shorter administration time than structured diagnostic interviews but do not as thoroughly provide information about the spectrum of diagnoses. Trained clinicians are needed.

Clinician-Administered PTSD Scale (CAPS). The CAPS is one of the most widely used PTSD interviews and has been used for a variety of traumatized populations, including war veterans and sexual assault survivors (Blake et al., 1990). The CAPS is a 34-item interview designed to evaluate the frequency and intensity of individual PTSD symptoms and associated features. It contains the 17 DSM PTSD symptom items as well as related symptoms such as depression, guilt, homicidality, memory impairment, and feelings of being overwhelmed. Items can be scored separately for frequency and intensity ratings as well as for dimensional and categorical scoring. Current and lifetime status of PTSD are obtained. A frequency rating of at least 1 on a 0–4 frequency scale and a severity rating of at least 2 on a severity scale from 0–4 are necessary to meet symptom criteria for diagnostic purposes. This scale was designed to be used by clinicians and lay personnel alike, an advantage over structured diagnostic interviews that require rigorous training for administration. The CAPS requires 40–60 minutes to administer.

The CAPS demonstrated good internal consistency (alphas ranged from .73–.85), and test-retest reliability (.90–.98) in a population of combat veterans. The agreement with the SCID PTSD module was moderate (kappa = .78). Sensitivity for the CAPS was .84; for specificity, .95. High reliability was supported in a study with a civilian population (Blanchard et al., 1995). This interview was found to be sensitive to treatment outcome (van der Kolk et al., 1994).

Other than one study, the published psychometric information for the CAPS is limited to Vietnam veterans, and further analysis in alternate traumatized populations would increase generalizability of the results. The extent of information questioned, such as the frequency and intensity of symptoms for both current and lifetime presence of PTSD, is time consuming yet does not add critical information for presence of a current diagnosis. The application of information collected regarding the eight related symptom areas is unclear and is not utilized in formulating a diagnosis. Finally, no questions elicit information about a traumatic event and its impact on the individual; instead, the CAPS presumes the presence of a PTSD-magnitude stressor.

PTSD Symptom Scale–Interview. The PTSD Symptom Scale–Interview (PSS-I; Foa, Riggs, Dancu, & Rothbaum, 1993) is a 17-item interview assessing the presence and severity of PTSD over the past two weeks. It was originally developed for use in a research program with rape victims. Items correspond to the 17 DSM symptom criteria for PTSD and are rated on a four-point scale ranging from "not at all" to "very much." Three subscales are scored: Reexperiencing, Avoidance, and Arousal. The interview can be administered by clinicians and lay interviewers and requires 20–30 minutes to administer.

Considerable psychometric evidence supports the reliability and validity of this instrument. The internal consistency coefficient was .85 for the total score, .69 for Reexperiencing, .65 for Avoidance, and .71 for Arousal. Test-retest reliability was .80 for the total scale score and ranged from .55–.77 for the three subscales. Concurrent validity was demonstrated by correlating the PSS-I with measures of depression, anxiety, and intrusion, with alphas ranging from .48–.72. Convergent validity was excellent. The PSS-I was compared to the PTSD module in the SCID and correctly classified 94 percent of the SCID-PTSD individuals. Sensitivity was .88 and specificity was .96. The PSS-I has been shown to be sensitive to treatment outcome (Foa et al., 1999; Rothbaum, 1997). Additional information about psychometric properties with other trauma populations and females would further validate the scale.

PTSD-Interview (PTSD-I). Like the PSS-I, the PTSD-I was developed to closely follow DSM guidelines, providing 17 symptom items answered on a seven-point frequency scale (Watson et al., 1991). Three questions inquire about the nature of the trauma and the duration of symptoms. The scale can be scored continuously and dichotomously. Clinicians and lay interviewers can use the PTSD-I. This interview demonstrated excellent reliability of .92 for internal consistency and .95 for test-retest reliability. Compared to the DIS-PTSD module, validity was supported with an agreement of .84. The overall hit rate of the PTSD-I for diagnosis was 92 percent, the sensitivity was .89, and specificity was .94. Further study of the instrument supported convergent validity with alternate measures of PTSD, with correlations ranging from .79 to .86 (Watson et al., 1994).

One caveat about the PTSD-I is that it cannot accurately assess Criterion A for PTSD because the nature of the trauma and its subjective impact on the individual are not assessed and therefore it cannot fully form a PTSD diagnosis. The use of this instrument and its psychometric properties with alternate trauma populations has not been published to establish sensitivity in populations beyond Vietnam veterans. Finally, the interview was based on the *DSM-III-R*, and it has not been updated for the *DSM-IV*.

Structured Interview for PTSD (SI-PTSD). This interview for PTSD is based on the *DSM-III* and uses continuous or dichotomous scoring to ascertain the severity of symptoms (Davidson, Smith, & Kudler, 1989). Current and lifetime diagnoses of PTSD can be obtained. The SI-PTSD was developed with veterans from the Korean War, Vietnam War, and World War II. The internal consistency was .94, and test-retest reliability was .71. Convergent validity was supported when compared to the SCID: The overall kappa coefficient was .79. The sensitivity of the SI-PTSD was 96 percent, and its specificity was 80 percent. Concurrent validity was only moderately supported, as the correlations with measures of anxiety, depression, and intrusion ranged from .51–.61. Overall, the validity of the scale requires further investigation, particularly with trauma populations other than veterans.

Self-Report Measures

Self-report instruments can be easily administered, thus providing time-efficient and cost-effective assessment of PTSD. Caveats to this form of assessment were mentioned earlier.

Post-traumatic Diagnostic Scale (PTDS). The PTDS (Foa, Cashman, Jaycox, & Perry, 1997) independently provides PTSD severity scores and yields a PTSD diagnosis according to *DSM-IV* criteria. It is a 49-item self-report instrument that assesses all *DSM-IV* criteria necessary to make a diagnosis of PTSD, including nature of the trauma (Criterion A), the 17 DSM symptoms items (Criteria B–D), duration of the symptoms (Criterion E), and inquiries regarding impairment in nine areas of functioning (e.g., work, friendships, household duties, sexual functioning, etc.) (Criterion F). The scale includes a checklist of 12 traumatic events and asks the respondent to mark the frequency with which each trauma was experienced or witnessed to indicate which event disturbed them the most in the past month; to briefly describe the event in space provided; and to refer to this event in completing the remainder of the scale. Symptom items are rated on a four-point frequency scale and correspond to the three clusters of PTSD: Reexperiencing, Avoidance, and Arousal. The PTDS yields both a diagnosis of PTSD as well as severity scores, obtained by summing scores of the 17 symptom items. A preliminary version of the scale was reviewed by 15 experts on PTSD. The PTDS offers the distinct advantage of being validated on 248 victims following a variety of traumas, including natural disaster, fire, sexual and nonsexual assault, imprisonment, and torture.

The internal consistency coefficient alphas for the PTDS were excellent, with the total symptom severity score evidencing an alpha of .92 and the subscales ranging from .78 to .84. Test-retest reliability for diagnosis revealed a kappa of .74 and a percentage agreement between diagnosis at the two time points of 87 percent. Test-retest reliability for the symptom severity scores ranged from .77–.85. The convergent validity of a PTSD diagnosis was obtained by comparing it with the diagnosis obtained from a structured diagnostic interview. A kappa of .65 was obtained, with 82 percent agreement between the two measures. The sensitivity of the PTDS was .89, whereas its specificity was .75. Concurrent validity was established for the severity scores, which demonstrated high correlations with measures of intrusion, avoidance, general anxiety, and depression.

The three subscales demonstrated high correlation with each other and the total score, calling into question the usefulness of each subscale beyond the information provided by the total score. Nonetheless, because each subscale corresponds to the three symptom clusters in the *DSM-IV*, they provide useful diagnostic information and were retained in the final version of the scale. Another caveat is that the measure correlated with measures of depression and anxiety, questioning the extent to which this scale assesses a specific trauma-related construct. Finally, as convention calls for a skilled clinician to arrive at a diagnosis, the diagnosis obtained from self-report should be used mostly for screening purposes.

PTSD Symptom Scale–Self-Report (PSS-SR). The PSS-SR (Foa et al., 1993) is a self-report version of the PSS-I that contains 17 items measuring the severity of each *DSM-III-R* symptom criterion on a four-point scale. The scale requires

5–15 minutes to complete. The PSS-SR demonstrated highly satisfactory psychometric properties in female victims of assault. The internal consistency coefficient was .91 for the total symptom scale, .78 for Reexperiencing, .80 for Avoidance, and .82 for Arousal. The scale demonstrated moderate test-retest reliability of .74 for the total symptom scale and coefficients ranging from .56 to .71 for the subscales. Because the sample consisted of recent trauma victims, moderate test-retest reliability might be expected given the rate of recovery over the first months after a trauma. Convergent validity for the PSS-SR was established in relation to diagnoses from the SCID, and the PSS-SR correctly diagnosed 86 percent of those with PTSD. Specificity (1.0) was considerably higher than sensitivity (.62). Concurrent validity was evidenced by correlating the PSS-SR with measures of anxiety, PTSD, and depression, which ranged from .52–.81. A German version of the PSS-SR demonstrated adequate psychometric properties and application to different trauma and cultures (Stieglitz, Frommberger, Foa, & Berger, 2001).

One caveat of this scale is that it cannot arrive at a diagnosis. Second, the validity is questionable, since it correlated highly with measures of depression and general anxiety. Finally, it was validated with strictly females.

Trauma Screening Questionnaire (TSQ). The TSQ is a brief 10-symptom screening instrument based on the PSS-SR that has been validated with independent samples (Brewin et al., 2002). Respondents indicate the presence of reexperiencing and arousal symptoms in a Yes/No format. A cutoff of six out of the 10 symptoms endorsed in any combination maximized overall efficiency (90 percent), yielding a sensitivity of 86 percent and specificity of 93 percent in victims of a rail crash. Similar results were obtained in a separate sample of crime victims. The TSQ's performance was equivalent to that of diagnoses obtained from structured diagnostic interviews. The items of the TSQ are simple and easy to understand, the Yes/No format simplifies responses, and a single scale makes this measure very practical for use in health care settings.

Impact of Events Scale (IES). The IES (Horowitz, Wilner, & Alvarez, 1979) was one of the first scales developed to assess post-trauma psychopathology and hence has been widely used with a variety of trauma populations including combat veterans, assault survivors, and accident victims. It is a 15-item instrument that assesses two dimensions of trauma symptoms: Intrusion and Avoidance. Items are scored for frequency as 1 (not at all), 2 (rarely), 3 (sometimes), or 4 (often). Any subscale score over 19, or a combined score over 38, is considered to be clinically significant.

Reliability was supported for the IES, in that the internal consistency was .78 for the Intrusion subscale, and .82 for the Avoidance. The test-retest reliability at one week was .87 for the total score, .89 for the Intrusion subscale, and .79 for the Avoidance subscale. The two subscales correlated .42, indicating fair agreement, and supporting each subscale's individual use. Cluster analysis (Horowitz et al., 1979) and factor analysis (Zilberg, Weiss, & Horowitz, 1982) supported the independence of the two subscales. Split-half reliability was found to be .86 (Zilberg et al., 1982), and the internal consistency of the subscales was supported (alphas ranged from .79–.92). The IES was sensitive to treatment effects in rape victims (Foa, Rothbaum, Riggs, & Murdock, 1991; Resick et al., 1988).

A major drawback of the IES is that it does not assess all aspects of PTSD and therefore cannot yield direct information about diagnostic categorization or the severity of the disorder. In a revised version of the IES, hyperarousal symptoms were added and the revised scale was validated on several samples of emergency personnel and disaster victims (IES-R; Weiss & Marmar, 1997). This extended version of the scale demonstrated excellent internal consistency across the various samples: .87–.92 for Intrusion, .84–.86 for Avoidance, and .79–.90 for Hyperarousal. The IES-R evidenced high test-retest reliability with earthquake victims (alphas ranged from .89–.94), but poorer reliability with emergency personnel (alphas ranged from .51–.59). Despite these additional items, the instrument does not fully correspond to the *DSM-IV* symptoms and continues to suffer from the drawback of the inability to fully measure the extent of PTSD symptoms.

Mississippi PTSD Scale (M-PTSD). This scale was initially developed for combat-related PTSD (Keane, Caddell, & Taylor, 1988) and is composed of 35 items scored on a five-point response scale that varies. Items are based on *DSM-III* symptoms of PTSD and associated features and fall into four categories: re-experiencing, withdrawal/numbing, arousal, and self-persecution. Respondents are asked to respond to items based on the time interval since they served in the military. In Vietnam veterans, internal consistency coefficients ranged from .94–.96, and test-retest reliability was .97 (Keane et al., 1988; McFall, Smith, Mackay, & Tarver, 1990). Sensitivity and specificity ranged from 88–93 percent based on varying cutoff scores for the two studies. Convergent validity was moderately supported in that the M-PTSD correlated from .46–.66 with measures of PTSD (McFall et al., 1990).

The Mississippi Scale was later extended to include civilian populations (Vreven, Gudanowski, King, & King, 1995). Respondents answer questions based on the frequency of symptoms "in the past." Satisfactory, albeit lower, internal consistency was demonstrated with civilians (alpha = .86). Convergent validity was not as strongly supported, as the civilian version corresponded weakly with the DIS-PTSD module. Another study has brought into question the validity of this measure in civilians, with the M-PTSD correlating higher with measures of general anxiety and depression than with two measures of PTSD in university students (Lauterbach, Vrana, King, & King, 1997).

To address these shortcomings, a 30-item revised version of the civilian scale was developed by Norris and Perilla (1996), evidencing satisfactory internal consistency for volunteers and hurricane victims (.86 and .88, respectively). The three subscales that correspond to the reexperiencing, avoidance, and arousal clusters of PTSD evidenced moderate to good internal consistency, with alphas ranging from .52–.79 for volunteers and .64–.84 for hurricane victims. Finally, an abbreviated version has been reported, with preliminary internal consistency demonstrated (alphas ranged from .83–.87; Fontana & Rosenheck, 1994).

A disadvantage of the M-PTSD is that it does not fully assess all symptom criteria in the *DSM-III-R*, nor has it been updated for the *DSM-IV*, and therefore cannot yield severity scores for PTSD or diagnostic status. Several studies have attempted to establish a cutoff score to indicate the presence or absence of PTSD, yet studies have used widely varying cutoff scores for validation. The use of cutoff scores also provides information that varies with sample characteristics. Finally, further psychometric evaluation regarding the scale's convergent and divergent validity is necessary.

Revised Purdue PTSD Scale (PPTSD-R). This 17-item scale was designed to assess *DSM-IV* symptom criteria following a variety of traumatic events (Lauterbach & Vrana, 1996). The three PTSD symptom categories are scored on a five-point frequency scale for dimensional or dichotomous information. The PPTSD-R was validated with male and female undergraduates who reported a variety of traumatic events. High internal consistency was supported for the total scale score (alpha coefficient of .91), as well as for the subscales (.84 for reexperiencing, .79 for avoidance, and .81 for arousal). Test-retest reliability was poor to moderate. The total scale score had a correlation of .72, and the three subscales ranged from .48–.71. Concurrent validity was supported, since the PPTSD-R correlated highly with measures of PTSD (alphas ranged from .50–.66), and correlated lower with measures of depression.

This scale offers the advantage of validation across men and women as well as a variety of traumas. However, there was a lack of stability in the reexperiencing subscale (test-retest of .48), and low sensitivity of the avoidance measure, which did not differentiate between trauma and nontrauma groups.

Penn Inventory for Post-traumatic Stress (Penn). This 26-item scale measures PTSD severity according to the *DSM-III-R* as well as other post-trauma reactions (Hammarberg, 1992). Each item consists of four sentences, scored 0–3, that represent varying levels of frequency and severity. Respondents choose the sentence that best describes them. The Penn Inventory exhibited high internal consistency (.94) and test-retest reliability (.96) in a sample of male combat veterans and nonveterans. Since the scale cannot determine the diagnosis or severity of PTSD, it relies on a cutoff score of 35 to indicate diagnosis of PTSD. Although this cutoff score was found to provide high sensitivity (.90) and specificity (1.0), considerably lower specificity was reported upon replication (.61). Divergent validity was not supported because the Penn correlated more highly with measures of depression than those measuring a similar construct.

There exist several limitations to this inventory, including the use of cutoff scores that may vary across sample characteristics as discussed earlier. In addition, this inventory lacks complete correspondence with the *DSM-IV*. Little evidence supports its use with female trauma victims and nonveteran samples. The complexity of responding has not been assessed, and the format of presentation of items may be confusing to individuals with lower reading levels. Finally, additional variable specificity across samples of veterans would be beneficial.

MMPI Scales. Two scales to assess PTSD have been derived from the Minnesota Multiphasic Personality Inventory (MMPI; Hathaway & McKinley, 1951) and its revised version, the MMPI-2 (Butcher et al., 1989). The first is the Keane PTSD scale (PK scale; Keane, Malloy, & Fairbank, 1984) composed of 49 items that empirically discriminate between combat veterans with PTSD from those with alternate psychiatric disorders. A cutoff score is used to indicate the likely presence of PTSD. The PK correctly classified 82 percent of those diagnosed with PTSD. The PK scale has undergone extensive validity testing, given that the empirically derived nature of the scale does not explicitly measure symptoms of PTSD. It correlated significantly with measures of intrusion, arousal, and cognitive interference to establish concurrent validity with Vietnam veterans (Watson, Juba, Anderson, & Manifold, 1990). Sensitivity estimates for male war veterans range from .67 to .87 across studies (Query, Megran, & McDonald, 1986; Watson, Kucala, & Manifold, 1986), and specificity estimates range from .74–.94 (Orr et al., 1990; Watson et al., 1986). The scale's ability to differentiate individuals with and without PTSD is inconsistent, with estimates ranging from .53–.95 (Cannon, Bell, Andrews, & Finkelstein, 1987; Watson et al., 1986). The development of the MMPI-2 led to minor revisions of the PK scale, with moderate correlations between the two scales reported (.64–.80; Albrecht et al., 1994; Litz et al., 1991). In a traumatized and psychiatric civilian population, a cutoff score of 19 yielded correct classification of 89 percent of PTSD cases for traumatized civilians and 85 percent sensitivity with psychiatric conditions (Koretsky & Peck, 1990). Convergent validity was also examined in 70 trauma victims, mixed veterans and civilians. The PK scale correlated highly with the CAPS (.84) and the IES (.79). However, the correlation was just as high with a general distress measure (.82).

The second scale derived from the MMPI is the PS, composed of 60 items (Schlenger & Kulka, 1989). Much less psychometric validation is available for the PS scale. However, high correlations between the PK and PS scales have been noted, ranging from .92–.96 (Litz et al., 1991; Miller, Goldberg, & Streiner, 1995).

Several considerations should be noted when evaluating the PK and PS scales. First, the reliability and validity are especially vulnerable to the specific characteristics of the particular sample used due to the empirical, rather than clinical, development of the scales. These scales thus require repeated validation across a variety of populations. Second, the items of the two scales do not correspond to the DSM symptoms, so their conceptual relationship to PTSD is ambiguous. Third, the MMPI is a lengthy scale to complete, and shorter measures targeting PTSD symptoms would make more sense in screening environments that do not utilize the MMPI as a matter of routine assessment.

CONCLUSION

Accurate assessment is critical to all interventions, particularly those that are behaviorally oriented. Assessment and treatment procedures are closely linked, in that continuing evaluation of problem behaviors throughout an intervention guides treatment and monitors response. It also provides feedback to patients regarding progress and areas for continued work. Although useful information can be gained from self-monitoring and clinical interviews, it is important to incorporate the use of objective, standardized measures with established psychometric properties to provide accurate assessment of PTSD and related problems. Of the standardized measures, only structured diagnostic interviews and one self-report measure, the PTDS, provide information about all six criteria of PTSD in the *DSM-IV*. The PTDS has the advantage of validation across a wide variety of traumas. The other self-report measures reviewed do not fully establish a diagnosis of PTSD given either incomplete correspondence to the 17 symptom items or incomplete assessment of the other PTSD criteria. All of the self-report measures specify the presence or absence of certain symptoms, and the majority assess the severity of those symptoms. Information about the nature of the event, duration of symptoms, or interference of symptoms in daily functioning is not obtained. Several instruments were validated on a single trauma population, although the CAPS, PTDS, IES, and TSQ do offer the advantage of assessing PTSD symptomatology across a variety of trauma populations.

REFERENCES

Albrecht, N. N., Talbert, F. S., Albrecht, J. M., Boudewyns, P. A., Hyer, L. A., Touze, J., et al. (1994). A comparison of MMPI and MMPI-2 in PTSD assessment. *Journal of Clinical Psychology, 50,* 578–585.

American Psychiatric Association (APA). (1980). *Diagnostic and statistical manual of mental disorders* (3rd ed.). Washington DC: Author.

American Psychiatric Association (APA). (1987). *Diagnostic and statistical manual of mental disorders* (3rd ed., rev.). Washington DC: Author.

American Psychiatric Association (APA). (1994). *Diagnostic and statistical manual of mental disorders* (4th ed.). Washington DC: Author.

Blake, D. D., Weathers, F. W., Nagy, L. M., Kaloupek, D. G., Klauminzer, G., Charney, D. S., et al. (1990). A clinician rating scale for assessing current and lifetime PTSD: The CAPS-1. *The Behavior Therapist, 13,* 187–188.

Blanchard, E. B., Gerardi, R. J., Kolb, L. C., & Barlow, D. H. (1986). The utility of the anxiety disorders interview schedule in the diagnosis of post-traumatic stress disorder (PTSD) in Vietnam veterans. *Behaviour Research Therapy, 24,* 577–580.

Blanchard, E. B., Hickling, E. J., Taylor, A. E., Forneris, C. A., Loos, W., & Jaccard, J. (1995). Effects of varying scoring rules of the Clinician-Administered PTSD Scale (CAPS) for the diagnosis of post-traumatic stress disorder in motor vehicle accident victims. *Behaviour Research Therapy, 33,* 471–474.

Breslau, N., Davis, G. C. D., Andreski, P., & Peterson, E. (1991). Traumatic events and post-traumatic stress disorder in an urban population of young adults. *Archives of General Psychiatry, 48,* 218–222.

Brewin, C. R., Rose, S., Andrews, B., Green, J., Tata, P., McEvedy, C., et al. (2002). Brief screening instrument for post-traumatic stress disorder. *British Journal of Psychiatry, 181,* 158–162.

Butcher, J. N., Dahlstrom, W. G., Graham, J. R., Tellegen, A., & Kaemmer, B. (1989). *MMPI-2: Manual for administering and scoring.* Minneapolis: University of Minnesota Press.

Cannon, D. S., Bell, W. E., Andrews, R. H., & Finkelstein, A. S. (1987). Correspondence between MMPI PTSD measures and clinical diagnosis. *Journal of Personality Assessment, 51,* 517–521.

Davidson, J. R. T., Hughes, D., Blazer, D. G., & George, L. K. (1991). Post-traumatic stress disorder in the community: An epidemiological study. *Psychological Medicine, 21,* 713–721.

Davidson, J., Smith, R., & Kudler, H. (1989). Validity and reliability of the DSM-III criteria for post-traumatic stress disorder: Experience with a structured interview. *Journal of Nervous and Mental Disease, 177,* 336–341.

DiNardo, P. A., & Barlow, D. H. (1988). *Anxiety Disorders Interview Scale–Revised.* Albany, NY: Center for Phobia and Anxiety Disorders.

DiNardo, P. A., Moras, K., Barlow, D. H., Rapee, R. M., & Brown, T. A. (1993). Reliability of DSM-III-R anxiety disorder categories. *Archives of General Psychiatry, 50,* 251–256.

Ellis, E. M., Atkeson, B. M., & Calhoun, K. S. (1981). An assessment of long-term reaction to rape. *Journal of Abnormal Psychology, 90,* 263–266.

Foa, E. B., Cashman, L., Jaycox, L., & Perry, K. (1997). The validation of a self-report measure of post-traumatic stress disorder: The Post-traumatic Diagnostic Scale. *Psychological Assessment, 9,* 445–451.

Foa, E. B., Dancu, C. V., Hembree, E. A., Jaycox, L. H., Meadows, E. A., & Street, G. P. (1999). A comparison of exposure therapy, stress inoculation training, and their combination for reducing post-traumatic stress disorder in female assault victims. *Journal of Consulting and Clinical Psychology, 67,* 194–200.

Foa, E. B., Riggs, D. S., Dancu, C. V., & Rothbaum, B. O. (1993). Reliability and validity of a brief instrument for assessing post-traumatic stress disorder. *Journal of Traumatic Stress, 6,* 459–473.

Foa, E. B., Riggs, D. S., & Gershuny, B. S. (1995). Arousal, numbing, and intrusion: Symptom structure of PTSD following assault. *American Journal of Psychiatry, 152,* 116–120.

Foa, E. B., & Rothbaum, B. O. (1998). *Treating the trauma of rape: Cognitive-behavioral therapy for PTSD.* New York: Guilford Press.

Foa, E. B., Rothbaum, B. O., Riggs, D., & Murdock, T. (1991). Treatment of post-traumatic stress disorder in rape victims: A comparison between cognitive-behavioral procedures and counseling. *Journal of Consulting and Clinical Psychology, 59,* 715–723.

Fontana, A., & Rosenheck, R. (1994). A short form of the Mississippi Scale for measuring change in combat related PTSD. *Journal of Traumatic Stress, 7,* 407–414.

Frank, E., & Stewart, B. D. (1984). Depressive symptoms in rape victims. *Journal of Affective Disorders, 1,* 269–277.

Hammarberg, M. (1992). Penn Inventory for Post-traumatic Stress Disorder: Psychometric properties. *Psychological Assessment, 4*, 67–76.

Hathaway, S. R., & McKinley, J. C. (1951). *Minnesota Multiphasic Personality Inventory: Manual for administration and scoring.* New York: Psychological Corporation.

Helzer, J. E., Robins, L. N., & McEvoy, L. (1987). Post-traumatic stress disorder in the general population. *New England Journal of Medicine, 317*, 1630–1634.

Horowitz, M., Wilner, N., & Alverez, W. (1979). Impact of Event Scale: A measure of subjective distress. *Psychosomatic Medicine, 41*, 209–218.

Keane, T. M., Caddell, J. M., & Taylor, K. (1988). Mississippi Scale for Combat-Related Post-traumatic Stress Disorder: Three studies in reliability and validity. *Journal of Consulting and Clinical Psychology, 56*, 85–90.

Keane, T. M., Malloy, P. F., & Fairbank, J. A. (1984). Empirical development of an MMPI subscale for the assessment of combat-related post-traumatic stress disorder. *Journal of Consulting and Clinical Psychology, 52*, 888–891.

Keane, T. M., & Penk, W. (1988). The prevalence of post-traumatic stress disorder [Letter to the editor]. *New England Journal of Medicine, 318*, 1690–1691.

Kilpatrick, D. G., & Veronen, L. J. (1984). Treatment for rape-related problems: Crisis intervention is not enough. In L. Cohen, W. Claiborn, & G. Specter (Eds.), *Crisis intervention* (2nd ed.). New York: Human Sciences Press.

Kilpatrick, D. G., Veronen, L. J., & Resick, P. A. (1979). The aftermath of rape: Recent empirical findings. *American Journal of Orthopsychiatry, 49*, 658–659.

Koretsky, M., & Peck, A. (1990). Validation and cross-validation of the PTSD subscale of the MMPI with civilian trauma victims. *Journal of Clinical Psychology, 46*, 296–300.

Kulka, R. A., Schlenger, W. E., Fairbank, J. A., Jordan, B. K., Hough, R. L., Marmar, C. R., et al. (1990). *Trauma and the Vietnam War generation: Report of findings from the National Vietnam Veterans Readjustment Study.* New York: Brunner/Mazel.

Lauterbach, D., & Vrana, S. (1996). Three studies on the reliability and validity of a self-report measure of post-traumatic stress disorder. *Assessment, 3*, 17–25.

Lauterbach, D., Vrana, S., King, D. W., & King, L. A. (1997). Psychometric properties of the Civilian Version of the Mississippi PTSD Scale. *Journal of Traumatic Stress, 10*, 499–513.

Litz, B. T., Penk, W. E., Walsh, S., Hyer, L., Blake, D. D., Marx, B., et al. (1991). Similarities and differences between MMPI and MMPI-2 applications to the assessment of post-traumatic stress disorder. *Journal of Personality Assessment, 57*, 238–253.

McFall, M. E., Smith, D. E., Mackay, P. W., & Tarver, D. J. (1990). Reliability and validity of Mississippi Scale for Combat-Related Post-traumatic Stress Disorder. *Psychological Assessment, 2*, 114–121.

McFarlane, A. C. (1988a). The longitudinal course of post-traumatic morbidity: The range of outcomes and their predictors. *Journal of Nervous and Mental Disease, 176*, 30–39.

McFarlane, A. C. (1988b). The phenomenology of post-traumatic stress disorders following a natural disaster. *Journal of Nervous and Mental Disease, 176*, 22–29.

Miller, H. R., Goldberg, J. O., & Streiner, D. L. (1995). What's in a name? The MMPI-2 PTSD scales. *Journal of Clinical Psychology, 51*, 626–631.

Nadelson, C. C., Notman, M. T., Zackson, H., & Gornick, J. (1982). A follow-up study of rape victims. *American Journal of Psychiatry, 139,* 1266–1270.

Norris, F., & Perilla, J. (1996). Reliability, validity, and cross-language stability of the Revised Civilian Mississippi Scale for PTSD. *Journal of Traumatic Stress, 9,* 285–298.

Orr, S. P., Claiborn, J. M., Altman, B., Forgue, D. F., de Jong, J. B., Pitman, R. K., et al. (1990). Psychometric profile of post-traumatic stress disorder, anxious, and healthy Vietnam veterans: Correlations with psychophysiological responses. *Journal of Consulting and Clinical Psychology, 58,* 329–335.

Query, W. T., Megran, J., & McDonald, G. (1986). Applying post-traumatic stress disorder MMPI subscale to World War II POW veterans. *Journal of Clinical Psychology, 42,* 315–317.

Resick, P. A., Jordan, C. G., Girelli, S. A., Hutter, C. K., & Marhoefer-Dvorak, S. (1988). A comparative victim study of behavioral group therapy for sexual assault victims. *Behavior Therapy, 19,* 385–401.

Riggs, D. S., Rothbaum, B. O., & Foa, E. B. (1995). A prospective examination of symptoms of post-traumatic stress disorder in victims of non-sexual assault. *Journal of Interpersonal Violence, 2,* 201–214.

Robins, L. N., Helzer, J. E., Croughan, J. L., & Ratcliff, K. S. (1981). National Institute of Mental Health Diagnostic Interview Schedule: Its history, characteristics, and validity. *Archives of General Psychiatry, 38,* 381–389.

Robins, L. N., Helzer, J. E., Croughan, J. L., Williams, J. B., & Spitzer, R. L. (1981). *NIMH Diagnostic Interview Schedule, Version III* (Publication No. ADM-T-42-3 [5-81,8-81]). Rockville, MD: NIMH, Public Health Service.

Rothbaum, B. O. (1997). A controlled study of eye movement desensitization and reprocessing in the treatment of post-traumatic stress disordered sexual assault victims. *Bulletin of the Menninger Clinic, 61,* 1–18.

Rothbaum, B. O., Foa, E. B., Riggs, D., Murdock, T., & Walsh, W. (1992). A prospective examination of post-traumatic stress disorder in rape victims. *Journal of Traumatic Stress, 5,* 455–475.

Schlenger, W., & Kulka, R. A. (1989). *PTSD scale development for the MMPI-2.* Research Triangle Park, NC: Research Triangle Institute.

Solomon, Z., Mikulincer, M., & Benbenishty, R. (1989). Locus of control and combat-related post-traumatic stress disorder: The intervening role of battle intensity, threat appraisal and coping. *British Journal of Clinical Psychology, 28,* 131–144.

Spitzer, R. L., Williams, J. B. W., Gibbon, M., & First, M. B. (1990). *Structured Clinical Interview for DSM-III-R–Patient ed.* (SCID-P). New York: Biometrics Research Department, New York State Psychiatric Institute.

Stieglitz, R., Frommberger, U., Foa, E. B., & Berger, M. (2001). Evaluation of the German version of the PTSD Symptom Scale (PSS). *Psychopathology, 34,* 128–133.

van der Kolk, B. A., Dreyfuss, D., Michaels, M., Shera, D., Berkowitz, R., Fisler, R. E., et al. (1994). Fluoxetine in post-traumatic stress disorder. *Journal of Clinical Psychiatry, 55,* 517–522.

Vreven, D. L., Gudanowski, D. M., King, L. A., & King, D. W. (1995). The Civilian Version of the Mississippi PTSD Scale: A psychometric evaluation. *Journal of Traumatic Stress, 8,* 91–109.

Watson, C., Juba, M., Anderson, P., & Manifold, V. (1990). What does the Keane et al. PTSD Scale for the MMPI measure? *Journal of Clinical Psychology, 46,* 600–606.

Watson, C., Juba, M., Manifold, V., Kucala, T., & Anderson, P. (1991). The PTSD Interview: Rationale, description, reliability, and concurrent validity of a DSM-III based technique. *Journal of Clinical Psychology, 47*, 179–185.

Watson, C. G., Kucala, T., & Manifold, V. (1986). A cross-validation of the Keane and Penk MMPI scales as measures of post-traumatic stress disorder. *Journal of Clinical Psychology, 42*, 727–732.

Watson, C., Plemel, D., DeMotts, J., Howard, M., Tuorila, J., Moog, R., et al. (1994). A comparison of four PTSD measures' convergent validities in Vietnam veterans. *Journal of Traumatic Stress, 7*, 75–82.

Weiss, D. S., & Marmar, C. R. (1997). The Impact of Event Scale–Revised. In J. P. Wilson & T. M. Keane (Eds.), *Assessing psychological trauma and PTSD* (pp. 399–411). New York: Guilford Press.

Zilberg, N. J., Weiss, D. S., & Horowitz, M. J. (1982). Impact of Event Scale: A cross-validation study and some empirical evidence supporting a conceptual model of stress response syndromes. *Journal of Consulting and Clinical Psychology, 50*, 407–414.

PART III

MENTAL DISORDERS AND FORENSIC PSYCHOLOGY

CHAPTER 17

CONDUCT DISORDERS AND IMPULSE CONTROL IN CHILDREN

STEVEN G. LITTLE AND K. ANGELEQUE AKIN-LITTLE
UNIVERSITY OF THE PACIFIC

UTA H. MOCNIAK
HOFSTRA UNIVERSITY

On October 1, 1997, Luke Woodham, a high school student in Pearl, Mississippi, fatally stabbed his mother with a butcher knife before heading to his school, where he murdered two others and wounded many more. Within the next 20 months there were widely publicized school shootings in Paducah, Kentucky; Jonesboro, Arkansas; Edinboro, Pennsylvania; Springfield, Oregon; Richmond, Virginia; Fayetteville, Tennessee; Littleton, Colorado; and Conyers, Georgia. The most extreme of these took place at Columbine High School in Littleton, Colorado, where Eric Klebold and Dylan Harris opened fire on students and teachers on April 20, 1999, killing 13 and injuring many more. These incidents alarmed both politicians and citizens and led to calls for increased security in schools, adult punishment for juvenile offenders, and other similar actions. In reality, however, schools are one of the safest places for children, even in large cities such as Chicago and Los Angeles (Hyman & Snook, 1999). In addition, according to the FBI's *Uniform Crime Report*, juvenile arrests for serious crimes fell nearly 11 percent from 1997 to 1998, double the 5.4 percent drop seen for adults over the same time period (Youth Crime, 1999). What makes these statistics even more impressive is that the drop was seen at a time when the population of those under age 18 had grown. Although crime statistics indicate a drop in juvenile offenders, serious incidents such as those mentioned make the identification and treatment of those at risk for such behaviors of paramount importance. It is also clear that adult criminal behavior is often the result of a developmental progression from childhood behavior problems to delinquency in adolescence to adult offending (Babinski, Hartsough, & Lambert, 1999). The aim of this chapter is to identify and discuss conduct disorder and other disorders occurring in childhood involving difficulties in impulse control that increase an individual's likelihood of developing and following such a progression.

The *Diagnostic and Statistical Manual of Mental Disorders*, fourth edition (*DSM-IV*) (American Psychiatric Association, 1994) and the *International Classification of Diseases* (ICD-10) (World Health Organization, 1992) are the primary diagnostic references for mental health professionals, including psychologists, psychiatrists, and social workers. The *DSM-IV* provides a relatively brief description of each disorder along with diagnostic criteria. However, it provides relatively little information on assessment, treatment, and relevance to specific populations. Since the focus of this chapter is on children, those disorders that *DSM-IV* classifies as usually first diagnosed in infancy, childhood, or adolescence will be emphasized, with a specific focus on Conduct Disorder and Attention Deficit Hyperactivity Disorder.

CONDUCT DISORDER

Conduct Disorder (CD) encompasses an extensive range of repetitive and persistent antisocial behaviors that include aggressive acts, setting fires, running away, theft, vandalism, and deceitfulness. These behaviors are all considered to violate the basic rights of others or major age-appropriate societal rules or norms (American Psychiatric Association, 1994; Kazdin, 1998). However, it is important to note that many behaviors indicative of CD emerge over the normal course of development. For example, lying, aggression, or stealing may occur at different points in the typical development of a child or adolescent. Usually, these behaviors dissipate over time; do not interfere with normal academic, social, or occupational functioning; and do not forecast unfavorable outcomes in adulthood (Kazdin, 1998). However, these behaviors can, if left untreated, progress to severe antisocial acts and to the diagnosis of Conduct Disorder or, in adulthood, Antisocial Personality Disorder (Kazdin, 1995).

Loeber, Farrington, Stouthamer-Loeber, and Van Kammen (1998) suggest three criteria to assess whether or not problem behaviors fit the description of deviance. The first concern is the persistence of the deviant behavior. Clearly, if problem behaviors persist throughout a time period when most youngsters of the same age would have outgrown such behaviors, the problem behaviors would be labeled deviant. The second criterion labels a problem behavior as deviant based upon severity of the impairment (e.g., conduct disorder causes the child to be expelled from school). The third and final area to be considered is the result of the behavior. If the problem behavior results in harm to others (e.g., stealing another's property), that behavior is considered deviant.

Definition

The most commonly accepted definition of CD is that provided in the *DSM-IV* (American Psychiatric Association, 1994). According to the *DSM-IV*, the diagnostic criteria for CD are as follows:

A. A repetitive and persistent pattern of behavior in which the basic rights of others or major age-appropriate societal norms or rules are violated, as manifested by the presence of three (or more) of the following criteria in the past 12 months, with at least one criterion present in the past six months:
   Aggression to people and animals
   (1) often bullies, threatens, or intimidates others
   (2) often initiates physical fights
   (3) has used a weapon that can cause serious physical harm to others (e.g., a bat, broken bottle, knife, gun)
   (4) has been physically cruel to people
   (5) has been physically cruel to animals
   (6) has stolen while confronting a victim (e.g., mugging, purse snatching, extortion, armed robbery)
   (7) has forced someone into sexual activity
   Destruction of property
   (8) has deliberately engaged in fire setting with the intention of causing serious damage
   (9) has deliberately destroyed others' property (other than by fire setting)
   Deceitfulness or theft
   (10) has broken into someone else's house, building, or car
   (11) often lies to obtain goods or favors or to avoid obligations (i.e., "cons" others)
   (12) has stolen items of nontrivial value without confronting a victim (e.g., shoplifting, but without breaking and entering; forgery)
   Serious violations of rules
   (13) often stays out at night despite parental prohibitions, beginning before age 13 years
   (14) has run away from home overnight at least twice while living in parental or parental surrogate home (or once without returning for a lengthy period)
   (15) is often truant from school, beginning before age 13 years
B. The disturbance in behavior causes clinically significant impairment in social, academic, or occupational functioning.
C. If the individual is age 18 years or older, criteria are not met for Antisocial Personality Disorder. (pp. 90–91)

The *DSM-IV* further lists subtypes and severity specifiers. The two subtypes include Childhood-Onset Type, which is defined as "onset of at least one criterion characteristic of Conduct Disorder prior to age 10 years" (p. 91), and Adolescent-Onset Type, which is defined as "absence of any criteria characteristic of Conduct Disorder prior to age 10 years" (p. 91). Severity specifiers include mild, moderate, and severe. The *DSM-IV* additionally states that some features of CD are present in Oppositional Defiant Disorder (ODD), and when criteria for both CD and ODD are met, a diagnosis of CD *only* (emphasis added) should be made. Similarly, Attention-Deficit Hyperactivity Disorder (ADHD) behaviors may involve disruptive behaviors similar to CD behaviors. However, children exhibiting ADHD behaviors do not typically engage in the severe rule-violating behavior commonly associated with CD, and when both CD and ADHD criteria are met, both diagnoses should be made. The relationship between CD and depression in children has also been investigated. It has been suggested that some children may engage in antisocial behavior to mask depression (Baum, 1989). This is especially true for the male population (Puig-Antich, 1982).

Prevalence

CD constitutes the highest rates of child referrals to mental health facilities. Figures for the number of outpatient referrals range from one-third to two-thirds of the total number of child referrals to these facilities (Baum, 1989). The *DSM-IV* (APA, 1994) states that although factors related to the population sampled influence prevalence, males are consistently diagnosed at a higher rate than females. Specifically, males under the age of 18 exhibit rates ranging from 6 to 16 percent of the population, whereas female rates range from 2 to 9 percent. Geographical location also appears to play a role in the prevalence of CD, with urban rates approximately double rural rates for both boys and girls (Sholevar & Sholevar, 1995). In addition, a large percentage (84%) of individuals referred for antisocial behavior during childhood receive a psychiatric diagnosis in adulthood (Kazdin, 1998).

Research also suggests that the individual providing information may influence the rate of diagnosis (Baum, 1989). Teachers have been found more likely to rate a child as exhibiting CD-related behaviors than parents (Offord, Adler, & Boyle, 1986). Age also appears to be an important variable in the diagnosis of CD, with rates tending to be higher for adolescents (approximately 7%) than for children (approximately 4%) (Offord, Boyle, & Racine, 1991). Additionally, ethnicity may be a significant factor in predicting who will be diagnosed with CD. African-American children are more likely to exhibit antisocial behaviors and be diagnosed with CD than Caucasians (Gray-Ray & Ray, 1990; Fabrega, Ulrich, & Mezzich, 1993). Furthermore, it is important to note that African Americans constitute 12 percent of the population yet account for 21 percent of all juvenile arrests (McCoy, 1997). In conclusion, it appears that males, adolescents, individuals living in urban areas, and African Americans are most likely to be identified as CD.

Risk Factors

Kazdin (1998) has characterized risk factors for the onset of CD into three major categories: child factors, parent and family factors, and school-related factors. The operation of these risk factors is complex, with several factors interrelated and presenting simultaneously. In addition, risk factors may interact with one another either to exacerbate the problem (i.e., parental discord during early or mid childhood) (Wadsworth, 1979) or to minimize it (i.e., high SES and family size) (West, 1982).

Child Factors

Sholevar and Sholevar (1995) identify a child's temperament as being a major risk factor in the development of CD. Children who demonstrate oppositional patterns, a negative mood, and who are less adaptable to change are more likely to be referred than are children with other temperamental characteristics (Thomas & Chess, 1977). Biological and neuropsychological factors have also been shown to influence rates of CD. Van Goozen, Matthys, Cohen-Kettenis, Thijssen, and van Engeland (1998) found that children diagnosed with CD exhibited higher levels of adrenal androgens than normal controls. Neurodevelopmental impairment (i.e., deficits in verbal and executive functions) have been found to be indirect predictors of CD (Olds et al., 1998). Academic and intellectual functioning, early onset of antisocial behavior, and social skills deficits have all also been implicated as risk factors (Kazdin, 1998).

Parent and Family Factors

A wide variety of parent and family factors have been found to be related to the development and progression of CD. Parental factors such as psychopathology and criminal behavior, as well as ineffective and inconsistent parenting, are a major risk factor (Sholevar & Sholevar, 1995). Additionally, Kazdin (1998) has identified harsh and inconsistent parental punishment; poor monitoring of the child; low levels of parental warmth, affection, and emotional support; marital discord; family size (i.e., families with more children); siblings with antisocial behavior; and socioeconomic disadvantage as risk factors that contribute to the diagnosis of CD. Prenatal maternal behavior such as alcohol consumption, cigarette smoking, and use of illicit drugs may also contribute to the development of child antisocial behaviors (Olds et al., 1998).

School-Related Factors

Kazdin (1998) and Sholevar and Sholevar (1995) both discuss the correlation between school-related factors and CD. These factors include attending school where little emphasis is placed on academic work, the poor physical condition of the school building(s), infrequent use of teacher praise, low teacher expectancy, and teacher unavailability to deal with students' problems.

Developmental Progression

Because of the severity and persistence of CD-related behaviors across the lifespan, there is great concern about the causal circumstances that lead to such behaviors and how best to predict and impede their progress. Often behaviors associated with CD emerge in a gradual pattern, starting with less severe or more intermittent types of behavior (Lahey et al., 1995). Lahey and colleagues also found stability of CD behaviors, with 87.7 percent of boys diagnosed as CD maintaining this diagnosis over the subsequent three years. Similarly, Farrington (1992) found that 76 percent of boys between the ages of 10 and 16 who were convicted of criminal activity, a factor related to CD diagnosis, were reconvicted between ages 17 and 24.

Patterson and his colleagues have studied conduct disorder and antisocial behavior in children and adolescents for almost 30 years. Their research facility, the Oregon Social Learning Center (OSLC), has from the beginning asked two major questions: "What causes children's antisocial behavior?" and "What can be done to help families change these problem behaviors?" (Patterson, Reid, & Dishion, 1992, p. 1). Their research on maladaptive behavior in children and adolescents and their attempts to treat families and children with CD led Patterson and colleagues to create what they refer to as the *coercion model*.

The coercion model consists of four distinct stages labeled according to the developmental milestone inherent in each. The first developmental milestone is categorized as basic training. The central tenet is that training for antisocial behaviors takes place in the home and that family members are the trainers. In the home setting, the child discovers that aversive behaviors such as whining, crying, yelling, or having temper tantrums are effective. Specifically, the child learns that his or her unpleasant behaviors stop the aversive behaviors of other family members. Over the course of several hundred trials, the child's pattern of antisocial behaviors increases and becomes a fundamental component of his or her behavioral repertoire. Eventually, the child will have literally coerced the family into allowing him or her into unsupervised activities (i.e., street time) that may lead to more antisocial behavior, such as an association with a deviant peer group.

The second developmental milestone involves the reaction of the social environment. The major developmental hurdles in this stage are the development of successful peer relations and satisfactory academic progress. However, children exhibiting antisocial behaviors tend to be at grave risk for failure in both the social and achievement arenas. Furthermore, these children are often rejected by their parents at this stage because of their abrasive interactional style (Patterson, 1986). Peer rejection, parental rejection, and poor academic performance often lead to a depressed mood, with many of these children exhibiting recurring bouts of sadness (Patterson et al., 1992).

The third developmental milestone involves increased association with deviant peers and the resultant "polishing" of antisocial skills. At this stage children are typically 12 to 13 years of age and are continuing to experience failure in both the academic and social arenas. They are rejected by nondeviant peers and parents and they continue to exhibit negative attitudes toward school and authority. Dishion, McCord, and Poulin (1999) use the term *deviancy training* to describe how deviant friendships can have a powerful influence on escalations in problem behavior in adolescents. Patterson, Dishion, and Yoerger (cited in Dishion, McCord, & Poulin, 1999) examined the deviancy training process and found evidence to suggest that adolescent friendships based on deviant interests provide the mechanism by which problem behaviors intensify via peers' positive reactions contingent on deviant talk and behavior. These relationships undermine healthy development (Hartup, 1996) and play an important role in the development of delinquent behavior.

The fourth and final developmental milestone is the emergence of the career antisocial adult. This stage is characterized by a marginal existence in adulthood, unhappy marriages, divorce, chaotic employment career, and often institutionalization for crimes or mental disorders (Caspi, Elder, & Bem, 1987). Patterson and colleagues (1992) write that one of their primary goals in formulating this coercion model was to identify children at risk for the CD diagnosis and to aid in preventing antisocial behavior in children. Kazdin (1995, 1997, 1998) has consistently discussed this model as being the most prominent of possible environmental explanations for the development of CD.

The prognosis into adulthood for individuals with CD is not optimistic. Many studies have shown powerful effects into adulthood, including continued antisocial behavior. It has been known for a long time that aggressive behavior in childhood is very stable over time and conduct disorder is one of the most stable forms of child psychopathology (Robins, 1999). A diagnosis of CD in childhood or adolescence does not guarantee that the individual will qualify for a diagnosis of antisocial personality disorder after the age of 18 but a large number (25–40%; Robins, 1999) will.

Assessment

Because of the complexity and pervasive nature of CD, assessment requires a comprehensive evaluation of the child's functioning and psychosocial environment, involving multiple informants and multiple assessment techniques (Kamphaus & Frick, 1996). Kazdin (1995) recommends the utilization of self-report measures, reports of significant others, direct observations, and review of school and other records. Self-report measures are more likely to be of value with adolescents than with younger children because of children's inability to identify themselves as having problems (Sholevar & Sholevar, 1995). Reports of significant others (e.g., parents, teachers, peers) are the most widely used assessment tool (Kazdin, 1995). A number of standardized behavior rating scales (e.g., Child Behavior Checklist, Behavior Assessment Systems for Children) provide valid and reliable ratings of children's emotional and behavioral problems (McConaughy &

Ritter, 1995). Kazdin reports that studies have shown that parental evaluations of children correlate with clinicians' judgments of a child's dysfunction. The scales may be completed relatively quickly and can cover many symptom areas. In addition, behaviors such as fighting, yelling, arguing, and other overt behaviors are easily detected by parents and teachers and, consequently, are reported. More covert acts such as substance abuse or stealing may be more difficult to assess.

Direct observation of a child's behavior has been proven to be effective because observations do not depend on the interpretation of significant others. Further, these observations often lead to the discovery of important environmental contingencies that maintain inappropriate behavior. However, some limitations have been noted, such as reactivity, difficulty in assessing low-frequency behaviors such as fighting, and inability to assess cognitions and emotions (Kamphaus & Frick, 1996). Behavioral observations may take the form of event recording, duration recording, or time sampling. In conducting these observations, clinicians must specifically define target behaviors and train observers appropriately.

Evaluation of school records such as attendance, grades, detentions, and suspensions as well as police reports and juvenile records plays an important part of CD assessment. The nature of CD is such that it leaves its marks on societal institutions in which the individual is involved. Although official records can underestimate the incidence of antisocial behaviors, they also provide a necessary and important indicator of a possible CD diagnosis.

In addition, Sholevar and Sholevar (1995) recommend obtaining a careful and complete medical history. They note that CNS trauma is common among aggressive offenders and that overall, children with CD have far less favorable medical histories than nondelinquent children. When there are indications of possible trauma, assessment may include a neurological examination or neuropsychological testing. A detailed psychoeducational evaluation can also aid in identifying learning problems that may contribute to behavior problems, including school truancy.

Intervention/Treatment

Kazdin (1998) notes that a variety of approaches have been applied to the treatment of children and adolescents with CD. He identifies over 230 methods, including psychotherapy (individual and group), community-based treatments, residential treatments, pharmacotherapy, psychosurgery, and cognitive behavioral interventions. Unfortunately, many of these treatments have yet to be empirically validated. Kazdin does, however, present four approaches that meet his criteria for identifying promising treatments. These criteria include a theoretical rationale for etiology and treatment, research that supports this approach, and outcome data that illustrate that the treatment achieves behavior change. The following four treatments are identified by Kazdin as meeting his criteria: cognitive problem-solving skills training (PSST), parent management training (PMT), functional family therapy (FFT), and multisystemic therapy (MST).

Cognitive Problem-Solving Skills Training

Here the therapist assists in the development of interpersonal cognitive problem-solving skills. In this approach the client is taught a step-by-step problem-solving strategy using modeling, role play, and direct reinforcement. This treatment also usually combines a token or point system and gradually shapes increasingly more complex social responses.

Parent Management Training

PMT focuses on changing parental behavior in an attempt to alter the child's behavior. Many variations of PMT exist, but all models focus on providing treatment/training to parents, who then implement the procedures taught in their interactions with their child. The therapist rarely provides direct intervention with the child. Parents are trained in new ways to conceptualize problem behaviors and to respond more appropriately. The focus is frequently on developing parent-managed reinforcement programs for child behavior at home and behavior and performance at school.

Functional Family Therapy

FFT takes a systems, behavioral, and cognitive approach in attempting to understand and treat children and adolescents with CD. Child behavior is viewed in the context of the function that it serves in the family as a system. "The goal of treatment is to alter interaction and communication patterns in such a way as to foster more adaptive functioning" (Kazdin, 1998, p. 295). Social learning theories provide the conceptual framework for these approaches. Interventions developed based on Patterson and colleagues' (1992) coercion model would be examples of the FFT approach.

Multisystemic Therapy

MST is a family systems-based approach that maintains that behavior problems of the child develop within the context of the family and treatment should focus on the family. The intervention also affirms that the child is a member of multiple systems (e.g., family, peers, school, neighborhood, etc.) and intervention should include individual treatment of the child as well as family-based treatment and systematic intervention. Subsystem issues may also develop and also need to be dealt with. Because multiple influences are present, many different treatment techniques are utilized.

Dishion, McCord, and Poulin (1999) caution against the use of peer-training group interventions for early adolescents at high risk for delinquency. They present evidence from two intervention studies that suggests possible iatrogenic effects of treatment. Bringing these peers together provides subtle but powerful reinforcement for deviant talk and subsequent deviant behavior. They propose that reinforcement for verbalizations of deviant behavior in the form of laughter and attention will likely increase the frequency of that behavior and that these adolescents acquire meaning and value from this process that provides the cognitive motivation to engage in future incidents of delinquent behavior. They recommend against aggregating high-risk adolescents into intervention groups. As indicated in the examination of specific treatments, a program that focuses on parents or other adult caregivers may be a more efficacious treatment approach.

Forensic Considerations

By definition, children and adolescents diagnosed with Conduct Disorder are likely to eventually come into contact with the criminal justice system. Virtually every one of the 15 criteria listed in the *DSM-IV* for Conduct Disorder involves a behavior that, if manifested to a sufficient magnitude and chronicity, will eventually lead to arrest and possible incarceration. Otto, Greenstein, Johnson, and Friedman (1992, cited in Grisso, 1998) reviewed the epidemiological research with regard to the prevalence of childhood mental disorders in delinquent populations and found that Conduct Disorder is the most prevalent diagnosis with a rate "probably about 50% to 60%" (Grisso, 1998, p. 32).

Grisso warns that clinicians need to be aware of three issues in applying *DSM-IV* criteria for Conduct Disorder in the diagnostic process. First, there is a tendency to stop the diagnostic process when the criteria for CD are met. In reality, the rates of comorbidity with other disorders, especially ADHD, are high. Second, the *DSM-IV* (APA, 1994) states that "the Conduct Disorder diagnosis should be applied only when the behavior in question is symptomatic of an underlying dysfunction within the individual and not simply a reaction to the immediate social context" (p. 88). This suggests that not all individuals meeting the criteria for CD should be given the diagnosis. It is therefore important to investigate the relationship between social and cultural conditions in which past delinquent behavior has occurred before making a CD diagnosis. The third issue involves the relationship of CD to Antisocial Personality Disorder (APD) in adulthood. It is true that a "substantial portion" of CD children and youth will meet the criteria for APD in adulthood, but the *DSM-IV* also states that "in a majority of individuals, the disorder remits by adulthood" (APA, 1994, p. 89).

When delinquent youths exhibit behaviors indicative of CD or other mental disorders, it is important to identify the disorder so that this can be taken into consideration when decisions are being made about the individual's need for clinical services as part of rehabilitation. However, because so many delinquent youth meet the diagnostic criteria for CD, the usefulness of the diagnosis may be limited. It simply describes a repeated pattern of illegal, disruptive, or antisocial behaviors. One value of the diagnosis is in the subtypes, Childhood-Onset Type and Adolescent-Onset Type, since the prognosis is poorer when the onset of CD behavior is in childhood. It is also important to document the individual's responses to past rehabilitation efforts. It is likely that the individual's parents and schools as well as juvenile authorities have attempted some form of intervention. The courts may use information on the success of previous interventions in gauging the likelihood that future rehabilitation efforts will be worthwhile. Lack of previous success, however, does not mean that future treatment efforts should not be made. The clinician should be able to evaluate the appropriateness and treatment integrity of previous interventions in making recommendations to the court.

A final, but very important, issue to consider is the clinician's judgment of the individual's risk of harm to others. Grisso (1998) identifies critical factors that need to be considered. These include:

- *Past behavior*—Several dimensions of past behavior must be considered. The first is chronicity of the violent behavior. As mentioned earlier, aggressive behavior that predates adolescence suggests greater risk of the continuation of these behaviors. A second dimension is the context in which the aggressive behavior occurred. If violent and aggressive behaviors appear situation specific, and if those situations can be avoided and controlled, risk is diminished. Other important factors to consider are recency (more recent episodes indicating greater risk) and frequency (frequent aggression indicating greater risk).
- *Substance use*—Overall, substance use by violent and aggressive youths increases the risk of future violence.
- *Peers and community*—Individuals who have a history of associating with a violent peer group (i.e., gangs) are at higher risk for future violence because these groups place the individual in situations that may call for an aggressive response. They also provide the individual with greater accessibility to weapons.
- *Family conflict and aggression*—A history of aggression and conflict within the individual's family increases the risk of that individual engaging in future violence. In addition, it makes family approaches to treatment more difficult.
- *Social stressors and supports*—Factors in the family such as divorce, illness, or economic difficulties all place stress on the individual and family and place the individual at greater risk for future violence. It is important to consider potential future, as well as past, stress in evaluating risk.
- *Personality traits*—Anger, impulsivity, and lack of empathy are all personality traits that increase the risk of future violence.
- *Mental disorders*—Although the connection is not clear between mental disorders and risk for aggression, there are factors associated with a number of disorders such as depression, ADHD, schizophrenia, and Post-Traumatic Stress Disorder (PTSD) that may increase the risk for future aggression.
- *Opportunity*—Much violent behavior is situation or person specific. If that is the case, and those conditions have changed, risk may be diminished.

One must consider, however, that even in some situations where the target may no longer be available, aggression may be directed toward a substitute (e.g., a family member).

ATTENTION DEFICIT HYPERACTIVITY DISORDER

During the normal course of child development we expect children to be active, energetic, impulsive, and easily bored. That is part of what it means to be a child. In some children, however, these behaviors become persistent and far exceed the levels observed in peers. When activity levels remain high, when they have difficulty sustaining attention and interest in activities as well as their peers, when they have difficulty focusing on long-term goals, or when their impulse control and self-regulation are well below expectations for their age, we are no longer simply observing normal development (Barkley, 1996). These are behaviors that are characteristic of Attention Deficit Hyperactivity Disorder (ADHD) (APA, 1994). According to Loeber, Farrington, Stouthamer-Loeber, and Van Kammen (1998), "of all the psychiatric syndromes, attention deficit hyperactivity disorder (ADHD) and CD are the most closely related to delinquency" (p. 165).

Children with ADHD that is left untreated tend to be highly active, inattentive, and impulsive. These children have difficulty coping with the demands required for the successful development of self-regulation functions. They often experience frequent punishment and little positive reinforcement by parents and teachers, who may view them as lazy, unmotivated, selfish, thoughtless, and/or irresponsible (Barkley, 1996). They also frequently suffer from peer rejection and, as was discussed earlier in this chapter with regard to the development of CD, begin to associate with a deviant peer group who provide reinforcement for successively greater levels of deviant and delinquent behavior. Barkley (1996) describes this disorder as not just an attention deficit but "most likely a disorder of behavioral inhibition that interferes with self-regulation and the cross-temporal organization of behavior" (p. 64).

Definition

The most commonly accepted definition of ADHD is that provided in the *DSM-IV* (APA, 1994). According to the *DSM-IV*, the diagnostic criteria for ADHD is as follows:
- A. Either (1) or (2):
  - (1) Six or more of the following symptoms of **inattention** have persisted for at least 6 months to a degree that is maladaptive and inconsistent with developmental level:
      Inattention
      - (a) often fails to give close attention to details or makes careless mistakes in schoolwork, work, or other activities

(b) often has difficulty sustaining attention to tasks and play activities
(c) often does not seem to listen when spoken to directly
(d) often does not follow through on instructions and fails to finish schoolwork, chores, or duties in the workplace (not due to oppositional behavior or failure to understand instructions)
(e) often has difficulty organizing tasks and activities
(f) often avoids, dislikes, or is reluctant to engage in tasks that require sustained mental effort (such as schoolwork or homework)
(g) often loses things necessary for tasks or activities at school or at home (e.g., toys, school assignments, pencils, books, or tools)
(h) is often easily distracted by extraneous stimuli
(i) is often forgetful in daily activities

(2) Six (or more) of the following symptoms of **hyperactivity-impulsivity** have persisted for at least 6 months to a degree that is maladaptive and inconsistent with developmental level:

Hyperactivity
(a) often fidgets with hands or feet and squirms in seat
(b) often leaves seat in classroom or in other situations in which remaining seated is expected
(c) often runs about or climbs excessively in situations in which it is inappropriate (in adolescents or adults, may be limited to subjective feelings of restlessness)
(d) often has difficulty playing or engaging in leisure activities quietly
(e) is often "on the go" or often acts as if "driven by a motor"
(f) often talks excessively

Impulsivity
(g) often blurts out answers before questions have been completed
(h) has difficulty awaiting turn
(i) often interrupts or intrudes on others (e.g., butts into conversations or games)

B. Some hyperactive-impulsive or inattentive symptoms that caused impairment were present before age 7 years.
C. Some impairment from the symptoms is present in two or more settings (e.g., school [or work] and at home).
D. There must be clear evidence of clinically significant impairment in social, academic, or occupational functioning.
E. The symptoms do not occur exclusively during the course of a Pervasive Developmental Disorder, Schizophrenia, or other Psychotic Disorder and are not better accounted for by another mental disorder (e.g., Mood Disorder, Anxiety Disorder, Dissociative Disorder, or Personality Disorder). (pp. 83–85)

The definition of ADHD has been evolving over the past few decades. These behaviors were first thought of as having their origins in brain injury but without hard signs of brain damage or retardation. This assumption led to a diagnostic category of Minimal Brain Dysfunction. Interest in the specific behaviors of hyperactivity and impulse control in the 1960s led to a category in the *DSM-II* of Hyperkinetic Reaction of Childhood (APA, 1968). A growing body of research appeared in the 1970s that changed the understanding of the disorder to problems of sustained attention and impulsivity in addition to overactivity (Douglas, 1972). The term Attention Deficit Disorder (ADD) was first used with the publication of the *DSM-III* (APA, 1980). In addition, ADD had two types: with and without hyperactivity. The *DSM-III-R* (APA, 1987) had one classification of ADHD with a single threshold for diagnosis and no types. The diagnosis was geared toward children and the focus was on school and play. The *DSM-IV* returned to a conceptualization of the disorder that included subtypes and changed the wording of some diagnostic criteria to include examples to allow the diagnosis to be more easily made with adults.

Core Behavioral Difficulties in School

In school, children with ADHD often have difficulty sustaining attention to effortful tasks and their completion of independent seatwork is inconsistent. This occurrence frequently leads to poor classroom performance. Other associated academic problems include poor test performance; deficient study skills; disorganized notebooks, desks, and written reports; and so on. Externalizing behavior problems are often a teacher complaint as the child may often disrupt classroom activities by frequent calling out without permission, talking with classmates at inappropriate times, leaving their desk without permission, repetitive tapping of hands and feet, rocking in chairs, and the like (DuPaul & Stoner, 1994).

Related Difficulties

The most frequent correlate of ADHD is academic underachievement. Up to 80 percent of children with ADHD have been found to exhibit academic performance problems (Cantwell & Baker, 1991) and 20 to 30 percent are classified as also having a learning disability (DuPaul & Stoner, 1994). High rates of noncompliance and aggression are common, with Oppositional Defiant Disorder (ODD) being the most common codiagnosis with ADHD. Barkley, DuPaul, and McMurray (1990) report that up to 40 percent of children and 65 percent of adolescents with ADHD display significant ODD behaviors. Barkley, Fischer, Edelbrock, and Smallish (1990) report that serious antisocial behaviors such as stealing, physical aggression, or truancy are exhibited by 25 percent or more of students with ADHD, particularly at the secondary level. Disturbances in peer relations are also common, with sociometric studies finding high rates of peer rejection (DuPaul & Stoner, 1994). The most common deficiencies include inappropriate attempts to join peer activities, poor conversational skills (e.g., frequent interruptions, minimal attention to what others are saying), and employing aggressive solutions to interpersonal problems. Power and DuPaul (1996) indicated that individuals with a history of hyperactivity and impulsivity are at a much higher risk for antisocial outcomes, a result supported by longitudinal data (Babinski, Hartsough, & Lambert, 1999).

Prevalence of ADHD

The *DSM-IV* indicates a prevalence rate of 3–5 percent of school-age children, with rates in adolescence and adulthood unknown. That averages to a rate of about one child per classroom at the elementary and secondary levels. Barkley (1990) reports that as many as 40 percent of child referrals to clinics are for ADHD. In a review of six epidemiological studies, Szatmari (1992) found prevalence rates ranging from 2–6.3 percent but some studies have found prevalence rates as high as 20–24 percent (Offord et al., 1987). According to the *DSM-IV*, boys outnumber girls 3:1 to 9:1. The higher rates are with clinic-referred samples, which suggests that boys are more likely to be referred to clinics. This may be a function of the fact that boys exhibit a higher prevalence of additional disruptive behaviors (DuPaul & Stoner, 1994).

Risk Factors

Although no one clear etiology has been established for ADHD, a number of factors have been shown to be associated with an increased risk for ADHD. The majority of factors that have received research support are biological in nature. Although neurological factors have received the greatest attention, most children diagnosed with ADHD present no structural deficits in the central nervous system and structural brain damage is not considered to be a primary cause of ADHD (Barkley, 1990). Factors such as cerebral blood flow, underactivity in certain areas of the brain, and an imbalance or deficiency in the neurotransmitters dopamine and norepinephrine have all been implicated in ADHD (DuPaul & Stoner, 1994). Genetics has also been investigated as a contributing factor in the development of ADHD. Although no evidence exists for any chromosomal abnormalities or a specific gene as a cause for ADHD, studies have shown that 10–35 percent of immediate family members of children with ADHD are also likely to have the disorder, with the sibling concordance rate approximately 32 percent (Biederman, Faraone, & Lapey, 1992; Pauls, 1991).

Developmental Progression

By definition, ADHD is a disorder originating in childhood. The *DSM-IV* diagnostic criteria specifically state that hyperactive-impulsive or inattentive symptoms must have been present before the age of 7 years of age in order to make the diagnosis. Barkley, DuPaul, and McMurray (1990) note that the onset of symptoms is usually earlier than this, typically ages 3 to 4. Behaviors such as greater negativity, defiant behavior, emotional reactivity, disruptiveness, aggressiveness, impulsivity, and hyperactivity are all common in preschool children with ADHD (Barkley, 1996). In elementary school these behaviors usually continue, with difficulties in sustained attention becoming much more noticeable. The child with ADHD has difficulty completing work both in school and at home and tends to be disorganized. In addition, oppositional and socially aggressive behaviors become common, with these defiant and hostile behaviors developing into symptoms of CD in up to 50 percent of children with ADHD (Loeber, Green, Lahey, Christ, & Frick, 1992). Barkley, Fischer, Edelbrock, and Smallish (1990) report that in clinic-referred children with ADHD, 50–80 percent will continue to experience the disorder into adolescence. During adolescence, additional problems arise as adolescents take jobs (e.g., greater turnover) and receive a driver's license (e.g., higher rate of accidents and tickets) (Anastopoulos, 1999). In addition, they are more likely to become involved with the criminal justice system (Mannuzza, Gittleman-Klein, Konig, & Giampino, 1989). Furthermore, these problems are likely to continue into adulthood (Anastopoulos, 1999), with criminality most likely for those individuals with a history of hyperactivity-impulsivity and early conduct problems, both independently and jointly (Babinski et al., 1999).

Assessment

A thorough assessment for ADHD is complicated by a number of factors. These include the variability seen in behavior as a function of situational demands (i.e., degree of structure and how interested the individual is in what he/she is doing in a given situation) and the high risk of comorbidity with Oppositional Defiant Disorder and Conduct Disorder (Anastopoulos, 1999). DuPaul and Stoner (1994) offer a comprehensive five-stage model of ADHD assessment. In their model Stage I is screening, the next two stages involve assessment and diagnosis, and the final two stages involve the development of a treatment plan and treatment evaluation. For the purposes of this chapter, we will focus on Stage II (Multimethod Assessment of ADHD), but the reader is referred to DuPaul and Stoner (1994) for a more comprehensive discussion of ADHD assessment.

The comprehensive assessment begins with both parent and teacher interviews. As ADHD behavior is variable across settings, it is important that neither the parents nor the teacher is the sole source of information. Reviewing the *DSM-IV* criteria for ADHD, ODD, and CD may help to initially identify the presence of symptoms. It may also prove useful to review symptoms of anxiety disorders and depression to rule out the presence of these disorders. A review of school records, whenever possible, is also advised in order to obtain information related to the onset and course of classroom difficulties related to ADHD. A third essential component of ADHD assessment is to have teachers and parents complete behavior rating scales. Behavior rating scales that have been recommended for use (Anastopoulos, 1999; DuPaul & Stoner, 1994) include the Child Behavior Checklist (CBCL; Achenbach, 1991), the Teacher Report Form of the Child Behavior

Checklist (TRF-CBCL; Achenbach, 1991), the Behavior Assessment System for Children (BASC; Reynolds & Kamphaus, 1992), the Revised Conners Parent and Teacher Rating Scales (Goyette, Conners, & Ulrich, 1978), the ADHD Rating Scale (DuPaul, 1991), the Home Situations Questionnaire–Revised (HSQ-R; DuPaul & Barkley, 1992), the School Situations Questionnaire–Revised (SSQ-R; 1992), and the Social Skills Rating System (SSRS; Gresham & Elliott, 1990).

Direct observation of behavior is another important assessment tool. Both interviews and behavior rating scales have limitations, including the biases of those answering the questions (Barkley, 1988). Direct observation of behavior across settings and situations is the best way to provide a less biased, and potentially more accurate, measure of behavior. A number of observational coding systems have been developed, including systems for observing behaviors in clinic analogue situations (Roberts, 1990), classrooms (Abikoff, Gittelman-Klein, & Klein, 1977; Jacob, O'Leary, & Rosenblad, 1978), and clinic-based interactions (Mash & Barkley, 1986). A final recommended area of assessment is academic performance. In conducting this assessment, however, it is important to recognize that children with ADHD usually perform similar to their peers on traditional, individually administered achievement tests (Barkley, DuPaul, & McMurray, 1990). It is therefore important to get a measure of their classroom performance from the child's teacher in an attempt to document performance that is inconsistent and inferior relative to that of peers (Barkley, 1990).

Intervention/Treatment

A complete discussion of treatment approaches to ADHD are beyond the scope of this chapter and readers are referred to Barkley (1990) and DuPaul and Stoner (1994) for excellent comprehensive summaries of treatment approaches. We will, however, summarize popular and empirically validated approaches to treatment.

Pharmacotherapy

The use of stimulant medication is the most frequent treatment of ADHD, with methylphenidate (Ritalin), d-amphetamine (Dexedrine), and pemoline (Cylert) most frequently prescribed (Anastopoulos, 1999). Extensive research has been conducted on the efficacy of stimulant medication, and results consistently demonstrate their efficacy in reducing ADHD symptomology, including short-term improvement in behavioral, academic, and social functioning (DuPaul & Barkley, 1990). According to Rapport, Denney, DuPaul, and Gardner (1994) as many as 80–90 percent of children respond favorably to these medications. Not all individuals respond favorably to stimulant medication, however, and some success in ameliorating ADHD symptoms has been found with tricyclic antidepressants such as imipramine (Plizska, 1987). In spite of their effectiveness, stimulant medication effects are enhanced when combined with other effective treatment approaches such as behavior modification (Pelham & Murphy, 1986). In addition, one must consider the possible negative side effects of stimulant medication. These have been documented to include appetite reduction, irritability, headaches, stomachaches, and, occasionally, motor or vocal tics (DuPaul & Stoner, 1994).

Parent Training

As was previously mentioned, combining stimulant medication with other approaches appears to enhance treatment effects. In addition, factors such as high rates of comorbidity with ODD and CD, the stress parents face in living with a child with ADHD, the need for additional structure in the ADHD child's environment, and the overall efficacy of behavior parent training all argue for parent training as an important component of a treatment regimen for a child with ADHD. Anastopoulos (1998) presents a good description of the parent training program used by Barkley and his associates at the University of Massachusetts Medical Center. This program has been used in the clinical practice of the first author, who has found it to be of value. The program includes 10 sessions and presents a behavioral approach to parent training. See Anastopoulos (1998) or Anastopoulos and Barkley (1990) for details about this program.

Classroom Behavior Modification

A contingency management program focusing on positive reinforcement for appropriate academic and social behavior should be seen as a cornerstone of any treatment regimen for a child with ADHD (DuPaul & Stoner, 1994). Research supports a number of behaviorally based contingency management programs in enhancing classroom behavior. These include token reinforcement programs (Robinson, Newby, & Ganzell, 1981), contingency contracting (Jenson, Rhode, & Reavis, 1994–95), response cost procedures (Pfiffner, O'Leary, Rosen, & Sanderson, 1985), time out (Barkley, 1997), and school-home notes (Kelley, 1990).

Cognitive Behavior Therapy

A variety of cognitive behavioral approaches have been used with some success in ameliorating symptoms of ADHD. Cognitive behavior therapy, however, should not be considered a primary form of treatment because studies examining their effectiveness have been disappointing (DuPaul & Stoner, 1994). Instead this type of therapy should be considered an important component in a comprehensive treatment package to help children and adolescents deal with associated emotional difficulties. Interventions that have been used include self-monitoring (Shapiro & Cole, 1995), a combination of self-monitoring and self-reinforcement (Hinshaw, Henker, & Whalen, 1984), and self-instructional training (Abikoff & Gittleman, 1985; Bornstein & Quevillon, 1976).

Forensic Considerations

Several longitudinal research studies have identified ADHD as a risk factor for aggression and criminal behavior (Satterfield, Hoppe, & Schell, 1982; Mannuzza et al., 1989; Babinski et al., 1999). This is especially true of individuals who are primarily hyperactive-impulsive type (Babinski et al., 1999). Mannuzza and colleagues (1989) compared arrest records of 89 "16- to 23-year old white males who had been diagnosed as cross-situationally hyperactive between the ages of 6 and 12 years," with 100 controls without a history of problem behaviors (p. 1075). Results indicated significantly more arrests, convictions, and incarcerations in the hyperactive group. The hyperactive group had nearly double the arrests (39% vs. 20%), more than three times the number of individuals with multiple arrests (26% vs. 8%), and more than double the rate of arrests for aggressive offenses (18% vs. 7%). The ratio was greatest for incarcerations (8:1) and multiple convictions (10:1). The authors conclude that children with hyperactivity, independent of the presence of Conduct Disorder, are at an increased risk for criminal activities leading to arrest, conviction, and incarceration in late adolescence and early adulthood. They further concluded that the association between arrest history and childhood hyperactivity is mediated by the occurrence of antisocial disorders in young adulthood. The most recent longitudinal study investigating the role of ADHD and later criminal activity was conducted by Babinski, Hartsough, and Lambert (1999). They followed 230 males and 75 females from childhood (average age 9 years) to adulthood (average age 26 years) and found that "both hyperactivity-impulsivity and early conduct problems, independently as well as jointly, predict a greater likelihood of having an arrest record for males, but not for females" (p. 347). They concluded that hyperactive-impulsive symptoms, but not inattention, contribute to the risk of criminal involvement, and that comorbidity with conduct problems places an individual at the highest risk. Lynam (1996) has gone so far as to describe these individuals as "fledgling psychopaths."

Otto, Greenstein, Johnson, and Friedman (1992, cited in Grisso, 1998) estimated that more than 20 percent of delinquent youth manifest ADHD, and there is considerable evidence to indicate an increased risk for violent and aggressive behavior for individuals diagnosed with ADHD (Barkley, 1990). In addition, Hinshaw, Lahey, and Hart (1993) reviewed the literature and concluded that children with ADHD and comorbid CD have an earlier age of onset of the behaviors associated with CD, exhibit more physical aggression, and exhibit more persistent CD than individuals with CD without comorbid ADHD. It is clear then that ADHD must be considered an important factor in the development and maintenance of criminal behavior.

As ADHD increases the likelihood of violent and aggressive behavior independently and in conjunction with CD, it is important to understand how ADHD may play a role in estimating the risk of future aggression. First, the hyperactive and impulsive behaviors characteristic of ADHD, hyperactive-impulsive type, increase the likelihood that individuals will act impulsively to threats or challenges. Second, features associated with ADHD such as low frustration tolerance, temper outbursts, stubbornness, and poor self-efficacy all may contribute to difficulties managing their responses when they are frustrated or angered. Their likely experiences with peer rejection, problems within their families, and academic failure may contribute to poor social problem-solving skills. All of these factors need to be considered by clinicians in evaluating a child or adolescent with ADHD for the court and in making treatment and placement recommendations. One must also consider a history of, or potential for, substance abuse in making recommendations. Remember that the most frequently prescribed medication (i.e., methylphenidate) is a stimulant with a high potential for abuse. Medications need to be tightly controlled when prescribed to delinquent youth.

Conclusion

This chapter by no means exhausted the disorders that involve conduct and impulse control problems in children and adolescents. Oppositional Defiant Disorder and the Impulse-Control Disorders Not Elsewhere Classified (i.e., Intermittent Explosive Disorder, Kleptomania, Pyromania, Pathological Gambling, and Trichotillomania) may increase the likelihood that a child or youth will come into contact with the criminal justice system, but to a much lesser degree than CD and ADHD. It has been clearly demonstrated in a number of studies that there is a strong relationship between Conduct Disorder and Attention Deficit Hyperactivity Disorder and subsequent criminal activity, including violent and aggressive behavior, in adolescence and early adulthood.

Of utmost importance is the appropriate identification of these disorders early in childhood and the implementation of treatment before the magnitude of the behavior has reached the level of delinquency. None of the behaviors discussed that are indicative of CD or ADHD develop in isolation, and attention to risk factors, early developmental signs of behavior disorders, and proactive strategies may be best to curb the development of delinquent behavior. Recognition that early developmental signs of hyperactivity-impulsivity and Conduct Disorder is essential because this combination results in the poorest prognosis. Assessment needs to be comprehensive and multifaceted and should always include an evaluation of familial factors. When these individuals come to the attention of the court, it is important to be aware of and implement empirically validated treatments, and those treatments must always involve caregivers, whether those caregivers are the state or parents. Finally, it is imperative to take any and all instances of antisocial and violent/aggressive behavior seriously and not to assume the individual will "outgrow" the behaviors. Both Eric Harris and Dylan Klebold had been arrested and evaluated by the courts and deemed not a threat to society. It is better to err on the side of caution than to place potentially dangerous children and adolescents back into an environment that provides conditions favorable to future acts of aggression.

References

Abikoff, H., & Gittleman, R. (1985). Does behavior therapy normalize the classroom behavior of hyperactive children? *Archives of General Psychiatry, 41*, 449–454.

Abikoff, H., Gittelman-Klein, R., & Klein, D. (1977). Validation of a classroom observations code for hyperactive children. *Journal of Consulting and Clinical Psychology*, *45*, 772–783.

Achenbach, T. M. (1991). *Manual of the Child Behavior Checklist and the Revised Child Behavior Profile*. Burlington, VT: University of Vermont, Department of Psychiatry.

American Psychiatric Association (1968). *Diagnostic and Statistical Manual of Mental Disorders* (2nd ed.) Washington, DC: Author.

American Psychiatric Association (1980). *Diagnostic and Statistical Manual of Mental Disorders* (3rd ed.) Washington, DC: Author.

American Psychiatric Association (1987). *Diagnostic and Statistical Manual of Mental Disorders* (3rd ed., rev.) Washington, DC: Author.

American Psychiatric Association (1994). *Diagnostic and Statistical Manual of Mental Disorders* (4th ed.) Washington, DC: Author.

Anastopoulos, A. D. (1998). A training program for parents of children with attention-deficit/hyperactivity disorder. In J. M. Briesmeister & C. E. Schaefer (Eds.), *Handbook of parent training* (2nd ed.) (pp. 27–60). New York: Wiley.

Anastopoulos, A. D. (1999). Attention-deficit hyperactivity disorder. In S. D. Netherton, D. Holmes, & C. E. Walker (Eds.), *Child and adolescent psychological disorders: A comprehensive textbook* (pp. 98–117). New York: Oxford University Press.

Anastopoulos, A. D., & Barkley, R. A. (1990). Counseling and training parents. In R. A. Barkley (Ed.), *Attention-Deficit Hyperactivity Disorder: A handbook of diagnosis and treatment* (pp. 397–431). New York: Guilford Press.

Babinski, L. M., Hartsough, C. S., & Lambert, N. M. (1999). Childhood conduct problems, hyperactivity-impulsivity, and inattention as predictors of adult criminal activity. *Journal of Child Psychology and Psychiatry*, *40*, 347–355.

Barkley, R. A. (1988). Child behavior rating scales and checklists. In M. Rutter, A. H. Tuma, & I. S. Lann (Eds.), *Assessment and diagnosis of child psychopathology* (pp. 113–155). New York: Guilford Press.

Barkley, R. A. (1990). *Attention-Deficit Hyperactivity Disorder: A handbook of diagnosis and treatment*. New York: Guilford Press.

Barkley, R. A. (1996). Attention-deficit hyperactivity disorder. In E. J. Mash & R. A. Barkley (Eds.), *Child psychopathology* (pp. 63–112). New York: Guilford Press.

Barkley, R. A. (1997). *Defiant children: A clinician's manual for assessment and parent training*. New York: Guilford Press.

Barkley, R. A., DuPaul, G. J., & McMurray, M. B. (1990). A comprehensive evaluation of attention deficit disorder with and without hyperactivity. *Journal of Consulting and Clinical Psychology*, *58*, 775–789.

Barkley, R. A., Fischer, M., Edelbrock, C. S., & Smallish, L. (1990). The adolescent outcome of hyperactive children diagnosed by research criteria: I. An 8-year prospective follow-up study. *Journal of the American Academy of Child and Adolescent Psychiatry*, *29*, 546–557.

Baum, C. G. (1989). Conduct disorders. In T. H. Ollendick & M. Hersen (Eds.), *Handbook of child psychopathology* (2nd ed.) (pp. 171–196). New York: Plenum Press.

Biederman, J., Faraone, S. V., & Lapey, K. (1992). Comorbidity of diagnosis in attention-deficit hyperactivity disorder. In G. Weiss (Ed.), *Child and adolescent psychiatric clinics of North America: Attention-deficit hyperactivity disorder* (pp. 335–360). Philadelphia: Saunders.

Bornstein, P. H., & Quevillon, R. P. (1976). The effects of a self-instructional package on overactive preschool boys. *Journal of Applied Behavior Analysis, 9*, 179–188.

Cairns, R. B. (1979). *Social development: The origins and plasticity of interchanges.* San Francisco: W. H. Freeman.

Cantwell, D. P., & Baker, L. (1991). Association between attention-deficit hyperactivity disorder and learning disorders. *Journal of Learning Disabilities, 24*, 88–95.

Caspi, A., Elder, G. H., & Bem, D. J. (1987). Moving against the world: Life course patterns of explosive children. *Developmental Psychology, 23*, 308–313.

Dishion, T. J., McCord, J., & Poulin, F. (1999). When interventions harm: Peer groups and problem behavior. *American Psychologist, 54*, 755–764.

Douglas, V. I. (1972). Stop, look, and listen: The problem of sustained attention and impulse control in hyperactive and normal children. *Canadian Journal of Behavioural Science, 4*, 259–282.

DuPaul, G. J. (1991). Parent and teacher ratings of ADHD symptoms: Psychometric properties in a community based sample. *Journal of Clinical Child Psychology, 20*, 245–253.

DuPaul, G. J., & Barkley, R. A. (1990). Medication therapy. In R. A. Barkley (Ed.), *Attention-Deficit Hyperactivity Disorder: A handbook of diagnosis and treatment* (pp. 537–612). New York: Guilford Press.

DuPaul, G. J., & Barkley, R. A. (1992). Situational variability of attention problems: Psychometric properties of the revised home and school situations questionnaires. *Journal of Clinical Child Psychology, 21*, 178–188.

DuPaul, G. J., & Stoner, G. (1994). *ADHD in the schools: Assessment and intervention strategies.* New York: Guilford Press.

Fabrega, J. H., Ulrich, R., & Mezzich, J. E. (1993). Do caucasian and black adolescents differ at psychiatric intake? *Journal of the American Academy of Child and Adolescent Psychiatry, 32*, 407–413.

Farrington, D. P. (1992). Criminal career research in the United Kingdom. *British Journal of Criminology, 32*, 521–536.

Goyette, C. H., Conners, C. K., & Ulrich, R. F. (1978). Normative data on Revised Conners Parent and Teacher Rating Scales. *Journal of Abnormal Child Psychology, 6*, 221–236.

Gray-Ray, P., & Ray, M. C. (1990). Juvenile delinquency in the black community. *Youth and Society, 22*, 67–84.

Gresham, F. M., & Elliott, S. N. (1990). *Social skills rating system.* Circle Pines, MN: American Guidance Service.

Grisso, T. (1998). *Forensic evaluation of juveniles.* Sarasota, FL: Professional Resource Press.

Hartup, W. W. (1996). The company they keep: Friendships and their developmental significance. *Child Development, 67*, 1–13.

Hinshaw, S. P., Henker, B., & Whalen, C. K. (1984). Self-control in hyperactive boys in anger-inducing situations: Effects of cognitive-behavioral training and of methylphenidate. *Journal of Abnormal Child Psychology, 12*, 55–77.

Hinshaw, S. P., Lahey, B. B., & Hart, E. L. (1993). Issues of taxonomy and comorbidity in the development of conduct disorder. *Development and Psychopathology, 5*, 31–49.

Hyman, I. A., & Snook, P. A. (1999). *Dangerous schools: What we can do about the physical and emotional abuse of our children.* San Francisco: Jossey-Bass.

Jacob, R. G., O'Leary, K. D., & Rosenblad, C. (1978). Formal and informal classroom settings: Effects on hyperactivity. *Journal of Abnormal Child Psychology, 6*, 47–59.

Jenson, W. R., Rhode, G., & Reavis, H. K. (1944–1995). *The tough kid tool box*. Longmont, CO: Sopris West.

Kamphaus, R. W., & Frick, P. J. (1996). *Clinical assessment of child and adolescent personality and behavior*. Boston: Allyn & Bacon.

Kazdin, A. E. (1995). *Conduct disorders in childhood and adolescence* (2nd ed.). Thousand Oaks, CA: Sage.

Kazdin, A. E. (1997). Conduct disorders across the lifespan. In S. S. Luthar, J. A. Burack, D. Cicchetti, & J. R. Weisz (Eds.), *Developmental psychopathology: Perspectives on adjustment, risk, and disorder* (pp. 248–272) New York: Cambridge University Press.

Kazdin, A. E. (1998). Conduct disorders. In R. J. Morris & T. R. Kratochwill (Eds.), *The practice of child therapy* (3rd ed.) (pp. 199–230). Boston: Allyn and Bacon.

Kelley, M. L. (1990). *School-home notes: Promoting children's classroom success*. New York: Guilford Press.

Lahey, B. B., Loeber, R., Hart, E. L., Frick, P. J., Applegate, B., Zhang, Q., et al. (1995). Four year longitudinal of conduct disorder in boys: Patterns and predictors of persistence. *Journal of Abnormal Psychology, 104*, 83–93.

Loeber, R., Farrington, D. P., Stouthamer-Loeber, M., & Van Kammen, W. B. (1998). *Antisocial behavior and mental health problems: Explanatory factors in childhood and adolescence*. Mahwah, NJ: Lawrence Erlbaum.

Loeber, R., Green, S. M., Lahey, B. B., Christ, M. A. G., & Frick, P. J. (1992). Developmental sequences in the age of onset of disruptive child behaviors. *Journal of Child and Family Studies, 1*, 21–41.

Lynam, D. K. (1996). Early identification of chronic offenders: Who is a fledgling psychopath? *Psychological Bulletin, 120*, 209–234.

Mannuzza, S., Gittelman-Klein, R. G., Konig, P. H., & Giampino, T. L. (1989). Hyperactive boys almost grow up: IV. Criminality and its relationship to psychiatric status. *Archives of General Psychiatry, 46*, 1073–1079.

Mash, E. J., & Barkley, R. A. (1986). Assessment of family interaction with the Response-Class Matrix. In R. Prinz (Ed.), *Advances in behavioral assessment of children and families (Vol. 2)* (pp. 29–67). Greenwich, CT: JAI Press.

McConaughy, S. H., & Ritter, D. R. (1995). Best practices in mutidimensional assessment of emotional or behavioral disorders. In A. Thomas & J. Grimes (Eds.), *Best practices in school psychology-III*. Washington, DC: National Association of School Psychologists.

McCoy, M. G. (1997). *The potential mediating role of parenting practices in the development of conduct problems*. Unpublished master's thesis, University of Alabama, Tuscaloosa, Alabama.

Offord, D. R., Adler, R. J., & Boyle, M. H. (1986). Prevalence and sociodemographic correlates of conduct disorder. *American Journal of Social Psychiatry, 4*, 272–278.

Offord, D. R., Boyle, M. H., & Racine, Y. A. (1991). The epidemiology of antisocial behavior. In D. F. Keppler & K. H. Rubin (Eds.), *The development and treatment of childhood aggression* (pp. 31–54). Hillsdale, NJ: Lawrence Erlbaum.

Offord, D. R., Boyle, M. H., Szatmari, P., Rae-Grant, N. I., Links, P. S., Cadman, D. T., et al. (1987). Ontario Child Health Study: II. Six-month prevalence of disorder and rates of service utilization. *Archives of General Psychiatry, 44*, 832–836.

Olds, D., Pettitt, L. M., Robinson, J., Henderson, C., Eckenrode, J., Kaitzman, H., et al. (1998). Reducing risks for antisocial behavior with a program of prenatal and early childhood home visitation. *Journal of Community Psychology, 26,* 65–83.

Patterson, G. R., & Yoerger, K. (1991, August). *The development of antisocial behavior.* Paper presented at the NATO Advanced Study Institute, "Crime and Mental Disorder," Ciocco, Italy.

Patterson, G. R. (1986). Maternal rejection: Determinant or product for deviant child behavior? In W. W. Hartup & Z. Rubin (Eds.), *Relationships and development* (pp. 73–94). Hillsdale, NJ: Lawrence Erlbaum.

Patterson, G. R., Reid, J. B., & Dishion, T. J. (1992). *Antisocial boys.* Eugene, OR: Castalia.

Pauls, D. L. (1991). Genetic factors in the expression of attention-deficit hyperactivity disorder. *Journal of Child and Adolescent Psychopharmacology, 1,* 353–360.

Pelham, W. E., & Murphy, H. A. (1986). Attention deficit and conduct disorders. In M. Hersen (Ed.), *Pharmacological and behavioral treatment: an integrative approach* (pp. 108–148). New York: Wiley.

Pfiffner, L. J., O'Leary, S. G., Rosen, L. A., & Sanderson, W. C., Jr. (1985). A comparison of the effects of continuous and intermittent response cost and reprimands in the classroom. *Journal of Clinical Child Psychology, 14,* 348–352.

Plizska, S. R. (1987). Tricyclic antidepressants in the treatment of children with attention deficit disorder. *Journal of the American Academy of Child and Adolescent Psychiatry, 26,* 127–132.

Power, T. J., & DuPaul, G. J. (1996). Attention-Deficit Hyperactivity Disorder: The reemergence of subtypes. *School Psychology Review, 25,* 284–296.

Puig-Antich, J. (1982). Major depression in conduct disorder in prepuburty. *Journal of the American Academy of Child Psychiatry, 21,* 118–128.

Rapport, M. D., Denney, C., DuPaul, G. J., & Gardner, M. J. (1994). Attention deficit disorder and methylphenidate normalization rates, clinical effectiveness, and response prediction in 76 children. *Journal of the American Academy of Child and Adolescent Psychiatry, 33,* 882–893.

Reynolds, C. R., & Kamphaus, R. W. (1992). BASC: *Behavior Assessment System for Children manual.* Circle Pines, MN: American Guidance Service.

Roberts, M. A. (1990). A behavioral observation method for differentiating hyperactive and aggressive boys. *Journal of Abnormal Child Psychology, 18,* 131–142.

Robins, L. N. (1999). A 70-year history of conduct disorder: Variations in definition, prevalence, and correlates. In P. Cohen, C. Slomkowski, & L. N. Robins (Eds.), *Historical and geographical influences on psychopathology* (pp. 37–56). Mahwah, NJ: Lawrence Erlbaum.

Robinson, P. W., Newby, T. J., & Ganzell, S. L. (1981). A token system for a class of underachieving hyperactive children. *Journal of Applied Behavior Analysis, 14,* 307–315.

Satterfield, J. H., Hoppe, C. M., & Schell, A. M. (1982). A prospective study of delinquency in 110 adolescent boys with attention deficit disorder and 88 normal adolescent boys. *American Journal of Psychiatry, 139,* 795–798.

Shapiro, E. S., & Cole, C. L. (1995). *Behavior change in the classroom: Self-management interventions.* New York: Guilford Press.

Sholevar, G. P., & Sholevar, E. H. (1995). Overview. In G. P. Sholevar (Ed.), *Conduct disorders in children and adolescents* (pp. 3–26). Washington, DC: American Psychiatric Press.

Szatmari, P. (1992). The epidemiology of attention-deficit hyperactivity disorders. In G. Weiss (Ed.), *Child and adolescent psychiatric clinics of North America: Attention-deficit hyperactivity disorder* (pp. 361–372). Philadelphia: Saunders.

Thomas, A., & Chess, S. (1977). *Temperament and development.* New York: Brunner/Mazel.

van Goozen, S. H. M., Matthys, W., Cohen-Kettenis, P. T., Thijssen, J. H. H., & van Engeland, H. (1998). Adrenal androgens in aggression in conduct disorder prepubertal boys and normal controls. *Biological Psychiatry, 43,* 156–158.

Wadsworth, M. (1979). *Roots of delinquency: Infancy, adolescence and crime.* New York: Barnes & Noble.

West, D. J. (1982). *Delinquency: Its roots, careers and prospects.* Cambridge, MA: Harvard University Press.

World Health Organization (1992). *International Statistical Classification of Diseases and Related Health Problems, 1989 Revision.* Geneva: Author.

Youth crime drop exceeds adults'. (1999, October 18). *Newsday,* p. A5.

CHAPTER 18

WHAT EVERY FORENSIC PSYCHOLOGIST SHOULD KNOW ABOUT PSYCHOPATHIC PERSONALITY

ELLISON M. CALE
SOUTH CAROLINA DEPARTMENT OF JUVENILE JUSTICE

SCOTT O. LILIENFELD
EMORY UNIVERSITY

Although psychopathic personality (psychopathy) is one of the most extensively researched conditions in all of psychopathology, its etiology, prognosis, and treatment remain controversial and poorly understood (Lykken, 1995; Millon, Simonsen, & Birket-Smith, 1998). Found most frequently in prison and forensic populations (Hare, 1991, 1996), this condition comprises a subset of criminals with unique personality features (Cunningham & Reidy, 1998; Hare, 1998). In addition, psychopathy is primarily a disorder of men (Lykken, 1995), although the reasons for this sex difference are largely or entirely unknown.

Over the past several decades, psychopathy researchers have produced a large body of research that bears important implications for forensic psychology. Nevertheless, many psychologists, including those who work in forensic settings, are largely unaware of this increasingly consistent and clinically relevant body of literature. In this chapter we summarize this literature and outline a number of crucial findings concerning psychopathy that should be understood by all forensic psychologists. In addition, we discuss unresolved issues in the psychopathy literature that may point to important avenues for research on this still enigmatic condition.

CONCEPTUALIZATIONS OF PSYCHOPATHY

In the early nineteenth century, the French psychiatrist Phillipe Pinel described the psychopathic personality (which he termed *manie sans delire*, that is, insanity without delirium) as exhibiting irrational and antisocial behavior in the absence of psychosis. Benjamin Karpman (1941) distinguished between two "types" of psychopathy, which, although often confused, stem from markedly different etiologies. Primary ("idiopathic") psychopaths are callous and nonanxious criminal personalities, whereas secondary ("symptomatic") psychopaths are neurotic or psychotic individuals whose antisocial behaviors spring from preexisting psychopathology. In the mid-twentieth century, Hervey Cleckley provided the most comprehensive description of psychopathy (Gacono & Hutton, 1994) in his highly influential book *The Mask of Sanity* (1941/1988). In this work, Cleckley delineated 16 criteria for psychopathy, including superficial charm, lack of anxiety, unreliability, deceitfulness, lack of remorse, inadequately motivated antisocial behavior, failure to learn from punishment, egocentricity, lack of emotional bonds, absence of insight, and failure to plan ahead. The "Cleckley criteria" have formed the basis for a large number of subsequent efforts (e.g., Hare, 1991) to assess psychopathy systematically. The term *sociopathy* has also been used, particularly during the early twentieth century (Stevens, 1993), to refer to psychopathic individuals, although this term has more recently fallen out of favor.

The first *Diagnostic and Statistical Manual of Mental Disorders* (*DSM-I*) of the American Psychiatric Association (APA, 1952) contained the diagnosis of "sociopathic personality, antisocial reaction," which bore important similarities to Cleckley's conceptualization of psychopathy (Gacono & Hutton, 1994). *DSM-II* (APA, 1968) retained this conceptualization in its diagnosis of "antisocial personality," whose criteria included guiltlessness, lack of loyalty, irresponsibility, impulsivity, and failure to learn from punishment (Alterman, Rutherford, Cacciola, McKay, & Boardman, 1998).

Because the global descriptions of *DSM-I* and *DSM-II* were deemed by many to be subjective and largely unreliable, *DSM-III* (APA, 1980) and *DSM-III-R* (APA, 1987) provided explicit criterion lists for the diagnosis of Antisocial Personality Disorder (ASPD) in an effort to improve diagnostic reliability (Hare, 1996). The *DSM-III* and *DSM-III-R* criterion sets for ASPD greatly deemphasized the personality features outlined by Cleckley and others and replaced these features with relatively clear-cut behavioral criteria, such as a longstanding history of physical aggression, stealing, vandalism, arson, and irresponsible parenting (Hare, 1996, 1998; Lilienfeld, 1994). Although *DSM-IV* (APA, 1994) attempted to reincorporate at least some of the Cleckley features of psychopathy into its diagnostic criteria (Hare, Hart, & Harpur, 1991; Widiger et al., 1996), the current criteria for ASPD continue to identify individuals primarily by chronic antisocial and criminal behaviors and to neglect many of the core personality features of psychopathy, such as lack of empathy, grandiosity, and incapacity to form intimate attachments with others (Hare, 1996, 1998).

Some authors have distinguished between two major approaches to operationalizing psychopathy (Alterman et al., 1998; Lilienfeld, 1994, 1998). Cleckley's criteria emphasize personality traits as the core features of psychopathy, as did the *DSM-II* diagnosis of antisocial personality. Consequently, these conceptualizations are *personality-based* because they focus on a constellation of personality traits (e.g., manipulativeness, lack of remorse, egocentricity). Alternatively, the *DSM-III*, *DSM-III-R*, and *DSM-IV* diagnoses of ASPD are primarily *behavior-based* because they emphasize enduring antisocial and criminal behaviors as the core features of this condition (Lilienfeld, 1994, 1998). Although measures of the personality-based and behavior-based conceptualizations correlate moderately, they differ substantially in their correlates and assessment implications (Harpur, Hare, & Hakstian, 1989).

In this chapter we focus primarily on the clinical features and correlates of psychopathy, with particular emphasis on those characteristics relevant to forensic settings. In particular, we have chosen to focus on the more traditional personality-based operationalization of psychopathy delineated by Cleckley and others (e.g, Karpman, 1941). For reasons to become evident shortly, we will not focus on the current *DSM* diagnosis of ASPD because this diagnosis offers considerably less promise than the classical construct of Cleckley psychopathy for differentiating among criminal offenders with markedly differing personality traits and motivations. We will argue that a personality-based approach to psychopathy bears several important implications for the assessment, classification, prognosis, and treatment of criminal offenders.

PSYCHOPATHY'S RELATIONS TO ASPD AND CRIME

Although psychopathic traits predispose individuals to criminal behavior (Cleckley, 1941/1988; Hare, 1998), the highly restrictive behavioral criteria of the recent *DSM*s may be *underinclusive* in failing to identify psychopathic individuals who do not consistently manifest antisocial or criminal behavior (Lilienfeld, 1994, 1998; Stevens, 1993). Such "subclinical" or "successful" psychopaths (Widom, 1977) would be missed by the current behavioral criteria for ASPD. Conversely, behavior-based criteria for psychopathy may also be *overinclusive*, because they may comprise a heterogeneous group of antisocial conditions in addition to Cleckley psychopathy, such as neurotic psychopathy (i.e., antisocial behavior that presumably stems largely from anxiety, chronic overcontrol of anger, and related problems [see Lykken, 1995; Megargee, Cook, & Mendelsohn, 1967]) and dyssocial psychopathy (i.e., antisocial behavior that is posited to result from allegiance to a culturally deviant subgroup [McNeil, 1970]) (Lilienfeld, 1994, 1998).[1] Thus, compared with psychopathy, ASPD almost certainly encompasses a more

---

[1] Our use of the term *psychopathy* focuses exclusively on Cleckley (1941/1988), or "primary" psychopathy (see Karpman, 1941).

psychologically heterogeneous group of criminals (Cunningham & Reidy, 1998; Hare et al., 1991; Lykken, 1995), who may differ markedly in their motivations for antisocial behavior and in their interpersonal, affective, and personality characteristics (Hare et al., 1991). For these reasons, the *DSM* diagnosis of ASPD appears to possess weaker construct validity than the Cleckley concept of psychopathy (Hare et al., 1991; Lilienfeld, 1994).

The research literature further supports the contention that psychopathy and ASPD are not interchangeable concepts (Hare, 1998; Hare et al., 1991). In forensic settings, Hart and Hare (1989) and Hart, Forth, and Hare (1991) found some overlap between diagnoses of psychopathy and ASPD, but considerably fewer diagnoses of psychopathy than ASPD. Hart and Hare also found that diagnoses of psychopathy were significantly predictive of ASPD diagnoses, but not vice versa. Overall, research indicates that in prison and forensic populations the base rate of psychopathy (15–25%) (Hare, 1991, 1996, 1998; see also Rice & Harris, 1995) is considerably lower than the base rate of ASPD (50–75%) (Hare, 1996; Widiger & Corbitt, 1995).[2] Although most psychopathic prisoners meet criteria for ASPD, a smaller proportion of ASPD prisoners meet criteria for psychopathy (Hare, 1996; Hart et al., 1991).

Psychopathy in Various Forensic Populations

Studies of psychopathy have been based predominantly on studies of North American white male criminals (Hare, 1991; Lilienfeld, 1998). As a consequence, relatively little is known regarding the manifestation of psychopathy in females, nonwhite ethnic groups, cultural groups outside of North America, children, or adolescents. There have recently been promising advances in studying psychopathy among these groups (Lilienfeld, 1998), but many findings are equivocal and have not yet been replicated.

Relatively little is known about psychopathy in females (Cale & Lilienfeld, 2002; Salekin, Rogers, & Sewell, 1997; Salekin, Rogers, Ustad, & Sewell, 1998). Salekin and colleagues, however, have examined this condition in female inmate samples and have reported female psychopathy prevalence rates to be lower than those previously reported for male inmates (Salekin et al., 1997; Salekin et al., 1998). Some studies of female forensic samples suggest that psychopathy may be more related to Somatization Disorder (Cloninger & Guze, 1970b), and Histrionic Personality Disorder (Cloninger & Guze, 1970b; Salekin et al., 1997) in females than in males, although most of these findings are preliminary and warrant replication. Among studies that have examined psychopathy in forensic settings, none has compared the correlates of psychopathy across sex, and many

---

[2] Although we use the term *base rate* for the sake of convenience, this term should technically be reserved for conditions that are known to be taxonic (see the section "Psychopathy: Assessment issues" for a discussion of taxonicity).

are limited by small samples (e.g., Barack & Widom, 1978; Cloninger & Guze, 1970a, 1970b). Some reviewers (e.g., Carlen, 1985; Heidensohn, 1968; Widom, 1984) have suggested that because males and females differ in criminal behavior patterns (with males tending to exhibit higher rates of overt aggression than females), operationalizations of psychopathy should be sex specific (see Steffensmeier & Allan, 1996). To date, however, there is no compelling evidence to support this claim, which implies the existence of sex bias in current measures of psychopathy (see Widiger & Spitzer, 1991, for a discussion). There is a paucity of evidence regarding sex differences in psychopathy in forensic settings, and a better understanding of such differences is of considerable importance to forensic psychologists who work with female offenders.

Some researchers have recently begun to examine ethnic differences in psychopathy. Kosson, Smith, and Newman (1990) reported that the personality and psychopathological correlates of interviewer-assessed psychopathy were fairly similar in black and white inmates, although there was some indication that the chronic antisocial and criminal behaviors sometimes associated with psychopathy were less related to measures of impulsivity in blacks than in whites. In addition, Kosson and colleagues found some evidence for higher psychopathy scores among blacks than whites (see also Brandt, Kennedy, Patrick, & Curtin, 1997). These lattermost findings may reflect genuine ethnic differences, selection biases, interviewer bias (the interviewers in the Kosson et al. samples were all white), or some combination thereof (Lilienfeld, 1998). Kosson and colleagues' findings are preliminary and warrant replication, and the limited evidence regarding race differences in the correlates and mean levels of psychopathy calls for further investigation (Gacono & Hutton, 1994). Investigators have not examined differences in psychopathy among Hispanics or Asians (Cunningham & Reidy, 1998).

Compared with the limited literature on ethnic differences, even less is known about cultural differences in psychopathy (Lilienfeld, 1998). Some studies suggest that psychopathy is a valid diagnosis across cultures, but few have compared its prevalence rates in different countries. Cooke (1996) reported that Scottish prisoners had lower rates of psychopathy than their North American counterparts. This finding provides provisional evidence for cultural differences in psychopathy, although the possibility of selection bias is difficult to exclude (e.g., the criteria for incarceration in North America and Scotland may differ) (Cooke, 1995). Nevertheless, there is little evidence for cultural bias in psychopathy measures (Cooke, 1995, 1996; Hare, 1998; Lilienfeld, 1998). There are no systematic studies of psychopathy outside of North America and Europe (Cooke, 1995; Lilienfeld, 1998).

Several researchers have suggested that psychopathy, as measured by modifications of adult psychopathy instruments, can be meaningfully assessed in children and adolescents (Lilienfeld, 1998). Forth, Hart, and Hare (1990) examined psychopathy in adolescent offenders and found the personality and psychopathological correlates of psychopathic symptoms to be similar to those found in adult inmates. Subsequent studies have corroborated these findings (see Brandt et al., 1997; Forth, 1995; Toupin, Mercier, Déry, Côte, & Hodgins, 1995), although they are few in number. Research on psychopathy in children and adolescents supports the claim that psychopathy and ASPD (or Conduct Disorder in children) are not equivalent (Frick, O'Brien, Wootton, & McBurnett, 1994; Lynam, 1997). The extant evidence further suggests that psychopathy can be reliably assessed in childhood and that childhood psychopathy measures possess incremental validity above and beyond conduct disorder in predicting serious, consistent antisocial behavior (Frick et al., 1994; Lynam, 1997).

PSYCHOPATHY: ASSESSMENT ISSUES

For many decades, the state of the psychopathy assessment literature was in disarray. Many widely used measures of psychopathy were poorly validated, and these measures tended to exhibit low intercorrelations, suggesting that they were assessing only slightly overlapping aspects of the same construct (see Lilienfeld, 1994, for a review). Nevertheless, the past 15 years have witnessed significant methodological advances in the assessment of psychopathy.

The Psychopathy Checklist and Its Progeny

Since the 1960s, Robert Hare and colleagues have been engaged in a large-scale research program to investigate psychopathy's conceptualization and assessment. The major methodological achievements of this research are the Psychopathy Checklist (PCL) (Hare, 1985b), the Psychopathy Checklist-Revised (PCL-R) (Hare, 1991), and the PCL Screening Version (PCL:SV) (Hart, Cox, & Hare, 1995). The PCL and its progeny incorporate both personality and behavioral characteristics in their operationalizations of psychopathy (Hare, 1993, 1996; Salekin, Rogers, & Sewell, 1996). These three measures include many features of Cleckley's criteria for psychopathy, including superficial charm, callousness, manipulativeness, promiscuity, irresponsibility, and lack of remorse, while also assessing aspects of the *DSM* ASPD criteria, such as chronic antisocial behavior, early history of crime, and impulsivity.

Findings indicate that the PCL, the PCL-R, and perhaps the PCL:SV measure two moderately correlated (i.e., correlations are approximately $r = .50$ across most studies) factors, whereby Factor 1 assesses the core affective and personality features of psychopathy (e.g., lack of guilt, callousness, grandiosity) and Factor 2 assesses such qualities as poor behavioral controls and chronic social deviance (Hare et al., 1990; Harpur, Hakstian, & Hare, 1988). A number of researchers have contended that both Factor 1 and Factor 2 are critical in the assessment of psychopathy (Harpur et al., 1989) and that these two factors correspond to the personality-based and behavior-based approaches, respectively (Lilienfeld, 1994, 1998). Moreover, these two factors have been found to differ substantially in their personality, cognitive, and demographic correlates. For example, whereas Factor 1 tends to negatively correlated with trait anxiety measures, Factor 2 tends to be positively correlated with such measures. In addition, Factor 2 is negatively correlated with educational level and verbal intelligence, whereas Factor 1 is negligibly associated with these variables (Harpur et al., 1989).

Cooke and Michie (2001) recently proposed an alternative three-factor model of psychopathy that subdivides Factor 1 into separable affective and interpersonal facets. Nevertheless, because the research support for this still controversial model is provisional, we will not discuss it further here.

The PCL-R, which is very similar in both its content and psychometric properties to the earlier PCL (Hare et al., 1990), is the most extensively construct validated of all psychopathy measures. PCL-R scores are derived from an intensive semistructured interview in conjunction with a detailed review of institutional file information. For research purposes, at least two hours are typically required to complete the PCL-R (Grann, Långström, Tengström, & Stålenheim, 1998), although well-trained clinicians can often administer this measure in less time (Gacono & Hutton, 1994). Although the PCL:SV, a shorter version of the PCL-R, appears to possess similar psychometric properties (e.g., interrater reliability, construct validity) to the PCL-R (see Hart, Hare, & Forth, 1994), the PCL-R is recommended for use in criminal populations, whereas the PCL:SV should be reserved for research purposes or as a possible screening device for psychopathy (Hare, 1998; Hart et al., 1994).

The PCL-R is a reliable and construct valid measure of psychopathy. Its interrater reliabilities for total scores typically exceed .80 among inmates and forensic patients (Hare, 1998). The PCL-R was validated in samples of inmates and forensic psychiatric patients and was developed primarily for use in these individuals (Cunningham & Reidy, 1998; Serin, 1993). In addition, the PCL-R provides a more complete assessment of psychopathic personality traits than does the *DSM-IV* diagnosis of ASPD, which, as noted earlier, greatly deemphasizes such traits (Cunningham & Reidy, 1998; Hare et al., 1991). Hart and Hare (1989) found that PCL total scores correlated positively and significantly with antisocial, histrionic, and narcissistic personality disorder traits and nonalcohol substance abuse, negatively and significantly with avoidant personality disorder traits, and negligibly and nonsignificantly with schizophrenia. Hart and Hare reported similar associations for PCL Factor 1 scores, although PCL Factor 2 scores correlated only with ASPD. PCL and PCL-R scores are also positively correlated with laboratory measures of passive avoidance learning (i.e., the capacity to withhold responses that lead to punishment), which is traditionally believed to be a central deficit in psychopathy (Newman & Kosson, 1986). Moreover, as will be discussed later, PCL-R–defined psychopaths tend to commit more serious and more varied crimes, offend earlier and at higher rates, exhibit more disruptive prison behavior, and have poorer treatment response than nonpsychopaths (Hare, 1998).

Before administering the PCL-R in prison and forensic settings, a licensed clinician should possess an advanced degree in the social or behavioral sciences, have experience with criminal assessment, and receive formal training in PCL-R administration (Gacono & Hutton, 1994; Hare, 1998; Serin, 1992). The PCL-R should not be scored after administering only the interview (Gacono & Hutton, 1994; Hare, 1998), and assessments based solely on file review should be used for research purposes only (see Grann et al., 1998; Serin, 1993). In clinical reports, the information from the PCL-R can be used to supplement the *DSM* criteria for ASPD (Gacono & Hutton, 1994).

One should exercise caution in PCL-R interpretation and use in forensic testimony (Hare, 1998). Administrators and expert witnesses should not make judgments on the basis of PCL-R scores unless they are thoroughly familiar with the large and complex literature concerning this measure's reliability and construct validity (Hart et al., 1994). As highlighted earlier in this chapter, the research literature on psychopathy, as measured by the PCL-R, may be limited in its generalizability to nonincarcerated populations (Cunningham & Reidy, 1998; Salekin et al., 1996; Widom, 1977). There is also mixed evidence regarding the most appropriate PCL-R cutoff score for psychopathy (Hare, 1998; Hare et al., 1991; Salekin et al., 1996).

Perhaps more important, it is unclear whether psychopathy is underpinned by a taxon (i.e., a nonarbitrary class that exists in nature) or a dimension (see Harris, Rice, & Quinsey, 1994; Lilienfeld, 1998). If the latter, the use of a categorical cutoff score to diagnose psychopathy may be largely or entirely arbitrary from a scientific standpoint. Using taxometric methods developed by Meehl and his colleagues (e.g., Meehl & Golden, 1982), Harris and colleagues reported evidence consistent with the claim that a latent taxon underlies scores on the PCL-R. Nevertheless, their analyses yielded evidence of taxonicity only for PCL-R Factor 2 and only for childhood antisocial behaviors, suggesting that the core affective and interpersonal features of psychopathy may be underpinned by a latent dimension.

Self-Report Measures of Psychopathy

Many researchers have examined the use of self-report inventories for assessing psychopathy. Because the PCL-R and cognate measures are time and labor intensive, such inventories represent appealing alternatives to interview-based indices. Nevertheless, because psychopaths tend to be deceitful and to lack insight into the nature and extent of their difficulties (Cleckley, 1941/1988), and because self-report measures are potentially susceptible to impression management, malingering, and other response styles, some researchers have questioned whether psychopathy can be validly assessed by means of self-report (Hart et al., 1991; Hart et al., 1994). Unlike most or all interviews, however, self-report measures can assess these response biases systematically (Widiger & Frances, 1987).

It is clear, however, that until quite recently the self-report assessment of psychopathy was plagued by numerous methodological difficulties. Most self-report measures of psychopathy tend to correlate weakly or at best moderately with clinical ratings and PCL-R diagnoses of psychopathy (Hart et al., 1991). In addition, the correlations among commonly used self-report psychopathy measures tend to be lower than the correlations among interview measures (Hare, 1985a). Most self-report psychopathy measures correlate more strongly with measures of chronic antisocial behavior (i.e., PCL-R Factor 2) than with measures of the interpersonal and affective features of psychopathy (i.e., PCL-R Factor 1) (Harpur et al., 1989; Hart et al., 1991; Hart et al., 1994), suggesting that these self-report measures assess generalized behavioral deviance rather than the core personality traits that distinguish psychopathic offenders from other offenders. Here, we review several self-report measures of psychopathy and discuss their strengths and limitations as well as the implications of their use in forensic settings.

The Minnesota Multiphasic Personality Inventory (MMPI) and its revision, the MMPI-2, which are empirically constructed measures of psychopathology (see Graham, 1993), are commonly used to assess psychopathic features among forensic patients (Kennedy, 1986). The MMPI Psychopathic Deviate (Pd) Scale, often in conjunction with the Hypomania (Ma) Scale (McKinley & Hathaway, 1944), is sometimes used to diagnose psychopathy (Hare, 1985a) and to aid in treatment planning (Kennedy, 1986). However, the use of the MMPI in the assessment of psychopathy is problematic in several respects. Individuals' MMPI scores sometimes change over time, and responses may be influenced by state factors (e.g., imprisonment, impending trials) and incentives to malinger (Cunningham & Reidy, 1998). More important, because the MMPI Pd scale is highly heterogeneous and multifactorial (Graham, 1993), moderately high Pd scores are ambiguous in meaning and can reflect familial conflict, authority problems, alienation, interpersonal poise, or a complex admixture of several of these attributes (Lilienfeld, 1999). Research evidence suggests that the MMPI Pd scale, like most other self-report psychopathy measures, correlates moderately with PCL-R Factor 2 but negligibly with Factor 1 (Harpur et al., 1989). As a consequence, the Pd scale does not adequately assess many of the core affective and interpersonal features of psychopathy and therefore lacks utility in differentiating psychopaths from both other forensic subjects (Cunningham & Reidy, 1998) and nonpsychopaths in psychiatric settings (Hawk & Peterson, 1974). All of these findings underscore the point that clinicians should not rely on MMPI Pd scores alone in assessing psychopathy (Lilienfeld, 1999).

There is some evidence that the MMPI-2 Antisocial Practices (ASP) content scale (Butcher, Graham, Williams, & Ben-Porath, 1990) possesses incremental validity above and beyond the MMPI Pd scale in assessing certain psychopathic personality features, including manipulativeness (Lilienfeld, 1996). In addition, certain Harris-Lingoes (1955) Pd subscales, particularly Pd2 (Authority Problems), appear to be more associated with Cleckley psychopathy than others. Moreover, certain other Pd subscales, such as Pd3 (Social Imperturbability) may be only weakly related to Cleckley psychopathy (Lilienfeld, 1999). Because of the differential correlates of the MMPI Pd Harris-Lingoes subscales, reliance on Pd total scores alone can often result in misleading interpretations, particularly when Pd score elevations are moderate in magnitude.

In the hopes of delineating a comprehensive criminal classification system to facilitate treatment decisions (Kennedy, 1986; Wrobel, Wrobel, & McIntosh, 1988), Megargee and Bohn (1979) outlined a typology for classifying youthful adult offenders. Determined by various MMPI configurations, the 10-cluster, analytically derived "Megargee types" are distinguished by different social and demographic variables, personality traits, attitudes, and behaviors. Some of the Megargee types appear to be related to psychopathy. For example, the type "Able," which is identified by elevations in MMPI Pd and Ma scales and is described by Megargee and Bohn as superficial, charming, and manipulative, appears to embody a number of the Cleckley criteria for psychopathy. The results of several studies indicate that the Megargee typology is reliable across various correctional settings (see Edinger, 1979; Walters, 1986), although these findings warrant replication. Moreover, some researchers have found that the Megargee classifications do not adequately predict violent behavior (see Baum, Hosford, & Moss, 1984; Louscher, Hosford, Moss, 1983; Moss, Johnson, & Hosford, 1984). Overall, cross-validation of the Megargee types in criminal samples has yielded mixed results, and this typology's use in predicting violence, recidivism, and treatment response necessitates further investigation (Kennedy, 1986). The Megargee typology may be promising in differentiating various criminal types, but little is known about its construct validity in assessing psychopathy.

The California Psychological Inventory (CPI) Socialization (So) Scale (Gough, 1969) is a measure of socialization (i.e., the extent to which societal values are internalized) that is sometimes scored in reverse as a measure of psychopathy (Megargee, 1972). The So scale was developed to assess the role-taking deficits of psychopathy (see Gough, 1948) and was constructed by contrasting the responses of delinquents and nondelinquents. Subsequent research suggests, however, that this scale assesses a broader dimension reflecting individual differences in the internalization of societal norms, and rank-orders a variety of criterion groups along a hypothesized continuum of socialization (Gough, 1994). So scale scores exhibit high test-retest reliability (Megargee, 1972), and low So individuals are deceitful, defensive, irresponsible, mischievous, outspoken, and quarrelsome (Megargee, 1972). In addition, antisocial and criminal individuals typically receive low So scores (Kosson, Steuerwald, Newman, & Widom, 1994). Because it correlates more strongly with PCL-R Factor 2 scores than Factor 1 scores (Harpur et al., 1989), however, the So scale appears to be more a behavior-based than a personality-based measure of psychopathy. As a consequence, it is probably more useful as a general marker of behavioral deviance than as a specific indicator of the core personality traits of psychopathy. In addition, although many researchers have examined the correlates of So scores, they have generally compared forensic samples with normal samples and have not examined the So scale's ability to distinguish psychopaths from nonpsychopaths within criminal samples (Kosson et al., 1994).

Two newer psychopathy self-report measures are subscales of the Millon Clinical Multiaxial Inventory–II (MCMI-II) (Millon, 1987) and the Personality

Assessment Inventory (PAI) (Morey, 1991). The MCMI-II was designed to assess both acute clinical disorders and personality disorders according to *DSM-III-R* criteria. The second revision of this measure, the MCMI-III, has recently been published (Millon, 1997), although its construct validity among criminal offenders is less clear. Hart and colleagues (1991) found that several MCMI-II scales (i.e., Antisocial, Narcissistic, Aggressive/Sadistic) correlated significantly with measures of psychopathy and ASPD. Like most other self-report measures, however, these scales correlated more highly with the behavioral (i.e., PCL-R Factor 2) than interpersonal (i.e., PCL-R Factor 1) component of psychopathy. There is little research on the MCMI-II's use in forensic settings, and the existing findings warrant replication. The PAI antisocial scale (ANT) is based partly on the work of Cleckley (Salekin et al., 1998). The PAI-ANT egocentricity and stimulus seeking (ANT-E and ANT-S, respectively) subscales assess personality features of psychopathy, whereas the antisocial behaviors (ANT-A) subscale primarily assesses the behavioral features of *DSM* ASPD. Preliminary evidence suggests that the PAI-ANT scale correlates moderately with the MMPI Pd scale (Morey, 1991). There is little research, however, supporting the use of the PAI in forensic settings (Cunningham & Reidy, 1998) or its construct validity as a measure of psychopathy.

It therefore appears that most self-report measures of psychopathy correlate more strongly with PCL-R Factor 2 than Factor 1. This finding is problematic because many of these measures (e.g., the MMPI Pd scale) are commonly used by forensic psychologists to assess psychopathy even though they correlate weakly or negligibly with the core personality features of this syndrome. A few recently developed self-report measures, however, show promise in assessing Factor 1 traits. The Psychopathic Personality Inventory (PPI) (Lilienfeld & Andrews, 1996) was originally designed to assess psychopathic personality traits in noncriminal samples, although it has recently been extended to incarcerated samples. It differs from other self-report psychopathy measures in that it (1) focuses exclusively on psychopathic personality traits; (2) excludes items explicitly assessing antisocial and criminal behaviors; (3) yields both a total score and scores on eight analytically derived subscales (e.g., Machiavellian Egocentricity, Fearlessness, Blame Externalization) intended to assess various facets of psychopathy; and (4) contains three validity scales designed to assess malingering, inconsistent responding, positive impression management, and other response styles that are potentially problematic among psychopaths (Lilienfeld, 1998; Poythress, Edens, & Lilienfeld, 1998). The PPI total score correlates significantly and moderately to highly with other self-report measures of psychopathy, including those that seem to primarily assess behavioral aspects of psychopathy (e.g., MMPI Pd scale, CPI So scale) (Lilienfeld & Andrews, 1996). In addition, there is preliminary evidence that the PPI possesses construct validity in criminal samples. For example, Poythress and colleagues (1998) found that PPI total scores correlated significantly with PCL-R total, Factor 1, and Factor 2 scores in a prison sample. Unlike other psychopathy self-report measures, however, the PPI correlated more highly with PCL-R

Factor 1 scores ($r = .54$) than with Factor 2 scores ($r = .40$), although this difference fell short of significance. Although the PPI appears to be a promising measure of psychopathic traits in criminals, further investigation is needed to evaluate whether it possesses incremental validity over and above other self-report measures in the assessment of psychopathic characteristics (Lilienfeld & Andrews, 1996; Poythress et al., 1998). It is worth noting, however, that the PPI exhibited incremental validity above and beyond self-report measures in assessing observer-rated Cleckley psychopathy among undergraduates (Lilienfeld & Andrews, 1996).

Levenson, Kiehl, and Fitzpatrick (1995) rationally constructed primary and secondary psychopathy scales to assess the two conceptualizations of psychopathy delineated by Karpman (1941). According to Karpman, primary and secondary psychopaths are characterized by low and high trait anxiety, respectively. Levenson and colleagues' primary psychopathy scale assesses narcissistic qualities as well as a callous disregard for others' welfare, whereas the secondary psychopathy scale assesses impulsivity and socially deviant behaviors (Wilson, Frick, & Clements, 1999). These scales are posited to be roughly analogous to PCL-R Factor 1 and Factor 2, respectively. Nevertheless, several correlates of the Levenson and colleagues' scales raise questions concerning these scales' construct validity. For example, contrary to prediction, Levenson and colleagues (1995) found that the primary psychopathy scale was weakly but significantly *positively* correlated with trait anxiety. Further research is needed to clarify the construct validity of Levenson and colleagues' scales (Lilienfeld, 1998) and to ascertain their construct validity in criminal samples.

Observer Rating Measures

It is surprising that more research has not been conducted on the use of observer rating measures of psychopathy. Such measures may help to circumvent the "blind spots" that presumably characterize psychopaths, many of whom lack insight into the nature and severity of their symptoms (Grove & Tellegen, 1991; Lilienfeld, 1994). Shedler and Westen (1998) have conducted initial studies on a Q-sort rating method for assessing personality disorders and have reported promising results for this technique in clinical samples. Nevertheless, the construct validity of this method for assessing psychopathy remains to be determined.

Reise and Oliver (1994) have developed a Q-sort method specifically designed to assess psychopathy. This observer-based method, the Psychopathy Q-Sort (PQS), requires observers to describe each subject by sorting 100 cards, each bearing an adjectival statement regarding a personality characteristic, into a forced quasinormal distribution. PQS scores reflect the correlation between a subject's rating profile and an empirically derived psychopathy prototype profile (Reise & Oliver, 1994). There is preliminary support for the convergent and discriminant validity of the PQS in nonclinical populations. Reise and Wink (1995) reported that the PQS tended to correlate positively with measures of Antisocial, Borderline, Histrionic, and Narcissistic Personality Disorders, but negatively or negligibly with measures of other personality disorders. They also reported that the PQS correlated negatively with the CPI So scale among both males and females.[3] Additional research is needed to determine whether the PQS or other psychopathy rating measures (see Lilienfeld & Andrews, 1996, for an alternative rating measure of psychopathy) possess incremental validity over and above interviews or self-report inventories in the assessment of psychopathy (Lilienfeld, 1998). Moreover, to our knowledge there is virtually no research on the use of observer rating measures in the assessment of psychopathy in prison samples (cf., Craddick, 1962).

Projective Measures

A number of researchers have contended that the Rorschach Inkblot Test (Exner, 1993) can be used to assess psychopathy. Gacono and Meloy (1994) argued, for example, that the Rorschach is "ideally suited" for assessing psychopathy. They went on to assert that "we have validated the use of the Rorschach as a sensitive instrument to discriminate between psychopathic and nonpsychopathic subjects" (see also Gacono, 1995, 1998). Gacono and Hutton (1994) reviewed evidence suggesting that the Rorschach responses of PCL-R psychopaths reflect more borderline organization, more narcissism, less anxiety, and less attachment than the responses of nonpsychopaths. For example, a number of researchers have claimed that psychopaths consistently show fewer Texture responses on the Rorschach than nonpsychopaths (Gacono, Meloy, & Berg, 1992; Gacono, Meloy, & Heaven, 1990), presumably indicative of a lesser need for interpersonal intimacy among the former individuals.

Despite these strong claims, careful scrutiny of the extant literature does not lend support to the construct validity of the Rorschach in the assessment of psychopathy (Cunningham & Reidy, 1998). Meloy, Gacono, and their colleagues conducted a large number of correlational analyses in their studies, thereby increasing the probability of Type I error (Wood, Lilienfeld, Garb, & Nezworski, 2000). More important, several attempts by independent investigators (e.g., Murphy-Peaslee, 1995/1993) to replicate their original findings (including the finding of fewer Texture responses among psychopaths) have failed (Wood et al., 2000). It is also worth noting that the Rorschach, like self-report measures, is not immune from the problem of response distortion (Cunningham & Reidy, 1998).

It remains to be seen whether the Rorschach proves to be worth its time and effort in administration given the absence of replicated construct validity for any of its indices in the assessment of psychopathy. Moreover, to our knowledge there are no data indicating that the Rorschach possesses incremental validity for measuring psychopathy above and beyond more easily administered (e.g., self-report)

---

[3] Because low scores on the CPI So scale imply a lack of socialization and are indicative of deceitfulness, irresponsibility, and other psychopathy characteristics, this negative correlation with the So scale is in the predicted direction.

measures. At this point, we cannot recommend the Rorschach for clinical applications in the assessment of psychopathy, although further research is warranted to resolve the discrepancies in findings across different investigative teams. We are not aware of any convincing evidence that other projective techniques (e.g., the Thematic Apperception Test; Morgan & Murray, 1935) are of utility in the assessment of psychopathy (see Lilienfeld, Hess, & Rowland, 1996).

PSYCHOPATHY AND DISSIMULATION

Although psychopaths are notorious for their propensities toward dishonesty (Cleckley, 1941/1988), the relation between psychopathy and dissimulation has received surprisingly little research attention. We examine the association between psychopathy and both malingering and positive impression management ("faking good"), and address the question of psychopaths' ability and willingness to dissimulate in these domains.

Psychopathy and Malingering

The *DSM-IV* describes malingering as a nonpsychopathological condition in which an individual, motivated by an external incentive such as evading criminal prosecution, intentionally produces false or exaggerated physical or psychological symptoms (APA, 1994). The *DSM-IV* contends that malingering should be suspected if an individual is diagnosed with ASPD but provides no information regarding psychopaths' propensity towards malingering. Although acknowledging that psychopaths often malinger to escape punishment after being caught for committing antisocial acts, Cleckley (1941/1988) maintained that there was no unequivocal relationship between psychopathy and malingering. Cleckley also argued that whereas malingerers tend to persist in malingering, psychopaths do not typically malinger across situations. Nevertheless, the association between psychopathy and malingering has been clouded by numerous methodological problems (Clark, 1988). Edens, Buffington, Tomicic, and Parker (1999) observed that although research has not shown a consistent association between psychopathy and malingering, many studies have suffered from a lack of random sampling, inadequate control groups, and the use of inmates as proxies for psychopaths.

Gacono, Meloy, Sheppard, Speth, and Roske (1995) examined the clinical characteristics and institutional behaviors of 18 malingerers and 18 hospitalized insanity acquittees, and found that malingerers had significantly higher PCL-R total, Factor 1, and Factor 2 scores than insanity patients. In addition, all of the malingers in this study were diagnosed with psychopathy. It is unclear, however, whether psychopathy itself was predictive of malingering or whether the malingering group was incidentally composed entirely of psychopaths. In addition, the use of insanity acquittees as a comparison sample is potentially problematic, because psychotic individuals may have unusually low rates of psychopathy (Cleckley, 1941/1988).

Edens and colleagues (1999) examined the relation between psychopathy, as assessed by the PPI, and malingering of psychosis among undergraduates, and found that PPI total scores were not significantly correlated with either successful malingering or perceptions of success at recent malingering attempts. Nevertheless, psychopathy was significantly correlated with an increased willingness to malinger in the future and an increased perception of success at malingering. Although these results bear interesting implications for forensic psychology, they require replication with criminal samples.

Although the findings of Edens and colleagues suggest that psychopathic individuals may be more willing than other individuals to malinger, malingering in forensic contexts may often be related more to contextual incentives than to personality traits (Clark, 1988). Because convicted individuals may be inclined to feign illness to escape punishment, the association between psychopathy and malingering could result from the tendency of psychopaths to be incarcerated more often than nonpsychopaths (Edens et al., 1999). In addition, incarcerated psychopaths are not typically self-referred for psychological evaluations, and the probability of their malingering increases as the criminal justice system forces them to undergo evaluations that may affect impending treatment and punishment (Clark, 1988). Such considerations suggest that the use of the PCL-R and other psychopathy measures to assess malingering in criminal samples is questionable (cf., Gacono & Hutton, 1994). Additional research is needed to examine the utility of psychopathy measures in forensic malingering referrals.

Psychopathy and Positive Impression Management

There is surprisingly little research on the propensity or ability of psychopaths to fake good on psychological tests. Interestingly, there is some evidence that psychopaths tend to receive *low* scores on self-report measures of faking good (Lilienfeld, 1994), which implies that psychopaths are often willing to acknowledge at least some negative personality characteristics. In a study of prisoners and undergraduates, O'Mahony and Murphy (1991) found that "honest" CPI So scores were not significantly associated with gains made in So scores in a "fake good" condition. The researchers instead found that variations in prisoners' intelligence scores accounted for more variation in So "fake good" score gains than "honest" So scores (see also Alliger, Lilienfeld, & Mitchell, 1996, for evidence indicating that intelligence measures are positively associated with the ability to fake good on self-report "honesty" indices). As noted earlier, however, the So scale correlates only weakly with the core personality features of psychopathy, rendering the relevance of these findings to psychopathy per se unclear. In addition, because O'Mahony and Murphy asked participants to fake good in a context in which there were no clear incentives for success, these findings may not be applicable to real-life forensic situations (Lanyon, 1997).

Some researchers have postulated that psychopaths are better at "beating" the polygraph ("lie detector") test than nonpsychopaths. In examining this issue, it is imperative that one bear in mind the relatively weak validity of the polygraph test for assessing lying (Clark, 1988; Lanyon, 1997; Lykken, 1998), which in turn may constrain the interpretations of studies on the polygraph test. This problem notwithstanding, there is no convincing evidence that psychopaths are more adept at "beating" polygraphs than nonpsychopaths (see Patrick & Iacono, 1986; but see Waid & Orne, 1982).

PSYCHOPATHY: CONCURRENT AND PREDICTIVE RELATIONS WITH CRIMINAL BEHAVIOR

Numerous researchers have examined the association between psychopathy and crime. The literature strongly suggests that across all demographic groups psychopaths are more criminally active than nonpsychopaths (Hart & Hare, 1997). Regardless of race or psychiatric diagnosis, psychopaths possess strong and stable propensities toward a variety of crimes, including violent offenses (Hare et al., 1991). Moreover, psychopathic criminals commit more crimes involving weapons, robbery, assault, kidnapping, vandalism, and fighting than nonpsychopathic criminals (Hare & McPherson, 1984). The development of violent offender and sexual offender taxonomies that assimilate psychopathic traits in their categories (Serin, 1992) further attests to the links between psychopathy and criminal behavior. Here we briefly review the literature on psychopathy's concurrent and predictive associations with various crimes. We focus on psychopathy's relations with violence, sexual crimes, behaviors in forensic institutions, and criminal recidivism.

Violent Crimes

Although there is disagreement among researchers regarding how to operationalize violence (e.g., categorically or dimensionally) and measure violence (e.g., by means of self-report or interview measures) and regarding whether sexual and property crimes should be included in assessing violence (Hart, 1998), the relation between psychopathy and violence has been consistent across studies. This association has been confirmed by studies that have retrospectively examined the criminal behaviors of psychopaths and nonpsychopaths (see Hart, 1995, 1998; Simourd & Hoge, 2000; Valliant, Gristey, Pottier, & Kosmyna, 1999). In a sample of 87 inmates, Serin (1991) found that 100 percent of criminal psychopaths had a prior violence conviction, compared with 68 percent of criminal nonpsychopaths. In a sample of 663 male inmates, Hare and McPherson (1984) found that PCL-defined psychopaths were more likely than nonpsychopaths to have engaged in violent crimes prior to incarceration. In addition, the authors found that criminal psychopaths committed three and a half times more violent crimes than criminal nonpsychopaths.

Psychopaths also tend to engage in a greater variety of violent crimes than nonpsychopaths (Hart & Hare, 1997) and are more likely to engage in instrumental (i.e., purposeful and goal directed) than reactive (i.e., emotional) aggression (Cornell et al., 1996; Williamson, Hare, & Wong, 1987). Using the PCL-R and the PCL:SV to assess psychopathy, Cornell and colleagues (1996) found that instrumental violent offenders were more psychopathic than both reactive violent offenders and nonviolent offenders. Other researchers have replicated Cornell and colleagues' findings and reported that the association between psychopathy and instrumental violence held for Factor 1 but not Factor 2 scores (Hart & Hare, 1997). In general, however, both PCL Factor 1 and Factor 2 scores have been found to correlate with most forms of violent behavior (Hart et al., 1994). Finally, Williamson and colleagues (1987) reported that psychopaths were more likely to have murdered strangers, whereas nonpsychopaths were more likely to have murdered during a domestic dispute, when they were extremely emotional, or both. These findings are consistent with the clinical portrait of the psychopath as cold, unemotional, and predatory (Cleckley, 1941/1988).

Sexual Crimes

There is also evidence for an association between psychopathy and sexual crimes, including rape and other sexual offenses (Kosson, Kelly, & White, 1997; Porter, Campbell, Woodworth, & Birt, 2001). In a meta-analysis of the literature on psychopathy and violence, Salekin and colleagues (1996) reviewed three studies of psychopathy and sexual crimes, and found that the PCL and PCL-R significantly predicted sexual sadism and deviant sexual arousal. Several findings also indicate that psychopaths are more likely than nonpsychopaths to use violence in committing sexual offenses and are more likely to be sexually aroused by violent stimuli (Hart & Hare, 1997). Nevertheless, most of the positive findings regarding psychopathy and sexual crimes are provisional and based on few studies. In addition, forensic psychologists should cautiously apply these findings to nonwhites, females, and adolescents (Salekin et al., 1996).

PCL-R scores have been found to differentiate among various types of sexual offenders. Rapists tend to be more psychopathic than incest offenders and pedophiles (Hart & Hare, 1997; Porter et al., 2001). Although rape is characterized by both sexual and aggressive components, the relationships among psychopathy, aggression, and sexual arousal are poorly understood (Barbaree, Seto, Serin, Amos, & Preston, 1994). Barbaree and colleagues examined differences in psychopathy among specific categories of rapists and did not find significant differences in PCL-R scores between sexual rapists (i.e., those for whom sex is the principal motivation for their offending) and nonsexual rapists (i.e., those for whom aggressiveness, hostility, and/or a callous disregard for the victim are the principal motivators for their offending). In the nonsexual rapist group, the researchers did not find significant differences in PCL-R scores between vindictive and opportunistic rapists. They did find, however, that sexual sadistic rapists scored higher than sexual nonsadistic rapists on PCL-R Factor 2 scores, but that there were no differences between the groups in PCL-R total or Factor 1 scores. Barbaree and colleagues noted that sadistic rapists exhibit a greater history of impulsive antisocial behaviors than nonsadistic rapists, which may explain the difference between PCL-R Factor 2 correlates of sadistic rapist subtypes. In reviewing Barbaree and colleagues' study, Salekin and colleagues (1996) found that the average effect size (.73) for PCL-R Factor 2 scores in predicting sexual sadism was larger than the average effect size (.42) for Factor 1 scores. Firestone, Bradford, Greenberg, and Larose (1998) found that sexual homicide offenders had higher PCL-R total, Factor 1, and Factor 2 scores than incest offenders.

Kosson and colleagues (1997) examined the relations between PCL ratings and CPI So scores and sexual aggression in college males. After controlling for So scores, PCL Factor 1 ratings predicted individuals' reported use of force and threats in sexual acts. In addition, Kosson and colleagues reported significant correlations between PCL Factor 2 ratings and the reported use of force in sexual acts and between So scores and various forms of sexual aggression, such as use of sexual force. As noted previously, however, the So scale does not appear to adequately assess many of the core personality characteristics of psychopathy and may thus be limited in its capacity to discriminate among certain types of sexual offenders. Although it seems plausible that PCL Factor 1 characteristics (e.g., narcissism, dominance) contribute to sexual aggression (Kosson et al., 1997), the link between core psychopathic traits and sexual aggression has not been clarified empirically (see also Firestone et al., 2000; Serin, Mailloux, & Malcolm, 2001).

Institutional Misbehavior

The results of several retrospective and predictive studies suggest that psychopaths have high rates of disciplinary infractions in correctional institutions and forensic hospitals (Gacono, 1998; Hart, 1995, 1998; Heilbrun et al., 1998; Hill, Rogers, & Bickford, 1996; Rogers, Johansen, Change, & Salekin, 1997), although this association has not been entirely consistent across studies. Some researchers have reported that while in prison incarcerated psychopaths display more aggressive behaviors than nonpsychopaths and are frequently segregated for treatment (Ogloff et al., 1990). Psychopaths have also been found in some studies to be more likely than nonpsychopaths to engage in fights and aggressive homosexuality in prison (Hart & Hare, 1997). Gacono and colleagues (1995) reported that their sample of malingerers, all of whom were diagnosed with PCL-R psychopathy, were more likely than insanity acquittees to (1) be verbally or physically assaultive, (2) require specialized treatment plans for their aggressive behavior, (3) have sexual relations with female staff, (4) deal drugs, and (5) be considered at risk for escape. Moreover, psychopaths tend to exhibit aggressive behaviors relatively soon after admission (i.e., within two months) to correctional facilities and forensic hospitals (Hart & Hare, 1997; Heilbrun et al., 1998). Overall, the correlations between PCL-R scores and poor institutional behavior are generally weak to moderate, although PCL-R scores tend to be better predictors of institutional misbehavior than demographic variables and criminal histories (Hart, 1995).

These positive findings concerning the relation between psychopathy and institutional misbehavior have not, however, been uniformly replicated (Cunningham & Reidy, 1998; Serin, 1991). Moreover, many of these studies suffer from methodological flaws. For example, in several studies institutional infractions have been considered in making PCL-R Factor 2 ratings, resulting in criterion contamination (Cunningham & Reidy, 1998).

Furthermore, although the PCL-R has been found in several studies to be useful in predicting or postdicting institutional misbehavior, it may not be superior to other psychopathy measures in this regard (Edens, Poythress, & Lilienfeld, 1999). In their study of ethnically diverse youthful criminals, Edens and colleagues found that PCL-R total, Factor 1, and Factor 2 scores and PPI total scores correlated with the combined number of disciplinary reports of physical aggression (e.g., using a weapon, fighting) and verbal aggression/defiance (e.g., threats, disrespect to officials, disobeying officials) during the first year of incarceration, with significant correlations ranging from .24 to .30. None of the correlations between the psychopathy indices and occurrences of nonaggressive, physical aggression, or verbal aggression/defiance disciplinary reports was significant, however, except for those between PCL-R Factor 2 scores and physical aggression reports ($r = .24$) and PPI scores and verbal aggression/defiance reports ($r = .23$). Neither the PCL-R nor the PPI showed incremental validity above and beyond the other measure in predicting institutional disciplinary problems.

In general, there is limited research on the relation between psychopathy and correctional facility offending, although there is some evidence that psychopathy measures correlate weakly to moderately with disciplinary infractions. Until there is more consistent evidence on this issue, forensic psychologists should exercise caution when using the PCL-R or other psychopathy measures to predict institutional misbehavior (Cunningham & Reidy, 1998).

Recidivism

The relation between psychopathy and criminal recidivism is one of the best established findings in forensic psychology (Hare, 1996). PCL- and PCL-R–defined psychopathic criminals have consistently been found to be more prone to recidivism than nonpsychopathic criminals (Cornell et al., 1996). For example, Hart, Kropp, and Hare (1988) found that 80 percent of released inmates with high PCL scores, compared with 25 percent of inmates with low PCL scores, were imprisoned again within three years. High-PCL inmates were four times more likely to commit a violent crime after release than low-PCL inmates. Hart and colleagues' study was the first predictive study of psychopathy and violent recidivism, and corroborating evidence has been reported in many studies of the PCL and the PCL-R (Cornell et al., 1996; Cunningham & Reidy, 1998; Douglas, Ogloff,

Nicholls, & Grant, 1999; Glover, Nicholson, Hemmati, Bernfield, & Quinsey, 2002; Hart, 1998; Hart & Hare, 1997; Hemphill et al., 1998; Kroner & Loza, 2001; Rice & Harris, 1995; Salekin et al., 1996; Skilling, Harris, Rice, & Quinsey, 2002). In their review, Hemphill, Hare, and Wong (1998) reported that at one year after release, PCL-R–defined psychopaths were three times more likely to recidivate and four times more likely to recidivate violently than nonpsychopaths. Wong (1995) conducted the first large-scale (i.e., approximately 10-year) longitudinal study of the association between PCL ratings and recidivism and found that PCL scores significantly predicted violent and nonviolent recidivism. Although the prevalence of psychopathy is lower in forensic psychiatric samples than in correctional institutions, psychopathy has also been found to be significantly associated with recidivism in forensic patients (Hare, 1996).

Among sexual offenders, psychopathy is associated with both violent and sexual recidivism (Rice & Harris, 1995). In their reviews of PCL and PCL-R studies, Hemphill and colleagues (1998) and Salekin and colleagues (1996) reported that the PCL and PCL-R are consistent predictors of general, violent, and sexual recidivism. Furr (1993) reviewed studies of recidivism in released sex offenders and argued that it may be possible to obtain reasonably accurate predictions of sexual or violent recidivism among released violent sex offenders by using the PCL-R in conjunction with an actuarial measure of recidivism. Nevertheless, the relatively small corpus of research in this area suggests that further research examining the relation between psychopathy and sexual recidivism is necessary (Serin, 1992).

It is not clear whether the two PCL factors differentially predict recidivism. Hemphill and colleagues' review suggests that PCL and PCL-R Factor 2 scores are stronger predictors of general recidivism than Factor 1 scores but that both factors predict violent recidivism (Hemphill & Hare, 1995; Hemphill et al., 1998). Serin (1996) reported that PCL-R Factor 1 was a better predictor of violent recidivism than Factor 2 and suggested that the core affective and interpersonal features of psychopathy may contribute uniquely to the prediction of violent recidivism. In contrast, Salekin and colleagues' (1996) meta-analysis indicated that PCL Factor 2 scores predicted general *and* violent recidivism better than Factor 1 scores. The relation between PCL-R factor scores and recidivism has been inconsistent across studies and requires additional investigation.

The PCL-R has consistently been found to predict recidivism, particularly violent and sexual recidivism, above and beyond measures of criminal history, demographic variables, and personality disorder diagnoses (Hare, 1996; Hare et al., 1991). Actuarial measures, which typically use static demographic variables (e.g., marital status) in addition to offense history to generate predictions about an individual's likelihood of reoffending, are often better predictors of criminal behavior than personality traits (Hare, 1996). In several studies, however, the PCL-R has outperformed actuarial measures of recidivism (e.g., Nuffield's [1982] Statistical Index of General Recidivism Scale [SIR]) (Hart & Hare, 1997; Serin, 1992, 1996; see also Webster, Rice, Cormier, & Quinsey, 1994). Zamble and Palmer

(1995) outlined an approach for predicting recidivism that involves using the PCL-R in combination with other measures. They found that at two to four years after release the PCL-R was more accurate in predicting recidivism than the SIR.

In summary, the literature supports the PCL-R's use in clinical assessments of general and violent recidivism risk (Hemphill et al., 1998) and suggests that this measure possesses incremental validity above and beyond actuarial risk indices. Although the findings regarding psychopathy and recidivism, especially sexual recidivism, warrant replication in nonwhites and females, forensic psychologists can justifiably consider using the PCL-R in making rough probability statements regarding parole and conditional release decisions and community placements among white male inmates (Salekin et al., 1996).

THE PROGNOSIS OF PSYCHOPATHIC CRIMINALS

Relatively little is known about the long-term prognosis of psychopaths (Hare, 1998). Some evidence suggests, however, that psychopaths exhibit age-related patterns of offending that differ from those of criminal nonpsychopaths.

The Natural History of Psychopathy

Psychopaths begin their criminal careers at relatively young ages (Hart & Hare, 1997). Furthermore, the crime rates (particularly violent crime rates) of psychopathic criminals tend to decrease around the age of 40 (Hare, 1996). Harpur and Hare (1994) found that PCL-R-defined psychopathy was less prevalent in older than in younger inmates. After conducting cross-sectional and longitudinal analyses, Hare, McPherson, and Forth (1988) found that although nonpsychopaths' rates of nonviolent crime were relatively constant over the life span, psychopaths' rates of nonviolent crime were consistent until about age 40, after which they decreased substantially. These findings support the contention that around or shortly after the age of 40, psychopaths exhibit burnout with respect to nonviolent offending (e.g., Robins, 1966).

Harris, Rice, and Cormier (1991) examined violent recidivism in forensic patients and found that even beyond age 40 PCL-defined psychopaths engaged in more violent recidivism than nonpsychopaths. Overall, the findings concerning age and psychopathy suggest that after the age of 40 psychopaths' involvement in nonviolent crimes tends to decline and resemble that of nonpsychopaths, whereas psychopaths' rates of violent crime remain above those of nonpsychopaths throughout the life span. Wong's (1995) preliminary results in a longitudinal study of psychopathy and recidivism similarly indicated that criminal activities of psychopaths tend to decrease with age. Nevertheless, replication of these findings using additional longitudinal analyses are required before forensic psychologists can offer strong predictions regarding psychopaths' potential for violent and nonviolent crimes at different ages.

A decline in criminal behavior with age does not, however, necessarily imply a change in underlying personality traits. As psychopaths commit fewer crimes, they may manifest different antisocial behaviors (Hare, 1996) or channel their psychopathic tendencies into more prosocial or at least less overtly antisocial behaviors (Harkness & Lilienfeld, 1997). Harpur and Hare (1994) found that psychopaths' PCL Factor 1 scores were stable over time, whereas their Factor 2 scores decreased with age. The researchers suggested that core psychopathic traits (e.g., egocentricity, deceitfulness) do not parallel apparent age-related declines in impulsivity, social deviance, and antisocial behavior. Because Harpur and Hare's data are cross-sectional, however, their conclusions should be interpreted with caution. Overall, preliminary findings on the longitudinal course of psychopathy suggest that psychopaths' interpersonal and affective traits are more stable over time than their antisocial and criminal behaviors (Hart & Hare, 1997).

Because psychopathy researchers have typically examined recidivism in relatively young adult parolees, there is a paucity of research on the manifestations of the personality traits and antisocial behaviors of psychopathic criminals at older ages. This is a particular limitation in decisions regarding parole after multidecade incarceration periods because it is not clear whether psychopathic offenders tend to naturally cease committing certain crimes as they age (Cunningham & Reidy, 1998). Forensic psychologists should cautiously evaluate the evidence on psychopaths' age-related changes in affective and behavioral characteristics when making correctional placement and treatment decisions.

The Treatment of Psychopathy

Cleckley (1941/1988) depicted psychopaths as virtually incurable and recommended that they be continually monitored to prevent their violation of others. Craft (1969) argued that knowledge concerning psychopaths' treatment responsivity was hindered by a lack of long-term follow-up intervention studies. He further asserted that there was no empirical basis for forming appropriate treatment and after-care services for psychopathic offenders.

Unfortunately, over three decades later psychologists are scarcely further advanced in their understanding of psychopaths' amenability to treatment. Although no structured treatment or resocialization programs are clearly known to be effective in decreasing psychopaths' criminality, it is common for offenders to be labeled psychopathic and then sentenced to treatment in correctional institutions or be asked to participate in treatment programs (Hare, 1996). Furthermore, parole boards are more willing to consider a conditional release for an inmate who has received treatment than one who has not, regardless of whether the treatment was successful (Ogloff, Wong, & Greenwood, 1990). In some correctional institutions, offenders with high PCL-R scores are excluded from traditional treatment programs (Hare, 1998), but it is unclear how effective these traditional treatment programs are in treating psychopaths.

Only a handful of psychopathy treatment programs have been systematically evaluated. Some clinicians have argued that Therapeutic Community (TC) treatment, a corrections-based community program in which inmates are encouraged to learn to take responsibility for their behaviors, is helpful in treating psychopaths (Ogloff et al., 1990). Ogloff and colleagues examined treatment outcomes in federal inmate volunteers to a TC program and found that psychopathy correlated negatively with time spent in the TC before being discharged for failure to complete the program, for lack of motivation, or for being a security risk. The researchers also reported that PCL-defined psychopaths showed less motivation, effort, and clinical improvement than nonpsychopaths. TC appeared to be somewhat effective for inmates with moderate, but not high, PCL scores. Rice, Harris, and Cormier (1992) evaluated the efficacy of a maximum-security TC program among mentally disordered offenders, some of whom were psychopaths. Compared with no treatment conditions, TC treatment was generally found to have little impact on recidivism, although it was associated with lower recidivism among nonpsychopaths. Among psychopaths, general recidivism was equally high in treated and untreated groups, and violent recidivism was *higher* in the treated groups than in the untreated groups. Thus, TC actually appeared to be harmful among psychopathic offenders. The researchers speculated that group therapy and insight-oriented programs may help psychopaths learn to better manipulate and deceive others.

Garrido, Esteban, and Molero (1995) conducted a meta-analysis on controlled and pre-post studies of treatment efficacy among psychopaths. Their results suggested that psychopaths are less likely than nonpsychopaths to benefit from treatment, especially TC program treatment. In addition, psychopaths showed some evidence for improvement (1) when treatment was not designed to address drug abuse, (2) when they were younger than 30, (3) with increases in intervention length, and (4) when they had moderate rather than high levels of psychopathy. Nevertheless, these findings will require corroboration in controlled outcome studies. In a study of the PCL-R in a youthful offender sample, Brandt and colleagues (1997) found that the short-term treatment of psychopathic juvenile offenders did not prevent future offenses over an extended period of time. Most studies of treatment efficacy among psychopaths are limited by inadequate assessments, poorly defined interventions, a lack of post-treatment follow-up, and an absence of appropriate control/comparison groups (Hart & Hare, 1997).

In summary, as suggested by the extensive anecdotal literature indicating that psychopaths lack insight into their antisocial attitudes and behaviors and tend to seek treatment only when it is in their best interest (e.g., applying for parole) (Cleckley 1941/1988), the admittedly limited research literature suggests that psychopaths are not generally responsive to existing treatments (Hare, 1998). Some analyses hint that individuals with low to moderate levels of psychopathy (i.e., PCL-R scores of 10 to 29) are potentially treatable, but the overall findings on the efficacy of treatment for psychopaths are sparse and contradictory (Cunningham & Reidy, 1998).

Although there is little compelling evidence that psychopathy is treatable, there is no conclusive evidence that it is untreatable (Hart & Hare, 1997). Because psychopaths do not clearly benefit from treatment programs geared towards developing empathy, conscientiousness, and interpersonal skills, Hare and colleagues have suggested tailoring programs specifically to psychopaths. They argue that such programs should convince psychopaths that emotion is less important in controlling, directing, and inhibiting their behavior than in other individuals and that they must work toward developing motivating and guiding strategies that do not rely on emotion (Hare, 1998). Hare and others have further proposed that relapse-prevention techniques be supplemented by cognitive-behavioral correctional programs to help psychopaths understand that they are responsible for their behaviors and to learn prosocial ways of satisfying their desires (Hare, 1996; Hart & Hare, 1997). Extensive supervision during institutionalization and in the community following release has also been suggested. Nevertheless, such treatment programs have not been extensively examined for their effectiveness as treatment alternatives for psychopaths within criminal justice systems.

CONCLUSION: TEN TAKE-HOME MESSAGES FOR FORENSIC PSYCHOLOGISTS

In this chapter, we reviewed the literature on the classification, assessment, and correlates of psychopathy, with particular emphasis on findings of relevance to forensic psychologists. We delineated two approaches to operationalizing psychopathy (i.e., personality based and behavior based) and emphasized the limitations of using purely behavior-based criteria, such as the *DSM-IV* criteria for ASPD, to assess criminal offenders. We urge all forensic psychologists to bear the following 10 points in mind when assessing and working with psychopaths.

1. The classical construct of psychopathy, as delineated by Cleckley, is not synonymous with ASPD, although these two syndromes overlap moderately. There are good reasons to believe that the *DSM-IV* criteria for ASPD are both underinclusive and overinclusive compared with the Cleckley-type (i.e., personality-based) criteria for psychopathy and possess weaker construct validity than the latter criteria among criminal offenders.
2. Because most studies of psychopathy have examined this syndrome in samples of white male North American inmates, forensic psychologists should cautiously apply the research findings discussed in this chapter to other forensic samples. Although there is promising evidence that the psychopathy construct can be meaningfully assessed in women and blacks, these findings warrant replication. Moreover, the possibility that psychopathy measures exhibit sex, ethnic, or cultural biases cannot be excluded with confidence on the basis of extant data.

3. The PCL and its progeny are the most extensively construct-validated measures of psychopathy. These measures consist of two factors, one of which assesses the core affective and interpersonal features of psychopathy and the other of which assesses chronic antisocial and criminal behaviors. These two factors differ substantially in their correlates and assessment implications, and should be examined separately in all clinical applications and research studies.
4. Most commonly used self-report measures of psychopathy, including the MMPI and MMPI-2 Pd scale and CPI So scale, primarily assess the antisocial and criminal behavior sometimes associated with psychopathy rather than the core personality components of this syndrome. As a consequence, such measures should not be used in isolation to assess Cleckley psychopathy or to distinguish Cleckley psychopaths from other offenders in criminal samples. Although a few recently developed self-report measures, such as the PPI, show promise in assessing the affective and interpersonal traits of psychopathy, these measures require further construct validation, particularly in forensic samples.
5. Relatively little progress has been made in the development of observer rating measures of psychopathy, although such measures hold considerable promise in circumventing the "blind spots" that may characterize psychopaths' self-reports. One such measure, the PQS, has been found to possess encouraging validity in nonclinical samples, although its construct validity in criminal samples is unknown.
6. The Rorschach and other projective techniques have not demonstrated consistent construct validity in the assessment of psychopathy and cannot presently be recommended for distinguishing psychopathic from nonpsychopathic criminals.
7. There is no convincing evidence that psychopaths are better than nonpsychopaths at either malingering or faking good on psychological measures, and there is relatively little evidence bearing on psychopaths' proclivity toward engaging in these response styles. Much more research is needed to address the relations between psychopathy and various forms of dissimulation, and forensic psychologists should not assume that the PCL-R or other psychopathy measures can be validly used to detect malingering or other forms of dishonesty.
8. As typically assessed by the PCL and PCL-R, psychopathy has been found to be associated with violent offending, including instrumental violent offending and violent-sexual offending, criminal recidivism, and institutional misbehavior, although the latter association has generally been found to be only weak or moderate in magnitude. Moreover, the PCL and PCL-R possess incremental validity above and beyond actuarial risk indices for predicting criminal recidivism. The homicides of psychopathic criminals are more likely to involve strangers than those of nonpsychopathic criminals, whereas the homicides of the latter

criminals are more likely to occur during domestic disputes or intense emotional arousal.
9. Psychopathic criminals engage in less criminal offending, especially nonviolent offending, after age 40, although core psychopathic traits appear to remain stable with age. More research derived from longitudinal designs needs to be conducted on the relation between psychopathy and aging.
10. There is little compelling evidence that psychopaths are responsive to treatment, although further research on this issue is clearly warranted. The oft-cited conclusion that "psychopaths cannot be treated" is premature. Because there is some suggestion that certain treatments may produce harmful effects among psychopaths, however, forensic psychologists should not assume that "some treatment is always better than no treatment."

We believe that all forensic psychologists will benefit from a greater familiarity with the psychopathy literature, and that this extensive body of research provides valuable information regarding the assessment, diagnosis, correlates, course, and treatment of psychopaths. We encourage all forensic psychologists to integrate the scientific findings concerning psychopathy into their routine clinical assessment and practice.

REFERENCES

Alliger, G. M., Lilienfeld, S. O., & Mitchell, K. E. (1996). The susceptibility of overt and covert integrity tests to coaching and faking. *Psychological Science, 7*, 32–39.

Alterman, A. I., Rutherford, M. J., Cacciola, J. S., McKay, J. R., & Boardman, C. R. (1998). Prediction of 7 months methadone maintenance treatment response by four measures of antisociality. *Drug and Alcohol Dependence, 49*, 217–223.

American Psychiatric Association. (1952). *Diagnostic and statistical manual of mental disorders*. Washington, DC: Author.

American Psychiatric Association. (1968). *Diagnostic and statistical manual of mental disorders* (2nd ed.). Washington, DC: Author.

American Psychiatric Association. (1980). *Diagnostic and statistical manual of mental disorders* (3rd ed.). Washington, DC: Author.

American Psychiatric Association. (1987). *Diagnostic and statistical manual of mental disorders* (3rd–revised ed.). Washington, DC: Author.

American Psychiatric Association. (1994). *Diagnostic and statistical manual of mental disorders* (4th ed.). Washington, DC: Author.

Barack, L. I., & Widom, C. S. (1978). Eysenck's theory of criminality applied to women awaiting trial. *British Journal of Psychiatry, 133*, 452–456.

Barbaree, H. E., Seto, M. C., Serin, R. C., Amos, N. L., & Preston, D. L. (1994). Comparisons between sexual and nonsexual rapist subtypes: Sexual arousal to rape, offense precursors, and offense characteristics. *Criminal Justice and Behavior, 21*, 95–114.

Baum, M. S., Hosford, R. E., & Moss, C. S. (1984). Predicting violent behavior within a medium security correctional setting. *International Journal of Eclectic Psychotherapy, 3*, 18–24.

Brandt, J. R., Kennedy, W. A., Patrick, C. J., & Curtin, J. J. (1997). Assessment of psychopathy in a population of incarcerated adolescent offenders. *Psychological Assessment, 9*, 429–435.

Butcher, J. N., Graham, J. R., & Ben-Porath, Y. S. (1990). *Development and use of the MMPI-2 content scales*. Minneapolis: University of Minnesota Press.

Cale, E. M., & Lilienfeld, S. O. (2002). Sex differences in psychopathy and antisocial personality disorder: A review and integration. *Clinical Psychology Review, 22*, 1179–1207.

Carlen, P. (1985). Law, psychiatry, and women's imprisonment: A sociological view. *British Journal of Psychiatry, 146*, 618–621.

Clark, C. R. (1988). Sociopathy, malingering, and defensiveness. In R. Rogers (Ed.), *Clinical assessment of malingering and deception* (pp. 54–64). New York: Guilford Press.

Cleckley, H. (1941/1988). *The mask of sanity*. St. Louis, MO: Mosby.

Cloninger, R. C., & Guze, S. B. (1970a). Female criminals: Their personal, familial, and social backgrounds. *Archives of General Psychiatry, 23*, 554–558.

Cloninger, R. C., & Guze, S. B. (1970b). Psychiatric illness and female criminality: The role of sociopathy and hysteria in the antisocial woman. *American Journal of Psychiatry, 127*, 303–311.

Cooke, D. J. (1995). Psychopathy across cultures. *Issues in Criminological and Legal Psychology, 24*, 24–29.

Cooke, D. J. (1996). Psychopathic personality in different cultures: What do we know? What do we need to find out? *Journal of Personality Disorders, 10*, 23–40.

Cooke, D. J., & Michie, C. (2001). Refining the construct of psychopathy: Towards a hierarchical model. *Psychological Assessment, 13*, 171–188.

Cornell, D. G., Warren, J., Hawk, G., Stafford, E., Oram, G., & Pine, D. (1996). Psychopathy in instrumental and reactive violent offenders. *Journal of Consulting and Clinical Psychology, 64*, 783–790.

Craddick, R. (1962). Selection of psychopathic from non-psychopathic prisoners. *Psychological Reports, 10*, 495–499.

Craft, M. (1969). The natural history of psychopathic disorder. *British Journal of Psychiatry, 115*, 39–44.

Cunningham, M. D., & Reidy, T. J. (1998). Antisocial personality disorder and psychopathy: Diagnostic dilemmas in classifying patterns of antisocial behavior in sentencing evaluations. *Behavioral Sciences and the Law, 16*, 333–351.

Douglas, K. S., Ogloff, J. R. P., Nicholls, T. L., & Grant, I. (1999). Assessing risk for violence among psychiatric patients: The HCR-20 violence risk assessment scheme and the Psychopathy Checklist: Screening Version. *Journal of Consulting and Clinical Psychology, 67*, 917–930.

Edens, J. F., Buffington, J. K., Tomicic, T., & Parker, J. L. (1999). *An investigation of the relationship between psychopathy and malingering on the psychopathic personality inventory*. Unpublished manuscript, Sam Houston State University.

Edens, J. F., Poythress, N. G., & Lilienfeld, S. O. (1999). Identifying inmates at risk for disciplinary infractions: A comparison of two measures of psychopathy. *Behavioral Sciences and the Law, 17*, 435–443.

Edinger, J. D. (1979). Cross-validation of the Megargee MMPI typology for prisoners. *Journal of Consulting & Clinical Psychology, 47*, 234–242.

Exner, J. (1993). *The Rorschach: A comprehensive system, vol. 1: Basic foundations* (3rd ed.). New York: John Wiley.

Firestone, P., Bradford, J. M., Greenberg, D. M., & Larose, M. R. (1998). Homicidal sex offenders: Psychological, phallometric, and diagnostic features. *Journal of the American Academy of Psychiatry and the Law, 26*, 537–552.

Firestone, P., Bradford, J. M., McCoy, M., Greenberg, D. M., Curry, S., & Larose, M. R. (2000). Prediction of recidivism in extrafamilial child molesters based on court-related assessments. *Sexual Abuse: A Journal of Research and Treatment, 12*, 203–221.

Forth, A. E. (1995). Psychopathy in adolescent offenders: Assessment, family background, and violence. *Issues in Criminological and Legal Psychology, 24*, 42–44.

Forth, A. E., Hart, S. D., & Hare, R. D. (1990). Assessment of psychopathy in male young offenders. *Psychological Assessment, 2*, 342–344.

Frick, P. J., O'Brien, B. S., Wootton, J. M., & McBurnett, K. (1994). Psychopathy and conduct problems in children. *Journal of Abnormal Psychology, 103*, 700–707.

Furr, K. D. (1993). Prediction of sexual or violent recidivism among sexual offenders: A comparison of prediction instruments. *Annals of Sex Research, 6*, 271–286.

Gacono, C. B. (1995). The Rorschach and the diagnosis of antisocial and psychopathic personality. *Issues in Criminological and Legal Psychology, 24*, 52–56.

Gacono, C. B. (1998). The use of the Psychopathy Checklist–Revised (PCL-R) and Rorschach in treatment planning with antisocial personality disordered patients. *International Journal of Offender Therapy and Comparative Criminology, 42*, 49–64.

Gacono, C. B., & Hutton, H. E. (1994). Suggestions for the clinical and forensic use of the Hare Psychopathy Checklist–Revised (PCL-R). *International Journal of Law and Psychiatry, 17*, 303–317.

Gacono, C. B., & Meloy, J. R. (1994). *The Rorschach assessment of aggressive and psychopathic personalities*. Hillsdale, NJ: Lawrence Erlbaum.

Gacono, C. B., Meloy, J. R., & Berg, J. L. (1992). Object relations, defensive operations, and affective states in narcissistic, borderline, and antisocial personality disorder. *Journal of Personality Assessment, 59*, 32–49.

Gacono, C. B., Meloy, J. R., & Heaven, T. R. (1990). A Rorschach investigation of narcissism and hysteria in antisocial personality. *Journal of Personality Assessment, 55*, 270–279.

Gacono, C. B., Meloy, J. R., Sheppard, K., Speth, E., & Roske, A. (1995). A clinical investigation of malingering and psychopathy in hospitalized insanity acquittees. *Bulletin of the American Academy of Psychiatry and the Law, 23*, 387–397.

Garrido, V., Esteban, C., & Molero, C. (1995). The effectiveness in the treatment of psychopathy: A meta-analysis. *Issues in Criminological and Legal Psychology, 24*, 57–59.

Glover, A. J. J., Nicholson, D. E., Hemmati, T., Bernfeld, G. A., & Quinsey, V. L. (2002). A comparison of predictors of general and violent recidivism among high-risk federal offenders. *Criminal Justice & Behavior, 29*, 235–249.

Gough, H. A. (1948). A sociological theory of psychopathy. *American Journal of Sociology, 53*, 359–366.

Gough, H. G. (1969). *Manual for the California Psychological Inventory*. Palo Alto, CA: Consulting Psychologists Press.

Gough, H. G. (1994). Theory, development, and interpretation of the CPI Socialization Scale. *Psychological Reports, 24,* 23–30.

Graham, J. R. (1993). *MMPI-2: Assessing personality and psychopathology.* New York: Oxford.

Grann, M., Långström, N., Tengström, A., & Stålenheim, E. G. (1998). Reliability of file-based retrospective ratings of psychopathy with the PCL-R. *Journal of Personality Assessment, 70,* 416–426.

Grove, W. M., & Tellegen, A. (1991). Problems in the classification of personality disorders. *Journal of Personality Disorders, 5,* 31–42.

Hare, R. D. (1985a). Comparison procedures for the assessment of psychopathy. *Journal of Consulting and Clinical Psychology, 53,* 7–16.

Hare, R. D. (1985b). *The Psychopathy Checklist.* Unpublished manuscript, University of British Columbia, Vancouver, Canada.

Hare, R. D. (1991). *The Hare Psychopathy Checklist–Revised.* Toronto: Multi-Health Systems.

Hare, R. D. (1993). *Without conscience: The disturbing world of the psychopaths among us.* New York: Pocket Books.

Hare, R. D. (1996). Psychopathy: A clinical construct whose time has come. *Criminal Justice and Behavior, 23,* 25–54.

Hare, R. D. (1998). The Hare PCL-R: Some issues concerning its use and misuse. *Legal and Criminological Psychology, 3,* 99–119.

Hare, R. D., Harpur, T. J., Hakstian, A. R., Forth, A. E., Hart, S. D., & Newman, J. P. (1990). The Revised Psychopathy Checklist: Reliability and factor structure. *Psychological Assessment, 2,* 338–341.

Hare, R. D., Hart, S. D., & Harpur, T. J. (1991). Psychopathy and the DSM-IV criteria for antisocial personality disorder. *Journal of Abnormal Psychology, 100,* 391–398.

Hare, R. D., & McPherson, L. M. (1984). Violent and aggressive behavior by criminal psychopaths. *International Journal of Law and Psychiatry, 7,* 35–50.

Hare, R. D., McPherson, L. M., & Forth, A. E. (1988). Male psychopaths and their criminal careers. *Journal of Consulting and Clinical Psychology, 56,* 710–714.

Harkness, A. R., & Lilienfeld, S. O. (1997). Individual differences science for treatment planning: Personality traits. *Psychological Assessment, 9,* 349–360.

Harpur, T. J., Hakstian, A. R., & Hare, R. D. (1988). Factor structure of the Psychopathy Checklist. *Journal of Consulting and Clinical Psychology, 56,* 741–747.

Harpur, T. J., & Hare, R. D. (1994). Assessment of psychopathy as a function of age. *Journal of Abnormal Psychology, 103,* 604–609.

Harpur, T. J., Hare, R. D., & Hakstian, R. (1989). A two-factor conceptualization of psychopathy: Construct validity and implications for assessment. *Psychological Assessment, 1,* 6–17.

Harris, R., & Lingoes, J. (1955). Subscales for the Minnesota Multiphasic Personality Inventory. Mimeographed materials, The Langley Porter Clinic, San Francisco, CA.

Harris, G. T., Rice, M. E., & Cormier, C. A. (1991). Psychopathy and violent recidivism. *Law and Human Behavior, 15,* 625–637.

Harris, G. T., Rice, M. E., & Quinsey, V. L. (1994). Psychopathy as a taxon: Evidence that psychopaths are a discrete class. *Journal of Consulting and Clinical Psychology, 62,* 387–397.

Hart, S. D. (1995). Psychopathy and risk assessment. *Issues in Criminological and Legal Psychology, 24,* 63–67.

Hart, S. D. (1998). The role of psychopathy in assessing risk for violence: Conceptual and methodological issues. *Legal and Criminological Psychology, 3*, 121–137.

Hart, S. D., Cox, D. N., & Hare, R. D. (1995). *The Hare Psychopathy Checklist: Screening Version (PCL:SV)*. North Tonawanda, NY: Multi-Health Systems.

Hart, S. D., Forth, A. E., & Hare, R. D. (1991). The MCMI-II and psychopathy. *Journal of Personality Disorders, 5*, 318–327.

Hart, S. D., & Hare, R. D. (1989). Discriminant validity of the Psychopathy Checklist in a forensic psychiatric population. *Journal of Consulting and Clinical Psychology, 1*, 211–218.

Hart, S. D., & Hare, R. D. (1997). Psychopathy: Assessment and association with criminal conduct. In D. M. Stoff, J. Breiling, & J. P. Maser (Eds.), *Handbook of antisocial behavior* (pp. 22–35). New York: John Wiley.

Hart, S. D., Hare, R. D., & Forth, A. E. (1994). Psychopathy as a risk marker for violence: Development and validation of a screening version of the revised Psychopathy Checklist. In J. Monahan & H. J. Steadman (Eds.), *Violence and mental disorder: Developments in risk assessment* (pp. 81–98). Chicago: The John D. and Catherine T. MacArthur Foundation series on mental health and development.

Hart, S. D., Kropp, P. R., & Hare, R. D. (1988). Performance of male psychopaths following conditional release from prison. *Journal of Consulting and Clinical Psychology, 56*, 227–232.

Hawk, S. S., & Peterson, R. A. (1974). Do MMPI psychopathic deviancy scores reflect psychopathic deviancy or just deviancy? *Journal of Personality Assessment, 38*, 362–368.

Heidensohn, F. (1968). The deviance of women: A critique and an inquiry. *British Journal of Sociology, 19*, 160–175.

Heilbrun, K., Hart, S. D., Hare, R. D., Gustafson, D., Nunez, C., & White, A. J. (1998). Inpatient and postdischarge aggression in mentally disordered offenders: The role of psychopathy. *Journal of Interpersonal Violence, 13*, 514–527.

Hemphill, J. F., & Hare, R. D. (1995). Psychopathy Checklist factor scores and recidivism. *Issues in Criminological and Legal Psychology, 24*, 68–73.

Hemphill, J. F., Hare, R. D., & Wong, S. (1998). Psychopathy and recidivism: A review. *Legal and Criminological Psychology, 3*, 139–170.

Hill, C. D., Rogers, R., & Bickford, M. E. (1996). Predicting aggressive and socially disruptive behavior in a maximum security forensic psychiatric hospital. *Journal of Forensic Sciences, 41*, 56–69.

Karpman, B. (1941). On the need for separating psychopathy into two distinct clinical types: Symptomatic and idiopathic. *Journal of Criminology and Psychopathology, 3*, 112–137.

Kennedy, T. D. (1986). Trends in inmate classification. *Criminal Justice and Behavior, 13*, 165–184.

Kosson, D. S., Kelly, J. C., & White, J. W. (1997). Psychopathy-related traits predict self-reported sexual aggression among college men. *Journal of Interpersonal Violence, 12*, 241–254.

Kosson, D. S., Smith, S. S., & Newman, J. P. (1990). Evaluating the construct validity of psychopathy in Black and White male inmates: Three preliminary studies. *Journal of Abnormal Psychology, 99*, 250–259.

Kosson, D. S., Steuerwald, B. L., Newman, J. P., & Widom, C. S. (1994). The relation between socialization and antisocial behavior, substance use, and family conflict in college students. *Journal of Personality Assessment, 63*, 473–488.

Kroner, D. G., & Loza, W. (2001). Evidence for the efficacy of self-report in predicting nonviolent and violent criminal recidivism. *Journal of Interpersonal Violence, 16,* 168–177.

Lanyon, R. I. (1997). Detecting deception: Current models and directions. *Clinical Psychology and Practice, 4,* 377–387.

Levenson, M. R., Kiehl, K. A., & Fitzpatrick, C. M. (1995). Assessing psychopathic attributes in a noninstitutionalized population. *Journal of Personality and Social Psychology, 68,* 151–158.

Lilienfeld, S. O. (1994). Conceptual problems in the assessment of psychopathy. *Clinical Psychology Review, 14,* 17–38.

Lilienfeld, S. O. (1998). Recent methodological advances and developments in the assessment of psychopathy. *Behavior Research and Therapy, 36,* 99–125.

Lilienfeld, S. O. (1999). The relation of the MMPI-2 Pd Harris-Lingoes subscales to psychopathy, psychopathy facets, and antisocial behavior: Implications for clinical practice. *Journal of Clinical Psychology, 55,* 241–255.

Lilienfeld, S. O., & Andrews, B. P. (1996). Development and preliminary validation of a self-report measure of psychopathic personality traits in noncriminal populations. *Journal of Personality Assessment, 66,* 488–524.

Lilienfeld, S. O., Hess, T., & Rowland, C. (1996). Psychopathic personality traits and temporal perspective: A test of the short time horizon hypothesis. *Journal of Psychopathology and Behavioral Assessment, 18,* 285–314.

Louscher, P. K., Hosford, R. E., & Moss, C. S. (1983). Predicting dangerous behavior in a penitentiary using the Megargee typology. *Criminal Justice and Behavior, 10,* 269–284.

Lykken, D. T. (1995). *The antisocial personalities.* Hillsdale, NJ: Lawrence Erlbaum.

Lykken, D. T. (1998). *A tremor in the blood: Uses and abuses of the lie detector.* New York: Plenum Press.

Lynam, D. R. (1997). Pursuing the psychopath: Capturing the fledgling psychopath in a nomological net. *Journal of Abnormal Psychology, 106,* 425–438.

McKinley, J., & Hathaway, S. R. (1944). The MMPI: Hysteria, hypomania, and psychopathic deviate. *Journal of Applied Psychology, 28,* 153–174.

McNeil, E. B. (1970). *Neuroses and personality disorders.* Englewood Cliffs, NJ: Prentice-Hall.

Meehl, P. E. & Golden, R. R. (1982). Taxometric methods. In P. C. Kendall & J. N. Butcher (Eds.), *Handbook of research methods in clinical psychology* (pp. 215–231). New York: Guilford Press.

Megargee, E. I. (1972). *The California Psychological Inventory handbook.* San Francisco: Jossey-Bass.

Megargee, E. I., & Bohn, M. J. (1979). *Classifying criminal offenders.* Newbury Park, CA: Sage.

Megargee, E. I., Cook, P. E., & Mendelsohn, G. A. (1967). The development and validation of an MMPI scale of assaultiveness in overcontrolled individuals. *Journal of Abnormal Psychology, 72,* 510–528.

Millon, T. (1987). *Millon Clinical Multiaxial Inventory–II manual.* Minneapolis, MN: National Computer Systems.

Millon, T. (Ed.). (1997). *The Millon inventories: Clinical and personality assessment.* New York: Guilford Press.

Millon, T., Simonsen, E., & Birket-Smith, M. (1998). Historical conceptions of psychopathy in the United States. In T. Millon, E. Simonsen, M. Birket-Smith, &

R. D. Davis (Eds.), *Psychopathy: Antisocial, criminal, and violent behavior*. New York: Guilford Press.

Morey, L. C. (1991). *Personality Assessment Inventory: A professional manual*. Odessa, FL: Psychological Assessment Resources.

Morgan, C. D., & Murray, H. A. (1935). A method for investigating fantasies. *Archives of Neurology and Psychiatry, 34*, 289–306.

Moss, C. S., Johnson, M. E., & Hosford, R. E. (1984). An assessment of the Megargee typology in lifelong criminal violence. *Criminal Justice and Behavior, 11*, 225–234.

Murphy-Peaslee, D. M. (1995). An investigation of incarcerated females: Rorschach indices and Psychopathy Checklist scores (Doctoral dissertation, California School of Professional Psychology, Fresno, 1993). *Dissertation Abstracts International, 56*, 0531B.

Newman, J. P., & Kosson, D. S. (1986). Passive avoidance learning in psychopathic and nonpsychopathic offenders. *Journal of Abnormal Psychology, 95*, 252–256.

Nuffield, J. (1982). *Parole decision making in Canada: Research towards decision guidelines*. Ottawa: Solicitor General of Canada.

O'Mahony, P. D., & Murphy, P. G. (1991). Role-taking ability and Gough's theory of psychopathy. *International Journal of Offender Therapy and Comparative Criminology, 32*, 107–118.

Ogloff, J. R. P., Wong, S., & Greenwood, A. (1990). Treating criminal psychopaths in a therapeutic community program. *Behavioral Sciences and the Law, 8*, 181–190.

Patrick, C. J., & Iacono, W. G. (1986). The validity of lie detection with criminal psychopaths. *Psychophysiology, 23*, 452–453.

Porter, S., Campbell, M. A., Woodworth, M., & Birt, A. R. (2001). A new psychological conceptualization of the sexual psychopath. In F. Columbus (Ed.), *Advances in psychology research, Vol. 7* (pp. 21–36). Huntington, NY: Nova Science.

Poythress, N. G., Edens, J. F., & Lilienfeld, S. O. (1998). Criterion-related validity of the psychopathic personality inventory in a prison sample. *Psychological Assessment, 10*, 426–430.

Reise, S. P., & Oliver, C. J. (1994). Development of a California Q-Set indicator of primary psychopathy. *Journal of Personality Assessment, 62*, 130–144.

Reise, S. P., & Wink, P. (1995). Psychological implications of the Psychopathy Q-Sort. *Journal of Personality Assessment, 65*, 300–312.

Rice, M. E., & Harris, G. T. (1995). Psychopathy, schizophrenia, alcohol abuse, and violent recidivism. *International Journal of Law and Psychiatry, 18*, 333–342.

Rice, M. E., Harris, G. T., & Cormier, C. A. (1992). An evaluation of a maximum security therapeutic community for psychopaths and other mentally disordered offenders. *Law and Human Behavior, 16*, 399–412.

Robins, L. N. (1966). *Deviant children grown up*. Baltimore: Williams & Williams.

Rogers, R., Johansen, J., Change, J. J., & Salekin, R. T. (1997). Predictors of adolescent psychopathy: Oppositional and conduct-disordered symptoms. *Journal of the American Academy of Psychiatry and the Law, 25*, 261–271.

Salekin, R. T., Rogers, R., & Sewell, K. W. (1996). A review and meta-analysis of the Psychopathy Checklist and Psychopathy Checklist-Revised: Predictive validity of dangerousness. *Clinical Psychology: Science and Practice, 3*, 203–215.

Salekin, R. T., Rogers, R., & Sewell, K. W. (1997). Construct validity of psychopathy in a female offender sample: A multitrait-multimethod evaluation. *Journal of Abnormal Psychology, 106*, 576–585.

Salekin, R. T., Rogers, R., Ustad, K. L., & Sewell, K. W. (1998). Psychopathy and recidivism among female inmates. *Law and Human Behavior, 22*, 109–128.

Serin, R. C. (1991). Psychopathy and violence in criminals. *Journal of Interpersonal Violence, 6*, 423–431.

Serin, R. C. (1992). The clinical application of the Psychopathy Checklist-Revised (PCL-R). *Journal of Clinical Psychology, 48*, 637–642.

Serin, R. C. (1993). Diagnosis of psychopathology with and without an interview. *Journal of Clinical Psychology, 49*, 367–372.

Serin, R. C. (1996). Violent recidivism in criminal psychopaths. *Law and Human Behavior, 20*, 207–217.

Serin, R. C., Mailloux, D. I., & Malcolm, P. B. (2001). Psychopathy, deviant sexual arousal, and recidivism among sexual offenders. *Journal of Interpersonal Violence, 16*, 234–246.

Shedler, J., & Westen, D. (1998). Refining the measurement of Axis II: A Q-sort procedure for assessing personality pathology. *Assessment, 5*, 333–353.

Simourd, D. J., & Hoge, R. D. (2000). Criminal psychopathy: A risk-and-need perspective. *Criminal Justice and Behavior, 27*, 256–272.

Skilling, T. A. Harris, G. T., Rice, M. E., & Quinsey, V. L. (2002). Identifying persistently antisocial offenders using the Hare Psychopathy Checklist and DSM antisocial personality disorder criteria. *Psychological Assessment, 14*, 27–38.

Steffensmeier, D., & Allan, E. (1996). Gender and crime: Toward a theory of female offending. *Annual Review of Sociology, 22*, 459–487.

Stevens, G. F. (1993). Applying the diagnosis antisocial personality to imprisoned offenders. *Journal of Offender Rehabilitation, 19*, 1–26.

Toupin, J., Mercier, H., Déry, M., Côte, G., & Hodgins, S. (1995). Validity of the PCL-R for adolescents. *Issues in Criminological and Legal Psychology, 24*, 143–145.

Valliant, P. M., Gristey, C., Pottier, D., & Kosmyna, R. (1999). Risk factors in violent and nonviolent offenders. *Psychological Reports, 85*, 675–680.

Waid, W. M., & Orne, M. T. (1982). Reduced electrodermal response to conflict, failure to inhibit dominant behaviors, and delinquency proneness. *Journal of Personality and Social Psychology, 43*, 769–774.

Walters, G. D. (1986). Correlates of the Megargee criminal classification system. *Criminal Justice and Behavior, 13*, 19–32.

Webster, C. D., Harris, G. T., Rice, M. E., Cormier, C., & Quinsey, V. L. (1994). *The Violence Prediction Scheme: Assessing dangerousness in high risk men.* Toronto: Centre of Criminology, University of Toronto.

Widiger, T. A., Cadoret, R., Hare, R., Robins, L., Rutherford, M., Zanarini, M., et al. (1996). DSM-IV antisocial personality disorder field trial. *Journal of Abnormal Psychology, 105*, 3–16.

Widiger, T. A., & Corbitt, E. (1995). Antisocial personality disorder. In W. J. Livesley (Ed.), *The DSM IV personality disorders* (pp. 103–134). New York: Guilford Press.

Widiger, T. A., & Frances, A. (1987). Interviews and inventories for the measurement of personality disorders. *Clinical Psychology Review, 7*, 49–75.

Widiger, T. A., & Spitzer, R. L. (1991). Sex bias in the diagnosis of personality disorders: Conceptual and methodological issues. *Clinical Psychology Review, 11*, 1–22.

Widom, C. S. (1977). A methodology for studying noninstitutionalized psychopaths. *Journal of Consulting and Clinical Psychology, 45*, 674–683.

Widom, C. S. (1984). Sex roles, criminality, and psychopathology. In C. S. Widom (Ed.), *Sex roles and psychopathology* (pp. 183–217). New York: Plenum Press.

Williamson, S., Hare, R. D., & Wong, S. (1987). Violence: Criminal psychopaths and their victims. *Canadian Journal of Behavioural Science, 19*, 454–462.

Wilson, D. L., Frick, P. J., & Clements, C. B. (1999). Gender, somatization, and psychopathic traits in a college sample. *Journal of Psychopathology and Behavioral Assessment, 21*, 221–235.

Wong, S. (1995). Recidivism and criminal career profiles of psychopaths: A longitudinal study. *Issues in Criminological and Legal Psychology, 24*, 147–152.

Wood, J. M., Lilienfeld, S. O., Garb, H. N., & Nezworski, M. T. (2000). The Rorschach test in clinical diagnosis: A critical review, with a backward look at Garfield (1947). *Journal of Clinical Psychology, 56*, 395–430.

Wrobel, N. H., Wrobel, T. A., & McIntosh, J. W. (1988). Application of the Megargee MMPI typology to a forensic psychiatric population. *Criminal Justice and Behavior, 15*, 247–254.

Zamble, E., & Palmer, W. (1995). Prediction of recidivism using psychopathy and other psychologically meaningful variables. *Issues in Criminological and Legal Psychology, 24*, 153–156.

CHAPTER 19

SEXUAL DEVIANCE AND FORENSIC PSYCHOLOGY: A PRIMER

TAMARA PENIX SBRAGA
CENTRAL MICHIGAN UNIVERSITY

Sexual deviance is irresistible. No, the author is not an apologist for sexual offending. For the majority of people, it is observing sexual misbehavior from a safe distance that is captivating; they can be seduced by tales of serial rapists, child molesters, and exhibitionists. This is not to say that people like or accept deviant behavior. It is instead paradoxical. Sexual deviance at the criminal level is so against the natural rhythm of life, so horrifying that it is fascinating. To truly comprehend sexual deviance requires a suspension of belief that permits consideration of the inconceivable. This chapter addresses forms of such "unbelievable" sexual behavior that may bring sexual deviates into contact with the legal system. Though people are imaginative and may be arrested for the full range of sexual behaviors, sex that typically avoids police contact is not included.

The various forms of sexual deviancy are categorized and defined utilizing the *DSM-IV* descriptions (American Psychiatric Association, 1994), not because this classification system provides the most useful way of thinking about sexual deviance (see Laws and O'Donohue, 1997, for a discussion of deficits in the taxonomy), but because it is most frequently used in forensic settings. The category of rape has been added, though it is not included explicitly in the APA taxonomy. Adult sexual assault is an essential focus of forensic psychology, variously diagnosed as sexual sadism, paraphilia NOS (not otherwise specified), or undiagnosed. Other forms of sexual deviance presented here include voyeurism, exhibitionism, frotteurism, sexual sadism, rape, and pedophilia. Each category is briefly explored through its etiology, course, epidemiology, assessment, and treatment. The unique hurdles that must be cleared when mental health professionals attempt to provide assessment and treatment services in the criminal justice system are discussed.

Issues related to the risk assessment of sexual offenders will be examined, including a discussion of ethical issues in the assessment of risk, clinical and actuarial approaches, static and dynamic risk factors, and, briefly, various assessment instruments. Community safety is discussed through two modalities: imprisonment and the civil commitment of sex offenders. Trends in incarceration and the mandatory hospitalization of sexual deviates in the justice system are reviewed. The chapter concludes with a discussion of the Achilles heel of mental health professionals in forensic settings: remembering who the client is and acting within the bounds of evidence.

Adult male offenders are the focus of the chapter because they are the vast majority of sexual criminals and the bulk of our information about sexual deviance stems from studies of this population. Please see Hunter and Mathews (1997) for a review of female sexual deviance; Barbaree, Marshall, and Hudson (1993) and Murphy and Page (2000) for coverage of juvenile sex offenders; and Haaven and Coleman (2000) for an overview of developmentally disabled sexual offenders.

Sexual Deviance: A Socially Driven Problem

Politics at least partially determine what is considered sexually deviant at any particular time. What is considered to be sexually deviant has no permanence in either the psychological or legal realm.

Changes with Time

Sexual deviance is in some way a socially constructed phenomenon that shifts over time with public opinion, thereby altering the criteria that classify one as a sexual deviate. Comparisons may be drawn throughout history: Nathaniel Hawthone provides a classic fictional account of the price of sexual deviance in early America in *The Scarlet Letter*. Hester Prynne's offense was adultery. Her punishment and treatment were remaining in the community while wearing a scarlet letter A on her clothing, thereby permitting the townspeople to identify her, recall her offensive behavior, and dole out their punishments. In the early 21st century, adultery is no longer considered a problem of sufficient magnitude to be considered sexual deviancy in broad American society.

A more recent example is homosexuality. The first two editions of the *Diagnostic and Statistical Manual* of the American Psychiatric Association identified homosexuality as a mental disorder (APA, 1952; APA, 1968). Homosexuality is now officially considered to fall within the range of sexually acceptable behavior. Did these behaviors change over the years? Did the definitions of adultery and homosexuality change? No, what changed were values, political opinions, psychological and legal constructs, and, eventually, definitions of deviance.

Variability

Beyond this shift in what is considered to be sexually deviant behavior, there is, within the continuum of what currently rates as deviance (from fetishism to sexual sadism), variability in which activities are considered to be worthy of attention in the psychological and legal realms. Frotteurism, for example, is unwanted sexual behavior that involves an assault (touching another person without permission); however, frotteurism is negligibly addressed by both psychology and the courts. There are no known treatment programs for frotteurs, no significant research of exclusive frotteurs, and there are few legal repercussions for the behavior (Krueger & Kaplan, 1997). If frotteurs engaged in the same behaviors in the workplace, they would often face greater penalties as sexual harassers than they do rubbing their genitals against unsuspecting strangers in crowded trains and elevators.

Normative Behavior

There is no authority on normal sexual behavior. Sexual behavior does not appear to conform to a typical pattern, level, or type across people. The "natural" expression of sexuality is unknown (Laws & O'Donohue, 1997). The usual state, form, amount, or degree of sexuality is unclear. There are individual differences in the perception of what is normal, and beyond those ideas there are significant variations in sexual behavior. It seems that most people consider normal to be whatever they do sexually, and maybe some range of behaviors around their accepted activities. Despite the best intentions of researchers such as the Kinsey Institute and Masters and Johnson, what constitutes normality remains a mystery. Studies have identified statistical averages of activities, frequency of sex, number of partners, and other relevant statistics (Masters, Johnson, & Kolodny, 1982), but it is not clear that average is normal, particularly if *normal* implies some sort of healthfulness.

Majority opinion (and political clout) has dictated acceptable social and sexual behavior. In the instance of homosexuality, for example, the shift in whether it was or was not a mental disorder did not seem to be fueled by research that refuted the idea that it was a mental disorder; the change appeared to be motivated rather by the political pressure of gay activist organizations (Bayer, 1981). These ideas have trickled down the political path to influence our psychological and legal views of sexual deviance.

Definitions

It is necessary to distinguish between the way researchers and the legal system approach deviant sexual behavior.

Psychological Conceptualizations

Many different aspects of sexuality could be considered pertinent variables in the definition of deviant sexual behavior. Frequency, numbers of partners, time spent engaged in sex, the level of distress produced by the behavior, and interference with other aspects of life are just a few examples. The *DSM-IV* authors have chosen to define sexual deviance according to the types of activities, length of time spent pursuing them, and whether the sexual behavior creates distress in the individual or life problems. These may or may not be reasonable criteria for identifying behavioral disorders, depending on the uses of the system. That debate remains for others to address.

Regardless of criteria and purported function, the taxonomy is difficult to apply because of its inconsistencies. Excessive masturbation, use of pornography, calls to 900 sex numbers, rape, and stalking are sexual behaviors that may endure over long periods of time, cause distress in the individual, impair one's ability to function in the world, and victimize others. They meet the broad *DSM-IV* criteria but are not included in the classification system. At the same time, other behaviors clearly meet the spirit of the diagnostic criteria but do not produce distress in the individual and may not impair daily functioning, and therefore are not diagnosable. For example, some types of child molesters are exceptions to the *DSM-IV* pedophilia criteria because they do not experience distress or functional impairments as a result of these activities (Marshall, 1997). The *DSM-IV* fails to define healthy sexual behavior and inconsistently defines mentally disordered behavior in order to make the sexual deviance disorders fit neatly into the broader nosological system. I argue, as have others more eloquently elsewhere (Hudson & Ward, 1997; Marshall, 1997, O'Donohue, Regev, & Hagstrom, 2000), that it is a poor fit. That being said, the criteria are as follows.

The *DSM-IV* (APA, 1994) defines a *mental disorder* as a significant behavioral or psychological syndrome or pattern that occurs in an individual and is associated with distress; impairment in functioning; or increased risk of suffering, death, pain, disability, or an important loss of freedom. It is a manifestation of a behavioral, psychological, or biological dysfunction *in* the individual (pp. xxi–xxii). Sexually deviant behavior and conflicts that are primarily between the individual and society are not mental disorders unless the deviance is a symptom of dysfunction in the individual (paraphrased). Thus, the problem cannot be that society simply does not like the behavior of the individual. The behavior must somehow be evidence of disorder within the individual.

The paraphilias in particular are generally characterized as follows. Criterion A is recurrent, intense, sexually arousing fantasies, sexual urges, or behaviors involving (1) nonhuman objects, (2) the suffering or humiliation of oneself or one's partner, or (3) children or other nonconsenting partners over a period of at least six months. These behaviors, sexual urges, or fantasies must cause clinically significant distress or impairment in social, occupational, or other important areas of functioning (Criterion B) (pp. 522–523). Each paraphilia is further defined by the peculiarities of the sexual act:

- *Voyeurism* (302.82) is the act of observing an unsuspecting person who is naked, in the process of disrobing, or engaging in sexual activity.
- *Exhibitionism* (302.4) is the exposure of one's genitals to an unsuspecting stranger.
- *Frotteurism* (302.89) is touching and rubbing against a nonconsenting person.
- *Sexual sadism* (302.84) is acts (real, not simulated) in which the psychological or physical suffering (including humiliation) of the victim is sexually exciting to the person.
- *Pedophilia* (302.2) is sexual activity with a prepubescent child or children (generally age 13 or younger). The person is at least 16 years old and five years older than the child or children in Criterion A (Criterion C).
- *Paraphilia NOS* (302.9) is a general category for sexual behaviors that may be considered to be deviant but do not fit into one of the other categories of paraphilia. Behaviors may include telephone scatologia, necrophilia, and many others. Preference for sex with nonconsenting persons (rape) is often included in this classification.

Whether sexually deviant behavior is a mental disorder in the classic disease sense remains to be seen, though investigations of biological bases of sexual deviance are underway (Langevin, 1990). What is evident is that sexual deviance does not fit nicely into the *DSM* system, a taxonomy with a distinctly physiological slant.

Legal Conceptualizations

Although psychological criteria for sexual deviance attend to the particular sexual thoughts and behaviors of paraphiliacs, the law focuses on the effects of behavior on other people. Psychological criteria for sexual deviance include internal behaviors such as clinically significant distress and sexual fantasies. These do not enter into legal conceptualizations of deviancy. The legal system defines sexually deviant behavior by the details of the behavior and by the ages of the perpetrator and victim. At the point of sentencing, consequences of the aberrant behavior are also considered. Specific categories of criminal sexual behavior vary from state to state, but most penal codes include:

- Rape
- Incest
- Communication with a minor for immoral purposes
- Sexual misconduct
- Child molestation
- Sodomy
- Oral copulation
- Penetration with a foreign object
- Indecent exposure
- Voyeurism

- Lewd or lascivious acts with a child
- Contributing to the delinquency of a minor
- Frotteurism
- Attempted sex offenses

Psychological distress and impairments in the lives of the perpetrators are not pertinent to the legal classification of sexually deviant behavior. Sexually offensive behaviors are evaluated relative to their effect on a victim or victims.

FORENSIC PSYCHOLOGY AND SEXUAL DEVIANCE: WHERE THE TWAIN MEET

Psychology meets the legal system around the issue of sexual deviance at several points following the alleged commission of a sexual crime. These junctures include (1) the determination of trial competency, (2) during a trial to determine sanity at the time of the crime, (3) during sentencing to make recommendations, (4) making the determination of where an inmate should serve his sentence, (5) making parole decisions, (6) the prediction of risk, (7) determining the appropriateness for civil commitment, and (8) treatment decisions.

Traditional Mental Illness

Responsibility, dangerousness, and appropriateness for treatment are the major issues psychology is asked to address throughout the legal process. For the first four points, it is ordinarily the presence of a major mental disorder that may have produced sexually deviant behaviors that is in question. These early phases of the legal system are not reviewed in this chapter because they are better covered in Chapter 8 in this volume. The basic issues that face the court in trial competency, insanity, sentencing, and placement are no different for sex crimes than for the other types of crime described by these authors. The presence of a bona fide mental illness is the issue, not sexual deviance.

The Paraphilias

The paraphilias come into play in the latter phases of the legal system. Once an inmate has been sentenced, the issue of sexual deviance treatment is raised relative to rehabilitation. In order to evaluate movement toward rehabilitation, the courts seek information about inmates' skill and pro-social behavior deficits. One potential area of assessment is sexual deviance. Forensic mental health questions at this stage include the following: Is there a paraphilia? How severe is it? At what stage in the punishment/rehabilitation process should the inmate receive treatment? And, does the paraphilia render the inmate so dangerous that treatment is mandatory prior to release? Once the inmate has entered treatment, the queries turn toward treatment gains, least restrictive alternatives for treatment, and risk of reoffending. Psychologists and psychiatrists take on the role of evaluator for the courts in order to address questions of diagnosis, prognosis, amenability to treatment, appropriate treatment, dangerousness, progress toward treatment goals, and risk. In addition to the role of evaluator, mental health professionals act as treatment providers for sexual deviates in outpatient settings, prisons, and inpatient facilities. In order to maintain objectivity and a positive therapeutic relationship with the inmate in assessment and treatment, it is recommended that the same professional does not fulfill both roles with the same client.

Sexual deviance becomes a categorization device that is used to determine whether a crime has been committed, appropriate punishments, type of penal institution, treatment considerations, and what happens toward the end of the sentence and/or treatment—that is, release, parole, extensive monitoring, or civil commitment.

FORENSIC ATTENTION: THE BIG SIX

This section provides the most basic information about each of the six major forms of sexual deviance that make contact with the legal system. For each type of paraphilia, descriptions of the behaviors, etiology, course, epidemiology, assessment, and treatment are offered. The descriptions are followed by a discussion of the problems inherent in assessing and treating sex offenders in the criminal justice system.

Voyeurism

Description

Voyeurism is seeking sexual pleasure from watching nude people. For some, the viewing occurs while the strangers are disrobing or having sex. There appear to be three distinct groups of voyeurs (Kaplan & Krueger, 1997). The first is composed of those who engage in voyeurism as their sole sexual outlet. The second is the preferred voyeur who additionally participates in other sexual activities. And last, there are voyeurs who engage in voyeuristic activities primarily when they are under increased stress. For all types of voyeurs, masturbation may occur during the peeping or later, as perpetrators fantasize about their experience (APA, 1994). Voyeurism is sometimes a precursor or adjunctive behavior to contact sexual offenses (Abel, Mittelman, & Becker, 1985).

Etiology

Voyeurism usually begins prior to age 15 and continues throughout the life span (APA, 1994).

Psychoanalytic Theory. Psychoanalysts maintain that sexual deviance is the result of unresolved conflicts in psychosexual development and a regression to earlier developmental levels in an attempt to reenact individuation from the mother and resolve castration anxiety (Meyer, 1995). Psychodynamic theory extends this idea as converting childhood trauma into adult triumph through sexually deviant behavior (Stoller, 1991).

Social Learning Theory. Sexual behaviors are acquired and maintained through classical and operant conditioning. They are learned through observation and shaped through contingent reinforcement, according to Laws and Marshall (1990). Higher-order conditioning is produced by masturbation, thereby reinforcing and strengthening the deviant behavior.

Sociobiological Theory. Voyeurism is also believed to be part of the natural selection process. Symons (1979) hypothesizes that seeking and watching nude females can maximize male reproductive opportunities.

Biological Theory. Androgens, neuropsychological deficits, and sex chromosome abnormalities are hypothesized to contribute to sexual deviance; however, there is little empirical support for these suppositions at this time (Langevin, 1990).

Course and Epidemiology

The course of voyeurism appears to be chronic. The epidemiology is unknown (Kaplan & Krueger, 1997). Voyeurism often goes undetected; when it comes to the attention of the authorities, it may be mistaken for trespassing or loitering (Kaplan & Krueger, 1997). In a study that gathered epidemiological data for a variety of paraphilias, Abel (1989) found that the median number of voyeuristic acts for his subjects was 17. Abel and Rouleau (1990) also reported that voyeurs tend to have other paraphilias and report a high frequency of sexually deviant acts.

Assessment

Assessment must always be conducted with the referral question in mind, often diagnosis and treatment recommendations. The first goal of assessment of voyeurs is to understand the parameters of the behavior for a given individual. A functional analysis of the behavior is the key to understanding the stimuli that elicit, maintain, and reinforce the behavior (Hanson & Harris, 1997). Because of the high cooccurrence of voyeurism with other paraphilias (Abel & Rouleau, 1990), it is also important to assess for other sexually deviant behavior and fantasies. Useful assessment tools may include the following:

- *The Erotic Preferences Examination Scheme (EPES; Freund, Watson, & Rienzo, 1988).* A self-report measure that contains six items pertaining to voyeurism. These items discriminated between voyeurs and nonvoyeurs in that 85 percent of the former endorsed all six, whereas only 20 percent of nonvoyeur sex offenders as well as student and nonstudent controls endorsed all of them.

- *The Clarke Sexual History Questionnaire (SHQ; Langevin, Paitich, Russon, Handy, & Langevin, 1990).* A self-report measure that contains a six-item Peeping scale. This has not been used to compare known voyeurs with other types of sex offenders or nonoffenders; however, the internal consistency of the whole scale for a diverse sample of paraphiliacs is between .76 and .84.
- *The Multiphasic Sex Inventory (MSI; Nichols & Molider, 1984).* A self-report measure containing nine items that assess voyeuristic activity. The scale has not been tested to discriminate voyeurs from other offenders and nonoffenders.
- *The Sexual Fantasy Questionnaire (SFQ; O'Donohue, Letourneau, & Dowling, 1997).* A self-report measure that assesses the range of sexual fantasy content. This scale demonstrated adequate test-retest reliability, internal consistency, and convergent validity in initial investigations of its psychometric properties. The scale discriminates between deviant and nondeviant content; however, subjects with sexually deviant fantasies acknowledge similar numbers of nondeviant sexual fantasies.

Phallometric procedures (male genital measures of sexual arousal) have not yet been developed and tested specifically to discriminate between voyeurs and nonvoyeurs.

Treatment

Voyeurism has not been the target of treatment development independent of the other paraphilias. Therefore, all treatments for voyeurism should be considered experimental at this time. Case study reports indicate that treatment providers have used a variety of approaches to attempt to reduce the peeping of voyeurs. These include orgasmic reconditioning (Jackson, 1969), aversion therapy (Gaupp, Stern, & Ratcliff, 1977; Rangaswamy, 1987; Tollison & Adams, 1979), satiation (Konopacki & Oei, 1988), and drug therapy (fluoxetine) (Emmanuel, Lydiard, & Ballenger, 1991). In each of these cases, the therapy was pronounced successful in significantly reducing the voyeuristic behavior.

Exhibitionism

Description

Exhibitionism is exposing one's genitals to an unsuspecting stranger. Exhibitionists are a heterogeneous group (Hall, 1990), closely matching the general population in intelligence, education, and vocations (Blair & Lanyon, 1981). No specific psychological impairment or personality disorder appears to distinguish exhibitionists from others, though the body of research in this area reflects poor research standards and conflicting results (Murphy, 1997). It is primarily a male disorder, though there have been nominal reports of female exposers (Murphy, 1997). Exhibitionists expose themselves to victims of all ages (Maletzky, 1998). It is not clear if those who exhibit to children have pedophilic proclivities or if the exposure is simply indiscriminate (Murphy, 1997).

Etiology

The onset of exhibitionism tends to occur in the mid-teens and mid-twenties (Berah & Myers, 1983; Mohr, Turner, & Jerry, 1964).

Psychoanalytic Theory. Psychoanalysts surmise that exhibitionism is caused by the oedipal conflict and castration anxiety relative to the mother (Allen, 1980).

Behavioral and Cognitive-Behavioral Theory. Exhibitionist behavior develops through operant and classical conditioning (Laws & Marshall, 1990).

Biological Theory. Exposing the genitals is a sexual signal among certain types of apes (Bailey, 1991). Male exposure of the genitals could be viewed as a normal sexual drive that is displaced or disinhibited, according to Bailey.

Course and Epidemiology

The natural course, incidence, and prevalence of the disorder are unknown (Murphy, 1997). Limited community and college samples indicate that between 40 and 60 percent of women report being victims of exhibitionism (Murphy, 1997). Abel and Rouleau (1990) reported that the 142 exhibitionists in their sample acknowledged 72,974 victims, indicating that the behavior is frequent. Moreover, exhibitionists account for approximately one-third of all identified offenders in early sex offender research (Mohr, Turner, & Jerry, 1964). In Abel's sample, 93 percent of these offenders had more than one paraphilia and 73 percent had more than three paraphilias (Abel & Rouleau, 1990).

Assessment

There are no assessment studies of exhibitionism alone (Maletzky, 1997). Assessments are data-gathering enterprises focused on culling information regarding characteristics of the offense, sexual history, mental status, the function of the behavior, the related issues of what elicits and maintains the exposure, and deviant sexual arousal. Collateral information is particularly valuable with exhibitionists. They are more likely than other offenders to underreport the frequency of their offending (McConaghy, 1993). No particular psychological measures are recommended for gathering the pertinent information because none has been normed and validated exclusively with this population. However, sexual inventories with strong psychometric properties that have included exhibitionists in their populations may be utilized, including the Clarke Sexual History Questionnaire (SHQ; Langevin, Paitich, Russon, Handy, & Langevin, 1990) and the Multiphasic Sex Inventory (MSI; Nichols & Molinder, 1984). Personality testing does not distinguish any type of sex offender from other offender types or nonoffenders, according to Marshall and Hall (1995).

Phallometric testing is of limited utility with exhibitionists. The majority of exhibitionists demonstrate sexual arousal similar to that of nonoffenders (Langevin & Lang, 1987; Maletzky, 1980). Deviant arousal to exhibitionist scenes has been demonstrated by some exhibitionists when the stimuli are verbal instead of visual, whereas nonexhibitors rarely produce sexual arousal to these scenes (Howes, 1995; Maletzky, 1980). Thus, if phallometry is to be used in a tentative manner in order to preliminarily investigate deviant sexual arousal, the use of verbal stimuli is recommended. Please see Maletzky, 1991 and Hall, Proctor, and Nelson, 1988, for reviews of the pros and cons of phallometric testing.

Treatment

A variety of treatment techniques have been used with exhibitionists. There is no standard treatment for the disorder. Techniques with empirical and clinical support include:

Treating Deviant Sexual Arousal
- Aversive conditioning pairs an unconditioned aversive stimulus with a deviant response in order to reduce the likelihood of it occurring. Aversive stimuli have included electroshock (Maletzky, 1991), olfactory conditioning (Maletzky, 1980), covert sensitization (McConaghy, 1990), and vicarious sensitization (Maletzky, 1994). Covert sensitization involves relaxation, visualizing exposure scenes that produce deviant arousal, imagining negative consequences, and escape that is paired with not exposing. Vicarious sensitization involves viewing scenes of negative outcomes for sex offenders, some of them extreme.
- Conditioning procedures have included alternative behavior completion (McConaghy, 1993). This involves having the offender generate alternative behaviors for different points in the chain of behaviors that leads to offending. He imagines being caught up in that chain, enacting a behavioral alterative, and imagining how he would feel having escaped without reoffending.
- Biofeedback has been used as a treatment technique using the plethysmograph (Maletzky, 1991; McConaghy, 1993).
- Directed masturbation techniques have been useful with some exhibitionists. Specific approaches include fantasy change (Maletzky, 1986), masturbatory satiation (Laws & Marshall, 1991), and directing the client not to masturbate to exposure fantasies (Maletzky, 1997). Fantasy change involves masturbating to deviant fantasies to nearly the ejaculation point and then switching to nondeviant fantasy. Masturbatory satiation involves masturbating to ejaculation using only nondeviant fantasies and continuing to fantasize after ejaculation, using deviant fantasies only in the flaccid state.
- Chemical castration through the use of medroxyprogesterone acetate (MPA) and cyproterone acetate (CPA) appears to be an effective treatment

for exhibitionists through the reduction of the sex drive (Hall, 1995; Langevin et al., 1979). Issues with the treatment include offender opposition to the use of the hormones, return of the same sex drive if the hormones are discontinued, and the anger (not sexual) basis of many sex crimes (Bradford, 1990; Maletzky, 1991). As a result, antiandrogen therapy is typically offered in conjunction with a comprehensive cognitive-behavioral treatment program, including many of the aforementioned treatment techniques.
- The use of pharmacological agents that affect serotonin levels has also been examined in the reduction of sexual drive in sex offenders. Preliminary studies of drugs such as fluoxetine, clomipramine, fluvoxamine, and sertraline have shown decreased sexual activity in subjects with sexual disorders (Bradford, et al., 1996; Coleman, Cesnik, Moore, & Dwyer, 1992; Stein, Hollander, Anthony, Schneider, Fallon, & Liebowitz, 1992). Investigations of these and other selective serotonin reuptake inhibitors (SSRIs) are ongoing.

Treating Cognitive Distortions
- Altering cognitive distortions is an approach common to many treatment programs. Exhibitionists often carry false beliefs regarding their offending behavior such as, "I'm not hurting anyone because I am not touching anyone." Helping offenders to identify their distortions and to view evidence that these thoughts are inaccurate may aid them in altering the pro-offending attitudes and behaviors these thoughts promote (Maletzky, 1980).

Enhancing Victim Empathy
- Victim empathy training is another technique that is common to sex offender treatment programs and may be particularly important to exhibitionists because they tend to deny the harm they cause their victims (Cox & Maletzky, 1980).

Treatment outcome studies for exhibitionists alone are rare. Programs vary significantly in their results; however, the best outcomes appear to be produced by cognitive-behavioral programs that include a number of the above elements. Maletzky (1987) and Wolfe (1989) reported reoffense rates of 14 percent and 15 percent, respectively, for patients who were followed from one to 14 years. Langevin and colleagues (1979) reported a reoffense rate of 41 percent, and Marshall and Barbaree (1990b) reported a reoffense rate of 48 percent for their treated offenders. It is difficult to determine the source of these vast differences in treatment outcome, yet it seems notable that the two former studies were conducted in private settings and the latter studies were conducted in institutions. Population differences seem likely. In a study that followed untreated exhibitionists for six years, 41 percent had reoffended after one year. Of those with a history of multiple arrests, 57 percent had reoffended (Frisbie & Dondis, 1965).

Frotteurism

Description

Frotteurs derive sexual pleasure from rubbing against unsuspecting strangers. They are not usually arrested and, if they are, they do not serve much time in jail (Krueger & Kaplan, 1997). This classification is included in a forensic chapter because of the high comorbidity of frotteurism with the paraphilias that capture the attention of the criminal justice system. Very little is known about offenders who engage exclusively in frotteurism. There are no published accounts of females who engage in the behavior.

Etiology

Psychoanalytic Theory. Frotteurism is viewed along with the other paraphilias as a lingering expression of childhood sexuality (Gillespie, 1964).

Behavioral Theory. Frotteurism is produced through classical and operant conditioning (Laws & Marshall, 1990). Laws and Marshall point out that because deviant arousal is only one element that contributes to offending behavior and is only found in approximately a third of offenders, other behaviors must be conditioned concurrently or there must be an adjunctive theoretical explanation to account for offending behavior in those without a deviant sexual arousal pattern.

Pathological Imprinting. Binet (1887) hypothesized that children develop a fetish through attachment to their caregivers and that touching and smelling that person strengthens the attachment to the object.

Neurological Deficits. Recent neurological studies are investigating the idea that paraphilic behavior stems from brain abnormalities, an idea that stems from the work of Kolarsky, Freund, Machek, and Polak (1967).

Courtship Disorder. The idea that the paraphilias reflect a problem in progressing through the normal phases of courtship originated with Albert Ellis (Ellis & Brancala, 1956). Noting the high degree of comorbidity among the paraphilias, Freund (1990) and his colleagues (Freund, Seto, & Kuban, 1997) elaborated on the theory. They view the paraphilias as a disorder of phasing in the sexual behaviors that precede intercourse. Hypotheses that drive the theory include (1) human courtship is regulated by natural preferences for certain erotic activities that occur in a sequential fashion; (2) courtship disorder occurs when, in the normative sequence, an intensification or distortion of a particular phase occurs; and (3) these problems reflect the preference of the paraphiliac for an instant conversion of sexual arousal into orgasm (Freund, Seto, & Kuban, 1997). These authors count voyeurism, exhibitionism, frotteurism, and preferential rape as different reflections of this disorder.

Course and Epidemiology

The true course and epidemiology of frotteurism are unknown. An epidemiological study by Abel, Becker, Cunningham-Rathner, Rouleau, and Murphy (1987) with nonincarcerated subjects found that the mean number of acts of frottage for subjects with frotteurism as the primary diagnosis was 849.5. Because of the high co-occurrence of frotteurism with the other paraphilias (Abel & Rouleau, 1990; Bradford, Boulet, & Pawlak, 1992; Freund, Sher, & Hucker, 1983), it is suggested that offenders with frottage in their history may be at risk of developing additional paraphilias.

Assessment

The assessment of frotteurs progresses similarly to that of any sex offender. It is imperative to gather data regarding what elicits and maintains the touching behavior and the conditions under which it occurs. Along with conducting a thorough functional analysis, useful historical information includes age of onset, frequency, the presence of other paraphilic interests, and the use of substances prior to engaging in the behavior (Abel, 1989). Krueger and Kaplan (1997) offer further guidelines for assessment such as discovering the context of the offenses, including environmental factors, victim characteristics, emotional states, impulsivity or planning, and the overall criminal and sexual histories.

Again, no psychological measures have been developed to discriminately assess frottage. Psychometrically sound instruments that may be useful in gathering a thorough sexual history have been mentioned. No reports of plethysmography with exclusive frotteurs are found in the literature.

Polygraphy is sometimes used in the assessment and treatment of sexual offenders (Abrams, 1991). The "lie detector" tests are controversial for reasons including a lack of standardized procedures, inadmissibility in courts, poor predictive performance, and the coercive properties they bear (Brett, Phillips, & Beary, 1986). However, with the appropriate informed consent, the polygraph may be a useful tool, not for the purpose of revealing lies, but as a motivational instrument that may aid in guiding the client toward revealing more about his history of offending.

Treatment

The special treatment needs of frotteurs are unknown and there are no treatment modalities that focus specifically on frottage. More general treatment approaches for the various paraphilias are described throughout this chapter. These are experimental methods of treatment that are being used with frotteurs. Frotteurism is a form of deviance with significant research and treatment development needs.

Sexual Sadism

Description

Sexual sadism is extracting sexual pleasure from causing pain to another living being. Fromm (1977) conceptualizes sadism as the drive to have absolute control over another person or animal. Sadism is commonly seen in individuals with additional paraphilias. Abel, Becker, Cunningham-Rathner, Mittelman, & Rouleau (1988) found that 18 percent of their sample of sex offender sadists were also masochistic, 46 percent had raped, 21 percent had exposed themselves, 25 percent had engaged in voyeurism, 25 percent had engaged in frotteurism, and 33 percent had engaged in pedophilia. The FBI collected data on 30 sexual sadists (Dietz, Hazelwood, & Warren, 1990). Their most interesting findings include that 43 percent of their sample had a history of homosexuality, more than 50 percent had no prior criminal record, and 50 percent had a history of drug abuse beyond alcoholism. Dietz and his colleagues also found these men to be profoundly narcissistic. Although some sadists appear to stay within the realm of consensual sadomasochistic activities with a masochistic partner (Hucker, 1990), others seem to thrive on inflicting pain on a nonconsenting person.

Etiology

Seventy-five percent of sadistic males report having been aware of their deviant interests prior to adulthood (Breslow, Evans, & Langley, 1985; Spengler, 1977). Sadistic females tend to become involved in the behaviors through adult relationships with masochistic men, discovering pleasure in sadism through its practice, according to Scott (1983).

Psychoanalytic Theory. Freud hypothesized that sadism originates when a child misinterprets sex as painful by observing his parents having sexual relations (1961).

Behaviorial Theory. Conditioned sexual arousal followed by masturbation and sexual fantasies that are reinforced encapsulates behaviorist thought on the basic origins of sadistic behavior (McGuire, Carlisle, & Young, 1965).

Biological Theory. It has been hypothesized that neurological abnormalities may be responsible for sexual sadism. Several studies have found mild associations between sadism and temporal lobe abnormalities (Graber, Hartmann, Coffman, Huey, & Golden, 1982; Gratzer & Bradford, 1995; Hucker, et al., 1988). It seems possible that these abnormalities could also be the result of physiologically and psychologically painful sex or an unidentified third variable. Other studies have examined hormonal differences between sexual sadists and controls without finding any significant differences (Bain, Langevin, Dickey, & Ben-Aron, 1987).

Course and Epidemiology

The course and prevalence of sexual sadism are unknown (Hucker, 1997). Several studies have attempted to gather prevalence information using community samples. Hunt (1974) found that 5 percent of men and 2 percent of women received sexual gratification from causing pain to their partners, while Arndt,

Foehl, and Good (1985) found that a third of women and half of men in their study had sexual fantasies of restraining a sex partner.

Assessment

Understanding what elicits and maintains sexual sadism involves assessing four major areas, according to Holmes and Holmes (1994). These four areas include having fantasies about inflicting pain, being attached to an inanimate object or body part, engaging in ritualism that focuses on the suffering of others, and feeling a compulsion to act out sadistic fantasies. Some of this information may be gathered through the self-report of the perpetrator and psychological testing, while plethysmography and thorough records reviews (particularly accounts of the crimes) provide useful supplemental data.

Psychological tests that may have investigative or treatment utility with sexual sadists are those that include both sexual and aggressive factors. Examples include the Aggressive Sexual Behavior Inventory (ASB; Mosher, 1988), the Coercive Sexual Fantasies Questionnaire (Greendlinger & Byrne, 1987), the Attraction to Sexual Aggression Scale (ASA; Malamuth, 1989), and the Multidimensional Assessment of Sex and Aggression (MASA; Knight, Prentky, and Cerce, 1994). Of these four instruments, the ASA and MASA have the strongest psychometric properties. The ASA was designed to measure the appeal of sexual aggression. All scales have an internal consistency ranging from .78 to .92 with high test-retest reliability. The MASA was designed to measure aggressive and sexual fantasies, cognitions, and behaviors. The internal consistency is in the acceptable range, with all scales at least .60 and 89 percent of them higher than .80. Test-retest reliability is also acceptable.

Fedora, Reddon, Morrison, Fedora, Pascoe, and Yeudall (1992) found a distinctive phallometric profile for sexual sadists. Sexual sadists in their study became sexually aroused to slides of nonsexual violence against fully clothed women, unlike comparison participants. In addition to finding a distinct pattern of responding that corresponds to physical violence against women, a separate sadistic profile demonstrates deviant arousal to the domination and humiliation of women (Thornton, 1993).

Treatment

Treatment targets for sexual sadists include controlling deviant sexual arousal, increasing victim empathy, modifying cognitive distortions, and increasing social competency and balance in the lifestyle.

Techniques for modifying deviant sexual arousal were described above. They include electroshock, olfactory aversion, covert sensitization, vicarious sensitization, masturbatory satiation and reconditioning, and chemical castration.

Victim empathy training includes elements such as meeting with victims of sexual aggression, hearing audiotaped 911 calls from frantic victims, watching videos of victims describing their experiences, writing unsent letters to victims, and discussing personal victimization experiences while relating one's experience to the experience of other victims.

Changing cognitive distortions involves the identification of distorted thinking and issuing challenges to those thoughts, typically in a group therapy format.

Increasing social competency may mean different skills training for different offenders based on individual deficits. Some offenders may be inept in general communication. Others may have problems with assertiveness, intimacy, or anger, for example.

Lifestyle balance also implies different needs for different offenders. Some offenders have problems with substance abuse, and others do not. Others may need treatment for other types of unbalanced behavior that establishes or maintains their deviance, such as viewing pornography, gambling, or isolating themselves from others. Established adjunctive treatments may be necessary to meet the unique needs posed by a particular presentation of sexually deviant behavior.

Rape

Description

Rape is sexual contact with a nonconsenting person. Because rape is legally defined and is not considered a paraphilia in the prevalent diagnostic system, the conceptualization is somewhat different from region to region. Which sexual behaviors constitute sexual assault, the criteria for nonconsent, and ages of the victim and perpetrator vary. Sometimes rape refers to vaginal penetration with a penis; in other contexts rape refers to any type of sexual penetration, including vaginal intercourse, anal intercourse, penetration with foreign objects, and oral copulation (Hudson & Ward, 1997).

Rape is difficult to research and treat because of the heterogeneity of the offenders and offenses that are classified as sexual assaults. Incarcerated rapists tend to be similar to the general prison population with low socioeconomic status, low educational attainments, and unstable employment as unskilled laborers (Bard, Carter, Cerce, Knight, Rosenbert, & Schneider, 1987). They additionally mirror similar rates of psychiatric problems (Barbaree, Marshall, & Lanthier, 1979). However, little is known about the offenders who are never reported or incarcerated. It is possible that rapists who are partners of their victims (the majority of rapists, Gavey, 1991; Koss, 1992) are more representative of the general population and are less frequently incarcerated. Prentky, Knight, Sims-Knight, Straus, Rokous, and Cerce (1989) found four developmental antecedents to sexual aggression and nonsexual aggression in adulthood. Caregiver inconsistency and sexual deviance in the family were related to the severity of sexual aggression, whereas institutional history and physical abuse predicted the severity of nonsexual aggression.

Etiology

Psychoanalytic Theory. Freud (1953) viewed deviant sexual behavior as a problem of infantile sexual desires that continues into adulthood. Psychodynamic theorists expand on this idea with feelings of anxiety that are linked to personal inadequacy. These emotions interact with aggression toward the mother that is displaced onto the victim, resulting in a sexual assault (Cohen, Garofalo, Boucher, & Seghorn, 1971; Groth, Burgess, & Holmstrom, 1977).

Behavioral Theory. Two popular behavioral theories have been proposed for sexual aggression. The first posits that sexual arousal in the presence of rape cues produces sexual assaults (Amir, 1971; Abel, Barlow, Blanchard, & Guild, 1977; Quinsey, Chaplin, & Upfold, 1984). However, this theory has been largely discarded because of increasing evidence that the sexual arousal patterns of rapists are similar to those of nonoffenders (Baxter, Barbaree, & Marshall, 1986). Laws and Marshall presented their comprehensive conditioning theory in 1990, discussed earlier in the chapter.

Feminist Theory. Rape is viewed as a "pseudosexual act which is primarily motivated by male sociopolitical dominance" (Hudson & Ward, 1997, p. 341). In this model, rape is viewed as a method of social control through fear and intimidation.

Social-Cognitive Theory. Biased processing of sex-related information may lead to sexual offending, in the view of Marshall and Barbaree (1989), Stermac and Segal (1989), and Ward, Hudson, Marshall, and Siegart (1995). At least some sexual assaulters appear to think differently about sex-related constructs than nonoffenders and nonsexual offenders. Rapists appear to misinterpret information in rape scenarios as positive from the victim's perspective (Scully, 1988).

Sociobiological Theory. Ellis (1989, 1991) argued that sexual aggression is favored in the scheme of natural selection. Men who sexually assault women have greater evolutionary advantages because they are maximizing their reproductive potential, according to Ellis.

Comprehensive Theory. Comprehensive theories of sexual aggression reflect the idea that at least several, if not many, factors come together, creating multiple pathways to sexually assaultive behavior. Various authors have proposed contributing factors and ways in which they merge to produce the behaviors.

- Malamuth, Heavey, and Linz (1993) consider deviant sexual arousal to rape, domination, hostility toward women, acceptance of rape myths, antisocial personality characteristics, and sexual experience in the etiology of rape.

- Marshall and Barbaree (1990a) stress developmental antecedents such as poor parenting, severe physical discipline, underdeveloped social controls, poor social skills, intimacy deficits, negative attitudes, and an impaired ability to distinguish between sex and aggression.
- Hall and Hirschman (1991) include four components in their model, in which physiological sexual arousal, cognitions that support sexual violence, affective dyscontrol, and characterological problems interact to produce sexual assault.
- Ward and Hudson (2000) propose that there are multiple pathways to similar sexual offenses. They attend to the interactions of cognitive, behavioral, affective, and contextual factors in the development and maintenance of sexually deviant behaviors. Theirs is a phase theory that considers nine phases including: contacting a life event, desiring deviant sex, establishing offense-related goals, selecting an offense strategy, entering a high-risk situation, lapsing, relapsing, evaluating the offense, and developing an attitude toward future offending.

Course and Epidemiology

The true epidemiology of rape is unknown because of underreporting (Koss, 1992). Approximately 25 percent of adult women report having been sexually assaulted (Gavey, 1991; Koss, Gidycz, & Wisniewski, 1987; Russell, 1984). Koss found that women are four times more likely to be sexually assaulted by someone they know than a stranger (1992). Gavey's 1991 data were consistent. She found over 82 percent of the sexual assaults in her sample were perpetrated by a partner, ex-partner, or acquaintance of the victims. Untreated rapists have a low recidivism rate compared with other sex offenders, ranging from 6 to 35 percent (Marshall & Barbaree, 1990b). Hanson and Bussiere's meta-analysis (1996) found a recidivism rate of 18.9 percent across 61 studies including 1,839 rapists.

Assessment

The assessment of rapists is a data-gathering enterprise that examines the context in which offending develops and is maintained. The evaluator gathers a wealth of information pertaining to the offender's history, psychological characteristics, sexual arousal pattern, and offense variables in order to discern diagnostic characteristics, issues that may be amenable to treatment, and, later, items that may determine the risk potential for reoffending. Ward, McCormack, Hudson, and Polaschek (1997) present a comprehensive list of areas that may be relevant to the assessment including family, educational, occupational, social, and sexual history, denial, cognitive processes, empathy, social competence, sexual preference/sexual arousal, psychopathology, religiosity, affective and motivational factors, offense antecedents, planning, victim characteristics, and the nature of the offense. As with any assessment endeavor, a multimethod approach is recommended in order to have multiple data points for integration as well as to avoid relying too heavily on any one fallible instrument. Utilization of a clinical interview, psychological testing, physiological testing, and a thorough records review are recommended for the most objective outcome.

A number of measures that were referred to earlier in the chapter are also of use with rapists including the MSI (Nichols & Molinder, 1984), SHQ (Langevin et al., 1990), MASA (Knight, Prentky, & Cerce, 1994), and ASA (Malamuth, 1989). Additional psychological tools that may be useful in gathering pertinent information from rapists include:

- Sexual Experiences Survey (SE; Koss & Oros, 1982). This instrument was designed to assess unreported rape and sexual aggression in nonincarcerated samples.
- Burt Rape Myth Acceptance Scale (RMAS; Burt, 1980). This instrument was developed to assess beliefs supportive of sexually aggressive behavior.
- Hostility Toward Women Scale (HTW; Check, 1985). This instrument was designed to identify hostile beliefs about women.
- Attitudes Toward Women Scale (ATW; Spence, Helmreich, & Stapp, 1973). This instrument was developed to assess beliefs about women's roles.
- Rape Empathy Scale (Deitz, Blackwell, Daley, & Bentley, 1982). This instrument was designed to tap into empathic feelings for rapists and victims of rape.
- Revised UCLA Loneliness Scale (Russell, Peplau, & Cutrona, 1980). This instrument was designed to assess feelings of loneliness in relation to other people.
- State-Trait Anger Expression Inventory (STAXI; Spielberger, 1988). This instrument was designed to measure anger and its expression.
- Psychopathy Checklist–Revised (PCL-R; Hare, 1980). This instrument was designed to measure levels of psychopathy in incarcerated and forensic hospital patients.

Treatment

Factors requiring treatment overlap for rapists and other sexual offenders. Important targets for treatment, depending on the idiographic offending pattern of the rapist, include denial and minimization, controlling deviant sexual arousal, victim empathy, cognitive distortions, understanding offending behavior chains, anger and stress management, and social skills training. A combination treatment approach including antiandrogen therapy and the appropriate cognitive-behavioral treatment components appears to be most promising. Hall (1995) conducted a meta-analysis of 12 treatment outcome studies that used a comparison or control group. He found that cognitive-behavioral and hormonal treatments produced larger effect sizes than strictly behavioral programs, larger effect sizes were found for studies that included higher recidivism base rates, and outpatient treatment studies fared better than those that focused on inpatient treatment. Hall found that over an average of 6.9 years at risk of reoffending, 19 percent of treated offenders and 27 percent of the comparison or control groups recidivated. More recently, Grossman, Martis, and Fichtner (1999), in a key review of sex offender treatment outcome studies from 1970–1998, reported that the literature suggests a reduction in recidivism of 30 percent over seven years, with comparable effectiveness for hormonal and cognitive-behavioral treatments. They acknowledged that design flaws interfere with the accuracy of results in these studies, as other researchers have previously discussed (Furby, Weinrott, & Blackshaw, 1989). However, they conclude that these limitations are not a barrier to cautious interpretation of the available data.

A problem with the treatment literature for rapists is that it is often the case that few rapists are included in the studies. That is, they comprise a small subset of the sex offender group that is treated. Typically, treatment programs have been developed with child molesters and have been offered to rapists unchanged, or simply modified from their original version. Marshall (1993) proposed the idea that the real treatment needs of rapists have not been thoroughly researched but have been inadequately accommodated by existing approaches. One difficulty in studying rapists exclusively is that they are difficult to engage in treatment (Marques, Day, Nelson, & West, 1994; Marshall, 1993).

Pedophilia

Description

The *DSM-IV* diagnosis of this disorder is controversial for a number of reasons. It describes *pedophilia* as being distinguished by fantasies, urges, or behaviors involving sex with a prepubescent child or children that must cause distress or impairment in the individual's functioning (APA, 1994). Problems arise in that some individuals exhibit pedophilic behaviors and experience no distress or impairment relative to their abuses and are thus not classified as pedophiles. Others may lead fairly normal lives and never act on (or even disclose) sexual fantasies about children; these individuals *are* considered to be pedophiles. Some adults enjoy having sex with young teenagers who may or may not have reached puberty. They *are not* considered to be pedophiles, according to the *DSM-IV* criteria, because their sexual choices do not cause them distress or social difficulties. See O'Donohue, Regev, and Hagstrom for a complete review of the problems with the *DSM-IV* diagnosis of pedophilia (2000).

Pedophilic behavior is exhibited by both males and females (Fehrenbach & Monastersky, 1988; Knopp & Lackey, 1987; Johnson & Shrier, 1987; Mathews, Matthews, & Speltz, 1989), though it is more prevalent in males (American Humane Association, 1988). Victims of pedophilia include both genders. Victims are typically known to their offenders as relatives or acquaintances (Fehrenbach & Monastersky, 1988; Mathews et al., 1989). Mathews and colleagues (1989) found that nearly as many females acknowledged using force in their crimes as their male counterparts; however, females are more likely to act out sexually with a male co-offender than are males. Hunter and Mathews (1997) found that three-quarters of victims of female pedophiles are eight years or younger. Few pedophiles suffer from any type of psychological disorder, including the personality disorders and psychopathy (Abel, Rouleau, Cunningham-Rathner, 1986; Marshall & Hall, 1995; Serin, Malcolm, Khanna, & Barbaree, 1994).

Etiology

In a sample of incarcerated pedophiles, Marshall, Barbaree, and Eccles (1991) found that over half did not offend until adulthood, and most of these late-onset offenders denied that they had fantasized about children prior to adulthood, despite the clinical lore that pedophilia always begins at a young age. Matthews, Hunter, and Vuz (1997) reported that in their sample of female pedophiles the behavior appeared to have a juvenile onset.

Little is known about the risk factors that predispose one to sexually offend against children (Marshall, 1993). When strong associations are found between characteristics such as intimacy deficits or a lack of empathy and offending, the chicken-and-egg problem arises. Professionals rely heavily on the self-reports of pedophiles, asking them to accurately recall and disclose whether these characteristics were present prior to their offending, or if they came in conjunction with the offending or thereafter. For example, more than 50 percent of molesters report having had no deviant fantasies prior to their initial offenses (Abel et al., 1987; Pithers et al., 1989; Marshall, Barbaree, & Eccles, 1991). It is not known if these data reveal a recall problem, low motivation to disclose incriminating information, or represent an accurate reflection of historical events.

More reliable predictors of pedophilic behavior appear to be early developmental experiences, though the data are again self-reported and retrospective in nature. Disruptive parent-child relationships seem to be related to later pedophilic behavior (Pithers et al., 1989; Marshall, Hudson, & Hodkinson, 1993). Hanson and Slater (1988) reported that in the sex offender literature the range of perpetrators who were victims of child sexual abuse varies from 0 to 67 percent. Dhawan and Marshall (1996) found significant differences in the sexual abuse histories of their incarcerated sample of offenders; 50 percent of sex offenders and 20 percent of incarcerated nonsexual offenders reported a history of sexual abuse in their study.

Another finding that appears to consistently separate some pedophiles from the crowd is a pattern of deviant sexual arousal. Nonfamilial child molesters display greater sexual arousal to children than do other sex offenders, nonsexual offenders, and community controls (Freund, 1981; Freund, Heasman, & Roper, 1982; Marshall, Barbaree, & Christophe, 1986; Quinsey, Chaplin, & Carrigan, 1979). There are conflicting reports of the deviant arousal profiles of incestuous offenders (Marshall et al., 1986; Quinsey et al., 1979).

Theory

The most prevalent hypothesis regarding the etiology of pedophilia is the conditioning theory popularized by Laws and Marshall (1990); see O'Donohue and

Plaud (1994) for a critique. As noted previously, its utility has been questioned because not all pedophiles demonstrate deviant sexual arousal physiologically and it is difficult to test the mental aspects of arousal. The theory is inadequate for what is currently known about pedophilic behavior.

In the previous section the growth of various comprehensive conceptualizations of sexual offending was presented. These are generally more complex and multifaceted theories than their predecessors. Marshall, his colleagues (Hudson, Marshall, Wales, McDonald, Bakker, & McLean, 1993; Marshall, Hudson, Jones, & Fernandez, 1995; Marshall, Jones, Hudson, & McDonald, 1993; Marshall & Maric, 1996), and other scholars are generating theory at a variety of levels in an attempt to explain the extant versions of sexual deviance. However, the heterogeneity of offenders makes the task challenging. Catching all sexual deviates in the same theoretical net is proving to be difficult.

Course and Epidemiology

The National Victim Center (1993) estimated the prevalence of child sexual abuse to be approximately 25 percent for females and 15 percent for males in the United States. Finkelhor (1994) made a more conservative estimate of at least 7 percent of females and 3 percent of males. The American Humane Association (1988) estimated 300,000 cases of child sexual abuse per year. These data additionally identified 77 percent of victims as females with an average age of 9.2 years. Eighty-two percent of perpetrators in this study were male.

A national survey conducted by Herman in 1980 estimated that between 4 and 17 percent of males had molested children. In a mixed sample of untreated sexual offenders, 41 percent reoffended in the six years following their release and 57 percent of repeat offenders had recidivated again in that time (Frisbie & Dondis, 1965). Hanson, Steffy, and Gauthier (1993) found that 42 percent of their sample of 197 child molesters committed a new offense in the average 19-year follow-up period (released between 1958 and 1974).

Assessment

Assessment recommendations for pedophilia have much in common with those offered throughout the chapter for the other paraphilias. It is essential to (1) understand the referral question and be sure that it is an appropriate one for the patient, setting, and evaluator; (2) use only those psychological instruments, interviewing strategies, and other methodologies that have sound empirical and clinical support for the purposes for which they are being used; (3) make the assessment useful, that is, link it to desired outcomes such as treatment goals, as opposed to simply diagnosing a disorder; (4) act ethically in the assessment process by obtaining a fully informed consent; and (5) write nothing in a report that could not be adequately defended in court.

Beyond these cardinal rules of assessment, the endeavor is really about gathering data on the variables that control these unwanted behaviors. Because important variables will differ from patient to patient, it is essential to engage in hypothesis testing around the relationships between variables and the deviant behaviors of interest. Based on the client's record, what are the best ideas about what caused or maintained the deviant behaviors? Notice how these behaviors are described in interviews and testing. How do they show up in physiological tests? Where are the inconsistencies, and how may they be understood? An evaluator must be willing to abandon early hypotheses with disconfirming evidence and not accept any single piece of evidence as the whole.

In addition to the instruments that have been suggested for data gathering, the Abel Child Cognitions Scale (Abel, Gore, Holland, Camp, Becker, & Rathner, 1989) may be useful with suspected pedophiles. This instrument assesses child-related cognitions in child molesters.

Phallometric testing is more standardized with child molesters than other sexual offenders. Penile Plethysmography (PPG) results consistently discriminate between nonfamilial child molesters and other populations of offenders and nonoffenders (Freund & Watson, 1991; Malcolm, Andrews, & Quinsey, 1993; Murphy, Haynes, Stalgaitis, & Flanagan, 1986), although there is heterogeneity in responding within the population as well. See O'Donohue, Letourneau, and Dowling (1997) for a review of phallometric testing.

If the purpose of a sex offender evaluation is to make broad-based diagnoses and treatment recommendations, it may be of some use to include in the battery instruments such as the Minnesota Multiphasic Personality Inventory, second edition (MMPI-II; Hathaway & McKinley, 1943), or the Millon Clinical Multiaxial Instrument, third edition (MCMI-III; Millon, 1983). Prior to investing resources in these procedures, there should be some indication that a major mental illness or personality disorder is present. The use of these tests in diagnosing a paraphilia, discriminating a sexual deviate from any other individual (Marshall & Hall, 1995), or developing a paraphilic profile for courtroom purposes is not indicated.

Treatment

The most popular treatments for pedophiles are cognitive-behavioral treatment (CBT) programs and antiandrogen interventions because they have the best reported outcomes (Grossman, Martis, & Fichtner, 1999; Hall, 1995). See the meta-analyses by Furby, Weinrott, and Blackshaw (1989) and Rice, Quinsey, and Harris (1991) for the limitations of these interventions.

Cognitive-behavioral treatments focus on altering deviant sexual arousal, changing offense-supportive environmental cues, finding alternative behaviors, and identifying/altering thoughts and feelings related to offending. Many of the approaches have been described earlier. The most popular combination treatment and maintenance program for sexual offenders in general, and pedophiles in particular, is the relapse prevention (RP) model (Laws, 1989; Pithers, 1990). Relapse prevention uses and extends the skills that are gained in sex offender treatment by helping the offender to recognize chains of internal and external events that led to each offense, identify high-risk situations that are related to those offense chains, recognize the short- and long-term consequences of offending behavior, and learn alternative coping skills in order to exit from the behavioral chain at any link prior to a relapse (Laws, 1989). The reader is directed to *Remaking Relapse Prevention*, edited by Laws, Hudson, and Ward (2000), for current, in-depth information about RP for sexual offenders.

The use of antiandrogens with pedophiles may be indicated if deviant sexual arousal is manifested, the offender is willing to participate in hormonal therapy, and there are no medical contraindications to the use of a pharmacological intervention.

Assessment and Treatment in Forensic Settings

A problem plaguing assessment and treatment endeavors in any environment that is exacerbated in forensic settings is access to pertinent information. From the general stigmatization of having a mental illness to specific sexual disorders to sexual *deviance* disorders, reasons for patients to be reluctant to completely disclose information to evaluators and treatment providers multiply. Sex is behavior that is not typically observed naturalistically. Sexual activity and information are generally private and become even more so when deviance is involved. There is consequently an unfortunate reliance on the self-reports of patients.

In forensic settings several issues interfere with full disclosures of relevant information. The first factor is embarrassment, shame, or guilt. Despite the bravado with which sex crimes are often committed, sex offenders may appear embarrassed and report feeling uncomfortable with the topic of sex. A second factor that impedes the collection of accurate information is the offender's fear of further criminal prosecution. Quite simply, sexually deviant offenders do not want to incur more punishment for their aberrant behaviors. Increased disclosure may result in increased punishment. Because assessment and treatment providers are part of the justice system and are mandatory reporters of sexual abuse, they may be the persons least likely to secure detailed information about sexually deviant behavior. Another factor that affects access to information is time. Sex offenders often receive treatment years after the commission of their crimes. Memory plays a part in the disclosure of relevant information for crimes that may be twenty years past. There is first a question of whether the patient initially attended to relevant details of the offense chain and crime. Second, the issue of accurately recalling those details years later arises. Couple the basic problems of memory with substance abuse, which is often involved in sexual crime (Abel, 1989), and the information dilemma is compounded. Delaying treatment until the period of incarceration is complete (or near complete) may have implications for the assessment and treatment of sexual deviance. This is a question in need of empirical investigation. It seems to be a corollary to the problem that the penal system sometimes views treatment as coddling prisoners. Treatment is often unavailable until the punishment phase of the sentence has been served. It may be questioned whether this policy is in the best interest of community safety, in that this practice may interfere with successfully treating sexually offensive behavior. Assessment and treatment without the relevant facts may be a futile task. An "as if" treatment may be produced in which offenders fill in the blanks artificially because they must do so in order to progress through treatment. Otherwise, they may face indefinite incarceration or treatment because they do not produce the details.

As a result of the access to information problem, assessment and treatment providers may rely on the versions of crimes that are presented in the records and the behaviors inmates admit to having done, with an eye toward statistical probabilities and implied information in the records. Hints may include time in the community with no treatment and no reported victims, dropped charges, and related charges (such as breaking and entering for a rapist). Unfortunately, accessing the truth is difficult. The product of missing data, lies, and inaccuracies is an "as if" assessment or treatment experience, and it is not clear that such an experience is useful in the reduction of risk to reoffend. If treatment is the way out of prison, patients will say and do the right things in order to appear to be fully assessed and treated.

Risk Assessment

Mental health professionals in forensic settings are often required to assess risk of reoffending for their patients. The assessments that have been discussed thus far have dealt with past and present behavior. Sex offender risk assessment involves estimating the likelihood of future sexual violence based on factors that are demonstrated predictors of reoffending. The most common conceptualization of risk in the literature is the simplest one, stated earlier as the likelihood of committing a new sexual offense. This way of thinking about risk is straightforward and permits the application of actuarial methods of prediction. It is a concept that may be quantified. However, the more qualitative aspects of risk—including the nature, severity, frequency, and imminence of the risk—are largely ignored in this type of analysis.

Throughout the chapter it is recommended that multiple methods be utilized to gather data about any particular psychological or forensic question in order to enrich the analysis. Records reviews, clinical interviews, and psychological and physiological testing were suggested assessment tools. In the area of risk assessment, experts differ in their opinions of whether multiple methods are most useful. There is a growing body of literature debating the accuracy of clinical judgment (see Janus & Meehl, 1997, for a relevant introduction to the topic). Some psychologists believe that clinical judgment is so poor that it detracts from the predictive accuracy of actuarial information alone (Quinsey, Harris, Rice, & Cormier, 1998). As a result, some professionals advocate only the use of risk assessment instruments, whereas others recommend a multimethod approach.

Two problems are inherent in using a purely actuarial approach as it is available at this time. First, any approach is only as strong as the instruments on which it relies. Although current risk assessment instruments have been shown to produce results more accurate than unstructured clinical judgment alone, they still account for only about 10 percent of the variance (Hanson & Thornton, 1999). A second problem is that the best available risk assessment instruments include only static risk factors in their estimates of risk. Static risk factors are characteristics that cannot be altered, such as the history of prior sex offenses (Hanson & Bussiere, 1998). If risk is gauged on static factors alone, it can never change. A whole realm of dynamic factors that are known to influence the risk propensity of an individual is not considered (such as being under the influence of alcohol). It is in the dynamic factors that there is potential for behavior change and a reduction in risk to reoffend. Investigations of dynamic risk factors such as victim empathy and cognitive distortions are in progress (Hanson & Harris, 2000; Seidman, Marshall, Hudson, & Robertson, 1994); however, nothing definitive has been reported at this writing. While these dynamic factors are being investigated, it has been proposed that evaluators use an actuarial approach supplemented by a structured clinical judgment approach that uses information about dynamic factors in an organized and more standardized fashion (Grubin, 1998). The actuarial information is used as an anchor, and the judgment is free to vary somewhat based on idiographic information about the patient's strengths and deficits, involvement in treatment, and treatment gains. A framework for considering all of the relevant information is David Thornton's Structured Anchored Clinical Judgment-Minimum (Grubin, 1998).

Actuarial instruments that are designed for general criminal offenders or those with violence only have not been found to be useful in predicting recidivism for sexual offenders (Bonta, Harman, Hann, & Cormier, 1996; Quinsey et al., 1998). Instruments that may be useful in estimating risk of sexual reoffending include:

- Minnesota Sex Offender Screening Tool–Revised (MnSOST-R; Epperson, Kaul, & Hesselton, 1998) uses 16 items to assess the recidivism potential of rapists and child molesters.
- Rapid Risk Assessment for Sexual Offense Recidivism (RRASOR; Hanson, 1997) predicts sex offender recidivism using only four items.
- Structured Anchored Clinical Judgment-Minimum (SACJ-Min.; Grubin, 1998) predicts sexual offending by entering static variable data into the analysis in stages. It was designed as a screening device for sex offender recidivism.
- Sex Offender Risk Assessment Guide (SORAG; Quinsey et al., 1998) a 14-item instrument that includes both static and dynamic risk factors but was developed with a narrow sample of sex offenders.
- STATIC 99 (Hanson & Thornton, 1999), a 10-item scale that is a combination of the RRASOR and SACJ items, is under revision. It was found superior to both in the prediction of sex offense recidivism ($r = .33$). Hanson and Thornton reported that the STATIC 99 identified approxi-

mately 12 percent of offenders whose likelihood to recidivate was greater than 50 percent as well as a group of offenders whose observed recidivism rates were 10 percent over a period of 15 years.

Trends in the Management of Sexual Deviates

Sexual deviates are under the microscope in the twenty-first century. The long-term supervision of sexual offenders has become an obvious priority of the justice system, as judged by its investment in the management of this subset of criminals. This interest is reflected in the numerous ways in which supervision has been temporally extended and intensified. Truth in sentencing laws, intensive parole systems, community notification, three-strikes laws, and civil commitment are the contemporary responses to sexual offending.

Incarceration

Sexual offenders are often violent offenders and therefore face enhanced penalties for their crimes, particularly in the United States. The "hard on crime" stance that fueled political campaigns in the 1980s and 1990s resulted in significantly increased penalties for violent offenders and fewer benefits for positive behavior during the penalty period. Many of these changes fall under the rubric of *truth-in-sentencing laws*. The terminology refers to different edicts in different states. However, the general approach to sentencing to which the phrase refers is for violent offenders to serve a substantial portion of their sentences prior to being released. By 1999, 27 states required offenders to serve at least 85 percent of their sentences, an increase from five percent of states in 1993 (U.S. Department of Justice, 1999). Prison releases have decreased and the prison population is growing nationwide (U.S. Department of Justice, 2002).

Inmates who are released are often under intensive supervision in the community in the form of supervised or conditional release programs and community notification (Megan's) laws. The rules of being on parole are becoming more stringent in many states. Intensified requirements often include maintaining work activities, mandatory involvement in treatment programs such as substance abuse and sex offender treatment, prohibitions against being in certain areas and having certain possessions (such as being near schools and having children's toys for pedophiles), and more meetings with a parole officer, both planned and unexpected. In addition to more intensive parole requirements, most states have enacted community notification laws, which extend the supervision of convicted sex offenders beyond parole. Again, the details of the laws vary from state to state. However, as of 1998, all states required sex offenders to register their names and addresses with their local law enforcement agencies whether they were on parole or were released with other conditions (Lieb & Matson, 1998). Forty-nine states required community notification or community access to the registration information as of 1998. Community notification is a controversial practice in that some communities have refused to allow released sex offenders to live in them, whereas in others sex offenders have faced threats and violence as a result of community awareness of their criminal histories.

Another trend in incarceration that affects sexual offenders is the three-strikes laws. Legislation was enacted in 24 states between 1993 and 1995 to increase penalties for habitual violent offenders. The essence of these laws is that offenders convicted of a third felony offense would be removed from society for a significant period of time. The sentences vary from state to state. The Washington statute requires a life term in prison without parole, and the California law exacts a sentence of 25 years-to-life for the third serious offense. The data have not borne out the efficacy of these laws in deterring or reducing crime in the states in which they were enacted (Macallair & Males, 1999). Even so, few politicians are interested in introducing legislation that would repeal these laws for fear of appearing soft on crime.

Civil Commitment

In addition to legislation that has violent offenders as its focus, special laws that authorize the confinement and treatment of sex offenders following the completion of their prison sentences have been enacted in many states. These laws are often referred to as *sexually violent predator (SVP) statutes*. The term *sexually violent predator* was created in Washington state in 1990 to describe sex offenders that are likely to reoffend (Lieb & Matson, 1998). The Washington State Institute for Public Policy (1998) offers the following history of this legislation: Laws enacted between the 1930s and 1960s authorized civil commitment for sexual offenders who were considered to be psychopathic and in need of treatment. As support for these statutes waned, by the 1990s the laws remained in only 13 states. New legislation was enacted in the 1990s that differed from the early sexual psychopath laws. Whereas the earlier statutes supported civil commitment instead of a prison sentence, the new laws called for civil commitment following incarceration. The current targets of SVP laws are repeat offenders, not the first-time offenders of the former legislation. In addition, sexually violent predators are ineligible for release until they are perceived to be a lesser risk to the community. The SVP statutes vary from state to state. Some states require that a mental illness or personality disorder be present in order to meet criteria; others dictate that the sexually violent behavior may not be attributable to a mental disorder.

Controversy surrounds the sexually violent predator laws. It has been argued that these statutes fly in the face of the original intention of civil commitment in that many of those who are detained with the laws are not mentally ill and divert resources from those who are (Janus, 2000). The safety of other types of civilly committed patients has been questioned when they are housed in locked facilities with SVPs. Lawyers for SVPs have cited these laws as examples of ex post facto sentencing and double jeopardy, stating that their clients are being punished twice for the same crime (Janus, 2000). SVPs themselves have also argued that treatments for sexual offending are ineffective; therefore, they are untreatable and cannot be legally detained for involuntary treatment.

Despite vehement arguments, the U.S. Supreme Court upheld the constitutionality of these laws in 1997 (*Kansas v. Hendricks*). The Court emphasized that the laws must touch only the most dangerous offenders, it must distinguish those in need of civil commitment from those that do not require this level of involvement, there must be evidence that the patient was not able to control his sexual behavior, and the patient does not have to be amenable to treatment in order to be civilly committed under these laws (Janus, 2000). Factors including whether assessment and treatment can be adequately provided under these involuntary and not confidential conditions, the questionable accuracy of risk assessments and minimal use of dynamic risk factors (the mode of being released from civil commitments), and the enormous cost of hospitalizing these offenders (approximately $100,000 per year per patient; Lieb & Matson, 1998) are growing concerns. As civil commitments are extended, the difficulties of risk assessment, treatment efficacy, and cost will have to be reckoned with. The containment and rehabilitation of sexual offenders is an inexact science at best. Societies are constantly searching for a better way to increase safety while balancing those needs with so many resource demands. It is safe to predict that the tension of managing the most dangerous offenders will remain while researchers scramble to answer questions of risk and rehabilitation. The field of sex offender research and treatment is growing rapidly, but it is not keeping up with the demands for answers.

Conclusion

Sexual violence strikes a chord that resonates powerfully in many people. The criminal justice response to that uncomfortable sound is expanding. More criminal justice contacts, longer sentences, and involuntary treatment for the most dangerous offenders mean that sexual deviates are in the judicial system in increasing numbers. Is containment achieving the goal of increased community safety? The jury is still out.

The majority of funding is invested in a minority of these offenders *after* they have offended repeatedly. It is only after they have multiple victims and a practiced pattern of dangerous behavior that sex offenders receive the most intensive treatment. This seems to be an ill-fated approach for several reasons. First, the field does not know definitively what separates sexually violent offenders from other people. It has been shown that people who do not appear to have a sexual offending problem report a range of sexual fantasies (O'Donohue, Letourneau, & Dowling, 1997): 30 percent of males report fantasies of tying up and raping a woman (Crepault & Couture, 1980), and between 35 and 60 percent of male college students reported some likelihood that they would rape a woman if they were not discovered (Briere & Malamuth, 1983; Malamuth, 1981). Psychology does not understand normative sexual behavior and therefore does not begin to understand what it is that makes some individuals cross the line into harmful sexual behaviors. This lack of comprehension of the etiology of sexual offending leaves the available assessment and treatment methods bereft of elements that are essential to maximally change behavior. As a result, the therapeutic technologies that are being applied may include unimportant elements that waste valuable treatment time and may lack elements that are essential to correcting the problem. Furthermore, the least is known about treating the worst offenders. It is possible to reasonably conjecture that the most resources are going into treatments-as-usual with a population for which their efficacy is unknown.

The allocation of some of these resources into new research and theory development seems warranted if the field is to better understand how to manage sexually deviant behaviors. Understanding the etiology of sexually normative and deviant practices is essential if we expect to develop a science of sexual deviance. At the same time, treatment-dismantling studies are needed to evaluate the active components of sex offender treatment, particularly for offenders who appear to be treatment resistant, such as psychopathic offenders, and youthful offenders whose behaviors are potentially more accessible and malleable. Risk for reoffense needs to be better understood, particularly dynamic risk factors. In addition, new theory that encompasses the heterogeneity of offenders and suggests innovative treatment strategies is needed. Along with improved research funding and theory development, the criminal justice system may benefit from an examination of how its limited resources might be best utilized. As discussed earlier in the chapter, treatment is often offered years after the crime has been committed, possibly impeding effective treatment applications. It has also been demonstrated that treatment is more effective when it is offered on an outpatient basis (Hall, 1995). It seems possible that offering sex offender treatment at the first signs of sexual deviance on an outpatient basis may be a more effective use of resources than ignoring the behavior until someone is seriously injured and the patient is incarcerated. Funneling resources into avenues with the most potential for societal gains opens a political discussion, one that is more and more timely in this age of ballooning containment and treatment costs and needs.

Last, mental health professionals are challenged to remember their roles in forensic settings. Mental health workers face the difficulties of understanding the agencies for which they work and the implications of their duties. Acting ethically with the inmates who are assessed and treated, particularly around issues of confidentiality and informed consent, is a difficult task in a system that is by nature adversarial. Psychologists and psychiatrists are pushed to examine their allegiances to the courts, agencies, and patients, recognizing that there may be pressures to arrive at certain conclusions that do not correspond with the clinical and research data or its absence. Acting within the scope of professional practice, as well as taking care not to answer ultimate legal questions while offering the most objective interpretations of mental health research and practice, is a dicey business. Those in the mental health professions must be willing to say, "I do not know," in response to some questions posed by inmates, attorneys, and the courts. This is perhaps the least desirable of all responses, but it is the ethical one. Mental health professionals who work with sexual deviates in forensic settings walk a fine line as assessors, treatment providers, and expert witnesses advancing the understanding and management of sexual deviance.

REFERENCES

Abel, G. G. (1989). Paraphilias. In H. I. Kaplan & B. J. Sadock (Eds.), *Comprehensive textbook of psychiatry VI, Vol. 1* (6th ed.) (pp. 1069–1085). Baltimore: Williams & Wilkins.

Abel, G. G., Barlow, D. H., Blanchard, E. B., & Guild, D. (1977). The components of rapists' sexual arousal. *Archives of General Psychiatry, 34*, 895–903.

Abel, G. G., Becker, J. B., Cunningham-Rathner, J., Mittelman, M., & Rouleau, J. L. (1988). Multiple paraphilic diagnoses among sex offenders. *Bulletin of the American Academy of Psychiatry and the Law, 16*, 153–168.

Abel, G. G., Becker, J. B., Mittelman, M., Cunningham-Rathner, J., Rouleau, J. L., & Murphy, W. D. (1987). Self-reported sex crimes of nonincarcerated paraphiliacs. *Journal of Interpersonal Violence, 2*, 3–25.

Abel, G. G., Gore, D. K., Holland, C. L., Camp, N., Becker, J. V., & Rathner, J. (1989). The assessment of the cognitive distortions of child molesters. *Annals of Sex Research, 2*, 135–153.

Abel, G. G., Mittelman, M., & Becker, J. B. (1985). Sexual offenders: Results of assessment and recommendations for treatment. In M. M. Ben-Aron, S. I. Huckers, & C. D. Webster (Eds.), *Clinical criminology: Current concepts* (pp. 191–205). Toronto: M & M Graphics.

Abel, G. G., & Rouleau, J. L. (1990). The nature and extent of sexual assault. In W. L. Marshall, D. R. Laws, & H. E. Barbaree (Eds.), *Handbook of sexual assault: Issues, theories, and treatment of the offender* (pp. 9–21). New York: Plenum Press.

Abel, G. G., Rouleau, J. L., & Cunningham-Rathner, J. (1986). Sexually aggressive behavior. In W. Curran, A. L. McBarry, & C. A. Shah (Eds.), *Forensic psychiatry and psychology: Perspectives and standards for interdisciplinary practice* (pp. 289–313). Philadelphia, PA: Davis.

Abrams, S. (1991). The use of polygraphy with sex offenders. *Annals of Sex Research, 4*, 239–263.

Allen, D. W. (1980). A psychoanalytic view. In D. J. Cox & R. J. Daitzman (Eds.), *Exhibitionism: Description, assessment, and treatment* (pp. 59–82). New York: Garland Press.

American Humane Association. (1988). *Highlights of official child neglect and abuse reporting, 1986*. Denver, CO: Author.

American Psychiatric Association. (1952). *Diagnostic and statistical manual of mental disorders*. Washington, DC: Author.

American Psychiatric Association. (1968). *Diagnostic and statistical manual of mental disorders* (2nd ed.). Washington, DC: Author.

American Psychiatric Association. (1980). *Diagnostic and statistical manual of mental disorders* (3rd ed.). Washington, DC: Author.

American Psychiatric Association. (1987). *Diagnostic and statistical manual of mental disorders* (3rd ed., rev.). Washington, DC: Author.

American Psychiatric Association. (1994). *Diagnostic and statistical manual of mental disorders* (4th ed.). Washington, DC: Author.

Amir, M. (1971). *Patterns of forcible rape*. Chicago: University of Chicago Press.

Arndt, W., Foehl, J., & Good, F. (1985). Specific fantasy themes: A multidimensional study. *Journal of Personality and Social Psychology, 48*, 472–480.

Bailey, K. G. (1991). Human paleopsychopathology: Implications for the paraphilias. *New Trends in Experimental and Clinical Psychiatry, 7*, 5–16.

Bain, J., Langevin, R., Dickey, R., & Ben-Aron, M. (1987). Sex hormones in murderers and assaulters. *Behavioral Sciences and the Law, 5*, 95–101.

Barbaree, H. E., Marshall, W. L., & Hudson, S. M. (1993). *The juvenile sex offender*. New York, NY: Guilford Press.

Barbaree, H. E., Marshall, W. L., & Lanthier, R. D. (1979). Deviant sexual arousal in rapists. *Behaviour Research and Therapy, 17*, 215–222.

Bard, L. A., Carter, D. L., Cerce, D. D., Knight, R. A., Rosenberg, R., & Schneider, B. (1987). A descriptive study of rapists and child molesters: Developmental, clinical, and criminal characteristics. *Behavioral Sciences and the Law, 5*, 203–220.

Baxter, D. J., Barbaree, H. E., & Marshall, W. L. (1986). Sexual responses to consenting and forced sex in a large sample of rapists and nonrapists. *Behaviour Research and Therapy, 24*, 513–520.

Bayer, R. (1981). *Homosexuality and American psychiatry: The politics of diagnosis*. New York: Basic Books.

Bereh, E. F., & Myers, R. G. (1983). The offense records of a sample of convicted exhibitionists. *Bulletin of the American Academy of Psychiatry and Law, 11*, 365–369.

Binet, A. (1887). Fetishism in love. *Revue Philosophie, 24*, 143–167.

Blair, C. D., & Lanyon, R. I. (1981). Exhibitionism: Etiology and treatment. *Psychological Bulletin, 89*, 439–463.

Bonta, J., Harman, W. G., Hann, R. G., & Cormier, R. B. (1996). The prediction of recidivism among federally sentenced offenders: A revalidation of the SIR scale. *Canadian Journal of Criminology, 38*, 61–79.

Bradford, J. M. W. (1990). The antiandrogen and hormonal treatment of sex offenders. In W. L. Marshall, D. R. Laws, & H. E. Barbaree (Eds.), *Handbook of sexual assault: Issues, theories, and treatment of the offender* (pp. 297–310). New York: Plenum Press.

Bradford, J. M. W., Boulet, J., & Pawlak, A. (1992). The paraphilias: A multiplicity of deviant behaviors. *Canadian Journal of Psychiatry, 37*, 104–108.

Bradford, J. M. W., Martindale, J. J., Lane, R., Greenberg, D., Gojer, J., Curry, S., et al. (1996). Sertraline in the treatment of pedophilia: An open label study. Unpublished manuscript.

Breslow, N., Evans, N., & Langley, J. (1985). On the prevalence and roles of females in sadomasochistic sub-culture: Report of an empirical study. *Archives of Sexual Medicine, 14*, 303–317.

Brett, A. S., Phillips, M., & Beary, J. F. (1986). Predictive power of the polygraph: Can the "lie detector" really detect liars? *Lancet, 1*, 544–547.

Briere, J., & Malamuth, N. M. (1983). Self-reported likelihood of sexually aggressive behavior: Attitudinal versus sexual explanations. *Journal of Research in Personality, 17*, 315–323.

Burt, M. R. (1980). Cultural myths and supports for rape. *Journal of Personality and Social Psychology, 38*, 217–230.

Check, J. V. P. (1985). The Hostility Toward Women Scale. Unpublished doctoral dissertation. University of Manitoba, Winnipeg, Canada. A study of incarcerated rapists and child molesters. Report to the Solicitor General of Canada. Ottawa: Office of the Solicitor General.

Cohen, M. L., Garofalo, R., Boucher, R., & Seghorn, T. (1971). The psychology of rapists. *Seminars in Psychiatry, 3*, 307–323.

Coleman, E., Cesnik, J., Moore, A. M., & Dwyer, S. M. (1992). An exploratory study of the role of psychotropic medications in the treatment of sexual offenders. *Journal of Offender Rehabilitation, 18*, 75–88.

Cox, D. J., & Maletzky, B. M. (1980). Victims of exhibitionism. In D. J. Cox & R. J. Daitzman (Eds.), *Exhibitionism: Description, assessment, and treatment* (pp. 289–293). New York: Garland Press.

Crepault, C., & Couture. M. (1980). Men's erotic fantasies. *Archives of Sexual Behavior, 9*, 565–581.

Dhawan, S., & Marshall, W. L. (1996). Sexual abuse histories of sexual offenders. *Sexual Abuse: A Journal of Research and Treatment, 8*, 7–15.

Deitz, S. R., Blackwell, K. T., Daley, P. C., & Bentley, B. J. (1982). Measurement of empathy toward rape victims and rapists. *Journal of Personality and Social Psychology, 43*, 372–384.

Dietz, P., Hazelwood, R. R., & Warren, J. (1990). The sexually sadistic criminal and his offenses. *Bulletin of the American Academy of Psychiatry and the Law, 18*, 163–178.

Ellis, A., & Brancala, R. (1956). *The psychology of sex offenders.* Springfield, IL: Charles C Thomas.

Ellis, L. (1989). *Theories of rape: Inquiries into the causes of sexual aggression.* New York: Hemisphere.

Ellis, L. (1991). A synthesized (biosocial) theory of rape. *Journal of Consulting and Clinical Psychology, 59*, 631–642.

Emmanuel, N. P., Lydiard, R. B., & Ballenger, J. C. (1991). Fluoxetine treatment of voyeurism. *American Journal of Psychiatry, 148*, 950.

Epperson, D. L., Kaul, J. D., & Hesselton, D. (1998, October). Final report of the development of the Minnesota Sex Offender Screening Tool-Revised (MnSOST-R). Presentation at the 17th Annual Research and Treatment Conference of the Association for the Treatment of Sexual Abusers, Vancouver, BC, Canada.

Fedora, O., Reddon, J. R., Morrison, J. W., Fedora, S. K., Pascoe, H., & Yeudall, C. T. (1992). Sadism and other paraphilias in normal controls and aggressive and nonaggressive sex offenders. *Archives of Sexual Behavior, 21*, 1–15.

Fehrenbach, P. A., & Monastersky, C. (1988). Characteristics of female adolescent sexual offenders. *American Journal of Orthopsychiatry, 55*, 148–151.

Finkelhor, D. (1994). The international epidemiology of child sexual abuse. *Child Abuse and Neglect, 14*, 409–417.

Freud, S. (1953). Three essays on the theory of sexual deviation. In J. Strachey (Ed.), *The complete psychological works of Sigmund Freud.* London: Hogarth Press. (Original work published 1905.)

Freud, S. (1961). *On sexuality.* Markham, ON: Penguin.

Freund, K. (1981). Assessment of pedophilia. In M. Cook & K. Howells (Eds.), *Adult sexual interest in children* (pp. 139–179). London: Academic Press.

Freund, K. (1990). Courtship disorder. In W. L. Marshall, D. R. Laws, & H. E. Barbaree (Eds.), *Handbook of sexual assault: Issues, theories, and treatment of the offender* (pp. 195–207). New York: Plenum Press.

Freund, K., Heasman, G. A., & Roper, V. (1982). Results of the main studies on sexual offenses against children and pubescents (a review). *Canadian Journal of Criminology, 24,* 387–397.

Freund, K., Seto, M., & Kuban, M. (1997). The theory of courtship disorder. In D. R. Laws & W. O'Donohue (Eds.), *Sexual deviance: Theory, assessment, and treatment* (pp. 111–130). New York: Guilford Press.

Freund, K., Sher, H., & Hucker, S. (1983). The courtship disorders. *Archives of Sexual Behavior, 12,* 369–379.

Freund, K., & Watson, R. (1991). Assessment of the sensitivity and specificity of a phallometric test: An update of phallometric diagnosis of pedophilia. *Psychological Assessment, 3,* 254–260.

Frisbie, L. U., & Dondis, E. H. (1965). Recidivism among treated sex offenders. California Mental Health Research Monograph no. 5. Sacramento, CA: Department of Mental Hygiene.

Fromm, E. (1977). *The anatomy of human destructiveness.* Markham, ON: Penguin.

Furby, L., Weinrott, M. R., & Blackshaw, L. (1989). Sex offender recidivism: A review. *Psychological Bulletin, 105,* 3–30.

Gaupp, L. A., Stern, R. M., & Ratcliff, R. G. (1971). The use of aversion-relief procedures in the treatment of a case of voyeurism. *Behavior Therapy, 2,* 585–588.

Gavey, N. (1991). Sexual victimization prevalence among New Zealand university students. *Journal of Consulting and Clinical Psychology, 59,* 464–466.

Gillespie, W. H. (1964). The psychoanalytic theory of sexual deviation with special reference to fetishism. In I. Rosen (Ed.), *The pathology and treatment of sexual deviation: A methodological approach.* Oxford: Oxford University Press.

Graber, B., Hartmann, K., Coffman, J., Huey, C., & Golden, C. (1982). Brain damage among mentally disordered sex offenders. *Journal of Forensic Sciences, 27,* 127–134.

Gratzer, T., & Bradford, J. (1995). Offender and offense characteristics of sexual sadists: A comparative study. *Journal of Forensic Sciences, 40,* 450–455.

Greendlinger, V., & Byrne, D. (1987). Coercive sexual fantasies of college men as predictors of self-reported likelihood to rape and overt sexual aggression. *Journal of Sex Research, 23,* 1–11.

Grossman, L. S., Martis, B., & Fichtner, C. G. (1999). Are sex offenders treatable? A research overview. *Psychiatric Services, 50,* 349–361.

Groth, A. N., Burgess, A. W., & Holmstrom, L. L. (1977). Rape: Power, aggression, and sexuality. *American Journal of Psychiatry, 134,* 1239–1243.

Grubin, D. (1998). *Sex offending against children: Understanding the risk.* Police Research Series Paper 99. London: Home Office.

Haaven, J. L., & Coleman, E. M. (2000). Treatment of the developmentally disabled offender. In D. R. Laws, S. M. Hudson, & T. Ward (Eds.), *Remaking relapse prevention with sex offenders* (pp. 369–388). Thousand Oaks, CA: Sage.

Hall, G. C. N. (1990). Prediction of sexual aggression. *Clinical Psychology Review, 10,* 229–245.

Hall, G. C. N. (1995). Sexual offender recidivism revisited: A meta-analysis of treatment studies. *Journal of Consulting and Clinical Psychology, 63,* 802–809.

Hall, G. C. N., & Hirschman, R. (1991). Toward a theory of sexual offending: A quadripartite model. *Journal of Consulting and Clinical Psychology, 59*, 662–669.

Hall, G. C. N., Proctor, W. C., & Nelson, G. M. (1988). Validity of the physiological measures of pedophilic sexual arousal in a sexual offender population. *Journal of Consulting and Clinical Psychology, 56*, 118–122.

Hanson, R. K. (1997). *The development of a brief actuarial risk scale for sexual offense recidivism*. Report no. 1997-04. Ottawa: Office of the Solicitor General of Canada.

Hanson, R. K., & Bussiere, M. T. (1996). Predictors of sex offender recidivism: A meta-analysis. Report No. 1996-04. Ottawa: Office of the Solicitor General of Canada.

Hanson, R. K., & Harris, A. J. R. (1997). Voyeurism: Assessment and treatment. In D. R. Laws & W. O'Donohue (Eds.), *Sexual deviance: Theory, assessment, and treatment* (pp. 311–331). New York: Guilford Press.

Hanson, R. K., & Harris, A. J. R. (2000). Where should we intervene? Dynamic predictors of sex offense recidivism. *Criminal Justice and Behavior, 27*, 6–35.

Hanson, R. K., & Slater, S. (1988). Sexual victimization in the history of child sexual abusers: A review. *Annals of Sex Research, 1*, 485–499.

Hanson, R. K., Steffy, R. A., & Gauthier, R. (1993). Long-term recidivism of child molesters. *Journal of Consulting and Clinical Psychology, 61*, 646–652.

Hanson, R. K., & Thornton, D. (1999). *STATIC 99: Improving actuarial risk assessments for sex offenders*. Report No. 1999-02. Ottawa: Office of the Solicitor General of Canada.

Hare, R. D. (1980). A research scale for the assessment of psychopathy in criminal populations. *Personality and Individual Differences, 1*, 111–119.

Hathaway, S. R., & McKinley, J. C. (1943). A multiphasic personality schedule (Minnesota): III. The measurement of symptomatic depression. *Journal of Psychology, 14*, 73–84.

Herman, J. L. (1980). Sex offenders: A feminist perspective. In W. L. Marshall, D. R. Laws, & H. E. Barbaree (Eds.), *Handbook of sexual assault: Issues, theories, and treatment of the offender* (pp. 177–193). New York: Plenum Press.

Holmes, R. M., & Holmes, S. T. (1994). *Murder in America*. Thousand Oaks, CA: Sage.

Howes, R. J. (1995). A survey of plethysmographic assessment in North America. *Sexual Abuse: A Journal of Research and Treatment, 7*, 9–24.

Hucker, S. J. (1990). Necrophilia and other unusual paraphilias. In R. Bluglass & P. Bowden (Eds.), *Principles and practice of forensic psychiatry* (pp. 723–728). London: Churchill Livingstone.

Hucker, S. J. (1997). Sexual sadism: Psychopathology and theory. In D. R. Laws & W. O'Donohue (Eds.), *Sexual deviance: Theory, assessment, and treatment* (pp. 194–210). New York: Guilford Press.

Hucker, S. J., Langevin, R., Wortzman, G., Dickey, R., Bain, J., Jandy, L., et al. (1988). Cerebral damage and dysfunction in sexually aggressive men. *Annals of Sex Research, 1*, 33–47.

Hudson, S. M., Marshall, W. L., Wales, D., McDonald, E., Bakker, L. W., & McLean, A. (1993). Emotional recognition skills of sex offenders. *Annals of Sex Research, 6*, 199–211.

Hudson, S. M., & Ward, T. (1997). Rape: Psychopathology and theory. In D. R. Laws & W. O'Donohue (Eds.), *Sexual deviance: Theory, assessment, and treatment* (pp. 332–355). New York: Guilford Press.

Hunt, M. (1974). *Sexual behavior in the 1970's*. New York: Playboy Press.

Hunter, J., & Mathews, R. (1997). Sexual deviance in females. In D. R. Laws & W. O'Donohue (Eds.), *Sexual deviance: Theory, assessment, and treatment* (pp. 465–480). New York: Guilford Press.

Jackson, B. T. (1969). A case of voyeurism treated by counter conditioning. *Behaviour Research and Therapy, 7*, 133–134.

Janus, E. S. (2000). Sex predator commitment laws: Constitutional but unwise. *Psychiatric Annals, 30*, 411–420.

Janus, E. S., & Meehl, P. E. (1997). Assessing the legal standard for predictions of dangerousness in sex offender commitment proceedings. *Psychology, Public Policy, and Law, 3*, 33–64.

Johnson, R. L., & Shrier, D. (1987). Past sexual victimization by females of male patients in an adolescent medicine clinic population. *American Journal of Psychiatry, 144*, 650–652.

Kansas v. Hendricks, 117 SCt 2072 (1997).

Kaplan, M., & Krueger, R. (1997). Voyeurism: Psychopathology and theory. In D. R. Laws & W. O'Donohue (Eds.), *Sexual deviance: Theory, assessment, and treatment* (pp. 297–310). New York: Guilford Press.

Knight, R., Prentky, R. A., & Cerce, D. D. (1994). The development, reliability, and validity of an inventory for the multidimensional assessment of sex and aggression. *Criminal Justice and Behavior, 21*, 72–94.

Knopp, F. H., & Lackey, L. D. (1987). *Female sexual abusers: A summary of data from 44 treatment providers.* Brandon, VT: Safer Society Press.

Kolarsky, A., Freund, K., Machek, J., Polak, O. (1967). Male sexual deviation: Association with early temporal lobe damage. *Archives of General Psychiatry, 17*, 735–743.

Konopacki, W. P., & Oei, T. P. S. (1988). Interruption in the maintenance of compulsive sexual disorder: Two case studies. *Archives of Sexual Behavior, 17*, 411–419.

Koss, M. P. (1992). The underdetection of rape: Methodological choices influence incidence estimates. *Journal of Social Issues, 48*, 61–75.

Koss, M. P., Gidycz, C. A., & Wisniewski, N. (1987). The scope of rape: Incidence and prevalence of sexual aggression and victimization in a national sample of higher education students. *Journal of Consulting and Clinical Psychology, 55*, 162–170.

Koss, M. P., & Oros, C. J. (1982). Sexual Experiences Survey: A research instrument investigating sexual aggression and victimization. *Journal of Consulting and Clinical Psychology, 50*, 455–457.

Krueger, R., & Kaplan, M. (1997). Frotteurism: Assessment and treatment. In D. R. Laws & W. O'Donohue (Eds.), *Sexual deviance: Theory, assessment, and treatment* (pp. 131–151). New York: Guilford Press.

Langevin, R. (1990). Sexual anomalies and the brain. In W. L. Marshall, D. R. Laws, & H. E. Barbaree (Eds.), *Handbook of sexual assault: Issues, theories, and treatment of the offender* (pp. 103–113). New York: Plenum Press.

Langevin, R., & Lang, R. A. (1987). The courtship disorders. In G. O. Wilson (Ed.), *Variant sexuality: Research and theory* (pp. 202–228). London: Croom Helm.

Langevin, R., Paitich, D., Hucker, S., Newman, S., Ramsay, G., Pope, S., et al. (1979). The effect of assertiveness training, Provera, and sex of therapist in the treatment of genital exhibitionism. *Journal of Behavior Therapy and Experimental Psychiatry, 10*, 275–282.

Langevin, R., Paitich, D., Russon, A. E., Handy, L., & Langevin, R. (1990). *The Clarke Sexual History Questionnaire for Males: Manual.* Toronto: Juniper Press.

Laws, D. R. (Ed.). (1989). *Relapse prevention with sexual offenders.* New York: Guilford Press.

Laws, D. R. (1995). Verbal satiation: Notes on procedure with speculations on its mechanism of effect. *Sexual Abuse: A Journal of Research and Treatment, 7,* 155–166.

Laws, D. R., Hudson, S. M., & Ward, T. (Eds.). (2000). *Remaking relapse prevention with sex offenders: A sourcebook.* Thousand Oaks, CA: Sage.

Laws, D. R., & Marshall, W. L. (1990). A conditioning theory of the etiology and maintenance of deviant sexual preferences and behavior. In W. L. Marshall, D. R. Laws, & H. E. Barbaree (Eds.), *Handbook of sexual assault: Issues, theories, and treatment of the offender* (pp. 209–227). New York: Plenum Press.

Laws, D. R., & Marshall, W. L. (1991). Masturbatory reconditioning with sexual deviates: An evaluative review. *Advances in Behavior Research and Therapy, 13,* 13–25.

Laws, D. R., & O'Donohue, W. (1997). Fundamental issues in sexual deviance. In D. R. Laws & W. O'Donohue (Eds.), *Sexual deviance: Theory, assessment, and treatment* (pp. 1–21). New York: Guilford Press.

Lieb, R., & Matson, S. (1998). Sexual predator commitment laws in the United States: 1998 update. Olympia, WA: Washington State Institute for Public Policy.

Macallair, D., & Males, M. (1999). Striking out: The failure of California's "Three strikes and you're out" law. San Francisco, CA: Justice Policy Institute.

Malamuth, N. M. (1981). Rape proclivity among males. *Journal of Social Issues, 37,* 138–157.

Malamuth, N. M. (1989). The attraction to sexual aggression: Part One. *Journal of Sex Research, 26,* 26–49.

Malamuth, N. M., Heavey, C. L., & Linz, D. (1993). Predicting men's antisocial behavior against women. In G. C. N. Hall, R. Hirschman, J. R. Graham, & M. S. Zaragoza (Eds.), *Sexual aggression: Issues in etiology, assessment, and treatment* (pp. 63–97). Washington, DC: Taylor & Francis.

Malcolm, P. B., Andrews, D. A., & Quinsey, V. L. (1993). Discriminate and predictive validity of phallometrically measured sexual age and gender preference. *Journal of Interpersonal Violence, 8,* 486–501.

Maletzky, B. M. (1980). Assisted covert sensitization. In D. J. Cox & R. J. Daitzman (Eds.), *Exhibitionism: Description, assessment, and treatment* (pp. 187–251). New York: Garland Press.

Maletzky, B. M. (1986). Orgasmic reconditioning. In A. S. Bellack & M. Hersen (Eds.), *Dictionary of behavior therapy techniques* (pp. 57–58). New York: Pergamon Press.

Maletzky, B. M. (1987, October). Data generated by an outpatient sexual abuse clinic. Paper presented at the annual conference of the Association for the Treatment of Sexual Abusers, Newport, OR.

Maletzky, B. M. (1991). *Treating the sexual offender.* Newbury Park, CA: Sage.

Maletzky, B. M. (1994). Exhibitionism. In C. G. Last & M. Hersen (Eds.), *Adult behavior therapy casebook* (pp. 235–257). New York: Plenum Press.

Maletzky, B. M. (1997). Exhibitionism: Assessment and treatment. In D. R. Laws & W. O'Donohue (Eds.), *Sexual deviance: Theory, assessment, and treatment* (pp. 40–74). New York: Guilford Press.

Maletzky, B. M. (1998). The paraphilias: Research and treatment. In P. E. Nathan & J. M. Gorman (Eds.), *A guide to treatments that work* (pp. 474–500). New York: Oxford University Press.

Marques, J. K., Day, D. M., Nelson, C., & West, M. A. (1994). Effects of cognitive-behavioral treatment on sex offender recidivism. Preliminary results of a longitudinal study. *Criminal Justice and Behavior*, *21*, 28–54.

Marshall, W. L. (1993). A revised approach to the treatment of men who sexually assault adult females. In G. C. N. Hall, R. Hirschman, J. R. Graham, & M. S. Zaragoza (Eds.), *Sexual aggression: Issues in etiology, assessment, and treatment* (pp. 143–165). Washington, DC: Taylor & Francis.

Marshall, W. L. (1997). Pedophilia: Psychopathology and theory. In D. R. Laws & W. O'Donohue (Eds.), *Sexual deviance: Theory, assessment, and treatment* (pp. 152–174). New York: Guilford Press.

Marshall, W. L., & Barbaree, H. E. (1989). Sexual violence. In K. Howells & C. R. Hollin (Eds.), *Clinical approaches to violence* (pp. 205–246). New York: Wiley.

Marshall, W. L., & Barbaree, H. E. (1990a). An integrated theory of the etiology of sexual offending. In W. L. Marshall, D. R. Laws, & H. E. Barbaree (Eds.), *Handbook of sexual assault: Issues, theories, and treatment of the offender* (pp. 257–275). New York: Plenum Press.

Marshall, W. L., & Barbaree, H. E. (1990b). Outcome of comprehensive cognitive behavioral treatment programs. In W. L. Marshall, D. R. Laws, & H. E. Barbaree (Eds.), *Handbook of sexual assault: Issues, theories, and treatment of the offender* (pp. 363–385). New York: Plenum Press.

Marshall, W. L., Barbaree, H. E., & Christophe, D. (1986). Sexual offenders against female children. Sexual preferences for age of victims and type of behaviours. *Canadian Journal of Behavioural Sciences*, *18*, 424–439.

Marshall, W. L., Barbaree, H. E., & Eccles, A. (1991). Early onset and deviant sexuality in child molesters. *Journal of Interpersonal Violence*, *6*, 323–336.

Marshall, W. L., & Hall, G. C. N. (1995). The value of the MMPI in deciding forensic issues in accused sexual offenders. *Sexual Abuse: A Journal of Research and Treatment*, *7*, 205–219.

Marshall, W. L., Hudson, S. M., & Hodkinson, S. (1993). The importance of attachment bonds in the development of juvenile sex offending. In H. E. Barbaree, W. L. Marshall, & S. M. Hudson (Eds.), *The juvenile sex offender* (pp. 164–181). New York: Guilford Press.

Marshall, W. L., Hudson, S. M., Jones, R., & Fernandez, Y. M. (1995). Empathy in sex offenders. *Clinical Psychology Review*, *15*, 99–113.

Marshall, W. L., Jones, R., Hudson, S. M., & McDonald, E. (1993). Generalized empathy in child molesters. *Journal of Child Sexual Abuse*, *2*, 61–68.

Marshall, W. L., & Maric, A. (1996). Cognitive and emotional components of generalized empathy deficits in child molesters. *Journal of Child Sexual Abuse*, *5*, 101–110.

Masters, W., Johnson, V., & Kolodny, R. (1982). *Human sexuality*. Boston: Little Brown.

Mathews, R., Hunter, J. A., & Vuz, J. (1997). Juvenile female sex offenders: Clinical characteristics and treatment issues. *Sexual Abuse: A Journal of Research and Treatment*, *9*, 187–199.

Mathews, R., Matthews, J. K., & Speltz, K. (1989). *Female sexual offenders: An exploratory study*. Orwell, VT: Safer Society Press.

McConaghy, N. (1990). Sexual deviation. In A. S. Bellack, M. Hersen, & P. E. Kazdin (Eds.), *International handbook of behavior therapy and modification.* (2nd ed.) (pp. 565–580). New York: Plenum Press.

McConaghy, N. (1993). *Sexual behavior: Problems and management*. New York: Plenum Press.

McGuire, R. J., Carlisle, J. M., & Young, B. G. (1965). Sexual deviation as a conditioned behavior: A hypothesis. *Behavior Research and Therapy, 2*, 185–190.

Meyer, J. K. (1995). Paraphilias. In H. I. Kaplan & B. J. Sadock (Eds.), *Comprehensive textbook of psychiatry VI, Vol. 1* (6th ed.) (pp. 1334–1347). Baltimore: Williams & Wilkins.

Millon, T. (1983). *Millon Clinical Multiaxial Inventory Manual* (3rd ed.). Minneapolis, MN: National Computer Systems.

Mohr, J. W., Turner, R. E., & Jerry, M. B. (1964). *Pedophilia and exhibitionism*. Toronto: University of Toronto Press.

Mosher, D. L. (1988). Aggressive Sexual Behavior Inventory. In C. M. Davis, W. L. Yarber, & S. L. Davis (Eds.), *Sexuality related measures: A compendium* (pp. 9–10). Lake Mills, IA: Graphic.

Murphy, W. D. (1997). Exhibitionism: Psychopathology and theory. In D. R. Laws & W. O'Donohue (Eds.), *Sexual deviance: Theory, assessment, and treatment* (pp. 22–39). New York: Guilford Press.

Murphy, W. D., Haynes, M. R., Stalgaitis, S. J., & Flanagan, B. (1986). Differential sexual responding among four groups of sexual offenders against children. *Journal of Psychopathology and Behavioral Assessment, 8*, 339–353.

Murphy, W. D., & Page, I. J. (2000). Relapse prevention with adolescent sex offenders. In D. R. Laws, S. M. Hudson, & T. Ward (Eds.), *Remaking relapse prevention with sex offenders* (pp. 353–368). Thousand Oaks, CA: Sage.

National Victim Center. (1993). *Crime and victimization in America: Statistical overview*. Arlington, VA: Author.

Nichols, H., & Molinder, I. (1984). *Manual for the Multiphasic Sex Inventory*. (Available from the authors at 437 Bowes Dr., Tacoma, WA 98466.)

O'Donohue, W., Letourneau, E., & Dowling, H. (1997). The measurement of sexual fantasy. *Sexual Abuse: A Journal of Research and Treatment, 9*, 167–178.

O'Donohue, W., & Plaud, J. (1994). The conditioning of human sexual arousal. *Archives of Sexual Behavior, 23*, 321–344.

O'Donohue, W., Regev, L., & Hagstrom, A. (2000). Problems with the DSM-IV diagnosis of pedophilia. *Sexual Abuse: A Journal of Research and Treatment, 12*, 95–105.

Pithers, W. D. (1990). Relapse prevention with sexual aggressors: A method for maintaining therapeutic gains and enhancing external supervision. In W. L. Marshall, D. R. Laws, & H. E. Barbaree (Eds.), *Handbook of sexual assault: Issues, theories, and treatment of the offender* (pp. 343–362). New York: Plenum Press.

Pithers, W. D., Beal, L. S., Armstrong, J., & Petty, J. (1989). Identification of risk factors through clinical interviews and analysis of records. In D. R. Laws (Ed.), *Relapse prevention with sex offenders* (pp. 77–87). New York: Guilford Press.

Prentky, R. A., Knight, R. A., Sims-Knight, J. E., Straus, H., Rokous, F., & Cerce, D. D. (1989). Developmental antecedents of sexual aggression. *Development and Psychopathology, 1*, 153–169.

Quinsey, V. L., Chaplin, T. C., & Carrigan, W. F. (1979). Sexual preferences amongst incestuous and nonincestuous child molesters. *Behavior Therapy, 10*, 562–565.

Quinsey, V. L., Chaplin, T. C., & Upfold, D. (1984). Sexual arousal to nonsexual violence and sadomasochistic themes among rapists and non-sex-offenders. *Journal of Counseling and Clinical Psychology, 52*, 651–657.

Quinsey, V. L., Harris, G. T., Rice, M. E., & Cormier, C. A. (1998). *Violent offenders: Appraising and managing risk.* Washington, DC: American Psychological Association.

Rangaswamy, K. (1987). Treatment of voyeurism by behavior therapy. *Child Psychiatry Quarterly, 20,* 73–76.

Rice, M., Quinsey, V., & Harris, G. (1991). Sexual recidivism among child molesters released from a maximum security psychiatric institution. *Journal of Consulting and Clinical Psychology, 59,* 381–386.

Russell, D. E. H. (1984). *Sexual exploitation: Rape, child sex abuse, and workplace harassment.* Thousand Oaks, CA: Sage.

Russell, D., Peplau, L. A., & Cutrona, C. E. (1980). The revised UCLA Loneliness Scale. *Journal of Personality and Social Psychology, 39,* 472–480.

Scott, G. G. (1983). *Dominant women, submissive men.* New York: Praeger.

Scully, D. (1988). Convicted rapists' perceptions of self and victim: Role-taking and emotions. *Gender and Society, 2,* 200–213.

Seidman, B. T., Marshall, W. L., Hudson, S. M., & Robertson, P. J. (1994). An examination of intimacy and loneliness in sex offenders. *Journal of Interpersonal Violence, 9,* 518–534.

Serin, R. C., Malcolm, P. B., Khanna, A., & Barbaree, H. E. (1994). Psychopathy and deviant sexual arousal in incarcerated sexual offenders. *Journal of Interpersonal Violence, 9,* 3–11.

Spence, J., Helmreich, R., & Stapp, J. (1973). A short version of the Attitudes Toward Women scale. *Bulletin of the Psychonomic Society, 2,* 219–220.

Spengler, A. (1977). Manifest sadomasochism of males: Results of an empirical study. *Archives of Sexual Behavior, 6,* 441–456.

Spielberger, C. D. (1988). *Stait-trait Anger Expression Inventory (STAXI) professional manual.* Odessa, FL: Psychological Assessment Resources.

Stein, D. J., Hollander, E., Anthony, D. T., Schneider, F. R., Fallon, B. A., & Leibowitz, M. R. (1992). Serotonergic medications for sexual obsessions, sexual addictions, and paraphilias. *Journal of Clinical Psychiatry, 53,* 267–271.

Stermac, L. E., & Segal, S. V. (1989). Adult sexual contact with children: An examination of cognitive factors. *Behavior Therapy, 20,* 573–584.

Stoller, R. (1991). The term perversion. In G. Fogel & W. Myers (Eds.), *Perversions and near perversions in clinical practice.* New Haven, CT: Yale University Press.

Symons, D. (1979). *The evolution of human sexuality.* New York: Oxford University Press.

Thornton, D. (1993). Sexual deviancy. *Current Opinion in Psychiatry, 6,* 786–789.

Tollison, C. D., & Adams, H. E. (1979). *Sexual disorders: Theory, treatment, and research.* New York: Gardner Press.

U. S. Department of Justice. (1999). Justice statistics. Washington, DC: Bureau of Justice Statistics.

U. S. Department of Justice. (2002). Justice statistics. Washington, DC: Bureau of Justice Statistics.

Ward, T., & Hudson, S. M. (2000). A Self-regulation model of relapse prevention. In D. R. Laws, S. M. Hudson, & T. Ward (Eds.), *Remaking relapse prevention with sexual offenders: A sourcebook* (pp. 79–101). Thousand Oaks, CA: Sage.

Ward, T., Hudson, S. M., Marshall, W. L., & Siegart, R. J. (1995). Attachment style and intimacy deficits in sex offenders: A theoretical framework. *Sexual Abuse: A Journal of Research and Treatment, 7,* 315–335.

Ward, T., McCormack, J., Hudson, S. M., & Polaschek, D. (1997). Rape: Assessment and treatment. In D. R. Laws & W. O'Donohue (Eds.), *Sexual deviance: Theory, assessment, and treatment* (pp. 356–393). New York: Guilford Press.

Wolfe, R. (1989). Novel techniques in treating the sexual offender. Workshop presented at the annual conference of the Association for the Treatment of Sexual Abusers, Seattle, WA.

CHAPTER 20

DISORDERS OF IMPULSE CONTROL

STEPHEN J. HUCKER

MCMASTER UNIVERSITY

Currently accepted diagnostic criteria for a number of psychiatric disorders include some form of impulsive behavior, although the latter is usually not precisely defined. Nonetheless, the term *impulsive* generally refers to acts carried out without reflection or forethought (Reber & Reber, 2001). Obviously, such behavior can occur in individuals with no formal psychiatric diagnosis, though certain of the latter conditions may be particularly associated with impulsive behavior (Moeller, Barratt, Dougherty, Schmmitz, & Swann, 2001).

IMPULSIVITY AND PERSONALITY DISORDERS

Borderline personality disorder, in which affective instability and identity disturbance are prominent features, is also characterized by impulsive behavior. The latter may include suicide attempts, gestures, and threats as well as other forms of self-harm. It may also include other potentially self-damaging behaviors such as excessive spending, sexual promiscuity, substance abuse, reckless driving, and binge eating.

Impulsivity is a central feature in the diagnosis of Borderline Personality Disorder and one that links it with Antisocial Personality Disorder (ASPD). However, impulsivity, as defined by the *Diagnostic and Statistical Manual of Mental Disorders* (*DSM-IV-TR*) (American Psychiatric Association, 2000) is only a possible, but not essential, criterion for the disorder. In fact, individuals with ASPD vary considerably in the degree to which they demonstrate impulsivity. Some studies suggest that there is a biological basis for impulsivity in these conditions. Linnoila and colleagues (1983) found that among 36 violent individuals with personality disorders, subjects with impulsive violence had significantly lower levels of the serotonin metabolite 5-hydroxyindoleacetic acid in their cerebrospinal fluid than individuals who had displayed premeditated violence. Also among individuals with personality disorders, those with a tendency to impulsive aggression show a significant prolactin response to the serotonin-releasing agent fenfluramine.

IMPULSIVITY AND CEREBRAL DAMAGE

Some individuals who have suffered traumatic brain injuries may be prone to impulsive behavior. Damage to the frontal cortex especially may result in impulsive behavior (Jentsch & Taylor, 1999), and head-injured patients have been described who show an acquired ASPD (Blair & Cipolotti, 2000).

IMPULSIVITY AND SUBSTANCE ABUSE

Although not a required diagnostic criterion in the *DSM-IV-TR*, many substance abusers behave impulsively, and individuals who exhibit other impulsive disorders are particularly prone to abuse substances (Brady, Myrick, & McElroy, 1998). Moreover, multiple substance abusers tend to be more impulsive that those who abuse single substances (McCown, 1988; O'Boyle & Barratt, 1993). Children with conduct disorders are particularly prone to become substance abusers (Disney, Elkins, McGue, & Iacono, 1999; Young et al., 1995). Attention Deficit Hyperactivity Disorder (ADHD) alone does not appear to increase the risk of substance abuse, but the presence of concomitant Conduct Disorder does do so (Disney et al., 1999; Molina, Smith, & Pelham, 1999).

IMPULSIVITY AND MAJOR MENTAL DISORDERS

Among psychotic disorders, Bipolar Disorder is the most usually associated with impulsive behavior. This is particularly the case with manic episodes (Swann et al., 2001). Depressive episodes may also be characterized by impulsivity, especially suicidal behavior (Corruble, Damy, & Guelfi, 1999).

IMPULSIVITY AND CHILDHOOD PSYCHIATRIC DISORDERS

Children with Attention Deficit Hyperactivity Disorder show hyperactivity, inattention, and impulsive behavior among their symptoms. In the impulsive/

hyperactive subtype, though not the inattentive subtype, there are high rates of comorbid Oppositional Defiant Disorder and Conduct Disorder symptoms (Willcutt, Pennington, Chhabildas, Friedman, & Alexander, 1999). Also, adults who show hyperactive/impulsive symptoms and Conduct Disorder symptoms as children are more likely to become adult criminals, though those with inattention symptoms alone do not (Babinski, Hartsough, & Lambert, 1999).

SPECIFIC DISORDERS OF IMPULSE CONTROL

In addition to the major psychiatric disorder categories already described, contemporary psychiatric classification systems include groups of disorders particularly characterized by impulsive behavior. The *DSM-IV-TR* (APA, 2000) includes a category of "Impulse Control Disorders Not Elsewhere Classified" (the 312 Codes, pp. 663–677). The ICD 10 has a corresponding category referred to as "Habit and Impulsive Disorders" (Code F63) (World Health Organization, 1992). Although the terminology is somewhat cumbersome, many of the conditions have been recognized by clinicians for at least two centuries and have been given time-honored names even though the conditions, if such they are, have been little studied. Those disorders named specifically in the section of *DSM-IV-TR* are Pathological Gambling, Kleptomania, Pyromania, Trichotillomania, and Intermittent Explosive Disorder. A residual category, "Impulse Control Disorder, Not Otherwise Specified" includes those conditions that do not meet the official criteria for the specific diagnoses or others elsewhere in the classification system. Although the criteria will be described in broad outline, these are not a substitute for the complete descriptions provided in the *DSM-IV-TR*.

Pathological Gambling

Individuals who are unable to resist the impulse to gamble, in contrast to more typical recreational gamblers, may be characterized by the term *pathological gamblers*. Characteristically, the tendency interferes with other aspects of their lives because they are unable to refrain from gambling, whether they are winning or losing. Jobs may be lost, personal and family relationships disrupted, and criminal behavior may be resorted to in order to support the habit. At least in the early stages, these individuals find the experience a pleasurable one, and for this reason some authorities have preferred the term *pathological* to *compulsive* gambling (Moran, 1970). Further, the condition is usually not regarded as ego-alien by the individual.

Unlike some of the other specific impulse control disorders, pathological gambling has only been recognized in the official classification of the American Psychiatric Association since the third edition of the *DSM* (APA, 1980). The currently accepted criteria require that five or more of the list of subcriteria are met including: preoccupation with gambling; illegal acts to obtain money for gambling; gambling to escape from problems or negative feelings such as depression, etc.; persistence in gambling, even after losing, in order to recover losses; soliciting money from others in desperation; betrayal of others by lying over current predicament; loss of jobs and other opportunities and important relationships because of gambling; increased amounts of money to gain excitement; and inability to stop gambling despite attempts to do so. The second requirement is that the individual's behavior is not better explained by a manic episode.

Some authorities have regarded pathological gambling as akin to a compulsive disorder (DeCaria & Hollander, 1993) or as an addiction (Dickerson, 1984). The problem appears to occur in between 0.1 to 2.3 percent of the population in the United States (Volberg & Steadman, 1988, 1989). Almost 7 percent of adult psychiatric inpatients (Lesieur & Blume, 1990) are affected, as are 8–25 percent of alcohol and other substance abusers (Lesieur, Blume, & Zoppa, 1986). The typical North American pathological gambler is a white, middle- to upper-middle-class male aged 40 to 50 years by the time they come to professional attention. Typically, pathological gamblers follow a progressive course of increasing loss of control along with substantial monetary losses. Like substance-dependent individuals, most develop tolerance (i.e., increase in size of debts and odds to obtain the same arousal levels) and show withdrawal symptoms (irritability, restlessness, depressed mood, and poorer concentration) when their gambling pattern is interrupted. With men, pathological gambling typically begins in adolescence, whereas women tend to develop it later in life (and there may be a history of a specific stress or major loss at the time of onset).

Classical studies of gambling behavior recognize four phases (Custer & Milt, 1985). The first phase, *winning*, is seen mainly in men who report "a big win" early in the course of the disorder, which fosters overconfidence in future gambling. Women, on the other hand, tend to develop the disorder in response to some emotional problem. In the second, *losing* phase, the gambler is unable to accept a run of bad luck and tries to win his or her money back ("chasing"). Heavier and more frequent betting follows, with consequent increase in debts. Many gamblers become superstitious and resort to "magical" practices, such as blowing on dice or carrying a lucky charm, or develop irrational beliefs, as in "lucky streaks," or ignore the simple probabilities, thinking that after losing several bets in a row their luck will change (the "Gambler's Fallacy"; Wagenaar, 1988). Gamblers begin to cover up their problem, resulting in occupational and relationship problems; a sense of urgency develops. When they run out of money, they often turn to friends and relatives to bail them out. The *desperation* phase results in uncharacteristic, sometimes illegal, behavior, including writing bad checks and embezzling from work. It is reported that about two-thirds of pathological gamblers will be driven to this extreme, rationalizing their behavior so that it becomes easier each time. As their gambling increases and personal relationships fail, gamblers become increasingly depressed and enter the fourth, *hopeless*, phase (Rosenthal, 1992), in which risk of suicide and stress-related illnesses dramatically increases. Despite the negative consequences, however, the gambling behavior continues.

Three-quarters of gamblers justify a diagnosis of Major Depressive Disorder and one-third suffer from bipolar disorders (Linden, Pope, & Jones, 1986). Fifty percent also develop problems with alcohol abuse (Smart & Ferris, 1996), and 17 to 24 percent attempt suicide (Ciarrocchi & Richardson, 1989). Personality disorders, especially narcissistic and antisocial types, are commonly noted in pathological gamblers (Blaszczynski, McConaghy, & Frakova, 1989). More recently, Black and Moyer (1998) used standardized diagnostic interviewing and specially developed impulsivity questionnaires to study 30 pathological gamblers. Sixty percent had a mood disorder, 64 percent a substance abuse disorder, and 40 percent an anxiety disorder, over the course of their lifetime. Eighty-seven percent had a personality disorder, the most common being obsessive-compulsive, avoidant, schizotypal, and paranoid disorders, as well as a relatively high rate of ASPDs. Other impulse control disorders were common, including compulsive buying and compulsive sexual behavior. These authors favored the continued inclusion of pathological gambling in the diagnostic category of Impulse Control Disorders. Large numbers report also dissociative experiences, including "trances," "memory blackouts," and the like during gambling sprees (Jacobs, 1988, p. 31).

Also, using structured clinical interviews with the *DSM-IV*, Grant and Kim (2001) recently found that most gamblers have severe financial, social, and legal problems and 58 percent had at least one first-degree relative who also showed problematic gambling behavior.

Lack of insight is typical in pathological gamblers and this, together with comorbid psychopathology such as substance abuse, makes treatment difficult (Ibanez et al., 2001). Although some authorities have claimed that pathological gambling is an eminently treatable disorder (e.g. Rosenthal, 1992, p. 77), there are few well-designed studies to support the claim. Some gamblers may find that attendance at Gamblers Anonymous, with its twelve-step approach, is sufficient to help them abstain. However, behavior therapy and psychodynamic psychotherapy have shown limited success. Newer cognitive behavioral approaches show greater promise, although clinicians must specifically address cognitive distortions and employ other specialized techniques (Tavares, Zilberman, & el-Guebaly, 2003). With the high comorbidity of mood and anxiety disorders and substance abuse, treatment of these underlying conditions will typically be necessary.

Trichotillomania

Trichotillomania is a chronic maladaptive and irresistible urge to pluck out one's hair. Usually it is scalp hair that is removed, although eyebrows and eyelashes and even body hair may be completely removed (Krishnan, Davidson, & Guajardo, 1985). Some have regarded the condition as a simple bad habit (Jillson, 1983), whereas others view it as a symptom of major mental illness (Oguchi & Miura, 1977) or as a variant of obsessive-compulsive disorder (Swedo, 1993) instead of an impulse control disorder. Typically, tension increases before the hair is pulled out or when the individual is trying to refrain from pulling, and relief or pleasure is obtained when the hair is being pulled out. In addition, to fulfill *DSM-IV-TR* criteria, the problem is not better explained by an alternative mental or medical disorder; clinically meaningful complications occur in social, vocational, and other areas; and hair loss is noticeable.

In most cases the condition may be concealed or not reported, but surveys suggest that 0.6 to 1.5 percent of males and 0.6 to 3 percent of females are affected (Christenson, Pyle, & Mitchell, 1991). Female patients, in fact, present more often to clinicians than males. The condition may begin very early in childhood and at this stage may respond to simple remedies or remit spontaneously. It may be accompanied by thumb sucking and dismissed as normal. Onset during the teens is more common in females, who conceal any disfigurement with wigs, hair styling, or cosmetics but may lead to avoidance of social contacts and impaired self-esteem. Despite these impairments, many never consult a mental health professional. Individuals may eat the plucked hairs and cause the formation of hair balls, which may cause medical complications.

Hair loss is variable but may be complete; when the hair grows again, it usually appears normal though may appear coarser and curlier. Usually the hair is pulled in private, though family members may be privileged to observe the act. The condition may increase at times of stress or, paradoxically, during relaxation. The episodes may be brief or prolonged. After the hair is plucked, the individual may stroke it against the cheek and lips or eat it, sometimes in a quite ritualistic fashion. The process of plucking is rarely described as painful and many are unaware that they are, in fact, doing it. On the other hand, attempts to inhibit the behavior may be accompanied by dramatic increase in anxiety and tension. Denial of the behavior is common in both the patients and their families.

Common comorbid conditions include major depressive disorder, generalized anxiety disorder, substance abuse, eating disorders, and excessive compulsive disorder (Swedo, 1993; Christianson, Pyle, & Mitchell, 1991). Personality disorders, usually histrionic, borderline, or passive-aggressive types, are often noted, but many patients otherwise appear perfectly normal (Winchell, 1992).

This strange phenomenon remains to be adequately explained, though there is currently a tendency to regard it as an atypical variant of obsessive-compulsive disorder. Various types of treatment have been proposed, including stress reduction and other behavioral therapies, hypnotherapy, dynamic psychotherapy, and self-help groups, all with variable success (Winchell, 1992). Medications that are used to treat both depression and obsessive-compulsive disorders—namely, the selective serotonin reuptake inhibitors (SSRIs, such as Prozac)—have been used successfully, although it has been noted that in some the underlying depression improves while the trichotillomania persists (Winchell, 1992).

Pyromania

The term *pyromania* has been used to identify fire setting for which there is no clear motive (Koson & Dvoskin, 1982; Lewis & Yarnell, 1951), although more obvious motives such as financial gain, concealment of some other crime, or expression of anger or revenge are easily concealed or overlooked. According to current criteria in *DSM-IV-TR* (APA, 2000), the person obtains relief, gratification, or pleasure from setting fires, watching them, or playing a role in the aftermath. Monetary gain is not the intent, and the fires are not set for political or criminal reasons or because of poor judgment induced by a mental disorder. Affect or tension is aroused before the act and the problem is not better explained by antisocial personality disorder, a manic episode or conduct disorder. The intent to set fires is deliberate and is repeated. Attraction to or fascination with fire is evident.

Although earlier studies suggested that pyromania was a common disorder, more recent research has suggested that it is in fact quite rare (APA, 2000, p. 670). Most pyromaniacs are male. Arousal and pleasure from setting fires may be explicitly sexual, but such "fire fetishes" are very rarely encountered despite their prominence in literature on fire setting. Indeed, there is little good research on pyromaniacs as distinct from fire setters in general. Many pyromaniacs also meet *DSM* criteria for intermittent explosive disorder, and the majority suffer from a mood disorder and alcohol abuse (Virkkunen et al., 1989). Common motives for fire setting are anger and vengeance (Prins, 1994). Classical psychoanalytic authors (Stekel, 1924; Freud, 1932/1964; Fenichel, 1945) suggested that pyromania is the result of unresolved sexual feelings though the one empirical study that explored this hypothesis failed to confirm it (Quinsey, Chaplin, & Upfold, 1989).

Low levels of serotonin metabolites have been found in the cerebrospinal fluid of "impulsive arsonists" (Roy, Virkkunen, Guthrie, & Linnoila, 1986) and recidivistic arsonists also have lower levels of these metabolites than nonrecidivists (Virkkunen et al., 1989). An underlying serotonergic or adrenergic disturbance may be present, leading some authors to suggest that the disorder be considered part of the "Affective Disorder Spectrum" (McElroy et al., 1995).

Systematic studies of treatments have rarely been carried out, and most reports are of single cases. Lack of insight, denial, and refusal to accept responsibility, together with comorbid alcohol problems, makes these patients difficult to treat (Mavromatis & Lion, 1977), although behavioral techniques have been successfully used. Multimodular programs have also claimed low recidivism rates of 1.4 to 6.3 percent (Kolko, 1988). An interesting personal account by a young woman who was a compulsive fire setter and diagnosed as having a Borderline Personality Disorder indicates that she responded well to intensive biofeedback therapy, social skills training, and treatment with clomipramine (Wheaton, 2001).

Intermittent Explosive Disorder

Despite its inclusion in several editions of the *Diagnostic and Statistical Manual*, many researchers and clinicians have doubted the existence of this disorder as an independent entity and it was almost excluded from the current edition (Bradford, Geller, Lesieur, Rosenthal, & Wise, 1994). Indeed, anger and aggression are extremely common in a wide range of psychiatric conditions. For example, Posternak and Zimmerman (2002) reported that about half of a sample of 1300 psychiatric outpatients reported currently experiencing moderate to severe levels of subjective anger and about a quarter had shown aggressive behavior in the preceding week. Anger levels correlated with depressed mood and anxiety. Although major depression disorder, bipolar I disorder, and cluster B personality disorders contributed to problems with anger and aggression in this sample, there were 40 individuals who met criteria for intermittent explosive disorder. However, clinicians usually apply the label very loosely to patients with a history of severe explosive outbursts (APA, 2000; Monopolis & Lion, 1983). Few studies use rigorous *DSM* criteria and as a result of using stringent methodology, Felthous, Bryant, Wingerter, and Barrett (1991) could identify only 13 cases. Strictly defined, therefore, the condition seems to be rare. In a review of over 800 possible cases in the preparation of *DSM-IV*, only 17 likely cases were identified (Bradford et al., 1994).

DSM-IV-TR criteria essentially require that impulses of aggression are uncontrolled in several separate episodes and result in serious assaults or destruction, that episodic violence is disproportionate to the provocation, and that disorders listed elsewhere in the *DSM* are insufficient to account for the episodes. Thus, currently the disorder is essentially defined by exclusion of other conditions. Problems with relationships, job loss, criminal behavior, alcohol abuse, and injuries resulting from fights and accidents are commonly seen in such patients. Early studies suggested that the violent outbursts may have some kind of subtle organic basis and terms such as *episodic dyscontrol* (Menninger & Mayman, 1956; Monroe, 1970) were used. Many textbooks suggest that a full neurological and neuropsychological assessment is required in these cases though discrete organic pathology is usually not identifiable.

In clinical practice it is often difficult to disentangle the features of intermittent explosive disorder from the typical background of antisocial or borderline personality characteristics, substance abuse, and deliberate violence for some specific end. Chronic aggression is typical of many patients with cluster B personality disorders and several studies show an overlap with Intermittent Explosive Disorder (Virkkunen, 1976; Pattison & Kahnan, 1983).

In addition to the possible significance of minor neurological abnormalities (Stein, Towey, & Hollander, 1995), interest in recent years has focused on serotonergic and adrenergic abnormalities in violence-prone individuals (Brown et al., 1989; Virkkunen et al., 1989). Serotonergic medications have been added to traditional psychodynamic behavioral and social therapies, but these have usually been heterogeneous populations so it is difficult to evaluate the true efficacy of these substances in intermittent explosive disorders. In fact, medication alone is usually quite insufficient to manage these patients and many of them have a tendency to abuse drugs in any case.

Kleptomania

The core notion of *kleptomania* is that the individual repeatedly gives in to the impulse to steal when he or she has sufficient money and no need for what is stolen. The *DSM-IV-TR* requires that the person be unsuccessful in resisting impulses to steal and has no other obvious motives such as anger, delusional ideas, and the like that might explain the behavior. Various other disorders or episodes must be excluded, and it is necessary that the person experiences gratification, relief, or pleasure when carrying out the theft and that the tension immediately increases prior to the act of stealing.

The validity of kleptomania as a discrete disorder has been questioned, although in recent years there have been a number of studies using *DSM*-defined subjects. Most of the literature on the topic refers in fact to shoplifters in general, most of whom likely would not fulfill the required criteria. Indeed, studies of shoplifters suggest that perhaps fewer than 5 percent would fulfill such criteria (APA, 2000). Nonetheless, the condition may be more common, particularly as it has been noted that many sufferers tend to be exceptionally secretive about their behavior (Goldman, 1991). Most reported cases of kleptomania have been female (McElroy, Pope, Hudson, Keeck, & White, 1991).

Though well aware they are committing a crime, most kleptomaniacs do not steal for personal gain. As required by the official criteria, they typically describe a feeling of increasing tension and pressure to steal followed by immediate pleasure or relief though subsequently often with residual guilt and shame as well.

Many kleptomaniacs develop self-control strategies, such as avoiding shopping malls or going shopping only when accompanied by other individuals. Some stop shopping altogether and become socially isolated. McElroy and her colleagues found kleptomania to be strongly associated with mood disorders (especially depression) and anxiety disorders, eating disorders, substance abuse, and other impulse control disorders (McElroy et al., 1991). Grant and Kim (2002a) more recently studied 22 kleptomaniacs identified using the structured clinical interview for the *DSM-IV* (SCID) and found that most had an average age of onset of 16 years with an average of 21 years duration of symptoms. Seventy-three percent reported specific triggers of their urges to steal, and 77 percent qualified for a lifetime diagnosis of various Axis I disorders, including major depressions, alcoholic dependence, and so on. More than 40 percent justified a current Axis I diagnosis. Sixty-eight percent reported intense shame or guilt following the thefts. Other impulse specific disorders of impulse control are reported in 18 percent. As with other recent studies, kleptomania is described by these authors as "a distressing and disabling disorder associated with high rates of psychiatric comorbidity."

Findings of this kind have led some researchers to suggest that kleptomania, and possibly other impulse control disorders as well, form part of the "affective spectrum disorders" linked by some common neurochemical abnormality involving low brain serotonin levels (McElroy, Hudson, Pope, Keck, & Aizley, 1992).

Psychoanalytic writers have tended to view compulsive stealing as a compensation for lack of affection in early life or as a defense against "castration anxiety." However, these elaborate speculations are difficult to evaluate and explore empirically. Cupchick and Atcheson (1983) suggested that some otherwise noncriminal shoplifters steal to compensate symbolically for some real or anticipated loss. Others, in line with the common observation of depression in shoplifters, have argued that stealing may have antidepressant effects by temporarily relieving feelings of anxiety (Fishbain, 1987; Goldman, 1991).

It is clear that many sufferers from kleptomania do not seek professional assistance and the natural history of the disorder is not known. Clinical studies do, however, suggest that it follows a chronic course (McElroy et al., 1991). Other than the work of McElroy and her colleagues, most research on the area of treatment is extremely difficult to evaluate as it is not applied to strictly defined cases. Behavioral strategies have been reported as successful (Glover, 1985; Guidry, 1975), though the soundest research points to promising results with the use of antidepressant medication, supporting the idea that these patients are suffering from some variant of a mood disorder (Hudson & Pope, 1990; McElroy et al., 1991; McElroy, Keck, Pope, Smith, & Strakowski, 1994). In particular, the serotonergic group of drugs such as fluoxetine and trazodone are reported as producing various degrees of remission. Recently, Naltrexone, an opioid antagonist, was found to be effective in the treatment of a small group of strictly defined kleptomaniacs (Grant & Kim, 2002b).

IMPULSE CONTROL DISORDER, NOT OTHERWISE SPECIFIED

As elsewhere in the *DSM-IV* classification scheme (APA, 2000), there is a residual category for those impulse control disorders that do not fulfill either the criteria for specific disorders outlined earlier or those other mental disorders with impulsive characteristics covered in other sections of the *DSM-IV-TR*. For example, substance abuse and paraphilia are not placed in this residual category because they are classified elsewhere in the manual.

Increasing attention has been paid to compulsive masturbation, habitual promiscuity, pornography dependence, compulsive use of telephone sex lines, and other behaviors. Some authors have referred to these as "nonparaphilic sexual disorders" or "paraphilia-related disorders" (Kafka, 1995; Travin, 1995). Other authors have referred to these as "sexual addictions" (Carnes, 1989, 2001) or "sexual compulsions" (Coleman, 1991, 1992; Anthony & Hollander, 1993). Some have suggested that these phenomena are related to mood disorders (Kafka, 1991; Kafka & Prentky, 1992), and in fact there have been encouraging reports indicating that not only these behavioral problems but also more discrete paraphilias may respond to antidepressant medications (Kafka, 1995). However, in the current *DSM-IV-TR* scheme, a diagnosis of Sexual Disorder Not Otherwise Specified (Code 302.9) rather than the corresponding Residual Impulse Control Disorder diagnosis (312.30) is to be preferred.

REPETITIVE SELF-MUTILATION

As with impulsivity in general, *self-mutilation* can occur in a wide range of psychiatric disorders. It is particularly associated with borderline personality disorder, the *DSM-IV* criteria that includes repetitive self-mutilation. Many authors have described individuals who episodically cut, carve, or burn their skin; interfere with healing of their wounds; and so on. Such people describe tension relief and other positive affects as a result of the self-mutilation (Favazza, 1987, 1992, 1995).

Usually the behavior begins in early adolescence, and self-harmful behavior becomes the individual's habitual way of dealing with personal distress. Between the episodes of self-harm there are periods of calm, though eating disorders, alcoholism, and substance abuse or kleptomania may also complicate the clinical picture. These patients are preoccupied with, and repeatedly fail to resist, harming themselves. As in other impulse control disorders, they experience feelings of tension immediately before hurting themselves, followed by feelings of relief or pleasure subsequently. The behavior is not suicidal and not a response to psychotic experiences. It has much in common with trichotillomania and some forms of nail biting and skin picking (Arnold, McElroy, Mutasim, Dwight, Lamerson, & Morris, 1998).

Once again, considerable interest has been focused on possible abnormalities of serotonin metabolism in these patients (Coccaro et al., 1989; Coccaro, Aspill, Herbert, & Schute, 1990). Psychotherapy is regarded as central to the management of repetitive self-mutilation (Walsh & Rosen, 1988), but there have been encouraging reports that selective serotonin reuptake inhibitors such as Prozac may help these patients even when there is no evidence of concomitant major depression (Markovitz, Calebresi, Schultz, & Meltzer, 1991).

COMPULSIVE SHOPPING

This behavioral problem, also referred to as *compulsive spending* or *oniomania* (Kraepelin, 1915; Bleuler, 1924) shows many affinities to kleptomania (McElroy, Keck, Pope, Smith, & Strakowski, 1994). Women appear to be more often afflicted than men (Faber, 1992; O'Guinn & Faber, 1989). In common with kleptomania, there is substantial comorbidity with mood and anxiety disorders (Christianson et al., 1994; McElroy et al., 1994). The relationship between compulsive buying and depression is well shown in the study of 119 depressed patients, 38 of whom were diagnosed as compulsive buyers. The latter tended to be associated with recurrent depression, comorbid with kleptomania and bulimia as well as benzodiazepine abuse or dependence (Lejoyeux, Tassain, Solomon, & Ades, 1997). Mood regulation is therefore a major determinant in impulse buying (Faber, 1992; O'Guinn & Faber, 1989), and these patients experience shopping or buying as exciting and mood enhancing. However, as with kleptomania, the behavior is followed later by remorse and regret. Once again, there is evidence that treatment with antidepressants may be helpful in alleviating the problem (McElroy, Satlin, Pope, Keck, & Hudson, 1991).

Conclusion

Although the specific category of Impulse Control Disorders has become firmly entrenched in the official diagnostic classification scheme in North America (APA, 2000), strictly defined cases are nonetheless relatively uncommon, with a result that large scale studies of homogeneous populations have been few. However, over the past decade more research has appeared that has stressed the substantial comorbidity of these disorders with mood disorders, anxiety disorders, eating disorders, substance abuse, personality disorders, and other specific impulse control disorders. Sometimes the features of individual diagnostic entities may in fact be clinically difficult to disentangle from one another, with a result that the impulsivity at the core of the disorders is obscured. Some disorders, such as compulsive buying, compulsive sexual behavior, and repetitive self-mutilation appear to show considerable similarities with other more traditional impulse control disorders and indeed may be more common. Certainly, clinicians have widely appreciated that these behavioral problems may cause significant distress for individuals and their families and may justify further study and attempts at treatment. In the future, other problem behaviors may well become included in this category and justify further study. At the present time, for example, there has been increasing interest in so-called Internet addiction, as a result of which individuals spend most of their waking hours in front of a computer screen. Similarly, other individuals may be observed to compulsively use their mobile telephones.

Finally, interest in a possible neurochemical basis for impulsive behaviors continues to proliferate with the eventual hope that newer pharmacological therapies may be available. Meanwhile, advances in cognitive behavioral treatment suggests that, as with other psychiatric conditions, pharmacotherapy and cognitive behavioral treatment in combination may mutually enhance each other's benefits.

REFERENCES

American Psychiatric Association. (1980). *Diagnostic and Statistical Manual of Mental Disorders: DSM-III 3rd edition.* Washington, DC: Author.

American Psychiatric Association. (2000). *Diagnostic and Statistical Manual, Fourth Edition–Textual Revision.* Washington, DC: Author.

Anthony, D. T., & Hollander, E. (1993). Sexual compulsions. In E. Hollander (Ed.), *Obsessive-compulsive related disorders.* Washington, DC: American Psychiatric Press.

Arnold, L. M., McElroy, S. E., Mutasim, D. F., Dwight, M. M., Lamerson, C. L., & Morris, E. M. (1998). Chracteristics of 34 adults with psychogenic excoriation. *Journal of Clinical Psychiatry, 59*, 509–514.

Babinski, L. M., Hartsough, C. S., & Lambert, N. M. (1999). Childhood conduct problems, hyperactivity-impulsivity, and inattention as predictors of adult criminal activity. *Journal of Child Psychology and Psychiatry, 40*, 347–355.

Black, D. W., & Moyer, T. (1998). Clinical features and psychiatric comorbidity of subjects with pathological gambling behavior. *Psychiatric Services, 49*, 1434–1439.

Blair, R. J., & Cipolotti, L. (2000). Impaired social response reversal: a case of "acquired psychopathy." *Brain, 123*, 1122–1141.

Blaszczynski, A., McConachy, N., & Frankova, A. (1989). Crime, antisocial personality, and pathological gambling. *Journal of Gambling Behavior, 5*, 137–152.

Bleuler, M. (1924). *Textbook of psychiatry* (A. A. Brill, trans.). New York: Macmillan.

Bradford, J., Geller, J., Lesieur, H., Rosenthal, R., & Wise, M. (1994). Impulse control disorders. In T. A. Widiger, A. J. Frances, H. A. Pincus, M. B. First, R. Ross, & W. Davis (Eds.), *DSM-IV Sourcebook*. Washington, DC: American Psychiatric Press.

Brady, K. T., Myrick, H., & McElroy, S. (1998). The relationship between substance abuse disorders, impulse control disorders, and pathological aggression. *American Journal of Addiction, 7*, 221–230.

Brown, G. L., Goodwin, F. K., Ballenger, J. C., Goyer, P. F., & Major, L. F. (1989). Aggression in humans: Correlates with CSF amine metabolites. *Psychiatry Research, 1*, 131–139.

Carnes, P. (1989). *Contrary to love: Helping the sex addict.* Minneapolis: CompCare.

Carnes, P. (2001). *Out of the shadows: Understanding sexual addiction* (3rd ed.). Center City, MN: CompCare.

Christenson, G. A., Faber, R. J., deZwann, M., Raymond, N., Specker, S. M., Ekern, E., et al. (1994). Compulsive buying: Descriptive characteristics and psychiatric comorbidity. *Journal of Clinical Psychiatry, 55*, 5–11.

Christenson, G. A., Pyle, R. L., & Mitchell, J. E. (1991). Estimated lifetime prevalence of trichotillomania in college students. *Journal of Clinical Psychiatry, 52*, 415–417.

Ciarrocchi, J., & Richardson, R. (1989). Profiles of compulsive gamblers in treatment: Update and comparison. *Journal of Gambling Behavior, 5*, 53–65.

Coccaro, E. F., Astill, J. L., Herbert, J. L., & Schut, A. G. (1990). Fluoxetine treatment of impulsive aggression in DSM-III-R personality disorder patients. [Letter]. *Journal of Clinical Psychopharmacology, 10*, 373–375.

Coccaro, E. F., Siever, L. J., Klar, H. M., Freidman, R. A., Moskowitz, A., & David, K. L. (1989). Serotonergic studies in patients with affective and personality disorders: Correlates with suicides and impulsive aggressive behavior. *Archives of General Psychiatry, 46*, 587–599.

Coleman, E. (1991). Compulsive sexual behavior. *Journal of Psychology and Human Sexuality, 4*, 37–52.

Coleman, E. (1992). Is your patient suffering from compulsive sexual behavior? *Psychiatric Annals, 22*, 320–325.

Corruble, E., Damy, C., & Guelphi, J. D. (1999). Impulsivity: a relevant dimension in depression regarding suicide attempts? *Journal of Affective Disorders, 53*, 211–215.

Cupchick, W., & Atcheson, D. (1983). Shoplifting: An occasional crime of the moral majority. *Bulletin of the American Academy of Psychiatry and Law, 11*, 343–354.

Custer, R. L., & Milt, H. (1985). *When luck runs out.* New York: Facts on File.

DeCaria, C. M., & Hollander, E. (1993). Pathological gambling. In E. Hollander (Ed.), *Obsessive-compulsive related disorders* (pp. 151–178). Washington, DC: American Psychiatric Press.

Dickerson, M. G. (1984). *Compulsive gamblers.* London: Longman.

Disney, E. R., Elkins, I. J., McGue, M., & Iacono, W. G. (1999). Effects of ADHD, conduct disorder, and gender on substance use and abuse in adolescence. *American Journal of Psychiatry, 156*, 1515–1521.

Faber, R. J. (1992). Money changes everything: Compulsive buying from a biopsychosocial perspective. *American Behavioral Scientist, 35*, 809–819.

Favazza, A. (1987). *Bodies under siege.* Baltimore: Johns Hopkins University Press.

Favazza, A. (1992). Repetitive self-mutilation. *Psychiatric Annals, 22*, 60–63.

Favazza, A. (1995). Self-mutilation. In E. Hollander (Ed.), *Impulsivity and aggression* (pp. 185–200). New York: Wiley.

Felthous, A. R., Bryant, S. G., Wingerter, C. B., & Barratt, E. (1991). The diagnosis of intermittent explosive disorder in violent men. *Bulletin of the American Academy of Psychiatry and Law, 19*, 71–79.

Fenichel, O. (1945). *The psychoanalytic theory of neurosis.* New York: Norton.

Fishbain, D. A. (1987). Kleptomania as risk-taking behavior in response to depression. *American Journal of Psychotherapy, 41*, 598–603.

Freud, S. (1964, orig. 1932). The acquisition and control of fire. In J. Strachey (Ed. and Trans.), *The standard edition of the complete psychological works of Sigmund Freud, Vol. 22* (pp. 183–193). London: Hogarth Press.

Glover, J. H. (1985). A case of kleptomania treated with covert sensitization. *British Journal of Clinical Psychology, 24*, 203–204.

Goldman, M. J. (1991). Kleptomania—making sense of the nonsensical. *American Journal of Psychiatry, 148*, 986–996.

Grant, J. E., & Kim, S. W. (2001). Demographic and clinical features of 131 adult pathological gamblers. *Journal of Clinical Psychiatry, 62*, 957–962.

Grant, J. E., & Kim, S. W. (2002a). Clinical characteristics and associated psychopathology of 22 patients with kleptomania. *Comprehensive Psychiatry, 43*, 378–384.

Grant, J. E., & Kim, S. W. (2002b). An open-label study of Naltrexone in the treatment of kleptomania. *Journal of Clinical Psychiatry, 63*, 349–356.

Guidry, L. S. (1975). Use of covert punishing contingency in compulsive stealing. *Journal of Behavior Therapy and Experimental Psychiatry, 6*, 169.

Hudson, J. I., & Pope, H. G. (1990). Affective spectrum disorder: Does antidepressant response clearly identify a family of disorders with a common pathophysiology? *American Journal of Psychiatry, 147*, 552–564.

Ibanez, A., Blanc, C., Donahue, E., Lesieur, H. R., Castro, I., Fernandez-Piqueras, J., & Saiz-Ruiz, J. (2001). Psychiatric comorbidity in pathological gamblers seeking treatment. *American Journal of Psychiatry, 158*, 1733–1735.

Jacobs, D. F. (1988). Evidence for a common dissociative-like reaction among addicts. *Journal of Gambling Behavior, 4*, 27–37.

Jentsch, J. D., & Taylor, J. R. (1999). Impulsivity resulting from frontostriatal dysfunction in drug abuse: implications for the control of behavior by reward-related stimuli. *Psychopharmacology* (Berl.), *146*, 373–390.

Jillson, O. T. (1983). Alopecia, II: Trichotillomania (trichotillohabitus). *Cutis, 31*, 383–389.

Kafka, M. (1991). Successful antidepressant treatment of of non-paraphilic sexual addictions and paraphilias in men. *Journal of Clinical Psychiatry, 52*, 60–65.

Kafka, M. (1995). Sexual impulsivity. In E. Hollander & D. Stein (Eds.), *Impulsivity and aggression* (pp. 221–228). New York: Wiley.

Kafka, M., & Prentky, R. (1992). Fluoxetine treatment of non-paraphilic sexual disorders and paraphilias in men. *Journal of Clinical Psychiatry, 53*, 351–358.

Kolko, D. J. (1988). Community intervention for juvenile firesetters: A survey of two national programs. *Hospital & Community Psychiatry, 39*, 973–979.

Koson, D. F., & Dvoskin, J. (1982). Arson: A diagnostic study. *Bulletin of the American Academy of Psychiatry & Law, 10*, 39–49.

Kraepelin, E. (1915). *Psychiatrie* (8th ed.). Leipzig: Barth.

Krishnan, K., Davidson, J., & Guarjardo, C. (1985). Trichotillomania: A review. *Comprehensive Psychiatry, 26*, 123–128.

Lejoyeux, M., Tassain, V., Solomon, J., & Ades, J. (1997). Study of compulsive buying in depressed patients. *Journal of Clinical Psychiatry, 58*, 169–173.

Lesieur, H. R., & Blume, S. B. (1990). Characteristics of pathological gamblers identified among patients on a psychiatric admissions service. *Hospital and Community Psychiatry, 41*, 1009–1012.

Lesieur, H. R., Blume, S. B., & Zoppa, R. M. (1986). Alcohol, drug use and gambling. *Alcoholism, 10*, 33–38.

Lewis, N., & Yarnell, H. (1951). *Pathological firesetting (pyromania)*. New York: Coolidge Foundation.

Linden, R. D., Pope, H. D., & Jones, J. M. (1986). Pathological gambling and major affective disorder: Preliminary findings. *Journal of Clinical Psychiatry, 47*, 201–203.

Linnoila, M. (1983). Low cerebrospinal fluid 5-hydroxyindoleacetic acid concentration differentiates impulsive from non-impulsive violent behavior. *Life Sciences, 33*, 2609–2614.

Markovitz, P. J., Calabrese, J. R., Schulz, S. C., & Meltzer, H. Y. (1991). Fluoxetine in the treatment of borderline and schizotypal personality disorders. *American Journal of Psychiatry, 148*, 1064–1067.

Mavromatis, M., & Lion, J. (1977). A primer on pyromania. *Diseases of the Nervous System, 38*, 954–955.

McCown, W. G. (1988). Multi-impulsive personality disorder and multiple substance abuse: evidence from members of self-help groups. *British Journal of Addiction, 83*, 431–432.

McElroy, S., Hudson, S., Pope, H., Keck, P., & Aizley, H. (1995). The DSM-III-R impulse control disorders not elsewhere classified: Clinical characteristics and relationships to other psychiatric disorders. *American Journal of Psychiatry, 149*, 318–327.

McElroy, S., Keck, P., Pope, H., Smith, J. N., & Strakowski, S. (1994). Compulsive buying: A report of 20 cases. *Journal of Clinical Psychiatry, 55*, 242–248.

McElroy, S., Pope, H., Hudson, J., Keck, P., & White, K. (1991). Kleptomania: A report on 20 cases. *American Journal of Psychiatry, 148*, 652–657.

McElroy, S., Pope, H., Keck, P., & Hudson, J. (1995). Disorders of impulse control. In E. Hollander & D. Stein (Eds.), *Impulsivity and aggression* (pp. 109–136). New York: Wiley.

McElroy, S. E., Satlin, A., Pope, H. G., Keck, P. E., & Hudson, J. I. (1991). Treatment of compulsive shopping with antidepressants: A report of three case studies. *Annals of Clinical Psychiatry*, *3*, 199–204.

Menninger, K., & Mayman, M. (1956). Episodic dyscontrol: A third order of stress adaptation. *Bulletin of the Menninger Clinic*, *20*, 153–165.

Moeller, F. G., Barratt, E. S., Dougherty, D. M., Schmitz, J. M., & Swann, A. C. (2001). Psychiatric aspects of impulsivity. *American Journal of Psychiatry*, *158*, 1783–1793.

Molina, B. S. G., Smith, B. H., & Pelham, W. E. (1999). Interactive effects of attention deficit hyperactivity disorder and conduct disorder on early adolescent substance use. *Psychology and Addictive Behavior*, *13*, 348–358.

Monopolis, S., & Lion, J. (1983). Problems in the diagnosis of intermittent explosive disorder. *American Journal of Psychiatry*, *140*, 1200–1202.

Monroe, R. R. (1970). *Episodic behavioral disorders.* Cambridge, MA: Harvard University Press.

Moran, E. (1970). Varieties of pathological gambling. *British Journal of Psychiatry*, *166*, 593–597.

O'Boyle, M., & Barratt, E. S. (1993). Impulsivity and DSM-III-R personality disorders. *Personality and Individual Differences*, *14*, 609–611.

O'Guinn, M., & Faber, R. J. (1989). Compulsive buying: A phenomenological exploration. *Journal of Consumer Research*, *16*, 147–157.

Oguchi, T., & Miura, S. (1977). Trichotillomania: Its psychological aspects. *Comprehensive Psychiatry*, *18*, 177–182.

Pattison, M., & Kahan, J. (1983). The deliberate self-harm syndrome. *American Journal of Psychiatry*, *140*, 867–872.

Posternak, M. A., & Zimmerman, M. (2002). Anger and aggression in psychiatric outpatients. *Journal of Clinical Psychiatry*, *63*, 665–672.

Prins, H. (1994). *Fire-raising: Its motivation and management.* London: Routledge.

Quinsey, V. L., Chaplin, T., & Upfold, D. (1989). Arsonists and sexual arousal to firesetting; correlation unsupported. *Journal of Behavior Therapy and Experimental Psychiatry*, *20*, 203–209.

Reber, A. S., & Reber, E. (2001). *The Penguin Dictionary of Psychology* (3rd ed.). Harmondsworth, UK: Penguin Books.

Rosenthal, R. J. (1992). Pathological gambling. *Psychiatric Annals*, *22* (2), 70–72.

Roy, A., Virkkunen, M., Guthrie, S., & Linnoila, M. (1986). Indices of serotonin and glucose metabolism in violent offenders, arsonists and alcoholics. *Annals of the New York Academy of Sciences*, *489*, 202–220.

Smart, R. G., & Ferris, J. (1996). Alcohol, drugs and gambling in the Ontario adult population, 1994. *Canadian Journal of Psychiatry*, *41*, 36–45.

Stekel, W. (1924). *Peculiarities of behavior: Wandering mania, dipsomania, cleptomania, pyromania, and impulsive acts, Vol. 2.* New York: Livewright.

Stein, D., Towey, J., & Hollander, E. (1995). The neuropsychiatry of impulsive aggression. In E. Hollander & D. J. Stein (Eds.), *Impulsivity and aggression* (pp. 91–108). New York: Wiley.

Swann, A. C., Janicak, P. L., Calabrese, J. R., Bowden, C. L., Disalver, S. C., Morris, D. D., et al. (2001). Structure of mania: depressive, irritable, and psychotic clusters with different retrospectively assessed course patterns of illness in randomized clinical trial participants. *Journal of Affective Disorders, 67*, 123–132.

Swedo, S. E. (1993). Trichotillomania. In E. Hollander (Ed.), *Obsessive-compulsive related disorders* (pp. 93–112). Washington, DC: American Psychiatric Press.

Tavares, H., Zilberman, M. L., & el-Guebaly, N. (2003). Are there cognitive and behavioural approaches specific to the treatment of pathological gambling? *Canadian Journal of Psychiatry, 48*, 22–27.

Travin, S. (1995). Compulsive sexual behaviors. *Psychiatric Clinics of North America, 18*, 155–169.

Virkkunen, M. (1976). Self-mutilation in antisocial personality (disorder). *Acta Psychiatric Scandinavica, 54*, 347–352.

Virkkunen, M., Dejong, J., Bartko, J., & Linnoila, M. (1989). Psychobiological concomitants of history of suicide attempts among violent offenders and impulsive firesetters. *Archives of General Psychiatry, 46*, 604–606.

Volberg, R. A., & Steadman, H. J. (1988). Refining prevalence estimates of pathological gambling. *American Journal of Psychiatry, 145*, 604–606.

Volberg, R. A., & Steadman, H. J. (1989). Porevalence estimates of pathological gambling in New Jersey and Maryland. *American Journal of Psychiatry, 146*, 1618–1619.

Wagenaar, W. A. (1988). *Paradoxes of gambling behavior.* Hillsdale, NJ: Erlbaum.

Walsh, B. W., & Rosen, P. (1988). *Self-mutilation.* New York: Guilford Press.

Wheaton, S. (2001). Memoirs of a compulsive firesetter. *Psychiatric Services, 52*, 1035–1036.

Willcut, E. G., Pennington, B. F., Chhabildas, N. A., Friedman, M. C., & Alexander, J. (1999). Psychiatric morbidity associated with *DSM-IV* ADHD in a non-referred sample of twins. *Journal of American Academy of Child and Adolescent Psychiatry, 38*, 1355–1362.

Winchell, R. (1992). Trichotillomania: Presentation and treatment. *Psychiatric Annals, 22*, 84–89.

World Health Organization. (1992). *The ICD-10 Classification of Mental and Behavioral Disorders: Clinical descriptions and diagnostic guidelines.* World Health Organization: Geneva.

Young, S. E., Mikulich, S. K., Goodwin, M. B., Hardy, J., Martin, C. L., Zoccolillo, M. S., & Crowley, T. J. (1995). Treated delinquent boys' substance use: Onset, pattern, relationship to conduct and mood disorders. *Drug and Alcohol Dependence, 37*, 149–162.

CHAPTER 21

DEVELOPMENTAL DISABILITIES AND MENTAL RETARDATION

W. LARRY WILLIAMS, PATRICK M. GHEZZI, AND ERIC BURKHOLDER
UNIVERSITY OF NEVADA, RENO

We begin this chapter by briefly describing the nature of developmental disabilities (DD) and mental retardation (MR) as well as the historical development and current prevalence of DD and MR. We also discuss the diagnostic, assessment, and treatment methods associated with DD and MR. We indicate, where appropriate, areas of needed research concerning assessment of persons with DD or MR. We also discuss issues of competence as related to persons with DD or MR. Finally, we review the current rights and contemporary social issues associated with persons with DD and MR.

THE NATURE OF DEVELOPMENTAL DISABILITIES AND MENTAL RETARDATION

There are many possible biomedical events in the life of a person that can result in considerable deviation from the normal or typical development (Simonoff, 1996). Currently, there are many known genetic, neurological, anatomical, medical, and psychological conditions or syndromes that as a group have become labeled as Developmental Disabilities (e.g., cerebral palsy, Tourette's syndrome, autism, pervasive developmental disorder, Down syndrome). Persons diagnosed with one or more of these conditions may also meet the criteria for the condition known as Mental Retardation (MR). Although MR as a term has been in the vernacular much longer than DD, the two are often erroneously used interchangeably. With the evolution in knowledge and practice during the later half of the twentieth century, several new terms have come to replace or draw attention away from the historical and general concept of mental subnormality or retardation in an attempt to deemphasize disabilities and to emphasize a person's abilities. The term *developmental disability* has become widely used as a result of this evolution. In this sense, *mental retardation* has become established as a term to describe a condition of intellectual and adaptive behavior functioning that results in an incomplete or altered development or a current developmental disability. Public Law 95-602 (1978) defines developmental disability as "a disability attributable to a mental or a physical impairment, manifested before 22 years of age, likely to continue indefinitely, resulting in a substantial limitation in three or more specified areas of functioning, and requiring specific and lifelong or extended care." Thus, DD does not necessarily include MR. (In the United Kingdom, the term most prevalent is *learning disabilities*, which is used in North America to describe specific deficiencies in reading, arithmetic, and other abilities.)

A Brief History

Numerous historical sources document how society has approached DD and MR as a social phenomenon and as a personal affliction (e.g., Hickson, Blackman, & Reiss, 1995; Pessotti, 1984; Sheerenberger, 1987; Williams, 1999). For example, throughout the Middle Ages, persons with what later would be termed mental illness (MI) or MR were punished out of fear and ignorance or for pleasure, or were alternatively protected as "lightning rods" to keep evil spirits away from others.

No significant progress toward understanding DD and MR or MR alone occurred until after the French Enlightenment and the famous "unshackling" of the patients by Pinel. Itard, Pinel, and other early pioneers of special education, such as Seguin and Montessori, sought to systematically study, care for, and educate persons with DD and MR or MR alone (Pessotti, 1984; Sheerenberger, 1987).

In 1848, Seguin moved to the United States and assisted S. G. Howe in establishing an experimental wing for ten "idiot" children at the Perkins Institute for the Blind. Subsequently, several northeastern states established institutions for the education and treatment of persons with DD and MR. In 1876, the Association of Medical Officers of American Institutions for Idiotic and Feebleminded Persons, now known as the American Association on Mental Retardation, was formed.

The early institutions were relatively small structures, located in rural areas with healthy food sources. Their charge was to provide sequenced training in basic skills and the study of effective methods to do so. They were to maintain relations with the communities to which their residents would be returned after training. Unfortunately, by the end of the century many institutions had become large and overcrowded. The situation for persons with DD and MR deteriorated further when Sir Francis Galton introduced the concept in 1901 of intelligence as an inherited trait.

Classification of persons in terms of their intellectual capacity gained initial scientific momentum with the advent of intelligence test construction at the beginning of the twentieth century. Goddard, interested in the classification of different levels of ability in the residents at the Vineland Training School in New Jersey, applied a test by Binet and Simon that would evolve into the Stanford-Binet Intelligence Test. As statistical methods and genetic developments in agriculture indicated that specific features of plants and animals were inherited, interest in the inheritability of intelligence increased. The eugenics movement was born, promoting the identification of persons who were "subnormal" with the intention of preventing them from procreation. These developments led to a widespread practice of isolation and sterilization of persons with DD and MR. Such practices continued during much of the first half of the twentieth century.

Advocacy for persons with DD and MR increased drastically during the 1950s. In 1952, the National Association of Parents and Friends of Mentally Retarded Children was founded. This organization became the National Association for Retarded Citizens in 1974, the Association for Retarded Citizens of the United States in 1980, and the ARC in 1991. In 1958, the first federal law specific to DD and MR, PL85-926, was enacted, providing for the training of teachers and other professionals to work with persons with DD and MR.

Prompted by the recommendations of President John Kennedy's Panel on Mental Retardation in 1962, advances in treatment and educational methods soon resulted in providing previously custodial residents in facilities with a variety of self-care skills, permitting greater independence in the areas of dressing, feeding, and toileting. There was a renewed commitment to more humane treatment that was accelerated with legal actions sparked by the civil rights movement. The Scandinavian movement of normalization (Wolfensburger, 1972), which became well known during the 1970s, advocated for deinstitutionalization. Litigation to gain basic rights for persons with DD and MR eventually resulted in rulings that reduced the numbers of institutionalized persons and eliminated many large facilities. During this time the amendments to the Vocational Rehabilitation Act (PL93-112) in 1973 and the establishment of the Education for All Handicapped Children Act (PL94-142) in 1975 irreversibly changed the course of services and treatment for persons with DD and MR. By the 1980s, all children, regardless of the severity of their disability, were entitled to free and appropriate public education with participation by parents in establishing learning objectives through a regular, individualized, interdisciplinary process. In 1990, the Individuals with Disabilities Education Act (IDEA) reaffirmed and amended the 1975 act to include persons with autism and acquired brain injury.

IDEA mandated transition planning by age 16 and addressed the special needs of minorities with disabilities. The Americans with Disabilities Act (ADA) of 1990 (PL101-336) provided for guarantees of civil rights, public services, public accommodations, transportation, and telecommunication. Bruyere and O'Keeffe (1994) have provided an extensive resource for the implications of the ADA for a variety of disabilities and contact points with business and society. Table 21.1 provides a list of the relevant legislation that has evolved.

TABLE 21.1
Federal Laws of Relevance to Mental Retardation

Public Law	Enactment	Relevance
83-531	7/26/54	Authorized cooperative research in education (in MR)
85-926	9/6/58	Establishment of the Institute of Child Health and Human Development (MR priority area); training of teachers of children with MR
88-156	10/24/63	Social Security Act Amendment; implementation of the Kennedy mental retardation program
88-164	10/31/63	Mental Retardation Facilities and Community Mental Health Centers Construction Act of 1963
89-10	4/11/65	Elementary and Secondary Education Act
89-97	7/30/65	Social Security Act Amendments: state plan funding to combat MR
89-105	8/4/65	Mental Retardation Facilities and Community Mental Health Centers Construction Act of 1965
89-313	11/1/65	Federal assistance to state-operated schools for the handicapped
90-170	12/4/67	MR amendments
91-695	1/13/71	Lead-based paint elimination support
93-112	9/26/73	Rehabilitation amendments
93-151	11/9/73	Lead-based paint poisoning prevention amendments
93-380	8/21/74	Education of the Handicapped Amendments of 1974
94-142	11/28/75	Education for all Handicapped Children Act; free appropriate education for all
98-199	12/2/83	Amendments to the Education of the Handicapped Act
99-457	10/8/86	Amendments to the Education of the Handicapped Act; extension of PL94-142 to preschool; incentives to infants, toddlers, transition, technology programs for persons with disabilities
101-336	7/26/90	Americans with Disabilities Act (ADA); civil rights assurance for people with disabilities in employment, public service and accommodation, and telecommunications
101-476	10/30/90	Individuals with Disabilities Education Act (IDEA); renaming and amending Education of the Handicapped Act; emphasized minorities with disabilities

For information on resources in your community, contact the following organizations:
    state or local chapter of the ARC
    state protection and advocacy organizations
    state mental health/mental retardation agencies
    independent living centers
    residential programs for offenders
    State Office of Vocational Rehabilitation

From Linda Hickson, Leonard S. Blackman, and Elizabeth M. Reis. *Mental Retardation: Foundations of Educational Programming.* © 1995. Published by Allyn and Bacon, Boston, MA. Copyright © 1995 by Pearson Education. Reprinted by permission of the publisher.

DEVELOPMENTAL DISABILITIES, MENTAL RETARDATION, AND THE LAW

Forensic psychology concerns itself with the measurement and analysis of components of the law from a psychological perspective (Batrol & Barton, 1994). Within the field of forensic psychology the analysis of a person's functioning level and his or her ability to make sound decisions is determined by a competency assessment. Judgment of competence in a court of law is conducted to determine if a defendant or witness is able to help in his or her defense, understand the charges, has the ability to act as his or her own lawyer, and either understands the consequences of pleading guilty or is competent to testify.

Defendants with MR are often inadequately represented because court officials do not understand the meaning of this diagnosis, or because appropriate steps have not been taken to understand the capabilities and limitations of an individual who has MR. Defendants with MR are often tried without sufficient assessment of their competence to stand trial. Although competence is specifically discussed in Chapters 10 and 11 this volume, we will summarize competence and its assessment for persons with MR.

Incidence

Genetic Factors

Many types of DD are associated with specific genetic and biological conditions (Simonoff, 1996). The incidence of these conditions and the type of DD that is typically observed are reasonably well known. These disorders include (1) inborn errors of metabolism that are inherited; (2) single-gene abnormalities where the abnormality is known to be related to a specific gene (e.g., tuberous sclerosis), with Mendelian inheritance and variable expression (following the mathematical probabilities of occurrence in offspring given the occurrence in a parent; (3) chromosomal abnormalities (chromosomal material being absent or in the wrong location (e.g., Down syndrome, fragile X syndrome) (APA, 1994). Approximately 30–40 percent of persons with MR have no clear etiology. Additionally, approximately 3 percent of the population will have MR but no identifiable medical or genetic condition. This is known as *cultural familial* MR and reflects the lower 3 percent of the assumed normal distribution of intellectual ability in the population. Table 21.2 lists some of the major genetic syndromes and their associated features.

Prenatal and Perinatal Factors

A second major contribution to DD and MR (30%) results from conditions that can occur to a developing fetus during pregnancy. A wide variety of influences such as physical trauma, significant exposure to drugs such as alcohol (e.g., fetal alcohol syndrome), deficiencies in the nutritional state of the mother, or extreme physical or emotional stress in the mother can result in conditions in the baby

TABLE 21.2
Environmental-Biological Causes of MR

Hemophilus influenzae–B	A bacteria causing meningitis, the most significant cause of MR in the U.S.
Congenital cytomegalovirus	Occurs in up to 2% of all live births with a mortality rate of 30%. Survivors show microcephaly, seizures, visual and hearing problems, and MR.
Toxoplasmosis	Microcephaly or hydrocephalus, cerebral palsy, epilepsy, or MR.
Rubella	Visual, auditory, cardiac, and neurological damage, resulting in MR.
Pediatric HIV and AIDS	High rates of mortality. Survivors commonly show encephalopathy, seizure disorders, motor dysfunctions, cortical atrophy, 70–90% central nervous system damage resulting in MR.
Fetal alcohol syndrome	Occurs in 7 in 10,000 live births. Growth deficiencies, facial abnormalities, brain and heart malformations, MR.
Low birth weight	From a variety of causes (smoking, malnutrition during pregnancy). Survivors have a higher incidence of cerebral palsy, autism, MR, developmental delay, sensory impairments, learning disabilities, hyperactivity, attention deficit.
Lead poisoning	Decreased intellectual functioning, central nervous system damage, learning disabilities, behavior problems.

that do not allow it to develop in the typical fashion. Damage can be caused to the fetus from extreme cranial pressure caused by instrumentation during birth, abnormal positioning of the fetus immediately prior to birth, or the permanent brain damage that can result when oxygen is limited to the brain caused, for example, by umbilical cord strangulation at birth. Table 21.2 describes several prominent perinatal factors.

Postnatal Factors

A third contributor to DD and MR consists of the effects of the postnatal environment on the developing neonate. A number of known diseases and traumas (e.g., shaken baby syndrome) can result in damage to the structure and function of the central nervous system during development. Measles, polio mellitus, scarlet fever, and a variety of other childhood illnesses can cause irreversible damage to the nervous system. Additionally, it is now known that the nervous system develops rapidly throughout the first few years of life. For example, a process called myelination that occurs early in the life of a developing child involves establishing nerve tracts that enable later normal neurotransmission. This process can be disrupted or stopped completely because of insufficient protein and essential amino acids. Malnutrition is the culprit in these cases, resulting in central nervous system impairment.

DD can also occur as a result of a wide variety of noxious substances (for example, lead or mercury poisoning); prolonged lack of oxygen to the brain, as may occur in suffocation or drowning; acquired brain injury from accidents; or permanent brain damage caused by ingestion of a variety of chemicals. Interestingly, although all incidents of DD and MR in the general population of

TABLE 21.3
Common Genetic Syndromes Associated with MR

Syndrome	Incidence	Features
Single gene defects		
Tuberous sclerosis	1 in 10,000	Epilepsy, facial spots, sclerotic brain nodules, lung cysts, retinal lesions, all levels of MR
Apert's syndrome		Elongated skull, abnormal fingers and toes, protuberant eyes; some have MR
Crouzon's syndrome		Elongated skull, protuberant eyes; some have MR
Ataxia telangiectasia Louis-Bar syndrome		Cerebella ataxia, extrapyramidal signs, predisposed to malignancy, variable MR after age 3–5
Laurence-Moon-Bredi syndrome		Obesity, hypogenitalism, pigmentary retinopathy, spastic paraplegia, variable MR
Virchow-Seckel Dwarf		Short stature, facial abnormalities, variable MR
Williams' syndrome	1 in 20–25,000	"Elfin" like, renal, cardiac and skeletal abnormalities, moderate-severe MR
X-linked disorders		
Aicardi's syndrome	only female (200)	Xp22, Agenesis of corpus callosum, chorioretinopathy, microphthalmia, seizures, lethal in males, varying MR
Duchenne's muscular dystrophy	1 in 35,000 males	Xp21.2, Hypertropic muscular dystrophy, varied MR in about 30% of cases, onset before age 6, loss of locomotion by age 12, death by age 20
Lesch-Nyan syndrome	1 in 10–380,000	Almost exclusively males, choreoathetosis, self-mutilation, hyperuricemia, spacticity, severe MR
Lowe's syndrome	1 in 200,000	Rickets (vitamin D deficiency), cataracts, hypotonia, severe MR
Nephrogenic diabetes		Polyuria, excessive thirst, vomiting, convulsions, MR secondary to dehydration
Norrie's disease		Cataracts, blindness, epilepsy, hearing impairment
Chromosomal abnormalities		
Down syndrome	1 in 1000	Trisomy 21, most common genetic cause of MR; flat forehead, oval face, large tongue, cataracts, hypothyroidism respiratory infections, leukemia, all levels of MR
Clinodactyly, congenital heart risk, Angelman syndrome	1 in 20,000	Stiff movements, ataxia, seizures, unprovoked laughter, severe MR; associated with a chromosome 15 (15q11–13) of maternal origin
Deletion of gene material on		
Cri-du-chat syndrome	1 in 50,000	Deletion (5p); spasticity, facial abnormalities, characteristic cry (catlike), all levels of MR
Edward's syndrome	1 in 8000	Trisomy 18; lowered, large ears, micrognathia, abnormal feet, all levels of MR
Fragile X syndrome	1 in 1250 (males) 1 in 750 (females)	Macro-orchidism, large ears, elongate face (60–80% males), speech, language and social difficulties, attention deficits, autistic features, psychiatric difficulties, mild to moderate MR
Klinefelter's syndrome	1 in 1000	47XXY, males, associated with difficulty in verbal skills, associated with normal intelligence

continued

TABLE 21.3
continued

Syndrome	Incidence	Features
Patau's syndrome	1 in 10,000	Trisomy 13, facial abnormalities, polydactyly, all levels of MR
Prader-Willi syndrome	1 in 25,000	Obesity, hyperphagia, hypogonadism, short stature, 40% mild MR associated with a deletion of gene material on chromosome 15 (15q12) of paternal origin
Turner's syndrome	1 in 2500	46XO-females, short stature, webbed neck, lack of secondary sexual characteristics, usually normal IQ
XXX syndrome	1 in 1000	47XXX, possible mild MR, no usual physical abnormalities
XYY syndrome	1–2 in 2000	Above-average height, mean IQ below that of general population; errors of metabolism
AdaGaucher's disease		Bone lesions, skin pigmentation, hypersplenism, varied MR
Hartnup disease	1 in 14,000	Cerebellar ataxia, photosensitive skin, intellectual deterioration, renal aminoacidurias
Homocystinuria	1 in 300,000	Skeletal abnormalities, epilepsy, lever degeneration, poor peripheral circulation, varied MR
Mucopolyhsaccharidoses	1 in 10,000	Gargoylism, deafness, hepatosplenomegaly, varied MR Type I Hurler's
Mucopolyhsaccharidoses	1 in 10,000	Gargoylism, deafness, hepatosplenomegaly, varied MR Type II Hunter's
Mucopolyhsaccharidoses	1 in 10,000	Mild physical signs, severe MR; Type III Sanfilippo's
Type IV	1 in 10,000	Corneal clouding, skeletal and aortic valve disorders, normal intellect
Maple syrup urine	1 in 120–200,000	Epilepsy, spasticity, characteristic urine odor, varied MR
Niemann-Pick disease		Spasticity, seizures, hepatosplenomegaly, varied MR
Phenylketonuria (PKU)	1 in 10,000	A phenylalanine hydroxylase deficiency, slowed growth, microcephaly, epilepsy, hyperactivity, autistic features, varied MR
Tay-Sachs disease	1 in 2500	Early regression, cherry "red spot" of macula, blindness, early death; Ashkenazi Jews

Adapted from Thapar, Gottesman, Owen, O'Donovan, and McGuffin (1994). The genetics of mental retardation. *British Journal of Psychiatry, 164.* Adapted with permission from the publisher.

the United States is around 3 percent, this prevalence is higher in populations associated with the criminal justice system. This difference is significant in that it may represent an inadequate understanding and assessment of persons with DD and MR within the criminal justice system.

FREQUENT QUESTIONS AND ANSWERS

How often are people with DD and MR involved in the criminal justice system? Based on the 1990 census, between 6.2 and 7.5 million people in the United States are diagnosed with mental retardation. Studies have estimated that between 2 and

10 percent of the prison population has mental retardation. For example, a survey by Denkowski and Denkowski (1985) found that about 2 percent of all inmates in either state or federal correctional facilities have mental retardation (about 14,000 people). New York state conducted a similar survey that produced comparable results: between 1.8 percent and 2.2 percent of people with MR were imprisoned (Sundram, 1990). Residential programs that house offenders with MR support another 12,500 people who have been convicted, or suspected, of committing a crime (Noble & Conley, 1992).

Surveys that set the total number of people with MR in prisons and residential programs (26,500 to 32,500) underestimate the extent of the problem by ignoring the number of people who are on probation, in local jails, or placed in programs for people with mental illness. Even though those in the criminal justice system constitute a small portion of all people with this disability, the number is significant enough to warrant the attention and concern of self-advocates, parents, criminal justice personnel, and policymakers. Standardization of nationwide data collection procedures are necessary before a more accurate assessment of the number of people with mental retardation involved in the criminal justice system can be determined (Noble & Conley, 1992).

Do people with DD and MR commit crimes more often than people without this disability? Some people with mental retardation may commit crimes, not because they have below-average intelligence, but because of their unique personal experiences. During the early 1900s, professionals believed that individuals with DD and MR were predisposed to becoming criminals because of their disability. This "alarmist" view lost support during the 1930s and its proponents rescinded their original beliefs. By the 1950s and since that time, any findings suggesting a significant link between DD and MR and criminal behavior have been proven incorrect and, consequently, rejected (Ellis & Luckasson, 1985).

For what crimes are people with DD and MR usually charged? The misconception that people with DD and MR usually commit serious crimes is unwarranted. Data taken from state and federal prisons reveal that people with DD and MR are more likely to commit serious felonies, but this information is misleading because prisons typically house inmates who commit serious crimes (Brown & Courtless, 1971). On the other hand, data gathered from a specialized community program for offenders with DD and MR revealed that most offenders were arrested for committing misdemeanors and other less serious felonies (White & Wood, 1986). Research also shows that people with MR commit less serious crimes, such as misdemeanors and public disturbances (Illinois Mentally Retarded and Mentally Ill Task Force, 1988).

What disadvantages do people with DD and MR face in the criminal justice system? As more people with DD and MR move out of institutions and into the community, their susceptibility to becoming involved in the criminal justice system as a victim, witness, or suspect of a crime increases. Individuals with DD and MR who do not understand their involvement in a crime or the consequences of their involvement are frequently used by others to assist in law-breaking activities. For example, they may be drawn to crime by the positive attention received from others or by the pressure not to displease others. In either case, they may agree to help with criminal activities in order to gain or maintain relationships. Many individuals unintentionally give "misunderstood responses" to officers, which increases their vulnerability to arrest, incarceration, and possibly execution, even if they committed no crime (Perske, 1991).

Either to be maintained by social attention (approval) or to hide their disability, upon arrest individuals with DD and MR usually answer affirmatively when asked if they understand their rights, even when they do not understand. Law enforcement officers often receive little or no training in the area of DD and MR and have difficulty recognizing a person who has this disability. They may be mistaken as someone who is drunk, on drugs, or who has a psychopathology (see later section on dual diagnosis and psychopathology). Court officials face the same dilemma. Attorneys may represent people with DD and MR without realizing that a disability exists, and judges may impose sentences without taking DD and MR into account. Considering such extreme disadvantages, it is not surprising that people with DD and MR are more likely to be arrested, convicted, sentenced to prison, and victimized in prison (Santamour, 1986). Once in the criminal justice system, these individuals are less likely to receive probation or parole and tend to serve longer sentences because of an inability to understand or adapt to prison rules.

Some common responses from persons with DD and MR that may affect their ability to protect their rights during police contact include (1) not wanting their disability to be recognized (leading them to try to cover up their disability); (2) not understanding their rights (but pretending anyway to understand them); (3) not understanding commands given by the police; (4) being upset by police presence; (5) acting upset at being detained and/or trying to run away; (6) saying what he or she thinks others want to hear; (7) having difficulty describing facts or details of offense; (8) being the first to leave the scene of the crime, and the first to get caught; (9) being confused about who is responsible for the crime and "confessing" even though innocent.

Some researchers have found that people with disabilities are roughly twice as likely as others to be victimized (Sobsey & Doe, 1991). Crimes committed against people with MR are often labeled as abuse and neglect, which understates the criminal victimization problem. Factors such as impaired cognitive abilities and judgment, physical disabilities, insufficient adaptive behaviors, constant interactions with "protectors" who exploit them, lack of knowledge about how to protect themselves, and living and working in high-risk environments increase the vulnerability of people with mental retardation to victimization (Luckasson, 1992). Many victims with MR may not report crimes because of their dependency on the abuser for basic survival needs. When victims do report crimes, police and court officials may not take the person's allegations seriously or may be reluctant to get involved. Additionally, people with MR often lack the resources necessary to prosecute (Sobsey, 1994).

COMPETENCE ASSESSMENTS OF PEOPLE WITH DEVELOPMENTAL DISABILITIES

Two types of competency are generally acknowledged: legal competence and clinical competence. All adults are considered legally competent until declared otherwise by a court, whereas those under the age of 18 are considered legally incompetent. Declaration of legal incompetence is a separate action from hospitalization, requiring a separate hearing and specification of distinct aspects or areas of incompetence.

Whereas legal competence is an all-or-none issue, *clinical competence*, or capacity to make decisions, can be variable in degree. Thus, "a person can have different levels or degrees of ability to function in a particular area, which are not fixed over time and situation. A person who is considered 'competent' may be said to have a sufficient, or threshold amount of, capacity to perform a given task under specified circumstance" (Wiener & Wettstein, 1993, p. 275). These authors provide a detailed description of 18 different procedures and considerations involved in performing evaluations of legal competence as well as seven common clinical criteria for determining legal competence. A declaration of incompetence will typically result in the appointment of a legal guardian for the purposes of decision making on behalf of the individual. Legal guardians may be appointed for a person's estate decisions (conservator), personal decisions (e.g., medical or psychiatric treatment), or both (plenary). For persons with DD judged incompetent, other protective services exist, such as a representative payee, adult protective services, and public guardians.

Although competency standards vary from state to state, the North Carolina statute on competency summarizes nicely how criminal law relates to persons with developmental disabilities: "No person may be tried, convicted, sentenced, or punished for a crime when by reason of mental illness or defect he is unable to understand the nature and object of the proceedings against him, to comprehend his own situation in reference to the proceedings, or to assist in his own defense in a rational or reasonable manner."

A diagnosis of a mental illness or of mental retardation alone is insufficient for determining a person's competency to stand trial. The role of the forensic psychologist is to evaluate a person's competence in a manner consistent with the clinician's own training and theoretical orientation. This evaluation is conducted depending on the person's functioning abilities by methods such as a standardized clinical interview with both projective and direct measurement psychological tests, interview information, direct observation, and background history evaluations (Bartol & Barton, 1994, p. 124). What follows are very brief descriptions of the information needed to be assessed to establish a person's competence to stand trial, to confess, to plead guilty, and to testify. Competence is not an all-or-none concept in the law. A person may be found incompetent to confess but competent to stand trial, so often multiple assessments may be necessary. (For a complete description of the subareas of competence, see Luckasson & Vance, 1995.)

In assessing competency to stand trial for a crime, a person must be assessed to determine his or her capacity to consult with a lawyer at some reasonable level, and to establish if that person has a factual understanding of the charges. In assessing the person's capacity to consult a lawyer, the forensic psychologist should consider the person's level of understanding of both the complexity and consequences of a conviction for the crime.

The assessment of an individual with DD who wants to confess to a crime should be conducted by a review of the records of school and other previous evaluations, intelligence testing, achievement testing, an interview with the defendant, interviews with others who know the defendant, and an analysis of the statement and its reflection of the abilities of the defendant (Luckasson & Vance, 1995). In addition, the forensic psychologist must assess the defendant's understanding of the warnings given in the Miranda rights, the concepts contained in the warnings, the ability to comprehend long-term consequences, and the ability to provide accurate and reliable information.

If a defendant with DD and MR wishes to plead guilty, it is the job of the forensic psychologist to determine if the accused can understand the relevant information given by the attorney, the consequences of this action, the meaning of his or her constitutional rights, and ability to make choices that have long-term consequences (Luckasson & Vance, 1995).

For a person with DD and MR to be competent as a witness, he or she must be able to observe, remember, relate, or express the experience and have the capacity to currently understand the oath (*United States v. Pryce*, 1991). The victim or witness with DD and MR who meets these criteria may then testify.

Diagnostic Assessments for DD and MR and MR Alone

The *Diagnostic and Statistical Manual* (*DSM-IV*) of the American Psychiatric Association (APA, 1994), the *International Classification of Diseases* (*ICD-9*; WHO, 1995) of the World Health Organization, the *Mental Retardation Definition, Classification, and System of Supports* (Luckasson et al., 1992) of the American Association on Mental Retardation (AAMR), and the *Manual of Diagnosis and Professional Practice in Mental Retardation* (Jackobson & Mulick, 1996) of the American Psychological Association (APA) provide currently used definitions of MR alone and DD and MR. These sources describe MR from different perspectives. For example, the *DSM-IV* perspective is a psychopathological and medical diagnosis approach along five "axes" of pathology: clinical disorders, personality/mental retardation, general medical condition, psychosocial and environmental, and global assessment of functioning. The AAMR and APA perspective is an intellectual, psychopathological, and skill functioning assessment (to arrive at a determination of needed educational, vocational, or living supports). However, there is general agreement between these two perspectives on a definition of MR in terms of a person's level of functioning.

Mental retardation, as a diagnosis, is defined as: (1) the presence of a significant intellectual deficiency (typically defined as having a standard intelligence test score that falls at or below approximately 70, when the average for the overall population is 100, and approximately 95 percent of all people would have a score between 70 and 130); (2) a concurrent significant limitation in "adaptive behavior" (for the AAMR and *DSM-IV* definitions, this means any two of ten typical "domains," such as communication, self care, and social skills, as measured by standard adaptive behavior tools such as the Adaptive Behavior Scales [Lambert, Nihira, & Leland, 1992], or the Vineland Adaptive Behavior Scales [Sparrow, Balla, & Cichetti, 1984]); and (3) demonstrating such deficiencies during the normal development period that ends at 18 (*DSM-IV* and AAMR) to 22 (MDPP) years of age. (Deficiencies that come about after this point, for someone who did not show them previously, are defined as resulting from environmental trauma such as acquired brain injury and are not defined as MR.)

According to Luckasson and Vance (1995), four assumptions are essential to the application of the definition of mental retardation: (1) Valid assessment considers cultural and linguistic diversity as well as differences in communication and behavioral factors; (2) the existence of limitations in adaptive skills occurs within the context of the community environments typical of the individual's age peers and is indexed to the person's individualized needs for supports; (3) specific adaptive limitations often coexist with strengths in other adaptive skills or personal capabilities; and (4) with appropriate supports over a sustained period, the life functioning of the person with mental retardation will generally improve.

Except for the AAMR (Luckasson et al., 1992) definition, MR has historically been specified into four levels of intellectual impairment: mild MR (IQ of 50–55 to approximately 70); moderate MR (IQ level 35–40 to 50–55); severe MR (IQ 20–25 to 35–40); and profound MR (IQ below 20–25). Persons diagnosed with *mild* MR represent about 85 percent of all persons with MR. Historically, this group was referred to as "educable" because they developed social and communication skills during preschool years, had normal sensory-motor development, progressed to about the sixth-grade level, and were able to enjoy independent or supervised community living.

Persons with *moderate* MR (historically and by today's practices prejudicially referred to as "trainable") represent about 10 percent of all persons with MR. They may acquire communication skills during early childhood and may succeed in vocational training and be taught independent self-care skills. Persons with moderate MR generally will not progress academically beyond approximately the grade two level. Some social skill deficiencies may interfere with peer relationships in adolescence. They may be able to perform unskilled or semiskilled jobs and adapt well to community living, usually in supervised settings.

Persons with *severe* MR constitute 3–4 percent of all persons with MR. Language development and basic self-care skills usually occur only with extensive and prolonged training. Basic preacademic skills such as letter recognition and counting may also be acquired with training. Persons with severe MR may also participate in supervised community living.

Persons with *profound* MR comprise 1–2 percent of all persons with MR. Eventual development of basic communication and self-care is realized through highly structured individual training and supervision. Community living is typically in supervised settings.

In contrast to the other definitions, the AAMR definition and classification system replaces the four levels of severity (mild, moderate, severe, and profound) with four levels of "intensity of support" that an individual with MR may require in his or her integrated life in the community. These levels of support are (1) *intermittent*: provided on an episodic or as-needed basis; (2) *limited*: supports occurring along some dimension on a regular basis for a short period of time; (3) *extensive*: ongoing regular support involvement in some environments and not time limited; and (4) *pervasive*: constant, high-rate support in several environments that are potentially life-sustaining in nature.

The AAMR system additionally provides an attempt to generate new practices in the field of MR by proposing a new "three-step" procedure in diagnosing and classifying a person with MR. The first step, Diagnosis, provides a diagnosis in a similar fashion to other systems, using intellectual function and adaptive behavior level. One controversial difference here, however, is a suggested IQ cutoff score of 75 (as opposed to the traditional 70) (see MacMillan et al., 1993, for a description of the detrimental effects of such a change).

The second step, Classification and Description, provides an assessment of psychological and emotional status and medical condition, including possible etiology (cause) of MR, and environmental (living) situation. Information is gathered through observation, interviews, applications of standard psychopathology instruments, and medical and psychiatric examination to expose any possible mental illness that a person may have in addition to the MR (since 1980 persons with MR have been considered three to four times more likely than others to suffer from psychopathology).

The third step, Profile and Intensities of Needed Supports, uses the prior information to plan the nature and intensities of supports that a person will require. This is the context within which the previously mentioned intensities of support are used.

The AAMR system provides a clear example of the changes that are occurring in the MR field. It promotes a person-centered, person-first approach that emphasizes the support needs for a member of society to live like any other person as opposed to a simple classification of a person's "deficiencies."

Dual Diagnosis: Psychopathology and Mental Retardation

As mentioned earlier, persons with MR are also vulnerable to psychopathology. This issue is extremely relevant for those with MR because the presence of psychopathology often reduces independence and may involve institutionalization.

Although not yet formally understood, it is ordinary to observe higher levels of stress, emotion, and insecurity in a population with lowered intellectual and social competencies. The prevalence of dual diagnosis results from changes since the early 1980s in the *DSM* classification system, which placed psychopathology and MR on two separate axes. Before this time, one could only receive a diagnosis of either MR or psychopathology. The detection and treatment of psychopathology in persons with MR can be difficult in the face of their diminished language and communication skills as well as a longstanding lack of medical and related professionals' knowledge and experience in both areas as opposed to one or the other.

Although all psychopathologies may be found at all levels of MR, persons with mild MR tend to be more frequently diagnosed with traditional psychiatric disorders, whereas those with severe or profound MR will be more often observed to show severe behavioral disturbances. Obsessive-compulsive disorder, panic disorder, and post-traumatic stress disorder have been diagnosed with less prevalence in persons with MR than those in the general population. Pathologies related to emotional disorders such as anxiety and bipolar disorder (manic-depressive) are often encountered. If personality disorders and maladaptive behavior disorders are not counted, psychopathology incidence is about the same for those with MR as for the general population.

Comprehensive instruments for assessing psychopathology are not numerous. They attempt to capture a broad range of conditions such as the Reiss Screen for Maladaptive Behavior (Reiss, 1988), the Psychopathology Instrument for Mentally Retarded Adults (PIMRA; Matson, Kazdin, & Sanatore, 1985, 1990), and the Diagnostic Assessment for the Severely Handicapped (DASH; Matson, Gardner, Coe, & Sovner, 1991). The Reiss screen is completed by a caregiver or family member who knows the person. The PIMRA is intended to help develop a psychiatric diagnosis for persons with MR and can be self-administered or informant-administered. The DASH provides a survey of psychiatric disorders for the MR population.

Two more focused instruments are based on direct observation of behavior as opposed to an assumed taxonomy of mental illness. They are the Aberrant Behavior Checklist (ABC; Aman, Singh, Stewart, & Field, 1985; Aman, Burrow, & Wolford, 1994) and the Strohmer-Prout Behavior Rating Scale (BRS; Strohmer & Prout, 1989).

Because of the difficulty in detecting pathologies in a largely nonvocal population, extreme caution should be taken in assuming the existence of an internal pathology as opposed to external causes. Direct observation of problem behaviors, elimination of medical reasons, and examination of current living and quality-of-life issues should be conducted before assuming pathology or undertaking a specific pharmacological regime to treat it (Health Care Financing Administration, 1996). Further development of valid and reliable assessment tools is sorely needed, especially those that might emphasize direct behavioral assessment and the relationship between observed performance and environmental events, as well as tools for accurate prediction of service placement outcomes.

TREATMENT AND SERVICE ASSESSMENTS

In addition to epidemiological and diagnostic assessments, there is a wide variety of specialized treatment assessment tools that provide clinicians and educators with information relevant to effective treatment strategies. Such assessments have been considered part of the "right to effective behavioral treatment" of persons with DD and MR (Van Houton et al., 1988).

Training Assessments

There are a number of teaching and training tools that provide professionals with information relevant to service placement and curriculum design. Early examples of these were the Portage Guide (Shearer & Shearer, 1972), and the Objective Behavior Assessment (OBA; Hardy, Martin, Yu, Leader, & Quinn, 1981). These are typically direct observation, criterion-based performance measures that allow assessment of a person's current skill level for training purposes. (For a review of such tests for use in special education settings, see Hickson, Blackman, & Reiss, 1995.)

Environmental and Functional Analyses of Behavior Disorders

Tremendous advances in the understanding of learning processes and the use of behavioral technology over the past thirty years have resulted in the development of teaching and clinical treatment strategies and procedures for a wide variety of learning problems and behavior disorders. These methods collectively come from the area of psychology known as applied behavior analysis and have become widely recognized and employed in the teaching and care of persons with DD and MR.

The earliest applications of behavior analysis were focused in institutional settings in the 1950s and 1960s. Often the extremely challenging cases in which persons had developed longstanding behaviors such as self-mutilation or aggression were undertaken by behavior analysts because the approaches and knowledge of the time could not help these people. An understanding of the significant role that the environment plays in determining the acquisition and maintenance of human behavior (in terms of the situations in which behavior occurs, and the consequences that immediately follow a given behavior) has developed into a sophisticated technology of teaching and clinical treatment. Along the path of this development, the field also had to suffer through the ethical dilemmas of using known "default" invasive methods to reduce extremely harmful behavioral excesses rather than allowing such behaviors to continue at considerable harm to individuals or others. Fortunately, the accumulation of knowledge has resulted in methods that focus on accurate assessment of the environmental functions of behavior problems, such that constructive teaching and intervention strategies can be accurately applied to change performance in positive and less restrictive ways.

Perhaps the greatest contribution that behavior analysis has provided to the field has been its hallmark feature of accurately describing and measuring actual performance and the situations in which that performance occurs. This has allowed for true interdisciplinary problem solving and the ability to assess teaching and treatment outcomes from all areas of specialization.

In addition to the now-standard functional assessment of severe behavior in order to detect the relationship between the behavior and its maintaining consequences (Iwata et al., 1982, 1994; O'Neil et al., 1990; Touchette & Howard, 1984), there are now a variety of reinforcer assessments (Fisher et al., 1996) that indicate a person's most recent preference for specific activities or consumables as well as curriculum assessments (Koegel & Koegel, 1986; Horner, 1994) that allow for a better fit between a person's functioning level and what is being taught.

Even more recent is the development of direct assessment of a person's learning abilities in terms of the types of discrimination learning he or she is capable of (Martin & Yu, 2000; Yu, Martin, & Williams, 1989). This information is central to the development of alternative communication skills and to the treatment and prevention of the development of aberrant behavior resulting from nonability to respond to regular instruction methods involving spoken language. The implications of these types of assessments for traditional service placement tools (e.g., Inventory for Client and Agency Planning (ICAP) (Elwinger, 1986) (Aman, Burrow, & Wolford, 1994) are only now being investigated (Williams & Collins, 1999). One early indication, however, is that such service placement tools can overestimate the abilities of many persons with DD and MR, resulting in inappropriate placements and services for a person's true functioning level. Further refinement in this area is one direction for future research. There are implications of these developments for assessing competence as determined from an individual's current communication and language ability and comprehension of basic concepts.

CONCLUSION

Historically, society has mistreated and misunderstood persons with DD and MR. There may be an overrepresentation of persons with DD and MR in the criminal justice system. Persons with DD and MR are at risk within the system for incompetency, misunderstanding, and abuse. Current legislation reflects advancements in the understanding of DD and MR and in appropriate methods for assessment, treatment, and education of persons with this condition. Several standard diagnostic instruments are used to diagnose DD and MR based upon performance on standard intelligence tests and adaptive behavior scales. There is controversy concerning the recent AAMR (Luckasson et al., 1992) diagnostic and classification system because it appears founded in social reform of treatment for persons with DD and MR as opposed to traditional psychological variables.

Persons with DD and MR are at risk for psychopathology. Few methods exist for diagnosing such disorders in the DD and MR population, especially those with poor or no communication abilities. Recent advances in behavioral (functional) assessments and treatment methods as well as current work on actual learning ability limitations represent an area of future research and development of more accurate tools for prediction of treatment and service outcomes. Functional assessment and learning ability methods as a whole have implications for competency assessments.

REFERENCES

Aman, M. G., Burrow, W. H., & Wolford, P. L. (1994). The Abberant Behavior Checklist–Community: Factor validity and effect of subject variables for adults in group homes. *American Journal of Mental Retardation, 100*, 283–292.

Aman, M. G., Singh, N. N., Stewart, A. W., & Field, C. J. (1985). The Abberant Behavior Checklist: A behavior rating scale for the assessment of treatment effects. *American Journal of Mental Deficiency, 89*, 485–491.

American Psychiatric Association. (1994). *Diagnostic and statistical manual of mental disorders* (4th ed.). Washington, DC: Author.

Association for Retarded Citizens. (1992). *Position statements of the Arc*. Arlington, TX: Author.

Association for Retarded Citizens. (1995). *Access to justice national resource list*. Arlington, TX: Author.

Bartol, C., & Bartol, A. (1994). *Psychology and the law: Research and application*. Pacific Grove, CA: Brooks/Cole.

Brown, B. S., & Courtless, T. (1971). *The mentally retarded offender*. DHEW Pub. No. (HSM) 72-90-39. Washington, DC: U.S. Government Printing Office.

Bruyere, S. M., & O'Keeffe, J. O. (1994). *Implications of the Americans with Disabilities Act for psychology*. New York: Springer.

Denkowski, G. C., & Denkowski, K. M. (1985). The mentally retarded offender in the state prison system: Identification, prevalence, adjustment, and rehabilitation. *Criminal Justice and Behavior, 12*, 53–70.

Drope v. Missouri, 420 U.S. 162 (1974).

Ellis, J., & Luckasson, R. (1985). Mentally retarded criminal defendants. *George Washington Law Review, 53* (3–4), 414–493.

Elwinger, E. S. (1986). Inventory for client and agency planning (ICAP). *Education and Training of the Mentally Retarded, 21*, 301–302.

Fisher, W., Piazza, C. C., Bowman, L. G., Hagopian, L. P., Owens, J. C., & Slevin, I. (1992). A comparison of two approaches for identifying reinforcers for persons with severe and profound disabilities. *Journal of Applied Behavior Analysis, 25*, 491–498.

Hall, H., & Sbordone, R. (1998). *Disorders of executive functions: civil and criminal law applications*. Boca Raton, FL: St. Lucie Press.

Hardy, L., Martin. G., Yu, D., Leader, C., & Quinn, G. (1981). *Objective behavioral assessment of the severely and moderately mentally handicapped: The OBA*. Springfield, IL: Charles C Thomas.

Health Care Financing Administration. (1996). *Psychopharmacological medications: Safety precautions for persons with developmental disabilities: A resource for training and education.* Columbus, OH: Nisonger Center, Ohio State University.

Hickson, L., Blackman, L. S., & Reis, E. M. (1995). *Mental retardation: Foundations of educational programming.* Boston: Allyn & Bacon.

Horner, R. H. (1994). Functional assessment: Contributions and future directions. *Journal of Applied Behavior Analysis, 27,* 401–404.

Illinois Mentally Retarded and Mentally Ill Offender Task Force. (1988, July). *Mentally retarded and mentally ill offender task force report.* Springfield: Author.

Iwata, B. A., Dorsey, M. F., Slifer, K. J., Bauman, K. E., & Richman, G. S. (1982). Toward a functional analysis of self-injury. *Journal of Applied Behavior Analysis, 27,* 197–209.

Iwata, B. A., Dorsey, M. F., Slifer, K. J., Bauman, K. E., & Richman, G. S. (1994). Toward a functional analysis of self-injury. *Analysis and Intervention in Developmental Disabilities, 2,* 3–20.

Jackobson, J. W., & Mulick, J. A. (1996). *Manual of diagnosis and professional practice in mental retardation.* Washington, DC: American Psychological Association.

Koegel, L. K., & Koegel, R. L. (1986). The effects of interspersed maintenance tasks on academic performance in a severe childhood stroke victim. *Journal of Applied Behavior Analysis, 19,* 425–430.

Lambert, N., Nihira, K., & Leland, H. (1992). *AAMR Adaptive Behavior Scales–School* (2nd ed.). Austin, TX: ProEd.

Luckasson, R. (1992). People with mental retardation as victims of crime. In R. W. Conley, R. Luckasson, & G. N. Bouthilet (Eds.), *The criminal justice system and mental retardation* (pp. 209–220). Baltimore, MD: Paul H. Brookes.

Luckasson, R., Coulter, D. L., Polloway, E. A., Reiss, S., Shalock, R. L., Snell, M. E., Spitalnik, D. M., & Stark, J. A. (1992). *Mental retardation: Definition, classification and system of supports* (9th ed.). Washington, DC: American Association on Mental Retardation.

Luckasson, R., & Vance, P. (Eds.) (1995). *Defendants, victims, and witnesses with mental retardation: An instructional guide for judges and judicial educators.* Reno, NV: The National Judicial College.

MacMillan, D., Gresham, F. G., & Siperstein, G. (1993). Conceptual and psychometric concerns about the 1992 AAMR definition of mental retardation. *American Journal on Mental Retardation, 98* (3), 325–335.

Martin, G. L., & Yu, D. (2000). The assessment of Basic Learning Abilities: A review of the literature. *Journal on Developmental Disabilities, 7* (2), 10–36.

Matson, J., Gardner, W. I., Coe, D. A., & Sovner, R. (1990). *Diagnostic Assessment for the Severe Handicapped (DASH) Scale* (user manual). Unpublished manuscript. Louisiana State University.

Matson, J., Gardner, W. I., Coe, D., & Sovner, R. (1991). A scale for evaluating emotional disorders in severely and profoundly mentally retarded persons: Development of the Diagnostic Assessment for the Severely Handicappe (DASH) scale. *British Journal of Psychiatry, 159,* 404–409.

Matson, J. L., Kazdin, A. E., & Senatore, V. (1985). Psychometric properties of the Psychopathology Instrument for Mentally Retarded Adults. *Applied Research in Mental Retardation, 5,* 81–89.

Noble, J., & Conley, R. (1992). Toward an epidemiology of relevant attributes. In R. W. Conley, R. Luckasson, & G. N. Bouthilet (Eds.), *The criminal justice system and mental retardation* (pp. 17–53). Baltimore: Paul H. Brookes.

Norley, D. (1976). *Police training in the recognition and handling of retarded citizens: Guidelines and materials for local and state Arc units.* Arlington, TX: Arc National Headquarters.

O'Neil, R. E., Horner, R. H., Albin, R. W., Storey, K., & Sprague, J. R. (1990). *Functional analysis of problem behavior: A practical assessment guide.* Pacific Grove, CA: Brookes/Cole.

Pate v. Robinson, 383 U.S. 375 (1966).

Penry v. Lynaugh, 492 U.S. 302 (1989).

Perske, R. (1991). *Unequal justice? What can happen when persons with retardation or other developmental disabilities encounter the criminal justice system.* Nashville, TN: Abingdon Press.

Pessotti, I. (1984). *Deficiencia mental: da supersticao a ciencia.* São Paulo: EDUSP.

Reiss, S. (1988). *Reiss Screen for Maladaptive Behavior.* Worthington, OH: International Diagnostic Systems.

Roesch, R., & Golding, S. (1980). *Competency to stand trial.* Chicago, IL: University of Illinois Press.

Santamour, M. (1986, Spring–Summer). The offender with mental retardation. *Prison Journal, 66* (7), 3–18.

Scheerenberger, R. C.(1987). *A history of mental retardation: A quarter century of promise.* Baltimore, MD: Paul H. Brookes.

Shearer, M. S., & Shearer, D. E. (1972). The Portage Project: A model for early childhood education. *Exceptional Children, 36,* 210–217.

Simonoff, E. (1996). Mental retardation: Genetic findings, clinical implications and research agenda. *Journal of Child Psychology and Psychiatry, 37,* 259–280.

Sobsey, D. (1994). *Violence and abuse in the lives of people with disabilities.* Baltimore, MD: Paul H. Brookes.

Sobsey, D., & Doe, T. (1991). Patterns of sexual abuse and assault. *Journal of Sexuality and Disability, 9* (3), 243–259.

Sparrow, S. S., Balla, D. A., & Cichetti, D. V. (1984). *Vineland Adaptive Behavior Scales.* Circle Pines, MN: American Guidance Service.

Strohmer, D. C., & Prout, H. T. (1989). *Strohmer-Prout Behavior Rating Scale.* Schenectady, NY: Genium.

Sundram, C. (1990, November). Inmates with developmental disabilities in New York correctional facilities. Albany: New York State Commission of Quality Care for the Mentally Disabled.

United States v. Pryce, 938 f. 2d 1343 (D.C. Cir.) (1991).

Thapar, A., Gottesman, I., Owen, M. J., O'Donovan, M. C., & McGuffin, P. (1994). The genetics of mental retardation. *British Journal of Psychiatry, 164.*

Touchette, P. E., & Howard, J. S. (1984). Errorless learning: Reinforcement contingencies and stimulus control transfer in delayed prompting. *Journal of Applied Behavior Analysis, 17,* 175–188.

Van Houton, R., Axelrod, S., Bailey, J. S., Favell, J. E., Fox, R. M., Iwata, B. A., & Lovaas, O. I. (1988). The right to effective behavioral treatment. *Journal of Applied Behavior Analysis, 21,* 381–384.

Weiner, B. A., & Wettstein, R. M. (1993). *Legal issues in mental health-care*. New York: Plenum.

White, D., & Wood, H. (1986). The Lancaster County, Pennsylvania, Mentally Retarded Offenders Program. *Prison Journal, 65* (1), 77–84.

Williams, W. L. (1999). *An introduction to mental retardation and developmental disabilities*. Champagne, IL: High Tide Press.

Williams, W. L., & Collins, J. (May 1999). The appropriateness of the Inventory for Client and Agency Planning (ICAP) assessment instrument for estimating community living support needs of persons with developmental disabilities from a perspective of the Assessment of Basic Learning Abilities (ABLA): A preliminary study. Paper presented at the anual meeting of the Association for Behavior Analysis, Chicago.

Wolfensberger, W. (Ed.) (1972). *Normalization. The principle of normalization in human services*. Toronto: National Institute on Mental Retardation.

World Health Organization. (1995). *International classification of diseases: Clinical modifications* (9th ed.). Geneva, Switzerland: Author.

Yu, D., Martin, G. L., & Williams, W. L. (1989). Expanded assessment for discrimination learning with mentally retarded persons: A practical strategy for research and training. *American Journal of Mental Retardation, 94*, 161–169.

Part IV

Special Topics

CHAPTER 22

ISSUES IN EYEWITNESS TESTIMONY

SIMONA GHETTI
RESEARCH INSTITUTE ON JUDICIAL SYSTEMS, NATIONAL RESEARCH COUNCIL, BOLOGNA, ITALY

JENNIFER M. SCHAAF
UNIVERSITY OF NORTH CAROLINA, CHAPEL HILL

JIANJIAN QIN
CALIFORNIA STATE UNIVERSITY, SACRAMENTO

GAIL S. GOODMAN
UNIVERSITY OF CALIFORNIA, DAVIS

Eyewitness accuracy has been the subject of controversy for thousands of years. Ancient societies were often concerned with witnesses' willingness to tell the truth and tried to develop methods to detect liars (Kleinmuntz & Szucko, 1984). Although such concerns exist today as well, an increasing focus is on witnesses who make honest mistakes rather than those who willfully mislead authorities.

The success of the criminal justice system relies critically on the accuracy of eyewitness testimony. On the one hand, for many crimes, such as physical assault, child abuse, and rape, eyewitness testimony is often key to prosecution of guilty suspects. Without reliance on eyewitness reports, vicious killers, sadistic rapists, or demented child abusers might go free to victimize others. On the other hand, inaccurate eyewitness testimony can send an innocent person to jail. To wit, after reviewing 28 cases in which defendants were wrongfully convicted by juries but later exonerated by DNA evidence, authors of a report issued by the National Institute of Justice (Connors, Lundregan, Miller, & McEwan, 1996) concluded that the most compelling evidence in the majority of the cases was (inaccurate) eyewitness testimony presented at trial (also see Huff, 1987). The number of defendants who have been exonerated by DNA evidence currently exceeds 100. Of these individuals, about 75% were mistakenly identified by witnesses (Wells et al., 1998; Scheck, Neufeld, & Dwyer, 2000).

The accuracy of eyewitness testimony is determined by a complex interaction of perception, memory, and socioemotional factors. Because extensive reviews of eyewitness testimony already exist (e.g., Goodman et al., 1999; Sporer, Malpass, & Koehnken, 1996), we focus in this chapter on a number of issues that are important enough to warrant separate discussion. These topics include stress and eyewitness accuracy, eyewitness identification, interviewing techniques, and children's eyewitness memory. We also include a section on topics currently emerging in the field that, we believe, deserve further attention from researchers. Before we turn to these specific issues, however, we present a brief overview of basic memory processes to provide a foundation for our discussion.

BASIC MEMORY PROCESSES

Memory is typically divided into three stages: encoding, retention, and retrieval. In situations relevant to eyewitness testimony, *encoding* happens when a victim experiences or a bystander witnesses a criminal act. Once in the memory system, information is stored for later use (i.e., *retention* stage). In the *retrieval* stage, a witness attempts to retrieve information about the event—for example, during a forensic interview or in a court of law.

Researchers emphasize that memory is reconstructive in nature (e.g., Bartlett, 1932; Loftus, 1979); that is, memory functioning cannot be equated to that of a tape recorder, which passively records and stores information and then plays it back later precisely as recorded. For example, during the encoding stage, instead of recording an exact copy of the encountered event, witnesses typically encode both the information from the witnessed event and their interpretations of the event. During the retention stage, information from other sources (e.g., descriptions made by another witness, media coverage of the incident) may enter memory and blend with the original memory trace. Eventually, what one retrieves may include information from the original event, interpretations of such occurrences, inferences about what must have happened, and information from other sources. Thus, reconstruction is present at each stage of memory.

Given eyewitness memory's reconstructive nature, it is not surprising that it is imperfect. Although memories can be quite accurate and fairly detailed (e.g., Baker-Ward, Gordon, Ornstein, Larus, & Clubb, 1993; Rudy & Goodman, 1991; Saywitz, Goodman, Nicholas, & Moan, 1991), errors and inaccuracies can be introduced at each stage of the memory process. A variety of factors can influence what and how much information enters memory, and the accuracy with which that memory can later be retrieved.

The Three Stages of Memory

Encoding

Eyewitness accuracy is constrained first of all by the conditions under which information was encoded. Many variables influence the probability that an event was properly encoded, such as observation conditions and exposure duration. For example, a witness to a robbery may have a better chance to identify the suspect later if the robbery occurred in bright daylight and if the culprit was visible for several minutes than if the robbery occurred in darkness and the culprit was observed only for a few seconds. Indeed, there is evidence that at least for one-time occurrences, better levels of illumination and longer exposure to the event are associated with better eyewitness memory (e.g., Clifford & Richards, 1977; Gross & Hayne, 1996; MacLin, MacLin, & Malpass, 2001; Yarmey, 1986).

Quality of encoding is also constrained by limits in attentional resources. Because attention is typically directed toward the central or core aspect of an event rather than the peripheral details of it, witnesses of crimes are typically more likely to encode and remember the core event, such as the actions involved in a crime, rather than the culprit's precise physical features. For example, the culprit's hitting another person is likely to be better attended than the color of the culprit's shirt. Clifford and Scott (1978) found that adults who had just viewed a videotape of a violent incident (physical assault) or a nonviolent incident (verbal exchange) recalled more about the assailants' actions than about their physical appearance. However, Christianson and Loftus (1991) found that the advantage of central versus peripheral information depended on the content of the material. They examined the quality of adults' memories of a thematic series of slides. The content of one critical slide in the middle of the series was varied as either emotional or neutral. Their findings indicate that when the critical slide was emotional, individuals remembered a central detail better than a peripheral detail. In contrast, when the central stimulus was unusual but not emotionally charged, the advantage of central information disappeared. In fact, stimuli that cause great emotion and that are also (hopefully) unusual, such as a gun pointed at one's head, may result in such focused attention that other details that might normally be attended are not, a phenomenon called *weapon focus* (Loftus, Loftus, & Messo, 1987).

People often presuppose that if someone is able to provide a description of peripheral details of a crime scene, she or he must have been attending closely to the central events as well or must have an exceptional memory. In contrast to laypeople's beliefs, someone's testimony can be accurate about central issues without being accurate about peripheral detail, and vice versa. Results from Wells and Leippe's (1981) research exemplify this point. Participants watched a man steal a calculator. Those who attended to the culprit's face and later recognized him accurately were less likely to remember minor details about the room. Thus, a negative correlation between the ability to recognize a perpetrator and the ability to recall trivial details was uncovered. Unfortunately, jurors are often impressed by memory for peripheral detail and may be less willing to believe a witness who cannot remember such information. Witnesses are also less likely to be believed if their testimony includes inconsistencies, even when they are limited to peripheral details only (Berman, Narby, & Cutler, 1995).

Encoding can also be affected by the way an observer interprets the event. In fact, it is fair to say that what we remember is not so much the original event itself, but rather, in important ways, our interpretation of the event, which is influenced by knowledge and expectations. When an event is predictable, expectations can lead to accurate information acquisition but can also lead to errors as well. Expected information present in the event may be recalled accurately, but expected information not actually present may be inaccurately recalled as well (Bartlett, 1932; Holst & Pezdek, 1992; List, 1986). Expectations may be used to confirm the presence of expected information but at the same time to supersede detailed analysis, so that a person might remember seeing a car, for example, but be unable to say what it looked like aside from prototypical features (Friedman, 1979). Expectations may also bias an observer so that she or he fails to notice detail that seems irrelevant or fails to match the encoding scheme, as when supporters of a football team see all the infractions made by the other side but none made by their own team (Hastorf & Cantril, 1954). Moreover, stereotypical expectations can bias eyewitness reports in both adults (Chen & Geiselman, 1993; but see Treadway & McCloskey, 1989) and children (Leichtman & Ceci, 1995).

Expectations are especially likely to lead to inaccuracies when an event is viewed under ambiguous, fast-moving circumstances. For example, hunting accidents often occur when a hunter's expectations lead to the misperception of a person as prey (Loftus, 1979; Sommer, 1959). Laboratory studies confirm the important role expectations play in biasing perceptions and memory when ambiguous information is briefly viewed (e.g., Bruner & Postman, 1949). When longer processing time is possible, however, expectations can cause increased attention to be paid to unexpected details. To interpret an unexpected event, attention may quickly shift to detailed encoding of the novel event (Friedman, 1979; Loftus & Mackworth, 1978). As a consequence, unexpected information may later be recognized with heightened accuracy (Friedman, 1979; Grasser, 1981; Maki, 1990). In summary, new information is encoded when an event occurs. This acquisition of new information is an active process that is constrained or bolstered by many factors, including the witness's attentional resources, knowledge, and expectations, as well as situational factors such as length of exposure to the to-be-remembered event.

Retention

There exists a consensus that, given the reconstructive nature of memory, stored information may undergo processes of change during the retention phase. Important for eyewitness testimony is the notion of retroactive interference. Retroactive interference occurs when a new piece of information disrupts the ability to remember a previously learned piece of information. For example, one may encounter some difficulty remembering a former phone number after having learned the new one. Relevant to eyewitness testimony, witnesses may encounter new information that may interfere with the originally stored information.

A deluge of research has been conducted to establish the effects that presenting new (and incorrect) information has on memory of the original event. Pioneering work on postevent misinformation was conducted by Loftus and colleagues (Loftus, 1977; Loftus et al., 1978). The Loftus paradigm involved showing adults a series of slides depicting some event (e.g., a car accident). After viewing the slides, some participants (the misled group) were exposed to misinformation about the event, whereas others were not (the control group). In the later recognition memory test, participants chose between the original slide and a slide consistent with the presented misinformation. The misled adults were less able than control adults to correctly identify the slide that they had seen before. It was originally suggested (Loftus, Miller, & Burns, 1978) that this effect might be caused by *overwriting* (i.e., misleading information replacing original information) or *coexistence* (i.e., misleading information being more easily accessible than original information). Overwriting would destroy the original information, but coexistence would simply make it less accessible. In contrast, McCloskey and Zaragoza (1985) noted that, using the original recognition test devised by Loftus, even if the misinformation had no effect at all on the adults' original event memory, misled participants would still perform worse on the recognition test for two reasons. First, like many of the participants in the control condition, the misled participants may not have encoded the original target information. Failure to encode the original information systematically disadvantages participants in the misinformation condition because they are later offered the opportunity to encode misinformation. Because the recognition task is a choice between two items, misinformed participants who had not encoded the target information would be more likely than control participants to choose the item that they were misled about, believing that the misinformation presented to them was an accurate representation of the original event.

The second reason cited by McCloskey and Zaragoza (1985) for the poorer performance of misled adults is related to demand characteristics. Because postevent misinformation is presented by the researchers conducting the study, participants might reasonably assume that the misinformation was meant to be an accurate representation of the original event. Thus, even if misled participants accurately remember the item from the original slides, they may answer at test with the information that they remember from the narrative, choosing to believe that the researcher is more accurate than their own memory.

McCloskey and Zaragoza (1985) concluded that the original procedure was not sufficient to test the memory impairment hypothesis and proposed that a modified test be used. In a series of experiments using their modified test, they found no differences between control and misled groups. Further research using McCloskey and Zaragoza's suggested modifications supported the existence of an attenuated misinformation effect (Payne, Toglia, & Anastasi, 1994) and spawned a new explanatory hypothesis (Lindsay & Johnson, 1989). Lindsay and Johnson (1989) proposed that postevent misinformation may cause a misinformation effect without altering or interfering with the original memory. They suggested that postevent misinformation may create confusion regarding which information (original information or misleading information) is from which source. This confusion has been termed *source-monitoring difficulty*. Source-monitoring difficulty may make it appear as though the original memory is lost when in fact both original memory and misinformation memory are available, but the appropriate context is not. When a person attempts to recall the original information, she or he may instead mistakenly access the more recent misinformation and assume that it is from the original event. Utilizing a more stringent criterion (e.g., carefully considering the context of retrieved memories) can minimize source-monitoring errors (Johnson, Hashtroudi, & Lindsay, 1993).

Research on the effects of postevent misinformation indicates that, although originally encoded information may not be completely lost, it may become difficult to access. The implication of this general finding is that the conditions under which retrieval of original information is attempted are crucial for successful recovery. We discuss such conditions in the following paragraphs as well as in the section on interviewing techniques.

Retrieval

Retrieval is the process by which information stored in memory is brought back to consciousness. Typical retrieval situations for witnesses include reporting to the police, viewing lineups, recounting experiences to friends and mental health professionals, and testifying in court. In all these different contexts, witnesses are generally provided with a series of cues (i.e., questions) to guide their reports. Because the conditions under which individuals retrieve information play a fundamental role in predicting the accuracy of the reported information, we will devote a separate section to the efficacy of interviewing techniques. In this section, we discuss an important general principle affecting the probability that original information is successfully retrieved—namely, the encoding-specificity principle.

The encoding specificity principle dictates that the extent to which the retrieval environment matches the encoding environment is an important determinant of a person's ability to provide accurate and complete eyewitness testimony (see Tulving, 1983, for a theoretical account). The more cues shared at acquisition and retrieval, the better retrieval will be. This principle has important implications for interviewers because it implies that testimony may be greatly enhanced as more and more retrieval cues can be found. Thus, increasing the cues available to the interviewee, including contextual cues, can help to increase recall. Although the physical site of an event can provide some helpful cues, many aspects of the original event will not be present when the site is revisited (e.g., sounds, other participants, emotions). The mental reinstatement of context, however, can provide these types of cues, thus improving memory recall. Mental reinstatement of context is an important component of the Cognitive Interview, discussed in a later section.

The use of guided memory procedures can provide additional cues. In guided memory procedures, witnesses are asked to mentally reinstate the context of the event, and their memory recall is guided with probing questions. Malpass and Devine (1981) used this interview procedure to enhance eyewitness identification of adult witnesses who had viewed a staged vandalism five months earlier. Adults were helped to visualize the classroom where the incident took place, their position in it, the suspect, the vandalism itself, and their reaction to it. When presented with a photo lineup that included the culprit, 60 percent of the witnesses were correct in their identifications. In comparison, only 40 percent of the witnesses who were not given the guided-memory task correctly identified the culprit. The guided-memory procedure did not lead to more false identifications or false rejections of the culprit. However, as Loftus (1994) points out, there are potential risks in using visualization together with other kinds of "memory work"—namely, these techniques seem to enhance the probability of creating false memories (e.g., Qin, 2000).

STRESS AND EYEWITNESS ACCURACY

Because of the nature of criminal acts, victims and bystanders often experience elevated levels of stress during a crime. Despite the existence of a large body of literature concerning memory for stressful events, the relation between stress and memory is yet to be fully understood. The notion that stressful events are meaningful and salient, and thus well-remembered, has been proposed. For example, the observation that people often report having particularly vivid memories (i.e., flashbulb memories) of events that surround a highly emotional event (e.g., the assassination of President Kennedy or the explosion of the space shuttle *Challenger*) led researchers to the speculation that perhaps emotionally charged memories are handled by a mechanism that differs from the mechanisms that control ordinary memory (Brown & Kulik, 1997). This mechanism would allow the exact details of a scene to become indelible parts of memory. More recent research revealed, however, that although individuals are more confident about their flashbulb memories than about memory for more ordinary events, flashbulb memories are subject to forgetting and distortion (Christianson, 1989, 1992; McCloskey, Wible, & Cohen, 1988; Neisser & Harsch, 1993; Weaver, 1993).

Consistent with the idea of a positive relation between stress and memory, trauma survivors often describe their memories of traumatic events as enduring and intruding. For instance, the principal symptoms of Post-Traumatic Stress Disorder (PTSD), according to the *DSM-IV* (American Psychiatric Association, 1994), are memory-related and speak to the endurance of traumatic memories. PTSD patients commonly describe experiences of intrusive thoughts and recollections of the events as well as emotional and physiological reactions upon being presented with reminders of trauma (e.g., Rothbaum, Foa, Riggs, Murdock, & Walsh, 1992).

On the other hand, in line with the Freudian tradition introducing the idea that repression shields individuals from conscious access to memories of threatening experiences, several researchers have explored the possibility that memory for stressful (and traumatic) events is inhibited by special psychological mechanisms. Numerous studies have found that a significant proportion of adults who report a trauma history also describe periods of time when they did not recall their experience (e.g., Briere & Conte, 1993; Elliot & Briere, 1995; Epstein & Bottoms, 1998; Loftus, Polonsky, & Fullilove, 1994).

Contrasting hypotheses concerning the relation between stress and memory have been reflected in the theoretical accounts advanced to date. In the early 1900s, the Yerkes-Dodson law stipulated that the relation between stress and performance could be modeled as an inverted-U-shaped function; stress improves performance at low to optimal stress levels, but once it has passed the optimal level, stress decreases performance. Some have attempted to apply the Yerkes-Dodson law to the relation between stress and eyewitness memory (e.g., Deffendbacher, 1983). Although intuitively appealing, the main problems with the Yerkes-Dodson law are that it is not clear what constitutes the optimal level, and the law fails to address the finding that at high levels of stress memory for emotionally charged details is enduring, with fear-provoking details being particularly encoded (Metcalfe & Jacobs, 2000).

An alternative view stems from the Easterbrook hypothesis (1959) that as stress increases in intensity, the individual's attention is progressively restricted to the relevant, salient features of an event. Under high arousal conditions, attentional focus is further narrowed and even some salient features are not attended. If this hypothesis is true, one consequence is that central (being relevant and salient) information may be attended to and remembered better, but at the expense of decreased memory for information that falls outside of the range of attention. Thus, the Easterbrook hypothesis implies that the relation between stress and memory depends on the centrality of information. Consistent with this proposition is the phenomenon called weapon focus, which was mentioned briefly earlier in this chapter. Research has illustrated that when a witness sees an offender wielding a weapon, the witness will later remember the weapon well but memory for the facial features of the offender will be compromised (e.g., Loftus et al., 1987; Maass & Koehnken, 1989; Pickel, 1999). Because weapons are one source of stress in many criminal situations, memory for the weapon would result in enhanced attention for it and reduced attention to other details of the crime scene.

The results of some laboratory studies that have been used to argue for a negative effect of stress on memory may be explained by Easterbrook's account (Loftus & Burns, 1982; Merritt, Ornstein, & Spicker, 1994; Peters, 1991). In one of the classic studies in the field, Loftus and Burns showed undergraduate student participants a film depicting a bank robbery. For half of the participants, the film ended in a violent scene in which a boy was shot in the face. For the other half of the participants, the film had a nonviolent ending. Participants who viewed the violent version remembered less about the film than those who saw the nonviolent version. However, only memory for details that were not directly related to the shooting was impaired, whereas memories of the shooting were well retained.

Consistent with predictions based on Easterbrook's hypothesis, memory for central information appears to remain strong despite high levels of stress. Studies of eyewitness accounts of adult rape victims suggest that memories for such experiences are reasonably accurate and well retained for long periods, especially for central details, whereas inaccuracies are mainly found for peripheral details (Koss, Tromp, & Tharan, 1995; Tromp, Koss, Figueredo, & Tharan, 1995; for a review, see Christianson, 1992). Memory for central events also appears to be enduring. Christianson and Hubinette (1993) compared bystander witnesses with victim witnesses of bank robberies after 4- to 15-month intervals. The authors found that memories of central features of robberies (e.g., actions, weapon) were highly consistent with information originally obtained in the police reports. However, memory for other information such as dates and times was not as consistent. Additionally, victims' reports were more accurate than bystanders' reports.

Nevertheless, it is often argued that memory for trauma may become completely forgotten (e.g., Williams, 1994). One potential explanation for what appears to be complete loss of memory for trauma may be the state-dependent hypothesis that suggests that the memories encoded under extreme circumstances may not be lost but become inaccessible because people rarely encounter the opportunity to experience a traumatic mental state similar enough to the original one to serve as an appropriate retrieval cue (Bower, 1981). In addition, recent advancements in the neurobiology of memory have emphasized that high levels of prolonged stress may have adverse effects on brain functioning, specifically on the hippocampus, a structure directly linked to the consolidation of new memories (e.g., Bremner, 1999, 2001; Sapolsky, 1996). Although this damage has been associated with episodic memory deficits, it has not been related to complete loss of memory (or knowledge) of having experienced a traumatic event. As Bremner (2001) emphasizes, Vietnam veterans often experience trouble remembering their appointments with doctors or what they had for breakfast that morning, but they remember their shocking experience in war in great detail. Furthermore, the recent *hot-cool systems* hypothesis (Metcalf & Jacobs, 2000) suggests that although high levels of stress may hinder the functioning of the emotionally neutral and cognitive (i.e., cool) hippocampus-based system, high levels of stress may not impair the emotional (i.e., hot) amygdala-based system, which would lead to hyperencoding of the emotionally charged events.

While attempting to comprehend the complex relation between stress and memory, researchers have begun to investigate the role of individual differences. For example, attachment style has been related to memory for stressful events in both adults (e.g., Fraley, Garner, & Shaver, 2000; Kirsh, 1996; Miller & Noirot,

1999) and children (Goodman, Quas, Batterman-Faunce, Riddlesberger, & Kuhn, 1997; Quas, Goodman, Bidrose, Pipe, Craw, & Ablin, 1999). Other individual differences explored are dissociation and coping styles (e.g., Briere, 1992; Nemiah, 1995).

Summary

The relation between stress and memory has fascinated a number of scholars over the years. Yet despite a number of candidate theoretical accounts, the nature of this relation has yet to be fully clarified. Important variables in explaining such relations may be the emotional nature and type of detail of the to-be-remembered event as well as factors related to individual differences.

EYEWITNESS IDENTIFICATION

One of the areas of greatest concern for those interested in eyewitness memory is eyewitness identification. Eyewitness identification is one of the most direct kinds of evidence of guilt because it links the suspect and the crime specifically. Other types of evidence, such as fingerprints or fiber evidence, may link the suspect with an item or location but not necessarily with the crime, and may be therefore considered less direct (Wells et al., 1998). Because of its importance, eyewitness identification has been the focus of many research programs since the 1970s (Buckhout, 1974; Wells, 1978). By the 1980s and 1990s, research in this area flourished and researchers had discovered much about how and why eyewitnesses come to make identification errors. Psychologists attempted to influence public policy with their findings, but their attempts through expert testimony and media pressure were met with only limited success (Wells et al., 2000).

Not until the advent of DNA evidence did the dramatic number of individuals who were wrongfully convicted of crimes based on mistaken eyewitness identifications became apparent (Connors et al., 1996; Wells et al., 1998). For example, Wells and colleagues (1998) examined 40 cases of people wrongly convicted and later vindicated by DNA testing. The cases were selected because they were the first available cases in which DNA evidence was used to exonerate convicted prisoners. Of importance, 90 percent of the cases involved inaccurate eyewitness identification. In several of the cases, victim or witness identifications were the sole or primary evidence leading to conviction. It is worthwhile to note that five of these falsely convicted people were sentenced to death, a sobering fact that underlies the importance of coming to greater understanding of why witnesses make errors and studying ways to reduce those errors. Such evidence was instrumental in causing the U. S. Department of Justice to solicit information from eyewitness researchers (along with others in the criminal justice system) in drafting a national guide for collecting eyewitness evidence (Technical Working Group for Eyewitness Evidence, 1999). This guide incorporated many, but not all, of the recommendations advocated by the eyewitness researchers and supported by research findings (see Wells et al., 2000, for a discussion of the history, accomplishments, and shortcomings of the report). In addition to some of the specific issues mentioned here, the national guide offers specific advice to law enforcement agencies on topics such as building rapport, avoiding leading questions, cautioning against guessing, and avoiding leading statements prior to and after an identification (see also Wells et al., 1998, for a more detailed description of specific steps that may be taken to improve the accuracy of identifications in lineups).

Because many factors that affect the accuracy of eyewitness identification cannot be controlled in real-life situations (known as estimator variables; e.g., lighting, opportunity to observe, and appearance of subject), research has focused on factors that can be controlled by the justice system, known as system variables. These include all factors associated with the lineup or identification procedures used by police after a crime has been committed. The manner in which identifications are conducted in forensic investigations can greatly affect the accuracy of the identification.

Lineup Fairness

It is common practice for witnesses to be required to select a culprit from a lineup. Lineups should constitute a fair procedure leading to accurate identification of a suspect, but many factors must be taken into consideration to create a fair lineup. The way the lineup procedure is conducted can greatly affect the accuracy of eyewitness identification. Increasing the number of persons in the lineup is just one obvious way of helping to create a lineup that will promote an unbiased identification process. If a lineup consisted of only two individuals, the chance that a suspect would be identified is 50 percent (or 33% if "not present" is an option) by chance alone, even if the witness truly remembers nothing about what the perpetrator looked like. By increasing the number of persons in the lineup, the chance of accidental identification decreases. In a lineup of six people, the chance that a suspect will be identified purely by accident is only 1 in 6, if a selection is made and if the other foils are appropriate.

Devising systems to measure lineup fairness has been an active area of research. Researchers have proposed several ways of measuring the fairness of specific lineups (Malpass, 1981; Malpass & Devine, 1981; Wells et al., 1979; for a discussion of the various methods, see Brigham, Meissner, & Wasserman, 1999). These methods typically involve the use of "mock witnesses," that is, persons who have never seen the perpetrator but who are provided with descriptions and then asked to view a lineup and identify a suspect. The response patterns of mock witnesses can reveal bias in lineups; if the lineup is fair and all members fit the description, mock witnesses should choose each member of the lineup with equal probability.

Lineups may be conducted either with live participants or by photo array. The photo array has several advantages and several drawbacks to the live lineup. The photo array is portable, and it offers maximum flexibility in choosing foils and increasing the number of individuals in the array. However, care must be taken to match the pose and expression of the photos presented in an array (Buckhout, 1974). Clearly, if some pictures were selected from smiling faces at a birthday party and others from the mug shots of scowling and recently arrested persons, the lineup would be unfair. The fairness of photo identification is perhaps a particularly important consideration because unlike live lineups, defendants do not have a right to have counsel present during photo lineup procedures (*United States v. Ash*, 1973).

Errors in Lineup Procedures

Multiple person lineups have long been preferred to "showups" in which only one person is presented as the possible suspect. However, there are some fairly obvious ways in which the benefits of a multiple person lineup can be eliminated. One is if only one member of the lineup matches the verbal description of the perpetrator. If the witness has previously described the perpetrator as blonde and muscular and only one person fitting that description appears in the lineup, then in effect the lineup size is reduced from six to one (Brigham, Ready, & Spier, 1990; Wells, 1993).

Perhaps even more problematic is the effect that an unbalanced lineup may have on the confidence of a witness. Wells, Rydell, and Seelau (1993) conducted a staged-crime experiment. In examining the results of lineups in which the culprit was not present, Wells and colleagues found that when only one lineup member fit the description of the culprit, witnesses selected the lineup member with the most resemblance to the suspect. Witnesses were also more confident in their selection than they were if the other lineup members more closely resembled the suspect. A more detailed discussion of the relation between witness confidence and accuracy will follow this section.

More subtle errors can also reduce the fairness of a lineup—for instance, if the witness is allowed to view the lineup members arriving and see that only one of them wears handcuffs. Giving eyewitnesses positive feedback after they make a lineup identification (e.g., "Good. You identified the actual suspect.") also is detrimental because it inflates witnesses' recollections of how confident they were at the time of the identification and also affects other testimony-relevant judgments, such as how well they could see the culprit, how much attention they paid during the event, and how quickly they were able to identify the suspect (Wells & Bradfield, 1999). In addition, indicating to the witness that the suspect is in the lineup is detrimental because it reduces the chances that a witness would choose none of the lineup members and encourages the witness to use a relative judgment process to make an identification.

Relative Judgments

Empirical evidence suggests that witnesses commonly use a relative judgment process to identify someone from a lineup—that is, witnesses simply select from the lineup the person who most resembles the perpetrator (Wells, 1984, 1993). Although this judgment process may have little consequence when the perpetrator is present in the lineup, it may lead to miscarriage of justice when the culprit is actually not present. In the case of a culprit-absent lineup, a relative-judgment process leads to a false identification. The lineup member who most resembles the perpetrator will be selected and identified. Reliance on relative judgment can be reduced by specifically warning the witnesses that the actual perpetrator may not be present in the lineup (Malpass & Devine, 1981; Wells, 1993). When individuals receive such a warning, they seem to become more likely to rely on absolute judgments, in which the eyewitness compares each lineup member to her or his memory for the perpetrator of the crime.

Malpass and Devine (1981) conducted a staged-crime experiment and found that 78 percent of the adult participants made identifications from culprit-absent lineups. When an explicit instruction regarding the possibility that the culprit might not be in the lineup was given, only 33 percent of participants made identifications in culprit-absent lineups. The Malpass and Devine study, as well as later meta-analysis, reveals that such an instruction appears to reduce false identifications from culprit-absent lineups without damaging witnesses' ability to identify the correct perpetrator in culprit-present lineups (Malpass & Devine, 1981; Steblay, 1997).

Another method recommended to reduce witness reliance on relative-judgment processes is the sequential lineup (Levi, 1999; Lindsay & Wells, 1985). In a sequential lineup, in contrast to a traditional lineup, witnesses view the lineup members only one at a time. Because only one individual is available for viewing at any one time, witnesses are more likely to compare the individual to their memory of the perpetrator rather than simply comparing him or her to the other individuals in the lineup. A sequential lineup can be conducted with live members or via a photo array.

Other-Race Identifications

Although the race of the witness and the race of the suspect by themselves are not associated with eyewitness identification accuracy, there does appear to be an interaction such that own-race recognitions tend to be more accurate than other-race recognitions (Bothwell, Brigham, & Malpass, 1989; Malpass & Kravitz, 1969; Platz & Hosch, 1988; Wright, Boyd, & Tredoux, 2001; see Meissner & Brigham, 2001, for meta-analysis). For instance, Wright and colleagues (2001) conducted studies in South Africa and England. Participants were approached by confederates and later asked to identify the confederate. In both countries, participants were better able to recognize confederates of their own race. The own-race bias appears to begin somewhere between 7 to 9 years of age and may actually dissipate somewhat by adulthood (Chance, Turner, & Goldstein, 1982; Goodman, Hirschman, Hepps, & Rudy, 1991; Lee & Goodman, 2003), but see Pezdek, Blandon-Gitlin, & Moore, in press. Probably depending upon exposure to other racial/ethnic individuals, some people may show less of an own-race bias than do others (e.g., Asian Americans versus European Americans, when both live in a society where Caucasians are the majority; Lee & Goodman, 2001).

Of course, the justice system cannot control which witnesses are needed to testify about which suspects, and thus cannot control the occurrence of other-race identifications. The own-race bias, however, appears in lineup construction as well as in identification, thus bringing the issue into the realm of system variables (Brigham et al., 1990). For example, Brigham and Ready (1985) found that both African-American and Caucasian participants asked to construct lineups spent more time evaluating own-race faces than other-race faces. To counteract the effects of own-race bias in lineup procedures, the justice system can employ tactics such as using individuals the same race as the suspect to conduct lineups and using larger lineups in other-race cases (Wells & Olson, 2001). The own-race bias may have implications for psychological research as well. In a series of two studies investigating own-race bias in lineup fairness measures, Lindsay and colleagues (Lindsay, Ross, Smith & Flanigan, 1999) found mixed results. Nevertheless, because some of their results indicated that the race of witnesses (who provided a description of a suspect) and mock witnesses (who judged photo lineups based on the witnesses' descriptions) had important effects, the authors concluded that researchers investigating real-world cases should match the race of mock witnesses to the race of the suspect.

Summary

Many factors can affect the fairness of lineups and the accuracy of witness identification. Foils for lineups must be chosen carefully to ensure that suspects do not stand out for any reason. Witnesses must not be permitted to see obvious differences between lineup members (such as handcuffs or clothing differences). Additionally, steps such as informing witnesses that the suspect may not in fact be present in the lineup, or presenting lineup members to witnesses one at a time, can help prevent witnesses from relying on relative judgments. Cross-racial effects can be mitigated by such techniques as having a same-race person (as the suspect) construct the lineup.

THE RELATION BETWEEN ACCURACY AND CONFIDENCE

The confidence with which a statement is delivered is probably the most important predictor of testimony believability (Cutler, Penrod, & Dexter, 1990; Leippe, Manion, & Romanczyk, 1992; Wells et al., 1979). For instance, Cutler and colleagues (1990) manipulated several factors that jurors might consider when assessing eyewitness identification evidence. Such factors were disguise, weapon focus, violence of the crime, instruction bias, foil bias, and witness confidence. Results showed that high versus low witness confidence was the most powerful manipulation in affecting jurors' verdicts. Leippe and colleagues (1992) found that the correlation between perceived accuracy and perceived confidence extended from identification tasks to more complex memory reports, such as descriptions of events elicited during forensic interviews.

In 1972, the U.S. Supreme Court (*Neil v. Biggers*, 1972) recommended that jurors consider the level of certainty demonstrated by witnesses in facing identification tasks; apparently, the court assumes that confidence is a reliable indicator of accuracy. Although witnesses' level of confidence is only one of the factors that the court recommended that jurors should take into consideration in assessing eyewitness testimony (other factors include the conditions under which the criminal was observed, the witnesses' level of attention at the time of the observation, and the time interval between witnessing the event and testifying), the U.S. Supreme Court decision clearly underlines both the fact that confidence plays an important role in the assessment of witness credibility and the fact that the court believes that witness confidence is a reliable indicator of eyewitness accuracy.

Are more confident witnesses really more accurate? In the present section, selected research findings on the confidence/accuracy (CA) relation are discussed. Because the majority of relevant research has been conducted with recognition memory measures, we first focus on these results. We then report studies on the CA relation when other memory measures, such as recall, are used.

CA Relation in Recognition Memory

The vast majority of studies regarding the CA relation have been conducted using recognition memory tasks, particularly face recognition. In 1987, Bothwell and colleagues (Bothwell, Deffenbacher, & Brigham, 1987) conducted the first meta-analysis of 35 staged-event studies examining the CA relation in identification experiments. They uncovered an overall $r = .25$, with a 95 percent confidence interval of .08 to .42. Thus, confidence should probably not be recommended as a systematic indicator of accuracy. Why are these correlations so low? Researchers have tried to identify factors that might increase or decrease the CA correlation.

Deffenbacher (1980) proposed that the CA relation is affected by the conditions under which the information is processed, with higher correlations being associated with better processing conditions. This proposition has been traditionally called the optimality hypothesis. Shapiro and Penrod (1986) found evidence in favor of the optimality hypothesis. In their study, the duration of witness exposure to target faces (a measure of quality of encoding) was significantly correlated with the CA relation, $r = .48$. Thus, when individuals were exposed longer to the target faces, confidence was more strongly related to accuracy than when individuals viewed the faces for less time. The optimality hypothesis, however, has not received consistent support.

For instance, Lindsay, Read, and Sharma (1998) found that the CA relation was more substantial when scores were collapsed across different levels of quality of encoding conditions. Specifically, adult participants watched two videotapes either for 10 seconds with no warning about the subsequent identification task, for 10 seconds with warning about the subsequent identification task, for 1 minute with warning about the subsequent identification task, and for 3 minutes with warning about the subsequent identification task. Within each encoding condition, participants were required to identify one person per videotape, that is, either a female or a male. Although the CA relation was significant in several conditions (i.e., in all encoding conditions when participants identified the male and in the 10-seconds with warning condition when participants identified the female), such a relation was no higher when participants could observe the to-be-identified individual longer (i.e., the 3 minutes condition). Instead, it was higher when data for the CA relations for each encoding condition were collapsed across warning condition ($r = .51$ for female identification and $r = .68$ for male identification). Lindsay and colleagues concluded that when conditions of witnessing were held constant, the CA relation is limited. One explanation for this finding may be that the conditions that lead to higher confidence in correct identifications also lead to higher confidence in false identifications.

Another factor that affects the CA relation concerns the characteristics of the target. For example, Brigham (1990) tested the hypothesis that the distinctiveness of the target may enhance the CA relation. Brigham exposed adults to distinctive, unusual faces as opposed to more prototypical faces and also to attractive versus unattractive faces. Consistent with his hypothesis, Brigham found that the CA relation was higher when the target faces were distinctive on some dimension rather than prototypical and when they were unattractive rather than attractive.

Researchers also investigated the CA relation by examining factors that differentially affect accuracy and confidence. Leippe (1980) proposed that eyewitness accuracy and confidence could be controlled by different mechanisms "capable of altering memory and confidence in orthogonal directions" (p. 271). One factor is the similarity between the target stimulus and distractors. For instance, Tulving (1981) found a double dissociation between adults' accuracy on a forced-choice recognition test and the confidence they expressed for their choice. Participants were shown pictures of nature scenes. The recognition test forced participants to choose which of two presented scenes was old. In each pair was one old scene, paired with either a completely new scene or an unseen portion of an old scene. Adults performed best and had the highest confidence when discriminating between seen and completely new pictures. When the two portions of the picture belonged to different nature scenes (one previously seen portion, one unseen portion of a previously viewed scene), participants had relatively low accuracy but high confidence in their choice. In this case, the familiarity elicited by both pictures may have increased errors. In contrast, when the two portions of the picture belonged to the same nature scene, participants had higher accuracy but low confidence. In this case, probably because participants scrutinized the images more carefully, they were more accurate but, because they were aware of the difficulty of the task, they reported low confidence. These results might have implications in the legal context: For instance, when an eyewitness must identify someone in the legal context, the degree of similarity between individuals included in the lineup may differentially influence accuracy and confidence.

There are other factors that affect accuracy and confidence in different ways and therefore could potentially have an effect on the CA relation. For instance, Luus and Wells (1991) tested the hypothesis that confidence in an identification task may be affected by knowing the outcome of the identification of other witnesses. The authors had pairs of naïve participants witness staged thefts. Participants were then requested to identify the culprit from a lineup. Unknown to the participants, however, the actual thief was not included in the lineup. After each participant made a choice, they were informed of the choice of the cowitness: Either they were told that the cowitness chose the same person or that the cowitness chose someone else. Results indicated that with accuracy held constant (all the participants who made an identification were by definition inaccurate), confidence could be either augmented or reduced by the type of available information regarding another witness's choice. Another factor relevant to the CA relation is postevent questioning. Shaw (1996) showed that questioning adults after viewing slides of a crime differentially affected accuracy and confidence on a forced-choice recognition task. Postevent questioning had no impact on accuracy when it was compared to a control condition. However, postevent questioning produced higher confidence ratings for incorrect responses.

Attempts to increase the CA relation have resulted in inconsistent results. Factors such as accountability (e.g., adults were led to believe that their decisions were monitored by others) and context reinstatement have been found to have positive influences on the CA relation (e.g., Kassin, Rigby, & Castillo, 1991; Krafka & Penrod, 1985). However, in Robinson and Johnson's (1998) research, these factors and others (for instance, public self-consciousness, retrospective narration of the event, hypothesis generation and disconfirmations regarding the goodness of identification) did not produce the expected enhancement of the CA relation. Robinson and Johnson (1998) speculated that sophisticated mental operations may differentially affect recognition abilities and confidence judgments, resulting in a failure to enhance the CA relation. Robinson and Johnson argue, for instance, that when individuals are engaged in sophisticated mental operations such as retrospective narration of the event or hypothesis generation, their recognition abilities may be negatively affected (possibly resulting from inadvertently committing source-monitoring errors), whereas these operations would not affect confidence ratings. The authors concluded that augmenting the salience of relatively automatic decision processes might be more likely to facilitate the CA relation.

In summary, meta-analyses indicate that the CA relation for recognition memory is fairly low. Also, manipulations of factors such as quality of encoding and type of target enhanced the CA relation in some studies; however, the magnitude of the CA relation for recognition is typically not large, certainly not high or reliable enough to justify the use of witness confidence as an indicator of accuracy. This conclusion is supported by the fact that several factors (e.g., similarity between target stimulus and distractor, feedback, postevent questioning) may differentially affect accuracy and confidence, thereby reducing the CA relation.

CA in Recall

A few studies have investigated the CA relation regarding crime-relevant information other than the identity of the offender. Results indicated a small CA relation when recognition tests were used, but a substantially higher CA relation when recall (usually cued recall) was introduced. For example, Robinson and Johnson (1996) conducted an experiment in which memory for details of a simulated crime was measured either with recall or recognition. In both conditions, adults made confidence ratings, thus allowing a comparison of the CA relation in recognition and recall. The authors found that recall memory performance was characterized by a higher CA correlation than forced-choice recognition performance. The authors argued that because a recall test generally puts higher cognitive demands on individuals than does a recognition test, individuals normally assess the amount of effort they had spent on retrieving information. The amount of effort may be an important indicator of accuracy. Thus, these findings are explained as a function of the availability of an ease-of-retrieval cue in recall memory. That is, the ease with which a memory trace is retrieved is directly reflected in confidence for that memory.

Even when recall measures are used, however, factors exist that seemingly differentially influence accuracy and confidence. One such factor is the acquisition of postevent information. Ryan and Geiselman (1991), for example, studied participants' accuracy and confidence of memory of a videotaped crime scenario. After one week, participants received a written passage describing the crime scene. Such descriptions contained either leading, misleading, or no supplemental information. Ryan and Geiselman found that after one week accuracy decreased particularly for participants who received misleading information. However, confidence did not vary in the same way: Participants were more confident when reporting the misinformation received in the written passage than when relying on their own memories.

The salience of information may also interfere with the CA relation. Weaver (1993) had a group of college students complete a memory questionnaire after having been exposed to an ordinary event. On the same day, by coincidence, the bombing of Iraq in the Gulf War started. Participants were therefore asked to fill out a similar memory questionnaire about the bombing. After a three-month interval and one-year interval, students completed both questionnaires again. The results showed that although the level of accuracy of memories for the two events did not differ, students attributed higher levels of confidence to their memories of the Iraq bombing than to their memories for the ordinary event. Thus, although the CA relation in recall is usually higher than in recognition, it is still affected by variables exerting a different influence on confidence and accuracy.

Summary

Whether information reported more confidently by witnesses is more accurate than information reported less confidently is of interest for applied but also theoretical reasons. However, despite its intuitive appeal, the relation between accuracy and confidence is not a simple one: Both eyewitness testimony research (for a review, see Luus & Wells, 1994) and basic memory research (for example, Tulving, 1981; Chandler, 1994; Weaver, 1993) reveal that confidence and accuracy can be, under certain conditions, dissociated. These results contradict the simplistic view that memory accuracy and confidence directly reflect the strength of a memory trace.

INTERVIEWING TECHNIQUES

Eyewitness memory plays an integral part in many forensic investigations. Although other evidence, such as fiber or DNA, can provide powerful evidence of guilt or innocence, these types of evidence may not be available or may become important at a later stage of the investigation, such as after a suspect has been identified. To initially identify suspects or in cases where other evidence is unavailable, eyewitnesses often must be relied on. Eyewitness memory, however, can be problematic in forensic investigations. The memory of witnesses may be incomplete or in error. In cases involving multiple eyewitnesses, individuals' accounts may contradict each other.

Remembering and recalling specifics in crime situations can be different from remembering other situations in several ways. Crimes are often witnessed in a state of intense stress, especially when the witness is also the victim or has reason to fear for his or her own safety, as do bystanders to armed bank robbery. In addition, witnesses may focus on certain items that are salient at the time (like weapons) rather than information that may be useful for later investigation of the crime, such as identifying marks on the perpetrator. Certainly, in the pressure of potentially terrifying moments, eyewitnesses are unlikely to deliberately use mnemonic strategies to remember information. Despite the shortcomings that may exist in eyewitness memory, the information that is retained by eyewitnesses is unique and valuable. Thus, interest in maximizing eyewitness memory reports has been high, and forensic and experimental psychologists have made significant progress in specifying ways to increase the amount of information eyewitnesses recall, and the accuracy of that information.

Hypnotic Interview

Hypnotic interviews have been used by investigators in the hope of increasing the amount of information that can be solicited from witnesses. Despite a relatively long history of use in clinical settings as well as in many forensic applications (Reiser & Neilson, 1980), the usefulness of hypnosis in forensic interviews is questionable mainly because of increased confabulation (the inclusion of false information in otherwise accurate recollection) under hypnosis. People tend to remember more information under hypnosis than when they are not hypnotized (Stager & Lundy, 1985). This increase in recalled information, however, may be achieved at the expense of accuracy. Additional information provided under hypnosis is as likely to be incorrect as to be correct (Gibbon, 1982). Without independent corroborating evidence, it is impossible to determine the veracity of additional remembered information, and thus the value of the additional information is greatly compromised.

Because of the controversial nature of the procedure, statements obtained under hypnosis may be inadmissible in court. As early at 1897, the Supreme Court of California disallowed the introduction of evidence uncovered by hypnosis in state court (*People v. Ebanks*). California, among other states, still adheres to a restrictive policy on hypnotic testimony, disallowing such testimony and only permitting a witness to testify to information that was remembered before being hypnotized. Other courts are less restrictive on the issue, some allowing hypnotized testimony (Diamond, 1980; *Harding v. State of Maryland*, 1968), offering guidelines for admission of hypnotic testimony (*State v. Hurd*, 1981), or evaluating it on a case-by-case basis (*People v. Hughes*, 1983).

Cognitive Interview

With a view towards bringing the principles of cognitive psychology to bear in the eyewitness interview situation, Geiselman and colleagues (Fisher & Geiselman, 1992; Geiselman et al., 1984; Geiselman, Fisher, Cohen, Holland, & Surtes, 1986) developed the *cognitive interview* (CI). The CI incorporated four retrieval techniques designed to bolster memory, but not increase confabulation. The first two techniques acted to increase the similarity between the states of encoding and retrieval: (1) mentally reconstructing the environment of the target event prior to recall; and (2) reporting all information, even information believed not to be useful. The latter two techniques encouraged witnesses to use multiple paths of retrieval: (3) recounting the events in multiple orders (such as backwards); and (4) reporting events from more than one perspective (for instance, from the perspective of another bystander or that of the perpetrator). In addition to utilizing specific retrieval techniques, the CI also emphasizes the importance of building rapport (Fisher & Geiselman, 1992).

The CI has been shown to be effective in a number of studies (Geiselman et al., 1984; Geiselman, Fisher, MacKinnon & Holland, 1986). For example, Aschermann, Mantwill, and Koehnken (1991) compared the CI to questioning without special instructions. All participants viewed a film and then were questioned first with free recall and then with specific questions after an approximately six-day delay. Participants who received CI instructions remembered significantly more correct information than those who received no specific instructions. Both groups produced more correct details in response to specific questions. However, specific questions also led to recall of more incorrect details in both interview conditions. There was no significant difference in recall of incorrect details across question types between the two interview conditions. Thus, the CI was shown to improve memory without significantly increasing the amount of incorrect information recalled.

The CI has also been shown to improve recall in children (Chapman & Perry, 1995; Hayes & Delamothe, 1997; McCauley & Fisher, 1995), although increased errors were also sometimes noted (Milne, Bull, Koehnken, & Memon, 1995; but see Fisher, Brennan, & McCauley, 2002). In addition, the CI may be ineffective or detrimental when used with children under 6 years old. Some specific CI techniques may be less easy to adapt for use with young children (see Hayes & Delamothe, 1997; Memon & Bull, 1991). Children may also have difficulty using some of the CI strategies, such as the direction to recount the event from a different perspective. In fact, it is recommended that the change-perspective portion not be used with young children (Geiselman, 1999).

Despite its usefulness, the CI does have limitations. Theoretically, it is not known which of the specific features of the CI confer the most benefit, whether all are equally important, or whether they operate together to increase memory (Memon & Higham, 1999). Unfortunately, although the CI can be effective in eliciting additional information that can be used to develop a suspect (e.g., identifying marks, clothing descriptions), the CI does not improve person identification performance (Clifford & Gwyer, 1999). The CI also may have some practical limitations because it requires more time and effort on the part of law enforcement officials, both for training and for administration. The precise amount of training needed prior to administering CIs, however, is not clear (Memon & Higham, 1999).

Summary

Although eyewitness memory has limitations, those in law enforcement must rely on it, sometimes in the absence of other types of evidence. By integrating findings from cognitive psychology into methods for use in forensic situations, special interview techniques, such as the cognitive interview, can be effective in improving the amount of information provided in the reports of witnesses. This technique offers an advantage over other methods, such as hypnosis, because it does not tend to increase the amount of incorrect information remembered. Because of the importance of eyewitness testimony to the justice system, improving witnesses' reports is critical.

THE CHILD WITNESS

The involvement of children in the legal system as witnesses has increased dramatically in the recent past, mainly as a result of society's heightened awareness of the problem of sexual and physical abuse and the subsequent removal of several legal impediments to children's testimony. The increased interaction between children and the legal system helped to create research interest in the area of children's eyewitness capabilities. Several sensational cases in the 1980s and 1990s in which children were interviewed with highly suggestive tactics, thus compromising their credibility, raised concerns about children's suggestibility and ability to provide accurate testimony.

Compared to earlier turn-of-the-century studies on children's eyewitness ability, more recent studies, especially studies conducted in the last decade, represent several advances in research methodology. For example, more recent studies have included children of younger ages (e.g., preschoolers), examined children's memory for personally significant and salient events (e.g., memory for invasive medical procedures, memory for emergency room visits for personal injuries), and assessed the effects of interview techniques that more closely resemble the actual interviewing techniques used in forensic settings. These studies have identified both strengths and weaknesses in children's eyewitness testimony (see Bruck & Ceci, 1999; Ceci & Bruck, 1993; Goodman, Emery, & Haugaard, 1997, for reviews).

Children's Suggestibility

Although many studies have indicated that younger children are more susceptible to misinformation than older children and adults (Ceci, Loftus, Leichtman, & Bruck, 1995; Leichtman & Ceci, 1995; Poole & Lindsay, 1995), children may also be very accurate, especially in response to questions concerning abuse-related acts (Goodman, Rudy, Bottoms, & Aman, 1990; Saywitz et al., 1991). Children, however, do sometimes become misled by misinformation, and younger children may be especially vulnerable.

Ceci, Ross, and Toglia (1987) were among the first researchers to examine misinformation effects in children. Children heard a story that was accompanied by black-and-white illustrations and then were presented with misinformation after a day. Children ranging in age from 3 to 12 years showed misinformation effects. However, in a series of studies by Zaragoza and colleagues (Zaragoza, 1987; Zaragoza, 1991; Zaragoza, Dahlgren, & Muench, 1992), no misinformation effect was found for children, even when the stimuli were the same as those used by Ceci and colleagues (1987).

Further studies have demonstrated that children may be misled about information from experienced events as well as for information in books, pictures, or videos (Portwood & Reppucci, 1996; Roberts & Blades, 1999; Schwartz-Kenney & Goodman, 1999). For example, Poole and Lindsay (1995) found that children were quite accurate in an immediate nonsuggestive interview about a science demonstration they had participated in with a researcher. After a delay and repeated exposure to misleading information, however, children often included misinformation in their responses (see also Poole & Lindsay, 2001).

As with adults, source-monitoring errors have been implicated as playing a major role in the suggestibility of children (Ackil & Zaragoza, 1995; Cassel, Roebers, & Bjorklund, 1996; Lindsay, Johnson, & Kwon, 1991; Quas, Goodman, Schaaf, & Luenberger, 1997). Source-monitoring errors occur when individuals forget or misattribute the source of a memory (e.g., mistakenly attributing misinformation presented in an interview to an experienced event). If a child reports misinformation in later free recall, then it is likely that the child has incorporated that information into his or her original event representation, making a source-monitoring error. For instance, Bjorklund and colleagues (1998) showed children a brief video of a theft and then repeatedly asked them either misleading or unbiased questions. Children were later given both free recall and multiple-choice recognition questions. Correct free recall of the central items declined across time, whereas levels of incorrect free recall, while remaining low overall, showed an increase over the testing sessions.

Several studies indicate that social demands also play a large role in the suggestibility of children. Support for the role of social demands comes from studies indicating that misinformation effects drop significantly when a new interviewer and unbiased questions are used (Ceci et al., 1994; Quas and Schaaf, 2002). Additional evidence of the role of social demands comes from studies indicating that misinformation is more likely to be reported when it comes from a more authoritative source (Ceci et al., 1987). Paradigms designed to minimize the social demands of the testing situation also cause reduced suggestibility in children (Lindsay, Gonzales, & Eso, 1995; Schaaf & Ghetti, 2001).

Interviewing Child Witnesses

One factor that is detrimental to the accuracy of child eyewitness reports is the delay that often exists between the alleged crime in question and the time that children are interviewed or testify about that incident. In some cases, delay may be caused by a delay in reporting the crime—for instance, when a child is abused but fails to disclose that abuse until much later. In other cases, though, the delay may simply be caused by the slowness of the justice system. Although studies on the long-term memories of children are relatively rare, there is evidence to suggest that long delays may be particularly harmful to the reports of younger children (Flin, Boon, Knox, & Bull, 1992; Follmer & Furtado, 1997). For instance, Salmon and Pipe (1997) interviewed 3- and 5-year-old children three days and again one year after a quasimedical event (examining a "sick" teddy bear). Though the reports of the older children remained equally accurate at the one-year delay as they were at the three-day delay, the reports of the younger children were more susceptible to errors over time.

A number of practices within an interview may also be harmful to accuracy of child witnesses. Past research has indicated that children's accuracy may be compromised when children are informed that a trusted adult confirmed the truth of an event (Ceci, Huffman, Smith, & Loftus, 1994). Questioning in a multiply suggestive manner or using coercion may also seriously degrade children's reports (Garven, Wood, Malpass, & Shaw, 1998). Children may also be less accurate when they are questioned about events in which they were not directly involved (Tobey & Goodman, 1992), and when they hold a stereotype that conforms to inaccurate suggested information (Leichtman & Ceci, 1995).

Another factor that may hinder accuracy of child witnesses is repeated multiply suggestive interviews. Although nonmisleading repeated interviews may help refresh and maintain accurate memory (e.g., Brainerd & Ornstein, 1991), highly suggestive repeated interviews can have a detrimental effect on children's ability to provide accurate eyewitness reports.

Repeated misleading questioning can heighten suggestibility, especially in younger children (Leichtman & Ceci, 1995). In addition, repeated questions may be detrimental to children's accuracy because children may interpret the repetition of a question as an indication that their previous answer was wrong. Thus, children who are asked questions repeatedly may change an answer simply to comply with the perceived wishes of the interviewer. For instance, in Cassel, Roebers, and Bjorklund's (1992) study in which children were questioned about their memory for a film of a bicycle theft, many children changed their answers in response to repeated questions. However, in some studies, the change of answer was to "don't know" rather than to a commission error.

Research has also indicated several interview techniques that can help increase the accuracy of children's reports and maximize the amount of information provided. A common recommendation for interviews with children is that open-ended rather than specific questions be used, at least initially, because children's answers to open-ended questions ordinarily have a high degree of accuracy (Dent & Stephenson, 1979; Goodman & Reed, 1986; Oates & Shrimpton, 1991). This recommendation is similar to training for the cognitive interview, which reminds interviewers to let the witness tell the story in free narrative and not to interrupt with specific questions. However, one limitation of open-ended questions is that children often provide only limited narratives in response to such questions (Nelson, 1986). Thus, interviewers are frequently obligated to probe for necessary information using more specific questions.

Interviewing by a kind and friendly interviewer can have a positive effect on children's accuracy and, conversely, interviewing by a stern and cold interviewer can have a negative effect (Goodman, Bottoms, Schwartz-Kenney, & Rudy, 1991). For instance, Carter, Bottoms, and Levine (1997) interviewed 60 children aged 5 to 7 years. Interviewers behaved either in a warm, supportive manner, or in a detached, cool, and therefore somewhat intimidating manner. Children who were interviewed by a supportive interviewer were more resistant to misleading questions than were children interviewed by a detached interviewer.

Scripted Protocols for Interviews

Most researchers and professionals agree that when an individual, particularly a child, is questioned during a crime investigation, the interviewers should begin with rapport building and then open-ended questions. Later in the session, the interviewer may use more focused and specific probes, if necessary. However, these specific probes or questions should be followed by open-ended questions to elicit narratives that are as free as possible from the constraints of the question form (Alexander, Redlich, Christian, & Goodman, 2003; Poole & Lamb, 1998). In reality, however, investigative interviewers may fail to follow recommendations and rely heavily on specific questions to elicit information, even after interviewers received special training specifically focused on the structure of the interview (e.g., Aldridge & Cameron, 1999; Warren, Woodall, Hunt, & Perry, 1996). What can be done to ensure that interviews are conducted in an effective manner?

Sternberg, Lamb, Esplin, and Baradaran (1999) proposed a promising approach. In addition to having experienced forensic interviewers participate in a training program, they asked them to follow a scripted protocol when interviewing real alleged victims of sexual offenses. Two types of scripted protocols, differing only in their introductory phase, were used. The open-ended introduction relied on open-ended prompts, whereas the direct introduction used specific questions. Thus, although both types of introduction dealt with similar contents—the child's family and school life—they used different question types. After completion of the introductory phase, the interviews focused on the issues of interest for the investigation.

The scripted protocol laid out well-established guidelines and specified the form of the questions to be asked. For instance, the interviewers started by asking: "I understand that something may have happened to you. Tell me everything that happened from the very beginning to the very end, as best as you can remember." Interviewers were also provided with a list of four nonleading prompts to encourage the child to disclose as much information as possible. Once the child disclosed sexual abuse, the interviewers were allowed to ask whether it happened once or more than one time. If the child reported experiencing the abuse once, the interviewer prompted the child about that time in an open-ended way. If the child reported multiple experiences, the interviewers prompted the child to report, in turn, on the last time, the first time, the best remembered time, and possibly another time, always using open-ended questions. Examples were also provided of possible specific nonsuggestive questions.

Results showed that in comparison with a control condition, interviewers who used the scripted protocols spent significantly more time introducing themselves, establishing rapport, and talking about a neutral topic. Additionally, interviewers in the scripted conditions gave permission more often to the child to correct them or to reply "I don't know." Finally, interviewers who used scripted protocols more often introduced relevant topics in a nonsuggestive manner.

Interestingly, in response to the first general substantive question, children disclosed more details when interviewed with the scripted protocols than in the control conditions, particularly children in the open-ended introduction condition. This result indicates that children "learned" to provide detailed responses to open-ended prompts in the introductory phase of the interview. Across the entire interview, children in the scripted conditions did not provide more information than did children in the control conditions. However, information provided in the scripted conditions was more often provided in response to open-ended prompts, which are more likely to elicit accurate information than specific prompts.

Although encouraging, these results are not conclusive, and additional research is recommended. First, of the 65 interviews conducted for Sternberg and colleagues' (1999) study, 25 had to be excluded because the interviewers did not adhere to the instructions. This suggests that the scripted protocols procedure in its current form is not easy to implement. In addition, as the authors pointed out, the exclusion of so many cases undermines the generalizability of the results. Further research may establish methods to increase the ease of use of the scripted protocol and provide further information about its generalizability.

Reports after Exposure to Misinformation

Despite attempts to ensure high-quality interviewing of children (e.g., by the establishment of Children's Advocacy Centers, where specially trained interviewers use nonsuggestive questioning), children may encounter misinformation when interviewed. This information may subsequently be incorporated into their later reports. The effect may be magnified when misinformation is presented repeatedly (Zaragoza & Mitchell, 1996). Researchers have begun to investigate whether children can recover original information after exposure to misinformation.

A study was recently conducted to investigate whether children can disregard misleading information when given an instruction to do so and whether they are able to later recall the original information (Schaaf, 2000; Schaaf & Ghetti, 2001). Specifically, 4- and 6-year old children participated in a play session. All children were later read a storybook by their parents that described aspects of the play session, using the child's name. Two-thirds of the children heard storybooks that provided incorrect information about the play session. The remaining one-third of the children served as the control group. Two weeks later, all children were interviewed about the event in a nonsuggestive manner. Before being interviewed, children who received misinformation were either given logic of opposition instructions (Jacoby, Woloshyn, & Kelley, 1995; Lindsay, Gonzales, & Eso, 1989) or no special instructions. The logic of opposition instruction specifically informed children that misinformation had been provided in the storybooks and directed them to exclude the storybook details from their reports. Results indicated that children were misled by the incorrect information but that the children who received the logic of opposition instruction were able to dismiss the misinformation and instead retrieve the correct details from their original memory. These results suggest that there are conditions under which children can exclude incorrect answers from their reports, even after having potentially accepted misinformation. However, because in the real world there is no way to establish the extent to which information discussed or suggested prior to the forensic interview was accurate or inaccurate, children cannot be simply instructed to refrain from reporting all information previously talked about. In consideration of this important issue, Poole and Lindsay (2002) recently extended this line of work in a significant manner. Similar to previous research, Poole and Lindsay had children experience a science demonstration and then receive misinformation through a storybook read by their parents. Of importance, at the time of the interview, children in the instruction condition were instructed to differentiate between things they had simply heard and things that they had experienced without making any explicit reference to the source of misinformation. Results showed that compared to a control condition, 7- to 8-year-olds but not 3- to 4- and 5- to 6-year-olds were more likely to exclude suggested false events. Future research should establish whether this ability may extent to more forensically relevant situations.

Whether children can retrieve original memory after exposure to misinformation is of relevance to the courts. If children are subjected to improper and inappropriate interview techniques, their accuracy can be greatly compromised. In at least one case, interview techniques were ruled improper and the children interviewed using those techniques were barred from further testimony (*State of New Jersey v. Michaels*, 1994). If in fact children are able to recover original memories after misleading interviewing, barring further testimony would be unwarranted in many situations. The extent to which the special instructions may help children dismiss previously encountered interviewers' suggestions or children's own previous incorrect statements in favor of retrieval of the original event information should be investigated in future studies. It is particularly important to extend our knowledge of the potentially different contributions of social demands and memory distortions to inaccurate statements and to clarify the extent to which original versus suggested information can be distinguished.

Summary

Children are subject to many of the same errors as are adults. Young children, however, may be especially vulnerable to poor interviewing techniques, including those that are suggestive. Because children are often interviewed in cases of suspected child abuse, including sexual abuse, the accuracy of their testimony is a serious consideration. Thus, special care should be taken when children are being interviewed in forensic situations. If possible, children should be interviewed relatively quickly after alleged events occur. Like adults, children should be interviewed by those trained in effective interviewing techniques.

EMERGING RESEARCH THEMES

In recent years, new areas of inquiry relevant to eyewitness memory have emerged. In the following paragraphs, we report findings and suggest potential directions for further research in two of these areas, eyewitness abilities in individuals with developmental disabilities and accuracy of hearsay testimony.

Eyewitness Abilities in Individuals with Developmental Disabilities

Although methodological and sampling problems in existing literature complicate generalizations, it is consistently suggested that 1 in 3 people with developmental disabilities (DD) are sexually abused before the age of 18 (Perlman & Ericson, 1992). Because individuals with DD may be likely to become involved in the legal system as victims of crime, their abilities as eyewitnesses need to be assessed and understood.

Despite a paucity of research conducted in this area, there are a few important exceptions. Dent (1986) included 33 mildly handicapped children in a study, which entailed witnessing a live event. Participants were then interviewed in one of three ways: free recall, general questions, or specific questions. When a similar procedure was employed with children of normal intelligence (Dent & Stephenson, 1979), reports were most accurate (although less complete) in the free-recall condition. In contrast, with mentally handicapped children, free recall produced relatively poor accuracy levels (as did specific questions), whereas the general questions elicited the best performance in terms of both accuracy and completeness.

This differential pattern of performance between individuals with DD and individuals of normal intelligence has not been confirmed in other studies, although the general performance level is usually worse for the former compared to the latter (Cardone & Dent, 1996; Perlman, Ericson, Esses, & Isaacs, 1994). For example, Perlman and colleagues had individuals with DD and with normal intelligence watch a film. Participants were subsequently asked to respond to five types of questions about the film: free recall, very general, short answer, specific, and statement questions. Misleading or leading questions were also asked. In response to free-recall and very general questions, individuals with DD provided fewer correct pieces of information than did individuals without DD, although the information provided by both groups was generally accurate. Both groups, but particularly individuals with DD, were less accurate when asked focused short-answer recall questions. Further, individuals with DD were more susceptible to fabrication on misleading short-answer questions and more prone to errors to misleading specific and statement questions, but both groups responded similarly to correct leading specific and statement questions.

Although this research suggests that individuals with DD may be generally less reliable witnesses than individuals without such a diagnosis, it remains unclear whether DD individuals' reports differ from reports of typically developing individuals' only quantitatively or if, instead, there are qualitative differences between them. If the differences were strictly quantitative, the performance of individuals with DD should be enhanced by the same interviewing techniques as performance of typically developing individuals. This principle might not apply if individuals with DD were sensitive to different forces than individuals without DD. The results of a recent study by Michel, Gordon, Ornstein, and Simpson (2000) appear consistent with a quantitative view of differences in memory performance. In their study, memory for a mock health checkup of 20 children with mental retardation was compared to that of 20 typically developing children matched on chronological age and 20 typically developing children matched on mental age. Michel and colleagues found that performance of children with mental retardation could not be distinguished from that of children matched in mental age in both measures of memory and suggestibility, but it was significantly worse than performance of children matched on chronological age on all memory variables except for recall.

The increased contact with the criminal justice system by individuals with DD as a result of their increased vulnerability to sexual abuse or assault should encourage researchers to investigate further these individuals' abilities as witnesses. For example, researchers have thus far compared individuals with DD to typically developing individuals on memory for neutral events, but not on memory for stressful events. Stress may differentially impact the experience and the memory of these two groups of individuals. Additionally, researchers have thus far included short-time delays in their experiments. It is possible that time affects the testimony of individuals with DD differently than individuals without such diagnosis. Finally, given that skepticism about the witness competency of people with DD remains among members of the legal system (Ericson, Perlman, & Isaacs, 1994), professionals should become competent interviewers of people with developmental disabilities by taking their developmental/cognitive difficulties into account when questioning them.

Accuracy of Hearsay (Secondhand) Testimony

It is common knowledge that children disclose sexual abuse and victimization experiences to a potentially wide variety of individuals, such as parents, relatives, teachers, friends, and other trusted adults. Any one of these individuals may be called to testify regarding children's disclosures. Although in the United States such out-of-court statements are considered hearsay and would not generally be accepted as evidence in court, there are many exceptions to the hearsay exclusion rule. At times, therefore, it becomes possible for adults to testify about the contents of their conversations with children (McGough, 1994; Myers, 1996). Whether these secondhand witnesses provide accurate testimony regarding the child's allegations is an empirical question that has recently been addressed by researchers.

To examine whether secondhand witnesses are accurate and unbiased, Bruck, Ceci and Francoeur (1999) involved 24 mothers with children aged 3 and 5 years in a study. Mothers were told that the study investigated mother-child conversations and were asked to converse with their children about a laboratory play event that children had experienced while the mothers were absent. Mothers were asked to interview their children about the event with the help of a list of 10 activities that may have taken place (six of these activities had in fact occurred, whereas four had not). Three to four days after mothers talked to their children about the play event, mothers' memory for the interview they conducted was tested. Mothers were asked free-recall, recognition, and source (whether information was elicited through prompts or reported spontaneously by children) questions.

Results showed that mothers' memory for the gist (i.e., the core meaning) of the conversation was better than for the precise wording of the conversation. The biggest difficulty for mothers was discerning the source of the information they were reporting. The results suggest that mothers were able to report accurately the core of the conversation with their child, demonstrating that they could reliably and accurately report the main theme of the conversation. However, mothers were not as able to reliably discriminate between prompted and spontaneously provided information. This distinction may be important in forensic situations, where it is desirable to know how information was solicited.

Warren and Woodall (1999) conducted another study with results consistent with Bruck and colleagues' (1999). A group of 27 experienced child interviewers questioned children about two events, a magic show and a mock doctor visit. Immediately after conducting the interviews, participants were asked to recall the contents of the conversation. Results showed that interviewers recounted accurately approximately 80 percent of the primary activities and 65 percent of the event details. However, interviewers were rarely able to report the exact wording of the questions or the contents of the specific questions they asked. Less than 20 percent of this type of information was reported accurately.

These results should be viewed with caution for a number of reasons. First, the type of information the secondhand witnesses reported in Bruck and colleagues' (1999) and Warren and Woodall's studies (1999) concerned positive, ordinary, and harmless events. Probably for this reason, mothers as well as interviewers did not repeatedly ask their children to provide more and more specific pieces of information, as would likely occur in a situation of disclosure of abuse, and they were not as motivated to remember the details of the conversation with the children. Additionally, it is possible that mothers' and interviewers' ability to discriminate between spontaneous and prompted information would change as a function of whether children exhibit a wider variety of disclosure behaviors and when mothers are more motivated to obtain certain information. Thus, this line of research needs to continue to investigate more ecologically valid interviewing endeavors and other factors (e.g., motivation to obtain information) that may influence the accuracy of secondhand information.

CONCLUSION

Eyewitness evidence often plays a crucial role in the process of uncovering the truth about a crime, ideally resulting in prosecution and conviction (and mental health treatment) of guilty criminals but not innocent people. For this reason, it is vital that researchers as well as law enforcement agencies understand the conditions under which eyewitness evidence can be accurate and reliable. It is thanks to the progress made by many researchers over the past decades that then Attorney General Janet Reno strongly endorsed the activities of the Technical Working Group for Eyewitness Evidence. During a one-year-period, psychologists and other professionals worked together to develop a guide for law enforcement on how to gather eyewitness evidence. Psychological research has therefore reached the community in an important manner, although there is still much more work to be done.

REFERENCES

Ackil, J. K., & Zaragoza, M. S. (1995). Developmental differences in eyewitness suggestibility and memory for source. *Journal of Experimental Child Psychology, 60*, 57–83.

Aldridge, J., & Cameron, S. (1999). Interviewing child witnesses: Questioning techniques and the role of training. *Applied Developmental Science, 3*, 136–147.

Alexander, K., Redlich, A. D., Christian, P., & Goodman, G. S. (2003). Interviewing children. In M. Peterson & M. Durfee (Eds.), *Child abuse and neglect: Guidelines for the identification, assessment, and case management* (pp. 17–19). Volcano, CA: Volcano Press, Inc.

American Psychiatric Association. (1994). *Diagnostic and statistical manual of mental disorders: Primary care version* (4th ed.). Washington, DC: Author.

Aschermann, E., Mantwill, M., & Koehnken, G. (1991). An independent replication of the effectiveness of the Cognitive Interview. *Applied Cognitive Psychology, 5*, 489–495.

Baker-Ward, L., Gordon, B. N., Ornstein, P. A., Larus, D. M., & Clubb, P. A. (1993). Young children's long-term retention of a pediatric examination. *Child Development, 64*, 1519–1533.

Bartlett, F. C. (1932). *Remembering*. Cambridge, UK: Cambridge University Press.

Bell, B. E., & Loftus, E. F. (1988). Degree of detail of eyewitness testimony and mock juror judgments. *Journal of Applied Social Psychology, 18*, 1171–1192.

Berman, G. L., & Cutler, B. L. (1996). Effects of inconsistencies in eyewitness testimony on mock-juror decision making. *Journal of Applied Psychology, 81*, 170–177.

Berman, G. L., Narby, D. J., & Cutler, B. L. (1995). Effects of inconsistent eyewitness statements on mock-juror's evaluations of the eyewitness, perceptions of defendant culpability and verdicts. *Law & Human Behavior, 19*, 79–88.

Bjorklund, D. F., Bjorklund, B. R., Brown, R. D., & Cassel, W. S. (1998). Children's susceptibility to repeated questions: How misinformation changes children's answers and their minds. *Applied Developmental Science, 2*, 99–111.

Bothwell, R. K., Brigham, J. C., & Malpass, R. S. (1989). Cross-racial identification. *Personality and Social Psychology Bulletin, 15*, 19–25.

Bothwell, R. K., Deffenbacher, K. A., & Brigham, J. C. (1987). Correlation of eyewitness accuracy and confidence: Optimality hypothesis revisited. *Journal of Applied Psychology, 72*, 691–695.

Bower, G. H. (1981). Mood and memory. *American Psychologist, 36*, 129–148.

Brainerd, C. J., & Ornstein, P. A. (1991). Children's memory for witnessed events: The developmental backdrop. In J. Doris (Ed.), *The suggestibility of children's recollections* (pp. 10–20). Washington, DC: American Psychological Association.

Bremner, J. D. (1999). Does stress damage the brain? *Biological Psychiatry, 45*, 797–805.

Bremner, J. D. (2001). Hypotheses and controversies related to effects of stress on the hippocampus: An argument for stress-induced damage to the hippocampus in patients with post-traumatic stress disorder. *Hippocampus, 11*, 75–81.

Briere, J. N. (1992). *Child abuse trauma: Theory and treatment of the lasting effects.* Thousand Oaks, CA: Sage.

Briere, J. N., & Conte, J. R. (1993). Self-reported amnesia for abuse in adults molested as children. *Journal of Traumatic Stress, 6*, 21–31.

Brigham, J. C. (1990). Target person distinctiveness and attractiveness as moderator variables in the confidence-accuracy relationship in eyewitness identifications. *Basic & Applied Social Psychology, 11*, 101–115.

Brigham, J. C., & Bothwell, R. K. (1983). The ability of prospective jurors to estimate the accuracy of eyewitness identifications. *Law & Human Behavior, 7*, 19–30.

Brigham, J. C., Meissner, C. A., & Wasserman, A. W. (1999). Applied issues in the construction and expert assessment of photo lineups. *Applied Cognitive Psychology, 13*(Spec Issue), S73–S92.

Brigham, J. C., & Ready, D. J. (1985). Own-race bias in lineup construction. *Law and Human Behavior, 9*, 415–424.

Brigham, J. C., Ready, D. J., & Spier, S. A. (1990). Standards for evaluating the fairness of photograph lineups. *Basic and Applied Social Psychology, 11*, 149–163.

Brown, R., & Kulik, J. (1977). Flashbulb memories. *Cognition, 5*, 73–99.

Bruck, M., & Ceci, S. J. (1999). The suggestibility of children's memory. *Annual Review of Psychology, 50*, 419–439.

Bruck, M., Ceci, S. J., & Francoeur, E. (1999). The accuracy of mothers' memories of conversations with their preschool children. *Journal of Experimental Psychology: Applied, 5*, 89–106.

Bruner, J. S., & Postman, L. (1949). Perception, cognition, and behavior. *Journal of Personality, 18*, 14–31.

Buckhout, R. (1974). Eyewitness testimony. *Scientific American, 231*, 23–31.

Cardone, D., & Dent, H. (1996). Memory and interrogative suggestibility: The effects of modality of information presentation and retrieval conditions upon the suggestibility scores of people with learning disabilities. *Legal and Criminological Psychology, 1*, 165–177.

Carter, C. A., Bottoms, B. L., & Levine, M. (1996). Linguistic and socioemotional influences on the accuracy of children's reports. *Law & Human Behavior, 20*, 335–358.

Cassel, W. S., Roebers, C. E. M., & Bjorklund, D. F. (1996). Developmental patterns of eyewitness responses to repeated and increasingly suggestive questions. *Journal of Experimental Child Psychology, 61*, 116–133.

Ceci, S. J., & Bruck, M. (1993). Suggestibility of the child witness: A historical review and synthesis. *Psychological Bulletin, 113*, 403–439.

Ceci, S. J., Huffman, M. L., Smith, E., & Loftus, E. F. (1994). Repeatedly thinking about a non-event: Source misattributions among preschoolers. *Consciousness and Cognition, 3*, 388–407.

Ceci, S. J., Loftus, E. F., Leichtman, M. D., & Bruck, M. (1994). The possible role of source misattributions in the creation of false beliefs among preschoolers. *International Journal of Clinical and Experimental Hypnosis, 42*, 304–320.

Ceci, S. J., Ross, D. F., & Toglia, M. P. (1987). Suggestibility of children's memory: Psycholegal implications. *Journal of Experimental Psychology: General, 116*, 38–49.

Chance, J. E., Turner, A. L., & Goldstein, A. G. (1982). Development of differential recognition for own- and other-race faces. *The Journal of Psychology, 112*, 29–37.

Chandler, C. C. (1994). Studying related pictures can reduce accuracy, but increase confidence, in a modified recognition test. *Memory & Cognition, 22*, 273–280.

Chapman, A. J., & Perry, D. J. (1995). Applying the cognitive interview procedure to child and adult eyewitnesses of road accidents. *Applied Psychology: An International Review, 44*, 283–294.

Chen, Y. Y., & Geiselman, R. E. (1993). Effects of ethnic stereotyping and ethnically-related cognitive biases on eyewitness recollections of height. *American Journal of Forensic Psychology, 11*, 13–19.

Christianson, S. A. (1989). Flashbulb memories: Special, but not so special. *Memory and Cognition, 17*, 435–443.

Christianson, S. A. (1992). Emotional stress and eyewitness memory: A critical review. *Psychological Bulletin, 112*, 284–309.

Christianson, S. A., & Hubinette, B. (1993). Hands up: A study of witnesses' emotional reactions and memories associated with bank robberies. *Applied Cognitive Psychology, 7*, 365–379.

Christianson, S. A., & Loftus, E. F. (1991). Remembering emotional events: The fate of detailed information. *Cognition and Emotion, 5*, 81–108.

Clifford, B. R., & Gwyer, P. (1999). The effects of cognitive interview and other methods of context reinstatement on identification. *Psychology, Crime, and Law, 5*, 61–80.

Clifford, B. R., & Richards, V. J. (1977). Comparison of recall by policemen and civilians under conditions of long and short durations of exposure. *Perceptual and Motor Skills, 45*, 503–512.

Clifford, B. R., & Scott, J. (1978). Individual and situational factors in eyewitness testimony. *Journal of Applied Psychology, 63*, 352–359.

Connors, E., Lundregan, T., Miller, N., & McEwan, T. (1996). *Convicted by juries, exonerated by science: Case studies in the use of DNA evidence to establish innocence after trial*. Alexandria, VA: National Institute of Justice.

Cutler, B. L., Penrod, S. D., & Dexter, H. R. (1990). Juror sensitivity to eyewitness identification evidence. *Law & Human Behavior, 14*, 185–191.

Deffenbacher, K. A. (1980). Eyewitness accuracy and confidence: Can we infer anything about their relationship? *Law & Human Behavior, 4*, 243–260.

Deffenbacher, K. A. (1983). The influence of arousal on reliability of testimony. In S. Lloyd-Bostock & B. R. Clifford (Eds.), *Evaluating witness evidence* (pp. 235–254). Chichester, UK: Wiley.

Dent, H. R. (1986). An experimental study of the effectiveness of different techniques of questioning mentally handicapped child witnesses. *British Journal of Clinical Psychology, 25*, 13–17.

Dent, H. R., & Stephenson, G. M. (1979). An experimental study of the effectiveness of different techniques of questioning child witnesses. *British Journal of Social and Clinical Psychology, 18*, 41–51.

Diamond, B. L. (1980). Inherent problems in the use of pretrial hypnosis on a prospective witness. *California Law Review, 68*, 313–349.

Easterbrook, J. A. (1959). The effect of emotion on cue utilization and the organization of behavior. *Psychological Review, 66*, 183–201.

Elliott, D. M., & Briere, J. (1995). Post-traumatic stress associated with delayed recall of abuse: A general population study. *Journal of Traumatic Stress, 8*, 629–647.

Epstein, M. A., & Bottoms, B. L. (1998). Memories of childhood sexual abuse: A survey of young adults. *Child Abuse and Neglect, 22*, 1217–1238.

Ericson, K., Perlman, N., & Isaacs, B. (1994). Witness competency, communication issues and people with developmental disabilities. *Developmental Disabilities Bulletin, 22*, 101–109.

Fisher, R. P., Brennan, K. H., & McCauley, M. R. (2002). The cognitive interview method to enhance eyewitness recall. In M. Eisen, J. Quas, & G. Goodman (Eds.), *Memory and suggestibility in the forensic interview* (pp. 265–286). Mahwah, NJ: Lawrence Erlbaum.

Fisher, R. P., & Geiselman, R. E. (1992). *Memory enhancing techniques for investigative interviewing: The cognitive interview*. Springfield, IL: Charles C Thomas.

Flin, R., Boon, J., Knox, A., & Bull, R. (1992). The effect of a five-month delay on children's and adults' eyewitness memory. *British Journal of Psychology, 83*, 323–336.

Follmer, A., & Furtado, E. A. (1997, April). Children's long-term retention: Using hierarchical linear models to estimate recall functions over time. Paper presented at the Biennial Meeting of the Society for Research in Child Development, Washington DC.

Fraley, R. C., Garner, J. P., & Shaver, P. R. (2000). Adult attachment and the defensive regulation of attention and memory: Examining the role of preemptive and postemptive defensive processes. *Journal of Personality and Social Psychology, 79*, 816–826.

Friedman, A. (1979). Framing pictures. The role of default knowledge in automized encoding and memory for gist. *Journal of Experimental Psychology: General, 108*, 315–355.

Garven, S., Wood, J. M., Malpass, R. S., & Shaw, J. S. (1998). More than suggestion: The effect of interviewing techniques from the McMartin Preschool case. *Journal of Applied Psychology, 83*, 347–359.

Geiselman, R. E. (1999). Commentary on recent research with the cognitive interview. *Psychology, Crime, and Law, 5*, 197–202.

Geiselman, R. E., Fisher, R. P., Cohen, G., Holland, H., & Surtes, L. (1986). Eyewitness responses to leading and misleading questions under the cognitive interview. *Journal of Police Science and Administration, 14*, 31–39.

Geiselman, R. E., Fisher, R. P., Firstenberg, I., Hutton, L. A., Sullivan, S. J., Avetissian, I. V., & Prosk, A. L. (1984). Enhancement of eyewitness memory: An empirical evaluation of the cognitive interview. *Journal of Police Science and Administration, 12*, 74–80.

Geiselman, R. E., Fisher, R. P., MacKinnon, D. P., & Holland, H. L. Eyewitness memory enhancement in the police interview: Cognitive retrieval mnemonics versus hypnosis. *Journal of Applied Psychology, 70*, 401–412.

Gibbon, H. B. (1982). The use of hypnosis in police investigations. *Bulletin of the British Psychological Society, 35*, 138–142.

Goodman, G. S., Bottoms, B. L., Herscovici, B. B., & Shaver, P. (1989). Determinants of the child victims' perceived credibility. In S. J. Ceci, D. F. Ross, & M. P. Toglia (Eds.), *Perspectives on the child witness* (pp. 1–22). New York: Springer-Verlag.

Goodman, G. S., Bottoms, B. L., Schwartz-Kenney, B. M., & Rudy, L. (1991). Children's testimony about a stressful event: Improving children's reports. *Journal of Narrative & Life History, 1*, 69–99.

Goodman, G. S., Emery, R. E., & Haugaard, J. J. (1997). Developmental psychology and law: Divorce, child maltreatment, foster care, and adoption. In I. Sigel & A. Renninger (Eds.), *Handbook of child psychology: Vol. 4. Child psychology in practice* (5th ed.) (pp. 775–874). New York: Wiley.

Goodman, G. S., Hirschman, J. E., Hepps, D., & Rudy, L. (1991). Children's memory for stressful events. *Merrill-Palmer Quarterly, 37*, 109–157.

Goodman, G. S., Golding, J. M., Helgeson, V. S., & Haith, M. M., & Michelli, J. (1987). When a child takes the stand: Jurors' perceptions of children's eyewitness testimony. *Law & Human Behavior, 11*, 27–40.

Goodman, G. S., Myers, J. E. B., & Redlich, A. D. (1997). *Children's evidence: Effects of hearsay on jurors' decisions in child sexual abuse cases.* Paper presented at the International Conference on Applied Psychology, San Francisco.

Goodman, G. S., Pyle-Taub, E., Jones, D. P. H., England, P., Port, L. P., Rudy, L., & Prado, L. (1992). *Emotional effects of criminal court testimony on child sexual assault victims.* Monographs of the Society for Research in Child Development, 57, no. 22.

Goodman, G. S., Quas, J. A., Batterman-Faunce, J. M., Riddlesberger, M., & Kuhn, J. (1997). Children's reactions to and memory for a stressful experience: Influences of age, knowledge, anatomical dolls, and parental attachment. *Applied Developmental Sciences, 1*, 54–75.

Goodman, G. S., Redlich, A. D., Qin, J. J., Ghetti, S., Tyda, K., Schaaf, J. M., & Hahn, A. (1999). Evaluating eyewitness testimony in adults and children. In A. K. Hess & I. B. Weiner (Eds.), *The handbook of forensic psychology* (2nd ed.) (pp. 218–272). New York: Wiley.

Goodman, G. S., & Reed, R. (1986). Age differences in eyewitness testimony. *Law and Human Behavior, 10*, 317–332.

Goodman, G. S., Rudy, L., Bottoms, B. L., & Aman, C. (1990). Children's concerns and memory: Issues of ecological validity in the study of children's eyewitness testimony. In F. Robyn & J. Hudson (Eds.), *Knowing and remembering in young children, Emory symposia in cognition, Vol. 3* (pp. 249–284). New York: Cambridge University Press.

Goodman, G. S., Tobey, A. E., Batterman-Faunce, J. M., Orcutt, H., Thomas, S., Shapiro, C., & Sachsenmaier, T. (1998). Face-to-face confrontation: Effects of closed-circuit technology on children's eyewitness testimony and jurors' decisions. *Law & Human Behavior, 22*, 165–203.

Grasser, A. (1981). *Prose comprehension beyond the world.* New York: Springer.

Gross, J., & Hayne, H. (1996). Eyewitness identification by 5- to 6-year-old children. *Law and Human Behavior, 20*, 359–373.

Harding v. State [of Maryland], 5 Md. App. 230, 246 A2d 302 (1968). 252 Md. 731, Cert. Denied, 395 U.S. 949, 89 S.Ct. 2030, 23 L. Ed.2d 468 (1969).

Hastorf, A. H., & Cantril, H. (1954). They saw a game: A case study. *Journal of Abnormal and Social-Psychology, 49*, 129–134.

Hayes, B. K., & Delamothe, K. (1997). Cognitive interviewing procedures and suggestibility in children's recall. *Journal of Applied Psychology, 82*, 562–577.

Holst, V. F., & Pezdek, K. (1992). Scripts for typical crimes and their effects on memory for eyewitness testimony. *Applied Cognitive Psychology, 6*, 573–587.

Huff, C. R. (1987). Wrongful conviction: Societal tolerance of injustice. *Research in Social Problems and Public Policy, 4*, 99–115.

Jacoby, L. L., Woloshyn, V., & Kelley, C. M. (1989). Becoming famous without being recognized: Unconscious influences of memory produced by dividing attention. *Journal of Experimental Psychology: General, 118*, 115–125.

Johnson, M. K., Hastroudi, S., & Lindsay, D. S. (1993). Source monitoring. *Psychological Bulletin, 114*, 3–28.

Johnson, M. K., & Raye, C. L. (1981). Reality monitoring. *Psychological Review, 88*, 67–85.

Kassin, S. M. (1997). The psychology of confession evidence. *American Psychologist, 52*, 221–233.

Kirsh, S. J. (1996). Attachment style and recognition of emotionally-laden drawings. *Perceptual and Motor Skills, 83*, 607–610.

Kleinmuntz, B., & Szucko, J. J. (1984). Lie detection in ancient and modern times: A call for contemporary scientific study. *American Psychologist, 39*, 766–776.

Koss, M. P., Tromp, S., & Tharan, M. (1995). Traumatic memories: Empirical foundation, forensic, and clinical implications. *Clinical Psychology: Science and Practice, 2*, 111–132.

Krafka, C., & Penrod, S. (1985). Reinstatement of context in a field experiment on eyewitness identification. *Journal of Personality & Social Psychology, 49*, 58–69.

Lee, J., & Goodman, G. S. (2003). *The development of memory for own- and other-racial/ethnic faces.* Paper submitted for publication.

Leichtman, M. D., & Ceci, S. J. (1995). The effects of stereotypes and suggestions on preschoolers' reports. *Developmental Psychology, 31*, 568–578.

Leippe, M. R. (1980). Effects of integrative memorial and cognitive processes on the correspondence of eyewitness accuracy and confidence. *Law & Human Behavior, 4*, 261–274.

Leippe, M. R., Manion, A. P., & Romanczyk, A. (1992). Eyewitness persuasion: How and how well do fact finders judge the accuracy of adults' and children's memory reports? *Journal of Personality & Social Psychology, 63*, 181–197.

Leippe, M. R., & Romanczyk, A. (1989). Reactions to child (versus adult) eyewitnesses: The influence of jurors' preconceptions and witness behavior. *Law & Human Behavior, 13*, 103–132.

Levi, A. M. (1999). An honourable discharge for line-up fairness measurement. *Applied Cognitive Psychology, 13*(Spec Issue), S121–S124.

Lindsay, D. S., Gonzales, V., & Eso, K. (1995). Aware and unaware uses of memories of postevent suggestions. In M. S. Zaragoza, J. R. Graham, G. C. N. Hall, R. Hirschman, & Y. S. Ben-Porath (Eds.), *Memory and testimony in the child witness* (pp. 86–108). Thousand Oaks, CA: Sage.

Lindsay, D. S., & Johnson, M. K. (1989). The eyewitness suggestibility effect and memory for source. *Memory and Cognition, 17*, 349–358.

Lindsay, D. S., Johnson, M. K., & Kwon, P. (1991). Developmental changes in memory source monitoring. *Journal of Experimental Child Psychology, 52*, 297–318.

Lindsay, D. S., Read, J. D., & Sharma, K. (1998). Accuracy and confidence in person identification: The relationship is strong when witnessing conditions vary widely. *Psychological Science, 9*, 215–218.

Lindsay, R. C. L., Ross, D. F., Smith, S. M., & Flanigan, S. (1999). Does race influence measures of lineup fairness? *Applied Cognitive Psychology, 13*(Spec Issue), S109–S119.

Lindsay, R. C., & Wells, G. L. (1985). Improving eyewitness identifications from lineups: Simultaneous versus sequential lineup presentation. *Journal of Applied Psychology, 70,* 556–564.

Lindsay, R. C., Wells, G. L., & O'Connor, F. J. (1989). Mock-juror belief of accurate and inaccurate eyewitnesses: A replication and extension. *Law & Human Behavior, 13,* 333–339.

List, J. A. (1986). Age and schematic differences in the reliability of eyewitness testimony. *Developmental Psychology, 22,* 50–57.

Loftus, E. F. (1977). Shifting human color memory. *Memory and Cognition, 5,* 696–699.

Loftus, E. F. (1979). *Eyewitness testimony.* Cambridge, MA: Harvard University Press.

Loftus, E. F. (1994). The repressed memory controversy. *American-Psychologist, 49,* 443–445.

Loftus, E. F., & Burns, T. E. (1982). Mental shock can produce retrograde amnesia. *Memory and Cognition, 10,* 318–323.

Loftus, E. F., Loftus, G. R., & Messo, J. (1987). Some facts about "weapon focus." *Law and Human Behavior, 11,* 55–62.

Loftus, E. F., Miller, D. G., & Burns, H. J. (1978). Semantic integration of verbal information into a visual memory. *Journal of Experimental Psychology: Human Learning & Memory, 4,* 19–31.

Loftus, E. F., Polonsky, S., & Fullilove, M. T. (1994). Memories of childhood sexual abuse: Remembering and repressing. *Psychology of Women Quarterly, 18,* 67–84.

Loftus, G. R., & Mackworth, N. H. (1978). Cognitive determinants of fixation location during picture viewing. *Journal of Experimental Psychology: Human Perception and Performance, 4,* 565–572.

Luus, C. A. E., & Wells, G. L. (1991). Eyewitness identification and the selection of distracters for lineups. *Law & Human Behavior, 15,* 43–57.

Luus, C. A. E., & Wells, G. L. (1994). Eyewitness identification confidence. In D. F. Ross, J. D. Read, & M. P. Toglia (Eds.), *Adult eyewitness testimony: Current trends and developments* (pp. 348–361). New York: Cambridge University Press.

Maass, A., & Koehnken, G. (1989). Eyewitness identification: Simulating the "weapon effect." *Law and Human Behavior, 13,* 397–408.

Maki, R. H. (1990). Memory for script actions: Effects of relevance and detail expectancy. *Memory and Cognition, 18,* 5–14.

Malpass, R. S. (1981). Effective size and defendant bias in eyewitness identification lineups. *Law and Human Behavior, 5,* 299–309.

Malpass, R. S., & Devine, P. G. (1981). Eyewitness identification: Lineup instructions and the absence of the offender. *Journal of Applied Psychology, 75,* 506–510.

Malpass, R. S., & Kravits (1969). Recognition for faces of own and other race. *Journal of Personality and Social Psychology, 13,* 330–334.

Marquis, K. H., Marshall, J., & Oskamp, S. (1972). Testimony validity as a function of question form, atmosphere, and item difficulty. *Journal of Applied Social Psychology, 2,* 167–186.

McCauley, M. R., & Fisher, R. P. (1995). Facilitating children's eyewitness recall with the revised cognitive interview. *Journal of Applied Psychology, 80,* 510–516.

McCloskey, M., Wible, C. G., & Cohen, N. J. (1988). Is there a special flashbulb-memory mechanism? *Journal of Experimental Psychology: General, 117,* 171–181.

McCloskey, M., & Zaragoza, M. (1985). Misleading postevent information and memory for events: Arguments and evidence against memory impairment hypotheses. *Journal of Experimental Psychology: General, 114*, 1–16.

McGough, L. S. (1994). *Child witnesses: Fragile voices in the American legal system.* New Haven, CT: Yale University Press.

MacLin, O. H., MacLin, M. K., & Malpass, R. S. (2001). Race, arousal, attention, exposure and delay: An examination of factors moderating face recognition. *Psychology, Public Policy, & Law, 7*, 134–152.

Meissner, C. A., & Brigham, J. C. (2001). Thirty years of investigating the own-race bias memory for faces: A meta-analytic review. *Psychology, Public Policy, and Law, 7*, 3–35.

Memon, A., & Bull, R. (1991). The cognitive interview: Its origins, empirical support, evaluation and practical implications. *Journal of Community and Applied Social Psychology, 1*, 291–307.

Memon, A., & Higham, P. A. (1999). A review of the cognitive interview. *Psychology, Crime, and Law, 5*, 177–196.

Merritt, K. A., Ornstein, P. A., & Spicker, B. (1994). Children's memory for a salient medical procedure: Implications for testimony. *Pediatrics, 94*, 17–23.

Metcalfe, J., & Jacobs, W. J. (2000). "Hot" emotions in human recollection: Toward a model of traumatic memory. In E. Tulving (Ed.), *Memory, consciousness, and the brain*: The Tallinn Conference (pp. 228–242). Philadelphia, PA: Taylor & Francis.

Michel, M. K., Gordon, B. N., Ornstein, P. A., & Simpson, M. A. (2000). The abilities of children with mental retardation to remember personal experiences: Implications for testimony. *Journal of Clinical Child Psychology, 29*, 453–463.

Miller, J. B., & Noirot, M. (1999). Attachment memories, models and information processing. *Journal of Social and Personal Relationships, 16*, 147–173.

Milne, R., Bull, R., Koehnken, G., & Memon, A. (1995). The cognitive interview and suggestibility. In G. M. Stephenson & N. K. Clark (Eds.), *Criminal Behaviour: Perceptions, Attrivutions and Rationale.* BPS Division of Criminological and Legal Psychology Occasional Papers, no. 22 (pp. 21–27). Leicester, UK: British Psychological Society.

Myers, J. E. B. (1996). A decade of international reform to accommodate child witnesses: Steps toward a Child Witness Code. In B. L. Bottoms & G. S. Goodman (Eds.), *International perspectives on child witnesses* (pp. 221–265). Thousand Oaks, CA: Sage.

Neil vs. Biggers, 409 U.S. 188 (1972), cert. denied, 444 U.S. 909 (1979).

Neisser, U., & Harsch, N. (1993). Phantom flashbulbs: False recollections of hearing the news about Challenger. In E. Winograd & U. Neisser (Eds.), *Affect and accuracy in recall: Studies of "flashbulb" memories* (pp. 9–31). New York: Cambridge University Press.

Nelson, K. (1986). *Event knowledge: Structure and function in development.* Hillsdale, NJ: Lawrence Erlbaum.

Nemiah, J. C. (1998). Early concepts of trauma, dissociation, and the unconscious: Their history and current implications. In J. D. Bremner & C. R. Marmar (Eds.), *Trauma, memory, and dissociation* (pp. 1–16). Washington, DC: American Psychiatric Press Series.

Oates, K., & Shrimpton, S. (1991). Children's memories for stressful and non-stressful events. *Medical Science and Law, 31*, 4–10.

Payne, D. G., Toglia, M. P., & Anastasi, J. S. (1994). Recognition performance level and the magnitude of the misinformation effect in eyewitness memory. *Psychonomic Bulletin and Review, 1*, 376–382.

People v. Ebanks, 117 Cal. 652; 49 P. 1049; 40 LAR 269 (1897).

People v. Hughes, 453 N. E.2d 484 (N.Y. App. 1983).

Perlman, N. B., & Ericson, K. (1992). Issues related to sexual abuse of persons with developmental disabilities: An overview. *Journal on Developmental Disabilities, 1*, 19–23.

Perlman, N. B., Ericson, K. I., Esses, V. M., & Isaacs, B. J. (1994). The developmentally handicapped witness: Competency as a function of question format. *Law & Human Behavior, 18*, 171–187.

Peters, D. P. (1991). The influence of stress and arousal on the child witness. In J. Doris (Ed.), *The suggestibility of children's recollections* (pp. 60–76). Washington, DC: American Psychological Association.

Pezdek, K., Blandon-Gitlin, I., & Moore, C. (in press) Children's face recognition memory: More evidence for the cross-race effect. *Journal of Applied Psychology*.

Pickel, K. L. (1999). The influence of context on the "weapon focus" effect. *Law and Human Behavior, 23*, 299–311.

Platz, S. J., & Hosch, H. M. (1988). Cross-racial/ethnic eyewitness identification: A field study. *Journal of Applied Social Psychology, 18*, 972–984.

Poole, D. A., & Lamb, M. E. (1998). *Investigative interviews of children: A guide for helping professionals*. Washington, DC: American Psychological Association.

Poole, D. A., & Lindsay, D. S. (1995). Interviewing preschoolers: Effects of nonsuggestive techniques, parental coaching, and leading questions on reports of nonexperienced events. *Journal of Experimental Child Psychology, 60*, 129–154.

Poole, D. A., & Lindsay, D. S. (2001). Children's eyewitness reports after exposure to misinformation from parents. *Journal of Experimental Psychology: Applied, 7*, 27–50.

Poole, D. A., & Lindsay, D. S. (2002). Reducing child witnesses' false reports of misinformation from parents. *Journal of Experimental Child Psychology, 81*, 117–140.

Portwood, S. G., & Reppucci, N. D. (1996). Adults' impact on the suggestibility of preschoolers' recollections. *Journal of Applied Developmental Psychology, 17*, 175–198.

Quas, J. A., & Schaaf, J. M. (2002). Children's memories of experienced and nonexperienced events following repeated interviews. *Journal of Experimental Child Psychology, 83*, 304–338.

Quas, J. A., Goodman, G. S., Bidrose, S., Pipe, M. E., Craw, S., & Ablin, D. S. (1999). Emotion and memory: Children's long-term remembering, forgetting, and suggestibility. *Journal of Experimental Child Psychology, 72*, 235–270.

Quas, J. A., Goodman, G. S., Schaaf, J. M., & Luenberger, J. (1997, April). Individual differences in preschoolers' suggestibility: Identifying the source. Paper presented at the meeting of the Society for Research in Child Development, Washington, DC.

Qin, J. (2000). Adults' memories of childhood: True versus false reports. *Dissertation Abstracts International: Section B: The Sciences and Engineering, 61*, 5021 (UMI Number AA19987507).

Reiser, M., & Neilson, M. (1980). Investigative hypnosis: A developing specialty. *American Journal of Clinical Hypnosis, 23*, 75–83.

Roberts, K. P., & Blades, M. (1999). Children's memory and source monitoring of real-life and televised events. *Journal of Applied Developmental Psychology, 20*, 575–596.

Robinson, M. D., & Johnson, J. T. (1996). Recall memory, recognition memory, and the eyewitness confidence-accuracy correlation. *Journal of Applied Psychology, 81,* 587–594.

Robinson, M. D., & Johnson, J. T. (1998). How not to enhance the confidence-accuracy relation: The detrimental effects of attention to the identification process. *Law & Human Behavior, 22,* 409–428.

Ross, D. F., Hopkins, S., Hanson, E., Lindsay, R. C., Hazen, A. L., & Eslinger, C. (1994). The impact of protective shields and videotape testimony on conviction rates in a simulated trial of child sexual abuse. *Law & Human Behavior, 18,* 553–566.

Rothbaum, B. O., Foa, E. B., Riggs, D. S., Murdock, T., & Walsh, W. (1992). A prospective examination of post-traumatic stress disorder in rape victims. *Journal of Traumatic Stress, 5,* 455–475.

Rudy, L., & Goodman, G. S. (1991). Effects of participation on children's reports: Implications for children's testimony. *Developmental Psychology, 27,* 527–538.

Ryan, R. H., & Geiselman, R. E. (1991). Effects of biased information on the relationship between eyewitness confidence and accuracy. *Bulletin of the Psychonomic Society, 29,* 7–9.

Salmon, K., Bidrose, S., & Pipe, M. E. (1995). Providing props to facilitate children's event reports: A comparison of toys and real items. *Journal of Experimental Child Psychology, 60,* 174–194.

Salmon, K., & Pipe, M. E. (1997). Recalling an event one year later: The impact of props, drawing and a prior interview. *Applied Cognitive Psychology, 14,* 99–120.

Sapolsky, R. M. (1996). Why stress is bad for your brain. *Science, 273,* 749–750.

Saywitz, K. J., Goodman, G. S., Nicholas, E., & Moan, S. F. (1991). Children's memories of a physical examination involving genital touch: Implications for reports of child sexual abuse. *Journal of Consulting and Clinical Psychology, 59,* 682–691.

Schaaf, J. M. (2000). Do children believe misleading information? Investigating the effects of postevent misinformation using the logic of opposition instruction. *Dissertation Abstracts International: Section B: The Sciences & Engineering, 60,* 5240 (UMI Number AA19987507).

Schaaf, J. M., & Ghetti, S. (2001, April). Investigating the effects of post event misinformation using the logic of opposition instruction. In S. Ghetti & J. Schaaf (Chairs). *Developmental differences in false memory formation: Errors as by-products of a functional system?* Symposium presented at the Biennial Conference of Society for Research in Child Development, Minneapolis, MN.

Scheck, B., Neufeld, P., & Dwyer, J. (2000). *Actual innocence.* New York: Random House.

Schooler, J. W., Gerhard, D., & Loftus, E. F. (1986). Qualities of the unreal. *Journal of Experimental Psychology: Learning, Memory, & Cognition, 12,* 71–181.

Schwartz-Kenney, B. M., & Goodman, G. S. (1999). Children's memory of a naturalistic event following misinformation. *Applied Developmental Science, 3,* 34–46.

Shapiro, P. N., & Penrod, S. (1986). Meta-analysis of facial identification studies. *Psychological Bulletin, 100,* 139–156.

Shaw, J. S. III. (1996). Increases in eyewitness confidence resulting from postevent questioning. *Journal of Experimental Psychology: Applied, 2,* 26–146.

Sommer, R. (1959). The new look on the witness stand. *Canadian Psychologist, 8,* 94–99.

Sporer, S. L., Malpass, R. S., & Koehnken, G. (Eds.) *Psychological issues in eyewitness identification.* Hillsdale, NJ: Lawrence Erlbaum.

Sporer, S. L., Penrod, S., Read, D., & Cutler, B. (1995). Choosing, confidence, and accuracy: A meta-analysis of the confidence-accuracy relation in eyewitness identification studies. *Psychological Bulletin, 118,* 315–327.

Stager, G. L., & Lundy, R. M. (1985). Hypnosis and the learning and recall of visually presented material. *International Journal of Clinical and Experimental Hypnosis, 33,* 38–39.

State [of New Jersey] v. Hurd, 432 A.2d 86 (N.J. 1981).

State [of New Jersey] v. Michaels, 136 N.J. 299, 642 A.2d 1372 (1994).

Steblay (1997). Social influence in eyewitness recall: A meta-analytic review of lineup instruction effects. *Law and Human Behavior, 21,* 283–298.

Stern, L. B., & Dunning, D. (1994). Distinguishing accurate from inaccurate eyewitness identifications: A reality monitoring approach. In D. F. Ross & J. D. Read (Eds.), *Adult eyewitness testimony: Current trends and developments* (pp. 273–299). New York: Cambridge University Press.

Sternberg, K. J., Lamb, M. E., Esplin, P. W., & Baradaran, L. P. (1999). Using a scripted protocol in investigative interviews: A pilot study. *Applied Developmental Science, 3,* 70–76.

Swim, J. K., Borgida, E., & McCoy, K. (1993). Videotaped versus in-court witness testimony: Does protecting the child witness jeopardize due process? *Journal of Applied Social Psychology, 23,* 603–631.

Technical Working Group for Eyewitness Evidence. (1999). *Eyewitness evidence: A guide for law enforcement* [Booklet]. Washington, DC: U.S. Department of Justice, Office of Justice Programs.

Tobey, A. E., & Goodman, G. S. (1992). Children's eyewitness memory: Effects of participation and forensic context. *Child Abuse & Neglect, 16,* 779–796.

Treadway, M., & McCloskey, M. (1989). Effects of racial stereotypes on eyewitness performance: Implications of the real and the rumoured Allport and Postman studies. *Applied-Cognitive Psychology, 3,* 53–63.

Tromp, S., Koss, M. P., Figueredo, A. J., & Tharan, M. (1995). Are rape memories different? A comparison of rape, other unpleasant, and pleasant memories among employed women. *Journal of Traumatic Stress, 8,* 607–627.

Tulving, E. (1981). Similarity relations in recognition. *Journal of Verbal Learning & Verbal Behavior, 20,* 479–496.

Tulving, E. (1983). *Elements of episodic memory.* Oxford, UK: Clarendon Press.

United States v. Ash, 413 U.S. 300 (1973).

Warren, A. R., & Woodall, C. E. (1999). The reliability of hearsay testimony: How well do interviewers recall their interviews with children? *Psychology, Public Policy, and Law, 5,* 355–371.

Warren, A. R., Woodall, C. E., Hunt, J. S., & Perry, N. W. (1996). "It sounds good in theory but": Do investigative interviewers follow guidelines based on memory research? *Child Maltreatment, 1,* 231–245.

Weaver, C. A. (1993). Do you need a "flash" to form a flashbulb memory? *Journal of Experimental Psychology: General, 122,* 39–46.

Wells, G. L. (1978). Applied eyewitness-testimony research: System variables and estimator variables. *Journal of Personality & Social Psychology, 36,* 1546–1557.

Wells, G. L. (1984). The psychology of lineup identifications. *Journal of Applied Social Psychology, 14,* 89–103.

Wells, G. L. (1993). What do we know about eyewitness identification? *American Psychologist, 48,* 553–571.

Wells, G. L., & Bradfield, A. L. (1999). Distortions in eyewitnesses' recollections: Can the postidentification-feedback effect be moderated? *Psychological Science, 10,* 138–144.

Wells, G. L., & Leippe, M. R. (1981). How do triers of fact infer the accuracy of eyewitness identifications? Using memory for peripheral detail can be misleading. *Journal of Applied Psychology, 66,* 682–687.

Wells, G. L., Lindsay, R. C., & Ferguson, T. J. (1979). Accuracy, confidence, and juror perceptions in eyewitness identification, *Journal of Applied Psychology, 64,* 440–448.

Wells, G. L., Malpass, R. S., Lindsay, R. C. L., Fisher, R. P., Turtle, J. W., & Fulero, S. M. (2000). From the lab to the police station: A successful application of eyewitness research. *American Psychologist, 55,* 581–598.

Wells, G. L., & Olson, E. A. (2001). The other-race effect in eyewitness identification: What do we do about it? *Psychology, Public Policy, and Law, 7,* 230–246.

Wells, G. L., Rydell, S. M., & Seelau, E. P. (1993). On the selection of distractors for eyewitness lineups. *Journal of Applied Psychology, 78,* 835–844.

Wells, G. L., Small, M., Penrod, S., Malpass, R. S., Fulero, S. M., & Brinacombe, C. A. E. (1998). Eyewitness identification procedures: Recommendations for lineups and photospreads. *Law and Human Behavior, 22,* 603–647.

Williams, L. M. (1994). Recall of childhood trauma: A prospective study of women's memories of child sexual abuse. *Journal of Consulting and Clinical Psychology, 62,* 1167–1176.

Wright, D. B., Boyd, C. E., & Tredoux, C. G. (2001). A field study of own-race bias in South Africa and England. *Psychology, Public Policy, and Law, 7,* 119–133.

Yarmey, A. D. (1986). Verbal, visual, and voice identification of a rape suspect under different levels of illumination. *Journal of Applied Psychology, 71,* 363–370.

Yuille, J. C., & Cutshall, J. L. (1986). A case study of eyewitness of a crime. *Journal of Applied Psychology, 71,* 291–301.

Zaragoza, M. S. (1987). Memory, suggestibility and eyewitness testimony in children and adults. In S. J. Ceci, M. P. Toglia, & D. F. Ross (Eds.), *Children's eyewitness memory* (pp. 53–78). New York: Springer-Verlag.

Zaragoza, M. S. (1991). Preschool children's susceptibility to memory impairment. In J. Doris (Ed.), *The suggestibility of children's recollections* (pp. 27–39). Washington, DC: American Psychological Association.

Zaragoza, M. S., Dahlgren, D., & Muench, J. (1992). The role of memory impairment in children's suggestibility. In M. L. Howe, C. J. Brainerd, & V. F. Reyna (Eds.), *The development of long-term retention* (pp. 184–216). New York: Springer-Verlag.

Zaragoza, M. S., McCloskey, M., & Jamis, M. (1987). Misleading postevent information and recall of the original event: Further evidence against the memory impairment hypothesis. *Journal of Experimental Psychology: Learning, Memory, and Cognition, 13,* 36–44.

Zaragoza, M. S., & Mitchell, K. J. (1996). Repeated exposure to suggestion and the creation of false memories. *Psychological Science, 7,* 294–300.

CHAPTER 23

IN SEARCH OF RECOVERED MEMORIES

AMY C. TSAI
UNIVERSITY OF WASHINGTON

SARAH K. MORSBACH
UNIVERSITY OF SOUTH CAROLINA

ELIZABETH F. LOFTUS
UNIVERSITY OF CALIFORNIA, IRVINE

While the general public can casually refer to a "repressed memory" and have little disagreement about its meaning, researchers have struggled for a long time to determine what it means to have a "repressed" memory and how such a memory might function. Freud used the term *repression* throughout his career, and although his definition changed over time, at one point he described it simply as "turning something away and keeping it at a distance from the conscious" (Erdelyi, 1990).

As the term *repressed memory* is used today, it supposedly originates when a child is a victim of a trauma such as sexual abuse. Because of this extreme trauma, the child presumably employs a defense mechanism such as repression or dissociation, which results in an inability to recall the traumatic event. Memory of the event is buried deep in the unconscious, which then causes mental and behavioral symptoms. The unconscious memory lies there for many years until it resurfaces in response to some triggering cue or event, such as therapy or hypnosis (Kihlstrom, 1996). These *recovered memories* have three components: (1) trauma, (2) inability to recall as a coping mechanism, and (3) recovery of the memory. In order to establish whether repression in fact exists, studies of recovered memories must consider each of these components. As we discuss later, numerous efforts to establish the existence of repression as a psychological mechanism have been published, including retrospective studies, prospective studies, and case histories.

The study of recovered memories took on new urgency in the 1990s with a rise in the number of lawsuits brought under claims of recovered memories of childhood sexual abuse. While researchers still debated the existence of repression, courts and legislatures across the country were being forced to determine the merit of such allegations. The Washington state supreme court first addressed the issue of whether such a claim should be heard in *Tyson v. Tyson* (1986). At that time the court was unwilling to extend the statute of limitations, but a few years after *Tyson* the Washington state legislature extended the child sexual abuse statute of limitations to claims involving repression.

Numerous court cases and media attention in the 1990s, which spotlighted celebrities and notables such as Roseanne Barr and Cardinal Bernardin, helped turn the relatively unheard-of phenomenon of repressed memory into a common household word. Do repressed memories exist? If so, how prevalent are they? If there are true cases of repressed memory out there, how does one separate them from any false ones inspired by the media frenzy? Stuck within the legal and scientific morass generated by this debate are the alleged victims and their families, torn apart by new memories of abuse that weren't there just moments before.

For this chapter, we survey the legal status of repression and the current trends toward third-party liability for clinicians diagnosing (or misdiagnosing) repression. The scientific evidence for the phenomenon will also be reviewed. This evidence can be broken down into studies on participants alleging repressed memories and studies on false memory creation using nonabused populations. If a claim of repression gets to trial, other issues arise, such as jury decision making. Finally, suggestions for practice and research are proposed.

LEGAL HISTORY OF REPRESSION

The question of whether repressed memories exist is not just one of scientific interest. Real lives are affected when people claim to recover such memories of childhood abuse. Inevitably, some of those cases find their way into the legal system. The adversarial truth-finding procedure adopted by the legal system is not unlike that of scientific disputes. Each side has its own theories, they battle it out in an arena, and the side with the most convincing arguments and evidence wins. Somewhere in that struggle it is hoped that the truth will come out.

At trial, a jury may have to decide whether abuse, and repression of that abuse, occurred or not. Before the case is brought to trial, however, the court must first determine whether the repressed memory claim can be heard at all. A repressed memory claim might involve allegations of a recovered memory of abuse dating back twenty or more years, well after the statute of limitations would have expired. Whether through the court system or legislative statutes, states have reached different conclusions about whether the statute of limitations should be put on hold in such cases.

Delayed Discovery Doctrine

Most types of claims have a statute of limitations that bars plaintiffs from filing suit beyond a specified statutory period after the action occurred. Statutes of limitation exist to protect defendants from old claims in which the alleged act occurred so far in the past that it may be difficult to prove, and perhaps even more difficult to disprove. In a case often cited by courts, *Order of Railroad Telegraphers v. Railway Express Agency, Inc.* (1944), it was noted that: "Statutes of limitation . . . are designed to promote justice by preventing surprises through the revival of claims that have been allowed to slumber until evidence has been lost, memories have faded, and witnesses have disappeared."

Nevertheless, although this statement makes sense in the context of a plaintiff who delayed bringing suit as a result of matters within his or her own control, the issue is more clouded for situations in which the plaintiff was clearly unable to bring the suit any sooner. For such cases, courts and legislatures have not readily agreed that the defendant's right to be free of stale claims outweighs the plaintiff's right to prosecution.

In recognition of this problem, in some areas a delayed discovery doctrine has been applied in which the statute of limitations does not begin to run until the plaintiff discovers or reasonably should have discovered the cause of action. The delayed discovery doctrine was traditionally used where evidence of clear wrongdoing surfaced after the statute of limitations has expired. For example, in *Ruth v. Dight* (1969), a patient found a surgical sponge left in her abdomen many years after an operation and was able to bring a suit for medical malpractice under the delayed discovery rule.

States have differed in their willingness to apply the discovery rule to childhood abuse cases. This is complicated by a distinction that has been drawn between nonrepressed (Type 1) and repressed (Type 2) claims. In a Type 1 case, the plaintiff claims to have remembered the abuse all along but only recently recognized that her physical and psychological problems stemmed from the early childhood incident; thus, until now she was unable to realize the existence of a cause of action. The Type 2 case is the classic repressed memory scenario, in which the plaintiff claims to have repressed all memory of the abuse until recently. States have come down on both sides of the issue in whether to apply the discovery rule to Type 1 or Type 2 cases. Whether by statute or case law, as of 1995 at least 29 states and the District of Columbia had adopted the discovery rule for cases of childhood sexual abuse, some allowing Type 1, Type 2, or both and some adding additional restrictions such as requiring repression of all memory of the abuse or independent corroboration of the abuse (Ferrante, 1995).

Admissibility of Repression Cases

Common law rulings (court decisions) have played a visible part in the repressed memory debate. Court opinions give insight into the rationales behind allowing or disallowing repressed memory claims in the courtroom, unlike statutes that may or may not have descriptive legislative histories.

As mentioned, the Washington state supreme court first spoke on the issue of repression in a 1986 case, *Tyson v. Tyson*. In a motion for summary judgment based on expiration of the statute of limitations, a district court asked the state supreme court to certify whether the discovery rule applied to an intentional tort involving a repressed memory of abuse. Nancy Tyson alleged that her father sexually abused her from ages 3 to 11 and that she recovered memories of the abuse during therapy at the age of 25. She filed suit at the age of 26. In its reasoning the state supreme court noted the imprecise and subjective nature of psychological therapy. Balancing the risk of spurious claims against the probability of determining the truth, the court stated that because there was no way to independently verify the allegations, the discovery rule should not apply. The decision was superseded by statute in 1989 (RCW 4.16.340). Washington state currently allows suit within three years of discovery of the abuse or three years after the age of 18, whichever is later.

Several cases in California highlight some of the difficult considerations that arise in the repressed memory debate. In *DeRose v. Carswell* (1987), the court of appeal affirmed a dismissal of a Type 1 case in which the plaintiff alleged abuse from ages 4 to 11 and brought suit 13 years later. The court stated that the delayed discovery doctrine only applies when the plaintiff "has not discovered all of the facts essential to the cause of action" (at 371). The court noted that in a repressed memory claim, on the other hand, the plaintiff allegedly does not even realize the abuse occurred.

In the Type 2 case of *Mary D. v. John D.* (1990), the California court reversed a summary judgment ruling that the case was time barred by the statute of limitations. The plaintiff alleged that she was abused at 5 years old and younger and that memories of the abuse surfaced in group therapy at the age of 24. The court noted that cases in other states have applied the delayed discovery doctrine to toll the statute of limitations when there were supporting affidavits from mental health professionals (e.g., *Johnson v. Johnson*). Even though there was no such supporting evidence offered in this case, the court nevertheless held that the plaintiff's complaint was sufficient to overcome a motion for summary judgment because the defendant only argued that the plaintiff's claim was time barred and did not negate the repressed memory claim. Therefore, the plaintiff's mere statement that she was a victim of repressed memories of abuse was sufficient to defeat the defendant's motion for summary judgment. One danger that arises from a court allowing one type of claim but not the other is that it could encourage plaintiffs to allege characteristics that meet the criteria of that jurisdiction.

Among the states that have allowed Type 2 claims, Michigan has employed a stiff standard of acceptance, requiring that the plaintiff must make a case for repression and also provide corroboration that the abuse occurred before the discovery rule will apply (*Meiers-Post v. Schafer*, 1988). In *Meiers-Post*, corroboration of the abuse was an easy call because the defendant, a high school teacher, admitted to a sexual relationship with the plaintiff, his student.

Similarly, Nevada required "clear and convincing" proof of abuse in *Peterson v. Bruen* (1990). In that case there were photographs and criminal convictions of Bruen, who had abused Peterson in a Big Brother program. Five years later, Peterson alleged that he recovered memories of the abuse in therapy (the normal statute of limitations for abuse was two years). The court noted that the concern of stale evidence did not apply where there was "clear and convincing" evidence of abuse, so there was no reason to give defendants the benefit of the statute of limitations. The court noted concern for plaintiffs who do not meet a standard of "clear and convincing" but left the issue for the state legislature to address. In 1991, the Nevada legislature extended the statute of limitations for childhood sexual abuse to within 10 years after the plaintiff either reached the age of 18 or within 10 years of when the plaintiff "discovers or reasonably should have discovered that his injury was caused by the sexual abuse" (Nev. Rev. Stat. §11.215(1)).

Similarly, after *DeRose v. Carswell* and *Mary D. v. John D.*, California statutorily tolled the limitations period for childhood sexual abuse claims. In California, childhood sexual abuse cases must be commenced "within eight years of the date the plaintiff attains the age of majority or within three years of the date the plaintiff discovers or reasonably should have discovered that psychological injury or illness occurring after the age of majority was caused by the sexual abuse, whichever period expires later" (Ca. Civ. Proc. Code §340.1). For plaintiffs 26 years of age or older, California also requires that the plaintiff file "certificates of merit," one from the attorney stating that the claim has merit, and one from an independent mental health professional stating that there is a reasonable basis to believe that the plaintiff experienced childhood sexual abuse.

In those states allowing Type 2 claims, the battle over repression does not necessarily end once a case survives summary judgment. The New Hampshire supreme court applied the discovery rule to repressed memories of abuse in *McCollum v. D'Arcey* (1994) but left with the plaintiff the burden of proving the abuse and validating the phenomenon of repression if challenged.

In a case involving alleged repressed memories of childhood sexual abuse dating back 33 years, the Utah supreme court held that the therapist's methods were not proven to be scientifically reliable and thus evidence derived from the recovered memories was inadmissible (*Franklin v. Stevenson*, 1999). After having panic attacks and hearing voices, Franklin began seeing a therapist who employed techniques such as relaxation and asking a question with one hand and answering with the other. Franklin subsequently recovered memories of her cousin Stevenson abusing her as a child and successfully sued him for $750,000 but the district judge granted a judgment notwithstanding the verdict. Franklin appealed and lost. In its decision, the court noted: "Neither the record nor our research indicate that these techniques enjoy a general acceptance within the field," and further added in a footnote that "In fact, our research suggests that the idea of memory repression itself, let alone the methods of recovery, is a point of disagreement within the medical, psychiatric, and psychological communities."

Courts have faced similar issues in the criminal context. The superior court of New Hampshire was called upon to judge the admissibility of memories of assault in cases of aggravated felonious sexual assault. Testimony by the alleged victims regarding memories recovered during psychotherapy was deemed inadmissible because of the scientific unreliability of the phenomenon of repression and because under New Hampshire's rules of scientific evidence it lacked general acceptance in the field of psychology. This decision was affirmed by the New Hampshire supreme court in 1997 (*State v. Hungerford*, 1997).

As an important side note, in *People v. Frazer* (1999), the California supreme court allowed criminal prosecution of sexual molestation well past the statute of limitations for a crime that allegedly occurred 12 years earlier. The California Penal Code allows prosecution of certain sexual crimes to be brought within one year after the victim reports an independently corroborated crime to the police (Cal. Penal Code § 803(g)). The U.S. Supreme Court later ruled that California's law cannot be used to prosecute individuals whose statute of limitations for their alleged crimes had expired prior to passage of the new law (*Stogner v. California*, 2003). Nevertheless, the law arguably sets the stage for criminal prosecutions of repressed memory claims of childhood abuse in the future.

The great legal and scientific controversy over the validity of the phenomenon of repression also has implications for clinical practice. Clinicians need to create an accepting environment in which a client can safely recall and work through sensitive and difficult issues, but must do so in a manner that minimizes the possibility of wild confabulations. Juries have substantiated this concern in third-party lawsuits.

Traditionally, only a patient could sue a therapist for malpractice because the therapist had a duty of care to the patient arising out of their relationship (Rock, 1995). But in *Tarasoff v. Regents of the University of California* (1976), the supreme court of California stated that a clinician also owes a duty to protect any person whom the clinician determines is endangered by his client. In *Tarasoff*, parents of a murder victim were permitted to sue therapists whose client had confided an intent to kill the victim. Since then, courts have also extended third-party liability to cases involving allegations of repressed memories.

In a highly publicized case in California, Holly Ramona's father was awarded $500,000 against her therapists for negligent infliction of emotional distress (*Ramona v. Isabella*, 1995) when claims of childhood sexual abuse arose out of Holly's initial treatment for bulimia and he lost his $300,000/year job as a result (Carro & Hatala, 1996). On the other hand, the supreme court of Illinois, in reversing an appellate court decision, affirmed the dismissal of a father's suit against his daughter's therapist in *Doe v. McKay* (1998). John Doe alleged that the therapist was negligent in diagnosing his daughter's problems as being the result of repressed memories of childhood sexual abuse. The court held that because the plaintiff did not have a therapeutic relationship with the therapist, the therapist did not owe a duty of care to him. In declining to find a duty of care to nonpatient third parties, the court noted that allowing such liability would "place therapists in a difficult position, requiring them to answer to competing demands and to divide their loyalty between sharply different interests. . . . This would be fundamentally inconsistent with the therapist's obligation to the patient."

The disagreement over third-party liability in repressed memory cases emphasizes the difficult situation facing clinicians. However, one need not necessarily resort to a callous assessment of appropriate practices based solely on the jurisdiction in which one practices. Instead, clinicians can balance the needs of the patient against potential harms both to the patient and others by minimizing those practices most likely to lead to the creation of false memories, some of which we discuss later in this chapter.

SCIENTIFIC EVIDENCE FOR REPRESSION

How widespread are claims of repression? Researchers' estimates of claims of repression have ranged from extremely low to well above 50 percent. For example, Melchert (1996) found that 9 percent of undergraduates reporting sexual abuse said that they had previously forgotten the abuse because of repression, whereas Herman and Shatzow (1987) found that 64 percent of women in a therapy group for sexual abuse survivors reported having had at least some degree of amnesia for their abuse. Other repressed memory studies (e.g., Briere & Conte, 1993; Williams, 1994) have yielded estimates somewhere in between those found by Melchert and by Herman and Shatzow. Clinician reports provide another source for estimating the prevalence of repression claims. Pope and Tabachnick (1995) surveyed 382 clinicians and found that 73 percent had at least one patient who claimed to have recovered a memory of being sexually abused.

In the face of so many reports and studies claiming to document repression, some have argued that it is foolhardy to deny the existence of true cases of repressed memory (Bowman & Mertz, 1996). Others have argued that these numbers merely reflect a nationwide hysteria that began in the late 1980s and is already in decline as courts and researchers continue to question the scientific validity of repression (Johnston, 1996). This nation is not unfamiliar with cases of mass hysteria, such as the Salem, Massachusetts, witch trials of 1692. In order to evaluate the validity of repression as a phenomenon, it is insufficient to rely solely on the existence of widespread reports. Rather, one must evaluate the scientific validity of each documentation of repression. Only after examining the evidence thoroughly can one decide whether one believes that there is a sufficient basis for concluding that repression exists.

The Scientific Study of Repression

Pope and Hudson (1995) outlined two criteria necessary for a study to establish the existence of repressed memories. First, the researcher must produce evidence confirming that the traumatic event occurred. Second, it must be established that the participant developed psychogenic amnesia. *Psychogenic amnesia* is an inability to remember caused by psychological factors and does not include amnesia caused by biological factors, childhood amnesia, ordinary forgetting, consciously trying to forget the abuse, or alleging abuse for secondary gain. The most direct way to investigate repressed memories would be to cause participants to experience a traumatic event in the lab and longitudinally study their memory of this traumatic experience. Clearly, however, this approach is unethical. Instead, researchers have used retrospective methods, prospective methods, and case histories.

Retrospective Methods

Retrospective studies examine claims of prior childhood sexual abuse. Upon identifying a possible history of childhood sexual abuse, researchers then assess whether repression ever occurred. In one of the first of such studies, Herman and Shatzow (1987) examined 53 female incest survivors in therapy groups. Of these women, 14 (26%) were classified as having severe amnesia for their abuse and 39 (74%) were reportedly able to corroborate having been abused. The majority of clients (64%) reported some degree of amnesia. The authors therefore concluded that traumatic memories of abuse can be repressed and recovered. However, it is unclear from the study's report how many of the 14 women classified with severe amnesia were among the corroborated cases. It is possible that the corroborated cases all came from patients who had either partial amnesia or no amnesia for their abuse and that, therefore, none of the "severe" amnesia cases were corroborated. In addition, corroboration was defined quite loosely, ranging from the perpetrator's admission to statements by other family members suggesting that they too may have been abused. Thus, Herman and Shatzow did not conclusively establish that trauma occurred. In addition, women in survivor support groups may experience social pressures to retrieve abuse memories, increasing the likelihood of false memory creation.

Briere and Conte (1993) also used a retrospective methodology, surveying 468 patients with self-reported sexual abuse. Fifty-nine percent of the patients responded yes to the question "During the period of time between when the first forced sexual experience happened and your eighteenth birthday was there ever a time when you could not remember the forced sexual experience?" Briere and Conte concluded that amnesia for abuse is a common occurrence among patients with sexual abuse histories. This study has been criticized for the ambiguous meaning of the term *remember*. Participants could have responded yes for other reasons besides repression: simple forgetting, a consciously avoided memory, or an amorphous script of frequently occurring abuse with little memory for individual incidents. Another difficulty with the study is that patients were not asked to corroborate the self-reported abuse. Third, it is unknown whether the sample was adversely affected by any "suggestive" therapist biases. All participants were seeing a particular network of therapists and some could have recovered false memories of abuse.

Another retrospective study by Melchert (1996) attempted to address the problem of the ambiguity of the term *remember*. Out of 553 students, Melchert asked 149 who reported having been sexually, physically, or emotionally abused whether there was a time when they couldn't remember the abuse. He included several options for why the participant may not have remembered the abuse, including repression, simple forgetting, organic causes, or conscious avoidance. Seven participants who reported sexual abuse claimed they forgot the abuse because of repression. Of those participants who reported physical and emotional abuse, seven and four, respectively, claimed to have repressed memories. Unfortunately, no corroboration of abuse was required of participants.

One major difficulty with the retrospective methodology is the need to dip into the past to ascertain abuse. Thus, the first prong of Pope and Hudson's (1995) criteria can be hard to prove. In retrospective studies this has been compounded by the use of self-report measures. Moreover, in virtually all of these cases corroboration is poorly assessed or documented.

Prospective Methods

Williams (1994) employed a longitudinal prospective method to first identify individuals known to have been abused in childhood and then later asked them if they remembered the abuse. She used 129 participants who had been examined in a hospital for sexual abuse as children. Seventeen years after their appearance at the hospital, participants were interviewed about any sexual abuse that they experienced in childhood. Thirty-eight percent of participants did not report the index abuse event (the hospital-documented event) and 12 percent failed to report ever having been abused. Although Williams did not draw any specific conclusions about repression, this study has been used in courts as proof that repression of abuse memories occurs. However, many critics of this study (e.g., Pope & Hudson, 1995) have pointed out that not reporting the index event is different from not remembering the event. Some women may not have wanted to disclose abuse to a stranger conducting an interview. In addition, one-third of the events involved fondling only, which, depending on its severity, may not have been characterized as abuse by some women. Other alternative explanations for not remembering abuse exist besides repression. For example, a woman who was abused throughout childhood may have simply forgotten any one particular incident. Alternately, those participants who were under the age of 3 when seen at the hospital may not have been able to remember the abuse because of childhood amnesia.

Case Histories

Although statistically the least conclusive, case histories provide a different perspective on the question of whether repressed memories exist. Is it possible to find at least one documented case of true repression? One benefit of using case studies is that the therapist generally knows a lot of information about the patient. Problems include the potential influence of therapist biases and the fact that the therapist may need to mask critical details of the case study in order to protect the confidentiality of the patient.

A case history of a 40-year-old man with possible repressed memories was presented by Nash (1994). The client entered therapy with complaints of sexual dysfunction, depression, and violent outbursts. Through hypnosis, he recalled childhood abuse by a cousin and his friends; they masturbated while looking at his buttocks. When he confronted his cousin, the cousin admitted that the incident took place. The corroboration of abuse in this case history is compelling. However, one alternative to a recovered memory explanation is that amnesia for the event was caused by alcohol or drug use and not the traumatic nature of the event; the client was a recovered alcoholic and had used drugs. Another possibility involves encoding specificity. If the client somehow forgot that the event occurred, therapy for sexual dysfunction could have brought to mind sexually related memories, including the memory involving his cousin.

In another case history, Corwin and Olafson (1997) published transcripts from videotaped interviews with "Jane Doe" at ages 6 and 17. At age 6 Jane disclosed sexual abuse by her mother to Corwin. At age 17, Jane remembered making abuse allegations as a child but appeared to Corwin to have no memory of the abuse itself. During an interview with Corwin, she seemed to spontaneously remember the sexual abuse. This case is currently being used in court as evidence of the existence of repressed memories. However, several factors conspire to raise doubt as to whether or not Jane was abused. The main evidence that Jane was abused came from clinical evaluations by Corwin and other professionals and from Jane's statements at age 6, but children's statements can be extremely vulnerable to outside suggestion (Bruck, Ceci, & Hembrooke, 1998). In fact, at age 6 Jane also alleged and later retracted an accusation that her father abused her, suggesting that her testimony is not entirely reliable. In addition, abuse allegations occurred in the midst of a custody battle, and professionals who saw Jane were divided as to whether or not she was abused.

Schooler, Ambadar, and Bendiksen (1997) presented four case studies involving what they term "discovered" memories. One case in particular, that of "DN," appeared to contain quite compelling evidence of forgetting. DN was sexually abused as a child and never forgot these memories. She was later raped at age 22 and successfully convicted her attacker shortly thereafter. Sometime after that, she was believed to have repressed the memory of being raped. At age 35 DN joined a childhood sexual abuse survivors support group and was told during one session that child sex abuse survivors are often also abused as adults. While driving home from that session, her rape memory came back to her. When asked in retrospect by the authors about the rape memory, she stated that she was totally unaware of this memory until she discovered it at age 35. A phone call by the authors to the lawyer involved in the rape case served as corroborative evidence; the lawyer verified that DN's rapist had been tried and convicted. The corroboration in this case seems particularly strong, and there do not appear to be any biological causes for amnesia. Using Pope and Hudson's (1995) criteria, this case study successfully established a trauma, forgetting, and retrieval, but some questions remain pertaining to the nature of the amnesia. Was DN really completely unable to recall the rape post trial? At what point did she "forget," and would she have been able to recall the rape if prompted? Was the experience simply forgotten and then triggered later by a retrieval cue? Or was there some process beyond ordinary forgetting and remembering that was involved in DN's case?

Retractors

Accounts from retractors provide another source of evidence about the legitimacy of repressed memories in that they offer proof that recovered memories of sexual abuse can be false. In short, retractors are people who truly believed that they were abused and had vivid memories of the abuse but later came to the conclusion that these beliefs and memories were false.

One such retractor was described with the pseudonym "Lynn" (Loftus & Ketcham, 1994). Lynn entered therapy with depression, anxiety, and an eating disorder. She always remembered being raped by her uncle, but her therapist suggested to her that she had repressed memories of abuse by her parents. Although Lynn denied that such abuse had taken place, she was asked to perform exercises such as imagination and dream analysis in order to "remember" abuse by her parents. She did not, however, recover abuse memories until she entered a therapy group with other women trying to recover memories. Lynn confronted her parents about the abuse and refused any contact with them when they denied that the abuse took place. In the next year, Lynn attempted suicide five different times and was admitted to a hospital. When her insurance ran out and she was forced to leave the hospital, Lynn slowly began to put the pieces of her life back together. She came to realize that her memories of abuse by her parents were false.

Accounts from retractors such as Lynn provide examples of false recovered memories and indicate that estimates of the prevalence of repression may be overinflated. What is particularly compelling is that people can be adamant that their recovered memories are true at the time of their recovery yet later come to realize they are false. This misplaced confidence shows the power that a false memory can hold over a person. To further confuse the issue, however, there is the possibility that a retractor might be under pressures to falsely retract memories of abuse, just as some patients may be under pressure to falsely retrieve them.

It is possible that repression is a real phenomenon, but the quantitative studies that have been done to date have methodological problems that make their results inconclusive. Pope and Hudson (1995) are not the only ones who have failed to find support for the phenomenon of repression. For example, Holmes (1994) also reviewed the laboratory research on repression and concluded that the existence of repression has never been demonstrated. Some case studies offer compelling evidence of repressed and recovered memories. However, some the dangers of relying on case studies alone are that the authors generally provide only part of the information, may change facts to preserve confidentiality, and are subject to confirmation biases. These inconclusive findings are ironic considering the popular belief that repression is widespread and experienced by many. Retractor accounts offer individual proof that recovered and repressed memories can be false, but the phenomenon of false memory creation has been scientifically studied as well.

Evidence on False Memory Creation

The flip side of the research coin of whether repressed memories exist is whether false memories can be implanted. That is, if researchers have been unable to conclusively establish the phenomenon of repressed memories to everyone's satisfaction, at least answering the question of whether recovered memories can be false lends some evidence to the debate.

Unlike evidence for the existence of repressed (and subsequently recovered) memories, evidence for the malleability of memory is quite strong. Research on the suggestibility of memory has followed two main types of designs: misinformation and repeated imagination. In the *misinformation* paradigm, a participant is fed misleading information about a previously presented critical item and may later recall the misinformation instead of the true original information. In the *repeated imagination* paradigm, a participant is presented with a false event and through repeated exposure may eventually come to believe that the event happened or at least increase belief in the likelihood of its occurrence.

Misinformation Studies

The *misinformation effect* is where introduction of misleading information about an event can lead to subsequent distortions in memory reports about that event. In an early study, Loftus, Miller, and Burns (1978) showed participants a slide show involving a car accident and a stop sign. In one condition a subsequent narrative mentioned the presence of a yield sign instead. Participants made significantly more errors in the misinformation condition than when accurate or irrelevant postevent information was introduced. The misinformation effect has been demonstrated in children as well. For example, Ceci, Ross, and Toglia (1987) found that children's memory recognition of a story was hampered by introduction of misleading postevent information about details in the story.

Applied implications for the misinformation effect have largely been discussed in terms of eyewitness suggestibility. The concern is raised that the eyewitness recall of a person presented with leading questions may be unduly swayed by the content of the questions. This has been a hallmark of misinformation studies: The presentation of seemingly innocuous questions that make erroneous assumptions about the facts (assuming the presence of a yield sign) leads to a distortion in recall of the true event (whether a yield sign was in fact present).

The process of recovering repressed memories contains similar elements. If a therapist asks a patient to think back on or imagine a possible scenario of childhood sexual abuse, the patient now has two potentially conflicting events to reconcile: what happened in his or her childhood and what he or she was asked to imagine in the therapy session. Under the right circumstances, memory for these two separate situations may become confused in the patient's mind. In subsequent imagination studies, rather than presenting a misleading item about a prior event, researchers turned to investigating whether erroneous memories for whole events could be created.

Imagination and Repeated Suggestion

In one of the first studies of false autobiographical memories, Loftus and Coan (described in Loftus and Pickrell, 1995) successfully established a false memory of being lost in a mall in a single 14-year-old participant. The boy was give three true events from his early childhood and one false event (getting lost in a mall), and asked to record details of the events over five days. Over the five days he began to recall more and more details about the fictitious event. In a final interview he rated the false event as more likely than two of the three true events, and in the debriefing he was also reluctant to believe the event never happened.

After this initial success, many studies using a similar methodology followed. For example, as a more extreme test of false memory creation, Hyman, Husband, and Billings (1995) introduced events that were more implausible, including spilling a punchbowl on parents of the bride at a wedding, overhead sprinklers activating in a grocery store, and releasing a parking brake and causing the car to roll into something. After three interviews spaced every other day, they found that true events increased from 89 percent to 95 percent recalled and false events increased from none to 25 percent recalled by the third interview. In addition, participants who described related information in their background (e.g., attended weddings) were more likely to create false recalls. Hyman and colleagues suggested that schematic knowledge may give people a basis around which to construct false memories. They also suggested that experimental demands to recall details increased the manipulation's effectiveness. In terms of false recovered memories, Hyman and colleagues extrapolated that events in childhood such as unwanted hugging or physical discipline might contribute "building blocks" for recall of abuse and that repeated questioning by therapists, as well as directly suggesting matches between self-knowledge and possible events, could encourage the creation of a false recall.

On the other end of the spectrum, it has been demonstrated that something as mild as imagining an event a single time can impact one's beliefs about the likelihood of an event's occurring. Garry, Manning, Loftus, and Sherman (1996) asked participants to rate the likelihood that certain events happened to them before the age of 10. Two weeks later, participants imagined and were questioned about four of the events and again rated the likelihood of the events under the pretext that the experimenters had lost the first survey. Garry and colleagues found that likelihood ratings increased more for the imagined items (34%) than the nonimagined items (25%). If a single imagination session is enough to generate differences in a person's subjective beliefs that an event occurred, then clinicians must be even more cautious in treating their clients.

Getting to Trial: Juror Attitudes Toward Repression

Although no conclusive proof of repression has been offered, courts are still left with claims of repression and the thorny problem of what to do with them. From the standpoint of attorneys, an important practical question other than whether repression exists is: How will jurors respond to claims of repression? Several researchers have used the mock juror paradigm in attempting to answer this question. Mock juror studies involving repressed memories usually have both a repressed condition, where the plaintiff repressed and recovered abuse memories, and a nonrepressed condition, where the plaintiff remembered the abuse all along. Participants are presented with a legal scenario and asked to judge the case on various dimensions (e.g., verdict, credibility of the parties, etc.).

Some findings suggest that participants are more skeptical of a repressed than a nonrepressed memory case. In the first of a series of three studies, Loftus, Weingardt, and Hoffman (1993) presented participants with a scenario in which a daughter accused her father of childhood sexual abuse in a civil court case. In the repressed condition she recovered the memory 10 years later in therapy, and in the nonrepressed condition she remembered the abuse but did not realize the damage it caused her until she was in therapy 10 years later. Overall, participants favored the daughter's claim over the father's, but more so in the nonrepressed than repressed condition. Key, Warren, and Ross (1996) used a scenario in which the plaintiff did not sue the alleged abuser until 20 years after the abuse took place. They found that the defendant was convicted more in the nonrepressed than in the repressed case. In other words, when the plaintiff's case involved a repressed memory, the defendant was less likely to be convicted. Thus, once again the repressed memory claim appeared to be viewed with greater skepticism. Tsai, Morsbach, and Loftus (1999) used a case scenario involving a stepdaughter accusing her stepfather of either sexual or physical abuse. They found that in both the physical and sexual abuse case scenarios the plaintiff was viewed more skeptically by mock jurors when she repressed the memory of her abuse.

Other studies show no difference in the degree of skepticism with which the plaintiff's case is viewed in repressed versus nonrepressed claims. Golding, Sego, Sanchez, and Hasemann (1995) used a scenario in which a 26-year-old woman claimed sexual abuse by her father at the age of 6. Unlike Loftus and colleagues' (1993) study, believability of the parties between repressed and nonrepressed cases showed no significant differences. That is, participants showed neither more nor less skepticism toward the plaintiff in a repressed memory case as compared to a nonrepressed memory case. Tetford and Schuller (1996) had participants read a scenario where a 29-year-old woman accused her father of sexually abusing her between the ages of 6 and 10. Consistent with Golding, Sego, Sanchez, and Hasemann (1995), whether or not her memory was repressed did not affect participants' evaluations of the case.

Thus, there are ambiguous findings for juror reactions to claims of repression. Some studies have found no differences in juror assessments of repressed and nonrepressed claims, whereas other studies have found differences. In none of these studies did participants view the repressed memory claim with *less* skepticism than the nonrepressed memory claim. The repression effect, when found, tended to go in the other direction, with jurors showing more skepticism towards repressed memories.

SUGGESTIONS FOR PRACTICE

The Courage to Heal, often called the bible of the incest recovery movement, mentions several signs of childhood abuse in the absence of memory of abuse, such as being scared by certain words or facial expressions, sleeping with clothes on in junior high school, or repeated vaginal infections (Bass & Davis, 1994, p. 26). It can be dangerous to draw conclusions of abuse from such vague symptoms, yet the needs of a safe, healing, therapeutic relationship sometimes diverge from the truth. As Bass and Davis (1994) note, "To say 'I was abused,' you don't need the kind of proof that would stand up in a court of law" (p. 26). The situation becomes more complicated when people act on such beliefs of abuse, necessitating court intervention.

Validity of Indicators of Childhood Sexual Abuse

Several studies discuss the various symptoms found in patients (e.g., Claridge, 1992; Herman & Shatzow, 1987). Some of the main symptoms include eating disorders, depression, low self-esteem, promiscuous sex, sexual dysfunction, panic attacks, difficulty with intimate relationships, and nightmares. Loftus and Ketcham (1994) issue a warning against such lists, pointing out that they include relatively harmless parts of a normal personality. Other researchers have analyzed these symptoms and determined that they are not necessarily indicative of sexual abuse. Pope and Hudson (1992) examined six studies exploring the relationship between childhood sexual abuse and bulimia. They found that four of the six studies showed no difference in rates of bulimia between adult sexual abuse survivors and members of the general population and that the methodology in all six studies tended to skew in favor of a connection between child sex abuse and bulimia. Kendall-Tackett, Williams, and Finkelhor (1993) did a meta-analysis of forty-five studies in which the prevalence of various symptoms of childhood abuse was compared with the prevalence of symptoms in the general population. They found that those who were sexually abused as children had more symptoms than those who were not abused, but no one symptom was exhibited by a majority of the sexually abused children. In addition, they found that approximately 33 percent of victims showed no symptoms. Rind, Tromovitch, and Bauserman (1998) conducted a meta-analysis on a sample of college students. They found a small positive correlation between childhood sexual abuse and a number of symptoms. However, when controlling for dysfunctional family environments, the relationship was reduced to almost zero. Thus, it appears that although many abused children showed more symptoms than did those who were not abused, the relationship between childhood sexual abuse and specific sexual abuse sequelae was weak or nonexistent, depending on the symptom. The lack of a clearly defined set of symptoms creates the potential for many false positives of recovered memories in adults exhibiting "symptoms" of childhood abuse. Potential clinicians' biases in interpreting these symptoms could make the task of correctly identifying a sexual abuse history based on symptoms even more difficult.

Biases in Decision Making

If there is no core set of symptoms that can accurately predict when someone has been abused, then clinicians face a formidable task if they wish to ascertain whether a patient might have a repressed memory of abuse. This is a different problem from determining how best to treat someone who has known from the beginning that he or she was abused, where the malleability of memory may be a nonissue. In diagnosing "repressed" memories of abuse, the lack of valid indicators leaves clinicians more susceptible to several kinds of decision-making biases.

The phenomenon of *illusory correlations* can lead clinicians to pay more attention to invalid than valid signs of a disorder; they may see a correlation between certain behaviors and diagnosticity that simply is not there. Chapman and Chapman (1969) gave undergraduates Rorschach responses paired with symptom statements in which some of the Rorschach responses were set up to correlate with symptoms of homosexuality. They found that students ignored these and instead saw illusory correlations between intuitive but invalid Rorschach signs and homosexuality. They observed a similar trend in 32 clinicians' perceptions of symptoms displayed by their homosexual patients; clinicians tended to list having seen signs of homosexuality in their homosexual patients that were in fact not valid predictors but that were strongly associated verbally with homosexuality by an independent group of undergraduates. In the area of childhood sexual abuse, a clinician might see an illusory correlation between childhood abuse and a "symptom" that seems like a logical sign of abuse. For instance, poor relationships was one of the most commonly agreed-upon indicators of childhood sexual abuse in a study by Poole, Lindsay, Memon, and Bull (1995), reported by about 15 percent of U.S. psychologists, yet marital relationship problems were also reported as one of the most frequent presenting complaints of adult female clients in general (81%).

In a similar vein, Shweder and D'Andrade's (1980) systematic distortion hypothesis proposes that in making memory judgments of behavior people mistake similarity in meaning for observed occurrences. Twenty undergraduates watched a tape of a family interview, then immediately rated family members on behavior categories from memory. They tended to misremember having seen behaviors that were closely related in meaning to each other rather than the behaviors that were actually on the videotape. Although one can argue that these were untrained undergraduates, still a clinician should make sure he or she does not overreport symptoms conceptually related to other observed symptoms but that did not occur.

A third phenomenon that may influence clinician diagnoses is confirmation bias. Confirmation bias is a predisposition to look for confirming rather than disconfirming evidence. For example, on a variety of rule discovery tasks, people tend to test hypotheses that would confirm what they think the rule is, even when a disconfirming strategy would be more effective or even necessary (Wason & Johnson-Laird, 1972). For example, if a clinician strongly believes in the prevalence of repression of childhood sexual abuse, he may be predisposed to look for evidence that confirms that diagnosis and discredit, reinterpret, or fail to consider evidence that disconfirms the diagnosis. A clinician who is aware of such predispositions can take steps to minimize its impact on his or her practice. One possible strategy, if a diagnosis of repression looked imminent, would be for the clinician to take a step back and explore alternative explanations that fit the same behavior profile that the patient is exhibiting.

In short, the absence of empirically validated and agreed-upon indicators of abuse opens the door for many biases. If a clinician believes childhood sexual abuse (CSA) is a likely diagnosis, she may be affected by confirmation bias and interpret a presenting symptom as a sign of CSA, discounting other possible diagnoses for which that symptom occurs. Hypothetically, a focus on confirmatory symptoms may also lead to an overestimation of the number of related symptoms observed, which will further confirm the diagnosis. She may also employ a positive test strategy, focusing on techniques designed to elicit memories of abuse. In the long term, as she diagnoses patients with CSA, this can perpetuate illusions that certain behaviors co-occur with and are diagnostic of CSA. Awareness of such potential biases can go a long way toward defusing them. Active consideration of alternative explanations for symptoms would help as well.

Therapeutic Techniques

Decision-making biases have an ongoing impact on a clinician's effectiveness, but the therapeutic techniques used have a direct impact on the patients themselves. As false memory research has shown, people can be susceptible to suggestion, and few may be as vulnerable to suggestion as a patient in a close clinician-patient relationship. What this means for a clinician is that even if he or she takes special care to avoid any biases in judgment, the patient may still be unduly swayed by suggestions that arise in the therapeutic process.

Some of the main techniques used by therapists to bring out allegedly repressed memories include hypnosis, age regression, dream interpretation, guided imagery and imagination, journaling and writing assignments, and interpreting body symptoms. Poole, Lindsay, Memon, and Bull (1995) surveyed 202 therapists and found that 71 percent had used at least one of these techniques to recover patients' memories and that 58 percent reported using two or more. In addition, 25 percent reported a number of beliefs and practices consistent with a focus on helping patients recover memories. It is worth noting, however, that the study by Poole and colleagues was published in 1995, and the frequency of use of such techniques and practices to bring out repressed memories may be different today. In the next section we discuss potential dangers associated with some of the practices and techniques seen in recovered memory therapy, including the use of leading questions, hypnosis, dream interpretation, and imagination exercises.

Leading Questions

Although technically not a form of therapy, it is quite possible that a clinician would employ leading questions to try to elicit responses from a reticent patient. This practice by itself is not inherently harmful. Problems arise only if the leading information is erroneous; unfortunately it can often be hard for both clinician and therapist to separate what is and isn't the truth. In a manner akin to the misinformation paradigm, erroneous information can be subtly incorporated into a patient's memory through implicit suggestion. Consider a hypothetical scenario in which a clinician might ask a patient to assume he or she was abused for the purposes of working out a sexual dysfunction probem: "When you were abused, do you remember what you were thinking?" Over time, reinforcement of the assumption of abuse may take on a different meaning than it had at the beginning of therapy.

One need only turn to the third-party lawsuits that have been brought successfully against mental health professionals to see examples of the power a clinician holds over patients in shaping their memories and beliefs. A clinician has the difficult task of making sure that patient-centered truths arrived at in the therapeutic process for the patient's treatment do not have adverse real-world consequences.

Hypnosis

Poole, Lindsay, Memon, and Bull (1995) surveyed two U.S. and one British population of psychologists. The second group of U.S. psychologists were asked more directly about repressed memory cases, so discussion of the first group will be omitted here. It was found that hypnosis was used by 34 percent of U.S. psychologists and 5 percent of British psychologists for memory recovery purposes. Despite this large percentage, many other therapists were skeptical of its use. Thirty-three percent of U.S. psychologists and 44 percent of British psychologists disapproved of the use of hypnosis.

Lynn and Nash (1994) noted that the imagination aspects of hypnosis and a belief in its ability to improve recall may encourage confusion between fantasy and reality. In a review of the scientific evidence on hypnosis, a report from the AMA Council on Scientific Affairs (1985) cautioned that hypnosis increases the number of both correct and incorrect statements and that there are no reliable means of discriminating between those that are true and those that are false.

Repeated questioning about the memories in the context of hypnosis as a recall-enhancement technique can also strengthen belief in the memories regardless of their accuracy (Lynn & Nash, 1994). Thus, a clinician who uses hypnosis runs the risk that the patient will generate a false memory; furthermore, if the clinician touts hypnosis as an accurate strategy of memory retrieval, it may strengthen the patient's confidence in memories both true and false. Use of hypnotically induced or refreshed memories can also create problems of legal admissibility.

The AMA (1985) makes several recommendations for the prudent use of hypnosis, including restricting its use to investigative procedures with proper safeguards. The subject's psychological history should first be ascertained and informed consent obtained dispelling misconceptions about hypnosis, and hypnosis should be performed by a qualified psychiatrist or psychologist aware of the legal implications in his or her jurisdiction.

Dream Interpretation

Dream interpretation is another technique sometimes used by therapists to recover memories. One theory behind dream interpretation is that dreams come from the unconscious mind and that dream interpretation may thus provide insight into memories that exist only in the unconscious mind. Poole, Lindsay, Memon, and Bull (1995) found that 37 percent of U.S. psychologists and 25 percent of British psychologists used dream interpretation to help clients recover abuse memories.

Using dream interpretation as a memory recovery technique can be a potentially problematic practice. An individual's dreams are often related to his or her day's events or thoughts. Therefore, a patient could have dreams involving sexual or abuse-related experiences not because he or she was abused, but simply because he or she was engaging in therapy, memory work, or thinking about the topic of abuse. Dreams containing sexual or abuse-related experiences could reinforce both the patient's and the therapist's belief that the patient repressed memories of abuse. Research by Mazzoni and Loftus (1998) has shown that individuals may increase their confidence that a particular event took place if an authority figure, such as a therapist, states that the individual's dreams are suggestive of that event. Thus, a therapist interpreting a patient's dream as symbolic of abuse could conceivably influence that patient to believe he or she was abused.

Imagination

Imagination can be used as a tool for memory recovery in a wide variety of ways. Poole, Lindsay, Memon, and Bull (1995) identified two techniques involving imagination, guided imagery related to abuse situations and instructions to give free rein to the imagination. They found that guided imagery was used by 32 percent of U.S. psychologists and 14 percent of British psychologists, whereas 22 percent and 18 percent, respectively, gave patients instructions to give free rein to the imagination.

Given the evidence that imagining a childhood event can increase one's confidence that such an event occurred (Garry et al., 1996), imagining abuse may increase a patient's belief that the abuse occurred regardless of whether or not it actually did. It is also possible that a patient who repeatedly imagines being abused may begin to have trouble differentiating between what is imagined and what is real.

In many respects, cautions against suggestive techniques of memory recovery are common sense. It is up to the clinician to ensure that he or she maintains objectivity, especially in encouraging the client to explore subjective impressions.

FUTURE DIRECTIONS

One of the most convincing documentations of some sort of forgetting of abuse is Williams's (1994) prospective study. By Pope and Hudson's (1995) criteria, Williams was able to establish abuse and provide modest evidence for failure to recall the abuse. Nevertheless, as we have discussed, this study is not without its own problems in interpretation. Future studies may return to the longitudinal design and attempt to obtain corroboration of the abuse beyond hospital records, such as interviewing other family members, including family members in the study so that discussions of the abuse with the victim can be monitored over time, and interviewing the victims who forget the abuse with successively greater degrees of prompting to ascertain the nature of their inability to remember the abuse. Those failing to recall any aspect of the abuse would need to be monitored indefinitely until the memory was in fact "recovered" in order to distinguish the phenomenon from normal forgetting.

Thus far, the body of research on repression has relied on defining it by its consequences, whether memory of a trauma was ever forgotten for a period of time, then later recalled. Yet almost all people can relate to misplacing their keys, being unable to recall where they are despite numerous promptings by themselves and others, and then spontaneously remembering the keys' location in response to a triggering cue. If the research is to move ahead, proponents of recovered memories will eventually have to develop a testable theory of the mechanisms of repression that distinguishes it from ordinary forgetting and recall. Otherwise it may turn out to be a catchy idea that in the long run has barely advanced our understanding of memory beyond what we already knew about it.

REFERENCES

American Medical Association Council on Scientific Affairs (1985). Scientific status of refreshing recollection by the use of hypnosis. *JAMA, 253* (13), 1918–1923.

Bass, E., & Davis, L. (1994). *The courage to heal: A guide for women survivors of child sexual abuse.* New York: Harper & Row.

Bowman, C. G., & Mertz, E. (1996). What should the courts do about memories of sexual abuse? Toward a balanced approach. *The Judges' Journal, 35* (4), 7–17.

Briere, J., & Conte, J. (1993). Self-reported amnesia for abuse in adults molested as children. *Journal of Traumatic Stress, 6,* 21 31.

Bruck, M., Ceci, S. J., & Hembrooke, H. (1998). Reliability and credibility of young children's reports: From research to policy and practice. *American Psychologist, 53,* 136–151.

Carro, J. L., & Hatala, J. V. (1996). Recovered memories, extended statutes of limitations and discovery exceptions in childhood sexual abuse cases: Have we gone too far? *Pepperdine Law Review, 23,* 1239–1275.

Ceci, S. J., Ross, D. F., & Toglia, M. P. (1987). Suggestibility of children's memory: Psycholegal implications. *Journal of Experimental Psychology: General, 116,* 38–49.

Chapman, L. J., & Chapman, J. P. (1969). Illusory correlation as an obstacle to the use of valid psychodiagnostic signs. *Journal of Abnormal Psychology, 74,* 271–280.

Claridge, K. (1992). Reconstructing memories of abuse: A theory-based approach. *Psychotherapy, 29,* 243–251.

Corwin, D. L., & Olafson, E. (1997). Videotaped discovery of a reportedly unrecallable memory of child sexual abuse. *Child Maltreatment, 2,* 91–112.

DeRose v. Carswell, 242 Cal.Rptr. 368 (Ca. App. 1987).

Doe v. Mckay, 700 N.E.2d 1018 (Ill. 1998).

Erdelyi, M. H. (1990). Repression, reconstruction, and defense: History and integration of the psychoanalytic and experimental frameworks. In J. L. Singer (Ed.), *Repression and dissociation*. Chicago: University of Chicago Press.

Ferrante, R. (1995). The discovery rule: Allowing adult survivors of childhood sexual abuse the opportunity for redress. *Brooklyn Law Review, 61,* 199–233.

Franklin v. Stevenson, 987 P.2d22 (Utah 1999).

Garry, M., Manning, C. G., Loftus, E. F., & Sherman, S. J. (1996). Imagination inflation: Imagining a childhood event inflates confidence that it occurred. *Psychonomic Bulletin & Review, 3,* 208–214.

Golding, J. M., Sego, S. A., Sanchez, R. P, & Hasemann, D. (1995). The believability of repressed memories. *Law and Human Behavior, 19,* 569–592.

Herman, J. L., & Schatzow, E. (1987). Recovery and verification of memories of childhood sexual trauma. *Psychoanalytic Psychology, 4,* 1–14.

Holmes, D. (1994). Is there evidence for repression? *Harvard Mental Health Letter, 10,* 4–6.

Hyman, I. E., Husband, T. H., & Billings, F. J. (1995). False memories of childhood experiences. *Applied Cognitive Psychology, 9,* 181–197.

Johnson v. Johnson, 701 F.Supp 1363 (Ill. 1988).

Johnston, M. (1996). Spectral evidence. *The Judges' Journal, 36* (4), 75–76.

Kendall-Tackett, K. A., Williams, L. M., & Finkelhor, D. (1993). Impact of sexual abuse on children: A review and synthesis of recent empirical studies. *Psychological Bulletin, 113,* 164–180.

Key, H. G., Warren, A. R., & Ross, D. F. (1996). Perceptions of repressed memories. *Law and Human Behavior, 20,* 555–563.

Kihlstrom, J. F. (1996). The trauma-memory argument and recovered memory therapy. In K. Pezdek & W. P. Banks (Eds.), *The recovered memory/false memory debate*. San Diego, CA: Academic Press.

Loftus, E. F., & Ketcham, K. (1994). *The myth of repressed memory: False memories and allegations of sexual abuse.* New York: St. Martin's Press.

Loftus, E. F., Miller, D. G., & Burns, H. J. (1978). Semantic integration of verbal information into a visual memory. *Journal of Experimental Psychology: Human Learning & Memory, 4*, 19–31.

Loftus, E. F., & Pickrell, J. E. (1995). The formation of false memories. *Psychiatric Annals, 25*, 720–725.

Loftus, E. F., Weingardt, K., & Hoffman, H. (1993). Sleeping memories on trial: Reactions to memories that were previously repressed. *Expert Evidence: The International Digest of Human Behaviour Science and Law, 2*, 51–59.

Lynn, S., & Nash, M. (1994). Truth in memory: Ramifications for psychotherapy and hypnotherapy. *American Journal of Clinical Hypnosis, 36*, 194–208.

Mary D. v. John D., 264 Cal.Rptr. 633 (Cal. App. 1990).

Mazzoni, G. A. L., & Loftus, E. F. (1998). Dream interpretation can change beliefs about the past. *Psychotherapy, 35*, 177–187.

McCollum v. D'Arcey, 638 A.2d 797 (N.H.1994).

Meiers-Post v. Schafer, 427 N.W.2d 606 (Mich. App. 1988).

Melchert, T. (1996). Childhood memory and a history of different forms of abuse. *Professional Psychology: Research and Practice, 27*, 438–446.

Nash, M. R. (1994). Memory distortion and sexual trauma: The problem of false negatives and false positives. *The International Journal of Clinical and Experimental Hypnosis, 42*, 346–362.

Order of Railroad Telegraphers v. Railway Express Agency, Inc. 645 Ct. 582, 586 (1994).

People v. Frazer, 982 P.2d 180 (Cal. 1999).

Peterson v. Bruen, 792 P.2d 18 (Nev. App. 1990).

Poole, D. A., Lindsay, D. S., Memon, A., & Bull, R. (1995). Psychotherapy and the recovery of memories of childhood sexual abuse: U.S. and British practitioners' opinions, practices, and experiences. *Journal of Consulting and Clinical Psychology, 63*, 426–437.

Pope, H. G., & Hudson, J. I. (1992). Is childhood sexual abuse a risk factor for bulimia? *American Journal of Psychology, 149*, 455–463.

Pope, H. G., & Hudson, J. I. (1995). Can memories of child sexual abuse be repressed? *Psychological Medicine, 25*, 121–126.

Pope, K. S., & Tabachnick, B. G. (1995). Recovered memories of abuse among therapy patients: A national survey. *Ethics and Behavior, 5*, 237–248.

Ramona v. Isabella, C 61898, Napa, Calif., Super. Ct., 1995.

Rind, B., Tromovitch, P., & Bauserman, R. (1998). A meta-analytic examination of assumed properties of child sexual abuse using college samples. *Psychological Bulletin, 124*, 22–53.

Rock, S. F. (1995). A claim for third party standing in malpractice cases involving repressed memory syndrome. *William and Mary Law Review, 37*, 337–379.

Ruth v. Dight, 453 P.2d 631 (Wash. 1969).

Schooler, J. W., Ambadar, Z., & Bendiksen, M. (1997). A cognitive corroborative case study approach for investigating discovered memories of sexual abuse. In D. Read and S. Lindsay (Eds.) *Recollections of Trauma: Scientific Research and Clinical Practices* (pp. 379–388). New York: Plenum.

Shweder, R., & D'Andrade, R. G. (1980). The systematic distortion hypothesis. In R. A. Shweder (Ed.), *Fallible judgment in behavioral research* (pp. 37–58). San Francisco: Jossey-Bass.

Spadaro, J. A. (1998). An elusive search for the truth: The admissibility of repressed and recovered memories in light of *Daubert v. Merrell Dow Pharmaceuticals, Inc., Connecticut Law Review, 30*, 1147–1198.

State v. Hungerford, 697 A.2d 916 (N. H. 1997).

Stogner v. California, 123 S.Ct. 2446 (2003).

Tarasoff v. Regents of the University of California, 551 P.2d 334 (Cal. 1976).

Tetford, I., & Schuller, R. A. (1996). Mock jurors' evaluation of child sexual abuse. *Behavioral Sciences and the Law, 14*, 205–218.

Tsai, A. C., Morsbach, S. K., & Loftus, E. F. (1999, June). The importance of the nature of the crime in repressed memory studies. Poster Session presented at 11th Annual American Psychological Society Conference, Denver, CO.

Tyson v. Tyson, 727 P.2d 226 (Wash. 1986).

Wason, P. C., & Johnson-Laird, P. N. (1972). *Psychology of reasoning: Structure and content*. Cambridge, MA: Harvard University Press.

Williams, L. M. (1994). Recall of childhood trauma: A prospective study of women's memories of child sexual abuse. *Journal of Consulting & Clinical Psychology, 62*, 1167–1176.

CHAPTER 24

A *DAUBERT* TESTING OF HYPNOTICALLY REFRESHED TESTIMONY IN THE CRIMINAL COURTS

EARL F. MARTIN
TEXAS WESLEYAN UNIVERSITY SCHOOL OF LAW

Any discussion of hypnotically refreshed testimony should begin by defining hypnosis. Unfortunately, this is easier said than done. A list of the various definitions that have been offered for the term could easily take up a couple of pages of text (Brown, Scheflin, & Hammond, 1998; Scheflin & Shapiro, 1989), but such an exercise is unnecessary for present purposes. Instead, this chapter will proceed under the influence of a rather broad definition of hypnosis, that is, a state of consciousness that entails the concentration of attention on a specific theme or image with an accompanying diminished interest in one's surroundings (Scheflin, Spiegel, & Spiegel, 1999; Ofshe & Watters, 1994; Scheflin & Shapiro, 1989).

The roots of hypnosis can be traced to late eighteenth- and nineteenth-century physicians who used the technique in their clinical and scientific practices. Toward the end of this period, hypnosis caught the attention of Sigmund Freud, who used it with his patients before abandoning it in favor of free association. The modern interest in the practice developed at the end of World War II, when it was discovered that soldiers suffering from war stress disorders responded favorably to hypnosis (Brown, Scheflin, & Hammond, 1998; Kanovitz, 1992; Scheflin & Shapiro, 1989). From that time until now, the use of hypnosis has become more pervasive. In fact, in a survey that sought to gather information about psychotherapists' attitudes towards hypnosis and the prevalence of its use in their practices, over one-half of the 869 respondents said that they used hypnosis in their work, and greater than one-third said that they used it at least occasionally to retrieve memories from their patients (Yapko, 1994).

Following the lead of clinicians, the use of hypnosis in criminal investigations has increased over the last few decades (McConkey, 1995; Fleming, 1990), and this use will be the focus of the following discussion. Specifically, this chapter will look at the reliability of hypnotically refreshed testimony in the criminal courts. We will first review how the common law has responded to the questions raised by hypnotically refreshed testimony. With this background in mind, we will proceed to consider the impact that the U. S. Supreme Court case of *Daubert v. Merrell Dow Pharmaceuticals* (1993) may have on this evidence. We will discuss *Daubert* and the more recent case of *Kumho Tire Co., Ltd. v. Carmichael* (1999) in an effort to detail the construct that the Supreme Court has created to test the reliability of scientific evidence. From there, we will employ this construct as a means of investigating whether the behavioral science literature can support the forensic application of hypnotically refreshed testimony in criminal prosecutions.

Before proceeding further, one important caveat needs to be stated. The typical scenario that serves as the background for this chapter is that of a subject being put under hypnosis as a means of retrieving a memory that is otherwise unavailable to the subject because of traumatic amnesia. Generally, although not well defined and differentiated, the psychological defense mechanisms of repression, suppression, and dissociation are invoked as the explanations that justify the use of hypnosis to extract unavailable memories (Frankel & Covino, 1997). The validity of the concept of psychological defense and the specific mechanisms just mentioned are part of the controversy surrounding the use of hypnotic techniques, especially when the case is one involving the phenomenon of "recovered memories" (Lindsay & Read, 1995; McConkey, 1995). Therefore, as a precursor to litigating the reliability of any particular strand of hypnotically refreshed testimony, one should anticipate the possibility of a reliability battle surrounding these psychological mechanisms. A debate, however, on the reliability of the science that underlies these mechanisms is beyond the scope of this chapter.

THE COMMON-LAW APPROACH TO HYPNOTICALLY REFRESHED TESTIMONY

For the vast majority of this country's history the courts refused to allow hypnotically refreshed testimony into evidence (Scheflin, Spiegel, & Spiegel, 1999). However, that changed in 1968 when the Maryland Court of Special Appeals in *Harding v. State* (1968) upheld the admission of hypnotically refreshed testimony from the victim of a sexual assault who recalled under hypnosis that it was the defendant who had attacked her. Even though the victim provided different accounts of her attack over time and achieved her in-court version of events only after being hypnotized, the *Harding* court said that any questions regarding the reliability of the hypnotically refreshed testimony went to the weight of the testimony and not its admissibility.

Following *Harding*'s lead, other courts began to admit hypnotically refreshed testimony in criminal cases and this precedent encouraged police agencies to expand their use of hypnosis as an investigative technique (Shaw, 1991; Fleming, 1990). This, perhaps inevitably, led to investigative abuses and to increased scrutiny and criticism of the use of hypnotically refreshed testimony from courts, legislatures, professional groups, and scholars (Moriarty, 1999; Shaw, 1991; Scheflin & Shapiro, 1989; Diamond, 1980). Eventually, this heightened consideration of the issue resulted in four different approaches to the admissibility of hypnotically refreshed testimony, ranging from liberal admission to absolute prohibition. Between these two extremes, a number of courts have tried to fashion tests that limit the admissibility of hypnotically refreshed testimony to situations where its reliability has been sufficiently established.

At one end of the spectrum lies the *per se* admissible approach to hypnotically refreshed testimony. Jurisdictions that follow this path hold that the effect of a hypnotic session on the reliability of a witness's recall goes to the weight and credibility of the witness's testimony and not to its admissibility or the witness's competence (Moriarty, 1999; Shaw, 1991; Fleming, 1990). These jurisdictions place great faith in the ability of the jury to evaluate the testimony accurately in light of cross-examination, expert testimony, and jury instructions (Wright & Gold, 1990). As one court put it regarding the first of these safeguards, "skillful cross-examination will enable the jury to evaluate the effect of hypnosis on the witness and the credibility of his testimony" (*State v. Brown*, 1983, p. 151). The *per se* admissible approach "has sparsely been followed since 1980" (*People v. Zayas*, 1989, p. 516).

At the opposite end of the spectrum lies a larger number of jurisdictions that hold that hypnotically refreshed testimony is *per se* inadmissible (*Roark v. Commonwealth*, 2000). Some of these jurisdictions will not allow a witness who has been hypnotized regarding the matter under consideration to take the stand at all. Others will not allow a witness to take the stand and testify about memories that were recovered as a result of a hypnotic session. In this second category of cases, if a party wants to put a witness on the stand who has been hypnotized in connection with the substance of his testimony, the court must be convinced that the subject matter of the witness's testimony is based entirely upon recollections that were available to the witness before he or she was hypnotized (Moriarty, 1999; Wright & Gold, 1990; Fleming, 1990).

A rationale given by many of the *per se* inadmissible jurisdictions is that, consistent with the requirements of the test first enunciated in *Frye v. United States* (1923), hypnosis has not achieved general acceptance within the relevant scientific community as a means of extracting accurate memories (Moriarty, 1999; Wright & Gold, 1990; Fleming, 1990). Furthermore, there are jurisdictions that have adopted an absolute bar to the testimony based upon the claim that its admission would violate a criminal defendant's constitutional right to confront the witnesses against him because of the tendency of hypnosis to lead to memory hardening, that is, overconfidence on the part of the witness regarding those matters recalled under hypnosis (Moriarty, 1999; Wright & Gold, 1990; Fleming, 1990). Finally, some jurisdictions embrace the *per se* inadmissible approach on the grounds that the prosecution's use of hypnotically refreshed testimony violates due process. These jurisdictions claim that a defendant is deprived of a fair trial when the state hypnotizes a witness, because the resulting suggestion and confabulation on the witness's memory is equivalent to tampering with or manufacturing evidence (Wright & Gold, 1990). Such tainting can result from the fact that an individual under hypnosis is susceptible to suggestion from verbal and nonverbal cues planted by the hypnotist, and from the fact that a hypnotized person may fill in the gaps in her memory, or "confabulate," as a means of making her recollection of an event more comprehensible (Moriarty, 1999; Wright & Gold, 1990).

Before leaving the *per se* inadmissible approach, a U.S. Supreme Court case from the 1980s needs to be discussed because of its undeniable impact on this issue. In *Rock v. Arkansas* (1987), the Court held that Arkansas's rule that a criminal defendant's hypnotically refreshed testimony was *per se* inadmissible was unconstitutional. Although it acknowledged that the dangers of memory hardening, suggestibility, and confabulation all created the potential for hypnosis to generate inaccurate memories, the Supreme Court still concluded that certain procedural safeguards could reduce the likelihood of error in posthypnotic testimony. Therefore, because the right to testify on one's behalf is so rooted in the Constitution, the Court found Arkansas's inflexible approach to a criminal defendant's hypnotically refreshed testimony to be an "arbitrary restriction on the [defendant's] right to testify in the absence of clear evidence by the State repudiating the validity of all post-hypnosis recollections" (*Rock v. Arkansas*, p. 61). Even though the Court explicitly limited the reach of its holding by refusing to express an opinion on the appropriate rule of admissibility for testimony from previously hypnotized witnesses other than criminal defendants, the case has caused a number of jurisdictions around the country to at least reconsider their *per se* ban on hypnotically refreshed testimony (*Burral v. State*, 1999; Wright & Gold, 1990).

In contrast to the two polar opposite treatments of hypnotically refreshed testimony, a number of jurisdictions employ one of two schemes that require the proffered testimony to satisfy a certain level of reliability before a judge will allow it to be considered for its substance. The first of these traces its roots to a New Jersey Supreme Court case from 1981 called *State v. Hurd*.

In *Hurd*, the court was called upon to review the admissibility of hypnotically refreshed testimony that implicated the defendant in a knife attack on his ex-wife. By casting the inquiry in terms of whether hypnosis was generally accepted by the scientific community as a means of overcoming amnesia and restoring the memory of a witness instead of requiring that it be generally accepted as a means of reviving historically accurate recall, the court found that the process satisfied its formulation of the *Frye* test. For a number of reasons, however, the court was concerned about the reliability of hypnotically refreshed testimony within the context of specific cases (*State v. Hurd*, 1981).

Relying upon the trial court testimony of Dr. Martin Orne and other authorities available to it, the *Hurd* court listed several features of the hypnotic experience that it believed called its ability to obtain accurate recall into question. First, persons undergoing hypnosis are extremely vulnerable to suggestions that can take the form of intentional or inadvertent cues. Second, persons under hypnosis are susceptible to a loss of critical judgment, in that they are more willing to speculate and will respond to questions with a confidence they would not have as a waking person. Third, in response to a posthypnotic suggestion that they will remember what they have recalled under hypnosis after they awake from the trance, persons coming out of hypnosis may indiscriminately confound or mix their hypnotic recall together with their waking memory. And fourth, persons coming out of hypnosis will have strong subjective confidence in the validity of their new recall (i.e., the aforementioned "memory hardening"), making it difficult for an expert or a jury to assess the credibility of their memory (*State v. Hurd*, 1981).

Although the *Hurd* court was troubled by these potential problems, it believed that a rule of *per se* inadmissibility was unnecessarily broad and would result in the exclusion of evidence that was as trustworthy as other eyewitness testimony. Therefore, it held that "testimony enhanced through hypnosis [was] admissible in a criminal trial if the [judge found] that the use of hypnosis in a particular case was reasonably likely to result in recall comparable in accuracy to normal human memory" (*State v. Hurd*, 1981, p. 95). Consistent with this case-by-case approach, the court fashioned a test that put the burden on the proponent of the hypnotically refreshed testimony to prove its reliability to a clear and convincing standard, taking into account both the kind of memory loss that hypnosis was used to restore and the specific technique employed.

As for the first part of its test, the *Hurd* court said that a trial judge must consider the appropriateness of using hypnosis for the kind of memory loss encountered. The court found that "hypnosis often is reasonably reliable in reviving normal recall where there is a pathological reason, such as a traumatic neurosis, for the witness's inability to remember," but "the likelihood of obtaining reasonably accurate recall diminishes if hypnosis is used simply to refresh a witness's memory concerning details where there may be no recollection at all, or to 'verify' one of several conflicting accounts given by a witness" (*State v. Hurd*, 1981, pp. 95–96). The court also noted that a related factor to be considered was whether the witness had any discernible motivation for not remembering or for "recalling" a particular version of events.

Turning to the second part of its test, the *Hurd* court said that if "a case is of a kind likely to yield normal recall if hypnosis is properly administered, then it is becomes necessary to determine whether the procedures followed were reasonably reliable" (*State v. Hurd*, 1981, p. 96). The court said the priority must be to guard against contamination of the witness's testimony, and thus a trial judge should be particularly sensitive to the manner of questioning, the presence of cues or suggestions, and the amenability of the subject to hypnosis. Furthermore, in order to provide an adequate record for evaluating the reliability of the hypnotic procedure, the *Hurd* court adopted several procedural requirements based on the testimony of Dr. Orne and what was prescribed by the trial court. These requirements are:

1. A psychiatrist or psychologist experienced in the use of hypnosis must conduct the session.
2. The professional conducting the hypnotic session should be independent of and not regularly employed by the prosecutor, investigator, or defense.
3. Any information given to the hypnotist by law enforcement personnel or the defense prior to the hypnotic session must be recorded, either in writing or another suitable form.
4. Before inducing hypnosis, the hypnotist should obtain from the subject a detailed description of the facts as the subject remembers them.
5. All contacts between the hypnotist and the subject must be recorded.
6. Only the hypnotist and the subject should be present during any phase of the hypnotic session, including the prehypnotic testing and the posthypnotic interview.

Over time, some jurisdictions have adopted the *Hurd* guidelines verbatim, while others have followed *Hurd* with their own additions and subtractions from its requirements. For example, courts have relaxed the prohibition against the presence of third parties during any phase of the hypnotic session, have added a corroboration factor, and/or have required that the hypnotic session take place at a neutral site (Moriarty, 1999; Shaw, 1991).

The second case-by-case admission scheme for hypnotically refreshed testimony, which has found most of its adherents in the federal system, employs a "totality of the circumstances" test to assess the reliability of the disputed testimony. Unlike the *Hurd* approach, this scheme does not profess to offer a laundry list of relevant factors; rather, it follows the more fungible practice of allowing each case to be judged based upon its unique facts, with the litigants being given great freedom in the range of their arguments regarding the reliability or unreliability of the hypnotically refreshed testimony. Ultimately, the trial court is called upon to balance the risk of unreliable testimony against the value of the testimony if reliable, with the question being whether the testimony is more likely than not to advance accurate fact finding (Wright & Gold, 1990). Not surprisingly, however, over time certain factors have been recognized as particularly important in assisting judges in making this determination. Specifically, courts have highlighted "the use of procedural safeguards, the presence of suggestive statements or other cues . . . , the quality of the witness's subsequent testimony, whether the testimony is corroborated by independent evidence, the nature of the witness's memory loss, the consistency of the testimony with prehypnosis recollection, the importance of the testimony to the case, and the availability of evidence concerning the hypnotist and the hypnotic session" (Wright & Gold, 1990, p. 171–172).

Putting the four common-law approaches into reliability terms, the *per se* admissible camp has decided that hypnotically refreshed testimony is reliable enough so that a witness's testimony that is at least partially the product of hypnosis will not generally be kept away from the fact finder. On the other hand, the *per se* inadmissible approach holds that hypnosis is such a potentially contaminating exercise that no witness's hypnotically refreshed testimony is trustworthy enough to allow that witness to be heard on the merits. This camp simply rejects, as a matter of course, the reliability of hypnotically refreshed testimony.

Those jurisdictions that follow one of the two conditional admission approaches do not bar the receipt of hypnotically refreshed testimony as too unreliable, but neither do they turn a blind eye to the issue. Instead, each approach states that in the right situation hypnotically refreshed testimony can be reliable enough to allow the fact finder to use that testimony in reaching its decision. A finding of reliability in any particular case depends upon a court either holding that a list of *Hurd*-inspired factors are present or holding that the totality of the circumstances satisfies the threshold standard of reliability. A similar, although more in-depth, case-by-case inquiry into the reliability of scientific evidence has been called for by the Supreme Court in *Daubert v. Merrell Dow Pharmaceuticals* (1993), and that Court's treatment of the general reliability issue in that case is the subject of the next section of this chapter.

THE *DAUBERT* TEST FOR SCIENTIFIC RELIABILITY

In *Frye v. United States* (1923), the U.S. Court of Appeals for the District of Columbia, in a short and citation-free opinion, created the "general acceptance" test for determining the admissibility of novel scientific evidence. Although not in quick fashion, over time the *Frye* test became the test of choice for both federal and state courts in determining the admissibility of scientific evidence (Giannelli & Imwinkelried, 1999). In June 1993, however, that changed in the federal courts and began to change in the state courts with the publication of the U.S. Supreme Court's *Daubert v. Merrell Dow Pharmaceuticals* opinion. Based upon the adoption of the Federal Rules of Evidence (hereinafter FRE), specifically FRE 702 regarding expert testimony, the *Daubert* Court rejected *Frye's* general acceptance test as an absolute prerequisite to the admissibility of scientific evidence and instead called for a more liberal and flexible standard of admissibility that would be grounded in the principles of relevance and reliability.

Daubert's insistence on relevance flows directly out of the language in FRE 702 that requires that evidence or testimony "assist the trier-of-fact to understand the evidence or to determine a fact in issue" (*Daubert v. Merrell Dow Pharmaceuticals*, 1993, p. 591). This part of FRE 702 demands that any offered evidence or testimony be relevant to the proceeding, which means that the information has the "tendency to make the existence of any fact that is of consequence to the determination of the action more probable or less probable than it would be without the evidence" (FRE 401). The *Daubert* Court used the word *fit* to describe what it was talking about, and in doing so it said that "[fit] is not always obvious and ... scientific validity for one purpose is not necessarily scientific validity for other, unrelated purposes" (*Daubert v. Merrell Dow Pharmaceuticals*, 1993, p. 591). The key to the inquiry is to determine whether the offered evidence or testimony would be helpful to the trier of fact. This will only be the case when there is a valid scientific connection between the offered evidence or testimony and the pertinent inquiry at hand.

Focusing on the expert scientific testimony that was the subject of the case (i.e., whether Bendectin was a human teratogen), the Court said that in order for this testimony or any scientific evidence to be admissible, it must be not only relevant but also reliable. Given its dependence on science for its substance, the *Daubert* Court explained that this meant that for the testimony to satisfy evidentiary reliability, it must be based upon scientific validity; that is, the underlying principle must support what it purports to show.

Offering what it called "some general observations," the *Daubert* Court then discussed some nonexclusive factors that could bear on the ultimate inquiry. The first of these is whether a theory or technique can be and has been tested, because scientific methodology is based on generating hypotheses and testing them to see if they can be falsified. The second is whether the theory or technique has been subjected to scrutiny by others in the field through peer review and publication. The Court said that "submission to the scrutiny of the scientific community is a component of 'good science,' in part because it increases the likelihood that substantive flaws in methodology will be detected" (*Daubert v. Merrell Dow Pharmaceuticals*, 1993, p. 593). The third and fourth factors concern whether, in respect to a particular technique, there is a high known or potential rate of error, and whether there are standards controlling the technique's operation. The fifth and final factor reinvigorates the *Frye* test by asking whether the theory or technique enjoys general acceptance within a relevant scientific community. The Court did not want a return to the dominance of *Frye*, but it recognized that "[w]idespread acceptance can be an important factor in ruling particular evidence admissible, and 'a known technique which has been able to attract only minimal support within the community' ... may properly be viewed with skepticism" (*Daubert v. Merrell Dow Pharmaceuticals*, 1993, p. 594).

Since *Daubert*, the lower courts have frequently struggled with two specific issues. First, even though FRE 702 speaks of "scientific, technical, or other specialized knowledge," many courts that have otherwise adopted *Daubert* have limited its application only to scientific expert testimony and evidence (Graham, 2001; Krebs & Tray, 1999; Graham, 1998). Second, notwithstanding the qualifiers that the *Daubert* Court put on its list of reliability factors, some courts have applied these as if they are exclusive and mandatory factors that must be satisfied before expert testimony or other scientific evidence is admissible (Graham, 2001; Graham, 1998). In an effort to address these concerns and bring clarity to the field, the Supreme Court revisited the issue in its March 1999 opinion of *Kumho Tire Co., Ltd. v. Carmichael*.

On the question of *Daubert*'s reach, the *Kumho Tire* opinion stated that *Daubert*'s general holding that discussed "the trial judge's 'gatekeeping' obligation—applies not only to testimony based on 'scientific' knowledge, but also to testimony based on 'technical' and 'other specialized' knowledge" (*Kumho Tire Co., Ltd. v. Carmichael*, 1999, p. 141). *Daubert*'s fixation on the issue of scientific testimony had been driven by its facts, but the plain language of FRE 702 does not draw a distinction among expert testimony based upon scientific, technical, or other specialized knowledge.

Turning to the confusion regarding *Daubert*'s reliability factors, the Court in *Kumho Tire* reiterated *Daubert*'s declaration in favor of flexibility by stating that "*Daubert*'s list of specific factors neither necessarily nor exclusively applies to all experts or in every case" (*Kumho Tire Co., Ltd. v. Carmichael*, 1999, p. 141). Instead, the Court noted that trial courts are granted the same broad latitude when they decide how to determine reliability as they enjoy in respect to their ultimate reliability determination. The Court pointed out that there are many different kinds of experts and many different kinds of expertise, and thus, "[t]he factors identified in *Daubert* may or may not be pertinent in assessing reliability, depending on the nature of the issue, the expert's particular expertise, and the subject of his testimony" (p. 150). The *Kumho Tire* majority opinion said that the Court could "neither rule out, nor rule in, for all cases and for all time the applicability of the factors mentioned in *Daubert*, [because] [t]oo much depends upon the particular circumstances of the particular case at issue" (p. 150). The Court took pains, however, to reiterate that the underlying objective was to ensure the relevancy and reliability of expert testimony and scientific evidence, and this means that trial judges must be diligent in meeting *Daubert*'s basic gatekeeping requirement, whatever factors prove ultimately to be decisive.

It is clear that if *Daubert* stands for anything, it stands for the proposition that scientific evidence must be reliable to be admissible. For purposes of the present discussion, this brings us to the question of whether hypnotically refreshed testimony should be subject to a *Daubert*-inspired reliability screening in those jurisdictions that follow its guidance. If it should, then we must go further and decide what that screening should look like, and then determine whether hypnotically refreshed testimony is up to the test. These issues are the focus of the next and final section of this chapter.

HYPNOTICALLY REFRESHED TESTIMONY AND THE *DAUBERT* TEST

The issue, for our purposes, becomes the effect, if any, that *Daubert* should have on the admissibility of hypnotically refreshed testimony. In other words, assuming a case is brought in the federal court system where the dictates of *Daubert* are binding or in a state court that has adopted *Daubert* and rejected either of the *per se* approaches to hypnotically refreshed testimony, should that testimony be required to pass through a *Daubert*-inspired reliability gate before it gets to the fact finder? Furthermore, if it must pass through that gate then what should it look like?

The short response to the first question could be to say no and simply cite a 1995 U.S. Second Circuit Court of Appeals opinion called *Borawick v. Shay*. In that case, the court of appeals held that the challenged hypnotically refreshed testimony was not subject to the rigors of *Daubert* because the issue did not concern the admissibility of data derived from scientific techniques or expert opinions; rather, the issue was whether Borawick was a competent lay witness. Therefore, the court held that the earlier discussed "totality of the circumstances" test was the appropriate test for the occasion. Even though the *Borawick* court held that *Daubert* did not provide direct guidance, it said that its decision was informed by the principles underlying that earlier Supreme Court opinion, and it noted that nothing in *Daubert* was inconsistent with its outlined approach. This last comment from the court drew a parallel between the purpose of its totality of the circumstances test and *Daubert*'s search for evidentiary reliability.

Commentators have offered support for *Borawick*'s refusal to apply the *Daubert* gatekeeping function to hypnotically refreshed testimony on a couple of grounds. First, *Borawick*'s straightforward assertion that hypnotically refreshed testimony is an issue of lay witness competency and not scientific evidence has been endorsed (Fenner, 1996; Wright & Gold, 1990). Second, a more practical concern has been advanced that claims that "trials would grind to a halt under the weight of *Daubert* if the courts were obligated to treat as scientific evidence all lay testimony that could be considered, in the broadest sense, the product of some scientific process" (Wright & Gold, 1997, p. 284).

Notwithstanding the outcome in *Borawick* and the arguments that have been advanced in support of its conclusion, for reasons of history, commonsense, and policy, a behavioral scientist who finds herself involved in a criminal case in a *Daubert* jurisdiction that includes hypnotically refreshed testimony should be prepared to support the admissibility of that testimony in terms that fit within *Daubert*'s framework. As a matter of history, a large number of courts have treated the admissibility of hypnotically refreshed testimony as a matter to be regulated by the rules governing the admissibility of scientific evidence or testimony (*Burral v. State*, 1999; *State v. Weston*, 1984; *State v. Collins*, 1983). This is, of course, part of the same evidentiary paradigm that *Daubert* is intended to control. Furthermore, in keeping with this historical treatment of the issue, many courts continue to label hypnotically refreshed testimony as scientific evidence subject to the rules those jurisdictions employ in screening that type of evidence (Moriarty, 1999; Wright & Gold, 1990; Fleming, 1990), with a number of courts explicitly rejecting a *Borawick*-like approach of making hypnotically refreshed testimony immune from a scientific reliability screening (*State v. Tuttle*, 1989).

Common sense also compels the conclusion that hypnotically refreshed testimony should be subject to the rigors of *Daubert* in those jurisdictions that have adopted its test. Lay witness testimony that has been refreshed by hypnosis is as much a form of scientific evidence as is testimony that explains the results of DNA testing. This conclusion does not require that "scientific evidence" be defined in an overly broad fashion, as the former testimony flows directly from, and indeed owes its existence to, the scientific discipline that is psychology (*State v. Tuttle*, 1989; *People v. Zayas*, 1989; *Polk v. State*, 1981), just as the latter testimony flows directly from and owes its existence to the scientific discipline that is genetics. But for the direct application of psychology through a hypnotic session, the hypnotically refreshed lay witness would not be in possession of the information that he or she is being called upon to relate to the court. To treat hypnotically refreshed testimony differently from DNA evidence is to perpetuate an approach in our courts that tends to judge the admissibility of evidence derived from the so-called hard sciences (e.g., chemistry and physics) more stringently than evidence derived from the application of the so-called soft sciences (e.g., psychology and sociology) (McCord, 1987).

Like history and common sense, policy concerns also support a *Daubert* screening of hypnotically refreshed testimony in *Daubert* jurisdictions. First, efficiency would be enhanced by such a holding. Instead of having two or more tests to screen this scientific evidence, *Daubert* offers a single test of admissibility. To the extent it is claimed that this is too rigid an approach, one only needs to recall the Supreme Court's admonition in *Daubert* and *Kumho Tire* that the process is meant to be flexible, taking into account the specifics of the case and the form of the evidence being offered. Second, insisting that hypnotically refreshed testimony meet *Daubert*'s requirements would enhance the reliability of the process, because the linchpin to admissibility under *Daubert* is evidentiary reliability. Third, coherence would be enhanced and confusion reduced by bringing hypnotically refreshed testimony under *Daubert* in those jurisdictions that have embraced its guidance. Again, the fixation on evidentiary reliability would generally serve both of these ends. Additionally, requiring this testimony to meet the rigors of a *Daubert*-inspired test as a condition of admissibility would avoid a potentially incongruous result. If hypnotically refreshed testimony were allowed to be heard without a *Daubert* screening but then were attacked on the ground that the use of hypnosis rendered the testimony unreliable, the opportunity would present itself for a court to deny a defense of that testimony by a psychologist on the ground that this expert testimony could not meet the requirements of *Daubert*. If a psychologist were to take the witness stand to offer testimony in support of admitting hypnotically refreshed testimony under attack, she may explicitly, and would at least implicitly, invoke the mantle of science (i.e., psychology), and thus an inquiry into the scientific validity of the reasoning and methodology underlying that expert's testimony would be appropriate and logical (Shuman & Sales, 1998). However, it is conceivable that a court would conclude that the expert's testimony does not satisfy *Daubert*'s requirements, and thus deny the expert the opportunity to be heard by the fact finder even though the court has already admitted the lay witness testimony under challenge. The far better practice would be to require the hypnotically derived testimony to survive a *Daubert* screening as a condition of its admissibility.

The possibility that hypnotically refreshed testimony will be have to pass through a *Daubert*-constructed gate before it makes its way to the fact finder brings us to the second question: What should that reliability gate look like for this testimony? Even though the Supreme Court in both *Daubert* and *Kumho Tire* went out of its way to stress the flexibility of its reliability screening process, a defense of hypnotically refreshed testimony would be well served to articulate that defense in terms reflective of *Daubert*'s factors. Therefore, the issues would be whether the validity of hypnosis can be, and has been, tested; whether research results on hypnosis have been subjected to peer review and publication; whether, in respect to hypnosis, there is a high known or potential rate of error; whether there are standards controlling its use; and whether hypnosis enjoys general acceptance within the relevant scientific community.

A key, if not the key, to answering these questions is to be certain about just what is being asked of hypnosis in the context of criminal cases. As mentioned earlier, a significant variation between many of those jurisdictions holding hypnotically refreshed testimony to be *per se* inadmissible versus those that have remained open to its admissibility is that different things are expected of hypnosis in different jurisdictions. In the *per se* inadmissibility jurisdictions, the inquiry has predominantly focused on the ability of hypnosis to revive historically accurate recall. On the other hand, in those jurisdictions that admit the evidence at least part of the time, the issue has often been cast in terms of the ability of hypnosis to overcome amnesia and restore the memory of a witness. This same debate will come up in a *Daubert* screening of hypnotically refreshed testimony because of that Court's adherence to the relevance requirement in FRE 702. That is, the testimony must assist the trier of fact to understand the evidence or to determine a fact in issue. The *Daubert* opinion said that this condition goes primarily to relevance or "fit," which means that there has to be a connection between the scientific knowledge offered and the contested issue in the case.

The easier position to defend is obviously the one that revolves around the ability of hypnosis to overcome amnesia and restore the memory of a witness, because hypnosis is frequently used in the clinical setting for just this purpose. A behavioral science expert, however, should not count on a court's framing the issue in this way. Whether or not hypnosis is a proper clinical technique to use with patients who are having memory problems would seem to be beside the point when the issue is, for example, whether or not the defendant is a rapist. The primary function of a criminal trial is to uncover the truth about a pending allegation of misconduct, and the successful accomplishment of this goal depends upon objectively accurate testimony. Therefore, a behavioral science expert who is called upon to defend hypnotically refreshed testimony is well advised, in keeping with *Daubert*'s insistence on "fit," to be prepared to address the ability of hypnosis to achieve historically accurate recall.

The first *Daubert* reliability factor, put in terms relevant to our present inquiry, would ask whether the ability of hypnosis to extract historically accurate recall can be and has been tested. Indeed, numerous studies of both the quantity and quality of recall facilitated by hypnosis have been carried out. For example, Dywan & Bowers (1983) tested the ability of hypnosis to help subjects recall line drawings that they were shown a week prior to being hypnotized. These researchers found that subjects who were highly hypnotized recalled more than twice the number of new items as the controls when they were put under hypnosis; however, they also made almost three times as many new errors as the controls, whose recall was facilitated only by task-motivated conditions. Similarly, Sanders and Simmons (1983) tested the effect of hypnosis on the ability of subjects to recall the particulars of a 20-second film depicting a pickpocketing incident. These researchers divided their subjects into two groups, one that would undergo hypnosis and one that would not, and showed both groups the same film. A week later, in connection with viewing a videotape of a lineup related to the theft and answering 10 specific questions about the event, both groups were invited to "'replay' the incident on an internal, mental TV screen, complete with slow-down and speed-up features, stop-action and zoom-in," with one group viewing the lineup and answering the questions while under hypnosis. Sanders and Simmons reported that the subjects who were under hypnosis at the time of viewing the lineup tape and responding to questions about that tape made more errors than those who were not hypnotized during these same exercises, largely because of the tendency of the hypnotized subjects to choose a decoy in the lineup who was wearing the distinctive jacket that the pickpocket wore in the original film.

Although the studies just mentioned claimed that hypnosis invites some level of recall error, they did not, in any significant way, seek to uncover the cause behind that conclusion. As the reader may recall, in the *Hurd* (1981) case three explanations were given for why hypnotically refreshed testimony may produce recall error: a hypnotized person is extremely vulnerable to suggestions from intentional or inadvertent cues; a person under hypnosis is susceptible to a loss of critical judgment in being more willing to speculate and will respond to questions with a confidence he or she would not have as a waking person; and the hypnotic experience can cause a person to confound memories evoked under hypnosis with prior recall. Given that the first of these explanations would entail the injection of external stimuli into the hypnotic session, which is something that can be controlled and tested, a number of studies have looked specifically at the ability of a hypnotist to suggest or implant a false memory into a hypnotized subject's recall.

Laurence and Perry (1983) suggested to hypnotized subjects, all of whom were highly hypnotizable, that one night during the previous week their sleep had been disturbed by a loud sound. After the hypnotic session was terminated, 13 of 27 subjects persisted in their belief, in contrast to their prehypnosis reports, that some sleep-disturbing sound had occurred. In fact, all 13 of the subjects maintained this erroneous belief even after being told that the hypnotist had suggested the sounds to them while they were under hypnosis.

Laurence and Perry, along with Louise Labelle and Robert Nadon (1990), repeated the sleep disturbance experiment a few years after the original effort. While under hypnosis, 16 (one low, eight moderately highly, and seven highly hypnotizable) of 32 subjects responded positively when asked whether, on a particular night in question, they heard a loud noise that may have sounded like a car backfiring or a door slamming. After the hypnotic session was terminated, 11 of these 16 subjects continued to maintain that the suggested noise actually happened. This final group was made up entirely of highly and moderately highly hypnotizable subjects.

The studies referenced in the previous paragraphs, and others like them (see Brown, Scheflin, & Hammond, 1998, for a thorough discussion and critique of the research), have been subjected, as *Daubert*'s second factor would require, to the scrutiny of peer review, with two general conclusions being reached. First, the studies show a tendency for hypnosis in the experimental setting to facilitate greater recall of meaningful material, but the price paid for this greater quantity of information is more incorrect recall and an increased sense of confidence in that recall on behalf of the subjects (Sheehan & McConkey, 1993; Meyer, 1992; American Medical Association, 1985). Second, research has shown that experimental subjects can be influenced by a hypnotist to believe that they experienced something that was merely suggested to them, with the highly hypnotizable subjects being most at risk (Frankel & Covino, 1997; McConkey, 1995; Kanovitz, 1992). These conclusions, however, have not escaped criticism.

Many within the behavioral science community have warned against making too much out of research like that just discussed because of what they perceive to be a strained analogy between the laboratory and the forensic setting (Scheflin, Spiegel, & Spiegel, 1999; Brown, Scheflin, & Hammond, 1998). Specifically, one claim is that these studies generally focus only on the short-term effects of hypnosis on memory, whereas the forensic setting is much more concerned with the long-term impact on recall because of the time that it takes court cases to move through the system. The argument is that it has not been shown that contaminating effects, if any, of hypnosis on memory will retain strength over such a long period of time. Moreover, the point is made that many of the studies that support these criticisms of hypnosis included within their design demand characteristics like forced-choice responses and compelled guessing that increased the amount of inaccurate information reported by subjects. Critics also challenge the conclusions drawn from the research on the ground that the laboratory cannot adequately replicate the role and impact that emotion and content play in the use of hypnosis to extract memories grounded in real-world traumatic experiences. The criticism goes hand in hand with another, which argues that there is great disparity between the motivational factors at work in an experimental effort (e.g., a college student volunteering to serve as a research subject) and those at work in a criminal forensic setting (e.g., a witness or victim undergoing hypnosis in order to retrieve memories that may lead to the conviction of an alleged wrongdoer). Shifting the focus slightly, critics of the experimental studies also claim that an important variable in the success of hypnosis is a trusting and caring relationship between the hypnotist and the subject, and this is something that is rarely, if ever, replicated in the laboratory setting (Scheflin, Spiegel, & Spiegel, 1999; Brown, Scheflin, & Hammond, 1998; Hammond et al., 1995).

Another avenue of peer commentary attempts to bolster the acceptability of hypnotically refreshed testimony by comparing it to recall generated in other ways. The claim here is that hypnosis is not necessarily more contaminating to recall than any other memory retrieval effort because the dangers of confabulation and memory hardening are not unique to, nor exacerbated by, hypnosis. In other words, the argument is that hypnosis does not render one more likely to experience either of these detrimental outcomes when compared with recall generated by other means. This view perceives suggestion on the part of those in control of the hypnotic session as the relevant, externally generated threat to the reliability of a hypnotically refreshed memory, and thus claims that as long as that danger is abated the testimony should be admitted (Scheflin, Spiegel, & Spiegel, 1999; Brown, Scheflin, & Hammond, 1998; Hammond et al., 1995).

This "no more contaminating than" argument would appear to have relevance within a *Daubert* screening exercise. This is because it addresses the critical question of whether hypnosis can generate historically accurate recall. Adherents of this position acknowledge the possibility of error, but they claim that this possibility can be eliminated, or at least kept to an acceptable limit, so long as proper procedures are followed in carrying out the hypnotic session. This mention of the possibility of error and controlling the same through the implementation of selected procedures takes us into the third and fourth *Daubert* screening factors: What is the error rate of hypnotically refreshed testimony, and how, if at all, do we eliminate or at least control that error rate?

Putting *Daubert*'s error rate inquiry into terms that are relevant to the present effort, the issue is one of determining the rate at which hypnosis generates historically inaccurate recall. The general findings from the previously mentioned research regarding the tendency of hypnosis to increase the amount of inaccurate recall and the fact that false memories can be contaminated through suggestion during hypnosis establish that hypnosis does produce some memories. In light of this, the question becomes one of trying to determine the error rate, and this proves to be a very difficult task. The simple fact is that with hypnotically recalled memories one cannot necessarily tell what memories are true from what memories are false (Frankel & Covino, 1997; Yapko, 1994; Meyer, 1992; American Medical Association, 1985). One of the possible explanations for this, as demonstrated in the experimental research, is that subjects who recall details under hypnosis tend to experience an increase in their confidence in those details, to the extent that the story they now tell will appear to be compelling, even though it may not be true (Frankel & Covino, 1997; Sheehan & McConkey, 1993; Meyer, 1992; American Medical Association, 1985). Even keeping in mind that all memory suffers from a similar problem, albeit in a generally somewhat weakened form, this turn of events is troublesome for supporters of hypnotically refreshed testimony because, as the proponents of the evidence, they have the burden of proving its reliability, which can be a near, if not absolute, impossibility in regard to all of the details recalled. Therefore, the only hope for the proponents of hypnotically refreshed testimony is to encourage courts to take each case on its own merits rather than rejecting such testimony out of hand. This, of course, is the approach that the *Hurd* and "totality-of-the-circumstancess" jurisdictions have taken toward this testimony, and it is an inquiry that has its place in a *Daubert*-inspired reliability test.

Given that there is an error rate associated with hypnotically refreshed recall and given that this error rate will fluctuate from case to case, the question becomes: How can one control the hypnotic session so as to eliminate or reduce the error rate and increase the likelihood of extracting historically accurate memories? This question, in turn, brings us to the fourth step in a *Daubert* test of the reliability of hypnotically refreshed testimony—a step that requires focusing attention on the standards that are available for controlling the use of hypnosis. This step is reminiscent of the common-law *Hurd* and "totality-of-the-circumstancess" approaches to dealing with hypnotically refreshed testimony. Although neither of those two approaches would be sufficient, in and of themselves, to determine the admissibility of some challenged hypnotically refreshed testimony in a *Daubert* jurisdiction, they can serve as guides when applying *Daubert*'s fourth reliability factor to that type of testimony.

As we have seen, the *Hurd* and "totality-of-the-circumstances" jurisdictions have fashioned a list of practices that are specifically aimed at controlling or eliminating contaminating influences from the hypnotic session. These practices were originally developed by behavioral scientists, and these researchers and commentators have continued to agree that these requirements are necessary to enhance the reliability of hypnotically refreshed testimony (Sheehan & McConkey, 1993; Meyer, 1992; Relinger & Stern, 1983).

In addition to generally vouching for the *Hurd* and "totality-of-the-circumstances" reliability-enhancing practices, behavioral science researchers and commentators have consistently spoken to other requirements that should be included as part of good hypnotic technique. There is a strong consensus in this community in favor of assessing the hypnotizability of a subject who is going to be put into a trance (Scheflin, Spiegel, & Spiegel, 1999; Sheehan & McConkey, 1993). Hypnotizability is a stable and measurable trait, and those with higher levels of hypnotizability have been found to be better able to use vivid mental imagery as a means of enhancing and expanding their recall (Scheflin, Spiegel, & Spiegel, 1999; Frankel & Covino, 1997). Because hynotizability correlates positively with suggestibility and the suspension of critical judgment, the more hypnotizable a subject is the greater the risk that the accuracy of his or her recall will be compromised (Scheflin, Spiegel, & Spiegel, 1999; Frankel & Covino, 1997). Therefore, the failure to test for hypnotizability could be a definitive block to the admissibility of any hypnotically refreshed testimony. On the other hand, if the hypnotizability of a witness whose hypnotically refreshed testimony is under consideration has been measured, then, generally speaking, a finding that the witness falls in the highly hypnotizable range would be a factor weighing against the reliability of the testimony, whereas the fact that the witness falls in the moderate or low hypnotizable range would be a factor in favor of admitting the testimony.

In conjunction with emphasizing the hypnotizability issue, behavioral science researchers and commentators have also highlighted two other practices that are designed to protect the integrity of hypnotically refreshed testimony. The first of these is the need to make sure that a witness whose testimony has allegedly been refreshed under hypnosis was in fact hypnotized. Because hypnosis is a condition that can be faked with some success (Sheehan & McConkey, 1993; Meyer, 1992; Orne, 1977), and because this issue has on occasion caught the attention of the courts (Zitter, 1993), an expert witness should be prepared to discuss whether that danger is present in any particular case. The best practice would be one that, as a matter of routine, administers one or more tests during the hypnotic session to determine if the subject is actually in trance (Sheehan & McConkey, 1993; Meyer, 1992).

Another reliability-enhancing practice highlighted by the scientific community is the need to avoid the "television technique" of hypnosis. This technique, which has been used widely by police departments in the past, involves telling hypnotized subjects that their memories are analogous to a videotape, complete with freeze-frame, pause, and reverse, and that hypnosis can help them provide additional details of which they are not aware. Unfortunately, this particular hypnosis tactic has the effect of encouraging subjects to guess and be creative in the absence of actual memories, and it causes subjects to develop an artificial sense of certainty about the veracity of their memories (Scheflin, Spiegel, & Spiegel, 1999; Meyer, 1992).

It is here, within the *Daubert*'s fourth factor, that a behavioral science defender of hypnotically refreshed testimony would want to focus a reviewing court's attention in order to maximize the likelihood that the testimony will be admitted. The defender cannot afford to rest solely on the science because, as we have seen, the science would leave the court at the point of a uncertain error rate attaching to the testimony. Instead, relying upon the fact that the Supreme Court in both *Daubert* and *Kumho Tire* stressed the flexibility of its reliability screening, the defender would need to convince the court that the standards available for controlling the use of hypnosis can eliminate, or least heavily mitigate, the error rate. In other words, the proponent must prove that because care was taken in extracting the hypnotically refreshed testimony in question, it is sufficiently reliable to justify its admission into evidence (Frankel & Covino, 1997; Sheehan & McConkey, 1993; Meyer, 1992).

In order to be in a strong position to carry this burden, the proponent of the evidence will have to demonstrate strict compliance with the standards that the courts and the scientific community have identified as critical to the reliability of the outcome. The ultimate goal is to end up with hypnotically refreshed testimony that is as free as possible of contaminating influences. Keeping in mind all of the specific details discussed about good hypnotic practice in this chapter, some general guidelines have emerged that can serve as markers of good practice in the forensic use of hypnosis. First, in order to increase the likelihood of an unassailable outcome, the hypnotist should be an independent, qualified psychiatrist or psychologist (Sheehan & McConkey, 1993; Meyer, 1992). Second, the use of hypnosis must be appropriate for the kind of memory loss encountered. Generally speaking, hypnosis is a more useful tool when it is used to overcome a memory block that can be traced to a highly emotional event (Scheflin, Spiegel, & Spiegel, 1999; Sheehan & McConkey, 1993). Third, the subject must be an appropriate candidate for the use of hypnosis. This requirement covers the issue of hypnotizability, which has already been discussed, and it includes the need to be sensitive to the different motivating factors that various subjects (e.g., witness, victim, or suspect) may bring to the hypnotic session (Scheflin, Spiegel, & Spiegel, 1999; Sheehan & McConkey, 1993). Fourth, as already mentioned, the totality of the hypnotic session must be controlled so as to eliminate suggestive influences. And fifth, the best practice would be to ensure that there is a detailed record, preferably a videotape record, of the entire hypnotic process that can be reviewed independently by the court (Meyer, 1992). Given the point at which the science rests regarding the reliability of hypnotically refreshed testimony, a court will need to see that those things that present a danger to reliability have not been allowed to impact the hypnotically refreshed testimony being offered.

The fifth and final *Daubert* factor requires a *Frye*-type inquiry, which asks whether hypnosis as a means of extracting historically accurate recall enjoys general acceptance within the behavioral science community. As mentioned earlier, the *Daubert* Court did not intend a return to the dominance of *Frye*, but it did believe that widespread acceptance, or rejection, can be an important factor in ruling particular evidence admissible or not. In the context of hypnotically refreshed testimony, the picture is not all that clear when it comes to its status within the behavioral science community. There are those who, focusing largely upon the empirical data, have concluded that hypnosis is as yet an unproven technique when it comes to the recovery of true memory (Frankel & Covino, 1997). At the same time, however, there are many who maintain that when proper guidelines are followed, hypnosis can be effective in retrieving otherwise unavailable, accurate information (Scheflin, Spiegel, & Spiegel, 1999; Brown, Scheflin, & Hammond, 1998; Hammond et al., 1995).

In the end, the *Frye* debate over hypnotically refreshed testimony comes to the same place as did the analysis of the previous four *Daubert* factors. Whether one looks with favor upon hypnotically refreshed testimony depends upon the extent to which one is strictly wedded to experimental research results versus the extent to which one will be willing to place faith in good technique. A court that insists upon it being scientifically proven that hypnosis produces either only historically accurate recall or the ability to tell the difference between accurate and inaccurate recall is not going to be receptive to hypnotically refreshed testimony. On the other hand, a view that recognizes the limitations of the technique as established by the science, but that still holds that it can produce sufficiently reliable testimony if done properly, will accept its admission into court. As already stated, the latter view is more in keeping with the Supreme Court's call in *Daubert* and *Kumho Tire* for a more liberal and flexible standard of admissibility for scientific evidence that is grounded in the principles of relevance and reliability.

Conclusion

> Experts wishing to practice competently in a well-conducted *Daubert/Kumho* hearing will find the new environment a spur to improving their testimony about complex science issues. By contrast, careless experts in *Daubert/Kumho* cross-examinations may reveal culpable technical and ethical errors. It is up to experts to uphold the highest standards of their respective professions, disclose fully and fairly the bases for their opinions, rely to the greatest extent possible on solid scientific findings, explain in understandable terms the uncertainties in their opinions, and be frank about the degree to which their theories and methods meet, or fail to meet, *Daubert* requirements (Grove & Barden, 1999, p. 238).

Taking Grove and Barden's general guidance and specifically applying it to a defense of hypnotically refreshed testimony in a *Daubert* jurisdiction, one can see rather clearly the path that must be followed if that defense is going to succeed. Rather than running away from research results that call the reliability of hypnotically refreshed testimony into question, a behavioral science expert must be prepared to speak intelligently about that research, its strengths and its limitations. It is not going to be enough to simply say that the research does not have applicability in the forensic setting, because this leaves the proponent with a blank slate in the face of bearing the burden to support the admissibility of the testimony. The expert is going to have to speak candidly to the court about the possibility of inaccurate testimony flowing from the hypnotic session, but then, while highlighting *Daubert*'s intended flexibility, stress that the likelihood of that inaccuracy has been severely diminished by technique specifically aimed at eliminating any possibility of suggestive influences. Of course, this assumes that the practices for controlling the use of hypnosis were indeed employed to such a rigorous degree, and this has at least two potentially serious implications.

The first implication that could be drawn is that hypnosis should be used on an individual who faces the potential of becoming a witness in a criminal case only as a last resort (Frankel & Covino, 1997; Hammond et al., 1995; Meyer, 1992). Other alternative, less intrusive techniques such as reassurance, relaxation, and review should be attempted before proceeding to hypnosis (Frankel & Covino, 1997). The second implication is that clinicians who use hypnosis in their practice must be aware of the possibility that if a patient recalls something that would have significance in the criminal setting, the opportunity for a court to hear testimony flowing from that memory may very well be lost unless standards for eliminating suggestive influences were in place and followed when the patient was put under trance. Of course, it is unlikely, and perhaps even impossible, in the clinical setting for those standards to be followed with great rigor. Although a full discussion of the ethical and practical problems this raises is beyond the scope of this chapter, generally speaking the patient and the clinician must both be fully informed as to the costs and benefits of undergoing hypnotic therapy. The patient in particular must understand that his or her ability to testify at some later date in a criminal proceeding may be compromised by consenting to having his or her memory refreshed through hypnosis (Meyer, 1992).

ACKNOWLEDGMENTS

The author would like to thank Shannon Pritchard and Nancy Gordon for their valuable research assistance. This chapter was previously published in 2003 in volume 9 of the *Texas Wesleyan Law Review* on pages 151–179.

REFERENCES

American Medical Association, Council on Scientific Affairs. (1985). Scientific status of refreshing recollection by the use of hypnosis. *Journal of the American Medical Association, 253*, 1918–1923.

Borawick v. Shay, 68 F.3d 597 (2nd Cir. 1995).

Brown, D., Scheflin, A. W., & Hammond, D. C. (1998). *Memory trauma treatment, and the law.* New York: Norton.

Burral v. State, 724 A.2d 65 (Md. 1999).

Daubert v. Merrell Dow Pharmaceuticals, 509 U.S. 579 (1993).

Diamond, B. L. (1980). Inherent problems in the use of pretrial hypnosis on a prospective witness. *California Law Review, 68*, 313–349.

Dywan, J., & Bowers, K. (1983). The use of hypnosis to enhance recall. *Science, 222*, 184–185.

Fenner, G. M. (1996). The *Daubert* handbook: The case, its essential dilemma, and its progeny. *Creighton Law Review, 29*, 939–1089.

Fleming, T. M. (1990). Admissibility of hypnotically refreshed or enhanced testimony. *American Law Reports (4th), 77*, 923–983.

Frankel, F. H., & Covino, N. A. (1997). Hypnosis and hypnotherapy. In P. S. Appelbaum, L. A. Uyehara, & M. R. Elin (Eds.), *Trauma and memory* (pp. 344–359). New York: Oxford University Press.

Frye v. United States, 293 F. 1013 (D.C. Cir. 1923).

Giannelli, P. C., & Imwinkelried, E. J. (1999). *Scientific evidence, Vol 1.* Charlottesville, VA: Matthew Bender.

Graham, M. H. (1998). The *Daubert* dilemma: At last a viable solution? *Federal Rules Decision, 179*, 1–18.

Graham, M. H. (2001). *Handbook of federal evidence* (5th ed.). St. Paul, MN: West.

Grove, W. M., & Barden, R. C. (1999). Protecting the integrity of the legal system: The admissibility of testimony from mental health experts under *Daubert/Kumho* analyses. *Psychology, Public Policy, and the Law, 5*, 224–242.

Hammond, D. C., Garver, R. B., Mutter, C. B., Crasilneck, H. B., Frischholz, E., Gravitz, M. A., et al. (1995). *Clinical hypnosis and memory: Guidelines for clinicians and for forensic hypnosis.* Des Plaines, IL: American Society of Clinical Hypnosis Press.

Harding v. State, 246 A.2d 302 (Md. Ct. Spec. App. 1968).

Kanovitz, J. (1992). Hypnotic memories and civil sexual abuse trials. *Vanderbilt Law Review, 45,* 1185–1262.

Krebs, P. A., & De Tray, B. J. (1999). *Kumho Tire Co. v. Carmichael*: A flexible approach to analyzing expert testimony under *Daubert. Tort and Insurance Law Journal, 34,* 989–1007.

Kumho Tire Co., Ltd. v. Carmichael, 526 U.S. 137 (1999).

Labelle, L., Laurence, J. R., Nadon, R., & Perry, C. (1990). Hypnotizability, preference for an imagic cognitive style, and memory creation in hypnosis. *Journal of Abnormal Psychology, 99,* 222–228.

Laurence, J. R., & Perry, C. (1983). Hypnotically created memory among highly hypnotizable subjects. *Science, 222,* 523–524.

Lindsay, D. S., & Read, J. D. (1995). "Memory work" and recovered memories of childhood sexual abuse: Scientific evidence and public, professional and personal issues. *Psychology, Public Policy, and the Law, 1,* 846–908.

McConkey, K. M. (1995). Hypnosis, memory, and the ethics of uncertainty. *Australian Psychologist, 30,* 1–10.

McCord, D. (1987). Syndromes, profiles and other mental exotica: A new approach to the admissibility of nontraditional psychological evidence in criminal cases. *Oregon Law Review, 66,* 19–108.

Meyer, R. G. (1992). *Practical clinical hypnosis: Technique and applications.* New York: Lexington Books.

Moriarty, J. C. (1999). *Psychological and scientific evidence in criminal trials.* St. Paul, MN: West Group.

Ofshe, R., & Watters, E. (1994). *Making monsters.* New York: Scribner's.

Orne, M. T. (1977). The construct of hypnosis: Implications of the definition for research and practice. *Annals of the New York Academy of Science, 296,* 14–33.

People v. Zayas, 546 N.E.2d 513 (Ill. 1989).

Polk v. State, 427 A.2d 1041 (Md. Ct. Spec. App. 1981).

Relinger, H., & Stern, T. (1983). Guidelines for forensic hypnosis. *Journal of Psychiatry and Law, Spring,* 69–74.

Roark v. Commonwealth, 90 S.W.3d 24 (Ky. 2002).

Rock v. Arkansas, 483 U.S. 44 (1987).

Sanders, G. S., & Simmons, W. I. (1983). Use of hypnosis to enhance eyewitness accuracy: Does it work? *Journal of Applied Psychology, 68,* 70–77.

Scheflin, A. W., & Shapiro, J. L. (1989). *Trance on trial.* New York: Guilford Press.

Scheflin, A. W., Spiegel, H., & Spiegel, D. (1999). Forensic uses of hypnosis. In A. K. Hess & I. B. Weiner (Eds.), *The handbook of forensic psychology* (pp. 474–498). New York: Wiley.

Shaw, G. M. (1991). The admissibility of hypnotically enhanced testimony in criminal trials. *Marquette Law Review, 75,* 1–77.

Sheehan, P. W., & McConkey, K. M. (1993). Forensic hypnosis: The application of ethical guidelines. In J. W. Rhue, S. J. Lynn, & I. Kirsch (Eds.), *Handbook of clinical hypnosis* (pp. 719–738). Washington, DC: American Psychological Association.

Shuman, D. W., & Sales, B. D. (1998). The admissibility of expert testimony based upon clinical judgment and scientific research. *Psychology, Public Policy, and the Law, 4*, 1226–1252.
State v. Brown, 337 N.W.2d 138 (N.D. 1983).
State v. Collins, 464 A.2d 1028 (Md. 1983).
State v. Hurd, 432 A.2d 86 (N.J. 1981).
State v. Tuttle, 780 P.2d 1203 (Utah 1989).
State v. Weston, 475 N.E.2d 805 (Ohio Ct. App. 1984).
Wright, C. A., & Gold, V. J. (1990). *Federal practice and procedure, Vol. 27*. St. Paul, MN: West.
Wright, C. A., & Gold, V. J. (1997). *Federal practice and procedure, Vol. 29*. St. Paul, MN: West.
Yapko, M. D. (1994). Suggestibility and repressed memories of abuse: A survey of psychotherapists' beliefs. *American Journal of Clinical Hypnosis, 36*, 163–187.
Zitter, J. M. (1993). Sufficiency of evidence that witness in criminal case was hypnotized, for purposes of determining admissibility of testimony given under hypnosis or of hypnotically enhanced testimony. *American Law Reports (5th), 16*, 841–854.

CHAPTER 25

A CRITICAL ANALYSIS OF THE POLYGRAPH

ERIN M. OKSOL AND WILLIAM T. O'DONOHUE

UNIVERSITY OF NEVADA, RENO

The ability to detect deception and discriminate between honest and deceptive responses has been an important goal throughout history (Ben-Shakhar, 1991). Historically, it has been important from both a criminal justice stance (i.e., to determine the guilt of a person regarding a specific criminal event) and from a personnel selection perspective (i.e., to discriminate truthtellers from deceivers in a group of job applicants). Recently, we have seen interesting trends in the use of polygraphy with sex offenders. There is a newfound interest in the usefulness of polygraphy as a tool in the treatment of sexual abusers. In essence, many probation officers are convinced they cannot sufficiently supervise sex abusers without polygraphy; therapists state that therapy cannot be adequately conducted without the use of the polygraph because they need to have accurate self-report in order to properly treat; and judges feel that they cannot protect society adequately without polygraph surveillance (Abrams, 1991).

Polygraphy is the evaluation of physiologic reactions that purportedly occur in response to the emotions of fear or conflict or are in some other way associated with lying. The polygraph measures a number of subtle and involuntary changes in physiological functions such as heart rate, skin resistance, and blood pressure. The changes in these autonomic functions are detected by amplifying and recording the functions on a multichannel instrument, the polygraph. It is so named because it has many (poly) pens, with each pen measuring and recording (graphing) a different physiological response. Some of these physiologic responses are recorded on a polygraph chart, and the polygrapher interprets these changes as indicative of truthfulness or deception.

Typically, some variation of four channels, or pens, is measured. One physiologic function measured is the *galvanic skin response*, or GSR, the short-term change in skin resistance. A second channel, known as the *cardio*, measures systolic and diastolic blood pressure via a pressure cuff on the arm. A third function is *respiration*, in which small changes in amplitude and frequency are measured. The fourth channel records the blood flow in the tip of the index finger. This is called the *vasomotor response* (VMR) and is similar to the GSR in that it changes depending on stimulation (Furedy & Heslegrave, 1988).

Over the years polygraph examinations have played an important role in many settings. These settings include criminal investigations of suspects accused of theft, rape, murder, or lesser crimes. District attorneys at times will not prosecute a complaint unless the victim of the crime agrees to a lie detector test. Recently, a number of criminal justice and treatment professionals have been advocating for the increased use of polygraph tests to assess child sexual abuse allegations or have implemented polygraph testing in their practices or treatment programs (Abrams, 1991; Abrams, Hoyt, & Jewell, 1991; Ansley, 1989; Jensen & Jewell, 1988; as cited in Cross & Saxe, 1991).

The Employee Polygraph Protection Act (EPPA) of 1988 eliminated much of the most widespread application of polygraph testing, the periodic screening of employees to verify their good behavior, and the preemployment screening of potential hires to see if they possess the qualities (e.g., honesty) desired by the employer. However, the government exempted itself from coverage by this law (Iacono & Patrick, 1999), resulting in more widespread use of polygraph tests by the government for these purposes.

Results from a polygraph can have significant consequences for the test taker. Families may be separated, police and prosecutors may be influenced to prosecute, litigation may either continue or cease, and the judgments and perceptions of jury members may be swayed (Kleinmuntz & Szucko, 1982). An individual's life can be fundamentally altered by the polygraph test. Knowing both the assets and limitations of this technique is therefore paramount.

Polygraphers, including those with scientific training, claim that polygraph tests have greater than 90 percent accuracy, that this claim is supported by scientific literature, that their techniques are based on sound scientific principles, and that scientists agree with these claims (Iacono & Patrick, 1999). They further argue that these techniques have great value and advocate their use in criminal and court proceedings, as well as to screen out undesirable employees. In this chapter we critically examine the empirical literature and arguments used to support these claims.

POLYGRAPH TEST PROCEDURES

The central element of any polygraph examination is a test of a subject's responses to a set of questions. The purpose of most polygraph tests is to elicit physiological reactions to questions that are referred to as *relevant* questions and compare these reactions to those that result when other questions, typically called *control* questions, are asked. Relevant questions are directly related to the focus of the investigation ("Did you steal the typewriter?"). Control questions are not related to the focus of the investigation. They are, however, believed to be emotionally arousing (e.g., "Have you ever stolen anything before the age of 18?"). A third type of question is an *irrelevant* question, one that is not related to the focus of the investigation and is believed to have little emotional impact ("Is your name . . . ?").

A Typical Polygraph Procedure

A typical polygraph test lasts between 3 to 4 hours, with less than 15 minutes actually spent obtaining physiological recordings (Saxe et al., 1985). The first phase, the *pretest interview*, lasts 30 to 60 minutes (Furedy, 1991). In this phase, the examiner seeks to convince the examinee of the polygraph's infallibility. The examiner discusses the relevant issues that will be tested and also discusses formulations of both relevant and control questions. The relevant questions are reformulated until they are unambiguous to the examinee so that he or she can clearly answer "no" to them (i.e., indicating innocence). The control questions are reformulated until they produce a physiological response, thus proving that the subject is capable of responding. The examiner wants the subject to experience considerable doubt about his or her truthfulness when responding to a control question. According to Kircher and Raskin (1983; as cited in Saxe et al., 1985), control questions are intentionally vague and extremely difficult to answer truthfully with an unqualified no. An example of such a control question might be, "Have you ever stolen anything in your life?"

Stimulation Tests

The actual test phase is often preceded by the card, or *stim*, test. Here the examiner uses the polygraph to detect, from a number of cards, the card the examinee has in mind. Sometimes the cards are secretly marked so that the examiner is sure to know the correct answer (Reid & Inbau, 1977). The purpose of the stim test is to convince the examinee of the polygraph's infallibility.

Test Phase Proper

Following the demonstration of "infallibility" during the stim test, the test proper is administered. This usually consists of 10 questions. Typically, at least three of the 10 questions are relevant questions and three are control questions. The questions are usually separated by about 30 seconds, and each repetition through the list of questions is called a *chart*. Typically, after three charts, the examiner can decide whether or not to conclude or administer more charts (Furedy, 1991).

Posttest Interview

At the end of the examination, the examiner will often assess whether a subject has responded in an honest or deceptive manner. Should the subject be thought to be deceptive, the examiner will administer the *posttest interview*. The purpose of this interrogatory phase (the existence of which most examinees are unaware of when they agreed to be "tested" by the polygraph) is to induce a confession. The interrogatory phase can last from 10 minutes to several hours and ends when the examinee confesses or the examiner decides a confession cannot be obtained (Furedy, 1991).

EXAMINING THE EVIDENCE

In examining the validity of polygraphic methods, it is necessary to consider separately the validity that can be achieved in detecting deception strictly on the basis of the polygraph charts. The only way to assess the validity of a polygraphic lie test, independent of clinical impressions, is to have the polygraph charts scored blindly by a second polygrapher who did not observe the subject and is unfamiliar with the case facts. Since polygraph charts are seldom scored this way in practice, however, it should be remembered that most lie detector "tests" are really clinical examinations (subject to the problems and limitations discussed earlier). In addition to this requirement of blind scoring, validity studies must be conducted in the field, in real-life testing situations. Volunteer subjects in laboratory experiments are not under the same emotional pressure that affects criminal suspects or persons being screened for employment purposes. Deceptive subjects may be less reactive in the laboratory than when lying about real crimes at the police station. Truthful subjects will almost certainly be more reactive in the field situation and, for this reason, more likely to be misclassified by the polygraphic lie test.

One psychometric issue concerns what kind of assessment methodology the polygraph typifies and therefore by what criteria it should be judged. The first possibility is that the polygraph is a norm-referenced test in which results from one examinee are compared to the results obtained by some reference group to ascertain whether the examinee's score deviates from that of the group. The second possibility is that the polygraph is a criterion-referenced test in which the examinee's responses are compared to some criterion of healthy or deviant responding (i.e., truthful or deceptive). The third possibility is that the polygraph should not be classified as a "test" but rather as a form of direct observation of behavior. If this were the case, autonomic arousal, as evidenced by movement of the pens on the polygraph, are a sample of behavior. This sample of behavior must be a representative sample if valid inferences are to be made to other domains of behavioral functioning. Recognizing that the question of which criteria are most relevant remains controversial, we will assume that traditional psychometric criteria (American Psychological Association, 1985) are relevant to this methodology.

The Validity of the Polygraph

How valid, or *accurate*, is the polygraph? This is a complicated question without a simple answer. One leader in the field asserts, "The notion that the polygraph can separate truth from falsity at high (or even moderately high) levels of accuracy is one of the great urban legends of popular psychology" (Scott Lilienfeld, personal communication, January 1999). Since the word *accurate* can be vague and a true "polygraph test" does not exist, the question perhaps needs to be reworded.

When polygraphers are asked to give a single percentage figure on the validity or "accuracy" of polygraphy, it seems as though errors in determining accuracy are of a single type or that differences between error types are unimportant. On the contrary, it is critical to distinguish between at least two major types of errors: false negative and false positive. To state, then, that "polygraphy is x percent accurate" is too simplistic (Furedy & Heslegrave, 1988).

Many would agree that for a test to be useful, its accuracy should be greater than chance levels, or 50 percent. But how accurate *ought* the polygraph be remains unanswered. Because the polygraph is so often used to make important life decisions, it seems that one should be certain that the results are very accurate indeed.

Complicating matters is that accuracy estimates of polygraph techniques depend on a great many factors. The skill level of the examiner, the psychological state of the subject, the scoring procedures, the questioning techniques, and the particular physiological variables measures are but a few of the variables that must be taken into account when one is attempting to determine the accuracy or validity of the procedure. It must be stated that most studies have provided insufficient control over the many factors that can influence the accuracy of polygraph procedures. Accordingly, the validity of these procedures remains an unresolved issue, and estimates of accuracy range from chance to perfection (Furedy & Heslegrave, 1988).

False Negatives and False Positives

What is important to recognize is that as long as the polygraph is not 100 percent accurate, everyone is at risk. The risk, moreover, is an "inverse function of the accuracy rate, as well as a direct function of the ever increasing fishing-expedition use of polygraph" (Furedy, 1987, p. 148). To persuade a suspect to take the polygraph, examiners often tell the examinee that "if you are innocent you have nothing to worry about." This assertion may sound reasonable to the suspect, especially when made under circumstances that are inherently worrisome (i.e., being under police suspicion for a serious crime). However, it is a patently false statement because it requires the assumption (and the evidence) that the polygraph is 100 percent accurate in classifying innocent persons. On the contrary, a review of the four most recently published field validity studies indicates that the combined false negative rate (guilty subjects diagnosed as innocent) is 5 percent and the false positive rate (innocent subjects misdiagnosed as guilty) is 10 percent (Raskin, Honts, Amato, & Kircher, 1999). Psychophysiological scientists disagree on actual accuracy rates, but let us grant for the sake of argument that Lykken's (1998) 70 percent estimate is incorrect. If, in one's career, one is subjected to three polygraph examinations, there is approximately a one in three chance that a single examination will produce a false positive result. One inaccurate conclusion is all it takes to ruin one's life (Furedy, 1987).

In this section we shall briefly review some of the literature pertinent to the accuracy and validity of current polygraph techniques. Ever since use of physiological recordings to detect the deceptiveness of criminal suspects was proposed by Marston (1917), controversy over polygraphic "lie tests" has raged. Polygraph tests have been debated in the U.S. Congress, courtrooms, and in a plethora of scientific and nonscientific forums (Saxe et al., 1985). Although much of the public debate about polygraph tests concerns ethical issues, at the heart of the controversy is validity—the relatively simple question of whether the polygraph can accurately discriminate honest and deceptive responses. This review does not attempt to exhaustively cover the vast literature, but rather to cover several of the more important issues related to determining the validity of the polygraph techniques described. Our intention is to provide the reader with information that will facilitate a critical examination of claims of accuracy.

The literature relevant to the validity of polygraph testing has been reviewed repeatedly in the past decade. Consequently, there are many sources the interested reader can turn to for insights and perspectives that extend the reviews presented here (Abrams, 1989; Bashore & Rapp, 1993; Ben-Shakur & Furedy, 1990; Furedy & Heslegrave, 1988; Honts & Quick, 1996; Honts, Raskin, & Kircher, 1994; Iacono, 1995, 1999; Iacono & Lykken, 1997a, 1997b, 1997c; Iacono & Patrick, 1988, 1997; Lykken, 1998; Saxe, 1991).

What Critics Have to Say. Critics of traditional polygraph procedures have argued that the assumptions on which they are based are flawed and there is essentially no sound scientific support for their validity (Bashore & Rapp, 1993). These critics contend that the traditional procedures have not been subjected to rigorous scientific evaluation and that claims of the power of these techniques by their proponents are based on subjective and impressionistic observations. Moreover, the critics claim that the vast majority of reports on the efficacy of these procedures have been done by the advocates themselves, who presumably have a vested interest in promoting their trade. These critics also assert that among those trained in traditional lie detection procedures, there are very few behavioral scientists or psychophysiologists with advanced academic degrees who are competent to conduct the type of research needed to assess the validity of these procedures. Another fundamental criticism made by opponents is that there is no physiological or behavioral response pattern indicative of lying, despite claims made by its proponents (Bashore & Rapp, 1993). Still other critics assert that the polygraph test neither meets the required criteria of standardization nor the established criteria of reliability and validity for psychological tests (Kleinmuntz & Szucko, 1984; Lykken, 1981; Szucko & Kleinmuntz, 1981). These views are nicely summarized by Furedy and Heslegrave (1988):

> It is also important to recognize the important role played by the attitudes of evaluators toward accepting errors, and weighing these errors depending upon the circumstances. Because the circumstances are known by the evaluator prior to the administration of the polygraph, and because the test is not standardized, it is likely that not only will the outcome be judged on the basis of examinee circumstance and examiner attitude, but also the administration of the test will be shaped by these prejudices. Because the test is psychological in the sense of involving a complex interview-like interaction between the examiner and examinee, any biases in designing and administering the test are likely to produce outcomes that are consistent with those biases. So different individuals accused of different crimes may be given quite different tests, even though all of those tests are called by a single name—a polygraph test. Indeed, the term test is potentially misleading because it suggests relatively standardized instruments such as IQ tests, that, although controversial, give essentially the same results across competent operators. (p. 224)

Some have stated that it is plausible to state there is no criterion at the present time that can completely verify or refute the validity of the polygraph. A polygrapher once testified before the Minnesota legislature that in 20,000 cases he had never been wrong (Lykken, 1998). One might ask, has he ever been proven to be right? To further emphasize the confidence that examiners have in the polygraph, a president of the American Polygraph Association wrote that he had never seen a truthful subject diagnosed as deceptive (Simpson, 1986).

The empirical evidence for the polygraph's validity can be divided into laboratory and field studies. The distinction is important. Giving lie detector tests to students or other mock-theft suspects who have enacted crimes does not provide grounds for adequate predictions of what can be expected in real-life criminal investigations (Kleinmuntz & Szucko, 1984). The main limitation is that the genuine motives that operate in real life are presumably missing. However, the advantage is knowing ground truth. Field studies, on the other hand, use real suspects, persons who are being truthful or deceptive about committing a crime. Here, the disadvantage is not knowing ground truth.

Evidence from Field Studies. There are, perhaps, 250 empirical reports of the validity of the polygraph (Iacono & Patrick, 1999). Most reports, however, do not include a independent assessment of ground truth and are case reports (Saxe et al., 1985). Only 10 of these studies meet criteria established from field studies in the Office of Technology Assessment (OTA), an organization designed to provide an assessment of current scientific knowledge about polygraph tests. A great deal of variability exists across results of these studies. Correct guilty decisions ranged from 70 to 98 percent. Correct innocent decisions ranged from a low of 12 percent to a high of 94 percent. False negatives ranged from zero to 29 percent, whereas false positives ranged from zero to 75 percent. Inconclusives ranged from zero to 25 percent (Saxe et al., 1985).

We shall now present a field study in which the authors were fortunate to be able to conduct the study as outsiders who obtained access to records in a leading polygraph firm (Kleinmunttz & Szucko, 1984). They selected the polygraph charts of 50 innocent subjects and 50 guilty subjects, all of whom were tested with regard to some theft-related investigation. Subjects who confessed to the full amount of the theft were considered to be guilty and subjects were considered to be innocent if others had confessed to the offense.

The polygraph charts of these 100 subjects were then submitted for interpretation to six polygraph trainees at the end of their internship training period. The judges were asked to rate each subjects chart on an 8-point scale (1 = definitely truthful, 8 = definitely untruthful). A critical finding in this study was that, on average, the polygraph interpreters misclassified 37 percent of the innocent subjects as guilty. This high false positive rate includes, among six judges, one who misclassified as many as 50 percent of innocent suspects, and another, clearly the best of the group, who misclassified only 18 percent of his innocent cases as guilty. Similar findings were found in a field study conducted by Horvath (1977), whose polygraphers called nearly half (50%) of the innocent respondents guilty. Barland and Raking (1976), in an unpublished paper, similarly reported that more than half (55%) of their truthful subjects were misclassified as deceptive (as cited in Saxe et al., 1985).

Regardless of the procedure to score the charts, the field examiner normally has been exposed to extrapolygraphic cues such as the case facts, the behavior of the suspect during the examination, and sometimes a confession from the examinee. For an investigation to provide a useful estimate of the accuracy of the psychophysiological test, the original examiner's charts must be reinterpreted by blind evaluators who have no knowledge of the suspect or case facts. Even though those trained in numerical scoring are specifically taught to ignore extrapolygraphic cues, Patrick and Iacono (1991) showed that they nevertheless did attend to them in their field study of Royal Canadian Mounted Police (RCMP) polygraph practices.

RCMP examiners are trained in numerical scoring and disdain the global approach. To determine if these examiners were indeed uninfluenced by extrapolygraphic cues, Iacono and colleagues compared the examiners' verdicts contained in their written reports with the verdicts they should have obtained given their own numerical scores for 276 examinations. For 59 subjects, the examiners contradicted the conclusions dictated by their own numerical scores by offering written verdicts that were not supported by the polygraph charts. It is of considerable interest that in 93 percent of these cases, they offered written opinions favoring the truthfulness of the subjects by assigning inconclusive verdicts to charts numerically scored as deceptive and truthful verdicts to charts numerically scored inconclusive. These charts were then blindly rescored by different examiners. By comparing these blind scores to the original scores, it was possible to determine if the original examiners were more likely to generate numerical scores indicating truthfulness than the blind examiners. This was indeed the case (Iacono, 1999), suggesting that the numerical scoring of the original examiners was also influenced by their belief that suspects were more likely to be innocent than was indicated by the physiological data.

Collectively, these findings have a number of interesting implications for determining the validity of the polygraph. First, they indicate that examiners are indeed influenced by extrapolygraphic data and that these data affect both their ultimate decisions and their numerical scores. Second, they suggest that at some level the examiners are aware that the psychophysiological assessment is biased against the innocent, so they tend not to trust their numerical scores that do not indicate truthfulness. Third, they indicate that examiners can improve their accuracy when they rely on case facts and other extraneous information rather than basing their decisions entirely on the polygraph chart tracings. The fact that these data show that the original examiner is more accurate when he or she overrides the charts speaks to the invalidity of the polygraph when used to determine truthfulness (Iacono & Patrick, 1999).

Evidence from Analogue (Lab) Studies. Most analogue studies have been conducted with college students (Saxe et al., 1985). This creates a potential external validity problem, because students are likely to be less concerned with the outcome of the test and, in various ways, are different from typical polygraph examinees. Raskin found that CQT experiments using students tended to have lower accuracy rates than other studies (cited in U.S. Congress, 1983).

Twelve analogue studies using CQT techniques were examined and included in a meta-analysis conducted by Saxe and colleagues (1985). As with field studies, there is a great deal of variability among the results. Correct guilty decisions ranged from 35.4 to 100 percent. Correct innocent decisions range from 31.6 to 91 percent. The range of false positives was 2 to 50.7 percent, whereas that of false negatives was zero to 28.7 percent.

We shall now present a lab study in which 30 undergraduate volunteers participated in a polygraph experiment using a mock theft paradigm in which the guilty subjects were required to participate in the theft of some items from an office. It should be noted that this paradigm typifies those most commonly employed in polygraph lab studies. This study is more extensively described elsewhere (Szucko & Kleinmuntz, 1981) and will be summarized here.

Fifteen subjects were assigned to the theft condition and 15 were assigned to the no-theft condition. Those in the former condition were given instructions for locating an office in which they were to search through the desk and then steal anything they desired. The no-theft subjects were instructed to simply walk around campus and return to the experimenter's office. After completing their tasks, all were given a standard CQT polygraph to determine their guilt or innocence. The polygraph tracings from these examinations were then given to six experienced polygraph examiners. The examiners did not know what was stolen or by whom or that the polygraph charts were obtained from experimental subjects. The prior experience of the six polygraphers ranged from three months to eight years.

The results showed that the polygraph examiners were highly fallible. What was highly discouraging was the false positive rate (ranging from 18–55%). In other words, the proportion of truthful subjects incorrectly classified as untruthful was 18 percent for the best interpreter and 55 percent for the worst. It was even more discouraging to learn that the highest false positive rate was achieved by the most experienced (i.e., eight years) polygrapher (Saxe et al., 1985).

These field and laboratory study examples demonstrate that polygraph judges have high rates of misclassification. Particularly damaging are the high rates of false positive judgments in which more than 50 percent of the innocent suspects are wrongly classified as guilty. This false positive rate almost renders the toss of a coin equal to the judgments of some professional polygraphers.

The Problem of No Criterion Ground Truth

On the basis of their experiences, it is not uncommon to hear polygraphers proudly make such assertions as, "On the basis of my experience of administering nearly 10,000 polygraph examinations, I am confident that it is very accurate," or "I have administered hundreds of polygraphs and I have never been shown to have made a mistake." Nearly every polygraph examiner boasts of high accuracy rates, with 95 percent usually the conservative estimate and 99 percent more likely the norm (Lykken, 1998). One must realize that it makes sense for a person who is highly devoted to the polygraph technique and financially dependent upon it for his or her livelihood to be strongly motivated to believe that these tests are accurate. Nevertheless, in most examinations the polygrapher never knows if he or she was right or wrong (Lykken, 1998).

What is perhaps most telling about the wide range of accuracy rates is a close examination of how those rates are calculated. Upon examination, one quickly realizes that making accurate statements of validity is often very difficult. The validity of the polygraph is measured by the agreement between the results of the polygraph "test" on the one hand and the "ground truth" on the other hand. However, the "ground truth"—which respondents are in fact lying and which are truthful—is rarely available in criminal cases, for the simple reason that many crimes remain unsolved, and many suspects never go to jail. Even when a suspect confesses, no real check on test accuracy can be completed. One would bet, however, that in cases such as those the examiner would categorize the result as a positive, a "hit." However, admissions never tell us anything about the accuracy of that polygraph test!

Take, for example, a group of 20 suspects who are administered a polygraph to determine who stole a television. In many cases, the examiner will hold all final judgment until either all 20 tests have been administered *or* until one of the 20 has confessed. If the twentieth confesses, the first 19 will most likely be recorded as valid negatives (i.e., persons truthfully tested as innocent).

One logical criterion of ground truth could be confessions. Although they are perhaps the best criterion available for published field studies, even confessions fall short of the ideal. First, rarely do persons confess to crimes they did not commit. Second, suspects who eventually confess are unlikely to be representative of deceptive persons in general. Third, reasons for confession may vary from one person to another. For example, one might confess because the stress of continued denial is more than he or she can bear. Some may lie simply because of the anticipation of a forthcoming polygraph. What this all means is that studies using confession as the truth criterion are less likely to include the type of guilty suspects who produce a false-negative lie test. These types of persons, having "beaten" the test, are much less likely to ultimately confess in the future. These studies are biased in the direction of showing inflated validities (accuracies) for the group that is the criterion—those that eventually confess (Lykken, 1998).

Another problem is that the percentage of cases that agree with the criterion is not an adequate measure of test validity. This is because even a totally invalid test might agree with the criterion in a high proportion of cases. Some have tried to circumvent this problem by calculating validity in another way. Instead of using total agreement between test and criterion, which may be influenced by factors unrelated to test accuracy, some compute the test's performance with the criterion-truthful and the criterion-deceptive subjects separately and then average these two percentages. So for a test that achieved accuracy of 90 percent for the criterion-truthful subjects and was correct only 10 percent for the criterion-deceptive subjects, these two numbers averaged yield an accuracy of 50 percent. Such an accuracy rate is expected on the basis of chance alone!

Another concern often ignored is that an amazingly high accuracy rate may at the same time be an amazingly *wrong* accuracy rate. Basically, what this means is that even if the accuracy number is high, the polygrapher may still have the wrong person. In the example used with the 20 persons suspected of stealing the television, if the 20th test results in a confession, the first 19 are recorded as valid negatives. However, for the various reasons just explicated, this 95 percent accuracy rate might be wrong; suspect 15 might very well have successfully "beaten" the polygraph, suspect 20 might have reluctantly confessed to a crime he did not actually commit, and the polygrapher is left wrongly convinced in the veracity of the outcome.

A fairly common application of the polygraph is the single-culprit paradigm, in which a crime has been committed and numerous individuals are potential suspects, only one of whom is guilty. Suppose a polygrapher tests 52 employees to try and determine which one stole the television from the employee lounge. As a result of testing, one employee is identified as responsible for the theft. Assuming that this person was falsely accused and that some other employee was responsible, we would find that even though the polygraph test wrongly identified an innocent person and failed to identify the actual culprit, the total accuracy of the procedure could be evaluated as 48/50, or 96 percent accuracy!

The Problems of Analogue Research

The majority of polygraph research is *analogue*, performed in the laboratory using college students. A plethora of literature indicates that the subject's level of motivation can greatly influence his or her physiological reactions (Gustafson & Orne, 1965). It makes sense, then, that strong physiological reactions to many questions are less likely for those college students who have little to nothing to lose as a result of their polygraph results.

It is well documented that most of the field research is methodologically poor, whereas laboratory studies may be methodologically sound but not generalizable outside the laboratory (Pink & Kotzan, 1986). In addition to the criteria of blind scoring, validity studies must be conducted in the field in real-life testing situations. Volunteer college students are not under the same pressure as are criminal suspects or persons being screened for employment purposes. Deceptive persons may be less reactive in the laboratory setting than when they are lying about real crimes at the police station. Truthful subjects will almost certainly be more reactive in the field situation and, for this reason, are more likely to be misclassified by polygraphic lie test methods.

Lack of Blind Scoring

When attempting to consider the validity of the polygraph, the truest measure would be having a second polygrapher score the charts who did not observe the subject and was unfamiliar with the case facts. Polygraph charts are seldom scored this way, however.

In summary, based on the evidence and what has been discussed here, it is plausible to state that no criterion at the present time can completely verify or refute the validity of the polygraph.

How Reliable are Polygraph Techniques?

The reliability of a test is simply the consistency with which it measures that which it is measuring. In terms of the relationship between reliability and validity, a test can be highly reliable but have low validity. However, it is impossible for a test to have low reliability and high validity.

Many psychological tests measure the amount of some trait possessed by the respondent. In assessing the reliability of intelligence tests, for example, one would be interested in how consistently the trait of intelligence was measured from one occasion to another. The reliability of the polygraph, then, might be estimated by having the same person or group of persons tested twice, by two different examiners. If the test were perfectly reliable, the agreement between the two examiners would be 100 percent. If the reliability of the polygraph were zero, then the two examiners would be expected to agree 50 percent of the time. Suppose, for example, that the polygraph "test" were just the flipping of a coin: heads you are truthful, tails you are deceptive. Such a "test" would have no reliability at all. How one was classified the first time has no relationship to how one is classified the second time.

Typically, in polygraph reliability studies reliability estimates are calculated using a widely used procedure termed *total percent agreement*. This figure is calculated by dividing the number of cases agreed on by the total number of cases. However, the total percent of agreement is a very poor way of assessing the reliability of a polygraph test. The correct way to find the polygraph's reliability is to find one polygrapher's percent agreement with another polygrapher's on those cases called truthful and on those cases called deceptive. The next step is to average these two percentages. With this method, 50 percent agreement represents chance expectation, perfect reliability is indicated by 100 percent agreement, and the reliability of actual polygraph tests will fall between 50 and 100 percent. This method will now be illustrated using an example. Suppose two examiners both test 100 people to decide which one is guilty of having stolen a television. Under such circumstances, each examiner will naturally expect to find only one person guilty. We shall further assume that examiner A finds a different guilty person than examiner B. Notice that even when the examiners choose different culprits, their total agreement, figured in the usual way of calculating percent agreement, would be 98/100, or 98 percent! Calculated in the proposed correct way, however, their agreement (reliability) is 49.9 percent, close enough to 50 percent (i.e., chance levels) for our purposes (Lykken, 1998).

The problem in trying to determine the reliability of the polygraph test is that the examiner's subjectivity can greatly influence the outcome. Two racist examiners, for example, might have perfect reliability merely by agreeing to classify one racial group as deceptive and another as truthful. If we want to assess the reliability of the polygraph test by itself, uninfluenced by clinical impressions, then it is necessary that test results are based solely on the polygraph charts. This can easily be done by having independent polygraphers who did not administer the polygraph and are blind to all background information score the polygraph chart(s). This procedure, however, is rarely, if not ever, done (Lykken, 1981).

A Look at the Polygraph: The Methods

Contrary to lay opinion, there is no such thing as a typical polygraph test. Procedures differ by the type of question asked, the type of information sought by the polygrapher, the methods by which the polygrapher seeks that information, and perhaps most important, the theoretical assumptions surrounding their effectiveness in detecting deception. Polygraphers choose from at least eight different question formats of lie detection. Thus, each has its own psychometric properties. Which format is used depends on the polygrapher's training and the problem at hand (Saxe et al., 1985). Each of these *polygraphic lie tests* will be briefly described, including the assumptions inherent in each technique and any empirical findings surrounding the validity of inferences based on each technique.

Another type of lie detection method is called the *clinical lie test*. Here, information in addition to the polygraph recordings is allowed. The polygrapher becomes the "lie detector," subjectively examining all information available. There are no means by which to evaluate what role the actual polygraph results play in the examiner's conclusion. One cannot speak to the validity of the polygraph test but to the validity of the particular examiner's conclusions.

Last, a relatively new technique employed in lie detection is assessing "stress." In assessing stress, the polygrapher infers deception in the *voice* of the subject. These *voice stress analyzers* can be used exclusively or in conjunction with other lie detection methods.

Polygraphic Lie Tests

Although a plethora of lie detection methods exist, the two most commonly employed techniques are the *control question test* (CQT) and the *guilty knowledge test* (GKT).

The Control Question Test (CQT)

Three different versions of the CQT exist. These include the directed lie test (DLT), the positive control test (PCT), and the truth control test (TCT).

The CQT typically consists of 10 questions: three relevant, three control, and several filler questions, with standard practice to repeat these questions at least three times in different orders. The assumption behind the CQT is that a person who is guilty of a crime will respond physiologically when asked a (relevant) question about that crime (Reid & Inbau, 1977; Lykken, 1998; Raskin & Kircher, 1992). Innocent persons, on the other hand, are hypothesized to be more concerned about appearing deceptive when answering the control questions and therefore show stronger physiological responses to them compared to the relevant questions (Faigman, Kaye, Saks, & Sanders, 1997).

There are several ways to score the CQT polygraph, ranging from informal *ocular analyses* to using cutoff scores. A CQT can be globally evaluated (Reid & Inbau, 1977), in which all of the information available to the polygrapher (i.e., the plausibility of the subject's account, his or her demeanor during the polygraph examination, impressions, behavior symptoms, and information from the investigative file available) is used to determine deception.

The most common method of scoring is numerical scoring using cutoff scores (Lykken, 1998). The examiner is trained to ignore any additional information that might be used in global scoring methods and to base the decision solely on the physiological data recorded by the polygraph pen(s). When a numerical scoring procedure is used, adjacent control and relevant questions are compared for each separate physiological reading. A score from +1 to +3 is assigned if the physiologic response to the control question is larger, with the magnitude of the score determined by the size of the difference. The assignment of scores is subjective, arbitrary, and qualitative in nature. A score from –1 to –3 is assigned if the physiological response to the relevant question is larger than the response to the control question. A total score is obtained by summing these values over all charts, with a score less than –5 indicating deception, a score greater than +5 indicating truthfulness, and scores between –5 and +5 indicating an inconclusive examination. When the examination is determined to be inconclusive, it is common procedure for the polygrapher to conduct a posttest interview, with the purpose of eliciting a confession.

CQT Validity Studies. The studies that have achieved publication, although none of them meets the criteria set out by Iacono & Patrick (1999), do permit certain limited conclusions to be drawn. First, there are a number of studies in which volunteers, usually college students, are required to commit a mock crime and then to lie about it during the CQT examination. The volunteers are not motivated by the fear that failing the CQT will lead to punishment (prison) but rather are motivated by a monetary prize. In these highly artificial experiments, CQT successfully discriminates between truthful and deceptive subjects.

When the circumstances are made more realistic, the accuracy of the CQT decreases. Using prison inmate volunteers, Iacono and Patrick, for example, led their subjects to suppose that their failing the CQT might result in the loss of a group reward and thus incur the "enmity of their potentially violent and dangerous comrades" (1999 p. 607). Under these circumstances, nearly half of the truthful subjects were wrongly classified as deceptive. In another study, Foreman and McCauley (1986) permitted their volunteer subjects to choose for themselves whether to be guilty or innocent. Those who chose to be truthful knew that their reward would be smaller but that they were more likely to earn the reward. This manipulation is analogous to crime situations in which an individual is confronted with an opportunity to commit a crime with little likelihood of getting caught and must decide whether to take the opportunity (Iacono & Patrick, 1999). By increasing the realism of the experiment, Foreman and McCauley found that half of their truthful subjects were erroneously classified as deceptive.

Thus, although mock crime studies with volunteer subjects clearly do not permit any confident extrapolation to the real-life conditions of criminal investigation, it does appear that the designs that approximate more real-life scenarios demonstrate that the CQT identifies truthful responding with only chance accuracy (Iacono & Patrick, 1997).

Of the field studies conducted prior to 1987, two distinct groups exist. The first set of studies was conducted by proponents of the polygraph and published in police trade journals. These investigations all reported high levels of accuracy for the CQT (90% for both innocent and guilty subjects). The other set consisted of studies published in peer-reported scientific journals. Interestingly, these studies report much lower levels of accuracy (about 57% for innocent subjects and 76% for guilty subjects). Both studies had serious methodological shortcomings in that they either failed to establish ground truth or they selected cases because a confession followed a deceptive verdict (confession bias) (Iacono & Patrick, 1999).

Of the field studies conducted on the CQT after 1987, one of the most illuminating is that conducted by Patrick and Iacono (1991). In this study, the authors attempted to circumvent the confession bias by reviewing police files for ground truth (collected outside of the context of the polygraph). Independent evidence of ground truth was uncovered for 24 criterion-innocent suspects and one criterion-guilty suspect. For these suspects, the blind rescoring of their polygraph charts produced a hit rate of 57 percent, indicating that the CQT has little better than chance levels of accuracy for the innocent (chance levels being 50%). It was not possible to estimate the accuracy of the CQT for guilty persons because only one was identified in this study.

Although no scientifically credible data exist regarding the accuracy of the CQT with guilty persons (as concluded by Iacono & Patrick, 1999), there is good reason to doubt the validity of truthful polygraph verdicts. Honts, Raskin, and Kircher (1994) showed that with less than a half hour of instruction on how to "beat" the polygraph (i.e., recognize control and relevant questions) a majority of guilty subjects in a mock crime experiment learned to escape detection by using countermeasures.

Prior to 1970, there was no scientific research available on the reliability and validity of the CQT. By 1983, 14 laboratory and 10 field studies had been reported. The strength of the laboratory approach is having control over the situation and knowing the criterion "ground truth" (i.e., whether the subject is guilty or innocent—at least in some analogue studies). In field studies the experimenter does not have control over the testing situation and often cannot verify the accuracy of the polygraph results with a known truth criterion.

Kircher, Horowitz, and Raskin conducted a meta-analysis of the laboratory studies of the CQT available up to 1988 (as cited in Faigman et al., 1997) and identified three variables that predicted accuracy rates reported in those studies. The three variables comprising "high-quality" laboratory studies included the following: laboratory mock crime studies that used explicit incentives associated with test outcomes, realistic field testing and scoring procedures, and nonstudent subject populations. Results of the meta-analysis indicate that in the high-quality laboratory studies the CQT is accurate approximately 90 percent of the time, with equivalent false positives (innocent subjects misclassified as guilty) and false negative rates (guilty subjects misclassified as innocent) for innocent and guilty subjects.

In 1983, 10 field studies were identified that met minimal standards for acceptability (Faigman et al., 1997). Overall, the results of those studies suggest that the CQT in the field is accurate approximately 85 percent of the time. However, it should be noted that none of these 10 studies met all four of the proposed criteria for an adequate study (see Faigman et al., 1997, for criteria). Subsequent to 1983, there have been reports of four other field studies of the CQT that have met the criteria for an adequate field study. The results of these studies suggest that the CQT is accurate 90.5 percent of the time (Faigman et al., 1997).

The Directed Lie Test (DLT). The *directed lie test* (DLT) is one of the three versions of the CQT. In the DLT the subject is instructed to give false answers when asked each control question. For example, a control question might be, "Have you ever told a lie," a question that everyone would answer truthfully as yes. Here the subject would be instructed to answer this question as no. The polygrapher then uses those responses as a gauge of how the subject reacts when lying. Some believe the DLT is an improvement on the standard CQT because, unlike the CQT, the control questions in the DLT can be the same for everyone, thereby increasing standardization of the technique. The main assumption of the DLT is that an innocent person will be more disturbed when told to lie about some past misdeed than when truthfully denying an accusation about the crime of which he or she is accused.

One of the problems with this technique is that the subject, after lying on instruction, is misled into believing that the polygrapher now has a formal criterion of how the subject responds when lying. This may lead the subject to conclude that the procedure has a scientific basis.

Horowitz and colleagues (as cited in Lykken, 1998) conducted the only DLT study published in a scientific journal. This study was conducted in a laboratory. Half of the volunteer subjects committed a mock crime and then were told to deny committing that crime in the polygraph examination. The other subjects were "innocent" and were told to be truthful on the test. Eighty percent of the volunteers were correctly classified.

In evaluating the DLT evidence, it is important to keep in mind that because these are mock crimes, with no penalty for failing the polygraph, they provide very little information that can be generalized safely to real-life situations of criminal interrogation (Lykken, 1998). It is surprising, also, how one study has caused leaders in the field of polygraphy to conclude that the DLT is a *significant* advance over the CQT.

The Positive Control Test (PCT). The positive control test (PCT) used by some polygraphers involves using the relevant question as its own control. The subject is asked each relevant question twice and instructed to answer truthfully on one presentation and falsely on the other. Therefore, it is argued that the only variable that should influence size of the physiological response is that one of the answers is deceptive and the other is not.

The first assumption of the PCT is that people will be more aroused when lying spontaneously compared to answering the same question truthfully (even when they believe the truthful answer is untrue). The second assumption is that people become more aroused in giving a false answer upon instruction than in answering the same question truthfully (Lykken, 1998). The most plausible reason that the PCT is sometimes preferred by examiners is that getting the respondent confused is a good way of inducing confessions. The respondent becomes confused so that "no" become confused with "yes" and vice versa, and the confession is procured.

Only one empirical study of the validity of the PCT has been published (Foreman & McCauley, 1986). This study used a mock crime design in which subjects were allowed to choose for themselves whether they wanted to be guilty or innocent. Those who chose to be "guilty" had to lie on the PCT, and those who chose to be "innocent" had to be truthful on the PCT. Each subject was given a short PCT along with a CQT and a three-item GKT. All three techniques produced accuracies that ranged from 68 to 78 percent.

The Truth Control Test (TCT). The truth control test (TCT) is based upon an entirely fictitious crime (Crime Y) that is similar to the crime under investigation (Crime X). Crime Y is made to appear very realistic to the subject. If a subject is innocent, it is assumed that the polygrapher can make the suspect think he or she is in equal jeopardy with respect to both crimes. After all, in both cases, the suspect knows he or she is innocent. It is assumed that a similar reaction to questions regarding both Crime Y and Crime X would be indicative of telling the truth. On the other hand, a deceptive subject should show much larger physiological responses to the relevant questions than to the control questions. In other words, a strong response to the actual crime question, coupled with the absence of a response to the fictitious crime question or a reaction considerably less than that to the actual crime questions, would indicate deception.

The primary assumption of the TCT is that the polygrapher is able to convincingly persuade the subject to be equally fearful of being prosecuted for a fictitious crime as he or she is for the real crime under investigation. Another assumption is that an innocent person will feel that both accusations are equally threatening to his or her well-being and will be equally aroused by both relevant and control questions (Lykken, 1981). A third assumption is that a guilty subject should be more disturbed by the relevant than by the control questions. Therefore, a polygraph chart showing small irrelevant responses, moderate control responses, and large relevant responses would suggest the subject is lying about the actual crime.

The ethical problem raised by this technique is that its accuracy hinges on the polygrapher's ability in deceiving the examinee. A polygraph test based solely on evidence from a TCT has never been administered (Lykken, 1998). Its greatest weakness is the unethical deception necessary for its use. In short, for this technique to work, the polygrapher must be a very good liar! Clearly, lying to an examinee while administering a psychological test is unethical for any professional.

The Guilty Knowledge Test (GKT)

The second most commonly used polygraph technique is the *guilty knowledge test* (GKT; Lykken, 1959; Faigman et al., 1997). In the GKT polygraph, subjects are asked about details of a crime or incident that supposedly only a guilty person would know. The subject is asked a series of questions about the crime or incident posed in multiple-choice format, with each question asking one specific detail about the crime or incident. An example of a GKT question concerning one detail of a shoplifting incident is as follows: "If you were the one who shoplifted from the department store, then you would know what was shoplifted. Was it (a) a shirt? (b) a pair of shoes? (c) some perfume? (d) a pair of pants? (e) a sweater?" The GKT assumes that guilty subjects will have stronger physiological reactions to the correct alternative, whereas innocent persons who know nothing about the incident would be expected to respond randomly, having similar physiological reactions to all response alternatives (Bashore & Rapp, 1993; Lykken, 1998).

There are several methods of scoring the GKT. The simplest method is to assign one point for each item on which the relevant alternative produced a larger physiological response than did any of the controls. The respondent is said to have "hit" on that item. The GKT normally consists of ten questions. The innocent subject should hit on fewer than three items while more than half of guilty subjects should be expected to hit on eight or more items (Lykken, 1981). For a more detailed review of the CQT and the GKT, interested readers are referred to the following sources: Bashore and Rapp (1993), Honts (1991), Honts and Perry (1992), Lykken (1981), Podlesny and Raskin (1977), and Raskin (1986).

GKT Validity Studies. Laboratory demonstrations of simulated crimes have shown the GKT to be highly accurate. A comprehensive review of mock-crime investigations conducted between 1959 and 1987 revealed mean hit rates of 85 percent for guilty participants and 95 percent for innocent participants (Iacono & Patrick, 1988). The GKT was 100 percent accurate in classifying innocent subjects in 6 of 11 studies. False negative errors are consistently more common than false positives, indicating that the GKT may be biased in favor of guilty suspects (Ben-Shakur & Furedy, 1990; Lykken, 1998; Raskin et al., 1997).

It should be noted that laboratory studies of the GKT are likely to overestimate its accuracy, more so for guilty than innocent individuals. Well-designed laboratory experiments construct a scenario in which guilty participants must attend to details of the crime that the examiner expects perpetrators to know and which are used to construct the questions on the GKT. In real life, a criminal may not attend to the aspects of a crime that an investigator views as being salient and important, and many details may be forgotten.

Because the GKT is virtually never used in the United States, no field studies have been conducted here. However, two studies have been reported by investigators in Israel. In one of these two studies, Elaad (1990) examined skin resistance tracings from the GKT records of 50 innocent and 48 guilty criminal suspects. Using blind chart evaluation, 98 percent of the innocent and 42 percent of the guilty examinees were correctly classified. In their second and follow-up study, Elaad and colleagues (1992) found that hit rates for innocent and guilty examinees were 94 percent and 75 percent, respectively. The results of these two studies indicate, consistent with laboratory research on the GKT, that the GKT is highly accurate with innocent suspects but that it has a very high false-negative error rate in real-life cases.

However, there are two prominent methodological weaknesses in these studies that constrain the conclusions that can be drawn (Iacono & Patrick, 1999). The first is that the GKTs in these studies contained an average of only two questions. This can lower test sensitivity because it lowers the odds that information salient to the perpetrator will be represented in the test. A second problem is that the GKTs in these studies were administered as an addendum to a full-length CQT. It can be argued that the physiological response habituation resulting from repeated presentations of relevant and control questions on the CQT might have diminished differential responding between critical and non-critical items on the GKT for guilty examinees (Iacono & Patrick, 1999).

Another factor to be considered when evaluating the potential of the GKT as a polygraph technique to be used in the field is the applicability of the technique to real-life cases. In order to conduct a GKT, the examiner must have a number of key items of information about the crime to develop and conduct the test. A researcher, Podlesny, studied information available in FBI case files and estimated that the GKT could be used in only 13–18 percent of the cases examined. The results of his study point to the limited applicability of the GKT in the field even if it has a high level of validity in the field (Iacono & Patrick, 1999).

A Caveat: Cutting Scores

It is important to recognize that, unlike objective scoring procedures employed in the science of psychophysiology, the objectivity of scoring methods used in polygraphy is severely limited. One problem is that scores are often derived from subjective and qualitative means. What one polygrapher may deem to be a clear 2 may be seen as a 1 to another. A second problem (and perhaps more psychometrically problematic) is that cutoff points are completely arbitrary. The actual scoring procedures vary from one method to another, as do the appropriate cutoff points indicating "deception" and "truthtelling."

The Relevant/Irrelevant (R/I) Test

The *relevant/irrelevant test* (R/I) compares responses to relevant questions and irrelevant questions. To remind readers, an irrelevant question is one that is unrelated to the subject matter under investigation and is nonstressful, such as, "Are you a man?" or "Is today Friday?" In addition to relevant and irrelevant questions, the subject is asked a control question. Confusingly, the R/I test uses "control" questions that are entirely different in function than those used in the CQT and GKT. In the R/I test, the control question is irrelevant but provocative, such as, "Have you been drunk sometime in the past year?" The sole purpose of these questions is to produce some sort of polygraphic response and thus prove that the examinee is capable of responding under the present conditions. The R/I test typically, but not invariantly, consists of three relevant questions, each preceded and followed by irrelevant questions, with a control question at the end. The subject is classified as deceptive if stronger polygraphic responses occur in response to the relevant questions as compared with the irrelevant questions.

There are two basic assumptions of the R/I test (Faigman et al., 1997). The first assumption is that a guilty person will produce stronger physiologic arousal to relevant questions compared to irrelevant questions and that this difference will be detectable on the polygraph chart. One can easily think of exceptions, however. Some individuals can be so fearless or lacking in conscience that they are not aroused when talking about a crime they may have committed. Also, if the individual has discussed the crime at length or on numerous occasions, they may have become habituated to talking about the case and no arousal is detected. A second assumption is that an innocent person will not become aroused by the relevant questions and will not show a differentially larger response to them. This second assumption is often implausible, as one can easily imagine an innocent subject being terribly frightened of being accused, especially if the crime is associated with negative consequences.

R/I Validity Conclusions. In over 50 years of use, only two empirical studies using "blind" evaluations of charts obtained from criminal suspects have tested the accuracy of the R/I method (Lykken, 1981; Faigman et al., 1997), one by Larson in 1938 and one by Horvath in 1968. A third study was conducted by Horowitz and colleagues (as cited in Faigman et al., 1997). In Larson's study, only one of 62 subjects had actually lied on the polygraph. Larson asked nine judges to read and score the charts. The number of suspects who were scored as deceptive ranged from 50 to 30, indicating very poor reliability. The average judge scored about one-third of the innocent suspects as deceptive. In Horvath's study, *all* of the innocent suspects were erroneously classified as deceptive by the R/I test, an increase from Larson's reported false positive error rate of 33 percent. Horowitz, Raskin, Honts, and Kircher (as cited in Faigman et al., 1997) recently reported that only 22 percent of the innocent subjects in their experiment were able to produce truthful outcomes. In summary, the R/I test is based on a "flagrantly implausible assumption" (Lykken, 1998, p. 113). The R/I test has been shown to be strongly biased against truthful suspects, even with one of the three studies conducted by the inventor of the R/I himself.

The Relevant Control Test (RCT)

The relevant control test (RCT) is most widely used for employment screening purposes. A typical RCT contains three irrelevant questions and thirteen relevant questions concerning various areas of interest to the prospective employer. In the screening situation, the examiner will go over the questions with the subject before attaching any polygraphic apparatus. The subject understands that he or she is to be able to answer every relevant question truthfully in the negative. The proper comparison, then, is between responses to the different relevant questions. If the subject shows greater polygraphic reactions in one or two content areas, the examiner would conclude that he or she has been deceptive regarding those content areas.

The main assumption of this technique is that all of the relevant questions seem about equally threatening and disturbing to the truthful subject (Faigman et al., 1997). The problem with this assumption is that it is very difficult to imagine a case in which three questions all have exactly equal stimulus value. This is compounded by the dilemma that the typical polygrapher is asked to create 10 or 15 questions of this sort.

RCT Validity Conclusions. There has been no published research on the accuracy of tests of this type.

The Peak-of-Tension Test (POT)

The peak-of-tension test (POT) is not a lie detection method per se but a guide to investigation. The POT is designed not to detect lying but to detect *guilty knowledge*. For the POT to work, the investigator must have knowledge of the details of the crime that a suspect would recognize if he or she is guilty. Suppose a subject was accused of robbing a bank. The subject would be asked a series of questions such as: "How much money did you steal from the bank? Did you steal $100? $200? $300? $400? or $500?" If the subject responded strongly to some figure in the series, this might indicate guilt. This type of examination is not a lie detection method but rather an investigatory tool. The POT, or guilty knowledge test, is designed not to detect lying, but to detect *guilty knowledge*. Lykken, a strong proponent of this method, says, "When it works, it provides its own verification" (1998, p. 148).

One assumption of this technique is that a subject will have a physiological response to the knowledge he or she possesses. A second assumption is that the subject knows the answer (i.e., the amount of money stolen). This test can be useful if and when it leads to the discovery of useful physical evidence or when it elicits a valid confession.

POT Validity Conclusions. The POT test has not yet been empirically tested.

Clinical Lie Test: The Examiner as "Lie Detector"

In the *clinical lie test*, the polygrapher is the lie detector, and he or she combines polygraphic information with impressions and behavioral observations to arrive at a decision. The polygrapher is to take all sources of information into account. This information may include what have been termed the "behavior symptoms" of the subject. Although vague and not operationally defined, these behavior symptoms have commonly been referred to in the literature as including, but not being limited to, the following: signs of covering up; the demeanor, actions and appearance of the subject; how the subject behaved in the waiting room; postponing the appointment; mental blocks; appearing to be shocked; having a dry mouth; describing oneself as religious; moving restlessly; being overly polite; being eager to leave the examination; and poor eye contact. These behaviors have been called "symptoms of lying" by some (Reid & Arthur, 1953; as cited in Lykken, 1981). Many of these behavior symptoms cannot be directly observed but must be inferred by the examiner (e.g., "subject is nervous" or "subject is sincere").

The assumption is that all polygraphers are skilled enough to make accurate inferences across all subjects they test and that they can observe all of these behaviors at the same time. Another assumption is the examiner will be able to convince each subject that his or her polygraph examination will produce accurate results. This assumption rests on the other assumption that the deceptive subject will feel stress. This is only plausible if those subjects actually believe in the test's ability to reveal the truth. Another assumption is that truthful subjects exhibit certain behavior symptoms that are different from those behavior symptoms exhibited by deceptive subjects. Some say, "This sort of claim makes a psychologist's hair stand on end" (Lykken, 1981, p. 95) because there is no convincing empirical evidence for such a distinction. Last, it is assumed that when a behavior symptom cannot be directly observed but must be inferred by the examiner (e.g., "subject is nervous"), all examiners will be skilled enough to make correct inferences in dealing with all varieties of subjects (Lykken, 1998). Without great discussion here, this assumption has to be rejected on the basis of many empirical studies concluding that we, as psychologists especially, are not nearly as accurate as we think (Lykken, 1998).

Clinical Lie Test Validity Conclusions. In the millions of clinical lie tests that have been administered, only one empirical study investigating this method's validity has been conducted, Bersh's (1969) army study. Bersh wanted to assess the accuracy of polygraph examinations done by U.S. Army polygraphers. Bersh gathered 323 representative cases, in which the polygrapher had scored the test as truthful or deceptive. These case files were then given to a panel of four army attorneys who were asked to study them (unhindered by technical rules or evidence) and decide which suspects they believed to be guilty and innocent. Eighty cases were discarded on the basis of insufficient evidence. Of the 243 remaining cases, the panel of attorneys reached unanimous agreement on 157, split three to one on 59 of the cases, and deadlocked two to two on 27 cases. Bersh then used the panel's decision as the criterion of ground truth. When the panel was unanimous, the polygraphers agreed with the panel on 92 percent of the cases. Agreement fell to 75 percent when the panel was split three to one.

Bersh stressed that based on this study, it is impossible to tell what role if any the actual polygraph results played in the levels of agreement obtained. Some warn that unless the result of a polygraph examination is based solely on the chart—the polygraph recording—then the result will be influenced to an unknowable extent by the examiner's clinical impressions, personal attitudes, and the like. The clinical judgment of a polygraph is presumably no more accurate than any other observer, is just as subject to bias and prejudice, and as some believe, is "probably wrong nearly 50% of the time" (Lykken, 1998, p. 107).

Voice Stress Analysis

In 1970, the *Psychological Stress Evaluator* (PSE) was introduced. The theory behind the PSE is that muscles in the throat or larynx exhibit microvibrations when stimulated or aroused. The exportability of the PSE could be staggering. If it worked, it would allow one to detect deception over the telephone, the radio, or on television.

Few would argue that the voice changes under stress. We have all heard it in our own voices and in the voices of others when we are angry, frightened, or scared. However, several important questions remain. How does the voice change? Of the many aspects of the voice that might change under stress, which ones do? Which stressors produce which changes in which person's voice? Does the same stressor result in the same voice change across persons? Also, do other stimuli (i.e., like the ones that would produce excitement) produce the same vocal changes as one experiences when lying?

Voice Stress Analysis Validity Conclusions. There is no empirical evidence that the PSE can reliably measure differences in "stress" as reflected by the human voice. Rather, there is evidence that the PSE used in conjunction with other lie detection methods discriminate truthful from deceptive subjects at only chance levels of accuracy (Lykken, 1998).

Summary of Methodologies

A common fallacy is that the polygraph "test" is indeed a standard test and that one can easily provide an accurate review of the general state of the polygraph. Two reasons make this task virtually impossible. First, there is no such thing as a polygraph "test." As just explicated, an assortment of different polygraph techniques exist, each involving different theoretical and metric assumptions. The different techniques vary considerably depending on what methodology is used, by whom, for whom, and under what circumstances. Second, a lack of standardization of the polygraph techniques makes it difficult to summarize their psychometric properties since psychometrics historically exist for those techniques that have standardized procedures and scoring methodology.

It seems appropriate at this point to discuss both the lack of standardization and the many choice points available in deciding how to measure physiological arousal during a polygraph test.

Lack of Standardization

A major source of confusion arises from the term *test* as used in the expression "polygraph test." This usage suggests relatively standardized instruments of psychological assessment like IQ and personality tests. Although those psychological assessment instruments are, to be sure, controversial as regards to their validity (e.g., there is the question of whether an IQ test is sufficiently culture-free), at least their interrater reliability is high, because they are standardized in the sense that their administration is the same from (competent) operator to operator (Furedy, 1991). In contrast, the polygraph examination varies immeasurably from operator to operator and does not, therefore, deserve the term *test* in the sense of being a standardized instrument of psychological assessment; it is, rather, a complex and highly variable conglomerate of choice points and interview situations. From formulating the questions that will be asked of the suspect to scoring the results of the physiological responses, polygraph techniques are not standardized. Instead, the polygraph represents an honorarium of sorts.

Choice Points

There exists a seemingly infinite number of choice points available to the polygrapher presented with an examinee suspected of some misdeed or deception. First, the polygrapher must choose which type of lie detection method to use. The polygrapher chooses between the many polygraphic lie tests described earlier.

Number of Questions Asked. The total number of questions asked varies from one method to another. The polygrapher not only has the freedom to decide the total number of questions asked but can also decide the total number of control questions and relevant questions asked. This can be significant when one realizes what may transpire with extra questions. By and large, more questions equal more opportunities to "catch" a deceptive subject. More questions could mean more stress for the examinee, which in turn could lead to more false confessions—those confessions caused by fatigue or an escape from further interrogation. More questions also could mean more time, and with more time the examinee might easily become more physiologically aroused (more time to worry about being falsely accused, etc.).

Scoring Procedures. Once a polygraph chart is available, the examiner can then choose whether to use an objective scoring procedure (i.e., cutoff scores) or a subjective scoring procedure (i.e., ocular analysis). It makes logical sense that if the polygrapher were to choose an ocular analysis, the amount of training would be yet another confounding variable affecting the accuracy of the analysis. It also makes logical sense that, although it has not been empirically tested, there is the possibility that diagnostic outcomes could be differentially related to the type of scoring procedure employed. In other words, it is not guaranteed that a polygrapher scoring a chart with ocular analysis would reach the same conclusion if he or she scored the same chart using cutoff scores.

Channels Used. A polygraph examiner is afforded the freedom of choosing what channels (i.e., blood flow, respiration, blood pressure, galvanic skin response) will be used to detect physiological responses to the questions presented in the examination.

Number of Channels. Polygraphers have the freedom to determine how many channels to measure. The number of permutations for the common four channels is staggering. Interestingly, two polygraphers could be employing the same technique but could be measuring different responses, based on the channels they chose to measure.

Although it is true that typically three or four channels are monitored and that the number of tests usually varies from three to five, this still remains a problem, at least mathematically speaking. The chances of scoring a polygraph administration test as inconclusive decrease as a function of the sum of the number of channels used and tests administered. This fact is likened to group significance testing in experimental psychology, where the likelihood of finding significant differences increases to near perfect levels as the sample size increases.

How big a response? As described earlier, the primary assumption of most polygraph methods is that physiological responses to relevant questions should be larger in magnitude than responses to control questions. The question remains, however: How large a response is required to be differentially larger? What change in magnitude accompanies a score of 2 or 3?

Combining Results. Yet another source of variability is how the polygrapher combines results from multiple channels. For example, how does the polygrapher make sense of a polygraph chart in which one channel increased (where an increase indicates deception) and the other channels remained constant? Where several channels increased and others decreased?

Interpreting "Noise." In discussing the validity of tests, one must be aware of the possible threats to the validity of the test, where a *valid* test is defined as one that measures what it purports to measure. Threats to the validity of a test can be thought of as "noise," or artifacts of testing that have the potential of decreasing the accuracy of one's conclusions. It seems that there is a substantial amount of noise that could potentially interfere with valid interpretations of a polygraph chart. For example, when galvanic skin responses are measured, a simple movement of the hand or finger could introduce movement artifacts that may be difficult to ignore or interpret. Another validity threat could be the temperature of the testing room. If, over time, the room increases in temperature, the subject may begin to sweat, affecting his GSR channel. Another threat to the test's validity is the individual differences of respondents. One person may be more physically susceptible to sweating, regardless of whether he is feeling threatened or being deceptive, whereas another individual may fail to sweat at all. The problem is that if the polygrapher chose not to include that channel for the person who sweats when lying, the polygrapher may "miss" that response and inaccurately label a guilty person as truthful. The suspect's age is also a confounding variable. An elderly person suffering from Parkinson's disease, for example, could potentially present with more uncontrollable movements compared with a suspect of the same age without Parkinson's.

Interpreting Charts: Absolute Levels or Change Scores? Another choice point is the decision of how and what to interpret on the polygraph charts. Does the polygrapher measure magnitude changes from baseline or from the most recent relevant question, and why? Some physiological responses take longer than others to return to baseline. Does the polygrapher allow a rest period to return to baseline? In measuring heart rate, does the polygrapher measure the suspect's maximal heart rate or realize there was an interval between questions and take an average?

THE ETHICS OF USE OF THE POLYGRAPH: TRANSGRESSIONS AND CONCERNS

Polygraphy as Psychological Testing

Now we will explore the ethics of polygraphy. The polygraph is a psychological test in the same sense that the Stanford-Binet, Weschler tests, and the Minnesota Multiphasic Personality Inventory are psychological tests. Like these other tests, polygraphy is designed to obtain a sample of a person's behavior (Kleinmuntz & Szucko, 1984). As a psychological test, then, the polygraph must meet the same criteria that are prescribed for all other psychological tests, criteria stipulated by the American Psychological Association's Standards for Educational and Psychological Tests. We argue that the use of the polygraph, as a psychological testing procedure, is in violation of a number of American Psychological Association (APA, 1992) ethical principles.

- *Principle 2.06: "Psychologists do not promote the use of psychological assessment techniques by unqualified persons"* (APA, 1992).

There are several organizations that set standards for the polygraph. The Department of Defense Polygraph Institute (DODPI) is the nation's premier polygraph education and research center. It develops and publishes criteria for use by polygraphers. However, it lacks any enforcement capabilities. In addition to DODPI, there are two national organizations representing members of the polygraph community. The American Polygraph Association has about 1,850 members and the American Association of Police Polygraphists has approximately 1,000 members. Interestingly, there are an estimated 2,000 polygraph examiners who do not belong to either society. Although both organizations publish standards for the polygraph, neither has the authority to force members to comply with them (Faigman et al, 1997). Also, there are no standardized requirements for a polygrapher's training, including no requirement that he or she even complete high school.

- *Principle 2.04 (b): "Psychologists recognize the limits to the certainty with which diagnoses, judgments, or predictions can be made about individuals."*

Because the polygraph lacks important psychometric data, it can be argued that the polygraph violates Principle 2.04 (b). We suggest that if the false positive and false negative rates were recognized for what they are, the polygraph would be banned for use by psychologists and polygraphers.

- *Principle 2.04 (c): "Psychologists attempt to identify situations in which particular interventions or assessment techniques or norms may not be applicable or may require adjustment in administration or interpretation because of factors such as an individual's gender, age, race, ethnicity, national origin, religion, sexual orientation, disability, language or socioeconomic status."*

There is some research evidence indicating that this requirement is not being met. First, with the majority of polygraph studies conducted using college students, the extent to which results are applicable to real-life criminal suspects remains limited. Second, several theories in psychophysiology indicate the polygraph does not possess adequate validity, most being described in the *Handbook of Psychophysiology* (Greenfield & Sternbach, 1972). The nervous system and physiologic loops of humans have been found to be influenced by genetics and experiential factors. Furthermore, individual patterns change from day to day and can be influenced by the simplest of variables, such as a toothache or a headache. One study indicated that joggers who go without jogging for a day are more likely to be interpreted as false positives on the polygraph (Thaxton, 1982). Racial differences have also been documented (Thaxton, 1982), indicating a potential for the polygraph to result in racial discrimination. In conclusion, there is an existing research base suggesting a high probability that Principle 2.04 (c) is being consistently violated by polygraphers.

- *Principle 2.05: "[Psychologists] take into account the various test factors and characteristics of the person being assessed that might affect psychologists' judgments or reduce the accuracy of their interpretations. They indicate any significant reservations they have about the accuracy or limitations of their interpretations."*

First, if this were truly the case, the number of inconclusive polygraphs would be substantially larger and the number of posttest interviews would be zero. On the contrary, polygraphers are highly invested in the results of the polygraphs they administer. After all, employers and law officials hire them with the purpose of gathering additional corroborating and incriminating evidence. If there are no negative consequences for the polygrapher who elicits false confessions from his or her subject during the postinterview and great positive reinforcers (i.e., being hired in the future, reputation, and income) for conclusive results, it seems obvious what choice a polygrapher will make. Second, the way in which polygraph tests are routinely administered makes it impossible for the administrator to remain objective. The polygrapher's lack of blindness, both to the administration of the polygraph and to the scoring of the results, posits serious ethical considerations. The polygrapher constructs the test questions to suit the particular case, often knowing intimate details about the crime under investigation. The polygrapher's manner will no doubt influence the emotional atmosphere in the interrogation room, and likewise his or her predispositions regarding the case will undoubtedly determine scoring decisions, especially those that are inconclusive or marginal.

Reid and Inbau (1977) have written *Truth and Deception*, the standard text used and studied by polygraph examiners. In addition, they operate one of the largest and best known polygraph schools in the nation. In their book they urge polygraphers to remain objective and never to appear accusatory during administration. Ironically, they also suggest that polygraphers be cognizant of the subjects' mannerisms and "behavioral symptoms"; these, they suggest, should be weighed by the polygrapher. Based on their instructions in their book, those behavior symptoms indicating guilt are to be weighed more heavily than those symptoms indicative of truth telling. It seems only ethical, then, that upon reaching a decision the polygrapher not only provide his or her verdict, but also the way in which the decision was reached. Stated in a court of law, those aspects of the decision that were blatantly subjective and a result of personal opinion might be more easily recognized for what they are—one person's opinion. Last, given the plethora of conflicting opinions about the polygraph's validity data, it seems that ethical psychologists and polygraphers should have much to disclose in the informed consent process.

False Confessions and Coercive Tactics

The interrogative features of most polygraph tests often elicit false confessions. Polygraphers who use confessions as a "ground truth" criterion are implicitly asserting that all confessions are true! Simple motivation principles should lead us to question the veracity of such an assumption. It seems more than plausible that under some conditions, the psychological pressure to terminate such an interrogation would be impetus enough to elicit a false confession. This issue remains to be tested empirically, as the rate of false confessions remains unknown (Furedy, 1993).

Many proponents of the polygraph agree that police and polygraphers often engage in coercive and unacceptable tactics when they administer polygraphs. They support their position by stating that to deny police and polygraphers the use of confessions when there is no question about the validity of these confessions is to abandon our ethical responsibilities to society. Research tells us that a subject's expectancies regarding the effectiveness of the polygraph partly determines their responsiveness (Meyer & Youngjohn, 1991). Evidence shows expectancies can also influence the actual verbal responses of the subject. Polygrapher proponents as well as opponents may agree that one of the greatest advantages of the polygraph lies not in its ability to detect lies but its ability to induce confessions from guilty persons.

Informed Consent

As previously stated, the accuracy of the polygraph is not 100 percent. Telling subjects that they can be confident of the polygraph's infallibility is a blatant lie. In what other psychological assessment or test is it standard practice to provide false information as part of informed consent? We would argue that the number would and should be small.

Second, informed consent means that the test taker (i.e., the suspect being polygraphed) is fully, not selectively, informed about the limitations of the test as well as its strengths. Polygraph examiners have long maintained that the purpose of the pretest interview is to convince the subject of the polygraph's infallibility (Rogers, 1988; Szucko & Kleinmuntz, 1981). We conjecture that the probability that an accused suspect would sign informed consent for the polygraph would be extremely low if that suspect was told he or she would be detained until a full confession was provided. Nor would the likelihood be high for consent if that suspect were told that the polygraph has a substantially high false-positive rate, a high false-negative rate, and is only slightly better than chance in discriminating guilty from innocent persons.

The Treatment Utility of the Polygraph and the Therapeutic Relationship

Many have argued that the real value of the polygraph does not lie in its ability to catch people in lies, but in helping them tell the truth. The argument is that the therapist (or law official) needs the whole truth and nothing but the whole truth for meaningful treatment. However, we would argue that not only is a coerced disclosure unethical, it may actually prove to have iatrogenic effects for the individual's treatment plan. We argue that a coerced disclosure may in fact disrupt the therapeutic relationship in very harmful ways. For example, let us imagine a man is convicted of four sexual offenses and ten other offenses remain undetected. Cannot the therapist get a good picture of that man's risk factors, offense cycle, cognitive distortions, and the like based on the four offenses? The added value of the coerced disclosure (which is in fact what you get) of the other offenses remains unclear. Although this is an empirical question, it seems that the level of trust between the man and his therapist might be greatly reduced as a result of the polygraph interrogation, and hence the possibility of meaningful treatment might be severely limited.

CONCLUSION

The purpose of this chapter has been to present a critical analysis of the polygraph. First, a brief review of the uses of lie detection illustrates the importance of knowing how accurate the polygraph is in classifying truthful from deceptive persons. Second, we have presented the many methods available to the polygrapher and have critically questioned the assumptions upon which each method rests. Third, we have argued that lie detection is a psychological test based on psychological principles and that a lack of standardization of the polygraph makes it difficult, if not impossible, to adequately summarize its psychometric properties. We have illustrated the many choice points each polygrapher makes, maintaining that it is virtually impossible to determine the validity, or accuracy, of the polygraph's conclusions because of the lack of standardization. Last, we asserted that the polygraph transgresses many ethical and standards for psychological testing.

Polygraph testing has thrived despite the weak theoretical and empirical foundation for its techniques. This state of affairs exists for several reasons. First, there is no dispute about the utility of polygraph testing. The fact that many criminal suspects confess as a result of a polygraph helps prosecutions resolve cases that would go unprosecuted and unresolved. In employee screening, the admissions employees make about their alcohol use, sex lives, and other suspect behavior provides the government or employers with valuable information that they often feel would be unattainable through other means.

As our review highlights, there is little evidence to support the use of the various polygraph techniques described. What little evidence does exist for the accuracy of the control question test, coupled by the weaknesses in CQT theory, indicates that the CQT has little more than chance accuracy with innocent persons and can be easily defeated by guilty persons through the use of countermeasures.

The GKT, by contrast, is somewhat more scientifically sound. Unfortunately, well-designed field research is needed. Without such evidence, it is premature to advocate its general use.

The polygraph has been used consistently in criminal investigations for over half a century. Nevertheless, both its validity and the ethical considerations involved in its administration continue to be debated. If this chapter has fostered a healthy skepticism about the utility, validity, and ethical properties of the polygraph, it will have accomplished its objectives.

REFERENCES

Abrams, S. (1989). *The complete polygraph handbook.* Lexington, MA: Lexington Books.

Abrams, S. (1991). The use of polygraphy with sex offenders. *Annals of Sex Research, 4,* 239–263.

American Psychological Association. (1992). *Ethical principles of psychologists and code of conduct.* Washington, DC: Author.

American Psychological Association. (1985). *Standards for educational and psychological testing.* Washington, DC: Author.

Backster, C. (1962). Methods of strengthening our polygraph technique. *Police, 6* (5), 61–68.

Bashore, T. R., & Rapp, P. E. (1993). Are there alternatives to traditional polygraph procedures? *Psychological Bulletin, 113* (1), 3–22.

Ben-Shakhar, G. (1991). Clinical judgment8 and decision-making in CQT-polygraphy. *Integrative Physiological and Behavioral Science, 26* (3), 232–240.

Ben-Shakur, G., & Furedy, J. J. (1990). *Theories and applications in the detection of deception.* New York: Springer-Verlag.

Bersh, P. M. (1969). A validation study of polygraph examiner judgments. *Journal of Applied Psychology, 53,* 399–403.

Campbell, D. T., & Fiske, D. W. (1959). Convergent and discriminant validation by the multitrait-multimethod matrix. *Psychological Bulletin, 56,* 81–105.

Carroll, D. (1991). Lie detection: Lies and truths. In R. Cochrane & D. Carroll (Eds.), *Psychology and social issues: A tutorial test.* New York: Falmer Press.

Cronbach, L. J., & Meehl, P. E. (1955). Construct validity in psychological test. *Psychological Bulletin, 52,* 281–302.

Cross, T. P., & Saxe, L. (1992). A critique of the validity of polygraph testing in child sexual abuse cases. *Journal of Child Sexual Abuse, 1* (4), 19–33.

Elaad, E. (1990). Polygrapher examiner awareness of crime-relevant information and the guilty knowledge test. *Law and Human Behavior, 21* (1), 107–120.

Elaad, E., Ginton, A., & Jungman, N. (1992). Detection measures in real-life criminal guilty knowledge tests. *Journal of Applied Psychology, 77* (5), 757–767.

Faigman, D. L., Kaye, D. H., Saks, M. J., & Sanders, J. (Eds.). (1997). *Modern scientific evidence: The law and science of expert testimony.* St. Paul, MN: West.

Foreman, R. F., & McCauley, C. (1986). Validity of the positive control test using the field practice model. *Journal of Applied Psychology, 71,* 691–698.

Furedy, J. J. (1987). Evaluating polygraphy from a psychophysiological perspective: A specific effects analysis. *Pavlovian Journal of Biological Science, 22* (4), 145–153.

Furedy, J. J. (1991). Symposium: On the validity of the polygraph. *Integrative Physiological and Behavioral Science, 26* (3), 211–213.

Furedy, J. J. (1993). The "control" question "test" (CQT) polygrapher's dilemma: Logico-ethical considerations for psycho-physiological practitioners and researchers. *International Journal of Psychophysiology, 15,* 263–267.

Furedy, J. J., & Heslegrave, R. J. (1988). Validity of the lie detector: A psychophysiological perspective. *Criminal Justice and Behavior, 15* (2), 219–246.

Greenfield, N. S., & Sternbach, R. A. (Eds.). (1972). *Handbook of Psychophysiology.* New York: Rinehart and Winston.

Gustafson, L. A., & Orne, M. T. (1965). Effects of heightened motivation on the detection of deception. *Journal of Applied Psychology, 47* (6), 408–411.

Honts, C. R. (1991). The emperor's new clothes: Applications of polygraph test in the American workplace. *Forensic Reports, 4,* 91–116.

Honts, C. R., & Perry, N. (1992). Polygraph admissibility: Changes and challenges. *Law and Human Behavior, 16,* 357–379.

Honts, C. R., & Quick, B. D. (1996). The polygraph in 1995: Progress in science and the law. *North Dakota Law Review, 71,* 987–1020.

Honts, C. R., Raskin, D. C., & Kircher, J. C. (1994). Mental and physical countermeasures reduce the accuracy of polygraph tests. *Journal of Applied Psychology, 79* (2), 252–259.

Horvath, F. S. (1977). The effect of selected variables on interpretation of polygraphy records. *Journal of Applied Psychology, 62,* 127–136.

Iacono, W. G. (1991). Can we determine the accuracy of polygraph tests? In J. R. Jennings, P. K. Ackles, & M. G. H. Coles (Eds.), *Psychology and Policing* (pp. 155–171). Hillsdale, NJ: Laurence Erlbaum.

Iacono, W. G. (1995). Offender testimony: Detection of deception and guilty knowledge. In N. Brewer & C. Wilson (Eds.), *Psychology and policing* (pp. 155–171). Hillsdale, NJ: Laurence Erlbaum.

Iacono, W. G. (1999). The detection of deception. In L. G. Tassinary, J. T. Cacioppo, & G. Berntson (Eds.), *Handbook of psychophysiology*. New York: Cambridge University Press.

Iacono, W. G., & Lykken, D. T. (1997a). The scientific status of research on polygraph techniques: The case against polygraph tests. In D. L. Faigman, D. Kaye, M. J. Saks, & J. Sanders (Eds.), *Modern scientific evidence: The law and science of expert testimony* (pp. 582–618). St. Paul, MN: West.

Iacono, W. G., & Lykken, D. T. (1997b). A response to professors Raskin, Honts, and Kircher. In D. L. Faigman, D. Kaye, M. J. Saks, & J. Sanders (Eds.), *Modern scientific evidence: The law and science of expert testimony* (pp. 627–629). St. Paul, MN: West.

Iacono, W. G., & Lykken, D. T. (1997c). A rejoinder to Raskin, Honts, and Kircher. In D. L. Faigman, D. Kaye, M. J. Saks, & J. Sanders (Eds.), *Modern scientific evidence: The law and science of expert testimony* (pp. 631–633). St. Paul, MN: West.

Iacono, W., & Patrick, C. (1988). Assessing deception: Polygraph techniques. In R. Rogers (Ed.) *Clinical assessment of malingering and deception* (pp. 205–233). New York: Guilford Press.

Iacono, W., & Patrick, C. (1997). Polygraphy and integrity testing. In R. Rogers (Ed.) *Clinical assessment of malingering and deception* (2nd ed.) (pp. 252–281). New York: Guilford Press.

Iacono, W. G., & Patrick, C. J. (1999). Polygraph ("lie detector") testing: The state of the art. In A. K. Hess & I. B. Weiner (Eds.), *The handbook of forensic psychology* (2nd ed.). New York: Wiley.

Kleinmuntz, B., & Szucko, J. J. (1984). Lie detection in ancient and modern times: A call for contemporary scientific study. *American Psychologist, 39* (7), 766–776.

Lykken, D. T. (1959). The GSR in the detection of guilt. *Journal of Applied Psychology, 43*, 385–388.

Lykken, D. T. (1960). The validity of the guilty knowledge technique: The effects of faking. *Journal of Applied Psychology, 44*, 258–262.

Lykken, D. T. (1981). *A tremor in the blood.* New York: McGraw-Hill.

Lykken, D. T. (1998). *A tremor in the blood: Uses and abuses of the lie detector* (2nd ed.). New York: McGraw-Hill.

Marston, W. M. (1917). Psychological possibilities in the deception tests. *Journal of Criminal Law and Criminology, 11*, 551–570.

McFall, R. M., & Townsend, J. T. (1998). Foundations of psychological assessment: Implications for cognitive assessment in clinical science. *Psychological Assessment, 10* (4), 316–330.

Meyer, R. G., & Youngjohn, J. R. (1991). Effects of feedback and validity expectancy on responses in a lie detection interview. *Forensic Reports, 4*, 235–244.

Patrick, C. J., & Iacono, W. G. (1991). Validity of the control question polygraph test: The problem of sampling bias. *Journal of Applied Psychology, 76* (2), 229–238.

Pink, L. A., & Kotzan, J. A. (1986). Polygraph testing: A comprehensive literature review of an ethical dilemma. *American Journal of Pharmaceutical Education, 50*, 175–180.

Podlesny, J., & Raskin, D. (1977). Physiological measures and detection of deception. *Psychological Bulletin, 84*, 782–799.

Raskin, D. C. (1986). The polygraph in 1986. *Utah Law Review, 1*, 29–73.

Raskin, D., & Kircher J. (1992). Polygraph techniques: History, controversies, and prospects. In P. Suedfeld (Ed.) *Psychology and social policy* (pp. 295–308). New York: Hemisphere Publishing Corporation.

Raskin, D. C., Honts, C. R., Amato, S. L., & Kircher, J. C. (1999). The scientific status of research on polygraph techniques: The case for the admissibility of the results of polygraph examinations. In D. L. Faigman, D. H. Kaye, M. J. Saks, & J. Sanders (Eds.), *Modern scientific evidence: The law and science of expert testimony* (pp. 117–135). St. Paul, MN: West.

Reid, J. E., & Inbau, F. E. (1977). *Truth and deception, the polygraph technique* (2nd ed.). Baltimore, MD: Williams & Wilkins.

Rogers, R. (1988). *Clinical assessment of malingering and deception.* New York: Guilford Press.

Rogers, R. (Ed.) (1988). *Clinical assessment of malingering and deception.* New York: Guilford Press.

Saxe, L. (1991). Science and the CQT polygraphy: A theoretical critique. *Integrative Physiological and Behavioral Science, 26* (3), 223–231.

Saxe, L., Dougherty, D., & Cross, T. (1985). The validity of polygraph testing. *American Psychologist, 40* (3), 355–366.

Simpson, B. A. (1986). The polygraph: Concept, usage, and validity. *Psychology, a Quarterly Journal of Human Behavior, 23* (1), 42–45.

Szucko, J. J., & Kleinmuntz, B. (1981). Statistical versus clinical lie detection. *American Psychologist, 36*, 488–496.

Thaxton, L. (1982). *Journal of Sports Psychology, 4*, 73.

U.S. Congress (1983). *Scientific validity of polygraph testing: A research review and evaluation.* Technical Memorandum OTA-TM-H-15. Washington, DC: Office of Technology Assessment, U.S. Congress.

CHAPTER 26

NONVERBAL DETECTION OF DECEPTION IN FORENSIC CONTEXTS

MARK G. FRANK
RUTGERS, THE STATE UNIVERSITY OF NEW JERSEY

PAUL EKMAN
UNIVERSITY OF CALIFORNIA, SAN FRANCISCO

Forensic science is about a search for the truth. This means that a lie injected into the legal system poses one of the largest threats to finding the truth. It is therefore essential to know the extent to which the people or processes involved in the legal system can unmask a lie. In order to begin to answer this question, we need to examine four precursor questions: (1) What do we mean by a lie? (2) What happens when someone lies? (3) How good are people at spotting lies? and (4) How do the processes involved in a trial help or hinder our abilities to spot these lies?

WHAT IS A LIE?

There are a number of ways in which testimony can be misleading. People can have an honest difference of opinion, they can have mistaken recall, they can have a false memory, or they can lie (Haugaard & Repucci, 1992). Two people can view the same traffic accident and have very different accounts. People forget facts, names, and license plates. The fact that innocent people have been convicted on the basis of erroneous eyewitness accounts testifies to this problem (Dwyer, Neufeld, & Scheck, 2000). What distinguishes a lie from these other forms of inaccurate testimony is that only a lie involves the *deliberate* presentation of information that a witness hopes will mislead. This aspect of a lie is the cornerstone of Ekman's definition of a lie as a deliberate attempt to mislead, without the implicit or explicit prior consent or notification of the target (Ekman, 2001). In other words, for purposes of this chapter *lying* is synonymous with established legal definitions of perjury. If a witness truly believes he or she saw the ghost of Elvis Presley rob a convenience store, that person would not be lying. If the witness knew it wasn't the ghost of Elvis, then he or she would be lying.

Lies can occur in many different forms, from outright fabrication, denial, distortion, evasion, and concealment, to even "telling the truth falsely" (Ekman, 2001). In a forensic context, it is clear that to fabricate information or to deny an allegation that the suspect or witness knows is true are lies. They are lies no matter where they appear, be it on the street, in the police station, or in the courtroom—where they are clearly perjury. However, clever liars can use distortion or evasion strategies in which they push the limits of what we mean by fabrication and denial. For example, if a murder suspect is asked whether he or she had a relationship with the victim, a clever suspect may say, "There *is* no relationship between us." This would be technically true, since the victim is dead and so there cannot be a current relationship, but it evades the actual thrust of the question, which is whether there *had been* a relationship. The extent to which this type of lie would be perjury is unclear because the statement is accurate, but it is not responding to the intent of the question.

Similar to this type of lie is the *concealment lie*, which typically involves concealing the truth in situations where it is implicit or explicit that the person should not conceal it. For example, children who get in trouble at school are expected to tell their parents without being asked; if they do not, they are concealing information that they are obligated to divulge—which, according to Ekman (2001), would constitute a lie. It strikes us that, like the evasion lie earlier, a concealment lie would not *practically* be a lie in a courtroom or police station, although *technically* one could argue that "the truth, the *whole* truth, and nothing but the truth" oath taken in a courtroom requires persons under oath to expand upon their testimony to ensure that it is not misleading or misunderstood, thus rendering these lies perjury. However, informal and unsystematic observations of courtroom trials by ourselves and others (e.g., Curriden, 1995) suggest that a person who did not answer a question beyond the immediate question presented would not be considered lying as long as he or she answered the immediate question. So if witnesses are never asked whether they saw the shooting, they are technically not lying about it and in all likelihood would not face perjury charges.

A final method of lying involves *telling the truth falsely* (Ekman, 2001). For example, a murderer trying to conceal his or her actions might say, "Oh sure, I definitely shot the victim with my own little gun" in a very sarcastic tone, so as to make others think that he or she is being ironic when this information is factually correct. This lie strategy has been observed in lying suspects on occasion during police questioning (e.g., Inbau, Reid, & Buckley, 1986). However, if a witness or defendant in a trial were to tell the truth falsely by saying in a sarcastic tone that he or she shot someone, any alert attorney would ask this person to clarify that statement to force him or her to commit to a denial lie or make a true admission.

Thus, although fabrications, distortions, evasions, concealments, and telling the truth falsely are all lies, it appears that only fabrications and distortions leave defendants or witnesses liable for perjury.

What Happens When Someone Lies?

The evidence suggests that in day-to-day life most lies are betrayed by factors or circumstance surrounding the lie, and not by behavior (Park, Levine, McCornack, Morrison, & Ferrar, 2002). This applies to forensic contexts as well, since juries and investigators often have a variety of other information, including videotapes, DNA evidence, phone records, and so forth, to help them ferret out the truth. For example, a suspect in a convenience store robbery may claim that he was at home during the hours in which the robbery occurred when in fact a hidden video camera clearly shows him holding a gun to the head of the clerk and fingerprint evidence shows that he had been in this store at some point. However, there are times where behavior is the only information that a lie catcher has to make his or her decision. A recent example includes the notorious "hockey dad" trial in Massachusetts, in which two fathers got into a fight after their children's hockey practice and during this fight one father killed the other. This trial did not need to determine whether one father killed the other, but instead the jury had to judge the motive and state of mind of the killer. They did this almost exclusively through the testimony of a parade of eyewitnesses to the fight, many of whom contradicted each other over what they saw (Butterfield, 2002).

In this instance, like many in the legal world, various technologies could have been applied to detect the truth; for example, the polygraph ("lie detector machine"), voice stress analyzer, P300 brain wave analysis, and other techniques were not applied. The validity of these machines and techniques as lie detectors is beyond the scope of this chapter, which will focus on detecting deception from behavior. Thus we will only discuss the situations in which lies are betrayed from individual behavior—that is, lies that are betrayed by what people say, how they say it, and how they appear as they say it—just like in the "hockey dad" trial.

This research suggests that two families of behavioral clues betray deception—clues related to liars' thinking about what they are saying and clues related to liars' feelings and feelings about deception (Ekman, 2001; Ekman & Frank, 1993; Hocking & Leathers, 1980).

Thinking Clues

In order to mislead someone deliberately, a liar must create facts, describe events that did not happen or that were not witnessed, or suppress critical information. However, the process of thinking about, or creating, this misinformation leaves behavioral signs. These signs range from hesitation in speech or a misplaced word or contradictory statement to very vague accounts with less logical structure (see DePaulo, Lindsay, Malone, Muhlenbruck, Charlton, & Cooper, 2003, for a review). These types of clues are particularly evident in situations in which liars should know exactly what they have done without having to think too much about it. A witness who claims to have been present at a crime scene should be able to tell the court where he or she was standing while witnessing the event without too much thought. A witness who was not present at that scene would have to create the details necessary to convince someone that he or she was there. This on-the-spot thinking, research has shown, often manifests itself in many speech hesitations, speech disfluencies, and errors, often with fewer of the hand or facial gestures that typically illustrate speech (DePaulo, Stone, & Lassiter, 1985; Ekman, Friesen, & Scherer, 1976).

Moreover, choice of words can also betray on-the-spot thinking (e.g., Stiff & Miller, 1986). Liars are less immediate, use words that are more general and simple to recall and generate, and less concrete (reviewed by Zuckerman & Driver, 1985). On top of this, deceptive witnesses have to be very careful to not contradict their statements made during the discovery period.

Feeling Clues

Not only do witnesses, defendants, or victims who are lying have to think out the lie and maintain a consistent story, but often emotions are aroused within them that are associated with these lies. Emotions can enter into the lie process in one of two ways—first, the person testifying could be lying about his or her feelings or emotions, or second, the act of lying may produce feelings or emotions within the liar.

Lying About Feelings

There are situations in which lies are betrayed by the false portrayal of an emotion. One of the most controversial aspects of the Menendez case in California—where two brothers killed their well-to-do parents but claimed to have been driven to that act by their parents' relentless physical and sexual abuse—involved whether the displays of sadness by the two brothers when they described their actions were real or feigned. We can ask whether their sadness was a genuine display of remorse over being forced, because of the years of abuse, to kill these monstrous parents before their parents killed them—or was it the simulated sadness of two culpable siblings designed to gain sympathy from the judge and jury so they could collect their sizeable inheritance?

Research has shown that when emotions are aroused, changes are unbidden and occur automatically. Subjectively, people report feeling that emotions *happen* to them and not that they *choose* which emotions to feel (imagine what would happen to the psychological profession if this were the case!). We know this phenomenon through our own experience. For example, during times when we may feel blue, we do things that we hope will make us feel better—we go for a walk, eat some forbidden food, rent a comedy video—but the emergence of the emotion of happiness is never a guarantee. Likewise, if we are walking down a dark alley and then notice we are being followed by people dressed in gang clothing, we will typically feel fear, despite our efforts to not do so. These changes occur within a split-second and are considered fundamental features of an emotional response (Ekman, 1984; Frijda, 1986).

Part of this emotional response, besides changes in heart rate, blood pressure, and so forth (Ekman, Levenson, & Friesen, 1983; Levenson, Ekman, Heider, & Friesen, 1992), is a facial expression of that emotion (Ekman, 1994; Izard, 1994). Research has shown that emotions such as anger, contempt, disgust, fear, happiness, sadness, and surprise appear on people's faces during an emotional experience, often despite their efforts to hide them (e.g., Ekman, Friesen, & O'Sullivan, 1988). Our research has shown that facial expressions that are driven by actual felt emotion have different characteristics than those that are mimicked emotions, including subtle differences in the muscles used in the expression (Ekman & Friesen, 1982; Frank & Ekman, 1993; Frank, Ekman, & Friesen, 1993). These subtle differences have been called "reliable" behavioral signs of emotion (Ekman, 2001), because few people can actually mimic them. For example, when people feel the emotion of happiness, their facial expression involves the contraction of the large muscles that surround the eyes (producing a "crow's feet" appearance) along with an upward contraction of the lip corners (Ekman & Friesen, 1982). When people are faking happiness or enjoyment, they will contract their lip corners, but do not—or cannot—contract the large muscles that surround the eyes (Frank & Ekman, 1993). Although a large-intensity smile will also generate the "crow's feet" appearance, at lower intensities "crow's feet" would be a reliable sign of actual felt enjoyment.

If the situation involves assessing the true feelings of a witness, then the lie catcher should try to observe the presence or absence of as many of these reliable clues to the emotion as possible. Reliable signs include the narrowing of the red margins of the lips in anger, the upward and inward contraction of the area between the eyebrows in fear, and the upward raise of the inner corners of the eyebrows in sadness (the reader is referred to Ekman [2001] for a more complete list of these behavioral signs of emotions). For example, a case in Australia featured a man who was trying to convince a detective that he was despondent (sad) over allegedly discovering the body of his dead father, but he could not deliberately move his inner corners of his eyebrows upward. Although he was feigning sadness, his facial behavior showed he was not actually feeling sadness, and he later confessed to the murder. Likewise, a sheriff's deputy described how a man claimed he would not harm his wife if she were to return to their apartment; as he was doing so, the red margins of his lips became more and more narrow. The deputy at the time noted this but did not interpret it correctly, because he allowed the wife to enter. When she did, the man struck her in the presence of the deputy. In the former case, the absence of the reliable sign betrayed the true emotion, whereas in the latter the presence of the reliable sign did.

These behavioral signs are often obvious but at other times are so fleeting as to be micromomentary. Ekman and Friesen (1969) called these micromomentary expressions of emotion *microexpressions*, and the evidence suggests that they can be as brief as one-quarter of a second. It also appears that only expert lie catchers detect these microexpressions with any accuracy, whereas average to poor lie catchers miss them (Ekman & O'Sullivan, 1991; Ekman, O'Sullivan, & Frank, 1999; Frank & Ekman, 1997; Frank, 2003).

The voice is also implicated in emotion (Scherer, 1984). There are particular patterns in fundamental frequency and amplitude that distinguish anger from fear and these emotions from others, and some limited evidence suggests that these vocal profiles for emotions are universal across cultures (Scherer & Walbott, 1994). For example, in anger the fundamental frequency gets lower (lower pitch), and the amplitude higher (i.e., louder), whereas in fear the fundamental frequency gets higher (higher pitch) and the amplitude softer (i.e., quieter).

Feelings About Lying

Not all lies involve concealing or falsifying emotions. A witness may conceal the fact that her friend actually threw the first punch in an assault, or the witness may conceal the fact that she never saw the dispute but was simply parroting the alleged victim's account. However, this witness may feel guilt about making up the account of the assault or may feel fear of being jailed for perjury, or may feel enjoyment at the fact that she has outsmarted the police into believing her account of the assault. Thus, lies can produce emotions independent of the act in which the lie was designed to conceal or falsify. Once these emotions are involved, they must be concealed if the lie is not to be betrayed. There are many emotions that could be involved in deception, but three seem most intertwined with deceit—fear of being caught in the lie, guilt about lying, and delight in having duped someone (Ekman, 2001).

Fear of Being Caught

Low levels of fear may help liars get away with their deceptions by maintaining their alertness. In its moderate and high levels, fear can produce behavioral signs that can be noticed by the skilled lie catcher (e.g., DePaulo et al., 2003; Ekman, O'Sullivan, & Frank, 1999; Frank & Ekman, 1997). There are a number of factors that can influence fear of being caught—for example, if the lie catcher has a reputation for being tough to fool, the liar may feel more fear. If the liar has not had much practice at telling and getting away with the lie, then his fear of being caught would increase. Conversely, a lying witness who has been able to convince police investigators of his fictional account of a crime would gain confidence and would not feel as fearful of being caught (after all, he has not been caught yet). Likewise, this practice enables the liar to anticipate other possible questions and thus further reduce the fear of getting caught. Finally, besides the fear of being caught, a lying witness may show fear of punishment—that is, punishment for the act upon which the lie was designed to conceal. In other words, the stronger the punishments for the crime, or for perjury, or getting caught in general, the more fear a deceptive witness is likely to show (e.g., Frank & Ekman, 1997).

Deception Guilt

Deception guilt refers to a feeling about lying and not the legal issue of whether someone is guilty or innocent. Deception guilt refers to the guilt felt when lying; for example, a witness may feel happiness at helping out a friend by claiming that the defendant threw the first punch but later may feel guilty about lying. This situation can be reversed as well—she may feel guilt about helping out the friend but feel no guilt about lying about it (or some can feel guilt for both, and some for neither). What is important is that it is not necessary to feel guilty about the content of a lie in order to feel guilty about lying. Like fear of being caught, deception guilt can vary in strength. For example, severe guilt can be a tortuous experience, undermining the sufferer's most fundamental feelings of self-worth (Ekman, 2001).

A number of factors function to increase the amount of guilt a liar might feel. First, it seems that some people are particularly prone to guilt—for example, those who suffer from generalized anxiety disorders. These individuals often have very strict upbringings, have been severely punished for lying, or have been led to believe that lying is one of the most severe sins. Conversely, psychopaths—who have been reported to show no remorse, shame, and an incapacity for love—may be much harder to detect than the average person because of their limited capacity to feel guilt (Hare, 1970). Second, a close relationship between the liar and the target of the lie (if they share values, respect each other, and so forth) also functions to augment guilt feelings. Conversely, a liar who does not share values with the target would feel less guilt; a witness who despises the legal system may not feel guilty about lying in court, much the same way in which a spy or terrorist feels no guilt about lying to a representative of an enemy government. Finally, if the target of the lie is impersonal or anonymous, then less deception guilt is generally felt. A witness who lies to a videotape camera or in an affidavit may feel less guilt than in lying to an actual person. However, guilt often causes people to rationalize their deceits; witnesses may convince themselves that the defendant had always been a troublemaker and deserved to be arrested, even though the defendant was not responsible for initiating the current altercation.

Duping Delight

Lying can produce positive as well as negative emotions. The lie may be viewed as a proud accomplishment. Peter Sutcliffe, the man convicted of being the Yorkshire Ripper, expressed his delight while he was twice interrogated and then dismissed by police before ultimately being caught. A number of factors may cause an increase in duping delight—if the target is hard to fool, or if there is an audience who is aware of the deception and enjoying the performance. Thus, a lying witness may enjoy the fact that he is sitting in center stage of the courtroom, in front of his friends, while he regales them with his bogus account of an assault.

It should be noted that these emotions can occur simultaneously or in any combination. For example, witnesses may feel guilt over producing a bogus account of the assault or fear being caught perjuring themselves, as well as a certain delight in being able to pull off the lie in front of all these supposedly important legal professionals.

Cautions

It must be noted that these thinking and feeling clues are just that—clues that witnesses, defendants, and victims are thinking, or clues that they are feeling or concealing some emotion. To date, no one has been able to identify a human equivalent of a *Pinocchio response*—that is, there is no one behavioral sign or constellation of signs that, across every person, in all situations, indicates that a person is lying. Thus, a lie catcher who identifies those behavioral clues described earlier must always infer why a witness would show guilt, or fear, or delight, or why a witness would mull something over. In particular, two types of mistakes are commonly made in judging deception. The first Ekman (2001) called the *Othello error*. Like Shakespeare's tragic hero, lie detectors who *dis*believe truthful witnesses may make the latter appear anxious and fearful—and hence appear as if they are being deceptive. This means lie catchers must decide whether the signs of fear that they believe they see are the fear of a person caught lying or the fear of a truthful person who is afraid of being disbelieved.

The second type of mistake Ekman (2001) called the *idiosyncrasy error*. This type of error is caused by a failure to observe a person's typical style of behavior. For example, research has shown that most people believe that liars do not make eye contact when they speak (DePaulo et al., 1985; Zuckerman, DePaulo, & Rosenthal 1981); however, there are some people who, either because of their shy nature or low self-esteem, never make eye contact in everyday conversation. To interpret a witness's lack of eye contact as evidence that the witness is lying, without knowing the witness's typical behavioral style, would clearly make it more likely that one would commit an error. Culture enters into this equation as well; for example, in some cultures it is considered a sign of respect to not look an authority figure in the eye.

Implications

Taken together, the research suggests that there is no single behavior or behaviors that, across all people or in all situations, guarantees that a person is lying. However, there is evidence in the face and voice that someone is lying, particularly in high-stake lies in which the liar faces benefits for successful lying and punishments for unsuccessful lying (DePaulo et al., 2003; Ekman, 2001). For example, research has shown that facial expressions of fear, distress, and disgust distinguish liars and truthtellers at over 76 percent accuracy (Frank & Ekman, 1997); when voice measures are added, this accuracy rises to 86.5 percent (Ekman, O'Sullivan, Friesen, & Scherer, 1991). Thus, it is possible to do a reasonably accurate job of sorting the liars from the truthtellers using behavioral measures, although to date it is not perfect or even 90 percent accurate.

An accuracy rate of less than 90 percent has huge forensic implications, chiefly concerning a key point of contention between science and the law—the distinction between probabilistic versus particular evidence (Bartol, 1983). Behavioral science often relies upon *probabilistic evidence*—that is, evidence that can tell you what are the odds that anyone drawn from a given population might show this pattern of behavior or have a certain characteristic. In contrast, the law is usually dependent upon *particular evidence*—that is, evidence concerning the abilities or characteristics of this specific person on the stand. This is best seen in debates over the applicability of research on eyewitness memory to actual courtroom situations. Researchers can predict the proportion of eyewitnesses who may succumb to a memory distortion technique in the laboratory but cannot identify in a courtroom whether a particular witness who has testified has actually succumbed (e.g., Loftus, 1979). They are left to reason that under the specific conditions in which witnesses saw the event, a certain percentage of them will have an inaccurate memory. They cannot say whether this witness is in the group who will have an inaccurate recall or the group who had an accurate recall. Judging a lie will pose a similar problem. If a witness showed signs of distress in the face and voice, and had hesitating speech replete with speech errors, is this person in the 80 percent of people who under this configuration of behaviors are likely to be lying, or is the witness in the remaining 20 percent of people who are truthful but nervous? The extent to which we can claim that a particular pattern of behavior suggests an 80 percent likely chance that a witness is lying does not tell us precisely whether a particular witness is lying, assuming there is no other unimpeachable corroborating evidence.

We are not fully confident that we are only capable of achieving 80 or 85 percent accuracy in lie catching from behavior because there has not been enough research examining the behaviors exhibited by people under high-stakes lie conditions, which are of course the situations that most interest forensic scientists. Moreover, of the work that has been done, more has been focused on the behavioral signs of emotions in the face and voice than on speech indicators and bodily signs (see Ekman, 2001, for a review). This means there may be areas of good lie clues in behavior that we just have not discovered yet. But we do know that it seems that the extent to which these behavioral signs are correlated with a lie is often the extent to which the lie will be caught. But can people detect them?

HOW GOOD ARE WE AT SPOTTING LIES?

There are a number of people involved in forensic settings who may be asked to detect a lie, including laypeople involved in the dispute or crime, the officer conducting the investigation, expert clinicians assessing a suspect or witness, and the jury and/or judge involved in the trial.

The evidence shows that laypeople are pretty poor at detecting lies. Research on people's accuracy at detecting deception from behavior shows that the typical person is around 55–58 percent accurate, despite the fact that a person who would simply guess who was lying would get approximately 50 percent correct (DePaulo et al., 1985; Kraut, 1980). The typical range of accuracy found in individual research studies, and the reviews that summarized them, is that individuals are 45–60 percent accurate (e.g., DePaulo et al., 1985; Ekman, 2001; Feeley & Young, 1998; Zuckerman, DePaulo, & Rosenthal, 1981; Zuckerman & Driver, 1985). The only deviations from this pattern happen under specific conditions and occur for specific subject groups. For example, people with left hemisphere brain damage, who thus could not process speech, could accurately detect the lies of nursing students who viewed an unpleasant film and tried to convince an interviewer that the film was pleasant (Etcoff, Ekman, Magee, & Frank, 2000). This accuracy was limited to judgments made from the facial channel and was superior to the performance of matched right-hemisphere-damaged patients and patient controls. Likewise, children who were abused and raised in institutions also showed a superior skill in lie detection from the face made from the same stimulus videotapes described above (Bugental, Shennum, Frank, & Ekman, 2001). This superiority is likely honed in these children's life history in which they had to make accurate judgments of caregivers' emotions in order to avoid an abusive encounter. More explanations have been generated to account for such poor performance in laypeople, including the lack of appropriate and timely feedback (e.g., Zuckerman, Koestner, & Alton, 1984) or social pressures to not identify deceptions that occur in daily life (e.g., the "truth bias," McCornack & Parks, 1986; Levine, Park, & McCornack, 1999).

When it comes to law enforcement personnel, the evidence is mixed. Some studies show that police officers are not any better than laypeople at detecting lies from behavior, although police are more confident in their abilities (DePaulo & Pfeifer, 1986). Customs officers were not seen as being better than college students at detecting smuggling-associated lies (Kraut & Poe, 1980). Other studies showed that typical "beat cop" police are not better than laypeople (Ekman &

O'Sullivan, 1991; Ekman et al., 1999), although others have argued that this outcome applies to all police (Bull, 1989; Garrido & Masip, 1999; Kohnken, 1987).

Within this literature, however, we have found that some groups of law enforcement officers clearly outperform not only chance levels of accuracy but other law enforcement personnel. In these studies, groups such as the U.S. Secret Service detected lies concerning concealed emotions at up to 64 percent accurate (Ekman & O'Sullivan, 1991), whereas detectives identified as top interviewers achieved 67 percent accuracy in a U.S. sample (Ekman et al., 1999), and up to 69 percent accuracy in a U.K. sample (Frank, 2003), which was significantly better than the 51 percent accuracy of other police. A sample of U.S. federal agents also achieved up to 73 percent accuracy at distinguishing liars from truthtellers (Ekman et al., 1999). These groups seemed to outperform laypeople and other groups because they were more motivated, which meant they were more attentive and worked harder at developing their skills. They also spent more time focusing on emotions that don't fit the prevailing situation, and our research has shown that those who are better at identifying microexpressions of emotion are better lie catchers (Ekman & O'Sullivan, 1991; Frank & Ekman, 1997; Frank, 2003). This accuracy may also result from the fact that the base rate for lying that they dealt with was lower than for "beat cops," which makes it easier to develop and identify patterns associated with lying. For example, if the base rate for lying is high, one merely has to judge everyone as lying to become as accurate as the base rate. So if the base rate for lying is 75 percent, then to judge everyone as lying would produce a 75 percent accuracy rate. But this strategy of judging everyone as lying will become less and less successful as the base rate drops. Thus, law enforcement personnel who deal with a lower base rate must develop some other judgment algorithms or heuristics to outperform that base rate, and it appears that these high-accuracy groups have done that.

The evidence suggests that most people involved in a trial, such as most expert clinicians, trial attorneys, and judges, are also no better than laypeople at detecting deception. But some were better. Once again, motivation seemed to be the key, as strongly motivated judges and clinical psychologists, defined as those willing to give up a day's pay to attend a workshop on detecting lies, distinguished lies and truths at rates above 60 percent. Motivated clinical psychologists were 68 percent accurate, and motivated judges were 62 percent accurate, compared with 56 percent for less motivated judges and other psychologists (Ekman & O'Sullivan, 1991; Ekman et al., 1999).

Finally, it is assumed in the American judicial system that because each side is allowed to advocate its position, an impartial jury will sift through the opposing arguments and distill the truth (Bartol, 1983). Unfortunately, we are aware of only one study that looked at a jury's ability to distinguish liars from truthtellers, and this study found that juries were not statistically significantly better than laypeople at catching lies, but that they as a group were more likely to judge an individual as lying as compared to individual lie catchers who did not discuss their judgments. Moreover, the juries were more confident in their judgments than individual lie catchers (Frank, Feeley, Servoss, & Paolantonio, 2003).

How the Legal Process Affects Catching Lies Through Behavioral Clues

The types of lies that occur in a forensic context, the model of how lies are betrayed, and our examination of human lie catchers makes it quite clear that the triers of fact in the courtroom have their work cut out for them when it comes to spotting lies. But we can also examine how the processes involved in a trial might help or hinder their abilities to unmask a lie. To see this, one must look at the structural features of that situation and how they interact with the processes described earlier concerning how lies are betrayed (Frank, 1992). Some appear to hinder our abilities to detect lies from behavior, and others help.

Hindering Factors

Ekman (2001) speculated that there are four ways in which the legal system works against a judge or jury's abilities to infer deception from a witness, defendant, or victim's testimony, and to this we can add two more. First, Ekman (2001) argued that a deceptive witness is allowed weeks and even months to prepare and rehearse lies before he or she has to present them in court. This rehearsal allows a deceptive witness to become more confident and thus reduces fear of detection. Moreover, during the course of rehearsal a deceptive witness may in fact convince himself that what he is saying is true, or that what he will say will "set things right"; these rationalizations would certainly work to reduce deception guilt as well as the fear of being caught.

Second, Ekman (2001) reasoned that, given this long delay between the event and the testimony, any emotions associated with the event may be blunted or diminished considerably—thus, any emotions that may betray true feelings may not appear by the time the witness takes the stand.

Third, Ekman (2001) suggested that witnesses may be coached and questioned in such a way by attorneys that they have to provide only "yes" or "no" answers; these answers are often harder to judge because they feature less speech information, so there is less behavior upon which judges and juries can assess whether a lie has occurred.

Fourth, Ekman (2001) argued that a truthful witness or defendant who appears in court will probably be quite anxious about being disbelieved. In the case of a truthful defendant, this would be particularly likely—after all, if the police interrogators, psychologists, and other did not believe the defendant, why should a judge and jury? Under these conditions, an innocent defendant may show more signs of fear than a guilty one, and a judge and jury stand a much greater chance of committing the Othello error.

Fifth, we have noticed that it is possible that defendants or witnesses may be on various medications that dampen their emotional reactions. This may take the form of benzodiazepines, like Valium or Xanax, or even the use of Botox injections to mask the facial expression specifically (as in a high-profile Australian murder case a few years ago). These medical interventions would make defendants and witnesses much more inscrutable to the jury, which would seem to confound rather than assist any identification of liars or truthtellers. But we do not know this for sure.

Sixth, recent physical and technological modifications allow a witness or victim to testify from behind screens or over closed-circuit television. Although the use of a screen was ruled unconstitutional in *Coy v. Iowa* (1988), the court did not explicitly rule out other techniques like closed-circuit television for witnesses and victims in cases like *Maryland v. Craig* (1990). However, the U.S. Supreme Court has ruled that the Sixth Amendment to the U.S. Constitution explicitly states that defendants have a right to confront their accusers in the presence of a jury, a jury whose duty is to judge the credibility of witnesses for and against a defendant. Writing for the majority about the importance of a witness's testifying face to face with a defendant, U.S. Supreme Court Justice Antonin Scalia wrote in *Coy v. Iowa* (1988):

> It is always more difficult to tell a lie about a person *to his face* than *behind his back*. In the former context, even if the lie is told, it will often be told less convincingly. The Confrontation Clause does not, of course, compel the witness to fix his eyes upon the defendant; he may studiously look elsewhere, but the trier of fact will draw its own conclusions.... That face-to-face presence may, unfortunately, upset the truthful rape victim or abused child; but by the same token it may confound and undo the false accuser, or reveal the child coached by a malevolent adult. (pp. 1019–1020, italics added)

This assumption originates in *Mattox v. United States* (1895), where the Court wrote that "the accused has an opportunity, not only of testing the recollection and sifting the conscience of the witness, but of compelling him to stand face to face with the jury in order that they may look at him, and *judge by his demeanor upon the stand and the manner in which he gives his testimony whether he is worthy of belief*" (cited in *Coy v. Iowa*, 1988, pp. 1026; italics added).

Research has only recently examined what, if any, are the effects of one particular physical barrier—testimony presented on closed-circuit television—on the judgments of jurors. When it comes to child witnesses, the data suggest that testimony over closed-circuit television does not affect a jury's ability to spot a child's lie (Orcutt, Goodman, Tobey, Batterman-Faunce, & Thomas, 2001), nor does it seem to affect overall jury verdicts in general (Davies, 1999). The data from Frank and colleagues' (2003) study showed that juries had about the same level of accuracy as individuals when they were shown adults testifying over television. However, most of these situations did not involve high-stakes lies, and the one study that did failed to compare closed-circuit television presentations with live presentations. So although it appears as if closed-circuit TV doesn't make that much of a difference, we cannot yet be 100 percent certain about what the effect of testifying over television, or from behind other physical barriers, will have on the ability of a jury to detect a lying witness, defendant, or victim as compared to live testimony offered in court.

Helping Factors

There appears to be three factors that might assist in lie catching in court. Ekman (2001) noted that this is half the number of factors that may hurt our abilities to catch them.

First, judges have a unique status in most legal systems. They are often seen as the only impartial person in the room and as such can develop a fair relationship with jurors and defendants, witnesses, and victims. A judge who establishes this fairness clearly in the minds of all, who may even have defendants, witnesses, and victims give the oath to him or her personally, may increase the odds that a person lying in court may feel guilt about it.

Second, a courtroom is a high-stakes situation in which there are stiff penalties for lying. This fact makes it more likely that a lying defendant, witness, or victim will display signs of their fear of getting caught. However, as described earlier, people in court may show fear for other reasons as well.

Third, if police, psychologists, attorneys, and judges view these behaviors as signs of thinking and signs of emotion, they can identify them as *hot spots*. This means that a particular line of questioning has elicited a physiological response from the person offering testimony. This reaction is useful because it suggests a topic area to pursue, although it does not guarantee that the person is lying about it. By doing this, however, the person is laying open more behavioral evidence that a jury can use to make their decisions. It also lays open more evidence that might enable a jury to compare against other more diagnostic evidence, such as fingerprints, DNA, videotape, and so forth.

Hot spots are revealed through a variety of modalities: facial expressions; voice pitch; voice tone; spoken words; or statements that are inconsistent, illogical, or are delivered hesitantly and with errors. Thus, when a particular line of questioning causes a calm, collected witness to subtly hesitate, show a slight rise in voice pitch, and display brief signs of fear in his or her eyebrow region—or, conversely, when this line of questioning causes an irascible witness to become calm and collected—then one must infer that the witness is thinking over a response or is feeling an emotion. A trier of fact can become even more confident that this is a hot spot when these changes in behavior occur across more than one modality (i.e., voice, face, body posture, speech errors, etc.), and occur only for particular topics (Ekman, 2001). To be further confident that one has hit a hot spot, the interrogator should temporarily change his or her line of questioning, observe the witness's changes in behavior, and then return to the emotion-eliciting topic and observe whether the hot spot reemerges. Once a hot spot is discovered, that discovery needs to be followed up with questions designed to elucidate the actual reason that the witness may be feeling that emotion or was carefully measuring words. Important in this process is that a courtroom lie catcher must seriously consider alternative explanations besides lying for the thinking or feeling behaviors shown by a witness. It may be the case that the witness who suddenly shows signs of emotion is afraid of being disbelieved. Or it may be that describing a blood-splattered murder causes a witness great anxiety. Or it may be that describing genitalia and personal sexual behaviors to a courtroom full of strangers causes a witness to show signs of fear, disgust, shame, or guilt. Thus, there are myriad reasons why a witness or defendant would show behaviors that suggest deception when in fact the person is telling the truth.

The evidence suggests that it is possible to train professionals to improve their abilities to detect these hot spots (Frank & Feeley, 2003). We found that even when laypeople were trained for less than an hour using poor training techniques or failing to identify actual distinguishing clues, meta-analyses suggest that lie-catching skills improve. We and others can only imagine how accurate people might become if adequate training techniques were employed (e.g., DePaulo, 1994).

Conclusion

It seems quite clear that the Pinocchio response does not happen when human beings lie. Because there is no unique lie behavior or behaviors, it would be impossible to create a foolproof lie detection device or strategy to apply to most forensic settings such as the courtroom. This is in addition to the fact that the mechanics of the legal process is such that more of it works against than for detecting lies from demeanor. To add insult to injury, research shows that most people associated with a trial are not any better at detecting lies from behavior than anyone else; thus, the finders of fact in the courtroom are not as good as the system has led us to believe. There are simply lots of other reasons that a witness would show signs of thinking or feelings that are unrelated to lying.

However, some individuals are quite excellent at distinguishing liars from truthtellers. The difficult part is identifying who these experts are. We cannot ask people how good they are at catching lies, since the research shows that people's confidence in their ability to catch lies is uncorrelated with their actual ability to catch lies (e.g., DePaulo, Charlton, Cooper, Lindsey, & Muhlenbruck, 1997). We could select from particular groups that tend to be good lie catchers, but then we would be only probabilistically certain about those individuals' abilities and not know for sure their actual ability. This problem takes on added gravity given the *Daubert v. Merrell Dow* (1993) decision of the U.S. Supreme Court, which ruled that the standard for admissibility of scientific evidence was dependent upon Federal Rule of Evidence 702, which stated that it was up to the trial judge to decide whether introduced scientific evidence or expert testimony was both relevant to the case and based upon reliable science.

This second prong—is it reliable science?—is a difficult decision for any judge to make, particularly given the fact that many are not trained in scientific techniques. The old standard for scientific evidence in the courtroom—that it is generally accepted by the scientific community (known as the Frye test)—seemed easier because it took a bit more burden off the trial judge (Goodman-Delahunty,

1997). We know we can reliably measure facial behavior, voice tone, body behavior, and analysis of words. What we don't know is exactly how reliable our conclusions about the nature of those behaviors are. We are reliable when inferring that someone is engaged in feeling emotions or thinking, but we are not nearly as reliable about inferring accurately that a lie has occurred. We simply do not know all that we really need to know about what happens to people behaviorally in these high-stakes situations to know with a level of certainty that would make this information particular and probative rather than probabilistic and prejudicial.

Thus it appears that, to mangle an analogy from Winston Churchill, the adversarial system is the worst system for detecting deceit from demeanor. It seems, however, better than any other system. The only way to improve this system is to improve the quality and usability of evidence that comes before the court, because in the end the only way to definitively detect lies from behavior, either inside or outside the courtroom, must be to gather unimpeachable corroborating evidence supporting or disproving a witness's testimony—which to some extent was what the adversarial system was designed to do in the first place.

REFERENCES

Bartol, C. (1983). *Psychology and American law*. Belmont, CA: Wadsworth.

Bugental, D. B., Shennum, W., Frank, M. G., & Ekman, P. (2001). "True lies": Children's abuse history and power attributions as influences on deception detection. In V. Manusov & J. H. Harvey (Eds.), *Attribution, communication behavior, and close relationships* (pp. 248–265). Cambridge, UK: Cambridge University Press.

Bull, R. (1989). Can training enhance the detection of deception? In J.C. Yuille (Ed.), *Credibility assessment*. NATO ASI Series. Dordrecht: Kluwer Academic.

Butterfield, F. (2002, January 26). Father in killing at hockey rink is given sentence of 6 to 10 years. *New York Times*, p. A1.

Coy v. Iowa, 108 S. Ct., 2798 (1988).

Curriden, M. (1995, May). The lies have it. *ABA Journal*, 68–72.

Daubert v. Merrell Dow Pharmaceuticals, Inc., 113, S. Ct. 2786 (1993).

Davies, G. (1999). The impact of television on the presentation and reception of children's testimony. *International Journal of Law and Psychiatry*, *22*, 241–256.

DePaulo, B. M. (1994). Spotting lies: Can humans learn to do better? *Current Directions in Psychological Science*, *3*, 83–86.

DePaulo, B. M., Charlton, K., Cooper, H., Lindsay, J. J., & Muhlenbruck, L. (1997). The accuracy-confidence correlation in the detection of deception. *Personality and Social Psychology Review*, *4*, 346–357.

DePaulo, B. M., Lindsay, J. J., Malone, B. E., Muhlenbruck, L., Charlton, K., & Cooper, H. (2003). Cues to deception. *Psychological Bulletin*, *129*, 74–112.

DePaulo, B. M., & Pfeifer, R. L. (1986). On-the-job experience and skill at detecting deception. *Journal of Applied Social Psychology*, *16*, 249–267.

DePaulo, B. M., Stone, J., & Lassiter, D. (1985). Deceiving and detecting deceit. In B. R. Schlenker (Ed.), *The self and social life* (pp. 323–370). New York: McGraw-Hill.

Dwyer, J., Neufeld, P., & Scheck, B. (2000). *Actual innocence: Five days to execution and other dispatches from the wrongly convicted.* New York: Doubleday.

Ekman, P. (1984). Expression and the nature of emotion. In K. Scherer & P. Ekman (Eds.) *Approaches to Emotion* (pp. 319–343). Hillsdale, NJ: Lawrence Erlbaum.

Ekman, P. (1992). Facial expressions of emotion: New findings, new questions. *Psychological Science, 3,* 34–38.

Ekman, P. (1994). Strong evidence for universals in facial expression: A reply to Russell's mistaken critique. *Psychological Bulletin, 115,* 268–287.

Ekman, P. (2001). *Telling lies: Clues to deceit in the marketplace, politics, and marriage.* New York: Norton.

Ekman, P., & Frank, M. G. (1993). Lies that fail. In C. Saarni & M. Lewis (Eds.), *Lying and deception in everyday life.* New York: Guilford.

Ekman, P., & Friesen, W. V. (1969). Nonverbal leakage and clues to deception. *Psychiatry, 32,* 88–105.

Ekman, P., & Friesen, W. V. (1982). Felt, false, and miserable smiles. *Journal of Nonverbal Behavior, 6,* 238–252.

Ekman, P., Friesen, W. V., & O'Sullivan, M. (1988). Smiles when lying. *Journal of Personality and Social Psychology, 54,* 414–420.

Ekman, P., Friesen, W. V., & Scherer, K. (1976). Body movement and voice pitch in deceptive interaction. *Semiotica, 16,* 23–27.

Ekman, P., Levenson, R. W., & Friesen, W. V. (1983). Autonomic nervous system activity distinguishes between emotions. *Science, 221,* 1208–1210.

Ekman, P., & O'Sullivan, M. (1991). Who can catch a liar? *American Psychologist, 46,* 913–920.

Ekman, P., O'Sullivan, M., & Frank, M. G. (1999). A few can catch a liar. *Psychological Science, 10,* 263–266.

Ekman, P., O'Sullivan, M., Friesen, W. V., & Scherer, K. (1991). Invited article: Face, voice, and body in detecting deceit. *Journal of Nonverbal Behavior, 15,* 125–135.

Etcoff, N. L., Ekman, P., Magee, J. J., & Frank, M. G. (2000). Superior lie detection associated with language loss. *Nature, 405* (11 May), 139.

Feeley, T. H., & Young, M. J. (1998). Humans as lie detectors: Some more second thoughts. *Communication Quarterly, 46,* 109–126.

Frank, M. G. (1992). On the structure of lies and deception experiments. In S. J. Ceci, M. DeSimone-Leichtman, and M. E. Putnick (Eds.), *Cognitive and social factors in early deception* (pp. 127–146). Hillsdale, NJ: Lawrence Erlbaum.

Frank, M. G. (2003). Detecting deception and emotion in Americans and Australians. Manuscript submitted.

Frank, M. G., & Ekman, P. (1993). Not all smiles are created equal: The differences between enjoyment and nonenjoyment smiles. *Humor: The International Journal for Research in Humor, 6,* 9–26.

Frank, M. G., & Ekman, P. (1997). The ability to detect deceit generalizes across different types of high stake lies. *Journal of Personality and Social Psychology, 72,* 1429–1439.

Frank, M. G., Ekman, P., & Friesen, W. V. (1993). Behavioral markers and recognizability of the smile of enjoyment. *Journal of Personality and Social Psychology, 64,* 83–93.

Frank, M. G., & Feeley, T. H. (2003). To catch a liar: Challenges for research in lie detection training. *Journal of Applied Communication Research, 35,* 78–93.

Frank, M. G., Feeley, T. H., Servoss, T. N., & Paolantonio, N. (2004). Detecting deception by jury: I. Judgmental accuracy. *Journal of Group Decision and Negotiation, 13*.

Frijda, N. H. (1986). *The emotions.* Cambridge, UK: Cambridge University Press.

Garrido, E., & Masip, J. (1999). How good are police officers at spotting lies? *Forensic Update, 58,* 14–21.

Goodman-Delahunty, J. (1997). Forensic psychological expertise in the wake of Daubert. *Law & Human Behavior, 21,* 121–140.

Hare, R. D. (1970). *Psychopathy: Theory and research.* New York: Wiley.

Haugaard, J. J., & Repucci, N. D. (1992). Children and the truth. In S. J. Ceci, M. DeSimone-Leichtman, and M. E. Putnick (Eds.), *Cognitive and social factors in early deception.* Hillsdale, NJ: Lawrence Erlbaum.

Hocking, J. E., & Leathers, D. G. (1980). Nonverbal indicators of deception: A new theoretical perspective. *Communication Monographs, 47,* 119–131.

Inbau, F. E., Reid, J. E., & Buckley, J. P. (1986). *Criminal interrogation and confessions.* Baltimore: Williams & Wilkins.

Izard, C. E. (1994). Innate and universal facial expressions: Evidence from developmental and cross-cultural research. *Psychological Bulletin, 115,* 288–299.

Kohnken, G. (1987). Training police officers to detect deceptive eyewitness statements: Does it work? *Social Behaviour, 2,* 1–17.

Kraut, R. E. (1980). Humans as lie detectors: Some second thoughts. *Journal of Communication, 30,* 209–216.

Kraut, R. E., & Poe, D. (1980). Behavioral roots of person perception: The deception judgments of customs inspectors and laymen. *Journal of Personality and Social Psychology, 39,* 784–798.

Levenson, R. W., Ekman, P., Heider, K., & Friesen, W. V. (1992). Emotion and autonomic nervous system activity in the Minangkabau of West Sumatra. *Journal of Personality and Social Psychology, 62,* 972–988.

Levine, T. R., Park, H. S., & McCornack, S. A. (1999). Accuracy in detecting truths and lies: Documenting the "veracity effect." *Communication Monographs, 66,* 125–144.

Loftus, E. F. (1979). *Eyewitness testimony.* Cambridge, MA: Harvard University Press.

Maryland v. Craig, 110, S. Ct. 3157 (1990).

McCornack, S. A., & Parks, M. (1986). Deception detection and the other side of trust. In M. L. McLaughlin (Ed.), *Communication Yearbook 9* (pp. 377–389). Beverly Hills, CA: Sage.

Orcutt, H. K., Goodman, G. S., Tobey, A. E., Batterman-Faunce, J. M., & Thomas, S. (2001). Detecting deception in children's testimony: Factfinders' abilities to reach the truth in open court and closed-circuit trials. *Law & Human Behavior, 25,* 339–372.

Park, H. S., Levine, T. R., McCornack, S. A., Morrison, K., & Ferrara, M. (2002). How people really detect lies. *Communication Monographs, 69,* 144–157.

Scherer, K. (1984). On the nature and function of emotions: A component process approach. In K. Scherer & P. Ekman (Eds.), *Approaches to emotion* (pp. 293–317). Hillsdale, NJ: Lawrence Erlbaum.

Scherer, K. R., & Wallbott, H. G. (1994). Evidence for universality and cultural variation of differential emotion response patterning. *Journal of Personality and Social Psychology, 66,* 310–328.

Stiff, J. B., & Miller, G. R. (1986). "Come to think of it . . .": Interrogative probes, deceptive communication, and deception detection. *Human Communication Research, 12,* 339–357.

Zuckerman, M., DePaulo, B. M., & Rosenthal, R. (1981). Verbal and nonverbal communication of deception. In L. Berkowitz (Ed.), *Advances in experimental social psychology. Vol. 14* (pp. 1–59). San Diego, CA: Academic Press.

Zuckerman, M., & Driver, R. E. (1985). Telling lies: Verbal and nonverbal correlates of deception. In W. A. Siegman & S. Feldstein (Eds.), *Multichannel integration of nonverbal behavior* (pp. 129–147). Hillsdale, NJ: Lawrence Erlbaum.

Zuckerman, M., Koestner, R. E., & Alton, A. (1984). Learning to detect deception. *Journal of Personality and Social Psychology, 46*, 519–528.

CHAPTER 27

FORENSIC ISSUES IN SEXUAL HARASSMENT

CLAUDIA AVINA, ADRIAN H. BOWERS, AND WILLIAM T. O'DONOHUE
UNIVERSITY OF NEVADA, RENO

Sexual harassment has become recognized as an increasingly important social problem over the last two decades. Highly public legal battles and settlements, empirical studies documenting high prevalence rates, and the fact that sexual harassment is a gendered problem, where men are predominantly the perpetrators and women the victims, all may account for growing public awareness of this social problem. In light of the evolution of women's rights and women's increased immigration into the workforce, social policies have made attempts to minimize the prejudicial and hurtful practices of sexual harassment. Consequently, scholars have focused attention on understanding causes of the problem, conducting adequate investigations of harassment allegations, assessing and treating psychological functioning of victims, developing interventions for perpetrators, and incorporating these findings into organizational structures.

The purpose of this chapter is to illustrate important forensic issues related to sexual harassment. We will review legal and psychological definitions of sexual harassment, including important federal cases, epidemiological data, characteristics of victims and perpetrators of sexual harassment, and common psychological effects on sexual harassment victims. Finally, we will discuss issues related to assessment of sexual harassment allegations.

WHAT IS SEXUAL HARASSMENT?

The difference between the legal and psychological definitions of sexual harassment is that legal definitions may not account for all events that victims experience as sexually harassing (Fitzgerald, Gelfand, & Drasgow, 1995). The legal definition of sexual harassment takes into account several factors, such as the perspective of the victim; the specific behaviors engaged in by the perpetrator; the frequency, duration, and severity of the behaviors; and the desirability of the behaviors. The legal decision will depend on the entirety of the situation, the specific jury involved, the state of sexual harassment laws, as well as some degree of randomness (Fitzgerald, Swan, & Magley, 1997). However, the psychological definition is determined solely by the experience of the victim. Given the influential role that the psychological study of sexual harassment has on judicial decisions, Fitzgerald, Swan, and colleagues (1997) claim that there is significance in evaluating "the interface between psychological and legal frameworks, taking care to articulate where they overlap, where they diverge, and the implications that each holds for the other" (p. 25). We will discuss both definitions and highlight some critical issues to be addressed:

Legal Definition of Sexual Harassment

The case of *Williams v. Saxbe* (1976) was the first to recognize sexual harassment as a type of sex discrimination protected under Title VII of the Civil Rights Act (1964). Title VII states:

> It shall be unlawful employment practice for an employer (1) to fail or refuse to hire or to discharge any individual, or otherwise to discriminate against any individual with respect to [her or] his compensation, terms, conditions, or privileges of employment, because of such individual's ... sex ... ; or (2) to limit, segregate, or classify [her or] his employees or applicants for employment in any way which would deprive or tend to deprive any individual of employment opportunities or otherwise adversely affect [her or] his status as an employee, because of such individual's ... sex.

In this case Diane Williams alleged that she was harassed, humiliated, and fired for refusing to comply with her supervisor's sexual requests. The presiding judge ruled against the employer's argument that the condition of being fired for refusing to have sex could be applied equally to either gender. It was decided that the discriminatory behavior does not need to depend on a characteristic specific to one sex or the other, only that the behavior be applied to one and not the other (Fitzgerald, Swan, et al., 1997).

The 1980 guidelines issued by the U.S. Equal Employment Opportunity Commission (EEOC) define sexual harassment as

> unwelcome sexual advances, requests for sexual favors, and other verbal or physical conduct of a sexual nature when cooperation or submission was an implicit or explicit condition of employment-related decisions; or when the conduct has the purpose or effect of unreasonably interfering with a person's work performance or creating an intimidated, hostile or offensive working environment.

These guidelines describe two types of sexual harassment: *quid pro quo* and hostile environment. In *quid pro quo* sexual harassment, an individual's work conditions are either implicitly or explicitly based on that individual's submission to, or rejection of, sexual requests. In hostile environment sexual harassment, an individual's work performance is disrupted because of a sexualized environment.

Quid pro quo as an illegal condition in the work environment was recognized in *Williams v. Saxbe* (1976) mentioned earlier and continued to receive recognition in other cases. It was not until a decade later, in *Meritor Savings Bank v. Vinson* (1986), that hostile environment was acknowledged as a form of sexual harassment. Vinson alleged that her supervisor, Sidney Taylor, had continuously sexually harassed her during the four years she worked for him. She claimed that he made frequent sexual requests to which she complied because of her fear of being fired. She also alleged he fondled her in front of coworkers and raped her. The U.S. Supreme Court ruled that creating a sexually hostile work environment is a form of sex discrimination protected under Title VII. In 1993, the court supported the Supreme Court's recognition of hostile environment as an illegal employment practice in *Harris v. Forklift Systems, Inc.* (1993) and decided that the plaintiff does not need to demonstrate psychological harm in order to prove that sexual harassment occurred.

Legal Issues of *Quid Pro Quo*

In order for judicial decisions to be made in the plaintiff's favor, it must be demonstrated that were it not for the sex of the victim, the behavior would not have occurred. Allegations of *quid pro quo* can be made based on a single incident and do not require continuous actions on behalf of the employer, as is in the case of hostile environment claims. Plaintiffs involved in *quid pro quo* litigation must demonstrate that a job benefit was withheld or changed because of the victim's noncompliance with sexual requests and that he or she was otherwise qualified to receive such benefit. This type of sexual harassment may involve the suspension of benefits until the victim agrees to comply with the requested sexual favors, the denial of benefits even though the victim has acquiesced, or supervisor retaliation against the victim's noncompliance. Retaliation may occur in the form of negative reviews of work performance, defamation of character, termination, transfer, and/or withholding or denying the promised benefit. The employer must prove that these responses are justified by plaintiff behaviors, such as absenteeism, lack of work, violation of employment policies, poor performance, and the like.

In *quid pro quo*, only a superior with the ability to alter the employee's status can commit the sexual harassment. Employers, and not just the perpetrator, have repeatedly been held liable for the actions of their employees. For example, an organization may be found responsible for the sexual harassment committed by one of its managers. Organizations are legally liable for the harassment, especially when the behaviors have occurred in the work setting.

Legal Issues of Hostile Environment

Hostile environment sexual harassment accounts for behaviors that are unwelcome and unwanted and produce an intimidating and unfriendly work environment. It involves either verbal or nonverbal behaviors of a sexual nature that create an environment that interferes with an employee's work performance. The offensive conduct could take the form of multiple sexual requests, sexually suggestive looks, unwanted sexual comments (e.g., jokes, teasing, remarks, innuendos), or the displaying of sexual materials. Hostile environment also includes being in an environment where coworkers are promoted for granting sexual favors, as was the case in *Broderick v. Ruder* (1988).

The assertion that the sexual conduct is sufficient enough to be considered hostile environment depends on the totality of the circumstances (Conte, 1997). Fitzgerald, Swan, and colleagues (1997) suggest that when *Meritor* acknowledged hostile environment as a form of sexual harassment it raised, but did not answer, the following issues: How hostile must an environment be to trigger the statute? What evidence is required to demonstrate it? What determines whether or not a behavior is sexual in nature? Whose standard of severity should be invoked?

Any supervisor, employee, coworker, client, or customer can behave in a sexually offensive way and create the intimidating and hostile environment. Employers are generally liable when they have some knowledge of the conduct or should have had this knowledge (Conte, 1997). In *Meritor*, the Supreme Court denied a definitive rule regarding strict liability. Employers may still be liable even when they are not informed about the sexually harassing behavior and even though a discrimination policy exists in the organization.

HOW FREQUENTLY DOES SEXUAL HARASSMENT OCCUR?

Fitzgerald (1990) pointed to several problematic issues in existing measures that attempt to assess the occurrence and frequency of sexual harassment. First, measurement development has focused little on psychometric characteristics. Validity and reliability data have rarely been documented. Also, the items included in the surveys could be interpreted in different ways and are often ambiguous. Fitzgerald (1990) also claimed that surveys have not included an exhaustive compilation of those behaviors that can be categorized as sexual harassment.

Similarly, Gruber (1990) acknowledged that those measures that inquire about similar forms of sexual harassment are not used across different researchers. Another problematic issue is the underrepresentation of hostile environment types of sexual harassment in harassment studies (Gruber, 1992). Fitzgerald and Shullman (1993) suggest that surveys should assess the complete range of behaviors considered to be sexually harassing, avoid the term "sexual harassment" when inquiring about these experiences, and employ items that ask about specific behaviors. They also propose using additional scales to assess frequency, duration, and offensiveness of specific behaviors.

Gruber (1997) suggests that research assessing victims' perspectives on harassment has facilitated the construction of valid and comprehensive harassment surveys, such as Fitzgerald's Sexual Experiences Questionnaire (Fitzgerald et al., 1988). Perception research has helped refine the discrimination between types of sexual harassment and expanded the range of behaviors that qualify as harassment. The U.S. Merit Systems Protection Board conducted the first national sexual harassment study and found that 42 percent of the women sampled endorsed at least one of six forms of sexual harassment (USMSPB, 1981). A study that used the same survey as that used in the 1981 Merit Systems study reported similar results; 46 percent of women reported that they had experienced harassment (Pryor, LaVite, & Stoller, 1993). The U.S. Merit Systems Protection Board conducted another study in 1995 and reported that 44 percent of women and 19 percent of men experience some form of unwelcome or unwanted sexual attention in their workplace (USMSPB, 1995).

Gruber (1990) reviewed 18 harassment studies conducted before 1987. The list of harassing behaviors reported from most to least endorsed was as follows: sexual comments, sexual posturing, sexual touching, pressure for social/sexual relationships, and sexual assault. Studies using samples of female students and working women have reported that sexual comments are more frequently endorsed and that sexual bribery and sexual assault are infrequent (Fitzgerald et al., 1988; Hagman, 1988; Hogbacka, Kandolin, Haavio-Mannila, & Kauppinen-Toropainen, 1987). These results suggest that more severe forms of sexual harassment occur least frequently. Moreover, studies have reported a rate of 46 percent and 44 percent of subjects experiencing sexual jokes or comments, whereas 2–5 percent of American and European sampled women experienced a sexual assault at work and 3–7 percent experienced sexual bribery (Gruber, 1990; Gruber, Smith, & Kauppinen-Toropainen, 1996; Fitzgerald et al., 1988). O'Hare and O'Donohue (1998) found similar results where gender harassment was the most prevalent form of sexual harassment reported by women in their study, followed respectively by unwanted sexual attention and sexual coercion.

WHO ARE THE TARGETS OF SEXUAL HARASSMENT?

There is limited research regarding predictors of sexual harassment. Studies have shown that young and/or single women are frequently the targets of sexual harassment (Baker, 1989; Gruber & Bjorn, 1982; Gutek, 1985). Age and marital status have been found to be stronger predictors than education status (Fain & Anderton, 1987; Hogbacka et al., 1987; USMSPB, 1981). Correlational studies that examine organizational factors have reported that women in male-dominated work environments and in male-dominated occupations are more likely to be sexually harassed than other women (Baker, 1989; Gutek, 1985; Gutek, Cohen, & Konrad, 1990; Hagman, 1988; Hogbacka et al., 1987; Rubenstein, 1992). It has been hypothesized that these groups of women are victimized more frequently because of the norms and activities practiced in male-dominated environments and occupations, such as sexual aggression, sexual posturing, and deprecation of what is feminine (Gruber, 1997). Studies have also shown that women who work in a sexualized environment are more likely to be harassed (Gutek, 1985; Haavio-Mannila, 1992). In contrast, sexual harassment is less prevalent when employers have explicit policies against sexual harassment and where organizational officials implement and enforce such policies (Pryor, LaVite, & Stoller, 1993).

O'Hare and O'Donohue (1998) proposed a four-factor model to explain sexual harassment. The model assumes that in order for sexual harassment to occur the conditions of the following factors must be met: (1) motivation; (2) overcoming internal inhibitors; (3) overcoming external inhibitors; and (4) overcoming victim resistance. The model attempts to account for individual factors of the harasser and victim, sociocultural factors, and organizational factors. O'Hare and O'Donohue (1998) found that the strongest organizational risk factor for sexual harassment was lack of knowledge about grievance procedures for sexual harassment, an unprofessional atmosphere, and sexist attitudes.

WHAT ARE THE PSYCHOLOGICAL EFFECTS ON VICTIMS OF SEXUAL HARASSMENT?

The psychological effects resulting from sexual harassment may be multiply determined by factors such as stress related to gossip around the harassment, lowered pay, and disrupted work history, and not just by the harassment itself (Gutek & Koss, 1993). Women commonly hesitate to report sexual harassment because of a fear of not being believed, being retaliated against, having their career damaged, or being humiliated (Fitzgerald et al., 1988; Gutek, 1985; Gutek & Koss, 1993; Martindale, 1990). Moreover, women report experiencing such negative consequences as being transferred or fired, receiving lowered evaluations, and being denied promotions when they have reported the sexual harassment (Loy & Stewart, 1984). These experiences and fears of potential consequences may influence the psychological impact on victims of sexual harassment.

Studies have found that victims of sexual harassment frequently experience anxiety, fear of rape (Holgate, 1989; Murphy, 1986), depression (Gutek, 1985), difficulties with interpersonal relationships, irritability, and anger (Gutek, 1985; Loy & Stewart, 1984; Paludi & Barickman, 1991). In 1997, Dansky and Kilpatrick of the Crime Victims Research and Treatment Center at the Medical University of South Carolina conducted a national study of sexual harassment victims. They found that 10 percent of sexual harassment victims—that is, women who reported experiencing behaviors that met the EEOC guidelines—experienced symptoms of Post-Traumatic Stress Disorder (PTSD) at the time of the study. Additionally, this group of women was more likely to meet the symptom criteria for lifetime PTSD behaviors than women who did not report experiencing any sexual harassment, women who reported being exposed to potentially sexually harassing behaviors, and women who reported experiencing potentially sexually harassing behaviors and perceived it as sexual harassment but did not indicate that it had a deleterious effect on their job. Additionally, they found that victims experienced some interference with their job as a result of experiencing sexually harassing behaviors. Other researchers have also demonstrated that victims of sexual harassment experience PTSD symptoms as well as decreased psychological well-being and decreased satisfaction with life (Glomb, Munson, Hulin, Bergamn, & Drasgow, 1999). Fitzgerald, Drasgow, Hulin, Gelfand, and Magley (1997) found that higher levels of sexual harassment (e.g., sexual coercion) were related to higher psychological distress assessed by symptoms of distress (e.g., anxiety and depression), symptoms of PTSD, and a global assessment of well-being.

WHEN DOES SEXUAL HARASSMENT OCCUR?

We have a limited understanding of why certain persons are more likely to engage in sexually harassing behavior. One reason for this limited knowledge is that research on this topic is sparse and fragmented because scholars study this phenomenon in the context of individualized typologies of sexual harassment. For example, Pryor and colleagues investigate men who are likely to sexually exploit, whereas Abbey (1982, 1987) focuses on sexual miscommunication and misperception. In addition, research findings have narrow implications for actual behavior. Studies that have examined sexual misperceptions have generally found that men are more likely to improperly perceive women's behavior as sexual when it is not than the reverse (Abbey, 1982; Saal, Johnson, & Weber, 1989; Shotland & Craig, 1988). However, these findings do not make clear the relationship between males' misperceptions and sexual harassment, nor how we are to identify sexual harassers. Similarly, scales developed to assess sexist attitudes have not been empirically validated and, as of yet, are not appropriate for making predictions about behavior (Pryor & Whalen, 1997).

Pryor and Whalen (1997) hypothesize that sexual harassment occurs within a Person × Situation model where certain person factors constitute a proclivity to sexually harass, but the environment must provide the necessary conditions for it to occur. Sexual exploitation is most likely to occur in social environments that provide opportunity and support for such behavior. As mentioned before, reports of sexual harassment occur less often in environments that take action against harassers than in sexist work settings.

Pryor (1987) developed the Likelihood to Sexually Harass (LSH) scale to examine how a man's proclivity to sexually exploit may underlie certain forms of sexual harassment. The scale inquires about a respondent's likelihood of engaging in *quid pro quo* type behaviors in 10 scenarios where they could exploit women with minimal punishment. Men who score high on the LSH also score high on measures that have been associated with a tendency towards sexual violence, such as the Rape Myth Acceptance Scale (Burt, 1980) and the Attraction to Sexual Aggression Scale (Malamuth, 1989). These men also score highly on instruments that measure stereotypic masculinity (Brannon & Juni, 1984) and sexual dominance (Pryor & Stoller, 1994).

Other studies have shown a relationship between harassing attitudes and actual sexually harassing behaviors. Pryor and colleagues (1993) found that men with high LSH scores were more likely to sexually harass a confederate female trainee after being exposed to a harassing role model. In another study, men with high LSH scores were also more likely to engage in harassing physical and verbal behaviors after witnessing their male peers harass a female confederate (Pryor, Giedd, & Williams, 1995).

THE SEXUAL HARASSMENT INVESTIGATION

It is essential that organizations conduct thorough and competent sexual harassment investigations given the negative consequences that may occur if a problematic investigation transpires. The consequences of sexual harassment include psychological effects for the accuser and the accused, legal problems for all involved including the organization itself, and systematic problems such as deterioration of work morale, increased absenteeism, and high employee turnover—all of these negative consequences can be exacerbated by a poorly conducted investigation. A competent investigation can decrease the likelihood and severity of the aforementioned problems. Furthermore, a competent investigation can avoid legal problems such as liability claims of failure to take corrective action, character defamation, and wrongful discharge. This is an important consideration since employers are required by law to be responsible for taking steps to remedy the situation when a harassment complaint has been made (Bloch, 1995). Additionally, the sexual harassment investigation and appropriate organizational response may prevent other sexual harassment occurrences.

Another consideration is how behaviors relevant to harassment allegations psychologically impact alleged victims and perpetrators. For example, unethical behaviors on behalf of the investigator, the employer's response to the allegations, organizational actions taken to remedy the situation, and coworkers' responses to having a harassment investigation conducted (e.g., gossip, isolation of a specific coworker) can all negatively affect the individuals involved in sexual harassment claims. A competent investigation can help to decrease the severity of all of these problems. Furthermore, a competent investigation may further prevent the "revictimization" of an individual by alleviating psychological costs associated with the sexual harassment. A poorly conducted investigation may feasibly increase the harm to everyone involved in sexual harassment charges.

One problem with the forensic issues surrounding sexual harassment investigations is that much of the effort associated with understanding and preventing sexual harassment has focused on the harassment policy versus the harassment investigation. Often the actual investigation is conducted as an afterthought with little planning of the investigation, scant training of the investigators, and based on questionable practices.

The investigation is a vital adjunct to a company's sexual harassment policy. Policies should explicitly proscribe sexual harassment and train employees to recognize and report it. There should be a seamless transition between sexual harassment policy and sexual harassment investigation in which the policy will help to both prevent harassment and facilitate the enactment of a competent investigation. The investigation should promptly follow any sexual harassment complaint and result in a well-conceived finding that leads to mediation. An organization must determine which staff members will be responsible for conducting the investigation. Appropriate training or background for investigators may include experience in investigating accidents in the workplace, training in human behavior, knowledge of causes and effects of socially deviant behavior, and training in crisis intervention (Head & Head, 1992). Others have also suggested that in addition to being able carry out a systematized investigation, investigators should also be trained in how to make sound decisions by knowing how to weigh evidence, how to judge the credibility of witnesses, and how to minimize perceptual distortions (Legnick-Hall, 1992).

Sexual harassment investigations raise a number of complex problems such as: (1) where is the burden of proof (innocent till proven guilty, beyond a reasonable doubt, preponderance of evidence, guilty until proven innocent), (2) necessary training and expertise of the investigator, (3) collection and handling of evidence, (4) disposition of interested parties while the investigation is occurring, (5) permissibility of legal representation, (6) valid ways of interpreting and synthesizing evidence, (7) arriving at reasonable outcomes.

There is no research that describes the current state of sexual harassment investigations. It is unclear how sexual harassment investigations are conducted or how they ought to be optimally conducted. There seems to be a wide range of practices such as hiring outside legal firms, having in-house trained or untrained human resources staff conduct the investigation or, in small firms, having a high-ranking individual such as the chief executive officer conduct the investigation. Currently, there is a complete lack of research on these investigative practices and their accuracy. However, some of these investigations might be quite good, whereas other investigations are likely to be "off the cuff" and amateurish. Since so much rides on these investigations, more work needs to be conducted to bring this topic into the research and quality improvement domain.

Although some have made recommendations for conducting an appropriate investigation, the suggestions are often vague, limited, and at times discrepant. Jayne (1994) makes the following recommendations for investigators: (1) identify the alleged harasser, (2) ascertain all facts in connection with the alleged incident, (3) ask how the complaining party responded and determine if efforts at informal resolution were made, (4) inform the charged party of all allegations made, (5) determine the frequency and type of the alleged harassment, (6) develop an understanding of the degree of control, amount of interaction, and relationship between the parties, (7) interview witnesses, and (8) remind all of the need for confidentiality. However, recommendations for systematically accomplishing these steps are lacking.

In addition, the literature describing the use of potential techniques (e.g., non-threatening questions, implementing behavior-provoking questions to elicit affirmative responses, and establishing dominance and control early on during the interview) is sparse and often lacking empirical support. Bowers and O'Donohue (1999) have developed a comprehensive and systematic protocol that addresses some of these limitations; the protocol is called the Sexual Harassment Investigation Protocol, or SHIP. This protocol is part of a scientific research program that aims to increase the forensic understanding of how best to conduct a sexual harassment investigation and how best to train individuals to be competent sexual harassment investigators. The model is predicated on a harm-reduction model that involves preventing further harm and reducing the harm that has already occurred. The protocol also addresses legal definitions of sexual harassment, common issues and problems during the investigative process, and how to incorporate mediation.

The SHIP serves as a preliminary step in the standardization of a content-valid sexual harassment investigation. Both standardization and content validity are important to the beginning process of empirical research. Standardization allows for replicability and consistency across conditions, whereas content validity buttresses the eventual determination of construct validity. With continued attention paid to standardization and to the inclusion of appropriate content in sexual harassment investigations, the path to a clearer determination of what are and what are not optimal sexual harassment investigation procedures will be illuminated with the help of empirical research that focuses on tangible measures of investigative outcomes.

The procedures outlined in the Bowers and O'Donohue SHIP offer many suggestions about how to reduce variability across investigations and improve the handling of sexual harassment investigations. Currently these recommendations are based on practical considerations and hypothesized best practices surrounding a sound sexual harassment investigation.

Background considerations of conducting a sound sexual harassment investigation include: (1) properly understanding the concept of sexual harassment, (2) explicitly choosing a balance of potential investigative errors, and (3) orienting toward a mediational stance throughout the investigation.

1. Understanding the Concept of Sexual Harassment

Investigators should have a thorough understanding of the concept of sexual harassment. This understanding is crucial to the investigative process because it allows investigators to orient toward relevant aspects of the case. Consequently, this understanding also allows for a more parsimonious investigation because extraneous factors associated with the investigation are quickly bypassed.

Although there is no absolute agreement on defining sexual harassment, there is a general consensus based on laws, legal precedents, psychological research, and general opinion that is quite consistent.

Basically, sexual harassment is viewed as falling under two legal categories—*quid pro quo* and hostile environment harassment. *Quid pro quo* is Latin for "this for that." It refers to the explicit or implicit communication that the employee must endure various types of workplace sexualization in order to stay employed or get certain job perks. Whether or not the employee participates or endures the sexual acts is irrelevant to *quid pro quo* harassment. What is relevant is whether there was sexual propositioning or sexualized behaviors that were *related* to some sort of employment status.

A hostile environment sexual harassment claim is established when an employee's workplace is sexualized in such a way or for the "purpose or effect of unreasonably interfering with a person's work performance or creating an intimidating, hostile, or offensive working environment" (EEOC, 1980). Usually for hostile environment claims a pattern of offensive behavior must be established (unless the offensive behavior was severe, such as unwanted touching of the accuser or the accused exposing his/her genitals).

The legal concept of *welcomeness* is important to both *quid pro quo* and hostile environment claims. Such that if the accuser welcomed the sexualized environment or behaviors, then sexual harassment did not take place. However, welcomeness or unwelcomeness can be difficult to establish. In fact, in *Meritor Savings Bank v. Vinson* (1986), Taylor, the alleged harasser, claimed that participation in all sexual behaviors was voluntary (i.e., implicitly claiming welcomeness) and therefore not harassing. However, Taylor lost the case, which is not surprising given the fact that the Supreme Court described what Vinson endured as having to "run a gauntlet of sexual abuse" (as reported in Fitzgerald, Swan, & Magley; 1996). Clearly, one difficulty with establishing welcomeness is the strong possibility that the behaviors were in fact not welcome.

The EEOC's 1990 *Policy Guidance on Sexual Harassment* somewhat clarifies this murky area by specifying some considerations to determining welcomeness: (1) Was a timely complaint made? (2) What behaviors did the accuser engage in? (3) Was it a consensual relationship? Answers to these questions may help an investigator weigh the welcomeness evidence.

Behavioral Representations of Sexual Harassment

Although legal representations and EEOC guidelines are helpful in delineating the realm of sexual harassment, behavioral representation and classification of sexually harassing behaviors are crucial to the determination of sexual harassment.

The Concept of the Reasonable Woman Standard

This concept refers to court precedent and psychological research that partially determines the realm of sexual harassment by determining what is and is not harassment based on what a normal, "reasonable" woman would find to be innocuous or offensive. The reasonable woman standard concentrates on individuals; our current understanding of sexual harassment, however, must also take into account societal norms of harassment.

Gruber's 1992 Typology of Sexual Harassment is designed to describe sexual harassment based on behavioral typology. Gruber divides types of sexual harassment into three behaviorally referenced subcategories: (1) Verbal requests, (2) verbal comments, and (3) nonverbal displays. Within each of these subcategories the severity of the sexual harassment is ranked from more to less severe. Remember that the subcategories themselves are not ranked in severity; only the behaviors *within* the respective subcategories are ranked.

    A. Verbal Requests (more to less severe)
        1. *Sexual bribery*—with threat and/or promise of reward (*quid pro quo*)
        2. *Sexual advances*—no threat, seeking sexual intimacy
        3. *Relational advances*—no threat, repeatedly seeking social relationship
        4. *Subtle pressures/advances*—no threat, goal or target is implicit or ambiguous
    B. Verbal Comments (more to less severe)
        1. *Personal remarks*—unsolicited and directed *to* a woman (or man)
        2. *Subjective objectification*—rumors and/or comments made *about* a woman (or man)
        3. *Sexual categorical remarks*—about women (or men) "in general"
    C. Nonverbal Displays (more to less severe)
        1. *Sexual assault*—aggressive contact involving coercion
        2. *Sexual touching*—brief *sexual* or contextually *sexualized* touching
        3. *Sexual posturing*—violations of personal space or attempts at personal contact
        4. *Sexual materials*—pornographic materials, sexually demeaning objects, profanation of women's (or men's) sexuality (Fitzgerald, Swan, and Magley, 1996)

Also, the supposed or real intention of a harasser is irrelevant to the legal determination of sexual harassment. This said, depending on the circumstances, investigators and company officials may want to take into account intention when disciplining employees found guilty of sexual harassment. In less severe cases, education may be a necessary main component of the punishment.

Conducting a competent investigation involves a process of referencing investigator/mediator actions to corresponding investigative goals. In other words, the investigator is constantly looking to see the correspondence of their actions with the following goals of: (1) preventing further harm, and (2) reducing harm that has already occurred. Personal ethics will be involved in the application of mediation towards these goals. It is important for the investigator to consider the following: Why do I view this situation this way? What is motivating my behavior? Are there other acceptable solutions that are more palatable to others? Can

I verbally justify why I see things this way? Can I convince others to see things my way on this issue? Consider these criteria—how to be fair and complete, how to reduce harm, and how to use mediation—when trying to adapt or expand guidelines to deal with unique situations.

Remember that many parties are intensely interested in every detail of how this investigation is conducted. Consider that the investigator will need to be held accountable, perhaps in a court of law. Therefore, the investigator should have good justifications for each of the moves he or she makes as an investigator. One way to do this is to thoroughly outline all reasonable possibilities at each choice point. Outline all positives and negatives of each possibility and make a decision about which has the best set of positives and the least worst set of negatives.

2. Explicitly Choosing a Balance of Potential Investigative Errors

Choosing an a priori estimate of error rates is a crucial background consideration in a sexual harassment investigation. Unfortunately, many individuals who conduct sexual harassment investigations are not aware of the problems of neglecting this step. The concept of error rates is related to test theory. Test theory states that every test that is not 100 percent accurate has some rate of error associated with it. Furthermore, error is partitioned into two types: Type I (false positives) and Type II (false negatives). All error, or mistakes that the test makes, are necessarily either false positives or false negatives.

In sexual harassment cases, a false positive or a false negative can be devastating. A false positive means that someone is wrongly accused of harassment—the investigator finds that the individual harassed someone when in fact he or she did not. Being wrongly accused of a crime (or of hurting someone else in general) can have serious negative psychological effects on an individual, along with the negative practical effects of potential loss of wages or being fired from a job.

A false negative, in a sexual harassment case, means that the accused individual actually did harass someone but that the investigator found the allegation to be false or "unfounded." This is a horrible situation: A harasser has navigated the system in such a way as to not be found guilty of the harassment that he or she carried out. The harasser could continue to harass others and may even increase the severity and/or frequency of harassment because he or she "got away with it" or "beat the system." Furthermore, the person who made the claim is now not only still susceptible to harassment but is seen as a liar or someone who cannot be trusted. This predicament can have a hugely negative psychological impact on the individual, and the individual may suffer more immediate consequences as well, such as demotion or loss of a job.

The problems that false positives and false negatives create in sexual harassment investigations are not discrete occurrences. These errors can create long-standing intractable problems for individuals. Furthermore, problems that are caused by these errors may radiate out in numerous directions. People's families will often bare the brunt of the stresses that these errors create. The workplace atmosphere can deteriorate rapidly and extensively. It becomes very difficult to accurately estimate the harm that these errors create and even more difficult to repair the damage that continues to spiral outward.

One more point to consider in determining an a priori estimate of error rates is that the error rates associated with sexual harassment investigations are simply not known. No research is available presently that indicates the percentage of Type I or Type II errors associated with conducting sexual harassment investigations. The only thing that is certain is that both of these types of errors do exist and they exist at some unknown rate. Furthermore, the investigator's explicit or implicit belief in the need to guard against Type I or Type II errors will largely determine the rate of these errors. For example, an investigator who thinks that virtually all claims of sexual harassment are founded will probably commit more Type I errors. However, an investigator who is highly skeptical of all claimants' accusations will probably commit more Type II errors.

Choosing a priori estimate of error rates for the investigation should include considerations of false positives and false negatives. It is our opinion that both types of errors are equally tragic; therefore, error rates should be estimated to be the same for false positives and false negatives. The practical implication of this belief is that investigators should always equally guard against both types of errors: falsely accusing the alleged harasser *and* falsely coming to an erroneous conclusion of no harassment when the harassment did in fact take place. The specifics of this conclusion are related to the decision of how to weigh the burden of proof in a sexual harassment investigation that is intricately connected to the investigator's desire to minimize Type I and Type II errors.

Burden of Proof and Sexual Harassment Investigations

Typical criminal investigations place the burden of proof on the claimant or the state prosecutors. Our country's justice works on the premise that someone is innocent until proven guilty. In most situations this premise works well to guard against abuses of the criminal justice system and to prevent innocent people from being erroneously punished for crimes that they did not commit. Our country has tacitly adopted the view that it is "better to let a guilty person go free than to punish someone who is innocent." As a societal edict this seems to make sense. We can all think about the horror of being incarcerated or even put to death for a crime that we did not commit—this scenario is truly frightening. And most of us accept the fact that to guard against this outcome some genuinely guilty people will not be convicted of crimes. The justice system works to minimize both Type I and Type II errors but protects against Type I errors more thoroughly. Again, Type I errors represent an outcome in which someone is judged to commit a crime that he or she did not do (a false positive). Type II errors refer to situations in which someone is not convicted of a crime that he or she did do (a false negative). By proving "beyond a reasonable doubt" that someone committed a crime, the courts support this bias towards minimizing Type I errors.

Although the bias towards minimizing Type I errors is crucial, sexual harassment investigations must grapple with how this decision rule materializes, given the peculiar circumstances of a sexual harassment investigation. In most cases in the criminal justice system, there is hard physical evidence that a crime took place and the claimant stands to lose only from whatever the accused supposedly did. For example, if someone is physically attacked, that person usually displays physical evidence of the attack, and being attacked physically is considered to be highly unpleasant by the vast majority of people. The accusation is both difficult to falsify (e.g., there is physical evidence) and there is usually no motive for doing so.

Now, in considering a typical sexual harassment investigation compared with a typical criminal investigation, our predicament can be seen more thoroughly. In many cases there is no physical evidence in a sexual harassment charge, and the claimant may have many significant reasons to fabricate the account of the sexual harassment. For example, the claimant's account is about remarks that were said to her or him by the accused when no witnesses were present. And if the accused is fired, the claimant will move into the accused's work position and receive a substantial pay raise. Because of these problems in sexual harassment investigations, a new understanding of burden of proof must be developed.

Burden of proof must deal with both the claimant and the accused. And because the claimant and the accused stand in direct opposition to each other, neither receives precedence of being considered innocent until proven guilty. A sexual harassment investigation must view its responsibility as two separate subinvestigations: (1) Did the alleged harasser sexually harass? and (2) Is the claimant giving an accurate account of the alleged harassment? Both the accused and the claimant should be thought of as innocent until the final conclusion of the investigation.

Although a sexual harassment investigation concerns two separate sub-investigations of the alleged harassment and the claimant's veracity, the investigator should handle the dissemination of this information with the utmost care. The claimant very well might not cooperate with the investigation if he or she feels on trial like the accused. This is an understandable reaction given the previous discussion of criminal investigations (i.e., investigations that focus solely on the accused). Furthermore, one can easily imagine the experience of divulging sensitive and possibly embarrassing information to investigators who are near strangers, only to be treated as a liar and another person to interrogate. Although the investigator will be investigating both the claimant and the accused, it is crucial to convey the message that the investigator is focusing his or her efforts on the accused. Investigators should also minimize distress to the claimant by stating early on that some inquiry will focus on the claimant in the investigation. The claimant should also be told that this is routine procedure and in no way suggests that his or her side of the story is false (if applicable, the revelation of a spurious charge should only be handed down at the conclusion of the investigation).

Another important consideration in estimating Type I and Type II errors is consideration of the investigative behaviors and participant psychology that would lend themselves to increasing the likelihood of a Type I or Type II error. Type II errors generally fall on the side of the investigators, whereas Type I errors generally relate to the psychology of the participants. For example, a Type II error or false negative, in which harassment did in fact take place but was missed by the investigation, often is caused by investigator mistakes. One example may be insufficient questioning of relevant witnesses that may lead to an erroneous conclusion that the harassment did not take place. These investigative mistakes are addressed and remedied in the Bowers and O'Donohue (1999) Sexual Harassment Investigation Protocol.

The causes of Type I mistakes, or false positives, are more perplexing. Investigator mistakes remain an avenue to Type I errors as well as Type II errors. For example, an investigator could synthesize collected evidence incorrectly leading to an erroneous conclusion of sexual harassment—a Type I error. However, another avenue to Type I errors relates to the psychology of participants in the investigation. There are various psychological reasons that participants may make false allegations of harassment. O'Donohue (2003) has described eleven pathways to false allegations. A brief overview of some of these pathways follows.

1. *Lying*. All participants are capable of lying to avoid some bad consequence or gain some good consequence. Lying is particularly problematic in sexual harassment investigations since there is often no hard physical evidence to fall back on.

2. *False interpretation*. In this pathway an act that was not actually sexually harassing is misconstrued to be something that is sexually harassing. This pathway is complex because interpretation is part of what determines sexual harassment but does not represent the entirety of what determines sexual harassment.

3. *False memory*. The creation of false memories has been demonstrated in laboratory settings (Loftus, 2000), and although false memory research has focused on memories of childhood sexual abuse, the paradigm can fit false memories of sexual harassment. However, this phenomenon is usually associated with certain types of questionable psychotherapist behaviors. The investigator should question whether allegations were uncovered in therapy or leading or biased interviewing.

4. *Biased interviewing*. There is a large body of research showing that children, and to a lesser extent adults, can be influenced to make false accusations of abuse when problematic interviewing techniques such as leading questions, disconfirmation, differential reinforcement, and conformity press are used (O'Donohue, Fanetti, & Elliott, 1998; Schacter, 1995). Although this research has not been directly applied to sexual harassment, the robustness of the effect warrants the use of caution in any interviewing situation.

5. *Gender politics*. Extreme gender political beliefs (e.g., all men are sexual predators; males exploit women; males "sexualize" all women) can lead to the view

that a particular instance is an example of sexual harassment when it is not. An example of this could be a male who comments on liking a particular commercial where the commercial is seen as involving women as sex objects by the listener, who then claims hostile environment sexual harassment. One's political viewpoint could flavor acts to be interpreted as sexual harassment when they are actually innocuous.

6. *Acute psychopathology and personality disorders.* A number of acute psychiatric conditions can precipitate an increased likelihood of making false allegations. In particular, delirium and substance intoxication can result in making false allegations because of the cognitive and perceptual distortions that are associated with these conditions.

A number of psychiatric personality disorders can also predispose individuals to making false allegations. In particular, antisocial personality disorder, borderline personality disorder, and histrionic personality disorder all contain elements that could increase the likelihood of making false allegations. According to the *Diagnostic and Statistical Manual of Mental Disorders* (*DSM-IV*; APA, 1994), "deceit and manipulation are central features of Antisocial Personality Disorder . . . deceitfulness or theft, or serious violations or rules" (pp. 645–646). People with this disorder "are frequently deceitful and manipulative in order to gain personal profit or pleasure (e.g., to obtain money, sex, or power). . . . They repeatedly lie . . . [and] con others" (p. 646).

Borderline personality disorder is characterized by the *DSM-IV* as having a "pervasive pattern of instability of interpersonal relationships, self-images and affects, and marked impulsivity" (p. 650). Moreover, individuals with borderline personality disorder "may idealize potential caregivers or lovers at the first or second meeting, demand to spend a lot of time together, and share the most intimate details early in a relationship. However, they may switch quickly from idealizing other people to devaluing them" (pp. 650–651). And they often "express inappropriate, intense anger or have difficulty controlling their anger" (p. 651).

Histrionic personality disorder is characterized by "emotionality and attention-seeking behavior" according to the *DSM-IV* (APA, 1994, p. 665). Individuals with this disorder often attempt to be the center of attention and may create some sort of drama to ensure that this occurs. Further,

> the appearance and behavior of individuals with this disorder are often inappropriately sexually provocative or seductive. . . . beyond what is appropriate for the social context . . . [and] consistently use physical appearance to draw attention to themselves. Individuals with Histrionic Personality Disorder have a high degree of suggestibility. Their opinions and feelings are easily influenced by others and by current fads. . . . They may "fish for compliments" regarding appearance . . . Individuals with this disorder often consider relationships more intimate than they actually are . . . Flights to romantic fantasy are common. (APA, 1994, p. 655)

As these descriptions of personality disorders indicate, psychopathology may have either a direct or indirect effect on either the perception of sexual harassment or the fabrication of false allegations of sexual harassment. Investigators should understand that various psychiatric conditions and the behaviors that these individuals display may increase the likelihood of false allegations of sexual harassment. This is not to say that individuals with this acute psychopathology or more chronic psychopathology, such as the personality disorders described, are necessarily fabricating accounts of sexual harassment; rather, psychopathology should be part of the equation in determining the legitimacy of sexual harassment allegations.

It is our recommendation that until there is empirical evidence to support our understanding of the true state of affairs concerning Type I and Type II errors, investigators should levy an equal burden of proof on both the claimant and the accused.

3. Orienting toward a Mediational Stance throughout the Investigation

Many investigations will not afford the level of evidence that is necessary to make an objective decision of culpability (i.e., often only the accuser and the accused have direct knowledge of the alleged events). The investigative procedure must be flexible. For cases where facts do not lead to a decision, the use of an iterative and mediational process will be crucial. Leave the door open for mediation. Investigators should not become frustrated because their investigative efforts fail to produce a definitive picture of what happened. The investigation will always imperfectly reflect the reality of what occurred. Investigators should expect to have to formulate a resolution based on incomplete, imperfect, and conflicting information. The job of the investigator is to collect as much information as reasonably possible and to analyze that information with an open and fair mind. The inability to perfectly mirror reality is yet another reason to always approach a sexual harassment investigation methodically, carefully, and fairly. Usually, such an investigation will entail plenty of hard work. The best strategy is to be fair to everyone, and approach the investigation always in both roles—as an investigator and as a mediatior.

Once the investigator orients toward the background issues of (1) understanding the concept of sexual harassment, (2) explicitly choosing an a priori estimate of error rates, and (3) maintaining a mediational stance throughout the investigation, the investigator can concentrate on the specifics associated with conducting a sound sexual harassment investigation. The following is a list of the most important aspects of conducting a sound sexual harassment investigation. Although this list is not exhaustive, it is designed to address a number of the issues that will be encountered during a sexual harassment investigation. Furthermore, the background considerations included with the list also are designed to solve some of the most serious and seemingly common mistakes that are made during sexual harassment investigations.

The Investigation Procedure

First, one should interview individuals in an order that will provide the most information in an efficient manner. Interviews should begin with the accuser, then any witnesses who have any knowledge about the alleged incidents, and finally the accused. Gather relevant information that will quickly lead to a valid conclusion. This may include assessing whether an individual is harassed because of his or her sexual history and ruling out the erroneous belief that an individual's sexual history makes the harassing behaviors acceptable. Moreover, an investigation should only inquire about sexual history that is relevant to that person's work life. See Bowers and O'Donohue (1999) for a complete explication of specific behaviors that may facilitate or impede the attainment of valid and useful evidence such as building rapport, the right interview style, and avoiding the use of leading questions and differential reinforcement.

If a satisfactory conclusion cannot be made based on the information gathered, mediation should be employed. The two primary goals of mediation are to prevent further harm and to reduce already incurred harm so that suffering is alleviated for all involved parties. As such, although mediation will be mainly used when culpability is unclear, it should be employed for any conclusion. A mediational framework can help determine remedial responses that are the most satisfactory for all sides and can attempt to mitigate foreseeable problems. It is important to remember that a mediator represents different views and perspectives and works to find an outcome that will benefit the accused as well as the accuser.

The investigation should take into account unfounded sexual harassment claims in the accuser's history and in the past of the accused. When there exists unfounded claims in the accuser's past, the investigator will have to determine whether these prior investigations were competently conducted such that a correct conclusion was reached, whether there was insufficient evidence to conclude that the sexual harassment actually occurred, or whether the accuser is an individual who is more likely than others to be harassed. Unfounded sexual harassment claims against the accused may indicate that a poor investigation was conducted or that the accused has a pattern of harassing coworkers but has not been caught. The investigator must also evaluate the believability of both parties and consider what the accuser could gain from making a false accusation.

When deciding whether sexual harassment actually occurred, the investigator should avoid reasoning from symptoms displayed by the accused or accuser. Symptoms are not valid evidence given that not all victims of sexual harassment show symptoms. Additionally, there is not a standard set of symptoms from which one could make conclusions about the occurrence of sexual harassment. The symptoms could be feigned by any of the parties involved, including witnesses, and do not necessarily indicate an individual's psychological state. Last, symptoms may be caused by some problem other than the sexual harassment.

In addition to the goals of collecting information and concluding whether or not sexual harassment occurred, the investigator has other responsibilities, such as managing ancillary risk, preventing and managing retaliation, and alleviating victimization. The investigator should inquire about the possible ancillary risks that would deter the investigation and ask questions that reduce risk to the company and all parties (e.g., questions about whether the company has mistreated the accuser or the accused, whether either party has been discriminated against). The investigator should inform all witnesses about what retaliation is and the disciplinary actions that will be taken in response to such behavior. A retaliation audit, which involves asking employees whether retaliation is occurring during an investigation, may also be necessary. Retaliation seems to be one of the most prevalent (yet potentially easily rectifiable) occurrences in sexual harassment cases. One common stumbling block with retaliation is its ability to look innocuous. For example, if a manager fires a subordinate for a number of work infractions after a charge of sexual harassment is made, the timing of the fire may be enough evidence to substantiate a case of retaliation. Were the work infractions current? Or did they occur years ago? Or were the work infractions a direct result of the consequences of sexual harassment, such as absenteeism because of medical or psychological problems? Because of the potential for victims of sexual harassment to experience the negative psychological consequences previously reviewed, the investigator may utilize particular strategies to ensure that the investigation itself does not add to or create this victimization. The investigator should not belittle an individual for his or her response to harassment nor attempt to change an individual's response by debate or argument. The investigator should be able to listen attentively and empathetically.

In concluding the investigation, investigators must determine culpability. Bowers and O'Donohue (1999) state that "a sexual harassment investigation must view its responsibility as two separate sub-investigations: (1) did the alleged harasser sexually harass, and (2) is the accuser giving an accurate account of the alleged harassment" (pp. 103) in which both the accused and accuser are considered innocent until the final conclusion is made. The investigator should attempt to synthesize information into a coherent whole by remaining open to ideas about what evidence means and how it is relevant; not punishing individuals for their contributions; and also taking a critical stance that allows the investigator to look for discrepancies, inconsistencies, and logical fallacies. The investigator should communicate the findings to the respective parties and respond appropriately to individual reactions to the investigative findings. The final segment of the investigation will always focus on mediation. The investigator/mediator should determine overlapping areas of acceptable solutions for the interested parties. Furthermore, mediation can be seen in the harm-reducing framework as a process that can create long-lasting solutions that benefit (or at least do not unjustly punish) the accuser, the accused, and the organization as a whole regardless of the confidence levels associated with the investigative findings.

Sexual Harassment Treatment

It is important to deliver appropriate psychological treatment to both the victim and the perpetrator when sexual harassment occurs.

Victim Treatment

It is evident that victims of sexual harassment experience psychological and somatic symptoms similar to victims of other forms of trauma such as natural disasters and sexual assault. Like other forms of trauma, sexual harassment affects victims during the time it occurs and has lasting effects because trauma-associated stimuli elicit responses exhibited during the trauma itself (Follette, Ruzek, & Abueg, 1998). Whereas victims have greater medical and psychological health claims after enduring sexual harassment (O'Hare & O'Donohue, 1998), there are no current treatment protocols developed specifically for dealing with psychological and organizational effects of sexual harassment. Those treatment protocols may be valuable in identifying and addressing specific needs relevant to sexual harassment victims.

Conversely, there exist a number of empirically supported manualized treatments for some of the more common individual psychological problems that may result from a trauma. Barlow, Esler, and Vitali (1998) have evaluated the effectiveness of treatments for panic and anxiety disorder. Beck and colleagues (Beck, 1976; Beck, Rush, Shaw, & Emery, 1979) have developed a cognitive-behavioral treatment manual for depression. There are also treatment guidelines and protocols for managing sexual difficulties (Leiblum & Rosen, 2000; Wincze & Carey, 1991).

Treatments specifically tailored to problems of trauma victims have also been implemented. Treatment manuals for trauma-relevant relapse prevention training (TRRPT; Abueg & Fairbank, 1992; Abueg & Kriegler, 1990; Abueg et al., 1994) address substance abuse in trauma victims. Additionally, Najavits and colleagues (Najavtis, Weiss, & Liese, 1996; Najavits, Weiss, Shaw, & Muenz, 1998) have shown that their treatment decreased substance abuse in trauma victims exhibiting Post-Traumatic Stress Disorder (PTSD). A PTSD diagnosis is only appropriate for individuals exposed to some form of traumatic event. There is some controversy about the appropriateness of this diagnosis and consequently about the treatment for this disorder in sexual harassment victims (Avina & O'Donohue, 2002). One should note that some forms of sexual harassment are sexual assaults, which are already recognized as constituting legitimate trauma. It has been argued that other lesser forms of sexual harassment can also constitute diagnosable trauma (Avina & O'Donohue, 2002; Hamilton, Alagna, King, & Lloyd, 1987). Moreover, treatments effective for other trauma victims are also appropriate for sexual harassment victims who meet qualifying diagnostic criteria, such as cognitive processing therapy and cognitive behavioral therapy for rape victims (Foa & Olasov Rothbaum, 1998; Resick & Schnicke, 1993).

The dearth of treatment packages tailored specifically for sexual harassment victims has two advantages: (1) turning clinicians' attention to the function of specific symptoms, which are numerous and complexly related to each other (Follette, Ruzek, & Abueg, 1998); and (2) the consequent development and dissemination of very specific and potentially effective therapies. A more appropriate conceptualization for any trauma victim, including sexual harassment, would be one in which etiology is not assumed from symptoms, a trauma victim is not considered as part of a homeogenous group, and specific individual and environmental variables are identified (Naugle & Follette, 1998). This kind of assessment leads to information that has direct treatment implications, since the identification of controlling variables facilitates the development of a treatment plan that is specific and precise for each individual client and his or her psychological problems. (Please see Naugle and Follette, 1998, for a review of important clinical issues relevant to functional assessment and treatment.)

Perpetrator Treatment

Sexual harassment allegations are generally managed within the organization itself or adjudicated in civil courts (Conte, 1997). The resulting effects for the harasser frequently include financial losses caused by termination of employment, demotion, mandated leave of absence, and difficulties obtaining appropriate employment that match levels of experience and education. It is unlikely that civil courts require harassers to receive treatment in the form of psychotherapy. Consequently, the harasser is able to engage in the same criminal behavior in new work settings unless the individual receives an appropriate and effective treatment for the problem. However, there is no currently validated treatment for sexual harassers (O'Donohue, 1997) despite sexual harassment's documented history and public recognition. As mentioned, this problem has generally been dealt with in financial, not psychological, terms.

The efficient delivery of effective treatment for harassers can be an important prevention strategy because it thwarts further victimization of other individuals. Brunswig and O'Donohue (2000) have developed a treatment protocol based on relapse prevention for offenders of other forms of sexual misconduct, such as sexual assault and exhibitionism (Laws, 1989; Laws & O'Donohue, 1997). Brunswig and O'Donohue (2000) state that their treatment is grounded in relapse prevention because sexual harassment is similar to other forms of sexual offending in the following ways: (1) It involves a problem of self-control, (2) it occurs in specific situations with specific individuals; (3) harassers exhibit cognitive distortions and have difficulties delaying immediate gratification; (4) harassment involves some elements of fantasy; (5) lapses can be defined in terms of fantasies, willful elaborations, formulated plans for the proscribed behavior, and relapses in terms of overt engagement in that behavior. Additionally, relapse prevention has been shown to be effective in treating other forms of sexual offending (Laws & O'Donohue, 1997).

Specifically, relapse prevention is a cognitive-behavioral treatment that targets cognitive and overt undesired behavior that is defined as lapses or relapses. The Brunswig and O'Donohue (2000) protocol has modified traditional relapse prevention treatments to be more appropriate for sexual harassers who likely consist of an outpatient population. This is an important distinction to recognize since sexual harassers, unlike sexual abusers, are not imprisoned and thus live in an unstructured environment; they are not constrained by notification laws whereby surrounding community members and coworkers are informed about their history and potential to engage in future harassment; and they are usually not obligated to receive treatment, which may be indicative of an individual's willingness and motivation to solve this problem.

There are circumstances in which it is possible that a sexual harasser will seek treatment even though not willing or motivated to do so. As a result of substantiated sexual harassment allegations, treatment may be a condition of employment. Also likely in a few cases, a civil court may "strongly recommend" treatment for the harasser. However, research has shown that relapse prevention is not usually effective for clients who are unmotivated (Laws, 1989) and/or who deny their offenses (Maletzky, 1997). Clients who meet one or both of these conditions should remain in pretreatment until these conditions are altered. Brunswig and O'Donohue (2000) refer the treatment provider to other therapies that delineate how to target these particular conditions that interfere with successful treatment.

The Brunswig and O'Donohue (2000) treatment protocol for sexual harassers provides a rationale for the appropriateness of relapse prevention for this specific problem; lists specific assessment instruments to be used in conjunction with the treatment and the information generated by each instrument; and outlines each session, including how much time to spend on each topic and specific homework assignments. The specific treatment targets of the Brunswig and O'Donohue (2000) treatment protocol are (1) establishing adequate motivation to engage in treatment; (2) overcoming denial and minimization; (3) decreasing sexual harassment myth acceptance and hostile attitudes toward women; (4) increasing victim empathy; (5) identifying high-risk situations, including emotional, physiological, and environmental conditions and skills for effectively navigating high-risk situations; (6) enhancing the harasser's repertoire of social skills and coping skills; (7) addressing outcome expectancies and the problem of immediate gratification (PIG, Marlatt, 1989); and (8) increasing the identification of seemingly irrelevant decisions. (Please see the Brunswig and O'Donohue [2000] protocol for a more detailed description of the treatment.)

FUTURE DIRECTIONS

Evidently, the problem of sexual harassment is one that affects a significant proportion of individuals across a great number of organizational domains. Although women are largely the victims and men the perpetrators, psychological, structural, and financial costs do not discriminate among genders. Once sexual harassment has occurred, it is costly for an organization to conduct an investigation; terminate an employee and train another in his or her place; pay legal fees; reimburse and/or accommodate work load around psychotherapy for the victim or perpetrator; and manage increased absenteeism, decreased productivity, and lowered employee morale. Psychological effects include those resulting from a perceived and actual traumatization of being exposed to sexual harassment, being labeled a "perpetrator," and recognizing uncontrollable and maladaptive sexual behavior.

Organizational responses to sexual harassment should include a two-pronged approach that targets primary and tertiary prevention. First, an organization should have policies in place to prevent sexual harassment from occurring. Employees should clearly know proscribed sexual behavior in the workplace, the company's sexual harassment policies for handling allegations and grievance procedures, and the level of expected professionalism. Second, an organization's sexual harassment policies should clearly delineate how to investigate allegations, determine culpability, and deliver penalties to offenders. Clearly explicated organizational policies will help manage sexual harassment incidents and prevent further occurrences.

These policies should be guided by empirically supported guidelines that are effective in meeting the desired goal of decreasing victimization by reducing the incidence of potentially traumatizing events and thwarting future reoccurrences. To date, there exists a paucity of sound empirical studies evaluating pathways of prevention, assessment, and treatment for sexual harassment. Fitzgerald (1990) has pointed out the difficulties in assessing the frequency of sexual harassment because of the lack of validity and reliability data for current measures and because instruments do not include an exhaustive set of possible sexually harassing behavior. Additionally, there are few studies examining predictors and risk factors for sexual harassment. We have a limited understanding of why certain persons are more likely than others to engage in sexually harassing behavior. It is also crucial that a thorough and competent sexual harassment investigation be conducted once allegations are made. However, existing investigation protocols have not been empirically tested and there does not exist any standard for conducting a sexual harassment investigation.

Too often, legal, organizational, and mental health professionals are faced with the task of evaluating the validity of sexual harassment allegations, assessing victims and perpetrators of sexual harassment, and treating these same individuals in the absence of practical guidelines for how to do so. Unfortunately, the extant research does not reveal a clear understanding of why sexual harassment occurs, nor whether current practices are effective in dealing with this problem (e.g., produce reliable and satisfactory investigation outcomes, decrease psychological and medical problems in victims of sexual harassment, prevent harassment reoffending, etc.). While reviewing the existing empirical literature directed at managing the problem of sexual harassment, this chapter attempts to highlight gaps in the current body of knowledge. Much effort has been put forth toward the understanding and management of sexual harassment. Unfortunately, much of this effort has not been guided by scientific inquiry. It is therefore essential that scientific research efforts continue to fill the remaining gaps in our understanding and management of sexual harassment. Without continued scientific research to guide this process, our understanding and management of the forensic aspects of sexual harassment will be resigned to conjecture and speculation.

REFERENCES

Abbey, A. (1982). Sex differences in attribution for friendly behavior: Do males misperceive females' friendliness? *Journal of Personality and Social Psychology, 42*, 830–838.

Abbey, A. (1987). Misperceptions of friendly behavior as sexual interest: A survey of naturally occurring incidents. *Psychology of Women Quarterly, 11*, 173–194.

Abueg, F. R., & Fairbank, J. A. (1992). Behavioral treatment of co–occurring PTSD and substance abuse: A multidimensional stage model. In P. A. Saigh (Ed.), *Posttraumatic stress disorder: A behavioral approach to assessment and treatment.* Boston: Allyn & Bacon.

Abueg, F. R., & Kriegler, J. A. (1990). *A 12-session manual for treatment of Vietnam veterans with PTSD and alcoholism.* Menlo Park, CA: National Center for PTSD.

Abueg, F. R., Lang, A. J., Drescher, K. D., Ruzek, J. I., Aboudarham, J. F., & Sullivan, N. (1994). *Enhanced relapse prevention training for post-traumatic stress disorder and alcoholism: A treatment manual.* Menlo Park, CA: National Center for PTSD.

American Psychiatric Association (1994). *Diagnostic and statistical manual of mental disorders* (4th ed.). Washington, DC: Author.

Avina, C., & O'Donohue, W. (2002). Sexual harassment and PTSD: Is sexual harassment diagnosable trauma? *Journal of Traumatic Stress, 15*, 69–75.

Baker, N. L. (1989). Sexual harassment and job satisfaction in traditional and nontraditional industrial occupations. Unpublished doctoral dissertation, California School of Professional Psychology, Los Angeles.

Barlow, D. H., Esler, J. E., & Vitali, A. E. (1998). Psychosocial treatments for panic disorders, phobias, and generalized anxiety disorder. In P. E. Nathan & J. M. Gorman (Eds.), *A guide to treatments that work* (pp. 288–318). New York: Oxford University Press.

Beck, A. T. (1976). *Cognitive therapy and the emotional disorders.* New York: International University Press.

Beck, A. T., Rush, A. J., Shaw, B. F., & Emery, G. (1979). *Cognitive therapy of depression.* New York: Guilford Press.

Bloch, G. D. (1995). Avoiding liability for sexual harassment. *HR Magazine, 40* (4), 5.

Bowers, A., & O'Donohue, W. (1999). Protocol for the standardization of sexual harassment investigations. Unpublished manuscript.

Brannon, R., & Junni, S. (1984). A scale for measuring attitudes about masculinity. *Psychological Documents, 14*, 6–7.

Broderick v. Ruder, 685 F. Supp. 1269 (1988).

Brunswig, K. A., & O'Donohue, W. (2000). A relapse-prevention therapy for sexual harassment. Unpublished manuscript.

Burt, M. (1980). Cultural myths and supports for rape. *Journal of Personality and Social Psychology, 38*, 217–230.

Civil Rights Act of 1964, Title VII, 42 U.S.C. 2000e *et. seq.*

Conte, A. (1997). Legal theories of sexual harassment. In W. O'Donohue. (Ed.), *Sexual harassment: Theory, research, and treatment* (pp. 50–83). Needham Heights, MA: Allyn & Bacon.

Dansky, B. S., & Kilpatrick, D. G. (1997). Effects of sexual harassment. In W. O'Donohue (Ed.), *Sexual harassment: Theory, research, and treatment* (pp. 152–174). Needham Heights, MA: Allyn & Bacon.

Equal Employment Opportunity Commission (1980, April). "Title 29-Labor, Chapter XIV-Part 1604-Guidelines on Discrimination Because of Sex Under Title VII of the Civil Rights Act, as Amended Adoption of Interim Interpretive Guideline," Washington, DC: U.S. Government Printing Office.

Fain, T., & Anderton, D. (1987). Sexual harassment: Organizational context and diffuse status. *Sex Roles, 16*, 291–311.

Fitzgerald, L. F. (1990). Sexual harassment: The definition and measurement of a construct. In M. Paludi (Ed.), *Ivory power: Sexual and gender harassment in academia*. Albany, NY: SUNY Press.

Fitzgerald, L. F., Drasgow, F., Hulin, C. L., Gelfand, M. J., & Magley, V. J. (1997). Antecedents and consequences of sexual harassment in organizations: A test of an integrated model. *Journal of Applied Psychology, 82* (4), 578–589.

Fitzgerald, L. F., Gelfand, M. J., & Drasgow, F. (1995). Measuring sexual harassment: Theoretical and psychometric advances. *Basic and Applied Psychology, 17*, 425–445.

Fitzgerald, L. F., & Shullman, S. L. (1993). Sexual harassment: A research analysis and agenda for the 90's. *Journal of Vocational Behavior, 42*, 5–29.

Fitzgerald, L. F., Shullman, S. L., Bailey, N., Richards, M., Swecker, J., Gold, Y., Ormerod, M., & Weitzman, L. (1988). The incidence and dimensions of sexual harassment in academia and the workplace. *Journal of Vocational Behavior, 32*, 152–175.

Fitzgerald, L. F., Swan, S., & Magley, V. J. (1997). But was it really sexual harassment? Legal, behavioral, and psychological definitions of the workplace victimization of women. In W. O. Donohue (Ed.), *Sexual harassment: Theory, research, and treament*. Needham Heights, MA: Allyn & Bacon.

Foa, E. B., & Olasov Rothbaum, B. (1998). *Treating the trauma of rape: Cognitive-behavioral therapy for PTSD*. New York: Guilford Press.

Follette, V. M., Ruzek, J. I., & Abueg, F. R. (1998). A contextual analysis of trauma: Assessment and treatment. In V. M. Follette, J. I. Ruzek, & F. R. Abueg (Eds.), *Cognitive-behavioral therapies for trauma* (pp. 3–14). New York: Guilford Press.

Glomb, T. M., Munson, L. J., Hulin, C. L., Bergman, M. E., & Drasgow, F. (1999). Structural equation models of sexual harassment: longitudinal explorations and cross-sectional generalizations. *Journal of Applied Psychology, 4* (1), 14–28.

Gruber, J. E. (1990). Methodological problems and policy implications in sexual harassment research. *Population Research and Policy Review, 9*, 235–254.

Gruber, J. E. (1992). A typology of personal and environmental sexual harassment: Research and policy implications for the 1990's. *Sex Roles, 26*, 447–464.

Gruber, J. E. (1997). An epidemiology of sexual harassment: Evidence from North America and Europe. In W. O'Donohue (Ed.), *Sexual harassment: Theory, research, and treatment*. Needham Heights, MA: Allyn & Bacon.

Gruber, J. E., & Bjorn, L. (1982). Blue-collar blues: The sexual harassment of women autoworkers. *Work and Occupations, 9*, 271–298.

Gruber, J., Smith, M., & Kauppinen-Toropainen, K. (1996). Sexual harassment types and severity: Linking research and policy. In M. Stockdale (Ed.), *Women and work V: Sexual harassment* (pp. 151–173). Thousand Oaks, CA: Sage.

Gutek, B. A. (1985). *Sex and the workplace: The impact of sexual behavior and harassment on women, men organizations*. San Francisco: Jossey-Bass.

Gutek, B. A., Cohen, A. G., & Konrad, A. M. (1990). Predicting social-sexual behavior at work: A contact hypothesis. *Academy of Management Journal, 33*, 560–577.

Gutek, B., & Koss, M. P. (1993). Changed women and changed organizations: Consequences of and coping with sexual harassment. *Journal of Vocational Behavior, 42*, 28–48.

Haavio-Mannila, E. (1992). *Work, family, and well-being in five North- and East-European capitals*. Helsinki: Soumalainentiedeakatemia.

Hagman, N. (1988). *Sexual harassment on the job*. Helsinki: Wahlstrom & Widstrand.

Hamilton, J. A., Alagna, S. W., King, L. S., & Lloyd, C. (1987). The emotional consequences of gender-based abuse in the workplace: New counseling programs for sex discrimination. *Woment & Therapy, 6*, 155–182.

Harris v. Forklift Systems, Inc., 114 S Ct. 367 (1993).

Head, A. A. R., & Head G. L. (1992). Investigator is key to sex harassment cases. *National Underwriter Property & Casualty–Risk & Benefits Management, 45*, 2.

Hogbacka, R., Kandolin, I., Haavio-Mannila, E., & Kauppinen-Toropainen, K. (1987). *Sexual harassment in the workplace: Results from a survey of Finns*. Helsinki: Ministry for Social Affairs and Health.

Holgate, A. (1989). Sexual harassment as a determinant of women's fear of rape. *Australian Journal of Sex, Marriage, and the Family, 10*, 21–28.

Jayne, B. C. (1994). Interviewing strategies that defeat deceit. *Security Management, 38* (2), 5.

Laws, D. R. (1989). *Relapse prevention with sex offenders*. New York: Guilford Press.

Laws, D. R., & O'Donohue, W. T. (Eds.). (1997). *Sexual deviance*. New York: Guilford Press.

Legnick-Hall, M. L. (1992). Checking out sexual harassment claims. *HR Magazine, 37*, p. 77.

Leiblum, S. R., & Rosen, R. C. (Eds.) (2000). *Principles and practice of sex therapy* (3rd ed.). New York: Guilford Press.

Loftus, E. J. (2000). Suggestion, imagination and transformation of reality. In A. Stone & J. Turkkan (Eds.), *The science of self-report: Implications for research and practice*, (pp. 201–210). Mahway, NJ: Lawrence Erlbaum.

Loy, P. H. & Stewart, L. P. (1984). The extent and effects of the sexual harassment of working women. *Sociological Focus, 17*, 31–43.

Malamuth, N. M. (1989). The Attraction to Sexual Aggression Scale: Part one. *Journal of Sex Research, 26*, 26–49.

Maletzky, B. M. (1997). Exhibitionism: Assessment and treatment. In D. R. Laws & W. T. O'Donohue (Eds.), *Sexual deviance*. New York: Guilford Press.

Marlatt, G. A. (1989). Feeding the PIG: The problem of immediate gratification. In D. R. Laws (Ed.), *Relapse prevention with sex offenders*. New York: Guilford Press.

Martindale, M. (1990). *Sexual harassment in the military: 1988*. Arlington, VA: Defense Manpower Data Center.

Meritor Savings Bank v. Vinson, 477 U.S. 57 (1986).

Murphy, S. S. (1986). How the victim pays the prices. *RN, 10,* 48.

Najavits, L. M., Weiss, R. D., & Liese, B. S. (1996). Group cognitive-behavioral therapy for women with PTSD and substance abuse disorder. *Journal of Substance Abuse Treatment, 13,* 13–22.

Najavits, L. M., Weiss, R. D., Shaw, S. R., & Muenz, L. R. (1998). "Seeking safety": Outcome of a new cognitive-behavioral psychotherapy for women with post-traumatic stress disorder and substance dependence. *Journal of Traumatic Stress, 11,* 437–456.

Naugle, A. E., & Follette, W. C. (1998). A functional analysis of trauma symptoms. In V. M. Follette, J. I. Ruzek, & F. R. Abueg (Eds.), *Cognitive-behavioral therapies for trauma* (pp. 48–73). New York: Guilford Press.

O'Donohue, W. (1997). Introduction. In W. O'Donohue (Ed.), *Sexual harassment: Theory, research and practice.* Boston: Allyn & Bacon.

O'Donohue, W. T. (2003). Pathways to false allegations of sexual harassment. Unpublished manuscript.

O'Donohue, W., Fanetti, M., & Elliott, A. (1998). Trauma in children. In V. Follette, J. Ruzek, & F. Abuge (Eds.). *Cognitive-behavioral therapies for trauma.* New York: Guilford Press.

O'Hare, E. A., & O'Donohue, W. (1998). Sexual harassment: Identifying risk factors. *Archives of Sexual Behavior, 27* (6), 561–580.

Paludi, M. A., & Barickman, R. B. (1991). *Academic and workplace sexual harassment: A manual of resources.* Albany, NY: SUNY Press.

Pryor, J. B. (1987). Sexual harassment in organizations. *Employee Responsibilities and Rights Journal, 1,* 273–282.

Pryor, J. B., Giedd, J. L., & Williams, K. B. (1995). A social psychological model for predicting sexual harassment. *Journal of Social Issues, 51* (1), 69–84.

Pryor, J., LaVite, C., & Stoller, L. (1993). A social psychological analysis of sexual harassment: The person/situation interaction. *Journal of Vocational Behavior, 42,* 68–81.

Pryor, J. B., & Stoller, L. (1994). Sexual cognition processes in men who are high in the likelihood to sexually harass. *Personality and Social Psychology Bulletin, 20,* 163–169.

Pryor, J. B., & Whalen, N. J. (1997). A typology of sexual harassment: Characteristics of harassers and the social circumstances under which sexual harassment occurs. In W. O. Donohue (Ed.), *Sexual harassment: Theory, research, and treatment.* Needham Heights, MA: Allyn & Bacon.

Resick, P. A., & Schnicke, M. K. (1993). *Cognitive processing therapy for rape victims: A treatment manual.* Newbury Park, CA: Sage.

Rubenstein, M. (1992). Combating sexual harassment at work. *Conditions of Work Digest, 11,* 7–285.

Saal, F. E., Johnson, C. B., & Weber, N. (1989). Friendly or sexy? It depends on whom you ask. *Psychology of Women Quarterly, 13,* 263–276.

Schacter, D. L. (Ed.) (1995). *Memory distortions: How minds, brains and societies reconstruct the past.* Cambridge, MA: Harvard University Press.

Shotland, L., & Craig, J. (1988). Can men and women differentiate between friendly and sexually interested behavior? *Social Psychology Quarterly, 34,* 990–999.

U.S. Merit Systems Protection Board (1981). *Sexual harassment in the federal workplace: Is it a problem?* Washington, DC: U.S. Government Printing Office.

U.S. Merit Systems Protection Board (1995). *Sexual harassment in the federal workplace: Trends, progress, continuing challenges.* Washington, DC: U.S. Government Printing Office.

Williams v. Saxbe, 413 F. Supp. 654 (1976).

Wincze, J. P., & Carey, M. P. (1991). *Sexual dysfunction: A guide for assessment and treatment.* New York: Guilford Press.

CHAPTER 28

LEGAL ISSUES IN CHILD ABUSE AND NEGLECT

SANDRA T. AZAR
THE PENNSYLVANIA STATE UNIVERSITY

NINA OLSEN
CLARK UNIVERSITY

THE WEIGHING OF CHILDREN'S NEEDS: NEW ASSESSMENT ROLES FOR MENTAL HEALTH PROFESSIONALS

The balancing of children's rights in relationship to those of parents has shifted over time in the legal system (Dredeyn, 1976).[1] In early times, parental rights were paramount and children were, for the most part, viewed as chattel (e.g., children could be given to others to work off parental debts; Kadushin, 1967). Over the last century, however, some specification of parents' responsibility to children began to be articulated. For instance, custody cases began to consider whether a parent would provide for a child's physical needs. As the rights of women evolved, so did those of children. The invoking of *tender years* as a rationale for awarding custody of young children to mothers signaled another shift in which children's needs beyond purely basic survival were considered. With these changes, courts began to take a closer look at the quality of care parents provide children and to deliver punishment for violations of children's rights to proper care by enacting child protection laws. Globally, as well, greater consideration to children as having rights separate from parents has begun to occur (UN General Assembly, Convention on Children's Rights, 1989). With this trend has come further

---

[1] It might be argued that there has been a simultaneous shift historically as well to giving the concept of "childhood" itself special privilege and protection (Radbill, 1980). This privileged status may vary also by cultural group, as might the range of ages over which it occurs.

broadening of applications of child protection laws and increasing willingness to terminate parental rights with the Adoption and Safe Families Act (1997).

With this shift in focus, psychologists have increasingly been asked to make contributions to the legal process involved in protecting children. The goal of this chapter is to highlight three focal areas around which we may be asked to make contributions. Our discussion is not intended to serve as a sole source of information. This area of practice is evolving quickly and further training and "upgrading" of ones' skills continuously is crucial.

AN OVERVIEW OF THE LEGAL PROCESS

Psychologists become involved most often around three legal decision points: reporting, risk assessment, and evaluation of parental fitness. We will describe the assessment roles that clinicians play within each. Standards for answering the legal questions in each phase are discussed where appropriate. It must be reiterated that legal statutes vary considerably (e.g., different laws exist in military and Native American communities and across states) and statutes are constantly changing. Thus, the material provided may become obsolete before this chapter even goes to print. In addition, we have artificially separated the phases in the legal process. In practice, multiple questions are put before most clinicians by the courts and initial referral questions may change in the midst of a legal proceeding. Clinicians, therefore, need to delineate clearly the areas of knowledge on which they can legitimately comment at the outset, in written reports, and during testimony. Resisting efforts to comment on areas outside this "territory" of expertise is crucial. If "educated" comments are possible, limits to their validity should be stated. Even with these restrictions, testimony may be used in a manner not intended (e.g., treatment planning report being used as baseline for terminating parental rights).

Mandated Reporting

Consensus regarding the behaviors that constitute maltreatment does not exist within our field and some debate occurs legally as well.

Psychology vs. the Law: Disparate Definitions of Child Maltreatment—A Point of Tension

Early attempts at definition were guided by the goals of case identification and prosecution. These definitions, therefore, focused narrowly on the intent of the perpetrator or the extent of physical consequences to the child (e.g., broken bones). These areas are still where the emphasis lies in the legal system. Because such definitions were not useful for treatment planning, clinicians utilize different and broader approaches to definition. This strategy may result in disparities in our views that have repercussions not only for reporting, but also for all three areas we discuss and can be a source of tension in our interactions with legal personnel.

Our field tends to view maltreatment as specific acts of omission or commission by perpetrators that are judged by a mixture of community values and professional expertise to be inappropriate or damaging (Garbarino & Giliam, 1980). Although such a definition is "socially mediated," it allows for a narrow versus a broad continuum in thinking about impact (e.g., demonstrable harm versus endangerment) and encompasses a broad continuum of actions (e.g., from failure to supervise appropriately to use of a gun or knife to being emotionally rejecting). In clinical practice, even broader definitions have emerged, including seeing maltreatment as part of a more general breakdown in caregiver capacities (Azar, Barnes, & Twentyman, 1988) or as part of a larger set of events labeled as trauma (Terr, 1991). These broader views are often viewed as too broad for the legal system.

Four types of maltreatment are typically recognized by the legal system: physical abuse, neglect, sexual abuse, and emotional maltreatment. *Physical abuse* involves the use of aversive or inappropriate control strategies with a child (e.g., beatings). *Neglect* is an act of omission of actions that leads to harm or endangerment of children's health or well-being, including a failure to provide minimal caregiving in the areas of medical care, education, nutrition, supervision, emotional contact, and safety, as well as providing inadequate environmental stimulation and structure. Definitions of *sexual abuse* typically focus on the element of sexual exploitation (based on an inequality of power) involving anal, oral, genital, or breast contact between a child and another person (Cohen & Mannarino, 1993). Often, perpetrators are people known to children (e.g., fathers, stepfathers, other relatives). The last, *emotional abuse*, is the hardest to define. It has been seen both as central to all types of maltreatment and as occurring as a distinct entity. Acts of emotional abuse are ones that are psychologically damaging to a child's behavioral, cognitive, affective, or physical functioning (e.g., rejecting, terrorizing, isolating, degrading, missocializing; Brassard, Germain, & Hart, 1987). Because of identification problems, emotional abuse is not typically a sole factor in legal cases. These four types often co-occur.

Clinically, other dimensions are important, including severity, frequency/chronicity, and the child's age when maltreatment occurs. One last factor discussed only recently is the meaning that the child takes from his or her experience (Azar & Bober, 1999). Children may incorporate elements of their abuse into schema regarding the self, others, and the world that are distorted and influence later functioning. The legal system may not see this factor as relevant, but the child's view may be the best predictor of outcome (McGee, Wolfe, Yuen, & Wilson, 1995).

Maltreatment is also often linked with a series of events, any one of which might derail development (e.g., poverty, domestic violence) or act in a compensatory way (e.g., nonperpetrator parent's supportive reactions). Although our field considers contextual factors as relevant, courts may weigh them differently in decision making, which is another source of tension.

Finally, ethnic, racial, and class differences exist in parenting practices (Azar & Benjet, 1994; Azar & Cote, 2002). Thresholds for labeling such behavior as "abuse" or "neglect" thus varies with the group under consideration. Whereas some acts (e.g., breaking a child's bones) may be viewed by any culture as abusive, others may not. Sibling care (e.g., an 8-year-old caring for siblings), for example, is common in some cultures (Korbin, 1994) but is viewed as risky in our culture and may be labeled as "neglect." Such gray areas add to the tension of reporting and impact work in the other areas we discuss (e.g., what is fit parenting).

Reporting Laws

In the early 1960s, all 50 states enacted laws regarding the mandatory reporting by professionals of suspected child maltreatment. These laws have not been completely immune from the definitional issues just outlined. State statutes vary as to what types of behaviors are covered and who may be labeled a perpetrator. In Massachusetts, the statute requires that abuse be done by "a caretaker" and thus, abuse by someone not in this role would not be covered under reporting laws but by more general assault ones. Acts either suspected of or causing substantial risk of serious physical or emotional injury to a child are considered abuse (either physical or sexual) and ones that involve the intentional withholding of necessary food, clothing, shelter, or medical care are considered neglect. Again, the breadth of acts covered vary (e.g., some states cover educational neglect such as truancy within such statutes and others do not).

Laws indicate who must report, to whom abuse must be reported, and the form and content of the report. The fact that parents seek treatment does not absolve the professional of the duty to report. Reporters' anonymity is typically protected and "good-faith" reporters are generally immune from civil liability and criminal penalty. A wide variety of professionals are required to report. In Massachusetts, mandated reporters include psychologists, physicians, dentists, osteopaths, chiropractors, nurses, podiatrists, school personnel, social workers, police officers, and any other person responsible for the care of children. Penalties exist for failure to report (e.g., imprisonment [5 days to 1 year]; fines from $100 to $1,000; Besharov, 1987).

Key to most statutes are words like *suspected* or *risk* of harm. Definitive proof is not required. Prompt reporting can be crucial. Documentation of abuse is difficult and if physical evidence is not present at the time of investigation, action may not be taken. Even if proof is not strong, reporting is advised as subsequent reports may be taken more seriously.

Over the last few decades, reporting has continued to increase (e.g., overall increase of 331% in the rate of substantiated reports since 1976, with the majority of this increase in reporting of physical abuse [up 58%] and sexual abuse [up 300%; NCCAN, 1995]). Underreporting, however, still occurs. A national survey, for example, estimated that only 28 percent of the cases found through community settings (e.g., hospital, schools) that met criteria for abuse were known to child protective services (CPS) (Sedlak & Broadhurst, 1996). Many reasons have been given for failures to report. Thresholds for reporting vary by professional status of the reporter (Giovanonni & Becerra, 1979), the family's minority and/or socioeconomic status (SES) (Turbett & O'Toole, 1980), the social attractiveness of the potential perpetrator and victim child (Jensen & Nicholas, 1984), and child age (Pagelow, 1989). Fears of legal entanglement (e.g., having to testify), threat to the therapeutic relationship, and/or potential for trauma to the child and parents may also prevent it. How other professionals react may also be an obstacle. Supervisors may discourage reporting in an institutional setting. Some states have statutes protecting employees from retaliation for reporting (Besharov, 1987).

The mandate of CPS and the courts is to protect children and, where possible, to help families stay intact (e.g., provide services, therapeutic help). For many parents, therefore, being reported may provide some relief. Yet despite potential positive outcomes of reporting, the possibility for negative impact on families has also received attention (Emery & Billings, 1998). Concerns include the iatrogenic impact of labeling (e.g., increasing resistance to intervention), failures of the system to provide real interventions once families are identified, and subjecting children to further trauma (e.g., foster care). Some evidence supports such concerns. For example, Schene (1991) noted that despite an increase of 55 percent in abuse reporting from 1980 to 1985, there was only a 2 percent increase in resources at federal, state, and local levels combined (U.S. House of Representatives Select Committee, 1987). More recent surveys have suggested a dearth of services in most states (Berkowitz & Sedlak, 1993). Finally, children have often been left to languish in foster care, without appropriate adoptive homes being found. Of the more than 450,000 children who were in the foster care system in 1994, 100,000 could not return home, with only 27,000 of these being legally freed and placed for adoption (a portion of these adoptions also fail). Nonetheless, the impact of failing to report and the possibility of further injury to the child should take precedence. A vulnerable child is left unprotected. Reporters dissatisfied with the outcome of reporting can speak with the CPS supervisor in charge and in some states can bring the case to the attention of juvenile court, where further protective actions may be ordered (McKittrick, 1981).

A final warning is needed for clinicians working with already identified abusive families. Recidivism rates in maltreatment are high (from 20–70% of cases; Hansen, Steffy, & Gauthier, 1993; Williams, 1983). It is easy to become desensitized to risk when abusive families are one's entire caseload. Treatment teams may safeguard against such failures to report.

What Happens Once the Report Is Made?

In some states, the police are immediately involved; in others, except where a perpetrator is charged (e.g., rape of a child), only child welfare staff are involved. Reporters are typically interviewed over the phone to determine children's immediate risk, with a more detailed follow-up interview at a later time. (Some cases are screened out at this juncture as not fitting mandated reporting or outside the agency's jurisdiction. A record, however, is often still made in case another report should occur.) Many states then require reporters to file a written report stating briefly the cause for suspicion. Only information pertinent to the maltreatment suspicions should be shared. It is only here that confidentiality can be breached within legal and ethical mandates.

Most states require an investigation within a specified time period, and in extreme cases the response is immediate (e.g., temporary removal of the child from the home with a more long-term arrangement made when additional data has been elicited). Removal typically involves the legal system, but it is uncommon for clinicians to be involved in investigations or removal decision making. A recent exception is a role played in the investigation of sexual abuse. Although the old roles in the dispositional phase (e.g., evaluation of parental fitness for termination of parental rights) have limitations and pitfalls that will be discussed later, this new investigatory role has even more difficulties. Further, substantiation of abuse does not mean it will lead to a court action. Fewer than one-half of cases result in prosecution (Portwood, Reppucci, & Mitchell, 1997). Alternative or mandatory treatment is often substituted for criminal penalties such as probation or incarceration. Whether prosecution will occur, however, is not known at the time a clinician is asked to conduct an evaluation. Thus, any attempt to substantiate abuse needs to meet legal criteria (see Chapter 12 this volume for more information). A more common role in the legal process, risk assessment, is described next.

Risk Assessment

Risk questions emerge around three areas—risk of future acts of violence (physical or sexual abuse), risk of other harm (e.g., failure to supervise or provide medical care, exposure to domestic violence), and risk of critical failures in socialization of children (e.g., encouragement of antisocial behavior). The first of these, violence prediction, has been a topic of much discussion in adult forensic work, but this discussion has not focused on violence toward children. The latter two have received little attention, except for longitudinal studies of offspring of psychiatrically ill parents and other at-risk samples. The limited foundational literature makes risk testimony difficult.

Until recently, it was argued that violence prediction had limited scientific foundation (Monahan, 1981). More recent data, however, have shown some predictive validity in narrowly defined groups (e.g., psychiatric patients with specific diagnoses) in specific settings (e.g., hospitals) and within certain limited time frames (e.g., immediately after discharge) using primarily actuarial methods (e.g., Gardner, Lidz, Mulvey, & Shaw, 1996). Even then, risk statements can only be made regarding the probability that a given individual or class of individuals of which the individual is a member will reoffend and are only possible when a certain level of scientific data is available regarding recidivism for that class of individual (Grisso & Appelbaum, 1992).

Unfortunately, our scientific database in child maltreatment in many ways fails to meet these criteria, especially given the nature of risk involved (risk within a specific relationship) and the period over which prediction may be required (e.g., for a 2-year-old, it would be 16 years until adulthood). Further, even if actuarial general models of risk for violence were useful, these have not worked for females, making prediction for mothers more difficult (Lidz, Mulvey, & Gardner, 1993).

Only a small literature exists on predicting risk in abuse cases, and an even smaller one involving neglect (APWA, 1988). Risk assessment systems have begun to be used by CPS that use a variety of parent, child, family, and environmental characteristics as predictors as well as characteristics of the maltreatment identified to date (Milner et al., 1998; Pecora, 1991). These systems are still in the early stages of development and suffer from methodological flaws (Wald & Woolverton, 1990). For some of these systems, evidence of ability to predict length of time the case has remained open, response to services, substantiation rates, and to a limited extent further abuse has been found. Nonetheless, false positive rates are too high to be used for legal purposes.

Studies of recidivism have been done in hopes of finding risk indicators. In one study, children who were maltreated during a four-year period were studied through a review of 24,506 records of substantiated child abuse cases in the Colorado Child Abuse and Neglect Registry (Fryer & Miyoshi, 1994). The probability that a child would be revictimized was related to the child's age, gender, and the form of maltreatment. Younger children (0–12 years old) were at greater risk than adolescents (12–17 years old). Females aged 1 to 6 were the most vulnerable group, especially following emotional or sexual abuse. Another study has shown that females are more vulnerable than males in each age group (Finkelhor, Hotaling, Lewis, & Smith, 1990). Even with this data, however, large proportions of females will not be revictimized (86–89%). Offender factors for which some predictive validity has been found include violence in their own childhood; unrealistic expectations of children; and increased levels of stress, poverty, and social isolation (Hamilton & Browne, 1998). These factors, however, also have low specificity as risk predictors.

Further data exist regarding predictors based on examinations of responsivity to intervention. For example, Cohn and Daro (1987) identified initial severity of maltreatment as the strongest predictor of recidivism, with neglect cases more likely to repeat than sexual abuse. (This may be because the "treatment" for sexual abuse often includes the perpetrator's removal from the home.) A review by Jones (1991) identified six parental variables that related to responsivity to treatment, including the severity and type of abuse, denial of abuse, severe personality problems, noncooperation, mental illness, and substance abuse. As we will discuss later, some of these factors, however, produce mixed predictive findings when child outcomes are considered.

In cases of repeated abuse, Hamilton and Browne (1998) argue for an examination of patterns (typologies). Different risk indicators may exist in cases where a parent was the repeated perpetrator than in cases where a parent failed to monitor or protect a child from a series of perpetrators. They also argue for the use of child resiliency factors that have been found in response to child abuse in assessing risk (e.g., rapid responsivity to danger, information seeking, formation and utilization of relationships for survival). This approach is controversial. Yet considering such factors in conjunction with situational and perpetrator ones may provide a more comprehensive picture of a child's vulnerability.

Along with risk models, use of personality instruments to determine risk and specific child abuse risk prediction instruments have been discussed (e.g., MMPI-2, Child Abuse Potential Inventory; Milner, 1986). The sensitivity and specificity of risk prediction for both physical and sexual abuse are too poor as yet to justify use in court decision making (i.e., too many false positive and false negative classifications; Caldwell, Bogat, & Davidson, 1988; Milner et al., 1998). Models focusing on transactional indicators have not yet been explored and are worth examination (see the behavioral skills models discussed in the next section).

Although strong risk assessment models are not yet available, providing a picture of the number of independent risk factors may help courts in weighing a child's risk if returned to parents or if allowed to continue to remain with parents. Definitive statements of absolute risk for any individual, however, cannot be made at this point.

Before we leave this topic, risk assessment among groups that appear often in CPS caseloads is worthy of specific discussion. These include domestic violence cases, mentally retarded and psychiatrically ill parents, and substance abusers.

A literature has emerged regarding the direct and indirect consequences to children of exposure to domestic violence. Child abuse is committed at high rates by both batterers (between 47–54%) and victims of battering (between 28–35%) (Saunders, 1994). Exposure to domestic violence alone has also been associated with heightened levels of both internalized and externalized behavioral problems in children, although variations in outcomes have been observed (e.g., based on gender, appraisal of the conflict, level of involvement in the disputes). CPS and courts have, therefore, begun to ask questions regarding children's continued risk here (i.e., risk of continued exposure). Recidivism in domestic violence appears high; rates of cessation over two-year periods have been shown to be only 20 percent (Quigley & Leonard, 1996) to 40 percent (Aldarondo & Sugarman, 1996). Predictors of recidivism include severity of marital discord, the severity and frequency of marital violence, the chronicity or stability of prior violence, and the level of psychological aggression the husband exhibits toward the wife. These factors may provide some guidance but are based on small sample studies; thus, interpretations need to be offered cautiously.

Substance-abusing parents, psychiatrically ill parents, and mentally retarded parents are other groups commonly seen as placing children at risk for harm. These groups have been shown to have higher than average involvement with CPS and greater risk of losing custody of their children (Famularo, Stone, Barnum, & Wharton, 1986; Seagull & Scheurer, 1986). For example, it has been estimated that as many as 80 percent of mentally retarded parents will have their parental rights terminated once they enter the CPS system (Feldman, 1998). Biases have been documented affecting judgments regarding the risk these groups pose to others. Indeed, within community samples, in judging the domains most affected by a number of disabling conditions, emotional disorders were viewed as most detrimental to parenting (MacDonald & Hall, 1969). Legal writers have cited similar bias in the legal system. For example, one legal writer stated with regards to mentally retarded parents: "From the perspective of the law, the mentally retarded parent is an oxymoron-in-waiting" (Hayman, 1990, p. 1202). It may be difficult for decision makers to transcend schematic responses (Budd & Greenspan, 1984; Azar, Benjet, Furhmann, & Cavallero, 1995). Yet for each of these groups evidence exists of variation in risk level, and clinicians need to weigh the factors present in each case and assist courts in evaluating whether functional relationships exist between the disorder and parenting, as well as children's risk of harm.

Although there is some evidence supporting increased risk of aggression globally among the mentally ill (a two- to threefold increase; Swanson, 1994), the absolute risk is *not* high. Only 7 percent of those with a major mental disorder (but without substance abuse) engaged in any assaultive behavior in a given year. Higher rates have been found in substance-abusing individuals (Swanson, 1994), but data regarding females and violence specifically toward children are lacking.

When specific diagnostic groups are considered with regards to risk to children (either direct violence or indirect harm—inadequate parenting and neglect), the database is limited. Although links between parental diagnosis and parenting disturbances and negative child outcomes exist (McCombs, Thomas, & Forehand, 1991; Tymchuk, 1992; West & Prinz, 1988), they may be more complex than originally thought. For example, a portion of mentally retarded parents do provide satisfactory basic care (e.g., keeping children clean, adequately fed, clothed and supervised, and in regular school attendance; Mickelson, 1947) and with the exception of those with very low IQ scores (30–49), the absolute level of intellectual functioning may not be systematically related to the adequacy of the care provided. Also, problems have not been found in all areas (e.g., level of punitiveness toward children, decision-making skills in childrearing situations; Tymchuk, 1992). Evidence also exists that specific skill deficits (e.g., problem solving) coupled with contextual stress may distinguish those who show parenting problems (Azar, 1995). Heterogeneity of child outcomes have also been found (Martin, Ramey, & Ramey, 1990), again suggesting individual differences.

For substance abuse and other psychiatric disorders, whether the disorder is in an active phase or not produces differing levels of disturbances in parent-child interaction patterns (e.g., in substance abuse, Jacob, 1992; Rodning, Beckwith, & Howard, 1991; Seilhamer, Jacob, & Dunn, 1993). The contextual issues associated with disorders (e.g., strain) may be at fault for negative outcomes (Hammen, et al., 1987). Substance abuse can be associated with increased marital discord, disconnection from social supports, increased violence exposure, and incarcerations or other separations (Wasserman & Leventhal, 1994). The disorder and contextual factors may also interact. For example, marital discord has been linked to behavioral problems in children with depressed mothers, but not in children of schizophrenics (Emery, Weintraub, & Neal, 1982). It is also unclear whether heightened problems among offspring result from these ill parents' capacity to be "good enough" parents or to forces that have exerted their influence before the child was even born (e.g., genetic infuences; Gotessman & Shields, 1972). Further, child factors may temper risk. For example, depressed mothers who enjoyed interactions with their children or received positive responses from their children have been found to be more effective in sustaining positive interactions with them (Cox, Puckering, Pound, & Mills, 1987), suggesting that the nature of the child's behavioral style or temperament must be considered. Fisher and colleagues (1987), in examining competent offspring of mentally ill mothers, found these children more often to have a parent with a mood disorder as opposed to a schizophrenic parent, one whose disorder was not chronic, whose disorder occurred later in the child's life, and one who, if lacking in warmth and an active style, was balanced by a father who compensated for this lack in their interaction. In assessing risk, therefore, this complexity needs to be reflected in evaluations.

Issues such as parents' level of participation in the treatment of their disorder (e.g., consistency in taking medication) should also be assessed. If two parents are present, the skills of the nonaffected parent and the nature of extended family/friend support should be assessed as compensatory forces. Low-IQ parents with good supports appear to do better (Mickelson, 1947; Seagull & Scheurer, 1986). Also, family emotional climate affects relapse of disorders. Heightened criticism, hostility, and intrusiveness are linked to relapse (Brown, Monck, Carstairs, & Wing, 1962).

In summary, in cases where parents have cognitive impairments or psychiatric disorder or are substance abusers, our database varies in providing a basis for contingent statements of risk. It is crucial to identify exactly which parenting capacities were compromised in the past (e.g., self regulation, ability to maintain a consistent and helpful social support network, poor modeling of social conventions through criminal activities) and whether they have remained and will continue to remain compromised in the future. Expert witnesses must interpret the more fine-grained meaning of risk (e.g., interactive effects, effects over time) and the multitude of other factors that may exacerbate or temper the risk of parental diagnosis. Judgments should be based on empirical data with a statement as to their strength. Overall, these functional questions are much harder to answer than the court might presume.

Termination of Parental Rights and Evaluating Parental Fitness

Questions that arise during the evaluation of parental fitness are many and diverse. One of the core questions in termination of parental rights (TPR) cases is the determination of whether the parents' capacity to rear their children has fallen so far below community standards that the child is at significant risk of harm. The evidence must be "clear and convincing." Courts frequently employ mental health professionals as evaluators and experts witnesses in making this determination (Grisso, 1986; Melton et al., 1997; Schetky & Benedek, 1992). Because of a lack of detailed statutory guidelines ("community standards") and well-operationalized psychological definitions of the elements of "fit" parenting, evaluations are difficult to carry out and the task may feel ambiguous. Criticisms have occurred around similar issues in evaluating parenting in divorce cases (O'Donohue & Bradley, 1999). Our discussion will, therefore, focus on the issues involved in how we define competent or "fit" parenting.

Evaluating Parental Fitness: A Question of Match

Judgments regarding adequacy of parenting are typically not just ones regarding sheer skill at parenting, but rather the goodness of fit of the capacities of a particular parent or set of parents to the needs of a specific child. Often, because maltreated children have special needs (e.g., emotional problems, cognitive delays), this can be a complex queston and becomes even more complex when more than one child, each with different needs, is involved. Unfortunately, the field has been virtually silent on evaluation of parent-child match. Also, the interpretation of the term *fit parenting* is easily subject to personal and cultural biases (Azar & Benjet, 1994; Azar & Cote, 2002). The very use of the term *parenting* highlights a fundamental shift in our assessment task from the traditional role of assessing individuals (assessing *parents*) to assessing processes between individuals (i.e., assessing *parenting*). Society requires its members to parent their children—an active verb indicating a conscious regulation and mastery of an activity (Campion, 1995), as opposed to traditional beliefs that enactment of this role comes "naturally."

Studies have not evaluated systematically what factors mental health professionals typically consider in conducting TPR evaluations. Nonetheless, a preliminary list of factors commonly used by expert witnesses can be gleaned from an examination of the clinical literature (Azar, 1992; Azar, Lauretti, & Loding, 1998; Grisso, 1986; Schetkey & Benedek, 1992; Schoettle, 1984; Steinhauer, 1983). These factors include the nature of the original abuse/neglect report(s), an assessment of ongoing child risk (see the earlier section), the parents' mental status and their current parenting skills; any special-care needs of the child; consistency of visitation of the child while in foster care; maintenance of an appropriate home environment; compliance with service plans and cooperation with appointed caregivers (e.g., therapists, caseworkers); treatment progress; and last but not least, development of improved parenting skills. Many of these are part of the traditional practice of clinicians (e.g., mental status) or involve documenting facts (e.g., visitation patterns). Others involve new assessment skills. It is here that we will focus our discussion—assessing parenting capacities.

In current practice, clinicians eroneously seem to be continuing to use traditional assessment strategies to answer these more relational questions (e.g., personality tests, projectives) (Budd, Poindexter, Felix, & Polan, 1999). This state of affairs results in part from the fact that our scientific database for this new type of assessment task is more limited. Existing models of parenting focus on the ingredients of *optimal*, as opposed to *minimally adequate*, parenting. They also typically emphasize a *narrow* band of qualities (e.g., warmth and nurturance) and ignore qualities required to engage in more *basic child care* (e.g., proper hygiene, medical care). Also, the available literature emphasizes group differences (e.g., risk if a parent is a member of group A vs. group B) (a *nomethetic* view), as opposed to the individual perspective required in TPR cases (an *ideographic* view). Parents rarely fit dead center into a designated group, and it is the extent of variation from their group status that is crucial to determine (e.g., our discussion of parental diagnostic groups). Finally, measures of parenting are not as developed as traditional assessment methods. Many constructs have not been concretized into measures or if they have been, we do not have actuarial data or norms for diverse groups). A sample of potentially useful measures are presented in Figure 28.1 (Azar & Soysa, 2000). These are aimed at individual issues (e.g., screening for acohol and drugs, symptoms) and both interactional (e.g., behavioral observation schemes) and contextual ones (e.g., stress level, social support). Some have norms and standards for diverse groups. No one of these, however, meet the standards necessary for actuarial predictions. In combination, however, they may provide the basis for evaluating core areas crucial to parenting.

Next we provide examples of more sophisticated frameworks in which to place this material that we believe will foster future work in this area. We would like to focus on two models of parenting that hold promise to enhance our work in this area: behavioral approaches and Vygotskyian views on parents' roles in children's development (Azar, Benjet, Fuhrmann, & Cavallaro, 1995). First, because the foundation of behavioral work is the assessment of functional relationships (Baer, Wolfe, & Risley, 1968; Nelson & Hayes, 1986), parenting models that have grown out of this approach have the most promise to answer the functional questions before courts (i.e., linking parental capacities to child needs). Behavioral clinicians are adept at carefully describing behavior and the conditions under which functioning is strongest and weakest as well as describing contexts and the interaction between an individual's behavioral skills and such environments. Thus, they are uniquely skilled at assessing the current functioning of a parent and his or her children and outlining for courts, in clear behavioral language, the strengths and weaknesses of each. The behavioral approach's sensitivity to antecedent conditions, individual conditions, and unwillingness to go beyond observable data also minimizes the potential for biases to enter the process, avoiding treating individuals as a class and focusing on unique contingencies, learning histories, and skills. This is an important perspective in TPR cases. Finally, there is an emphasis on social validation (Wolf, 1978). One must be aware of the expected social behaviors of the clients' cultural group (e.g., "social comparison"; Kazdin, 1977), which fits with the law's use of "community standards" as a yardstick for decision making.

Self Report Inventories on Parenting

The Child Abuse Potential Inventory (Milner, 1986)
The Adult/Adolescent Parenting Inventory (Bavolek, 1984)
The Parenting Scale (Arnold, O'Leary, Wolff, & Acker, 1993)

Measures of Cognitive Distortions

Expectations (Parent Opinion Questionnaire; Azar, Robinson, Hekimian, & Twentyman, 1984)
Role reversal (Bavolek, 1984)
Problem solving (parenting, adult-adult relationships, and other areas; Hanson, et al., 1995; Wasik, Bryant, & Fishbein, 1981)
Negative intent attributions (Child Vignettes; Azar, 1990, unpublished)

Observational Protocols (see review by Mash, 1991)

For infants and toddlers:
    Nursing Assessment Satellite Training Instruments (Barnard et al., 1989; Farell et al., 1991)
    Home Observation for the Measurement of the Environment (Caldwell & Bradley, 1984)
    Behavioral ratings for basic child care skills (Feldman et al., 1992)
For preschoolers and school-aged children:
    The Dyadic Parent-Child Interaction Coding System (DPICS II, Eyberg et al., 1994)
    Oregon Social Learning Theory Center protocol (Dishion et al., 1984; Reid, 1978)
    Ratings of videotapes of discipline (Hoffman, Fagot, Reid, & Patterson, 1987)

Neglect Issues

    Home cleanliness (Rosenfield-Schlichter et al., 1983; Watson-Perczel et al., 1988)
    Home safety (Home Accident Prevention Inventory; Tertinger, Greene, & Lutzker, 1984)
    General family resources (Family Resource Scale; Dunst, 1986)
    Parent Outcome Interview (Magura & Moses, 1986)
    Emergency and medical care skills (Tymchuk, 1990; Delgado & Lutzker, 1985)

Symptom Checklists

    Symptom Checklist–90 (Derogatis, 1983)
    Anger (Anger Scale; Novaco, 1975)
    Depression (CESD, Radloff et al., 1977; Beck Depression Inventory, Beck et al., 1979)
    Alcoholism (Michigan Alcohol Screening Test; Selzer, Vinokur, & vanRooijan, 1975)
    Drug Abuse (Skinner, 1982)

Child Behavior Problems

    Child Behavior Checklist (Achenbach & Edelbrock, 1983)
    Eyberg Child Behavioral Inventory (Eyberg & Ross, 1978)
    The Issues Checklist (Robin & Foster, 1989)

Contextual Measures

    The Parenting Stress Index (Abidin, 1983; Lloyd & Abidin, 1985)
    The Life Stress Scale (Egeland, Breitenbucher, & Rosenberg, 1980)
    Perceived Social Support from Family and Friends (Procidano & Heller, 1983)
    Social Support Inventory (Cyrnic, Greenberg, Ragozin, Robinson, & Basham, 1983)

FIGURE 28.1 Potential Measures (Azar & Soysa, 2000)

The second valuable approach is Vygotskian theory (1934), which focuses on an ideographic view of adults' role in children's development. Competent parenting (i.e., parenting that facilitates development) in this view involves responses on the parent's part that are within a child's developmental reach (within what is called the "zone of proximal development"; Rogoff & Wertsch, 1984). The focus is on (1) the specific capacities of the child, and (2) the parents' ability to operate in a manner that is just above where the child is developmentally, moving them to higher levels of functioning. Thus, parents who are insensitive to their children's immaturity and respond in ways that are outside their range would be deemed less appropriate (e.g., expecting a 4-year-old to comfort them when they are sad and becoming enraged when they do not). Although this model is primarily focused on cognitive development, it can be easily applied to development in other domains and may ultimately provide a useful frame for the evaluation of a parent-child match.

An additional element, not currently considered in discussions in this area, is the context in which the parenting is to occur (Azar, 1992; Azar et al., 1998; Campion, 1995). Context has two components, the child and what he or she brings to interaction with the parent (e.g., health status, age, temperament, etc.) and the environmental context (e.g., extent of social supports, safety of the living environment). For example, the level of a parent's capacities might not place a *well-functioning* child at risk but would endanger a child who has *intensive medical care needs*. We will focus on this aspect of match later. The match of parent capacities to child needs is more of interest to the legal system than the fit of those capacities to the context in which they live, but the latter should be considered nonetheless, as its importance to parenting outcomes has begun to be documented. Cauce (1995), for example, argues that parenting in a high-crime, inner-city neighborhood may require more "precision" parenting than in a suburban, low-crime one. Also, some contextually based risks may be beyond parents' control and this fact needs to be considered. For example, housing quality available to lower SES parents may be more limited, increasing their children's risk (e.g., lead poisoning) through no fault of the parent. In such cases, the better assessment question is whether the parent recognizes these potential risks and the ways in which they attempt to cope with them to protect their children from obstacles to their development. The latter question is more relevant in considering "fitness" than the presence of the risk alone.

With these general models in mind, several behavioral frameworks have begun to appear in the literature for assessing parenting capacities that may act as a starting point for evaluations. Ones posited by Tymchuk (1998), Feldman (1998), and Greene and Kilili (1998) are similar in their emphasis on specific content areas of parenting (e.g., medical care skills, components of feeding of babies), whereas the model proposed by Azar and her colleagues (Azar & Twentyman, 1986; Azar, 1992; Azar, Lauretti, & Loding, 1998) has the added emphasis on the importance of more global cognitive and behavioral processes that cut across specific parenting tasks *and* the provision of an environment to support parenting and children's development (e.g., problem-solving capacities, capacities to maintain a support network to use for instrumental help in parenting, advocacy skills to deal with teachers) (Figure 28.2).

The model described by Tymchuk (1998) was developed for assessment and working with cognitively limited parents and thus speaks to the issues of the most basic of child care. It emphasizes parenting as consisting of four major skill areas: (1) fundamental knowledge and skills (effective coping strategies, grooming and

> 1. Parenting Skills
>   Problem-Solving Abilities
>   A Repertoire of Child Management Skills (Balance of Positive and Negative Strategies, Discipline Skills)
>   Medical Care and Physical Care Skills (e.g., Ability to Identify Needs for Medical Assistance; Capacity to Select Nutritious Foods)
>   Safety and Emergency Response Skills
>   Capacities for Warmth and Nurturance (e.g., Affective Recognition/Expression Skills)
>   Sensitive and Discriminant Interactional Response Capacities
> 2. Social Cognitive Skills
>   Perspective Taking
>   Problem-Solving Capacities
>   Appropriate Expectations Regarding Children's Capacities
>   Cognitive Reflectivity/Complexity
>   Balancing Short- and Long-Term Socialization Goals
>   Positive Attributional Style
>   Perceptual/Observational Skills
>   Self-Efficacy
> 3. Self-Control Skills
>   Impulse Control
>   Accurate/Adaptive Perceptions
>   A Positive Interpretive Bias
>   Self-Monitoring Skills
>   Assertiveness
> 4. Stress Management
>   Self-Care Skills
>   Relaxation Skills
>   Recreational Capacities
>   Ability to Marshal and Maintain Social Support Network
>   Positive Appraisal Style
>   A Breadth of Coping Capacities (Problem-Focused Coping, Emotion-Focused Coping, Avoidant Coping)
>   Financial Planning Skills
> 5. Social Skills
>   Interpersonal Problem-Solving Skills
>   Empathy
>   Affective Recognition/Expression Skills
>   Assertiveness
>   Social Initiation Skills
>   Capacities to Respond Effectively to a Breadth of Individuals (e.g., family, friends, employers, social workers, children's teachers)

FIGURE 28.2 Sampling of Skills Areas Required to Parent

hygiene skills, meal planning and management of finances, ability to create and maintain a support network), (2) health-related knowledge and skills (understanding bodily functions and body parts, knowledge of common health problems, illnesses and medicines, ability to recognize and evaluate severity of symptoms, ability to recognize and prevent life-threatening emergencies), (3) safety-related knowledge and skills (e.g., knowledge of potential dangers in the home and in the community), and (4) mutual parent-child enjoyment (e.g., playing together, reading and singing to the child). Feldman (1998) developed a similar framework (also for a treatment program with cognitively limited parents) with a focus on ages 0–3. He has task analyses of a set of basic parenting capacities, including skills such as feeding babies solids, washing hair, and bathing, along with a list of component responses required to do each successfully.

Azar and her colleagues (Azar & Twentyman, 1986; Azar, Barnes, & Twentyman, 1988; Azar, 1992; Azar, Lauretti, & Loding, 1998) have taken a different approach and argue for an evaluation of cognitive processes and behavioral skills that pervade all content areas of parenting, with the most fundamental being ones in the social cognitive realm (Figure 28.1). For example, parents' capacity to problem solve, have realistic expectancies of others (including their children), and perspective taking in relationships are all needed to engage in appropriate child care and the maintenance of an environment that is conducive to children's safety, health, and development. Moreover, in this model, these capacities are seen as evolving as the child's needs change. For example, cognitive coping strategies for dealing with an infant's prolonged crying and the oppositional behavior of an adolescent may have both common elements (e.g., self-calming capacities) and different ones (e.g., capacity to negotiate calmly in the face of verbal provoation) (Azar & Siegel, 1990).

Central to all these frameworks is an emphasis on the use of behavioral performance-based evaluation (e.g., task analyses, live role plays, and use of visual prompts to solicit responding, such as enactment of a grease fire to assess emergency skills). Though useful, these frameworks are not yet sufficiently developed or normed for the court process. They hold, however, tremendous promise. Beginning efforts have occurred to norm some of them, and these provide starting points for court assessments (Feldman, 1998). Selection of which capacities to assess should be based on parents' previous inadequacies and the concerns of key informants (e.g., caseworkers). As in all assessments, clarification of the assessment question is paramount.

As noted, parental fitness must be viewed in the context of the child's caretaking needs, requiring a thorough assessment of the child's functioning along with assessing parental skills. This might start with what is known regarding the potential areas of disturbed functioning found in children exposed to child abuse and neglect. Azar, Breton, and Ferraro (1997) highlight five areas of development that may be affected: (1) physical health and well-being; (2) cognitive functioning and academic performance; (3) emotional and social development; (4) stress management and anger control capacities, and (5) self-regulation.

Abused and neglected children show a heterogeneous set of symptoms and needs. As with parents, the child's functioning in all these domains also needs to be considered across contexts. For example, discrepancies in functioning may hint at environmental contingencies that negatively affect the child and that, if the biological parent is unable to protect against, may bode poorly for the child. For example, a highly chaotic environment may be detrimental to a child with attentional problems performing adequately. The consistency, quality, and content of the care a child requires needs to be considered (e.g., does he or she have special psychological or medical needs, such as care and monitoring of a chronic illness?); special safety needs (e.g., does the child engage in self-injurious behaviors requiring constant monitoring?); needs for stability and structure; and needs for higher than typical caregiver patience and responsiveness (e.g., in cases where the child exhibits high rates of provocative, oppositional behavior or, in contrast, is highly passive) (Azar et al., 1998).

Standard child assessment batteries form the starting point, including reports from multiple caregivers. (Reports by abusive and neglectful parents are not entirely accurate.) The data collected must then be linked to the present and future parenting needs of the child and the level of the parent's capacities in each need area. For special-needs children, this means a thorough review of appropriate literature for the problem area in question and what is known regarding the types of parenting capacities that are associated with better outcomes. For example, a diabetic child may require high levels of organizational skills and specific perceptual qualities. Children with certain forms of developmental disabilities may require a high level of initiation on the part of parents (e.g., an ability to persist in the face of less responsiveness). Dimensions that have been considered important in the literature on special-needs children include parental acceptance of the child's disorder, parents' knowledge of the care needs of the child and the role adjustments required of them, and elements of the child's responses that facilitate or hinder reciprocal relationships. For example, some child factors promote attachment (e.g., smiling, crying, vocalizing, visual searching, eye contact, locomotion around the room, demonstrating physical contact, tactile discrimination) and others discourage attachment (e.g., negative response to being handled, such as stiffening, tenseness, limpness, and lack of responsiveness; lowered or bland activity level; bizarre or unpleasant crying; hyperactivity; passivity; undifferentiated anger) (Blaher, 1984). The child's level of dependency, communicative ability, temperament, mobility, social skills, "cuddability" (hypo- or hypertonicity), physical attractiveness, sensory awareness, and role-taking ability are all important to understanding risks for the severely handicapped child (Blaher, 1984). Parental adaptations to any of these child elements must be evaluated. The child's capacity to compensate for parent inadequacies might also be considered. A highly engaging child might rouse a depressed parent and get his or her needs met despite the parent's mood state, whereas a passive child may be unable to do so.

Because the majority of TPR cases involve neglect, the match issues often occur in the more basic care areas (e.g., safety issues, health care, stability and level of chaos of the home setting, hygiene). Assessing such care has not been much addressed. "Basic" care may vary with child characteristics. Special-needs children may require specific skills or heightened levels of what would be considered average parenting skills. Areas important to consider include the consistency of care required (e.g., are there special psychological or medical needs, such as care of a chronic illness with injections, medication, or diet); needs for stability and consistency of structure; and needs for higher than typical caregiver patience (e.g., given slow progress in self-care abilities). An asthmatic child may need a cleaner home than the average child, whereas a diabetic child may need more intensive monitoring of eating habits and ongoing health care. Evaluators need to outline such needs and assess parents' capacities for meeting each.

Research in the area of special-needs children need to be used as a source of guidelines. Assessment studies delineating factors linked to good child outcome, as well as treatment studies that identify key skill areas for parenting work, can be helpful here. For example, research on children with attention deficit disorder has suggested that family cohesion, communication, and problem solving are important predictors of a child's outcome (Holderness, 1998). An assessment of the parents' knowledge of the disorder and positive reinforcement skills (including responding and ignoring skills, such as attending to appropriate behavior/compliance and ignoring inappropriate behavior) are other factors to consider in parenting of an ADHD child. Information relevant to match also comes out of treatment research. For instance, parent training programs with attention deficit disorder have found the best outcomes in children when the disorder has been less intense in symptoms, when parental stress has been lower, and when parents' self-esteem is higher (Anastopolous et al., 1993). This finding suggests factors important to consider in evaluations in predicting risk.

Parenting children with disabilities require a myriad of adaptations, not required in parenting a child who is developing normally. These include efforts to understand the child's disability, behaviors, and needs, continuing behavior management, and long-term cooperation with medical and educational caregivers. The parent must have a capacity to act as an advocate for a child in multiple settings (e.g., working with school personnel to provide the right learning environment for their behaviorally disordered child). Contact with teachers, pediatricians, and child therapists can provide information regarding parents' past efforts to advocate for the child. Again, it is crucial to consider that parents of different SES may vary in their advocacy style. For example, there are SES differences in how parents think they should be involved in their child's education (Chavkin & Williams, 1989). Baker and colleagues (1997) have developed a comprehensive table of parenting challenges that arise from having a child with developmental disabilities, as well as the adaptations required of parents in response to these challenges. How these change over development are also outlined (i.e., needs of infants who are developmentally disabled vary from those of adolescents).

Studies of families with special-needs children also emphasize the heightened level of parental stress in such families. For example, Clark, Azar, Hagberg, and Pollack (in preparation) found that mothers of children with congenital heart disease were significantly depressed and stressed and both conditions were related to their use of coping strategies. Similar high levels of stress have been found in parents of infants with cystic fibrosis or congenital heart disease (Goldberg et al., 1990); preschool children with developmental delays (Cameron, Dobson, & Day, 1991) or autism (Donenberg & Baker, 1993); and school-age children and adolescents with autism or Down syndrome (Wolfe, Noh, Fishman, & Speechley,

1993). Equally high levels of stress are also found in children with conduct disorder but no developmental delays (Donenberg & Baker, 1993; Webster-Stratton, 1988). An evaluation of parental coping capacities may be extremely important. Evidence of greater use of problem-focused coping (e.g., capacity to make specific plans, acting on the plan, reframing stressful events into ones that allow for positive growth) over emotional focused coping (e.g., venting emotions, denial, resignation, mental or behavior avoidance, or disengagement) is seen as more adaptive. Such strategies have been seen to lead to increased self-confidence and self-regard as well as less depression, stress, and illness (Callahan, 1996; Krauss & Seltzer, 1993).

Finally, it must be pointed out that much of the decision making in termination cases is at a gross level and might not require this fine-grained analysis. That is, a sophisticated evaluation is not required when a parent has beaten a child and broken limbs and has not been receptive to a single treatment provider over a five-year period. Not much subtle knowledge is required to say this is detrimental to children! Yet in other cases, where the responses involved are open to some question (e.g., neglect cases) and where the evidence is more ambiguous or open to discussion, a refined view of parent-child transactions may be very useful. Careful behavioral descriptions delineating under what circumstances the neglectful behavior occurs is extremely helpful. For instance, if we can identify that a parent is neglectful only when intoxicated and can also identify the conditions in which he or she is most likely to drink as well as the success rate of intervention attempts, then we have provided the *trier of fact* (the judge) with valuable information. The judge is then better able to weigh the cost of terminating parental rights and can make a data-based decision.

Generally, the caution that should be foremost in our minds in doing such work is to be careful not to overinterpret, but to observe and report behavior providing multiple possible interpretations. In this way, we can help courts make more informed judgments, since without our help it is possible they may make them on a more idiosyncratic basis.

Conclusion

The questions regarding defining maltreatment, child risk, and parenting needs placed before expert witnesses in the legal system are complex ones and require training and reflective practice on the part of clinicians. Too often, simple solutions (i.e., ones we are more comfortable with) have been substituted for more adequate ways to respond to such questions. Despite our questioning the basis of participation in legal processes, we believe clinicians with strong backgrounds in developmental psychology, systems theory, and measurement do have assets to offer while major decisions are made to protect children and determine their placement. Ultimately, the decision is based on community standards. Because it is a moral one, our role is to make a contribution, not the decision itself.

Acknowledgement

This chapter was written while the first author was a Liberal Arts Fellow at Harvard Law School.

References

Abidin, R. (1983). *Parenting Stress Index—Manual.* Charlottesville, VA: Pediatric Psychology Press.

Achenbach, T., & Edelbrock, C. S. (1983). *Manual for the child behavior checklist and revised child behavior profile.* Burlington, VT: University Associates in Psychiatry.

Aldarondo, E., & Sugarman, D. B. (1996). Risk marker analysis of the cessation and persistence of wife assault. *Journal of Consulting and Clinical Psychology, 64,* 1010–1019.

American Public Welfare Association (1988). Second national roundtable on CPS risk assessment. *Summary of highlights.* Washington, DC: Author.

Anastapolous, A. D., Shelton, T. L., DuPaul, G. J., & Guevremont, D. C. (1993). Parent training for attention-deficit hyperactivity disorder: Its impact on parent functioning. *Journal of Abnormal Child Psychology, 21* (5), 581–596.

Arnold, D. S., O'Leary, S. G., Wolff, L. S., & Acker, M. M. (1993). The Parenting Scale: A measure of dysfunctional parenting in discipline situations. *Psychological Assessment, 5,* 131–136.

Ayoub, G., Jacewitz, M. M., Gold, R. G., & Milner, J. (1982). Assessment of a program's effectiveness in selecting individuals at risk for problems in parenting. *Journal of Clinical Psychology, 39,* 334–339.

Azar, S. T. (1990). *Child Vignettes, unpublished measure,* Frances L. Hiatt School of Psychology, Clark University.

Azar, S. T. (1992). Legal issues in the assessment of family violence involving children. In R. T. Ammerman & M. Hersen (Eds.), *Assessment of family violence* (pp. 47–70). New York: Wiley.

Azar, S. T. (1995, April). *Is the intellectually low functioning parent at risk for child maltreatment?* Paper presented at the biennial meeting of the Society for Research in Child Development, Indianapolis.

Azar, S. T., Barnes, K. T., & Twentyman, C. T. (1988). Developmental outcomes in physically abused children: Consequences of parental abuse or the effects of a more general breakdown in caregiving behaviors? *Behavior Therapist, 11,* 27–32.

Azar, S. T., & Benjet, C. L. (1994). A cognitive perspective on ethnicity, race and termination of parental rights. *Law and Human Behavior, 18,* 249–268.

Azar, S. T., Benjet, C. L., Fuhrmann, G., & Cavallero, L. (1995). Child maltreatment and termination of parental rights: Can behavioral research help Solomon? *Behavior Therapy, 26,* 599–623.

Azar, S. T., & Bober, S. (1999). Children of abusive families. In W. K. Silverman & T. H. Ollendick (Eds.), *Developmental issues in the clinical treatment of children and adolescents* (pp. 371–392). Boston: Allyn & Bacon.

Azar, S. T., Breton, S., & Ferraro, M. (1997). Child abuse and neglect. In T. H. Ollendick & M. Hersen (Ed.), *Handbook of child psychopathology* (3rd ed.) (pp. 483–504). New York: Plenum.

Azar, S. T., & Cote, L. R. (2002). Sociocultural issues in the evaluation of the needs of children in custody decision-making: What do our current frameworks for evaluating parenting practices have to offer? *International Journal of Law & Psychiatry, 25,* 193–217.

Azar, S. T., Lauretti, A., & Loding, B. (1998). The evaluation of parental fitness in termination of parental rights cases: A functional-contextual perspective. *Clinical Child and Family Psychology Review,* 1, 77–99.

Azar, S. T., Robinson, D. R., Hekimian, E., & Twentyman, C. T. (1984). Unrealistic expectations and problem solving ability in maltreating and comparison mothers. *Journal of Consulting and Clinical Psychology, 52,* 687–691.

Azar, S. T., & Siegel, B. (1990). Behavioral treatment of child abuse: A developmental perspective. *Behavior Modification, 14,* 279–300.

Azar, S. T., & Soysa, K. (2000). How do I assess a caregiver's parenting attitudes, knowledge, and level of functioning? In H. Dubowitz & D. De Panfilis (Eds.) *The handbook of child protection* (pp. 308–313). Thousand Oaks, CA: Sage.

Azar, S. T., & Twentyman, C. T. (1986). Cognitive behavioral perspectives on the assessment and treatment of child abuse. *Advances in cognitive-behavioral research and therapy, Vol. 5* (pp. 237–267). New York: Academic Press.

Baer, D. M., Wolfe, M. M., & Risley, T. R. (1968). Some current dimensions of applied behavioral analysis. *Journal of Applied Behavioral Analysis, 1,* 91–97.

Baker, B. L., Blacker, J., Kopp, C. B., & Kraemer, B. (1997). Parenting children with mental retardation. *International Review of Research in Mental Retardation, 20,* 1–45.

Barnard, K. E., Hammond, M. A., Booth, C. L., Bee, H. L., Mitchell, S. K., & Spieker, S. J. (1989). Measurement and meaning of parent-child interaction. In F. Morrison, C. Lord, & D. Keating (Eds.), *Applied Developmental Psychology* (Vol. III, pp. 40–75). New York: Academic Press.

Bavolek, S. J. (1984). *Handbook of the Adolescent-Parenting Inventory.* Park City, UT: Family Development Resources, Inc.

Beck, A. T., Rush, A. J., Shaw, B. E., & Emery, G. (1979). *Cognitive therapy of depression.* New York: Guilford.

Berkowitz, S., & Sedlak, A. J. (1993). *Study of high risk: Child abuse and neglect groups. State survey report.* Washington, DC: National Center on Child Abuse and Neglect.

Besharov, D. J. (1987). Reporting out-of-home maltreatment: Penalties and protections. *Child Welfare, 66,* 399–408.

Blaher, J. (1984). A dynamic perspective on the impact of a severely handicapped child on the family. In J. Blaher (Ed.), *Severely handicapped young children and their families* (pp. 3–50). New York: Academic Press.

Brassard, M. R., Germain, R., & Hart, S. N. (1987). *Psychological maltreatment of children and youth.* New York: Pergamon.

Brown, G. W., Monck, E. M., Carstairs, G. M., & Wing, J. K. (1962). Influence of family life on course of schizophrenic illness. *British Journal of Preventive and Social Medicine, 16,* 55–68.

Budd, K. S., & Greenspan, S. (1984). Mentally retarded women as parents. In E. Blechman (Ed.), *Behavior modification with women* (pp. 477–506). New York: Guilford Press.

Caldwell, B. M., & Bradley, R. H. (1984). *Home observations for the measurement of the environment: Administration manual* (rev. ed). Little Rock: University of Arkansas.

Caldwell, R. A., Bogat, G. A., & Davidson, W. S. (1988). The assessment of child abuse potential and the prevention of child abuse and neglect: A policy analysis. *American Journal of Community Psychology, 16*, 609–624.

Callahan, E. J. (1996). Identifying coping mechanisms of parents of children with special needs. *Dissertation Abstracts International: Section B: The Sciences and Engineering 57(2-B)*.

Cameron, S. J., Dobson, L. A., & Day, D. M. (1991). Stress in parents of developmentally delayed and non-delayed preschool children. *Canada's Mental Health, 39*, 13–17.

Campion, M. J. (1995). *Who's fit to be a parent?* London: Routledge.

Cauce, A. M. (1995, June). *Slouching toward cultural competence in research.* Paper presented at the Family Processes Institute, Ogunquit, ME.

Chavkin, N. F., & Williams, D. L. (1989). Low income parents' attitudes toward parent involvement in education. *Journal of Sociology and Social Welfare, 16*, 17–28.

Cohen, J. A., & Mannarino, A. P. (1993). A treatment model for sexually abuse preschoolers. *Journal of Interpersonal Violence, 3*, 115–131.

Cohn, A., & Daro, D. (1987). Is treatment too late? What ten years of evaluative research tells us. *Child Abuse & Neglect, 11*, 433–442.

Cox, A. D., Puckering, C., Pound, A., & Mills, M. (1987). The impact of maternal depression on young children. *Journal of Child Psychology and Psychiatry, 28*, 917–928.

Crnic, K. A., Greenberg, M. T., Ragozin, S. A., Robinson, N. M., & Basham, C. (1983). Effects of stress and support on mothers and premature and full term infants. *Child Development, 54*, 209–217.

Delgado, A. E., & Lutzker, J. R. (1985, November). *Training parents to identify and report their children's illness.* Paper presented at the annual convention of the Association for Advancement of Behavior Therapy, Houston.

Derogatis, L. R. (1983). *SCL-90-R administration, scoring, and procedures manual-II.* Townson, MD: Clinical Psychometric Research.

Dishion, T., Gardner, K., Patterson, G., Reid, J., Spyrou, S., & Thibodeaux, S. (1984). *The family process code: A multidimensional system for observing family interactions.* Unpublished coding manual, Oregon Social Learning Center, Eugene, OR.

Donenberg, G., & Baker, B. L. (1993). The impact of children with externalizing behaviors on their families. *Journal of Abnormal Child Psychology, 21*, 179–198.

Dredeyn, A. P. (1976). Child custody contests in historical perspective. *American Journal of Psychiatry, 133*, 1369–1376.

Dunst, C. H. (1986). *Family resources, personal well-being, and early intervention.* Unpublished manuscript. Family Infant and Preschool Program, Western Carolina Center, Morganstown, NC.

Egeland, B. R., Breitenbucher, M., & Rosenberg, D. (1980). Prospective study of the significance of life stress in the etiology of child abuse. *Journal of Consulting and Clinical Psychology, 48*, 195–205.

Emery, R. E., & Billings, L. L. (1998). An overview of the nature, cases, and consequences of abusive family relationships. *American Psychologist, 53*, 121–135.

Emery, R. E., Weintraub, S., & Neale, J. M. (1982). Effects of marital discord on the school behavior of children of schizophrenic, affectively disordered, and normal parents. *Journal of Abnormal Child Psychology, 10*, 215–228.

Eyberg, S., Bessmer, J., Newcomb, K., Edward, D., & Robinson, E. (1994). *Dyadic parent-child interaction coding system II: A manual.* Unpublished manuscript, University of Florida, Gainesville, Department of Clinical/Health Psychology.

Eyberg, S. M., & Ross, A. W. (1978). Assessment of child behavior problems: The validation of a new inventory. *Journal of Clinical Child Psychology, 7*, 113–116.

Famularo, R., Stone, K., Barnum, R., & Wharton, R. (1986). Alcoholism and severe child maltreatment. *American Journal of Orthopsychiatry, 56*, 481–485.

Farell, A. M., Freeman, V. A., Keenan, N. L., & Huber, C. J. (1991). Interaction between high-risk infants and their mothers: The NCAST as an assessment tool. *Research in Nursing and Health, 14*, 109–118.

Feldman, M. A. (1998). Parents with intellectual disabilities. In J. R. Jutzker (Ed.), *Handbook of child abuse research and treatment* (pp. 401–420). New York: Plenum Press.

Feldman, M. A., Case, L., Garrick, M., MacIntyre-Grande, W., Carnwell, J., & Sparks, B. (1992). Teaching child-care skills to mothers with developmental disabilities. *Journal of Applied Behavior Analysis, 25*, 205–215.

Finkelhor, D., Hotaling, G., Lewis, I. A., & Smith, C. (1990). Sexual abuse in a national survey of adult men and women: Prevalence, characteristics, and risk factors. *Child Abuse & Neglect, 14*, 19–28.

Fisher, L., Kokes, R. F., Cole, R. E., Perkins, K., & Wynne, L. C. (1987). Competent children at risk: A study of well-functioning offspring of disturbed parents. In E. J. Anthony & B. J. Cohler, *The invulnerable child* (pp. 211–228). New York: Guilford Press.

Fryer, G. E., & Miyoshi, T. J. (1994). A survival analysis of the revictimization of children: The case of Colorado. *Child Abuse & Neglect, 18*, 1063–1071.

Garbarino, J., & Giliam, G. (1980). *Understanding abusive families*. Lexington, MA: Lexington Books.

Gardner, W., Lidz, C. W., Mulvey, E. P., & Shaw, E. C. (1996). Clinical versus actuarial prediction of violence in patients with mental illness. *Journal of Clinical Psychology, 64*, 602–609.

Giovanonni, J. M., & Becerra, R. M. (1979). *Defining child abuse*. New York: Free Press.

Goldberg, S., Morris, P., Simmons, R. J., & Fowler, R. S. (1990). Chronic illness in infancy and parenting stress: A comparison of three groups of parents. *Journal of Pediatric Psychology, 15*, 347–358.

Gottesman, I. I., & Shields, J. (1972). *Schizophrenia and genetics. A twin study vantage point*. New York: Academic Press.

Greene, B. F., & Kililil, S. (1998). How good does a parent have to be? In J. R. Jutzker (Ed.), *Handbook of child abuse research and treatment* (pp. 53–74). New York: Plenum Press.

Grisso, T. (1986). *Evaluating competencies*. New York: Plenum.

Grisso, T., & Appelbaum, P. S. (1992). Is it unethical to offer predictions of future violence? *Law and Human Behavior, 16*, 621–633.

Hamilton, C. E., & Browne, K. D. (1998). The repeat victimization of children: Should the concept be revised? *Aggression and Violent Behavior, 3*, 47–60.

Hammen, C., Adrian, C., Gordon, D., Burge, D., Jaenicke, C., & Hiroto, D. (1987). Children of depressed mothers: Maternal strain and symptom predictors of dysfunction. *Journal of Abnormal Psychology, 96*, 190–198.

Hansen, R. K., Steffy, R. A., & Gauthier, R. (1993). Long-term recidivism of child molesters. *Journal of Consulting and Clinical Psychology, 61* (1), 646–652.

Hanson, D. J., Pallotta, G. M., Christopher, J. S., Conaway, R. L., & Lundquist, L. M. (1995). The parental problem-solving measure: Further evaluation with maltreating and non-maltreating parents. *Journal of Family Violence, 10*, 319–336.

Hayman, R. L. (1990). Presumptions of justice: Law, politics, and the mentally retarded parent. *Harvard Law Review, 103*, 1201–1271.

Hoffman, D. A., Fagot, B., Reid, J. B., & Patterson, G. F. (1992). Parents rate the FCIS comparisons of problem and non-problem boys using parent derived behavior composites. *Behavioral Assessment, 9*, 131–140.

Holderness, S. L. (1998). *Parenting perceptives on family adaptation to ADHD: Effects of family style, coping, and stress on child outcomes.* Dissertation, Oklahoma State University.

Jacob, T. (1992). Family studies of alcoholism. *Journal of Family Studies, 5*, 319–338.

Jensen, R. F., & Nicholas, K. B. (1984). Influence of the social characteristics of both father and child on the tendency to report child abuse. *Professional Psychology, 15*, 121–128.

Jones, D. P. H. (1991). The effectiveness of intervention. In M. Adcock, R. White, & A. Hollows (Eds.), *Significant harm* (pp. 61–84). Croyden, UK: Significant Publications.

Kadushin, A. (1967). *Child welfare services.* New York: Macmillian.

Kazdin, A. E. (1977). Assessing the clinical and applied importance of behavior change through social validation. *Behavior Modification, 1*, 427–452.

Korbin, J. E. (1994). Sociocultural factors in child maltreatment. In G. B. Melton & F. D. Barry (Eds.), *Protecting children from abuse and neglect* (pp. 182–223). New York: Guilford.

Krauss, M. W., & Seltzer, M. M. (1993). Coping strategies among older mothers of adults with retardation: A life-span developmental perspective. In P. Turnbull, J. M. Patterson, S. K. Behs, D. L. Murphy, J. G. Marquis, & M. J. Blue-Banning (Eds.), *Cognitive coping, families and disability* (pp. 173–182). Baltimore: Books.

Lidz, C. W., Mulvey, E. P., & Gardner, W. (1993). The accuracy of predictions of violence to others. *Journal of the American Medical Association, 269*, 1007–1011.

Loyd, B. H., & Abidin, R. R. (1985). Revision of the parenting stress index. *Journal of Pediatric Psychology, 10*, 169–177.

MacDonald, A. P., & Hall, J. (1969). Perception of disability by the nondisabled. *Journal of Consulting and Clinical Psychology, 33*, 654–660.

Magura, S., & Moses, B. S. (1986). *The Parent Outcome Interview.* Washington, DC: Child Welfare League.

Martin, S. L., Ramey, C. T., & Ramey, S. (1990). The prevention of intellectual impairment in children of impoverished families: Findings of a randomized trial of educational day care. *American Journal of Public Health, 80*, 844–847.

Mash, E. H. (1991). Measurement of parent-child interaction in studies of maltreatment. In R. Starr & D. A. Wolfe (Eds.), *The effects of child abuse and neglect* (pp. 203–255). New York: Guilford.

McCombs, C., Thomas, A., & Forehand, R. (1991). The relationship between paternal depressive mood and early adolescent functioning. *Journal of Family Psychology, 4*, 260–271.

McGee, R. A., Wolfe, D. A., Yuen, S. A., & Wilson, S. K. (1995). The measurement of maltreatment: A comparison of approaches. *Child Abuse and Neglect, 19*, 233–249.

McKittrick, C. A. (1981). Child abuse: Recognition and reporting by health professionals. *Nursing Clinics of North America, 16*, 103–115.

Melton, G. B., Petrila, J., Poythress, N. G., & Slobogin, C. (1997). *Psychological evaluations for the courts: A handbook for mental health professionals* (2nd ed.). New York: Guilford Press.

Mickelson, P. (1947). The feebleminded parent: A study of 90 family cases. *American Journal of Mental Deficiency, 51,* 644–653.

Milner, J. S. (1986). *The Child Abuse Potential Inventory: Manual* (2nd ed.). Webster, NC: Psytec.

Milner, J. S., Murphy, W. D., Valle, L. A., & Tolliver, R. M. (1998). Assessment issues in child abuse evaluations. In J. R. Lutzker (Ed.), *Handbook of child abuse research and treatment* (pp. 75–116). New York: Plenum.

Monahan, J. (1981). *Predicting violent behavior: An assessment of clinical techniques.* Beverly Hills, CA: Sage.

National Center on Child Abuse and Neglect (1995). *Child maltreatment 1995. Reports from the states to the National Center on Child Abuse and Neglect.* Washington, DC: U.S. Department of Health and Human Services.

Nelson, R. O., & Hayes, S. C. (1986). *Conceptual foundation of behavioral assessment.* New York: Guilford Press.

Novaco, R. W. (1975). *Anger control: The development and evaluation of an experimental treatment.* Lexington, MA: Lexington Books.

O'Donohue, W., & Bradley, A. R. (1999). Conceptual and empirical issues in child custody evaluations. *Clinical Psychology, Science and Practice, 6,* 310–322.

Pagelow, M. D. (1989). The incidence and prevalence of criminal abuse of other family members. In L. Ohlin & M. Tonry (Eds.), *Family violence* (pp. 263–314). Chicago: University of Chicago Press.

Pecora, P. J. (1991). Investigating allegations of child maltreatment: The strengths and limitations of current risk assessment systems. *Child and Youth Services, 15,* 73–92.

Portwood, S. G., Reppucci, N. D., & Mitchell, M. S. (1998). Balancing rights and responsibilities: Legal perspective on child maltreatment. In J. R. Lutzker (Ed.), *Handbook of child abuse research and treatment* (pp. 31–52). New York: Plenum Press.

Procidiano, M., & Heller, K. (1983). Measures of perceived social support from friends and family: Three validation studies. *American Journal of Community Psychology, 11,* 1–24.

Quigley, R. M., & Leonard, K. E. (1996). Desistance of husband aggression in the early years of marriage. *Violence and Victims, 11,* 355–370.

Radbill, S. X. (1980). Children in a world of violence: A history of child abuse. In C. H. Kempe & R. E. Helfer (Eds.), *The battered child* (pp. 3–20). Chicago: University of Chicago Press.

Radloff, L. S. (1977). The CES-D Scale: A self report depression scale for research in the general population. *Applied Psychological Measurement, 1,* 385–401.

Reid, J. B. (1978). *A social learning approach to family intervention: II. Observation in the home settings.* Eugene, OR: Castalia.

Robin, A. L., & Foster, S. L. (1989). *Negotiating parent-child conflict: A behavioral-family systems approach.* New York: Guilford.

Rodning, C., Beckwith, L., & Howard, J. (1991). Quality of attachment and home environments in children prenatally exposed to PCP and cocaine. *Development and Psychopathology, 3,* 351–366.

Rogoff, R., & Wertsch, J. V. (1984). *Children's learning in the "zone of proximal development."* San Francisco: Jossey-Bass.

Rosenfield-Schlicter, M. D., Sarber, R. E., Bueno, G., Greene, B. F., & Lutzker. (1983). Maintaining accountability for an ecobehavioral treatment of one aspect of child neglect: Personal cleanliness. *Education and Treatment of Children, 6,* 153–164.

Saunders, D. G. (1994). Child custody decisions in families experiencing woman abuse. *Social Work, 39,* 51–59.

Schene, P. A. (1991). Intervention in child abuse and neglect. In J. C. Westman (Ed.), *Who speaks for the children?* (pp. 205–220). Sarasota, FL: Professional Resources Exchange.

Schetky, D. H., & Benedek, E. P. (1992). *Clinical handbook of child psychiatry and the law.* Baltimore: Williams & Wilkins.

Schoettle, U. C. (1984). Termination of parental rights: Ethical issues and role conflicts. *Journal of the American Academy of Child Psychiatry, 23,* 629–632.

Seagull, E. A., & Scheurer, M. D. (1986). Neglected and abused children of mentally retarded parents. *Child Abuse & Neglect, 10,* 493–500.

Sedlak, A. J., & Broadhurst, D. D. (1996). *Third national incidence study of child abuse and neglect.* Washington, DC: U.S. Department of Health and Human Services.

Seilhamer, R. A., Jacob, T., & Dunn, N. J. (1993). The impact of alcohol consumption on parent-child relationships in families of alcoholics. *Journal of Studies on Alcohol, 54,* 189–198.

Selzer, M. L., Vinokur, A., & vanRooijen, L. (1975). A self-administered Short Michigan Screening Test. *Journal of Studies of Alcohol, 36,* 117–126.

Skinner, H. A. (1982). The Drug Abuse Screening Test. *Addictive Behavior, 7,* 363–371.

Steinhauer, P. D. (1983). Assessing for parenting capacity. *American Journal of Orthopsychiatry, 53,* 468–481.

Swanson, J. W. (1994). Mental disorder, substance abuse, and community violence. In J. Monahan & H. J. Steadman (Eds.), *Violence and mental disorder: Developments in risk assessment* (pp. 101–136). Chicago: University of Chicago Press.

Terr, L. (1991). Childhood traumas: An outline and overview. *American Journal of Psychiatry, 148,* 10–20.

Tertinger, D. A., Greene, B. F., & Lutzker, J. R. (1984). Home safety: Development and validation of one component of an ecobehavioral treatment program for abused and neglected children. *Journal of Applied Behavior Analysis, 17,* 150–174.

Turbett, J. P., & O'Toole, R. (August, 1980). *Physicians' recognition of child abuse.* Paper presented at the annual meeting of the American Sociological Association, New York.

Tymchuk, A. J. (1990). Assessing emergency responses of people with mental handicaps. *Mental Handicap, 18,* 136–142.

Tymchuk, A. J. (1992). Predicting adequacy of parenting by people with mental retardation. *Child Abuse & Neglect, 16,* 165–178.

Tymchuk, A. J. (1998). The importance of matching educational interventions to parent needs in child maltreatment: Issues, methods, and recommendations. In J. R. Lutzker (Ed.), *Handbook of child abuse research and treatment* (pp. 421–448). New York: Plenum.

United Nations General Assembly, Convention on Children's Rights. (1989, November). *Adoption of the convention on the rights of the child* (U.N. Doc. A/Res/44/25). New York: Author.

U.S. House of Representatives Select Committee on Children, Youth, and Families (1987). *Victims of official neglect.* Washington, DC: U.S. Congress.

Vygotsky, L. S. (1934). *Thought and language.* Cambridge, MA: MIT Press.

Wald, M. S., & Woolverton, M. (1990). Risk assessment: The emperor's new clothes? *Child Welfare, 69,* 483–511.

Wasik, B. H., Bryant, D. M., & Fishbein, J. (1981, November). *Assessment of parent problem solving skills*. Paper presented at the Annual Meeting of the Association for the Advancement of Behavior Therapy, Toronto.

Wasserman, D. R., & Leventhal, J. M. (1994). Maltreatment of children born to cocaine-dependent women. *American Journal of Diseases of Children, 147*, 1324–1328.

Watson-Perczel, M., Lutzker, J. R., Greene, B. F., & McGimpsey, B. J. (1988). Assessment and modification of home cleanliness among families adjudicated for child neglect. *Behavior Modification, 12*, 57–87.

Webster-Stratton, C. (1988). Mothers' and fathers' perceptions of child deviance: Roles of parent and child behaviors and parent adjustment. *Journal of Consulting and Clinical Psychology, 56*, 909–915.

West, M. O., & Prinz, R. J. (1988). Parental alcoholism and child psychopathology. *Annual Progress in Child Psychiatry and Development*, 278–314.

Williams, G. (1983). The urgency of authentic prevention. *Journal of Clinical Child Psychology, 12*, 312–319.

Wolf, L. C., Noh, S., Fishman, S. N., & Speechley, M. (1989). Psychological effects of parenting stress on parents of autistic children. *Journal of Autism and Developmental Disabilities, 19*, 157–166.

Wolf, M. M. (1978). Social validity: The case for subjective measurement, or how applied behavior analysis is finding its heart. *Journal of Applied Behavior Analysis, 11*, 203–214.

CHAPTER 29

PARTNER VIOLENCE: ASSESSMENT, PREDICTION, AND INTERVENTION

ERIC R. LEVENSKY AND ALAN E. FRUZZETTI
UNIVERSITY OF NEVADA, RENO

In recent years, the number of partner violence cases in the nation's criminal justice courts has increased substantially (Roehl & Guertin, 1998). This increase results in large part from the fact that many states now require police to make mandatory arrests when responding to domestic violence calls, and further require that these cases be prosecuted regardless of victim consent (Sherman, Schmidt, & Rogan, 1992; Rebovich, 1996). With this increase in partner violence cases in the court system, psychologists and other mental health professionals are being called upon more frequently by the courts to conduct assessments and provide expert opinions in the area of domestic violence. Specifically, these professionals are often being asked to (1) describe the nature, frequency, severity, and consequences of previous violence; (2) make predictions about the likelihood and severity of future violence; (3) provide intervention recommendations for the batterer as well as for the victim; and (4) make predictions regarding the likely outcomes of these interventions. This chapter provides psychologists and other professionals working in forensic settings with a source of current and empirically based information to guide their work in partner violence cases. Specifically, it will discuss (1) the known prevalence and typical course and consequences of partner violence, (2) the assessment of past partner violence, (3) the prediction of future partner violence, and (4) intervention options and empirical outcomes in partner violence cases.

The scope of the chapter is limited to the issues of *male-to-female physical violence* and will touch only minimally on female-to-male physical violence and on emotional or psychological abuse in couples. Female-to-male violence and emotional abuse in couples result in criminal justice proceedings much less frequently than does male-to-female violence; female-to-male violence is often engaged in as a means of self-defense (Hamberger & Lohr, 1994; Saunders, 1986), and often does not result in physical injury to the male partner (Cascardi, Langhin-Richsen, & Vivian, 1992; Stets & Straus, 1990). Additionally, emotional or psychological abuse is often not considered an unlawful act. It is important to note, however, that although emotional or psychological abuse is not typically illegal, it does often have significant deleterious effects on its victims and almost always precedes and co-occurs with physical abuse (O'Leary, 2001).

Definition of Partner Violence

Although there is some variation in the definition of *partner violence* across states and legal jurisdictions, the National Association for Court Management (NACM) has provided a generally accepted legal definition of this term. The NACM definition of partner violence includes four different types of acts committed by one family or household member against another. These four types of acts are as follows:

1. Physical assault resulting in bodily injury
2. Sexual assault or abuse (e.g., engaging in unwanted sexual activity with a partner)
3. Forced imprisonment (e.g., preventing a partner from leaving the home)
4. Threats of any of the above

The NACM further defines "family or household members" as including the following:

1. Current or former spouses
2. Persons currently or formerly involved in a significant romantic or sexual relationship

Prevalence, Course, and Consequences of Male-to-Female Partner Violence

Male-to-female partner violence is a common social problem in the United States. In fact, national surveys found that approximately 11.6 percent of women reported being the victim of physical partner abuse in the last year, and 3.4% reported severe abuse during that time (Straus & Gelles, 1990). There are also data suggesting that (1) battering often begins early in relationships; (2) once a male begins to batter, he will likely continue to batter; and (3) this violence will often escalate in frequency, intensity, and severity without intervention (Holtzworth-Munroe, Beatty, & Anglin, 1995; Straus & Gelles, 1990; O'Leary et al., 1989; Feld & Straus, 1989; Pagelow, 1981).

Researchers have found that male-to-female partner violence is often associated with substantial increases in psychological and physical health problems in its victims. These problems include Post-Traumatic Stress Disorder, substance abuse, depression, low self-esteem, increased risk of suicide attempts, and increased physical injuries (Holtzworth-Munroe, Smutzler, Bates, & Sandin, 1997; Coben, Forjuoh, & Gondolf, 1999; Sharps & Campbell, 1999). These sequelae of partner violence will be reviewed in greater detail later in this chapter.

ASSESSMENT OF PAST PARTNER VIOLENCE

Thorough and accurate assessment of past violence is an extremely important part of effective and clinically responsible forensic work in partner violence cases. This is because testimony and recommendations provided to the courts in these cases will be based largely on assessment data obtained. However, conducting sound assessments in partner violence cases can often be a difficult and complex task because this type of violence occurs in many forms, occurs for many reasons, and has a variety of consequences. This multifaceted nature of partner violence makes understanding, predicting, and stopping it quite difficult. Adding to this complexity, the perpetrator and the victim of the partner violence are often reluctant to provide accurate or complete information about past violence (Heckert & Gondolf, 2000). The perpetrators of the violence often feel shame and guilt about their past violent behavior, fear the consequences of a negative evaluation, and are angry about being involved in legal proceedings and facing potentially negative consequences. The victims of partner violence often feel embarrassed about having remained in an abusive relationship and can worry about negative evaluations of their mental health. Additionally, victims of partner violence often worry about retaliation from their partners for reporting past violence, can feel a sense of loyalty to their partners, and may have reunited with the perpetrator.

The purpose of this section is to provide a number of guidelines that can make conducting assessments of past partner violence efficient and more likely to result in valid conclusions and effective recommendations. The first set of guidelines discussed is more stylistic (i.e., procedural considerations for conducting the assessment) than technical (i.e., what data to collect and how to collect them). These stylistic guidelines are intended to aid in the effective implementation of the more technical guidelines, which will be discussed later in this chapter. Holtzworth-Munroe, Beatty, and Anglin (1995) provide three such stylistic suggestions. First, before conducting an assessment of partner violence and its consequences, it is important to separate the partners and assess them individually. As already noted, many abused women are hesitant to speak candidly about the abuse in the presence of their partners because of fear of retributions, and research has shown that victims report more violence if they are interviewed separately from the perpetrator (Cantos, Neidig, & O'Leary, 1994). The perpetrator can also be reluctant to speak freely about past abuse with the victim present.

Second, in conducting an assessment of past partner violence, it is important to communicate in a respectful and nonjudgmental manner with both the perpetrator and the victim. It is likely that the perpetrator and the victim will be experiencing shame and defensiveness about the abuse, and conducting the assessment in a respectful and nonjudgmental manner may increase their willingness to provide detailed and accurate information regarding the violence and its consequences. Third, it is important that the assessor maintains awareness of his or her own reactions and beliefs about partner violence and how these reactions and beliefs may influence the assessment.

It is also important that before conducting the assessment of past violence, the assessor is straightforward with both the perpetrator and the victim about the purpose and structure of the assessment as well as the ultimate use of the assessment data and limits of confidentiality. This should include (1) explaining why the assessment is being conducted and what type of information is to be obtained, (2) describing how this information may be used, (3) describing the assessment procedures, (4) explaining the possible consequences of the assessment on the victim and on the perpetrator, (5) explaining who will and will not be provided with the assessment data collated, and (6) the circumstances under which assessment information would be provided to individuals other than those originally specified (e.g., mandatory reporting of danger to self or others).

In addition to these stylistic considerations, it is essential that the assessor come to the assessment session with specific targets in mind. That is, the assessor should have a clear understanding of what specific questions are to be answered in the assessment. These questions may cover (1) the nature (form), frequency, severity, and consequences of past violence; (2) the likelihood that violence will continue to occur with and without intervention; (3) the type of intervention (if any) that would be most appropriate for the perpetrator and the victim, and so forth.

The assessor should also come to an understanding of the "context" in which the assessment is occurring. That is, the assessor should understand contextual factors such as whether the partner violence is a known fact or is an allegation as well as the contingencies in place that may influence the victim's and perpetrator's reporting of past violence. With regard to these contingencies, both the victim and perpetrator should be assessed for what each may have to gain and lose from accurately reporting, and not accurately reporting, partner violence. For the victim, this assessment should include (1) the extent that the victim fears recrimination for reporting partner violence, (2) whether or not the victim wants to stay in the relationship, and (3) whether or not the victim wants the perpetrator to receive punishment or treatment. For the perpetrator, this assessment should include (1) what the perpetrator sees as the consequences for reporting and not reporting partner abuse, and (2) what he may have to gain from feigning contrition.

Finally, the assessor should be aware of, and work within, the limitations of current partner violence assessment methodologies. In the context of assessing past partner violence, this means that that assessor should be aware that (1) current assessment methods are limited in their ability to accurately and consistently assess the nature, frequency, severity, and consequences of past partner violence; and (2) the validity of these methods are highly influenced by under- and misreporting of past violence and by assessor biases and heuristics. It is hoped that this section of the chapter will aid clinicians in conducting responsible and effective assessments of past partner violence given these limitations.

Assessing the Nature, Frequency, and Severity of Past Partner Violence

Typically, a useful place to start an assessment of past partner violence is by identifying the nature, frequency, and severity of that violence. This can be a difficult task because, as mentioned earlier, victims and perpetrators of partner violence are often hesitant to provide accurate and detailed information about past abuse. Most often, this reporting problem is in the form of underreporting past violence by both of the perpetrator and the victim (Heckert & Gondolf, 2000). However, researchers have found that conducting direct, systematic, and behaviorally specific assessments of partner violence can substantially increase partners' reporting of violence. For example, O'Leary, Vivian, and Malone (1992) found that although only 6 percent of wives in a sample of 132 couples indicated partner violence as a major marital problem on intake forms for couples' therapy, 53 percent of these wives indicated the occurrence of physical aggression in a direct and behaviorally specific assessment for marital violence. The key here seems to be that direct questions were asked concerning very specific behaviors rather than using more vague or open-ended questions.

A commonly used tool for conducting a direct and behaviorally specific assessment of past partner violence is the Conflict Tactics Scale (CTS; Straus, 1979; Straus, Hamby, Boney-McCoy, & Sugarman, 1996). The original CTS is a 19-item self-report questionnaire designed to assess the frequency and severity of behaviors that partners may engage in during an argument. These items comprise four subscales: (1) Reasoning (e.g., "discussed the issue calmly" and "argued heatedly but short of yelling"), (2) Verbal Aggression (e.g., "insulted, swore, or yelled at the other one" and "threatened to hit or throw something at the other one"), (3) Physical Aggression (e.g., "pushed, grabbed, or shoved the other one" and "slapped the other one"), and (4) Severe Aggression (e.g., "kicked, bit, or hit with a fist" and "used a gun or knife"). Each partner indicates whether or not he or she has ever engaged in any of the behaviors described in the CTS over the past year as well as whether or not his or her partner has ever done so. Respondents then rate the frequency with which they, and their partners, have engaged in each of the endorsed items over the past year.

Recently, Straus and colleagues revised the CTS (CTS2; Straus, Hamby, Boney-McCoy, & Sugarman, 1996). The 39-item CTS2 is more comprehensive in its assessment of past abuse than is the original 19-item CTS. Specifically, in addition to assessing reasoning, verbal aggression, and physical aggression, the CTS2 has scales assessing sexual coercion and physical injury resulting from abuse.

Several items have also been added to the original scales, and several items in the original scales have been modified to enhance clarity.

It is important to note here that partners are often not reliable with one another in their reporting of partner violence on the CTS. Specifically, researchers have found that women report significantly more violence in the relationship than do their male partners (Browning & Dutton, 1990; Heyman & Schlee, 1997; Jouriles & O'Leary, 1985; Straus & Gelles, 1990). It is commonly believed that this discrepancy is often the result of underreporting by the male perpetrator (Heyman & Schlee, 1997). Therefore, although both partners' reports of violence on the CTS should be considered, a woman's report of violence on the CTS should be given primary consideration, even when it is not corroborated by the male partner's CTS reporting.

Although the CTS is widely used, researchers and clinicians have described several limitations of this instrument (e.g., Holtzworth-Munroe, Beatty, & Anglin, 1995). One such limitation is that some versions of the CTS assess only for violence that occurs during conflict and do not assess for violence that occurs outside the context of conflicts (e.g., if a male partner assaults his partner without a precipitating argument). Second, the items included in the CTS do not account for all possible aggressive acts that can occur between couples. The consequence of these limitations is that the assessor may not get a clear picture of the actual nature and frequency of violence that has occurred in the relationship. Third, the CTS does not assess for the function of past violence or the context in which it has occurred. That is, the CTS does not assess for the chain of events that led up to, occurred during, and followed the violence. An assessment of the function and context of violence can be extremely useful because it can allow the assessor to determine what environmental or relationship factors may have contributed to the occurrence of the violence and what purpose the violence may have served (Fruzzetti & Levensky, 2001).

To correct these potential limitations of the CTS, the assessor can (1) modify the instructions to the CTS to include having partners report on abuse that occurred outside the context of arguments, (2) instruct the partners to indicate on the CTS any abusive behaviors engaged in but not addressed in the instrument, and (3) follow up the CTS administration with a behavioral assessment of the violent behaviors endorsed in the instrument. With regard to this third recommendation, the assessor can conduct further assessment to determine the context, nature, and function (purpose) of the abuse, including the intent, severity, antecedents, and consequences of the abuse, if these factors are relevant to the purposes of the assessment (e.g., intervention recommendations).

Assessing the Consequences of Past Partner Violence

Once the nature, frequency, and severity (and possibly the function) of past partner violence have been determined, it is often appropriate to assess the consequences of that abuse to the victim. Of course, the same assessment limitations and recommendations just mentioned apply here as well.

Researchers have found that male-to-female partner violence is often associated with a substantial increase in psychological and physical health problems in its victims (see Holtzworth-Munroe, Smutzler, & Sandin, 1997; Holtzworth-Munroe, Smutzler, & Bates, 1997, for reviews of this literature). Before discussing these health problems and common means of assessing them, it is important to note that the vast majority of the studies on the psychological and physical health sequelae of partner violence have used a cross-sectional (as opposed to longitudinal) research design. Therefore, it can not be determined with certainty that the physical and psychological health problems found to be *associated* with partner violence are, in fact, *causally* related to this abuse. It is possible, for example, that in some cases, rather than being the direct consequence of partner violence, increased psychological and physical health problems in abused women preceded the abuse. It is also possible that both the partner violence and these correlates are linked by other factors (e.g., life stressors, other forms of marital discord, etc.). Despite the methodological limitations in many of these studies, however, it is generally accepted by researchers and clinicians that significant psychological and physical health problems are common consequences of partner violence (Holtzworth-Munroe, Smutzler, & Sandin, 1997). This assumption is supported by the finding that the severity of psychological and physical health problems in abused women is related to the severity and recency of the abuse (e.g., Astin, Lawrence, & Foy, 1993).

The following are the most commonly found psychological and physical health sequelae of partner violence as well as commonly used, and relatively easy to administer, standardized assessments that can be used to assess for these sequelae:

Post-Traumatic Stress Disorder (PTSD)

Researchers have found that many victims of partner violence suffer from PTSD. Golding (1999), for example, conducted a meta-analysis of studies examining mental health problems in women victims of partner violence, and found that across 11 studies examined, the average prevalence of Post-Traumatic Stress Disorder (PTSD) in these women was 63.8 percent. It is important to note here that although not all victims of partner violence meet criteria for PTSD, many do exhibit symptoms similar to those found in PTSD. Walker (1988) has termed this PTSD-like condition "battered woman syndrome" and has documented its debilitating features.

Commonly used, and relatively brief, instruments for assessing PTSD include: (1) the PTSD Symptom Scale-Interview (PSS-I; Foa, Riggs, Dancu, & Rothbaum, 1993), a 17-item interview assessing the presence and severity of PTSD, (2) the PTSD Symptom Scale-Self-Report (PSS-SR; Foa, Riggs, Dancu, & Rothbaum, 1993), a self-report version the PSS-I, (3) the Impact of Events

Scale (IES; Horowitz, Wilner, & Alvarez, 1979), a 15-item self-report scale measuring the PTSD dimensions of event-related intrusion and avoidance, and (4) the Trauma Symptom Checklist (TSC; Briere & Runtz, 1989), a 33-item self-report questionnaire measuring several dimensions of PTSD.

Depression

Abused women have also been found to have high rates of depression. Cascardi, O'Leary, and Schlee (1999) reviewed 14 studies of depression in women victims of partner violence and found rates of depression in these women ranging from 38 percent to 83 percent. In another study, these researchers found that approximately 50 percent of abused women exhibit depressive symptoms, and the majority have significantly lower self-esteems (Cascardi & O'Leary, 1992). In related work, Stark & Flitcraft (1988) estimate that battered women are at a five times greater risk of a suicide attempt than nonbattered women.

By far the most commonly used instrument for assessing depression is the Beck Depression Inventory, Revised (BDI-II; Beck, Steer, Ball, & Ranieri, 1996), a 21-item questionnaire-format measure of depression that has demonstrated good reliability and validity in several empirical studies. The BDI-II can also be used to assess for suicide ideation. A commonly used measure of general distress is the Symptom Checklist–90–Revised (SCL-90-R; Derogatis, Lipman, Rickels, Uhlenhuth, & Covi, 1974), a 90-item scale assessing general levels of psychological distress and psychopathology. The Brief Symptom Inventory (BSI; Derogatis & Melisaratos, 1983) is a widely used shorter version of the SCL-90.

Substance Abuse

A third common finding is that abused women have an increased risk for substance abuse problems. Gleason (1993), for example, compared rates of substance abuse in two samples of abused women (a shelter sample and a community sample) with rates of substance abuse in a normative population sample. Gleason found that 23 percent and 44 percent of the women in the abused samples, respectively, reported alcohol abuse (compared to 4% in the normative sample) and found that 10 percent and 25 percent, respectively, reported drug abuse (compared to 4% in the normative sample). In Golding's (1999) meta-analysis, she found that across 10 studies examined the average prevalence of alcohol abuse was 18.5 percent and that across four studies examined the average prevalence of drug abuse was 8.9 percent. Two commonly used questionnaire-format instruments for assessing substance abuse are the Michigan Alcohol Screening Test (MAST; Selzer, 1971) and the Drug Abuse Screening Test (DAST; Skinner, 1982).

Physical Health Problems

Researchers have also found a strong relationship between partner violence and physical health problems in its victims. One indicator of this relationship is that battered women have a significantly higher rate of medical utilization than do nonbattered women (Stark, Flitcraft, Zuckerman, Grey, Robinson, & Frazier,

1981). Another, and more direct, indicator of the impact of partner violence on victims' physical health is the finding that each year in the United States, over 1 million women seek medical care for injuries resulting from battering and that 20 percent of all women's emergency room visits are the result of battering (Stark & Flitcraft, 1982). Common injuries to victims of partner violence include acute and chronic pain, bruises, broken bones, and contusions (see Sharps & Campbell, 1999). Recently, Coben, Forjouh, and Gondolf (1999) interviewed 648 female partners of male batterers and found that 75 percent of these women reported a history of physical injury as a result of partner violence, with contusions the most frequently reported injury.

The SF-36 Health Status Survey (Ware & Sherbourne, 1992) is a widely used questionnaire-format instrument for assessing (1) limitations in physical activities because of health problems, (2) limitations in social activities because of physical or emotional problems, (3) limitations in usual role activities because of physical health problems, (4) bodily pain, (5) general mental health, (6) limitations in usual role activities because of emotional problems, (7) vitality, and (8) general health perception. The Conflict Tactics Scale–Revised (CTS2; Straus, Hamby, Boney-McCoy, & Sugarman, 1996) can also be used to assess physical injury resulting from partner violence.

PREDICTING FUTURE PARTNER VIOLENCE

Like assessing past partner violence, predicting future partner violence effectively is a difficult and often elusive task. This is because (1) there are many factors that affect the likelihood of future partner violence, (2) different individuals will often have different determining factors for future violence, (3) reliably identifying what these determining factors are for any given individual is difficult, and (4) even if these determining factors are identified for a given individual, obtaining a valid assessment of these factors for that individual is difficult.

A primary problem with currently available methods of predicting future partner violence is that there are no clear variables, instruments, or algorithms for predicting future violence that have *both* sufficient sensitivity and sufficient specificity. That is, current assessment methods do not accurately and reliably identify who *will* batter in the future (sensitivity) while also accurately and reliably identifying who *will not* batter in the future (specificity). It is important that a method of predicting future partner violence has both sensitivity and specificity because we do not want to falsely identify dangerous individuals as nondangerous and similarly we do not want to falsely identify nondangerous individuals as dangerous. Although quite different, the consequences both these types of mistakes are very serious.

A number of studies have found characteristics that statistically differentiate batterers from nonbatterers and moderately to strongly predict future violence in batterers as a *group* (for reviews of this literature, see Holtzworth-Munroe, Smutzler, & Sandin, 1997; Holtzworth-Munroe, Smutzler, & Bates, 1997;

Schumacher, Feldbau-Kohn, Slep, & Heyman, 2001). However, these characteristics have not been found to be highly accurate or reliable in predicting future violence in a given *individual*. Similarly, researchers have begun to develop and evaluate instruments that use these characteristics to predict future partner violence, and although a few of these instruments have shown promise in their ability to predict future violence in groups of batterers, they also are limited in their ability to accurately predict future violence in a given individual (see Goodman, Dutton, & Bennett, 2000, and Roehl & Guertin, 1998, for reviews of this literature). Therefore, although these characteristics indicate an increase in the probability that an individual will be violent in the future, they by no means indicate a certain outcome. Rather, these characteristics constitute *risk factors* for future violence and must be used in this manner.

Because of these limitations in currently available violence prediction methods, we must be careful in how we use these methods and must be careful not to make strong conclusions based on these methods. However, despite these limitations, the courts frequently demand that predictions of future violence be made by mental health experts testifying in court cases. Therefore, we must try to use our currently available methods of predicting future violence in the most responsible and valid ways possible.

There are a number of steps an assessor can take when attempting to predict the likelihood of future partner violence that may increase the validity and reliability of these predictions. One such step that can be taken is for the assessor to be aware of the heuristics that he or she uses in making predictions of future partner violence and to avoid making heuristic errors in these cases. Heuristics are "rules of thumb" or decision-making rules we use to help us quickly evaluate information and make decisions. Heuristic errors are errors of logic or decision making that result when a heuristic is misapplied. Two common heuristic errors that are worth noting here are (1) the *representativeness* heuristic error, which is the tendency to assume, despite compelling facts or odds to the contrary, that someone is a member of a group (e.g., actually dangerous persons) because he or she shares common elements with typical members of the group (e.g., substance abuse, low education, male gender, etc.); and (2) the *availability* heuristic error, which is the tendency to overestimate the likelihood of an event (e.g., a low-income male rebattering) because examples of this event readily come to mind (for a review of common heuristic errors and methods of avoiding them, see Nisbett & Ross, 1980).

A second step that can be taken is for the assessor to make a decision a priori about whether a false positive or a false negative would be most tolerable. As mentioned earlier, current methods of predicting future partner violence do not have both high sensitivity (i.e., the ability to accurately identify individuals who will batter in the future) and high specificity (i.e., the ability to accurately identify individuals who will not batter in the future). With the exception of extreme cases such as the chronic and severe batterer who states that he has no intention of stopping the violence, or the high-functioning first-time batterer who pushed his partner one time and who expresses a great deal of contrition and a strong commitment to being nonviolent in the future, current assessment methods are limited in their ability to predict with high accuracy whether an individual is likely to batter again. Therefore, given the relatively high possibility of error, it may be important for the assessor to decide which type of error (potentially falsely identifying someone as dangerous or falsely identifying someone as nondangerous) is more justified. Of course, this decision will often be made case by case and may be dictated by the courts. The rights of the perpetrator versus the rights of the victim, potential future victims, and the community must be balanced here.

Assessing Risk Factors of Future Battering

As mentioned, a number of characteristics have been found to be risk factors for future or repeat battering. Holtzworth-Munroe, Smutzler, and Sandin (1997); Holtzworth-Munroe, Smutzler, and Bates (1997); and Schumacher, Feldbau-Kohn, Slep, and Heyman (2001) provide excellent reviews of this literature and much of the information on characteristics of batterers presented here is taken from these sources. Additionally, several relatively easy to administer and standardized instruments have been developed to assess for these characteristics. It should be noted that the majority of studies examining factors differentiating batterers from nonbatterers used cross-sectional designs. Therefore, it cannot be concluded with certainty that the risk factors described here have a causal role in battering per se, but rather that they should be considered as factors that alert a clinician to a possible increase in the likelihood of future violence and should be used to inform hypothesis testing in these cases. Additionally, many of these characteristics are likely to be more *distal* risk factors for battering rather than *proximal* risk factors. That is, even if the characteristics are causal, or partially causal in future battering, they are likely to be neither directly causal nor highly influential in outcomes. An example would be the risk factor of low socioeconomic status (SES). It is clear that low SES does not directly cause battering, but rather contributes to overall levels of stress, which may be a more proximal cause of battering. Finally, in addition to these cautions, all of the stylistic and technical recommendations discussed in the "Assessment of Past Partner Violence" section of this chapter apply here as well. Although the assessment questions are somewhat different, the assessment issues are quite similar.

History of Battering

One of the strongest known predictors of future partner violence is past partner violence. In fact, researchers have generally found that two-thirds of batters reassaulted within one year (e.g., Straus, Gelles, & Steinmetz, 1980; Schulman, 1979). Furthermore, Straus, Gelles, and Steinmetz's (1980) national survey found that for batterers who do reassault within the next year, there is an average of approximately six battering episodes during that year. Another important finding along these lines is that the majority of battering men who leave their abused partners end up abusing partners in future relationships (Pagelow, 1981). It is also worth noting here that men's verbal (or psychological) abuse is a risk factor for battering. In a longitudinal study of battering in newlyweds, Murphy and O'Leary (1989) found that a husband's verbal abuse significantly predicted a first incident of physical abuse in the next year.

As mentioned previously, the most used and studied measure of past partner abuse is the Conflict Tactics Scale (CTS and CTS2; Straus, 1979; Straus et al., 1996). Psychological abuse can be assessed using a number of different instruments, including the Index of Spouse Abuse Scale (ISAS; Hudson & McIntosh, 1981), the Psychological Maltreatment of Women Scale (PMWI; Tolman, 1989), and the Abusive Behaviors Inventory (ABI; Shepard & Campbell, 1992).

Sociodemographic Variables

Age is inversely associated with partner violence. That is, younger men are more likely to be physically violent with their partners than are older men (Schumacher, Feldbau-Kohn, Slep, & Heyman, 2001). For example, Kantor, Jasinski, and Aldarondo (1994) studied 1,970 families and found that age decreased the odds of partner violence by a factor of .93. Additionally, low-income, under- or unemployed, and low-educated men are at a greater risk of partner violence (Hotaling & Sugarman, 1986; Holtzworth-Munroe, Smutzler, & Bates, 1997). The data on race as a risk factor for partner violence is mixed, but overall African-American and Hispanic men have been shown to be at a slightly higher risk of partner violence than Caucasian men (Schumacher, Feldbau-Kohn, Slep, & Heyman, 2001). It is important to note, however, that many of these sociodemographic risk factors most likely influence battering via general stress or other mediating factors rather than being causal themselves. Additionally, although many batterers fit these demographic characteristics, many individuals who fit these demographic criteria do not batter.

Violence in Family of Origin

Another distal risk factor for partner violence is a man being brought up in a family in which violence has occurred. This is the case for both men who witnessed family violence as children and those who were the victims of violence themselves as children. Men who experienced both are at the greatest risk of battering (Hotaling & Sugarman, 1986; Straus, 1980).

Psychopathology

Studies have consistently shown that domestically violent men have more symptoms of psychopathology than do nondomestically violent men. For example, batterers have been shown to score significantly higher on standard measures of depression than nonbatterers (Maiuro, Cahn, Vitaiano, Wagner, & Zegree, 1988). Pan, Neidig, and O'Leary (1994) found that battering men were not only significantly more depressed than nonbattering men, but that a greater severity of violence was associated with a greater severity of depression. Additionally, batterers have been found to exhibit more Axis II symptomatology, particularly antisocial and borderline personality disorder (Holtzworth-Munroe, Bates, Smutzler, & Sandin, 1997; Dutton, 1998). Widely used measures of psychopathology include the Beck Depression Inventory, Revised (BDI-II; Beck et al., 1996) and the Millon Clinical Multiaxial Inventory (MCMI; Millon, 1983).

Substance Abuse

Batterers also tend to have alcohol abuse problems. Tolman and Bennett (1990), for example, found that across 13 studies nearly 60 percent of batterers were alcohol abusers. Researchers have also found a positive correlation between alcohol abuse and partner violence in men (Stith & Farley, 1993; Schumacher, Feldbau-Kohn, Slep, & Heyman, 2001). A number of studies have also found drug use to be a risk factor for partner violence (Schumacher, Feldbau-Kohn, Slep, & Heyman, 2001). Pan and colleagues (1994), for example, found that having a drug problem increased the risk of partner violence by 121 percent in 11,870 white men enrolled in the U.S. army. The Michigan Alcohol Screening Test (MAST; Selzer, 1971) is a widely used questionnaire-format screening assessment for assessing alcohol abuse, and the Drug Abuse Screening Test (DAST; Skinner, 1982) is a similar instrument commonly used to determine drug abuse.

Anger

Battering men have been found to have more anger than nonbattering men, and anger has been shown to predict male battering in a number of studies (Saunders & Hanusa, 1986; Schumacher, Feldbau-Kohn, Slep, & Heyman, 2001). Novaco's Anger Index (Novaco, 1977) is a commonly used measure of the anger-arousing potential of various situations. Other measures of anger include the Buss-Durkee Hostility Inventory (BDHI; Buss & Durkee, 1957), the Multidimensional Anger Inventory (MAI; Siegel, 1986), and the State-Trait Anger Scale (Spielberger, Gorsuch, & Lushene, 1970).

Stress

Stress is not consistently related to battering, but some research has indicated that "external stress" (e.g., problems at work) is related to men's battering (Barling & Rosenbaum, 1986; Straus, 1980). In the area of stress in particular, however, it is difficult to determine cause and effect.

Social Skills Deficits

Battering men have been found to have difficulty being assertive in relationships as compared to nonviolent men, particularly in the area of making requests (Maiuro, Cahn, & Vitaliano 1986). Batterers have also been found to have "spouse-specific" assertiveness skill deficits as compared to nonbattering men (Rosenbaum & O'Leary, 1981), as well as fewer relationship communication skills (Cordova et al., 1993) and relationship problem-solving skills deficits (Dutton & Browning, 1988).

Beliefs

Battering men have been found to have a more positive attitude toward violence than nonbattering men (Kantor et al., 1994). Additionally, battering men are more likely to attribute negative intentions to their partners' behavior than nonbattering men (Holtzworth-Munroe & Hutchinson, 1993).

The obvious questions when confronted with this list is: Which of these characteristics are most important to consider in predicting future violence? To help answer this question, Saunders (1995) reviewed the literature on risk factors for future partner violence and categorized risk factors as either "Prominent," "Probable," or "Possible" based on the amount of empirical support for them as predictive variables. Based on this review, Saunders concluded that "Prominent" risk factors for future battering include (not necessarily in this order):

1. The male has grown up in a family that experienced battering (especially if the man both witnessed and experienced the violence).
2. The male has low education and income (especially if the female partner has more education and income than the male).
3. The male has alcohol abuse problems (especially chronic abuse).
4. The male is violent both inside and outside the home (i.e., generalized aggression).

In the "Probable" risk factors category, Saunders included:

1. The male has communication and assertiveness skills deficits (especially if the male feels a need for power in the relationship).
2. The male meets criteria for a personality disorder (especially antisocial or borderline personality disorders).
3. The male has a history of childhood physical abuse.
4. The male experiences high amounts of anger (particularly in relationship-specific situations).

Finally, in the "Possible" risk factors category, Saunders included:

1. The male is experiencing high levels of stress (especially an "external" stressor, e.g., stressful employment circumstances, etc.).
2. The male is experiencing elevated levels of depression (however, this may be a proxy variable for low self-esteem).
3. The male exhibits antisocial traits (particularly extensive criminal history and lack of remorse for prior battering).

Saunders (1995) noted that the majority of the studies from which these risk factors were derived examined batterers who were in treatment at the time of the studies and therefore may not have been representative of most batterers. Saunders (1995) also noted that the risk factors for the most severe forms of violence (e.g., beatings, hitting with objects, and the use of weapons) are generalized aggression, alcohol abuse problems, and violence in the male's family of origin. Although these statistically derived risk factors for battering are not highly accurate in predicting future violence, they likely provide more accurate predictions of battering than clinical-intuition based judgments of battering risk (Dawes, Faust, & Meehl, 1989). It is important to note, however, that Saunders' system of grouping these risk factors has not been evaluated in terms of its ability to increase the validity of predictions of future partner violence.

Recently, Schumacher, Feldbau-Kohn, Slep, and Heyman (2001) conducted an extensive review of the available research on risk factors for male-to-female partner violence and came to conclusions about important risk factors that are quite similar to the conclusions of Saunders (1995). These researchers examined the effect sizes of identified risk factors in the literature and found that risk factors that showed moderate to strong effects sizes overall included SES, education, history of childhood sexual abuse, history of childhood physical and/or verbal abuse, witnessing adult violence as a child, anger, psychopathology (particularly personality disorders and depression), drug and/or alcohol abuse, deficits in spouse-specific assertiveness, and attitudes that condone partner abuse.

A number of instruments have been developed to help mental health and legal professionals assess for the dangerousness of batterers (i.e., determine the likelihood of future violence; see Roehl & Guertin, 1998, for a review of these instruments). These instruments generally use some combination of the risk factors described here. Although little research has been conducted to date evaluating these instruments' abilities to predict future violence in batterers (they have been primarily evaluated retrospectively), there is some empirical support for the utility of the Danger Assessment Scale (DAS; Campbell, 1986, 1995) in predicting future violence. The DAS is one of the most commonly used risk assessment measures. It is composed of 15 items that have been drawn from research of risk factors for homicide and serious injury. The instrument is brief, easy to use and score, and elicits the information from the victim. The items ask about past physical abuse, psychological abuse, and threats, as well as availability of weapons and the use of alcohol and other drugs. Goodman, Dutton, and Bennett (2000) conducted a pilot study of the DAS's ability to predict the reoccurrence of battering in the next three months. These researchers found that the DAS was a fairly strong predictor of repeat battering and that the instrument was a stronger predictor of repeat violence than was a measure of past violence (the CTS) alone. Specifically, a logistic regression showed that for every one standard deviation increase in the DAS score, the likelihood of reabuse increased by 4.18 times (as compared to a likelihood increase of 2.77 times for every one standard deviation in the CTS). Although promising, it should be noted that research on the DAS (as well as other reoffending risk assessment instruments) is in its early stages and that further research is needed to verify this and other measures' validity in predicting future battering.

In another recent study, Hilton, Harris, and Rice (2001) evaluated the validity of the Violence Risk Appraisal Guide (VRAG) in predicting violent recidivism among 88 batterers with a history of partner abuse. The VRAG is a 12-item actuarial assessment tool that measures demographic, childhood history, criminal history, and psychological variables found to be related to recidivism. The VRAG has been shown to be psychometrically sound in several studies (e.g., Quinsey et al., 1998). Hilton, Harris, and Rice's (2001) prospective study followed the batterers for an average of 7 years and found that the VRAG had fairly strong predictive validity ($r = .42$), and that the VRAG had significantly better predictive power than a measure of psychopathology alone.

Using a different approach, Weisz, Tolman, and Saunders (2000) examined the utility of victim estimates of the likelihood for future violence versus the utility of statistical methods using established risk factors for future violence in predicting reoffending in batterers during a four-month follow-up period. These authors found that both methods were useful in predicting future violence in batters and found that when victim predictions of future violence were added to the risk factor model (utilizing both sources of data), the predictive ability of model was significantly improved. This study suggests that victim report of the likelihood of future violence should be considered seriously when assessing future dangerousness in batterers. However, victims are not always accurate in their predictions, and risk factors can alert clinicians to high-risk batterers even when victims are confident that future violence is unlikely (Weisz, Tolman, & Saunders, 2000).

In summary, research conducted to date on risk factors for future battering and on measurement tools used to predict dangerousness can aid the assessor in making predictions about future violence in partner violence cases. However, current methods of predicting future violence in these cases do not allow for high levels of specificity or sensitivity at level of individuals. Therefore, clinicians must use these risk factors and measurement tools with caution and make conclusions within the limitations of these methods.

INTERVENTIONS IN PARTNER VIOLENCE CASES

Most legal jurisdictions have three primary goals in partner violence cases: (1) stopping the violence, (2) enhancing victim safety, and (3) holding the abuser accountable. To meet these goals, the courts commonly use several different methods of intervention. Perpetrators of partner violence are often either ordered to serve jail time or ordered to attend a batterers' treatment programs (or both), and victims of partner violence are often provided with Protection Orders (POs), given referrals for domestic violence shelters, given referrals for group or individual counseling, or provided with some combination of all three. This section will describe these intervention options for the perpetrators and victims of partner violence and will discuss what is currently known about the efficacy of these interventions in reducing recidivism.

Interventions for Perpetrators of Partner Violence

Arrest of Perpetrators

Mandatory jail time for the perpetrator is a common intervention in partner violence cases. The effect of jail time on recidivism in batterers has been most thoroughly studied with batterers who have been arrested by police responding to partner violence calls. Although a number of these studies have been conducted, they do not paint a clear picture as to whether arrest serves to deter further battering. For example, Sherman and Berk (1984) evaluated the relative effectiveness of three different police responses to partner violence. Approximately 300 misdemeanor spousal assault cases were randomly assigned to be responded to by police with either (1) arresting the batterer, (2) mediation and advice, or (3) physical separation of the couple. Based on subsequent arrest records and interviews with the victims, the arrest response had about half the rate of recidivism compared to the no-arrest conditions over the next six months (10% vs. 20%). Shortly after these results were published, a mandatory arrest policy was adopted by 84 percent of the nation's large municipalities (Hirschel & Hutchinson, 1992; Holtzworth-Munroe et al., 1995).

In response to the encouraging results of this study, the U.S. National Institution of Justice sponsored a series of replications on the effect of arrest on recidivism in six different cities (Berk, Black, Lilly, & Rikoski, 1991; Dunford, Huizinga, & Elliot, 1990; Hirschel, Huchinson, Dean, Kelley, & Pesackis, 1990; Pate & Hamilton, 1992; Sherman et al., 1991). Unlike the original study, the conclusion from these studies was that arrest did not have a deterrent effect on recidivism overall. However, in subsequent analyses, arrest was found to be an effective deterrent of reabuse in men who were married or employed, presumably because they had a stake in social conformity. For unmarried and unemployed batterers, arrest was associated with a significant increase in subsequent assaults (Sherman, Smith, Schmidt, & Rogan, 1992; Berk, Campbell, Klap, & Western, 1992; Pate & Hamilton, 1992). Thus, mandatory arrest may be a useful deterrent only for batterers with a stake in conformity.

Psychosocial Treatments for Perpetrators

Batterer treatment programs are another commonly used intervention in partner violence cases. These programs typically treat male batterers using a group format with one male and one female co-therapist, and with the groups meeting weekly for $1\frac{1}{2}$ to 2 hours for periods ranging from 8 to 36 weeks. Most batterer treatment programs use cognitive-behavioral interventions, with a curriculum that includes core instruction in anger management and violence cessation skills (e.g., anger recognition, time out, self-talk, and relaxation). The curriculum also often includes feminist-based interventions, including sex-role education, resocialization, and discussions of patriarchal male power issues, as well as training in skills to improve relationship functioning, such as communication and conflict resolution skills, social skills, and assertion skills (Holtzworth-Munroe, Beatty, & Anglin, 1995).

Although the courts frequently mandate perpetrators of partner violence to these types of batterers' treatment programs, and despite the fact that a great deal of resources have gone into the development and implementation of these programs, there is not strong evidence that batterers' treatment programs are generally effective in significantly reducing rates of recidivism. One reason for this lack of support is that the vast majority of research studies evaluating the effectiveness of batterer treatment programs have been plagued with methodological problems that have prevented researchers from unambiguously interpreting and generalizing from their results (Hamberger & Hastings, 1993). Rosenbaum (1988) and Holtzworth-Munroe et al. (1995) note several such methodological problems, including that many batterers' treatment outcome studies (1) used small sample sizes (thereby limiting the experimental power of the studies), (2) did not use random assignment to control or comparison groups, (3) had high dropout rates (with completers differing substantially from noncompleters on important variables), (4) used short follow-up periods (e.g., less than six months, which is a problem with such a low base rate behavior), and (5) used widely varying operational definitions of outcome variables as well as variety of sources of outcome data, including batterer self-report, victim report, and police reports (which has made making between-study comparisons difficult).

A second reason that there is not strong support for the effectiveness of batterer treatment programs is that the outcome studies, to the extent that they can be interpreted, have not shown these programs to produce a significant reduction in rates of recidivism. In fact, reviews of the literature on batterer's treatment outcomes have generally found recidivism rates of approximately 30 to 40 percent in the six months to one year following treatment (e.g., Eisikovits & Edleson, 1989; Tolman & Bennett, 1990; Gondolf, 1991; Rosenfeld, 1992). For example, Rosenfeld (1992) reviewed 25 treatment outcome studies for court-ordered batterers and found that across the studies the average recidivism rate (i.e., at least one act of violence by the follow-up assessment) was 27 percent. Although Rosenfeld recognized the methodological problems in the studies that had been conducted to date and acknowledged the resulting limitations in this body of literature, he believed that some conclusions could be made. Specifically, Rosenfeld concluded that individuals who complete batterers' treatment have only slightly lower rates of recidivism than batterers who do not undergo treatment (e.g., not ordered to treatment, refuse treatment) or who drop out of treatment early. Additionally, Rosenfeld found that batterers who were arrested and not referred to treatment had no greater rates of recidivism than did batterers who were arrested and underwent batterer treatment. Rosenfeld also noted that these studies have shown only "modest gains" in reducing psychological abuse. It should be noted that the studies included in this review had rather short follow-up periods (i.e., less than 6 months) and that recidivism rates would surely be higher with longer follow-ups.

Batterer treatment outcome studies that have been conducted since those reviewed by Rosenfeld (1992) have, as a whole, improved somewhat methodologically as compared to their predecessors but have not demonstrated outcomes that are any more promising in terms of effectiveness in reducing recidivism rates. For example, Gondolf (1997), evaluating outcomes for 840 batterers who received treatment at four "well established" cognitive-behavioral batterer treatment programs, found that 39 percent reassaulted at least once during a 15-month follow-up, 70 percent engaged in verbal abuse, and 43 percent engaged in threats of violence during that time. It is likely that batterer treatment outcomes vary among treatment types, but it is not yet clear which type of batterer treatments are most effective, nor is it clear what type of treatment is most effective for particular types of batterers.

Batterer treatment programs also experience high dropout rates. In fact, Gondolf and Foster (1991) estimate that the dropout rate between initial contact with batterer treatment programs and program completion is greater than 90 percent. Researchers have also found that approximately 50 percent of batterers who actually begin treatment programs for partner violence drop out before program completion (see Hamberger & Hastings, 1989, and Pirog-Good & Stets, 1986, for reviews of this literature). In a recent evaluation of batterer treatment dropout, Babcock and Steiner (1999) examined 339 male batterers who had been court ordered to cognitive-behavioral group treatment. These authors found that only 31 percent the batterers actually completed the court-ordered treatment.

One possible reason for the apparent limited effectiveness of current batterer treatment programs is that these programs treat all batterers in the same manner, when in fact there may be several subtypes of batterers that require different types of treatments. This concern has been discussed by a number of partner violence researchers (e.g., Holtzworth-Munroe & Stuart, 1994). A body of research is beginning to emerge suggesting that there are different types of batterers who would benefit from different types of interventions. However, this research is too early in its development to be the basis for treatment recommendations. The batterer typology research has not yet produced treatment matching methods that would be useful in the forensic setting. Specifically, there are not currently appropriate assessment instruments, nor are there separate treatment packages for different typologies established at this time. Additionally, there is not a consensus in the field on the appropriate groupings of subtypes of batterers.

In addition to the concern that existing batterer treatment programs may not be effective in significantly reducing recidivism rates, there is reason to believe that in some cases these programs may actually be harmful to victims of partner violence. Gondolf (1988) found that the strongest predictor of whether or not a battered wife will return to her husband after leaving a shelter is whether or not the husband has undergone batterer treatment. Given the lack of strong evidence for the efficacy of batterers' treatment programs, these programs may inadvertently increase battering victims' risk of being reassaulted by giving the victims a false sense of security when their batterers have sought treatment (Holtzworth-Munroe, Beatty, & Anglin, 1995).

Based on these batter intervention data, it is not clear that the current treatments are effective in significantly reducing recidivism rates. Additionally, arrest seems be an effective deterrent of battering for only married and employed men. What is clear is that further development of batterers' treatments is warranted, as are methodologically sound evaluations of new and existing interventions.

Interventions for Victims of Partner Violence

Despite the fact that psychosocial and legal interventions are frequently used to aid victims of partner violence, there has been little research on the effectiveness of these interventions. Additionally, as is the case with batterer interventions, the research that has been conducted suffers from methodological problems that make interpretation of the data difficult. However, the following is a description of the current state of the literature on the effectiveness of these interventions.

Domestic Violence Shelters for Victims

A common intervention for victims of partner violence who are in danger of being reassaulted is a referral to a domestic violence shelter. Domestic violence shelters are typically run and staffed by women and are often in locations unknown to perpetrators. The services offered at these shelters typically include (1) a safe place to stay with or without children, (2) support groups for women victims of partner violence, (3) individual therapy and case management by shelter staff, (4) legal advising and referral, (5) referral and advocacy for additional services in the community, (6) assistance in negotiating through social services, and (7) safety plan development.

To date, only a few studies have been conducted examining the effectiveness of domestic violence shelters. One of the primary outcome variables examined in these studies has been whether or not the victim returns to her abuser after leaving the shelter. Studies examining this variable have found that 25–50 percent of women victims of partner violence return to their abuser after leaving a domestic violence shelter (Gondolf, 1988; Strube, 1988).

The one study that could be found that evaluated the effects of shelters on reassault rates had mixed results (Berk, Newton, & Berk, 1986). These authors followed 155 victims of partner violence who stayed at a domestic violence shelter and found that, overall, there was a small and nonsignificant reduction in battering for these women during a six-week follow-up. However, these authors also found that the women who sought help in addition to the shelter (e.g., from the prosecutor's office) experienced a significant reduction in violence during the six-week follow-up and that women who did not seek additional help had a slight increase in violence during this time.

Protection Orders (POs) for Victims

Another common intervention for victims of partner violence who are in danger of being reassaulted is the issuing of a Protection Order (PO; also commonly referred to as a "restraining order"). The primary function of a PO is to protect victims of partner violence by prohibiting the perpetrator from communicating with the victim or coming near the victim or her household (see Keilitz, 1994, for a description of the process of obtaining a PO). Only a few studies on the effects of POs in deterring reassault have been conducted, and the results of these studies have been mixed. Overall, these studies have found that between 24 and 60 percent of women who filed for POs were reassaulted in the next four months to two years (see Carlson, Harris, & Holden, 1999, for a review of this literature). Although at least one study found no difference in reassault rates between women with a PO and those without one, it is still not clear to what extent POs actually deter recidivism (Carlson, Harris, & Holden, 1999).

Psychosocial Treatments for Victims

Group therapy programs for women victims of partner violence are also widespread. These groups are often held at battered women's shelters and are free of change. The primary function of these groups is often to provide social, emotional, and practical support to women who are currently in, or who have recently left, an abusive relationship. Another goal of these groups is to assist women in leaving and achieving independence from their battering partners. These groups often supply women with assistance in obtaining social services or employment and in functioning within the legal system. Although little research has been conducted evaluating the outcomes of these groups, there is some evidence that they can have positive outcomes in terms of both psychological functioning and a reduction in future partner violence (for a review of this literature, see Abel, 2000).

Safety Plan Development for Victims and Perpetrators

Regardless of what interventions are used for the perpetrator and the victim, a safety plan should always be made with the victim for avoiding future violence. This safety plan should include several elements. First, the assessor should determine whether the victim is in imminent risk of harm. As discussed in the "Predicting Future Partner Violence" section of this chapter, this can be a difficult task. At the very least, however, the assessor should determine if the perpetrator (1) has made specific threats to harm the victim, (2) has indicated a specific plan to harm the victim, and (3) has the means to carry out this plan. Second, if there is immediate danger, steps should be taken to remove the victim from the danger (e.g., having her go to a shelter, having the batterer go to jail, etc.). Third, even if there is not immediate danger for the victim, the assessor should determine if there are any weapons in the home and, if there are, have them removed. Fourth, the victim should be told about (1) available community resources, (2) local domestic violence shelters, (3) possible legal actions (e.g., POs, prosecution of the batterer, etc.), and (4) how to get out of the house safely and where to go once she has left (see Eigenberg, 2001, for a thorough discussion of safety plan development for victims of partner violence).

It is also important to assess the victim's level of homicidal ideation toward the perpetrator given that, although rare, some victims kill their perpetrators (Campbell, 1995; Browne, 1987). This assessment should include identifying any homicidal thoughts the victim may have towards the perpetrator, as well as determining if the victim has a specific plan (or fantasy), or available means for committing homicide. The extent to which the victim believes that she has no alternatives to killing her perpetrator should also be assessed (Holtzworth-Munroe et al., 1995).

CONCLUSION

The purpose of this chapter is to provide psychologists and other professionals working in forensic settings with recommendations and empirically based information to guide their work in partner violence cases. Specifically, this chapter discussed (1) the assessment of past partner violence and its consequences, (2) the prediction of future violence, and (3) intervention options for both the victims and the perpetrators of partner violence.

An important task in many forensic partner abuse cases is to identify and describe the frequency, severity, and consequences of past partner abuse. However, obtaining accurate and complete information in these areas is quite difficult due to problems of under-reporting of violence and the complexity of identifying and determining the cause of psychological sequelae of violence. A number of steps can be taken to reduce reporting biases on the parts of the victim and perpetrator. Past violence and its consequences are most effectively assessed in a direct and behaviorally specific manner. Several methods and instruments are discussed to aid the clinician in conducting and interpreting these assessments.

Clinicians working in forensic settings are also frequently asked to predict the likelihood, frequency, and severity of future violence. A number of risk factors for partner violence have been identified, and several instruments have been developed to assess for these factors. However, current methods of predicting violent behavior do not provide high levels of sensitivity and specificity, and these methods must, therefore, be used judiciously. Specifically, the use of strong conclusions, overgeneralizations, and heuristic errors are discussed and cautioned against.

Several intervention options for perpetrators and victims of partner violence are widely used. The effectiveness of these interventions in preventing future violence is not clear because few methodologically sound evaluations of them have been conducted, and results have been conflicting. However, the data that are available, to the extent that they can be interpreted, do not provide strong support for the general effectiveness of these interventions in significantly reducing rates of recidivism. An extremely important task in working with partner abuse cases is assessing victims' immediate safety and taking steps to ensure it.

REFERENCES

Abel, E. M. (2000). Psychosocial treatments for battered women: A review of empirical research. *Research on Social Work Practice*, *10* (1), 55–77.

Astin, M. C., Lawrence, K. J., & Foy, D. W. (1993). Post-traumatic stress disorder among battered women: Risk and resiliency factors. *Violence & Victims*, *8* (1), 17–28.

Babcock, J. C., & Steiner, R. (1999). The relationship between treatment, incarceration, and recidivism of battering: A program evaluation of Seattle's coordinated community response to domestic violence. *Journal of Family Psychology*, *13* (1), 46–59.

Babcock, J. C., Waltz, J., Jacobson, N. S., & Gottman, J. M. (1993). Power and violence: The relation between communication patterns, power discrepancies, and domestic violence. *Journal of Consulting & Clinical Psychology*, *61* (1), 40–50.

Barling, J., & Rosenbaum, A. (1986). Work stressors and wife abuse. *Journal of Applied Psychology*, *71* (2), 346–348.

Beck, A. T., Steer, R. A., Ball, R., & Ranieri, W. F. (1996). Comparison of Beck Depression Inventories-IA and -II in psychiatric outpatients. *Journal of Personality Assessment*, *67* (3), 588–597.

Berk, R., Black, H., Lilly, J., & Rikoski, G. (1991). *Colorado Springs spouse assault replication project: Final report.* Unpublished manuscript, Colorado Springs Police Department, Colorado Springs, CO.

Berk, R., Campbell, A., Klap, R., & Western, B. (1992). The deterrent effect of arrest in incidents of domestic violence: A Bayesian analysis of four field experiments. *American Sociological Review*, *57*, 698–708.

Berk, R. A., Newton, P. J., & Berk, S. F. (1986). What a difference a day makes: An empirical study of the impact of shelters for battered women. *Journal of Marriage and the Family*, *48* (3), 481–490.

Briere, J., & Runtz, M. (1989). The Trauma Symptom Checklist (TSC-33): Early data on a new scale. *Journal of Interpersonal Violence*, *4* (2), 151–163.

Browne, A. (1987). *When battered women kill.* New York: Free Press.

Browning, J., & Dutton, D. (1986). Assessment of wife assault with the Conflict Tactics Scale: Using couple data to quantify the differential reporting effect. *Journal of Marriage and the Family*, *48* (2), 375–379.

Buss, A. H., & Durkee, A. (1957). An inventory for assessing different kinds of hostility. *Journal of Clinical and Consulting Psychology*, *21*, 343–349.

Campbell, J. C. (1986). Assessment of risk of homicide for battered women. *Advances in Nursing Science*, *8* (4), 36–51.

Campbell, J. C. (1995). Prediction of homicide of and by battered women. In J. C. Campbell (Ed.), *Assessing dangerousness: Violence by sexual offenders, batterers, and child abusers* (pp. 96–113). Thousand Oaks, CA: Sage.

Cantos, A. L., Neidig, P. H., & O'Leary, K. D. (1994). Injuries of women and men in a treatment program for domestic violence. *Journal of Family Violence*, *9* (2), 113–124.

Carlson, M. J., Harris, S. D., & Holden, G. W. (1999). Protective orders and domestic violence: Risk factors for re-abuse. *Journal of Family Violence, 14* (2), 205–226.

Cascardi, M., Langhin-Richsen, J., & Vivian, D. (1992). Marital aggression: Impact, injury, and health correlates for husbands and wives. *Archives of Internal Medicine, 152*, 1178–1184.

Cascardi, M., & O'Leary, K. D. (1992). Depressive symptomatology, self-esteem, and self-blame in battered women. *Journal of Family Violence, 7* (4), 249–259.

Cascardi, M., O'Leary, K. D., & Schlee, K. A. (1999). Co-occurrence and correlates of post-traumatic stress disorder and major depression in physically abused women. *Journal of Family Violence, 14* (3), 227–249.

Coben, J. H., Forjuoh, S. N., & Gondolf, E. W. (1999). Injuries and health care use in women with partners in batterer intervention programs. *Journal of Family Violence, 14* (1), 83–94.

Cordova, J. V., Jacobson, N. S., Gottman, J. M., Rushe, R., et al. (1993). Negative reciprocity and communication in couples with a violent husband. *Journal of Abnormal Psychology, 102* (4), 559–564.

Dawes, M. D., Faust, D., & Meehl, P. E. (1989). Clinical versus actuarial judgment. *Science, 243*, 1668–1674.

Derogatis, L. R., & Melisaratos, N. (1983). The Brief Symptom Inventory: An introductory report. *Psychological Medicine, 13* (3), 595–605.

Derogatis, L. R., Lipman, R. S., Rickels, K., Uhlenhuth, E. H., & Covi, L. (1974). The Hopkins Symptom Checklist (HSCL): A self-report symptom inventory. *Behavioral Science, 19* (1), 1–15.

Dunford, F. W., Huizinga, D., & Elliot, D. (1990). The role of arrest in domestic assault: The Omaha police experiment. *Criminology, 28* (2), 183–206.

Dutton, D. G. (1998). *The abusive personality.* New York: Guilford Press.

Dutton, D. G., & Browning, J. J. (1988). Power struggles and intimacy anxieties as causative factors of wife assault. In G. W. Russell (Ed.), *Violence in intimate relationships* (pp. 163–175). Costa Mesa, CA: PMA.

Eigenberg, H. M. (2001). *Women battering in the United States.* Prospect Heights, IL: Waveland Press.

Eisikovits, J. L., & Edleson, J. L. (1989). Intervening with men who batter: A critical review of the literature. *Social Service Review, 63*, 384–414.

Feld, S. L., & Straus M. A. (1989). Escalation and desistance of wife assault in marriage. *Criminology, 27*, 141–159.

Foa, E. B., Riggs, D. S., Dancu, C. V., & Rothbaum, B. O. (1993). Reliability and validity of a brief instrument for assessing post-traumatic stress disorder. *Journal of Traumatic Stress, 6* (4), 459–473.

Fruzzetti, A. E., & Levensky, E. R. (2001). Dialectical behavior therapy for domestic violence: Rationale and procedures. *Cognitive and Behavioral Practice, 7*, 435–447.

Giles-Sims, J. (1983). *Wife battering: A systems theory approach.* New York: Guilford Press.

Gleason, W. J. (1993). Mental disorders in battered women: An empirical study. *Violence and Victims, 8* (1), 53–68.

Golding, J. M. (1999). Intimate partner violence as a risk factor for mental disorders: A meta-analysis. *Journal of Family Violence, 14* (2), 99–132.

Gondolf, E. W. (1988). The effect of batterer counseling in shelter outcome. *Journal of Interpersonal Violence, 3*, 275–289.

Gondolf, E. W. (1991). A victim-based assessment of court-mandated counseling for batterers. *Criminal Justice Review, 16,* 214–226.

Gondolf, E. W. (1997). Patterns of reassault in batterer programs. *Violence and Victims, 12* (4), 373–387.

Gondolf, E. W., & Foster, R. A. (1991). Pre-program attrition in batterers' programs. *Journal of Family Violence, 6,* 337–349.

Goodman, L. A., Dutton, M. A., & Bennett, L. (2000). Predicting repeat abuse among arrested batterers: Use of the Danger Assessment Scale in the criminal justice system. *Journal of Interpersonal Violence, 15* (1), 63–74.

Hamberger, L. K., & Hastings, J. E. (1989). Counseling male spouse abusers: Characteristics of treatment completers and dropouts. *Violence and Victims, 4,* 275–286.

Hamberger, L. K., & Hastings, J. E. (1993). Court mandated treatment of men who assault their partner: Issues, controversies, and outcomes. In N. Z. Hilton (Ed.), *Legal responses to wife assault* (pp. 188–229). Newbury Park, CA: Sage.

Hamberger, L. K., & Lohr, J. M. (1994). The intended function of domestic violence is different for arrested male and female perpetrators. *Family Violence and Sexual Assault Bulletin, 10* (34), 40–44.

Hart, B. (1996). Battered women and the criminal justice system. In E. Buzawa and C. Buzawa (Eds.), *Do arrests and restraining orders work?* (pp. 98–114). Thousand Oaks, CA: Sage.

Heckert, D. A., & Gondolf, E. W. (2000). Assessing assault self-reports by batterer program participants and their partners. *Journal of Family Violence, 15* (2), 181–197.

Heyman, R. E., & Schlee, K. A. (1997). Toward a better estimate of the prevalence of partner abuse: Adjusting rates based on the sensitivity of the Conflict Tactics Scale. *Journal of Family Psychology, 11* (3), 332–338.

Hilton, N. Z., Harris, G. T., & Rice, M. E. (2001). Predicting violent recidivism by serious wife assaulters. *Journal of Interpersonal Violence, 16,* 408–423.

Hirschel, J. D., & Hutchinson, I. W. (1992). Female spouse abuse and the police response: The Charlotte, North Carolina experiment. *Journal of Criminal Law and Criminology, 83,* 73–119.

Hirschel, J., Hutchinson, I., Dean, C., Kelley, J., & Pesakis, C. (1990). *Charlotte spouse assault replication project: Final report.* Washington, DC: National Institute of Justice.

Holtzworth-Munroe, A., Bates, L., Smutzler, N., & Sandin, E. (1997). A brief review of the research on husband violence. Part I: Maritally violent versus nonviolent men. *Aggression and Violent Behavior, 2* (1), 65–91.

Holtzworth-Munroe, A., Beatty, S. B., & Anglin, K. (1995). The assessment and treatment of marital violence: An introduction for marital therapists. In N. S. Jacobson & A. S. Gurman (Eds.), *Clinical handbook of marital therapy* (pp. 317–339). New York: Guilford Press.

Holtzworth-Munroe, A., & Hutchinson, G. (1993). Attributing negative intent to wife behavior: The attributions of maritally violent versus nonviolent men. *Journal of Abnormal Psychology, 102* (2), 206–211.

Holtzworth-Munroe, A., Smutzler, N., & Bates, L. (1997). A brief review of the research on husband violence. Part III: Sociodemographic factors, relationship factors, and differing consequences of husband and wife violence. *Aggression and Violent Behavior, 2* (3), 285–307.

Holtzworth-Munroe, A., Smutzler, N., & Sandin, E. (1997). A brief review of the research on husband violence. Part II: The psychological effects of husband violence on battered women and their children. *Aggression and Violent Behavior, 2* (2), 179–213.

Holtzworth-Munroe, A., & Stuart, G. L. (1994). Typologies of male batterers: three subtypes and the differences among them. *Psychological Bulletin, 116*, 476–497.

Horowitz, M. J., Wilner, N., & Alvarez, W. (1979). Impact of Events Scale: A measure of subjective distress. *Psychosomatic Medicine, 41*, 209–218.

Hotaling, G. T., & Sugarman, D. B. (1986). An analysis of risk markers in husband to wife violence: The current state of knowledge. *Violence and Victims, 1*, 101–124.

Hudson, W. W., & McIntosh, S. R. (1981). The assessment of spouse abuse: Two quantifiable dimensions. *Journal of Marriage and the Family, 43* (4), 873–885.

Jouriles, E. N., & O'Leary, K. D. (1985). Interspousal reliability of reports of marital violence. *Journal of Consulting & Clinical Psychology, 53* (3), 419–421.

Kantor, G. K., Jasinski, J. L., & Aldarondo, E. (1994). Sociocultural status and incidence of marital violence in Hispanic families. *Violence & Victims. Special Issue: Violence against women of color, 9* (3), 207–222.

Keilitz, S. L. (1994). Civil protection orders: A viable justice system tool for deterring domestic violence. *Violence & Victims, 9* (1), 79–84.

Maiuro, R. D., Cahn, T. S., Vitaiano, P. P. (1986). Assertiveness deficits and hostility in domestically violent men. *Violence & Victims, 1* (4), 279–289.

Maiuro, R. D., Cahn, T. S., Vitaiano, P. P., Wagner, B. C., & Zegree, J. B. (1988). Anger, hostility, and depression in domestically violent versus generally assaultive men and nonviolent control subjects. *Journal of Consulting & Clinical Psychology, 56* (1), 17–23.

Millon, T. (1983). *Millon Clinical Multiaxial Inventory, Manual*. Minneapolis, MN: Interpretive Scoring Systems.

Murphy, C. M., & O'Leary, K. D. (1989). Psychological aggression predicts physical aggression in early marriage. *Journal of Consulting & Clinical Psychology, 57* (5), 579–582.

National Association for Court Management. *The courts' response to domestic violence*. Williamsburg, VA: Author.

Nisbett, R., & Ross, L. (1980). *Human inference: Strategies and shortcomings of social judgment*. Englewood Cliffs, NJ: Prentice-Hall.

Novaco, R. W. (1977). Stress inoculation: A cognitive therapy for anger and its application to a case of depression. *Journal of Consulting and Clinical Psychology, 45* (4), 600–608.

O'Leary, K. D. (2001). Psychological abuse: A variable deserving critical attention in domestic violence. In K. D. O'Leary & R. D. Maiuro (Eds.), *Psychological abuse in violent domestic relations* (pp. 3–28). New York: Springer.

O'Leary, K. D., Barling, J., Arias, I., Rosenbaum, A., Malone, J., & Tyree, A. (1989). Prevalence and stability of physical aggression between spouses: A longitudinal analysis. *Journal of Consulting and Clinical Psychology, 57*, 263–268.

O'Leary, K. D., Vivian, D., & Malone, J. (1992). Assessment of physical aggression against women in marriage: The need for multimodal assessment. *Behavioral Assessment, 14*, 5–14.

Pagelow, M. D. (1981). *Women-battering: victims and their experiences.* Newbury Park, CA: Sage.

Pan, H. S., Neidig, P. H., & O'Leary, K. D. (1994). Predicting mild and severe husband-to-wife physical aggression. *Journal of Consulting & Clinical Psychology, 62* (5), 975–981.

Pate, A., & Hamilton, E. (1992). Formal and informal deterrents to domestic violence: The Dade County spouse assault project. *American Sociological Review, 57,* 691–697.

Pirog-Good, M. A., & Stets, J. (1986). Programs for abusers: Who drops out and what can be done. *Response, 9,* 17–19.

Quinsey, V. L., Harris, G. T., Rice, M. E., & Cormier, C. A. (1998). *Violent offenders: Appraising and managing risk.* Washington, DC: American Psychological Association.

Rebovich, D. J. (1996). Prosecution response to domestic violence: Results of a survey of large jurisdictions. In E. S. Buzawa, & C. G. Buzawa (Eds.), *Do arrests and restraining orders work?* (pp. 176–191). Thousand Oaks, CA: Sage.

Roehl, J., & Guertin, K. (1998). *Current use of dangerousness assessments in sentencing domestic violence offenders: Final report.* Pacific Grove, CA: State Justice Institute.

Rosenbaum, B. D. (1988). Methodological issues in marital violence research. *Journal of Family Violence, 3,* 91–104.

Rosenbaum, A., & O'Leary, K. D. (1981). Marital violence: Characteristics of abusive couples. *Journal of Consulting & Clinical Psychology, 49* (1), 63–71.

Rosenfeld, B. D. (1992). Court-ordered treatment of spouse abuse. *Clinical Psychology Review, 12,* 205–226.

Saunders, D. G. (1986). When battered women use violence: Husband-abuse or self defense? *Violence and Victims, 1,* 47–60.

Saunders, D. G. (1995). Prediction of wife assault. In J. C. Campbell (Ed.), *Assessing dangerousness: Violence by sexual offenders, batterers, and child abusers* (pp. 68–95). Thousand Oaks, CA: Sage.

Saunders, D. G., & Hanusa, D. (1986). Cognitive-behavioral treatment for men who batterer: The short-term effects of group therapy. *Journal of Family Violence, 7,* 357–372.

Schulman, M. (1979). *A survey of spousal violence against women in Kentucky.* Washington, DC: U.S. Department of Justice, Law Enforcement.

Schumacher, J. A., Feldbau-Kohn, S., Slep, A. M., & Heyman, R. E. (2001). Risk factors for male-to-female partner physical abuse. *Aggression & Violent Behavior. Special Issue: Risk factors for family violence, 6* (2–3), 281–352.

Selzer, M. L. (1971). The Michigan Alcoholism Screening Test: The quest for a new diagnostic instrument. *American Journal of Psychiatry, 127* (12), 1653–1658.

Sharps, P. W., & Campbell, J. (1999). Health consequences for victims of violence in intimate relationships. In X. B. Arriaga, & S. Oskamp (Eds.), *Violence in intimate relationships* (pp. 163–180). Thousand Oaks, CA: Sage.

Shepard, M. F., & Campbell, J. A. (1992). The Abusive Behavior Inventory: A measure of psychological and physical abuse. *Journal of Interpersonal Violence, 7* (3), 291–305.

Sherman, L. W., & Berk, R. (1984). The specific deterrent effects of arrest for domestic assault. *American Sociological Review, 49,* 261–272.

Sherman, L. W., Schmidt, J. D., & Rogan, D. P. (1992). *Policing domestic violence: Experiments and dilemmas.* New York: Free Press.

Sherman, L. W., Schmidt, J. D., Rogan, D. P., Gartin, P. R., Cohn, E. G., Collins, D. J., & Bacich, A. R. (1991). From initial deterrence to long-term escalation: Short term custody for poverty ghetto violence. *Criminology, 29,* 821–849.

Sherman, L. W., Smith, D., Schmidt, J. D., & Rogan, D. P. (1992). Crime, punishment, and stake in conformity: Legal and informal control of domestic violence. *American Sociological Review, 57,* 680–690.

Siegel, J. M. (1986). The Multidimensional Anger Inventory. *Journal of Personality & Social Psychology, 51* (1), 191–200.

Skinner, K. A. (1982). The Drug Abuse Screening Test. *Addictive Behaviors, 7* (4), 363–371.

Spielberger, C. D., Gorsuch, R. L., & Lushene, R. E. (1970). *Manual for the State-Trait Anxiety Inventory.* Palo Alto, CA: Consulting Psychologist Press.

Stark, E., & Flitcraft, A. (1982). Medical therapy as repression: The case of the battered women. *Health and Medicine, 1* (3), 29–32.

Stark, E., & Flitcraft, A. (1988). Violence among intimates: An epidemiological review. In V. B. Van Hasselt, R. L. Morrison, A. S. Bellack, & M. Hersen (Eds.), *Handbook of family violence.* New York: Plenum Press.

Stark, E., Flitcraft, A., Zuckerman, D., Gray, A., Robinson, J., & Frazier, W. (1981). *Wife abuse in the medical setting: An introduction for health personnel.* Monograph No. 7. Washington, DC: Office of Domestic Violence.

Stets, J., & Straus, M. A. (1990). Gender differences in reporting marital violence and its medical and psychological consequences. In M. A. Straus & R. Gelles (Eds.), *Physical violence in American families.* New Brunswick, NJ: Transaction Books.

Stith, S. M., & Farley, S. C. (1993). A predictive model of male spousal violence. *Journal of Family Violence, 8* (2), 183–201.

Straus, M. A. (1979). Measuring intrafamily conflict and violence: The Conflict Tactics (CT) Scales. *Journal of Marriage and Family, 41,* 75–88.

Straus, M. A. (1980). Victims and aggressors in marital violence. *American Behavioral Scientist, 23,* 681–704.

Straus, M. A., & Gelles, R. J. (1990). How violent are American families? Estimates from the national family violence survey and other studies. In M. A. Straus & R. J. Gelles (Eds.), *Physical violence in American families: Risk factors and adaptations to violence in 8,145 families* (pp. 95–112). New Brunswick, NJ: Transaction Books.

Straus, M. A., Gelles, R. J., & Steinmetz, S. K. (1980). *Behind closed doors: Violence in the American family.* Garden City, NY: Anchor Press/Doubleday.

Straus, M. A., Hamby, S. L., Boney-McCoy, S., & Sugarman, D. B. (1996). The revised Conflict Tactics Scale (CTS2): Development and preliminary data. *Journal of Family Issues, 17,* 283–316.

Strube, M. J. (1988). The decision to leave an abusive relationship: Empirical evidence and theoretical issues. *Psychological Bulletin, 104* (2), 236–250.

Tolman, R. M. (1989). The development of a measure of psychological maltreatment of women by their male partners. *Violence & Victims, 4* (3), 159–177.

Tolman, R. M., & Bennett, L. W. (1990). A review of quantitative research on men who batter. *Journal of Interpersonal Violence, 5* (1), 87–118.

Walker, L. E. (1988). The battered woman syndrome. In G. T. Hotaling & D. Finkelhor (Eds.), *Family abuse and its consequences: New directions in research* (pp. 139–148). Thousand Oaks, CA: Sage.

Ware, J. E., & Sherbourne, C. D. (1992). The MOS 36-item short-form health survey (SF-36): Conceptual framework and item selection. *Medical Care, 30* (6), 473–483.

Weisz, A. N., Tolman, R. M., & Saunders, D. G. (2000). Assessing the risk of severe domestic violence: The importance of survivors' predictions. *Journal of Interpersonal Violence, 15* (1), 75–90.

CHAPTER 30

ELDER ABUSE: GUIDELINES FOR TREATMENT

DEBORAH HENDERSON AND DUANE VARBLE
UNIVERSITY OF NEVADA, RENO

JEFFREY A. BUCHANAN
MINNEAPOLIS VA MEDICAL CENTER

Since the mid-1970s, elder abuse has received recognition as a significant health problem in the United States and in other countries. Elder mistreatment was originally referred to in the medical literature as "granny battering" by G. R. Burston (1975) in the *British Medical Journal* and then by R. N. Butler (1975) as the "battered old person syndrome." Since the early 1970s, the United States began passing legislation on elder abuse; there are now elder abuse laws in every state that are designed to identify and allow for intervention in elder abuse cases.

The incidence of elder abuse is unclear because of wide variability in definitions from state to state on what constitutes elder abuse and barriers to identification such as social isolation of the victim(s) and a reluctance among professionals to report abuse. It is estimated, however, that between 4 and 10 percent of the elderly population (i.e., persons aged 65 years and above) has been or is currently being abused (Ansello, 1996). Given this estimate, it is important that we as clinicians become skilled at providing treatment for elder abuse victims and those responsible for the abuse, since it is quite likely that we will encounter this problem at some point in our professional lives.

Although there is no generally accepted definition of elder abuse, most definitions include the following categories of mistreatment: physical abuse, psychological or verbal abuse, financial abuse or exploitation, and neglect. In general, it can be stated that *physical abuse* of an elderly person includes such acts as striking, pushing, pinching, biting, or restraining a person with enough force to cause unnecessary pain or injury, or sexual abuse such as forced sexual contact or forcing the elderly person to look at sexual material or to engage in any sexualized behavior. *Psychological or verbal abuse* includes such acts as threatening or intimidating the elderly person, humiliating him or her, enforced isolation, name calling, or any behavior that results in fear or mental distress for the elderly person. *Financial abuse or exploitation* includes such acts as misusing the elderly person's money or taking control of possessions or property without permission or rights to do so, financial scams, or denying the elderly person access to his or her own money or property. *Neglect* of an elderly person includes such acts as refusing medical assistance, food, or required medications; failure to provide adequate care such as bathing; intentionally failing to meet the social or emotional needs of the elderly person; improper financial management; and (in the case of self-neglect) failing to perform adequate daily care activities such as bathing or eating (Penhale, 1993; Wolf, 1996).

The lack of a general consensus regarding what constitutes elder abuse is problematic in a number of different ways. For example, it creates confusion in discriminating between "normal" family conflict and abuse; there are difficulties in comparing findings across research studies regarding the possible causes and consequences of abuse; and it is difficult to determine what an effective course of treatment for the abused person and/or the perpetrator should include. Although it is beyond the scope of this chapter to resolve these difficulties, we will attempt to summarize what we do know about this problem and to make informed recommendations on the assessment and treatment of elder abuse victims and their perpetrators. These recommendations should be considered critically, however, since they are drawn from a literature that is at times contradictory and certainly incomplete.

THEORETICAL EXPLANATIONS FOR ELDER ABUSE

Theoretical models are important for several reasons. At a minimum, they allow us to focus our efforts in attempts to identify causal variables. Identifying these causal pathways is important because it allows us to generate strategies for intervention or prevention (Haynes, 1992). A sound theoretical model, however, will do more than this; it will make predictions that can be tested empirically. Unfortunately, theory building has encountered many obstacles in the field of elder abuse research. Among these obstacles are the differing definitions of elder abuse, the inability to randomly assign research subjects (i.e., elder victims and abusers) to groups for testing, findings that are incomparable across studies because of different criteria for what constitutes abuse and different outcome measures, and the covert nature of elder abuse. For these and other reasons (e.g., the likelihood that abuse arises from multiple causal pathways), the causes and effects of elder abuse have not been adequately studied. Nevertheless, from a review of the literature it is clear that a handful of theories predominate. These will briefly be reviewed here.

Transgenerational Violence

The theory of transgenerational violence holds that abuse is a learned behavior and that victims of child abuse are themselves more likely to become abusers than are individuals who were not child abuse victims (Kosberg, 1988; Janz, 1990). This has been called the *cycle of violence*. According to this theory, perpetrators have learned that behaving in an aggressive manner is an effective and/or acceptable way to respond to frustrating situations. Although some data supports this theory for spousal abuse (Hotaling & Sugarman, 1990) and child abuse (Straus, Gelles, & Steinmetz, 1980), as yet no convincing data support the extension of the transgenerational violence theory to elder abuse (Biggs, Kingston, & Phillipson, 1995).

Social Exchange Theory

Social exchange theory assumes that social interactions involve the exchange of rewards and punishments (Finkelhor, 1983; Phillips, 1989). According to this theory, rewards are achieved by receiving resources (e.g., money, support), services, or positive feedback, whereas punishments include the receipt of negative feedback or the withdrawal or loss of resources. This theory suggests that when relationships are unbalanced in the exchange of rewards and punishments (i.e., when one person delivers more rewards than he or she receives in return), an imbalance of power occurs that leads to abusive behavior. Interestingly, the social exchange theory predicts that abuse will occur regardless of the direction in which the imbalance occurs; that is, either the elderly victim or the caregiver may be in the "powerless" position. This theory has received support from the descriptive literature, which clearly shows that dependency of the abuser on the victim is a risk factor for elder abuse (Wolf, Strugnell, & Godkin, 1982).

Excessive Demands

The *excessive demands* or *"exhausted caregiver" theory* proposes that the stress of providing care to an elderly person increases the risk that the caregiver will behave in an abusive manner (Curry & Stone, 1995). Although some critics claim that this theory relieves the perpetrator of accountability (Pillemer & Finkelhor, 1989; Tomita, 1990), others claim that excess stress is in fact experienced by caregivers of elderly persons and therefore prevention efforts should be focused on relieving this stress for the benefit of the elderly victim (Eastman, 1984; Grafstrom, Nordberg, & Winblad, 1992). This theory has become quite popular among mental health practitioners and the public, possibly because it lends itself so easily to intervention strategies. Not coincidentally, many services (e.g., Meals on Wheels, home care services, etc.) supported by various governmental funding agencies are directed at decreasing the burden of caring for an elderly person.

External Stress

The *external stress theory* suggests that individuals who are experiencing excess stress not directly related to caregiving may be more likely to abuse an elderly care recipient than individuals who are not experiencing these external pressures (Block & Sinnot, 1979; Hudson, 1986). External stressors that may contribute to the probability of engaging in abusive behavior for these caregivers include job stress, marital stress, financial pressures, and so forth. Like the excessive demand theory, the external stress theory appears to shift accountability away from the perpetrator. However, it also suggests some interesting intervention strategies—job training, marital counseling, and stress management training, to name a few. Given that elder abuse is likely caused by a multitude of factors, a theory that suggests such novel intervention approaches may be well worth investigating further.

Ageism

Ageism refers to attitudes toward the elderly that are characterized by a lack of valuing. Such prejudicial attitudes, it has been suggested, may lead to abusive behavior because the needs or rights of the elderly are seen as less important than the needs or rights of other people, particularly the caregiver (Fulmer, 1989). In Western culture, in particular, elderly people tend to be regarded with less respect than their younger counterparts—perhaps because they are no longer viewed as "carrying their own weight" in a culture that is built around individual achievement. Caretaking of an elderly relative in this climate may be viewed more with resentment than with affection, thus making abuse a more likely occurrence.

RISK FACTORS ASSOCIATED WITH ELDER ABUSE

Because of the necessarily correlational nature of studies on elder abuse, risk factors (rather than "causal factors") for elder abuse are the focus of a great deal of attention. Risk factors are those characteristics of the victim, the perpetrator, or the environment that, when present, increase the probability that elder abuse will occur. The number of risk factors that have been associated with elder abuse is large, but most risk factors assume that there is some type of caregiving arrangement in place. We will identify some of the most common risk factors for elder abuse here. For a more comprehensive review, please see Johnson (1991) and Kosberg (1988).

Risk Factors for the Victim

Gender

Until fairly recently, it was accepted that most victims of elder abuse were women (Wolf, Strugnell, & Godkin, 1982; O'Malley, 1987). One of the explanations given for this gender factor was that there is a proportionately larger number of elderly women than there are elderly men, and therefore it is more likely that an abused elderly person will be female. Another possible explanation is that women tend to be physically weaker and more passive, thus leaving them more vulnerable to physical mistreatment. However, Tatara (1993) has reported more recently that there in fact are more male than female victims, stating that it is possible males are being "paid back" for previous abuses that they themselves inflicted, or that they are more likely to make inappropriate choices (e.g., gambling or drinking) that affect their ability to interact effectively with their caregivers. Although it is unclear whether men or women are more likely to be abused, it is clear that both men and women are abused and that both should be considered as potential victims of elder abuse.

Age

As elderly people age, the probability that they will be abused increases (Whittaker, 1993). Age is associated with more health problems and therefore greater impairment, which may make the elderly person more reliant upon and therefore more vulnerable to the abuser (who may be experiencing excessive stress). It has been clearly documented that the risk of abuse increases with physical or mental impairment (Block & Sinnot, 1979). This is especially the case when we consider individuals with a diagnosis of dementia, who tend to exhibit aggressive behaviors during caregiving tasks with some frequency (O'Malley, Everitt, O'Malley, & Campion, 1983). Caregivers may not understand this behavior as being a consequence of a medical condition and instead personalize the behavior, viewing it as uncooperativeness or retaliatory in nature (Garcia & Kosberg, 1993; Kosberg & Cairl, 1986). Alternatively, some caregivers state that even though they do understand that the elderly person's behavior is caused by an impairment and is not intentional, they still justify their own abusive behavior as resulting from anger toward the elderly person's behavior (Garcia & Kosberg, 1993).

Substance Abuse

Elderly people who abuse substances are at greater risk for being abused than those who do not (Kosberg, 1988). This may be because the elderly substance abuser is more likely to live in a situation that is less stable (e.g., financially, emotionally) than nonabusers, or perhaps because he or she may be less aware that the caregiving being received is inadequate or harmful. Other possibilities include provocative behavior by the elderly individual; very often, individuals addicted to drugs or alcohol behave in erratic, insensitive, or otherwise ineffective ways. It is possible that such behavior, directed toward a caregiver, may function to increase the probability of abusive behavior along with other relevant factors.

Psychological Problems

Psychological or emotional factors in victims that have been identified as risk factors for abuse include depression, anxiety, a tendency to blame oneself for problems, a tendency to excuse the behavior of family members, and apathy.

Individuals possessing these characteristics may be likely to deny abuse, take the blame for abuse, fail to take action to protect themselves from abuse, or isolate themselves from others—which is itself is a risk factor for abuse. That is, elderly people who are isolated from social contact are in a position that limits the possibility that an abusive situation will be identified as such by individuals outside the system (Grafstrom, Nordberg, & Winblad, 1992).

Risk Factors for the Perpetrator

Perpetrators of elder abuse are typically below 60 years of age and are living with or close to the elderly victim in a caregiving role (Quinn & Tomita, 1986). Abusers tend more often to be female than male, since caregiving tends to fall to the daughters of elderly persons rather than the sons.

Psychological Problems

Although psychopathology has been identified as a risk factor associated with elder abuse, it has not been shown that any particular diagnosis makes a person more likely to engage in abusive behavior (Tomita, 1990). However, it has been suggested (Kosberg, 1988) that when psychological problems are present, caregivers may have more difficulty interacting effectively with their elderly care recipients; that is, they may have difficulty controlling anger or frustration and take these feelings out on the elderly victim. It is also possible that caregivers suffering from psychological problems may have unrealistic expectations about the elderly person's abilities and/or the caregiving situation.

Substance Abuse

Like psychological problems, substance abuse has been documented as a risk factor that interferes with the ability to regulate one's behavior toward an elderly care recipient. Indeed, substance abuse is one of the better documented risk factors (Fulmer, 1989; Godkin, Wolf, & Pillemer, 1989; O'Malley, Segel, & Perez, 1979; Pillemer & Wolf, 1989). The increased risk associated with substance abuse may be caused by the cost of maintaining an alcohol or drug habit; that is, this cost may be an additional stressor. In addition, servicing this habit may take priority over providing for the needs of the elderly victim. Certainly, alcohol or drug use may impair judgment and lessen inhibitions, and this may result in increased incidences of abuse, intentional or not.

Inadequate Caregiving Skills

Caregivers tend most often to be family members of the elderly care recipient. As such, they tend to lack formal training in caregiving skills, an issue that can be particularly problematic when the care recipient is suffering from either physical or mental impairment and/or exhibits problem behavior, such as aggressiveness (common in dementia patients). Lacking these skills, caregivers may misinterpret the elderly person's behavior as being retaliatory or as an act of stubbornness and become angry or frustrated. These caregivers are unlikely to know the most effective way to gain control over the care recipient's behavior and may resort to aggressive means of gaining this control.

Stress

Caregivers who are experiencing excess stress, either from external sources or from the caregiving itself, are at greater risk for engaging in abusive behavior than those who are able to manage their stress effectively (Brody, 1985; Hudson, 1986). Unfortunately, those family members placed in the role of caregiver for an elderly relative often experience this caregiving task as an additional burden to an already stressful life; occupational stress, parenting, marital issues, health problems, and financial pressures are some of the other stressors that caregivers may be experiencing. Also, the more dependent the care recipient is in terms of physical, emotional, and/or financial needs, the more stressful the caregiving role becomes (Ansello, King, & Taler, 1986). One stressor that should not be ignored is the possibility that caregivers may themselves be elderly and suffering from dementia or a cognitive impairment. Giordano and Giordano (1983), Steinmetz (1983), and Ryden (1988) have documented that aggressive behavior on the parts of both the caregiver and the care recipient is associated with cognitive impairment.

Dependence

Dependence of the caregiver on the care recipient, typically financial, has been associated with an increased probability of physical and psychological abuse (Pillemer, 1985; Wolf & Pillemer, 1989). It has been generally assumed that it is the dependency of the victim, not the abuser, that determines the vulnerability of the older person to abuse. However, it appears that this is more often true in cases of neglect, where caregiving is seen as an unwanted obligation. When caregivers depend upon the elderly care recipient for financial or emotional support, they tend to report more feelings of anger, impotence, and frustration (Curry & Stone, 1995). These feelings may lead to an increased probability of abuse.

Contextual Risk Factors

Certain environments contribute more to the probability of elder abuse than others. Although these environmental, or contextual, factors do not exist separately from risk factors associated with the victim and the abuser, it is worthwhile to note them in order to aid in identifying which situations are more likely to lead to (or maintain) elder abuse. Caregiving environments that are more likely to lead to an abusive relationship are those that include financial difficulties, a history of family violence or family conflict, a scarcity of social support, and overcrowded living arrangements.

Financial Difficulties

Caregiving very often involves an increase in financial burden; caring for an elderly person who may require expensive medications or who has other special needs (such as constant supervision) can place pressure on an already strained situation. This is especially true when the caregiver has children in the household and/or a low-paying job. In this situation, both the caregiver and the care recipient (as well as other members of the household) may become frustrated, anxious, depressed, and/or resentful. To make matters worse, caregiving for an elderly person is a task that typically becomes more demanding over time, both financially and in terms of other resources. Therefore, feelings of hopelessness may arise as caregivers and care recipients alike see no end in sight. Such feelings on the part of either or both persons may result in provocative and/or abusive behavior.

Family Conflict

Family conflict, current or past, appears to lead to an increased probability of violence toward the elderly. In families where there is a history of harsh discipline or child abuse, adult children may carry over their childhood experiences into the caregiving situation. That is, they may "correct" the elderly care recipient aggressively or "pay back" the elderly person by treating him or her in a harsh manner. It is also the case that family conflicts that exist between children and their parents do not disappear simply because one (or both) of them are now elderly (Blenkner, 1965). Old conflicts (e.g., power struggles, personality differences) are likely to show up in the caregiving relationship, albeit with the positions of power often reversed. Family members who have not learned to communicate effectively with one another are likely to continue to communicate ineffectively, perhaps violently.

Inadequate Social Support

The support of family, friends, and others (e.g., a community service agency) can be of great importance in decreasing the burden of caregiving and the stress of coping with a multitude of pressures (Pillemer, 1986). This is true whether the support is directed toward the caregiver, the care recipient, or both. When caregivers have no one to turn to, they experience a decrease in the frequency with which they engage in pleasant activities; an increase in the stress associated with caregiving; a decrease in control over how their time is structured; a decrease in privacy; an increase in financial burden; and an increase in depression, anger, and related symptoms. A care recipient who is isolated from social support will typically experience more depression, more health problems leading to an increased demand on the caregiver (Gottlieb, 1991), and a lesser probability that abuse will be identified.

Overcrowded Living Arrangements

Overcrowded living arrangements are associated with conflict in many settings (Kosberg, 1988; Pillemer, 1985). In the caregiving setting, this often translates into tension and hostility on the part of the caregiver, some of which is likely to be directed toward the elderly person. When caregivers experience a lack of privacy and a sense of "invasion," they are more likely to blame the elderly person for this inconvenience verbally and possibly to punish them for it physically. The elderly victim in this situation may experience a great deal of stress and anxiety; often, elderly persons are reluctant to move in with their relatives for this reason or because they, too, experience the close living quarters as invasive.

Barriers to Identifying Elder Abuse

Although the information we have regarding risk factors for elder abuse may be helpful in identifying potentially abusive situations, it is also the case that there are many barriers to identifying elder abuse and subsequently reporting this abuse to the appropriate agency. Among these barriers are a reluctance among family members to seek outside assistance when it is needed; a reluctance among observers to intrude in family matters; ageist attitudes that assume fewer rights for the elderly; shame on the part of either the victim or the perpetrator; fear of reprisal or other negative consequences; feelings of self-blame; uncertainty about what ought to be regarded as abusive; lack of training on the part of professionals such as physicians in accurately identifying signs and symptoms of abuse; lack of familiarity with state reporting laws for elder abuse; an unwillingness to go against a patient's wishes by reporting abuse; and being unconvinced that reporting elder abuse will result in positive consequences for the victim.

It is important to be familiar with both the risk factors for elder abuse and the barriers to identifying elder abuse not only because they can alert us to potentially abusive situations (i.e., serve as a basis for screening), but also because they can help us to select appropriate assessment and treatment strategies. In the following section we will present some guidelines for the appropriate treatment of elder abuse victims and their abusive caregivers that take these risk factors into consideration.

Guidelines for the Treatment of Elder Abuse

In deciding what is "good practice" for the treatment of elder abuse, it is instructive to first consider what the goals of good practice ought to be. We propose that good practice with regard to elder abuse has as its goal the prevention and/or suspension of abuse in the most effective, least intrusive, and least time-consuming manner possible. In addition, good practice ought to take into consideration the financial cost of delivering treatment. Although many mental health professionals feel uncomfortable taking cost of treatment delivery into consideration in developing a treatment plan, the fact of the matter is that cost is almost always a constraint when a client enters into treatment: either from the standpoint of the client, the insurance carrier, and/or the treatment provider.

In this section, we will discuss strategies for screening, assessment, and intervention for elder abuse that we think are consistent with the goals of good practice as outlined here. We will also discuss special issues related to providing treatment in these cases. Although some of the strategies we will be discussing may appropriately and effectively be utilized by physicians or other health-care professionals, we will be focusing specifically on the role of the mental health professional throughout this section. In addition, we will be extending our guidelines to include the perpetrator of abuse as well as the victim. We will be doing this for essentially two reasons.

First, it is often not the case that there is only one victim in cases of elder abuse. Consider the situation where an elderly alcoholic man is cared for by his son. If the elderly man is verbally abusive (e.g., yells at, demeans, makes humiliating comments) toward his son and one day the son pushes the elderly man to the ground in anger, it is clear that elder abuse has occurred. However, it is also the case that the son has been the victim of verbal/psychological abuse by the father. Treatment here would focus not only on the psychological consequences of abuse for both parties but also on relationship issues and problem-solving skills of both parties in order to decrease the probability that abuse will continue to occur.

Second, even if it is clear that there is one perpetrator and one victim, it is not enough to simply treat the psychological consequences of abuse that the victim may display, particularly when the victim and perpetrator will continue to be in a caregiver/care recipient relationship. If the goal is to prevent abuse from occurring in the future, it is imperative that the possible causes of abuse, which may include substance abuse or excessive stress on the part of the caregiver, be addressed. Otherwise, it is quite possible that we could be in the position of being emotionally supportive of abuse victims while continually sending them back to an abusive situation. Such a strategy, which unfortunately is a popular form of treatment, is not consistent with good practice. Reasons for using this strategy (i.e., of excluding the perpetrator from treatment) include not wanting to "reward" the perpetrator with attention or services, not wanting to excuse the perpetrator from his or her behavior by giving the message that "it's not your fault, you have a problem," and the belief that punishment will be effective in ending abuse (Holmer & Gilleard, 1990). Though it is certainly understandable that some clinicians might prefer not to work with perpetrators of abuse, it is also the case that by excluding them from treatment we potentially lose the opportunity to effectively address factors that may be maintaining abusive behavior.

Guidelines for Screening

The purpose of screening is to determine whether an elderly person may be at risk for abuse. Pillemer and Finkelhor (1988) suggest that elder abuse occurs with enough frequency to justify regular screening by health-care professionals; in other words, physicians and others (including mental health professionals) ought to include in their regular assessment or intake procedure questions that are designed to determine whether an elderly person may be in an abusive situation. The screening procedure should take no more than two or three minutes and can be conducted by a physician, a nurse or other medical staff, a mental health worker, or (in cases where time limitations are severe) by paper-and-pencil self-report along with other forms the patient or client may be asked to complete.

Screening Potential Victims

There are several abuse screens available for use with elderly persons. Some examples of these include Hwalek and Sengstock's (1986) Elder Abuse Screening Test, Reis and Nahmiash's (1998) Indicators of Abuse screen, Tomita's (1982) protocol for the detection of elder abuse, and the American Medical Association's (1992) Diagnostic and Treatment Guidelines on Elder Abuse and Neglect. There are other screening instruments available that vary in length and ease of administration. It may also be acceptable to implement a screening procedure that is designed for the particular setting in which it will be used. The important thing to remember is that the screening instrument or procedure selected must be practical (i.e., brief and easy to administer) or it will not be utilized. It must also cover, to the greatest degree possible, all areas of abuse that may occur. In selecting or designing an elder abuse screening instrument, recall that the purpose of screening is simply to identify the presence of a potentially abusive condition so that the need for further assessment may be determined.

In Table 30.1, we have presented one example of an elder abuse screen. Here we list ten screening questions that may be asked in a yes-or-no format. Using this format, any yes responses should be explored in greater detail by someone trained to interview abuse victims (it should be noted that although a yes response to the first question in the screen may or may not indicate the presence of abuse, it may indicate psychological distress that warrants referral to a mental health professional).

In addition to employing screening instruments, it is often useful to note the quality of interactions between the elderly person and the caregiver, if he or she is present. For example, does the caregiver include the elderly person in conversations with others, touch him or her in an affectionate manner, include him or

TABLE 30.1
A Sample Elder Abuse Screen

1. Are you sad, or frightened of anyone?
2. Has anyone threatened you?
3. Has someone forced you to do something, or tried to force you to do something, that you did not want to do?
4. Does anyone in your family or anyone caring for you have a drinking or drug problem?
5. Has anyone hurt you, physically or emotionally?
6. Has anyone stolen from you, or used your possessions without your consent?
7. Has anyone taken advantage of you?
8. Has anyone refused to provide you with the care that you need?
9. Have you had any recent injuries?
10. Has anyone asked you to sign papers that you did not fully understand, or did not want to sign?

her in decision making, speak to him or her in a sharp or demeaning manner, or say threatening things? Does the elderly person appear withdrawn from the caregiver, display anxiety in the presence of the caregiver, talk comfortably with the caregiver, or ask the caregiver for assistance (Sengstock & Steiner, 1996)?

Interviewing Considerations. There are several issues to consider in screening for abuse with an elderly person. Some of these issues were referred to earlier in our discussion of barriers to identifying abuse and include feelings of shame, fear, self-blame, and uncertainty on the part of the elderly victim of abuse. In addition, elderly persons who are not victims of abuse may experience resentment or be offended by the suggestion that they might be victims. To minimize such reactions to an abuse screen, the person administering the screen should take care to introduce the reason for the screen and be sensitive to reactions that the elderly person may have.

In administering the screen, the treatment provider should inform the elderly person of the reason for the screen, normalize the process as much as possible, and inform the elderly person of confidentiality limits that may be present. One example of how these instructions may be given is presented below.

> Mr. Jones, I am Dr. Allison. I would like to ask you some questions that I ask every client who is age sixty or above. These questions are designed to see if you are experiencing any problems with other people that might be considered abusive or neglectful, or if you are having other kinds of problems. I ask these questions of everyone over sixty because it is very common for older adults to have problems with family members or other people and we would like to do something to help you if you are having some of these problems too. It is important that you know the limits of my legal ability to maintain your confidentiality when we talk about these things. Because I am a mandated reporter for elder abuse, if you tell me anything that causes me to believe that you are a victim of elder abuse, I must report this to an appropriate agency, such as the Division for Aging Services. In this state, elder abuse is defined as . . . [insert the legal definition for abuse in your state]. You are free to refuse to answer any of these questions, but I hope that you will answer them so that I can provide you with the help you need if in fact you do need help.

Privacy is crucial when screening for elder abuse, especially from the caregiver of the elderly person who may have accompanied him or her to the clinician's office. The person conducting the abuse screen should be careful not to make any blaming statements about either the victim or the perpetrator of abuse and should take care not to display shock or repugnance if a report of abuse is made. Patience is very important when interviewing an elderly person, and the interviewer should allow plenty of time for the elderly person to answer questions.

Caregiver Screening

As stated previously, the abuser of an elderly person is also most likely to be the caregiver of that person. Given this, it is recommended that individuals who are in a caregiving role with an elderly person be screened for abusive behaviors that he or she may display toward the care recipient. Caregivers should also be screened for risk factors that contribute to the probability of abuse, such as caregiver stress. Measures that may be used to screen caregivers include the Caregiver Abuse Screen (Reis & Nahmiash, 1995), the Screen for Caregiver Burden (Vitaliano, Russo, Young, & Becker, 1991), and the Caregiver Activity Survey (Davis et al., 1997).

Interviewing Considerations. As with elderly persons, there are issues to consider when screening a caregiver for potentially abusive behaviors. Caregivers are typically under a great deal of stress and may interpret the screen as insulting, invasive, humiliating, or invalidating of their attempts to provide care for an elderly person. In talking with caregivers, it is important to convey an understanding of the difficulties and frustrations of caregiving as well as a desire to help them in dealing with the stress they may be experiencing. Limits to confidentiality must be specified for the caregiver prior to administration of a screening instrument. Again, privacy for conducting this screen is important, as is avoiding placing blame for behaviors that may be abusive in nature. Though displaying empathy toward a potential abuser may be challenging for the clinician, it is important to keep in mind that in order to prevent future abuse the abuser must first be willing to discuss problematic issues and then to engage in treatment to address these issues; alienating the perpetrator is not likely to lead to this result.

Positive Screens for Abuse

When a screen for elder abuse is positive, more in-depth assessment should be conducted to determine the extent and circumstances surrounding the abuse. Depending upon the particular situation, this assessment may begin immediately (if time allows or if the severity of abuse is of sufficient concern) or another appointment may be made. Reports of elder abuse to the appropriate reporting agency should be made immediately, and the victim should be informed of—and included in, if possible—the process. Never send a victim home to a dangerous situation; if the abuse is severe or frequent enough to give the clinician reason to believe that it will occur again before an adult protective services (APS) worker intervenes, then the victim must be informed of this concern and encouraged to stay in the clinician's office or another location until an APS worker arrives or until other arrangements can be made.

Guidelines for Assessment

The purpose of assessment is to inform treatment. That is, by the end of the assessment process the clinician should have targets selected for treatment as well as ways to measure change for each of these targets. There is not one generally accepted protocol or guideline for assessment of elder abuse; the American Medical Association's Diagnostic and Treatment Guidelines on Elder Abuse and

Neglect (1992) is one example of a protocol that is available, and there are others that vary in length and in the way questions are presented. Whether you use one of the structured interviews or conduct an unstructured interview, a thorough assessment of the following domains should be conducted for both the elderly victim of abuse and the abuser:

A. Characteristics of the Abuse

This includes the type of abuse (e.g., physical, psychological, exploitation, etc.) as well as the level of intent if possible. Level of intent refers to whether the abuse is the result of an intention to do harm or the result of misguided intentions (such as when an elderly person is denied social interaction against his or her wishes because the caregiver believes social interaction to be distressing to the victim) or entirely unintentional (such as financial mismanagement resulting from a failure to understand the elderly person's wishes). In addition, the clinician should determine who the abuser is, if there is more than one abuser, and when and under what circumstances abuse occurs. It is also important to determine the immediate consequences of abuse (e.g., the discontinuation of an argument) and, relatedly, the function that the abuse serves. For example, the abuse could function to assert the caregiver's authority, to end aggressive behavior from the victim, to gain compliance, and so forth.

B. Living Environment

This refers to where, and with whom, the victim and caregiver live. Other information to gather includes the degree of privacy available in this environment, who is in charge of household tasks, the cleanliness and appropriateness of the environment, sleeping arrangements, and so forth.

C. Family Relationship History

The clinician should assess for current and past family conflicts, including spousal and child abuse history. In addition, it should be determined which family members, if any, the victim and caregiver consider themselves close to or estranged from.

D. Resources

Anything that has the potential to make life easier for the victim or caregiver and that they currently have access to should be considered a resource. Examples of resources include money, friendships, individual strengths, other people that can be counted on for help, flexible work hours, and so forth.

E. Needs

Anything that the victim or caregiver needs help with is considered a need. Examples of needs include financial aid, transportation, medical care, legal aid, child care, help with household tasks, a supportive social network, and so forth.

F. Substance Use

The clinician should determine the amount, type, and frequency of alcohol and drug use by both the victim and the abuser, as well as when substance use occurs (e.g., when under stress, constantly throughout the day). It should also be determined whether this substance use is problematic to the functioning of the client or caregiver.

G. Caregiving Skills

The caregiver's knowledge of the care recipient's physical and psychological needs should be assessed as well as his or her knowledge and ability to meet these needs. The caregiver should be asked which tasks are the most difficult or frustrating as well as which behaviors on the part of the care recipient are the most difficult to manage.

H. Activities of Daily Living

This refers to functional status, or the degree to which the victim or caregiver is able to perform activities of daily living, such as bathing, dressing, and shopping without assistance. The Activities of Daily Living (Katz, Downs, Cash, & Grotz, 1970) and Instrumental Activities of Daily Living (Lawton & Brody, 1969) measures are useful ways to assess these areas.

I. Problem-Solving Skills

Problem-solving skills refer to the techniques that individuals use to overcome difficulties. D'Zurilla (1986) states that problem solving consists of five steps: orienting to the problem, defining the problem and generating goals, generating solutions, decision making, and solution implementation. To assess each of these skills, it can be useful to ask the victim and caregiver to talk through how they solve disagreements or difficulties at home, including asking them to define one of the problems and to generate alternative solutions to the problem.

J. Depression

Depression is very common among both victims of abuse and caregivers. There are several brief self-report instruments that can be used to assess the severity of depression the client is experiencing. These include the Beck Depression Inventory (Beck, Steer, & Garbin, 1988), the Geriatric Depression Scale (Yesavage et al., 1983), and the Center for Epidemiologic Studies Depression Scale (Radloff, 1977). Assessment should include the length of time the individual has been experiencing feelings of depression, suicidal ideation, and past attempts to alleviate the depressive symptoms.

K. Stress

Like depression, stress is very common among both victims and caregivers. Useful self-report measures of stress include the State-Trait Anxiety Scale (Speilberger, Gorsuch, & Luchene, 1978), the Strain Questionnaire (Lefebvre & Sandford,

1985), and the Perceived Stress Scale (Cohen, Kamarck, & Mermelstein, 1983). In addition to assessing the degree of stressed experienced, clinicians should assess coping strategies that the individual employs. Lazarus and Folkman's (1984) Ways of Coping Checklist may be useful for this purpose.

L. Post-Traumatic Stress Disorder

PTSD is common among victims of elder abuse and less so among abusers; the clinician should use his or her own judgment to determine if a PTSD assessment is warranted for the abuser. PTSD symptoms can be assessed using any of a variety of measures; one such self-report measure is the PTSD Symptom Scale Self Report developed by Foa and her colleagues (Foa, Riggs, Dancu, & Rothbaum, 1993).

M. Other Psychological Problems

It is possible that psychological problems other than depression and PTSD are contributing to the behavior of the victim and/or the abuser. Obsessive-compulsive disorder, generalized anxiety disorder, and schizophrenia are just a few examples of psychological problems that the victim and/or the abuser may be struggling with.

N. Cognitive Functioning

The clinician must determine whether the victim and/or the abuser are cognitively impaired. This is especially important when the abuser as well as the victim is elderly, a not uncommon circumstance. Cognitive status can be assessed by means of a test such as the Mini-Mental State Exam (Folstein, Folstein, & McHugh, 1975) or the Short Portable Mental Status Questionnaire (Pfeiffer, 1975). It is important for the clinician assessing this domain not to confuse bad judgment with cognitive impairment or incompetence. The client has the right to make choices that others may consider foolish or even reckless. As long as the client understands the consequences of his or her decisions or actions, it most likely does not indicate incompetence.

O. Possible Barriers to Treatment

Many of the barriers to successful treatment of elder abuse victims and their abusers will have been identified while assessing the individual's needs. However, other barriers, such as low motivation to engage in treatment and a lack of belief that treatment will be successful, may exist. The clinician should attempt to identify the things that the client feels will get in the way of coming to treatment, finding it valuable, or being willing or able to trust the clinician and/or the process of treatment.

Once the assessment information is gathered, the clinician should summarize the findings for each domain. For each domain where intervention is indicated, the clinician should document the problem (e.g., inadequate caregiver skills) and a proposed solution (e.g., caregiver skills training) as well as possible barriers to the effectiveness of the proposed intervention (e.g., low motivation, time pressures). In addition, a way to measure change, or improvement, in the problem area should be selected and recorded (e.g., a test of caregiver knowledge and/or self-report by the caregiver and the victim about the caregiver's effectiveness in carrying out selected caregiving tasks).

Assessment Considerations

As with screening, the clinician should take care to present a nonblaming and validating attitude toward both the victim and the caregiver during the assessment process. Keep in mind that both the victim and the abuser may view the treatment process as punishing or as a sign that they have done something wrong or are inadequate. This is especially likely if treatment was court ordered, as is often the case. The clinician must be sensitive to these reactions from the client and be careful to present the treatment process in a way that the client will find acceptable—for example, as an opportunity to help a family member or to get some much-deserved relief from the burdens of caregiving. It should be conveyed to the client that the assessment process may take more than one, and sometimes several, sessions to complete and that the purpose of assessment is to identify the things that would be most helpful to work on. The client should also be made aware that this is a collaborative process—that together, the client and the clinician will develop a treatment plan that makes sense.

Guidelines for Intervention

The purpose of intervention is to effect change on targets identified in the assessment phase. In the beginning of the intervention phase, it is recommended that the therapist collaborate with the client to select the target(s) to address first in treatment. Including the client in the decision process in this way may help him or her to feel more in control over what is happening and thus more likely to participate fully. The importance of empowering the client at this and every stage of treatment cannot be overstated, particularly since it is within the client's rights to refuse treatment at any time, for any reason. To decrease the likelihood that discontinuation of treatment by the client will occur, it is a good idea to encourage the client to target treatment barriers early in the intervention process.

Once targets have been selected, it is important for the clinician to determine with the client how they will know when the goal with regard to this target has been successfully reached. For some targets, such as finding an adult day-care center that is affordable and acceptable to the elderly person, successful goal completion is clear. For other targets, such as overcoming depression, successful completion is less clear. Since everyone is depressed from time to time and mood can fluctuate hourly, the goal should be operationalized in such a way that it can be measured as clearly as possible (e.g., a BDI score of less than 10 for six weeks in a row).

Selecting an Intervention

Once the target has been operationalized into a measurable goal and a method of measurement (see guidelines for assessment) has been selected, an intervention may be implemented. When considering a particular intervention for use with a client, the clinician should consider (1) whether the intervention has sufficient empirical support to recommend its use; (2) whether the intervention is appropriate for use with this population (e.g., elderly); (3) whether the client has the skills necessary to take advantage of the intervention (e.g., cognitive skills); and (4) the length of the intervention, with briefer interventions being preferred. It is beyond the scope of this chapter to list all the interventions that are available for use with elderly abuse victims and their caregivers. However, for reference we have listed some of the interventions that we think can be useful in treating a few of the recurrent problems arising from caregiver/care recipient relationships:

Depression. There are several treatment manuals dealing with depression in the elderly. Among these are Scogin and McElreath's (1994) cognitive therapy for geriatric patients; Coon and colleagues' (1999) cognitive behavioral therapy for the treatment of late-life distress; Dick and colleagues' (1996) cognitive behavioral therapy; and Teri, Gallagher-Thompson, and Thompson's (1994) cognitive behavioral intervention for depression in Alzheimer's patients.

Caregiver Stress. Interventions designed at reducing stress experienced by caregivers include the "Coping with Frustration" and "Coping with the Blues" psychoeducational programs designed by Gallagher-Thompson (1994), Steffan's (2000) anger management for dementia caregivers, and Farran and Keane-Hagarty's (1994) multi-modal intervention strategies for distressed caregivers. Meichenbaum's (1985) Stress Inoculation Training may also be useful with this population.

Caregiver Skills. Barusch (1991) provides guidance for developing, implementing, and evaluating training and support programs for caregivers in her book, *Elder Care: Family Training and Support*. The training program she presents is drawn from the University of Utah's Caregiver Support Project and includes instructions for working with reluctant caregivers, legal concerns, medication management, and home safety.

Measuring Therapeutic Progress

As mentioned previously, it is important for the clinician to measure client progress in meeting treatment targets periodically (i.e., weekly or monthly) in order to determine if the selected intervention is effective and to provide reinforcement to the client (and the clinician). If no progress is indicated on the progress measures after an adequate period of time, the clinician should determine whether treatment was implemented and engaged in adequately by the client. If both of these conditions have been met, then selection of another intervention is indicated. In these cases (i.e., where another intervention is implemented because of treatment failure) it is important for the clinician to convey to the client that not every intervention works for every person and that failure to see progress with the first method does not indicate that the client will never see improvement.

In addition to assessment of client progress, the clinician must assess for new incidences of abusive behavior at every session and report all such incidents of abuse to the appropriate adult services agency. It is the clinician's responsibility to make the client aware of this limit to confidentiality. Unfortunately, under these circumstances it is not unusual for the client to feel that he or she should not admit to committing, or being subjected to, abusive acts. The clinician can validate the concerns that the client may have about the consequences of admitting that abusive behavior has occurred and assure the client that the priority is to help him or her, not to deliver punishment. In the end, however, the clinician cannot force a client to admit to abusive behavior nor should this be attempted, because it may lead only to the alienation of the client.

Follow-up assessment is a useful way for clinicians to determine if the treatment(s) they delivered were effective both in and of themselves (e.g., to decrease caregiver stress) and in terms of ending abusive behavior. We recommend that clinicians conduct follow-up assessment procedures one month, three months, six months, and one year following termination of treatment. With such continued contact, reengagement in treatment (if necessary) is likely to be easier following a failure of treatment gains to generalize or to be sustained outside of the clinician's office. In addition, treatment successes can be identified and appropriate reinforcement for making significant changes can be provided to the client.

Documentation

Documentation is an important part of all elder abuse cases and serves both a legal and a clinical function. Legally, documentation of screening and assessment procedures may be used to support a claim of elder abuse against a particular perpetrator. Treatment records, including screening and assessment summaries and standardized measures, should therefore be selected and completed with enough care to withstand legal scrutiny. Observations regarding the client's behavior should be described (e.g., "the client did not make eye contact at any time during the screening procedure, and placed her head in her hands three times when asked to answer questions regarding physical abuse directed toward her by her daughter") rather than interpreted (e.g., "the client was uncomfortable during the screening procedure"), and the client's responses to open-ended questions during screening and assessment procedures should be recorded in his or her own words when possible. All records should be legible and organized in a coherent fashion that demonstrates a thoughtful and thorough assessment procedure.

Clinically, clear and organized documentation is helpful not only to the current clinician (i.e., by way of helping the clinician to plan a thorough and systematic treatment approach as we have recommended in this chapter) but may also be helpful to future clinicians. That is, a therapist who is employed by the client in the future will be able to determine from the record the type of treatment delivered as well as the effectiveness of this treatment and plan his or her interventions accordingly. In short, the only downside to good documentation is the time investment it may require from the clinician; the use of standardized measures helps to address this issue to a certain degree. In any case, the potential legal considerations and typically complicated nature of elder abuse cases clearly justifies this time expenditure.

CONCLUSIONS AND FUTURE DIRECTIONS

Significant progress has been made in the past three decades both in terms of acknowledging elder abuse as a social problem and understanding some of the possible causes and consequences of elder abuse. However, it is clear that much more needs to be done in order to address the needs of the thousands of elderly persons who are being abused every year, as well as the caregivers who are being overwhelmed by the burdens associated with caring for an impaired elderly person. More research in the area of elder abuse treatment is needed. Specifically, we need more data on the effectiveness of intervention strategies that use a single definition of elder abuse. We also need more data not only on the effectiveness of screening tools, but on the most effective strategies for implementing these tools in the primary care setting. To do this we will need to create briefer instruments that can be administered with little or no training.

With more and more people approaching late adulthood, we can expect to see an increase in elder abuse and caregiver burden in the future. Mental health professionals will need to become as familiar with these populations as they have had to become with child abuse victims and their perpetrators. In each case, specialized knowledge is called for as well as specialized skills both in interviewing and in administering treatment. Both also require at least a basic understanding of laws relating to abuse. In this chapter, we have attempted to provide an overview of the issues mental health professionals will need to understand in order to effectively treat victims and perpetrators of abuse. Elder abuse is a complex problem, however, and clinicians are encouraged to seek out opportunities for training with this population in order to become comfortable in screening, assessing, and treating elder abuse victims and perpetrators.

REFERENCES

American Medical Association. (1992). *Diagnostic and treatment guidelines on elder abuse and neglect*. Chicago: Author.

Ansello, E. F. (1996). Causes and theories. In L. A. Baumhover & S. C. Beall (Eds.), *Abuse, neglect and exploitation of older persons* (pp. 9–29). Baltimore, MD: Health Professions Press.

Ansello, E. F., King, N. R., & Taler, G. (1986). The environmental press model: A theoretical framework for intervention in elder abuse. In K. A. Pillemer & R. S. Wolf (Eds.), *Elder abuse: Conflict in the family* (pp. 314–330). Dover, MA: Auburn House.

Barusch, A. (1991). *Elder care: Family training and support*. Newbury Park, CA: Sage.

Beck, A. T., Steer, R. A., & Garbin, M. G. (1988). Psychometric properties of the Beck Depression Inventory: Twenty-five years of evaluation. *Clinical Psychology Review, 8*, 77–100.

Biggs, S., Kingston, P. A., & Phillipson, C. (1995). *Elder abuse perspectives*. Buckingham, UK: Open University Press.

Blenkner, M. (1965). Social work and family relationships in later life with some thoughts on filial maturity. In E. Shanas & G. Streib (Eds.), *Social structure and family generational relations* (pp. 46–59). Englewood Cliffs, NJ: Prentice-Hall.

Block, M. R., & Sinnot, J. D. (1979). *The battered elder syndrome: An exploratory study*. College Park: University of Maryland Centre on Ageing.

Brody, E. (1985). Parent care as normative family stress. *Gerontologist, 25*, 19–29.

Burston, G. R. (1975). Letter: Granny-battering. *British Medical Journal, 3* (5983), 592.

Butler, R. N. (1975). Psychiatry and the elderly: An overview. *American Journal of Psychiatry, 132* (9), 893–900.

Cohen, S., Kamarck, T., & Mermelstein, R. (1983). A global measure of perceived stress. *Journal of Health and Social Behavior, 24*, 385–396.

Coon, D. W., Rider, K., Gallagher-Thompson, D., & Thompson, L. (1999). Cognitive-behavioral therapy for the treatment of late-life distress. In M. Duffy (Ed.), *Handbook of counseling and psychotherapy with older adults* (pp. 487–510). New York: John Wiley.

Curry, L. C., & Stone, J. G. (1995). Understanding elder abuse: The social problem of the 1990s. *Journal of Clinical Geropsychology, 1* (2), 147–156.

Davis, K. L., Marin, D. B., Kane, R., Patrick, D., Peskind, E. R., Raskind, M. A., & Puder, K. L. (1997). The Caregiver Activity Survey (CAS): Development and validation of a new measure for caregivers of persons with Alzheimer's disease. *International Journal of Geriatric Psychiatry, 12* (10), 978–988.

Dick, L. P., Gallagher-Thompson, D., & Thompson, L. W. (1996). Cognitive-behavioral therapy. In R. T. Woods (Ed.), *Handbook of the clinical psychology of aging* (pp. 509–544). Chichester, UK: John Wiley.

D'Zurilla, T. J. (1986). *Problem solving therapy*. New York: Springer.

Eastman, M. (1984). At worst just picking up the pieces. *Community Care*, 20–22.

Farran, C. J., & Keane-Hagarty, E. (1994). Multi-modal intervention strategies for caregivers of persons with dementia. In E. Light, G. Niederehe, & B. D. Lebowitz (Eds.), *Stress effects on family caregivers of Alzheimer's patients: Research and interventions* (pp. 242–259). New York: Springer.

Finkelhor, D. (1983). Common features of family abuse. In D. Finkelhor, R. Gelles, G. Hotaling, & M. Strauss (Eds.), *The dark side of families: Current family violence research*. Beverly Hills, CA: Sage.

Foa, E., Riggs, D., Dancu, C., & Rothbaum, B. (1993). Reliability and validity of a brief instrument for assessing post-traumatic stress disorder. *Journal of Traumatic Stress, 6*, 459–474.

Folstein, M., Folstein, S., & McHugh, P. (1975). Mini-Mental State: A practical method for grading the cognitive state of patients for the clinician. *Journal of Psychiatry Research, 12*, 289–298.

Fulmer, T. T. (1989). Mistreatment of elders: Assessment, diagnosis, and intervention. *Nursing Clinics of North America, 23* (3), 707–716.

Gallagher-Thompson, D. (1994). Clinical interventions for distressed caregivers: Rationale and development of psychoeducational approaches. In E. Light, G. Niederehe, & B. D. Lebowitz (Eds.), *Stress effects on family caregivers of Alzheimer's patients: Research and interventions* (pp. 260–277). New York: Springer.

Garcia, J. L., & Kosberg, J. I. (1993). Understanding anger: Implications for formal and informal caregivers. *Journal of Elder Abuse and Neglect, 4* (4), 87–99.

Giordano, N. H., & Giordano, J. A. (1983). *Family and individual characteristics of five types of elder abuse: Profiles and predictors*. Paper presented at the annual meeting of the Gerontological Society of America, San Francisco.

Godkin, M. A., Wolf, R. S., & Pillemer, K. A. (1989). A case-comparison analysis of elder abuse and neglect. *International Journal of Aging and Human Development, 23* (3), 207–225.

Gottlieb, B. H. (1991). Social support and family care of the elderly. *Canadian Journal on Aging, 10* (4), 359–375.

Grafstrom, M., Nordberg, A., & Winblad, B. (1992). Abuse is in the eye of the beholder. *Scandinavian Journal of Social Medicine, 21* (4), 247–255.

Haynes, S. N. (1992). *Models of causality in psychopathology: Toward dynamic, synthetic, and nonlinear models of behavior*. New York: Macmillan.

Holmer, A. C., & Gilleard, C. (1990). Abuse of elderly people by their caregivers. *British Medical Journal, 301*, 1359–1362.

Hotaling, G. T., & Sugarman, D. B. (1990). Prevention of wife assault. In R. T. Ammerman & M. Hersen (Eds.), *Treatment of family violence*. New York: John Wiley.

Hudson, M. F. (1986). Elder mistreatment: Current research. In K. A. Pillemer & R. S. Wolf (Eds.), *Elder abuse: Conflict in the family* (pp. 125–166). Dover, MA: Auburn House.

Hwalek, M., & Sengstock, M. (1986). Assessing the probability of elder abuse: Toward the development of a clinical screening instrument. *Journal of Applied Gerontology, 5* (2), 153–173.

Janz, M. (1990, September–October). Clues to elder abuse. *Geriatric Nursing*, 220–222.

Johnson, T. F. (1991). *Elder mistreatment: Deciding who is at risk*. Westport, CT: Greenwood Press.

Katz, S., Downs, T. D., Cash, H. R., & Grotz, R. C. (1970). Progress in the development of the index of ADL. *Gerontologist, 1*, 20–30.

Kosberg, J. I. (1988). Preventing elder abuse: Identification of high risk factors prior to placement decisions. *Gerontologist, 28* (1), 43–50.

Kosberg, J. I., & Cairl, R. E. (1986). The Cost of Care Index: A case management tool for screening informal care providers. *Gerontologist, 26*, 273–278.

Lawton, M. P., & Brody, E. M. (1969). Assessment of older people: Self-monitoring and instrumental activities of daily living. *Gerontologist, 9*, 179–186.

Lazarus, R. S., & Folkman, S. (1984). *Stress, appraisal, and coping.* New York: Springer.

Lefebvre, R. C., & Sandford, S. L. (1985). A multi-modal questionnaire for stress. *Journal of Human Stress, 11*, 69–75.

Meichenbaum, D. (1985). *Stress inoculation training.* New York: Pergamon Press.

O'Malley, T. A. (1987). Abuse and neglect of the elderly: The wrong issue? *Pride Institute Journal of Long Term Health Care, 5*, 25–28.

O'Malley, T. A., Everitt, D. E., O'Malley, H. C., & Campion, E. W. (1983). Identifying and preventing family-mediated abuse and neglect of elderly persons. *Annals of Internal Medicine, 98*, 998–1005.

O'Malley, H. C., Segel, H. D., & Perez, R. (1979). *Elder abuse in Massachusetts: Survey of professionals and paraprofessionals.* Boston: Legal Research and Services to the Elderly.

Penhale, B. (1993). The abuse of elderly people: Considerations for practice. *British Journal of Social Work, 23*, 95–112.

Pfeiffer, E. (1975). A Short Portable Mental Status Questionnaire for the assessment of organic brain deficit in elderly patients. *Journal of the American Geriatrics Society, 23*, 433–441.

Phillips, L. R. (1989). Issues involved in identifying and intervening in elder abuse. In R. Finlinson & S. Ingman (Eds.), *Elder abuse: Practice and policy* (pp. 197–217). New York: Human Sciences Press.

Pillemer, K. A. (1985). The dangers of dependency: New findings on domestic violence of the elderly. *Social Problems, 33*, 146–158.

Pillemer, K. A. (1986). Risk factors in elder abuse: Results from a case control study. In K. A. Pillemer & R. S. Wolf (Eds.), *Elder abuse: Conflict in the family* (pp. 239–264). Dover, MA: Auburn House.

Pillemer, K. A., & Finkelhor, D. (1988). The prevalence of elder abuse: A random sample survey. *Gerontologist, 28*, 51–57.

Pillemer, K. A., & Wolf, R. S. (1989). *Helping elderly victims: The reality of elder abuse.* New York: Columbia University Press.

Quinn, M. J., & Tomita, S. K. (1986). *Elder abuse and neglect: Causes, diagnoses, and intervention strategies.* New York: Springer.

Radloff, L. S. (1977). The CES-D Scale: A self-report depression scale for research in the general population. *Applied Psychological Measurement, 1* (13), 385–401.

Reis, M., & Nahmiash, D. (1995). Validation of the Caregiver Abuse Screen (CASE). *Canadian Journal on Aging, 14* (2, Suppl 2), 45–60.

Reis, M., & Nahmiash, D. (1998). Validation of the Indicators of abuse (IOA) screen. *Gerontologist, 38* (4), 471–480.

Ryden, M. (1988). Aggressive behavior in persons with dementia living in the community. *Alzheimer Disease and Associated Disorders: International Journal, 2* (4), 342–355.

Scogin, F., & McElreath, L. (1994). Efficacy of psychosocial treatments for geriatric depression: A quantitative review. *Journal of Consulting and Clinical Psychology, 62* (1), 69–73.

Sengstock, M. C., & Steiner, S. C. (1996). Assessing nonphysical abuse. In L. A. Baumhover & S. C. Beall (Eds.), *Abuse, neglect and exploitation of older persons* (pp. 105–122). Baltimore, MD: Health Professions Press.

Speilberger, C. D., Gorsuch, R. L., & Lushene, R. E. (1978). *Manual for the State-Trait Anxiety Inventory.* Palo Alto, CA: Consulting Psychologists Press.

Steffan, A. M. (2000). Anger management for dementia caregivers: A preliminary study using video and telephone interventions. *Behavior Therapy, 31* (2), pp. 281–299.

Steinmetz, S. K. (1983). Dependency, stress and violence between middle-aged caregivers and their elderly parents. In J. I. Kosberg (Ed.), *Abuse and maltreatment of the elderly: Causes and interventions* (pp. 134–149). Littleton, MA: John-Wright-PGS.

Strauss, M., Gelles, R., & Steinmetz, S. (1980). *Behind closed doors: Violence in the American family.* New York: Doubleday.

Tatara, T. (1993). *Summaries of the statistical data on elder abuse in domestic settings for FY90 and FY91: A final report.* Washington, DC: National Aging Resource Center on Elder Abuse.

Teri, L., Curtis, J., Gallagher-Thompson, D., & Thompson, L. W. (1994). Cognitive-behavior therapy with depressed older adults. In L. S. Schneider, C. F. Reynolds, B. D. Lebowtiz, & A. J. Friedhoff (Eds.), *Diagnosis and treatment of depression in late life: Results of the NIH Consensus Development Conference* (pp. 279–291). Washington, DC: American Psychiatric Press.

Tomita, S. K. (1982). Detection and treatment of elderly abuse and neglect: A protocol for health care professionals. *P.T. and O.T. in Geriatrics, 2* (2), 37–51.

Tomita, S. K. (1990). The denial of elder mistreatment by victims and abusers: The application of neutralization theory. *Violence and Victims, 5* (3), 171–184.

Vitaliano, P. P., Russo, J., Young, H. M., & Becker, J. (1991). The screen for caregiver burden. *Gerontologist, 31* (1), 76–83.

Whittaker, T. (1993). Rethinking elder abuse: Towards an age and gender integrated theory of elder abuse. In P. Decalmer & F. Glendenning (Eds.), *The mistreatment of elderly people* (pp. 116–128). London: Sage.

Wolf, R. S. (1996). Elder abuse and family violence: Testimony presented before the U.S. Senate Special Committee on Aging. *Journal of Elder Abuse & Neglect, 8* (1), 81–96.

Wolf, R. S., & Pillemer, K. (1989). *Helping elder victims: The reality of elder abuse.* New York: Columbia University Press.

Wolf, R. S., Strugnell, E. P., & Godkin, M. A. (1982). *Preliminary findings from the model projects on elderly abuse.* Worcester: University of Massachusetts Center on Aging.

Yesavage, J. A., Brink, T. L., Rose, T. L., Lum, O., Huang, V., Adey, M., & Leirer, V. O. (1983). Development and validation of a geriatric screening scale: A preliminary report. *Journal of Psychiatric Research, 17,* 37–49.

CHAPTER 31

INVOLUNTARY COMMITMENT

BRADLEY R. JOHNSON
PRIVATE PRACTICE
TUCSON, ARIZONA

Civil commitment is the process of involuntarily hospitalizing or requiring outpatient psychiatric treatment of an individual because of mental illness. Psychiatric illnesses may differ from general medical illnesses. That is, individuals who suffer from a mental illness may have difficulties with judgment and insight to the degree, at times, that they may not realize that they are causing harm to themselves or others and need to seek treatment. Alternatively, persons with mental illness may not have good judgment and refuse treatment during times of decompensation. However, mental health specialists do not have the legal right to force hospitalization upon an individual merely because they think it would be in the person's best interest. Rather, in the United States, the process of involuntary hospitalization is governed by the law.

Although there are current criteria that are used to determine whether an individual is able to be civilly committed or not, society's view on the appropriateness of and the situations under which an involuntary hospitalization can occur has undergone a great deal of change. Case law has now set the minimum standards that must be followed in each state in order to involuntarily hospitalize or force treatment upon an individual. This chapter will address the history of civil commitment in the United States, the landmark cases that have helped determine the criteria for commitment, current criteria for commitment, the therapist's obligation toward his or her patient and others, and how the concept of civil commitment is being used in modern-day psychiatric and psychological practices.

The History of Involuntary Commitment

In American history during colonial times, the nonviolent mentally ill were placed in poorhouses and the violent mentally ill were jailed. In the mid-eighteenth century, facilities began to be established where family members could bring the mentally ill based on a doctor's judgment and the family's ability to pay. The first such facility was established in 1750 at the Pennsylvania Hospital in Philadelphia. By the mid 1800s, there were 48 hospitals for the mentally ill in operation throughout the United States housing approximately 8,500 individuals (Katz, 1989). The state hospitals and the private asylums that were built at that time were settings where hospital superintendents and families could mandate admission if it was felt the patient was in need of treatment. That is, patients were confined involuntarily to these psychiatric institutions with little recourse (Gutheil and Appelbaum, 2000).

The mental institutions of the mid-1800s were basically asylums where the mentally ill were confined; they were not settings for actual psychiatric treatment. This period predated the time when individuals could voluntarily admit themselves to a psychiatric hospitalization for intensive treatment. Allegations of abuse arose in many instances, and consequently criminal style procedures with judicial hearings were introduced to determine the need for confinement. Cases began to appear in the courts, which then helped set the stage for developing the rights of the mentally ill.

One of the first and most well-known cases regarding patient rights and civil commitment was the matter of Josiah Oakes. In 1844, Mr. Oakes was detained in a Massachusetts asylum after becoming engaged to a young woman "of unsavory character" at the same time that his first wife was dying. It was believed that he suffered from a mental illness. He challenged his confinement based on the common-law right of *habeas corpus*. The state supreme court held that an individual could not be restrained or detained against his will without procedural or legal safeguards. With this case, there appeared to be a gradual erosion of the prior standards for detention and specific criteria began to be used in determining the ability to involuntarily hospitalize an individual. Therefore, the concept of hospitalizing individuals for treatment rather than merely detaining the violent mentally ill for the protection of society began to become an important concept.

In 1864, a second well-known case helped shape the history of civil commitment. At that time, Mrs. E. P. W. Packard was involuntarily committed by her husband to the Illinois State Hospital for three years. The Illinois statute, which provided for commitment of married women and infants, stated that those women and infants who, "in the judgment of the medical superintendent are evidently insane and distractive, may be received and detained at the request of the husband . . . without the evidence of insanity and distraction required in other cases." Because of Mrs. Packard's crusade three years after her release, Illinois eventually enacted a personal liberty bill that required a jury trial to determine the commitment of an individual to a psychiatric hospital setting.

In the mid-1800s, Dorothea Dix traveled through much of the United States visiting psychiatric facilities, asylums, and jails and exposing the terrible conditions in which many of the mentally ill were housed. Many of the individuals who were being held had not been convicted of any crime, causing her to believe that their liberty had been inappropriately curtailed. In many cases, the mentally ill were not being offered any type of treatment. Because of her efforts, many hospitals were created that provided the mentally ill with appropriate treatment and better housing facilities, and a number of states improved their provisions for the mentally ill.

By the end of the nineteenth century, most jurisdictions had adopted a judicial review of commitment. There continued to be some alternation during the early twentieth century between periods of criminalization of commitment procedures and periods of efforts to protect patients who were in need of treatment including hospitalization. By the 1970s, as part of the civil rights movement in the United States, the concept of civil commitment once again changed drastically. No longer were the criteria for commitment based on the need for treatment. Rather, the reason for civil commitment began to be based on dangerousness. The duration of involuntary hospitalization changed from undefined or indefinite to time limited. Patient rights were finally being watched closely by the courts and legislatures. Therefore, although recriminalization of the commitment process was occurring, limited safeguards were put in place.

Presently, many states differ slightly on the criteria and process for civil commitment for forced psychiatric treatment. However, there are many similarities in procedural safeguards. For example, it is not unusual that an individual be committed for psychiatric hospitalization or forced outpatient treatment for renewable periods of six to twelve months under the order of a judge. The patient's rights can include the notice of proceedings, a full hearing (often with a jury if requested), and the right to a legal counsel at the state's expense if necessary. The individual may then have periodic reviews to determine the need for continued confinement or recommitment.

In the past, civil commitment was considered the same as involuntary hospitalization. The patient would then be allowed to have trial discharges with the ability to rehospitalize the individual if he or she began to refuse treatment or decompensate. However, the concept of the least restrictive alternative has become more popular. In many states, outpatient commitment frequently is used when there is a need for treatment but hospitalization is not necessary. These days, almost every state has some provision authorizing outpatient commitment.

Historically, the major diagnoses of candidates for civil commitment have been schizophrenia, mania, depression, or other types of psychosis (Hiday, 1988). However, depending on local statutes, civil commitment could be considered in other cases, such as persons with Munchausen's syndrome, to prevent imminent self-harm (Johnson & Harrison, 2000, Schlesinger et al., 1989). Cleveland and colleagues (1989) have concluded that persons whom psychiatrists consider highly in need of treatment, no matter what the underlying psychiatric cause, either voluntarily admit themselves or need to be considered dangerous enough to themselves or others to be committed under a dangerousness standard. Recently, a new interpretation of civil commitment has been used by some U.S. states in order to require dangerous sexual offenders to receive treatment if, because of a mental disorder, they are at a high propensity to reoffend.

The Legal Basis of Civil Commitment

The legal basis for involuntary hospitalization and civil commitment consists of two concepts, police powers and *parens patriae*. The concept of police powers state that the government has the authority to prevent harm to the community, including harm to mentally ill individuals. That is, it is interpreted under police powers that the government could intervene when a person's behavior or condition leads to a danger to that person or to the public at large.

Parens patriae denotes the state acting in place of the parent and therefore taking responsibility for those unable to care for themselves (Miller, 1992). *Parens patriae* is often interpreted to mean that the government acts for the infirmed, incompetent, and mentally ill, who are unable to act in their own interest to care and provide for themselves in a safe and capable manner (Zeman & Schwartz, 1994). Involuntarily hospitalizing an individual solely because of a mental illness would be an act based purely on the principal of *parens patriae*.

Current commitment laws require that such individuals be mentally ill in addition to being a danger to themselves or others. A non-mentally ill person who might be dangerous would not be committed because hospitalization would not benefit that individual. Therefore, components in deciding civil commitment include mental illness, dangerousness, and treatability. Additionally, Reisner (1985) clarifies that both concepts, police powers and *parens patriae*, are limited by the U.S. Constitution in both the First and Fifth Amendments, addressing specific civil rights of individuals. These amendments clarify that the government does not have unlimited prerogative to take actions to protect other individuals or society.

Involuntary Commitment Procedures

Most states allow emergency commitments for short-term hospitalization until a court hearing is held. Within days to weeks, a formal hearing is conducted to decide commitment for hospital-based or outpatient psychiatric care (Miller, 1992). The standard of commitment in most or all states include the following as a result of mental illness: danger to others, danger to self, or inability to care for self (grave disability). Gutheil and Appelbaum (2000) described additional criteria for civil commitment used in some states, such as danger to property, the concept of being in need of treatment, and the concept of being at risk of deterioration.

When an individual is being held on an emergency basis awaiting a hearing for actual civil commitment, a physician or psychologist generally must sign the commitment certificate. In some states, more than one professional is required to sign. Also, in some states the police or the courts can sign the commitment certificate when a mental health professional is not available (Gutheil & Appelbaum, 2000).

During the time that the individual is being held and awaiting a commitment hearing, psychological or psychiatric evaluations are conducted to more accurately determine whether an individual is at need of being civilly committed. At some point in the procedure the holding facility must determine whether the individual meets the criteria for civil commitment or not. Individuals who are judged not to meet criteria may be released. However, if probable cause is believed to exist, the individual can then be held involuntarily until a hearing or trial takes place to determine actual civil commitment for a specified period of time.

U.S. Legislative and Case Law Decisions

A number of landmark legal cases have established modern-day criteria used for civil commitment in the United States. Following is a summary of the most important of these cases.

Lake v. Cameron

The landmark case of *Lake v. Cameron* (1966) addressed the issue of the least restrictive alternative for treatment. Catherine Lake was an elderly woman considered senile and homeless. In 1962, she was civilly committed to St. Elizabeth's Hospital. Judge David Bazelon of the District of Columbia Circuit Court of Appeals addressed the issue of least restrictive alternative for treatment, requiring that the entire spectrum of services be available to a patient needing civil commitment, including outpatient treatment, halfway houses, and nursing homes (Hoge, Applebaum, & Geller 1989). It was considered that a more restrictive environment than was deemed necessary would deprive the individual of his or her liberty, going beyond what was necessary for the individual's own protection. However, some argue that the least restrictive alternative may not be the most appropriate setting from a therapeutic standpoint for many individuals, depending on the type of mental illness.

Lessard v. Schmidt

In *Lessard v. Schmidt* (1972), the Federal District Court in Wisconsin established due process safeguards for civil commitment. The Lessard decision established the right to a jury trial, no hearsay evidence, patient privilege, the patient's right to an attorney, and the patient's right to be proved beyond a reasonable doubt both mentally ill and dangerous. Up to this point, the standard of proof of "beyond a reasonable doubt" had only been applied to criminal procedures.

Jackson v. Indiana

In 1972, the U.S. Supreme Court reviewed the case of a deaf-mute individual who had been charged with criminal offenses. The individual had been committed to a mental hospital secondary to being found incompetent to stand trial. The case was overturned by the U.S. Supreme Court, which claimed that the defendant had been denied equal protection and due process. Under the existing law at the time, persons who had been charged with, but not been convicted of, a criminal offense, could be involuntarily hospitalized in order to restore their competence. Hospitalization could have continued indefinitely if the staff had been unable to restore the individual to competency. Because of this case, many states have since passed laws that limit the amount of time that an individual can be committed in order to restore competency to stand trial. This case is important in a discussion of civil commitment because it addresses the issue of placing time limitations on involuntary hospitalization.

O'Connor v. Donaldson

In 1975, the U.S. Supreme Court reviewed the case of *O'Connor v. Donaldson*. Mr. Donaldson had been held in a Florida state hospital from 1957 to 1972 and had never been shown to be dangerous. Although his friends had been willing to take responsibility for him, the superintendent of the state hospital refused to discharge him. The Supreme Court declared that a nondangerous mentally ill individual could not be confined in a psychiatric hospital "without more." This has been interpreted to mean that the finding of dangerousness was necessary in order to justify involuntary hospitalization and that a mental disease alone does not qualify a person for civil commitment (Stromberg & Stone, 1982).

Fasulo v. Arafeh

In 1977, the Connecticut Supreme Court decided in the case *Fasulo v. Arafeh* that there needed to be further regulation of the commitment procedures. This case addressed the situation of an individual who was civilly committed for long-term psychiatric care without periodic review for continued hospitalization. The court ruled that if there were no regular reviews of individuals civilly committed, due process was considered violated. Based on this case, many other states have now enacted statutes that prevent civil commitment without periodic review for the need for continued hospitalization or outpatient treatment.

Addington v. Texas

In *Addington v. Texas* (1979), the Supreme Court resolved the issue of the standard of proof debate previously brought up in *Lessard v. Schmidt*. The possible standards included a preponderance of the evidence (more likely than not), clear and convincing evidence (roughly greater than a 75% chance or better), and beyond a reasonable doubt (roughly a 90–95% chance or greater). The court ruled that the preponderance standard was insufficient when an individual's liberties were at stake, but that the "beyond a reasonable doubt" standard would be too difficult to prove in many cases. Therefore, the "clear and convincing" standard was established, as required by constitutional law. The "clear and convincing" standard was set as a minimum. However, some states have opted to continue to use a "beyond a reasonable doubt" standard.

Landmark Court Decisions on the Commitment of a Minor

In re Gault

In 1967, the U.S. Supreme Court established many of the procedures used for the juvenile court system in the case *In re Gault*. Gault was a 14-year-old adolescent from Arizona who had been found guilty of making obscene phone calls and was placed in a state industrial school until his adulthood. The Supreme Court, recognizing the injustice in the handling of this case, established due process requirements as part of all adjudicatory hearings on delinquency petitions. *In re Gault* helped set the stage for the civil commitment reform by bringing the issue of due process for juveniles into account.

Parham v. J.R

In *Parham v. J.R.* (1979), the Supreme Court established the constitutional minimum for civil commitment procedures for minors. It established that there was no requirement for an adversarial hearing in commitment procedures for minors. Rather, a "neutral fact finder" would review and oversee cases. *Parham v. J.R.* was seen as a victory for parental authority, and emphasis was placed on medical rather than judicial decision making. In fact, the case was seen to some degree as a retreat from the procedural safeguards that were articulated in the *Gault* decision.

Criteria for Involuntary Commitment

Danger to Self

The evaluation for suicide is difficult and challenging. It is difficult to predict events that occur infrequently, as is the case with suicide. Many feel that evaluators may overpredict potential suicide, creating a large number of false positives. It is important to conduct a comprehensive assessment of the patient's suicide risk. A number of standard approaches to the assessment of suicide risk have been described in the psychiatric literature (Blumenthal, 1990; Chiles & Strohasall, 1995; Maris et al., 1992). It is considered that short-term suicide risk assessments, such as predicting danger to self for a period of 24 to 48 hours, are much more reliable than longer-term predictions (Binder, 1999).

It is generally accepted to be a standard of care that evaluation of suicide should be part of most, if not all, psychiatric or psychological evaluations. In fact, the most common legal action involving psychiatric care is the failure to provide reasonable protection to patients from harming themselves. If the patient is foreseeably suicidal, then appropriate steps should be taken through civil commitment to protect them from the possibility of death. This does not set a standard, however, that the mental health specialist can prevent all suicides. Many times suicides occur that might have been preventable but were not foreseeable. Therefore, the law tends to assume that suicide is preventable only if it is foreseeable.

Occasionally, mental health professionals will receive a *no self-harm contract* from the patient. Although these contracts may be helpful in establishing a therapeutic alliance, they cannot be used in place of an adequate suicide assessment (Simon, 1999). Rather, contracts may give the therapist a sense of false security, allowing them to feel that hospitalization may not be necessary.

The criteria for being dangerous to one's own self addresses suicide or severely self-destructive behavior (Applebaum & Gutheil, 1991). Other requirements often included are the immediacy of the harm and the direct evidence of the threat or attempt. Wexler (1981) argues that danger to self does not need to be restricted to suicide but can be broadened in interpretation to encompass other physical harm. An interesting interpretation of "the danger to self" standard could be applied in the instance of factitious disorder. In factitious syndrome (Munchausen's syndrome), suicidality is conspicuously absent. However, the behaviors utilized to feign symptoms and to achieve the sick role may at times be significantly life threatening (Nichols et al., 1990). Houck (1992) concluded that some individuals who suffer from factitious disorder may be at such severe danger that there could be grounds to warrant civil commitment. There are only a few cases documented in the literature in which an individual is referred for civil commitment based on complications secondary to factitious disorder (Houck, 1992; Johnson & Harrison, 2000, Miller et al., 1985; Yassa, 1978).

Danger to Others

The assessment of dangerousness to others brings up the issue of the ability to predict future violence toward others. Threats against others might be extremely common, but it is the actual dangerousness to others that would make one committable rather than mere threats alone. Nonetheless, legal decisions such as *Tarasoff v. Regents of the University of California* have ruled that the therapist has a "duty to protect." Therefore, the mental health professional has to walk a fine line between ignoring threats or mere potential violent behaviors and actually seeking for civil commitment in order to protect. In some cases, possible criminal legal intervention is more appropriate or the only alternative.

It is frequently agreed that a history of previous violence or aggression is the strongest risk factor in predicting future violence or aggression. The situation becomes more difficult, however, when the individual being assessed has no history of previous violence. However, Applebaum and Gutheil (1991) have used common sense in stating that the "longer the period of time that the present balance has existed, the stronger the possibility that it represents a stable equilibrium." They concluded that when the situation appears to be changing more rapidly, however, one may need to err on the side of safety. Clearly, there needs to be a relationship between the potential dangerousness and actual mental illness for an individual to be civilly committed. Nonetheless, in many situations such diagnoses as explosive disorder, alcoholism, or antisocial personality disorder may not be an appropriate basis for civil commitment. Rather, these may present for situations that are again more appropriately referred for criminal rather than civil commitment.

In the past, it was often felt that mental health professionals overpredicted the future risk of a person's becoming violent. However, the ability to assess the risk for future violence has improved in recent years (Johnson, 2000). The evaluator who outlines identified risk factors for violence and understands what is currently happening with the patient is often able to predict violence in the short term with moderate accuracy. This is especially true these days, when actuarially derived scales such as the Violence Risk Appraisal Guide (Quinsey, Harris, Riu, & Cormier 1998) and the Psychopathy Check List (Hare, Hart, & Harpur, 1991) can be used to help predict future risk of violence. These and other similar scales not only help one outline the risk factors that may apply to their patient but may also be helpful in predicting low, medium, or high risk of future violent behaviors with the individual in question.

Actuarial scales are becoming increasingly helpful in the assessment of a person's dangerousness to others. Some mental health professionals believe that these scales should not be used alone to make predictions but in combination with clinical judgment. Also, no single actuarially derived scale is universally accepted to predict violence.

Inability to Care for Self

The standard of inability to care for oneself (commonly referred to as *grave disability*) refers to individuals' failure to provide for themselves basic essentials secondary to their mental illness. Such essentials could include basic food, clothing, and shelter, the lack of which could place such individuals at serious physical harm or danger to themselves. These criteria are not meant to be interpreted to mean that all individuals with mental illness must reach the average level of ability in general society to care for themselves. Rather, they are intended to address the issue of individuals who cannot even provide the mere basics for themselves because of mental illness. This, in turn, causes them to be gravely disabled. In such cases, individuals are frequently committed for outpatient treatment because hospitalization is frequently unnecessary. However, they would be required to follow up with case managers, therapists, and psychiatrists in helping set up the appropriate provisions that are necessary to survive in the community.

Other Standards for Civil Commitment

As mentioned, some states have considered other criteria for civilly committing an individual for required treatment. In 1979, Washington state permitted civil commitment if the individual was at risk for severe deterioration secondary to his or her mental illness. Some states have attempted using the standard of danger to property for civil commitment. Generally, this has been found unconstitutional and is not usually considered grounds for civil commitment. Other criteria that have been tried have included the standard of "in need of treatment" based on the *parens patriae* standard. However, as previously discussed, this concept alone is not considered constitutional and is not used as grounds for civil commitment in today's society.

Forced Treatment of Incarcerated Prisoners

Usually considered a landmark case regarding the right to refuse treatment, *Washington v. Harper* (1990) also addresses the issue of forced treatment of prison inmates. The U.S. Supreme Court reviewed the case in which prisoners objected to treatment when it was recommended to be in their best interest by their treating psychiatrist. In this situation, forced treatment was based on a different legal basis than that for forced medication under civil commitment laws. For incarcerated prisoners, it was decided that a three-person panel including both clinical and administrative individuals would review the case and determine whether the inmate would be required to be forcibly medicated or not. The inmate has the right to present evidence, to have lay representation, to appeal, and to have regular review at specific time intervals as part of his or her prisoner's rights. Basically, the interpretation of *Harper* has been that if prisoners have met the state's regular civil commitment criteria and treatment was in their interest, then medication could be administered against their will.

A court hearing as used in a civil commitment setting is not necessary, according to *Harper*. Additionally, in some states the need to prove dangerousness to self or others has not been necessary either. Some argue that this approach does not protect patient rights in an incarcerated setting. However, others argue that prisoners do not have the same rights as individuals who are not incarcerated and that not only the patient's interest, but the interest of the institution in which they reside is important and must be accounted for.

CIVIL COMMITMENT OF SEXUAL OFFENDERS

In recent years there has been a new interpretation of civil commitment laws used for individuals who are at a high risk of repeating sexual offenses. The basis for civil commitment of sexual offenders is the assumption that some sexual offenders suffer from mental illness that predisposes them to be a danger to others in society. These individuals were first described as "sexually violent predators." In the landmark case *Kansas v. Hendricks* (1997), the legislature concluded that "the treatment needs of this population are very long term and the treatment modalities for this population are very different than the traditional treatment modalities for people appropriate for commitment under the [general Involuntary Civil Commitment Statute]."

The Kansas civil commitment of sexual offenders law was based upon a situation in which Leroy Hendricks, an inmate with a long history of convictions for child molestation, was scheduled to be released from prison. The state filed a petition to seek civil commitment of Mr. Hendricks, referring to him as a "sexually violent predator." Mr. Hendricks filed to dismiss the petition, but probable cause was found and he requested and was granted a jury trial. Mr. Hendricks had been diagnosed with passive-aggressive personality disorder and pedophilia, and expert witnesses testified that he was likely to commit further sexual offenses if he was not committed. An expert for Hendricks argued that it was not possible to predict future dangerousness of a sexual offender. The jury found beyond a reasonable doubt that Hendricks was a sexually violent predator. Therefore, this case defined pedophilia legally as a "mental abnormality."

Hendricks appealed the outcome of this case to the Kansas supreme court, arguing that pedophilia was different than the usual civil commitment criteria for mental illness. It was also argued that civil commitment of a sexual offender would constitute double jeopardy. That is, civilly committing an individual after incarceration would mean that in essence the individual was serving time twice for the same offense. He argued therefore that involuntary commitment was basically the same as a criminal conviction and sentence.

The U.S. Supreme Court upheld the state's decision, arguing that in certain circumstances, the state has the right to civilly detain individuals who are unable to control their behavior and therefore pose a danger to others in society. The act requires proof of more than just a mere predisposition to violence. It requires evidence based on risk factors and past behaviors that the individual is at a likelihood to repeat offenses. The court also agreed that a mental illness must be coupled with the dangerousness. To address the issue of double jeopardy, an individual would need to be offered treatment for the mental illness that predisposes him or her to commit repeat sexual offenses. Therefore, the issue of civil commitment is tantamount to treatment rather than mere incarceration. In fact, the U.S. Supreme Court concluded that it was unnecessary to consider Hendricks's double jeopardy argument since the state of Kansas was not establishing a criminal proceeding (Grudzinskas & Henry, 1997).

Since the establishment of *Kansas v. Hendricks*, a number of states have enacted similar "sexually violent predator" or "sexually violent person" laws. Specially designed civil commitment programs for sexually violent individuals have been established in a number of states. In an attempt not to ignore the issue of double jeopardy, it is only appropriate that civil commitment programs for sexual offenders offer actual treatment and therapy that has been found effective for treating sexual offenders.

Civil commitment programs for sexual offenders are located on the grounds of some state psychiatric hospitals. In other states, they are connected with departments of correction. However, civil commitment of sexual offenders is not considered a criminal proceeding nor a function of corrections. Rather, it is similar to the commitment of mentally ill individuals, as previously described. That is, they are placed in a hospital setting where they are provided appropriate treatment rather than being merely housed or incarcerated. The mental illnesses that are often considered to predispose an offender for recidivism may include paraphilias or personality disorders.

Like civil commitment proceedings in general, the establishment of sexually violent predator laws in some states has required that the treatment of civilly committed sex offenders be provided in the least restrictive setting. Therefore, some sexual offenders may be civilly committed into an outpatient or halfway house setting. Others who are considered more dangerous or in need of more intense treatment, however, would need to be placed in a locked hospital setting until they are ready for a less restrictive setting.

It is likely that there will be a number of issues to be worked out legally regarding the civil commitment of sexual offenders. Among these issues include the standard of proof that will likely be established in each state in which there is a civil commitment law. Other issues being addressed in current civil commitment programs include the standards by which civil committees are reevaluated on a regular basis to determine the need for continued treatment and the criteria that need to be established to determine when an individual might be ready for discharge from a treatment program.

Since sexual paraphilias are considered incurable, treatment programs for civil committees are considered facilities where appropriate skills to reduce the risk of reoffense can be taught. They do not give treatment that permanently cures the offender. Therefore, in many cases it may be recommended that individuals who are discharged from a civil commitment program be placed on lifetime probation so that they could be recommitted for hospitalization or incarcerated again under criminal proceedings for repeat offenses or high-risk behavior.

Conclusion: Ethical Issues

Civil commitment often presents a number of ethical dilemmas for clinicians. Many physicians are understandably uncomfortable about denying their patients their personal liberties by involuntarily committing them to forced medication treatment under civil commitment. However, it is often difficult to balance this conflict with the knowledge that the patient may not do well psychiatrically without treatment. Frequently, the patient's family is wanting their mentally ill relative to seek treatment and will take whatever means is necessary to make treatment a reality. Clinicians may worry that committed individuals may attempt to bring suit for improper detainment or commitment. Additionally, clinicians may become concerned that they will destroy their therapeutic alliance and relationship with their patients by committing them.

Often the need for civil commitment is more clear in situations of danger to self or danger to others. However, these ethical concerns can be more difficult in situations under the "grave disability" criterion. Although the patient's rights to confidentiality and to refuse treatment generally must be honored, the clinician needs to also recall that there are situations resulting from the patient's mental illness that places them or others at such grave danger that confidentiality needs to be waived. In these situations and in the better interest of the patient, civil commitment procedures must be started. Clinicians can find solace in the fact that family members are usually in support of their efforts to force hospitalization, and frequently patients are able to express their gratitude for being forced into treatment or hospitalization once they are appropriately treated and back to their regular psychiatric baseline.

REFERENCES

Addington v. Texas, 441 U.S. 418 (1979).

Appelbaum, P. S., & Gutheil, T. G. (1991). *Clinical handbook of psychiatry and the law* (2nd ed.). Baltimore, MD: Williams & Wilkins.

Binder, R. L. (1999). Are the mentally ill dangerous? *Journal of American Academy of Psychiatry Law, 27*, 189–201.

Blumenthal, S. J. (1990). An overview and synopsis of risk factors, assessment, and treatment of suicidal patients over the life cycle. In S. J. Blumenthal & D. J. Kupfer (Eds.), *Suicide over the life cycle* (pp. 685–733). Washington, DC: American Psychiatric Press.

Chiles, J. H., & Strohsall, K. (1995). *The suicidal patient: Principles of assessment, treatment and case management*. Washington, DC: American Psychiatric Press.

Cleveland, S., Mulvey, E. P., Appelbaum, P. S., & Lidz, C. W. (1989). Do dangerousness-oriented commitment laws restrict hospitalization of patients who need treatment? A test. *Hospital and Community Psychiatry, 40*, 266–271.

Fasulo v. Arafeh, 173 Conn. 473, 373 A. 2d 553 (1977).

Grudzinskas, A. J., & Henry, M. G. (1997). Analysis and commentary: Kansas v. Hendricks. *Journal of the American Academy of Psychiatry Law, 25*, 607–612.

Gutheil T. G., & Appelbaum, P. S. (2000). *Clinical handbook of psychiatry and the law* (3rd ed.). Philadelphia: Lippincott Williams & Wilkins.

Hare, R. D., Hart, S. D., & Harpur, T. J. (1991). Psychopathy and the proposed DSM-IV criteria for antisocial personality disorder. *Journal of Abnormal Psychology, 7*, 35–50.

Hiday, V. A. (1988). Civil commitment: A review of empirical research. *Behavioral Sciences and the Law, 6*, 15–43.

Hoge, S. K., Appelbaum, P. S., & Geller, J. L. (1989). Involuntary treatment. *Review of Psychiatry, 8*, 432–450.

Houck, C. A. (1992). Medicolegal aspects of factitious disorder. *Psychological Medicine, 10*, 105–116.

In re Gault, 387 U.S. 1 (1967).

Jackson v. Indiana, 406 U.S. 715 (1972).

Johnson, B. R. (2000). Assessing the risk for violence. *New Directions for Mental Health Services, 86*, 31–35.

Johnson, B. R., & Harrison, J. A. (2000). Suspected Munchausen's syndrome and civil commitment. *Journal of the American Academy of Psychiatry Law, 28*, 74–76.

Kan. Stat. Ann. 59–29a01 (1994).
Kansas v. Hendricks, 521 U.S. 346 (1997).
Katz, S. E. (1989). Hospitalization in the mental health service system. In H. I. Kaplan & B. Sadock (Eds.), *Comprehensive textbook of psychiatry* (5th ed.) (pp. 2083–2090). Baltimore, MD: Williams & Wilkins.
Lake v. Cameron, 364 F. 2d 657 (1966).
Lessard v. Schmidt, 349 F. Supp 1078 E. D. Wis (1972).
Maris, R. W., Berman, A. L., Maltsberger, J. T., et al. (1992). *Assessment and prediction of suicide*. New York: Guilford Press.
Miller, R. D. (1992). An update on involuntary civil commitment to outpatient treatment. *Hospital and Community Psychiatry, 43*, 79–81.
Miller, R. D., Blancke, F. W., Doren, D. M., & Maier, G. J. (1985). The Munchausen patient in a forensic facility. *Psychiatric Quarterly, 57*, 72–76.
Nichols, G. R., Davis, G. J., & Covey, T. S. (1990). In the shadow of the baron: Sudden death due to Munchausen's syndrome. *American Journal Emergency Medicine, 8*, 216–219.
O'Connor v. Donaldson, 422 U.S. 563 (1975).
Parham v. J. R., 42 U.S. 584 (1979).
Quinsey, V. L., Harris, G. T., Riu, M. G., & Cormier, C. A. (1998). *Violent offenders: Appraising and managing risk*. Washington DC: American Psychological Association.
Reisner, R. (1985). *Law and the mental health system*. St. Paul, MN: West.
Schlesinger, R., Daniel, D. G., Robin, P., et al. (1989). Factitious disorder with physical manifestations: Pitfalls of diagnosis and management. *Southern Medical Journal, 82*, 210–214.
Simon, R. I. (1999). The law and psychiatry. In R. E. Hales, S. C. Yudofsky, & J. A. Talbott (Eds.), *The American Psychiatric Press textbook of psychiatry* (3rd ed.) (pp. 1493–1502). Washington, DC: American Psychiatric Press.
Stromberg, C. D., & Stone, A. (1982). A model state law on civil commitment of the mentally ill. *Harvard Journal on Legislation, 20*, 275–396.
Tarasoff v. Regents of the University of California, 17 Cal. 3d 425, 551 P. 2d 334 (1976).
Washington v. Harper, 1105 Ct. 1028 (1990).
Wexler, D. B. (1981). *Mental health law*. New York: Plenum Press.
Yassa, R. (1978). Munchausen's syndrome: A successfully treated case. *Psychosomatics, 19*, 242–243.
Zeman, P. M., & Schwartz, H. I. (1994). Hospitalization: Voluntary and involuntary. In R. Rosner (Ed.), *Principals and practice of forensic psychiatry* (pp. 111–116). New York: Chapman & Hall.

CHAPTER 32

JURORS *CAN* BE SELECTED: NONINFORMATION, MISINFORMATION, AND THEIR STRATEGIC USES FOR JURY SELECTION

DEBORAH DAVIS AND WILLIAM C. FOLLETTE

UNIVERSITY OF NEVADA, RENO

> *The verdict is in when the jury's selected.*
>
> Trial attorneys everywhere

Trial attorneys enter the first day of trial facing a jury panel of strangers who hold in their hands not only the fate of the attorney's client, but also potentially the fate of the attorney's own job, reputation, and/or financial outcomes, up to millions of dollars. Somehow attorneys must diagnose who among these strangers will fulfill their dreams and who will devastate their hopes. Yet even those who successfully diagnose jurors' favorability cannot then *select* the jurors they want (conventional wisdom dictates)—they can only *deselect* the worst of the lot.

Our purpose in this chapter is to show that this conventional assumption of attorneys and trial consultants alike is literally, but not functionally, true. The attorney and his or her trial team can exert much more control over the jury selection process than is usually assumed. Through proper use of both their own scientific jury research and science-based jury selection strategy and the opposition's mistaken assumptions, stereotypes, and pseudoscientific aids, attorneys can not only *deselect* jurors through preemptory challenge, they can also significantly increase the odds that favorable jurors will go unchallenged—in a way *selecting* those they want.

SCIENCE AND NONSCIENCE IN JURY SELECTION

The importance of trial outcomes, in combination with high uncertainty about how to diagnose individual juror biases and verdict leanings, has led attorneys to seek aid from sources ranging from professional lore, psychics, private investigators, and graphologists to modern scientific jury selection services. The uninformed attorney may be easily misled by unfounded predictions of juror behavior. In fact, however, with carefully crafted strategy all of these sources can be used to the attorney's advantage—albeit somewhat differently than one might expect. This chapter explicates the manner in which both scientific and nonscientific diagnostic criteria may be used to help the attorney actually seat the most desirable jury. That is, we show how the skillful trial consultant can use *scientific* jury selection processes to *diagnose* juror favorability and *nonscientific* intuition, professional lore, and other nonscientific sources to *misdirect* opposing attorneys so that they will tend to use their own preemptory challenges to their own disadvantage. In fact, we show that the common reminder that one cannot *select* a jury—only *de*select individual jurors—is an exaggeration. In fact, science-based strategy in *voir dire* can—at a minimum—increase the odds that particular prospective jurors will be seated on the trial jury.

We begin the chapter with a review of scientific jury research procedures, with emphasis on those designed to develop accurate diagnostic criteria for juror favorability (i.e., those designed to identify juror attitudes, experiences, and demographic characteristics that actually predict verdict/damage/sentencing decisions). We then consider how this information may be used, in combination with noninformation (i.e., juror characteristics and behaviors during *voir dire* that are not actually diagnostic but are likely to be thought diagnostic by one's opponent) and misinformation (i.e., characteristics and behaviors that are actually diagnostic but in the opposite direction than one's opponent is likely to expect), to produce the best outcome (i.e., the most favorable seated jury) during *voir dire*. That is, we show how the traditional services of trial consultants to aid identification of jurors for challenge can be expanded to offer *voir dire* strategy designed to protect desirable prospective jurors from challenge and seat them on the trial jury.

USES OF SCIENTIFIC JURY RESEARCH

Scientific jury research is employed for three general purposes: (1) to *evaluate* an existing jury venue (eligible jurors in the community) or venire (pool of potential jurors from which the specific trial jury is selected) *as a whole*, (2) to aid in *selection* of the trial jury, and (3) to *adjust trial strategy* to fit the seated jury. Evaluation of the jury venue or venire is typically done either in cases involving extensive pretrial publicity (to evaluate the necessity of a change of venue) or in cases involving racial issues (to evaluate whether the racial composition of the trial jury pool or venire is representative of the community, and perhaps aid in a composition challenge). Jury selection research is done for the more familiar purpose of facilitating selection of the most favorable trial jury.

Finally, in addition to its uses for case evaluation and general strategy development, mock jury or trial simulation research is done in part to identify the differential persuasiveness of alternative themes, analogies, trial stories, analytical versus emotional arguments, and so on to *categories* of jurors. Once the jury is seated, the attorney may use this information to adjust the presentation of the case to fit what has been determined as maximally persuasive to the predominant juror type or to the jurors expected to be most influential. We discuss these techniques in the order in which they most typically arise, with primary emphasis on the jury selection procedures and *voir dire* strategy for actually seating the most desirable jury. In each case, we describe the relevant purposes and general procedures, referring the reader to sources of more detailed procedural guidelines.

Generally, however, the reader is directed to the recently published *Handbook of Jury Research* (Abbott & Batt, 1999) and to the American Society of Trial Consultants, which maintains archives of articles, technological manuals, example questionnaires, and other materials written by members. These materials, which cover a large variety of subjects and types of trials, can be very helpful to those assisting with a particular procedure or case type for the first time. The annual meetings also provide useful instruction and updates in most areas of trial consulting.

EVALUATION/SELECTION OF THE JURY POOL

Jury consultants are often engaged well before trial to evaluate the jury pool, for one of two purposes—either to support remedies for pretrial publicity (such as a change of venue (location) for the trial), or to support a composition challenge (a challenge to the racial/demographic composition of the venire). In effect, the trial consultant is asked to aid with determination of the entire jury venue or venire prior to selection of individual jurors.

Remedies for Pretrial Publicity

An extensive scientific literature has documented adverse effects of pretrial publicity on juror decision making (Linz & Penrod, 1992; Ogloff & Vidmar, 1994; Otto, Penrod, & Dexter, 1994; Studebaker & Penrod, 1997). In the case of criminal trials, for example, there is a significant association between guilty verdicts and the amount of evidence known to jurors prior to trial. The pretrial information appears both to provide extensive facts (or alleged facts) supporting the assumption of guilt and to set up initial schemas, trial stories, and/or attitudes toward the defendant through which new information is filtered. Thus, such predetermined opinions are not readily overcome by remedies during jury selection or by trial presentations, and serve the further biasing purpose of providing ammunition for persuasion of other (unexposed) jurors during deliberation. Further, jurors are unable to identify and accurately report their biases, making their representations regarding impartiality during *voir dire* unreliable. Trial consultants may be asked to aid with two kinds of remedies for this situation.

First, in recognition of the biasing effects of pretrial publicity, the trial judge may grant a *change of venue*, moving the trial to a location less blanketed with trial-relevant publicity. The trial consultant may be asked to conduct a *change of venue survey*, the purpose of which is to document the extent of awareness within the community of case parties and facts as well as bias toward the defendant. The purpose of such a survey is to evaluate/support the attorney's argument that a fair trial in the existing venue is unlikely, particularly in relation to alternative venues. Successful change of venue research will typically survey residents of the home venue and several other locations in order to demonstrate both that substantial awareness/prejudice exists in the home venue and that less awareness/prejudice exists in alternate locations, varying as a function of their distance from the home venue.

Questions in the change-of-venue survey first screen participants for jury eligibility (to include only members of the pertinent jury venue[s]). They proceed from questions assessing general knowledge of crimes (civil cases) in the community by way of relatively open-ended questions and proceed through general, open-ended questions concerning the case and parties at hand to increasingly closed-format, specific, and leading questions. These are intended to assess both the ease with which a case and case-relevant information comes to mind and the extent of case-relevant knowledge. This section should include assessment of knowledge of evidence that would be *inadmissible* in trial (which is deemed particularly damaging by the courts). The case-relevant questions end with *assessment* of the case, including the respondent's assessment of the strength of evidence favoring one or both sides and their probable verdict or damage decisions.

Finally, questions are included that may be useful for jury selection. Generally, profiling questions are discussed later in the profiling section. Such questions are included in a change-of-venue survey to essentially "profile" jurors who are most likely to have been exposed to, and biased by, the pretrial publicity. These include questions regarding where the person heard about the case (TV, newspapers, friends, neighbors, and so on—and the reading/viewing and other habits that tend to be associated with exposure to the publicity). For detailed explication of pertinent survey methods see Abbott and Batt (1999), Abbott, Hall, and Linville (1993), Nietzel and Dillehay (1986), Nietzel, Dillehay, and Abbott (1999), and Starr and McCormick (1985; 2000).

Secondary Uses of Change-of-Venue Research. In the event attempts to obtain a change of venue fail, the trial consultant may work with the attorney to better evaluate the degree of bias (due to pretrial publicity) in venire members. This is done through development of supplementary questions for extended *voir dire*, which are designed to examine current knowledge and attitudes about the case among members of the jury venire. Such questions attempt to assess potential for juror bias by asking directly about venire members' media habits and familiarity with key persons in the case and by asking open-ended questions about what jurors may know of the case at hand (including statements by the attorneys, reports of physical evidence, confessions, prior criminal records of the parties, results of lie detector tests, or evidence pertinent to high-profile civil litigation). Information acquired through such extended *voir dire* questions may be used to establish the basis of challenges for cause or for the attorney's choice of preemptory challenges.

Judges will not uniformly or automatically allow extended *voir dire*, even where extensive pretrial publicity is well documented. However, change-of-venue research—even when not successful in leading to a change of venue—may often be used to support arguments in favor of extended *voir dire*. Although not the intended use, this secondary benefit of change-of-venue research is useful, since research has shown a positive relationship between extended forms of *voir dire* and successful challenges of biased venire members (e.g., Moran, Cutler, & Loftus, 1990; Nietzel & Dillehay, 1982; Nietzel, Dillehay, & Himelein, 1987).

Further, in some cases, where change of venue research and/or supplemental questions to the trial venire show extensive awareness of the case among the venire, demonstration of this potential for bias can support motions for other remedies. Continuances, for example, have been shown to attenuate factual, but not emotional, pretrial publicity (e.g., Otto, Penrod, & Dexter, 1994).

Finally, in the event that all motions have failed (and the trial attorney must try the case in the home venue, with no continuance and without extended *voir dire*), the results of the change-of-venue survey may be used to create a "profile" of jurors most likely to be biased by pretrial publicity. This profile would consist of those respondent characteristics shown by the survey to correlate with the degree of case-relevant knowledge and verdict bias and may be used as one basis for preemptory challenges during *voir dire*.

Composition Challenge

In the event the entire venue (the jurors selected by the jury commissioner to serve as the pool for all trials) and/or the specific venire (panel selected from the pool from which the case specific jurors are further selected) appear conspicuously discrepant from the ethnic composition of the community, the composition of the array of jurors may be challenged. This kind of challenge is infrequent and varies widely by region. However, if the attorney believes a defendant's Fifth and Sixth Amendment rights (currently interpreted by the courts to mean the right to a jury that does not systematically exclude any cognizable group; see Weeks, 1999) are violated by significant underrepresentation or exclusion of specific demographic groups (most often racial), he or she may submit a motion to quash the jury venire.

The jury consultant may aid in this process by providing an empirical comparison of the demographics of the jury venue or venire and those of the community from which they are drawn. Support for the attorney's motion will depend upon the extent to which discrepancies are large and statistically significant. An excellent and detailed analysis of the mechanisms through which nonwhite racial groups tend to be excluded from jury service is provided by Fukurai, Butler, and Krooth (1993). Statistical reasoning and tests on which to base composition challenges are provided by demographer John Weeks (1999).

DIAGNOSTIC PROFILING: IDENTIFYING (UN)DESIRABLE JURORS

Once the trial venue is determined, the attorney and trial consultant next attempt to develop a "profile" of desirable and undesirable jurors. This is done in a series of steps, typically by using both scientific and nonscientific methods.

Developing Working Hypotheses

The first step is to formulate *working hypotheses* regarding which juror characteristics might be expected to predict verdict decisions. Typically this is done in strategic sessions between attorneys and trial consultants in which they consider the potential impact of demographic characteristics along with case-relevant attitudes and experiences. Hypotheses regarding how these variables may relate to verdicts are based on each professional's trial experience and intuition, and the trial consultant's examination of available scientific literature on predictive characteristics for the type of case at hand.

For an interesting discussion of common old wives' tales concerning desirable jurors, see Hastie, Penrod, and Pennington (1983) or Fulero and Penrod (1990), who have catalogued some of the common stereotypes of "good" and "bad" jurors among attorneys. Most of these stereotypes the average trial consultant has repeatedly encountered in clients' contributions to the working hypotheses.

The scientific literature has provided some guidance for both criminal and civil cases in general and for some specific case types within each category (e.g., Cutler, 1990; Fulero & Penrod, 1990; Goodman, Loftus, & Greene, 1990; Penrod, 1990). Two characteristics, for example, have been shown to affect verdicts in a variety of criminal trials. Both *authoritarianism* (see, for example, Batt, 1999; Dillehay, 1999; Narby, Cutler, & Moran, 1993; Peterson, Doty, & Winter, 1993) and *death qualification* (e.g., Allen, Mabry, & McKelton, 1998; Ellsworth, 1991; Nietzel, McCarthy, & Kerr, 1999; Hans, 1988) have been associated with antidefendant attitudes, greater tendency toward prosecution verdicts, and harsh sentencing as has the Juror Bias Scale (Kassin & Wrightsman, 1983) and the revised version of this scale by Myers and Lecci (1998). *Legal authoritarianism* (Kravitz, Cutler, & Brock, 1993), a measure of authoritarianism specific to the legal system, may be more valuable to those constructing jury questionnaires, since the items obviously pertain to the legal system and may be more easily justified to the judge for *voir dire* or supplemental juror questionnaires (see below). *Due process* orientation has also shown potential for use in criminal cases, particularly those involving the death penalty, minority defendants, and procedural violations/protections (e.g., Fitzgerald & Ellsworth, 1984; Liu & Shure, 1993), including issues of entrapment (Davis & Lewis, 2000).

Other bodies of literature have identified characteristics associated with case-relevant attitudes and verdicts in specific areas such as rape (e.g., Allison & Wrightsman, 1993; Olsen-Fulero & Fulero, 1997; Ward, 1995), sex abuse (e.g., Vidmar, 1997), sexual harassment (e.g., Wiener, Hurt, Russell, Mannen, & Gasper, 1997), murder among battered women (e.g., Schuller, 1992; Schuller & Hastings, 1996), or entrapment (e.g., Davis & Lewis, 2000). Considerably less data have been amassed for the civil arena. However, Abbott (1987; 1999a; 1999b) has provided evidence of the role of several demographic variables and "economic conservatism."

Notwithstanding the existence of some literature documenting associations of specific characteristics with verdicts for general case types, it has typically been the case that predictors of verdict, sentencing, or damages tend to be quite case specific (see review in Kovera, Dickinson, & Cutler, 2003). Hence, it is inadvisable to rely on this literature in the absence of case-specific profiling research.

Empirical Development of the Profiles

Once the set of working hypotheses is developed, several forms of empirical jury research may be performed to establish which among the proposed variables are actually predictive of verdicts (and, secondarily, of reactions to specific arguments, parties, or case facts). The first step for each procedure is to develop a *jury profiling questionnaire* (or a *profiling section* of a larger survey) containing questions to assess the demographic, attitudinal, and experiential variables hypothesized to relate to verdicts.

Developing the Jury Profiling Questionnaire

Most jury consultants have a standard set of questions regarding demographics and general attitudes toward civil or criminal cases that forms the standardized beginning of their case-specific questionnaires. Both standard questionnaires and case *type*–specific questionnaires are available from the archives of the American Society of Trial Consultants. (See also Abbott, 1999b, and Starr, 1996, for suggestions for standard juror profiling questions.)

Demographic Questions. The demographic section of the questionnaires contains variables such as age, race, sex, income, profession, marital status, family variables (number and age of children, living at home or not, etc.), education, rural versus central city residence, and the like. These questions may request both *current* (e.g., current residence) and *historical* (where the person grew up) information. This section of the questionnaire will typically contain mostly standard questions, which may be supplemented if more detailed demographics (for example, family constellation or work history) seem pertinent. For reviews of the impact of pertinent demographics, see Bothwell (1999), Golash (1992), or Simon (1999b) on race; Dillehay and Nietzel (1999) on prior jury service; Rothman, Dunlop, and Rambali (1999) on age; Simon (1999b) on gender; and Wrightsman, Nietzel, and Fortune (1998, Chapter 14) for a discussion of a variety of other characteristics.

Case-Relevant Attitudes. The attitudinal sections of the questionnaires assess both attitudes considered generally relevant to either the civil (attitudes toward corporations, attitudes toward lawsuits or verdict size, etc.) or criminal (i.e., authoritarianism, due process versus crime control orientation, death qualification) arenas; and those hypothesized to be relevant to the case at hand (such as those toward medicine, doctors, health behavior, etc., for a medical malpractice case).

Walter Abbott (1987, 1999a,b) has developed standardized demographic and attitudinal questions termed "The Analytic Juror Rater," which he suggests is predictive for a variety of criminal and civil cases. It includes demographic questions and attitudinal questions to assess "authoritarianism," "corporatism" (economic conservatism), "cosmopolitanism," "tolerance," "anomia," and "wordpower." He offers suggestions concerning the use of the Analytic Juror Rater for profiling and selection during *voir dire*. Among these, Abbott considers authoritarianism, economic conservatism, and racial tolerance key to verdict prediction across a wide variety of cases. He offers published juror ratings, available to those who cannot afford to do case-specific jury research. These should be used with some caution, however, because they are not necessarily predictive for the case at hand.

Case-Relevant Experiences. The third category of questions to be included in the profiling questionnaires are case-relevant *experiences*. These should include *knowledge* (or self-perceived knowledge) level regarding technology, skills, and experiences at issue; *training* that may predict relevant knowledge; *relatives* in related professions (for example, doctors' families when the case involves a claim of malpractice); and direct personal experience (and those of close friends or family) with relevant events, technologies, professions, and so on (including those that affect either case relevant knowledge or attitudes).

Case-Relevant Habits or Personality. Finally, many trial consultants and/or attorneys include questions regarding personal habits that are assumed to *indirectly* assess attitudes, knowledge, leadership potential, or relevant personality characteristics. These often include such behaviors as hobbies; memberships in various political, social, or fraternal organizations; and reading and movie/television viewing habits, including amounts and selection (e.g., are they Rush Limbaugh fans?). They may also include questions regarding distant personal history—such as where they grew up; what their parents did for a living; details about brothers, sisters, and other family members; and so on.

These questions will be intended to indirectly assess attitudes, values, and personality characteristics the trial team expects to be crucial to the case (or generally to a specific case type). For example, Jo-Ellan Dimitrius (the consultant many will recognize as having worked on the O. J. Simpson case) looks in responses to these questions (and others) for evidence of three characteristics she considers vitally important—compassion, socioeconomic background, and satisfaction with life (Dimitrius & Mazzarella, 1998).

There is also growing awareness of the importance of the fit between *affective* versus *cognitive* individual processing styles, affectively based versus cognitively based attitudes, and the advantage of tailoring affectively based arguments to affective processors or affectively based attitudes on one hand and cognitively based arguments to cognitive processors or cognitively based attitudes on the other (e.g., Fabrigar & Petty, 1999; Rusting & Larsen, 1998).

Testing the Profile

Once developed, juror profiles may be tested by presentation of the case to jury-eligible adults who have responded to the profiling questions. Reactions to the case facts, parties and witnesses, and verdict/sentencing/damage decisions are analyzed for statistically significant associations with profile questions. Two general techniques for testing the profile are commonly employed: the *community survey* and the *trial simulation/mock jury*. These general techniques vary in (1) whether they are conducted over the phone or in person, (2) the level of detail of the case presentation, and (3) sample size. Generally, there is a tradeoff between sample size (and thus statistical power in testing the profile) and detail/realism of the case presentation (and thus the validity of results). Detailed critical and instructional discussions of both methods and appropriate statistical analyses may be found in Abbott and Batt (1999) or Starr and McCormick (1985; 2000).

The Community Survey. For the community survey, a large sample of community residents is interviewed by telephone. Respondents listen to a brief synopsis of the case and then respond to a series of questions eliciting their opinions concerning the primary issues, parties, and evidence of the case; likely verdict/damage/sentencing decisions; and the reasons for these opinions/decisions. Finally, they respond to the profiling questions. The strength of the community survey lies in numbers. Hundreds of participants may be interviewed by phone for the same or lesser cost than that of a mock jury involving 30–40 participants.

However, the disadvantage of community research lies in the tradeoff between sample size and quality of the case presentation and the implications for validity of the results. The well-known warning that "the devil is in the details" is clearly reflected in the fact that more detailed case presentations lead to more predictive (valid) results—both with respect to profiling and to predicting verdicts.

Hence, it is our view that the community attitude survey is most useful under two circumstances.

First, when the nature and facts of the case are extremely simple (i.e., when there is little detail to be lost by a brief presentation), predictive validity will more closely approximate that of a more comprehensive case presentation. Thus, the power gained by larger sample size may well outweigh the less comprehensive presentation.

Second, the community survey may be restructured such that it profiles those likely to have favorable or unfavorable *case-relevant attitudes, knowledge, or experience* instead of those likely to favor a particular verdict/damage decision. The survey, in this case, would not include presentation of the case or questions regarding reactions to the case and instead would include assessment of attitudes believed to predict case reactions. This is particularly useful where *attitudes, knowledge, or experiences* related to verdicts have already been identified (through existing literature or mock jury research, for example). The community survey would then be conducted to try to identify demographic characteristics (or other characteristics of members of the trial venire likely to be visible/accessible to the trial team) that are *associated* with verdict-relevant attitudes. Although indirect, this strategy avoids the problems associated with invalid results caused by inadequate case presentation.

It is crucial to note, however, that such an indirect strategy is only as good as the links between (1) characteristics knowable to the trial team and the case-relevant attitudes, and (2) the case-relevant attitudes and verdict/damage decisions. We have consistently found in our practice that although some attitudes are typically predictive, most attitudes expected to predict verdicts in fact do not—a finding consistent with experimental tests of such links (see review in Kovera et al., 2003). Hence, the indirect strategy is very risky when the relationship between attitudes and verdicts has not been established via mock jury research or existing literature. In the absence of this knowledge, the use of presumed indirect links may lead the trial team to rely on irrelevant (at best) or misleading information. Further, at best, indirect predictors are less related to verdict than direct predictors. Hence, the indirect strategy, per force, relies on weaker predictors of verdicts/damages and should be used only when more powerful strategies are unavailable.

The Trial Simulation/Mock Jury. In a full trial simulation, surrogate jurors witness an event that resembles the expected trial procedures as closely as possible, including as many of the actual attorneys and witnesses for the case (or videotapes of them) as possible and actor standins for unavailable parties (such as the opposing attorneys), *voir dire*, opening and closings, and judicial instructions. Less complete simulations leave out some or most of these. Perhaps the most common version restricts the presentation to an argument (an amalgamation of opening and closing) for each side. The results of trial simulations are broadly useful for both jury selection and trial strategy. For a discussion of these uses, see, for example, Abbott and Batt (1999), Davis (1989), Bennett, Hirschhom, and Dimitrius (1995), Starr and McCormick (1985; 2000), and Vinson (1986).

Uses of the trial simulation for jury selection lie in the relationships between juror characteristics assessed in the jury profiling questionnaire and various case reactions. Surrogate jurors fill out jury profiling questionnaires prior to the case presentations, fill out individual case reaction/verdict questionnaires afterward, and finally deliberate in groups to a verdict. More technologically sophisticated procedures also include computer-coded continuous reactions from jurors during the presentation, which are amalgamated to track the overall sentiment of the jurors moment by moment.

Data analyses then associate individual juror characteristics (or constellations of characteristics) with a range of variables—including pre- and postdeliberation verdict/damage decisions and reactions to individual parties or witnesses as well as specific evidence or arguments.

In some cases (with more substantial resources), two or more versions of the presentation may be included, both to test which strategy is more successful overall and to examine the interaction of strategy with juror characteristics (to see which strategy is most successful with which groups of jurors). The latter results become useful once the jury is seated, such that strategy may be tailored to the characteristics of the seated jury (or to the most probably influential seated jurors).

GETTING THE JURORS YOU WANT: THE DIPP METHOD

Once the profiling results are in and the trial team has determined which kinds of jurors they do and do not want, attention must turn to the twin goals of (1) collecting diagnostic information on the jury venire members, and (2) executing *voir dire* strategy that will both exclude undesirable jurors from the final seated jury and retain desirable jurors. Since one is not allowed to select jurors, but only to challenge (*de*select) them, traditional approaches to jury selection have focused on identification and challenge of undesirable jurors—assuming that there is no effective strategy for retaining those that are desirable.

Davis (1996) has described a means to accomplish both goals—what she called the DIPP strategy for *voir dire*. The acronym refers to four central functions served by *voir dire*: (1) *Diagnosis* of juror favorability, (2) *Ingratiation* of the attorney and client to the jury, (3) *Persuasion* (creating favorable disposition toward your side of the case, setting up schemas and trial story structures for further favorable processing of arguments and evidence, etc.), and (4) *Procuring* desirable jurors (i.e., challenging effectively and protecting favorable jurors from opposition challenge). As we shortly demonstrate, the diagnostic, persuasive, and procuring functions are all central to the process of jury selection, whereas ingratiation and persuasion are intended to facilitate eventual favorable verdict decisions.

Davis (1996) further described the strategic use of *misdirection*, *misinformation*, and *noninformation* to accomplish these strategic goals. It is in our review and elaboration of this strategy of misdirection that we fulfill our promise to show how the skillful trial team can use scientific jury selection processes to diagnose juror favorability and (through the use of science-based strategy) take advantage of *nonscientific* intuition, professional lore, and other nonscientific sources (i.e., noninformation and misinformation) to misdirect opposing attorneys so that they will tend to use their own preemptory challenges to their own disadvantage—and thereby help the trial team to actually get (procure/select) the jurors it wants.

We illustrate the DIPP method (excluding the Ingratiation function) and associated strategic misdirection in the sections that follow. However, we first define three important terms. First, *diagnostic* criteria refer to those juror characteristics that have been empirically linked (either through existing scientific literature or through the trial team's case-specific profiling research) to verdicts.

Second, *nondiagnostic* criteria (also referred to as *noninformation*) refer to those criteria that are *not* empirically linked to verdicts. These fall into two categories. First, nondiagnostic criteria may be identified through jury profiling research. That is, they are criteria included in the profiling research questionnaire but found to have no significant relationship with verdict decisions. Our own experience with profiling research is that of all the juror characteristics anticipated by the trial team to predict verdicts, many more are actually nondiagnostic than are diagnostic. Thus, there are always a number of nondiagnostic profiling criteria that may be used for strategic misdirection.

Nondiagnostic criteria may also include attitudes expressed during *voir dire* in response to persuasive or coercive questions from attorneys or the judge. These, and the rationale for their nondiagnosticity, are discussed further in the *voir dire* section that follows.

Finally, *reverse diagnostic* criteria (also referred to as *misinformation*) are those that *are* empirically linked to verdicts but in a manner opposite to that expected. In other words, these are criteria for which intuition, folklore, and in some cases even some scientific literature would have suggested a particular link to verdict decisions. However, a significant relationship was obtained in the jury profiling research—but in the exact opposite of the expected direction. Reverse diagnostic criteria have appeared less frequently (in our experience) than nondiagnostic criteria but are exceptionally useful when they do.

Our proposed methods of strategic misdirection rely on the proposition that the average trial attorney (in the absence of concrete knowledge/jury profiling research results to the contrary) will typically rely on intuitively plausible but factually incorrect (either nondiagnostic or reverse diagnostic) criteria for diagnosis of juror favorability. These may include intuition, folklore, unreliable techniques such as graphology, and so on. The trial team may take advantage of this tendency through *apparent* emphasis on these non- or reverse diagnostic criteria (which will tend to make them salient to, and thus more likely to be used by, the opposition). To the extent that opposing attorneys employ nondiagnostic criteria, their challenges will be at best ineffective. If they use reverse diagnostic criteria, their challenges will be counterproductive. Either ineffective or counterproductive opposition challenges are advantageous to the trial team.

Pretrial Diagnosis

Diagnosis of juror favorability occurs in several stages before and during trial. Prior to trial, the trial team may have access to the following information regarding individual prospective jurors: (1) standard jury questionnaires (those filled out by venire members for all cases in that jurisdiction), (2) supplemental jury questionnaires (detailed, case-specific questionnaires designed by one or both trial teams), (3) investigative reports of detectives, or (4) a "network analysis" (Bonora & Krauss, 1979) using community contacts to gain personal knowledge of the prospective jurors. Each of these sources provides information that may be compared to the profiles developed from profiling research as a basis for favorability ratings of each prospective juror.

The final diagnostic stage occurs during *voir dire*, when the judge and attorneys question the individual jurors either individually or in open court. At this stage, the trial team may attempt to further assess juror favorability by questions following up on information obtained in the pretrial phase and by observation of nonverbal responses. Where little or no pretrial information is available, the attorney will have to question the individual jurors as thoroughly as the judge permits (addressing as many diagnostic criteria as possible).

In the sections that follow, we briefly review the pretrial diagnostic tools and then move on to focus more extensively on *voir dire*. In each case we point to the potential for strategic use of misdirection.

Standard and Supplemental Juror Questionnaires

Prior to trial, jurors fill out *standard* jury questionnaires in which they provide a few, primarily demographic, family, and litigation history self-descriptors. A *supplemental* juror questionnaire refers essentially to a profiling questionnaire (in that it contains essentially the same categories of questions, both general and case specific, typically included in profiling research). However, it is given to the actual jurors before trial (or in court before the trial begins). Judges will tend to allow such questionnaires in cases where lengthy *voir dire* is anticipated; those with limited or no attorney-conducted *voir dire*; those where large numbers of jurors will have to be questioned in order to pass enough for cause to try the case; and those involving sensitive (potentially personally embarrassing) issues, extensive pretrial publicity, well-known parties, heinous crimes, or highly charged issues. In such cases, the judge may allow the supplemental questionnaire to save time during *voir dire* and/or to facilitate honesty from (and avoid contamination between) jurors. Diane Wiley (1999) of the National Jury Project has provided an excellent summary of the nature and purpose of supplemental questionnaires, how to convince a judge to allow them, and questionnaire design (including example questions for specific case issues).

Supplemental juror questionnaires are highly desirable for the trial team. They provide much more extensive and sensitive assessment of diagnostic criteria developed in jury research than either standard questionnaires or questioning in open court. They are, in fact, the only means by which each and every member of the venire can respond to the exact questions included in the jury profiling research in exactly the same format—and thereby provide the means to compare each juror directly to the desirable and undesirable profiles. Thus, the supplemental questionnaire provides a crucial diagnostic tool for the trial team.

It is also important to note that while some jurisdictions permit almost unlimited attorney *voir dire*, others permit little to none. Judges enjoy wide discretion with regard to *voir dire*, and even within the same jurisdiction judges may vary widely in the amount and type of attorney questioning they permit. To the chagrin of trial consultants and attorneys alike, judges in federal courts tend to ask most, if not all, questions of the jurors, and to permit very restricted questions, if any, from the attorneys. Questions tend to be restricted in both number and content in federal courts, and the attorney cannot effectively carry out much of the *voir dire* strategy recommended here. Hence, when faced with a more restrictive judge, the best hope of the trial team for obtaining the most useful juror information is to persuade the judge to permit a supplemental juror questionnaire.

Strategic Misdirection and the Supplemental Questionnaire. The supplemental questionnaire provides the first opportunity for *strategic misdirection* through use of noninformation and misinformation. This is accomplished through deliberate inclusion of questions that the other trial team will likely believe to be diagnostic but that your team has determined (in its jury research) to actually be either nondiagnostic or reverse diagnostic. This will be most effective, of course, when the other team either has not done jury profiling research or has done it poorly. Unable to focus on truly diagnostic criteria in developing their ratings of the venire members, the opposition's judgment will be at least diluted by inclusion of "noise" from the nondiagnostic criteria and perhaps led astray through focus on those that are reverse diagnostic.

Jury Investigation and Network Analysis

Jury investigations, by private investigator or by network analysis, have in common the fact that they assess jurors by means other than self-report. Further, both are able to assess characteristics the judge may have excluded from supplemental questionnaires or from questioning during *voir dire*. Whereas the judge will often restrict both supplemental questionnaires and *voir dire* to questions that are apparently relevant to the case, the trial team's investigations are not restricted in this manner and thereby provide an additional source of information for comparison of individual jurors to the profiles.

Hence, the trial team may obtain information to verify and/or expand upon self-reports from questionnaires and *voir dire*. The investigations may uncover dishonesty (for example, we have not infrequently found venire members to fail to report criminal records or involvement in previous litigation and to overreport income/education/professional status, etc.). Reports from the detectives or network analysis have also identified hobbies, group memberships, political party membership, case-relevant attitudes, and even conclusions formed on the basis of pretrial publicity. For an interesting (if horrifying) account of the potential excesses of these techniques (and more generally of extreme abuse of trial tactics), see the account of the Cullen Davis murder trials, *Final Justice: The True Story of the Richest Man Ever Tried for Murder*, by Steven Naifeh and Gregory White Smith (1993).

Comparing Jurors to Profiles: Rating the Jury Venire

Once the trial team has gathered all available information prior to trial, the jury consultant may provide desirability ratings for each venire member based on comparison of data on that juror to the profiles. These profile analyses/ratings should include not only an index of likely favorability, but also an index of leadership potential and probable role in deliberations. It is typical for trial consulting companies to provide ratings including indices of at least (1) favorability (indicating probable verdict leaning and/or damage/sentencing decisions), (2) leadership potential, and (3) an overall desirability rating, based on the combination of the previous two. The most dangerous juror is one with negative verdict leanings and strong leadership potential. Some include more indices, including such things as sympathy, emotionality, authoritarianism, conservatism, and many others.

Although used primarily for jury selection, juror ratings (along with others one may be asked to provide—such as probable cognitive style) may also be valuable for trial strategy decisions. The common admonition, "Know your audience," cannot be overemphasized. The more one knows about the specific individuals one must persuade, the more effectively they can be persuaded.

Diagnosis in *Voir dire*

Recall that questions during *voir dire* serve the four DIPP functions of Diagnosis, Ingratiation, Persuasion, and Procuring. Hence, it is crucial to *voir dire* strategy for the trial consultant and attorney to clearly understand which kinds of questions and interaction with the jury serve which function. Answers to persuasive questions, for example, are rarely diagnostic, and the trial team must be careful not to consider them when diagnosing juror favorability.

The trial consultant may assist the attorney in both (1) formulation of questions to serve each function of *voir dire*, (2) determination of which questions to use on each individual venire member, and (3) selection of jurors for preemptory challenge (the most common service). In the sections that follow, we discuss how to formulate questions to serve each of the four functions of *voir dire* and identify which questions are appropriate for which jurors.

Developing Diagnostic Questions for Voir dire

Diagnostic questions during *voir dire* fall into two categories: those asked of the entire venire and those asked only of specific prospective jurors.

Questions for the Entire Panel. It is vital to ask each and every juror questions during *voir dire*. As most trial consultants will tell you, the most likely person to end up on the seated jury is the person who has said nothing during *voir dire*. The person who says nothing scares no one (assuming no negative pretrial information), and thus goes unchallenged. Hence, in the vast majority of trials, the prospective jurors about whom the attorneys know the least are those who end up deciding the case. Particularly when no pretrial investigations and no supplemental questionnaires are available, the trial team must guard against this possibility.

When no pretrial information is available (and to the extent the judge permits), *voir dire* questions should include the same question types recommended for jury profiling and supplemental questionnaires. The attorney should take care to ask all jurors the same questions to facilitate comparisons between jurors.

Where possible, diagnostic questions should be in open format: "Can you tell me about . . . ?" "How do you feel about . . . ?" "You responded in your questionnaire that . . . ?" "Could you tell me what you meant by . . . ?" "a little more about . . . ?" "Why you chose . . . ?" "What you were planning to . . . ?" and so on. Much more can be learned about prospective jurors when they are allowed and encouraged to talk freely about attitudes, experiences, feelings, behaviors, and so on. Such open responses also provide more information regarding how jurors think and their reactions to the attorney.

Questions for Individual Jurors. Diagnostic questions may relate to something identified in the particular juror's questionnaire or responses to previous questions. Again, even where extensive pretrial information is available, it is desirable to hear jurors talk about their attitudes and experiences in the open format just illustrated. The more the trial team can listen to the jurors' thoughts, feelings, and reasoning, the better judgments they can make of jurors' potential biases, information processing styles, and likely roles in group deliberations.

Observation of Nonverbal Responses. Most jury consultants recommend focus on the nonverbal behavior of venire members in contexts ranging from waiting in the hallways, sitting in the "peanut gallery" when they are not yet in the jury box for questioning, questioning during *voir dire*, and even after the case presentation has begun. During *voir dire*, it is desirable, where possible, to have one consultant focus on the person being questioned and another on those not being questioned. Jurors' nonverbal responses while not the center of attention are often very revealing, because they are less careful to control their responses.

These observations are intended to assess such varied issues as potential relationships between jurors (potential leadership roles, friendships, etc.), reactions to attorneys and case parties, personality characteristics, and deception (see Starr & McCormick, 1985; 2000; Dimitrius & Mazzarella, 1998, for specific suggestions for reading these variables from nonverbal behavior). Caution is in order, however, since many of the common recommendations for reading personality, attitudes, and the like from nonverbal cues are untested and may be misleading to the trial team.

The Primacy of Diagnosis. Diagnosis is first in *voir dire*, both in importance and in order. One must first identify the jurors who will tend to favor and oppose one's case before proceeding to challenge those deemed unfavorable and protect those deemed favorable. Hence, when planning *voir dire* the trial team must plan to diagnose first and then proceed with *persuasive/lure* and *deflection* questions designed to seat the jury it wants.

Misdirection with Non- and Reverse Diagnostic Questions

Diagnostic questions during *voir dire* provide the second opportunity to misdirect the opposition into counterproductive challenges. Just as questions regarding nondiagnostic and reverse diagnostic criteria are included in supplemental jury questionnaires in order to mislead the opposition, they should also be included with other (actually diagnostic) questions in open court. To the extent that opposing attorneys have failed to do adequate profiling research, they will be lured into challenges based on their (probably) inaccurate assumptions regarding the predictive value of these criteria.

Persuasion in *Voir dire*

The trial consultant may help the attorney to formulate persuasive questions and plan their use for misdirection of the opposition. Persuasive questions during *voir dire* are recommended for two purposes: (1) to *indoctrinate* the jury, or predispose them to favor one side; and (2) to *lure* the opposition into challenging jurors who would actually tend to favor their side of the case. In other words, persuasive questions may be used to lure the opposition into challenging jurors the trial team would actually want to challenge itself (or who the team considers undesirable but does not expect to challenge because others must be challenged with higher priority).

This lure strategy relies once again on the power of noninformation to deceive the opponent into making useless or damaging challenges. This is true because jurors' responses to persuasive questions do not typically reflect attitudes predictive of verdict decisions, as we will shortly explain.

Attribution theorists have identified a number of common errors in understanding of the causes of behaviors. Most prominent among them is the *fundamental attribution error*, or the *correspondence bias* (e.g., Jones & Harris, 1967;

Humphrey, 1985; Ross, 1977), which refers to the general failure to recognize the power of the situation to influence behavior. In other words, in perceiving the cause of others' behavior and explaining to ourselves why they behave the way they do (and say the things they do), we tend to be "personality" psychologists. We assume that people behave and say things in the manner they do because of the kinds of people they are rather than the kinds of situations they are in. We also suffer lack of awareness of *perceiver-induced constraint*—meaning our own influence on others and the way we constrain their behavior by our own actions.

In the courtroom setting, these errors of attribution cause attorneys and trial consultants to overestimate the diagnostic value of juror responses to what are essentially coercive questions that leave them few to no options of how to respond. Jurors are confronted with a number of powerful situational constraints on their behavior. They are asked leading ("Do any of you feel that . . . ?"), and coercive ("Wouldn't you agree with me that . . . ?" "Can you put aside that attitude and follow the law the judge gives you?") questions from the judge and attorneys that certainly constrain the answers they can or will give. Jurors are strongly affected by what they think they are supposed to say or what they think the questioner wants to hear. These situational forces are certain to compromise the diagnostic value of jurors' expressions of attitudes and feelings. Yet just as certainly, those hearing them will be victims of the fundamental attribution error—and tend to overestimate the correspondence between what jurors say in such powerfully constraining circumstances and what they truly feel.

The Coercive Power of Persuasive Questions

Persuasive or *indoctrinating* questions are designed to either make a particular point or argument, to establish the elements of the attorney's trial story, or to instantiate a particular schema or structure for understanding and evaluating the case through which jurors will filter and evaluate the evidence to come. However, persuasive questions tend to share common features. Generally, whereas diagnostic questions should be structured much like *direct examination* of witnesses (i.e., more open ended and allowing the witness more flexibility in response), good persuasive questions should be structured much like *cross-examination* of witnesses (i.e., closed format and allowing the witness only one reasonable response). Since the attorney asks the jurors persuasive, indoctrinating questions to help make particular points, he or she must ask them in such a way that the juror cannot help but provide a helpful answer. An attorney who gets an initial answer in line with expectations may ask the juror to explain *why* the juror answered as he or she did and thereby cause the juror to help the attorney argue the point. Again, the juror is almost guaranteed to give a helpful explanation because the questions are structured so that reasonable people can answer only one way.

For example, we worked on a case where a pilot who poorly maintained his plane, and who had ample signs and warning that the left engine was compromised (difficult to start and leaking fluids), suffered an engine out on takeoff. He crashed, killing his wife and seriously and permanently injuring several passengers—and later sued the manufacturer of the airplane. During *voir dire*, our client asked jurors a number of persuasive questions intended to lay the fault at plaintiff's door. He asked each juror about vehicles or equipment they might own. Then when the juror identified something (their car, a tractor or large truck, lawnmowers, and so on), he asked about what they would do if something appeared about to break—preferably something that would be dangerous if it did. For example, several jurors were asked if they would continue to drive a car if one of the tires appeared to be wobbling or if the tire was threadbare and might cause a blowout. If not, the juror was asked to explain why not. Finally, the juror was asked if he or she did drive and there was an accident, whose fault would that be, and why.

Like all good persuasive lines of questions, these questions clearly conveyed the point to jurors, with their full participation but without allowing them any real freedom of response. These and other effective persuasive questions constrain jurors' responses to the point where they offer no useful diagnostic indication of case-relevant attitudes. However, given observer susceptibility to the fundamental attribution error, responses to such coercive questions can *appear* diagnostic. It is this mistake in inference that can be used to the trial team's advantage in *voir dire*. That is, by asking persuasive, indoctrinating questions that in effect force the juror to respond with answers that *appear* favorable to the trial team's side of the case, the juror is made to *appear* dangerous to the opposition (though they actually may or may not be). In this way, the opposition can often be "lured" into challenging the wrong jurors—those the trial team finds undesirable. To accomplish this goal, however, it is important to remember the following.

Use Persuasive-Lure Questions on Jurors Your Team Does Not Want. All jurors will hear and be affected by the persuasive questions and their answers. However, because jurors who respond to these questions will appear dangerous to the opposing attorney, they should be used only on jurors your team *wants the opposition to challenge*. Use of persuasive questions on jurors your team wants risks luring the opposition into challenging them.

Don't Be Hoist by Your Own Petard. It is important to remember that one's own team will be susceptible to the fundamental attribution error as well and to be aware of this potential to be caught in one's own trap. *Jurors' responses to persuasive (or any other coercive questions) are not diagnostic*. The trial team must remember that a good persuasive script is truly coercive and constraining, leaving the juror few to no response options. If the trial team believes a juror is bad before the persuasive questions, it should stick with that opinion. Diagnosis should occur *before* the persuasive questions begin, and persuasive or deflecting questions (see below) should serve strictly the persuasive or protection/procuring functions of *voir dire*.

Deflection: Keeping the Jurors You Want

The opposition can simultaneously be lured into challenging jurors essentially for one's own trial team and deflected from challenging those the team wants to keep—thus serving the fourth function of *voir dire*, procuring the jury you want. Both strategies rely on the fundamental attribution error and the tendency of observers to believe in the diagnostic significance of coercive questions. The difference lies in the *direction* of the coercive questions.

In essence, in order to *deflect* the opposition from challenges of desirable jurors, one must (mis)lead them into believing the jurors are good for them. As we will illustrate, this is most effectively accomplished through use of questions made to appear as if intended to discover attitudes that might be unfavorable for your case. Clearly, one would not want to ask persuasive questions against one's own interests. However, it is perfectly appropriate to ask questions to *find out about (diagnose)* unfavorable attitudes.

To execute the deflection function, the trial team must first identify several areas in which a number of jurors are likely to have attitudes that will *appear* unfavorable to its own side. Second, the jury as a whole must be questioned to identify those who hold these attitudes. When a desirable juror expresses an apparently undesirable attitude, he or she must be drawn out and led to express that attitude fully. This should make the juror appear dangerous to your team (and desirable to the other attorney), and protect the juror from challenge. Finally, once the undesirable attitudes are fully expressed, other jurors who have expressed the same attitude (but whom your team *does not want*) must be asked persuasive/coercive questions designed to counter the undesirable attitude. This tactic should simultaneously (1) protect the desirable juror, (2) lure the opponent into striking the undesirable juror, and (3) make your team's persuasive point.

For this strategy to be effective, however, the deflection questions must address truly nondiagnostic attitudes. For example, a plaintiff's attorney might ask the question, "Is there anyone who believes there are too many lawsuits in this country?" Many, if not most, jurors will raise their hands. We have found, in jury research across a number of cases, that this attitude does *not* predict antiplaintiff bias. The same jurors who believe there are too many lawsuits also believe that people should have a right to sue, that there are many legitimate lawsuits, that corporations should be held accountable, that a person who is genuinely injured through another's wrongdoing should be compensated, and so on. However, skillful questioning can lead such jurors to appear to have an antiplaintiff bias when none exists—and thus protect them from defense challenges. Similarly, other jurors can be led to elaborate on the right to sue, corporate responsibility, and the like, thereby (1) arguing the plaintiff attorney's case for him, (2) appearing to possess an antidefendant bias, and (3) increasing the odds of challenge from the defense. Used skillfully together, persuasive and deflection questions can very effectively mislead the opposing attorney to make challenges exactly opposite to those in his or her interest. For a more detailed description of this strategy, see Davis (1996), who provided a script illustrating the persuasive/lure and deflection process for civil lawsuits.

CONCLUSION

Traditional wisdom regarding jury selection, and the role of trial consultants in assisting attorneys, has restrictively assumed that the trial team is limited to *de*-selection of undesirable jurors. This view is unnecessarily pessimistic. While it is true that one cannot ensure the selection of any particular juror, it is also true that well-crafted strategy prior to and during *voir dire* can significantly either increase or decrease the odds that a particular juror will be seated—independently of one's own preemptory challenges. The sophisticated trial team can, in effect, increase the number of its own challenges (by *luring* the opposing attorney into counterproductive challenges), and protect desirable jurors (by *deflecting* the opponent's challenges of these jurors), all the while indoctrinating and beginning to persuade the jurors.

To understand and help the attorney to implement these strategies, the trial consultant should be thoroughly familiar both with standard procedures for jury research and with the literatures (at least) on cognitive processing, persuasion, and jury behavior. Both diagnosis of juror favorability and selection strategy should be firmly grounded in scientific findings—either existing literature or case-specific jury research. Guesses and assumptions regarding juror favorability are too often completely inaccurate. In fact, our strategy recommendations depend on it. Better to be the team working with real information rather than assumption, stereotypes, superstition, and pseudoscience.

REFERENCES

Abbott, W. F. (1987). *Analytic juror rater*. Philadelphia: ALA-ABA.
Abbott, W. F. (1999a). The analytic juror rater: Towards an unobtrusive *voir dire* technique. In W. F. Abbott & J. Batt (Eds.), *A handbook of jury research* (pp. 15:1–15:38). Philadelphia: ALA-ABA.
Abbott, W. F. (1999b). The juror questionnaire: Quantitative and narrative forms. In W. F. Abbott & J. Batt (Eds.), *A handbook of jury research* (pp. 27:1–27:24). Philadelphia: ALA-ABA.
Abbott, W. F. (1999c). Designing and implementing mock trials: A checklist. In W. F. Abbott & J. Batt (Eds.), *A handbook of jury research* (pp. 28:1–28:40). Philadelphia: ALA-ABA.
Abbott, W. F. (1999d). *Voir dire*: Applying the analytic juror rater. In W. F. Abbott & J. Batt (Eds.), *A handbook of jury research* (pp. 30:1–30:18). Philadelphia: ALA-ABA.
Abbott, W. F., & Batt, J. (1999). *A handbook of jury research*. Philadelphia: ALA-ABA.
Abbott, W. F., Hall, F., & Linville, E. (1993). *Jury research: A review and bibliography*. Philadelphia: ALA-ABA.

Allen, M., Mabry, E., & McKelton, D. (1998). Impact of juror attitudes about the death penalty on juror evaluations of guilt and punishment: A meta-analysis. *Law and Human Behavior*, *23*, 715–732.

Allison, J. A., & Wrightsman, L. A. (1993). *Rape: The misunderstood crime*. Newbury Park, CA: Sage.

Batt, J. (1999). Enemy of the criminal defense team: The narcissistic authoritarian juror—with special attention to the trial of Orenthal James (O.J.) Simpson. In W. F. Abbott & J. Batt (Eds.), *A handbook of jury research* (pp. 14:1–14:29). Philadelphia: ALA-ABA.

Bennett, C. E., Hirschhorn, R. B., & Dimitrius, J. (1995). *Bennett's guide to jury selection and trial dynamics*. San Francisco: West.

Bonora, B., & Krauss, E. (Eds.) (1979). *Jurywork: Systematic techniques*. Berkeley, CA: National Jury Project.

Bothwell, R. K. (1999). The ethnic factor in *voir dire*. In W. F. Abbott & J. Batt (Eds.), *A handbook of jury research* (pp. 10:1–10:10). Philadelphia: ALA-ABA.

Bottoms, B. L., & Goodman, G. S. (1994). Perceptions of children's credibility in sexual assault cases. *Journal of Applied Social Psychology*, *24*, 702–732.

Cutler, B. L. (1990). The status of scientific jury selection in psychology and law. *Forensic Reports*, *3*, 227–232.

Davis, D. (1989). Flying with radar: Use of mock jury research to target critical issues and fine tune trial strategy. *Inter Alia: Journal of the State Bar of Nevada*, *54*, Forum 4–12.

Davis, D. (1996). Jury selection in the 90's: Perspectives of a trial consultant. *Torts, Insurance and Compensation Law Section Journal* (*State Bar of New York*), *25*, 18–26.

Davis, D., & Follette, W. C. (2001). "*DIPP*ing" in the jury pool: Designing voir dire questions to *D*iagnose, *I*ngratiate, *P*ersuade, and *P*rocure the jury you want. *Proceedings of the Journal of Air Law and Commerce Symposium*.

Davis, D., & Lewis, E. (2000). Determinants of perceptions of entrapment: The roles of juror characteristics, repeated police solicitation, incentives and defendant record. Unpublished manuscript, University of Nevada, Reno.

Dillehay, R. C. (1999). Authoritarianism and jurors. In W. F. Abbott & J. Batt (Eds.), *A handbook of jury research* (pp. 13:1–13:18). Philadelphia: ALA-ABA.

Dillehay, R. C., & Nietzel, M. (1999). Prior jury service. In W. F. Abbott & J. Batt (Eds.), *A handbook of jury research* (pp. 11:1–11:16). Philadelphia: ALA-ABA.

Dimitrius, J., & Mazzarella, M. (1998). *Reading people*. New York: Ballantine.

Ellsworth, P. C. (1991). To tell what we know or wait for Godot? *Law and Human Behavior*, *15*, 77–90.

Fabrigar, L. R., & Petty, R. E. (1999). The role of the affective and cognitive bases of attitudes in susceptibility to affectively and cognitively based persuasion. *Personality and Social Psychology Bulletin*, *25*, 363–381.

Fitzgerald, R., & Ellsworth, P. C. (1984). Due process vs. crime control: Death qualification and jury attitudes. *Law and Human Behavior*, *8*, 81–93.

Fukurai, H., Butler, E. W., & Krooth, R. (1993). *Race and the jury*. New York: Plenum Press.

Fulero, S. M., & Penrod, S. D. (1990). Attorney jury selection folklore: What do they think and how can psychologists help? *Forensic Reports*, *3*, 233–259.

Golash, D. (1992). Race, fairness and jury selection. *Behavioral Sciences and the Law*, *10*, 155–177.

Goodman, J., Loftus, E. F., & Greene, E. (1990). Matters of money: *Voir dire* in civil cases. *Forensic Reports*, *3*, 303–329.

Hans, V. P. (1988). Death by jury. In K. C. Haas & J. A. Inciardi (Eds.), *Challenging capital punishment* (pp. 149–175). Beverly Hills, CA: Sage.

Hastie, R., Penrod, S., & Pennington, N. (1983). *Inside the jury*. Cambridge, MA: Harvard University Press.

Humphrey, R. (1985). How work roles influence perception: Structural-cognitive processes and organizational behavior. *American Sociological Review*, *50*, 242–252.

Jones, E. E., & Harris, V. A. (1967). The attribution of attitudes. *Journal of Experimental Social Psychology*, *3*, 1–24.

Kassin, S. M., & Wrightsman, L. S. (1983). The construction and validation of a juror bias scale. *Journal of Research in Personality*, *17*, 423–442.

Kovera, M. B., Dickinson, J. J., & Cutler, B. L. (2003). Voir dire and jury selection. In A. M. Goldstein & I. B. Weiner (Eds.), *Handbook of psychology: Vol. 11: Forensic Psychology* (161–175). Hoboken, NJ: Wiley.

Kovera, M. B., Gresham, A. W., Borgida, E., Gray, E., & Regan, P. C. (1997). Does expert testimony inform or influence juror decision-making? A social cognitive analysis. *Journal of Applied Psychology*, *82*, 178–191.

Kovera, M. B., McAuliff, B. D., & Hebert, K. S. (1999). Reasoning about scientific evidence: Effects of juror gender and evidence quality on juror decisions in a hostile work environment case. *Journal of Applied Psychology*, *84*, 362–375.

Kravitz, D. A., Cutler, B. L., & Brock, P. (1993). Reliability and validity of the original and revised legal attitudes questionnaire. *Law and Human Behavior*, *17*, 661–678.

Linz, D., & Penrod, S. (1992). Exploring the First and Sixth Amendments: Pretrial publicity and jury decision making. In D. E. Kagehiro & W. S. Laufer (Eds.), *Handbook of psychology and law* (pp. 1–20). New York: Springer-Verlag.

Liu, J. H., & Shure, G. H. (1993). Due process orientation does not always mean political liberalism. *Law and Human Behavior*, *17*, 343–360.

Myers, B., & Lecci, L. (1998). Revising the factor structure of the Juror Bias Scale: A method for the empirical evaluation of theoretical constructs. *Law and Human Behavior*, *22*, 239–256.

Moran, G., Cutler, B. L., & Loftus, E. A. (1990). Jury selection in major controlled substance trials: The need for extended voir dire. *Forensic Reports*, *3*, 331–348.

Naifeh, S., & Smith, G. W. (1994). *Final justice : The true story of the richest man ever tried for murder*. New York: Dutton.

Narby, D. J., Cutler, B. L., & Moran, G. (1993). A meta-analysis of the association between authoritarianism and jurors' perceptions of defendant culpability. *Journal of Applied Psychology*, *78*, 34–42.

Nietzel, N. R., & Dillehay, R. C. (1982). The effects of variations in *voir dire* procedures in capital murder trials. *Law and Human Behavior*, *6*, 1–13.

Nietzel, N. T., & Dillehay, R. C. (1986). *Psychological consultation in the courtroom*. New York: Pergammon Press.

Nietzel, M., Dillehay, R. C., & Abbott, W. F. (1999). Legal surveys. In W. F. Abbott & J. Batt (Eds.), *A handbook of jury research* (pp. 6:1–6:35). Philadelphia: ALA-ABA.

Nietzel, M. T., Dillehay, R. C., & Himelein, M. J. (1987). Effects of voir dire variations in capital trials: A replication and extension. *Behavioral Sciences and the Law*, *5*, 467–477.

Nietzel, M. T., McCarthy, D. M., & Kerr, M. J. (1999). Juries: The current state of empirical literature. In R. Roesch, S. D. Hart, & J. R. P. Ogloff (Eds.), *Psychology and law: State of the discipline* (pp. 23–52). New York: Kluwer Academic/Plenum.

Ogloff, J. R. P., & Vidmar, N. (1994). The impact of pretrial publicity on jurors: A study to compare the relative effects of television and print media in a child sex abuse case. *Law and Human Behavior, 18,* 507–525.

Olsen-Fulero, L., & Fulero, S. M. (1997). Commonsense rape judgments: An empathy-complexity theory of rape juror story making. *Psychology, Public Policy, and Law, 3,* 402–427.

Otto, A. L., Penrod, S. D., & Dexter, H. R. (1994). The biasing impact of pretrial publicity on juror judgments. *Law and Human Behavior, 18,* 453–470.

Penrod, S. D. (1990). Predictors of jury decision making in criminal and civil cases: A field experiment. *Forensic Reports, 3,* 261–277.

Peterson, B. E., Doty, R. M., & Winter, D. G. (1993). Authoritarianism and attitudes toward contemporary social issues. *Personality and Social Psychology Bulletin, 19,* 174–184.

Ross, L. (1977). The intuitive psychologist and his shortcomings: Distortions in the attribution process. In L. Berkowitz (Ed.), *Advances in experimental social psychology, Vol. 10* (pp. 174–221). New York: Academic Press.

Rothman, M. B., Dunlop, B. D., & Rambali, C. (1999). The older juror. In W. F. Abbott & J. Batt (Eds.), *A handbook of jury research* (pp. 9:1–9:19). Philadelphia: ALA-ABA.

Rusting, C. L., & Larsen, R. J. (1998). Personality and cognitive processing of affective information. *Personality and Social Psychology Bulletin, 24,* 200–213.

Schuller, R. A. (1992). The impact of battered woman syndrome evidence on jury decision processes. *Law and Human Behavior, 16,* 597–620.

Schuller, R. A., & Hastings, P. A. (1996). Trial of battered women who kill: The impact of alternative forms of expert evidence. *Law and Human Behavior, 20,* 167–187.

Simon, R. (1999a). Is there an effect of pre-trial publicity on jury verdicts? In W. F. Abbott & J. Batt (Eds.), *A handbook of jury research* (pp. 5:1–5:11). Philadelphia: ALA-ABA.

Simon, R. (1999b). Women in the jury room. In W. F. Abbott & J. Batt (Eds.), *A handbook of jury research* (pp. 8:1–8:8). Philadelphia: ALA-ABA.

Starr, V. H. (1996). *Jury selection: Sample* voir dire *questions*. Boston: Little Brown.

Starr, V. H., & McCormick, M. (1985). *Jury selection*. Boston: Little, Brown.

Starr, V. H., & McCormick, M. (2000). *Jury selection* (3rd ed.). New York: Aspen.

Studebaker, C. A., & Penrod, S. D. (1997). Pretrial publicity: The media, the law, and common sense. *Psychology, Public Policy, and Law, 3,* 428–460.

Vidmar, N. (1997). Generic prejudice and the presumption of guilt in sex abuse trials. *Law and Human Behavior, 21,* 5–26.

Vinson, D. E. (1986). *Jury trials: The psychology of winning strategy.* Charlottesville, VA: Michie.

Ward, C. A. (1995). *Attitudes toward rape: Feminist and social psychological perspectives.* Thousand Oaks, CA: Sage.

Weeks, J. R. (1999). Jury representativeness: Challenging the array. In W. F. Abbott & J. Batt (Eds.), *A handbook of jury research* (pp. 7:1–7:30). Philadelphia: ALA-ABA.

Wiener, R. L., Hurt, L., Russell, B., Mannen, K., & Gasper, C. (1997). Perceptions of sexual harassment: The effects of gender, legal standard, and ambivalent sexism. *Law and Human Behavior, 21,* 71–93.

Wiley, D. (1999). Pre-*voir dire*, case specific supplemental juror questionnaires. In W. F. Abbott & J. Batt (Eds.), *A handbook of jury research* (pp. 16:1–16:43). Philadelphia: ALA-ABA.

Wrightsman, L. S., Nietzel, M. T., & Fortune, W. H. (1998). *Psychology and the legal system*. New York: Brooks/Cole.

CHAPTER 33

ISSUES OF ETHNICITY IN FORENSIC PSYCHOLOGY: A MODEL FOR HISPANICS IN THE UNITED STATES

MARTHA B. MAHAFFEY

PRIVATE PRACTICE, RENO, NEVADA

Hispanics are a fast-growing group in the United States. According to the 2000 census (U.S. Census Bureau, 2001), there are 35.3 million Hispanics in the United States, representing 12.5 percent of the total population of the country. This is a 58 percent increase from the 1990 census. The actual number of Hispanics in the United States is much higher considering the number of illegal Hispanic immigrants. Statistics in California, provided by the Immigration and Naturalization Service, describe that approximately 1.6 million illegal immigrants reside in California and 125,000 more enter the state each year (Cowan, Martinez, & Mendiola, 1997). Considering the continuing legal and illegal migration of Hispanics, legalization of illegal immigrants, and population growth in general, the number and percentage of Hispanics in the United States is expected to be much higher in the twenty-first century. Projections of Hispanic growth in the United States have yielded estimates of 55 million Hispanics, or 17 percent of the population, by the year 2020 and 98 million Hispanics, or 24.3 percent of the population (one out of four United States residents), by the year 2050 (U.S. Census Bureau, 2002).

A great number of Hispanics in the United States are involved in the legal system, particularly the criminal justice system. Consequently, competence in combined Hispanic psychology and forensic psychology will be in great demand in the twenty-first century. Despite such demand, books on forensic psychology published in the past few years have virtually ignored or given scant attention to the issue of race and ethnicity in the forensic arena. This chapter attempts to address issues of Hispanic psychology pertinent to the forensic psychologist.

COMPETENCE

There are guidelines, adopted by the American Psychological Association (APA), or its divisions, that are of value to the forensic psychologist working with Hispanics. The *Ethical Principles of Psychologists and Code of Conduct* (APA, 2002) state:

> Respect for People's Rights and Dignity
> Psychologists are aware of and respect cultural, individual, and role differences, including those based on age, gender, gender identity, race, ethnicity, culture, national origin, religion, sexual orientation, disability, language, and socioeconomic status, and consider these factors when working with members of such groups. (Principal E, p. 1063)

> Boundaries of Competence
> Where scientific or professional knowledge in the discipline of psychology establishes that an understanding of factors associated with age, gender, gender identity, race, ethnicity, culture, national origin, religion, sexual orientation, disability, language, or socioeconomic status is essential for effective implementation of their services or research, psychologists have or obtain the training, experience, consultation, or supervision necessary to ensure the competence of their services, or they make appropriate referrals. (Standard 2.01b, p. 1063)

> Use of Assessments
> Psychologists use assessment instruments whose validity and reliability have been established for use with members of the population tested. When such validity or reliability has not been established, psychologists describe the strengths and limitations of test results and interpretations. (Standard 9.02b, p. 1071)

> Interpreting Assessment Results
> When interpreting assessment results, including automated interpretations, psychologists take into account the purpose of the assessment as well as the various test factors, test-taking abilities, and other characteristics of the person being assessed, such as situational, personal, linguistic, and cultural differences, that might affect psychologists' judgments or reduce the accuracy of their interpretations. They indicate any significant limitations of their interpretations. (Standard 9.06, p. 1072)

On the matter of competence, the *Specialty Guidelines for Forensic Psychologists* (Committee on Ethical Guidelines for Forensic Psychology, 1991), state: "Forensic psychologists provide services only in areas of psychology in which they have specialized knowledge, skill, experience, and education" (Guideline 3, p. 658). The *Guidelines for Child Custody Evaluations in Divorce Pro-

ceedings (APA, 1992) promote awareness of personal and societal biases and engagement in nondiscriminatory practice:

> The psychologist engaging in child custody evaluations is aware of how biases regarding age, gender, race, ethnicity, national origin, religion, sexual orientation, disability, language, culture, and socioeconomic status may interfere with an objective evaluation and recommendations. The psychologist recognizes and strives to overcome any such biases or withdraws from the evaluation. (Guideline 6, p. 678)

The *Guidelines for Providers of Psychological Services to Ethnic, Linguistic, and Culturally Diverse Populations* (APA, 1993) provide comprehensive principals for working with diverse populations:

1. Psychologists educate their clients to the processes of psychological intervention, such as goals and expectations; the scope and, where appropriate, legal limits of confidentiality; and the psychologists' orientations.
2. Psychologists are cognizant of relevant research and practice issues as related to the population being served.
3. Psychologists recognize ethnicity and culture as significant parameters in understanding psychological processes.
4. Psychologists respect the roles of family members and community structures, hierarchies, values, and beliefs within the client's culture.
5. Psychologists respect clients' religious and/or spiritual beliefs and values, including attributions and taboos, since they affect world view, psychosocial functioning, and expressions of distress.
6. Psychologists interact in the language requested by the client and, if this is not feasible, make an appropriate referral.
7. Psychologists consider the impact of adverse social, environment, and political factors in assessing problems and designing interventions.
8. Psychologists attend to as well as work to eliminate biases, prejudices, and discriminatory practices.
9. Psychologists working with culturally diverse populations should document culturally and sociopolitically relevant factors in the records.

The recently published *Guidelines on Multicultural Education, Training, Research, Practice, and Organizational Change for Psychologists* (APA, 2003) provide guidelines to ensure commitment to cultural awareness and knowledge of self and others: "Psychologists are encouraged to recognize that, as cultural beings, they may hold attitudes and beliefs that can detrimentally influence their perceptions of and interactions with individuals who are ethnically and racially different from themselves" (Guideline 1, p. 382); and "Psychologists are encouraged to recognize the importance of multicultural sensitivity/responsiveness to, knowledge of, and understanding about ethnically and racially different individuals" (Guideline 2, p. 385). For practice: "Psychologists are encouraged to apply culturally appropriate skills in clinical and other applied psychological practices" (Guideline 5, p. 390).

To meet these guidelines, Hispanics in the forensic arena should be evaluated by bilingual, bicultural Hispanic psychologists with expertise in Hispanic psychology and forensic psychology. The importance of bilingualism is self-explanatory. Spanish-speaking individuals should be evaluated in their primary language. A monolingual English-speaking psychologist may be acceptable for monolingual English-speaking Hispanics born in the United States, although bilingual skills may still be needed when interviewing family or other collateral individuals. Biculturalism is important in providing firsthand cultural knowledge, experience, and sensitivity to both the minority and majority culture. An Anglo-American practitioner who has personal and/or professional experience with Hispanic individuals may be culturally sensitive but still lacks optimal cultural experience. Finally, it is not enough to have a bilingual, bicultural Hispanic practitioner. The psychologist must be culturally competent in Hispanic psychology and competent in forensic psychology as evidenced by training and experience. The psychologist must integrate clinical findings of Hispanics with legally relevant criteria. A bilingual, bicultural Hispanic psychologist should attain supervision from an expert psychologist in Hispanic psychology and/or forensic psychology if competencies in these two latter areas have not yet been attained. LaCalle (1986) warns that monolingual English-speaking mental health professionals should not perform evaluations on monolingual Spanish-speaking litigants in cases where life and civil liberty are at stake. The forensic examiner of Hispanics must truly be qualified to speak to the defendant in his or her own language and truly understand the defendant's cultural and ethnic background.

Pope, Butcher, and Seelen (1993) caution that expert witnesses must be alert to their own historical, cultural, and personal experiences, influences, and viewpoints that may potentially limit or bias their work. This is particularly pertinent to the Hispanic forensic psychologist, who must be clear about his or her role as expert witness and not lean toward advocacy of the Hispanic individual. Such a role is clearly distinct from the role of Hispanic practitioner.

Sources of Bias in the Legal System

There are several sources of bias specific to Hispanics in the legal system that the forensic psychologist should be aware of. The expert may not be able to directly impact these issues nor be directly affected by them, but it is important that he or she be aware of such biases and educate attorneys so they can best plan legal strategy.

Overrepresentation of Hispanics in the Criminal Justice System

Tonry (1995) has suggested that ethnic minorities are disproportionately overrepresented at virtually every stage in the criminal justice system and they are increasingly overrepresented in incarcerated populations. He attributes such disparity to the confounding factors of poverty and unemployment. Cultural factors, poverty, unemployment, and socioeconomic status are special circumstances for psychologists to alert judges and juries to in order to potentially lessen sentencing disparities attributable to ethnicity.

In the twentieth century, young men of ethnic minority cultures have been overrepresented as perpetrators and victims of violent crime, gang members, substance abusers, and sellers of illicit drugs. They also have been the group most frequently arrested for robberies, burglaries, and motor vehicle thefts (Yung & Hammond, 1997). Statistics show an overrepresentation of minority youth in juvenile detention and correctional facilities (Schwartz, 1989). In the 1980s, Hispanic youth accounted for almost 25 percent of the total juvenile arrests for murder at a time when their representation in the U.S. population was about 8 percent (Ewing, 1990). The overall rate of incarceration for Hispanic youth was 60 percent greater than that of Caucasian youths although less than half that of African-American youths (Jones & Krisberg, 1994). Female offenders are typically poor, uneducated, unskilled, and disproportionately from ethnic and racial minority groups (Feinman, 1994). Hispanic women are the fastest-growing group in federal and state prisons, primarily for drug offenses. In 1993, racial and ethnic statistics from the Federal Bureau of Prisons (FBP) revealed that 24.9 percent of the females in custody of the FBP were Hispanic, and 64.2 percent were members of minority groups (Kline, 1992).

Sentencing Disparity

Sentencing disparity potentially leading to overrepresentation of Hispanics in correctional facilities has been extensively studied. Studies on sentencing disparity have yielded mixed results, perhaps because of analysis of different settings and varying levels of methodological rigor (Wooldredge, 1998). Some investigators have concluded that Hispanics and African Americans are at risk of receiving harsher sentences than Caucasians convicted of the same kinds of offenses (Lopez, 1995; Williams, 1995). Combining race or ethnicity of offenders and victims in a study of the death penalty and discrimination in Arizona, Thomson (1997) concluded that Hispanics and African Americans were overrepresented in death sentencing when accused of killing Caucasians and underrepresented in death sentencing when accused of killing minorities.

Different jurisdictions report variations in sentencing of Hispanic defendants. LaFree (1985) discovered that Hispanic and Caucasian defendants in Tucson received comparable types of adjudication, verdicts, and sentences. In El Paso, however, Hispanic defendants were more likely than Caucasian defendants to receive less favorable pretrial release outcomes, be convicted in jury trials, and receive more severe sentences when found guilty at trial. It is helpful for forensic psychologists to be aware of research within their jurisdiction if trends have been identified.

The Death Penalty

Despite the fact that litigation has challenged the use of tests in employment selection and promotion and educational settings when the result was on overall pattern of discrimination, the courts have not scrutinized the death penalty in the same fashion. In *McCleskey v. Kemp* (1987), social science statistical data of capital sentencing in Georgia was produced in support of the African-American plaintiff's claim that the Georgia capital sentencing process was administered in a racially discriminatory manner in violation of the Eighth and Fourteenth Amendments. The Supreme Court accepted the statistical validity of the social science data, which demonstrated racial disparity in Georgia's capital sentencing particularly with regard to race of the victim, but rejected the claim that purposeful discrimination was made against the defendant.

A noteworthy consequence of the *McCleskey v. Kemp* decision is that it put an end to statistical challenges by social scientists to the administration of the death penalty. Instead, researchers and litigants working on issues of arbitrariness and discrimination in capital sentencing have shifted to alternative approaches for documenting the underlying sources of race-of-victim and race-of-defendant discrimination, for example, juror factors that influence decisions or the manner in which prosecutors handle their cases (Baldus, Woodworth, & Pulaski, 1992).

Ethnicity in the Courtroom

Although the U.S. Constitution contends that a defendant is entitled to be tried by a cross-section of one's community, or a jury of one's peers, as to whether such promotes fairness and impartiality is debatable. The impact of defendant ethnicity, juror ethnicity, and judge's ethnicity upon sentencing decision and civil trial verdicts warrants consideration when assisting counsel in a case involving a Hispanic defendant or Hispanic litigant. An analysis of jury decision in 317 non-capital felony cases in El Paso, Texas, revealed no relation between defendant ethnicity and conviction (Daudistel, Hosch, Holmes, & Graves, 1999). However, Anglo-American defendants received sentences that were approximately twice as severe as those of Hispanic defendants. Sentences imposed by juries were significantly related to defendant ethnicity and type of crime for which they were tried. Sentences were also influenced by defendant ethnicity in interaction with jury ethnic composition. Important differences appeared when there was a critical mass of six or more Hispanics jurors. Another study examined the sentencing of felony defendants by Anglo and Hispanic judges in El Paso, Texas (Holmes, Hosch, Daudistel, Perez, & Graves, 1993). Results indicated that Hispanic judges were not influenced by defendant ethnicity. However, Anglo judges sentenced non-Hispanic defendants less severely than their Hispanic counterparts, who received sentences similar to those granted by Hispanic judges.

CULTURALLY COMPETENT FORENSIC ASSESSMENT

Culturally competent assessment practice is now mandated by the 2002 APA ethical code. The books *Handbook of Multicultural Assessment* (2nd ed.; Suzuki, Ponterotto, & Meller, 2001), *Psychological Testing of Hispanics* (Geisinger, 1992), *Handbook of Cross-Cultural and Multicultural Personality Assessment* (Dana, 2000), and *Handbook of Multicultural Mental Health* (Cuellar & Paniagua, 2000) provide valuable information to the forensic psychologist on culturally responsible assessment of Hispanics.

The latest two editions of the American Psychiatric Association's (APA) *Diagnostic and Statistical Manual of Mental Disorders*, the *DSM-IV* (APA, 1994) and *DSM-IV-TR* (APA, 2000), the primary tools in the United States to diagnose mental disorders, provide an appendix that includes an *Outline for Cultural Formulation*. The outline is meant to supplement the multiaxial diagnostic formulation and facilitate and systematize the assessment of cultural factors in diagnostic evaluations. It suggests a summary of the following categories: (1) cultural identity of the individual; (2) cultural explanation of the individual's illness; (3) cultural factors related to psychosocial environment and levels of functioning; (4) cultural elements of the relationship between the individual and the clinician; and (5) overall cultural assessment for diagnosis and care.

Silva and his colleagues (Silva, Leong, Weinstock, Yamamoto, & Ferrari, 1996; Silva, Leong, Yamamoto, Weinstock, & Ferrari, 1997; Silva, Leong, Dassori, Ferrari, Weinstock, & Yamamoto, 1998) perceived the *DSM-IV Outline for Cultural Formulation* as an effective tool in providing biopsychosociocultural evaluation and identifying potentially legally mitigating and aggravating issues in parent child-killing behavior. They propose that available taxonomies of child-killing behavior vary in the extent to which they consider psychosocial, cultural, and ecological factors. Those that focus primarily upon motives for homicidal behavior do not provide an optimally comprehensive understanding of child-killing behavior and are at risk of failing to identify all aggravating and mitigating factors related to the homicidal behavior. Less comprehensive assessments lead not only to inequitable delivery of justice but also to suboptimal clinical interventions during incarceration and failure to diminish the risk of violence recidivism upon reentry into the community (Silva et al., 1998).

Dana (1995) has proposed that culturally competent assessment requires an understanding of the client's cultural history and beliefs, cultural identity/acculturation status, health-illness beliefs, appropriate language skills, and knowledge of culture-specific tests and when and how to use "corrections" applied to standard tests, including moderator variables, special scales, special norms, translations, and aids to test interpretation. Moderator variables that apply to all individuals include age, gender, education, and socioeconomic status. For the Hispanic individual additional moderator variables must be addressed.

Cultural Heterogeneity

Hispanics in the United States share a commonality of language and culture, but they are generally a heterogeneous group originating from 22 different countries. The largest subgroups of Hispanics are Mexicans, Puerto Ricans, Cubans, and other Hispanics or Latinos, accounting for 58 percent, 10 percent, 4 percent, and 28 percent, respectively, of the total U.S. Hispanic population (U.S. Census, 2001). There are distinct differences in group identity among subgroups representing generations of well-established residents to new immigrants. Each group has a distinct history of migration because of economics, industrialization, revolution, war, and other factors that has accounted for educational, economic, and geographic disparity among Hispanic immigrants (Dana, 1993). Hispanics are more geographically concentrated than the total population, with 85 percent residing in twelve states (U.S. Census Bureau, 2002). Forensic psychologists in New York, New Jersey, and Massachusetts are more likely to work with Puerto Ricans; those in Florida with Cubans; and those in California, Arizona, New Mexico, Colorado, Texas, Washington, Illinois, and Georgia with Mexicans. It is important for the forensic psychologist to be aware of cultural features specific to the Hispanic subgroup with which they are most likely to work, although invariably the expert will be exposed to a variety of Hispanic subgroups.

Hough, Canino, Abueg, and Gusman (1996) highlight the distinct experiences of trauma among Hispanic immigrants from varying countries, including political persecution, torture, massacre, detainment, earthquakes, volcanoes, flooding, and war. Such trauma will color one's view of the world, affect the development of defense mechanisms and personality style, and lead to serious mental health disorders. It is important to obtain an understanding of the immigrant's unique personal, social, cultural, and historical experiences prior to arriving in the United States.

Puente (1990) has argued that within-minority group analysis is as important as minority versus majority group comparisons. Forensic psychologists need to be alert to differences between Hispanic groups that may be relevant to forensic evaluation. Research on the Diagnostic Interview Schedule (DIS) with Puerto Ricans, Mexicans, and Mexican Americans (Anduaga, Fortez, & Lira, 1991); the Holtzman's Ink Blot Test with Hispanics from the United States, Argentina, Mexico, Panama, Venezuela, and Colombia (Holtzman, 1988); domestic violence with Puerto Ricans, Mexicans, and Cubans (Kantor, Jasinski, & Aldarondo, 1994); and locus of control with Mexican Americans, Central Americans, and South Americans (Mahaffey, 1986) underscore the cultural heterogeneity among Hispanic subgroups.

Acculturation

All forensic evaluations of Hispanics should include a measure of acculturation to determine the degree to which Anglo-American interpretations versus Hispanic/Hispanic-American interpretations should be made. A linear model of acculturation would suggest that the more acculturated a person is to the United States culture, the greater the likelihood that U.S. standardized norms can be applied with confidence. The more acculturated a person is to the Hispanic culture, the greater the likelihood that cultural variables will suppress or amplify test results as compared to the normative sample. However, a linear model may not discern the more complex relations characterizing multidomain constructs such as personality and acculturation, with an orthogonal model of acculturation potentially capturing such nuances in more effective manner (Cuellar, 2000). Cuellar (2000) identifies select research studies showing the relationship between acculturation and personality on a variety of personality measures and addresses the mechanics for moderating test scores for acculturation.

Dana (1993) and Zane and Mak (2003) analyzed 10 and 13 acculturation measures for Hispanic Americans, respectively. In a forensic setting, where a mere classification of acculturation level may be sufficient, the brief 12-item Short Acculturation Scale for Hispanics, which focuses upon language and social affiliation (SAS; Marin, Sabogal, Marin, Otero-Sabogal, & Perez-Stable, 1987), or the 10-item Brief Acculturation Scale (Norris, Ford, & Bova, 1996), which was derived from the language subscale of the SAS, may be sufficient.

The acculturation scale that is most widely used and has received the most research attention is the Acculturation Rating Scale for Mexican Americans (ARSMA; Cuellar, Harris, & Jasso, 1980). The ARSMA was revised in 1995 (ARSMA-II; Cuellar, Arnold, & Maldonado, 1995). The ARSMA-II focuses upon multiple acculturation variables that may serve as useful moderator variables in forensic assessments, including cultural practices, language proficiency and preference, social affiliation, ethnic identity, and attitudes and behavior. Other acculturation measures that look at multiple acculturation variables include the Bidimensional Acculturation Scale (Marin & Gamba, 1996), Cultural Life Styles Inventory (Mendoza, 1989), Biculturalism/Multicultural Experience Inventory (Ramirez, 1983), and Bicultural Involvement Questionnaire (Szapocznik, Kurtines, & Fernandez, 1980).

There are acculturation measures specific for Cuban Americans, including the Behavioral Acculturation Scale (Szapocznik, Scopetta, Kurtines, & de los Angeles, 1978), Value Acculturation Scale (Szapocznik et al., 1978), and Cuban Behavioral Identity Questionnaire (CBIQ; Garcia and Lega, 1979). Acculturation measures for children and adolescents include the Children's Hispanic Background Scale (Martinez, Norman, & Delaney, 1984), Children's Acculturation Scale (Franco, 1983), and Multidimensional Scale of Cultural Differences (Olmedo, Martinez, & Martinez, 1978).

Related to acculturation is the concept of acculturation stress (e.g., Hispanic Stress Inventory; Cervantes, Padilla, & Salgado de Snyder, 1990; Saldana, 1995). Acculturation stress is the result of the adaptation process of acculturation for first-generation ethnic minority immigrants and a response to the pulls of maintaining ethnic ties in second and later generations (Roysircar-Sodowsky &

Maestas, 2000). It may or may not be pathological in nature. Understanding acculturation stress specific to the Hispanic individual is helpful to the forensic psychologist who is attempting to identify mitigating or aggravating factors in a criminal case or issues of proximate cause, pre- and postfunctioning, resiliency, and vulnerability in a personal injury case.

Culturally Distinct Expressions of Psychopathology

The forensic psychologist working with Hispanics usually assumes the role of evaluator and diagnostician. Consequently, the question arises as to whether there are culture-bound disorders or culture-bound ways of viewing disorders in Hispanics.

It is a challenge to arrive at universal criteria for mental health disorders and attain cultural sensitivity utilizing culturally distinctive epistemologies and paradigms, considering the differences in cultural conventions about the self, reality, social rules, and patterns of emotional expression (Fabrega, 1987). It is a fallacy to develop nosological categories for a particular cultural population and apply that category to members of another culture without establishing its validity for that culture (Rogler, 1989). One must disentangle psychopathology from cultural material, as, for example, whether endorsements involving spirits are reflective of psychopathology or cultural beliefs.

The diagnostic nosologies within the *DSM-IV* (APA, 1994) and *DSM-IV-TR* (APA, 2000), as compared to earlier editions, are more sensitive to cultural issues in diagnosis. Each diagnostic category has a subsection labeled *Specific Culture, Age, and Gender Features*, which provides guidance for clinicians concerning variations in the presentation of the disorder that may be attributable to the individual's culture, developmental stage, or gender, including differential prevalence rates related to culture, age, and gender. The *DSM-IV* and *DSM-IV-TR* also provide a Glossary of Culture-Bound Syndromes, which may or may not be linked to a particular diagnosis. Paraphrased, such syndromes that apply to Hispanics include:

> *Nervios*: It includes a wide range of symptoms of emotional distress, somatic disturbances, and inability to function. Common symptoms include headaches and "brain aches," irritability, stomach disturbances, sleep difficulties, nervousness, easy tearfulness, inability to concentrate, trembling, tingling sensations, and *mareos* (dizziness with occasional vertigolike exacerbations). It spans the range from cases free of a mental disorder to presentations resembling Adjustment, Anxiety, Depressive, Dissociative, Somatoform, or Psychotic Disorders.
>
> *Ataque de nervios*: Symptoms include uncontrollable shouting, attacks of crying, trembling, heat in the chest rising into the head, and verbal or physical aggression. Dissociative experiences, seizurelike or fainting episodes, and suicidal gestures may be present. A general feature of an *ataque de nervios* is a sense of being out of control. *Ataques* span the range from normal expressions of distress not associated with having a mental disorder to symptom presentations associated with the diagnoses of Anxiety, Mood, Dissociative, or Somatoform Disorders.

Bilis and *Colera*: The underlying cause of these syndromes is thought to be strongly experienced anger or rage. Symptoms can include acute nervous tension, headache, trembling, screaming, stomach disturbances, and, in more severe cases, loss of consciousness. Chronic fatigue may result from the acute episode.

Locura: It refers to a severe form of chronic psychosis. Symptoms include incoherence, agitation, auditory and visual hallucinations, inability to follow rules of social interaction, unpredictability, and possible violence.

Mal de ojo: Individuals are susceptible when exposed to someone's "evil eye." Symptoms include fitful sleep, crying without apparent cause, diarrhea, vomiting, and fever in a child or infant.

Susto: It is a fright-induced reaction that causes the soul to leave the body and results in unhappiness and sickness. Typical symptoms include appetite disturbances, inadequate or excessive sleep, troubled sleep or dreams, feelings of sadness, lack of motivation to do anything, and feelings of low self-worth or dirtiness. Somatic symptoms include muscle aches and pains, headache, stomachache, and diarrhea. *Susto* may be related to Major Depressive Disorder, Post-Traumatic Stress Disorder, and Somatoform Disorder.

Ataque de nervios has been well addressed in the literature (De La Cancela, Guarnaccia, & Carrillo, 1986; Guarnaccia, Rubio-Stipec, & Canino, 1989; Low, 1981; Rivera-Arzola & Ramon-Grenier, 1997; Zea, Quezada, & Belgrave, 1997). Using the Diagnostic Interview Schedule (DIS) in Puerto Rico, Guarnaccia and colleagues (1989) demonstrated how the symptoms of *ataques* fail to be diagnosed or were categorized under symptoms of depressive, anxiety, or panic disorders.

Studies have suggested that there are commonalities and differences in the manner that symptoms cluster in Hispanics and Anglos. Factor analyses have noted a difference in the factor structure of depression symptoms on the Center for Epidemiologic Studies Depression (CES-D) scale between Mexican Americans and Anglo Americans (Garcia & Marks, 1989) and a difference in the factor structure of phobia and psychotic symptoms on the DIS between Puerto Ricans and Anglo Americans (Rubio-Stipec, Shrout, Bird, Canino, & Bravo, 1989).

Research has strongly suggested that Hispanics tend to manifest psychological distress in terms of physical distress, consistent with somatization. Studies with Mexican Americans (Escobar, 1987; Escobar, Burnam, Karno, Forsythe, Landsverk, & Golding, 1986; Escobar, Burnam, Karno, Forsythe, & Golding, 1987; Escobar, Randolph, & Hill, 1986; Escobar, Rubio-Stipec, Canino, & Carno, 1989; Kolody, Vegg, Meinhardt, & Bensussen, 1986), Puerto Ricans (Angel & Guarnaccia, 1989), and Latin Americans (Escobar, Gomez, & Tuason, 1983; Mezzich & Rabb, 1980) suggest that Hispanics, primarily those from a lower social class, tend to express psychological distress through physical distress or somatization. This tendency toward somatization is potentially caused by an interplay between culture and emotions and is distinct from the manner in which Anglo Americans manifest psychological distress. Expressing symptoms physically rather than psychologically is more socially acceptable and less stigmatizing than acknowledging mental illness (Angel & Guarnaccia, 1989; Fabrega, 1995; Low, 1981).

For Hispanics, language barriers, lack of acculturation, lack of education, limited work skills, employment barriers, lower socioeconomic levels, poverty, discrimination, illegality, history of political persecution in their country of origin, history of civil war, or exposure to other catastrophic trauma in their country of origin greatly contribute to psychological stress, which in turn is likely to be manifested in physical distress. Hispanics are also more likely to interpret work-related "nervous" conditions as physical illness and seek treatment with a medical professional rather than a mental health professional (Karno & Edgerton, 1969).

In personal injury and worker's compensation cases, culturally induced emotional distress, physical distress, and medically treated problems combined with a tendency to somatize are likely to be interpreted by defense attorneys as reflective of exaggeration or malingering, poor premorbid adjustment, or preexisting conditions and be used to disprove damages consequent to the injury. Utilizing profiles from the Minnesota Multiphasic Personality Inventory (MMPI; Hathaway & McKinley, 1983) of Hispanics and Caucasians who had filed worker's compensation claims for psychiatric disability, DuAlba and Scott (1993) found that Hispanics were more likely to report emotional distress in terms of physical symptoms but were no more likely to malinger than were Caucasians. The forensic psychologist plays a crucial role in educating attorneys, judges, and juries about the different ways in which Hispanic and Caucasian individuals manifest stress, particularly as measured by psychometric instruments with Caucasian norms.

Specific Cultural Moderators

Marin and Marin (1991) identified Hispanic response styles that need to be taken into account in analyzing and interpreting Hispanic data, including the tendency to provide extreme, acquiescent, socially desirable, less self-disclosing responses; the possibility that responses do not reflect reality; and the presence of incomplete responses or missing data. The concept of *simpatia* (the cultural value among Hispanics to promote smooth and pleasant social relationships, be congenial, conform to expectations, and defer to authority), and the concept of collectivism or allocentrism (the cultural value among Hispanics to be more group oriented than individualistically oriented) are perceived by Marin and Marin (1991) as contributing to the previously mentioned response styles of Hispanics.

Although not addressed in forensic literature, *simpatia* and collectivism have potential implications in forensic psychology. Such tendencies toward social desirability might lead Hispanics to waive their Miranda rights or more readily accept plea bargains. Research on the MMPI has determined that the elevation most likely encountered by Hispanics as compared to Caucasians is an elevation on the L scale (Greene, 1991; Zalewski & Green, 1996). Such an elevation may be interpreted by attorneys as indicative of questionable validity and of the Hispanic respondent attempting to "fake good." For the Hispanic individual who is more acculturated to the Hispanic culture, an elevated L scale is more likely reflective of the cultural tendency not to be self-disclosing about psychological difficulties and provide acquiescent or socially desirable responses.

Language and Reading Skills

Language is among the first issues that must be addressed in forensic evaluations of Hispanic individuals. Interviews should be done in the language in which the individual is most fluent. Studies have demonstrated that when primarily Spanish-speaking individuals are interviewed in English, psychopathology can be either underestimated (Del Castillo, 1970; Sabin, 1975) or overestimated (Marcos, 1976; Marcos, Alpert, Urcuyo, & Kesselman, 1973; Marcos, Urcuyo, Kesselman, & Alpert, 1973). Bilingual individuals frequently state that they have no language preference. This is true for the genuinely bilingual individual, but such a statement may be made out of *simpatia* (a tendency to promote smooth, pleasant social relationships and conform to expectations) or reflect pride or embarrassment in one's language attainment. For the Hispanic who has spent several years in both a Latin American country and the United States, the interview may fluidly flow between Spanish and English.

Formalized testing should be done in the language in which the person is best able to read. Reading level should be assessed, particularly for the Hispanic who has questionable command of the spoken and written English or Spanish language. Considering the fact that some individuals are educated in Latin America and the United States, reading level in either language may not be sufficient for reliable test administration. In such cases, audiotapes of tests are preferable to having test items read aloud. If both language and educational skills are compromised, as in the frequent cases of immigrant field and service laborers, alternative forms of assessment are more appropriate.

Use of Translators

In a forensic evaluation within a community in which there are Spanish-speaking, Hispanic forensic psychologists, the use of translators should be avoided. Butcher (1995) notes that the use of interpreters or translators promote a type of procedural alteration that cannot be defended in forensic assessments. The inherent problems of having a bilingual person translate items simultaneously to the client include risk of interpretation rather than translation, lack of accurate translation for specific terminology, change in item meaning, change in item difficulty level, change in standardized administration, and potential change in reliability and validity. To be alert to verbal and nonverbal cues from both the English-speaking evaluators and Spanish-speaking translator is a difficult task. Inevitably, the Hispanic defendant focuses more upon and develops a relationship with the Spanish-speaking translator as opposed to the forensic examiner.

LaCalle (1986) notes that the presence of a certified court translator does not guarantee that such a translator has suitable ability to understand fully the nature, procedures, and terminology of a psycholegal evaluation. Frequently the forensic psychologist obtains a linguistic translation together with an interpretation added by the translator. LaCalle (1986) presented a case example in which a translation of the word *violar* as rape ignored the alternative Spanish interpretations of less serious sexual violations and led to the signing of an erroneous confession.

The *Guidelines for Providers of Psychological Services to Ethnic, Linguistic, and Culturally Diverse Populations* (APA, 1993) note that translators who have a dual role with the client, such as family, therapists, and probation officers, should not be retained to avoid jeopardizing the validity and effectiveness of the evaluation. The *Ethical Principals of Psychologists and Code of Conduct* (APA, 2002) promote:

> Delegation of Work to Others
> Psychologists who ... use the services of others, such as interpreters, take reasonable steps to (1) avoid delegating such work to persons who have a multiple relationship with those being served that would likely lead to exploitation or loss of objectivity; (2) authorize only those responsibilities that such persons can be expected to perform competently on the basis of their education, training, or experience, either independently or with the level of supervision being provided; and (3) see that such persons perform these services competently. (Standard 2.05, p. 1064)
>
> 9.03 Informed Consent in Assessments
> (c) Psychologists using the services of an interpreter obtain informed consent from the client/patient to use that interpreter, ensure that confidentiality of test results and test security are maintained, and include in their recommendations, reports, and diagnostic or evaluative statements, including forensic testimony, discussion of any limitations of the data obtained. (Standard 9.03c, p. 1071)

Use of Translated Tests

Only tests that have been formally translated into Spanish and validated should be used to ascertain linguistic and construct equivalence (Dana, 1993), that is, back-translation (Brislin, 1970). Early studies comparing English and Spanish translations of the MMPI suggested that translations cannot be used interchangeably with the English form (Fuller & Malony, 1984). More recent translations are much improved in terms of linguistic and cultural equivalence, although differences in the Spanish spoken by the variety of Hispanic subgroups make universal usage of one translation a challenge.

Spanish translations of multilevel personality tests have been criticized for being made clinically available and commercially promoted prior to sufficient validation (Fantoni-Salvador & Rogers, 1997; Rogers, Flores, Ustad, & Sewell, 1995).

Validation studies of Spanish translations of the MMPI-2 (Butcher, Dahlstrom, Graham, Tellegen, & Kaemmer, 1989) and Personality Assessment Instrument (PAI; Morey, 1991) have recently been conducted (Butcher, 1994; Fantoni-Salvador & Rogers, 1997; Rogers et al., 1995). A review of the literature did not identify a validation study of the Millon Clinical Multiaxial Inventory-III (MCMI-III; Millon, 1994) Spanish translation or the adolescent translated versions of the MMPI and Millon inventories.

One of the limitations of the Spanish translations is that reading comprehension levels of the Spanish versions of the cited personality measures have not been established and cannot be assumed to be comparable to their English counterparts considering the linguistic nuances that occur in translation. Forensic examiners are left to estimate the reading level of Spanish-speaking examinees and the reading level of translated tests.

PSYCHOLOGICAL TESTING

The Supreme Court decisions in *Daubert v. Merrell Dow Pharmaceuticals* (1993), *Kumho Tire Co. v. Carmichael* (1999) and *General Electric v. Joiner* (1997) have increased the scrutiny regarding the degree of scientific reliability and validity of assessment measures used in a forensic setting. Whether or not psychological testing of Hispanics meets the *Daubert* standard is a crucial factor to consider when choosing a particular test and a particular normative sample.

The expert witness should also be well aware that the courts have expressed judicial concern regarding the use of psychologist tests in decision making when (1) the individual's racial or ethnic status is not represented in the norming process (Blau, 1998); and (2) the use of testing leads to a disproportionate number of individuals being chosen from one ethnic group over another, even if the difference in test results could be explained in terms of the characteristics of the ethnic minority group (Bersoff, 1988). When statistical data has shown that a test to hire had disproportionate impact on minority individuals, the court held that such practice was discriminatory and actionable regardless of whether the test was fair (Koocher & Keith-Spiegel, 1998). Donlon (1992) provides a review of litigation affecting educational and employment testing of Hispanics. Blau (1998) writes: "Although the bulk of research and commentary relates to fairness of tests in selection, promotion, and educational issues, it is in the forensic arena that the individual and society may suffer the most extensive unfairness and damage if test results are not applied with careful recognition of sources of bias based on race, gender, or ethnicity" (p. 65).

Choca and Van Denburg (1997) have proposed that differences between ethnic groups do not necessarily need to be seen as a flaw of the test but as data with which psychologists must be familiar. Similarly, Matarazzo (1970) distinguished between psychological testing and psychological assessment and proposed that problems lie in overreliance upon test scores instead of comprehensive assessment. Gynther (1989) proposed a conservative approach to interpretation that involves underinterpretation of test elevations. In tests of psychopathology and personality, it may be appropriate at times to dismiss marginally elevated scores, explain elevations as reflective of culturally determined defense mechanisms, understand when elevations are best accounted for by culturally bound traits or symptoms, and identify the presence or absence of true psychopathology.

Forensic examiners of Hispanics that include psychological tests should (1) use standardized tests that have Hispanic norms; (2) use tests that have sufficient research to distinguish differences between Hispanic subjects and the standardization sample; (3) address the limitations of utilizing tests that do not have Hispanic norms or research distinguishing the response style of Hispanics and the standardization sample and propose modified interpretations when appropriate; or (4) acknowledge the absence of standardized assessment measures applicable to Hispanics when there is such an absence. Canter, Bennet, Jones, and Nagy (1994) note that although adjustments of linguistically and culturally distinct individuals may be appropriate, conclusions or generalizations drawn from such adjustments must be stated tentatively and with relevant limitations described. It is the responsibility of the forensic examiner to ascertain that psychological tests and assessments not be used in a manner detrimental to the examinee, society, or forensic setting.

Despite the radical and cross-examinatory posture of Ziskin (1995), in many ways he is a champion of sensitivity to Hispanic issues in the courtroom when he writes: "It seems obvious that evaluations of members of ethnic groups should be viewed with caution in the court of law with its usually rigorous safeguards to determine insofar as possible that evidence offered has a reasonable probability of trustworthiness and relevance" (p. 1048). I disagree with Ziskin (1995) that assessment of minorities on the basis of Caucasian normative date is inappropriate. I propose culturally sensitive forensic assessment that utilizes standardized tests within a comprehensive assessment model that considers the previously mentioned issues of culturally competent assessment and identifies limitations.

Cognitive Testing

Intelligence testing is frequently used in the forensic arena when the question of cognitive capacity is at question. Revisions of the Wechsler standardized intelligence tests—the Wechsler Adult Intelligence Scale–III (WAIS-III; Wechsler, 1997), the Wechsler Intelligence Scale for Children–III (WISC-III; Wechsler, 1991), and the Wechsler Preschool and Primary School of Intelligence–Revised (WPPSI-R; Wechsler, 1989)—include a U.S. census–stratified number of racial and ethnic minorities in their normative samples. Test performance of English-speaking Hispanics born in the United States may resemble the performance of the normative samples when socioeconomic factors are controlled. In a review of Wechsler studies analyzing racial or ethnic group differences, Suzuki, Vraniak, and Kugler (1996) concluded that the WAIS-R (Wechsler, 1981) is valid and reliable with respect to different racial or ethnic minority groups when used appropriately but that the factor structure of the WAIS-R and WISC-R (Wechsler, 1974) may vary across different racial or ethnic groups. The more distinct the individual is in terms of language, culture, country of origin, and acculturation to U.S. culture, the more likely test scores will be an underrepresentation of intellectual capacity.

In cases where intelligence testing of Spanish-speaking Hispanics may be appropriate, the on-the-spot translation of the WAIS-III is invalid, unreliable, and unethical. The forensic psychologist could utilize the WAIS (Wechsler, 1955) adaptation, the *Escala de Inteligencia Wechsler para Adultos* (*EIWA*; Wechsler, 1968), whose standardization sample is Puerto Rican residents primarily from rural areas with less than eight years of schooling. However, researchers (Lopez & Nunez, 1987; Lopez & Romero, 1988; Melendez, 1994) have noted significant differences between the *EIWA* and WAIS, specifically pertaining to the demographic characteristics of the standardization sample, administration, content, scoring, and conversion of raw scores to scale scores. Its publisher, Psychological Corporation (2003), includes in its ordering catalogue the disclaimer, "The test was normed in Puerto Rico and, thus, is not representative of individuals on the mainland" (p. 142). The distinctions between the WAIS and the *EIWA* make the *EIWA* a more lenient test, leading to a potentially inflated intelligence quotient (IQ) and overrepresentation of intellectual capacity. Lopez and Romero (1988) recommend using the *EIWA* only with monolingual Spanish-speaking individuals from a rural background, a low education, and a low occupational status and with communication about the normative sample and potential lack of generalizability to WAIS intelligence scores.

The *Escala de Inteligencia Wechlser para Ninos* (*EIWN*; Wechsler, 1951) is a Puerto Rican translation and revision of the WISC (Wechsler, 1949) which utilizes United States norms and like its English counterpart is at risk of underestimating the IQ scores of Hispanic children. The *Escala de Inteligencia Wechsler para Ninos-Revisada* (*EIWN-R*; Martin, 1977) is a "Florida" translation of the WISC-R with norms based primarily upon Spanish-speaking Cuban children in Florida rather than a representative sample of Hispanic children in the United States. The *Escala de Inteligencia Wechsler para Ninos—Revisada de Puerto Rico* (*EIWN-R PR*; Herrans & Rodriguez, 1992) is a Puerto Rican translation and revision of the WISC-R which utilizes Puerto Rican norms and so is not representative of Hispanic children in mainland United States.

Alternatives to the Spanish-language Wechsler adaptations in the United States are translations from other Spanish-speaking countries such as Mexico and Spain. The forensic psychologist who uses such versions must be aware of the limitations inherent in transporting tests from other countries. Some translations preserve the Wechsler structure, whereas other translations significantly change it. Some translations utilize the Wechsler United States norms in such a way that the likelihood of underestimation of intellectual functioning remains high. Other translations are normed on Mexican or Spanish nationals so that, like the *EIWA* and *EIWN-R PR*, the generalizability of such norms to Hispanics in the United States is questionable. The latter norms, however, may be appropriate for newly immigrated Hispanic individuals who match the same level of education and socioeconomic status as the normative sample in their country of origin.

Whichever version of the Wechsler intelligence scales are utilized, it is important that the forensic expert makes his or her audience aware of how the standardization sample is similar or distinct from the Spanish-speaking individual being tested, the potential limitations in the test, and the tendency toward overestimation or underestimation of intellectual functioning. A reliable score may not be feasible, in which case the forensic psychologist may have to rely upon other clinical and behavioral indices to illustrate cognitive capacity and certainly a measure of adaptive behavior if contemplating a diagnosis of mental retardation.

Alternatives to the Wechsler scales for Spanish- and English-speaking Hispanics in forensic settings are cognitive screening measures or nonverbal tests of intelligence. Such tests include the Raven's Standard Progressive Matrices (SPM; Raven, Court, & Raven, 1938, 1947, 1977) and Coloured Progressive Matrices (CPM; Raven, 1977) and the Test of Nonverbal Intelligence, Third Edition (TONI-3; Brown, Sherbenou, & Johnson, 1997). The SPM is the most widely used and researched culture-reduced, nonverbal, cognitive assessment instrument (Harris, Reynolds, & Koegel, 1996). The SPM, CPM, and TONI-3 have been identified as useful instruments for testing individuals from different linguistic and cultural backgrounds in a more nonbiased manner (Llabre, 1984; Harris et al., 1996). The TONI-3 has been viewed as a fairer measure of intellectual ability for ethnic minorities because of its nonverbal item content and pointing response adaptation (Harris et al., 1996). The SPM and CPM norms were updated in 1990 including ethnic norms. The TONI-3 was standardized on individuals stratified on a variety of factors, including race and ethnicity.

Neuropsychological Testing

Neuropsychology and the Hispanic Patient: A Clinical Handbook (Ponton & Leon-Carrion, 2001) is an excellent resource for the forensic psychologist called to render opinions about the cognitive and neuropsychological status of Hispanic individuals. There are two neuropsychological test batteries that have derived Hispanic norms. The first is the Neuropsychological Screening Battery for Hispanics (NeSBHIS; Ponton, Satz, Herrera, Ortiz, Furst, & Namerow, 1996), a standardized battery in Spanish modeled on a battery successfully used by the World Health Organization to assess cognition across various cultures. It utilizes well-known neuropsychological tests, including the Raven Standard Progressive Matrices; WHO-UCLA Auditory Verbal Learning Test; Rey Osterrieth Complex Figure Test; FAS Test; Color Trails Test; and subtests from the *Escala de Inteligencia Wechsler para Adultos (EIWA)*—namely, digit span, digit symbol, and block design. It is normed on 300 monolingual and bilingual Spanish-speaking Hispanics in the United States from Mexico, Central America, and other countries.

Norms are stratified by gender, age, and education. Another neuropsychological test battery is the Neuropsi (Ostrosky, Ardila, & Roselli, 1997), a brief standardized neuropsychological test battery in Spanish normed on 800 monolingual Spanish-speaking Mexican nationals from the Mexican Republic. Norms are stratified by age and education. A limitation of both the NeSBHIS and Neuropsi is their limited sample sizes, with need to add to their existing body of normative data. A limitation of the Neuropsi is its generalizability to Hispanic Americans, although the normative sample is applicable to newly immigrated Mexican nationals.

Minnesota Multiphasic Personality Inventories (MMPI/MMPI-2)

The MMPI-2 is the most widely used personality assessment instrument for evaluating individuals in forensic settings (Lees-Haley, 1992; Pope et al., 1993). With respect to forensic requirements for normative data, the MMPI-2 is presently better developed and more adequate than most if not all measures of personality (Weiner, 1995). As compared to the MMPI, the MMPI-2 improved its semantics to be more culturally unbiased and included ethnic minority individuals within its normative or standardization sample representative of the 1980 census. The sample size of Hispanics (N = 35) and percentage (3%; Butcher, Dahlstrom, et al., 1989) is considerably light given the growing number of Hispanics in the United States. Proportional sampling with such small sample size is not sufficient to ensure nonbiased testing of Hispanics. The current norms remain more highly indicative of Anglo-American response styles.

During the past four decades, there have been ample studies of the MMPI/MMPI-2 and MMPI-Adolescent version (MMPI-A; Butcher, Williams, et al., 1992). In a comprehensive bibliography of MMPI, MMPI-2, and MMPI-A research with Hispanics, Velasquez, Ayala, and Mendoza (1998) identified 170 such studies. Reviews of MMPI/MMPI-2 studies comparing Caucasian and Hispanic profiles yielded a variety of opinions. Campos (1989) conducted a meta-analytic review of 16 MMPI studies and concluded that the only consistent finding was that Hispanics scored higher than Caucasians on the L scale. Greene (1991) surmised that the literature examining Hispanic-Caucasian differences has not yielded a definite pattern, but a few support the contention that Hispanics frequently score higher on the L scale and lower on scale 5. Zalewski and Green (1996) concluded that the MMPI research on Hispanic-Caucasian comparisons identified no scale to distinguish Hispanics and Caucasians in every study, but higher L scale scores in Hispanics as compared to Caucasians was the most consistent finding. Hall, Bansal, and Lopez (1999) performed a meta-analytic review of 13 MMPI/MMPI-2 studies of Hispanic and Caucasian males and found that Hispanics exhibited greater scores than Caucasians on some scales and lower scores on others; however, aggregate effect sizes were not statistically robust. The largest aggregate effect size was on scale 5, with male Hispanics scoring lower on the scale than their Caucasian counterparts. Graham (2000) concluded that there have been more similarities than differences on MMPI/MMPI-2 scores of Hispanics and Caucasians, with reported differences between the two groups being difficult to interpret because of small sample size, heterogeneity among Hispanics, and lack of adequate controls for socioeconomic status and acculturation.

Butcher and Williams (1992) reported the normative means and standard deviations for MMPI/MMPI-2 validity and clinical scales for male and female Caucasians, African Americans, Native Americans, Hispanics, and Asians and concluded that the MMPI-2 norms apply equally well regardless of ethnic group background and that no special considerations need to be made with regard to race. Hall and Phung (2001) conclude that examination of the literature of MMPI/MMPI-2 ethnic differences yielded no substantive ethnic differences on these measures but that no conclusions could be made in regard to Hispanic-American females, Asian Americans, and American Indians, considering the paucity of MMPI/MMPI-2 studies on these groups. Graham (1993) felt that it is still uncertain to what extent MMPI-2 scores of African Americans, Hispanics, and Native Americans can be interpreted similarly to those of Caucasians.

Anderson (1995) suggested guidelines for interpreting Hispanic MMPI and MMPI-2 profiles. For nonpsychiatric populations, profiles of English-speaking Hispanics who are acculturated more to the United States culture can be interpreted like Anglo-American profiles, with likely elevations on scales L and 5. For nonacculturated Hispanic immigrants for whom Spanish is the primary language, MMPI interpretations should be made cautiously, with likely elevations on a variety of validity and clinical scales. For psychiatric populations, Hispanic-American profiles may reflect pathology in the same manner as Anglo-American profiles. For substance abuse populations, the MMPI profiles of Hispanic Americans may be lower than those of Anglo-American profiles. Anderson's (1995) MMPI/MMPI-2 interpretation guidelines are oversimplified considering the complexity of language and orthogonal factors of acculturation within the Hispanic population. Velasquez and colleagues (Velasquez, 1995; Velasquez, Gonzales, Butcher, Castillo-Canez, Apodaca, & Chavira, 1997; Velasquez, Ayala, & Mendoza, 1998; Velasquez, Ayala, Mendoza, Nezami, Castillo-Canez, Pace, Choney, Gomez, & Miles, 2000) have made recommendations for using the MMPI with Hispanics, including a list of guidelines for test administration, test interpretation, and consideration of language and acculturation. Dana (1995) suggested that behavioral and observational data should always supplement MMPI scale scores to ward against exaggeration of psychopathology. Clinical interviews should be used to determine whether elevations are a true reflection of psychopathology or merely a cultural aberrant.

To date, MMPI and MMPI-2 forensic studies addressing ethnicity or race have focused primarily on differences between Anglo American and African American offenders (Rogers & McKee, 1995). Studies of criminal offenders comparing Anglo-American, African-American, and Hispanic MMPI profiles in presentencing evaluations have yielded mixed results. McCreary and Padilla (1977) compared Caucasian, African-American, and Mexican-American male misdemeanor offenders referred to a legal psychiatry clinic for a presentencing, postconviction evaluation. Mexican Americans scored significantly higher on validity scales L and K, the overcontrolled hostility (OH) scale, and the hypochondriasis (HY) scale. The elevations on L, K, and OH were attributed to cultural factors, whereas the elevation on HY was attributed to socioeconomic factors. Mexican Americans were classified more often as psychiatric, whereas Caucasians and African Americans were more often classified as sociopathic. The latter finding was potentially explained in terms of distinctions in the referral process. Holland (1979) compared Caucasian, African-American, and Mexican-American felony offenders referred by judges for a presentencing, postconviction assessment of their suitability for probation. Mexican-American offenders, as compared with Caucasian and African-American offenders, scored significantly less pathological on a variety of clinical scales. Culturally determined values were identified as potentially accountable for such differences. Neither McCreary and Padilla (1977) nor Holland (1979) addressed the manner in which MMPI results and cultural factors affected expert opinion or sentencing.

The MMPI is used internationally in more than 65 countries with more than 115 translations (Dana, 1995). There are several translated versions of the MMPI and MMPI-2 from Puerto Rico, Mexico, Chili, Argentina, and Spain (Butcher, 1996). Early versions of MMPI translations (Puerto Rican version, Bernal et al., 1959; Mexican version, Nunez, 1967) received much criticism for lacking information on development, standardization data, and norms and for bearing language not universally understandable by all Hispanics. The latest Spanish translation of the MMPI-2 most widely used in the United States is a subsequent Puerto Rican translation published by the Psychological Corporation (Garcia-Peltoniemi & Chaviano, 1993). It continues to bear some of the problems found in the original translation but is a marked improvement. It has the appearance of linguistic and construct equivalence, but such attainment is a challenge among diverse subgroups of Hispanics. The forensic psychologist should interpret profiles from translated MMPIs or MMPI-2s with caution, again bearing in mind the important of clinical and behavioral correlates to supplement scale elevations.

Millon Clinical Multiaxial Inventories (MCMI/MCMI-II/MCMI-III)

The Millon inventories have received increased utilization in the clinical and forensic arenas. Additionally, there has been an attempt to reduce potential ethnic and racial biases in the MCMI-II (Millon, 1987) via replacement of MCMI (Millon, 1977) items that had significant ethnic-racial differences in item-endorsement and the development of preliminary norms, albeit small sample size, for African American and Hispanic patients. Despite such efforts and growing popularity, there has been a dearth of MCMI/MCMI-II/MCMI-III studies distinguishing the response styles of Caucasian and racially and ethnically distinct individuals. Rudd and Orman (1996) compared Caucasian, African-American, and Hispanic active duty male soldiers to a local normative male sample but did not assess for ethnic group differences. No MCMI/MCMI-II/MCMI-III study comparing Hispanic and Caucasian test responses was identified. Studies that have compared African-American and Caucasian-American individuals on the MCMI have suggested significant race differences, with African Americans scoring more pathological on a variety of personality and clinical scales (Choca, Shanley, Peterson, & Van Denburg, 1990; Donat, Walters, & Hume, 1992). The fact that race differences have been found on the MCMI highlights the need to explore whether Hispanic ethnic cultural difference exist within this measure of personality and clinical constructs.

Personality Assessment Inventory (PAI)

The PAI (Morey, 1991) is a relatively new self-report personality inventory that has become popular in correctional and forensic settings, with research support for the construct validity of the PAI in the forensic assessment context (Douglas & Hart, 1998; Edens, Hart, Johnson, & Johnson, 2000; Edens, Cruise, & Buffington-Vollum, 2001). The psychometric properties of the PAI have been investigated utilizing Hispanics with findings yielding mixed results (Alterman, Zaballero, Lin, Siddiqui, Brown, Rutherford, & McDermott, 1995; Fantoni-Salvador & Rogers, 1997; Rogers et al., 1995). Validation studies of the PAI Spanish version with Hispanics concluded that the PAI may be a useful instrument for screening because it can alert the examiner to potential problems worth exploring, but not a definitive measure of psychopathology for Hispanics (Fantoni-Salvador & Rogers, 1997; Rogers et al., 1995). Psychologists should be very circumspect in deriving any conclusions about malingering and defensiveness of Hispanics from the PAI validity scales.

Psychopathy Checklist–Revised (PCL-R)

The Psychopathy Checklist–Revised (PCL-R; Hare, 1991), in its assessment of psychopathy, has attained respect in the courtroom for its identification of habitual criminals and potentially violent or otherwise deviant offenders and has significantly impacted civil liberties. The standardization samples of the PCL-R and its newly released edition, the PCL-R, 2nd edition (Hare, 2003), have been primarily Caucasian Canadian or North American, with some African American, North American Native, Hispanic American, and other. The second edition includes statistics for white, African American, Native Canadian, British, and Swedish samples with data on other ethnic groups still needed. Hare (1991, 2003) considers that the PCL-R and PCL-R, 2nd edition, require evaluation of complex social, interpersonal, and behavioral factors and that ethnicity might influence the way in which they are scored, particularly in situations where the rater and subject are from different races or cultures. He recommends that clinicians be judicious when interpreting the PCL-R scores of groups for whom the instrument has not been well validated.

Research focusing upon Caucasian and African-American racial differences on the PCL/PCL-R has generated comparable results under well-controlled conditions. When PCL raters' race or ethnicity was not controlled, there was a similar correlation between psychopathy and criminality for Caucasian and African-American inmates, but a difference between the two groups in the distribution of psychopathy scores, relationship between psychopathy and personality scores, and congruence of the underlying factor structure (Kosson, Smith, & Newman, 1990). When PCL-R raters included Caucasian, African-American, and Latina raters, the factor structure of psychopathy was found to be the same for Caucasian and African-American inmates (Cooke, Kosson, & Michie, 2001). Hare (2003) found that the distribution of PCL-R scores, percentile ranks, and T-scores were comparable for his sample of white and African-American male and female offenders.

Cross-cultural studies comparing North American samples and Scottish samples demonstrated a degree of cross-cultural generalizability of the PCL-R (Cooke & Michie, 1999). However, Scottish inmates scored significantly lower than North American inmates on the PCL-R and a much smaller percent of Scottish inmates were classified as psychopaths compared with North American inmates. A study of a Spanish-translated version of the PCL-R in a Spanish prison population found a factor structure opposite to that found in the standardization sample (Molto, Carmona, Poy, Avila, & Torrubia, 1995). In a review of PCL-R data from 16 European samples, comparison of the overall mean in the European sample with the mean of the standardization sample indicated a substantial difference (Cooke, 1998).

Racial and cross-cultural findings emphasize the need to assess the generalizability of the use of the PCL-R, its second edition, and its screening version (PCL-SV). A study of the applicability of the PCL-R with a Hispanic federal inmate sample found that Cooke and Michie's (2001) three-factor hierarchical model produced better fit indices than did Hare's (1991) two-factor model. In a study assessing psychopathy among Mexican-American gang members, the PCL-SV was effective in distinguishing between gang members and nongang members, with gang members having significantly higher PCL-SV total, affective, and behavioral scores than nongang members (Valdez, Kaplan, & Codina, 2000). In a study that explored the generalizability of the PCL-R to a nonforensic ethnically diverse alcoholic inpatient sample, African Americans, Puerto Ricans, and Caucasians were found to have comparable factor structures (Windle & Dumenci, 1999). However, the alcoholic sample may have been more homogenous than a diverse forensic sample would be.

It is likely that Hispanic cultural factors may suppress or amplify the expression of psychopathy. Such factors may include collectivism and *simpatia* as opposed to individualism and competitiveness; the tendency not to be self-disclosing; culturally distinct expressions of affect and behavior; level of acculturation; overrepresentation of Hispanics in the criminal system; and rater ethnicity and language.

FORENSIC SPECIFIC MEASUREMENT

Forensic psychologists can serve a variety of roles as expert witnesses in cases involving Hispanics. Following is a description of areas in which psychologists frequently encounter the Hispanic litigants, primarily because of the question of psychopathology, concern for reoffense, and overrepresentation, as in workers' compensation and immigration cases. Areas of forensic psychology in which Hispanics are underrepresented include custody evaluations. Such disparity is potentially because of cultural issues of family unity, stereotypic determinants of mothers as the primary caregivers, and financial insufficiency.

Competency

The issue of competency permeates the judiciary. Competency to stand trial is by far the most frequently adjudicated competency issue (Melton, Petrila, Poythress, & Slobogin, 1997). Johnson and Torres (1992) note that language and cultural factors provide a challenge in the assessment of competencies of Hispanics. To assess competency to stand trial in a monolingual Spanish-speaking Hispanic individual, it is important to utilize a bilingual, bicultural evaluator who can adequately address language and cultural issues, utilize appropriate psychometric measures, and identify limitations of psychometric measures with Hispanics. Otherwise, defendants may erroneously be labeled as incompetent to stand trial because (1) the defendant's intelligence was underestimated utilizing an intelligence measure with Anglo-American norms; (2) the evaluator overly relied upon stereotypes of the Hispanic immigrant without adequate assessment to see if the individual met such stereotypes; or (3) issues relevant to malingering could not be adequately assessed without language ability and cultural understanding (Johnson & Torres, 1992).

Spanish-speaking Hispanic immigrants are frequently referred for evaluations of competency to stand trial because of language and cultural barriers to the client-attorney relationship rather than an actual mental insufficiency. An English-speaking Anglo-American defense attorney who relies upon a translator will inevitably find it challenging to communicate with an uneducated, nonacculturated Hispanic immigrant who is ignorant of the American criminal justice system. Intelligence screening and evaluation in the defendant's primary language frequently denote no intellectual deficit or mental disorder. Recommendations in those cases lie in educating the attorney and judge about the defendant's capabilities and encouraging very simplistic, concrete, and patient dialogue with the use of a translator and basic legal process education. For purposes of justice, a Spanish-speaking defendant should have a Spanish-speaking attorney. Unfortunately, the recommendation that the defendant have a Spanish-speaking attorney is not always a viable option in a community that is lacking in such resources.

Competency to waive Miranda rights has a threshold higher than competency to stand trial. It involves assessing if the defendant's behavior was knowing, intelligent, and voluntary (Melton et al., 1997). All three criteria are a challenge when issues of linguistics, cultural ignorance, judicial ignorance, passivity, and suggestibility (e.g. *simpatia* and tendency toward acquiescence and social desirability) potentially confound the behavior of Hispanic immigrants. Grisso's (1999) Instruments for Assessing Understanding and Appreciation of Miranda Rights hold promise for helping to determine if the Hispanic individual knowingly and intelligently comprehended his Miranda rights. A validated Spanish translation standardized on a variety of Hispanic subgroups or a variety of validated Spanish translations sensitive to subgroup differences in the Spanish language is a much needed instrument.

Criminal Responsibility

In a review of the use of the MMPI-2 in the assessment of criminal responsibility, Rogers and McKee (1995) note a scarcity of MMPI-2 research on insanity and pretrial evaluations. Interview formats (Shapiro, 1999) or instruments (Rogers Criminal Responsibility Scale; Rogers, 1984) providing models for evaluating criminal responsibility have been formulated. However, they lack reference to the importance of assessing factors of ethnicity and culture that may affect mental status at the time of the crime. Kunst and Reed (1999) present a case study of a Mexican-American woman who was found not guilty by reason of insanity for infanticide, the murder of her young son. They note the importance of identifying the psychodynamic operations that laid the foundation for the crime, including identity development and mitigating factors of gender, culture, and psychopathology in the evaluation for criminal responsibility.

Violence and Sexual Reoffense Prediction

Despite the growing attention granted risk assessment in the past two decades, there is a paucity of actuarial research exploring the factors that statistically predict violence and sex offense recidivism distinctly between standardization samples and racially and ethnically distinct individuals. The Hare Psychopathy Checklist–Revised (PCL-R; Hare, 1991) has been identified as a robust measure for future violence. However, the PCL-R and the psychopathy construct have been found to be distinct among populations culturally distinct from the primarily Canadian normative sample (Cooke, 1998; Cooke & Michie, 1999; Molto et al., 1995).

Actuarial and empirically validated measures of violence risk assessment and sexual offense risk assessment frequently utilize results from the PCL-R among their prediction variables. Four such measures include the Violence Risk Appraisal Guide (VRAG; Quinsey, Harris, Rice, & Cormier, 1998; Rice & Harris, 1995), the HCR-20 (Webster, Eaves, Douglas, & Wintrup, 1995; Webster, Douglas, Eaves, & Hart, 1997), the Sex Offense Risk Appraisal Guide (SORAG; Quinsey, Lalumiere, Rice, & Harris, 1995) and the Sexual Violence Risk–20 (SVR-20; Boer,

Hart, Kropp, & Webster, 1995). The actuarial measures, VRAG and SORAG, utilize normative samples from a maximum security forensic hospital in Penetanguishene, Ontario, which are likely more internationally diversified rather than racially or ethnically diversified in the same manner as in the United States. Restricted to a small number of risk factors that are thought to predict violence and sexual reoffense in their population in general, they ignore factors that are idiosyncratic to a specific case. An advantage of the empirically derived measures, HCR-20 and SVR-20, is that they allow for structured professional judgment and consideration of "other" factors that may include culture, ethnicity, and race.

There is concern that the PCL-R, VRAG, HCR-20, SORAG, and SVR-20 tend to utilize factors that may potentially bias Hispanics. The five measures look at violence history, violent criminal history, nonviolent criminal history, or criminal versatility. Considering the data noting conviction and sentencing disparity among Hispanics, research is needed to see if such factors or other factors lead to disparity of Hispanics in attributions of psychopathy and violence or sexual offense risk assessment.

In an account of his own experience working with monolingual Spanish-speaking Hispanic immigrants in California, LaCalle (1986) identified cultural and ethnic background as often mitigating elements in the case of sexual offenses and the motivation of defendants. He provided case examples of recent Hispanic immigrants who were surprised that their actions were labeled as illegal in this country or labeled with a stronger degree of criminality. A poor uneducated 18-year-old adult male Mexican national who grew up on a *rancho* may view it as culturally normal to urinate and defecate in public (albeit discreetly), strip naked to wash the only clothes he owns, pinch a girl's behind, enter into a relationship with a young 13- or 14-year-old pubescent girl, or take on a 17-year-old "wife" although not legally married. He is in culture shock when he is told he is being arrested for indecent exposure, soliciting, lewdness with a minor, rape, or kidnapping. Hispanic defendants in such cases are guilty of doing something illegal in this country, but their actions are motivated by cultural ignorance rather than sexual perpetration. In some cases, lessons on the American value system and law may be more appropriate than sex offender treatment (LaCalle, 1986).

Culture and ethnicity are also important in addressing mitigating and aggravating factors in criminal cases involving violence. In the case of the Hispanic gang youth, it is helpful for attorneys, jurors, and judges to understand the dynamics of gang participation that led to the illegal and violent behavior. Hispanic gang youth are frequently from single-parent families that are female centered and include inadequate parenting or supervision of the children; domestic violence from an aggressive father or male father figure; a mother who is powerless to protect her children; family histories of alcoholism and drugs; poverty; inadequate housing; low educational attainment; and pressures of acculturation, discrimination, and racism (Adler, Ovando, & Hocevar, 1984; Belitz & Valdez, 1995, 1997; Morales, 1992; Vigil, 1988a, 1988b). Hispanic youths frequently feel isolated and marginal within their families, helpless and powerless in a home environment that is unpredictable and violent, abandoned and betrayed, and ambivalent, angry, and without adequate identity. To protect themselves from their feelings, they identify with the abusive father figure and learn that aggression brings power and control (Belitz & Valdez, 1995). As the family becomes less capable of satisfying the youths' needs, the neighborhood street gang serves as a surrogate family and place from which to formulate a sense of identity, competency, purpose, status, and financial gain (Belitz & Valdez, 1995, 1997; Morales, 1992). Newly immigrated Hispanics may join gangs to help them acculturate and develop a Mexican-American identity, or some join gangs composed largely of newly immigrated Mexican nationals so they may adapt to the streets but maintain their ethnic identity (Belitz & Valdez, 1997). It is not uncommon for fathers, father figures, or older brothers to serve as role models of gang membership. Frequently neighborhoods in which the youths grow up are within the hub of a specific gang. Not to join the neighborhood group would in essence mean not surviving the streets of their own neighborhood. As gang affiliates, youths learn to master the streets.

Violence and crimes resulting from such gang affiliations are undoubtedly illegal and intolerable. Forensic psychologists may be enlisted to assess the gang youth to identify aggravating and mitigating factors related to the crime or to make presentencing recommendations regarding treatment and risk to the community. It is important for psychologists to have some knowledge of the gang culture in the local community and sociocultural stressors that affect minority youth to avoid the risk of overdiagnosing an adolescent's problems because of his gang affiliation and underdiagnosing genuine and serious mental health disorders (Belitz & Valdez, 1997). Experts can help the triers of fact attain understanding of how the youth entered into high-risk affiliations and behaviors and identify underlying depression, anxiety, history of trauma, and learning disabilities masked by hostility and aggression as well as psychiatric labels of oppositional-defiant and conduct disorder.

Mental Retardation and the Death Penalty

On June 20, 2002, the U.S. Supreme Court issued a landmark ruling in *Atkins v. Virginia* declaring the execution of persons with mental retardation unconstitutional. Forensic psychologists appointed as experts to evaluate potentially mentally retarded Hispanic or Hispanic-American death row inmates will face considerable challenges. They will be challenged by the risk of underreporting or overreporting the intellectual and adaptive behavioral functioning of Hispanic individuals. The most frequently utilized measures of intelligence and adaptive behavioral functioning are potentially biased because of a primarily Anglo-American standardization sample. With straightforward interpretation of such measures, there is a risk of underrepresentation of a Hispanic individual's intellectual and adaptive behavioral functioning, allowing an offender to escape execution. With utilization of translated measures and/or measures that have been renormed in a foreign

Hispanic culture, there is a risk of overrepresentation of a Hispanic individual's intellectual and adaptive behavioral functioning, potentially contributing to the erroneous execution of a genuinely mentally retarded individual.

The forensic psychologist evaluating a death row inmate for mental retardation is prudent to utilize a comprehensive assessment model that considers culturally competent assessment and limitations and includes a thorough psychosocial evaluation and review of academic, psychological, medical, legal, and other pertinent documents. Such a model will increase the likelihood that genuinely mentally retarded Hispanic and Hispanic American inmates will be accurately identified as mentally retarded. The risk still remains that nonmentally retarded Hispanic and Hispanic-American offenders who were previously erroneously identified as mentally retarded will become legitimate candidates for execution.

Employment Litigation

Hispanics constitute both a sizeable group of the blue-collar working class and a significant proportion of individuals seeking workers' compensation benefits for work-related injuries, with some areas reporting 90 percent of contested stress claims from Hispanic workers (DuAlba & Scott, 1993). There are many factors that may account for Hispanics' vast representation in employment litigation: (1) passage of a controversial immigration reform bill providing 350,000 "guest workers" from Mexico per year (Dana, 1993); (2) exposure to a large number of stressors (language barriers, lower socioeconomic status, lack of education, limited work skills, acculturation, and discrimination); (3) employment in the least sanitary, least health-conscious, and most dangerous jobs, particularly for undocumented Hispanic workers (Nogales, 1992); (4) exposure to stereotypes and discrimination on the job; (5) lack of language skills, knowledge of rights, and legal documents to enable them to make a complaint without embarrassment, fear of losing one's job, or fear of deportation; (6) less likelihood to report an injury or quit a job for fear of unemployment; and (7) tendency to somatize when under stress.

Nogales (1992) notes that workers' compensation cases of Hispanics include claims of emotional distress damages because of (1) excessive work demands, (2) inappropriate work tasks, (3) physical health/safety threatened, (4) medical treatment denied, (5) physical condition/recovery ignored/threatened, (6) fear of job loss generated by employer, (7) verbal abuse/harassment, (8) unfair employment practices, (9) racial discrimination/harassment, (10) excessive vigilance, and (11) physical assaults/harassment.

When performing psycholegal evaluations in workers' compensation cases, Nogales (1992) highlights the importance of addressing linguistic and cultural factors in the utilization of psychological testing, the limitations and possible underrepresentation of symptoms when using interpreters, and cultural factors that may hamper full self-disclosure of symptoms. Weisenberg, Kreindler,

Schachat, and Werbogg (1975) cite a number of studies that illustrate that the experience of pain is learned within the family and ethnic/cultural background. Sabin (1975) notes how translators may minimize the accuracy in assessment of affect, increase emotional distance from the pain of the patient, and underestimate the risk of suicide.

DuAlba and Scott (1993) examined the MMPI profiles of 60 Spanish-speaking Hispanic individuals and 60 Caucasian individuals who were referred for psychological testing as part of a medical-legal evaluation pursuant to filing a workers' compensation claim for psychiatric disability. Hispanics were administered a Spanish version of the MMPI. Results suggested that consistent with cultural expectation, the MMPI profiles of Hispanics suggested somatization more than the MMPI profiles of Caucasians, as assessed by elevations on the hypochondriasis, depression, and hysteria scales. Hispanics were no more likely to malinger than were Caucasians, as assessed by the MMPI dissimulation index of $F - K > +9$.

Post-Traumatic stress disorder (PTSD) is a diagnosis frequently encountered in employment litigation. Hough and colleagues (1996) reviewed the literature on PTSD among Hispanics, including Latin American refugees and immigrants, victims of natural and manmade disasters, and Vietnam veterans. They found inconclusive information concerning the hypothesis that Hispanics, Caucasians, and others differ significantly in their propensities to experience trauma and develop serious mental health consequences. The National Vietnam Veterans Readjustment Study (Kulka, Schlenger, Fairbank, Hough, Jordan, Marmar, & Weiss, 1991) provided convincing data of significant culturally endogenous reactions to trauma, with Hispanic veterans exhibiting higher rates of diagnosable PTSD than African-American or Caucasian veterans when controlling for a wide range of predisposing factors.

Immigration

The role of the forensic psychologist in immigration cases has been given little attention in forensic mental health literature. The Hispanic forensic expert can make valuable contributions in this unique forensic subspecialty. Frumkin and Friedland (1995) provide an excellent review of the immigration cases in which the forensic psychologist may have a role: (1) waiver of deportation for long-time lawful permanent residents who have been convicted of certain crimes; (2) suspension of deportation; (3) permanent residence for abused spouses and children; (4) asylum to persons who establish persecution or well-founded fear of persecution; (5) waiver of inadmissibility to the United States for certain health related reasons; and (6) parole for emergent reasons and reasons deemed to be in the public interest.

The psychologist is most likely to be retained for the first four immigration cases. In cases involving waiver of deportation for long-time lawful permanent residents who have been convicted of a certain crime, the expert witness may be able to address mitigating or aggravating circumstances surrounding the crime, rehabilitation, character, and hardship to the respondent, his or her spouse, and children if the respondent is deported and separated from his or her family or if the respondent's relocation forces the family's relocation to the respondent's country of origin.

The term *suspension of deportation* has been replaced with the term *cancellation of removal* (Immigration and Nationality Act, 1999). In such cases, the expert witness may be able to help counsel establish that removal of the inadmissible or deportable alien would result in "exceptional and extremely unusual hardship" to the alien's spouse, parent, or child who is a citizen of the United States or an alien lawfully admitted for permanent residence. "Exceptional and extremely unusual hardship" is a difficult standard to meet since it goes beyond the ordinary hardship that would be expected when a close family member leaves this country, such as loss of family contact, loss of employment, or decline in standard of living. Whether or not evidence of psychological hardship meets the legal criteria of "exceptional and extremely unusual hardship" is the ultimate issue.

Immigration judges are sensitive to potential hardships of the Hispanic family, primarily older U.S. citizen children, if the family were to be separated (as is usually the case when the respondent is deported and the other parent is a U.S. citizen or lawful permanent resident) or if the family were to relocate as a whole (as is usually the case when both parents are illegal). The psychologist can address a variety of psychological hardship issues posed by deportation leading to family separation, including dissolution of the marital and family units, single parenthood and consequent emotional burdens, loss of mother or father and consequent emotional and behavioral problems, and loss of support for elderly parents in this country who are solely dependent upon the applicant. Psychological hardships posed by relocation of the respondent and the family to the respondent's country of origin are numerous. Interviews, psychological testing, and review of academic, mental health, and/or medical records will alert the psychologist to the hardships older U.S. citizen children who are primarily English-speaking would encounter if forced to relocate to a foreign country. They would experience difficulty with language, reading and writing skills, acculturation stress, culture shock, and separation from family, friends, community, school, and customs. Children with learning disabilities, intellectual impairment, emotional disability, history of trauma, or medical disability might not find educational, mental health, or medical resources in the Latin American country comparable to U.S. resources. It is important for the expert to be aware of resources in the respondent's country of origin, preferably in the region to which they are likely to relocate, to knowledgeably compare and contrast resources. Immigration judges do not appreciate unfounded implications that the particular Latin American country to which the family would relocate has no resources.

In 1990 and 1995, the Immigration and Nationality Act was amended to allow an alien spouse and children to file a petition for permanent residence when she or her children are physically, emotionally, or sexually abused or exposed to threat of such abuse by a U.S. citizen or permanent resident spouse or parent (Frumkin & Friendland, 1995). Psychologists can be instrumental in documenting and assessing abuse and current and potential symptoms of such abuse. There is ample literature regarding battered Hispanic women that can be helpful to the forensic expert (Cox, 1992; Champion, 1996; Jasinski, 1998; Kantor et al., 1994; Perilla, 1999; Ptacek, 1999; Rodriguez, 1998; Sorenson & Telles, 1991; Straus & Smith, 1990; Torres, 1998).

Finally, in cases of asylum resulting from persecution on account of race, religion, nationality, or membership to a particular social group, the psychologist can be instrumental in summarizing the trauma experienced by the respondent and identifying the emotional consequences to the trauma, including the presence of PTSD or other mental health disorder.

CONCLUSIONS AND DIRECTIONS FOR FUTURE RESEARCH

Considering the anticipated growth of the U.S. Hispanic population in the twenty-first century and the overrepresentation of Hispanics in the legal system, there is a demand for competence in combined Hispanic psychology and forensic psychology. To meet the variety of ethical guidelines posed by the APA and its divisions, Hispanics in the forensic arena should be evaluated by bilingual, bicultural Hispanic psychologists with expertise in Hispanic and forensic psychology. Experts should be aware of potential sources of bias in the legal system against Hispanics, including overrepresentation in the criminal justice system, sentencing disparity, issues surrounding the death penalty, and juror perceptions of Hispanic defendants.

Models for culturally competent forensic assessment with Hispanics include the *DSM-IV* (APA, 1994) and *DSM-IV-TR* (APA, 2000) *Outline for Cultural Formulation*, a biopsychosociocultural model, and a model that is alert to cultural history, beliefs, and within-group heterogeneity; acculturation; culturally distinctive expressions of illness and culturally bound syndromes (e.g., *ataque de nervios* and tendency toward somatization); specific cultural moderators (e.g., *simpatia* and collectivism); and other moderator variables such as language, reading skills, use of translators, and use of translated tests.

Psychological testing of Hispanics, within a culturally sensitive forensic evaluation, can be a useful tool in supporting expert opinion. Examination should use standardized tests that have Hispanic norms; use tests that have sufficient research to distinguish differences between Hispanic subjects and the standardization sample; address the limitations of utilizing tests that do not have Hispanic norms or research distinguishing the response style of Hispanics and the standardization sample and propose modified interpretations when appropriate; or acknowledge the absence of standardized assessment measures applicable to Hispanics when there is such an absence. The Wechsler intelligence scales, nonverbal intelligence tests, MMPI/MMPI-2, Millon inventories, PAI, PCL-R, and their translations when applicable are scrutinized for their appropriate application with Hispanics in the courtroom.

There is a paucity of research with Hispanics utilizing forensic specific measurement. The forensic expert alert to linguistic and cultural variables can help the triers of fact identify true, nonexistent, and feigned psychopathology in cases of competency and criminal responsibility. A variety of cultural and associated variables can assist the forensic expert in identifying mitigating and aggravating factors related to the crime, make presentencing recommendations regarding treatment and risk to the community, and potentially lessen sentencing disparity attributable to ethnicity. Within employment litigation, the forensic psychologist needs to be alert to cultural factors that account for Hispanics' vast representation in such litigation and culturally bound health-illness factors that can challenge the forensic evaluation. Finally, psychologists can play a valuable role in the forensic subspecialty of immigration law, identifying extenuating circumstances for granting of permanent residency.

To date, the dearth of literature regarding Hispanics in the forensic arena is descriptive in nature. To most effectively isolate the role culture and ethnicity of Hispanics play in forensic psychology, we need studies that are truly comparative and, at the same time, culturally sensitive. Some researchers propose reconstructed and restandardized testing for Hispanics incorporating an acculturation validity scale (Dana, 1975), whereas others propose the development of alternative measures and procedures to facilitate the movement of the profession toward more culturally sensitive assessment practices (Melendez, 1994; Suzuki et al., 1996). Indicators of malingering, a concept of particular importance in the legal system, have yet to be validated with specific reference to race and ethnicity. Considering MMPI/MMPI-2 findings that Hispanics tend to produce elevated L scales potentially because of a cultural tendency to not be self-disclosing, further studies on validity measures and response tendencies within the forensic arena are needed for experts to assist the triers of fact in accurately addressing the absence or presence of malingering.

Research suggests that most courtroom decisions are based on the quality and clarity of the evidence. The forensic expert is in a key position to enhance this process through culturally sensitive assessment within the legal system.

REFERENCES

Adler, P., Ovando, C., & Hocevar, D. (1984). Familiar correlates of gang membership: An exploratory study of Mexican-American youth. *Hispanic Journal of Behavioral Sciences*, 6, 64–76.

Alterman, A. I., Zaballero, A. R., Lin, M. M., Siddiqui, N., Brown, L. S., Rutherford, & McDermott, P. A. (1995). Personality assessment inventory (PAI) scores of lower-socioeconomic African American and Latino methadone maintenance patients. *Assessment*, 2, 92–100.

American Psychiatric Association. (1994). *Diagnostic and statistical manual of mental disorders* (4th ed.). Washington, DC: Author.
American Psychiatric Association. (2000). *Diagnostic and statistical manual of mental disorders* (4th ed, text revision). Washington, DC: Author.
American Psychological Association. (1985). *Standards for educational and psychological testing.* Washington, DC: Author.
American Psychological Association. (1993). Guidelines for providers of psychological services to ethnic, linguistic, and culturally diverse populations. *American Psychologist, 48,* 45–48.
American Psychological Association. (1994). Guidelines for child custody evaluations in divorce proceedings. *American Psychologist, 49,* 677.
American Psychological Association. (2002). Ethical principles of psychologists and code of conduct. *American Psychologist, 57,* 1060–1073.
American Psychological Association. (2003). Guidelines on Multicultural Education, Training, Research, Practice, and Organizational Change for Psychologists. *American Psychologist, 58,* 377–402.
Anderson, W. (1995). Ethnic and cross-cultural differences on the MMPI-2. In J. C. Duckworth & W. P. Anderson (Eds.), *MMPI & MMPI-2 interpretation manual for counselors and clinicians* (4th ed.) (pp. 439–460). Bristol, PA: Accelerated Development.
Anduaga, J. C., Forteza, C. G., & Lira, L. R. (1991). Concurrent validity of the DIS: Experience with psychiatric patients in Mexico City. *Hispanic Journal of Behavioral Sciences, 13,* 63–77.
Angel, R., & Guarnaccia, P. J. (1989). Mind, body, and culture: Somatization among Hispanics. *Social Science and Medicine, 28,* 1229–1238.
Arnold, B. R., Montgomery, G. T., Castaneda, I., & Longoria, R. (1994). Acculturation and performance of Hispanics of selected Halstead-Reitan neuropsychological tests. *Assessment, 1,* 239–248.
Atkins v. Virginia, 122 S. Ct. 2242 (2002).
Baldus, D. C., Woodworth, G., & Pulaski, C. A. (1992). Law and statistics in conflict: Reflections on McCleskey v. Kemp. In D. K. Kagehiro & Laufer, W. S. (Eds.), *Handbook of psychology and law* (pp. 251–271). New York: Springer-Verlag.
Belitz, J., & Valdez, D. M. (1995). Clinical issues in the treatment of Chicano male gang youths. In A. M. Padilla (Ed.), *Hispanic psychology: Critical issues in theory and research* (pp. 148–165). Thousand Oaks, CA: Sage.
Belitz, J., & Valdez, D. M. (1997). A sociocultural context for understanding gang involvement among Mexican-American male youth. In J. G. Garcia & M. C. Zea (Eds.), *Psychological intervention and research with Latino populations* (pp. 56–72). Boston: Allyn and Bacon.
Bernal, M. E., Colon, A., Fernandez, E., Mena, A., Torres, A., & Torres, E. (1959). *Inventario Multifacico de la Personalidad.* New York: Psychological Corporation.
Bersoff, D. N. (1988). Should subjective employment devises be scrutinized? It's elementary, my dear Ms. Watson. *American Psychologist, 12,* 1016–1018.
Blau, T. (1998). *The psychologist as expert witness* (2nd ed.). New York: John Wiley.
Boer, D. P., Hart, S. D., Kropp, P. R., & Webster, C. D. (1997). *Manual for the Sexual Violence Risk–20.* Burnaby, British Columbia: Simon Fraser University.
Brislin, R. W. (1970). Back-translation for cross-cultural research. *Journal of Cross-Cultural Psychology, 1,* 185–216.

Brown, L., Sherbenou, R. J., & Johnson, S. K. (1997). *Test of Nonverbal Intelligence* (3rd ed.). Austin, TX: Pro-Ed.

Butcher, J. N. (1994). New developments in Spanish language versions of the MMPI-2 and MMPI-A. *MMPI-2 & MMPI-A News and Profiles, 5,* 5–6.

Butcher, J. N. (1995). Personality patterns of personal injury litigants. In Y. S. Ben-Porath, J. R. Graham, G. C. N. Hall, R. D. Hirschman, & M. S. Zaragoza (Eds.), *Forensic applications of the MMPI-2* (pp. 179–201). Thousand Oaks, CA: Sage.

Butcher, J. N. (Ed.) (1996). *International adaptations of the MMPI-2: Research and clinical applications.* Minneapolis: University of Minnesota Press.

Butcher, J. N., Dahlstrom, W. G., Graham, J. R., Tellegen, A., & Kaemmer, B. (1989). *Minnesota Multiphasic Personality Inventory-2 (MMPI-2): Manual for administration and scoring.* Minneapolis: University of Minnesota Press.

Butcher, J. N., & Williams, C. L. (1992). *Essentials of MMPI-2 and MMPI-A interpretations.* Minneapolis: University of Minnesota Press.

Butcher, J. N., Williams, C. L., Graham, J. R., Archer, R. P., Tellegen, A., Ben-Porath, Y. S., & Kaemmer, B. (1992). *MMPI-A (Minnesota Multiphasic Personality Inventory-Adolescent): Manual for administration, scoring, and interpretation.* Minneapolis: University of Minnesota Press.

Campos, L. P. (1989). Adverse impact, unfairness, and bias in the psychological screening of Hispanic peace officers. *Hispanic Journal of Behavioral Sciences, 11,* 122–135.

Canter, M. B., Bennet, B. E., Jones, S. E., & Nagy, T. F. (1994). *Ethics for psychologists: A commentary on the APA Ethics Code.* Washington, DC: American Psychological Association.

Cervantes, R. C., Padilla, A. M., & Salgado de Snyder, N. (1990). Reliability and validity of the Hispanic Stress Inventory. *Hispanic Journal of Behavioral Sciences, 12,* 76–82.

Champion, J. D. (1996). Woman abuse, assimilation, and self-concept in a rural Mexican American community. *Hispanic Journal of Behavioral Sciences, 18,* 508–521.

Choca, J., Shanley, L., Peterson, C., & Van Denburg, E. (1990). Racial bias and the MCMI. *Journal of Personality Assessment, 54,* 479–490.

Choca, J. P., & Van Denburg, E. (1997). *Interpretive guide to the Millon Clinical Multiaxial Inventory* (2nd ed.). Washington, DC: American Psychological Association.

Committee on Ethical Guidelines for Forensic Psychologists. (1991). Specialty guidelines for forensic psychologists. *Law and Human Behavior, 15,* 655–665.

Cooke, D. J. (1998). Cross-cultural aspects of psychopathy. In D. J. Cooke, A. E. Forth, & R. D. Hare (Eds.), *Psychopathy: Theory, research and implications for society* (pp. 13–45). Dordrecht, the Netherlands: Kluwer Academic.

Cooke, D. J., Kosson, D. S., & Michie, C. (2001). Psychopathy and ethnicity: Structural, item, and test generalizability of the Psychopathy Checklist-Revised (PCL-R) in Caucasian and African American participants. *Psychological Assessment, 13,* 531–542.

Cooke, D. J., & Michie, C. (1999). Psychopathy across cultures: North America and Scotland compared. *Journal of Abnormal Psychology, 108,* 58–68.

Cooke, D. J., & Michie, C. (2001). Refining the construct of psychopathy: Towards a hierarchical model. *Psychological Assessment, 13,* 171–188.

Cowan, G., Martinez, L., & Mendiola, S. (1997). Predictors of attitudes toward illegal Latino immigrants. *Hispanic Journal of Behavioral Sciences, 19,* 403–415.

Cox, E. S. (1992). The Mexican battered women's movement and the case for internalization. *Response to the Victimization of Women and Children: Journal of the Center for Women Policy Studies, 14,* 2–4.

Cuellar, I. (2000). Acculturation as a moderator of personality and psychological assessment. In R. H. Dana (Ed.), *Handbook of cross-cultural and multicultural personality assessment* (pp. 113–129). Mahwah, NJ: Lawrence Erlbaum.

Cuellar, I., Harris, I. C., & Jasso, R. (1980). An acculturation scale for Mexican American normal and clinical populations. *Hispanic Journal of Behavioral Science, 2*, 199–217.

Cuellar, I., Arnold, B., & Maldonado, R. (1995). Acculturation Rating Scale for Mexican Americans–II: A revision of the original ARSMA scale. *Hispanic Journal of Behavioral Sciences, 17*, 275–304.

Cueller, I., & Paniagua, F. A. (2000). *Handbook of multicultural mental health: Assessment and treatment of diverse populations.* San Diego: Academic Press.

Dana, R. H. (1993). *Multicultural assessment perspectives for professional psychology.* Boston: Allyn & Bacon.

Dana, R. H. (1995). Culturally competent MMPI assessment of Hispanic populations. *Hispanic Journal of Behavioral Sciences, 17*, 305–319.

Dana, R. H. (2000). *Handbook of cross-cultural and multicultural personality assessment.* Mahway, NJ: Lawrence Erlbaum.

Daubert v. Merrell Dow Pharmaceuticals, 509 U.S. 579 (1993).

Daudistel, H. C., Hosch, H. M., Holmes, M. D., & Graves, J. B. (1999). Effects of defendant ethnicity of juries' dispositions of felony cases. *Journal of Applied Social Psychology, 29*, 317–336.

De La Cancela, V., Guarnaccia, P., & Carrilo, E. (1986). Psychosocial distress among Latinos: A critical analysis of *ataques de nervios. Humanity and Society, 10*, 431–447.

Del Castillo, J. C. (1970). The influence of language upon symptomatology in foreign-born patients. *American Journal of Psychiatry, 127*, 242–244.

Donat, D., Walters, J., & Hume, A. (1992). MCMI differences between alcoholics and cocaine abusers: Effect of age, sex, and race. *Journal of Personality Assessment, 58*, 96–104.

Donlon, R. F. (1992). Legal issues in the educational testing of Hispanics. In K. F. Geisinger (Ed.), *Psychological testing of Hispanics* (pp. 55–78). Washington, DC: American Psychological Association.

Douglas, K. S., & Hart, S. D. (1998). *Validity of the Personality Assessment Inventory (PAI) in forensic assessment.* Paper presented at the annual meeting of American Psychological Association Convention, San Francisco, CA.

DuAlba, L., & Scott, R. L. (1993). Somatization and malingering for worker's compensation applicants: A cross-cultural MMPI study. *Journal of Clinical Psychology, 49*, 913–917.

Edens, J. F., Cruise, K. R., & Buffington-Vollum, J. D. (2001). Forensic and correctional applications of the Personality Assessment Inventory. *Behavioral Sciences and the Law, 19*, 519–543.

Edens, J. F., Hart, S. D., Johnson, D. W., Johnson, J., & Olver, M. E. (2000). Use of the PAI to assess psychopathy in offender populations. *Psychological Assessment, 12*, 132–139.

Escobar, J. I. (1987). Cross cultural aspects of the somatization trait. *Hospital Community Psychiatry, 38*, 174–180.

Escobar, J. I., Burnam, M. A., Karno, M., Forsythe, A., Landsverk, J., & Golding, J. M. (1986). Use of the Mini Mental State Examination (MMSE) in a community population of mixed ethnicity. *Journal of Nervous and Mental Disease, 174*, 607–614.

Escobar, J. I., Burnam, M. A., Karno, M., Forsythe, A., & Golding, J. M. (1987). Somatization in the community. *Archives of General Psychiatry, 44,* 713–718.

Escobar, J. I., Gomez, J., & Tuason, V. B. (1983). Depressive phenomenology in North and South American patients. *American Journal of Psychiatry, 140,* 47–51.

Escobar, J. I., Randolph, E. T., & Hill, M. (1986). Symptoms of schizophrenia in Hispanic and Anglo veterans. *Culture, Medicine, and Psychiatry, 10,* 259–276.

Escobar, J. I., Rubio-Stipec, M., Canino, G. J., & Carno, M. (1989). Somatic Symptom Index (SSI): A new and abridged somatization construct. *Journal of Nervous and Mental Disease, 177,* 140–146.

Ewing, P. (1990). *When children kill children: Dynamics of juvenile homicide.* Lexington, MA: Lexington Books.

Fabrega, Jr., H. (1995). Hispanic mental health research: A case for cultural psychiatry. In A. M. Padilla (Ed.), *Hispanic psychology: Critical issues in theory and research* (pp. 107–130). Thousand Oaks, CA: Sage.

Fantoni-Salvador, P. (1997). Spanish version of the MMPI-2 and PAI: An investigation of concurrent validity with Hispanic patient. *Assessment, 4,* 29–39.

Feinman, C. (1994). *Women in the criminal justice system* (3rd ed.). Westport, CT: Praeger.

Franco, J. N. (1983). An acculturation scale for Mexican-American children. *Journal of General Psychology, 108,* 175–181.

Frumkin, I. B., & Friedland, J. (1995). Forensic Evaluations in Immigration Cases: Evolving Issues. *Behavioral Sciences and the Law, 13,* 477–489.

Fuller, C. G., & Malony, H. N. (1984). A comparison of English and Spanish (Nunez) translations of the MMPI. *Journal of Personality Assessment, 48,* 130–132.

Garcia, M., & Lega, L. I. (1979). Development of a Cuban Ethnic Identity Questionnaire. *Hispanic Journal of Behavioral Sciences, 1,* 247–261.

Garcia, M., & Marks, G. (1989). Depressive symptomatology among Mexican American adults: An examination with the CES-D scale. *Psychiatry Research, 27,* 137–148.

Garcia-Peltoniemi, R. E., & Chaviano, A. A. A. (1993). *MMPI-2: Inventario Multifasico de la Personalidad-2-Minnesota.* Minneapolis: University of Minnesota Press.

Geisinger, K. F. (Ed.). (1992). *Psychological testing of Hispanics.* Washington, DC: American Psychological Association.

General Electric v. Joiner, 188 S. Ct. 512 (1997).

Graham, J. R. (1993). *MMPI-2: Assessing personality and psychopathology* (2nd ed.). New York: Oxford University Press.

Greene, R. L. (1991). *The MMPI-2/MMPI: An interpretative manual.* Boston: Allyn & Bacon, 1991.

Grisso, T. (1998). *Instrument for assessing understanding and appreciation of Miranda rights.* Sarasota, FL: Professional Resource Press.

Guarnaccia, P. J., Rubio-Stipec, M., & Canino, G. (1989). *Ataque de nervios* in the Puerto Rican diagnostic interview schedule: The impact of cultural categories on psychiatric epidemiology. *Culture, Medicine, and Psychiatry, 13,* 275–295.

Gynther, M. D. (1989). MMPI comparisons of blacks and whites: A review and commentary. *Journal of Clinical Psychology, 45,* 878–883.

Hall, G. C. N., Bansal, A., & Lopez, I. R. (1999). Ethnicity and psychopathology: A meta-analytic review of 31 years of comparative MMPI/MMPI-2 research. *Psychological Assessment, 11,* 186–197.

Hall, G. C. N., & Phung, A. H. (2001). Minnesota Multiphasic Personality Inventory and Millon Clinical Multiaxial Inventory. In L. A. Suzuki, J. G. Ponterotto, & P. J. Meller (Eds.), *Handbook of multicultural assessment* (2nd ed.). San Francisco: Jossey-Bass.

Hare, R. D. (1991). *Manual for the Hare Psychopathy Checklist–Revised.* Toronto, ON: Multi-Health Systems.

Hare, R. D. (2003). *Hare Psychopathy Checklist–Revised (PCL-R): 2nd edition.* Technical Manual. North Tonawanda, NY: Multi-Health Systems.

Harrington, R. G. (1985). Test of nonverbal intelligence. In D. J. Keyser & R. C. Sweetland (Eds.), *Test critiques, Vol. 2* (pp. 319–325). Kansas City, MO: Test Corporation of America.

Harris, A. M., Reynolds, M. A., & Koegel, H. M. (1996). Nonverbal Assessment: Multicultural Perspectives. In L. A. Suzuki, P. J. Meller, & J. G. Ponterotto (Eds). *Handbook of multicultural assessment* (pp. 223–252). San Francisco: Jossey-Bass.

Hathaway, S. R., & McKinley, J. C. (1983). *The Minnesota Multiphasic Personality Inventory manual.* New York: Psychological Corporation.

Herrans, L. L., & Rodriguez, J. M. (1992). *Escala de Inteligencia Wechsler para Ninos-Revisada.* San Diego, CA: Psychological Corporation.

Holland, T. R. (1979). Ethnic group differences in MMPI profile pattern and factorial structure among adult offenders. *Journal of Personality Assessment, 43,* 72–77.

Holmes, M. D., Hosch, H. M., Daudistel, H. C., Perez, D. A., & Graves, J. B. (1993). Judges' ethnicity and minority sentencing: Evidence concerning Hispanics. *Social Science Quarterly, 74,* 496–506.

Holtzman, W. H. (1988). Beyond the Rorschach. *Journal of Personality Assessment, 52,* 578–609.

Hough, R. L., Canino, G. J., Abueg, F. R., & Gusman, F. D. (1996). PTSD and related stress disorders among Hispanics. In A. J. Marsella, C. Chemtob, & R. Hamada (Eds.), *Ethnocultural aspects of post-traumatic stress disorder: Issues, research, and clinical applications* (pp. 301–338). Washington, DC: American Psychological Association.

Immigration and Nationality Act, as amended, 8, United States Code (U.S.C.), Sec. 1101 et seq. (1952).

Immigration and Nationality Act, 8 U.S.C. 1129b(b) (Supp. V), Sec. 240A(b) (1999).

Jasinski, J. L. (1998). The role of acculturation in wife assault. *Hispanic Journal of Behavioral Sciences, 20,* 175–191.

Johnson, M. B., & Torres, L. (1992). Miranda, trial competency and Hispanic immigrant defendants. *American Journal of Forensic Psychology, 10,* 65–80.

Jones, M., & Krisberg, B. (1994). *Images and reality: Juvenile crime, youth violence and public policy.* San Francisco: National Council on Crime and Delinquency.

Kantor, G. K., Jasinski, J. L., & Aldorondo, E. (1994). Sociocultural status and incidence of marital violence in Hispanic families. *Violence and Victims, 9,* 207–222.

Karno, M., & Edgerton, R. (1969). Perception of mental illness in a Mexican-American community. *Archives of General Psychiatry, 20,* 237–262.

Kline, S. (1992). A profile of female offenders in the Federal Bureau of Prisons. *Federal Prisons Journal, 3,* 33–34.

Kolody, B., Vegg, W., Meinhardt, K., & Bensussen, G. (1986). The correspondence of health complaints and depressive symptoms among Anglos and Mexican-Americans. *Journal of Nervous and Mental Disease, 174,* 221–228.

Koocher, G. P., & Keith-Spiegel, P. (1998). *Ethics in psychology: Professional standards and cases.* New York: Oxford University Press.

Kosson, D. S., Smith, S. S., & Newman, J. P. (1990). Evaluating the construct validity of psychopathy on black and white male inmates: Three preliminary studies. *Journal of Abnormal Psychology, 99,* 250–259.

Kulka, R. A., Schlenger, W. E., Fairbank, J. A., Hough, R. L., Jordan, B. K., Marmar, C. R., & Weiss, D. S. (1991). *Trauma and the Vietnam war generation: Report of findings from the National Vietnam Veterans Readjustment Study.* New York: Brunner/Mazel.

Kumho Tire Co., v. Carmichael, 199 S. Ct. 1167 (1999).

Kunst, J. L., & Reed, M. (1999). Cross-cultural issues in infanticide: A case study. *Cultural Diversity and Ethnic Minority Psychology, 5,* 147–155.

LaCalle, J. J. (1986). Hispanic defendants on sex offense charges: Primer for the expert witness. *American Journal of Forensic Psychology, 4,* 19–29.

LaFree, G. D. (1985). Official reactions to Hispanic defendants in the southwest. *Journal of Research in Crime and Delinquency, 22,* 213–237.

Lambert, N. M. (1981). Psychological evidence in Larry P. v. Wilson Riles. *American Psychologist, 36,* 937–952.

Larry P. v. Riles, 343 F. Supp. 1306 (N.D. CA. 1972) (preliminary injunction), *aff'd,* 502 F. 2d 963 (9th Cir. 1974), opinion issued No. C-71–2270 RFP (N.D. CA. October 16, 1979).

Lees-Haley, P. (1991). MMPI-2 F and F-K scores of personal injury malingerers in vocational neuropsychological and emotional distress claims. *American Journal of Forensic Psychology, 9,* 5–14.

Llabre, M. M. (1984). Standard progressive matrices. In D. J. Keyser & R. C. Sweetland (Eds.), *Test critiques, Vol. 1* (pp. 595–602). Kansas City, MO: Test Corporation of America.

Lopez, A. S. (Ed.) (1995). *Latinos in the United States: History, law, and perspective.* New York: Garland.

Lopez, S., & Nunez, J. A. (1987). Cultural factors considered in selected diagnostic criteria and interview schedules. *Journal of Abnormal Psychology, 96,* 270–272.

Lopez, S., & Romero, A. (1988). Assessing the intellectual functioning of Spanish-speaking adults: Comparison of the EIWA and the WAIS. *Professional Psychology: Research and Practice, 19,* 263–270.

Low, S. M. (1981). The meaning of *nervios*: A sociocultural analysis of symptom presentation in San Jose, Costa Rica. *Culture, Medicine, and Psychiatry, 5,* 25–47.

Mahaffey, M. B. (1986). Locus of control in Mexican, Central, and South American adults. (Doctoral dissertation, University of Nevada, Reno, 1986). *Dissertation Abstracts International, 47,* 12.

Marcos, L. R. (1976). Bilinguals in psychotherapy: Language as an emotional barrier. *American Journal of Psychotherapy, 30,* 549–553.

Marcos, L. R., Alpert, M., Urcuyo, L., & Kesselman, M. (1973). The effect of interview language on the evaluation of psychopathology in Spanish-American schizophrenic patients. *American Journal of Psychiatry, 130,* 549–553.

Marcos, L. R., Urcuyo, L., Kesselman, M., & Alpert, M. (1973). The language barrier in evaluating Spanish-American patients. *Archives of General Psychiatry, 29,* 655–659.

Marin, G., & Gamba, R. J. (1996). The new measurement of acculturation for Hispanics: The Bidimensional Acculturation Scale for Hispanics (BAS). *Hispanic Journal of Behavioral Sciences, 18,* 297–316.

Marin, G., & Marin, B. V. (1991). *Research with Hispanic populations.* Newbury Park, CA: Sage.

Marin, G., Sabogal, F., VanOss Marin, B. V., Otero-Sabogal, R., & Perez-Stable, E. J. (1987). Development of a short acculturation scale for Hispanics. *Hispanic Journal of Behavioral Sciences, 9*, 183–205.

Martin, P. C. (1977). *A Spanish translation, adaptation, and standardization of the Wechsler Intelligence Scale for Children-Revised.* Unpublished doctoral dissertation, University of Miami.

Martinez, R., Norman, R. D., & Delaney, H. D. (1984). A Children's Hispanic Background Scale, *Hispanic Journal of Behavioral Sciences, 6*, 103–112.

Matarazzo, J. D. (1990). Psychological assessment versus psychological testing: Validation from Binet to the school, clinic, and courtroom. *American Psychologist, 45*, 999–1016.

McClesky v. Kemp, 481 U.S. 279 (1987).

McCreary, C. P., & Padilla, A. E. (1977). MMPI differences among black, Mexican-American, and white male offenders. *Journal of Clinical Psychology, 33*, 171–177.

Melendez, F. (1994). The Spanish version of the WAIS: Some ethical considerations. *Clinical Neuropsychologist, 8*, 388–393.

Melton, G. B., Petrila, J., Poythress, N. G., & Slobogin, C. (1997). *Psychological evaluations for the courts: A handbook for mental health professionals and lawyers* (2nd ed.). New York: Guilford Press.

Mendoza, R. H. (1989). An empirical scale to measure type and degree of acculturation in Mexican-American adolescents and adults. *Journal of Cross-Cultural Psychology, 20*, 372–385.

Mezzich, J. E., & Rabb, E. S. (1980). Depression symptomatology across the Americans. *Archives of General Psychiatry, 37*, 818–823.

Millon, T. (1977). *Millon Clinical Multiaxial Inventory.* Minneapolis, MN: National Computer Systems.

Millon, T. (1987). *Manual for the MCMI-II* (2nd ed.). Minneapolis, MN: National Computer Systems.

Millon T. (1994). *Manual for the MCMI-III.* Minneapolis, MN: National Computer Systems.

Molto, J., Carmona, E., Poy, R., Avila, C., & Torrubia, R. (1995). Psychopathy Checklist–Revised in Spanish prison populations: Some data on reliability and validity. *Issues in Criminological and Legal Psychology, 24*, 109–114.

Morales, A. T. (1992). Latino youth gangs: Causes and clinical intervention. In L. A. Vargas & J. D. Koss-Chioino (Eds.), *Working with culture: Psychotherapeutic intervention with ethnic minority children and adolescents* (pp. 129–154). San Francisco: Jossey-Bass.

Morey, L. C. (1991). *Personality Assessment Inventory professional manual.* Odessa, FL: Psychological Assessment Resources.

Munoz, E. A., Lopez, D. A., & Stewart, E. Misdemeanor sentencing decisions: The cumulative disadvantage effect of "gringo justice." *Hispanic Journal of Behavioral Sciences, 20*, 298–319.

Nogales, A. (1992). Hispanic injured workers. *American Journal of Forensic Psychology, 10*, 67–80.

Norris, A. E., Ford, K., & Bova, C. B. (1996). Psychometrics of a brief acculturation scale for Hispanics in a probability sample of urban Hispanic adolescents and young adults. *Hispanic Journal of Behavioral Sciences, 18*, 29–38.

Nunez, R. (1967). *Inventario Multifasico de la Personalidad: MMPI-Espanol.* Mexico City: El Manual Moderno, S.A.

Olmedo, E. L., Martinez, J. L., Jr., & Martinez, S. R. (1978). Measure of acculturation for Chicano adolescents. *Psychological Reports, 42*, 159–170.

Ostrosky, F., Ardila, A., & Rosselli, M. (1977). *Neuropsi: Un examen neuropsicologico breve en Espanol* [Neuropsi: A brief neuropsychological exam in Spanish]. Mexico City: Bayer.

PACE v. Hannon, 506 F. Supp. 831 (N.D. IL. 1980).

Perilla, J. L. (1999). Domestic violence as a human rights issue: The case of immigrant Latinos. *Hispanic Journal of Behavioral Sciences, 21*, 107–133.

Ponton, M. O., & Leon-Carrion, J. (Eds.). (2001). *Neuropsychology and the Hispanic patient: A clinical handbook.* Mahway, NJ: Lawrence Erlbaum.

Ponton, M. O., Satz, P., Herrera, L., Ortiz, F., Furst, C., & Namerow, N. (1996). Normative data stratified by age and education for the Neuropsychological Screening Battery for Hispanics (NeSBHIS): Initial report. *Journal of the Internal Neuropsychological Society, 2*, 96–104.

Pope, K. S., Butcher, J. N., & Seelen, J. (1993). *The MMPI, MMPI-2, and MMPI-A in court.* Washington, DC: American Psychological Association.

Psychological Corporation. (2003). *The catalog for psychological assessment products.* New York: Psychological Corporation.

Ptacek, J. (1999). *Battered women in the courtroom: The power of judicial responses.* Boston: Northeastern University Press.

Puente, A. E. (1990). Psychological assessment with minority group members. In G. Goldstein & M. Hersen (Eds.), *Handbook of psychological assessment* (2nd ed.) (pp. 505–520). New York: Pergamon.

Quinsey, V. L., Harris, G. T., Rice, M. E., & Cormier, C. A. (1998). *Violent offenders: Appraising and managing risk.* Washington, DC: American Psychological Association.

Quinsey, V. L., Lalumiere, M. L., Rice, M. E., & Harris, G. T. (1995). Predicting sexual offenses. In J. C. Campbell (Ed.), *Assessment of dangerousness: Violence by sexual offenders, batterers, and child abusers* (pp. 114–137). Thousand Oaks, CA: Sage.

Ramirez, M., III. (1983). *Psychology of the Americas: Mestizo perspectives on personality and mental health.* New York: Pergamon.

Raven, J. C. (1956, 1962). *Coloured Progressive Matrices.* London: H. K. Lewis.

Raven, J. C., Court, J. H., & Raven, J. (1938, 1947, 1977). *Standard Progressive Matrices.* London: H. K. Lewis.

Rice, M. E., & Harris, G. T. (1995). Violent recidivism: Assessing predictive validity. *Journal of Consulting and Clinical Psychology, 63*, 737–748.

Rivera-Arzola, M., & Ramos-Grenier, J. (1997). Anger, *ataques de nervios*, and *la mujer Puertorriquena*: Sociocultural considerations and treatment implications. In J. G. Garcia & M. C. Zea (Eds.), *Psychological interventions and research with Latino populations.* Boston: Allyn & Bacon.

Rodriguez, R. (1998). Clinical interventions with battered migrant farm worker women. In J. C. Campbell (Ed.), *Empowering survivors of abuse: Health care for battered women and their children* (pp. 271–279). Thousand Oaks, CA: Sage.

Rogers, R. (1984). *Rogers Criminal Responsibility Assessment Scale, Interpretative Manual.* Odessa, FL: Psychological Assessment Resources.

Rogers, R., Flores, J., Ustad, K., & Sewell, K. W. (1995). Initial validation of the personality assessment inventory—Spanish version with clients from Mexican American communities: A brief report. *Journal of Personality Assessment, 64*, 340–348.

Rogers, S., & McKee, G. R. (1995). Use of the MMPI-2 in the assessment of criminal responsibility. In Y. S. Ben-Porath, J. R. Graham, G. C. N. Hall, R. D. Hirschman, & M. S. Zaragoza (Eds.), *Forensic applications of the MMPI-2* (pp. 103–126). Thousand Oaks, CA: Sage.

Rogler, L. H. (1989). The meaning of culturally sensitive research and mental health. *American Journal of Psychiatry, 146,* 296–303.

Rosado, J., & Elias, M. (1993). Ecological and psychocultural mediators in the delivery of services for urban, culturally diverse Hispanic clients. *Professional Psychololgy: Research and Practice, 24,* 450–459.

Roysircar-Sodowsky, G., & Maestas, M. V. (2000). Acculturation, ethnic identity, and acculturative stress: Evidence and measurement. In R. H. Dana (Ed.), *Handbook of cross-cultural and multicultural personality assessment* (pp. 131–172). Mahway, NJ: Lawrence Erlbaum.

Rubio-Stipec, M., Shrout, P., Bird, M., Canino, G., & Bravo, M. (1989). Symptom scales of the Diagnostic Interview Schedule: Factor results in Hispanic and Anglo samples. *Psychological Assessment: A Journal of Consulting and Clinical Psychology, 1,* 30–34.

Rudd, M. D., & Orman, D. T. (1996). Millon Clinical Multiaxial Inventory profiles and maladjustment in the military: Preliminary findings. *Military Medicine, 161,* 349–351.

Sabin, J. E. (1975). Translating despair. *American Journal of Psychiatry, 132,* 197–199.

Saldana, D. H. (1995). Acculturative stress: Minority status and distress. In A. M. Padilla (Ed.), *Hispanic psychology: Critical issues in theory and research.* Thousand Oaks, CA: Sage.

Schwartz, I. M. (1989). *Injustice for juveniles: Rethinking the best interests of the child.* Boston: Lexington Books.

Shapiro, D. L. (1999). *Criminal responsibility evaluations: A manual for practice.* Sarasota, FL: Professional Resource Press.

Silva, J. A., Leong, G. B., Weinstock, R., Yamamoto, J., & Ferrari, M. M. (1996). A biopsychosociocultural approach for the evaluation of parents who kill their children. *American Journal of Forensic Psychiatry, 17,* 25–36.

Silva, J. A., Leong, G. B., Yamamoto, J., Weinstock, R., & Ferrari, M. M. (1997). A transcultural forensic psychiatric perspective of a mother who killed her children. *American Journal of Forensic Psychiatry, 18,* 39–58.

Silva, J. A., Leong, G. B., Dassori, A., Ferrari, M. M., Weinstock, R., & Yamamoto, J. (1998). A comprehensive typology for the biopsychosociocultural evaluation of child-killing behavior. *Journal of Forensic Science, 43,* 1112–1118.

Sorenson, S., & Telles, C. (1991). Self-reports of spousal violence in a Mexican-American and non-Hispanic white population. *Violence and Victims, 6,* 3–15.

Straus, M. A., & Smith, C. (1990). Violence in Hispanic families in the United States: Incidence rates and structural interpretations. In M. A. Straus & R. J. Gelles (Eds.), *Physical violence in American families: Risk factors and adaptations to violence in 8,145 families* (pp. 341–367). New Brunswick, NJ: Transaction.

Suzuki, L. A., Ponterotto, J. G., & Meller, P. J. (Eds.). (2001). *Handbook of multicultural assessment* (2nd ed.). San Francisco: Jossey-Bass.

Suzuki, L. A., Vraniak, D. A., & Kugler, J. F. (1996). Intellectual assessment across cultures. In L. A. Suzuki, J. G. Ponterotto, & P. J. Meller (Eds.), *Handbook of multicultural assessment* (pp. 141–177). San Francisco: Jossey-Bass.

Szapocznik, J., Kurtines, W. M., & Fernandez, T. (1980). Bicultural involvement and adjustment in Hispanic-American youth. *International Journal of Intercultural Relations, 4,* 353–365.

Szapocznik, J., Scopetta, M. A., Kurtines, W., & de los Angeles Aranalde, M. (1978). Theory and measurement of acculturation. *Inter-American Journal of Psychology, 12,* 113–130.

Thomson, E. Discrimination and the death penalty in Arizona. (1997). *Criminal Justice Review, 22,* 65–76.

Tonry, M. (1995). *Malign neglect: Race, crime and punishment in America.* New York: Oxford University Press.

Torres, S. (1998). Intervening with battered Hispanic pregnant women. In J. C. Campbell (Ed.), *Empowering survivors of abuse: Health care for battered women and their children* (pp. 259–270). Thousand Oaks, CA: Sage.

Tubb, V. A. (2001). The factor structure and psychometric properties of the Psychopathy Checklist–Revised: Data from an Hispanic federal-inmate sample. (Doctoral dissertation, University of Texas at El Paso, 2001). *Dissertation Abstracts International, 62,* 5426.

U.S. Census Bureau. (2001). Profiles of general demographic characteristics: 2000. *http://www.census.gov/prod/cen2000/dp12kh00.pdf.*

U.S. Census Bureau. (2002). 2001 statistical abstract of the United States. *http://landview.census.gov/prod/2002pubs/01statab/stat-ab01.html.*

Valdez, A., Kaplan, C. D., & Codina, E. (2000). Psychopathy among Mexican American gang members: A comparative study. *International Journal of Offender Therapy and Comparative Criminology, 44,* 46–58.

Velasquez, R. J. (1995). Personality assessment of Hispanic clients. In J. N. Butcher (Ed.), *Clinical personality assessment: Practical approaches* (pp. 120–139). New York: Oxford University Press.

Velasquez, R. J., Ayala, G. X., & Mendoza, S. A. (1998). *Psychodiagnostic assessment of U.S. Latinos: MMPI, MMPI-2, and MMPI-A results.* East Lansing, MI: Julian Samora Institute.

Velasquez, R. J., Ayala, G. X., Mendoza, S. A., Nezami, E., Castillo-Canez, I., Pace, T., Choney, S. K., Gomez, Jr., F. C., & Miles, L. E. (2000). Culturally competent use of the Minnesota Multiphasic Personality Inventory–2. In I. Cuellar & F. A. Paniagua (Eds.), *A handbook of multicultural mental health* (pp. 389–417). San Diego: Academic Press.

Velasquez, R. J., Gonzales, R. J., Butcher, J. N., Castillo-Canez, I., Apodaca, J. X., & Chavira, D. (1997). Use of MMPI-2 with Chicanos: Strategies for counselors. *Journal of Multicultural Counseling and Development, 25,* 107–120.

Vigil, J. D. (1988a). Group processes and street identity: Adolescent Chicano gang members. *Ethos, 16,* 421–445.

Vigil, J. D. (1988b). Street socialization, locura behavior, and violence among Chicano gang members. In J. F. Kraus, S. B. Sorenson, & P. D. Juarez (Eds.), *Research conference on violence and homicide in Hispanic communities* (pp. 231–241). Los Angeles: UCLA Publication Services.

Webster, C. D., Douglas, K. S., Eaves, D., & Hart, S. D. (1997). *HCR-20: Assessing risk of violence, Version 2.* Burnaby, British Columbia: Simon Fraser University.

Webster, C. D., Eaves, D., Douglas, K. S., & Wintrup, A. (1995). *The HCR-20 scheme: The assessment of dangerousness and risk.* Vancouver: Simon Fraser University and British Columbia Forensic Psychiatric Services Commission.

Wechsler, D. (1949). *Wechsler Intelligence Scale for Children*. New York: Psychological Corporation.
Wechsler, D. (1951). *Escala de Inteligencia Wechsler para Ninos*. New York: Psychological Corporation.
Wechsler, D. (1955). *The Wechsler Adult Intelligence Scale*. New York: Psychological Corporation.
Wechsler, D. (1968). *Escala de Inteligencia Wechsler para Adultos*. New York: Psychological Corporation.
Wechsler, D. (1974). *The Wechsler Intelligence Scale for Children-Revised*. San Antonio, TX: Psychological Corporation.
Wechsler, D. (1989). *Manual for the Wechsler Preschool and Primary Scale of Intelligence–Revised*. San Antonio, TX: Psychological Corporation.
Wechsler, D. (1991). *Manual for the Wechsler Intelligence Scale for Children–Third edition*. San Antonio, TX: Psychological Corporation.
Wechsler, D. (1997). *Manual for the Wechsler Intelligence Scale for Adults–Third edition*. San Antonio, TX: Psychological Corporation.
Weiner, I. B. (1995). Psychometric issues in forensic applications of the MMPI-2. In Y. S. Ben-Porath, J. R. Graham, G. C. N. Hall, R. D. Hirschman, & M. S. Zaragoza (Eds.), *Forensic applications of the MMPI-2* (pp. 48–81). Thousand Oaks, CA: Sage.
Weisenberg, N., Kreindler, M. L., Schachat, R., & Werbogg, J. (1975). Pain: Anxiety and attitudes in black, white and Puerto Rican patients. *Psychosomatic Medicine*, *37*, 123–135.
Williams, J. J. (1995). Race of appellant, sentencing guidelines, and decisionmaking in criminal appeals: A research note. *Journal of Criminal Justice*, *23*, 83–91.
Windle, M., & Dumenci, L. (1999). The factorial structure and construct validity of the Psychopathy Checklist–Revised (PCL-R) among alcoholic inpatients. *Structural Equation Modeling*, *4*, 372–393.
Wooldredge, J. D. (1998). Analytic rigor in studies of disparities in criminal case processing. *Journal of Quantitative Criminology*, *14*, 155–179.
Yung, B. R., & Hammond, W. R. (1997). Antisocial behavior in minority groups: Epidemiological and cultural perspectives. In D. M. Stoff, J. Breiling, & J. D. Maser (Eds.), *Handbook of antisocial behavior*. New York: John Wiley.
Zalewski, C., & Green, R. L. (1996). Multicultural usage of the MMPI-2. In L. A. Suzuki, P. J. Meller, & J. G. Ponterotto (Eds.), *Handbook of multicultural assessment: Clinical, psychological, and educational applications* (pp. 77–114). San Francisco: Jossey-Bass.
Zane, N., & Mak, W. (2003). Major approaches to the measurement of acculturation among ethnic minority populations: A content analysis and an alternative empirical strategy. In K. M. Chun, P. B. Organista, & G. Marin (Eds.), *Acculturation: Advances in theory, measurement, and applied research* (pp. 39–60). Washington, DC: American Psychological Association.
Zea, M. C., Quezada, T., & Belgrave, F. Z. (1997). Limitations of an acultural health psychology for Latinos: Reconstructing the African influence on Latino culture and health-related behaviors. In J. G. Garcia & M. C. Zea (Eds.), *Psychological interventions and research with Latino populations* (pp. 255–266). Boston: Allyn & Bacon.
Ziskin, J. (1995). *Coping with psychiatric and psychological testimony* (5th ed.). Los Angeles: Law and Psychology Press.

CHAPTER 34

PSYCHOLOGY IN A SECURE SETTING

KIRK A. BRUNSWIG
UNIVERSITY OF NEVADA, RENO

ROBERT W. PARHAM
ARGOSY UNIVERSITY, SEATTLE

One of the most important decisions mental health professionals have to make about this career is the setting in which they choose to practice. Undergraduate and graduate practica, volunteering, internships, and postdoctoral trainings are an ideal way to experience and learn about these various settings. Of the many careers available to the psychologist, this chapter addresses that of working within correctional or other secure settings, such as a jail, prison, mental health hospital, secure forensic unit, or civil commitment facility, to name only a few. Many doctoral students avoid these particular fields of practice because of misconceptions or lack of information about working with this population. It is the aim of this chapter to inform psychologists and other mental health professionals about the practice of psychology in these settings.

We recognize the heterogeneity within and among these various institutions and hope that the reader will appreciate the limitations of such a broad grasp as describing the practice of psychology within a secure setting. A majority of the research in psychology in a secure setting is prison-based research. However, topographical and functional similarities across secure settings suggest that the results from prison research may extend to secure mental health settings. A key difference among these settings that may limit generalizability is the rights bestowed to and removed from residents of the institution.

Scott (1997) reports similarities between nursing homes and prisons. Although nursing home residents may liken their experience to prison, Scott highlights the following characteristics common to both: the staff (line staff, floor staff, and 24-hour staff) has the most contact with the inmates and clients, both avoid mental health identity (e.g., prisoner over mentally ill, physically disabled over mentally ill), and both complain of the food. The floor staff in both facilities are typically the lowest paid and least educated. Although Scott did not address other secure settings, such as competency restoration, civil commitment mental hospital, and civil commitment facilities for sexually violent persons, it is anticipated that similarities would continue to emerge. For example, it would be expected that if staff attend only to inmates, clients, customers, consumers, and stakeholders when they are disruptive, complaining, acting out, incontinent, or otherwise behaving problematically, these behaviors would continue. Thus, an experience in a geriatric setting may be informative for the clinician considering a career in a correctional or secure setting.

Boothby and Clements (2000, 2002) researched the actual and ideal task allocation of correctional psychologists. They provide several examples of what psychologists can expect to do, and Correia (2001) and this chapter provide specific examples of these duties, jobs, chores, and adventures. Psychologists in prison settings report spending most of their time in administrative duties (30%), treatment (26%), and assessment (18%; Boothby & Clements, 2000). However, psychologists report that their ideal time allocation includes more time in treatment, less time in administrative duties, and about the same amount of assessment.

In a follow-up study, Boothby and Clements (2002) surveyed job satisfaction in state and federal correctional psychologists. The survey consisted of 18 items related to peer interactions, acknowledgement, advancement, safety, job security, and professionalism. Federal psychologists indicated generally more satisfaction than state psychologists. Overall, the results indicate that psychologists are not satisfied with those items that they deem most important. Those items showing the least satisfaction were opportunity for advancement, professional atmosphere, recognition, and access to and influence upon decision making. The highest satisfaction ratings among both state and federal psychologists are related to job security, safety, and relationship with inmates. These data should be encouraging for those considering a career in a secure setting, since job and personal security considerations are among the first that psychologists address when considering a career in this field.

ENVIRONMENTAL ASPECTS OF CORRECTIONAL AND SECURE SETTINGS

One of the challenges facing the psychologist in a secure setting, before approaching any specific job, is the environment itself. The name of the facility may be telling; penitentiaries are designed to foster penitence, prisons are designed to detain, correctional centers to correct, reformatories to reform, and so on. Further, there may be differing objectives within the administrative, clinical, and line staff and outside influences such as families, courts, and attorneys (McDougall, 1996). Some staff may have a punishment mindset and not agree with the expenditure of resources on *criminals* to be educated, supported, or rehabilitated (emphasis in original, McDougall, 1996). Hollin and colleagues (1992) state that the organization must have rehabilitation as its principle guiding practice in order to succeed in this goal. Factors such as inmate motivation and staff attitudes can impact the environment's ability to foster and maintain change.

Clinicians are responsible not only for the direct service aspects of services, but also extend their skills into the larger treatment environment. Psychologists are specially equipped to "help correctional facilities interpret the overall climate in which institutional problems surface, are resolved, and can be altogether avoided" (Arrigo, 2000, p. 230). With this in mind, psychologists have the added responsibility of possessing an understanding of both criminal pathology and organizational psychology. Because this knowledge provides a unique perspective on workplace dynamics, psychologists must engage in the often political dance of how to facilitate change within an already established system. Hayes, Austin, Houmanfar, and Clayton's (2001) edited work includes several chapters relevant to the psychologist facing the challenge of motivating or implementing change in a correctional or secure setting. Several of the chapters in their text are based in educational or academic settings, but the principles described relating to increased performance, safety, satisfaction, and cohesion are applicable in secure settings.

Concerning this challenge, McDougall (1996) provides sound advice for new psychologists:

- The presence of a new specialist with qualifications can be threatening to the establishment. Remember this when circumstances arise to demonstrate superior skills. It is easy to reinforce the threat factor if you are not careful.
- A desire to bring about change in the program must be approached in the same manner you would approach change in a client.
- It is important to aim for high professional standards, both in personal behavior and in quality of work.
- Do the job that needs doing rather than the one you want to do.
- Be prepared to learn and listen.
- Respect the skills of other groups of staff and involve them in your work where possible.
- Enjoy what you do. Specialists have a great deal to offer secure institutions, a fact that is increasingly being recognized and welcomed. (p. 112–113)

Psychologist Roles in Correctional and Secure Settings

Correia (2001) provides a thorough overview for the psychologist considering, entering, entertaining, or enjoying a career in a correctional setting. This text is a must read for those considering entering the field, and its contents are summarized only briefly here. Correia describes several roles a psychologist may fill in a correctional setting. Generally the jobs can be grouped into administrative and direct services, with some roles requiring a combination of administrative and direct service.

Management/Supervisor

This role can include, but is not limited to, supervision of psychologists, interns, graduate and undergraduate volunteers/practicum students, bachelor's and/or master's level counselors, and line staff. Further, psychologists may be tasked to participate on organizational committees, such as morale or wellness, labor management, forms and documents, policy and procedures, and community liaison. Work with professionals from a variety of domains in these settings and on committees such as these highlights the multidisciplinary organization of prisons and secure mental health facilities. This organizational structure leads to the occasional oxymoron of the multidisciplinary team.

Multidisciplinary Team

This team can include psychologists, psychiatrists, administrators, nurses, social workers, physical therapists, occupational therapists, speech therapists, master's level counselors, line staff, educational staff, and other institution-specific jobs. Multidisciplinary teams are often organized around a specific group of inmates or clients restricted to a certain problem or difficulty (substance abuse, cognitive impairment), certain level in treatment program (beginning, intermediate, advanced), or location (Charlie unit, east minimum security, etc). As a member of this team, the psychologist may be the team leader or program manager for the area under purview, may be a vital and active teammate and contributor, and, in some facilities, may be a token representative whose ideas and contributions are ignored or ridiculed. There are very few graduate programs that emphasize the skill set required to work effectively with medical professionals. However, some programs, such as that at the University of Nevada, Reno, are emphasizing the role of the psychologist in multidisciplinary teams in medical settings.

As a member (or leader) of the multidisciplinary treatment team, the psychologist may be tasked with the creation or supervision of the development of multidisciplinary treatment plans. Typically treatment plans address some combination of the following domains: Axis I and II diagnoses, substance abuse, medical, nursing, living unit, criminogenic aspects, family, vocational, and discharge planning. Other aspects of treatment planning would be the development, implementation, monitoring, and revising of problem-specific treatment plans.

These can be for acute or chronic issues not otherwise addressed through the regular treatment planning process.

Management Consultant

Block (2000) summarizes the role of a consultant, though emphasizing the external consultant in deserting this role. If the psychologist were an outsourced consultant, Block's book would be a vital resource. For an internal consultant, Block's work is still helpful because the psychologist may find himself or herself doing several of the tasks described in this section. In this role, the psychologist may spend time "floating" around the institution conducting formal or informal climate audits. These audits can be related to the sexual harassment climate (Bowers & O'Donohue, 1999), job stress, morale (both staff and client), humane treatment, training needs, or other issues tasked by management (Arrigo, 2000).

Personnel Selection

At times, it seems that Groucho Marx had prison personnel in mind when he said he would not want to be a member of any club that would have him as a member. There are, and will likely continue to be, people involved in the custody and treatment of the convicted and mentally ill who, based on their histories and skill sets, are not well suited to work in such an environment. There are, and will likely continue to be, people involved in the custody and treatment of the convicted and mentally ill who are exceptionally well qualified, caring, professional, ethical, and a credit to their institutions, guild, and society. Discerning between the two types of people is difficult, given the limited number of applicants to work in these typically remote and challenging settings. There may limited opportunities for psychologists to consult, assess, inform, or participate in the hiring process. The psychologist can contribute positively to the employee selection process outside the bounds of testing and assessment, however. Psychologists often have strong interview skills and a fund of knowledge of benefit to the hiring process.

Staff Counselor/Employee Assistance

The psychologist may also be tasked to provide assistance to co-workers. At times this can place the psychologist in a role similar to that when they provide therapy to inmates; management may want to know, "Who's got problems?" The dual role in these situations is readily apparent and should be clarified with administrative supervisors before entering into the fray. The psychologist may also be called in for crisis counseling and debriefing for staff. In a secure setting, inmates and residents will fight, get assaulted, assault staff, be released, and/or die. All of these events can create a strain and even traumatize staff.

Pretermination Assessment/Counseling

Although these are rare occurrences, the media has relayed several stories of the terminated or pretermination employee wreaking violence in the workplace. Workplace violence has been an area of research interest for several years, with

Harley, Rigger, and Olivetti (2002) having recently reviewed work in this area. LeBlanc and Callaway (2002) report on challenging aspects of risk assessment in this area, and psychologists may be tasked to perform such assessments and interventions.

Investigator

Although investigations are often tasked to those trained in law enforcement or investigative techniques, there may be situations in which psychologists assist or conduct the investigations. A common example is the psychologist conducting the investigation into allegations of sexual harassment. Bowers and O'Donohue (1999) have highlighted the problems with sexual harassment investigations, and psychologists are not immune from these concerns.

Risk Assessment

This task requires the most continuing education of any role filled by psychologists of a secure setting. Here the psychologist is asked to provide an estimate of the inmate or resident's likelihood of reoffending, reoffending violently, or reoffending sexually. These sorts of risk assessments are best informed by clinical and actuarial judgment. Actuarial studies related to these domains are increasing yearly, as the data-driven decision trees of actuarial prediction have increasingly larger foundations of survival and recidivism data. Dawes, Faust, and Meehl (1989) and Litwack (2001) describe the pros and cons of actuarial and clinical judgment. Typically, risk assessment involves one or more actuarial measures, in conjunction with a semistructured clinical interview. Cannon and Quinsey (1995) review some of the challenges in risk assessment (e.g., bias, rater drift). As data are continually added to the collective knowledge fund, the following recommendations may not be applicable into the distant future. However, the merits of the approaches may be extended into selection of measures for future use.

Several authors have reviewed measures or procedures derived for the assessment of risk. In Chapter 6 of this text, Dempster has done an exceptional job summarizing the various issues in risk assessment, techniques, measures, strengths and weakness in risk assessment. This section will address the issues only briefly, and readers are encouraged to refer to Chapter 6 for a more thoughtful explication and discussion of risk assessment.

Several authors have reviewed or compared various risk assessment tools (cf., Dempster, Chapter 6). Silver, Smith, and Banks (2000) discuss the strengths and weaknesses of traditional and recently developed classification tools. Glover, Nicholson, Hemmati, Bernfeld, and Quinsey (2002) compare several predictors of general and violent recidivism. Likewise, Barbaree, Seto, Langton, and Peacock (2001) made several comparisons among tools used to predict risk for sex offenders, whereas Rice and Harris (1995) examine violent reoffense prediction.

Quinsey, Rice, Harris, and Cormier (1998) wrote the essential text for psychologists called upon to perform these types of risk assessment. In this text, the VRAG (Violence Risk Appraisal Guide) and SORAG (Sex Offender Risk Appraisal Guide) are described. In preparing risk assessments, it is often useful, and in some cases required, to complete the Hare Psychopathy Checklist–Revised (PCL-R; Hare, 1991; cf., Hare, Clark, Grann, & Thornton, 2000; Hart, 1998; Hart, Cox, & Hare, 1995). The VRAG, SORAG, and PCL-R are often the three most commonly used tools in risk assessment.

Risk assessments may be an annual requirement, end-of-sentence requirement, or informative treatment planning assessment. Hudson, Wales, Bakker, and Ward (2002), Dempster and Hart (2002), Thornton (2002), Beech, Friendship, Erikson, and Hanson (2002), and Dempster (Chapter 6 of this text) provide the leading works in the area of adult risk assessment in sex offender research. The current work in sex offender risk assessment emphasizes the importance of dynamic risk factors. Dynamic factors also play a role in the prediction of future violence and future reoffense. Static and dynamic risk assessments, as well as the role of clinical and actuarial judgment, are worthy of extensive attention.

End-of-Sentence/Sexually Violent Persons Assessment

For psychologists working in a correctional setting, this is a critical task requiring thorough review of the inmate's behavior while incarcerated compared with treatment efforts and historical/static factors that led to incarceration. The psychologist may have the opportunity to make recommendations for the court that could have a significant impact on potential recidivism, as well as the quality of life for the newly released prisoner.

Parole

Like the end-of-sentence evaluation informing civil commitment, the parole hearing often requires the psychologist to review relevant data, participate in a panel interview, and make recommendations as a member of the board. Roberts (2001) provides a perspective on the role of psychology in sentencing and parole. Risk assessment tools, including some of those just described, are also used to inform decision making in parole settings (Serin, 1992). Bonham, Janeksela, and Bardo (1986) assessed the relative impact of a variety of factors on parole decision making. While it is difficult to assess the impact of these decisions because ethics prevent the random assignment of parole versus nonparoled, Bonham and colleagues indicate that recidivism risk, inmate age at time of hearing, and class of felony were related to parole decision.

Intake Assessment

The psychologist conducting intake assessment may find similarities between their university-clinic training and a secure setting. Assessing depression and anxiety, common complaints in the university clinic, are also the leading complaints among prisoners. Further, intake assessment may require intellectual assessment to inform educational or custodial placement decisions. Boothby and Clements (2000) report typical areas of clinical attention are depression, anger, and substance abuse. Adjustment issues may be present and assessed, though inmates and residents are likely to have been in other secure settings previously (e.g., city or county jail). A comprehensive and thorough intake assessment should provide the treatment team with specific target areas of therapeutic need and direct the treatment planning process. The most commonly used assessment tools in prison are the WAIS and the MMPI, with 87 percent reporting using the MMPI and 69 percent using the WAIS (Boothby & Clements, 2000).

Substance Abuse Assessment, Prevention, and Intervention

In addition to anxiety and depression, substance abuse is often a primary complaint among those in secure settings (Boothby & Clements, 2000). In prisons, drugs and alcohol are available; either manufactured within the facility (brew, pruno) or brought into the facility through mail, visitors, or compromised staff. Prisoners, the mentally ill, and civilly committed sex offenders often describe substances as maladaptive coping skills, disinhibitors for their offending, or both. Twelve-step programs are common in secure settings, and the psychologist may be asked to provide an adjunctive role for those not succeeding in these programs or requiring more intensive intervention. Several institutions have or are mandating tobacco-free policies, and the psychologist may be called upon to develop and implement tobacco-cessation programs.

Suicide Assessment, Prevention, and Intervention

Psychologists are often called upon to assess, predict, or interdict in the area of suicide. Its relative low-base rate makes the prediction of suicide a difficult undertaking. However, sharing this knowledge with facility administrators does little to dissuade their directives to make such predictions. Typically, institutions will have self-harm policies that limit the discretion of psychologists to intervene on the functional aspects of self-injury. Inmates have been known to self-injure to avoid other tasks, increase access to staff, or create a change in residence (e.g., infirmary). In these settings, psychologists may have their hands tied in terms of initial response but often can influence follow-up care for the self-injurious. Inmates and residents meeting diagnostic criteria for Borderline Personality Disorder can highlight the problems with self-injury policies (e.g., attention-maintained self-injury may be maintained by mandated responses). Several forensic and correctional institutions are researching or implementing variants of Dialectical Behavior Therapy (DBT) for the treatment of problems consistent with the diagnostic criteria of borderline personality disorder and other problems seen in correctional settings (Ivanoff, 2002). Psychologists may be called to develop in-service trainings for staff to recognize common precursors to suicidality or to train others on DBT.

Isolation Placement

Psychologists and psychiatrists often carry the burden of treatment oversight of placement in isolation, segregation, or punitive detentions. Psychologists may be asked to assess an inmate or resident for placement in isolation (brief or extended stays), their mental status during isolation, or readiness for return to general population. In addition to oversight of isolation areas, psychologists are often tasked to evaluate and report on the consistency of conditions of confinement with psychological principles and standards in the larger detention and treatment facility.

Sexual Assault Assessment, Prevention, and Intervention

Correia (2001) reports that the common lore of rampant sexual assaults in prison may overestimate the problem. However, the "con code" prevents accurate reporting for fear of being labeled a "snitch," which would likely result in retaliatory assaults. That it occurs is without question, however; only the incidence and prevalence are uncertain. Psychologists can expect to perform rape counseling for the victims of these attacks and counseling for the vicarious trauma for any witnesses or first responders. As with suicide, psychologists may be tasked to develop and implement in-service trainings for staff and inmates on the signs and symptoms of sexual assault, the prevention of sexual assault, and interventions for victims of sexual assault.

Malingering

Psychologists in correctional and secure settings will encounter attempts to malinger by their clientele. Clients may malinger to attempt to avoid prosecution, avoid placement in certain settings, gain access to certain privileges, or avoid stigma (e.g., in prison settings it may be better to be "crazy" than a pedophile). Rogers (1997; as cited in Correia, 2001) reports several clinical signs of malingerers.

1. Malingerers tend to overact. They may believe that the more bizarre they act, the more psychotic they will appear.
2. Malingerers are often quick to call attention to their illness, whereas true schizophrenics are reluctant to discuss their symptoms.
3. Malingerers do not display loosening of associations and other related cognitive signs of schizophrenic illness.
4. Claimed symptom picture in malingerers often does not correspond with any standard diagnostic entity.
5. Malingerers often claim a sudden onset of delusions/hallucinations, whereas in real cases onset is usually gradual over a period of weeks.
6. Malingerers are more likely to make contradictory claims about their symptoms. When challenged, they may sulk or laugh.
7. Malingerers may accuse the interviewer of thinking they are faking, whereas psychotics rarely do.
8. Malingerers are more likely to repeat questions about their "illness," to answer slowly, or to pause before responding. They are also more likely to give "don't know" answers.
9. Malingerers do not typically show signs of residual symptoms such as impaired relatedness, blunted affect, or peculiar thinking.
10. Real hallucinations are associated with congruent delusions in the vast majority of cases (88%).
11. Schizophrenic hallucinations tend to be intermittent rather than continuous. Malingerers may claim that their voices never cease for long periods of time.

12. In the cases of true auditory hallucinations, both male and female voices are heard 75 percent of the time. In only 7 percent of the cases is the message vague and undecipherable. Malingerers are more likely to have difficulty describing voices and content of message.
13. Schizophrenic patients usually have developed superstitious behaviors to make voices go away or to reduce influence through distractions such as engaging in certain activities, changing posture, listening to radio, and the like. Malingerers typically will claim, "Nothing helps."

For example, malingerers have been observed to generate a fake-bad profile on the MMPI-2, while at the same time scoring so poorly on the WAIS they should not have been able to generate an interpretable MMPI-2 profile. Correia (2001) provides extensive examples of clinical presentation and evaluation of malingering. Psychologists are often called upon to (1) detect malingering, (2) assess motivation for malingering, and (3) develop interventions related to malingering.

Crisis Intervention and Hostage Negotiation

The hostage situation is one that correctional psychologists hope to prevent though, when called upon, offer their services to assist in. Inmates and residents outnumber the staff in almost every secure setting. At any one time, the inmates and residents could take control of aspects of the institution based solely on numbers. In these settings, prevention truly is the best medicine because training, education, and guidance may prepare staff to interact in such a way as to prevent a hostage situation. Climate morale audits are an essential component of prevention. Should a hostage situation arise, however, psychologists trained in negotiation and crisis situations may be able to offer valuable resources to the institutional response team (Bahn & Louden, 1999; Butler, Leitenberg, & Fuselier, 1993; Fuselier, 1988; Greenstone, Kosson, & Gacono, 2000). Further, several resources exist that may be of assistance to psychologists both before and after a hostage situation (cf., Fuselier, 1986; Lewicki, Saunders, & Minton, 1999; Soskis & Van Zandt, 1986). Likewise, other crises may arise in which psychologists may be valued members of the response team. Inmate or staff assault and inmate or staff death are two situations in which tempers flare, and violence is often seen as a coping response. Psychologists may be called upon to diffuse intense encounters. Palm, Smith, and Follette (2002) provide a reminder about the need for psychologist self-care in crisis settings and situations allowing the possibility of vicarious trauma.

Individual and Group Psychotherapy

Boothby and Clements (2000) indicate that psychologists spend about 25 percent of their time in service delivery, with about equal shares of individual and group psychotherapy (Morgan, Winterowd, & Ferrell, 1999). Boothby and Clements (2000) report the modal therapeutic approach is cognitive, with over half of respondents indicating a behavioral orientation and 40 percent endorsing a rational-emotive approach. Brodsky (1996), in his review of the founding and early history of *Criminal Justice and Behavior*, notes that the early notion of group and individual therapy as a cure for recidivism has fallen to the wayside, with a current emphasis on treatment within and outside the secure setting for men and women in need of intensive intervention. Thus, the inpatient psychologist will set up the necessary treatment plan for aftercare with the intent of fostering generalization upon return to the community. However, research on dynamic risk factors indicates that a return to an environment with similar dynamic cues may lead to recidivism.

From the economic standpoint, groups may be a more efficient deployment of resources. With this ever-growing shift to group psychotherapy comes unique considerations for group composition, confidentiality, and safety. Psychologists delivering services in group must attend to the "convict code" and the threats to confidentiality, as the notion of "what happens in group stays in group" is easily violated when groups members are coerced, threatened, or cajoled into sharing information from group with a member outside the group. Furthermore, information revealed in group settings may be relevant to administrative or security staff, pressing the psychologist into an ethical gray area. Training in group dynamics in the correctional setting is a vital aspect of preparation for the psychologist in a secure setting.

Sex Offender Treatment

The most common primary intervention for the treatment of sexual offenders is relapse prevention (RP). Initially developed as an adjunct to enhance aftercare, it has become a stand-alone intervention for the problem of sexual offense. Brunswig and colleagues have described RP in general and its application to the treatment of sex offenders (Brunswig, Penix, & O'Donohue, 2002; Brunswig, Penix Sbraga & Harris, in press). Steen (2001) provides a workbook for sexual offenders using relapse prevention skills. Brunswig and O'Donohue's Relapse Prevention for Sexual Harassers (2002) provides a treatment manual for sexual harassment that provides treatment techniques for relapse prevention. Their description of RP techniques allows for the application of these techniques to other problem behaviors. Laws (1989) and Laws, Hudson, and Ward (2000) review the development, implementation, theory, and research behind RP as applied to sexual offenders. Hanson and colleagues' (2002) analysis of a compendium of data from varied sources indicate that sex offender treatment reduces sexual reoffense.

Family Counseling

At times psychologists may be asked, especially if they have training or specialize in this, to provide family counseling. An inmate new to the facility may want assistance in transitioning to the new lifestyle and his or her support group may need assistance as well. Likewise, an inmate who has spent several years incarcerated may need assistance in renewing and relearning life and family skills once on the "outs." The psychologist (or social worker) may also be called upon for grief and bereavement counseling if a family member of an inmate or resident dies, requests divorce, or has some other profound life change (birth of child, grandchild, graduations, marriages, etc.).

Research Coordinator

Boothby and Clements (2000) report a limited role for psychologist-researchers in secure settings. Often research in such a setting is performed by faculty and dissertation-seeking graduate students from nearby universities. In this case, the psychologist may be asked to review the study for the institutional review board, coordinate or collaborate with the university-based researchers, oversee the adherence of the study to institution rules and requirements, and, in the case of their study, be a participant. Other studies may involve the psychologist in the study as a treatment provider (e.g., outcome research on the impact of psychological treatment in a secure setting).

ETHICAL ISSUES IN THE CORRECTIONAL AND SECURE SETTINGS

The multiple mindsets in correctional and secure settings often create potential ethical problems. An ethical dilemma often cited by psychologists in secure settings is that of the apparent dual role of being a mental health treatment provider as well as a security worker (Weinberger & Sreenivasan, 1994). Weinberger and Sreenivasan provide an example of a psychologist who is tasked to perform the job of a correctional officer (e.g., pat search, cell search). In this example, the psychologist has become a "cop" in the inmate's eyes, and the damage to the therapeutic frame would likely be severe. Weinberger and Sreenivasan provide other vignette examples in which the role of the psychologist as therapist is blurred in performing duties within a secure setting (e.g., administrative reviews for punishment of discipline) or in conducting assessments outside the bounds of APA ethical standards (e.g., using a test for purposes other than its intended and empirically supported use).

Weinberger and Sreenivasan (1994) provide examples in which behaviors consistent with Axis II diagnoses would likely have different interpretations and interventions by psychological staff and correctional staff. Further complicating matters is that often within correctional and secure settings the psychologist's chain of command rarely zeniths at the ultimate decision maker and instead peaks under the supervision of the associate warden or superintendent, who more often than not are not trained in psychology. Weinberger and Sreenivasan conclude that to address these ethical dilemmas and role conflicts, mental health should be delivered through departments of health or mental health, that corrections be handled by departments of corrections, and in situations where mental health and security both need be addressed that departments of health and mental health provide for both.

A small number of states have indefinite civil commitment for those adjudicated to be sexually violent persons. Typically, statutes require that in order to be deemed sexually violent, a person must have a history of sexual violence and a mental illness or some characterological aspects that predisposes the person to commit future acts of sexual violence. For the forensic psychologist who may conduct assessments for the various sexually violent predator programs around the United States, there are some ethical concerns to consider. For example, it is typically the job of one branch of state government (mental health, human services, health) to both assess and treat those who are civilly committed under the sexually violent persons statute. The state attorney general's office, also a state agency, is responsible for the prosecution of these cases. The prosecuting attorneys depend heavily on the results of the assessments in order to make their case for the state. Although the forensic psychologists employed by the department of mental health, human services, or health may not provide direct care services such as individual or group therapy, there remains a potential conflict of interest.

Greenberg and Shuman (1997, p. 57) adapted from Greenberg and Moreland (1995) a list of ten differences between therapeutic and forensic relationships.

	CARE PROVISION	FORENSIC EVALUATION
1. Whose client is the patient/litigant?	The mental health practitioner	The attorney
2. The relational privilege that governs disclosure in each relationship	Therapist-patient privilege	Attorney-client and attorney–work product privilege
3. The cognitive set and evaluative attitude of each expert	Supportive, accepting, empathic	Neutral, objective, detached
4. The differing areas of competency of each expert	Therapy techniques for treatment of the impairment	Forensic evaluation techniques relevant to the legal claim
5. The nature of the hypothesis tested by each expert	Diagnostic criteria for the purpose of therapy	Psychological criteria for the purpose of legal adjudication
6. The scrutiny applied to the information utilized in the process and the role of historical truth	Mostly based on information from the person being treated with little scrutiny of that information by the therapist and the court	Litigant information supplemented with that of collateral sources and scrutinized by the evaluator
7. The amount and control of structure in each relationship	Patient structured and relatively less structured than forensic evaluation	Evaluator structured and relatively more structure than therapy
8. The nature and degree of "adversarialness" in each relationship	A helping relationship; rarely adversarial	An evaluative relationship; frequently adversarial
9. The goal of the professional in each relationship	Therapist attempts to benefit the patient by working within the therapeutic relationship	Evaluator advocates for the results and implications of the evaluation for the benefit of the court
10. The impact on each relationship of critical judgment by the expert	The basis of the relationship is the therapeutic alliance, and critical judgment is likely to impair that alliance	The basis of the relationship is evaluative, and critical judgment is unlikely to cause serious emotional harm

The correctional psychologist will likely face several ethical dilemmas in the practice of psychology in a secure setting. Fortunately, the correctional psychologist is supported by several ethical standards, including those developed by the American Psychological Association and the American Association for Correctional Psychology. The American Association for Correctional Psychology's (1999) second edition of the standards for psychology services in jails, prisons, correctional facilities, and agencies provides the following standards, which strengthen the psychologist's ability to deliver services in a secure setting:

> 13. The minimum ratio of full-time psychology staff to adult inmates is 1 for every 150 to 160 inmates. In specialized units (e.g., drug treatment and special management units for mentally ill inmates), the minimally acceptable ratio is 1 full-time psychologist for every 50 to 75 adult inmates. The minimum ratio in facilities for juvenile offenders is 1 full-time psychologist for every 60 to 75 juveniles in general population and 1 full-time psychologist for every 20 to 25 juveniles in a special management unit. (p. 449)
> 17. Psychologists shall limit their functioning to their demonstrated areas of professional competence. (p. 452)
> 28. The collection of psychological evaluation/screening data is performed only by psychological services staff personnel or facility/agency staff trained in them. . . . *At no time is the responsibility for test administration, scoring, or filing of psychological data given to inmate workers.* (emphasis in original, p. 463)
> 36. Only those treatment methodologies recognized and accepted by the state and general psychological community are employed in a facility unless specifically prohibited by facility or organizational administration policies. (p. 469)
> 41. Correctional facilities must ensure that security staff who are assigned to special management units are screened and trained to interact with mentally ill offenders. (p. 473)

These are but some of the ethical standards that guide psychological practice in a correctional setting. However, conflicts may arise when administrators unfamiliar with the ethical standards request psychologists to perform outside these limitations. Psychologists entering a secure setting would likely benefit from reviewing the ethical standards and comparing those standards to the standards of practice within the setting they are considering.

Research in Correctional and Secure Settings

Clearly, the need for research in correctional settings is a pressing concern. Research into the efficacy of treatment interventions as well as research into the complicated interplay between mental health staff and correctional staff is still underdeveloped. Reppucci and Clingempeel (1978) highlight problems in research with correctional populations. Although 25 years have passed since this publication, their concerns still inform research within secure settings. They provide five areas of concern: the intrusion of values, trait-derived methodologies, external validity, recidivism, and ethics. Their thrust, though applicable to research in general, emphasizes the frequent omission of strengths and contextual factors influencing crime.

Reppucci and Clingempeel (1978) assert that this values-based approach emphasizes characterological factors, especially negative factors, implying that these factors are explanatory and predictive. They also ask that researchers in correctional settings heed Campbell and Fiske's (1959) recommendations for multitrait-multimethod assessment in terms of participant descriptions, recidivism, and contextual factors (e.g., multiple definitions of recidivism). They ask for the researcher to attend to person by situation interactions: in the criminal acts, in the research interaction (both inmate's and researcher's demand characteristics and social desirability), and in the behavior observed in the institution. Reppucci and Clingempeel argue that contextual variables impact all these situations and that ignoring these variables weakens the research. Their final concern is that the procedures common in outpatient research be included in the reports of research with inmate populations (e.g., they indicate that informed consent should be included in the conduct and reporting of research in correctional settings).

Megargee (1995) extends the concerns presented by Reppucci and Clingempeel (1978) and provides problems, issues, difficulties, and challenges in the applied aspect of research in a secure setting. Megargee likens research in correctional settings to cross-cultural research. Those who have not spent time (professionally or otherwise) in a correctional setting look to the media for their impression of secure settings. While several documentaries capture the experience—and books, television, and films exaggerate aspects of the setting—Megargee emphasizes the contextual culture of corrections. Further, within the larger culture of a secure or correctional setting, there are often cultures in the administration and the staff as well as several cultures among inmates, residents, and patients.

Megargee makes several recommendations for the researcher new to the secure setting. First, he recommends the researcher spend time in the correctional setting and time with the correctional setting literature; getting to know the data, staff, and procedures is valuable in forming research questions and research partnerships. Megargee provides examples of inroads to the research such as trainings, consultations, workshops, and collaborations with correctional psychologists.

Megargee reviews three aspects of research and highlights how research in a secure setting complicates the already challenging aspects of research. First, limited access to the population constricts the kind of research that can be conducted. Second, journals in which relevant research may be found may be unfamiliar to the researcher. Megargee recommends the National Criminal Justice Reference Service as an extensive resource of published and unpublished reports. Third, literature on (typically) prisoners, inmates, or convicts varies across jurisdictions because state-to-state differences and state-to-federal differences exist concerning what constitutes a crime (and criminal). Further complicating the notion of "participant" is the overrepresentation of minorities in correctional settings and heterogeneity within the inmate population. Thus, there is often limited access to the population and a lack of consistency across settings as to who constitutes an "inmate" or "prisoner" in correctional research.

Additional concerns are found in the methods and materials used in correctional settings. Department of Correction review boards are often reluctant to permit tasks, procedures, or materials that could be construed as cruel and unusual punishment. For example, litigious prisoners or clients could construe exposure and response prevention, or any intervention employing an extinction procedure, as cruel and unusual. Further, it can be argued that informed consent may be compromised by factors influencing participation (e.g., escape from punitive tasks, access to researcher, etc.). Megargee (1995) reports that lengthy or invasive procedures are also unlikely to be approved. He also indicates that several questionnaires are not designed for use in a secure setting because behaviors assessed by the questionnaires may not be possible within the institution (e.g., how often do you drink, when was your last airplane flight, etc.).

Researchers in a secure setting are often confronted by the institutional and organizational challenges involved in obtaining approval for the research. Typically, research in a prison setting involves approval at the local level within the institution (the warden), at a regional level within the department of corrections, and in some cases further approval by a special board at the state level of the department. The university or agency out of which the research is based also often requires review in addition to any funding agencies involved. At a minimum, a researcher in this setting can expect at least three levels of review, with changes by any one level often necessitating approval by the other boards. Including representatives from all levels, and their input, will likely expedite the review process (Megargee, 1995). Further complicating this already challenging process is turnover in the department of corrections. If a warden is promoted, demoted, retired, transferred, or dies, the new warden will most likely want to start the review process anew.

Megargee also cautions the researcher to stay in contact with the staff and personnel involved in the research process. Although the project may be paramount to the student completing her dissertation or the professor working on "that big grant," it is reasonable to expect that the warden and associate wardens will have other pressing concerns (e.g., budget, labor management, security) that may override continued attention to the project. Generally, not all members of the institution will likely support the project, and without the continued cooperation and support of line staff, administrations, and participants it is unlikely the project will have continued success (Megargee, 1995).

Harkening back to the earlier advice of spending time in the setting, Megargee (1995) emphasizes some subtle yet important factors in research in these institutions. Dress, demeanor, and disposition are all variables that influence a researcher's (or research assistant's) success in an institution. We have observed staff last less than a day in this setting and know of others who have been sent home for dress inconsistent with standards or because they have failed background checks. As far as possible, knowing of these requirements and difficulties ahead of time may speed up the process.

Once the project is approved, other aspects of research in secure settings arise. Typically, the participants and researchers will need to be escorted to the research location. If no escorts are available, all parties wait until such escorts are available. Certain materials may not be permitted, such as ink pens of a certain color, cell phones, credit cards, and pocket knives. Staff may be required to attend emergency response training and facility orientation. And access to bathrooms, food, and water may be limited, so plan ahead!

Megargee also provides recommendations for the analysis and publication of research in a secure setting (1995). Megargee reports several problems having to do with the writing of research results based upon research in a secure setting (e.g., adequate description of population; appropriateness of statistics used, such as nonparametric statistics when the assumptions of parametric statistics are not met; cross-validation; and the use of materials not standardized for the population). He also expresses concerns about the level of generalization based upon the limited number of inmates available in research studies in comparison with the larger population onto which the study results are implied. Finally, Megargee reminds the investigator to share the results with those who helped contribute the to study's success: the line staff, administrators, and participants.

CONCLUSION

Although there are specific issues that need to be considered before venturing into the field of correctional psychology, the good news is that it offers a wealth of opportunities for practicum and internship students as well as for practicing psychologists. This view is supported by a study conducted by Pietz and colleagues (1998) that surveyed current and former interns in federal and state prisons. Respondents indicated having had a rewarding experience, with many opportunities for training and experience. Students expressed an overall satisfaction, with an increased interest in the field after completing an internship. This study also reports graduates with training and experience in these settings found employment within three months of the end of their internship.

The desire of correctional psychologists to spend more time in treatment and less in administrative duties is not unique to the secure setting. Many mental health professionals would endorse this position. The implications are that psychologists may need more training in administrative functions and that there is room for the development of more efficient ways to perform these duties. There is something to be learned from federal programs in that psychologists report having more satisfaction in these settings versus state programs. Contributing factors to this discrepancy and the transfer of effective strategies to the state correctional system are areas worth further study.

Staff cohesion in most inpatient settings is often problematic and provides opportunities for the organizational psychologist to conduct research into what works and provide direction for those in administrative positions who wish to find a solution to this ongoing problem. Psychologists have much to offer administrators on organizational change in facing these challenges. New psychologists in these settings can be positive role models for all staff to follow if they will approach their work with the understanding that they are only one piece of an interdependent system.

As noted in this chapter, psychologists serve a variety of functions in secure settings. What is clear from the literature is that interns report having had exposure to many of these functions and are better able to identify their specific interests. Whether that is research, assessment, treatment, or administration, the result is marketability upon graduation. These various functions and roles are also conducive to challenges in ethics. Dual roles and conflicts of interest are only two of the many hurdles one may face in this type of setting. There are several professional organizations that provide codes of ethics and standards of care to turn to for guidance in these areas. Being aware of the potential dilemmas and what the codes and standards say will prepare the psychologist for confrontation by others or defending their own actions.

Practicing psychology in secure settings is a promising field with plenty of challenging opportunities. This chapter was intended to provide an overview for the psychologist or psychologist in training about the multitude of options available for the psychologist in a secure setting. Just as there is broad diversity in the populations within our prisons, forensic units, secure mental health centers, and civil commitment programs for sexually violent persons, there is great diversity in the jobs and opportunities for psychologists in these settings.

REFERENCES

American Association for Correctional Psychology. (1999). Standards for psychology services in jails, prisons, correctional facilities and agencies, second edition. *Criminal Justice and Behavior, 27* (4), 433–494.

Arrigo, B. A. (2000). *Introduction to forensic psychology: Issues and controversies in crime and justice*. San Diego, CA: Academic Press.

Barbaree, H. E., Seto, M. C., Langton, C. M., & Peacock, E. J. (2001). Evaluating the predictive accuracy of six risk assessment instruments for adult sex offenders. *Criminal Justice and Behavior, 28*, 490–521.

Bahn, C., & Louden, R. J. (1999). Hostage negotiation as a team enterprise. *Group, 23* (2), 77–85.

Beech, A., Friendship, C., Erikson, M., & Hanson, R. K. (2002). The relationship between static and dynamic risk factors and reconviction in a sample of U.K. child abusers. *Sexual Abuse: A Journal of Research and Treatment, 14* (3), 155–168.

Block, P. (2000). *Flawless consulting: A guide to getting your expertise used* (2nd ed.). San Francisco: Jossey-Bass Pfeiffer.

Bonham, G., Janeksela, G. M., & Bardo, J. (1986). Predicting parole decisions in Kansas via discriminate analysis. *Journal of Criminal Justice, 14* (2), 123–133.

Boothby, J. L., & Clements, C. B. (2000). A national survey of correctional psychologists. *Criminal Justice and Behavior, 27* (6), 716–732.

Boothby, J. L., & Clements, C. B. (2002). Job satisfaction of correctional psychologists: Implications for recruitment and retention. *Professional Psychology: Research and Practice, 33* (3), 310–315.

Bowers, A. H., & O'Donohue, W. (1999). Conducting a sexual harassment investigation. Paper presented at symposium on Sexual Harassment as Sexual Abuse: Current Research, Treatment and Issues. Association for the Treatment of Sexual Abusers, 18th annual conference, Buena Vista, Florida.

Brodsky, S. L. (1996). Twenty years of criminal justice and behavior: Observations from the beginning. *Criminal Justice and Behavior, 23* (1), 5–11.

Brunswig, K. A., & O'Donohue, W. T. (2002). *Relapse prevention for sexual harassers.* New York: Kluwer Academic Plenum.

Brunswig, K. A., Penix, T. M., & O'Donohue, W. (2002). Relapse prevention. In M. Hersen and W. Sledge (Eds.), *Encyclopedia of psychotherapy.* New York: Academic Press.

Brunswig, K. A., Penix Sbraga, T., & Harris, C. D. (In press). Relapse prevention. In W. O'Donohue, J. E. Fisher, & S. C. Hayes (Eds.), *Handbook of empirically supported treatments.* Thousand Oaks, CA: Sage.

Butler, W. M., Leitenberg, H., & Fuselier, G. D. (1993). The use of mental health professional consultants to police hostage negotiation teams. *Behavioral Sciences and the Law, 11,* 213–221.

Campbell, D. T., & Fiske, D. W. (1959). Convergent and discriminate validation by the multitrait-multimethod matrix. *Psychological Bulletin, 56,* 81–105.

Cannon, C. K., & Quinsey, V. L. (1995). The likelihood of violent behaviour: Predictions, postdictions, and hindsight bias. *Canadian Journal of Behavioral Science, 27,* 92–106.

Correia, K. M. (2001). *A handbook for correctional psychologists: Guidance for the prison practitioner.* Springfield IL: Charles C Thomas.

Dawes, R. M., Faust, D., & Meehl, P. E. (1989). Clinical versus actuarial judgment. *Science, 243,* 1668–1674.

Dempster, R. J., & Hart, S. D. (2002). The relative utility of fixed and variable risk factors in discriminating sexual recidivists and nonrecidivists. *Sexual Abuse: A Journal of Research and Treatment, 14* (3), 121–138.

Ferrell, S. W., Morgan, R. D., & Winterowd, C. L. (2000). Job satisfaction of mental health professionals providing group therapy in state correctional facilities. *International Journal of Offender Therapy and Comparative Criminology, 44* (2), 232–241.

Fuselier, G. D. (1986). A practical overview of hostage negotiations. *FBI Law Enforcement Bulletin, 55,* 1–4.

Fuselier, G. D. (1988). Hostage negotiation consultant: Emerging role for the clinical psychologist. *Professional Psychology: Research and Practice, 19,* 175–179.

Glover, A. J. J., Nicholson, D. E., Hemmati, T., Bernfeld, G. A., & Quinsey, V. L. (2002). A comparison of predictors of general and violent recidivism among high-risk federal offenders. *Criminal Justice and Behavior, 29* (3), 235–249.

Greenberg, S. A., & Moreland, K. (1995). Forensic evaluations and forensic applications of the MMPI/MMPI-2. Unpublished manuscript, University of Minnesota, Minneapolis, and The American Academy of Forensic Psychology.

Greenberg, S. A., & Shuman, D. W. (1997). Irreconcilable conflict between therapeutic and forensic roles. *Professional Psychology: Research and Practice, 28* (1), 50–57.

Greenstone, J. L. (1995). Tactics and negotiating techniques (TNT): The way of the past and the way of the future. In M. I. Kurke, & E. M. Scrivner (Eds.), *Police psychology in the 21st century* (pp. 357–371). Hillsdale, NJ: Erlbaum.

Greenstone, J. L., Kosson, D. S., & Gacono, C. B. (2000). Psychopathy and hostage negotiation: Some preliminary thoughts and findings. In C. B. Gacono (Ed.), *The clinical and forensic assessment of psychopathy: A practitioner's guide. The LEA series in personality and clinical psychology* (pp. 385–403). Mahwah, NJ: Lawrence Erlbaum.

Hanson, R. K., Gordon, A., Harris, A. J. R., Marques, J. K., Murphy, W., Quinsey, V. L., & Seto, M. C. (2002). First report of the collaborative outcome data project on the effectiveness of psychological treatment for sex offenders. *Sexual Abuse: A Journal of Research and Treatment, 14* (3), 169–194.

Hare, R. D. (1991). *The revised Psychopathy Checklist*. Toronto, ON: Multi-Health Systems.

Hare, R. D., Clark, D., Grann, M., & Thornton, D. (2000). Psychopathy and the predictive validity of the PCL-R: An international perspective. *Behavioral Sciences and the Law, 18*, 623–645.

Harley, D. A., Riggar, T. F., & Jolivette, K. (2002). Violence in work settings: Understanding risk and developing solutions. *Journal of Rehabilitation Administration, 26* (2), 111–122.

Hart, S. D. (1998). The role of psychopathy in assessing risk for violence: Conceptual and methodological issues. *Legal and Criminological Psychology, 3*, 123–140.

Hart, S. D., Cox, D. N., & Hare, R. D. (1995). *The Hare PCL:SV. Psychopathy Checklist: Screening Version*. Toronto, ON: Multi-Health Systems.

Hayes, L. J., Austin, J., Houmanfar, R., & Clayton, M. C. (Eds.) (2001). *Organizational change*. Reno, NV: Context Press.

Hudson, S. M., Wales, D. S., Bakker, L., & Ward, T. (2002). Dynamic risk factors: The Kia Marama evaluation. *Sexual Abuse: A Journal of Research and Treatment, 14* (3), 103–120.

Ivanoff, A. M. (2002). Forensic, correctional, and not-so-civil DBT: More data, more mountains to climb. Clinical roundtable at the 36th Annual Convention of the Association for Advancement of Behavior Therapy, Reno, Nevada.

Laws, D. R. (Ed.) (1989). *Relapse prevention with sex offenders*. New York: Guilford Press.

Laws, D. R., Hudson, S. M., & Ward, T. (Eds.) (2000). *Remaking relapse prevention with sex offenders: A sourcebook*. Thousand Oaks, CA: Sage.

LeBlanc, M. M., & Kelloway, E. K. (2002). Predictors and outcomes of workplace violence and aggression. *Journal of Applied Psychology, 87* (3), 444–453.

Lewicki, R. J., Saunders, D. M., & Minton, J. W. (1999). *Negotiation*. Singapore: McGraw-Hill.

Litwack, T. R. (2001). Actuarial versus clinical assessments of dangerousness. *Psychology, Public Policy, and the Law, 7* (2), 409–443.

Marlatt, G. A., & Gordon, J. R. (Eds.) (1985). *Relapse prevention*. New York: Guilford Press.

McDougall, C. (1996). Working in secure institutions. In C. R. Hollin (Ed.), *Working with offenders: psychological practice in offender rehabilitation*. New York: John Wiley.

Megargee, E. I. (1995). Assessment research in correctional settings: Methodological issues and practical problems. *Psychological Assessment, 7* (3), 359–366.

Morgan, R. D., Winterowd, C. L., & Farrell, S. W. (1999). A national survey of group psychotherapy services in correctional facilities. *Professional Psychology: Research and Practice, 30* (6), 600–606.

Palm, K. M., Smith, A. A., & Follette, V. M. (2002). Trauma therapy and therapist self-care. *Behavior Therapist, 25* (2), 40–42.

Pietz, C. A., DeMier, R. L., Dienst, R. D., Green, J. B., & Scully, B. (1998). Psychology internship training in a correctional facility. *Criminal Justice and Behavior, 25* (1), 99–108.

Quinsey, V. L., Harris, G. T., Rice, M. E., & Cormier, C. A. (1998). *Violent offenders: appraising and managing risk*. Washington, DC: American Psychological Association.

Reppucci, N. D., & Clingempeel, W. G. (1978). Methodological issues in research with correctional populations. *Journal of Consulting and Clinical Psychology, 46* (4), 727–746.

Rice, M. E., & Harris, G. T. (1995). Violent recidivism: Assessing predictive validity. *Journal of Consulting and Clinical Psychology, 63*, 737–748.

Roberts, J. V. (2001). Sentencing, parole, and psychology. In R. A. Schuller & J. R. P. Ogloff (Eds.), *Introduction to Psychology and Law: Canadian Perspectives* (pp. 188–213). Toronto, ON: University of Toronto Press.

Rogers, R. (Ed.) *Clinical assessment of malingering and deception* (2nd ed.). New York: Guilford Press.

Scott, E. M. (1997). A prison and a nursing home: Any similarities? *International Journal of Offender Therapy and Comparative Criminology, 41* (3), 298–301.

Serin, R. C. (1992). The clinical application of the Psychopathy Checklist–Revised (PCL-R) in a prison population. *Journal of Clinical Psychology, 48* (5), 637–642.

Silver, E., Smith, W., & Banks, S. (2000). Constructing actuarial devices for predicting recidivism: A comparison of methods. *Criminal Justice and Behavior, 27* (6), 733–764.

Soskis, D. A., & Van Zandt, C. R. (1986). Hostage negotiation: Law enforcement's most effective nonlethal weapon. *FBI Management Quarterly, 6*, 1–8.

Steen, C. (2001). *The adult relapse prevention workbook*. Brandon, VT: Safer Society Press.

Thornton, D. (2002). Constructing and testing a framework for dynamic risk assessment. *Sexual Abuse: A Journal of Research and Treatment, 14* (3), 139–154.

Weinberger, L. E., & Sreenivasan, S. (1994). Ethical and professional conflicts in correctional psychology. *Professional Psychology: Research and Practice, 25* (2), 161–167.

Wooldredge, J. D. (1999). Inmate experiences and psychological well-being. *Criminal Justice and Behavior, 26* (2), 235–250.

CHAPTER 35

EVALUATION OF YOUTH IN THE JUVENILE JUSTICE SYSTEM

RANDY OTTO AND RANDY BORUM

FLORIDA MENTAL HEALTH INSTITUTE, UNIVERSITY OF SOUTH FLORIDA

The relationship between forensic clinical psychology and the juvenile courts and juvenile justice system is a special one. Psychologists and other mental health professionals have been involved in the juvenile courts since their inception a little over 100 years ago, and some commentators have offered that forensic psychology can trace its roots to psychologists' involvement in juvenile matters (Otto & Heilbrun, 2002). In this chapter, after providing an overview of the juvenile justice system and its history, we review a number of clinical issues critical to understanding adolescents and their involvement in the juvenile justice system, and we finish with a discussion of the law and clinical factors surrounding evaluation in this context.

BRIEF HISTORY OF THE JUVENILE JUSTICE SYSTEM

The juvenile court and juvenile justice system are relatively new legal institutions, having just celebrated their 100-year anniversaries a few years ago. The first juvenile court came into existence in Illinois in 1899, and other states rapidly adopted the concept thereafter (Grisso, 1998a). Indeed, the impact of the first juvenile court has even expanded beyond the borders of the United States since special courts for juveniles exist in almost all developed nations (Zimring, 2000). Prior to the establishment of juvenile courts, minors age 14 and older who were accused of criminal acts were processed through (adult) criminal court and received adult sanctions (Tanenhaus, 2000). Children between the ages of 7 and 14 were presumed incapable of forming criminal intent, but this was a rebuttable presumption. Those who were found to have such capacity were also adjudicated in criminal court, while those without such capacity were not sanctioned. Children below the age of 7 were considered simply to lack capacity to form the requisite criminal intent and were not subject to criminal sanctions.

The juvenile court is considered to be the product of two separate but related developments in the United States. With the transition from an agrarian to an industrial economy, implementation of compulsory education laws, and adoption of child labor laws at the beginning of the twentieth century, the age at which persons took on adult tasks, roles, and responsibilities was delayed. These changes were accompanied by formal and scientific recognition (some have suggested invention) of the developmental stage of adolescence. Adolescents, though they clearly showed greater cognitive, emotional, and behavioral capacities than their younger counterparts, were considered not to possess the same capacities as adults. Whereas the law presumed adults to possess free will, to be in control of their behavior, and to fully appreciate the nature and consequences of their actions, developmental psychologists and others argued that adolescents' capacities in these areas were more limited. Accordingly, providing adolescents with the same legal privileges and responsibilities as adults was considered inappropriate, as was holding them equally responsible or culpable for their criminal acts. The juvenile court was to consider criminal behavior of minors in its developmental context, with a greater emphasis on rehabilitation and a diminished emphasis on punishment (Zimring, 2000).

The juvenile court and the juvenile justice system have undergone significant changes over time. Because the juvenile court was to be more rehabilitation focused and less punitive than adult courts, psychologists, social workers, and other mental health professionals played a significant role in all aspects of adjudication and disposition, and the legal proceedings were less formal than in (adult) criminal court. Indeed, such procedural formalities were considered by some to be counterproductive (Mnookin, 1978). The lack of strict legal procedures was not seen as problematic and was considered to constitute something of a tradeoff in return for the goals of the proceedings, which were ostensibly rehabilitative rather than punitive. However, beginning in the 1960s, questions were raised about whether the rehabilitative ideal of the juvenile justice system was being met. Some claimed that the juvenile court and juvenile justice system were, in some ways, no less punitive than the adult criminal justice system.

The Supreme Court offered its opinion of the juvenile justice system in a series of cases in which the constitutional protections that were due children in juvenile proceedings were at issue. Its commentary was not positive. In a 1966 case in which the Court considered the appropriateness of transferring a minor to be tried in the criminal court without benefit of any hearing (see later for further discussion of transfer provisions), the majority offered that a child involved in the juvenile court "gets the worst of both worlds: that he gets neither the (procedural legal) protections accorded to adults nor the solicitous care and regenerative treatment postulated for children" (*Kent v. United States*, 1966, p. 556). The next term, in the case of *In re Gault* (1967), the Supreme Court had the opportunity to delineate the constitutional rights afforded to juveniles who were subject to delinquency proceedings. The Court, noting that a minor appearing in juvenile court was not provided with many of the basic rights granted to adult defendants appearing in criminal court, including the right to notice of the charges, the right to counsel, the right to confront and cross-examine adverse witnesses, and the right to avoid self-incrimination, compared the juvenile court operating in Arizona to a "kangaroo court." In its decisions in *Gault*, *Kent*, and *In re Winship* (1970), the Supreme Court took notice that the rehabilitative ideal of the juvenile court and juvenile justice system might have been diminished, and it made clear that juveniles accused of offenses were entitled to most of the same procedural rights and safeguards granted to their adult counterparts. In response, juvenile proceedings became somewhat more formal and structured, although overall they remain less formal than adult proceedings.

Perhaps the next significant development in the administration and operation of the juvenile court and the juvenile justice system occurred in the late 1980s, when the majority of states revised their juvenile codes in response to increased public fear of juvenile crime (Grisso, 1996). Although the specific changes adopted by different jurisdictions varied, their net effect was to emphasize the punitive and incapacitating roles of the juvenile justice system and diminish the emphasis on rehabilitation (Bonnie & Grisso, 2000). Despite these changes, however, the juvenile justice system continues to devote more resources to rehabilitation than the adult criminal justice system, and intervention and treatment remain priorities in many juvenile justice systems.

CLINICAL ISSUES RELEVANT TO JUVENILE FORENSIC EVALUATION

Central to forensic assessments of juveniles charged with an offense are three substantive clinical issues: (1) psychosocial maturity and developmental status, (2) risk for future offending or violence, and (3) the nature and extent of the juvenile's antisocial behavior and character. We review each of these areas, then discuss the specific psycholegal questions to which they most frequently are applied.

Maturity and Development

Children and adolescents—by definition—are in a constant state of change. Their capacities and characteristics are evolving physically, cognitively, socially, and emotionally. This fluid developmental status is part of what sets them apart from adults (Borum, in press; Borum & Verhaagen, in press; McCord & Spatz-Widom, 2001; Rosado, 2000; Griffin & Torbet, 2002; Grisso, 1998a).

In criminal and juvenile justice matters, the law is often interested in a juvenile's degree of "sophistication" or "maturity" to inform decisions about culpability and disposition (see *Kent v. United States*, 1966). The issue of how those inferences should be made, however, has been much less clear. Too often, a youth's maturational status is imputed based on his or her age, physical development, or severity of the alleged offense. None of these factors, however, serves as a reliable proxy for true psychosocial capacities (Grisso, 1998; Steinberg & Schwartz, 2000).

It is true that most developmental psychology textbooks have some type of chart or matrix that shows the ostensible age at which certain characteristics typically emerge. The reality of human development, though, is that there is great variability in the age and rate at which different cognitive, social, or emotional capacities develop (Grisso, 1996; Steinberg & Cauffman, 1996, 1999). And charts that purport to display a "typical" or "average" progression may have even more limited applicability to youth who are in the justice system. Those normative estimates often are based on Caucasian middle-class children, whereas minority youth living in poverty are the ones most disproportionately represented in the justice system. Research has demonstrated that economic disadvantage may delay or inhibit certain developmental capacities, so the "average" trajectory of these youth may be expected to differ (Grisso, 1996, 1998a).

Physical development, while easy to gauge, is an unreliable marker of psychosocial maturity (Steinberg & Schwartz, 2000). Different capacities and characteristics in physical, cognitive, social, and emotional realms emerge and develop at different rates that are not necessarily related to one other. It is easy (and problematic) to assume that a young person who is physically well developed and looks older that his age (e.g., tall, mature features, facial hair) must have all the concomitant cognitive and social capacities that one would expect of an older person (Cauffman & Steinberg, 2000a, 2000b).

The severity of the index offense is similarly a poor marker of a youth's developmental status. Philosophies and slogans such as "adult time for adult crime" belie an assumption that a youth who commits a more serious offense (e.g., homicide) must have cognitive, social, and emotional capacities that are more adultlike, thereby warranting parity in culpability and punishment. In reality, the index offense is not a good predictor of recidivism, nor is it a reliable sign of one's level of maturity (Cauffman & Steinberg, 2000a, 2000b). Although past behavior is predictive of future behavior, incidence rates of violent behavior—even serious violence—in adolescence are so high as to almost be considered common. For example, approximately 40 percent of males and between 16 and 32 percent of females in three regional samples (Denver, Pittsburgh, and Rochester) reported engaging in at least one act of serious violence—such as aggravated assault, robbery, rape, and gang fights—*before age 16* (Tatem-Kelley, Huizinga, Thornberry, & Loeber, 1997). Yet most youth who engage in violence during adolescence do not continue offending into adulthood. In fact, about 80 percent commit no further acts of violence after age 21 (Elliott, 1994).

If a juvenile's age, physical development, and index offense do not reveal his or her level of maturity and developmental status, how should that status be assessed or measured? First, it is useful to define psychosocial maturity as it relates to legally relevant decision making in juveniles. Cauffman and Steinberg (2000a) have described it as "the complexity and sophistication of the process of individual decision-making as it is affected by a range of cognitive, emotional, and social factors" (p. 743). Specifically, they outline three developmental capacities that combine to shape that decision-making process. The first of these developmental capacities is responsibility. This is the ability to be self-reliant and unaffected by external pressure or influence in making decisions. The second is perspective. This capacity has two components; one is temporal (i.e., the ability to see and consider both short- and long-term implications of a decision) and the other is interpersonal (i.e., the ability to take another's perspective and understand a different point of view). The third developmental capacity is temperance. This is the ability to exercise self-restraint and to control one's impulses (Cauffman & Steinberg, 2000b; Steinberg & Schwartz, 2000).

The evaluator should assess directly those specific capacities relevant to psychosocial maturity, and not simply infer them from other characteristics or factors that actually may not be related. Considering and presenting forensic issues in developmental context will facilitate a more sophisticated juvenile forensic psychological examination (Grisso, 1998a).

Violence Risk

Whether juvenile offenders are processed in the adult or juvenile justice system, issues regarding the risk for future violence are present at almost every stage (Borum, 2000, in press; Borum & Verhaagen, in press; Grisso, 1998a). Initially, there is a decision about whether an arrestee can be released into the community pending a trial or hearing. At a sentencing or disposition hearing, the offender's violence risk often is a key factor in determining the level of security needed. And if a juvenile is sentenced or released to community supervision, the supervision plan must account for violence potential and how to prevent it.

Assessments of violence risk in children and adolescents differ from parallel assessments with adults. As noted, the key reason for this difference is that juveniles are in a significant and simultaneous state of transition in multiple spheres of development. Their patterns of behavior and personality generally are less stable across time and contexts (Borum, 2002, in press; Grisso, 1998). Nevertheless, some assessment is necessary in order to manage risk and prevent future violent behavior.

There are two distinguishable types of assessments for violence risk (Borum, 2000, in press; Borum & Reddy, 2001). The first is a general risk assessment, in which the question is whether, and the extent to which, this juvenile might engage in violent behavior toward anyone within a specified period of time. The second, sometimes referred to as a "threat assessment," is conducted when a youth has engaged in some behavior or communication that has brought him or her to official attention and caused someone be concerned or to raise the issue of potential risk (Borum, Fein, Vossekuil, & Berglund, 1999; Fein, Vossekuil, Pollack, Borum, Reddy, & Modzeleski, 2002; Fein & Vossekuil, 1998). In this circumstance, the question is whether, and the extent to which, this juvenile might be on a pathway toward (e.g., planning or preparing for) a violent attack directed at an identified or identifiable target (Fein et al., 2002). Each type of assessment requires a somewhat different approach; however, we focus here on the general risk assessment since it is more common to juvenile justice issues.[1]

The risk assessment should be tailored to its purpose, but most referral questions involve some implications for risk management or risk reduction (Borum, in press). Because the ultimate goal is to *prevent* violent behavior, assessment and management should be interactive and interdependent functions (Heilbrun, 1997). Lessons learned from decades of early research led to a clear conclusion that assessments of violence risk must go beyond an assessment of the individual–either as a source of information or as a focus of the evaluation.

Regarding sources of information that may prove of some value in conducting a risk assessment, although just having "more" is not necessarily better, certainly information that goes beyond the examinee's self-report is a good start (Borum, 2000; Borum & Verhaagen, in press). The examiner should consider the feasibility and usefulness of reviewing available records and interviewing collateral informants. A juvenile might have records from prior involvement with the justice system or previous evaluations. Interviewing family members might provide additional information or a new perspective on the juvenile's history and family or living environment. In some circumstances, this information may be limited, but the value is that an evaluator with multiple sources is often better able to gauge the quality and reliability of the information presented. Not all examinees will intentionally distort information, but being able to corroborate key facts and hypotheses across multiple sources is beneficial, and better data lead to more valid conclusions (Borum, Otto, & Golding, 1993).

Regarding the focus of the assessment, the field has moved from an exclusive focus on the individual as the subject of the assessment and toward a broader appraisal and weighing of situational factors (Borum, 1996, 2000). The nature and degree of "risk" being assessed is dynamic and highly dependent on context, situations, and circumstances (National Research Council, 1989). This means that a competent risk assessment of a juvenile must involve a careful review of social and contextual risk factors as well as individual and historical ones.

To facilitate a systematic, comprehensive evaluation, an assessment model—with accompanying instruments—has been developed and is referred to as *struc-*

---

[1] For a more detailed description of a Threat Assessment model and its applicability with juveniles, particularly in a school context, please see Borum, Fein, Vossekuil, & Berglund, 1999; Fein, Vossekuil, Pollack, Borum, Reddy, & Modzeleski, 2002; Fein & Vossekuil, 1998; Fein, Vossekuil, & Holden, 1995.

tured professional judgment (SPJ). In the SPJ model, an evaluator conducts a systematic assessment of predetermined risk factors that have strong, empirically established relationships with criterion violence. The evaluator considers the applicability of each risk factor to the case and classifies its severity, but the ultimate determination of risk level is not based on a particular cutting score derived from summing the items. The summary risk appraisal is based on the examiner's professional judgment, informed by a systematic appraisal of the relevant factors. In this way, the SPJ model draws on the strengths of both the clinical and actuarial (formula-driven) approaches to decision making, and attempts to minimize their respective drawbacks (Borum & Douglas, 2003).

The development of SPJ instruments for children and adolescents is a relatively new enterprise. Two instruments appear quite promising: the EARL (Early Assessment Risk List), for use with children under age 12, and the SAVRY (Structured Assessment of Violence Risk in Youth), for use with adolescents.

EARL[2]

The *EARL-20B* (Early Assessment Risk List for Boys) (Augimeri, Koegl, Webster, & Levene, 2001) is an SPJ tool designed to aid evaluators in making judgments about future violence and antisocial behavior among boys under the age of 12—particularly those who exhibit behavioral problems and are considered to be at high risk. Like most of the adult instruments, the protocol contains 20 risk items, each of which is assigned a score of 0, 1, or 2 depending on the certainty and severity of the characteristic's presence in a given case. The 20 items are divided into three categories, including six Family Items (e.g., Household Circumstances); twelve Child Items (e.g., Developmental Problems); and two Responsivity Items. In a preliminary research investigation with 378 boys and 69 girls in a court-based intervention program for young offenders, the EARL demonstrated good interrater reliability and validity, with "high" scorers being much more likely than "low" scorers to have a subsequent criminal conviction after age 12. The developers of this tool have created a parallel measure for assessing risk in young girls, called the *EARL-21G*. The domain names are the same, but a few of the risk factors are different than those included in the version for boys.

SAVRY[3]

The *SAVRY* (Structured Assessment of Violence Risk in Youth) (Bartel, Borum, & Forth, 2000; Borum, Bartel, & Forth, 2003) focuses specifically on violence risk in adolescents. The SAVRY protocol is composed of 24 Risk items that are

---

[2] Copies of the EARL-20B and EARL-21G can be ordered from Earlscourt Child and Family Centre, 46 St. Clair Gardens, Toronto, Ontario, Canada M6E 3V4. 416-654-8981. Email: mailus@earlscourt.on.ca. Web: www.earlscourt.on.ca.

[3] More information on the SAVRY can be found on the Web at http://www.fmhi.usf.edu/mhlp/savry/statement.htm Copies of the SAVRY can be ordered from Specialized Training Services, 9606 Tierra Grande, Suite 105, San Diego, CA 92126. Telephone: (800) 848-1226. Web: www.specializedtraining.com.

divided into three categories (Historical, Individual, and Social/Contextual), and six Protective items. The risk items each have a three-level coding structure (High, Moderate, and Low), and the protective items have a two-level structure (Present or Absent). Specific coding guidelines are provided for each level. Preliminary estimates of reliability and validity have been consistently encouraging, even across diverse and high-risk samples. Numerous studies in at least six different countries are currently in progress.

Antisocial Behavior and Character

Since at least 1990, there has been a surge of interest in understanding and assessing antisocial processes and personality traits in children and adolescents. In the late 1970s, Robert Hare began working on an assessment scale to measure the construct of psychopathy as conceived by Herve Cleckley (1976). Research on the instrument (ultimately known as the Hare Psychopathy Checklist or PCL) progressed quickly and infused new energy in the study of antisocial personality. By 1990, Hare and Adele Forth began to modify the items to explore whether they might be applicable to adolescents (Forth & Burke, 1998). The preliminary results were promising and spawned a generation of research on the developmental psychopathology of psychopathy and its measurement (Forth & Burke, 1998; Frick, 2002; Frick, Barry, & Boudin, 2000; Salekin, Rogers, & Manchin, 2001).

As conceptualized in adults, there are two distinctive dimensions that characterize the construct of psychopathy (Vincent & Hart, 2002). The first, Interpersonal/Affective, pertains to interpersonal transgressive disregard and deficiencies in emotional experience such as conning, manipulation, and lack of guilt and empathy. Frick (2002) has referred to these as "callous/unemotional" traits. The second, Social Deviance, pertains to antisocial lifestyle and behavioral patterns such as impulsivity and early behavioral problems. The construct is stable across time and has been linked consistently with risk for violence and general criminal behavior.

As this line in inquiry with juveniles has evolved, there have been serious concerns about the ascription of a psychopathic diagnosis or label to persons in an active state of developmental transition. These concerns typically involve one or more of three assertions: (1) personality disorders should only be diagnosed in adulthood; (2) psychopathy cannot be reliably assessed in childhood/adolescence because of developmental overlap; and (3) labeling a youth as a "psychopath" is ethically problematic because of the potential consequences of such a pejorative moniker (Edens, Skeem, Cruise, & Cauffman, 2001; Seagrave & Grisso, 2002).

Borum and Verhaagen (in press) propose four conceptual distinctions that help to frame the discussion and evaluation of these arguments. The first is whether the construct-related traits can even be measured in youth. A number of empirical studies using the modified version of the PCL and other newly developed instruments have attempted to measure these traits and processes in child and adolescent samples. Largely, these efforts have met with success. The items were assessed with consistency across examiners. The scales cohered psychometrically and their scores correlated significantly with related measures and constructs (Edens et al., 2001; Seagrave & Grisso, 2002). Overall, studies conducted to date suggest at least that features of psychopathy can be reliably assessed in children and adolescents (Frick, 2002; Salekin, Rogers, & Machin, 2001; Vincent & Hart, 2002).

The second distinguishable question is whether that cluster of traits can be used as a risk marker for violence risk. Much attention has been given to the Hare PCL-R in forensic assessments, in part because of its robust utility in predicting future violence. The instrument, however, was not developed as a measure of violence risk, but of the clinical construct of psychopathy. It just happens that the construct is strongly related to violence-related outcomes. Thus, if a cluster of traits are identifiable and can reliably be assessed in juveniles, that cluster may have certain correlates or serve as a reliable risk marker for certain outcomes, even if it does not represent the Cleckley construct of psychopathy. Indeed, most studies that have explored the correlates of psychopathic traits (or the instruments that purport to measure them) in youth have found that the identified grouping of traits is significantly related to risk for conduct problems and violent offending (Christian, Frick, Hill, & Tyler, 1997; Gretton, 1999; Frick, 1995; Frick, O'Brien, Wootten, & McBurnett, 1994; Lynam, 1998). In one of the earliest studies, Forth, Hart, and Hare (1990), for example, modified the PCL-R to apply to youth and found that scores correlated with a number of relevant variables, including number of postrelease violent offenses ($r = .26$) (Forth & Burke, 1998).

The third distinctive level is whether the identified cluster of traits actually measures the construct of psychopathy itself, as developed by Cleckley and refined by Hare. Contemporary conceptualizations of psychopathy suggest that it is a chronic syndrome with symptoms that typically begin to emerge in childhood. If that is true, then "true psychopaths," or those who will show many traits of psychopathy across the lifespan, should—at some level—be identifiable before adulthood. The challenge, however, is that some young people may demonstrate traits and behaviors consistent with psychopathy that are *not* stable and do *not* persist into adulthood. Perhaps, then, those characteristics do not represent early signs of nascent psychopathy (Edens et al., 2001; Seagrave & Grisso, 2002; Lynam, 2002). While recent research has measured psychopathy-related traits in young people, there has been far less evidence that those traits are stable and persist into adulthood or that those juveniles whose behaviors do persist are reliably distinguishable from those who do not. Not all "psychopathic traits" evidenced in childhood and adolescence are evidence of "fledgling psychopathy" (Lynam, 2002).

The fourth and final level pertains to the applicability of the label. That is, whether, or in what circumstances it is appropriate to apply the label *psychopath* to someone before adulthood. The empirical element of this discussion rests on the nature and quality of evidence for the construct validity of psychopathy, including, as noted earlier, its longitudinal stability. There is also a more practical element, however, that recognizes the pejorative nature of the term *psychopath* and the potential for that label to assume "master identity" status for a juvenile. The term and its derivatives carry connotations of extreme dangerousness and untreatability that could negatively and unfairly affect perceptions of, and decisions about, a young person (Edens et al., 2001; Seagrave & Grisso, 2002).

In light of these distinctions, what is the state of empirical evidence pertaining to arguments for and against the study and application of psychopathic traits with juveniles? Borum and Verhaagen (in press) have described the state of affairs as follows:

1. *Argument: Personality disorders should only be diagnosed in adulthood.* The *DSM-IVTR* offers a clinical guideline—although not an absolute rule—that personality disorders generally should not be diagnosed until an individual reaches age 18 (American Psychiatric Association, 2000). This does not imply, however, that associated traits and behavioral patterns do not emerge until adulthood, but rather, that there should be sufficient time to determine that the symptoms observed are lifelong, maladaptive, and consistent across contexts, and that they do result in functional impairment and/or significant distress. Accordingly, it is not unreasonable to investigate or research psychopathic traits in preadulthood to understand better the developmental course of the disorder (Frick, 2002; Lynam, 2002). Empirical studies conducted to date suggest that a cluster of traits, similar to those that characterize psychopathy in adults, can reliably be identified—at least cross-sectionally—in children and adolescents (Edens et al., 2001; Frick, 2002; Frick, Barry, & Boudin, 2000).

2. *Argument: Psychopathy cannot be reliably assessed in childhood/adolescence because of developmental overlap.* Some argue that psychopathy-related traits such as impulsivity, egocentrism, or parasitic lifestyle virtually define the developmentally normal course of adolescence. The concern is that there may be too much overlap between normal and psychopathic personality traits and patterns to make a meaningful distinction, particularly among teens (Edens et al., 2001; Seagrave & Grisso, 2002). There is some merit to these arguments, but the implication seems to be a need for using age-appropriate bases of comparison. Empirical studies suggest not only that the traits are assessable in juveniles, but that it is possible to distinguish between those who are relatively "high" or "low" with regard to a given characteristic and between those with a greater or lesser number of them overall (Frick, 2002).

3. *Argument: Labeling a youth as a "psychopath" is ethically problematic.* The rational arguments on this score are fairly compelling. The connotations of the label are uniformly negative, and, as noted, the label itself is so powerful that any information about a youth as an individual may be lost once this language is applied. From an empirical perspective, the central fact to consider is that the long-term stability of psychopathic traits in youth has not been definitively estab-

lished. Thus, applying the label to a child or adolescent might not only be stigmatizing, it may be also inaccurate (Seagrave & Grisso, 2002). Some youth who exhibit psychopathic traits are or are becoming "psychopaths"—but some, perhaps many, are not. Without greater confidence in understanding the developmental course of the disorder and evidence that that the construct of psychopathy itself (not just associated traits) can be identified before adulthood, extreme prudence and caution are warranted in any clinical description or application.

PSYCHOLEGAL QUESTIONS INVOLVING YOUTH IN THE JUVENILE JUSTICE SYSTEM

Psychologists and other mental health professionals can work with delinquent youth in two primary ways. Psychologists can assist judges and attorneys who are charged with making important decisions about minors involved in the juvenile justice systems by conducting specific forensic evaluations of the subjects of their proceedings and providing them with important information about the youth's emotional, behavioral, and cognitive functioning that they would not otherwise have. This should result in more informed and better decision making and dispositions. Additionally, psychologists can provide treatment and other interventions to juveniles and their families, the purpose of which is to bring about an overall improvement in the youth's emotional and behavioral adjustment and functioning as well as to decrease the youth's likelihood of reoffending. A review of effective treatments for delinquent youth is beyond the scope of this chapter (see Borum, 2003a; Frick, 2002; Hoge, 2001; Lipsey & Wilson, 1998; and Dowden & Andrews, 1999, for such reviews). In the remainder of this chapter, we discuss forensic evaluation of juveniles.

Transfer[4] Evaluations

Although, since its inception a little over 100 years ago, the juvenile court has served as the primary venue for adjudicating minors charged with offenses, not all such youth remain under its jurisdiction. All states allow for some youth to be tried in (adult) criminal court (Zimring, 2000). The transfer process is based on the presumption that, although the majority of youth accused of law breaking may show significant potential for rehabilitation, there is a subset of youth whose criminal behavior is not primarily attributable to developmental factors, who are

---

[4] Although we use the term *transfer* throughout this chapter to refer to the process that allows for transfer of a minor to adult court for adjudication, it is noted here that other terms may be used by jurisdictions (e.g., *waiver, bindover, declination, certification*) and different terms may refer to different procedures in various jurisdictions.

likely to continue offending in a dangerous manner, and who present a special threat to the community. Transfer of this subset of youth to the criminal courts, which allows for imposition of more punitive sanctions and greater incapacitation, is considered necessary. Although some commentators have questioned whether the transfer process brings about its intended effects, such as decreased recidivism (see, e.g., Bishop & Frazier, 2000), and others have raised concerns about whether it is applied consistently across jurisdictions (Dawson, 2000) or in racially or sexually discriminatory ways (see, e.g., Bortner, Zatz, & Hawkins, 2000; Dawson, 2000), some form of juvenile transfer provision remains in place in all jurisdictions.

Although the process and conditions of transfer vary between jurisdictions, Clausel and Bonnie (2002) identified three ways in which youth may come under the jurisdiction of the adult criminal justice system (see Dawson, 2002; U.S. General Accounting Office, 1995, for reviews of state laws). *Judicial waiver* provides the judge with discretion in determining which cases should be transferred to criminal court; *legislative exclusion* removes any discretion from the judge and requires that certain classes of juveniles be tried in adult court; and *prosecutorial election* confers on prosecutors the discretion to decide whether to file charges in criminal or juvenile court for a specific subset of juveniles. Transfers via legislative exclusion and prosecutorial election are typically conditioned upon factors such as the youth's age (e.g., 16 and above), the youth's history (e.g., a particular number of prior delinquency adjudications), and the nature of the alleged offense (e.g., violent offenses against persons). For example, in Florida, the state attorney *must* charge in criminal court any 16- or 17-year-old who is charged with possessing or discharging a firearm during the commission of drug trafficking or a variety of violent offenses against persons (Florida Statutes 985.227 [2] [d], 2002). In judicial waiver transfers, the judge is obligated to consider a variety of factors identified by the specific state statute in making a decision about whether to waive a juvenile to criminal court for adjudication. In many jurisdictions, the judge is directed to consider certain factors that are psychological in nature, including the youth's maturity, amenability to treatment, and risk of reoffending (see, e.g., Florida Statute 985.226 [3] [c], 2002). It is for this subset of discretionary transfer cases that psychologists may be called on to evaluate a youth so as to better inform the legal decision maker about these factors. In some cases, the psychologist may submit a report summarizing his or her findings or testify at a hearing where the transfer decision is made.

As noted, psychologists are typically required to address three factors in most discretionary transfer cases: the youth's risk for future violent and nonviolent offending, the youth's maturity, and the youth's amenability to treatment. As discussed, because the ultimate goal is to *prevent* violent behavior, assessment and management should be interactive and interdependent functions (Heilbrun, 1997). Assessment must go well beyond assessment of the youth alone, given what we know about the role of peers, the environment, and social context in violent and nonviolent delinquent offending (Borum, 1996, 2000; also see above).

Assessment of a youth's amenability to treatment requires the examiner to identify (1) the factors that may contribute to the examinee's involvement in the juvenile justice system, (2) effective treatments and interventions, and (3) any impediments to effective treatment (Grisso, 1998a, 2002). Necessary for such an assessment is an understanding of the youth and his or her particular adjustment and needs, the youth's environment and context, and effective interventions. Andrews and Bonta (2003) provide a helpful template for evaluations of adult and youthful offenders that emphasizes assessment of (1) the examinee's relative risk for reoffending, so that the necessary intensity of treatments and interventions can be identified (risk principle); (2) the offender's particular needs, so that the specific treatments/interventions can be proposed (need principle); and (3) the learning style of the examinee, so that treatments/interventions can be offered in a way that the examinee can best understand and incorporate (responsivity principle) (see also Hoge, 2002).

Not all treatments are equally effective. In the past few years, a number of interventions have been developed that bring about clear reductions in delinquent behaviors (see Borum, 2003a; Frick, 2002; Hoge, 2001; Lipsey & Wilson, 1998; Dowden & Andrews, 1999, for a review and summary of some successful approaches), whereas some more traditional interventions such as "building self-esteem" have not performed so well. Evaluators must be knowledgeable about effective interventions and their availability in the community and recommend them when appropriate.

Finally, as discussed in detail, the evaluator must keep in mind how the adolescent's ongoing development may affect the assessment process, remembering that assessing a juvenile is akin to "hitting a moving target." The evaluator is assessing the juvenile as he or she is maturing emotionally, cognitively, and physically. Although a general progressive trend may be expected, capacities may wax and wane over time, and not all abilities or capacities may mature or develop uniformly (see above).

Competence Evaluations

Competence to Confess/Waive the Right against Self-Incrimination

In one of its best-known decisions, the U.S. Supreme Court, in *Miranda v. Arizona* (1967), ruled that the Sixth Amendment of the Constitution required that any confessions made by defendants and used against them in criminal proceedings must be preceded by warnings informing them of their constitutional rights. In *Fare v. Michael C.* (1979) the Supreme Court went on to hold that waiver of these rights must be done "voluntarily, knowingly and intelligently." In *Colorado v. Connolly* (1986), the Supreme Court decided that confessions will likely be considered voluntary as long as they are not the product of police coercion, as opposed to coercion from non-law enforcement actors.

Juveniles' ability to understand and meaningfully exercise their right against self-incrimination has received increasing attention for the past 25 years, beginning with publication of results of an NIMH-funded study examining these capacities in youth (Grisso, 1981). As in all forensic evaluations, examinations of the youth's ability to voluntarily, knowingly, and intelligently waive the right against self-incrimination and to confess require assessment of the juvenile's functional psycholegal abilities as they may have been affected by behavioral, emotional, cognitive, or situational factors. Unlike many forensic evaluations, however, competence to confess/waive Miranda rights evaluations are retrospective insofar as the focus of the evaluation is the youth's mental state at a point in time in the past—when the arrest and interrogation occurred. As such, the evaluator is required, as best he or she can, to reconstruct the youth's ability to understand, comprehend, and exercise his or her Sixth Amendment rights at the time they were ostensibly waived.

In these evaluations, the examiner must identify both developmental factors that might have affected the relevant psycholegal abilities at the time of the arrest and interrogation (e.g., cognitive, emotional, or behavioral problems or limitations) as well as situational factors that may have had an impact (e.g., time, nature, and condition of the interrogation; the presence or absence of parents; intoxication). A review of these factors reveals that although some factors affecting a youth's ability to understand and exercise his or her Sixth Amendment rights are more static and enduring in nature (e.g., intelligence), others are more dynamic and less stable over time (e.g., intoxication).

According to the Supreme Court, in considering the validity of a confession and the competence of a waiver of one's right to avoid self-incrimination, the courts are obligated to consider the "totality of the circumstances" (*People v. Lara*, 1967; *Fare v. Michael C.*, 1979). Indeed, courts typically consider a variety of factors, including those that are person centered (e.g., the youth's age, IQ, level of education, literacy, emotional and behavioral adjustment, level of intoxication, prior contact with law enforcement officers) as well as environmental/situational (e.g., when and where the interrogation took place, who was present during the interrogation, how the Miranda rights were presented to the detainee) (Oberlander, Goldstein, & Goldstein, 2002; Frumkin, 2000; Oberlander & Goldstein, 2001). Thus, although third-party information is critical in all forensic evaluations (Committee on Specialty Guidelines for Forensic Psychologists, 1991) accessing collateral information is particularly important in competence-to-confess evaluations given their retrospective nature and the variety of factors that must be considered. Examining police reports and documentation of the interrogation process; reviewing medical, academic, and mental health records; and interviewing the arresting and interrogating police officers and other third parties who are familiar either with the youth or the circumstance of the interrogation (e.g., parents) may provide critical information. Also important is a comprehensive assessment of the youth's emotional, cognitive, and behavioral functioning, based on review of relevant records, psychological testing, and interviews. Finally, the examiner should assess the youth's ability to understand and exercise the *Miranda* warnings via structured testing (Grisso, 1998b; Gudjonsson, 1984) and conduct an interview to gain an understanding of his or her experience of the arrest and interrogation process.

The examiner should always keep in mind that the youth's abilities and capacities at the time of the evaluation are not what is of interest to the court and may not be indicative of his or her abilities at the time of his or her arrest and interrogation. Thus, it is incumbent upon the examiner to make clear that any opinions offered about the youth's psycholegal abilities at the time of the arrest are inferred from his current capacities and accounts, as well as any relevant and available third-party information.

Competence to Proceed[5] with the Legal Process

The premise that persons accused of offenses must be competent to participate in legal proceedings against them can be traced to at least 17th century Common Law, and is well rooted in American law (Melton, Petrila, Poythress, & Slobogin, 1997; Stafford, 2002). In *Dusky v. United States* (1960), the Supreme Court ruled that the Constitution requires a defendant to have "sufficient present ability to consult with his attorney with a reasonable degree of rational understanding and a rational as well as factual understanding of proceedings against him" (p. 789; also see Chapter 9 in this volume for a review of criminal competence more generally).

The Supreme Court, however, has never addressed what capacities are required of juveniles participating in delinquency proceedings, and how factors such as mental disorder, mental retardation, and cognitive "limitations"[6] associated with normal development as they affect a youth's capacity are to be considered. Such issues, of course, are less pressing when the juvenile justice system is considered to be rehabilitative, non-adversarial, and a system that acts in the best interests of the child. The issue of juvenile competency, however, has received more attention in the past decade, likely in response to perceptions that the juvenile justice system has diminished its emphasis on rehabilitation and become more punitive.

Approximately half the states specifically address the issue of competence to proceed in juvenile court, and most states appear simply to have adopted *Dusky*-like criteria that are employed in adult proceedings (Grisso, 1998a, 2002). Contrary to what one might predict based on a review of the Supreme Court's decisions in *Gault*, *Kent*, and *Winship* (see above), at least one court has deter-

---

[5] We use the term *competence to proceed*, rather than *competence to stand trial*, since (a) the former is more inclusive and reflects the law's requirement that accused persons be competent throughout their involvement in the justice process, and (b) the large majority of accused adults and juveniles do not ever proceed to a trial or hearing; rather, some kind of plea or alternative adjudication is reached.

[6] We place "limitations" in quotations since they are not truly limitations, but simply reflect normal development.

mined that juveniles need not be competent to participate in juvenile proceedings since those proceedings are not punitive in nature (*G.J.I. v. State of Oklahoma*, 1989).

Principles for assessing juveniles' competence-related abilities have largely been drawn from the adult competence literature (see Chapter 9 in this volume for a review of criminal competence more generally). As in all forensic evaluations, the focus of the competence evaluation is the juvenile's functional psycholegal abilities as they may be affected by current mental, behavioral, and emotional functioning. Some of the more important functional abilities include both a factual and rational understanding of the charges, the allegations, possible sanctions, the adversarial nature of the legal process, and the roles of those involved in the process (e.g., judge, defense attorney, prosecutor, witnesses). Also crucial is assessment of the juvenile's ability to work with his or her attorney, both with respect to providing information of relevance (e.g., information regarding the juvenile's behavior and whereabouts at and around the time of the alleged offense, information designed to assist the attorney in challenging prosecution allegations and witnesses) and consider various legal strategies and options.

Important to remember is that the test of competence is one of capacity, as distinguished from knowledge or willingness. Thus, juveniles who simply are ignorant about the legal system and its operation, the charges and allegations, or possible sanctions are not incompetent to proceed providing they have the ability to incorporate and utilize such information in their decision-making process once it is presented to them. Similarly, a juvenile who is capable of working with his attorney or otherwise participating in the legal process but chooses not to do so for reasons other than those that might be attributed to mental disorder, mental retardation, or developmental "limitations" has the *capacity* to participate. Also important to note is that the capacity required to be competent to proceed is not absolute, as indicated by the Supreme Court's references to "*sufficient* present ability" and "*reasonable* degree of rational understanding" in *Dusky* (1960).

Although research indicates that older teenagers' factual understanding of the legal system and its operation is not much different from that of adults, research examining adolescents' decision-making processes and values suggests greater differences in these areas (Grisso, 2000; Bonnie & Grisso, 2000; Cauffman & Steinberg, 2000a; Cauffman & Steinberg 2000b). Thus, of particular importance when evaluating juveniles' competence to proceed is assessing their rational understanding and decision making in addition to their factual understanding. Not only should the examiner assess a youth's knowledge of the legal system and his or her case, but also how his or her emotional functioning and development affects his or her reasoning about the case. For example, although a youth may "know" that he faces a minimum of 30 years in prison for a charge of felony murder, what can be said about how he might decide whether to accept a plea agreement for 20 years (with a minimum of 17 in prison) and assess his chances of acquittal? Are his abilities and decision-making processes the same as those of a 32-year-old male who is charged with the same offense and who is presented with the same options? And if their decision-making processes and abilities are different, does this raise questions about the 16-year-old's capacity and competence to proceed?

As discussed earlier, evaluation of juveniles is complicated by their less than complete and ongoing cognitive, emotional, and physical development. Thus, when the examiner identifies specific deficits in a juvenile's competence-related abilities, the next task is to identify whether the deficit results from mental disorder, mental retardation, "limitations" associated with normal development, or a combination of these factors. Identifying the root cause(s) of competence-related abilities, of course, is crucial for determining the likelihood of "restoration" to competence and the type of intervention necessary (see Chapter 9; Grisso, 1998a; and Stafford, 2002, for a review of restoration issues).

Although a number of forensic assessment instruments have been developed for assessing trial competence–related abilities of adults, no such instruments have been developed for or normed on juveniles (see Grisso, 2002, and Stafford, 2002, for reviews of the instruments used with adults). Thus, examinations of juveniles' competence to proceed are necessarily clinical ones that are ideally tied to, or anchored in, the relevant state law.

Mental State at the Time of the Alleged Offense/Sanity Evaluations

The insanity defense is one of the most controversial aspects of criminal law and allows a select subset of persons to avoid criminal responsibility for what would otherwise be criminal actions upon a determination that their mental state affected their decision-making abilities or actions in some legally relevant and important way. Exculpation is based on the presumption that criminal adjudication and the sanctions that follow should only be applied to those persons who are in control and aware of their behavior. Almost all states employ some version of the insanity defense, the use of which can be traced to ancient times, and a number of different tests of insanity have been proposed (see Rogers & Shuman, 2000, and Chapter 31 for a more detailed review of the law of insanity and the evaluation process). Not all states provide for an insanity defense in juvenile proceedings (or adult proceedings, for that matter), and it is not clear that provision of such a defense for adults is required by the Constitution (Stephen Morse, personal communication, March 5, 2003).

Little has been written about the insanity defense as it applies to youth, presumably because the role of, or need for, the insanity defense with juveniles has never been apparent, at least since the inception of the juvenile court. As noted earlier, prior to establishing the juvenile court, youth ages 14 and older who were accused of criminal acts were entitled to the same privileges and sanctions as adults via the criminal justice system, presumably including the insanity defense (Tanenhaus, 2000). Children between the ages of 7 and 14 were presumed incapable of forming criminal intent, but this was a rebuttable presumption, and children below the age of 7 were simply considered to lack capacity to form the requisite criminal intent. Since the juvenile court is grounded in the presumption that minors do not possess the same capacities as adults and that dispositions are intended for rehabilitation, use of the insanity defense might be considered superfluous. Just as the juvenile justice system, at least historically and in theory, is designed to rehabilitate rather than punish, so too does the insanity defense allow for treatment, rather than punishment, of the individual. Thus, to provide a defense that precludes punishment and provides for treatment in a system already designed to treat rather than punish might be considered unnecessary. With movement toward a more sanction-oriented juvenile justice system, however, it could be argued that there is a place for the insanity defense in juvenile proceedings.

Assessment of a juvenile's mental state at the time of the offense will be similar in structure and format to evaluations of adults in the criminal justice system (see Chapter 8; Rogers & Shuman, 2000; Borum, 2003b, and Goldstein, Morse, & Shapiro, 2002, for further discussion of the general evaluation process). In conducting such evaluations of juveniles, however, the forensic psychologist must consider how the minor's delinquent actions might be related to, or explained by, adolescent development or psychopathology. Although a number of measures has been designed to assist in structuring mental state at the time of the alleged offense/sanity evaluations, none has been developed specifically for use with juveniles, nor have any such assessment techniques proven particularly valuable (see Borum, 2003b; Goldstein, Morse, & Shapiro, 2002; Melton, Petrila, Poythress, & Slobogin, 1997; Rogers & Shuman, 2000, for reviews). Thus, examinations of juveniles in this context are necessarily clinical ones that are ideally tied to, or anchored in, the relevant state law.

Dispositional Evaluations

Dispositional assessments are the evaluations most frequently performed by psychologists who assess youth in the juvenile justice system. This should not be surprising, since these evaluations are rehabilitation focused and identify any emotional, behavioral, environmental, or substance abuse problems that are related to the youth's offending, as well as appropriate interventions that will ultimately improve the youth's adjustment and decrease the likelihood of future involvement with the juvenile justice system. Indeed, it was for this very purpose that the juvenile court and juvenile justice system was established. Essentially any factor that may be related to the youth's involvement with the juvenile justice system is to be considered by the examiner, with interventions recommended as appropriate and necessary. Because dispositional assessments may look very different depending on the particular juvenile and his or her needs, no clear prescription for conducting such evaluations can be offered. However, all of the factors that are assessed in waiver evaluations (discussed earlier) may be relevant in disposition cases.

Conclusion

For a little over 100 years, the juvenile court has been in place to account for the special needs and concerns of youth who are involved with the legal system. Although their focus and purpose has changed over time and with varying political agendas, the juvenile court and the juvenile justice system continue to emphasize interventions designed to rehabilitate youth. Forensic psychologists have made, and continue to make, important contributions by giving legal decision makers a better understanding of youth involved in the juvenile justice system and their treatment needs and also by developing interventions designed to meet their needs and reduce the liklihood of future contact with the juvenile justice system.

References

American Psychiatric Association. (2000). *Diagnostic and statistical manual of mental disorders (4th ed.), Text revision*. Washington, DC: Author.

Andrews, D. A., & Bonta, J. (2003). *The psychology of criminal conduct* (3rd ed.). Cincinnati, OH: Anderson.

Augimeri, L., Webster, C., Koegl, C., & Levene, K. (1998). *Early Assessment Risk List for Boys: EARL-20B, Version 1-Consultation Edition*. Toronto: Earlscourt Child and Family Centre.

Bartel, P., Borum, R., & Forth, A. (2000). *Structured Assessment for Violence Risk in Youth (SAVRY)*. Tampa, FL: Louis de la Parte Florida Mental Health Institute, University of South Florida.

Bartel, P., Forth, A., & Borum, R. (2003). Development and validation of the Structured Assessment for Violence Risk in Youth (SAVRY). Manuscript under review.

Bishop, D., & Frazier, C. (2000). Consequences of transfer. In J. Fagan & F. E. Zimring (Eds.), *The changing borders of juvenile justice: Transfer of adolescents to the criminal court* (pp. 227–276). Chicago: University of Chicago Press.

Bonnie, R., & Grisso, T. (2000). Adjudicative competence and youthful offenders. In T. Grisso & R. G. Schwartz (Eds.), *Youth on trial: A developmental perspective on juvenile justice* (pp. 73–103). Chicago: University of Chicago Press.

Bortner, M. A., Zatz, M. S., & Hawkins, D. F. (2000). The impact of jurisdiction shifts. In J. Fagan & F. E. Zimring (Eds.), *The changing borders of juvenile justice: Transfer of adolescents to the criminal court* (pp. 277–320). Chicago: University of Chicago Press.

Borum, R. (1996). Improving the clinical practice of violence risk assessment: Technology, guidelines and training. *American Psychologist, 51*, 945–956.

Borum, R. (2000). Assessing violence risk among youth. *Journal of Clinical Psychology, 56*, 1263–1288.

Borum, R. (March, 2002). Why is assessing violence risk in juveniles different than in adults? Paper presented at the biennial conference of the American Psychology-Law Society, Austin, TX.

Borum, R. (2003a). Managing at risk juvenile offenders in the community: Putting evidence based principles into practice. *Journal of Contemporary Criminal Justice, 19,* 114–137.

Borum, R. (2003b). Not guilty by reason of insanity. In T. Grisso (Ed.), *Evaluating competencies: Forensic assessments and instruments* (pp. 193–227). New York: Kluwer/Plenum.

Borum, R. (in press). Assessing risk for violence among juvenile offenders. In S. Sparta & G. Koocher (Eds.), *The forensic assessment of children and adolescents: Issues and applications.* New York: Oxford University Press.

Borum, R., Bartel, P., & Forth, A. (2003). *Manual for the Structured Assessment for Violence Risk in Youth (SAVRY): Version 1.1.* Tampa, FL: Louis de la Parte Florida Mental Health Institute, University of South Florida.

Borum, R., & Douglas, K. (March, 2003). New directions in violence risk assessment. *Psychiatric Times, 20* (3), 102–103.

Borum, R., Fein, R., Vossekuil, B., & Berglund, J. (1999). Threat assessment: Defining an approach for evaluating risk of targeted violence. *Behavioral Sciences & the Law, 17,* 323–337. Available online at http://www.treas.gov/usss/ntac.

Borum, R., Otto, R., & Golding, S. (1993). Improving clinical judgment and decision making in forensic evaluation. *Journal of Psychiatry and Law, 21,* 35–76.

Borum, R., & Reddy, M. (2001). Assessing violence risk in Tarasoff situations: A fact-based model of inquiry. *Behavioral Sciences & the Law, 19,* 375–385.

Cauffman, E., & Steinberg, L. (1996).The cognitive and affective influences on adolescent decision-making. *Temple Law Review, 68,* 1763–1789.

Cauffman, E., & Steinberg, L. (2000a). (Im)maturity of judgment in adolescence: Why adolescents may be less culpable than adults. *Behavioral Sciences and the Law, 18,* 1–21.

Cauffman, E., & Steinberg, L. (2000b). Researching adolescents' judgment and culpability. In T. Grisso & R. G. Schwartz (Eds.), *Youth on trial: A developmental perspective on justice* (pp. 325–343). Chicago: University of Chicago Press.

Christian, R. E., Frick, P. J., Hill, N. L., Tyler, L., & Frazer, D. R. (1997). Psychopathy and conduct problems in children: II. Implications for subtyping children with conduct problems. *Journal of the American Academy of Child and Adolescent Psychiatry, 36,* 233–241.

Clausel, L. E. F., & Bonnie, R. J. (2000). Juvenile justice on appeal. In J. Fagan & F. E. Zimring (Eds.), *The changing borders of juvenile justice: Transfer of adolescents to the criminal court* (pp. 181–206). Chicago: University of Chicago Press.

Cleckley, H. (1976). *The mask of sanity* (5th ed.). St. Louis: Mosby.

Colorado v, Connolly, 479 U.S. 157 (1986).

Committee on Specilty Guidelines for Psychologists. (1991). Speciality guidelines for forensic psychologists. *Law and Human Behavior, 15,* 655–665.

Dawson, R. O. (2000). Judicial waiver in theory and practice. In J. Fagan & F. E. Zimring (Eds.), *The changing borders of juvenile justice: Transfer of adolescents to the criminal court* (pp. 45–82). Chicago: University of Chicago Press.

Dowden, C., & Andrews, D. (1999). What works in young offender treatment: A meta-analysis. *FORUM on Corrections Research, 11* (2), 21–24.

Dusky v. US, 362 U.S. 402 (1960).

Edens, J., Skeem, J., Cruise, K., & Cauffman, E. (2001). Assessment of "juvenile psychopathy" and its association with violence: A critical review. *Behavioral Sciences and the Law, 19,* 53–80.

Elliott, D. (1994). Serious violent offenders: Onset, developmental course, and termination. American Society of Criminology 1993 presidential address. *Criminology, 32,* 1–21.

Fare v. Michael C., 442 U.S. 707 (1979).

Fein, R., Vossekuil, B., & Holden, G. (1995). Threat assessment: An approach to prevent targeted violence. *National Institute Justice: Research in Action;* September: 1–7.

Fein, R., Vossekuil, B., Pollack, W., Borum, R., Modzeleski, W., & Reddy, M. (2002). *Threat assessment in schools: A guide to managing threatening situtations and creating safe schools climates.* Washington, DC: US Department of Education, Office of Elementary and Secondary Education, Safe and Drug-Free Schools Program and US Secret Service, National Threat Assessment Center.

Forth, A., & Burke, H. (1998). Psychopathy in adolescence: Assessment, violence and developmental precursors. In D. Cooke, A. Forth, & R. Hare (Eds.) *Psychopathy: Theory, research and implications for society* (pp. 205–229). New York: Kluwer Academic Publishers.

Forth, A., Hart, S., & Hare, R. (1990). Assessment of psychopathy in male young offenders. *Psychological Assessment: A Journal of Consulting and Clinical Psychology, 2,* 342–344.

Frick, P. (1995). Callous-unemotional traits and conduct problems: A two-factor model of psychopathy in children. *Issues in Criminological & Legal Psychology, 24,* 47–51.

Frick, P. (2002). Juvenile psychopathy from a developmental perspective: Implications for construct development and use in forensic assessment. *Law and Human Behavior, 26,* 247–253.

Frick, P., Barry, C., & Bodin, S. (2000). Applying the concept of psychopathy to children: Implications for the assessment of antisocial youth. In C. Gacono (Ed.), *The clinical and forensic assessment of psychopathy* (pp. 3–24). Mahwah, NJ: Lawrence Erlbaum.

Frick, P. J., O'Brien, B. S., Wooton, J. M., & McBurnett, K. (1994). Psychopathy and conduct problems in children. *Journal of Abnormal Psychology, 103,* 700–707.

Frumkin, B. (2000). Competence to waive Miranda rights: Clinical and legal issues. *Mental and Physical Disability Law Reporter, 24,* 326–331.

G.J.I. v. State of Oklahoma, 778 P.2d 485 (Okla. Crim. 1989).

Goldstein, A., Morse, S., & Shapiro, D. (2002). Evaluations of criminal responsibility. In A. Goldstein (Ed.), *Forensic psychology* (pp. 381–406). New York: John Wiley.

Gretton, H. (1999). Psychopathy and recidivism in adolescence: A ten-year retrospective follow-up. *Dissertation Abstracts International: Section B: the Sciences & Engineering, 59* (12-B), 6488.

Griffin, P., & Torbet, P. (2002). *Desktop guide to good juvenile probation practice.* National Center for Juvenile Justice, Pittsburgh, PA [producer]. Washington, DC: Office of Juvenile Justice and Delinquency Prevention.

Grisso, T. (1981). *Juveniles waiver of rights: Legal and psychological competence.* New York: Plenum Press.

Grisso, T. (1996). Society's retributive response to juvenile violence: A developmental perspective. *Law and Human Behavior, 20,* 229–247.

Grisso, T. (1998a). *Forensic evaluation of juveniles.* Sarasota, FL: Professional Resource Press.

Grisso, T. (1998b). *Assessing understanding and appreciation of Miranda rights: Manual and materials*. Sarasota, FL: Professional Resource Press.

Grisso, T. (2000). What we know about youths' capacities as trial defendants. In T. Grisso & R. G. Schwartz (Eds.), *Youth on trial: A developmental perspective on juvenile justice* (pp. 139–171). Chicago: University of Chicago Press.

Grisso, T. (2002). Forensic evaluations in delinquency cases. In A. Goldstein (Ed.), *Forensic psychology, Handbook of psychology* (pp. 315–344). New York: John Wiley.

Gudjonsson, G. (1984). A new scale of interrogative suggestibility. *Personality and Individual Differences, 5*, 303–314.

Hart, S., Watt, K., & Vincent, G. (2002). Commentary on Seagrave and Grisso: Impressions of the state of the art. *Law and Human Behavior, 26*, 241–245.

Heilbrun, K. (1997). Prediction vs. management models relevant to risk assessment: The importance of legal decision-making context. *Law and Human Behavior, 21*, 347–359.

Hoge, R. (2001). *The juvenile offender: Theory, research, and applications*. Norwell, MA: Kluwer/Plenum.

Hoge, R. (2002). Standardized instruments for assessing risk and need in youthful offenders. *Criminal Justice and Behavior, 29*, 380–396.

In re Gault, 387 U.S. 1 (1967).

In re Winship, 397 U.S. 358 (1970).

Kent v. United States, 383 U.S. 541 (1966).

Lipsey, M., & Wilson, D. (1998). Effective intervention for serious juvenile offenders: A synthesis of research. In R. Loeber & D. P. Farrington (Eds.), *Serious and violent juvenile offenders: Risk factors and successful interventions* (pp. 313–345). Thousand Oaks, CA: Sage.

Lynam, D. (2002). Fledgling psychopathy: A view from personality theory. *Law and Human Behavior, 26*, 255–259.

McCord, J., Widom, C. S., & Crowell, N. A. (Eds.) (2001). *Juvenile crime, juvenile justice*. Washington, DC: National Academy Press.

Melton, G. B., Petrila, J., Poythress, N., & Slobogin, C. (1997). *Psychological evaluations for the courts: A handbook for mental health professionals and lawyers*. New York: Guilford Press.

Miranda v. Arizona, 384 U.S. 436 (1966).

Mnookin, R. (1978). *Child, family, and state: Problems and materials on children and the law*. Boston, MA: Little, Brown.

National Research Council. (1989). *Improving risk communication*. Washington, DC: National Academy Press.

Oberlander, L., & Goldstein, N. (2001). A review and update on the practice of evaluating Miranda comprehension. *Behavioral Sciences and the Law, 19*, 453–471.

Oberlander, L., Goldstein, A., & Goldstein, N. (2002). Competence to confess. In A. Goldstein (Ed.), *Forensic psychology* (pp. 335–357). New York: John Wiley.

Otto, R. K., & Heilbrun, K. (2002). The future of forensic psychology: A look toward the future in light of the past. *American Psychologist, 57*, 5–18.

People v. Lara, 432 P.2d 202 (1967).

Rogers, R., & Shuman, D. (2000). *Conducting insanity evaluations* (2nd ed.). New York: Guilford Press.

Rosado, L. (Ed.) (2000). *Kids are different: How knowledge of adolescent development theory can aid decision-making in court*. Washington, DC: American Bar Association Juvenile Justice Center.

Salekin, R., Rogers, R., & Machin, D. (2001). Psychopathy in youth: Pursuing diagnostic clarity. *Journal of Youth and Adolescence, 30*, 173–194.

Seagrave, D., & Grisso, T. (2002). Adolescent development and the measurement of adolescent psychopathy. *Law and Human Behavior, 26*, 219–239.

Stafford, K. P. (2002). Assessment of competence to stand trial. In A. Goldstein (Ed.), *Forensic psychology* (pp. 359–380). New York: John Wiley.

Steinberg, L., & Cauffman, E. (1996). Maturity of judgment in adolescence: Psychosocial factors in adolescent decisionmaking. *Law and Human Behavior, 20*, 249–272.

Steinberg, L., & Cauffman, E. (1999, December). A developmental perspective on serious juvenile crime: When should juveniles be treated as adults? *Federal Probation*, 52–57.

Steinberg, L., & Schwartz, R. (2000). Developmental psychology goes to court. In T. Grisso and R. Schwartz (Eds.), *Youth on trial: A developmental perspective on juvenile justice* (pp. 9–31). Chicago: University of Chicago Press.

Tanenhaus, D. S. (2000). The evolution of transfer out of the juvenile court. In J. Fagan & F. E. Zimring (Eds.), *The changing borders of juvenile justice: Transfer of adolescents to the criminal court* (pp. 13–43). Chicago: University of Chicago Press.

Tatem-Kelley, B., Huizinga, D., Thornberry, T. P., & Loeber, R. (1997). *Epidemiology of serious violence.* Bulletin. Washington, DC: U.S. Department of Justice, Office of Justice Programs, Office of Juvenile Justice and Delinquency Prevention.

U.S. Department of Health and Human Services. (2001). *Youth violence: A report of the Surgeon General*. Rockville, MD: U.S. Department of Health and Human Services, Substance Abuse and Mental Health Services Administration, Center for Mental Health Services, National Institutes of Health, National Institute of Mental Health. Available online at http://www.surgeongeneral.gov/library/youthviolence

U.S. General Accounting Office. (1995). *Juveniles processed in criminal court and case dispositions*. Washington, DC: Author.

Vincent, G., & Hart, S. (2002). Psychopathy in childhood and adolescence: Implications for the assessment and management of multi-problem youths. In R. Corrado, R. Roesch, S. Hart, & J. Gierowski (Eds.), *Multi-problem violent youth: A foundation for comparative research on needs, interventions, and outcomes* (pp. 150–163). Amsterdam: IOS Press.

Zimring, F. E. (2000). The punitive necessity of waiver. In J. Fagan & F. E. Zimring (Eds.), *The changing borders of juvenile justice: Transfer of adolescents to the criminal court* (pp. 207–226). Chicago: University of Chicago Press.

CHAPTER 36

THE ROAD TO PERDITION: EXTREME INFLUENCE TACTICS IN THE INTERROGATION ROOM

DEBORAH DAVIS AND WILLIAM T. O'DONOHUE
UNIVERSITY OF NEVADA, RENO

> *That we have power . . . to give or withhold our assent at will is so evident that it must be counted among the first and most common notions that are innate in us.*
>
> Descartes (1644/1984, p. 205)

> *The strongest knowledge—that of the total unfreedom of the human will—is nonetheless the poorest in successes, for it always has the strongest opponent; human vanity.*
>
> Nietzsche (1886/1996)

The months of late 2002 and early 2003 were filled with newspaper, television, and magazine accounts of the case of the New York Jogger. The case had been closed nearly 13 years earlier when five Harlem teenagers confessed to the brutal bludgeoning, rape, and sodomization of a 28-year-old investment banker who was attacked while jogging in New York's Central Park. The teenagers entered Central Park on the night of April 19, 1989 looking for trouble. During their "wilding" in the park, the boys had attacked and roughed up other visitors, and police reasonably viewed them as likely suspects for the jogger attack, which occurred during the time the boys were engaged in their own separate rampage. The boys were held in custody for 14 to 30 hours and faced lengthy rounds of questioning before finally confessing in lurid and convincing detail to the crime.

Yet this seemingly successful resolution of the case was blown wide apart by the recent DNA identification of Matias Reyes, a convicted serial rapist and murderer, as the real perpetrator. Reyes confessed to the crime, insisted he had acted alone, and denied any involvement of the five teenagers who had confessed 13 years ago. No evidence—other than their shockingly detailed confessions—ever connected the five teenagers to the crime. Reyes's identification as the real attacker provoked extensive commentary by the media, attorneys, police, and psychologists on the issue of what could have provoked such a clearly false confession from not just one, but five separate criminal suspects.

In hindsight, the confessions appear hopelessly confused, inconsistent, and inaccurate (Dwyer, 2003; Ingrassia, 2002; Kassin, 2002; Dwyer & Saulny, 2002a, 2002b). Yet at the time the extensive and vivid detail with which the boys told their story was convincing to police, prosecutors, and, most important, to the juries that tried them. The confessions were compelling even though the boys retracted their confessions when freed from the pressures of interrogation and continued to maintain their innocence to the day they were vindicated by Reyes's own confession—and the DNA tests that validated it (Dwyer & Saulny, 2002, October 16).

It may seem at first glance that the New York jogger case is a highly unusual instance, perhaps explained by unique characteristics of the boys who confessed. Surely, no normal innocent person—or *group* of persons—could be made to confess to such a horrific crime! Nonetheless, it is clear that false confessions can and do occur at an alarming rate. The Innocence Project (www.innocenceproject.org), for example, maintains a webpage listing cases of *proven* false confessions which includes over 60 cases. Further, as documented on their website, of the first 70 innocent prisoners freed by the Innocence Project staff, 21.4 percent were imprisoned at least in part as a result of false confession. Other studies have similarly shown that false confession is among the most common causes of wrongful conviction (e.g., Bedau & Radelet, 1987; Borchard, 1932; Brandon & Davies, 1973; Frank & Frank, 1957; Huff, Rattner, & Sagarin, 1986; Radin, 1964; Rattner, 1988).

Since innocence can only be proven either if the true culprit is found and confesses or is proven guilty, or if it is later proven through additional evidence that the innocent person could not possibly be guilty, the vast majority of confessions deemed probably false and coerced cannot be firmly proven to be so. Moreover, since police routinely consider the case solved once they have obtained a confession, further investigation that might otherwise uncover proof of innocence is rare. Hence, known proven cases of false confessions can be taken as only the tip of the iceberg.[1]

---

[1] Unfortunately, precise estimates of the incidence of false confessions in our society are not available (Leo & Ofshe, 1998). Neither the absolute number of false confessions nor the proportion of all confessions that are false can be established absent certain knowledge of guilt in all cases.

As we will shortly explore, neither mysterious circumstances, nor abnormal targets, nor extraordinary influence tactics are necessary to elicit a false confession. Instead, the manner in which common interrogation procedures elicit false confessions can be understood in terms of everyday tactics of social influence and persuasion. In the context of criminal interrogation, these procedures can nevertheless be viewed as "extreme influence" tactics, simply because the combined tactics are sufficient to elicit such an extremely consequential behavior as a confession so extremely discrepant from the defendant's initial intentions and best interests, and from his core beliefs about himself and his own behavior.

Modern theoretical accounts of the interrogation process provide a way to understand how false confessions such as those elicited in the New York jogger case can be obtained from innocent (as well as guilty) suspects (e.g., Gudjonsson, 1989, 1992a, 2003; Hilgendorf & Irving, 1981; Jayne, 1986; Kassin, 1997a,b; Kassin & Wrightsman, 1985; Leo, 1996a,b; Leo & Ofshe, 2001; Ofshe & Leo, 1997a,b; Wrightsman & Kassin, 1993). Central to these accounts is the idea that the interrogation process compromises decision-making capabilities, such that the decision to confess falsely is based on a flawed but rational analysis of what will be the least damaging choice in circumstances presenting no good choice. In other words, the person is considered to choose what is *perceived* as the least of all evils. Ofshe and Leo (1997a) describe the process as follows:

> Psychological interrogation is effective at eliciting confessions because of a fundamental fact of human decision-making—people make optimizing choices given the alternatives they consider. Psychologically based interrogation works effectively by controlling the alternatives a person considers and by influencing how these alternatives are understood. The techniques interrogators use have been selected to limit a person's attention to certain issues, to manipulate his perceptions of his present situation, and to bias his evaluation of the choices before him. (p. 985)

The interrogation tactics themselves are designed to both constrain and falsify the information suspects use to analyze their situations. Furthermore, the entirety of the interrogation can effectively impair cognitive resources and information processing capacity such that the person cannot effectively evaluate and employ even the information he is constrained to use and is therefore even less able to "think outside the box"—that is, the *cognitive box* the person has been constrained to. That is, depleted processing resources render the person less able to access other information from memory that is crucial to evaluating current circumstances and options.

Further, no data are currently collected cataloging the number of interrogations conducted, along with evaluations of the tactics employed, proportion of interrogations that elicit confessions, and reliability of the confessions they do elicit. Unfortunately, because most interrogations remain unrecorded, evaluation of tactics employed and their potential to have elicited a false confession is not possible.

Moreover, although suspects are clearly guided by their attempts to rationally analyze their options, they are also affected by attempts to manage physical and emotional consequences of the interrogation, by their ability to control their actions (i.e., self-regulatory capacity), by the strong emotions generated by the accusatory situation itself and the police tactics specifically intended to manipulate emotions, and by other less rational reactions to the social situation. Finally, criminal suspects are confronted with a battery of powerful social/motivational influence tactics that induce them to confess in much the same way a salesman motivates the purchase of his product.

In the sections that follow, we explore the "road to perdition"—the nature and typical sequence of interrogative strategies and events leading to false confession as well as the underlying psychological principles through which they exert their influence. In recognition of the various contributory causes of false confession, we first consider several classification schemes for confessions and their underlying causes. Following this, we provide a brief summary of common sequences of police tactics—beginning with selection of a suspect, and following the interrogation of that suspect through the production of the full confession and account of the crime. We then consider basic psychological processes through which specific interrogative tactics exert their effects. Next, we turn to individual differences that render specific individuals particularly vulnerable to influence and false confession. Finally, we consider the consequences of confession evidence for eventual disposition of the case.

Throughout, we base our discussion and analysis on interrogation tactics that have been observed in published analyses of actual interrogations (e.g., Gudjonsson, 1992a, 2003; Leo, 1996a,b), our own case analyses as expert witnesses, and tactics specifically recommended in popular police interrogation manuals (e.g., Inbau, Reid & Buckley, 1986; Inbau, Reid, Buckley, & Jayne, 2001). The manual by Inbau and colleagues is perhaps the most well-known and widely used such manual. In view of this popularity, we devote considerable attention to the psychological implications of its recommended tactics.

FORKS IN THE ROAD: VARIETIES OF CONFESSION

A variety of classification schemes have been offered to distinguish between *true* and *false* confessions, whether they may be considered *voluntary* or *involuntary*, and whether they are elicited via *persuasion* or *compliance* (that is, whether the person is actually persuaded of guilt or the desirability of confession vs. complies for other reasons) (e.g., Gudjonsson, 2003; Kassin & Wrightsman, 1985; McCann, 1998; Ofshe & Leo, 1997a). As documented in Gudjonsson's (2003) very thorough review of these classification schemes, a host of causes may underlie both true and false confessions. These include, for example, those internal to the suspect such as guilt, desire for notoriety, desire to help the investigator, desire to protect someone else, or (paradoxically) desire to avoid incarceration; noncustodial external forces such as pressure or threats from friends, family, or enemies; physical and emotional stressors of the interrogation; threats and promises (explicit or implied) by the interrogator; conviction that the evidence of guilt is overwhelming, and other informational, social, and emotional influences of the interrogation. For full review of these causes as well as the various classification schemes, we refer the reader to the original sources, and to Gudjonsson's (2003) review.

For the purposes of this chapter, we focus upon the classifications for false confessions offered by Kassin and Wrightsman (1985) and Gudjonsson (2003). These authors offer a relatively simple three category classification of false confessions: (1) voluntary, (2) pressured-internalized (G) or coerced-internalized (K & W), and (3) pressured-compliant (G) or coerced-compliant (K & W). Ofshe and Leo (1997a) prefer to use the term "persuaded" rather than "internalized" since false confessions are associated with relatively temporary persuasion, whereas internalization is considered to be a more long-term form of persuasion.

Two differences underlie the three-category system: (1) whether the confession is essentially voluntary or involuntary (i.e., given freely for internally generated reasons versus either coerced or pressured through external forces); and (2) whether a coerced or pressured confession is based on causing the suspect either (a) to actually believe in his guilt (internalized/persuaded), or (b) to agree to confess for instrumental reasons (compliant).

Although category-based schemes for classification of confessions are common, it is important to note that both true and false confessions can occur for multiple, rather than single, reasons. For example, even though an innocent suspect may come to believe in his guilt as a result of false evidence provided by interrogators (coerced-internalized in categorical terms), he may decide to confess for instrumental reasons similar to those eliciting compliance from a guilty suspect—such as avoiding more serious charges or terminating the interrogation (either voluntary or coerced-compliant in categorical terms). Hence, although classification may better serve legal goals such as determinations of admissibility, it may be more appropriate for future psychological analyses of the causes of false confession to move to more scalar treatments acknowledging the multiple influences that jointly promote confession.

Following a brief review of interrogation tactics, we consider three general psychological sources of influence that can promote false confession. We begin with stress-inducing forces of the interrogation that can produce sufficient drive to escape the immediate situation as to overpower the need to maximize long-term outcomes. We then turn to the cognitive/decision-making and social/motivational forces that promote persuasion and compliance.

THE ROAD TO PERDITION: COMMON INTERROGATION PRACTICES

Choosing the Suspect

The road to false confession begins, as it must, with the police decision to target an innocent suspect. For any of a variety of reasons, such choices appear rational to police at the time the suspect is targeted. In some cases, only one suspect is possible—as, for example, when the "victim" accuses a particular person of date rape. In others, the suspect may simply be the most readily noticed person who fits a general description given by an eyewitness. Although many may fit the description, the target may be chosen simply because he happens to be available for police to notice—or perhaps because he was reported by someone who had seen a police sketch or was falsely identified from a mug book or lineup.

Often the suspect is identified based on widespread crime-related schemas held by police and public alike. Such schemas include likely motives for the crime as well as perpetrators likely to have such motives (e.g., Davis & Follette, 2002; Vanous & Davis, 2002). Family members, for example, have been led to confess falsely to murdering their wives, children, or parents, largely because police start with the assumption that most such murders are committed by family and proceed by ruling out family before looking for other suspects. Eighteen-year-old Peter Reilly, for example, was led to confess falsely to murdering his mother. Police targeted Peter immediately after he reported the murder and elicited the confession before investigation of any other possibilities had begun (Connery, 1977, 1995).

Sometimes police target the innocent suspect for reasons idiosyncratic to the case. Timothy Hennis, for example, was identified as a suspect in the triple murder of a mother and two of her three children simply because he had bought a dog from the family during the week before the murders (Loftus & Ketcham, 1991). However the innocent person is targeted, police interviews and interrogations of the suspect are henceforth guided by the presumption of guilt. During the initial interview or interrogation, the detective is unlikely to receive unequivocal evidence of innocence. The defendant may offer such evidence, but without independent verification of the defendant's claims or new exculpatory evidence found by police personnel, the detective may simply ignore the defendant's claims and proceed with the interrogation on the continuing assumption of guilt. The nature of interrogation tactics necessarily vary, however, as a function of whether the detective has strong versus weak or no evidence to support accusations against the suspect (Ofshe & Leo, 1997a,b).

Perhaps the best defense against interrogation-generated false confessions lies in criteria for interrogation—in effect, in probable-cause requirements for interrogation of a particular suspect. Ofshe and Leo (1997a,b) point out that if police are required to have significant evidence of a suspect's guilt prior to interrogation, the potential for inducing false confession from an innocent person is minimized.

The Wolf in Sheep's Clothing: False Pretenses to Circumvent Miranda and Get the Interrogation Underway

> *. . . a salesman, a huckster as thieving and silver-tongued as any man who ever moved used cars or aluminum siding, more so, in fact, when you consider that he's selling long prison terms to customers who have no genuine need for the product.*
> Simon, 1991, p. 213 (describing the police interrogator)

Perhaps the majority of interrogations begin under false pretenses—often with police appearing to merely interview the suspect as a possible witness or to enlist his aid in solving the crime (for detailed explanation of such tactics for circumventing *Miranda*, see Gudjonsson, 2003; Leo, 1996a,b, 2001; Leo & White, 1998; Ofshe & Leo, 1997a,b). One cannot help but be reminded of television's Lieutenant Columbo, who routinely lured his prime suspects into talking about the crime by pretending to enlist their aid in solving it. In cases involving custodial suspects, police may go so far as to conceal their identities, posing as a fellow prison inmate to induce the suspect to talk about the crime under the false appearance of friendship (Gudjonnson, 2003).

For noncustodial suspects, in the initial stages the detective may neither tell the person he is a suspect nor adopt a hostile accusatory tone. Instead, the investigator attempts to develop positive rapport with the suspect and appears to focus only on areas of knowledge the suspect may have that would aid the investigator. Unbeknownst to the suspect, however, the detective's primary goal may be to acquire information to be used against the suspect in the accusatory interrogation to come. Several kinds of information are of particular interest (see Inbau et al., 1986, 2001).

First, the detective may engage in what appears to be relatively informal, "getting to know you" chit-chat—a strategy shown to be effective in inducing compliance with later requests (e.g., Nawrat, 2001). The purposes of this stage are threefold: to establish positive rapport with and liking for the detective, to discover personal information about the suspect that can later be used for *theme development* (lines of argument to encourage confession; see later sections), and generally to facilitate willingness to talk with the detective.

Second, suspects are asked about such issues as their whereabouts at the time of the crime and potential as a "witness," or their own and others' relationships with the victim, or any additional information about the victim, other parties, or relevant circumstances that may explain the crime. In part, these questions are strictly informative for the investigator. However, the investigator carefully analyzes this information to detect any signs of inconsistency or lack of credibility that may later be used against the suspect in the accusatory stage of the interrogation. The detective may also pay close attention to any information pertinent to possible motives, relationship issues with the victim, and so on that may be useful for theme development and confrontation. Finally, the initial interview is used to form an initial assessment of the suspect's likely guilt and deceptiveness and to form impressions of the suspect's personality that would provide clues to how he will respond to various interrogation strategies.

In some cases, the detective may also conduct a preinterrogation polygraph examination. If the results are unfavorable, this fact, along with any other inconsistencies uncovered in the interview, may be used to confront the suspect with indications that he may be dishonest during the main interrogation. Short of confession, the polygraph results both provide more information about the suspect and offer the detective the opportunity to confront the suspect with his alleged failure of the test. This technique is often effective in eliciting confessions from both guilty and innocent suspects (Gudjonnson, 1992a, 2003).

Together, the interview and polygraph results (if any) provide the detective with a substantial armament of powerful weapons of influence. Very wisely, the wily detective begins, as he should, with efforts to *know his audience*. Perhaps the most fundamental principle of influence is that one should know the person one is trying to persuade—what he knows, what he thinks and why, what he values, how he usually behaves and why, what incentives would matter enough to change him, what kinds of influence strategies are likely to resonate with his particular personality, and much more.

The Accusatory Phase: The Reid Nine Steps of Interrogation

The 1986 edition of the Inbau and colleagues interrogation manual (Inbau, Reid, & Buckley, 1986) introduced a nine-step method for breaking down suspect resistance and inducing confession called the *Reid technique*. The nine steps of the Reid technique are summarized in Table 36.1. We list them here, as we refer to them throughout the remainder of the chapter. The authors state that the nine steps need not be enacted in the order presented, but may be employed as appropriate at the discretion of the detective. Broadly, these steps can be broken into three phases: two pre-confession stages and the final stage of the confession itself. Throughout the interrogation, the detective is to use tactics to command and maintain suspect attention (steps 5 and 6) in order to facilitate suspect processing of the interrogator's points. This is done through nonverbal means, voice tone and volume, posture, or invasion of personal space as well as through selection of attention-grabbing topics.

Phase 1: The Borg Maneuver

The first phase, we call *the Borg maneuver*. *Star Trek* fans among our readers will recognize the favorite pronouncements of the Federation's nemesis race known as the Borg—*"Resistance is futile!" "You will comply!"* The Borg expect their targets to recognize their power as overwhelming and impossible to resist—and therefore to make the only remaining choice and simply comply. Police interrogators hope to accomplish the same with their criminal suspects. The investigator's goal during the first phase is to move the suspect from confident denial to hopeless acceptance that he is caught—that is, that police already possess sufficient evidence of the suspect's guilt, that lying about guilt or details of the crime will be detected and hence futile, and that the suspect cannot hope to escape responsibility for the crime. To accomplish this goal, the investigator confidently confronts the suspect with the conclusion that he is the guilty party and that more than sufficient evidence exists to prove his guilt. The detective displays both verbal and nonverbal absolute confidence in the suspect's guilt and may cite support for that conclusion from other detectives, witnesses, polygraph or other test results, alleged statements of coconspirators, and other apparently damning evidence—much of it falsified (step 1). If the suspect

Text continues on page 913

TABLE 36.1
Recommended Interrogation Practices from *Criminal Interrogation and Confesions*, 4th ed.

PREINTERROGATION INTERVIEW

Purposes:
1. **To Develop Case-Relevant Facts**
   To interview outside *Miranda*
   Elicit investigation relevant information
   (e.g., alibi, motives, crime or victim-relevant knowledge, suspect's knowledge of other parties)
2. **To Gain Knowledge of Suspect**
   (To Facilitate Influence in Interrogation Phase)
   Assess behavior of suspect for emotionality
      (Interrogation tactics are later tailored to emotional vs. nonemotional style of suspect)
   Assess deceptiveness
   Establish "behavioral baseline" for comparison during accusatory phase
3. **To Establish Positive Rapport with Suspect Investigator Aims to Convey:**
   Expertise, trustworthiness, benevolence, objectivity

Tone:
Nonaccusatory, conversational, pleasant

Setting:
   Informal Settings:
   Suspect's home or work environment
   Squad car, street corner, or other
   Formal Settings:
   Police interview room

Suspect Understanding of Purpose:
Suspect is unaware of status as suspect
Understands interview as completely voluntary
May understand purpose is to eliminate him as suspect

THE REID NINE STEPS OF INTERROGATION

Purpose:
To break down resistance to confession
To positively motivate suspect to confess

Methods:
Nine step method below

Ability to Elicit False Confession:
"It must be remembered that none of the steps is apt to make an innocent person confess and that all the steps are legally as well as morally justifiable" (p. 212). ". . . the investigator must appreciate that the prescribed efforts to obtain a confession from a truly guilty person would, in no way, be apt to cause an innocent person to confess" (p. 365). "The self-preservation instincts of an innocent suspect during an interrogation conducted in accordance with the techniques taught in this text are sufficiently strong to maintain the suspect's stated innocence. When an innocent suspect accepts responsibility for a crime he did not commit, this strongly suggests that improper inducements, such as threats and promises, or deprivation of biological needs were used" (pp. 446–447).

continued

TABLE 36.1
continued

STEP 1:
Direct, Positive Confrontation

Purpose:
To convince suspect police have proof of guilt
To move suspect from confident denial to hopelessness

Methods:
State confidently that the results of investigation clearly indicate suspect committed offense
Pause briefly to observe suspect response to accusation
Restate confidence in suspect guilt
Tell suspect purpose of conversation is not to establish whether suspect committed offense, but rather to establish why, and what kind of person suspect is.

Ability to Induce False Confession:
"... an innocent suspect, even one who is uncertain of his possible involvement in a crime, is not apt to confess to a crime merely because the investigator expresses high confidence in his guilt ..." (p. 290). "It is our clear position that merely introducing fictitious evidence during an interrogation would not cause an innocent person to confess. It is absurd to believe that a suspect who knows he did not commit a crime would place greater weight and credibility on alleged evidence than his own knowledge of his innocence. Under this circumstance, the natural human reaction would be one of anger and mistrust toward the investigator. The net effect would be the suspect's further resolution to maintain his innocence" (p. 429).

STEP 2:
Theme Development

Purpose:
To reinforce suspect's own rationalizations and justifications for crime
To make it easier for suspect to confess by allowing him to save face
To offer themes suggesting proof of guilt
To increase sense of futility in denial

Methods:
Convey understanding and sympathetic attitude toward suspect to gain trust
Suggest themes to suspect
Evaluate whether suspect is "relating to investigator's theme, if not change themes"

Themes for Emotional Offenders:
"Emotional offender refers to an offender who would predictably experience a considerable feeling of remorse, mental anguish, or compunction as a result of his offense. This individual has a strong sense of moral guilt—in other words, a 'troubled conscience.' ... Because of the 'troubled conscience' feeling, the most effective interrogation tactics and techniques to use on such a suspect are those based primarily upon a sympathetic approach—expressions of understanding and compassion with regard to the commission of the offense as well as the suspect's present difficulty" (pp. 209–210).

> **Theme 1:** Sympathize with the suspect by saying that anyone else under similar circumstances might have done the same thing
> Suggest common behavior for many persons
> Anyone else under similar circumstances would do same thing
> Investigator under similar circumstances might well do same
> Tell suspect investigator has friends or relatives who have done same
> Convey sympathy and understanding for why it happened

TABLE 36.1
continued

Theme 2: Reduce suspect's feeling of guilt by minimizing the moral seriousness of the offense
    Suggest common behavior among many persons
    State investigator has had many offenders do far worse things
    Suggest investigator has experienced similar motives, and would have committed similar offense but for . . .
    Compare current offense with other more serious prior offense of suspect

Theme 3: Suggest a less revolting and more morally acceptable motivation or reason for the offense than that which is known or presumed
    Cast as accident
    Financial need versus greed
    Starting fire for entertainment versus to kill or destroy
    Suggest intoxication or drugs responsible
    Did not plan killing, but occurred in context of less serious crime
    Blame suspect's emotional state at time of crime
    (See Inbau et al. Exhibit 13-1, p. 250, for many such distorted motives)

Theme 4: Sympathize with suspect by condemning others
    Blame victim
    Blame coperpetrators
    Blame societal changes in values
    Blame others for financial burden leading to crime
    Blame parents, relatives of victim, home, suspect's neighborhood

Theme 5: Appeal to suspect's pride by well-selected flattery
    Flatter to increase positive rapport
    Flatter plan or execution of crime to motivate suspect to take credit

Theme 6: Point out the possibility of exaggeration on part of accuser or victim, or exaggerate nature and seriousness of the event itself
    Instill fear that others' claims might lead to more serious charge
    Instill desire to convey accurate picture of suspect and crime

Theme 7: Point out grave consequences and futility of continuation of criminal behavior
    Cast confession as way to avoid deterioration into life of criminality
    Point out how much worse crime could have been, how lucky suspect was to be caught early in the game
    Point to importance of learning from mistakes

Themes for Nonemotional Offenders:
"Nonemotional offender refers to a person who ordinarily does not experience a troubled conscience as a result of committing a crime . . . the suspect approaches arrest, prosecution, and possible conviction as an occupational hazard and experiences no regret or remorse as a result of exploiting victims—he psychologically insulates himself from victims. . . . The most effective tactic and techniques to use on the nonemotional offender are those based primarily upon a factual analysis approach . . . appealing to the suspect's common sense and reasoning rather than to his emotions; it is designed to persuade him that his guilt is established or that it soon will be established and, consequently, the intelligent choice to make is to tell the truth" (p. 210).

Tactic 1: Seek admission of lying about some incidental aspect of the occurrence
    Seek to minimize significance of sought admission
    Once admission is given, return to other themes to gain larger admission

continued

TABLE 36.1
continued

Tactic 2: Have the suspect place himself at the scene of the crime or in contact with the victim or occurrence
    Initial attempt to accomplish this should be in nonaccusatory interview

Tactic 3: Suggest a noncriminal intent behind the act
    Cause suspect to admit physical responsibility by initially relieving suspect of responsibility for criminal intent
    Suggest was accident
    Suggest extraneous circumstances caused the suspect to behave out of character
    Suggest self-defense
    Find inconsistencies in initial admission to move toward more accurate account

Ability to Induce False Confession:
"It is our contention, however, that an innocent suspect operating within normal limits of competency would not accept physical responsibility for an act he knows he did not commit. Furthermore, since this interrogation tactic is merely a stepping-stone approach to eventually elicit the complete truth, this approach would not cause an innocent person to provide false evidence concerning his involvement in a crime" (p. 286).

Tactic 4: Point out the futility of resistance to telling the truth
    "Argue against self-interest"
    State investigator has nothing to gain by continuing
    Sole purpose is to allow suspect to explain what happened
    Tell suspect conversation will be terminated soon, regardless of whether suspect confesses
    Cause suspect to worry about whether coconspirator may confess first
    State evidence shows suspect is quilty

Tactic 5: When co-offenders are being interrogated and previously described themes have been ineffective, "Play one against the other"
    Imply to one suspect that other has confessed or implicated him
    Explicitly tell suspect that other has confessed or implicated him

Themes for Juvenile Offenders:
Place blame on parent abuse, neglect, or on desire to get parent attention
Place blame on many temptations for today's youth, including alcohol or drugs
Place blame on youthful energy, boredom, and tendency to make mistakes
Place blame on suspect's neighborhood for not providing alternatives to misconduct
Suggest decision of whether to take responsibility will determine whether suspect learns lesson versus goes route of hardened criminal

Ability to Induce False Confession:
"As evidenced by the innocent suspect's rejection of the investigator's theme concepts, an interrogation theme does not plant new ideas in the suspect's head. . . . An innocent suspect will reject theme concepts because he has not justified the crime" (p. 233).

STEP 3:
Handle Denials

Purpose:
Anticipate denials before they are voiced
Prevent suspect from voicing denials
Evaluate denials that are voiced for indications of actual innocence

TABLE 36.1
continued

    Prevent suspect public commitment to innocence
    Convey absolute confidence in suspect guilt
    Reinforce suspect sense that he cannot successfully deny involvement

Methods:
    Interrupt suspect denials
    Reassert interrogator confidence in suspect's guilt
    Reassert that purpose of conversation is to establish reason crime was committed
    Tell suspect to listen to interrogator points
    Deny suspect eye contact, hold up hand to stop suspect utterances, change loudness and tone of voice to redirect attention to interrogator
    Don't acknowledge suspect attempts to leave room
    Present further evidence of suspect guilt
    Offer opportunity to take polygraph
    Do *not* tell suspect of all evidence against him, only suggest strength of evidence
    Use good-cop, bad-cop strategy. Nice interrogator leaves as a result of suspect uncooperativeness, whereupon harsh interrogator takes over. Later, nice interrogator returns.
    When suspect shifts from simple denial to trying to prove interrogator wrong, go to Step 4

Ability to Elicit False Confession:
"It must be made clear that the suspect was not physically restrained from offering denials, but rather, procedures were used to socially discourage the suspect from offering denials. Further, it can be emphasized that during interrogation an innocent suspect will not be concerned with social protocol and will vehemently state his case: it is the guilty suspect who allows his denial to be put off because he knows it is a lie" (p. 305). ". . . none of what is recommended is apt to induce an innocent person to offer a confession! . . . In the majority of instances, innocent suspects will not allow the investigator to stop their denials; in fact, the intensity and frequency of denials from the innocent will increase as the interrogation continues. An innocent suspect will become angry and unyielding and often will attempt to take control of the interrogation by not allowing the investigator to talk until the suspect has made clear the point that he did not commit the crime under investigation" (p. 313).

STEP 4:
Overcome Objections

Purpose:
    To refute any "proof" of innocence offered by suspect
    To further convince suspect of futility of resistance

Methods:
    Allow suspect to offer objection (proof of innocence), and draw out details
    Reinforce suspect for stating objection (e.g., "I understand how that feels.")
    Redefine meaning of objection and use it for further development of theme
    Sidestep difficult objections by acknowledgement and change of subject
    Continue to counterargue objections until suspect shows signs of withdrawal, and move to Step 5

Ability to Elicit False Confession:
Irrelevant:
"Objections . . . are heard, almost exclusively, from guilty suspects. . . . A suspect's move from a denial to an objection is a good indication of a concealment of the truth. An innocent suspect will usually remain steadfast with the denial alone and will feel no need to embellish it at all. He considers 'I didn't do it' to be entirely adequate" (p. 331).

continued

TABLE 36.1
continued

STEP 5:
Procure and Retain Suspect's Attention

Purpose:
    To recognize symptoms of psychological withdrawal
    To prevent suspect from withdrawing and ignoring interrogator's theme
    To retain suspect attention and focus on the theme
    To maintain psychological closeness to suspect

Methods:
    Move chair closer to suspect in small increments
    Move body to front edge of chair and lean forward
    Establish and maintain eye contact
    Touch suspect gently
    Use visual aids or vivid verbal imagery (e.g., Telling the truth will be like cutting out malignant cancer from his heart)
    Ask hypothetical questions to engage suspect in conversation

Ability to Induce False Confession:
    Irrelevant:
    "It is important to note that innocent suspects who have been accused of committing a crime will not psychologically withdraw. This response goes against every basic instinct for someone who realizes that he may be wrongly facing severe consequences. Provided the investigator has not threatened the innocent suspect, or offered promises of leniency, an innocent suspect will remain at the denial stage during an interrogation or, out of frustration and anger, terminate the interrogation by leaving the room or invoking his rights under Miranda" (p. 338).

STEP 6:
Handle the Suspect's Passive Mood

Purpose:
    To prevent suspect's sense of hopelessness from causing him to mentally withdraw from interaction
    To concentrate on core of selected theme
    To move from general theme (e.g., economic hardship) to specific theme (e.g., handling specific debts)
    To prepare groundwork for alternative questions (Step 7)

Methods:
    Focus suspect's mind on themes surrounding reason for offense
    Exhibit sympathy and understanding
    Convey absolute sincerity through verbal and nonverbal means
    Urge suspect to tell the truth:
        Bring up stress suspect places on victim by not telling the truth
        Suggest suspect will feel better after "clearing this up," taking responsibility, etc.
        Redirect fear of social consequences of admitting guilt to social consequences of not admitting guilt (taking responsibility for own actions)
        Appeal to decency, honor, or religion
    Bring up motives and actions that prepare suspect for alternative questions (Step 7)
    Go to Step 7 as soon as suspect shows signs of resignation

TABLE 36.1
continued

STEP 7:
Present the Alternative Question

Purpose:
Culmination of theme development
To trigger first small admission and begin "stepping-stone" approach to full admission
To produce initial psychological commitment to telling truth
To encourage admission by offering face-saving interpretations of crime
To instill fear in suspect that if he does not tell "his side of the story," others will believe something worse is true instead
Provide suspect opportunity to explain why crime was committed (Assume it is easier to admit wrongdoing if one can "explain")

Methods:
Begin when suspect exhibits symptoms of resignation in Step 6
Present suspect with two alternative versions of crime, and ask which is true
    Both involve admission of guilt
    Once is less heinous and more face-saving that the other
    One *implies* more serious legal consequences than the other (not acknowledged by authors)
To avoid charges of coercion, *do not*:
    Mention legal charges
    Threaten inevitable consequences
    Offer a promise of leniency

Ability to Elicit False Confession:
"... no innocent suspect, with normal intelligence and mental capacity, would acknowledge committing a crime merely because the investigator contrasted a less desirable circumstance to a more desirable one and encouraged the suspect to accept it.... Absent specific threats and promises, an innocent person certainly would not be apt to accept responsibility for committing a crime when offered contrasting reasons for committing it. The innocent person ... would reject both choices and maintain his innocence" (p. 365). "The key is that the suspect arrives at the reason through his own thought process. Perhaps of more importance, such an ambiguous statement ('If this is something that happened on the spur of the moment, that would be important to include in my report.') would not cause an innocent suspect to believe that it would somehow be in his best interest to confess" (p. 420). "An innocent suspect who is told that it is important to explain the reason behind committing the crime will predictably reject the investigator's entire premise and explain that he had no involvement in the crime whatsoever" (p. 421).

STEP 8:
Have Suspect Orally Relate Details of Offense

Purpose:
To draw suspect into previously primarily one-sided conversation
To correct admission in response to alternative question to reflect truth of motive, means, etc.
To elicit full details of crime
To elicit new information only guilty party would know

Methods:
Reinforce admission to alternative question
Ask for relatively unemotional additional details to draw suspect out
Once suspect has started to talk, ask for full details with open-ended questions
Avoid legalistic words such as rape, murder, etc., until suspect has supplied full details

continued

TABLE 36.1
continued

Avoid use of note taking, audio or video recording of confession
After suspect has offered confession of guilt, return to beginning of account to elicit details for further investigation and corroboration
Avoid revealing evidence to suspect, allow suspect to supply all information
Confront suspect with problems regarding initial admission to alternative question in order to elicit more accurate account. (Use new alternative question, but between two more serious alternatives than before—and continue until full extent of crime is admitted to)
Once basic admissions are secured, bring in witness to hear brief account from investigator and secure verification from suspect (To further commit suspect to confession, and to have witness in event suspect refuses to sign written confession)

STEP 9:
Convert Oral to Written Confession

Purpose:
To preserve confession as document admissible in court
To cause confession to withstand coming scrutiny in court

Methods:
Elicit written confession immediately after oral confession
Repeat *Miranda* warnings prior to writing confession and include in materials suspect signs
Do not place confessor under oath (viewed as coercive in some courts)
Elicit written confession in same room as oral confession (to avoid stimulus to retraction)
Either question-answer or narrative form
Only investigator, confessor and stenographer should be present
Elicit confession to only one crime at a time
Recommend against videotape
Have suspect sign confession ("A suspect who balks at signing the confession . . . may be told that his signature would demonstrate sincerity and that the suspect cooperated in the investigation") (p. 384).

To Increase Credibility of Confession:
Get acknowledgment of guilt early in confession
Use confessor's own language
Avoid leading questions (Allow suspect to provide details, rather than respond yes-no to interrogator-supplied details)
Include personal information throughout that can come only from confessor
Have stenographer put simple errors in text that confessor will have to correct in own writing
Have confessor initial all pages and sign last page
Use female stenographer and have her sign as witness (Presumably deters claims of police brutality)
Elicit details to converge with other evidence and witness testimony
Include statements that suspect was allowed food, drink, bathroom facilities, needed medications, and was not under influence of drugs or alcohol
Include statement that confession was given by suspect's own free will, without any threats or promises.

Source: Inbau, Reid, Buckley, and Jayne (2001).

tries to deny these allegations, the detective is to interrupt, overpower, or otherwise prevent the suspect from voicing the denial (step 3). If the suspect tries to refute or criticize the evidence, the detective is to listen to and confidently attack each of the suspect's points as inconsistent, implausible, contradicted by case evidence, or simply impossible—regardless of their actual merit (step 4).

Although such tactics are intended to convince a guilty suspect that he cannot hope to escape the legal consequences of his behavior, they also embody powerful influence weapons that can in some circumstances convince an innocent suspect that—despite having no memory of the offense—he *must have* committed the crime. Hence, he may give a *coerced-internalized* false confession. For this to occur, the suspect must first be induced to distrust his memory—which Gudjonsson (2003) has labeled *Memory Distrust Syndrome.* Unless convinced otherwise, an innocent suspect will be firmly committed to his innocence in part because he does not remember committing the crime—and perhaps does remember what he was doing instead, or how he discovered the completed crime.

Guilty suspects may likewise have no memory of the crime—particularly if it was committed while under the influence of drugs or alcohol (Herman, 1995; Taylor & Kopelman, 1984; Schacter, 1986). Hence, to convince the suspect that he is guilty the investigator must first *"unfreeze"* belief in innocence and reduce the person's commitment to this belief by providing a convincing explanation for this lack of memory. Although Inbau and colleagues (2001) recommend against this tactic, it has nevertheless played a role in many instances of documented false confession (see examples in Connery, 1977, 1995; Gudjonnson, 2003; Ofshe & Leo, 1997a,b; and the Innocence Project website).

An innocent suspect may also confess because he has become convinced via the Borg maneuver that he has been successfully framed in a way that will ensure conviction. In such cases, the suspect may give a *coerced-compliant* false confession if he is convinced his outcomes will be less severe if he confesses. Unfortunately, the tactics of the second general phase generally lead to inferences that confession will result in greater leniency (e.g., Leo, 2001; Ofshe & Leo, 1997a,b; Kassin & McNall, 1991).

Phase 2: The Carrot and the Stick

The second broad phase of the interrogation is intended to increase the suspect's desire to confess by convincing him that the benefits of confession outweigh the costs of denial. Hence, the suspect may be threatened (explicitly or implicitly) with dire consequences of refusal to confess—such as more serious charges, stiffer penalties (secular or spiritual), social disapproval, moral failure, or consequences for self-worth. Likewise, the suspect may be offered (again implicitly or explicitly) benefits of confessing, such as promises of leniency or other legal benefits, relief of guilt and anxiety, moral redemption, social approval, and restored self-esteem. Although explicit threats of more serious legal consequences or promises of leniency will typically cause the confession to be ruled inadmissible, those communicated via implication tend to be viewed as acceptable by the courts (e.g., Gudjonnson, 2003; Kassin, 1997b).

These incentives are conveyed during the process of *theme development* (steps 2 and 7). Leo (2001) offers a three-tier classification of inducements. *Low-end* inducements appeal to the suspect's self-image, to his social image with friends, family, or other associates, and to his conscience—implying that the suspect will expiate guilt, feel better about himself, and receive greater approval from significant others (or God) if he takes responsibility for his actions. Inbau and colleagues (2001) recommend such "themes" for *emotional* offenders who are susceptible to guilt, anxiety, remorse, or damaged self-esteem—and hence more receptive to moral or emotion-based influence.

Systemic inducements appeal to the suspect's hopes of more sympathetic treatment by those who handle his case (Ofshe & Leo, 1997a,b). Essentially, the detective conveys the impression that if the suspect confesses and displays remorse, his case is likely to be processed more favorably by all who handle it—beginning with the detective himself and following through the jury trial, should one occur. Most fundamentally, this tactic is embodied in Inbau and colleagues' (2001) recommendation that the detective should tell the suspect that the only reason he wants to talk to the suspect is to hear the suspect's "side of the story"—which of course includes admitting to the crime and explaining exactly how it happened. The detective implies that confessing at that point, and explaining the motive and details in full, will help to ensure that others (from the prosecutor to the jurors) hear the most sympathetic version of the case. Although clearly less acceptable in legal terms, the detective may also explicitly convey that he can help the suspect if the suspect confesses but will be unable to do so if the suspect continues to deny guilt.

High-end inducements carry such expectations even farther. That is, they communicate the message that the suspect will receive less harsh punishment or greater leniency as a result of confession or that continued denial may result in more serious charges. Again, such inducements may be either explicit or implicit. However, as long as the suspect understands the detective to communicate such consequences, he may base his rational analysis of the relative costs and benefits of confession on these anticipations.

Themes that tend to lead to such inferences are designed to alter suspect perceptions of the seriousness or legal definition of the crime—for example, by blaming the victim, casting the crime as accidental, self-defense, or otherwise justifiable. Such themes naturally lead the suspect to expect that the detective himself—and others who follow—will view the crime less seriously. In contrast, the detective may choose a theme that exaggerates the seriousness of the crime—to induce the suspect to confess in order to convince the detective it was less serious. For example, the detective may claim a coperpetrator revealed that the suspect was the mastermind of a robbery and the person who pulled the trigger to kill a guard. This is designed to cause the suspect to confess to a lesser crime in order to deny the murder part of the charge. Themes of this sort are assumed to be more effective with *nonemotional* offenders, who presumably will not react to inductions of guilt and anxiety or moral exhortations (Inbau et al., 2001).

In sweeping disregard of the pragmatic nature of communication, Inbau and collcagucs (2001) repeatedly deny that their theme development tactics will be interpreted as either threats or promises of leniency—and particularly that such inferences, should they occur, could lead an innocent person to confess (see Table 36.1, step 7). Strangely enough, they do state that "the solicitations of a sympathetic investigator may allow the suspect to believe that if the investigator can understand the reasons for his crime, others too may be more understanding" (Inbau et al., 2001, p. 242) and that "because of this, after a suspect confesses—even though he or she acknowledges committing the crime—this suspect is likely to believe that because the crime was somewhat justified, or could have been much worse, he or she should receive some special consideration" (Jayne & Buckley, 1991). Still, the authors somehow view these inferences as less than perceived promises or threats. Moreover, they fail to recognize that innocent suspects who are convinced they have been successfully "framed" for the crime may begin to consider how they can minimize the consequences in just the same way as a guilty suspect. Like guilty suspects, innocent suspects may expect that if they confess to the themes the interrogator suggests they will enjoy greater leniency—and hence confess to make the best of a hopeless situation. Lacking recognition of this possibility, the authors (Inbau et al., 2001) sum up their position as follows:

> In summary, the concept of pragmatic implication is meaningless unless it can be demonstrated that innocent criminal suspects would be likely to interpret the investigator's statement as such a significant incentive (a promise of leniency or threat of inevitable consequence or physical harm) as to cause a false confession. There are absolutely no data, empirical or statistical, to support such a claim. (p. 422)

Notwithstanding the authors' denials, however, empirical research has shown that such tactics do convey threats and promises via pragmatic implication (e.g., Kassin & McNall, 1991) and that innocent persons can and do confess based on rational analysis of the probable consequences of confession versus denial (see Ofshe & Leo, 1997a,b; Gudjonnson, 2003, for reviews of countless published accounts of such real-life cases of proven false confession).

Further, even for the legally unsophisticated, typical TV-watching American, the specific examples the authors give of how to phrase *alternative questions* related to their theme developments (step 7) are often quite explicit in their implications. Generally, their suggestions state the more serious version of the crime, followed by statements such as "if that's how it happened, I don't even want to talk to you," or "If you're that kind of person, I'm through talking to you," or "I'm wasting my time talking to you," and so on. This more serious version is followed by the less serious version, whereupon the detective states that if that version is true, "I can understand how that would happen," or "This kind of thing happens to lots of people," or "That would be important to know."

In addition to conveying probable consequences for the detective's esteem and potential assistance as well as probable reactions from others who follow in the legal system, the alternative questions also clearly imply different legal charges for the crime. For example, the following suggestion was made regarding alternative questions for a man accused of stabbing his wife to death:

"... You went over to her apartment with the intention of talking to her about the marriage separation and money settlement like normal human beings, but she probably started an argument with you, and she got so mad and unreasonable that she eventually backed you up to the kitchen table. Now, if you were backed up to the kitchen table, and she was raising complete hell with you, and your hand rested on a knife, and you used it without thinking (*implies less than first-degree murder*), **I can understand that, and I can easily see how this could happen**. That's one thing, but if you took the time to look in several drawers to find one and then you used it (*implies first-degree murder*), that's different; if that's what happened, **I don't want to talk to you further**. However, if it was on the table and not in the drawer, and in backing up while she was sticking her finger in your face and screaming at you, your hand then landed on it and you used it on her without thinking, **I can well understand how this happened. . . . This is a most important point**, Jack. Was it on the table or in the drawer? . . ." (Inbau et al., 2001, p. 363)

Although neither explicitly threatening punishment nor promising leniency, such alternative presentations clearly imply legally relevant consequences that can enter into the cost-benefit calculus of innocent and guilty suspects alike.

Phase 3: The Confession

Once the suspect has decided to admit to the crime, the detective is to have the suspect recount all details of the crime orally (step 8) and then convert the oral account into a written confession (step 9). Although it is not the focus of our analysis, others have suggested that the details of the confession provide the opportunity for later analysis of validity (e.g., Ofshe & Leo, 1997a,b). That is, the suspect's account can be examined for linguistic cues to validity and compared to the actual known details of the crime. A true confession, for example, should not only match known police evidence but should also convey knowledge unique to the perpetrator and offer leads to discovery of additional evidence.

Summary

The tactics recommended by Inbau and colleagues (2001) are truly sophisticated weapons of influence, embodying most of what is known about effective influence techniques. As we shortly explore, interrogation tactics make use of the same principles used by other influence professionals of all stripes. One of the authors of the Inbau manual acknowledges this fact, recounting his son's training in the five-step approach to selling newspapers:

> With just a few minor changes of terminology, the boys . . . got basic training in criminal interrogation. Indeed, the principles involved in selling a product door to door are similar to those described in this text for eliciting confessions from criminal suspects. The investigator's "product" is the truth, and a successful interrogator sells it in quite the same way as these boys were taught to sell newspaper subscriptions. (p. 211)

Just as Inbau and colleagues suggest, interrogative weapons of influence are commonplace but extremely powerful. Although they are morphologically similar to, and work via the same mechanisms as, the methods of "influence professionals" such as advertisers, salespersons, or even panhandlers, interrogation practices are conducted in the context of extreme discrepancy in power between the persuader and target, and circumstances which the target cannot escape, and tend to induce far more powerful emotions and stress-related decrements in will and cognitive functioning. Hence the potential for influence is significantly enhanced. In the sections that follow, we review the fundamental influence processes embodied in modern interrogation practices, and explicate characteristics of the interrogation and setting that magnify their power. We begin with stress-inducing forces of the interrogation, and follow with consideration of cognitive and social/motivational influences.

SIMPLE ESCAPE: PHYSICAL AND EMOTIONAL STRESS AS IMPETUS TO CONFESSION

Look over the annals of false confessions, and almost all of them say, "I just wanted to go home."

Saul Kassin (in Ingrassia, 2003)

While most theoretical models of the psychological underpinnings of confession consider relatively "rational" decision making on the part of the suspect, several prominently include purely stress-driven motivation to escape the interrogation itself or immediate confinement (e.g., Gudjonsson, 1992a; 2003; Ofshe & Leo, 1997a,b)—as reflected in the inclusion of the *stress-compliant* category in the Ofshe-Leo classification scheme. Thus, before turning to relatively cognitive/rational determinants of confessions, we consider the issue of how stress and the aversiveness of the interrogation may create an overwhelming immediate need for escape that can overpower other rational or social considerations.

The very fact of being interviewed about a crime often creates intense stress and anxiety—particularly if the crime is personally involving in some way as a result of actual guilt, emotional ties with a victim, the nature of what one may have witnessed (rather than committed), or other factors. Further anxiety and stress is created if the person is aware that police have identified him as a suspect or that important family, friends, and others are aware of the arrest and accusations. The person may be uncertain of the situation, fearful of what will happen at the police station, fearful of the social consequences of his arrest, and fearful of long-term consequences and possible confinement. Some may be suffering bereavement at the loss of a significant friend or family member—or emotional shock over the crime he has witnessed or learned of (Gudjonsson, 2003). Hence, the interrogation begins under conditions creating considerable initial stress and anxiety, which is in turn magnified by interrogative tactics that are, by design, inherently stressful and anxiety provoking. This stress derives from five essential features of the process: (1) confinement, (2) social isolation, (3) physical discomfort, (4) a sense of helpless and lack of control, and (5) the aversive nature of police verbal interrogation tactics.

For some suspects, the need for immediate escape from confinement may overwhelm the effects of any perceived long-term consequences of confession. In fact, many suspects appear to believe that confession will lead to immediate release. In part, this assumption can be caused by failure to understand that confession will result in being charged with the crime. Police often characterize the purpose of interaction as helping them "clear this up" or "straighten this out" (terminology recommended in Inbau et al., 2001) and their motives as trying to help the suspect. Consistent with these apparent motives, the detective may offer understanding and justifications for the crime that provide a way for the suspect to confess while saving face. These tactics can lead suspects (particularly those who are relatively inexperienced with the legal system) to believe the police don't think of the crime as serious and will let the suspects go when the matter is "cleared up" (see Kassin & McNall, 1991).

One of our Reno cases clearly involved such assumptions on the part of the suspect—a young man of low intelligence charged with molestation of an 8-year-old girl he was babysitting. Police never arrested him or apprised him of his rights until he had confessed. They asked him to come to the station voluntarily to help them "clear this up." During the interrogation, the detective characterized himself as trying to help the suspect (but repeatedly stated he could not help the suspect unless the suspect could help him understand what happened and "clear this up"). Then, as specified by the Reid nine-step method (Inbau et al., 2001), the detective suggested face-saving themes for how and why the suspect might have committed the offense. For example, he suggested that perhaps the inappropriate actions were performed when the suspect was not fully awake, dreaming of his girlfriend—and that in his sleepy state he confused the little girl with his girlfriend. Hence he had not intended to touch the girl, and the whole incident was an accident. The suspect confessed within less than an hour—at which point the detective *Mirandized* and arrested him. The suspect was clearly flabbergasted that he was being arrested. He sobbed uncontrollably and repeatedly protested that the detective had said he was trying to help and that they were going to clear the situation up right then. Clearly, he believed confession was the route to freedom.

Others may believe they will be released on bail pending trial or hearing. Indeed, empirical studies of reported reasons for confession have shown that the seemingly nonsensical and unrealistic motivation of desire for release from custody is among the most frequent causes of both true and false confessions (e.g., Dell, 1971; Bottoms & McClean, 1976). In a series of such studies, Gudjonnson and his colleagues found that fear of being locked up was reported as a very important reason for confession in over 20 percent of cases (see review in Gudjonnson, 2003).

Criminal defense attorney Diarmuid White believes the desire to go home was partially responsible for the confession of the Central Park jogger defendants.

White opined: "That is what's underlying all of these confessions and tapes: They believe if they just tell the detectives about the rape, they can go home." Defendant Wise's taped remarks clearly reflected this belief, White argued. In explaining why he elected to give a second statement implicating himself in the rape even more than his first account, Wise stated "I seen like from the first minute I stepped inside all I had to do was tell the truth and I would've probably been home by now" (Ingrassia, 2003).

In addition to fear of incarceration, motivation to confess can be fueled by motivation to escape the immediate stresses of the interrogation setting and tactics. For example, police manuals (e.g., Inbau et al., 2001) place considerable emphasis on the social isolation of a suspect—such that other sources of support or social influence can neither provide comfort nor buttress the suspect's resistance to confession—and on the physical discomfort of the interrogation setting. The room is typically bare with the exception of a table and uncomfortable chairs, is set at an uncomfortable temperature, and in some jurisdictions permit no access to food, drink, or toilet facilities.

Physical discomfort can be enhanced by preexisting conditions of the suspect—such as sleep deprivation, exhaustion, drug or alcohol withdrawal symptoms, or other conditions that can be remedied only through escape from the interrogation. Features of the interrogation—such as length and intensity—can create substantial physical discomfort and further exacerbate existing discomfort. A junkie who has been in confinement long enough to experience withdrawal, for example, may confess simply to get out on bail and score (Gudjonnson, 2003).

Motivation to escape may also be fueled by the sense of helplessness and lack of control over the interaction. Even those undergoing apparently voluntary interviews with police, under circumstances apparently unrelated to the crime or their own involvement, are likely to feel constrained in their options to control or terminate the interaction. The power of those in (even apparent) authority to elicit compliance with requests ranging from the mild to the extreme has long been recognized (e.g., Blass, 2000; Cialdini, 2001; Milgram, 1992). Hence, even when actually free to exert their right and leave, many suspects may fail to recognize that freedom and submit to an unwanted interview or interrogation. Often, however, the sense of lack of freedom and control is real and, for some, a source of intolerable stress.

The stresses associated with lack of control per se are compounded by the aversive natures of circumstances and events that are uncontrollable. These include the previously discussed emotional and physical discomforts inherent in the nature of the circumstances. However, police verbal tactics can also be strongly aversive, in part, because they continually wrest control of the interaction from the suspect. Just as an unpredictable or uncontrollable environment is stressful (e.g., Thompson, Cheek, & Grahma, 1988), so are uncontrollable verbal exchanges (e.g., Davis & Perkowitz, 1979; Davis, 1982). In addition, police tactics are deliberately designed to enhance anxiety (Gudjonnson, 2003).

In his process model for understanding the effectiveness of the Reid model of confession (Inbau et al., 1986, 2001), Jayne (1986) explicated the role of negative emotions in elicitation of confession, suggesting that it is most difficult to elicit a confession from suspects with high tolerance for anxiety and guilt manipulation. This enhanced difficulty is based in the nature of the Reid method, since one of the primary tactics is to motivate confession through enhancement of negative emotions such as fear, anxiety, and guilt. The investigator aims to lead the suspect to view confession as the route to relief of these emotions.

The combined stresses of the crime itself (whether one is the perpetrator or not), the fact of being interviewed or interrogated by police, being suspected of the crime, and being subjected to the interrogative setting and the aversive police interrogation tactics prove overwhelming to some individuals. Those suffering extreme stress or those with poor emotion regulation or low tolerance for stress—and who view confession as the best means to terminate the immediate intolerable stresses—are particularly vulnerable to confession for simple escape. In categorical terms, the confession may be *voluntary* (such as the drug addict who wants to get an immediate fix) or *involuntary stress compliant* (when the length, settings, or tactics of the interrogation are the source of stress).

ALPHA AND OMEGA: TWO BASIC APPROACHES TO PERSUASIVE INFLUENCE

If the suspect does not confess simply to escape custody or interrogation and does not readily comply with police demands to confess, the interrogator must then *persuade* him to confess. Typically, this involves two persuasive goals: first, to convince the suspect that police have overwhelming evidence of his guilt and that he will be unable to escape conviction; and second, to convince him that confession is the best course of action, in that it will result in the best legal, social, or moral outcomes for the suspect. Hence, in the following sections we consider the basic mechanisms of persuasive influence and how they are reflected in the tactics of criminal interrogation.

Eric Knowles and his colleague (Knowles & Linn, in press) have recently distinguished between two basic approaches to persuasive influence–which the authors term *alpha* and *omega* strategies. *Alpha strategies* influence attitudes and behavior by providing *incentives* to act or believe in a particular fashion. For example, one might make a person *want* to behave in a particular way by offering a material inducement, providing sound arguments for why the behavior is desirable, by making the person like the persuader and hence want to please him or her, or by explicit threats and promises. Similarly, one might motivate a target to change a belief through comparable strategies, such as providing sound arguments that the new belief is true or making the person want to please the persuader by changing the belief. *Omega strategies* work, instead, by disabling or overcoming sources of *resistance* to influence—that is, by disengaging or removing the person's reluctance to change or comply.

Alpha Strategies: Incentives to Change or Comply

The criminal interrogation process targets both beliefs and behavior. That is, the investigator aims to influence such crucial behaviors as willingness to talk with the investigator and eventually to confess to the crime and describe it in detail. To accomplish these behavioral goals, the investigator may employ both cognitive and social-motivational strategies to influence the suspect's beliefs in the wisdom of confession or sheer motivation to comply, and hence the behavior of confessing.

Theories of cognitively based influence and persuasion have identified two basic routes through which persuasive influence can occur. The person on the *central route* engages in systematic *active elaborative processing* by thinking carefully about the information and critically evaluating the arguments, evidence, or incentives favoring the belief, decision, or action. In contrast, the person on the *peripheral* or *heuristic* route engages in restricted processing of the quality of arguments, evidence, or incentives and responds primarily to cues that can be taken essentially as proxies for validity—such as communicator credibility, the *quantity* rather than *quality* of evidence, and so on (Chaiken, 1987; Petty & Cacioppo, 1986).

Moreover, influence can occur through *compliance* (e.g., Cialdini, 2001). *Compliance* is said to occur when the person acts in accordance with strong incentives unique to the situation in which the behavior occurs—often involving social motivations, such as when a request comes from an authority figure with power over the person, when the behavior might result in strong social reinforcers or punishments, or when the person does something contrary to his or her own preferences simply to please someone else. Clearly perceived incentives affect both persuasion and compliance. Hence the distinction lies primarily in several areas. First, persuasion more typically refers to beliefs and attitudes, whereas compliance refers to behavior. Second, persuasion (or internalization) refers to the degree to which the target comes to believe the incentives are more generally applicable, whereas compliance applies more uniquely to the specific immediate environment or persons—and hence is assumed to be less general and less permanent influence. Moreover, research described as investigating *compliance* typically concerns behavioral reactions to specific requests or demands from a particular person (see reviews in Cialdini, 2001; Wilson, 2002).

Elaborative Processing and the Central Route to Persuasion

Persuasion through central route processing is based primarily on the target's perception of the quality of information favoring a particular belief or course of action. Essentially, the person reviews the available information, evaluates the reliability and implications of that information, and forms a judgment or decision (Petty & Cacioppo, 1986). Thus, to influence a person in this manner the persuader must cause the target to consider what is perceived as credible information favoring the desired belief or action. This may be done in one of several ways.

Terms of Engagement: Defining the Issue

It is merciless, or rather psychologically wrong, to expect anyone boldly and directly to confess his crime. . . . We must smooth the way, render the task easy.

Hans Gross (1907, p. 120)

Pratkanis and Aronson (2001) suggest that one of the most important processes through which persuasion occurs is *pre-persuasion*—or the process of determining how an issue is structured and the decision is framed. This *framing* of the issue occurs at multiple stages of a criminal interrogation, in each case helping the investigator to "smooth the way" or "pre-persuade" the suspect of what is targeted at the time. First, by casting the initial interaction as a witness interview or as helping the police to solve the crime rather than as a suspect interrogation, the detective can more successfully induce the suspect to talk freely or voluntarily come to the police station. Later, the interrogator aims to structure the suspect's thinking such that he no longer thinks of the issue as whether he can get away with the crime, but rather how to minimize the consequences. Confession will certainly not serve the first goal but may serve the second. Then, to direct the suspect's attention away from the possibility of imprisonment (which would presumably deter confession), the investigator attempts to lead the suspect to think of confession in terms of its *moral* rather than *legal* consequences—for example, that the suspect will be a better person or a better role model for his children if he confesses.

Finally, through the process of *theme development* the investigator attempts to frame the issue as one of whether the suspect committed the crime for morally reprehensible reasons versus for relatively acceptable reasons (i.e., as *why* rather than *whether* the suspect committed the crime; see Inbau et al., 2001), or *what* the suspect did, rather than *whether* he did something (e.g., was it forcible rape or simply statutory rape?). Thus, the suspect is led to focus on how to make the crime appear less reprehensible rather than how to convince the interrogator he is innocent.

Inbau and colleagues (2001) argue that "guilty suspects generally require a face-saving excuse to tell the truth" (p. 236). Hence, part of the interrogator's strategy is to "frame" the crime in terms the suspect might be willing to accept. That is, the interrogator may interpret the crime for the suspect in a way that reduces resistance to confessing by causing the suspect to infer that (a) the punishment will be less severe, (b) he might actually be released without punishment, (c) social disapproval will be less, or (d) the implications for his self-concept are not as severe (e.g., Gudjonsson, 2003; Kassin, 1997b; Ofshe & Leo, 1997a).

In part, interrogators' attempts to minimize the seriousness of the crime, and/or redirect blame to the victim, and/or explain the crime in terms of drugs, alcohol, or other situational forces work through reduction in the *embeddedness* of the suspect's belief in innocence (or in the undesirability of confession) or in other important beliefs. In effect, such tactics either uncouple the commission of the crime from the individual's self-concept by casting the action as involuntary or redefine that link by casting it as justified and therefore consistent with a positive self-view. If commission of the crime is recast in a way that renders it consistent with other strongly held attitudes and self-views, the latter no longer present a significant source of resistance to change. The guilty person may be led to expect less severe social and legal consequences for a less heinous crime and the innocent person may be more willing to believe he *could have* committed such a crime, moving that much closer to the belief that he *did*.

THE POWER OF CONTRAST EFFECTS. The previous strategies serve to identify what issue the suspect is considering. However, once the issue is identified, a decision can also be framed by defining the choices. For example, once the suspect is led to focus on minimizing consequences rather than escaping altogether, the interrogator may seek to influence the perceived desirability of confessing through contrasting it with potentially disastrous consequences of going to trial. He hopes to lead the suspect to ask, "Would I rather confess and get a life sentence, or go to trial and die in the electric chair?" rather than "Would I rather confess or go free?" Clearly, confessing will seem more desirable in the former context.

Inbau and colleagues (2001) also make much of the use of contrast to allow the suspect to save face and make him feel comfortable enough to confess. The suspect may be asked, for example, "Did you steal the money just so you could get another fix? Or did you steal it so you could afford to feed your little boy?"—a technique called *posing the alternative question* (see Table 36.1, step 7). The authors suggest that stealing to feed one's son seems much more acceptable when contrasted to stealing for dope—and hence enables the suspect to face confessing to *something* even if the motive is not strictly accurate. The authors further suggest that framing the choices in such a manner leads the suspect to consider whether it would be more desirable to let all concerned (including detectives, prosecutors, judges, juries, and the suspect's social network) believe the crime was committed for the more reprehensible reason versus to tell his side of the story and inform these parties of the real (more justifiable) reason for the crime—thereby directing attention away from the third alternative of perhaps not admitting to or being convicted of the crime at all.

Erickson and Rossi (1975) refer to this sort of strategy as the *alternative choice double bind*. Although there is a choice to be made, both bind the person to the same outcome—in this case, admitting to the crime. Knowles and Linn (in press) suggest that the strategy works through focusing resistance on the clearly worse alternative—thus sidestepping resistance to the lesser evil.

Inbau and colleagues (2001) also recommend exaggeration of the seriousness of the offense (theme 6), again using contrast in an effort to cause the suspect to view confession to the less serious offense as relatively more desirable. Often this is done through false exaggeration of victim reports of the crime. For example, the suspect might be told that the victim claimed the suspect had committed a more serious crime (such as forcible rape of a minor), rather than the lesser crime of statutory rape. The authors note, "It is in human nature to find fault in another person's apparent 'unfounded accusations.' This instinct is so strong that, in an effort to prove the other person wrong, the person defending his position may make incriminating admissions" (p. 271).

Such a tactic is similar to what is known as the *door-in-the-face* technique in the compliance literature (Cialdini, Vincent, Lewis, Catalan, Wheeler, & Darby, 1975). The persuader makes a large or even outrageous request–which is likely to result in the "door in the face"—before backing down to the request he or she actually wanted to have accepted (e.g., "Dad, can I borrow the car and $200 to take Sally out tonight?" "No way!!" "Well can I just borrow the car and $20?"). Research has repeatedly shown that a smaller request is more likely to succeed when preceded by a larger, rejected request. Among other possible reasons for this effect, the smaller request simply seems smaller and more acceptable when contrasted with the larger one.

The interrogation tactic known as maximization (Kassin & McNall, 1991) essentially operates through similar processes of framing and contrast. *Maximization* refers to the use of scare tactics to lead the suspect to infer disastrous post-interrogation consequences if he fails to confess. The detective may present false witnesses or evidence to convince the suspect that going free is not an option, and then make use of the *contrast effect* by overstating the seriousness of the crime or magnitude of the charges to lead the suspect to view risking trial or being charged with a more serious crime as more dangerous than confession.

Contrast is also inherent to what Kassin & McNall (1991) refer to as the tactic of *minimization*—"a 'soft sell' tactic in which the detective tries to lull the suspect into a false sense of security by offering sympathy, tolerance, face-saving excuses, and moral justification; by blaming the victim or an accomplice; and by underplaying the seriousness or magnitude of the charges" (Kassin, 1997b, p. 223). These goals are accomplished through contrast-based tactics such as theme development (step 2) and the alternative question technique (step 7).

Inbau and colleagues (2001) endorse minimization rather than explicit maximization tactics—suggesting that the suspect should be prevented from thinking of the legal consequences of the crime or confession, as such thoughts are presumed to fuel resistance to confession. The manual goes so far as to instruct interrogators to avoid the use of words that define a crime—such as murder, arson, rape, and the like (which might remind the suspect of harsh legal consequences) and instead to refer to the crime in terms such as "this thing," "this situation," or "what happened" (e.g., p. 82). Instead of negative legal issues and consequences, the suspect is to be led to think of the positive moral and social consequences of confession, such as expiation of guilt, social approval for taking responsibility for his actions, and so on. Notwithstanding this recommendation, however, both tactics appear to be common (Leo, 1996a; Simon, 1991; Wald, Ayres, Hess, Schantz, & Whitebread, 1967).

Inbau and colleagues (2001) do, in effect, recommend maximization through implication. The effectiveness of the interrogation is predicated upon first convincing the suspect that he cannot escape responsibility for the crime. This is done by convincing that sufficient evidence exists to firmly establish his guilt. Further, although the authors repeatedly admonish the investigator not to *explicitly* threaten or promise legal outcomes as a result of the suspect's decision to confess or not, they do recommend procedures that lead the suspect to infer them—as in the preceding example, where the suspect is led to think the victim is claiming a more heinous crime than the suspect committed.

Control the Information the Target Considers. The central route to persuasion is fundamentally based on critical analysis of information. We tend to base judgments and decisions on information that is *available* (or easily brought to mind—the familiar *availability heuristic* [Tversky & Kahneman, 1973]). Hence, the most direct approach is to cause the target to focus on what he will perceive as very high-quality arguments or evidence favoring the desired outcome.

Police interrogators make use of this principle through such tactics as (1) forcefully commanding the suspect's attention to themselves and the arguments and evidence they present (e.g., through invasion of the suspect's personal space, nonstop accusations, overbearing demeanor, arousal of fear, loudness, etc.), (2) presenting apparently compelling (but often false) arguments and evidence, (3) using vivid and personally relevant imagery, (4) restricting access to potentially contradictory information (such as friends, family, attorneys, and other persons or sources of information), (5) interrupting and refusing to respond to attempts to change the subject, (6) attempting to induce suspects to focus on the consequences of the immediate interaction with the investigator for long-term outcomes rather than later reactions of the prosecutor, judge, or jury, or (7) allowing the suspect insufficient time and mental resources to access contradictory information from memory (see Gudjonnson, 2003; Kassin, 1997b; Ofshe & Leo, 1997a,b). Further, the investigator attempts to arouse emotions such as fear, anxiety, and guilt, which have the effect of narrowing attention to information relevant to mechanisms for managing the emotions (see later sections).

Control the Interpretation of Information. Information affects judgment and decision making only in light of the *interpretation* it is given. Hence, the effective persuader must not only control the information the target considers, but must also influence what the target makes of it. For example, in an attempt to convince the suspect that he cannot possibly convince a jury of his innocence (and therefore that he will get off lighter by confessing), the detective will typically present a set of "damning" evidence against him. In turn, the detective must convince the suspect both that the evidence is real and valid, and that it is sufficient to convict him in court. Alternatively, faced with a suspect's insistence that he does not remember the crime, the detective may present an *interpretation* the suspect might accept—such as an alcohol-induced blackout or post-traumatic repression.

Control Motivations and Emotions. Pratkanis and Aronson (2001) offered four central stratagems of influence, the fourth of which is to first arouse an emotion and then to offer the target a way of responding to that emotion that just happens to be the desired course of action. This stratagem is based on recognition of the fundamental motivating influence of emotions—a principle reflected in the growing interest in *motivated social cognition* among cognitive and social psychologists (see *Psychological Inquiry* [1999] entire issue for reviews). Essentially, emotions cause the person to *want* a specific outcome—such as to believe we are loved by our spouse, to have a particular object, to be safe from feared physical, social, or material harm, to feel better, to please another person, and so on. Such desires tend both to directly cause behaviors expected to produce these outcomes and to bias our interpretation of events and information or shift the expected consequences of behavior such that the desired outcome appears more certain.

For example, we might interpret a spouse's lack of interest in sex as related to stress and distraction in order to maintain the belief that we are still loved and sexually attractive. We might believe in the effectiveness of age-reversing herbs and medications because we want to stay forever young. Or a suspect may confess because the interrogator has aroused a sense of guilt and led the suspect to think he will feel better if he confesses. Indeed, the Inbau and colleagues (1986, 2001) interrogation manual specifically instructs the interrogator to use emotions to promote confessions. They are to arouse fear, anxiety, and guilt and to cast confession as the way to effectively diffuse these emotions. Empirical research has provided support for the effectiveness of such strategies.

THE ROLE OF FEAR. Fear can be an effective motivator for attitude change and compliance. Attitude research has shown that even though intense fear may cause a person to become defensive, to deny the importance of a threat, and to become unable to think rationally about the issue (e.g., Baron, Inman, Kao, & Logan, 1992; Janis & Feshback, 1953; Jepson & Chaiken, 1990; Liberman & Chaiken, 1992), if the fear-arousing threat is accompanied by clear instructions for avoiding the feared outcome, it can be quite effective in creating the desired change (e.g., Das, de Wit, & Stroebe, 2003; Leventhal & Cameron, 1994; see review in Petty, 1995). Thus, to use fear effectively, the interrogator must first arouse fear and then lead the suspect to expect that confession will help him avoid the outcome he most fears.

Fear has also been shown to affect decision making. For example, recent research has shown that persons experiencing emotions embodying uncertainty and lack of control (such as fear and anxiety) tend to adopt pessimistic risk assessments and to make risk-averse choices, whereas those experiencing emotions embodying certainty and control (such as happiness or anger) tend to adopt more optimistic risk assessments and to make risk-seeking choices (see Lerner & Keltner, 2000, 2002)—an effect that appears to be mediated primarily through the effects of emotional state on perception of control. This research supports the notion that interrogative practices that raise fear and anxiety (or otherwise promote a sense of helplessness) will promote confession through more pessimistic projections of the consequences of denial and failure to confess, along with reduced willingness to risk these consequences. Further, those dispositionally prone to fear and anxiety will be particularly reactive to such techniques. Consistent with Lerner and Keltner's findings (2000, 2002), Inbau and colleagues (2001) note that those with little anxiety or greater tolerance for anxiety present a greater challenge to the interrogator.

FEAR AND THE SCARCITY EFFECT. The police interrogator is prone to use another kind of fear—the fear of unavailability or lost opportunity—to motivate compliance. Pratkanis and Aronson (2001) recount the story of Catherine the Great's clever and very successful campaign to increase Russian consumption of potatoes. Potatoes offered a useful addition to the sparse Russian diet but were widely considered poisonous by Russian peasants. Catherine ordered fences built around potato fields, bearing posted warnings not to steal potatoes. Just as any 2-year-old who is told *not* to do something will surely immediately try, Catherine's prohibition turned the peasants from fearful avoidance to motivated acquisition—and the potato became a staple of the Russian diet. (See a modern illustration of the power of prohibition to fuel defiance by Pennebaker & Sanders, 1976—who found that strongly worded posted prohibitions of graffiti increased rather than decreased graffiti.)

Catherine's very early use of the *reverse psychology* inherent to the scarcity effect illustrates the persuasive motivating power of the fear that we might lose the freedom to choose how to act or believe, or to have certain objects, privileges, or benefits (e.g., Brehm, 1966; Brock, 1968). The power of scarcity is both cognitively and motivationally based.

Jack Brehm's theory of *psychological reactance* (1966; Brehm & Brehm, 1981) proposed that when our choices are limited or threatened, the powerful psychological motive to retain freedom of choice motivates us to desire the threatened alternative all the more. In turn, we tend to reassert that freedom by active attempts to acquire or reclaim the threatened alternative. In effect, our attention shifts from carefully considering whether the threatened choice is actually desirable compared to other competing choices to plotting how to maintain and even exercise that particular choice. Further, to make sense of our heightened desire, we begin to view it more positively (motivated cognition steps in).

Modern cognitive theories of influence further view scarcity as an heuristic cue to value. That is, since things that are difficult to come by are often more valuable, if something is scarce or difficult to acquire we tend to assume it is more valuable. Often, this assumption is valid—unless the scarcity is unnaturally created or even fabricated (Cialdini, 2001).

The scarcity technique is very effective, as reflected in its widespread use by compliance professionals (see reviews and a wealth of examples in Cialdini, 2001; Pratkanis & Aronson, 2001). A product may be depicted as rapidly selling out, as available only during a one-day sale or as a "limited edition." Particularly relevant to police tactics is the *time-limited offer*, whereby the target is enjoined to make an immediate decision before leaving the premises and is told that any delay will either result in a stiff price increase or inability to purchase at all.

Police interrogators use the time-limited offer technique to induce suspects to immediately take advantage of the investigator's (mostly illusory) abilities to negotiate a better deal for the suspect. The interrogator attempts to constrain the suspect's focus to the consequences of the immediate interaction with the investigator (e.g., "I want you to pay real close attention to what I'm going to tell you now. The decisions you make right here and right now in this room are going to affect the rest of your life.") and then proceeds to make a time-limited offer of help (e.g., "I know you want to do the best you can for yourself here—and I'm gonna try to help you. But I can't do anything for you once you leave this room. It'll be out of my hands then. And the district attorney will take over."). In this way, the interrogator plays on the suspect's fear of losing the interrogator's help and the prospect of facing a much bleaker outcome from those who follow later in the system. Hence, motivation turns to maintaining that opportunity, and attention to the means to do so (the detective's suggestion?—confession!).

The Power of Guilt. Guilt has also been shown to motivate compliance with requests—even when the source of guilt is unrelated to the person making the request. Carlsmith and Gross (1969), for example, found that those who had been led to transgress against a victim were subsequently more likely to comply with a request either from the victim or from an uninvolved third party. The authors suggested that guilt can motivate compliance with requests through three primary processes: (1) sympathy for a victim, (2) restitution or compensation for wrongdoing, and (3) repair of tarnished self-esteem. Presumably enhanced compliance to the person's victim can serve the first two processes, whereas either form of compliance can serve to repair damaged self-esteem.

Pratkanis and Aronson (2001) summarize the power of guilt as follows:

> The power of guilt to convince and to persuade stems, as with most emotional appeals, from its power to direct our thoughts and to channel our energies. When we feel guilty we typically pay little attention to the cogency of an argument, to the merits of a suggested course of action. Instead, our thoughts and actions are directed to removing the feeling of guilt—to somehow making things right or doing the right thing. (p. 229)

In fact, in line with the Reid method's recommended use of guilt to motivate confession, it appears to be a powerful tool. The series of studies by Gudjonnson and colleagues on reported causes of confessions found that across several countries 40 percent of guilty confessors reported confessing because they felt guilty about the offense, and more than 40 percent said they felt relief after confessing (see review in Gudjonnson, 2003).

Guilt and the Reciprocity Principle. Sometimes guilt works retroactively, motivating some kind of repair or reparation for one's lost self-image or damaged relationship with the victim. Other times it may work proactively, as when anticipatory guilt might prevent a person from committing a transgression or from taking advantage of another.

Powerful norms of reciprocity exist across cultures (e.g., Gouldner, 1960) and generally motivate people to reciprocate benefits offered by others—including material benefits as well as social benefits such as compliments. Although not typically cast in these terms, these normative pressures toward reciprocity may be viewed as motivating through anticipatory guilt. That is, compliance to the requests of those to whom we feel obligated may be motivated by anticipated feelings of guilt should we fail to meet those obligations. Mark Parisi (Atlantic Feature, 1991) illustrated this principle in his cartoon depicting a stingy restaurant patron who says to the hostess, "I'm a lousy tipper and I'd like your rudest waitress so I won't feel guilty about it" (reprinted in Cialdini, 2001).

As with other powerful weapons of influence, compliance professionals make full use of the reciprocity principle to sell their wares. Among the most common—and most effective—strategies is the offer of a free gift to prospective targets. Such a strategy has been pursued, for example, by the Hare Krishna, who offer a flower to targets to whom they wish to sell a book, or by the hostesses of Tupperware parties and other salespersons who offer their guests a free gift before the sales pitch. Likewise, the police interrogator takes advantage of pressures toward reciprocity to motivate the suspect to confess. By offering to "help" the suspect, he hopes to motivate the suspect to "help" him as well—that is, by helping him understand how and why the crime was committed (i.e., solving the case through confession).

THE IMPORTANCE OF INDIVIDUAL MOTIVES. Before leaving our discussion of motivational influences on persuasion and compliance, it is important to note that some individuals will be driven toward compliance by forces independent of the interrogation. Lower-IQ suspects, for example, have often learned to survive through compliance and trying to please others (Gudjonnson, 2003). When such motives are applied to a police interrogator, they can induce the person (guilty or not) to confess simply to be helpful and pleasing.

There is also evidence that felt inferiority in social rank is associated with the tendency to submit when threatened or criticized by those viewed as superiors. Social rank theory (Gilbert, 1992; Price, 2000; Price, Sloman, Gardner, Gilbert, & Sohde, 1994) suggests that social standing is associated with (1) the *appraisal* of threats from others in the social system, (2) *relative rank appraisal* of a potential adversary, and (3) *strategy selection* for dealing with the threat (e.g., aggression and defiance versus submission). Threat appraisal tends to be minimized, and strategy selection tends to be more aggressive among those of relatively higher social rank than their adversary. For example, those who view a critic as of equal or lesser social rank tend to quarrel with (attempt to refute) his or her criticisms, whereas those who view the critic as higher in rank tend to submit (as do those with a general feeling of inferiority—e.g., Fournier, Moskowitz, & Zuroff, 2002; for a recent review of the behavioral effects of relative social power, see Keltner, Gruenfeld, & Anderson, 2003). Thus, suspects who view the police in relatively exalted terms (or themselves in relatively negative terms) may less vigorously defend against the interrogator's assault on their self-esteem and innocence.

Promote Self-Persuasion. One of the most effective routes to influence is to induce the target to influence himself. This strategy was first illustrated in a wartime experiment by Kurt Lewin, considered to be the "father" of social psychology. Lewin was called upon during World War II by the Committee on Food Habits to help increase consumption of relatively unattractive but nutritious food products, including organ meats such as hearts, kidneys, liver, or intestines. Lewin conducted a relatively simple experiment in which housewives were either exposed to a 45-minute lecture emphasizing the importance of eating the meats for the war effort, their nutritional qualities, and their economic advantages, or were induced to spend 45 minutes in a group discussion essentially persuading themselves. The discussions began with an introduction by the leader on the problem of maintaining health during the war, whereupon the housewives were asked, "Do you think that housewives like yourselves could be persuaded to participate in the intestinal meat program?" The housewives then proceeded to discuss the utility of consuming organ meats and how to get housewives such as themselves to use them. Although the two alternative formats covered essentially the same information, the group discussion format was far more effective. Follow-up interviews revealed that whereas only 3 percent of those who heard the lecture later served organ meats, 32 percent of the discussion group participants did so.

Several large bodies of research have since shown that self-generated persuasion can be promoted by such techniques as inducing *motivation* for change (for example, inducing dissonance and need for self-justification through causing the target to engage in counterattitudinal behavior), promoting self-induced perspective change through role-playing an opponent's position; or inducing *imagery* consistent with the desired belief or behavior. Pratkanis and Aronson (2001) summarized the operation of tactics promoting self-generated persuasion as follows: "It gains its power from . . . directions that ask the target of influence, in effect, to 'think up as many positive cognitive responses about the issue as you can and, if you do happen to come up with some counterarguments, to be ready to refute them'" (2001, p. 168).

Police interrogators are trained to promote self-persuasion through each of these mechanisms. The interrogator attempts to enlist the suspect's help to solve the crime—first in the apparent role of helpful witness, and later in attempting to explain how the suspect could have and did commit the crime and why—thereby leading the suspect to actively construct plausible scenarios of his own guilt. Second, the suspect may be asked to think about the effects of his situation and actions on family and others in order to encourage the suspect to act as the interrogator suggests these significant others would wish (i.e., inducing the suspect to self-invoke the power of social norms and social approval needs to persuade). Finally, the interrogator often asks the suspect to picture (or imagine) aspects of the crime to help reconstruct how it could have happened (if it is assumed the suspect can't remember) or did happen. All of these are powerful promoters of self-generated persuasion.

THE SPECIAL POWER OF IMAGINATION. Perhaps the most widely investigated mechanism of self-persuasion today is that of imagination. Imagination is widely used by sales professionals to motivate product purchase. Targets who are asked to imagine experiencing the benefits of a particular behavior (such as subscribing to cable TV) are more likely to become convinced that the benefits are true and to perform the behavior than those who are simply told about the benefits. Likewise, those who are induced to imagine the costs of failing to perform a behavior (such as not purchasing insurance) come to believe the costs are more likely and are therefore more likely to perform the behavior (buy insurance) to avoid them (e.g., Gregory, Cialdini, & Carpenter, 1982; Gregory, Burroughs, & Ainslie, 1985). Hence, a suspect who is led to picture the potentially harsh social outcomes and legal penalties that may result if he fails to confess may come to view those outcomes as more likely and therefore become more likely to confess to avoid them.

Another effect of imagination is widely viewed as likely to contribute to the development of coerced-internalized false confessions (those in which the suspect comes to falsely believe that he indeed committed the crime). That is, imagining an event or action can lead to the development of false beliefs and even false "memories" that it did happen. Imagination can lead to false beliefs in and memories for such simple events as hearing a dog bark or having said something one only thought about—or something as complex as autobiographical events such as being lost in a mall or even sexual abuse (see review in Davis & Follette, 2001).

It is not uncommon for police interrogators to ask criminal suspects to imagine how the crime might have been committed (Gudjonnson, 2003; Ofshe & Leo, 1997a,b). Often this technique is used with suspects who claim no memory of the crime. After offering some reasons why the suspect might not remember committing the crime, the interrogator might ask the suspect to help him try to understand what happened by trying to picture how it might have happened. The suspect is led to understand that this process of imagining how things *might* have happened will help to uncover how they *did* happen.

Unfortunately, things one only imagines can easily become confused with things that have actually happened—particularly under conditions that encourage poor source monitoring (Johnson, Hastroudi, & Lindsay, 1993). In the interrogation situation, accurate *source monitoring* refers to accurate attributions for the source of a particular "memory": that is, accurately recognizing a vivid mental image as either a real memory for a real behavior or as a self-generated image of the behavior (i.e., as having imagined performing it).

Research examining the determinants of accuracy in source monitoring has shown that source confusion is more likely under conditions that generally impair encoding—including situational factors such as distraction, stress, or fatigue and personal impairments such as intoxication, attention disorders, or age-related cognitive decline (Johnson, Hastroudi, & Lindsay, 1993; Glisky, 2001; Koutstaal & Schacter, 2001; Raz, 2000). As we explore in subsequent sections, the physical and emotional stresses of the interrogation can strongly impair cognitive processing resources, and many of the specific behaviors of the investigator can disrupt cognitive processing even in unimpaired suspects. Thus, the conditions of the interrogation can directly impair what is known as the *binding* in memory of target information (for example, the image of stabbing the victim) with contextual features such as the source of the image (imagining versus doing) in memory. If the target information and context (or source) are not properly "bound" at encoding, they are susceptible to greater confusion upon retrieval.

The suspect who is operating under conditions of extreme physical and emotional stress, high levels of distraction, and genuine confusion over what may have happened and who, through imagination, develops vivid images of committing the crime is a prime candidate for *source confusion* and may come to believe these images are real memories—and that he did actually commit the crime.

When Elaborative Processing Fails: The Role of Heuristic Processes in Persuasion and Compliance

When elaborative processing is not possible, people rely on *heuristic processes*—or what might be regarded as *shortcut evidence* of accuracy. Both the *elaboration likelihood* (Petty & Cacioppo, 1986) and the *heuristic-systematic* (Chaiken, 1987) models of persuasion propose two routes to attitude change—the central systematic elaborative processing route we have discussed to this point and the *peripheral* or *heuristic* route. When a target of persuasive influence is either unmotivated or unable to process an influence attempt elaboratively, he or she will often rely on cues assumed to reflect accuracy—such as the credibility or trustworthiness of the would-be persuader, the *number* (rather than quality) of arguments offered to support the persuader's position, or the number of other people who appear to agree with the advocated position (see reviews in Chaiken, 1987; Chen & Chaiken, 1999; Petty & Cacioppo, 1986; Petty & Wegener, 1999).

Five heuristic cues are of particular relevance to the interrogative situation: (1) *likeability* of the interrogator, (2) *credibility/trustworthiness* of the interrogator or of the evidence he or she presents, (3) *communicator confidence,* (4) *social proof* of the interrogator's position (i.e., others who support the interrogator's position, such as real or alleged witnesses to the crime or the involvement of the suspect), and (5) the *number* of arguments, items of evidence, or sources of social proof presented to the suspect as evidence of his guilt.

The Likeable Communicator. Most of us, as a rule, prefer to say yes to requests from people we know and like (Cialdini, 2001) and, moreover, feel comfortable agreeing with those we like but somewhat uncomfortable agreeing with those we dislike (Heider, 1946, 1958). We are even more likely to comply with the requests of those with whom we have fleeting but pleasant encounters (e.g., Burger, Soroka, Gonzago, Murphy & Somervell, 2001). Consider the title of Dale Carnegie's famous book—*How to Win Friends and Influence People*—which essentially embodies the principle that making oneself liked creates fertile ground for influence.

Roger Ailes (1988)—public relations advisor for the Reagan and George Bush presidential campaigns, and later chair and CEO of Fox News—put it as follows:

> If you could master one element of personal communications that is more powerful than anything we've discussed, it is the quality of being likeable. I call it the magic bullet, because if your audience likes you, they'll forgive just about everything else you do wrong. If they don't like you, you can hit every rule right on target and it doesn't matter. (p. 81)

Compliance professionals make full use of the liking principle (see extensive discussions in Cialdini, 2001; Pratkanis & Aronson, 2001). Those operating at the mass communication level, such as advertisers and political campaigners, commonly employ popular sports figures, public figures, or actors to endorse their products or candidacy. Multilevel marketers such as Amway, ReLiv Nutritional Supplements, Mary Kay Cosmetics, and Tupperware make use of liking between friends to sell their products. In fact, studies of home party product sales have shown that the strength of the friendship bond between hostess and party guests is twice as likely to determine product purchase as is preference for the product itself (e.g., Frenzen & Davis, 1990).

Communicator likeability promotes influence through several routes. First, likeable communicators are expected to support desirable positions (Eagly & Chaiken, 1975). Hence, likeability serves as an heuristic cue to message quality and desirability and therefore affects persuasion more when the target is engaging in peripheral or heuristic processing rather than elaborative central route processing (e.g., Petty, Cacioppo, & Schumann, 1983).

Second, since we are more comfortable agreeing with liked communicators (Heider, 1946, 1958), we are less motivated to find flaws in their positions. Hence, *resistance* to influence is lessened (or even transformed to positive motivation) and the message is more persuasive. Similarly, we are more motivated to please those we like and consequently are more willing to comply with their requests. Finally, the beliefs we hold and the behaviors we choose serve to define who we are and are central to our sense of self and social identity (e.g., Pratkanis & Aronson, 2001). Similarity to those we like and admire serves to enhance our own self-esteem and to define our social identities in positive terms.

Given the power of liking to motivate persuasion and compliance, it is important to consider the mechanisms through which a compliance professional can ingratiate himself or herself to the target. Generally we tend to like others who are physically attractive, who appear to like us (as expressed through directly stating liking, positive nonverbal cues, compliments, etc.), who behave in a generally positive and friendly manner, who are similar to us, who are familiar to us, who tend to cooperate with us or generally behave consistently with our own interests, and who appear to possess positive traits such as intelligence, competence, kindness, honesty, and so on (see reviews in Cialdini, 2001; Pratkanis & Aronson, 2001).

The criminal interrogator often begins the interaction with the suspect in a friendly, cooperative, nonhostile mode that is designed to avoid resistance to talking with the investigator that might otherwise be created by the suspect's awareness of the interrogator's real attitude and intent. Later, when the interrogation turns to the accusatory and confrontational stage, the interrogator will often alternate confrontation with sympathy, flattery, and empathy and stress similarities between himself and the suspect in order to maintain some degree of positive bond. Alternatively, the interrogation may involve the "good-cop, bad-cop" double-teaming approach (referred to as the "Mutt and Jeff" approach by investigators) so that the resistance can be focused upon the "bad" cop, even as the "good" cop motivates acceptance and compliance.

Communicator Credibility and Authority. The criminal interrogator embodies a powerful package of apparent expertise, trustworthiness, and authority. He appears to possess considerable expertise regarding the law, criminal investigation, and evidence as well as the authority to set in motion both relatively positive or negative outcomes for the suspect. In addition to these factors inherent to the role, the detective also often appears to have access to much more information relevant to the suspect's individual situation than the suspect himself. Although in many instances this expertise and authority may be more apparent than real, it can nevertheless powerfully influence the suspect.

Both expertise and authority serve to command the attention of the target. In addition, expertise is perceived as an heuristic cue to the likely validity of the communicator's statements or to the advisability of complying with his request, whereas communicator authority leads to the perception that the communicator has the ability to affect the target's outcomes. Hence, both credibility and authority serve to enhance persuasion and compliance (see reviews in Cialdini, 2001; Milgram, 1992; Petty & Cacioppo, 1986; Pratkanis & Aronson, 2001)

As with other peripheral cues, source credibility exerts more influence on persuasion when the person is on the peripheral rather than the central route to persuasion. Petty, Cacioppo, and Goldman (1981), for example, showed that targets for whom an issue was of low personal relevance (which is known to encourage heuristic processing) were affected strongly by source expertise (but not by message quality), whereas those for whom the issue was highly relevant were affected strongly by message quality but not source expertise. Hence, once again, those suspects whose ability to analyze the detective's claims is compromised—either by lack of intelligence or impairment of cognitive resources, or by lack of relevant knowledge—will tend to be strongly affected by the apparent credibility of the detective or the sources of evidence he presents.

It should be noted that credibility includes both expertise and trustworthiness. The Inbau and colleagues (2001) manual advises the interrogator to project both:

> Basic to any theme application is confidence on the part of the investigator and, more important, a conveyance of sincerity in whatever is said. . . . The most effective attitude is generally one that reveals a calm confidence, wherein there is a patient display of a vital, intense interest to learn the truth, but one that, at the same time, implies an understanding, considerate and sympathetic feeling toward the suspect. (pp. 236, 237)

That is, the investigator is to project a very sincere concern for the suspect and the appearance of trustworthiness even as he deploys his full complement of weapons of influence to work against the suspect's best interests. Such trait projections can be particularly effective—particularly with an already trusting, perhaps innocent suspect who fails to imagine that police will systematically lie, deceive, and misrepresent evidence to achieve their goals.

Communicator Confidence. Communicator confidence can serve as yet another heuristic influence on persuasion. That is, confidence tends to be regarded as an indicator of accuracy. A large body of literature on eyewitness identification, for example, has shown that witness confidence is the strongest predictor of perceived accuracy (e.g., Cutler, Penrod, & Dexter, 1990; Cutler, Penrod, & Stuve, 1988). Further, nonverbal behaviors reflecting confidence—such as few speech errors, authoritative tone of voice, steady and upright body posture—are positively related to persuasion (e.g., Leippe, Manion, & Romanczyk, 1992).

Inbau and colleagues (2001) appear to recognize the importance of communicator confidence. Interrogators are advised to steadfastly maintain the appearance of absolute certainty in the suspect's guilt (e.g., Inbau et al., 2001)—through maintaining a strong, confident demeanor, through repeatedly stating belief in the suspect's guilt; and through absolute refusal to acknowledge the validity of the suspect's arguments. This strategy has at least two effects. It provides indirect evidence of the strength of the case against the suspect ("If he is that confident, he must have good reason [evidence]"), and it undermines the suspect's confidence in his ability to convince the detective (and hence others) of his innocence, thereby contributing to the sense that "resistance is futile." Further, it may contribute to the development of false internalized belief in one's guilt.

Social Proof. A particularly potent heuristic route to persuasion is the powerful human tendency to evaluate the correctness of an opinion through *social comparison*—that is, through comparison of one's opinion to those of others (e.g., Festinger, 1954). Others' support of the belief is regarded as *social proof*. In other words, we evaluate whether a particular action or belief is correct by finding out what other people think is correct—and we are particularly likely to use this *social consensus heuristic* route to belief when uncertain ourselves or when unwilling or unable to engage in more systematic processing (see review in Cialdini, 2001).

As Cialdini (2001) so eloquently describes it, the effectiveness of social proof is widely recognized by hucksters and businesses alike—as reflected in such strategies as the use of canned laughter for television shows, enthusiastic shills in public events or religious revivals, salting collection baskets and tip jars with apparent donations from others, or advertisers' descriptions of their products as the "fastest-growing" or "best-selling" product on the market.

Interrogators commonly employ the principle of social proof. Inbau and colleagues (2001), for example, specifically recommend what might be called an "illusory" social proof tactic designed to lend greater weight to the interrogator's confidence in the suspect's guilt and claims of strong evidence against him.

> Note that in the example of a direct confrontation, the investigator referred to "our" investigation. This carries the implication that several investigators have contributed evidence to the case and also share in the belief of the suspect's guilt. The statement, therefore, is more impressive than if the investigator merely had said: "It looks like you broke into . . ." or "I believe that you started that fire." (p. 220)

The investigator may also offer social proof through claims regarding testimony of either coperpetrators or other witnesses. The suspect might be told that others have confessed and implicated him, that a witness has testified against him—or the police may stage a spontaneous "lineup" in which a witness identifies him. Although often effective in eliciting true confessions from guilty suspects (e.g., Ofshe & Leo, 1997a), evidence exists to suggest that such tactics can be effective with innocent suspects as well.

Saul Kassin and Katherine Kiechel (1996; see also Forest, Wadkins, & Miller, 2002; Horselenberg, Merckelbach, & Josephs, 2003; Redlich & Goodman, 2003 for replications and extensions) devised a laboratory situation in which subjects could be falsely accused of an offense against the experimenter. Subjects were led to perform a computer task but were warned not to touch the ALT key, which would allegedly cause the computer to malfunction and erase all the experimenter's data. A confederate of the experimenter read a list of letters that the subject was to type in as quickly as possible. After 60 seconds, the computer appeared to crash and the apparently frantic experimenter rushed in to accuse the subject of having caused the crash (although all were actually innocent).

The authors varied two factors relevant to the principle of social proof. The first was the participant's *vulnerability*—or certainty regarding his or her innocence. This was done by varying the speed at which letters had to be entered (either 43 or 67 per minute). Presumably, the demands of working more quickly would render participants less able to monitor or remember key strokes—and therefore less certain of whether they may have accidentally hit the forbidden key. The second was the presentation of false testimony from the confederate. For half of the participants, the confederate said she saw the participant hit the forbidden key; for the other half, she said she did not see what happened.

Insisting that the participant had indeed committed the offense, the apparently extremely upset experimenter attempted to cause the participant to sign a handwritten confession. Subsequently, as participants left the lab, they encountered another confederate ostensibly waiting to participate in the experiment who asked about what had happened. Replies to this inquiry were coded in terms of whether participants apparently internalized and accepted the blame for the crash or not. Finally, the experimenter came out to ask the participants to return to the lab to see if they could reconstruct how and when they had hit the ALT key. This was done to see if they would manufacture details to fit the allegation.

Overall, the majority of participants signed the confession. However, the group of participants who were least certain of the keys they hit (those in the faster-paced group) *and* who were confronted with a false witness were most likely to confess (100%), to describe themselves as actually guilty to the confederate (65%), and to confabulate false details of how they had committed the offense (35%). Further, just as expected, the effect of the false witness was strongest when the falsely accused participant could be least certain of his or her innocence. Hence, Kassin and Ketchel's results clearly lend support to the proposition that the testimony of others can influence beliefs regarding one's own behavior—and willingness to confess to alleged misdeeds of which one is actually innocent.

The Importance of Quantity. Quantity, in various forms, tends to be perceived as an important cue to quality—ranging from the number of persons who endorse a product or position, the number of positive features it possesses, the number of items of evidence supporting an argument or alleged feature of a product, to the number of times one is exposed to a product or assertion. Since these aspects of quantity are often in reality associated with quality, they are often used as heuristic proxies for actual evidence of quality.

NUMBER OF SUPPORTERS. We have already discussed the heuristic of social proof. However, there is also evidence that the *social impact* of social proof becomes greater as a function of larger numbers of supporters for a particular position (e.g., Latane & Wolf, 1981). Hence, to the extent the detective offers multiple sources of evidence (such as other detectives) or witnesses (fact witnesses and other suspects) to support his confidence in the suspect's guilt, the suspect is likely to become more convinced of the hopelessness of convincing others of his innocence.

NUMBER OF ITEMS OF EVIDENCE. A clever study by Alba and Marmorstein (1987) illustrated the way in which the number (rather than quality) of items of evidence can exert disproportionate influence under conditions that encourage heuristic processing. Participants in their study were to choose one of two comparably priced cameras. Twelve features of each camera were presented in such a way that some participants were exposed to each feature for 2 seconds (allowing insufficient time for elaborative processing), others for 5 seconds (allowing more time for elaborative processing), and others for as long as they chose. Brand A was described as superior on just three of the twelve features—but the three were the most important (e.g., quality of the pictures). Brand B was described as superior on eight features—but these were relatively unimportant features (such as the presence of a shoulder strap). When given unlimited time to consider each feature, two-thirds of participants chose the better camera (with fewer but more crucial superior features), whereas only 38 percent of those given 5 seconds, and 17 percent of those given 2 seconds, did so. That is, the less time participants were given to consider the importance of each feature (the quality of the feature as evidence of superiority), the more they were affected by the number of features for which the camera was superior to its competitor (the number of pieces of evidence of superiority).

Similarly, number may become more important when heuristic processing is encouraged by lack of motivation for elaborative processing. Petty and Cacioppo (1984), for example, showed that for personally important issues (more likely to elicit elaborative processing), persuasion was affected by both the quality and number of arguments. High-quality arguments were more persuasive than low-quality arguments; and more high-quality arguments enhanced persuasion, whereas more low-quality arguments reduced it. In contrast, for issues with little personal relevance (more likely to elicit heuristic processing), persuasion was unaffected by argument quality—but was enhanced by greater numbers of both high- and low-quality arguments. To the extent that either characteristics of the suspect or of the interrogative situation prevent elaborative processing, the suspect will suffer enhanced susceptibility to influence via the sheer number of poor-quality arguments or evidence.

NUMBER OF CLAIMS. Even simple numerical *claims* may enhance persuasion—"There are 300 reasons you should confess," "Thirty thousand Americans have received relief by using this product" (Musweiler, 2000, 2002).

LENGTH. A related heuristic—*length equals strength*—leads those on the heuristic route to find longer messages more persuasive, regardless of quality (e.g., Caples, 1974; Ogilvy, 1983; Petty & Cacioppo, 1984). Since a primary interrogative strategy is to command the floor for long periods with tactics including the presentation of multiple items of evidence—some or all of it fabricated—susceptibility to the heuristic cue of length may contribute substantially to the suspect's perception of the strength of evidence against him and thereby to his evaluation of the wisdom of confession.

NUMBER OF REPETITIONS: FAMILIARITY AND THE "TRUTH EFFECT." People tend to rate familiar or often-repeated statements or claims as being more valid and believable than those presented less often (Arkes, Hackett, & Boehm, 1989; Boehm, 1994; Hertwig, Gigerenzer, & Hoffrage, 1997)—an effect known in the marketing and advertising literature as the *truth effect*. This tendency is assumed to result from the increasing sense of familiarity resulting from repetition combined with increased reliance on less effortful heuristic processing and failure of source memory (failure to remember whether the source of the information was credible). Presumably as a result of impairments in cognitive processing resources (including source memory), older persons are more susceptible to this effect (Law, Hawkins, & Craik, 1998), suggesting that older suspects may be more persuaded by oft-repeated claims, whether backed by good evidence or not. To the extent processing resources are similarly impaired by interrogation-related stresses, suspects may suffer enhanced susceptibility to the truth effect and thereby become susceptible to belief in frequently repeated accusations and evidence presented by interrogators.

Summary. A variety of heuristic cues are embodied in police interrogation tactics, substantially increasing the persuasive power of the interrogation. It should be noted, however, that persuasion that occurs via the peripheral or heuristic route is substantially less permanent, less likely to be reflected in behavior, and less resistant to counterpersuasion than influence that occurs via the careful elaborative processing of the central route (e.g., Chaiken, 1980; Mackie, 1987; Petty, Haugtvedt, & Smith, 1995; Petty & Wegener, 1998). It is not surprising, then, that confessions are so frequently retracted immediately after the interrogation is finished (see Ofshe & Leo, 1997a,b; Gudjonsson, 2003). Freed of the pressures of the interrogation, the person returns to central processing only to realize that confession was not wise (the guilty suspect), not valid (the innocent suspect), or both.

Omega Strategies: Overcoming Resistance to Influence

Although some suspects are eager to confess to their own (and even others') crimes, most suspects—innocent or guilty—will vigorously resist confession. The successful interrogator must therefore be the master of tactics for overcoming resistance. He must understand where resistance comes from and be able to overcome it at every step. Hence, before turning to consideration of the tactics for overcoming resistance, we first review the foundations of resistance (see Wegener, Petty, Dove, & Fabrigar, in press, for review of the foundations of resistance).

Sources of Resistance to Influence

Characteristics of Existing Attitudes and Beliefs. All attitudes are not equally resistant to persuasion. Generally, *stronger* attitudes are more resistant to change. A number of theorists have offered classifications of the properties characterizing strong attitudes (e.g., see reviews in Bassili, 1996; Boninger, Krosnick, & Berent, 1995; Brinol, Rucker, Tormala, & Petty, in press; Fuegen & Brehm, in press; Krosnick, Boninger, Chuang, Berent, & Carnot, 1993; Petty & Krosnick, 1995; Pomeranz, Chaiken, & Tordesillas, 1995; Wood, Rhodes, & Biek, 1995; Tormala & Petty, in press). We review several of the most pertinent of these, all of which are associated with enhanced resistance to change. As we will see, the attitudes underlying the innocent person's resistance to confession possess all of the features most strongly associated with attitude strength and resistance to persuasion—as do those of a guilty person who resists confession.

DIRECT EXPERIENCE. Attitudes formed on the basis of direct experience are more resistant to persuasion than those formed as a result of receiving relevant information (e.g., Wu & Shaffer, 1987). For example, one's opinion of a particular beer is stronger and more resistant to persuasion based on tasting it rather than on hearing the opinions of others. The innocent person faced with an interrogator's accusations has a variety of strong attitudes based firmly in experience. First, he knows he did not commit the crime. He has the experiences associated with what he *was doing* to contradict the accusation that he was committing the crime instead. Second, he has experience with his own memory to tell him that he would have remembered such a behavior had he committed it (although confidence in one's memory can vary as a function of both personality and circumstance). Third, he has experience with his own behavioral tendencies and, based on this, strongly held beliefs concerning what kinds of behaviors he will or will not perform. Fourth, he may have a long history of behaviors and feelings experienced in association with the alleged victim that form the basis of opinions regarding likely behavior toward that person. These and other relevant experience-based knowledge and beliefs form the basis of substantial resistance to persuasion that he actually did commit the crime. The guilty person may also have substantial experience in the legal system suggesting that confession is unwise.

IMPORTANCE. An attitude is considered personally *important* to the extent the individual cares deeply about, or has a vested interest in, the issue. Vested interest can be the result of either outcomes tied to the attitude (such as belief in the value of stock in which one has invested heavily), of the relationship of the attitude to valued social identities or group memberships, or of the relationship of the attitude to fundamental values. Clearly, the innocent suspect is personally invested and cares deeply about the issue of his innocence, and both guilty and innocent suspects will view the potential consequences of confession as well as the consequences of the crime for self-esteem, social identity, and social reactions from others as important.

It should be noted, however, that even though fundamental values are often more resistant to attack, they can be surprisingly vulnerable when the person does not possess substantial information to support and defend them against attack. Since some fundamental values (and very strong beliefs) are simply taken for granted and are rarely subject to attack, the person may possess no armament of evidence and arguments to support them and no experience with defending them: Hence, the person can find it difficult to defend these values when subjected to strong arguments or criticisms (e.g., McGuire & Papageorgis, 1961; Bernard, Maio, & Olson, 2003). The suspect who is confronted for the first time with an attack on the validity of his self-conceptions (as innocent), memory, or concepts of the legal system may have no armament of arguments and evidence to counter the attack.

INTENSITY. *Intensity* refers to the strength of emotion or feeling attached to the attitude in question (Fuegen & Brehm, in press). Clearly, a falsely accused suspect will have substantial emotion attached to belief in his innocence, as will the guilty suspect to beliefs regarding confession. Further, emotion- and value-based attitudes are very difficult to change via logic-based appeals (e.g., Sherman & Kim, 2002). Cognitively based attitudes are most effectively changed by rational logic-based appeals, whereas more emotional or affectively based attitudes are most effectively changed with emotional or value-based appeals (Edwards, 1990; Edwards & vonHippel, 1995; Fabrigar & Petty, 1999; Shavitt, 1989). Thus, to be effective in changing such attitudes, interrogation tactics must successfully diffuse emotion-based resistance or arouse other emotions with potential to promote confession.

The Reid nine steps of interrogation (see Inbau et al., 2001; Table 36.1) include separate instructions for how to handle emotional versus nonemotional suspects. Essentially, recommended tactics for emotional suspects consist of using the suspect's guilt, anxiety, needs to save face, and moral values to promote confession. Those for nonemotional suspects focus more strongly on evidence of guilt to convince suspects they are hopelessly caught, and on manipulation of suspects' perceptions of the consequences of resistance versus confession.

COMMITMENT. Resistance to persuasion is also fostered by *commitment* to the initial attitude (e.g., Pomeranz, Chaiken, & Tordesillas, 1995; Visser & Krosnick, 1998). That is, when (1) the person is more certain or confident the attitude is correct (Petty, Brinol, & Tormala, 2002; Tormala & Petty, in press), and (2) more sure he or she won't change it, (3) the position is more extreme (Fuegen & Brehm, in press), and (4) the person has publicly announced the position, the person is then considered more *committed* to the attitude or position. Just as the innocent person possesses substantial direct experience supporting his belief in his own innocence, he is also typically firmly committed to those beliefs. That is, he begins the interrogation with complete confidence in his total innocence (and his ability to convince others of it), cannot possibly imagine that he would change his mind, and repeatedly and publicly (to all he can) asserts his innocence. A guilty person may also be firmly committed to the position that confession is completely undesirable rather than to firm belief in innocence—and may have made a number of overt claims of innocence.

In recognition of the power of public commitment to fuel resistance to persuasion, the Inbau and colleagues (2001) interrogation manual specifically recommends strategies that prevent the suspect from overtly voicing too many statements of innocence (p. 229). The authors believe the suspect will be most willing to confess when it is possible to save face. Hence, the suspect who has made repetitious denials may find it impossible to reverse himself without substantial loss of face.

Embeddedness. An attitude or belief that is firmly *embedded* in (connected to) other strongly held attitudes and beliefs is much more resistant to persuasion—since changing this target attitude would require changes in the vast array of other knowledge, beliefs, attitudes, values, self-conceptions, social identities, and so on to which it might be related (Visser & Krosnick, 1998). An innocent person's conviction of his innocence is likely to be highly embedded in other strongly held beliefs—such as those regarding himself, the type of person he is, or the operation of memory—that are wholly inconsistent with the idea of guilt. Further, the suspect may hold a number of beliefs inconsistent with the idea that confession is wise under any circumstances—even if guilty.

Part and parcel of the concept of embeddedness is the extensiveness of knowledge in which the target attitude is embedded. Thus, one source of attitude strength is knowledge of the target area (e.g., Wood, Rhodes, & Biek, 1995). It is much more difficult to persuade a person to change a belief when that belief is embedded in a wide range of relevant knowledge—in part because knowledge increases the ability to critically evaluate persuasive messages (as we shortly discuss). In the interrogation context, knowledge of one's real activities (and, if guilty, evidence possibly left behind), of the technology relevant to police claims, of police tactics, and of long-term legal ramifications can all fuel resistance to deceptive police tactics.

Also central to the concept of embeddedness is the relationship of a given attitude or belief to the individual's social world—including his own social identities (e.g., father, professional, Christian, etc.) and his beliefs regarding how important others view the issues in question. Modern *expectancy-value* approaches to the relationship between attitudes and behavior (e.g., Ajzen, 1985, 1996; Fishbein & Ajzen, 1975) suggest that behavior is determined by the expected outcomes associated with the behavior (including social reactions of important others) and the value the individual attaches to those outcomes. Thus, the stronger or more important the anticipated social outcomes associated with a behavior (e.g., the embeddedness of an attitude in social identity/social approval concerns), the more influence such anticipated outcomes will have on behavior.

Confession to a crime is almost uniformly associated with both anticipated and actual negative legal outcomes, negative self-definitions, and negative social reactions of immense magnitude (e.g., Gudjonsson, 2003). Thus, as reviewed earlier, interrogators must employ tactics to distract attention from such concerns; to redefine the moral implications (and therefore implications for social reactions, self-concept, and by implication legal consequences) of the crime; to redirect focus to the immediate rather than extended social network and to immediate rather than long-term social consequences; and/or to deceive the suspect regarding likely long-term consequences (e.g., Ofshe & Leo, 1997a). The Inbau and colleagues (2001) manual instructs investigators that the recommended tactics do not communicate probable legal consequences. In fact, however, suspects are unlikely to fail to notice the pragmatic implications of such tactics as lengthy investigator theme development, whereby the investigator is instructed to help the suspect save face by redefining the moral repugnance of the crime. For example, he may tell the suspect he really needs to know why the suspect committed the crime—and that he wouldn't even want to waste his time on the suspect if it turns out the suspect committed theft out of simple greed but that it would be important to know if he had stolen to feed his family. Indeed, such redefinition tactics do produce expectations of less harsh legal consequences (see Kassin & McNall, 1991).

SUMMARY. It is difficult to imagine attitudes that would be stronger and more resistant to persuasion that the belief of an innocent person in his or her innocence. Even the belief of a guilty person that confession is unwise is likely to be unusually strong. Hence, the interrogator is faced with the necessity to *unfreeze* (e.g., Schein, Schneier, & Barker, 1961) these beliefs before he can hope to change them. Typically, this is accomplished through techniques designed (1) to convince the suspect that he has been successfully caught (or, if innocent, framed); (2) if needed, to provide an explanation of how the person could have committed the crime without remembering it; (3) to uncouple the commission of the crime from the person's strongly held self-views by providing *themes* (Inbau et al., 2001) that would render the crime less morally repugnant; and (4) to alter perceptions of the consequences of confession (Gudjonsson, 1992a; Kassin, 1997b; Ofshe & Leo, 1997a). Once the innocent person is convinced that he could have (or must have) committed the crime, the investigator can hope to convince him that he did commit it. Alternatively, once the guilty person is convinced that exoneration is unlikely and that confession is not always unwise, the investigator can hope to convince him it is the best alternative in his case. The latter goals are typically accomplished through presentation of false information and evidence designed to convince the person both that the police have proof of guilt and that confession will result in more favorable outcomes (moral, social, or legal) than denial. These goals are facilitated by interrogation procedures that actively impair the suspect's analytical and decision-making capabilities.

Active Processing Mechanisms and Resistance to Persuasion. Resistance to persuasion occurs largely through the ability to discount information inconsistent with current beliefs. In turn, the process of discounting occurs largely through three mechanisms: (1) control over attention and exposure to consistent versus inconsistent information, (2) active critical analysis and evaluation of incoming information, and (3) biased processing of attitude-inconsistent information.

SELECTIVE ATTENTION AND EXPOSURE. Persuasion research has documented a tendency toward *selective attention and exposure* to attitude-consistent information (e.g., Festinger, 1964; Jonas, Schulz-Hardt, Frey, & Thelen, 2001). In unrestrained circumstances, the person may choose to divert attention from inconsistent information when exposed to it or to avoid materials, circumstances, or persons expected to present such information. Further, in response to counterattitudinal information or persuasive attempts, the person can seek out information to check on the attitude-inconsistent claims or to support current attitudes—from additional social or nonsocial sources.

Police interrogations, however, are designed explicitly to prevent escape—either from the interrogation itself or from attention to the relentless police accusations and attempts to elicit a confession. Among the most important of such tactics, of course, are those designed to induce the suspect to waive his *Miranda* rights and undergo interrogation without the presence of an attorney, family member, or other potential sources of information supporting resistance to confession (e.g., Leo, 2001; Leo & White, 1999). If the suspect fails to assert his *Miranda* rights to remain silent and/or to have an attorney present, resistance to influence through avoidance of the interrogation itself is not effective, and voluntary seeking of relevant additional information to check on or evaluate police claims is not possible.

ACTIVE ELABORATIVE PROCESSING. The second active mechanism of resistance to persuasion is *active elaborative processing* of information. The cognitive response approach to persuasion suggests that the best predictor of change in response to persuasive communication lies not in the content of the persuasive message itself, but rather in the thoughts the target generates in response to the message (e.g., Greenwald, 1968; Petty & Cacioppo, 1986). Such thoughts (i.e., elaborative processing) may be either positive or negative in content, but *resistance* to persuasion is facilitated by critical evaluation of information and production of *counterarguments*. That is, the person may carefully process the information and critique its accuracy by noticing inconsistencies in the information itself, retrieving inconsistent information from long-term memory, perceiving flaws in the arguments or evidence presented, or discerning indications of dishonesty. The information retrieved from memory, inconsistencies and flaws noticed in the incoming information, and cues of dishonesty become the basis of counterarguments against the position being advocated.

The importance of elaborative processing of incoming information cannot be overemphasized—particularly with respect to its role in resistance to persuasion and particularly in the context of police interrogation. Suspects in criminal interrogations are faced with a great deal of false information—ranging from the nature of the options open to them to the evidence available to police. To resist pressure to confess, the suspects must have the wherewithal both to recognize flaws and falsity in that information and to integrate these assessments into their judgments and decisions (which, as we will shortly see, interrogation tactics are designed to impair).

THE TRUTHFULNESS BIAS. In the absence of careful scrutiny of incoming information, we tend to simply consider it true—an effect known as the *truthfulness bias*. Research on detection of deception has consistently shown that perceivers are biased toward believing others are telling the truth, even when they are not (e.g., DePaulo, Stone, & Lassiter, 1985; Zuckerman, DePaulo, & Rosenthal,

1981). This truthfulness presumption also extends to other sources of information (e.g., Gilbert et al., 1990, 1993).

The truthfulness bias is presumed to result from a dual-process sequence in which information is first simultaneously understood and believed, then subsequently corrected if necessary (e.g., Spinoza, 1677/1982; Gilbert, 1991, 1993). The philosopher Benedict Spinoza was first to propose this sequence—arguing that understanding and believing are simply two different words for the same mental operation. Spinoza presumed people to first believe all information they understand, but then, in a second reconsideration stage, to evaluate the information in light of relevant evidence—and to *unbelieve* information inconsistent with other knowledge. This proposition has been strongly supported by modern research on information processing, persuasion, and social judgment. In particular, this research has shown that when people are exposed to information under conditions that prevent elaborative processing, true information is still perceived as true, whereas false information is less likely to be recognized as false (e.g., Gilbert, Krull, & Malone, 1990; Gilbert, Tafarodi, & Malone, 1993). In other words, elaborative processing is not necessary to believe—only to "unbelieve."

This dual process has been shown with respect to information about oneself as well. Knowles and Condon (1999), for example, showed that subjects asked whether certain traits or descriptions applied to them when under a distracting cognitive load were more likely to answer "yes" than those not under such a distracting load. Thus, even suggestions regarding the self tend to be immediately accepted as true until corrected through more elaborative thought.

More generally, initial impressions of incoming information (social or otherwise), which may be biased by schemas, prejudices, presumptions, or other sources of *default assumptions*, are more likely to remain uncorrected under circumstances that inhibit more controlled elaborative processing (e.g., Chen & Chaiken, 1999; Devine, 1989; Kruglanski & Webster, 1996; Petty & Cacioppo, 1986; Petty & Wegener, 1999). In other words, if a person is prevented in any way from engaging in the second step of active evaluation of incoming information (particularly false information), he or she is more likely to accept it as true.

Unfortunately, the active evaluation stage is much more deliberative and effortful, and thus more easily disrupted by both situational and personal forces that impair cognitive resources or control. Hence, it is of interest to examine both personal and situational factors likely to impair elaborative processing—particularly those relevant to the interrogation setting—as they will in turn affect the suspect's ability to resist coercive influence. Two personal factors are assumed to promote active elaborative processing of information: (1) motivation, and (2) ability (see Chaiken, 1987; Petty & Caccioppo, 1986). We first consider these, then turn to situational determinants of elaborative processing.

MOTIVATION FOR ELABORATIVE PROCESSING. Motivation to carefully analyze information is a function of both individual differences such as personality variables (for example, *need for cognition*—the tendency to enjoy and engage in deliberative thought; e.g., Cacioppo, Petty, Feinstein, & Jarvis, 1996), or personal interest or involvement in the topic at hand (e.g., Petty, Cacioppo, & Goldman, 1981) and situational factors such as task importance or need for accuracy (e.g., Darke, Chaiken, Bohner, Einwiller, Erb, & Hazelwood, 1998; see reviews in Chen & Chaiken, 1999; Kruglanski & Webster, 1996; Petty & Cacioppo, 1986; Petty & Wegener, 1999). Those high in need for cognition, those for whom the issues are personally relevant or interesting, and those who need to hold accurate opinions on a particular issue in a particular circumstance tend to more carefully evaluate the quality and accuracy of arguments and evidence presented in support of a particular argument or course of action. Thus, it can be expected that a suspect facing interrogation and the myriad consequences of confession will be very high in motivation to carefully evaluate the arguments and evidence presented by the police. The issues of guilt, confession, and their potential consequences for the suspect's foreseeable future are clearly of extreme personal importance and interest. Given such consequences, the suspect will be highly motivated to accurately evaluate and choose among the various options open to him.

Motivation to carefully evaluate information may also derive from sheer desire to resist influence. In these circumstances, however, motivation to carefully evaluate information may become simply motivation to discount and resist the information—hence leading the person to engage in strenuous overt or covert counterarguing, thereby reducing persuasion. *Reactance theory* (Brehm, 1966) suggests that an individual who feels his freedom to believe or act as he chooses is threatened will tend to act in a manner that will restore that freedom. With respect to coercive influence attempts, restoration of a sense of freedom would occur through even more firm belief in, and commitment to, the original belief or behavior.

Motivation to resist influence is also affected by *liking* of the source of influence (see review in Cialdini, 2001), such that motivation to resist disliked sources is much higher. Thus, coercive persuasive attempts, particularly from a disliked source, can result in a *boomerang effect* whereby the original attitude or commitment to the originally planned course of action becomes even more extreme (e.g., Pennebaker & Sanders, 1976).

Police engaging in inherently coercive influence tactics will be at high risk of engendering both dislike and reactance. Hence, in order to avoid these effects and the resistance sure to accompany them, interrogation tactics are designed to create a more positive bond between the interrogator and suspect and to disguise their coercive nature.

ABILITY TO PROCESS ELABORATIVELY. Elaborative processing requires not only *motivation* to carefully evaluate incoming information, but also the *ability* to do so. Two general abilities are necessary: (1) ability to *understand* the information presented, and (2) ability to *critically evaluate* the information. Both, in turn, are dependent upon two general facets of the individual in question—intelligence and topic-relevant knowledge—and upon the ability to use these personal strengths in the circumstances in which the information is encountered (see review in Petty & Cacioppo, 1986).

The importance of topic-relevant knowledge has been illustrated in the context of police interrogations in that those who have had previous experience with the criminal justice system are less likely to confess than those who have not (Inbau et al., 2001; Ofshe & Leo, 1997a). Presumably, experienced felons are no longer fooled by police claims of sympathy, desire to help, fabricated evidence, and other deceptive tactics because they have direct knowledge of the falsity of specific claims of benevolent intent as well as of the general tendency toward falsification of evidence. General intelligence, analytical ability, and nonverbal decoding skills also allow the suspect to better understand the information, identify flaws in evidence and arguments, and detect deception. It is crucial to note, however, that neither knowledge nor abilities will enhance critical appraisal of information if circumstances prevent their use. Hence, in later sections we consider omega influence tactics, including strategies that disrupt critical elaborative processing.

Motivated Denial

For a man always believes more readily that which he prefers.
Francis Bacon (1620/1955, p. 111)

Much resistance to a particular belief or action is motivated by the sheer initial magnitude of its unattractiveness, unpleasantness, or discrepancy from the target's initial preference. The person may simply not want to believe or behave in the suggested manner. This desire motivates rejection of the influence attempt and may lead the person not only to refuse to budge, but also to engage in biased processing of the evidence relevant to the new belief or behavior. For example, people exposed to an influence attempt consistent with their current preferences tend to ask the question "Can I believe this?" and often engage in heuristic processing while failing to systematically inspect it for flaws. In contrast, those exposed to preference-inconsistent information tend to ask the question "Must I believe this?" and search for weaknesses and for counterarguments against it (see review in Dawson, Gilovich, & Regan, 2002).

Recall that investigators are trained to use emotions and motivation to their advantage. Essentially, they are trained to override the resistance fueled by motivations promoting denial—such as fear of jail—with other, more powerful fears and anxieties that promote confession—for example, fear of the death penalty.

Omega Strategies for Overcoming Resistance

Given the multiple sources of resistance that may otherwise derail the persuader's influence attempt, influence is best achieved via methods that incorporate both alpha and omega strategies, sweeping away resistance even as they offer compelling reasons for change.

Sidestep Resistance. Clearly, the most effective strategy to avoid the effects of resistance is to avoid raising it in the first place (Knowles & Linn, in press). Hence, a number of *omega strategies* are designed to avoid, minimize, or divert resistance.

WOLF IN SHEEP'S CLOTHING: DISGUISE PERSUASIVE INTENT. Resistance tends to begin as soon as the person is aware of the persuasive intent of another. For example, overheard communications (which are not intended to persuade the eavesdropper) are more persuasive that those directly addressed to him (which are intended to persuade; e.g., Walster & Festinger, 1962). Moreover, when forewarned that they will shortly hear a message inconsistent with their current attitudes, participants begin to develop *anticipatory counterarguments* before the speech begins (see reviews in Cialdini & Petty, 1981; Wood & Quinn, in press). Resistance is further enhanced if the anticipated influence attempt is perceived as favoring the speaker's interest and/or as potentially against one's own interest. In contrast, persuasion is enhanced if an action, argument, or admission is perceived as against the persuader's own self-interest (see review in Pratkanis & Aronson, 2001). To enhance persuasion, then, the persuader can disguise the true intent and personal interests (his own and those of his target) that would be affected by target compliance.

One strategy is to hide the true persuasive intent and persuasive goals of the interaction, or to *redefine the relationship* (Knowles & Linn, in press) as cooperative rather than adversarial. This principle is embodied in the common recommendation to salespersons to redefine the sales interaction as a cooperative interaction intended to identify and satisfy the best interests of the customer (Alessandra, 1993; Jolson, 1997; Knowles & Linn, in press; Straight, 1996). The salesperson is thereby identified as working in favor of the customer's best interest rather than his or her own, and thus resistance is not aroused by the perceived need to defend oneself against unwanted influence.

Not surprisingly, modern interrogation tactics are designed in part to accomplish just such a redefinition of roles, as noted earlier. This is first accomplished through disguising the true intent of the initial interview (for example, by asking the suspect's help as a witness as opposed to arresting him for interrogation). Later, when the suspect's status is made known, the interrogator presents himself as trying to help the suspect achieve the most favorable outcome for himself (i.e., ostensibly acting in the suspect's best interests) rather than as simply attempting to secure an arrest and conviction (i.e., actually acting in the suspect's worst interests).

Inbau and colleagues (2001) explained this strategy as follows:

> A central component of this tactic is for the investigator to "argue against self-interest." . . . the investigator should not appear anxious to get the suspect to confess or portray to the suspect that a confession is necessary in order to resolve the case. Quite to the contrary, the investigator wants to present the interrogation as an opportunity for the suspect to explain his side of the story or to offer the reasons for his commission of the crime." (p. 290)

The authors go on to provide an analogy with professional salespersons: "By removing himself from any personal benefit resulting from the customer's decision to buy his product, he tremendously increases, in the customer's mind, the few benefits his product offers. A forthcoming sale is likely" (p. 291). Hence, the investigator is advised to make such statements as, "Whether or not you acknowledge your involvement makes no difference to me; the evidence will speak for itself! My only reason for spending this time with you is to give you the opportunity to explain why this thing happened" (p. 291). In this way, the goals of the interaction are redefined as helpful to the suspect, rather than to the investigator.

THE BORG MANEUVER: "RESISTANCE IS FUTILE". Psychologist Elliot Aronson dubbed psychological and behavioral reactions to a sense of futility the *psychology of inevitability* and reviewed evidence to suggest that once an outcome is certain, cognitive and motivational forces are engaged to promote acceptance, compliance, and even approval of the unavoidable situation (Aronson, 1999). Motivational principles are central to theories of learned helpless (Seligman, 1975), self-efficacy (Bandura, 1997), and the theory of planned behavior (Ajzen, 1985). All such theories recognize that attempts to behave in a particular manner (or seek a particular outcome) are determined not only by the desirability of the behavior or outcome, but also by perceptions of one's *ability* to achieve success. A person is more likely to try when expecting success.

Police interrogators recognize that the decision to confess will typically be based, at least in part, on the suspect's expectations regarding both short- and long-term consequences of resistance versus confession. In recognition of the natural tendency for the suspect to try to optimize his outcomes, the investigator must strive to tilt the suspect's cost-benefit scale toward confession. To accomplish this goal, investigators make full use of the Borg maneuver and the psychology of inevitability.

Most central to a suspect's cost-benefit analysis of confession is subjective likelihood of conviction and imprisonment. An innocent suspect is likely to begin with the assumption that imprisonment is impossible (or nearly impossible)—and even that being formally charged with the crime is highly unlikely. Unfortunately, many also believe that even if they confess, they will be cleared as soon as their lawyer becomes involved or a more extensive investigation gets underway (Gudjonnson, 2003; Ofshe & Leo, 1997a,b). Guilty suspects, on the other hand, will typically be less certain but nevertheless often hopeful or even confident that they will not be caught and convicted. Hence, the primary goal of the police interrogator is to overcome the suspect's confidence that he will be exonerated. Unfortunately, the tactics by which this is accomplished can lead both guilty and innocent suspects to conclude that their situation is hopeless and therefore that confession offers the least undesirable of a set of terrible choices (Gudjonnson, 2003; Kassin, 1997b; Ofshe & Leo, 1997a,b)—thereby causing a *coerced-compliant* confession (either true or false). Perhaps more perniciously, the same "evidence" that can lead the suspect to conclude he will certainly be *perceived* as guilty, and therefore almost certainly be *convicted* in court, can also sometimes convince an innocent suspect that he *is guilty*—and thereby cause a *coerced-internalized* false confession.

Essentially, police attempt to convince suspects that resistance is futile through three fundamental processes: (1) exaggeration or falsification of evidence (steps 1, 3), (2) invalidation of suspect claims and arguments (step 4), and (3) simple refusal to listen to suspects' points or acknowledge their validity (step 3).

These tactics are designed to affect the suspect's rational analysis of the situation. However, the interrogator proceeds with these strategies under conditions that both restrict access to other relevant information (via confinement, social isolation, and circumvention of *Miranda* rights) and compromise the suspect's ability to carefully analyze available information (via physical and stress-related impairment of cognitive processes)—as discussed in subsequent sections. And, in addition, the interrogator sometimes employs verbal tactics—such as rapid-fire accusations, multiple interrogators, and the like—that essentially distract the suspect or produce time constraints that further interfere with elaborative and critical analysis of the information presented. The result is that the suspect uses compromised cognitive resources to analyze flawed, restricted, and falsified information.

EXAGGERATION/FALSIFICATION OF EVIDENCE. Clearly the most effective way to convince a suspect that he will be convicted in court is to "prove" the case against him by presenting apparently incontrovertible evidence of guilt. Some detectives provide a great deal of evidence, although Inbau and colleagues (2001) suggest that one should present only parts of the evidence to avoid giving the suspect a picture of the full evidence (or lack thereof) against him. Instead, the detective should provide enough evidence to make the suspect insecure and confidently assert that much more is available or forthcoming.

Although the suspect will often either know or suspect the "evidence" offered by the detective is false, consistent with the principles of *authority* and *social proof*, the apparent credibility of the police, the alleged witnesses, the scientific tests, or other aspects of the "evidence" can cause suspects to both feel a sense of hopelessness regarding their ability to discredit the evidence, and/or cause innocent suspects to begin to doubt their own innocence.

A wide variety of evidence may be offered by police, often including exaggerated or falsified evidence. Where multiple suspects are arrested, the detective may claim that another has confessed and implicated the target. The detective may claim that an eyewitness identified the suspect and claimed to have witnessed the crime (or to have placed him at the scene, seen him argue with the victim, or to have witnessed other incriminating behaviors)—and in some cases may go so far as to stage an elaborate mock lineup and fake eyewitness identification (Gudjonnson, 2003; Ofshe & Leo, 1997a). The investigator may also stage an elaborate scenario designed to convince the suspect that his coperpetrators have confessed and implicated him (Reid step 2, tactic 5).

Many such false claims involve trace evidence such as hair, fingerprints, DNA, fibers, car tracks, and so on—and often are so clearly false that it defies imagination that suspects nevertheless believe it. In a recent Reno case, for example, I (Davis) was asked to evaluate the confession of a young man who was accused of molesting his $1\frac{1}{2}$-year-old daughter. Among many other false items of evidence, the detective told the young man that they had found his DNA (from saliva) on his daughter's vagina—notwithstanding the passage of more than one week between the alleged abuse and the DNA "test," a daily bath, and multiple diaper changes. Unfortunately, the young man was unable to discount the obviously false evidence. He never claimed to remember the abuse, but eventually (in light of claims of multiple items of false evidence) began to question himself and how he might have done such a thing without remembering it. The detective, of course, had a ready explanation.

Police may also induce the suspect to submit to a polygraph examination—which innocent suspects are often only too eager to agree to. Unfortunately, the suspect may actually fail the test, as many innocent suspects do (Lykken, 1998), or, if not, the police may falsely inform the suspect he has failed. These inaccurate (or inaccurately portrayed) results can either serve to convince the suspect that the results will make it difficult or impossible to avoid conviction—or, in some cases, to cause the person to falsely believe in his own guilt.

Coerced-internalized false confessions are caused almost fully in this manner (e.g., Gudjonnson, 2003). The suspect is presented with evidence that seems to prove his guilt, under conditions in which he lacks the cognitive resources and external information necessary to invalidate it. His objections are invalidated (or apparently invalidated) by the interrogator. Hence, he comes to believe he must have committed the crime. Depending upon the use of other tactics, he may also come to falsely "remember" committing the crime as well.

The words of Thomas Sawyer reflect exactly this process of internalized false belief in guilt. After a grueling 16-hour interrogation, Sawyer confessed to the brutal murder of his neighbor. Police presented Sawyer with a variety of false evidence and convinced him that even though he didn't remember it, he could have committed the crime in an alcoholic blackout. Finally, when Sawyer confessed, in a perfect illustration of the persuasive power of these tactics, he said "I guess all the evidence is in, I guess I must have done it" (Jerome, 1995).

Vulnerability to the effects of presentation of evidence is enhanced among those lacking either the motivation or ability to critically evaluate the evidence and arguments presented by police. Motivation may be compromised, for example, by trust in the honesty and motives of the police. Peter Reilly, who, as previously discussed, confessed falsely to the murder of his mother (Connery, 1977, 1995), knew and admired some police officers—and even considered a career in law enforcement—prior to the murder. His general admiration for police and trust in their motives and honesty rendered him particularly unlikely to disbelieve police claims of the meaning of a failed polygraph examination against him or the existence of the evidence they claimed against him. Some, often the less intelligent (e.g., Gudjonsson, 2003), may be more motivated to help or please the police than to protect themselves.

To the extent that careful scrutiny of interrogator arguments and evidence (central route processing) is impaired by personal or situational factors, the person becomes more susceptible to heuristic (peripheral route) processing (Petty & Cacioppo, 1986). In this mode the suspect will be less affected by the actual quality of the interrogator's arguments or evidence and more affected by heuristic cues—or shortcuts to determining accuracy, such as the likeability, credibility, or trustworthiness of the communicator or type of evidence; the investigator's confidence; the sheer number of "facts" the interrogator presents as evidence; or others who appear to believe the suspect is guilty.

PREVENT OR REFUTE SUSPECT COUNTERARGUMENTS. Given that the suspect has been accused of the crime and presented with apparently incontrovertible evidence against him, the next task of the investigator is to convince the suspect that he will neither be able to refute that evidence nor to convince anyone of his innocence. To accomplish this, the investigator must either prevent or refute counterarguments by the suspect. Steps 3 and 4 of the Reid method (see Table 36.1) are designed to accomplish these goals. Step 3 instructs interrogators to interrupt and prevent suspect denials. Step 4, in contrast, suggests that suspects' attempts to offer arguments or evidence to "prove" their innocence should be drawn out, refuted where possible, and generally used to catch them in lies or inconsistencies that can be used against them. The interrogator is never to show any doubt in the suspect's guilt as a result of the suspect's arguments. Instead, he is to reinforce the suspect for bringing it up but to discount the suspect's "proof" in some way, and then twist and reinterpret it to integrate it into his theme development such that it now provides support for the desirability of confessing.

Successful resistance to persuasion tends to increase certainty in one's initial position (e.g., Tormala & Petty, 2002), thereby fueling further resistance. Wisely, the interrogator's strategies are designed to prevent any sense of successful resistance on the part of the suspect. Instead, they collectively promote a sense of helplessness and futility.

THE BORG MANEUVER LAMDA: "LYING IS FUTILE". Part and parcel of the above tactics is the detective's insistence that lying is futile—as it will certainly be detected. The Inbau and colleagues (2001) manual recommends that detectives convey to the suspect that they possess sufficient evidence about what happened to detect when the suspect is lying. The sense that he will be caught in any lies is presumed to inhibit lying and promote truth telling.

Indeed, evidence exists to support this recommendation. The *Bogus Pipeline* procedure developed by Edward Jones and Harold Sigall (Jones & Sigall, 1971) employed essentially the "lying is futile!" strategy to induce subjects to more accurately report socially undesirable social attitudes—such as racial prejudices. Essentially, the procedure is set up to convince participants that the Bogus

Pipeline apparatus can read their true responses to the questions asked. Hence, any attempt at misrepresentation is seen as futile. Research using the procedure has shown it to increase willingness to report undesirable attitudes and destructive behaviors such as alcohol or drug use or smoking (e.g., Aguinis, Pierce, & Quigley, 1995; Gimenes & Adame, 2002) as well as to decrease overreporting of desirable behaviors such as exercise (Tourangeau, Simith, & Rasinski, 1997). In other words, when lying seems futile, truth tends to take its place.

MINIMIZE RESISTANCE: GRADUAL ESCALATION AND THE POWER OF THE FOOT IN THE DOOR. Clearly one cannot completely sidestep resistance from criminal suspects. Nonetheless, one may still minimize it. The *foot-in-the-door* technique (Freedman & Fraser, 1966) minimizes resistance by employing small incremental sequential requests. Compliance research (see review in Cialdini, 2001), as well as research on obedience to authority (see review in Blass, 2000) and submission to cult-related demands to give up one's identity and financial assets (see review in Pratkanis & Aronson, 2001), has shown that people who are first led to agree to a series of much smaller, less offensive, requests (come to the Saturday cult-group meeting) can be led to agree to much more disagreeable and larger requests (quit your job, give your total assets to the cult leader, commit mass suicide) than those who are not first led through the smaller requests.

The criminal suspect can be similarly led through a series of escalating demands for compliance—first with a request for a noncustodial interview as a "witness," later to come to the station to help the investigator, still later to waive *Miranda* rights and submit to an accusatory interrogation, and finally to tell the interrogator exactly how the crime was committed and to put it in writing. The investigator may also first seek to induce the suspect to make a series of minor admissions that ultimately build up to full confession—by first admitting to being at or near the scene of the crime, later by admitting to talking to the victim, still later by admitting to stealing from her and finally to raping her as well. Inbau and colleagues (2001) recommend this escalating sequence of admission, wisely recognizing that the suspect will resist each individual step much less strongly than admitting to the full details of the crime straightaway. Discussing the theme development tactic of suggesting a noncriminal intent behind the act, for example, the authors described its purpose as follows: "The objective of this approach is to initially have the suspect accept personal responsibility for the physical act in committing the crime as a stepping stone approach to eventually learning the complete truth" (p. 286).

Similarly, the authors view the foot-in-the-door principle as crucial to the success of the alternative-question tactic to minimize the perceived seriousness of an admission: "A person is more likely to make a decision once he has committed himself, in a small way, toward that decision. This is precisely what the alternative question accomplishes during an interrogation. It offers the guilty suspect the opportunity to start telling the truth by making a single admission" (p. 353).

DIVERTING RESISTANCE. Diversionary tactics are standard operating procedure for conflictual interactions. Boxers feint in one direction to draw the opponent's punch, only to attack from another as the opponent is drawn in. Military strategists may send a small diversionary force to attack a peripheral target to draw defense resistance away from the true objective. A gang of thieves may cause a diversion to draw attention away from the target or perpetrator of the theft. Across multiple contexts and countless objectives, diversionary tactics are used to draw resistance away from the true target to leave it more vulnerable to attack.

Analogous tactics can be effective with targets of influence. In some cases, resistance is sure to occur—as, for instance, with the suspect who realizes that the interrogator wishes him to confess. Yet resistance to the persuader or to the desired outcome can still be sidestepped through diverting it, in effect, to a decoy. The *good-cop, bad-cop* strategy employs this principle to focus resistance on the bad cop, leaving the suspect more receptive to the good cop. Inbau and colleagues (2001) also recommend the strategy of exaggerating victim/accuser claims against the suspect (theme 6, discussed earlier). This strategy can serve to redirect resistance to the victim/accuser, leading the suspect to comply with investigator goals simply to discredit the other's accounts.

This theme and the other framing and contrast techniques previously described as alpha strategies directly affect judgment of severity through perceptual contrast effects—but also operate through diversion of resistance. That is, by leading the suspect to consider whether he would rather confess and go to prison or resist and die in the electric chair, the interrogator in effect focuses resistance on the electric chair, rendering the suspect less resistant to life in prison.

DIVERT RESISTANCE THROUGH CONFUSION. Psychiatrist Milton Erickson developed a "conversational" approach to hypnosis that offered mechanisms to disrupt resistance to hypnotic induction (Erickson, 1964; Gilligan, 1987). Essentially the approach relied upon the idea that the target will develop expectations regarding the source, timing, and mechanism of attempted induction (influence)—and that he is thereby primed to resist that particular source and an influence attempt fitting his expectations. Erickson's technique involved the use of unexpected sources, timing, and mechanisms so that the target's primed forces of resistance were not adjusted in time to resist the unexpected persuasive assault. This "disruption" or "confusion" technique has proven to induce compliance effectively in a variety of persuasive contexts, including hypnotic induction (e.g., Rosen, 1991), panhandling (Santos, Leve, & Pratkanis, 1994), attitude change (e.g., Vallacher & Wegner, 1985), and sales (e.g., Davis & Knowles, 1999).

Although a police interrogator might employ variations of this technique throughout the interrogation, his basic demeanor provides a fundamental departure from the scripted expectations of many suspects. The novice offender, in particular, may expect an overbearing, hostile, and perhaps physically abusive interrogator rather than a pleasant, ingratiating, understanding collaborator who hopes to "help" the suspect out. Hence, resistance primed to target the expected "bad cop" is disrupted by the apparent "good-cop" presentation.

DEPERSONALIZE THE MESSAGE. Milton Erickson also reported use of illustrative narrative stories to illustrate a point with resistant patients (Erickson, Rossi, & Rossi, 1976; Rosen, 1991). Erickson would tell stories (essentially therapeutic "parables") ostensibly involving other uninvolved people and events but invoking the essential issues of the patient's problem and providing a potential solution to the predicament. This strategy essentially sidestepped the resistance the patient might show to direct personal interpretations and recommendations (see also Dal Cin, Zanna, & Fong, in press; Green, Strange & Brock, 2002, for discussion of the power of stories to sidestep resistance).

Inbau and colleagues (2001) recommended strategies for *theme development* prominently include such third-party storytelling. The investigator might tell the story of how and why another suspect got involved in a crime as a result of peer pressure, for example, as a means to offer the suspect the opportunity to save face for his own crime by blaming others who drew him into it. Often, such narratives are offered to show how similar criminal behavior—or at minimum the desire to engage in it—can "happen to anyone." The manual generally encourages the interrogator to tell stories of how he, other suspects, and/or the interrogator's friends, family, or acquaintances found themselves in similar situations to the one he thinks triggered the suspect's crime and to expand on the feelings, emotions, and crime-related thoughts they experienced.

Disable Cognitive Resources or Prevent Their Use. Perhaps the most effective and fundamental strategy for overcoming resistance to influence is disruption of the basic cognitive processing resources that form the foundation of resistance. Such a strategy affects not only resistance, but all processes crucial to rational decision making. Thus, in the following sections we consider the role of cognitive resources in the broader context of decision making—including their role in resistance to persuasion.

It should come as no surprise that effective rational decision making requires cognitive competence. Such competence includes at least two factors: intact cognitive resources and full and correct relevant information. Interrogation tactics are designed to directly constrain and falsify information the suspect considers, as noted earlier. Less obvious, however, is the fact that interrogation-related impairment of basic cognitive processing resources not only causes decrements in processing of available information, it also affects what information is available. That is, intact cognitive resources are necessary for the person (1) to access and retrieve all relevant information from memory, (2) to accurately and efficiently process and store new relevant information, (3) to carefully evaluate new information in the context of relevant existing knowledge and information, (4) to hold all relevant information in mind while evaluating alternative choices of action, and (5) to *control attentional processes* to inhibit retrieval of or attention to irrelevant information while successfully using appropriate relevant information. These abilities are crucial to rational decision making *and* to the ability to resist social influence.

Hence, it is not surprising that theoretical analyses of interrogation tactics have long since noted the role of impaired cognitive processes in susceptibility to influence and false confessions. Although largely unsupported by empirical research at the time, theoretical analyses of the "show" trials and public confessions in Stalin's Russia (e.g., Beck & Godin, 1951; Leites & Bernaut, 1954; Hinkle & Wolff, 1956) and the *coercive persuasion* and *thought reform* techniques employed on American military and civilian personnel by Chinese communists (e.g., Lifton, 1956; 1961; Schein, 1956; Schein, Schneier & Barker, 1961), for example, emphasized the role of physical torture or discomfort, exhaustion, sleep deprivation, social isolation, and the like in production of cognitive impairment, confusion, enhanced suggestibility, and inability to resist influence—and hence in facilitation of confession, extreme attitude and value change, and compliance with other demands of their captors. Confessions elicited by extremes of such tactics are currently excluded as involuntary by American courts (Kassin, 1997b). Nevertheless, modern police interrogation procedures are often conducted under circumstances creating extreme physical exhaustion, emotional distress, social isolation, disruption of critical thinking, and other physical and emotional reactions that tend to compromise cognitive functioning.

Research in both cognitive and social psychology has now accumulated to show that cognitive resources and/or the ability to use them are impaired by at least five factors characteristic of the interrogation setting: (1) physical exhaustion/sleep deprivation, (2) anxiety and emotional stress, (3) social isolation, (4) disruption of elaborative processing (such as distracting the suspect, interrupting suspect statements, rapid-fire accusations), and (5) time constraints on decision processes. Further, interrogations are sometimes conducted in the context of extreme emotions generated by the nature of the crime itself. When interrogated as suspects, for example, family and friends of victims may be suffering bereavement that in itself can compromise both the will and cognitive abilities necessary to resist a coercive interrogation.

It is interesting to note that while the effects of stresses inherent to the interrogation on decision making often go unrecognized, the law has recognized that those *external* to the interrogation can render a confession essentially involuntary. In *Commonwealth v. Crawford* (1999), a Massachusetts appellate court held that the trial court should have allowed testimony regarding battered woman syndrome and substance abuse to support the defendant's claim that her confession was involuntary.

SLEEP DEPRIVATION/PHYSICAL EXHAUSTION. Physical exhaustion is considered to be a strong contributor to stress-induced confessions as well as to coerced-internalized false confessions (e.g., Gudjonsson, 2003). Defendants in the New York jogger case had been held for up to 30 hours before their confessions. Peter Reilly, who confessed falsely to the murder of his mother, returned from an evening church meeting to find his mother dead. Already at the end of the day when he found his mother, Peter called the police, accompanied them to the station voluntarily, and was interrogated for another 16 hours before confessing. He was both physically and emotionally exhausted and was suffering in addition from the emotional aftermath of his mother's death (Connery, 1977).

Both cognitive and self-regulatory functions may be compromised by exhaustion, impairing in turn the person's ability or motivation to resist influence. Mark Blagrove (1996; Blagrove, Alexander, & Horne, 1995; Blagrove, Cole-Morgan & Lambe, 1994) suggested that sleep deprivation and exhaustion may lead to greater interrogative suggestibility via deficits in speed of thinking, concentration, motivation, confidence, ability to control attention, and ability to ignore irrelevant or misleading information. Although he did not test these mediating mechanisms, Blagrove and his colleagues did find enhanced interrogative suggestibility among relatively sleep-deprived subjects.

ANXIETY/EMOTIONAL STRESS. Anxiety and stress tend to disrupt cognitive processing in at least two ways: (1) through diversion of attention, and (2) through depletion of processing resources. Research on anxiety has consistently documented performance decrements for tasks demanding of cognitive resources (see review in Sengupta & Johar, 2001). Anxiety is presumed to engage cognitive resources in worrying, thus leaving less capacity for the task at hand. Sengupta & Johar (2001) also showed that high anxiety biased processing of persuasive messages such that heuristic cues carried more weight. Stress has been shown to impair working memory capacity (e.g., Klein & Boals, 2001). In turn, impairment of working memory capacity is related to increased susceptibility to misinformation effects (e.g., Jaschinski & Wentura, 2002) as well as a variety of general decrements in information processing (e.g., David & Loftus, in press). Indeed, Forest et al. (2002) found that pre-existing stress from watching emotionally aversive pictures increased the tendency for men to confess in Kassin and Kiechel's (1996) laboratory false confession paradigm (athough, strangely, they did not find this effect for women).

Two views of the effects of emotion on attention have been offered—one based on the redirection of attention toward *internal* events (emotions) and emotion-regulation (Pratkanis & Aronson, 2001), and the other based on allocation of attention among emotion producing versus peripheral *external* events (Christianson & Safer, 1996). The former view was reviewed previously as among the alpha strategies of influence. Hence, we focus here on the latter.

Christianson and his colleagues have suggested a three-stage process by which stress or arousal affects attention and memory (Christianson & Safer, 1996). First, in the *preattentive* stage, emotion-eliciting stimuli, such as blood or personal threat, trigger an orienting response drawing attention to the emotion-eliciting stimuli. Then, in the second stage, active attentional mechanisms promote elaborative encoding focused on the emotional material. This selective attention and elaboration limits processing capacity for peripheral information not central to the emotional aspects of the event. In cases of very strong emotion, the person may become preoccupied by intrusive thoughts regarding the threatening event, further narrowing the focus of attention/processing.

Safer, Christianson, Autry, and Osterlund (1998) refer to the outcome of the narrowed attention and heightened psychological focus on the source of the emotional arousal as *tunnel memory*. Events witnessed under this narrow processing mode will tend to promote better processing and memory for *central* information, that is, the details of the emotion-provoking part of the event. In contrast, it will tend to inhibit processing and memory for *peripheral details*, or details that are either irrelevant or spatially peripheral to the core source of arousal (Easterbrook, 1959). A number of studies have supported this conclusion (e.g., Brown, 2003; see reviews in Christianson, 1992a,b; Christianson & Safer, 1996; Heuer & Reisberg, 1992).

Although this line of research has been concerned with processing of information inherent in the witnessed event itself, the effects of narrowed attentional processes extend to information that could otherwise be retrieved from memory. In the interrogation situation, for example, narrowing of attentional processes to the core of interrogation events—such as the questions, demands, and claims of the interrogator (or to internal efforts at emotion regulation, as suggested by the Pratkanis-Aronson view)—will tend to inhibit the use of deliberative attentional processes that could otherwise retrieve relevant information from memory and use it to provide context for evaluation of incoming information. In other words, stress-related inhibition of voluntary attentional processes can impair the person's ability to use stored knowledge, values, and beliefs to actively evaluate, critique, and resist the assertions and demands of the interrogator. The most potent defense against persuasion—the ability to critique and counterargue against incoming persuasive attempts—is thus effectively disabled.

Even with cognitive and self-regulatory resources unimpaired, elaborative processing may yet be prevented or impaired through various additional mechanisms affecting either the motivation or ability to process elaboratively.

SOCIAL ISOLATION. During the interrogation itself, suspects are isolated from social support (although juveniles in some jurisdictions can have a parent present). In some countries, suspects may be held in solitary confinement prior to or between interrogations (see Gudjonnson, 2003). Although little empirical research has addressed the effects of such isolation on cognitive functioning, Baumeister, Twenge, and Nuss (2002) examined the effects of *expectations* of social isolation on cognitive performance. The authors offered several theoretical bases for prediction of cognitive decrements caused by real or anticipated social isolation. Among them was the idea that real or anticipated social isolation is emotionally distressing. Efforts to regulate these emotions would consume self-regulatory capacity that would otherwise be available for cognitive tasks (see the discussion of research illustrating the ego-depletion model of self-regulation in later sections).

The authors gave half of their participants false personality test feedback indicating either that they were the sort of people who were highly likely to end up alone in life or that they were the sort of people who were likely to spend the rest of their life surrounded by people who cared about them. Those in a misfortune control group were informed that later in life they would become quite accident prone. Participants were subsequently given IQ tests, both difficult and easy sections from the reading comprehension section of the Graduate Record Exam, and problems from the Analytical section of the GRE. Results indicated that expected social isolation led to substantial impairment in the controlled processes and executive function necessary for more complex reasoning but not in the relatively simple and automatic processes needed for the less complex learning and recall involved in rote memory tasks. Further, the forecast of social exclusion led to both slower and less accurate performance.

Apparently, projected social isolation can also lead to self-defeating behaviors of various sorts (Twenge, Catanese, & Baumeister, 2002). Using the same manipulations as the preceding research, the authors found that those who were told to expect a future alone were more likely to take irrational self-defeating risks; to choose unhealthy, rather than healthy, behaviors; and to engage in procrastinating pleasurable activities rather than to study for an upcoming test. Again, the authors interpreted the results as reflecting the impact of depletion of self-regulatory capacity on controlled executive functions.

Although these studies did not assess cognitive functioning *during* social isolation, they do strongly suggest that a suspect will suffer decrements in cognitive functioning and behavioral control during interrogation. The effects of projected social isolation are theoretically mediated by emotional distress and its impact on self-regulatory capacity. Interrogative suspects can and do feel emotional distress as a result of both current isolation from social support, as well as worry about future isolation should they be incarcerated. Hence, the effects on cognitive functioning, as well as the ability to inhibit self-destructive behaviors should be comparable.

PREVENT ELABORATIVE PROCESSING THROUGH DISTRACTION. Distraction has been shown to prevent elaborative processing of persuasive messages (including critical analysis and counterargumentation). When the message is contrary to an existing opinion, distraction interferes with retrieval of relevant inconsistent information from memory, disrupts critical thoughts and counterarguments to the message, and thereby enhances persuasion (see review in Petty & Cacioppo, 1986).

The interrogator is specifically trained to disrupt counterargument and denials through a variety of means (see Inbau et al., 1986, 2001). Some of these distract the suspect from critical focus on the interrogator's points. The interrogator may simply refuse to listen to the suspect's refutations of one point, for example, and redirect attention to another item of his own agenda, thus distracting the suspect from thinking of flaws in the first point. Multiple investigators may fling accusations and evidence simultaneously or in rapid-fire sequence, thus preventing focus on any one argument long enough for critical analysis.

TIME CONSTRAINTS. Time constraints are also crucial for elaborative processing. If the person has insufficient time to counterargue, counterattitudinal information becomes more persuasive (e.g., Alba & Marmorstein, 1987; Ratneswar & Chaiken, 1991)—even that which the person has clearly been told is false (e.g., Gilbert et al., 1993). Gilbert and colleagues (1993) found that subjects whose processing capacities were overwhelmed by a taxing task (which left them with meager resources for counterarguing), or who were given insufficient time to counterargue, were persuaded even by information they knew was false (Gilbert, Tafarodi, & Malone, 1993). The effects of time restriction on elaborative processing have also been suggested to explain the fact that likeable communicators (e.g. Chaiken & Eagly, 1983) and U.S. presidents (e.g., Jorden, 1993) are better able to affect opinions only when their arguments are presented in audio or video rather than written format. Presumably counterargument is less possible when the pace of presentation is faster in audio or video format. Hence, peripheral cues such as attractiveness exert greater impact than argument quality.

Interrogative practices commonly pose significant time-related obstacles to careful information processing and decision making. The suspect is pressured into deciding whether to cooperate and confess during the interrogation itself rather than taking time to go home and consider what would be the best decision. Then, during the interrogation, questions and accusations may be paced so quickly, sometimes coming from multiple sources, that the person has no time to form effective counterarguments before being interrupted by new demands for response (e.g., Ofshe & Leo, 1997a).

Deplete Self-Regulatory Capacity. Resistance to the coercive influences of criminal interrogation requires considerable exertion of will—or *self-regulation*. The suspect must exert considerable effort to control both cognitive processes and behavior. That is, the suspect must attempt to control attention such that relevant incoming information is attended to, understood, and evaluated; relevant additional information is retrieved from memory; attention to immediate interrogator claims and demands does not overwhelm consideration of more important long-term consequences; and all relevant information is properly integrated to form judgments. Further, in the stressful circumstances posed by the interrogation, the suspect must exert control over his emotions such that they neither interfere with important cognitive processes nor inappropriately drive behavior—by, for example, leading the suspect to confess simply in order to terminate the aversive immediate situation or to alleviate guilt. Finally, in the service of his long-term best interests, the suspect must control impulses toward dysfunctional behaviors such as aggression, unwise disclosures, or ultimately full confession that are generated by the immediate pressures of the interrogation.

Essentially, self-regulation occurs when the person attempts to change the way he or she would otherwise think, feel, or behave (Muraven & Baumeister, 2000). The relatively *automatic* (e.g., Bargh & Chartrand, 1999) impulses generated by the immediate forces of the situation must be suppressed so that more *controlled* processes can guide responses. The nature of the interrogation situation and the tactics employed by interrogators generate a number of automatic responses—including initial acceptance of interrogator claims requiring effortful evaluation to "unbelieve"; emotional responses such as fear, anger, despair, hopelessness, embarrassment, and the like with potential to impel self-destructive or self-incriminating actions; and impulses to escape the immediate situation at the expense of long-term well-being, among others.

Criminal interrogation imposes unremitting demands on self-regulatory capacity through the demands of the interrogators, the need for self-regulation of emotions, and the escalating depletion of physical and mental resources as the length of the interrogation increases. Unfortunately, self-regulatory capacity appears to be a limited resource that becomes depleted with use (Baumeister, Muraven, & Tice, 2000; Muraven & Baumeister, 2000).

Muraven and Baumeister (2000) offer four propositions of their *ego-depletion* model: (1) that self-regulation is a limited resource; (2) that exercising self-control consumes this limited resource; (3) that self-regulatory energy can be replenished, but at a slower rate than it is consumed; and (4) that capacity for self-control can be enhanced through practice. The authors reviewed substantial evidence indicating that attempts at self-control are more likely to fail when they have been preceded by other actions or circumstances requiring self-control. Dieters who have just resisted eating attractive cookies, for example, were less likely to persist in attempts to solve difficult puzzles. Even more relevant for the interrogation setting, those who had attempted to suppress emotional reactions to a movie were less likely to persist in subsequent physical or cognitive efforts (Baumeister, Bratslavsky, Muraven, & Tice, 1998). Generally, exposure to stress and management of emotions appear to deplete self-regulatory capacity—as do previous efforts to resist impulses, to control thoughts, or to engage in unattractive tasks (Schmeichel, Vohs, & Baumeister, 2003; see review in Muraven & Baumeister, 2000). Similarly, environmental unpredictability has been shown to reduce self-regulatory function and enhance physiological stress (e.g., Pham, Taylor, & Seeman, 2001).

Knowles and Linn (in press) include *consuming resistance* among their omega influence strategies of undermining resistance, suggesting that because self-regulation becomes more difficult each time one must resist influence attempts, people should be less able to resist repeated than initial attempts. To test this hypothesis, Knowles, Brennan, and Linn (2002) exposed participants to a series of political ads. The position of the target ad varied so that it either was seen first (when capacity to resist influence was presumably greatest) or last (when capacity to resist would presumably be lowest). Further, for half of those seeing the ad last, it was preceded by a 12-minute unrelated travel advertising video. Subjects were either to criticize (presumed to continue depletion of capacity to resist influence) or to indicate what they liked about it (presumed to allow replenishing of critical capacity). Finally, participants were divided into those who rated themselves as skeptical and untrusting of political advertisements versus those who indicated little or no distrust.

The authors found mixed support for their hypothesis. Participants low in skepticism showed the expected pattern of failing resistance. They were least accepting of the target political ad when it was shown first or after their resources had been replenished by a 12-minute *accepting* viewing of the travel ad—and most accepting (indicating reduced capacity to resist influence) when it appeared last, either with no intervening video or with an intervening video they were required to critique. Thus, for those relatively lacking in skepticism, early resistance appeared to deplete their capacity for later resistance.

Interestingly, the skeptics became more, rather than less, resistant to the target ad when it was presented later in the sequence—regardless of the intervening travel video. At least within the relatively short time frame of the experiment, greater skepticism appeared to fuel and maintain resistance. Such an effect may partially explain greater resistance to interrogative tactics among those with greater experience in the legal system—who no doubt are much more skeptical of police claims of all sorts.

Although capacity to resist attitude change in response to persuasive attempts is important, it is only one of many crucial self-regulatory capacities of importance in the interrogation room. The ability to continue to control one's emotions, cognitive processes, and impulses to do anything to escape the aversive situation are also crucial. Unfortunately, the evidence reviewed by Muraven and Baumeister (2000) suggests that these capacities will increasingly fail as the cumulative self-regulatory load of the interrogation mounts.

Attitude Change without Persuasion: The Power of Simple Acknowledgment. Linn and Knowles (2002) have recently shown that the simple acknowledgment that one's target may disagree is sufficient to reduce resistance and increase persuasion. The authors tested the persuasive impact of arguments with and without prefaces such as "Most people don't think so, but . . . ," "It's really weird and sounds bizarre, but . . . ," "You're not going to believe this but . . . ," or "I know you will not want to agree with this, but. . . ." Strangely enough, those with the prefaces produced significantly more attitude change.

The Inestimable Power of Flattery. Inbau and colleagues (2001) quite rightly recognize the power of flattery to induce compliance. The Reid nine-step method is replete with recommendations to use flattery both to induce liking for the interrogator (which itself promotes compliance) and to directly influence compliance. The authors suggest that perhaps due to lack of sufficient love and approval from family, friends, or those in authority in their past, criminal suspects are, on the average, more susceptible to flattery than most (particularly those of low social status): "It is a basic human trait to seek and enjoy the approval of other persons. . . . However, those who engage in criminal activities, particularly those who operate alone, may seldom receive approving remarks and compliments; moreover, the need for such attention and status is just as great or even greater than it is with everyone else" (p. 268).

The authors go on to explain that flattery serves to diffuse the adversarial relationship between the suspect and investigator. It also helps to promote investigator themes designed to induce the suspect to take responsibility for the crime, such as: "I'm sure in my mind that you wouldn't deliberately do a thing like this. You're basically a good, honest person, who got drawn into this situation. You wouldn't do this under normal circumstances. You're not a common criminal motivated by greed and selfishness. You did this to protect your family, didn't you, Joe?"

The investigator may also use flattery to give the suspect positive motivation to take credit for what the investigator depicts as an unusually skillful crime. By praising the physical or tactical skill or the bravery involved, the investigator motivates the suspect to want to confess simply in order to own the flattering labels and claim the investigator's admiration for himself.

Knowles and Linn (in press) include *raising self-esteem* or *self-affirmation* among their omega influence strategies. Indeed, Zuwerinck-Jacks and O'Brien (in press) review evidence showing that people who have been praised, reminded of crowning accomplishments, or allowed to succeed at a previous task become less resistant to (more persuaded by) an unrelated message.

Summary

Interrogative strategies are designed to overcome resistance. As the preceding sections have made clear, the Reid method is replete with very powerful omega tactics that indeed sweep away resistance, even as equally powerful alpha strategies provide incentives to comply and confess. Though based on common everyday tactics of influence, these strategies are particularly powerful when employed in the interrogative situation—where the target is in a relatively powerless role and an inescapable influence situation. Further, although such strategies are widely effective in promoting influence and compliance, some individuals are particularly vulnerable to them—a topic to which we now turn.

THE ROLE OF PERSONALITY VARIABLES AND PSYCHOPATHOLOGY

In the previous sections we have discussed variables that are largely found in the interview situation that can lead to false confessions. Thus, strategies utilized by the police such as incentives, power of contrasts, false information, and the like are all either present to some degree or absent in the situation and either lead or do not lead to false confessions or reports. There are some short-term variables that may plausibly be labeled either situation or person variables. Fatigue is a case in point. Clearly it is the person who is fatigued, but fatigue may simply be a product of causal events in the situation, such as not allowing the individual to rest or sleep for an extended period. However, in general these factors are not enduring. A night's rest can completely change the individual's fatigue level. This section describes factors related to false confessions that the person clearly brings into the situation and that are more enduring traits of that person. Others have discussed the role of personality characteristics such as suggestibility, excessive compliance, and low self-esteem, and the interested reader is referred to this work (e.g., Gudjonsson, 2003; Oberlander, Goldstein, & Goldstein, 2003).

In this section we focus on mental disorders that may serve as diatheses (vulnerabilities) for false confessions. That is, certain individuals may be suffering from dysfunctions that harm these individuals in certain contexts by increasing the likelihood that they will make a false confession. This analysis suggests a diathesis-stress model in which certain mental disorders can create proclivities that, when combined with the situational variables discussed in the previous sections, result in a higher likelihood of false confessions. One advantage of this approach is that while personality variables generally cannot be used as grounds for ruling a confession inadmissible, documentable mental disorders have much more mitigation potential. Essentially, the individual's competency to confess was significantly diminished by the impairments associated with the individual's mental disorder.

The *DSM-IV* (American Psychiatric Association, 2000) defines a mental disorder as "A clinically significant behavioral or psychological syndrome or pattern that occurs in an individual and that is associated with present distress (e.g., a painful symptom) or disability (i.e., impairment in one or more important areas of functioning) or with significantly increased risk of suffering death, pain, disability, or an important loss of freedom" (p. xxi). For our purposes the questions become:

1. Can the distress associated with certain mental disorders be exacerbated by interview characteristics such that the individual will falsely confess in order to escape, reduce, or manage this distress? For example, will an individual with panic disorder and agoraphobia falsely confess in order to escape a small, enclosed interview room?
2. Can the disability associated with a mental disorder interact with interview characteristics such that the individual falsely confesses? For example, an individual with mental retardation can be cognitively impaired in such a way that he or she cannot process key information, thereby enhancing the likelihood of false confession (see Gudjonsson, 2003; Oberlander, Goldstein, & Goldstein, 2003, for reviews of the effects of mental retardation). This is by far the larger set of possibilities.

We consider these possibilities here. We list some of the major mental disorders and possible pathways associated with these disorders that could lead to false confessions:

1. *Mental retardation.* Individuals with mental retardation can have difficulties with recalling events, understanding questions, understanding the full range of consequences of his or her actions, and understanding the full meaning of utterances. These impairments increase with the severity of the retardation (mild, moderate, severe, profound). Some can have an exaggerated need to please, perhaps due to their social isolation or social fears. These cognitive impairments can lead to false confessions (see Gudjonsson, 2003).

2. *Communication disorders.* Individuals with communication disorders may have difficulty understanding words, sentences, or specific types of words. They may have problems with both receptive and expressive language and leave out key parts of sentences. Because confessions are verbal (oral or written), a disorder that interferes with, or produces errors in, communication can lead to false confessions.
3. *Pervasive developmental disorders.* One set of diagnostic criteria for these disorders is abnormalities in communication as well as abnormalities in other cognitive skills. Other related features may be impulsiveness and short attention span. Subtypes include autistic disorders, Rett's disorder, childhood disintegrative disorder, and Asperger's disorder. The cognitive, verbal, attention, and social abnormalities associated with these disorders can lead to false confessions.
4. *Attention deficit/hyperactivity disorder.* This set of disorders includes problems with attention, impulsivity, listening, not following through on instructions, distraction, forgetfulness, blurting out answers before questions have been completed, all of which could lead to false confessions.
5. *Oppositional/defiant disorder.* In this disorder the individual (child or adolescent) defies adult rules, is annoying to individuals, and is spiteful and vindictive. It is possible that situations can arise (e.g., to hurt parents and to defy the rule of always telling the truth) that an individual with this disorder may falsely confess.
6. *Separation anxiety disorder.* In this disorder children experience excessive distress when separated from home or major attachment figures. They also have excessive and persistent fear about possible harm befalling a major attachment figure. These motivations could lead to false confessions in order to escape from being separated from an attachment figure or to falsely implicate themselves to save an attachment figure.
7. *Delirium disorders.* In this set of disorders the individual has a disturbance of consciousness with reduced ability to focus or sustain attention, as well as a change in cognitive abilities, such as memory deficits, language impairments, or perceptual disturbances. Delirium may be caused by substance abuse or by other causes such as head trauma. False confessions may occur if the individual suffers from a delirium either at the time of the alleged crime or during the interview.
8. *Dementia disorders.* Dementias are associated with multiple cognitive impairments (particularly memory impairments). Individuals suffering from dementias may also exhibit language disturbances, agnosias (failure to recognize or identify objects), and disturbances in executive functioning that may result in disorientation and thereby false confessions. Dementias may include Alzheimer's disease; vascular dementias; dementias due to HIV disease; dementias due to head trauma; and dementias due to Parkinson's disease, Huntington's disease, Pick's disease, and Creutzfeldt-Jakob disease as well as other medical conditions.

9. *Amnesic disorders.* These disorders involve disturbance in memory that is due either to the physiological effects of a general medical condition or to the effects of a substance (drug of abuse). The memory deficits may allow confabulation of memories, which may result in false confessions.
10. *Substance abuse disorders.* Substance intoxication may result in cognitive impairments that can be associated with false confessions. Moreover, the withdrawal symptoms of some substance abuse disorders can be severe and could motivate an individual to falsely confess in an attempt to gain access to the substance and escape from the withdrawal symptoms. There are a wide variety of substances of abuse, including alcohol, amphetamines, cocaine, hallucinogens, and opioids, among others.
11. *Schizophrenia and other psychotic disorders.* These disorders can include abnormalities in perception, inferential thinking, language and communication, behavioral monitoring, and attention. *Delusions*, which are false beliefs, and *hallucinations*, which are false perceptions, are also associated with these disorders. These disorders can give rise to false confessions because these individuals often have a variety of beliefs that are not veridical.
12. *Mood disorders.* Depression can be associated with fatigue, problems in concentrating, inappropriate guilt, indecisiveness, and a sense of a foreshortened future that can give rise to false confessions. The manic episodes found in bipolar disorders can be associated with grandiosity, pressure to keep talking, flight of ideas, distractibility, and false beliefs that can be associated with false confessions.
13. *Anxiety disorders.* Anxiety disorders would not generally produce any cognitive impairment that would directly result in false confessions. The major pathway to false confessions associated with anxiety disorders is if the interview itself invoked sufficient anxiety (particularly panic) that the individuals would falsely confess to escape the panic-inducing situation.
14. *Dissociative disorders.* In these disorders the individual is characterized by inability to recall important personal information (dissociative amnesia), or by sudden, unexpected travel accompanied by an inability to recall his or her past (dissociative fugue), or by the presence of two or more distinct identities that result in an inability to recall personal information (dissociative identity disorder). The impairment of normal information processing associated with these disorders can result in false confessions.
15. *Personality disorders.* This group of disorders is associated with chronic patterns of inner experience and behavior that are abnormal. There are ten subtypes. Individuals with *schizotypal personality disorder* have cognitive and perceptual distortions that can result in eccentric behavior, including false confessions. These distortions include ideas of reference,

odd beliefs in their abilities, and bodily illusions. Individuals with *antisocial personality disorder* have a pattern of impulsivity, lying, and rule violation that is consistent with false confessions. Patients with *borderline personality disorder* have a pattern of instability, marked impulsivity, dissociative symptoms, and unstable self-image. Individuals with *histrionic personality disorder* have excessive needs for attention seeking, are highly suggestible, and may falsely confess in order to gain much desired notice. Finally, individuals with *narcissistic personality disorder* have a grandiose sense of importance (e.g., exaggerate achievements) and are preoccupied with fantasies of fame that may lead to false confessions.

Many of these disorders often go undiagnosed in the general population. It is useful upon reviewing suspected false confessions either to look at existing mental health records or to have the individual undergo a mental health diagnostic assessment in order to rule in or rule out the presence of these disorders. Once this is done, it is a separate question to see if the disorders contributed in any way to the false confession, or rendered a true confession voluntarily.

THE CONSEQUENCES OF FALSE CONFESSION

> *No other class of evidence is so profoundly prejudicial ... Triers of fact accord confessions such heavy weight in their determinations that the introduction of a confession makes the other aspects of trial in court superfluous, and the real trial, for all practical purposes, occurs when the confession is obtained.*
> Supreme Court Justice William Brennan
> (Colorado v. Connelly, 1986, p. 182)

Pretrial Consequences of Confession

Confessions, once given, are not easily retracted. Intuitions of police, prosecutors, judges, and jurors alike lead them to find the notion that an innocent person would confess falsely—particularly to horrific crimes—to be inherently lacking in credibility (Kassin & Sukel, 1997; Leo & Ofshe, 1998; Ofshe & Leo, 1997a,b). Indeed, criminal investigators are neither trained to believe that false confessions can be elicited from innocent witnesses nor trained to understand the processes by which this may occur. Nor are they trained to avoid tactics that have been shown to elicit false confession or to recognize them when they do occur. Indeed, some of the most popular criminal investigation manuals specifically instruct the reader that false confessions cannot be exacted from innocent persons.

For example, the third edition of the Inbau manual (Inbau, Reid, & Buckley, 1986) instructs the reader that "none of what is recommended will induce an innocent person to confess" (p. 147). Two of the authors (Jayne & Buckley, 1992) later argued in defense of common interrogation tactics that "none of these techniques, in and of themselves, is unique to interrogations, and none of them would cause an innocent suspect to confess to a crime" (p. 69). In the latest edition of the Inbau and colleagues manual (4th edition, 2001), the authors repeat their earlier claims: "It must be remembered that none of the steps is apt to make an innocent person confess and that all the steps are legally as well as morally justifiable" (p. 212). This edition does include a chapter addressing the possibility of false confessions but generally discounts much of the research illustrating the influence processes that contribute to them and appears to take the position that only suspects who are impaired in some way will falsely confess in response to such influences.

Although clearly false, this belief appears to be shared by those who follow the interrogators as the person who has confessed proceeds through the justice system. Those who confess are henceforth presumed guilty and judged and treated more harshly at every remaining stage of the case. Even though innocent, and even if he recants the confession, the defendant's chances of eventual acquittal plummet (see Gudjonsson, 2003; Kassin & Sukel, 1997; Leo, 1996; Ofshe & Leo, 1997a,b; Walker, 1998).

Because police assume the confession to be true, they are unlikely to pursue exculpatory evidence or follow leads to other suspects, and instead tend to consider the case solved (e.g. Leo, 1996). Failing to believe the confession could be false, they tend not to follow up evidence or leads the defendant or others may suggest will prove his innocence. Instead, police may so strongly pursue evidence of the defendant's guilt that evidence may become tainted in the process—for example, through inadvertent but powerful biasing of eyewitness identifications or accounts or even through alteration or deliberate falsification.

Judges tend to view a defendant who has confessed as guilty and refuse to grant bail, which then significantly reduces the chance of acquittal (Walker, 1998). On the strength of the confession, prosecutors tend to "charge high" (charge with a more serious offense) and to be less inclined to plea bargain—a reaction shared in some ways by defense attorneys, who, because of the anticipated impact of the confession, tend to pressure the client to plead guilty (Nardulli, Eisenstein, & Flemming, 1988).

Impact of the Confession at Trial and Beyond

Commonly, a defendant who has confessed will attempt to have the confession excluded from trial, claiming the confession was coerced. Before trial, the judge must rule on admissibility on the basis of whether the confession is deemed voluntary or coerced. Depending upon jurisdiction, confessions ruled to be voluntary are either simply admitted without special instruction or admitted with an instruction to the jury to come to an independent judgment of voluntariness and to disregard statements judged as coerced (Kamisar, LaFave, & Israel, 1994; Kassin, 1997b).

In *Miranda v. Arizona* (1966), the court established that the voluntariness of a waiver of rights is to be established through examination of the *totality of the circumstances* surrounding the interrogation—including such aspects as the characteristics of the accused, the conditions of the interrogation, and the conduct of the police (*Shneckloth v. Bustamonte*, 1973). The court must weigh the circumstances of pressure against the power of resistance of the person confessing (*Dickerson v. United States*, 2000). Under this test, interrogative pressures must be considered in light of suspect vulnerabilities such as retardation, youth, mental illnesses, and the like (see discussions in Brophy & Huang, 2000; Florian, 1999; Mcguire, 2000; Meyer, 1999; White, 1998). Hence, there is no simple explicit guideline for determining whether a confession is voluntary or coerced (White, 1998).

Most suspects waive their *Miranda* rights (DeFilippo, 2001; Rosenberg & Rosenberg, 1989; White, 2001). If the suspect is *Mirandized* but confesses anyway, the courts often automatically find the confession to be voluntary (White, 2001, p. 1220), despite evidence that suspects commonly fail to understand their rights even when apprised of them (e.g., Grisso, 1998a,b). Typically, however, it will be excluded if elicited via actual physical violence, threats of harm, promises of leniency, or without proper *Miranda* warnings (Kamisar, Lafave, & Israel, 1994; Mueller & Kirkpatrick, 1995; Wigmore, 1970). However, if the confession is obtained via the previously described *minimization* or *maximization* techniques, where threats and promises are merely implied, it is often ruled voluntary and admissible (Kassin, 1997b; Sasaki, 1988; Ofshe & Leo, 1997a,b; White, 1979). They are only a factor in the "totality of the circumstances" test of voluntariness (Leo & White, 1999).

Although some states have passed legislation requiring proof of voluntariness *beyond a reasonable doubt*, the standard by which the determination of voluntariness is to be judged was established by the Supreme Court in *Lego v. Twomy* (1972) as that of "preponderance of the evidence" rather than the stricter reasonable-doubt standard. The Court stated: "Our decision was not based in the slightest on the fear that juries might misjudge the accuracy of confessions" (p. 625) and went on to affirm its faith that jurors are able to identify and willing to discount coerced confessions. Apparently, the Court felt that if this looser standard led to the admission of questionable confession evidence, jurors would be able to recognize and discount it, thereby preventing it from exerting inappropriate prejudicial effects on verdicts. Unfortunately, as we shall shortly see, this optimism is clearly unfounded.

If a confession is admitted into evidence and the defendant is convicted, the defendant may appeal, arguing that the confession was actually coerced and inappropriately admitted (see Gudjonnson, 2003, for a discussion of case law regarding challenges of confessions). Prior to 1991, if the confession was deemed coerced, the conviction was routinely reversed. However, in the *Arizona v. Fulminante* (1991) decision, the U.S. Supreme Court ruled that in certain circumstances—for example, when the confession is cumulative or there is sufficient corroborating evidence—the admission of a coerced confession may be "harmless error." The appellate court is required to consider the confession in the context of all of the evidence to determine whether it exerted significant prejudicial effect upon the outcome. If not, the conviction will stand.

The various tasks of judges and juries require, at a minimum, (1) accuracy in understanding interrogation practices that are actually coercive, and their abilities to elicit both true and false confessions; (2) the ability to ignore a confession deemed involuntary and to eliminate both direct and indirect influences it may have on their judgments; and (3) the ability to ignore the trial jury verdict in evaluating the strength of evidence without the confession (for appellate judges). Substantial research suggests, however, that neither judges nor juries can meet these requirements.

Judging Coercion

First in the necessary chain of cognitive tasks is judgment of the confession as voluntary versus coerced. Accuracy thus requires the perceiver to understand the power of the situational forces affecting the decision to confess *as they interact with the personal vulnerabilities of the suspect*. Generally, psychological research has demonstrated that people fail to appreciate situational determinants of behavior. Instead, they fall prey to the "fundamental attribution error" (Ross, 1977) or "correspondence bias" (Gilbert & Jones, 1986)—the tendency to assume that behavior reflects internal causes such as personality, desires, moods, and so on, rather than external causes such as the behavior of others or other situational forces (see Jones, 1990; Gilbert & Malone, 1995 for reviews).

In other words, there is a well-documented and powerful tendency to assume that behavior is fundamentally voluntary. This assumption is reflected, for example, in the widespread belief among respondents to surveys on hypnosis that, even when hypnotized, people cannot be made to lie or to perform behaviors fundamentally inconsistent with their values (see review in Laurence & Perry, 1988). Unfortunately, many powerful influence tactics appear innocuous yet exert substantial influence on behavior. Thus, although perceivers may recognize the importance of physical torture or overt threats, they are less likely to recognize the influence of such tactics as isolation, controlling the conversation, apparent sympathy, repeated accusations, interruptions, the principle of reciprocity, and others with less obvious coercive effect.

Lay perceivers also generally lack awareness of the vulnerability of human information processing, memory, and decision-making capacities (see reviews in Davis & Follette, 2001; Davis & Loftus, in press). As reviewed earlier, the interrogation setting and tactics, along with excessive length and inherent stress, combine to deplete mental processing resources and render defendants unable to effectively analyze what they are being told, argue for their own innocence, or come to a reasonable decision. Further, particularly in such a depleted state, the person can be led to develop false memories of having committed the crime—again, an outcome that is wholly inconsistent with lay beliefs regarding memory. This near-complete lack of understanding among the lay public (including those in the judicial system) of the manner in which the interrogation setting and tactics affect cognitive processes renders judges and jurors fundamentally incapable of accurately perceiving the full range of coercive aspects present in any given interrogation.

Moreover, given the general lack of understanding of the coercive power of interrogation tactics, it is even less likely that judges and jurors can intuitively grasp the truly extreme influence such tactics can exert on more vulnerable suspects. As discussed earlier, such vulnerabilities may derive from obvious deficiencies such as low IQ but may also be the result of less obvious sources, such as extreme admiration or respect for police, a very compliant and dependent personality, or depleted self-regulatory resources.

Finally, as Kassin (1997b, 1998) and Ofshe and Leo (1997a,b) have argued, the innocent person may be led to understand his situation in such a way that knowingly confessing falsely appears to be the strategy that will produce the best outcome. Judges and jurors at the trial end of the process and beyond are unlikely to understand how a person could be convinced that confessing was the best strategy, and thus are unlikely to understand or believe the ways in which both explicit and implied threats and incentives can prompt an innocent person to reasonably believe his best outcomes are possibly only through false confession.

In this context, the conviction of interrogators and others in the judicial system that innocent persons are unlikely to confess, unless perhaps in response to extreme physical abuse or explicit threats of harm, are to be expected. Although perhaps able to appreciate the effects of physical abuse—or even explicit threats—they are genuinely unaware of the full extent of the power of interrogation tactics to influence the thought processes, beliefs, memories, and decision strategies of an innocent person. As Kassin (1998) noted with respect to such convictions among detectives, "The detective who boasts that 'I've never taken a false confession'—and who, when pressed for proof, notes that all of his or her confessors were later found guilty—demonstrates the pernicious effects of motivated reasoning built on a foundation of naiveté regarding the psychology of human behavior" (p. 320).

Not surprisingly, given these considerations, empirical research assessing the way in which lay perceivers evaluate interrogation tactics has shown that the full coercive impact of common interrogation tactics is not understood.

Preserving the Record: Problems of Assessing Coercion without a Full Record of Police-Suspect Interactions. It is more than obvious that the degree of coercion exerted by police interrogators cannot be accurately assessed in the absence of a full record of police-suspect interactions at all points prior to and through the completion of the confession itself. Unfortunately, it is rare for judges or jurors to have access to the complete record.

Inbau and colleagues (2001) adamantly oppose full recording of police interrogations in any format, recommending instead that the suspect be interrogated without the entire content being formally recorded. The investigator is advised to produce a concise summary, after the confession is obtained, using the suspect's own words as far as possible. The authors suggest that the use of recordings would result in fewer confessions and difficulties with court rulings. Essentially, they regard recordings as detrimental to their purposes.

Perhaps in part owing to the influence of this popular interrogation manual, full recordings of police-suspect interactions occur only in a minority of cases. Geller (1992) estimated that approximately one-third of all large police and sheriffs' departments in the United States videotape at least some interrogations—and that most cases that are videotaped involve more serious crimes such as homicide, rape, and aggravated assault. Thus, the vast majority of U.S. criminal interrogations remain unrecorded. (In contrast, since 1991 England and Wales have required tape-recording of interviews of any person suspected of an indictable offense; Gudjonnson, 2003.)

A further problem involves the extent to which all police-suspect interactions and interrogations are recorded, as opposed to a select sample. Some tapes may be "lost," and other crucial interrogations may remain unrecorded (Shuy, 1998), perhaps deliberately. Such a selective sample of the interactions renders assessment of coercion dependent upon the memories and honestly of the suspect and interrogators.

It is quite common for interrogators to record only the final segment of the interrogation, after the suspect has admitted guilt, where he provides his full confession and account of the crime (Geller, 1993). Kassin (1997a) noted two problems with this procedure (the *recap bias*). First, if jurors see the final confession without access to the coercive pressures leading up to it, they may be more likely to view the confession as voluntary. Second, after the pressures of the interrogation itself have eased as a result of his previous admissions and accounts of the crime, the suspect may show less emotion and appear unusually callous—which would tend to result in harsher judgments against him.

Empirical Studies of Perception of Coercion. Empirical research regarding perception of coercion in interrogation has been carried out almost exclusively in a series of mock jury studies by Saul Kassin and his colleagues—most of which have assessed both juror judgments of the degree of voluntariness of the confession as well as the impact of both voluntary and involuntary confessions on verdicts. Hence, we review these in the next section on ability to disregard confession evidence. In this section, however, we review evidence that judgments of coercion can be biased by the manner in which the interrogation itself is preserved. That is, we examine the subtle but powerful effects of the camera views of the parties to the interrogation.

In the previous section, we noted the widespread lack of full records of interviews and interrogations of suspects. Some have advanced the "simple" solution of videotaping all custodial interrogations. Although some police-suspect interactions would remain unrecorded with such a strategy, the primary interrogation, at least, would be fully recorded. Barry Scheck, cofounder of the Innocence Project, stated on ABC *World News Tonight* (May 11, 2000) that with videotaped interrogations "there's no dispute later—what did the person say, what didn't he say, was it coerced, was it not coerced?" Leo and Ofshe (1998) argued that "the existence of an exact record of the interrogation is crucial for determining the voluntariness and reliability of any confession statement, especially if the confession is internally inconsistent, is contradicted by some case facts, or was elicited by coercive methods or from highly suggestible individuals" (p. 494). Hence, they believe that in addition to evaluating voluntariness, the fact finders may also find clues to the veracity of the confession in the details of what is said. Some (Cassell, 1996) have gone so far as to suggest that *Miranda* warnings to suspects might be dispensed with if interrogations are routinely videotaped, since voluntariness can be reliably assessed from such recordings. Is such faith in the diagnostic and remedial power of videotaped interrogations justified, however?

Daniel Lassiter and his colleagues (see review by Lassiter, Geers, Munhall, Handley & Beers, 2001) have performed a series of studies showing that the way in which an interrogation is taped can bias perceptions of the coercive nature of the interrogation and the validity of the confession. Most interrogations are videotaped such that the camera is positioned behind the interrogator (so that he or she is either not visible or only the back of the head is visible), and directly focused on the suspect (Geller, 1992; Kassin, 1997b). This angle *seems* logical, as the fact finders presumably need to see the suspect clearly in order to assess voluntariness and truthfulness. In fact, this is a false assumption.

Unfortunately, as the extensive literature on detection of deception has shown, there are few reliable cues to deception (DePaulo, Lindsay, Malone, Muhlenbruck, Charlton, & Cooper, 2003). Hence, not surprisingly, perceivers are unable to detect deception at greater than chance levels (e.g., Ekman & O'Sullivan, 1991). Although some law enforcement professionals can outperform the average person (Ekman, O'Sullivan, & Frank, 1999), most perform at chance level (DePaulo & Pfeifer, 1986; Ekman & O'Sullivan, 1991; Elaad, 2003; Kraut & Poe, 1980; Mann, 2001; Meissner & Kassin, 2002; Porter, Woodworth, & Birt, 2000). Beliefs concerning how to detect deception among police, prosecutors, and judges are strikingly inaccurate (e.g., Akejurst, Kohnken, Vrij, & Bull, 1996; Porter, Campbell, Stapleton, & Birt, 2003; Stroemwall & Granhag, 2003; Vrij, 2001). For example, consistency in accounts over time is the cue used most by interrogators, whereas this cue is not actually related to accuracy (e.g., Granhag & Stroemwall, 2001), and generally the stories of liars actually tend to be more "perfect" than those of truth tellers (DePaulo et al., 2003).

Moreover, a recent meta-analysis of the literature on detection of deception has shown that the correlation between accuracy in detecting deception and confidence in ability to detect deception is essentially zero (DePaulo, Charlton, Cooper, Lindsay, & Muhlenbruck, 1997). Hence, although most interrogators are very confident of their ability to evaluate the truthfulness of their suspects, this confidence is wholly unrelated to accuracy. Finally, studies of real-life successful lie detection have shown that lies tend to be detected indirectly (e.g., Vrij, Edward, & Bull, 2001), over a period of days, weeks, or months (rather than in the course of a single interview, conversation, or interrogation) and that the lies are detected primarily on the basis of concrete evidence, third-party information, and other external sources—and not through accurate reading of the liar's deceptive communications (e.g., Johnson, Grazioli, Jamal, & Berryman, 2001; Park, Levine, McCornack, Morrison, & Ferrara, 2002; Vrij, 2001).

Although there is some evidence that proper training in lie detection can modestly raise accuracy (Frank & Feeley, 2003), Kassin and Fong (1999) have recently demonstrated that those who are taught to distinguish truth from deception using methods commonly taught to police interrogators were actually *less accurate* than untrained controls. Police interrogators appear to be biased by the presumption of guilt, some going so far as to claim that they *never* interrogate an innocent suspect (Kassin, 2002). Unfortunately, this presumption tends to engage biasing interrogation behaviors that lead the suspect to appear guilty. As recently shown by Kassin, Goldstein, and Savitsky (2003), interrogators who presumed their suspects were guilty asked more guilt-presumptive questions, used more interrogation techniques, judged the suspect as more likely guilty, and exerted more pressure to get a confession—*particularly when they were paired with an innocent suspect!* Independent observers who later listened to the tapes perceived suspects whose interrogators believed them guilty as more defensive and more guilty. Hence, the expectations of guilt first led the interrogator to behave differently, which in turn influenced the suspect's behavior and ultimately the judgments of neutral observers.

Thus, camera focus on the suspect is unlikely to serve the stated goal of helping to evaluate the suspect's truthfulness. On the other hand, as Lassiter and his colleagues have shown, judgments of voluntariness can be significantly biased by the camera perspective.

Jones and Nisbett (1972) first proposed that attribution might follow the focus of attention. That is, in attempting to attribute causality to an action, the perceiver will be unduly influenced by what is most perceptually salient. In the context of social interaction, this *salience effect* leads observers to overestimate the causal role of individuals who are seen most clearly (see Lassiter et al., 2001; McArthur, 1981; Taylor & Fiske, 1978 for reviews of this literature). As noted earlier, there is already a pervasive tendency of observers to fall prey to the *fundamental attribution error*—or the tendency to see behavior as much more voluntary than appropriate. This failure to fully appreciate the causal role of situational forces is exacerbated when these forces are rendered less salient by virtue of the observer's visual perspective (Lassiter et al., 2001). Hence a camera perspective that focuses fully on the suspect while failing to show the interrogator can be expected to bias the perceiver toward the attribution that the suspect's behaviors are voluntary—and away from the attribution that the suspect's behavior was coerced by the interrogator.

Across a series of studies, Lassiter and his colleagues had subjects judge videotaped, audiotaped, or transcribed interrogations, finding that (1) confessions were perceived as most voluntary when the camera focused exclusively on the suspect, next most voluntary when focused equally on interrogator and suspect, and least voluntary when focused on the interrogator; (2) confessions were seen as equivalently voluntary when raters saw a videotape focused equally on suspect and interrogator versus when they either listened to a tape or read a transcript; and (3) judgments of guilt were related to camera perspective in the same manner as judgments of voluntariness, as were sentencing recommendations. Further, the point-of-view bias was sufficiently strong that it was neither eliminated by jury deliberations nor by specific instructions to focus on the content of what was said or to avoid any bias due to camera perspective. Nor was it eliminated by anticipated review by a local judge (intended to simulate *accountability* for one's judgment).

Lassiter and his colleagues then went on to investigate the effects of camera perspective within the context of a full mock trial simulation. For example, Lassiter and colleagues (2001) exposed mock jurors to a trial simulation of the Peter Reilly case (Connery, 1977), including two prosecution and three defense witnesses, opening and closing arguments, Reilly's reenacted interrogation/confession, and legal instructions (approximately 2.5 hrs, including 40 minutes of the interrogation). All trial materials were held constant, except for the three camera perspectives from which the interrogation was videotaped. Again, when the interrogation was depicted with focus on the suspect, the confession was seen as more voluntary (and the suspect as more likely guilty) than when the interrogation was depicted with equal focus. Detective focus, as before, resulted in judgments of the least voluntariness and least guilt.

Finally, Lassiter and his colleagues (Lassiter, Geers, Handley, Weiland, & Munhall, 2002) investigated the issue of whether there exist circumstances under which judgments of voluntariness are more accurate for videotaped interrogations. Based on existing attribution literature, the authors argued that the most accurate judgments of the voluntariness of a confession may be obtained when the camera provides a viewpoint most similar to what the *suspect* actually saw during the interrogation. This literature has generally indicated that situational factors are more likely to affect causal attributions for behavior when they are somehow made more salient or obvious (see review in Lassiter et al., 2001). Storms (1973), for example, showed that the fundamental attribution error can be attenuated to some degree when observers see a videotape depicting exactly what the original actor saw. Does the ability to visually "occupy the suspect's shoes" enable one to better understand the situational forces driving confession?

Participants viewed a mock trial simulation of the trial of Bradley Page, who is considered to have provided a false coerced-internalized confession to the murder/rape of his girlfriend (Leo & Ofshe, 1998; Pratkanis & Aronson, 1991). Using a transcript of the actual interrogation, the authors reenacted portions of the interrogation considered most crucial to the production of the confession. The mock trial brought out numerous discrepancies between Page's confession and other facts that came out in the trial and included Page's own testimony about how the interrogators implored him to help them solve the case by imagining how the crime might have occurred if he were to have done it. Participants viewed the same evidence in all conditions and then deliberated in groups. Only the camera angle varied (detective focus vs. equal focus).

Based on previous accounts of the case (Leo & Ofshe, 1998; Pratkanis & Aronson, 1991), the authors deemed the Page confession to be false. Hence, jurors who viewed the confession as involuntary and Page as not guilty were considered "correct." As anticipated, jurors who viewed the interrogation from the suspect's original point of view (i.e., detective focus) were much more likely to see the confession as involuntary (and Page as not guilty) than those who viewed it from the equal focus view (more than 30% difference between conditions on both measures).

SUMMARY AND CONCLUSIONS. Lassiter's very systematic and detailed program of research has suggested several conclusions regarding the utility of videotaping interrogations. First, it is more than clear that the camera perspective from which an interrogation is recorded will have significant impact on judgments of both voluntariness and guilt. This result was obtained with both student and community samples, for individual judgments and group verdicts regardless of instructions or warnings regarding potential camera angle effects, and for both judgments of the isolated interrogation and verdicts in full trial simulations. Hence, this effect may be considered very reliable and robust.

The issue of which camera angle can be expected to produce the most "accurate" judgments is less well established. The attribution literature supports the hypothesis that accuracy will be enhanced when the fact finders view the video from the suspect's perspective. However, the one study addressing this hypothesis was not fully convincing because it relied on only one interrogation that was presumed coerced and one suspect presumed not guilty. Future research can better address this issue through use of a larger number of stimulus cases so that ability to discriminate voluntariness and validity can be assessed.

Meanwhile, the widespread practice of taping with suspect focus will surely exacerbate an already dangerous bias toward perception of voluntariness. That is, focus on the suspect can only serve to enhance the already powerful tendency to view his behavior (confession) as voluntary and to fail to appreciate the significant coercive force of the interrogator's behavior.

Can Judges and Jurors Disregard Involuntary Confessions?

Kassin and his colleagues have conducted a series of studies to evaluate the questions of (1) whether jurors can correctly evaluate the voluntariness of a confession and, if so, (2) whether they can successfully discount confessions deemed coerced, and finally, (3) whether a judge's instructions to disregard a coerced confession that has been introduced but then withdrawn reduce the impact of that confession on juror verdicts.

In the first of these studies, participants read criminal trial transcripts depicting an interrogation including either *explicit* threats of harm or promises of leniency. Unfortunately, although jurors were clearly able to discount confessions obtained via explicit threats (Kassin & Wrightsman, 1980), they failed to fully recognize the coercive power of promises of leniency. Participants fully rejected confessions obtained via threats of harm in that they both judged the confession as involuntary and did not allow it to influence their verdicts. On the other hand, confessions elicited via promises of leniency were not fully rejected.

Although most jurors viewed them as involuntary, more voted guilty compared to the no-confession control. This failure to fully recognize the coercive power of incentives—as compared to threats—has been dubbed the *positive coercion bias* (e.g., Kassin, 1997b) and has been replicated in a series of subsequent studies with both individual mock jurors and deliberating groups of six, and with both explicit threats and promises as well as implied incentives/threats communicated through the techniques of *minimization* and *maximization* described earlier (Kassin & Wrightsman, 1981, 1985; Kassin & McNall, 1991). Such findings are generally consistent with literature on causal attribution processes, which indicates that behaviors enacted in order to produce positive outcomes are viewed as more voluntary than those enacted to avoid negative outcomes (e.g., Bramel, 1969; Kelley, 1972; Steiner, Rotermund, & Talaber, 1974; Wells, 1980).

Kassin and Sukel (1997) provided a further test of the impact of confession evidence on juror judgments—and in addition addressed the question of whether judicial instructions to disregard the confession would mitigate its impact. Mock jurors in each of two experiments read transcripts of a murder trial that contained either no confession or a confession elicited under either high-pressure (physical discomfort and angry, aggressive yelling and waving of a gun in the air) or low-pressure (the defendant confessed immediately upon questioning but described himself as in a state of shock) interrogation. For both confession conditions, the confession was described as having been either admissible or inadmissible by the judge. The defense attorney objected to the admissibility of testimony regarding the confession, whereupon the judge either overruled the objection or upheld it, ordered the confession testimony to be stricken from the record, and instructed jurors to disregard it. Upon completion of the transcript, jurors rated the voluntariness of the confession and rendered verdicts.

Jurors generally recalled the judge's ruling correctly, were less likely to judge the confession elicited through high-pressure interrogation as voluntary than the confession elicited through low-pressure tactics, and were somewhat less likely to report that it had influenced their verdicts. Moreover, it is interesting to note that jurors were strongly affected by the judge's ruling, in that they were much more likely to report that the confession was voluntary and that it had influenced their verdicts if the judge ruled it admissible rather than inadmissible. However, as is often the case, jurors did not fully understand the impact of the evidence on their verdicts.

The majority of jurors failed to recognize the influence of confession evidence on their judgments (76% in experiment I and 52% in experiment II reported that the confession did not influence their judgment). Notwithstanding such denials, mock jurors rated the defendant as more likely guilty in all confession groups than in the no-confession control group (experiment I) and were significantly more likely to render a guilty verdict (experiment II)—whether or not they were instructed to disregard the confession by the judge.

The results of Kassin and his colleagues have cast considerable doubt on the argument that confession evidence can be considered harmless error—at least in the absence of overwhelming additional evidence of guilt. Subjects in Kassin and

Sukel's (1997) research, for example, failed to fully discount a confession, whether it was elicited under high or low pressure, whether the mock jurors viewed it as coerced or not, whether the judge had ruled it as admissible or not, and even when they reported that it did not influence their verdicts.

Hence, even coerced confession evidence exerts considerable power—apparently outside the awareness of the jurors who must judge it—and despite judicial instructions to disregard the confession. Further, it must be emphasized that the power of the confession is often sufficient to turn acquittal into conviction. Kassin and Sukel (1997; Experiment II), for example, found conviction rates of over 50 percent across the confession conditions as opposed to 19 percent in the no-confession control.

Limitations and Directions for Future Research. Although these studies of ability to judge coercion offer some support for the notion that jurors (and judges) can perceive the coercive nature of some of the more intuitively obviously coercive tactics, several important issues remain unaddressed.

First, there has been little attempt to assess the ability of judges or jurors to understand the full range of coercive influences inherent to police interrogations. Research has thus far focused upon such intuitively coercive tactics as explicit and implicit threats and promises, physical discomfort, or yelling and aggressive behavior. There have thus far been no tests of ability to recognize the coercive influence of most of the less obvious, but very powerful, influences reviewed earlier in this chapter.

Second, we know of no attempts to assess lay abilities to recognize the enhanced coercive force of a variety of interrogative pressures for vulnerable populations. Thus, much remains to be investigated regarding the ability of judges and jurors to recognize the full range of coercive influences—and likely ability to resist them—for both normal and vulnerable individuals.

Finally, as it is clear that judges and jurors will not appreciate the full range of such influences on their own, it will be important for future research to address the potential for expert testimony to influence reactions to evidence of both coercive influence and individual vulnerability.

Posttrial Appeal

Both legal scholars (e.g., Mueller & Kirkpatrick, 1995) and psychologists (e.g., Kassin, 1997b; Kassin & Sukel, 1997) have suggested that appellate judges cannot successfully judge the issue of whether confession evidence can be deemed harmless. In essence, such a judgment requires the appellate court to first assess whether the confession was indeed admitted in error (i.e., whether it should or should not be considered coerced), and if so, to then assess the strength of the prosecution case *without the crucial confession* in an effort to determine whether the confession exerted undue prejudicial impact. In other words, the appellate court is in the same position as jurors who are asked to judge the degree to which the confession was coerced or to disregard inappropriate confession evidence—and, in addition, must attempt to assess the prejudicial impact of the confession evidence accurately. Thus, there is substantial reason to doubt the effectiveness of the appellate process.

First, as noted earlier, lower court rulings do not reflect sufficient awareness of the coercive effects of a wide range of interrogation tactics. Instead, though they do tend to rule confessions elicited by explicit threats and promises to be coerced, lower court judges generally admit confessions elicited by the wide range of additional coercive techniques shown to elicit false confessions. Thus, there is no reason to expect appellate judges to evaluate such procedures differently.

Second, the nature of the appellate procedure invokes *hindsight biases* such that perceptions of the appropriateness of an existing verdict is affected by the very knowledge of the verdict. This problem was illustrated in a study by Galen Bodenhausen (1990). The author presented summaries of two cases (a high school teacher accused of molesting a student and a violent assault) to groups of mock jurors. At the end of the presentation of evidence, one group was told the defendant had been found guilty, the second was told he had been found not guilty, and the third was not told the verdict. Based on the evidence they saw, jurors were then asked to rate the likelihood that the defendant was actually innocent on a scale from 0 to 100 percent.

Overall, mock jurors were strongly affected by knowledge of the previous jury verdict, so that those who learned the defendant was convicted rated him as more likely to be factually guilty than those who were not told the verdict, whereas those who had been told the previous jury had acquitted the defendant rated him as more likely to be factually innocent than those who were not told the verdict. Clearly, the jurors were affected by knowledge of what the jury had found. Although Bodenhausen's research was not conducted with judges, judges are human and thus susceptible to most, if not all, of the same biasing influences affecting others.

The appellate process further subjects the judges to yet another bias in information processing—the inability to ignore unwanted or inappropriate information. The appellate judge essentially must ask: "Is there enough evidence to convict without the coerced confession?" or "Does the evidence prove guilt beyond a reasonable doubt without the confession?" That is, just as jurors are often asked to come to a verdict while ignoring one or more items introduced inappropriately, the judge must try to ignore knowledge of the confession and ask whether the remaining evidence is sufficient to convict. A vast body of research, both on the success of thought suppression generally (see reviews in Golding & MacLeod, 1998; Wegner, 1994) and on the ability to ignore inadmissible evidence specifically (e.g., Kassin & Sukel, 1997; Kassin & Studebaker, 1998; Sommers & Kassin, 2001), has shown that people are generally unsuccessful in such efforts.

Jurors can and do discount evidence if it is shown to be invalid or false—and thus might likewise discount a confession if it could be shown to be false (see Kassin & Studebaker, 1998). But if evidence is perceived as relevant and true, jurors tend to use it notwithstanding instructions to disregard. Even if the inadmissible evidence itself can be successfully discounted, it can still lead the perceiver to interpret other evidence differently (e.g., Johnson & Seifert, 1994). For example, an eyewitness may be perceived as more credible with than without the confession, and thus may exert more influence on verdicts. Thus, jurors and judges may attempt to discount the direct effect of the confession even as they fall prey to its indirect effects.

Finally, the appellate court's judgment of the strength of the prosecutor's case is used as one basis to determine the likely prejudicial impact of confession evidence. Unfortunately, there is reason to doubt that the courts appreciate the prejudicial power of confession evidence. The U.S. Supreme Court stated in *Arizona v. Fulminante* (1991) that admission of involuntary confession evidence is a "trial error" similar in magnitude and type to the erroneous admission of other types of evidence. This attitude flies in the face of substantial evidence that confession is highly likely to result in conviction—whether coerced or not. Further, Kassin and Neumann (1997) found that confession evidence exerted stronger effects on verdicts than eyewitness identification testimony (which has been repeatedly shown to powerfully affect verdicts). There are unlikely to be many, if any, trial errors with as seriously prejudicial effects as the inappropriate admission of confession evidence—and yet, this difference appears to be unappreciated by the courts.

Further, the previously reviewed mock jury studies of Kassin and his colleagues indicated that while jurors could recognize coercive interrogation behaviors as coercive, the majority did not recognize the influence of the confessions (whether coerced or not) on their own verdicts. Hence, it would be premature to conclude that perceivers are better able to identify the prejudicial impact of such evidence upon others.

In summary, then, it is quite unlikely that judges will reliably recognize coerced confessions or those elicited from a vulnerable individual who might reasonably be deemed not "competent to confess" (Oberlander, Goldstein, & Goldstein, 2003). Nor can judges be expected to more successfully disregard confession evidence or determine its true prejudicial value than jurors or any others. Once introduced, there will be no effective remedy for the prejudicial impact of confession evidence.

THE ROLE OF THE EXPERT WITNESS

For the foreseeable future, the problem of false confessions is likely to be reduced neither through alterations in police procedures that tend to elicit them nor through lessened prejudicial impact on the prosecutors, judges, and juries that react to them once elicited. Hence, it falls to the expert witness to provide context for judges ruling on admissibility and juries deciding culpability. Leo (2001) suggested the expert witness can aid these processes by (1) discussing the scientific literature documenting the fact of police-induced false confessions, (2) explaining how and why particular interrogation methods and strategies can induce false confession, (3) identifying the conditions that increase the risk of false confession (including personal vulnerability), and (4) explaining the generally accepted principles of postadmission narrative analysis.

Although research has not yet (to our knowledge) addressed the effectiveness of the testimony of influence experts, evidence from other areas of expert testimony suggests it will lead fact finders to more accurately understand the operation of coercive interrogative pressures—both explicit and implicit—and hence to adjust their decisions to reflect them. Testimony regarding the determinants of eyewitness accuracy, for example, has been shown to cause jurors to use more appropriate cues to distinguish between accurate and inaccurate eyewitnesses (see review by Leippe, 1995). It remains for future research to do the same for confessions.

REFERENCES

Aguinis, H., Pierce, C. A., & Quigley, B. M. (1995). Enhancing the validity of self-reported alcohol and marijuana consumption using a bogus pipeline procedure: A meta-analytic review. *Basic and Applied Social Psychology, 16,* 515–527.

Ailes, R. (1988). *You are the message.* New York: Doubleday.

Ajzen, I. (1985). From intentions to actions: A theory of planned behavior. In J. Kuhl & J. Beckmann (Eds.), *Action-control: From cognition to behavior* (pp. 11–39). Heidelberg, Germany: Springer-Verlag.

Ajzen, I. (1996). The directive influences of attitudes on behavior. In P. M. Gollwitzer & J. A. Bargh (Eds.), *The psychology of action: Linking cognition and motivation to behavior* (pp. 385–403). New York: Guilford Press.

Akehurst, L., Lohnken, G., Vrij, A., & Bull, R. (1996). Lay persons' and police officers' beliefs regarding deceptive behavior. *Applied Cognitive Psychology, 10,* 461–471.

Alba, J. W., & Marmorstein, H. (1987). The effects of frequency knowledge on consumer decision making. *Journal of Consumer Research, 14,* 14–25.

Alessandra, A. J. (1993). *Collaborative selling: How to gain the competitive advantage in sales.* New York: Wiley.

American Psychiatric Association. (2000). *Diagnostic and statistical manual of mental disorders* (4th ed. TR). Washington, DC: Author.

Arizona v. Fulminante, 499 US 279 (1991).

Arkes, H. R., Hackett, C., & Boehm, L. E. (1998). The generality of the relation between familiarity and judged validity. *Journal of Behavioral Decision Making, 2,* 81–94.

Aronson, E. (1999). *The social animal.* New York: Worth/Freeman.

Bacon, F. (1620/1955). Novum organum. In R. M. Hutchins (Ed.), *Great books of the Western world, Vol. 30* (pp. 105–195). Chicago: Encyclopedia Britannica.

Bandura, A. (1997). *Self-efficacy: The exercise of control.* New York: Freedman.

Bargh, J. A., & Chartrand, T. L. (1999). The unbearable automaticity of being. *American Psychologist, 54,* 462–479.

Baron, R. S., Inman, M., Kao, C., & Logan, H. (1992). Emotion and superficial social processing. *Motivation and Emotion, 16,* 323–345.

Bassili, J. N. (1996). Meta-judgmental versus operative indices of psychological attributes: The case of measures of attitude strength. *Journal of Personality and Social Psychology, 71,* 637–653.

Baumeister, R. F., Bratslavsky, E., Muraven, M., & Tice, D. M. (1998). Ego depletion: Is the active self a limited resource? *Journal of Personality & Social Psychology, 74,* 1252–1265.

Baumeister, R. F., Muraven, M., & Tice, D. M. (2000). Ego depletion: A resource model of volition, self-regulation, and controlled processing. *Social Cognition, 18,* 130–150.

Baumeister, R. F., Twenge, J. M., & Nuss, C. K. (2002). Effects of social exclusion on cognitive processes: Anticipated aloneness reduces intelligent thought. *Journal of Personality & Social Psychology, 83,* 817–827.

Beck, F., & Godin, W. (1951). *Russian purge and the extraction of confession.* London: Hurst and Blacknett.

Bedau, H. A., & Radelet, M. L. (1987). Miscarriages of justice in potentially capital cases. *Stanford Law Review, 40,* 21–174.

Bernard, M. M., Maio, G. R., & Olson, J. M. (2003). The vulnerability of values to attack: Inoculation of values and value-relevant attitudes. *Personality & Social Psychology Bulletin, 29,* 63–75.

Blagrove, M. (1996). Effects of length of sleep deprivation on interrogative suggestibility. *Journal of Experimental Psychology: Applied, 2,* 48–59.

Blagrove, M., Alexander, C. A., & Horne, J. A. (1995). The effects of chronic sleep reduction on the performance of cognitive tasks sensitive to sleep deprivation. *Applied Cognitive Psychology, 9,* 21–40.

Blagrove, M., Cole-Morgan, D., & Lambe, H. (1994). Interrogative suggestibility: The effects of sleep deprivation and relationship with field-dependence. *Applied Cognitive Psychology, 8,* 169–179.

Blass, T. (2000). *Obedience to authority: Current perspectives on the Milgram paradigm.* Mahwah, NJ: Lawrence Erlbaum.

Bodenhausen, G. V. (1990). Second guessing the jury: Stereotypic and hindsight biases in perceptions of court cases. *Journal of Applied Social Psychology, 20,* 1112–1121.

Boehm, L. E. (1994). The validity effect: A search for mediating variables. *Personality & Social Psychology Bulletin, 20,* 285–293.

Boninger, D. S., Krosnick, J. A., & Berent, M. K. (1995). Origins of attitude importance: Self-interest, social identification, and value relevance. *Journal of Personality and Social Psychology, 68,* 61–80.

Borchard, E. (1932). *Convicting the innocent: Errors of criminal justice.* New Haven, CT: Yale University Press.

Bottoms, A. E., & McClean, J. D. (1976). *Defendants in the criminal process.* London: Routledge and Kegan Paul.

Bramel, D. (1969). Determinants of beliefs about other people. In J. Mills (Ed.), *Experimental social psychology.* New York: Macmillan.

Brandon, R., & Davies, C. (1973). *Wrongful imprisonment.* London: Allen & Unwin.

Brehm, J. (1966). *A theory of psychological reactance.* New York: Academic Press.

Brehm, J. W., & Brehm, S. S. (1981). *Psychological reactance: A theory of freedom and control.* New York: Academic Press.

Brinol, P., Rucker, D. D., Tormala, Z. L., & Petty, R. E. (in press). Individual differences in resistance to persuasion: The role of beliefs and meta-beliefs. In E. S. Knowles & J. A. Linn (Eds.), *Resistance and persuasion.* Mahwah, NJ: Lawrence Erlbaum.

Brock, T. C. (1968). Implications of comodity theory for value change. In A. G. Greenwald, T. C. Brock & T. M. Ostrom (Eds.), *Psychological foundations of attitudes*. New York: Academic Press.

Brophy, E. E., Huang, W. W. (2000). Twenty-ninth annual review of criminal procedure. I. Investigation and police practices. Custodial interrogations. *Georgetown Law Journal, 88*, 1021–1043.

Burger, J. M., Soroka, S., Gonzago, K., Murphy, E., & Somervell, E. (2001). The effect of fleeting attraction on compliance to requests. *Personality and Social Psychology Bulletin, 27*, 1578–1586.

Cacioppo, J. T., Petty, R. E., Feinstein, J., & Jarvis, B. (1996). Dispositional differences in cognitive motivation: The life and times of individuals low versus high in need for cognition. *Psychological Bulletin, 119*, 197–253.

Caples, J. (1974). *Tested advertising methods*. Englewood Cliffs, NJ: Prentice Hall.

Carlsmith, J. M., & Gross, A. E. (1969). Some effects of guilt on compliance. *Journal of Personality and Social Psychology, 11*, 232–239.

Cassell, P. G. (1996). All benefits, no costs: The grand illusion of *Miranda's* defenders. *Northwestern University Law Review, 90*, 1084–1124.

Chaiken, S. (1980). Heuristic versus systematic information processing and the use of source versus message cues in persuasion. *Journal of Personality and Social Psychology, 39*, 752–766.

Chaiken, S. (1987). The heuristic model of persuasion. In M. P. Zanna, J. M. Olson & C. P. Herman (Eds.), *Social influence: The Ontario symposium* (pp. 3–39). Hillsdale, NJ: Lawrence Erlbaum.

Chaiken, S., & Eagly, A. (1983). Communication modality as a determinant of persuasion: The role of communicator salience. *Journal of Personality & Social Psychology, 45*, 241–256.

Chen, S., & Chaiken, S. (1999). The heuristic-systematic model in its broader context. In S. Chaiken & Y. Trope (Eds.), *Dual-process theories in social psychology* (pp. 73–96). New York: Guilford Press.

Christianson, S. A. (1992a). Emotional stress and eyewitness memory: A critical review. *Psychology Bulletin, 112*, 284–309.

Christianson, S. A. (1992b). Remembering emotional events: Potential mechanism. In S. A. Christianson (Ed.), *The handbook of emotion and memory: Research and theory* (pp. 305–340). Hillsdale, NJ: Lawrence Erlbaum.

Christianson, S. A., & Safer, M. A. (1996). Emotional events and emotions in autobiographical memories. In D. C. Rubin (Ed.), *Remembering our past: Studies in autobiographical memory* (pp. 218–243). Cambridge: Cambridge University Press.

Cialdini, R. B. (2001). *Influence: Science and practice*. Boston: Allyn & Bacon.

Cialdini, R. B., & Petty, R. E. (1981). Anticipatory opinion effects. In R. E. Petty, T. M. Ostrom & T. C. Brock (Eds.), *Cognitive responses in persuasion* (pp. 217–235). Hillsdale, NJ: Lawrence Erlbaum.

Cialdini, R. B., Vincent, J. E., Lewis, S. K., Catalan, J., Wheeler, D., & Darby, B. L. (1975). Reciprocal concessions procedure for inducing compliance: The door-in-the-face technique. *Journal of Personality and Social Psychology, 31*, 206–215.

Colorado v. Connelly 479 U.S. 157 (1986).

Commonwealth v. Crawford, 429 Mass. 60 (1999).

Connery, D. S. (1977). *Guilty until proven innocent*. New York: Putnam's.

Connery, D. S. (1995). *Convicting the innocent*. Cambridge, MA: Brookline.

Cutler, B. L., Penrod, S. D., & Dexter, H. R. (1990). Juror sensitivity to eyewitness identification evidence. *Law and Human Behavior, 14,* 185–229.

Cutler, B. L., Penrod, S. D., & Stuve, T. E. (1988). Juror decision making in eyewitness identification cases. *Law and Human Behavior, 12,* 41–55.

Dal Cin, S., Zanna, M. P., & Fong, G. T. (in press). Narrative persuasion and overcoming resistance. In E. S. Knowles & J. A. Linn (Eds.), *Resistance and persuasion.* Mahwah, NJ: Lawrence Erlbaum.

Darke, P. R., Chaiken, S., Bohner, G., Einwiller, S., Erb, H., & Hazlewood, J. D. (1998). Accuracy motivation, consensus information, and the law of large numbers: Effects on attitude judgment in the absence of argumentation. *Personality & Social Psychology Bulletin, 24,* 1205–1215.

Das, E. H. H. J., de Wit, J. B. F., & Stroebe, W. (2003). Fear appeals motivate acceptance of action recommendations: Evidence for a positive bias in the processing of persuasive messages. *Personality & Social Psychology Bulletin, 29,* 650–664.

Davis, D. (1982). Determinants of responsiveness in dyadic interaction. In W. Ickes & E. S. Knowles (Eds.), *Personality, roles and social behavior* (pp. 85–139). New York: Springer-Verlag.

Davis, D., & Follette, W. C. (2001). Foibles of witness memory in high profile/traumatic cases. *Journal of Air Law and Commerce, 66,* 1421–1549.

Davis, D., & Follette, W. C. (2002). Rethinking probative value of evidence: Base rates, intuitive profiling and the postdiction of behavior. *Law and Human Behavior, 26,* 133–158.

Davis, D., & Loftus, E. F. (in press). Aging in the legal system: Victims, witnesses, and jurors. In I. Noy & N. Karwowski (Eds.), *Handbook of forensic human factors and ergonomics.* New York: Taylor and Francis.

Davis, D., & Perkowitz, W. T. (1979). Consequences of responsiveness in dyadic interaction: Effects of probability of response and proportion of content-related responses on interpersonal attraction. *Journal of Personality and Social Psychology, 37,* 534–550.

Dawson, E., Gilovich, T., & Regan, D. T. (2002). Motivated reasoning and performance on the Wason selection task. *Personality and Social Psychology Bulletin, 28,* 1379–1387.

DeFilippo, M. (2001). You have the right to better safeguards: Looking beyond Miranda in the new millennium. *John Marshall Law Journal, 34,* 637–712.

Dell, S. (1971). *Silent in court: Occasional Papers on Social Administration No. 42.* London: Social Administration Trust.

DePaulo, B. M., Charlton, K., Cooper, H., Lindsay, J. J., & Muhlenbruck, L. (1997). The accuracy-confidence correlation in the detection of deception. *Personality & Social Psychology Review, 1,* 346–357.

DePaulo, B. M., Lindsay, J. J., Malone, B. E., Muhlenbruck, L., Charlton, K., & Cooper, H. (2003). Cues to deception. *Psychological Bulletin, 129,* 74–112.

DePaulo, B. M., & Pfeifer, R. L. (1986). On-the-job experience and skill at detecting deception. *Journal of Applied Social Psychology, 16,* 249–267.

DePaulo, B. M., Stone, J. L., & Lassiter, G. D. (1985). Deceiving and detecting deceit. In B. R. Schlenker (Ed.), *The self in social life* (pp. 323–370). New York: McGraw-Hill.

Descartes, R. (1644/1984). Principles of philosophy. In J. Cottingham, R. Stoothoff & D. Murdoch (Eds.), *The philosophical writings of Descartes, Vol. 1* (pp. 193–291). Cambridge, UK: Cambridge University Press.

Devine, P. G. (1989). Stereotypes and prejudice: Their automatic and controlled components. *Journal of Personality and Social Psychology, 56*, 5–18.

Dickerson v. United States, 530 US 428 (2000).

Dwyer, J. (2003, February 2). Police and prosecutors may never agree on who began jogger attack. *The New York Times*.

Dwyer, J., & Saulny, S. (2002, October 25). Hair evidence in jogger case is discredited. *New York Times*.

Dwyer, J., & Saulny, S. (2002, October 16). Youths' denials in '89 rape case cost them parole chances. *The New York Times*.

Eagly, A., & Chaiken, S. (1975). An attributional analysis of the effect of communicator characteristics on opinion change: The case of communicator attractiveness. *Journal of Personality & Social Psychology, 32*, 136–144.

Easterbrook, J. A. (1959). The effect of emotion on cue utilization and the organization of behavior. *Psychological Review, 66*, 183–201.

Edwards, K. (1990). The interplay of affect and cognition in attitude formation and change. *Journal of Personality & Social Psychology, 59*, 202–216.

Edwards, K., & von Hippel, W. (1995). Hearts and minds: The priority of affective versus cognitive factors in person perception. *Personality & Social Psychology Bulletin, 21*, 996–1011.

Ekman, P., & O'Sullivan, M. (1991). Who can catch a liar? *American Psychologist, 46*, 913–920.

Ekman, P., O'Sullivan, M., & Frank, M. (1999). A few can catch a liar. *Psychological Science, 10*, 263–266.

Elaad, E. (2003). Effects of feedback on the overestimated capacity to detect lies and the underestimated ability to tell lies. *Applied Cognitive Psychology, 17*, 349–363.

Erickson, M. H. (1964). The confusion technique in hypnosis. *American Journal of Clinical Hypnosis, 6*, 183–207.

Erickson, M. H., & Rossi, E. L. (1975). Varieties of double bind. *American Journal of Clinical Hypnosis, 17*, 143–157.

Erickson, M. H., Rossi, E. L., & Rossi, S. (1976). *Hypnotic realities: The induction of clinical hypnosis and forms of indirect suggestion*. New York: Irvington.

Fabrigar, L. R., & Petty, R. E. (1999). The role of the affective and cognitive bases of attitudes in susceptibility to affectively and cognitively based persuasion. *Personality & Social Psychology Bulletin, 25*, 363–381.

Fein, S. (1996). Effects of suspicion on attributional thinking and the correspondence bias. *Journal of Personality & Social Psychology, 70*, 1164–1184.

Festinger, L. (1954). A theory of social comparison processes. *Human Relations, 7*, 117–140.

Festinger, L. (1964). *Conflict, decision, and dissonance*. Stanford, CA: Stanford University Press.

Fishbein, M. F., & Ajzen, I. (1975). *Belief, attitude, intention, and behavior: An introduction to theory and research*. Reading, MA: Addison-Wesley.

Florian, A. S. (1999). Fifth amendment Miranda waiver and fourteenth amendment voluntariness. Doctrine in cases of mentally retarded and mentally ill criminal defendants. *Suffolk Journal of Trial and Appellate Advocacy, 4*, 271–293.

Forest, K. D., Wadkins, T. A., & Miller, R. L. (2002). The role of preexisting stress on false confessions: An empirical study. *Journal of Credibility Assessment and Witness Psychology, 3*, 23–45.

Fournier, M. A., Moskowitz, D. S., & Zuroff, D. C. (2002). Social rank strategies in hierarchical relationships. *Journal of Personality & Social Psychology, 83*, 425–433.

Frank, J., & Frank, B. (1957). *Not guilty*. London: Victor Gallancz.

Frank, M. G., & Feeley, T. H. (2003). To catch a liar: Challenges for research in lie detection training. *Journal of Applied Communication Research, 31*, 58–75.

Freedman, J. L., & Fraser, S. C. (1966). Compliance without pressure: The foot-in-the-door technique. *Journal of Personality & Social Psychology, 4*, 195–202.

Frenzen, J. R., & Davis, H. L. (1990). Purchasing behavior in embedded markets. *Journal of Consumer Research, 17*, 1–12.

Fuegen, K., & Brehm, J. W. (in press). The intensity of affect and resistance to social influence. In E. S. Knowles & J. A. Linn (Eds.), *Resistance and persuasion*. Mahwah, NJ: Lawrence Erlbaum.

Geller, W. A. (1993). *Videotaping interrogations and confessions. National Institute of Justice: Research in Brief*. Washington, DC: U.S. Department of Justice.

Gemenes, T. J. C., & Adame, M. L. (2002). Influence of message credibility and the pressure to hide tobacco consumption in the effectiveness of the "Bogus Pipeline" technique. *Drugs: Education, Prevention & Policy, 9*, 187–193.

Gilbert, D. T. (1991). How mental systems believe. *American Psychologist, 46*, 107–119.

Gilbert, D. T. (1993). The assent of man: The mental representation and control of belief. In D. M. Wegner & J. W. Pennebaker (Eds.), *Handbook of mental control* (pp. 57–87). Englewood Cliffs, NJ: Prentice Hall.

Gilbert, D. T. (1998). Ordinary personology. In D. T. Gilbert, S. T. Fiske, & G. Lindzey (Eds.), *The handbook of social psychology* (4th ed.) (pp. 89–150). New York: McGraw-Hill.

Gilbert, D. T., Krull, D. S., & Malone, P. S. (1990). Unbelieving the unbelievable: Some problems in the rejection of false information. *Journal of Personality & Social Psychology, 59*, 601–613.

Gilbert, D. T., & Malone, P. S. (1995). The correspondence bias. *Psychological Bulletin, 117*, 21–38.

Gilbert, D. T., Tafarodi, R. W., & Malone, P. S. (1993). You can't not believe everything you read. *Journal of Personality & Social Psychology, 65*, 221–233.

Gilbert, P. (1992). *Depression: The evolution of powerlessness*. New York: Guilford Press.

Gilligan, S. G. (1987). *Therapeutic trances: The cooperation principle in Ericksonian hypnotherapy*. New York: Brunner/Mazel.

Gimenes, T. J. C., & Adame, M. L. (2002). Influence of message credibility and the pressure to hide tobacco consumption in the effectiveness of the 'Bogus Pipeline' technique. *Drugs: Education, Prevention & Policy, 9*, 187–193.

Glisky, E. L. (2001). Source memory, aging, and the frontal lobes. In M. Naveh-Benjamin, M. Moscovitch & H. L. Roediger III (Eds.), *Perspectives on human memory and cognitive aging* (pp. 265–276). New York: Psychology Press.

Golding, J. M., & MacLeod, C. M. (Eds.). (1998). *Intentional forgetting: Interdisciplinary approaches*. Mahwah, NJ: Lawrence Erlbaum.

Gouldner, A. W. (1960). The norm of reciprocity: A preliminary statement. *American Sociological Review, 25*, 161–178.

Granhag, P. A., & Stroemwall, L. A. (2001). Deception detection: Interrogators' and observers' decoding of consecutive statements. *Journal of Psychology, 135*, 603–620.

Green, M. C., Strange, J. J., & Brock, T. C. (Eds.) (2002). *Narrative impact: Social and cognitive foundations*. Mahwah, NJ: Lawrence Erlbaum.

Greenwald, A. G. (1968). Cognitive learning, cognitive response to persuasion, and attitude change. In A. G. Greenwald, T. C. Brock & T. M. Ostrom (Eds.), *Psychological foundations of attitudes* (pp. 147–170). New York: Academic Press.

Gregory, S. W., Burroughs, W. J., & Ainslie, F. M. (1985). Self-relevant scenarios as indirect means of attitude change. *Personality & Social Psychology Bulletin, 11*, 435–444.

Gregory, S. W., Cialdini, R. B., & Carpenter, K. M. (1982). Self-relevant scenarios as mediators of likelihood estimates and compliance: Does imagining make it so? *Journal of Personality & Social Psychology, 43*, 89–99.

Grisso, T. (1998a). *Forensic evaluation of juveniles*. Sarasota, FL: Professional Resources.

Grisso, T. (1998b). *Instruments for assessing understanding and appreciation of Miranda rights*. Sarasota, FL: Professional Resources.

Gross, H. (1907). *Criminal investigation*.

Gudjosson, G. H. (1989). The psychology of false confessions. *Medico-Legal Journal, 57*, 93–110.

Gudjonsson, G. H. (1992a). *The psychology of interrogations, confessions and testimony*. New York: Wiley.

Gudjonsson, G. H. (1992b). *The psychology of interrogations, confessions, and testimony*. Unpublished manuscript, London.

Gudjonsson, G. H. (2003). *The psychology of interrogations and confessions: A handbook*. West Sussex, UK: Wiley.

Haugtvedt, C. P., & Petty, R. E. (1992). Personality and persuasion: Need for cognition moderates the persistence and resistance of attitude changes. *Journal of Personality & Social Psychology, 63*, 308–319.

Heider, F. (1946). Attitudes and cognitive organization. *Journal of Psychology, 21*, 107–112.

Heider, F. (1958). *The psychology of interpersonal relations*. Hillsdale, NJ: Lawrence Erlbaum.

Herman, J. L. (1995). Crime and memory. *Bulletin of American Academy of Psychiatry Law, 23*, 5–17.

Hertwig, R., Gigerenzer, G., & Hoffrage, U. (1997). The reiteration effect in hindsight bias. *Psychological Review, 10*, 194–202.

Heuer, F., & Reisberg, D. (1992). Emotion, arousal, and memory for detail. In S.-A. Christianson (Ed.), *The handbook of emotion and memory: Research and theory* (pp. 151–180). Hillsdale, NJ: Lawrence Erlbaum.

Hilgendorf, E. L., & Irving, B. (1981). A decision-making model of confessions. In M. A. Lloyd-Bostock (Ed.), *Psychology in legal contexts: Applications and limitations* (pp. 67–84). London: Macmillan.

Hilton, J. L., Fein, S., & Miller, D. T. (1993). Suspicion and dispositional inference. *Journal of Personality & Social Psychology, 19*, 501–512.

Hinkle, L. E., & Wolff, H. G. (1956). Communist interrogation and indoctrination of "enemies of the states." *American Medical Association Archives of Neurology and Psychiatry, 76*, 115–174.

Horselenberg, R., Merckelbach, H., Josephs, S. (2003). Individual differences and false confessions: A conceptual replication of Kassin and Kiechel (1996). *Psychology, Crime, & Law, 9*, 1–8.

Huff, R., Rattner, A., & Sagarin, E. (1986). Guilty until proven innocent. *Crime and Delinquency, 32*, 518–544.

Inbau, F. E., Reid, J. E., & Buckley, J. P. (Eds.) (1986). *Criminal interrogation and confessions* (3rd ed.). Baltimore: Williams & Wilkins.

Inbau, F. E., Reid, J. E., Buckley, J. P., & Jayne, B. C. (2001). *Criminal interrogations and confessions* (4th ed.). Gaithersburg, MD: Aspen.

Ingrassia, R. (2003, October 18). Are confessions valid? Three experts weigh in on teens' taped admissions. *Daily News.*

Jacks, J. Z., & O'Brien, M. E. (in press). Decreasing resistance by affirming the self. In E. S. Knowles & J. A. Linn (Eds.), *Resistance and persuasion*. Mahwah, NJ: Lawrence Erlbaum.

Janis, I. L., & Feshbach, S. (1953). Effects of fear-arousing communications. *Journal of Abnormal and Social Psychology, 49*, 78–92.

Jaschinski, U., & Wentura, D. (2002). Misleading postevent information and working memory capacity: An individual differences approach to eyewitness memory. *Applied Cognitive Psychology, 16*, 223–231.

Jayne, B. C. (1986). The psychological principles of criminal interrogation: An appendix. In F. E. Inbau, J. E. Reid & J. P. Buckley (Eds.), *Criminal interrogation and confessions* (3rd ed.) (pp. 327–347). Baltimore, MD: Williams & Wilkins.

Jayne, B. C., & Buckley, J. P. (1991). Criminal interrogation techniques on trial. The Prosecutor. *Journal of the National District Attorney's Association, 25/2.*

Jayne, B. C., & Buckley, J. P. III. (1992). Criminal interrogation techniques on trial. *Security Management. Arlington, 36*, 64–70.

Jepson, C., & Chaiken, S. (1990). Chronic issue-specific fear inhibits systematic processing of persuasive communications. *Journal of Social Behavior and Personality, 5*, 61–84.

Jerome, R. (1995, August 13). Suspect confessions. *The New York Times Magazine*, 28–31.

Johnson, H. M., Hastroudi, S., & Lindsay, D. L. (1993). Source monitoring. *Psychological Bulletin, 114*, 3–28.

Johnson, H. M., & Seifert, C. M. (1994). Sources of the continued influence effect: When misinformation in memory affects later inferences. *Journal of Experimental Psychology: Learning, Memory, and Cognition, 20*, 1420–1436.

Johnson, M. E., & Hauck, C. (1999). Beliefs and opinions about hypnosis held by the general public: A systematic evaluation. *American Journal of Clinical Hypnosis, 42*, 10–20.

Johnson, P. E., Grazioli, S., Jamal, K., & Berryman, R. G. (2001). Detecting deception: Adversarial problem solving in a low base-rate world. *Cognitive Science, 25*, 355–392.

Jolson, M. A. (1997). Broadening the scope of relationship selling. *Journal of Personal Selling and Sales Management, 17*, 75–88.

Jonas, E., Schulz-Hardt, S., Frey, D., & Thelen, N. (2001). Confirmation bias in sequential information search after preliminary decisions: An expansion of dissonance theoretical research on selective exposure to information. *Journal of Personality & Social Psychology, 80*, 557–571.

Jones, E. E. (1990). *Interpersonal perception.* New York: Freeman.

Jones, E. E., & Nisbett, R. E. (1972). The actor and the observer: Divergent perceptions of the causes of behavior. In E. E. Jones, D. E. Kanouse, H. H. Kelley, R. E. Nisbett, S. Valins & B. Weiner (Eds.), *Attribution: Perceiving the causes of behavior* (pp. 79–94). Morristown, NY: General Learning Press.

Jones, E. E., & Sigall, H. (1971). The bogus pipeline: A new paradigm for measuring affect and attitude. *Psychological Bulletin, 76*, 349–364.

Jorden, D. L. (1993). Newspaper effects on policy preferences. *Public Opinion Quarterly, 57*, 191–203.

Kamisar, Y. (1995). On the "fruits" of Miranda violations, coerced confessions, and compelled testimony. *Michigan Law Review, 93*, 929–1010.

Kamisar, Y., Lafave, W., & Israel, J. (1994). *Modern criminal procedure* (8th ed.). St. Paul, MN: West.

Kassin, S. M. (1997a). False memories against the self. *Psychological Inquiry, 8*, 300–302.

Kassin, S. M. (1997b). The psychology of confession evidence. *American Psychologist, 52*, 221–233.

Kassin, S. M. (1998). More on the psychology of false confessions. *American Psychologist, 53*, 320–321.

Kassin, S. M. (2002). The cooperating witness conundrum: Is justice obtainable? *Cardozo Law Review, 23*, 809–816.

Kassin, S. M. (2002, November 1). False confessions and the jogger case. *The New York Times*.

Kassin, S. M., & Fong, C. T. (1999). "I'm innocent!": Effects of training on judgments of truth and deception in the interrogation room. *Law and Human Behavior, 23*, 499–516.

Kassin, S. M., Goldstein, C. C., & Savitsky, K. (2003). Behavioral confirmation in the interrogation room: On the dangers of presuming guilt. *Law and Human Behavior, 27*, 187–203.

Kassin, S. M., & Kiechel, K. L. (1996). The social psychology of false confessions: Compliance, internalization, and confabulation. *Psychological Science, 7*, 125–128.

Kassin, S. M., & McNall, K. (1991). Police interrogations and confessions: Communicating promises and threats by pragmatic implication. *Law and Human Behavior, 15*, 233–251.

Kassin, S. M., & Neumann, K. (1997). On the power of confession evidence: An experimental test of the "fundamental difference" hypothesis. *Law and Human Behavior, 21*, 469–484.

Kassin, S. M., Reddy, M. E., & Tulloch, W. F. (1990). Juror interpretations of ambiguous evidence: The need for cognition, presentation order and persuasion. *Law and Human Behavior, 14*, 43–55.

Kassin, S. M., & Studebaker, C. A. (1998). Instructions to disregard and the jury: Curative and paradoxical effects. In J. M. Golding & C. M. MacLeod (Eds.), *Intentional forgetting: Interdisciplinary approaches* (pp. 413–434). Mahwah, NJ: Lawrence Erlbaum.

Kassin, S. M., & Sukel, H. (1997). Coerced confessions and the jury: An experimental test of the "harmless error" rule. *Law and Human Behavior, 21*, 27–46.

Kassin, S. M., & Wrightsman, L. S. (1980). Prior confessions and mock juror verdicts. *Journal of Applied Social Psychology, 10*, 133–146.

Kassin, S. M., & Wrightsman, L. S. (1981). Coerced confessions, judicial instruction, and mock juror verdicts. *Journal of Applied Social Psychology, 11*, 489–506.

Kassin, S. M., & Wrightsman, L. S. (1985). Confession evidence. In S. M. Kassin & L. S. Wrightsman (Eds.), *The psychology of evidence and trial procedure* (pp. 67–94). Beverly Hills, CA: Sage.

Kelley, H. H. (1972). Attribution in social interaction. In E. E. Jones, D. E. Kanouse, H. H. Kelley, R. E. Nisbett, S. Valins & B. Weiner (Eds.), *Attribution: Perceiving the causes of behavior* (pp. 1–26). Morristown, NY: General Learning Press.

Keltner, D., Gruenfeld, D. H., & Anderson, C. (2003). Power, approach, and inhibition. *Psychological Review, 110*, 265–284.

Kenrick, D. T., Neuberg, S. L., & Cialdini, R. B. (2002). *Social psychology: Unraveling the mystery* (2nd ed.). Boston: Allyn & Bacon.

Klein, K., & Boals, A. (2001). The relationship of life event stress and working memory capacity. *Applied Cognitive Psychology, 15,* 565–579.

Knowles, E. S., Brennan, M., & Linn, J. A. (2002). *Consuming resistance to political ads.* Unpublished manuscript, University of Arkansas; Fayetteville, AR.

Knowles, E. S., Butler, S., & Linn, J. A. (2001). Increasing compliance by reducing resistance. In J. P. Forgas & K. D. Williams (Eds.), *Social influence: Direct and indirect processes* (pp. 41–60). Philadelphia, PA: Psychology Press.

Knowles, E. S., & Condon, C. A. (1999). Why people say "yes": A dual-process theory of acquiescence. *Journal of Personality & Social Psychology, 77,* 379–386.

Knowles, E. S., & Linn, J. A. (in press). Approach-avoidance model of persuasion: Alpha and omega strategies for change. In E. S. Knowles & J. A. Linn (Eds.), *Resistance and persuasion.* Mahwah, NJ: Lawrence Erlbaum.

Koutstall, W., & Schacter, D. L. (2001). Memory distortion and aging. In M. Naveh-Benjamin, M. Moscovitch & H. L. Roediger III (Eds.), *Perspectives on human memory and cognitive aging: Essays in honour of Fergus Craik* (pp. 362–383). New York: Psychology Press.

Kraut, R. E., & Poe, D. (1980). On the line: The deception judgements of customs inspectors and laymen. *Journal of Personality & Social Psychology, 36,* 380–391.

Krosnick, J. A., Boninger, D. S., Chuang, Y. C., Berent, M. K., & Carnot, C. G. (1993). Attitude strength: One construct or many related constructs? *Journal of Personality and Social Psychology, 65,* 1132–1151.

Kruglanski, A. W., & Webster, D. M. (1996). Motivated closing of the mind: "Seizing" and "freezing." *Psychological Review, 103,* 263–283.

Lassiter, G. D., Geers, A. L., Handley, I. M., Weiland, P. E., & Munhall, P. J. (2002). Videotaped interrogations and confessions: A simple change in camera perspective alters verdicts in simulated trials. *Journal of Applied Psychology, 87,* 867–874.

Lassiter, G. D., Geers, A. L., Munhall, P. J., Handley, I. M., & Beers, M. J. (2001). Videotaped confessions: Is guilt in the eye of the camera? In M. P. Zanna (Ed.), *Advances in experimental social psychology, Vol. 33* (pp. 189–254). San Diego, CA: Academic Press.

Latane, B., & Wolf, S. (1981). The social impact of majorities and minorities. *Psychological Review, 88,* 438–453.

Laurence, J.-R., & Perry, C. (1988). *Hypnosis, will and memory: A psycho-legal history.* New York: Guilford Press.

Law, S., Hawkins, S. A., & Craik, F. I. M. (1998). Repetition-induced belief in the elderly: Rehabilitation age-related memory deficits. *Journal of Consumer Research, 25,* 91–107.

Lego v. Twomey, 404 US 477 (1972).

Leippe, M. R. (1995). The case for expert testimony about eyewitness memory. *Psychology, Public Policy, and Law, 1,* 909–959.

Leippe, M. R., Manion, A. P., & Romanczyk, A. (1992). Eyewitness persuasion: How and how well do fact finders judge the accuracy of adults' and children's memory reports. *Journal of Personality & Social Psychology, 63,* 191–197.

Leites, N., & Bernaut, E. (1954). *Ritual of liquidation.* Glencoe, IL: Free Press.

Leo, R. A. (1996a). Inside the interrogation room. *Journal of Criminal Law and Criminology, 86,* 266–303.

Leo, R. A. (1996b). Miranda's revenge: Police interrogation as a confidence game. *Law and Society Review, 30,* 259–288.

Leo, R. A. (2001). False confessions: Causes, consequences, and solutions. In S. D. Westervelt (Ed.), *Wrongly convicted: Perspectives on failed justice* (pp. 36–54). New Brunswich, NJ: Rutgers University Press.

Leo, R. A. (2001). Questioning the relevance of Miranda in the twenty-first century. *The Michigan Law Review, 99*, 1000–1029.

Leo, R. A., & Ofshe, R. J. (1998). The consequences of false confessions: Deprivations of liberty and miscarriages of justice in the age of psychological interrogation. *Journal of Criminal Law and Criminology, 88*, 429–496.

Leo, R. A., & Ofshe, R. J. (2001). The truth about false confessions and advocacy scholarship. *Criminal Law Bulletin, 37*, 293–370.

Leo, R. A., & White, W. S. (1999). Adapting to miranda: Modern interrogators' strategies for dealing with the obstacles posed By Miranda. *Minnesota Law Review, 84*, 397–472.

Lerner, J. S., & Keltner, D. (2000). Beyond valence: Toward a model of emotion-specific influences on judgment and choice. *Cognition and Emotion, 14*, 473–493.

Lerner, J. S., & Keltner, D. (2002). Fear, anger, and risk. *Journal of Personality and Social Psychology, 81*, 146–159.

Leventhal, H., & Cameron, L. (1994). Persuasion and health attitudes. In S. Shavitt & T. C. Brock (Eds.), *Persuasion* (pp. 219–249). Boston: Allyn & Bacon.

Lewin, K. (1947). Group decision and social change. In T. M. Newcomb & E. L. Hartley (Eds.), *Readings in social psychology* (pp. 330–344). New York: Holt.

Liberman, A., & Chaiken, S. (1992). Defensive processing of personally relevant health messages. *Personality & Social Psychology Bulletin, 18*, 669–679.

Lifton, R. J. (1956). "Thought reform" of Western civilians in Chinese prisons. *American Journal of Psychiatry, 110*, 732–739.

Lifton, R. J. (1961). *Thought reform and the psychology of totalism.* New York: Norton.

Linn, J. A., & Knowles, E. S. (2002, May). *Acknowledging target resistance in persuasive messages.* Paper presented at the Midwestern Psychological Association, Chicago.

Loftus, E. F., & Ketcham, K. (1991). *Witness for the defense.* New York: St. Martin's Press.

Lykken, D. T. (1998). *Tremor in the blood: Uses and abuses of the lie detector.* New York: Plenum.

Mackie, D. M. (1987). Systematic and nonsystematic processing of majority and minority persuasive communications. *Journal of Personality & Social Psychology, 53*, 41–52.

Mann, S. (2001). Who killed my relative? Police officers' ability to detect real-life high-stakes lies. *Psychology, Crime & Law, 7*, 119–132.

McArthur, L. Z. (1972). The how and what of why: Some determinants and consequences of causal attribution. *Journal of Personality and Social Psychology, 22*, 507–519.

McArthur, L. Z. (1981). What grabs you? The role of attention in impression formation and causal attribution. In E. T. Higgins, C. P. Herman, & M. P. Zanna (Eds.), *Social cognition: The Ontario symposium Vol. 1* (pp. 201–241). Hillsdale, NJ: Lawrence Erlbaum.

McCann, J. T. (1998). Broadening the typology of false confessions. *American Psychologist, 53*, 319–320.

McCann, J. T. (1998). A conceptual framework for identifying various types of confessions. *Behavioral Sciences and the Law, 16*, 441–453.

Mcguire, R. E. (2000). A proposal to strengthen juvenile Miranda rights: Requiring parental presence in custodial interrogations. *Vanderbuilt Law Review, 53*, 1355–1387.

McGuire, W. J., & Papageorgis, D. (1961). The relative efficacy of various types of prior belief defense in producing immunity against persuasion. *Journal of Abnormal and Social Psychology, 62*, 327–337.

Meissner, C. A., & Kassin, S. M. (2002). "He's guilty!": Investigator bias in judgments of truth and deception. *Law and Human Behavior, 26*, 469–480.

Meyer, T. (1999). Testing the validity of confessions and waivers of the self-incrimination privilege in the juvenile court. *University of Kansas Law Review, 47*, 1035–1078.

Milgram, S. (1992). Some conditions of obedience and disobedience to authority. In S. Milgram, J. Sabini, & M. Silver (Eds.), *The individual in the social world: Essays and experiments* (pp. 136–161). New York: McGraw-Hill.

Miranda v. Arizona 384 U.S. 336 (1966).

Mueller, C. B., & Kirkpatrick, L. C. (1995). *Modern evidence: Doctrine and practice.* Boston: Little, Brown.

Muraven, M., & Baumeister, R. F. (2000). Self-regulation and depletion of limited resources: Does self-control resemble a muscle? *Psychological Bulletin, 126*, 247–259.

Mussweiler, T. (2000). Overcoming the inevitable anchoring effect: Considering the opposite compensates for selective accessibility. *Personality & Social Psychology Bulletin, 26*, 1142–1150.

Mussweiler, T. (2002). The malleability of anchoring effects. *Experimental Psychology, 49*, 67–72.

Nardulli, P.-F., Eisenstein, J., & Flemming, R.-B. (1988). *The tenor of justice: Criminal courts and the guilty plea process.* Urbana, IL: University of Illinois Press.

Nawrat, I. R. (2001). Dialogue involvement as a social influence technique. *Personality & Social Psychology Bulletin, 27*, 1395–1406.

Nietzche, F. (1886/1996). *Human, all too human: A book for free spirits.* Lincoln, NE: University of Nebraska Press.

Oberlander, L. B., Goldstein, N. E., & Goldstein, A. M. (2003). Competence to confess. In A. M. Goldstein (Ed.), *Handbook of psychology: Forensic psychology* (Vol. 11, pp. 335–357). New York: Wiley.

O'Brian, J. A. (1993, September 23). Mother's killing still unresolved, but Peter Reilly puts past behind. *The Hartford Courant*, p. A1.

Ofshe, R. J. (1989). Coerced confessions: The logic of seemingly irrational action. *Cultic Studies Journal, 6*, 1–15.

Ofshe, R. J., & Leo, R. A. (1997a). The decision to confess falsely: Rational choice and irrational action. *Denver University Law Review, 74*, 979–1122.

Ofshe, R. J., & Leo, R. A. (1997b). The social psychology of police interrogation: The theory and classification of true and false confessions. *Studies in Law, Politics & Society, 16*, 189–251.

Ogilvy, D. (1983). *Ogilvy on advertising.* New York: Crown.

Ogletree, C. J. (1991). *Arizona v. Fulminante*: The harm of applying harmless error to coerced confessions. *Harvard Law Review, 105*, 152–175.

Park, H. S., Levine, T. R., McCornack, S. A., Morrison, K., & Ferrara, M. (2002). How people really detect lies. *Communication Monographs, 69*, 144–157.

Pennebaker, J. W., & Sanders, D. Y. (1976). American graffiti: Effects of authority and reactance arousal. *Personality & Social Psychology Bulletin, 2*, 264–267.

Petty, R. E. (1995). Attitude change. In A. Tesser (Ed.), *Advanced social psychology* (pp. 195–255). New York: McGraw-Hill.

Petty, R. E., Brinol, P., & Tormala, Z. L. (2002). Thought confidence as a determinant of persuasion: The self-validation hypothesis. *Journal of Personality & Social Psychology, 82,* 722–741.

Petty, R. E., & Cacioppo, J. T. (1984). The effects of involvement on responses to argument quantity and quality: Central and peripheral routes to persuasion. *Journal of Personality & Social Psychology, 46,* 69–81.

Petty, R. E., & Cacioppo, J. T. (1986). *Communication and persuasion: Central and peripheral routes to attitude change.* New York: Springer-Verlag.

Petty, R. E., Cacioppo, J. T., & Goldman, R. (1981). Personal involvement as a determinant of argument-based persuasion. *Journal of Personality & Social Psychology, 41,* 847–855.

Petty, R. E., Cacioppo, J. T., & Schumann, D. (1983). Central and peripheral routes to advertising effectiveness: The moderating role of involvement. *Journal of Consumer Research, 10,* 134–148.

Petty, R. E., Haugtvedt, C. P., & Smith, S. M. (1995). Elaboration as a determinant of attitude strength. In R. E. Petty & J. A. Krosnick (Eds.), *Attitude strength: Antecedents and consequences* (pp. 93–130). Hillsdale, NJ: Lawrence Erlbaum.

Petty, R. E., & Krosnick, J. A. (1995). *Attitude strength: Antecedents and consequences.* Mahwah, NJ: Lawrence Erlbaum.

Petty, R. E., & T., C. J. (1986). *Communication and persuasion: Central and peripheral routes to attitude change.* New York: Springer-Verlag.

Petty, R. E., & Wegener, D. M. (1998). Attitude change: Multiple roles for persuasion variables. In D. T. Gilvert, S. T. Fiske, & G. Lindzey (Eds.), *Handbook of social psychology, Vol. 1* (4th ed.) (pp. 323–390). New York: McGraw-Hill.

Petty, R. E., & Wegener, D. M. (1999). The elaboration likelihood model: Current status and controversies. In S. Chaiken & Y. Trope (Eds.), *Dual-process theories in social psychology* (pp. 41–72). New York: Guiford Press.

Pham, L. B., Taylor, S. E., & Seeman, T. E. (2001). Effects of environmental predictability and personal mastery on self-regulatory and physiological processes. *Personality & Social Psychology Bulletin, 27,* 611–620.

Pomeranz, E. M., Chaiken, S., & Tordesillas, R. S. (1995). Attitude strength and resistance processes. *Journal of Personality and Social Psychology, 69,* 408–419.

Porter, S., Campbell, M. A., Stapleton, J., & Birt, A. R. (2003). The influence of judge, target, and stimulus characteristics on the accuracy of detecting deceit. *Canadian Journal of Behavioral Science, 34,* 172–185.

Porter, S., Woodworth, M., & Birt, A. R. (2000). Truth, lies, and videotape: An investigation of the ability of federal parole officers to detect deception. *Law and Human Behavior, 24,* 643–658.

Pratkanis, A. R., & Aronson, E. (2001). *Age of propaganda.* New York: W. H. Freeman.

Price, J. (2000). Subordination, self-esteem, and depression. In L. Sloman & P. Gilbert (Eds.), *Subordination and defeat: An evolutionary approach to mood disorders and their therapy* (pp. 165–177). Mahwah, NJ: Lawrence Erlbaum.

Price, J., Sloman, L., Gardner, R., Gilbert, P., & Rohde, P. (1994). The social competition hypothesis of depression. *British Journal of Psychiatry, 164,* 309–315.

Psychological Inquiry (1999). *10*(1)

Radin, E. D. (1964). *The innocents.* New York: William Morrow.

Ratneshwar, S., & Chaiken, S. (1991). Comprehension's moderating role in persuasion: The case of its moderating effect on the impact of source cues. *Journal of Consumer Psychology, 18* (1), 52–63.

Rattner, A. (1988). Convicted but innocent: Wrongful conviction and the criminal justice system. *Law and Human Behavior, 12,* 283–293.

Raz, N. (2001). Aging of the brain and its impact on cognitive performance: Integration of structural and functional findings. In F. I. M. Craik & T. A. Salthouse (Eds.), *The handbook of aging and cognition* (2nd ed., pp. 1–90). Mahwah, NJ: Lawrence Erlbaum.

Redlich, A. D., & Goodman, G. S. (2003). Taking responsibility for an act not committed. *Law and Human Behavior, 27,* 141–156.

Reilly, P. (1995). When will it ever end? In D. S. Connery (Ed.), *Convicting the innocent* (pp. 84–86). Cambridge, MA: Brookline.

Rosen, S. (1991). *My voice will go with you: The teaching tales of Milton H. Erickson, M.D.* New York: W. W. Norton.

Rosenberg, I. M., & Rosenberg, Y. L. (1989). A modest proposal for the abolition of custodial confessions. *North Carolina Law Review, 68,* 69–115.

Ross, L. D. (1977). The intuitive psychologist and his shortcomings: Distortions in the attribution process. In L. Berkowitz (Ed.), *Advances in experimental social psychology* (Vol. 10, pp. 173–220). New York: Academic Press.

Safer, M. A., Christianson, S.-A., Autry, M. W., & Oesterlund, K. (1998). Tunnel memory for traumatic events. *Applied Cognitive Psychology, 12,* 99–117.

Santos, M. D., Leve, C., & Pratkanis, A. R. (1994). Hey buddy, can you spare seventeen cents? Mindful persuasion and the pique technique. *Journal of Applied Social Psychology, 24,* 755–764.

Sasaki, D. W. (1988). Guarding the guardians: Police trickery and confessions. *Stanford Law Review, 40,* 1593–1616.

Schacter, D. L. (1986). Amnesia and crime: How much do we really know? *American Psychologist, 41,* 286–295.

Scheck, B. (2000, May 11). *ABC World News Tonight.*

Schein, E. H. (1956). The Chinese indoctrination program for prisoners of war. A study of attempted "brainwashing" of American civilian prisoners by the Chinese Communists. *Psychiatry, 19,* 149–172.

Schein, E. H., Schneier, I., & Barker, C. H. (1961). *Coercive persuasion: A sociopsychological analysis of the "brainwashing of American civilian prisoners by the Chinese communists."* New York: W. W. Norton.

Schmeichel, B. J., Vohs, K. D., & Baumeister, R. F. (2003). Intellectual performance and ego depletion: Role of the self in logical reasoning and other information processing. *Journal of Personality & Social Psychology, 85,* 33–46.

Seligman, M. E. (1975). *Helplessness: On depression, development, and death.* Oxford, UK: W. H. Freeman.

Sengupta, J., & Johar, G. V. (2001). Contingent effects of anxiety on message elaboration and persuasion. *Personality & Social Psychology Bulletin, 27,* 139–150.

Shavitt, S. (1989). Operationalizing functional theories of attitude. In A. R. Pratkanis, S. J. Breckler, & A. G. Greenwald (Eds.), *Attitude structure and function* (pp. 311–337). Hillsdale, NJ: Lawrence Erlbaum.

Shuy, R. W. (1998). *The language of confession, interrogation, and deception.* Thousand Oaks, CA: Sage.

Sherman, D. K., & Kim, H. S. (2002). Affective perseverance: The resistance of affect to cognitive invalidation. *Personality & Social Psychology Bulletin, 28,* 224–237.

Shneckloth v. Bustamonte, 412 US 218 (1973).

Simon, D. (1991). *Homicide: A year on the killing streets.* New York: Ivy Books.
Sommers, S. R., & Kassin, S. M. (2001). On the many impacts of inadmissible testimony: Selective compliance, need for cognition, and the overcorrection bias. *Personality & Social Psychology Bulletin, 27*, 1368–1377.
Spinoza, B. (1677/1982). *The Ethics and selected letters.* Indianapolis, IN: Hackett.
Steiner, I. D., Rotermund, M., & Talaber, R. (1974). Attribution of choice to a decision maker. *Journal of Personality & Social Psychology, 30*, 553–562.
Storms, M. D. (1973). Videotape and the attribution process: Reversing actors' and observers' points of view. *Journal of Personality & Social Psychology, 27*, 165–175.
Straight, D. K. (1996). How to benefit by straight shooter selling. *American Salesman, 41*, 10–15.
Stroemwall, L. A., & Granhag, P. A. (2003). How to detect deception? Arresting the beliefs of police officers, prosecutors and judges. *Psychology, Crime & Law, 9*, 19–36.
Taylor, P. J., & Kopelman, M. D. (1984). Amnesia for criminal offenses. *Psychological Medicine, 14*, 581–588.
Taylor, S. E., & Fiske, S. T. (1978). Salience, attention, and attribution: Top of the head phenomena. In L. Berkowitz (Ed.), *Advances in experimental social psychology, Vol. 11* (pp. 249–288). New York: Academic Press.
Thompson, S. C., Cheek, P. R., & Grahma, M. A. (1988). The other side of perceived control: Disadvantages and negative effects. In S. Spacapan & S. Oshkamp (Eds.), *The social psychology of health* (pp. 69–93). Newbury Park, CA: Sage.
Tormala, Z. L., & Petty, R. E. (2002). What doesn't kill me makes me stronger: The effects of resisting persuasion on attitude certainty. *Journal of Personality & Social Psychology, 83*, 1298–1313.
Tormala, Z. L., & Petty, R. E. (in press). Resisting persuasion and attitude certainty: A meta-cognitive analysis. In E. S. Knowles & J. A. Linn (Eds.), Resistance and persuasion. Mahwah, NJ: Lawrence Erlbaum.
Tourangeau, R., Smith, T. W., & Rasinski, K. A. (1997). Motivation to report sensitive behaviors on surveys: Evidence from a bogus pipeline experiment. *Journal of Applied Social Psychology, 27*, 209–222.
Tversky, A., & Kahneman, D. (1973). Availability: A heuristic for judging frequency and probability. *Cognitive Psychology, 5*, 207–232.
Twenge, J. M., Catanese, K. R., & Baumeister, R. F. (2002). Social exclusion causes self-defeating behavior. *Journal of Personality & Social Psychology, 83*, 606–615.
Vallacher, R. R., & Wegner, D. M. (1985). *A theory of action identification.* Hillsdale, NJ: Lawrence Erlbaum.
Vanous, S., & Davis, D, (2001, April). Motive evidence: Probative or just prejudicial? Paper presented at the Rocky Mountain Psychological Association, Reno, Nevada.
Vanous, S., & Davis, D. (2002, April). Murder scripts: Perceived motives and means for spouse murder. Paper presented at the Rocky Mountain Psychological Association, Salt Lake City.
Visser, P. S., & Krosnick, J. A. (1998). Development of attitude strength over the life cycle: Surge and decline. *Journal of personality and Social Psychology, 75*, 1389–1410.
Vrij, A. (2001). Detecting the liars. *Psychologist: Special Issue: After the facts: Forensic special issue, 14*, 596–598.
Vrij, A., Edward, K., & Bull, R. (2001). Police officers' ability to detect deceit: The benefit of indirect deception detection measures. *Legal & Criminological Psychology, 6*, 185–196.

Wakefield, H., & Underwager, R. (1998). Coerced or nonvoluntary confessions. *Behavioral Sciences and the Law, 16*, 423–440.

Wald, M., Ayres, R., Hess, D. W., Schantz, M., & Whitebread, C. H. (1967). Interrogations in New Haven: The impact of *Miranda. Yale Law Journal, 76*, 1519–1648.

Walker, S. (1998). *Sense and nonsense about crime and drugs: Policy guide* (4th ed.). Belmont, CA: West/Wadsworth.

Walster, E., & Festinger, L. (1962). The effectiveness of "overheard" persuasive communications. *Journal of Abnormal and Social Psychology, 65*, 395–402.

Wegener, D. M. (1994). Ironic processes of mental control. *Psychological Review, 101*, 34–52.

Wegener, D. M., Petty, R. E., Dove, N. L., & Fabrigar, L. R. (in press). Multiple routes to resistance to persuasion. In E. S. Knowles & J. A. Linn (Eds.), *Resistance and persuasion*. Mahwah, NJ: Lawrence Erlbaum.

Wells, G. L. (1980). Asymmetric attributions for compliance: Reward vs. punishment. *Journal of Experimental Social Psychology, 16*, 47–60.

White, W. S. (1979). Police trickery in inducing confessions. *University of Pennsylvania Law Review, 127*, 581–629.

White, W. S. (1998). What is an involuntary confession now? *Rutgers Law Review, 50*, 2001–2057.

White, W. S. (2001). Miranda's failure to restrain pernicious interrogation practices. *Michigan Law Review, 99*, 1211–1247.

Wigmore, J. H. (1970). *Evidence, Vol. 3* (Revised by J. J. Chadbourn). Boston: Little, Brown.

Wilson, S. R. (2002). *Seeking and resisting compliance: Why people say what they do when trying to influence others.* Thousand Oaks: CA: Sage.

Wood, W., & Quinn, J. M. (in press). Forewarned and forearmed? A meta-analytic synthesis of forewarning experiments. In E. S. Knowles & J. A. Linn (Eds.), *Resistance and persuasion*. Mahwah, NJ: Lawrence Erlbaum.

Wood, W., Rhodes, N., & Biek, M. (1995). Working knowledge and attitude strength: An information-processing analysis. In R. E. Petty & J. A. Krosnick (Eds.), *Attitude strength: Antecedents and consequences* (pp. 283–313). Mahwah, NJ: Lawrence Erlbaum.

Wrightsman, L. S., & Kassin, S. M. (1993). *Confessions in the courtroom.* Newbury Park, CA: Sage.

Wu, C., & Shaffer, D. R. (1987). Susceptibility to persuasive appeals as a function of source credibility and prior experience with the attitude object. *Journal of Personality & Social Psychology, 52*, 677–688.

Zuckerman, M., DePaulo, B. M., & Rosenthal, R. (1981). Verbal and nonverbal communication of deception. In L. Berkowitz (Ed.), *Advances in experimental social psychology, Vol. 14* (pp. 1–59). New York: Academic Press.

CHAPTER 37

WHAT'S GOOD FOR THE GOOSE COOKS THE GANDER: INCONSISTENCIES BETWEEN THE LAW AND PSYCHOLOGY OF VOLUNTARY INTOXICATION AND SEXUAL ASSAULT

DEBORAH DAVIS
UNIVERSITY OF NEVADA, RENO

ELIZABETH F. LOFTUS
UNIVERSITY OF CALIFORNIA, IRVINE

On May 24, 1999, Jolene Medeiros's friends threw a party for her eighteenth birthday. The party entertainment included tequila and other mixed drinks, a male stripper named Josh Boykin, and Josh's friend Wes McDonald, who came along to keep Josh company. During the course of the evening, Jolene engaged in a number of sexualized behaviors with one or both men. She removed her clothes and danced naked or partially naked with both. She allowed Josh to lick whipped cream off her nipples, she fished for money in his G-string with her teeth, and, in front of the room of partiers, she allowed him to lie on top of her and hump her in mock intercourse.

Eventually, Jolene entered a bedroom with Wes and Josh, where she continued to dance naked, jumped up into Wes's arms, wrapping her legs around him, and finally had sex with both. Later that night, Jolene claimed to have been raped (*People v. Joshua Cody Boykin*, 2000). Notwithstanding the multitude of cues of consent Jolene displayed throughout the evening, if she proved able to support her claim of an incapacitating level of intoxication at the time of sexual activity, the two men would, by law, be guilty of *rape by intoxication*.

Perhaps alone among criminal acts, evaluation of the crime "rape" requires consideration of the victim's ability to form the specific intent/consent to engage in the act that is the focus of the crime. In effect, uniquely in the case of alleged rape, the concept of *mens rea*, or the state of mind necessary to form the intent to engage in the act, becomes relevant for both accused *and* accuser (see reviews by Falk, 2002; Rolfes, 1998; Wertheimer, 2001).

Effects of alcohol on judgment, including the ability to form voluntary intentions of all sorts, are similar for each sex and generally for accused and accuser. Nevertheless, current laws regarding rape specifically, and voluntary intoxication generally, treat these effects quite differently for the accused and accuser. That is, "an intoxicated woman is presumed not to have consented" to sexual activity (see Kramer, 1994, p. 3), thereby in many circumstances mandating a finding of guilt for the crime "rape by intoxication" (e.g., *People v. Giardino*, 2000; but see Falk, 2002, for discussion of jurisdictions that differentiate between voluntary and involuntary intoxication).

In contrast, for the defendant, in more than 20 percent of jurisdictions intoxication cannot be raised as evidence of *mens rea* or "diminished capacity" at all. Marlowe, Lambert, and Thompson (1999) summarized the law in the 50 states, the District of Columbia, the U.S. Virgin Islands, and Puerto Rico, finding that evidence of intoxication was then inadmissible as evidence of *mens rea* in 12 jurisdictions. Sixteen others restricted such evidence to address the issue of specific intent, still others admitted it to negate general intent (21), and the remainder admitted evidence of intoxication only to evaluate the degree of murder or other specific issues.

The conceptual distinction between *specific intent* and *general intent* is difficult to understand, poorly articulated in the law, inconsistently applied to particular crimes, and widely criticized as an arbitrary and meaningless distinction (Berner, 1971; Epstein, 1978; Ferguson, 1971; Kaplan & Weisberg, 1991; Marlowe, Lambert, & Thompson, 1999; Roth, 1979). Perhaps reflecting these difficulties, both general assault and sexual assault are sometimes treated as specific-intent and sometimes as general-intent crimes. Hence, evidence of an accused rapist's intoxication will not be admitted as evidence to mitigate or to negate *mens rea* in many jurisdictions (see Rolfes, 1998, for a review of the treatment of defendant intoxication in Canada and England). In stark contrast, however, evidence of the alleged victim's intoxication is always admissible and in many jurisdictions or circumstances, by law, will be considered definitive proof of rape.

Psychological literature on determinants of sexual assault has focused on the proposition that males tend to *overperceive* the extent to which use of alcohol indicates consent, thus promoting the idea that consumption of alcohol is "misperceived" or "overperceived" as an indication of consent (e.g., Abbey & Harnish, 1991; Abbey, McAuslan, & Ross, 1998; Abbey, Ross, McDuffle, & McAuslan, 1996; Schuller & Wall, 1998). Further, this literature has demonstrated that victim use of alcohol is associated with impaired ability to recognize risk and resist sexual assault as well as increased likelihood of actual sexual victimization. Paradoxically, however, alcohol use leads to greater blame of the victim while simultaneously reducing blame of the perpetrator.

Some scholars have taken the position that the documented tendency to blame intoxicated female victims for sexual assault and to exonerate their assailants is inappropriate and irrational, based in part on the arguments that consent to intoxication does *not* reflect greater likelihood of consent to sexual activity and, in fact, that intoxication renders true consent impossible. Thus, it also assumes both explicitly and implicitly that the documented association between victim use of alcohol and both victim blame and exoneration of perpetrators is unjust. It is perhaps in response to this literature regarding alcohol and sexual victimization that the laws of many states now presume that intoxication is related to *inability* to consent while simultaneously and paradoxically ruling that intoxication is *not* admissible in defense against criminal liability.

In this chapter, we examine the argument that the *psychology* of voluntary intoxication and sexual consent does *not* support the *law* that intoxicated alleged victims should be presumed unable to consent/raped. We will argue instead that alcohol use is *probative* but not *definitive* of both actual sexual intentions and displayed cues reflecting consent on the part of the "victim." In legal terms, "probative" means that a conclusion (for example, desire to have sex) is *more likely* given the evidence (for example, evidence of intoxication) than without the evidence. "Definitive" or "dispositive" means that if the evidence is true, the conclusion is *certain*.

This chapter will present evidence in support of the propositions that (1) consent may occur well before, as well as during, the actual act; (2) the decision to use alcohol is related to (is probative of) sexual intentions; (3) alcohol use is related to (probative of) cues of sexual consent displayed by the user; and therefore (4) intoxication should be considered in the context of all evidence, and should be regarded as (a) *probative* evidence of both sexual intentions and ability to consent, rather than as *definitive* negation of consent, and (b) as probative of both the alleged victim's *display*, and alleged perpetrator's reasonable *interpretation,* of cues of consent/nonconsent. In addition, we examine potential mechanisms through which an alleged victim's alcohol use may actually promote false allegations of rape.

To do so, we first review empirical research relevant to the relationship between voluntary alcohol use and sexual intentions in dating/couple contexts, addressing the following questions: (1) Does alcohol increase sexual motivation? (2) Do men and women *believe* alcohol promotes voluntary sexual activity? (3) Does alcohol actually promote voluntary sexual activity? (4) Are men and women aware of the link between alcohol use and sexual victimization? and (5) Does alcohol consumption depend in any way upon sexual intentions?

DOES ALCOHOL USE ENHANCE SEXUAL MOTIVATION/AROUSAL?

> *Let's drink to love—to wine that warms our kisses.*
> Giuseppe Verdi, *La Traviata*

Substantial evidence exists to support widespread cultural beliefs that alcohol enhances sexual motivation and arousal.

Alcohol Enhances Subjective Arousal/Enjoyment of Sex

Men and women report greater subjective arousal (Wilson & Lawson, 1976b; 1978) and orgasmic pleasure and intensity (Malatesta, Pollack, Wilbanks, & Adams, 1979) with increasing levels of blood alcohol, even though physiological response (including orgasm) tends to diminish with increasing levels of consumption (Heaton & Varrin, 1991; Rosen, 1991; Rosen & Ashton, 1993; see reviews by Beckman & Ackerman, 1995; Crowe & George, 1989; George & Stoner, 2000; Leigh, 1990; Norris, 1994). A survey of over 20,000 Americans asked whether drinking enhanced their sexual pleasure (Athanasiou, Shaver, & Tavris, 1970). Over 60 percent responded that it did, saying that alcohol helped "put them in the mood" for sex, with a significantly higher proportion of women providing this response. At least for some people, perhaps disproportionately women, the disinhibition of fear and guilt (e.g., Steele & Josephs, 1990) that can accompany alcohol use can result in benefits outweighing dampening of physiological arousal.

Alcohol is used for the specific purpose of enhancing sexual pleasure and/or reducing sexual inhibitions. Perhaps because alcohol does enhance sexual responding for many, it is also used by many for the specific purpose of reducing inhibitions and/or enhancing sexual pleasure (see reviews by Beckman & Ackerman, 1995; George & Stoner, 2000). Perhaps most frequently, alcohol is used for this purpose in what might be thought of as normal sexual encounters. However, alcohol or other intoxicating substances may also be used to reduce inhibitions for more deviant encounters, as in a recent case involving a young woman whom we'll call "Mary."

Mary met several men at a bar where she was a lap dancer. The men invited her to come to their place to "party." Mary agreed, and soon she and two of her new friends, "Jack" and "John," decided to make a pornographic film together. Mary stated in front of witnesses that she wanted to make the film, but needed to get really "f_____ed up" in order to do so. Apparently, Mary wanted to diffuse any inhibition and embarrassment that would interfere with the intended sexual activity/performance. She voluntarily became intoxicated specifically for that purpose and proceeded to make the film with her two friends. She spent the night with them and had breakfast with them the next morning, laughing about their filmmaking. Later, she accused them of rape by intoxication, and the two are now serving time.

The common use of alcohol for disinhibition or enhancement of relatively normal and of deviant sexual encounters bears directly on the legal presumption of negation of consent. Intentions to engage in sexual behavior can be made clear *ex ante*, before the first drink (as illustrated, for example, in the lyrics to the popular Jimmy Buffet song "Why don't we get drunk and screw?"), as can the specific intention to use alcohol to facilitate the encounter. Indeed, in the preceding example, consent was given specifically *contingent upon intoxication.* Why, then, should intent/consent be negated in the process of carrying out intentions that have been previously clearly stated? In such circumstances, would it not be more appropriate for a finding of rape to require explicit withdrawal of the previously given consent?

Alcohol Impairs Ability to Suppress Sexual Arousal

Even among those wishing to avoid sexual responding, alcohol appears to enhance motivation. Perhaps as a result of alcohol myopia (Steele & Josephs, 1990) and the tendency toward enhanced focus on sexual stimuli when intoxicated with a member of the opposite sex, alcohol appears to impair the ability to *suppress* or *inhibit* arousal. Laboratory demonstrations of this phenomenon have taken two forms. First, some authors have exposed men to erotic stimuli while instructing them to suppress sexual arousal. Measures of penile tumescence have shown that as intoxication increases, so does penile girth, despite instructions to avoid arousal.

Other studies have examined penile tumescence upon exposure to deviant sexual stimuli, such as rape or child molestation, among sex offenders and nonoffenders. Subjects are not instructed to suppress arousal; rather, desire to suppress arousal to such stimuli is assumed. For nonoffenders, nondeviant arousal increases when intoxicated, whereas arousal in response to deviant stimuli remains unchanged. In contrast, for offenders, arousal in response to deviant stimuli increases while intoxicated, whereas arousal in response to nondeviant stimuli remains unchanged. Thus, deviants, who would be expected to try to suppress arousal to deviant stimuli, are less able to do so when intoxicated (see review of this literature by George & Stoner, 2000).

George and Stoner (2000) suggest that the widely reported relationship between alcohol and sexual risk taking is in part the result of inability to suppress arousal while intoxicated. That is, they argue that alcohol-induced inability to suppress arousal renders the person insensitive and unresponsive to cues that might normally prevent sexual engagement (such as the risk of pregnancy, disease, sexual assault, etc.). Recent studies have supported this reasoning with respect to use of condoms (e.g., Derman & Cooper, 2000; MacDonald, MacDonald, Zanna, & Fong, 2000) and attraction to risky partners (e.g., Murphy, Monahan, & Miller, 1998).

Generally, the observed difficulties in suppression of arousal while intoxicated support prevailing alcohol expectancies of disinhibition of sexuality. Alcohol would be expected to render suppression of any instigated behavior (including sexual responding) more difficult among any who are otherwise inclined or led to want to engage in it, whether male or female.

Particularly pertinent to the sexual assault scenario, Steele and Josephs's (1990) alcohol myopia model specifies that intoxication drives disinhibition of behavior only in cases where the person faces high conflict between instigatory and inhibitory motives. It follows, then, that those who may otherwise wish to avoid sexual engagement will experience the greatest disinhibitory effects of alcohol—arguably later becoming more likely to attempt to avoid responsibility through claims of coercion or rape.

Intoxication Promotes Interest in Erotic Stimuli

Theoretically, interest in erotic materials reflects desire and willingness to experience sexual arousal. Thus, to the extent that alcohol promotes interest in erotica, it may be assumed to promote interest in sexual activity. Evidence from studies varying expected and/or actual alcohol consumption have indicated that interest in erotica is enhanced by both real and expected alcohol consumption, particularly when the person is with a co-participant believed to also be drinking (see review by George & Stoner, 2000).

Alcohol-Induced Sexual Motivation Promotes the Illusion of Interest in Others

Alcohol-induced sexual motivation is in part reflected in inability to perceive lack of interest in others. Marx and Gross (1995) developed an experimental procedure in which subjects were confronted with a hypothetical audiotaped vignette in which a woman is involved in a scenario depicting progressively more attempted sexual contact by her date. Subjects were to determine when her partner had become inappropriate. In their research, both males who had consumed alcohol and those who only believed they had consumed alcohol took longer to recognize situations in which a male should cease attempts for further sexual contact, and differences between sexually coercive and noncoercive males in recognition disappeared among those who had consumed alcohol (Gross, Bennett, Sloan, Marx, & Juergens, 2001; Marx & Adams, 1999; Marx, Gross, & Juergens, 1997, but see also Wydra, Marshall, Earls, & Barbaree, 1983, for different results). Norris, George, Davis, Martell, and Leonesio (1999) found that intoxicated men perceived less negative reactions in rape victims depicted in violent pornography. In part, the reduction in ability to know when sexual behavior should cease, or when it is causing pain and distress, may be the result of impaired perception. However, it is also arguably a matter of elevated personal sexual motivation coloring the interpretation of that of others (that is, a particular instance of the "false consensus bias").

DO MEN AND WOMEN BELIEVE ALCOHOL INCREASES INTEREST IN VOLUNTARY SEXUAL ACTIVITY?

Substantial evidence has accumulated to show that men and women *believe* alcohol increases interest in voluntary sexual activity. We review research from four separate areas illustrating these beliefs: (1) research on "alcohol expectancies" showing that men and women *expect to become sexually aroused* while consuming alcohol; (2) research showing that men and women *perceive others as more sexually aroused, willing to consent, and easy to seduce* when consuming alcohol; (3) research showing that men and women use alcohol as a strategy for seduction of reluctant partners; and (4) research illustrating the deliberate use of alcohol as a means to avoid responsibility for otherwise unacceptable sexual behaviors or partners.

Men and Women Expect to Become Aroused When Using Alcohol

Pervasive "alcohol expectancies" (beliefs about alcohol's effects on behavior and social judgments—e.g., Brown, Goldman, Inn, & Anderson, 1980; Critchlow, 1986; Hull & Bond, 1986; Lang, Searles, Lauerman, & Adesso, 1980; Southwick, Steele, Marlatt, & Lindell, 1981) and cultural portrayals of alcohol as a disinhibitor and aphrodisiac suggest that alcohol is associated with sexual arousal and motivation. The mere *belief* that one has consumed alcohol (even if not true), for example, has been shown to increase arousal (Briddell, Rimm, Caddy, Krawitz, Sholis, & Wunderlin, 1978; Crowe & George, 1989; George & Marlatt, 1986; Lang, 1985; Lang, Searles, Lauerman, & Adesso, 1980; Rapaport & Posey, 1991; Roehrich & Kinder, 1991; Wilson & Lawson, 1976a). A meta-analysis of nine balanced placebo design studies found that *expectancies* (beliefs that one had imbibed alcohol) had a significant positive effect on sexual arousal, whereas *actual alcohol consumption* did not (Hull & Bond, 1986). This *alcohol placebo effect* on arousal clearly demonstrates that people expect to be more sexually aroused when intoxicated, despite the reality that alcohol actually suppresses arousal in both sexes (though for a contrasting view regarding suppressive effects, see George & Stoner, 2000, for review of null findings of suppression of arousal). Further, the more positive an individual's expectancies of arousal, the greater the arousal experienced (see review by George & Stoner, 2000).

This belief has been more recently specifically articulated by college students who expressed the beliefs that alcohol enhances sociability, as well as sexual arousal and enjoyment, among other positive effects (Corbin, Bernat, Calhoun, McNair, & Seals, 2001; Gravitt & Krueger, 1998, Norris, Nurius, & Dimeff, 1996).

Men and Women Perceive Others as More Sexually Aroused, Willing to Consent, and Easy to Seduce When Consuming Alcohol

> *Alcohol removes inhibitions—like that scared little mouse who got drunk and shook his whiskers and shouted: "Now bring on that damn cat!!"*
>
> Eleanor Early, 1950

Expectancies regarding the link between alcohol and arousal apply to noninvolved parties as well. Evidence of these expectations comes from studies showing that men and women who have consumed alcohol are (1) rated as more sexually aroused/easy to seduce/likely to engage in sexual activity, (2) perceived as more likely to consent or to have consented to sexual activity, and (3) perceived as less credible when accusing a partner of rape.

Intoxicated Persons Are Perceived as More Aroused and Easy to Seduce

A number of studies have shown that persons who have, or are depicted as having, consumed alcohol are rated as more sexually aroused, easy to seduce, sexually available, having more sexual initiative and intentions, and/or likely to engage in foreplay or intercourse (Abbey & Harnish, 1995; Abbey, Ross, McDuffie, & McAuslan, 1996; Abbey, Zawacki, & McAuslan, 2001; Corcoran & Bell, 1990; Corcoran & Thomas, 1991; George, Coe, Lopez, Crowe, & Norris, 1995; George, Gournic, & McAfee, 1988; George, Lehman, Cue, Martinez, Lopez, & Norris, 1997; George, Stoner, Norris, Lopez, & Lehman, 2000; Leigh, 1995). One such study (George et al., 1997) found monotonic increases in perceptions of the target's sexual interest and availability with increasing intoxication. Further, several studies have shown that *mutual* alcohol consumption is perceived as suggesting sexual intent/consent (Abbey & Harnish, 1995; Corcoran & Thomas, 1991; Leigh, Aramburu, & Norris, 1992).

Intoxicated Women Are Perceived as More Likely to Consent to Sexual Activity

Evidence of the link between intoxication and perceptions of consent to sexual activity comes from several sources.

Professionals Perceive Intoxicated Women as More Likely to Consent. Lee and Cheung (1991) developed an Attitudes Toward Rape scale, including the item "Intoxicated women are usually willing to have sexual relations," which they administered to lawyers, counselors, doctors, and police. Agreement with this statement was generally high, with greatest agreement expressed by lawyers (51%) and doctors (53%) and least agreement by counselors and police (both 37%). It is noteworthy that such a high percentage of agreement with the idea that intoxication *usually* equals willingness to have sex was obtained in the professions most frequently confronted with issues of sexual assault—and in the context of a scale focusing on rape. Clearly, cultural beliefs in the link between intoxication and sexual interest and availability are strong and pervasive. Although such beliefs may be stronger in groups possessing rape-supportive attitudes or those with sexually coercive tendencies, they are in no way limited to such groups. Beliefs in the aphrodisiac qualities of alcohol are widespread among both sexes.

Intoxicated Victims of Alleged Rape Are Perceived as Less Credible. Perceptions of whether or not sexual coercion or rape has occurred are affected by alcohol consumption, such that sexual encounters lead to greater victim blame and derogation and are less likely to be perceived as coercion or rape when the victim is intoxicated or has gone to a bar alone (Bernat, Calhoun, & Stolp, 1998; Emmers-Sommer & Allen, 1999; Hammock & Richardson, 1997; LaFree, 1981; LaFree, Reskin, & Visher, 1985; Norris & Cubbins, 1992; Richardson & Campbell, 1982; Rose & Randall, 1982; Schuller & Wall, 1998; Stormo, Lang, & Stritzke, 1997; Wilsnack, 1991), or has a history of drug or alcohol abuse (Kerstetter, 1990)—particularly among males (e.g., Schuller & Stewart, 2000), or those scoring high for rape-related attitudes (e.g., Schuller & Wall, 1998), or on scales reflecting hypergender ideology (e.g., Norris et al., 1999; Ozman & Davis, 1999). (Interestingly, female victims of other violent encounters are held more responsible when intoxicated as well—e.g., Aramburu & Leigh, 1991; Harrison & Esqueda, 2000; Leigh & Aramburu, 1994; Richardson & Campbell, 1980; Stewart & Maddren, 1997; Wild, Graham, & Rehm, 1998.)

Some research has indicated a gender-based double standard regarding intoxication, in that a male perpetrator is sometimes found to be *less* culpable when intoxicated (e.g., Norris & Cubbins, 1992; Stormo et al., 1997; see discussion in section on alcohol and victimization). However, two studies (Aramburu & Leigh, 1991; Stewart & Maddren, 1997) have found that intoxicated male *victims* of sexual assault are, like their female counterparts, judged more harshly than male victims who are not intoxicated, perhaps a reflection of the relationship between alcohol use and perceived interest in sex.

Police investigators are likely to judge the complaints of intoxicated women as "unfounded." Indeed, of all rape complaints judged as "unfounded" in one investigation, 82 percent involved an intoxicated victim (Police discretion, 1968; see also Kerstetter, 1990; Kerstetter & Van Winkle, 1990). Suspects are also less likely to be prosecuted if the victim had been at a bar alone prior to the rape (LaFree, 1981), or if the victim had a history of drug or alcohol abuse (Kerstetter, 1990).

Schuller and Stewart (2000) presented over two hundred police officers with acquaintance-rape vignettes in which the alcohol consumption of both alleged victim and perpetrator varied. Surprisingly, the defendant's level of intoxication had no effect on any variable. In contrast, however, the complainant's level of intoxication was related to a variety of police perceptions of both complainant and defendant. The complainant was generally perceived more negatively. Her claim was perceived as less credible, she was blamed more, was seen as more interested in having sex and as less likely to have communicated nonconsent, and her expectations that the defendant should have refrained from sexual activity were seen as less reasonable. In contrast, the alleged perpetrator was perceived as less culpable and as more likely to have honestly believed that she had consented. He was also perceived as more reasonable to assume that she was interested in sex.

Despite the pervasive effects of alcohol on perceptions of the complainant's intentions and the defendant's perceptions of those intentions, however, alcohol did not influence reported likelihood of charging the perpetrator with rape (see also Frazier & Haney, 1996; Stewart & Maddren, 1997, for similar results). The authors suggested that although police judgments of the victim may be affected by intoxication, the decision to charge the defendant may be constrained by other legal and extralegal factors that prevent police from acting on their attitudes (see also Hoyle, 1998; Stewart & Maddren, 1997). Nevertheless, there is evidence from some studies that when the case reaches the prosecuting attorney, he or she is less likely to file charges if the victim has been drinking (Chandler & Torney, 1981; Kerstetter, 1990).

Overall, then, there is clear and consistent evidence that allegations of rape are perceived as less credible when the complainant is intoxicated. Some scholars have tended to regard this pattern as an unjustified bias (e.g., Abbey & Harnish, 1995; Abbey, McAuslan, & Ross, 1998; Allison & Wrightsman, 1993; Ward, 1995), perhaps characteristic only (or primarily) of those with flawed attitudes or character, such as those high in "Rape Myth Acceptance" (Burt, 1980), or other rape-supportive attitudes (see reviews by Anderson, Cooper, & Okamura, 1997; Olsen-Fulero & Fulero, 1997). However, it is worth noting that the truth may not always reflect what is politically correct at a given point in cultural history. As scientists, we should not automatically assume that judgments found to be culturally or politically unpalatable reflect errors or biases in judgment rather than valid perceptions.

The previously reviewed evidence of the relationship between alcohol use and the likelihood of actual consent clearly supports the view that it is reasonable and rational to assume that an intoxicated person is more likely to consent to sexual activity than one who is not intoxicated. While it would *not* be reasonable to assume in every such case that use of alcohol is definitive evidence of consent, it is certainly rational to view intoxication as one factor to consider when evaluating the likelihood of consent. It is arguably rational and appropriate for alcohol use to affect (but not fully determine) judgments of the ultimate issue of rape versus consensual sex.

Men Are Slower to Perceive Nonconsent Among Intoxicated Women

There is evidence that men perceive intoxicated women as more interested in sexual activity, and thus are slower to recognize nonconsent. Bernat, Calhoun, and Stolp (1998) used an experimental procedure to show that females' use of alcohol is linked to *perceptions* of consent among males (particularly among sexually coercive males). For example, sexually coercive males listening to a date scenario involving an increasingly coercive sexual sequence indicated a later point in the sequence as the appropriate stopping point for the male when the female had consumed alcohol than when she had not, whereas alcohol use did not affect the decision times of nonsexually coercive males.

Alcohol Is a Tool of Seduction for Both Sexes

Beliefs in the power of alcohol to promote voluntary sexual activity are translated into active seductive/coercive strategies in both sexes. Men who have committed sexual assault report getting their female companion drunk in order to facilitate seduction or coercion (Kanin, 1984; Mosher & Anderson, 1986; Wilson, Calhoun, & McNair, 2002), and female victims report having been "set up" for sexual seduction or coercion through either encouragement to drink or surreptitious spiking of drinks (e.g., Testa & Livingston, 1999). More generally, college students report frequent use of alcohol to facilitate sexual encounters (Anderson & Mathew, 1993; Corcoran & Thomas, 1991; George, Gournic, & McAfee, 1988; Gravitt & Krueger, 1988; Keeling, 1994; Montgomery, Benedicto, & Haemmerlie, 1993; Sanday, 1996; Ward, Chapman, Cohn, White, & Williams, 1991). Finally, studies of sexually coercive women and of male victims of sexual coercion indicate that sexually coercive women, like their male counterparts, use alcohol as a coercive tool (see reviews in Anderson & Struckman-Johnson, 1998).

Alcohol Is Used to Provide an Excuse for Otherwise Unacceptable Sexual Behavior

> *I walked into the bar and saw a woman sitting on a bar stool. She gave me the eye—and I knew it was gonna take a lotta beer to drink her pretty.*
> Comedian Kenny Bob Davis, Reno Comedy Club performance

Some have suggested that the disinhibiting effects of alcohol intoxication are viewed as a socially acceptable excuse for behavior that would be viewed more negatively under other circumstances (e.g., Critchlow, 1983, 1986; Sobell & Sobell, 1975; Workman, 2001). Gravitt and Krueger (1998) examined the use of alcohol as an excuse for sexual behavior among college students. The authors conducted campus focus groups to examine college student beliefs about the link between alcohol and sex. Their subjects revealed two beliefs relevant here. First, they indicated that alcohol promotes both coercive and noncoercive sexual encounters. Second, they reported that alcohol is widely used as an *excuse* for sexual behavior. That is, both men and women reported that they deliberately became intoxicated so that they could engage in various sexual behaviors without "taking the blame." Their subjects expounded rather dramatically . . . indicating that not only do many college students use alcohol as an excuse for sexual behaviors that they would not engage in while sober (e.g., having intercourse, engaging in unsafe sex, "beer goggling," "hooking up," and so on), but also that they are aware they are doing so . . . Operating with this awareness, many students intentionally use the excuse alcohol provides to avoid being held accountable for their behavior (Gravitt & Krueger, 1988, p. 185).

As one of their female subjects put it: "I think that's a pretty good excuse. You can say, 'I had sex with him, but I was drunk: so, I am not really a slut.' So it's probably the best [excuse] you can give instead of saying 'Oh, I slept with him because I felt like it'" (1988, p. 180). Women tended to use alcohol as an excuse for sleeping with casual partners, whereas men were more likely to use it as an excuse for "beer goggling" or sleeping with an unattractive partner. Each strategy, however, reflects the inherent belief that alcohol promotes consensual sexual encounters. Clearly, beliefs regarding the facilitating effects of alcohol on sexual interest are pervasive.

Similar results were reported by Norris, Nurius, and Dimeff (1996). Focus group discussions among their subjects revealed beliefs that alcohol enhances sociability and reports that alcohol was used as a rationalization for desired, but inappropriate, sexual behavior (see also Workman, 2001).

To summarize, both direct and indirect evidence supports the proposition that both sexes *expect* alcohol to increase interest in sexual activity. Subjects directly express such beliefs in surveys of alcohol expectancies and perceptions of intoxicated others and indirectly express them through judgment of consent in intoxicated individuals and through their strategic use of alcohol for seduction/coercion and for managing reactions to undesirable sexual behavior. To the extent that subjects believe alcohol will increase voluntary sexual activity, if they nevertheless choose to become intoxicated it can be reasonably inferred that (on the average) they find sexual activity more acceptable than those who choose not to.

DOES ALCOHOL USE ACTUALLY PROMOTE VOLUNTARY SEXUAL ACTIVITY?

Sobriety diminishes, discriminates, and says no; drunkenness expands, unites, and says yes.
William James, *The Varieties of Religious Experience* (1902)

Intoxicated women are admittedly more likely to become involved in coerced sexual activity, in part because of impaired judgment and ability to resist aggression effectively (Norris et al., 1996; Testa & Parks, 1996). However, there is also evidence of greater propensity toward voluntary sexual activity and sexual risk taking (unsafe sex, for example) among intoxicated men and women (Butcher, Manning, & O'Neal, 1991; Meilman, 1993; Meilman, Burwell, Smith, 1993; O'Leary, Goodhart, Jemmott, & Boccher-Lattimore, 1992; Radius, Joffe, & Gall, 1991; Wechsler & Isaac, 1992; Weinhardt & Carey, 2000). In the sections that follow, we review evidence from several areas of research documenting alcohol-induced enhancement of sexual activity.

Voluntary Sexual Activity Is Higher among Those Using Alcohol

Indirect evidence of the relationship of actual sexual consent to alcohol use comes from studies linking degree of sexual activity, sexual risk taking, having sexually permissive attitudes, and drinking alcohol (e.g., Tyler, Hoyt & Whitbeck, 1998; Weinhardt & Carey, 2000). Put another way, women who tend to use alcohol also tend to be sexually active and permissive, suggesting that use of alcohol is a predictor (if not a cause), across a number of encounters, of likelihood of consensual sex.

Event-based surveys, in which respondents report alcohol consumption during a specific date, have shown increased likelihood of intercourse during first dates among those consuming alcohol (e.g., Cooper & Orcutt, 1997; Dermen & Cooper, 2000). Intoxicated survey participants report greater likelihood of involvement in risk-prone behaviors (Testa, Livingston, & Collins, 2000) and reduced likelihood of using direct resistance to fend off sexual aggression (Norris, George, & Davis, 2000). Even within ultimately coercive sexual encounters, intoxicated women engage in more consensual sexual activity and resist sexual advances less immediately prior to the assault (Harrington & Leitenberg, 1994, Norris et al., 1996), suggesting that men will be faced with more receptive cues among both willing and reluctant intoxicated women as compared to their unintoxicated counterparts.

In summary, there is substantial evidence both (1) that men and women believe that alcohol increases sexual interest and availability, and (2) that alcohol actually does increase interest, availability, and (among women in particular) pleasure. Women are more likely to engage in sexual activity when drinking and tend to enjoy it more when they do (see reviews by Beckman & Ackerman, 1995; George & Stoner, 2000). These findings suggest that intoxication with a date is *probative* of intentions to have sex. That is, those who drink alcohol are *more likely* to be actually interested in sexual activity than those who do not. This does not imply that intoxication is *definitive* evidence of consent, however. A person may well be intoxicated and not wish to engage in sexual activity. In contrast to current popular and legal thinking, it is, however, rational to use intoxication as one clue to probable level of sexual interest.

ARE MEN AND WOMEN AWARE OF THE LINK BETWEEN INTOXICATION AND VICTIMIZATION?

The nature of the actual link between alcohol use and sexual victimization is clear. Up to 80 percent of instances of sexual victimization involve drug and/or alcohol intoxication of the victim, perpetrator, or both (e.g., Abbey, 1991; Abbey, Ross, McDuffie, 1994; Abbey, McAuslan, Zawacki, Clinton, & Buck, 2001; Abbey, Zawacki, Buck, Clinton, & McAuslan, 2001; Crowell & Burgess, 1996; Frintner

& Robinson, 1993; Harrington & Leitenberg, 1994; Koss, Gidyez, & Wisniewski, 1987; Miller & Marshall, 1987; Muehlenhard & Linton, 1987; Hindmarch & Brinkmann, 1999; Larimer, Lydum, Anderson, & Turner, 1999; Molitor, Ruiz, Klausner, & McFarland, 2000; Parkes & Miller, 1997; Pernanen, 1991; Seto & Barbaree, 1995; Testa & Dermen, 1999; Testa & Parks, 1996; Ullman, Karabatsos, & Koss, 1999a, b) and approximately one-half of victims are intoxicated, with estimates ranging from 30 to 79 percent (Abbey et al., 2001). Pre-assault victim use of alcohol has also been linked to greater likelihood of completed rape in both date and stranger rape situations (Abbey & Ross, 1992; Ullman, Karabatsos, & Koss, 1999a, b; Ullman & Knight, 1993), and pre-assault use by the perpetrator with more severe sexual abuse of victims (Abbey & Ross, 1992; Martin & Ronet, 1998; Testa & Livingston, 1999—but see Brecklin & Ullman, 2001, for inconsistent effects.), and more victim injuries (Brecklin & Ullman, 2001; Coker, Walls, & Johnson, 1998; Martin & Bachman, 1998). Further, individual propensity toward alcohol abuse is linked to lifetime sexual victimization (e.g., Burnam, Stein, Golding, Siegel, Sorenson, Forsythe, & Telles, 1988; Corbin, Bernat, Calhoun, McNair, & Seals, 2001; Greene & Navarro, 1998; Testa & Livingston, 2000; Wingfield, George, Swartz, & Blazer, 1990) as well as to the likelihood of perpetration of sexual assault (Abbey et al., 1994; Koss & Dinero, 1988).

Clearly, then, alcohol use increases the risk of sexual coercion. Do men and women understand this link, however? In fact, substantial evidence, both direct and indirect, suggests they do.

Direct Evidence

Direct evidence of understanding of the link between intoxication and sexual assault comes from two sources: (1) perpetrator reports of their own personal attempts to get their targets intoxicated for easier sexual seduction and coercion, and targets' reported experiences of perpetrator attempts to get them intoxicated to set them up for seduction or coercion (reviewed earlier); and (2) male and female reports of their beliefs concerning the general use and likely success of such strategies.

Earlier, we reviewed evidence that both men and women report use of alcohol for seduction or coercion, and both sexes report being set up for seduction or coercion by others promoting alcohol use (Finley & Corty, 1993; Kanin, 1984; Koss, 1988; Koss, Gidycz, & Wisniewski, 1987; Martin & Hummer, 1989; Mosher & Anderson, 1986; Testa & Livingston, 1999; Yegidis, 1986). Muehlenhard and Cook (1988), for example, reported that 11 percent of college women had engaged in unwanted sexual intercourse because their date got them drunk and took advantage of the situation.

A sizable minority of men and women *expect* a woman to be assaulted if she has either first consented to sex and then reneged, or is stoned or drunk (Cook, 1995). Women's view of their own risk for sexual victimization is linked to their own use of alcohol (e.g., Testa & Livingston, 2000). They also view other women who consume alcohol on a date as more vulnerable to sexual assault (e.g., Abbey,

McAuslan, Ross, & Zawacki, 1999; Cue, George, & Norris, 1996; Parks, Miller, Collins, & Zetes-Zanatta, 1998) and report use of active strategies to counteract the dangers of coercion while intoxicated. For example, Gravitt and Krueger's (1998) female subjects were widely aware of the danger of sexual victimization while intoxicated and reported using a "buddy system" for protection while intoxicated. At least one among a group of women would agree to remain sober in order to protect the others from exploitation during their intoxication. Men, of course, attempt to counter this strategy by their own strategies to separate an intoxicated woman from her protective buddy or group.

Hence, men explicitly acknowledge the strategy of getting women drunk in order to seduce or coerce them, and women explicitly acknowledge that men use that strategy and that they take steps to counteract it when they are unwilling to have sex. Both sexes are clearly aware that alcohol is used as an aid to coercion. It is perhaps partly for this reason that intoxicated victims tend to be perceived as more responsible or blameworthy. Jurors and others appear to believe that the woman who chooses to become intoxicated, particularly when alone with a man, has either actively consented by consuming alcohol, or "assumed the risk" of sexual coercion, as discussed in the next section.

Indirect Evidence

Indirect evidence of widespread cultural understanding of the link between intoxication and vulnerability to sexual aggression comes from research showing negative reactions to intoxicated victims (reviewed earlier).

The assumption of increased female vulnerability to assault when intoxicated can also be seen through examination of reactions to intoxicated *perpetrators* as well. Although many studies have shown that mock jurors assign less culpability to an intoxicated defendant and are less likely to find the defendant guilty of sexual assault (e.g., Allison & Wrightsman, 1993; Richardson & Campbell, 1982; Ward, 1995), two studies have shown that when *both* the man and woman are portrayed as drinking comparable levels of alcohol, respondents were more likely to question the validity of a claim of rape, and to view the victim more negatively and as more responsible and blameworthy—and the defendant as less blameworthy (Norris & Cubbins, 1992; Stormo, Lang, & Stritzke, 1997).

Some, however, have shown greater harshness in verdicts and judgments of culpability among intoxicated defendants (Aramburu & Leigh, 1991; Leigh & Aramburu, 1994), even when the victim was not intoxicated (Schuller & Wall, 1998; Wall & Schuller, 2000), but particularly if the victim was clearly *more intoxicated* than the defendant. Leigh and Arumburu (1994) suggested that the tendency of later studies to find increased blame for intoxicated perpetrators may reflect changing societal attitudes toward alcohol-related offenses.

A study by Stormo, Lang, and Stritzke (1997), for example, found that alcohol appeared to lessen culpability attributions to the male, only if he was as intoxicated as the female but not when the female was much more intoxicated (see also Norris & Cubbins, 1992), and some have found no relationship of alcohol consumption by victim or perpetrator to perceptions or verdicts (e.g., Fisher, 1995, although in her scenario the male used a knife). Overall, the findings seem to indicate that a woman will be blamed more (and the man less) for sexual victimization when she is drinking unless she drinks much more than the man. At that point, the male may be perceived as taking advantage of his intoxicated partner, causing the blame to shift in his direction (although the effects of relative intoxication need further examination). The clear implication of such findings is that cultural perceptions of the link between female intoxication and the potential for her victimization are strong. When she is *relatively* more incapacitated than her date, she is perceived as more easily victimized.

Similar implications can be drawn from studies of self-blame among sexual assault victims (e.g., Janoff-Bulman, 1979). Rape counselors in her survey reported that approximately 70 percent of victims blamed the assault at least in part on their own *behavior*, and 20 percent blamed the assault to some degree on their *character*. Thus, although estimates of prevalence of self-blame vary somewhat (e.g., McCombie, 1975; Meyer & Taylor, 1986; Sommerfeldt, Burkhaart, & Mandoki, 1989; Wyatt, Notgrass, & Newcomb, 1990), victims themselves commonly believe they engaged in behaviors that might be expected to increase the likelihood of sexual coercion (e.g., Koss, Dinero, & Seibel, 1988). Among these is use of alcohol. Smith and Ousley (1982), for example, reported that victims who were using drugs or alcohol at the time of the assault blamed themselves more than those who were not and expected greater blame from friends and family. Alcohol use is also among reported reasons of victims for failure to report rape (e.g., Stewart, Dobbin, & Gatowski, 1996).

Generally scholars have attributed such self-blame to inappropriate adoption of "false" cultural stereotypes regarding causes of sexual coercion (e.g., Bem, 1972; Janoff-Bulman, 1979; Ward, 1995). Another interpretation, however, is that women are accurately aware that intoxication increases the risk of sexual victimization. Although they may choose to ignore that risk or to believe that the level of risk is minimal with their particular date, when they are actually victimized while intoxicated they blame themselves, and expect blame from others, because they know they took a real risk by becoming intoxicated. Like many stereotypes, rape-related stereotypes are arguably based in part on fact, but overgeneralized, and often applied to individual cases in error.

DOES WOMEN'S ALCOHOL CONSUMPTION DEPEND UPON SEXUAL INTENTIONS?

Researchers addressing issues of alcohol, sexual coercion, and consent have to date been motivated and guided largely by victim advocacy. It would occur to few such researchers to ask if, in fact, willingness to drink or become intoxicated might actually be related to willingness to have sex, as such a finding would tend to undermine claims that intoxication is irrelevant to consent or that intoxication renders consent impossible. It stands to reason, however, that if women are widely aware of the arousing properties of alcohol for themselves and/or for their dates, the attempts of males to seduce women through intoxicating them, and/or the dangers of sexual coercion to intoxicated females, it would follow that the decision to drink or become intoxicated would depend, at least in part, on their sexual intentions. In the following sections, we will examine two questions: (1) Is alcohol use *probative* of sexual intentions? (i.e., are women more likely to consume alcohol when willing to have intercourse than when not willing?), and (2) Is alcohol use *definitive* evidence of sexual intentions? (i.e., do women consume alcohol if, and only if, willing to have intercourse?).

Are Women More Likely to Consume Alcohol When Willing to Have Intercourse Than When Not Willing?

Two types of findings support the proposition that women are more likely to consume alcohol when willing to have intercourse than when not willing. First, the previously discussed widely reported use of alcohol to "facilitate" sexual encounters, to "get in the mood," and the like implies greater likelihood of alcohol use when intending to have sexual encounters.

Second, Davis, Follette, and Merlino (1999) investigated this relationship in college students. Participants were asked to indicate for a variety of behaviors, including drinking with a date, getting drunk with a date, and doing drugs with a date, whether they were (1) more likely to do the behavior when *willing* to have sex than when not willing, (2) equally likely to do the behavior whether willing or not, or (3) more likely to do the behavior when *not willing* to have sex than when willing. Those who never drank or did drugs were instructed to answer (2).

Results revealed that large numbers of women report that they are more likely to use drugs (33%), have a few drinks (46%), or get drunk (61%) with their date when they are willing to have sex than when not willing. Among women who do drink or take drugs, the percentages would be even larger, as many students do not engage in those activities at all. Men also believe that women are more likely to use drugs (57%), have a few drinks (61%), or get drunk (75%) with their date when they are willing to have sex than when not willing.

It appears that women do base their decision of whether to drink or become intoxicated in part on their willingness to have sex. Women who are willing to have intercourse with their dates are, on the average, more likely to drink (and especially to become drunk) on their dates than those who are not. Thus, contrary to victim advocacy thinking, use of alcohol is relevant to and probative of sexual intentions and availability. Just as clearly, it is rarely definitive evidence of sexual intent, as shown in the next section.

Are Some Women Willing to Become Intoxicated with a Date If, and Only If, They Are Willing to Engage in Sexual Activity?

Clearly victim advocacy oriented scholars are correct in arguing that the fact of intoxication is not *definitive* evidence of consent in a particular case. That is, it is inappropriate to assume that because a woman chose to drink or become intoxicated, she was "asking for it" (i.e., that she wanted intercourse or that she knew or believed that intoxication would place her at risk with that partner in that circumstance). Some women, however, may nevertheless drink *only* when willing to have sex with their dates.

Davis, Follette, and Merlino (1999) also asked college students whether they (1) never (used drugs, drank, or got drunk) with a date at all; (2) performed the behavior if, and only if, willing to have sex; (3) sometimes performed the behavior when *not* willing to have sex; or (4) often performed the behavior when *not* willing to have sex. A clear majority of women reported having a few drinks with a date when not willing to have sex (84%) and getting drunk with a date when not willing to have sex (71%). However, a minority reported use of drugs when not willing to have sex (31%). Thus, these behaviors (particularly use of drugs with a date) are definitive for some women, in that they engage in them if and only if they are willing to have sex. However, drinking or getting drunk with a date are definitive indications of consent for a small minority. The majority of women drink and get drunk with dates when they have no intention at all to have sex.

Further, only a small minority of men viewed using drugs (28%), having a few drinks (8%), or getting drunk with a date (19%) as definitive evidence of willingness to have intercourse (i.e., responded that women do these things if, and only if, they are willing to have intercourse). Thus, reasonable men can be expected to know that drug or alcohol use is not definitive evidence that the woman is willing.

It is also noteworthy that drunkenness is both probative and definitive of sexual intentions for more women than is "having a few drinks"—and is perceived as such by men. Thus, in direct contrast to the law (which assumes greater intoxication equals greater negation of consent), greater drunkenness is more likely among women who are willing to consent.

Summary: What Is the Actual Relationship between Alcohol Use and Sexual Consent?

The empirical evidence clearly supports the conclusion that alcohol use is related to sexual intentions and sexual activity. Widespread beliefs among the population include the expectancies that alcohol enhances sexual motivation, arousal, and enjoyment and leads to greater voluntary and involuntary sexual activity. Thus, those who possess such expectancies and yet choose to drink can reasonably be expected to find such outcomes more acceptable, and even to desire them more, than those who choose not to. Further, alcohol does increase both sexual motivation and the likelihood of voluntary sexual activity. The majority of women acknowledge that they are more likely to get drunk with a date when they are willing to have intercourse than when not willing—and the majority of men believe this to be the case. Taken together, these findings clearly indicate that alcohol use is *probative* of sexual consent. That is, given that a person has consumed alcohol, the likelihood of voluntary sexual activity is greater than if that person has not consumed alcohol.

Just as clearly, however, alcohol use is not *definitive* evidence of consent. Sexual motivations and intentions are among many motivations for alcohol use. Others, such as anxiety reduction, easing social conversation, drowning troubles, and so on, may be primary motivators in the absence of any interest in sex. The majority of women report sometimes or often using alcohol with a date, even when they are unwilling to have sex, and men are aware of this. Hence, alcohol use is not definitive evidence of consent at the time it is consumed. Further, regardless of intentions at the time of initial consumption, they may later change.

Given that alcohol use is clearly, but not perfectly, associated with consensual sexual activity, it is inappropriate to conclude either that an intoxicated alleged victim has certainly consented (or "asked for it") or that she has certainly not consented.

IMPLICATIONS FOR THE LEGAL SYSTEM

The documented relationships between alcohol use and sexual motivation and behavior support six conclusions. First, consent may be properly viewed as a *process* unfolding over time rather than as a unitary event that must take place immediately prior to intercourse. Second, sexual activity with an intoxicated partner should *not* be presumed rape, as the decision to consume alcohol is probative of sexual intentions at the time of the decision as well as at the time of intercourse. Third, although intentions may change at any point, evidence of alcohol consumption is relevant to evaluation of the credibility of victim claims of coercion. Fourth, alcohol use is probative of what would be reasonable perceptions of both actual consent and ability to consent. Fifth, alcohol consumption may actually contribute to false claims of rape/coercion. Finally, regulation of sexual behavior while intoxicated presents a double-edged sword of protection from harm versus restriction of freedom.

Consent Is a *Process* Unfolding over Time

The process of consent to sexual encounters often unfolds in such a way that the woman first resists and later consents. This may happen because she is not interested at first, and later changes her mind, because she does not wish to appear too "easy," or for other reasons. However, as sequential interactions occur, or a specific interaction proceeds, cues given at each stage provide predictive utility for behaviors at the next. Some, such as holding hands, intimate discussions, or willingness to go to an isolated location, may provide only probabilistic cues for the recipient to interpret. Others may be offered in contractual format, such as promises to engage in intercourse if the partner obtains a condom, takes one to dinner first, or, as in our earlier example, if the person offering the commitment may first become intoxicated. Given adequate cues or explicit statements of consent (contingent or not), at some point a reasonable participant may conclude that consent is established (although it may later be withdrawn). Further, at any point, the reasonable participant might rationally assume that previous cues stand valid until contradicted by those occurring later in the process.

As it stands, the law presumes intoxication to negate the ability to rationally consent *at the time of intercourse*. Should it also negate intentions formed prior to intoxication, and reflected in behavior throughout the interaction preceding intercourse—including flirtation, various forms of foreplay, the decision to use alcohol, or even explicit verbal commitments to have intercourse?

Sexual Activity with an Intoxicated Partner Should Not Be Presumed Rape

Currently, rape law presumes the alleged victim's consent to sexual activity must consciously and rationally occur at or immediately prior to sexual engagement. Hence the presumption that if the victim is intoxicated at that time consent is not possible (and thus he or she is raped). This presumption stands in stark contrast to treatment of intoxication and criminal responsibility in some jurisdictions, specifying that the decision to consume alcohol confers responsibility for criminal actions taken later while under the influence (Marlowe et al., 1999).

This "responsibility claim" (Wertheimer, 2001) can be likewise applied to the intoxicated party to sexual relations. "It might be argued that if a woman is responsible for her intoxicated behavior, it follows that her intoxicated consent must be treated as valid" (p. 374). "In what might be regarded as the *flow through* view, we can justifiably ascribe responsibility to an agent for voluntary intoxicated behavior if she had the requisite volitional and epistemological capacities at the appropriate prior time. The main point is that moral responsibility does not chronologically track the agent's psychological capacities. If an agent has a fair opportunity at Time-1 to control or guide her behavior at Time-2, then our moral response to her use of those opportunities at Time-1 flows through to her behavior at Time-2, even if she is unable to guide or control her behavior at Time-2" (p. 383; see also Fischer & Ravizza, 1998).

Empirical evidence of widespread beliefs in the capacity of alcohol to stimulate sexual arousal and facilitate sexual encounters and of widespread knowledge of the relationship of intoxication to vulnerability to coercion and assault is consistent with the notion that women knowingly assume the risk of these outcomes when they voluntarily elect to become intoxicated in a particular social context. While arguably the intoxicated victim may not be responsible for her own mugging or rape by a stranger as she approaches her apartment door, the foreseeable consequences of intoxication are quite different in the context of a date or a drunken fraternity bash. When the woman can reasonably foresee the consequences of intoxication, and yet voluntarily chooses to become intoxicated, it is reasonable to consider that she may have found those consequences acceptable.

Further, the empirical evidence documenting the deliberate use of alcohol to promote or enjoy sexual encounters likewise suggests that the implications of alcohol consumption for consent or responsibility for sexual encounters should be evaluated, at least in part, at the point the person elects to use alcohol. As exemplified by our earlier example of "Mary" and her pornographic film, one may consume alcohol specifically in order to disinhibit oneself or to promote and enjoy a sexual encounter. In such a case, the person's desire or intent to engage in sexual activity is clear, even though clarity of thinking may diminish prior to intercourse.

Just as clearly, such intent/consent is not irrevocable. Denial or withdrawal of consent may occur at *any* time. Hence, if at any time the "victim" attempts to resist sexual engagement or explicitly says no, lack of consent has become clear, rendering earlier intentions and/or inferences based on alcohol use irrelevant. If no explicit physical or verbal denial of consent is offered, however, alcohol should not be considered to negate the intentions that set both the alcohol consumption and sexual engagement in motion. Consent may be given at any time and, in the absence of later withdrawal, may be presumed valid through what may reasonably be considered a continuous encounter between conscious participants. Since substantial evidence suggests that alcohol use is more likely among those intending/willing to have sex and that intent to have sex is more likely among those who have used alcohol, negation of intent because of intoxication will sometimes be inappropriate.

Alcohol Use May Reasonably Inform Judgments of Victim Credibility

Earlier we reviewed evidence that claims of coercion are viewed as less credible when involving an intoxicated victim. Such findings cannot be regarded as simply indicating inappropriate juror prejudice, rape "myths," or bias. Given the actual relationship between intoxication and enhanced likelihood of consensual sexual activity, it is reasonable and rational that, on the average, the rape claims of intoxicated women should be viewed as less credible than those of unintoxicated women.

In no way, however, does such a conclusion imply that a woman who consents to drink or become drunk should be presumed to have consented or to have "asked for it." Instead, alcohol use should be one clue among the entire array of evidence to be considered in arriving at a conclusion of consent or lack of consent.

As in any case, witness credibility in rape trials is crucial to juror decisions. Rape cases are unique, however, in that the evidence commonly consists mostly or solely of the testimony of alleged victim and perpetrator. Particularly when intercourse has occurred and consent is the issue, both physical evidence (presuming no evidence of injury to either party) and independent fact witnesses are often lacking. Thus, jurors' decisions depend largely upon assessment of the relative credibility of the alleged victim and defendant. Olsen-Fulero and Fulero (1997), for example, note that judgment that rape has occurred "necessarily involves inferential judgments about motives, intentions, and behavior beyond the evidence presented" (p. 405). They also state "the juror in a rape trial is faced with the dilemma of determining the relative responsibility and veracity of the victim and the defendant. Because the facts of the case would rarely make such judgments obvious, jurors must draw inferential conclusions about personal character, events, and intention" (p. 402).

Given the documented inability of laypersons and "experts" (such as judges, psychologists, attorneys, police, detectives, etc.) alike to judge truthfulness at greater than chance level (e.g., Ekman & O'Sullivan, 1991; Vrij, 1993), jurors are arguably unsuited to judge cases resting on witness credibility—particularly in the absence of other evidence. However, given that they must make the judgment, jurors are forced to rely, as Olsen-Fulero and Fulero note, on other indicators reflecting which of the parties is likely to be most truthful. To the extent that any given behavior is probative of sexual intentions/behaviors for either alleged victim or defendant, it can reasonably be used as evidence going to the credibility of either party's claims. Clearly the choice to use alcohol, and particularly to become intoxicated, is probative of sexual intentions at the time the choice is made. Indeed, in view of the documented association between chronic alcohol use and sexual permissiveness, intoxication is probative of the probability of consent in a specific encounter. Thus, jurors should be allowed to consider, in the context of the other evidence, the implications of voluntary intoxication for probable consent at the time of sexual engagement and for witness credibility, rather than be instructed to presume that intoxication negates consent.

Intoxication Is Probative of Reasonable Partner Understanding of Sexual Intentions/Consent

For cases involving allegations of rape by intoxication, two issues of perceived consent are relevant. First, an honest and reasonably held, but erroneous, belief that the alleged victim is not too intoxicated to give legal consent to intercourse is considered defense to rape by intoxication (see *People v. Giardino*, 2000; see review of Canadian Law regarding reasonable belief in consent and capacity to consent by Rolfes, 1998). Particularly in cases where the alleged victim has previously specifically connected her intention to use alcohol to sexual intentions, a reasonable person would not conclude that alcohol negated the consent tied to its use.

Second, given that the alleged victim is assumed able to offer legally valid consent, it must be determined whether he or she *actually* consented. Again, the defendant's honest and reasonably held belief that the alleged victim actually consented is considered defense to rape. Further, a finding of lack of consent requires that refusal of consent must be actively communicated, either verbally or physically (see *People v. Giardino*, 2000. See review of Canadian law regarding reasonable belief in consent by Rolfes, 1998). Thus, to the extent the alleged victim has engaged in behaviors predictive of actual consent and has *not* actively communicated nonconsent, these behaviors contribute to the reasonable interpretation of consent by the alleged perpetrator.

The previously reviewed evidence clearly established an association between alcohol use and actual consent. Further, research on the role of alcohol in sexual victimization suggests that intoxicated women tend to produce more behavioral cues of consent—thereby potentially causing their partners to more reasonably infer token resistance and/or consent. Even in ultimately coercive sexual encounters, intoxicated women engage in more foreplay before beginning to resist, and then resist less, and less forcefully, prior to the assault (Harrington & Leitenberg, 1994, Norris et al., 1996). Thus, arguably, the partner of an intoxicated woman, even an actually unwilling one, would be presented with fewer indications of nonconsent. In turn, it would be less likely that he could have or should have known that sexual activity was involuntary. Given these facts, jurors may reasonably use evidence of alleged victim intoxication as evidence of the defendant's probable understanding of the alleged victim's consent.

"Victim" Intoxication May Contribute to False Claims of Rape

Steele and Josephs's (1990) alcohol myopia model specifies that alcohol will produce the greatest disinhibiting effects on the sexual behavior of those who feel strong inhibitory forces in combination with sexual arousal. Such people might include those high in sex guilt and others who feel sex is inappropriate, those contemplating sex with inappropriate partners (see Murphy, Monahan, & Miller, 1998) or partners they do not really like, or those with no condoms or other protection. In other words, alcohol may be most likely to disinhibit sexual behavior for those most likely to feel guilt or regret upon regaining sobriety. For example, MacDonald, MacDonald, Zanna, and Fong (2000) found that alcohol enhanced the relationship between sexual arousal and intentions to have sex without condoms.

At high enough levels, alcohol will also impair memory for the event (e.g., Casbon, Curtin, Lang, & Patrick, 2003; Kirchner & Sayette, 2003; Rosen & Lee, 1976; Tracy & Bates, 1999; Yuille & Tollestrup, 1990), as can chronic alcohol use (e.g., Sullivan, Fama, Rosenbloom, & Pfefferbaum, 2002). Thus, when the person later attempts to reconstruct the events in question, their memories may be susceptible to the distorting influence of a self-concept inconsistent with their sexual behavior while intoxicated and/or expectations and opinions of their partner that are inconsistent with having engaged in voluntary intercourse with that person. In turn, such schemas and expectations may create first the belief and then the illusory "memory" of rape.

Although their application to false accusations of rape is speculative at this point, the individual processes proposed here have been repeatedly documented.

Alcohol clearly impairs memory. In turn, poor memory, in the context of other expectations and emotions, has been proven susceptible to substantial distortion based on schemas, expectations, self-protective and other motivations, and other sources of influence (see reviews in Schacter, 1996, 2001). Likewise, literature on autobiographical memory has documented the impact of these influences on memory for one's personal past (e.g., Smith, Leffingwell, & Pacek, 1999; Ross & Wilson, 2000). In addition, shame or guilt resulting from behavior while intoxicated may lead to deliberate false claims to avoid social censure or other consequences.

The Double-edged Sword: Protection from Harm Versus Restriction of Freedom

Finally, it is important to note that regulation of sexual relations under the influence of alcohol has both positive and negative implications for sexual autonomy. As Wertheimer (2001) points out:

> We do well to remember that there is both a positive and negative dimension to respecting an agent's autonomy. We respect an agent's negative autonomy when we protect her from interventions by others that do not reflect her will. We respect her positive autonomy when we allow her to render it permissible for others to engage in relationships with her. Although both dimensions of autonomy are important, we cannot always maximize both forms simultaneously. To the extent that we zealously protect an agent's negative autonomy by setting high standards for what qualifies as valid consent, we may encroach on her positive autonomy to realize her own goals and desires. (p. 376)

Clearly, the law is designed to protect us against circumstances in which intoxication results in sexual activity that would be rejected while sober. However, it is important for the law to recognize the deliberate use of alcohol to facilitate sexual goals that are fully consistent with our sober intentions and desires, and for our courts to permit the jury to evaluate the actual purpose of alcohol use and its relationship to these *ex ante* sober sexual intentions.

CONCLUSION

Epstein (1978) long ago described inconsistencies in the treatment of intoxication in English and American criminal law as "in reality controlled by the weight of perceived public opinion" (quoted in Critchlow, 1985, p. 453). Critchlow (1983, 1985; 1986) noted the existence of widely held ambivalent cultural attitudes toward alcohol use and its effects, which have produced both a long history of controversy and inconsistency in the law regarding alcohol and criminal responsibility (Epstein, 1978; Marlowe, Lambert, & Thompson, 1999; Levine, 1981; Rolfes, 1998; Singh, 1933) and similarly inconsistent and contradictory research illustrations of the effects of alcohol on lay judgments of responsibility. As Critchlow (1983) noted:

On the one hand, because alcohol is widely used and accepted as a pleasurable adjunct to sociability, antisocial acts committed under its influence may be taken less seriously. Because of alcohol's status as a disinhibitor, these acts can be attributed to alcohol rather than to the person. On the other hand, alcohol's reputation as destroyer of self-control leads to a derogation of those who do not control its use and therefore control themselves. Because these people should have "known better," their acts are seen as particularly blameworthy. Thus we have two views in our society: one an excuse of drunken deviant acts and one of moral blame. (p. 469)

Reflecting this ambivalence, the law has tended to shift between emphasis on responsibility for wrongdoing while intoxicated and understanding of alcohol-induced cognitive impairment and mitigation of responsibility for "behavior under the influence" or BUI, (e.g., Critchlow, 1983; Epstein, 1978; Marlowe et al., 1999; Levine, 1981; Singh, 1933)—perhaps, as Epstein (1978) suggested, in response to shifts in the weight of public preference.

Similarly, rape laws have shifted substantially in response to public outrage over failure to convict rapists and to arguments and research findings regarding what are viewed as prejudicial effects of evidence now excluded by rape shield laws. Current alcohol laws in many jurisdictions reflect polar opposite emphasis for alleged offender and victim—that is, punishment for wrongdoing for the alleged offender, but negation of responsibility (consent/intent) through cognitive impairment for the alleged victim. It remains to hope that the law will shift yet again, toward a more moderate and complex approach to the implications of complainant intoxication, recognizing the implications of the actual associations between alcohol use and sexual consent as well as the relevance of cues of consent conveyed prior to, as well as at the time of, intercourse. To reasonably evaluate the implications of the complainant's intoxication for consent, the jury should consider the degree to which intoxication was voluntary and the circumstances of the choice along with other complainant and defendant behavior and other contextual evidence. The presumption of negation of consent forces a decision based on incomplete information and is susceptible to arbitrary error.

Recall the case we began with, of Jolene and her two accused rapists. Jolene engaged in a variety of sexualized behaviors with the two defendants prior to the alleged rape. Perhaps more important, however, defense attorney Mary Lynn Belsher located witnesses who testified that Jolene and a friend had planned to set up a man to "rape" them in order to later sue him to make lots of money out of it. Notwithstanding Jolene's sexualized behavior and her intentions to falsely accuse someone of rape in order to profit, Josh and Wes would have been found guilty of rape by intoxication if the prosecution had been able prove Jolene was sufficiently intoxicated. Instead, alcohol expert Stanley Dorrance provided persuasive testimony that, based on her blood alcohol level by the time she reached the hospital, Jolene could not have been sufficiently intoxicated at the time of the alleged rape to negate consent. But for his testimony, Josh and Wes would likely now be in prison.

Although Josh Boykin and Wes McDonald were found innocent in this instance, their case, like the case of "Mary" and her pornographic movie, provides an example of the injustice that can result from failure to consider the entire context of intoxication along with other cues and predictors of consent.

REFERENCES

Abbey, A. (1991). Acquaintance rape and alcohol consumption on college campuses: How are they linked? *Journal of American College Health, 39,* 165–169.

Abbey, A., & Harnish, R. J. (1995). Perception of sexual intent: The role of gender, alcohol consumption, and rape-supportive attitudes. *Sex Roles, 32,* 297–313.

Abbey, A., McAuslan, P., & Ross, L. T. (1998). Sexual assault perpetration by college men: The role of alcohol, misperception of sexual intent, and sexual beliefs and experiences. *Journal of Social and Clinical Psychology, 17,* 167–195.

Abbey, A., McAuslan, P., Ross, L. T., & Zawacki, T. (1999). Alcohol expectancies regarding sex, aggression, and sexual vulnerability: Reliability and validity assessment. *Psychology of Addictive Behaviors, 13,* 174–182.

Abbey, A., McAuslan, P., Zawacki, T., Clinton, A. M., & Buck, P. O. (2001). Attitudinal, experiential, and situational predictors of sexual assault perpetration. *Journal of Interpersonal Violence, 16,* 784–807.

Abbey, A., & Ross, L. T. (1992). The role of alcohol in understanding misperception and sexual assault. Paper presented at the annual meeting of the American Psychological Association, San Francisco.

Abbey, A., Ross, L. T., & McDuffie, D. (1994). Alcohol's role in sexual assault. In R. R. Watson (Ed.), *Drug and alcohol abuse reviews: Volume 5, Addictive behaviors in women* (pp. 97–123). Totowa, NJ: Humana Press.

Abbey, A., Ross, L. T., McDuffie, D., & McAuslan, P. (1996). Alcohol, misperception, and sexual assault: How and why are they linked? In D. M. Buss & N. M. Malamuth (Eds.), *Sex power conflict: evolutionary and feminist perspectives* (pp. 138–161). New York: Oxford University Press.

Abbey, A., Zawacki, T. Buck, P. O., Clinton, A. M., & McAuslan, P. (2001). Alcohol and sexual assault. *Alcohol Health and Research World, 25,* 1–14.

Abbey, A., Zawacki, T., & McAuslan, P. (2001). Alcohol's effects on sexual perception. *Journal of Studies on Alcohol, 61,* 688–697.

Allison, J. A., & Wrightsman, L. S. (1993). *Rape: The misunderstood crime.* Newbury Park, CA: Sage.

Anderson, K. B., Cooper, H., & Okamura, L. (1997). Individual differences and attitudes toward rape: A meta-analytic review. *Personality and Social Psychology Bulletin, 23,* 295–315.

Anderson, P. B., & Mathieu, D. A. (1993, April). The relationship of alcohol consumption as a sexual disinhibitor to high risk social behavior: Gender differences. Paper presented at the Society for the Scientific Study of Sexuality, Western Region meeting, San Diego, CA.

Anderson, P. A., & Struckman-Johnson, C. (Eds.) (1998). *Sexually aggressive women: Current perspectives and controversies.* New York: Guilford Publications, Inc.

Aramburu, B., & Leigh, B. C. (1991). For better or worse: Attributions about drunken aggression toward male and female victims. *Violence and Victims, 6,* 31–41.

Athanasiou, R., Shaver, P., & Tavris, C. (1970, July). Sex. *Psychology Today*, 39–52.

Beckman, L. J., & Ackerman, K. T. (1995). Women, alcohol, and sexuality. *Recent Developments in Alcoholism*, *12*, 267–285.

Bem, D. (1972). Self-perception theory. In L. Berkowitz (Ed.), *Advance in experimental social psychology*, Vol. 6 (pp. 2–63). New York: Academic Press.

Berkowitz, A. (1992). College men as perpetrators of acquaintance rape and sexual assault: A review of the literature. *Journal of American College Health*, *40*, 175–181.

Bernat, J. A., Calhoun, K. S., & Stolp, S. (1998). Sexually aggressive men's responses to a date rape analogue: Alcohol as a disinhibiting cue. *Journal of Sex Research*, *35*, 341–348.

Brecklin, L. R., & Ullman, S. E. (2001). The role of offender alcohol use in rape attacks: An analysis of national crime victimization survey data. *Journal of Interpersonal Violence*, *16*, 3–21.

Briddell, D., Rimm, D., Caddy, G., Krawitz, G., Sholis, D., & Wunderlin, R. (1978). The effects of alcohol and cognitive set on sexual arousal to deviant stimuli. *Journal of Abnormal Psychology*, *87*, 418–430.

Brown, S. A., Goldman, M. S., Inn, A., & Anderson, L. R. (1980). Expectations of reinforcement from alcohol: Their domain and relation to drinking patterns. *Journal of Consulting and Clinical Psychology*, *48*, 419–426.

Burnam, M. A., Stein, J. A., Golding, J. M., Siegel, J. M., Sorenson, S. B., Forsythe, A. B., & Telles, C. A. (1988). Sexual assault and mental disorders in a community sample. *Journal of Consulting and Clinical Psychology*, *56*, 843–850.

Burt, M. R. (1980). Cultural myths and support for rape. *Journal of Personality and Social Psychology*, *38*, 217–230.

Butcher, A. H., Manning, D. T., & O'Neal, E. C. (1991). HIV-related sexual behaviors of college students. *Journal of the American College of Health*, *40*, 115–118.

Casbon, T. S., Curtin, J. J., Lang, A. R., & Patrick, C. J. (2003). Deleterious effects of alcohol intoxication: Diminished cognitive control and its behavioral consequences. *Journal of Abnormal Psychology*, *112*, 476–487.

Chandler, S. M., & Torney, M. (1981). The decisions and the processing of rape victims through the criminal justice system. *California Sociologist*, *4*, 155–169.

Coker, A. L., Walls, L. G., & Johnson, J. E. (1998). Risk factors for traumatic physical injury during sexual assaults for male and female victims. *Journal of Interpersonal Violence*, *13*, 605–620.

Cook, S. L. (1995). Acceptance and expectation of sexual aggression in college students. *Psychology of Women Quarterly*, *19*, 181–194.

Cooper, M. L., & Orcutt, H. K. (1997). Drinking and sexual experience on first dates among adolescents. *Journal of Abnormal Psychology*, *106*, 191–202.

Corbin, W. R., Bernat, J. A., Calhoun, K. S., McNair, L. D., & Seals, K. L. (2001). The role of alcohol expectancies and alcohol consumption among sexually victimized and nonvictimized college women. *Journal of Interpersonal Violence*, *16*, 297–311.

Corcoran, K. J., & Bell, B. G. (1990). Opposite sex perceptions of the effects of alcohol consumption on subsequent sexual activity in a dating situation. *Psychology*, *27*, 7–11.

Corcoran, K. J., & Thomas, L. R. (1991). The influence of observed alcohol consumption on perceptions of initiation of sexual activity in a college dating situation. *Journal of Applied Social Psychology*, *21*, 500–507.

Critchlow, B. (1983). Blaming the booze: The attribution of responsibility for drunken behavior. *Personality and Social Psychology Bulletin, 9*, 451–473.

Critchlow, B. (1985). The blame in the bottle: Attributions about drunken behavior. *Personality and Social Psychology Bulletin, 11*, 258–276.

Critchlow, B. (1986). The powers of John Barleycorn: Beliefs about the effects of alcohol on social behavior. *American Psychologist, 41*, 751–764.

Crowe, L. C., & George, W. H. (1989). Alcohol and human sexuality: Review and integration. *Psychological Bulletin, 105*, 374–386.

Crowell, N. A., & Burgess, A. W. (1996). *Understanding violence against women.* Washington, DC: National Academy Press.

Cue, K. L., George, W. H., & Norris, J. (1996). Women's appraisals of sexual assault risk in dating situations. *Psychology of Women Quarterly, 20*, 487–504.

Davis, D., Follette, W. C., & Merlino, M. L. (1999). Seeds of rape: Female behavior is probative for females, definitive for males. In *Psychological Expertise and Criminal Justice* (pp. 101–140). Washington, DC: American Psychological Association.

Derman, K. H., & Cooper, M. L. (2000). Inhibition conflict and alcohol expectancy as moderators of alcohol's relationship to condom use. *Experimental and Clinical Psychopharmacology, 8*, 198–206.

Early, E. (1950). *News summaries 30 Jan 50.* Cited in *Simpson's Contemporary Quotations* (1988), no. 6532.

Ekman, P., & O'Sullivan, M. (1991). Who can catch a liar? *American Psychologist, 46*, 913–920.

Emery, E. M., Ritter-Randolph, G. P., & Strozier, A. L. (1993). Using focus group interviews to identify salient issues concerning college students' alcohol abuse. *Journal of American College Health, 41*, 195–198.

Emmers-Sommer, T. M., & Allen, M. (1999). Variables related to sexual coercion: A path model. *Journal of Social and Personal Relationships, 16*, 659–678.

Epstein, T. (1978). A sociolegal examination of intoxication and the criminal law. *Contemporary Drug Problems, 7*, 401–471.

Falk, P. J. (2002). Rape by drugs: A statutory overview and proposals for reform. *Arizona Law Review, 44*, 131–212.

Finley, C., & Corty, E. (1993). Rape on campus: The prevalence of sexual assault while enrolled in college. *Journal of College Student Development, 34*, 113–117.

Fisher, G. J. (1995). Effects of drinking by the victim or offender on verdicts in a simulated trial of an acquaintance rape. *Psychological Reports, 77*, 579–586.

Fisher, J. M., & Ravizza, M. (1998). *Responsibility and control.* Cambridge: Cambridge University Press.

Frazier, P. A., & Haney, B. (1996). Sexual assault cases in the legal system: Police, prosecutor and victim perspectives. *Law and Human Behavior, 20*, 607–628.

Frintner, M. P., & Robinson, L. (1993). Acquaintance rape: The influence of alcohol, fraternity membership, and sports team membership. *Journal of Sex Education and Therapy, 19*, 272–284.

Fromme, K., & Wendel, J. (1995). Beliefs about the effects of alcohol on involvement in coercive and consenting sexual activities. *Journal of Applied Social Psychology, 25*, 2099–2117.

George, W. H., Coe, K. I., Lopez, P. A., Crowe, L. C., & Norris, J. (1995). Self-reported alcohol expectancies and postdrinking sexual inferences about women. *Journal of Applied Social Psychology, 25*, 164–186.

George, W. H., Gournic, S. J., & McAfee, M. P. (1988). Perceptions of postdrinking female sexuality: Effects of gender, beverage choice, and drink payment. *Journal of Applied Social Psychology, 15*, 1295–1317.

George, W. H., Lehman, G. L., Cue, K. L., Martinez, L., Lopez, P. A., & Norris, J. (1997). Postdrinking sexual inferences: Evidence for linear rather than curvilinear dosage effects. *Journal of Applied Social Psychology, 18*, 629–648.

George, W. H., & Marlatt, G. A. (1986). The effects of alcohol and anger on interest in violence, erotica, and deviance. *Journal of Abnormal Psychology, 95*, 150–158.

George, W. H., & Stoner, S. A. (2000). Understanding acute alcohol effects on sexual behavior. *Annual Review of Sex Research, 11*, 92–124.

George, W. H., Stoner, S. A., Norris, J., Lopez, P. A., & Lehman, G. L. (2000). Alcohol expectancies and sexuality. A self-fulfilling prophecy analysis of dyadic perceptions and behavior. *Journal of Studies on Alcohol, 61*, 168–176.

Gomberg, E. S. (1981). Women, sex roles, and alcohol problems. *Professional Psychology, 12*, 272–284.

Goodchilds, J. D., & Zellman, G. L. (1984). Sexual signaling and sexual aggression in adolescent relationships. In N. M. Malamuth & E. Donnerstein (Eds.), *Pornography and sexual aggression* (pp. 223–243). Orlando, FL: Academic Press.

Gravitt, G. W., Jr. & Krueger, M. M. (1998). College students' perceptions of the relationship between sex and drinking. *Sexuality and Culture, 1*, 175–190.

Greene, D. M., & Navarro, R. L. (1998). Situation-specific assertiveness in the epidemiology of sexual victimization among university women. *Psychology of Women Quarterly, 22*, 589–604.

Gross, A. M., Bennet, T., Sloan, L., Marx, B. P., & Juergens, J. (2001). The impact of alcohol and alcohol expectancies on male perception of female sexual arousal in a date rape analog. *Experimental and Clinical Psychopharmacology, 9*, 380–388.

Hammock, G. S., & Richardson, D. R. (1997). Perceptions of rape: The influence of closeness of the relationship, intoxication and sex of participant. *Violence and Victims, 12*, 237–246.

Harrington, N. T., & Leitenberg, H. (1994). Relationship between alcohol consumption and victim behaviors immediately preceding sexual aggression by an acquaintance. *Violence and Victims, 9*, 315–324.

Harrison, L. A., & Esqueda, C. W. (2000). Effects of race and victim drinking on domestic violence attributions. *Sex Roles, 42*, 1043–1057.

Heaton, J., & Varrin, S. (1991). The impact of alcohol ingestion on erections in rats as measured by a novel bio-assay. *Journal of Urology, 145*, 192–194.

Hindmarch, I., & Brinkmann, R. (1999). Trends in the use of alcohol and other drugs in cases of sexual assault. *Human Psychopharmacology Clinical & Experimental, 14*, 225–231.

Hull, J. G., & Bond, C. F., Jr. (1986). Social and behavioral consequences of alcohol consumption and expectancy: A meta-analysis. *Psychological Bulletin, 99*, 347–360.

James, W. (1902). *The varieties of religious experience.* Cited in *Columbia World of Quotations*, (1996), no. *30506.*

Janoff-Bulman, R. (1979). Characterological versus behavioral self-blame: Inquiries into depression and rape. *Journal of Personality and Social Psychology, 37*, 798–809.

Kanin, E. J. (1984). Date rape: Unofficial criminals and victims. *Victimology, 9*, 95–108.

Kaplan, J., & Weisberg, R. (1991). *Criminal law.* Boston: Little Brown.

Keeling, R. P. (1994). Changing the context: The power in prevention (alcohol awareness, caring, and community). *Journal of American College Health, 42*, 243–247.

Kerstetter, W. A. (1990). Gateway to justice: Police and prosecutorial response to sexual assaults against women. *Journal of Criminal Law and Criminology, 81*, 267–313.

Kerstetter, W. A., & Van Winkle, B. (1990). Who decides? A study of the complainant's decision to prosecute in rape cases. *Criminal Justice and Behavior, 17*, 268–283.

Kirchner, T. R., & Sayette, M. A. (2003). Effects of alcohol on controlled and automatic memory processes. *Experimental & Clinical Psychopharmacology, 11*, 167–175.

Koss, M. P. (1988). Hidden rape: Sexual aggression and victimization in a national sample of students in higher education. In A. Burgess (Ed.) *Rape and sexual assault II* (pp. 3–25). New York: Garland.

Koss, M. P., & Dinero, T. E. (1988). Predictors of sexual aggression among a national sample of male college students. *Annals of the New York Academy of Sciences, 528*, 133–147.

Koss, M. P., Dinero, T. E., & Seibel, C. A. (1988). Stranger and acquaintance rape: Are there differences in the victims' experience? *Psychology of Women Quarterly, 12*, 1–24.

Koss, M. P., Gidycz, C. A., & Wisniewski, N. (1987). The scope of rape: Incidence and prevalence of sexual aggression and victimization in a national sample of students in higher education. *Journal of Consulting and Clinical Psychology, 55*, 162–170.

Kramer, K. M. (1994). Rule by myth: The social and legal dynamics governing alcohol-related acquaintance rapes. *Stanford Law Review, 47*, 115–160.

LaFree, G. D. (1981). Official reactions to social problems: Police decision in sexual assault cases. *Social Problems, 28*, 582–594.

LaFree, G. D., Reskin, B., & Visher, C. (1985). Jurors' responses to victim's behavior and legal issues in sexual assault trials. *Social Problems, 32*, 389–402.

Landrine, H., Bardwell, S., & Dean, T. (1988). Gender expectations for alcohol use: A study of the significance of the masculine role. *Sex Roles, 19*, 703–712.

Lang, A. R. (1985). The social psychology of drinking and human sexuality. *Journal of Drug Issues, 15*, 273–289.

Lang, A. R., Searles, J., Lauerman, R., & Adesso, V. (1980). Expectancy, alcohol, and sex guilt as determinants of interest in and reaction to sexual stimuli. *Journal of Abnormal Psychology, 89*, 644–653.

Layton, C. J. (1997). No more excuses: Closing the door on the voluntary intoxication defense. *John Marshall Law Review, 30*, 535–1288.

Larimer, M. E., Lydum, A. R., Anderson, B. K., & Turner, A. P. Male and female recipients of unwanted sexual contact in a college student sample: Prevalence rates, alcohol use, and depression symptoms. *Sex Roles, 40*, 295–308.

Lee, H. B., & Cheung, F. M. (1991). The Attitudes toward Rape Victims Scale: Reliability and validity in a Chinese context. *Sex Roles, 24*, 599–603.

Leigh, B. C. (1989). In search of the seven dwarves: Issues of measurement and meaning in alcohol expectancy. *Psychological Bulletin, 105*, 361–373.

Leigh, B. C. (1990). Venus gets in my thinking: Drinking and female sexuality in the age of AIDS. *Journal of Substance Abuse, 2*, 129–145.

Leigh, B. C. (1995). A thing so fallen, and so vile: Images of drinking and sexuality in women. *Contemporary Drug Problems, 22*, 415–434.

Leigh, B. C., & Aramburu, B. (1994). Responsibility attributions for drunken behavior: The role of expectancy violation. *Journal of Applied Social Psychology, 24*, 115–135.

Leigh, B. C., Aramburu, B., & Norris, J. (1992). The morning after: Gender differences in attributions about alcohol-related sexual encounters. *Journal of Applied Social Psychology, 22,* 343–357.

Levine, H. G. (1981, January). The good creature of God and demon rum: Colonial American and nineteenth century ideas about alcohol, crime, and accidents. Paper presented at the Conference on Alcohol and Disinhibition, Berkeley, California.

Lonsway, K. A., & Fitzgerald, L. F. (1994). Rape myths: In review. *Psychology of Women Quarterly, 16,* 133–164.

Lopez, P. (1992). He said . . . she said . . . an overview of date rape from commission through prosecution through verdict. *Criminal Justice Journal, 13,* 275–302.

MacDonald, T. K., MacDonald, G., Zanna, M. P., & Fong, G. (2000). Alcohol, sexual arousal, and intentions to use condoms in young men: Applying alcohol myopia theory to risky sexual behavior. *Health Psychology, 19,* 290–298.

Malatesta, V., Pollack, R. H., Wilbanks, W. A., & Adams, H. E. (1979). Alcohol effects on the orgasmic-ejaculatory response in human males. *Journal of Sex Research, 15,* 101–107.

Marlowe, D. B., Lambert, J. B., & Thompson, R. G. (1999). Voluntary intoxication and criminal responsibility. *Behavioral Sciences and the Law, 17,* 195–217.

Marchell, T., & Cummings, N. (2001). Alcohol and sexual violence among college students. In A. J. Ottens & K. Hotelling (Eds.), *Sexual violence on campus* (pp. 30–52). New York: Springer.

Martin, C. M., & Hoffman, M. A. (1993). Alcohol expectancies, living environment, peer influence, and gender: A model of college student drinking. *Journal of College Student Development, 34,* 206–211.

Martin, P. Y., & Hummer, R. A. (1989). Fraternities and rape on campus. *Gender & Society, 3,* 457–473.

Martin, S. E., & Bachman, R. (1998). The contribution of alcohol to the likelihood of completion and severity of injury in rape incidents. *Violence against Women, 4,* 694–712.

Marx, B. P., & Gross, A. M. (1995). Date rape: An analysis of two contextual variables. *Behavior Modification, 19,* 451–463.

Marx, B. P., Gross, A. M., & Adams, H. E. (1999). The effect of alcohol on the responses of sexually coercive and noncoercive men to an experimental rape analogue. *Sexual Abuse: Journal of Research & Treatment, 11,* 131–145.

Marx, B. P., Gross, A. M., & Juergens, J. P. (1997). The effects of alcohol consumption and expectancies in an experimental date rape analogue. *Journal of Psychopathology and Behavioral Assessment, 19,* 281–302.

McCombie, S. L. (1975). Characteristics of rape victims seen in crisis intervention. *Smith College Studies in Social Work, 46,* 137–158.

Meilman, P. W. (1993). Alcohol-induced sexual behavior on campus. *Journal of American College Health, 4,* 27–31.

Meilman, P. W., Burwell, C., & Smith, K. E. (1993). Using survey data to capture students' attention: Three institutions look at alcohol-induced sexual behavior. *Journal of College Student Development, 34,* 72–73.

Meyers, C. B., & Taylor, S. E. (1986). Adjustment to rape. *Journal of Personality and Social Psychology, 50,* 1226–1234.

Miller, B., & Marshall, J. C. (1987). Coercive sex on the university campus. *Journal of College Student Personnel, 28,* 38–47.

Molitor, F., Ruiz, J. D., Klausner, J. D., & McFarland, W. (2000). History of forced sex in association with drug use and sexual HIV risk behaviors, infection with STDs, and diagnostic medical care. *Journal of Interpersonal Violence, 15*, 262–278.

Mosher, D. L., & Anderson, R. D. (1986). Macho personality, sexual aggression, and reactions to guided imagery of realistic rape. *Journal of Research in Personality, 20*, 77–94.

Montgomery, R. L., Benedicto, J. A., & Haemmerlie, F. M. (1993). Personal vs. social motivation of undergraduates for using alcohol. *Psychological Report, 73*, 960–962.

Mosher, D. L., & Anderson, R. D. (1986). Macho personality, sexual aggression, and reactions to guided imagery of realistic rape. *Journal of Research in Personality, 20*, 77–94.

Muehlenhard, C. L., & Cook, S. W. (1988). Men's self-reports of unwanted sexual activity. *Journal of Sex Research, 24*, 58–72.

Muehlenhard, C. L., & Linton, M. A. (1987). Date rape and sexual aggression in dating situations: incidence and risk factors. *Journal of counseling Psychology, 34*, 186–196.

Murphy, S. T., Monahan, J. L., & Miller, L. C. (1998). Inference under the influence: The impact of alcohol and inhibition conflict on women's sexual decision-making. *Personality and Social Psychology Bulletin, 24*, 517–528.

Norris, J. (1994). Alcohol and female sexuality: A look at expectancies and risks. *Alcohol Health and Research World, 18*, 197–201.

Norris, J., & Cubbins, L. A. (1992). Dating, drinking, and rape: Effects of victim's and assailant's alcohol consumption on judgments of their behavior and traits. *Psychology of Women Quarterly, 16*, 179–191.

Norris, J., George, W. H., Davis, K. C. (2000, August). Alcohol's effects on perceiving and responding to risk associated with acquaintance sexual assault. Paper presented at the Annual Convention of the American Psychological Association, Washington, DC.

Norris, J., George, W. H., Davis, K. C., Martell, J., & Leonesio, R. J. (1999). Alcohol and hypermasculinity as determinants of men's empathic responses to violent pornography. *Journal of Interpersonal Violence, 14*, 683–700.

Norris, J., Nurius, P. S., & Dimeff, L. A. (1996). Through her eyes: Factors affecting women's perception of and resistance to acquaintance sexual aggression threat. *Psychology of Women Quarterly, 20*, 123–145.

Nurius, P. S., & Norris, J. (1996). A cognitive-ecological model of women's response to male sexual aggression in dating. *Journal of Personality and Human Sexuality, 8*, 117–139.

O'Leary, A., Goodhart, F., Jemmott, L. S., & Boccher-Lattimore, D. (1992). Predictors of safer sex on the college campus: A social cognitive theory analysis. *Journal of the American College of Health, 40*, 254–263.

Olsen-Fulero, L., & Fulero, S. M. (1997). Commonsense rape judgments: An empathy-complexity theory of rape juror story making. *Psychology, Public Policy and the Law, 3*, 402–427.

Ozman, S. L., & Davis, C. M. (1999). Predicting perceptions of date rape based on individual beliefs and female alcohol consumption. *Journal of College Student Development, 40*, 701–709.

Parks, K. A., & Miller, B. A. (1997). Bar victimization of women. *Psychology of Women Quarterly, 21*, 509–525.

Parks, K. A., Miller, B. A., Collins, R. L., & Zestes-Zanatta, L. (1998). Women's descriptions of drinking in bars: Reasons and risks. *Sex Roles, 38*, 701–717.

People v. Joshua Cody Boykin, State of California: Merced County Superior Court Case #24135 (2000).

People v. Giardino 82 Cal.App.4th 454, 98 Cal. Rptr.2d 315 (2000).

Perkins, H. W. (1992). Gender patterns in consequences of collegiate alcohol abuse: A ten year study of trends in an undergraduate population. *Journal of Studies of Alcohol, 53*, 458–462.

Pernanen, K. (1991). *Alcohol in human violence.* New York: Guilford Press.

Police discretion and the judgment that a crime has been committed: Rape in Philadelphia (Comment). (1968). *University of Pennsylvania Law Review, 117*, 277–292.

Radius, S. M., Joffe, A., & Gall, M. J. (1991). Barrier versus oral contraceptive use: A study of female college students. *Journal of American College Health, 40*, 83–85.

Rapaport, K. R., & Posey, C. D. (1991). Sexually coercive college males. In A. Parrot & L. Bechhofer (Eds.), *Acquaintance rape: The hidden crime* (pp. 217–228). New York: Wiley.

Richardson, D., & Campbell, J. L. (1980). Alcohol and wife abuse: The effect of alcohol on attributions of blame for wife abuse. *Personality and Social Psychology Bulletin, 6*, 51–56.

Richardson, D., & Campbell, J. L. (1982). Alcohol and rape: The effect of alcohol on attributions of blame for rape. *Personality and Social Psychology Bulletin, 8*, 468–476.

Richardson, D. R., & Hammock, G. (1991). Alcohol and acquaintance rape. In A. Parrot & L. Bechhofer (Eds.), *Acquaintance rape: The hidden crime* (pp. 83–95). New York: Wiley.

Robinson, P. H. (1984 & 1997 Supp.). *Criminal law defense.* St Paul, MN: West

Roehrich, L., & Kinder, B. N. (1991). Alcohol expectancies and male sexuality: Review and implications for sex therapy. *Journal of Sex and Marital Therapy, 17*, 45–54.

Rolfes, B. (1998). The golden thread of criminal law: Moral culpability and sexual assault. *Saskatchewan Law Review, 61*, 87–125.

Rose, V. M., & Randall, S. C. (1982). The impact of investigator perceptions of victim legitimacy on the processing of rape/sexual assault cases. *Symbolic Interaction, 5*, 23–36.

Rosen, L. J., & Lee, C. L. (1976). Acute and chronic effects of alcohol use on organizational processes in memory. *Journal of Abnormal and Social Psychology, 85*, 309–317.

Rosen, R. (1991). Alcohol and drug effects on sexual response: Human experimental and clinical studies. *Annual Review of Sex Research, 2*, 119–179.

Rosen, R., & Ashton, A. (1993). Prosexual drugs: Empirical status of the "new aphrodisiacs." *Archives of Sexual Behavior, 22*, 521–541.

Ross, M., & Wilson, A. E. (2000). Constructing and appraising past selves. In D. L. Schacter & E. Scarry (Eds.), *Memory, brain and belief* (pp. 231–258). Cambridge, MA: Harvard University Press.

Ryan, K. M. (1988). Rape and seduction scripts. *Psychology of Women Quarterly, 12*, 237–245.

Sanday, P. R. (1996). Rape-prone versus rape-free campus environments. *Violence against Women, 2*, 191–208.

Schacter, D. L. (1996). *Searching for memory: The brain, the mind, and the past.* New York: Basic Books.

Schacter, D. L. (2001). *The seven sins of memory: How the mind forgets and remembers.* New York: Houghton Mifflin.

Schuller, R. A., & Stewart, A. (2000). Police responses to sexual assault complaints: The role of perpetrator/complainant intoxication. *Law and Human Behavior, 24,* 535–551.

Schuller, R. A., & Wall, A. (1998). The effects of defendant and complainant intoxication on mock jurors' judgments of sexual assault. *Psychology of Women Quarterly, 22,* 555–573.

Seto, M. C., & Barbaree, H. E. (1995). The role of alcohol in sexual aggression. *Clinical Psychology Review, 15,* 545–566.

Singh, R. U. (1933). History of the defence of drunkenness in English criminal Law. *Law Quarterly Review, 49,* 529–546.

Smith, R. E., Leffingwell, T. R., & Ptacek, J. T. (1999). Can people remember how they coped? Factors associated with discordance between same-day and retrospective reports. *Journal of Personality and Social Psychology, 76,* 1050–1061.

Smith, W. R., & Ousley, N. L. (1992, August). Social and psychological consequences of different types of sexual assault. Paper presented at the Annual Convention of the American Psychological Association, Washington, DC.

Sobell, L. C., & Sobell, M. B. (1975). Drunkenness, a "special circumstance" in crimes of violence: Sometimes. *International Journal of the Addictions, 10,* 869–882.

Sommerfeldt, T. G., Burkhart, B. R., & Mandoki, C. A. (1989, August). In her own words: Victims' descriptions of hidden rape effects. Paper presented at the Annual Convention of the American Psychological Association, New Orleans, LA.

Southwick, L., Steele, C. M., Marlatt, G. A., & Lindell, M. (1981). Alcohol-related expectancies: Defined by phase of intoxication and drinking experience. *Journal of Consulting and Clinical Psychology, 49,* 713–721.

Spigner, C., Hawkins, W., & Loren, W. (1992). Gender differences in perception of risk associated with alcohol and drug use among college students. *Women & Health, 20,* 87–97.

Steele, C. M., & Josephs, R. A. (1990). Alcohol myopia: Its prized and dangerous effects. *American Psychologist, 45,* 921–933.

Stewart, A. L., & Maddren, K. (1997). Police officers' judgment of blame in family violence: The impact of gender and alcohol. *Sex Roles, 37,* 921–934.

Stewart, M. W., Dobbin, S. A., & Gatowski, S. I. (1996). "Real rapes" and "real victims:" The shared reliance on common cultural definitions of rape. *Feminist Legal Studies, 4,* 159–177.

Stormo, K. J., Lang, A. R., & Stritzke, W. G. K. (1997). Attributions about acquaintance rape: The role of alcohol and individual differences. *Journal of Applied Social Psychology, 27,* 279–305.

Sullivan, E. V., Fama, R., Rosenbloom, M. J., & Pfefferbaum, A. (2002). A profile of neuropsychological deficits in alcoholic women. *Neuropsychology, 16,* 74–83.

Testa, M., & Collins, R. L. (1997). Alcohol and risky sexual behavior: Event-based analyses among a sample of high-risk women. *Psychology of Addictive Behaviors, 11,* 190–201.

Testa, M., & Dermen, K. (1999). The differential correlates of sexual coercion and rape. *Journal of Interpersonal Violence, 14,* 548–561.

Testa, M., & Livingston, J. A. (1999). Qualitative analysis of women's experiences of sexual aggression: Focus on the role of alcohol. *Psycholoty of Women Quarterly, 23,* 573–589.

Testa, M., & Livingston, J. A. (2000). Alcohol and sexual aggression: Reciprocal relationships over time in a sample of high-risk women. *Journal of Interpersonal Violence, 2000, 15,* 413–427.

Testa, M., Livingston, J. A., & Collins, R. L. (2000). The role of alcohol in women's vulnerability to sexual aggression. *Experimental and Clinical Psychopharmacology, 8*, 185–191.

Testa, M., & Parks, K. A. (1996). The role of women's alcohol consumption in sexual victimization. *Aggression and Violent Behavior: A Review Journal, 1*, 217–234.

Tracy, J. I., & Bates, M. E. (1999). The selective effects of alcohol on automatic and effortful memory processes. *Neuropsychology, 13*, 282–290.

Tyler, K. A., Hoyt, D. R., & Whitbeck, L. B. (1998). Coercive sexual strategies. *Violence and Victims, 13*, 47–61.

Ullman, S. E., Karabatsos, G., & Koss, M. P. (1999a). Alcohol and sexual assault in a national sample of college women. *Journal of Interpersonal Violence, 14*, 603–625.

Ullman, S. E., Karabatsos, G., & Koss, M. P. (1999b). Alcohol and sexual aggression in a national sample of college men. *Psychology of Women Quarterly, 23*, 673–689.

Ullman, S. E., & Knight, R. A. (1993). The efficacy of women's resistance strategies in rape situations. *Psychology of Women Quarterly, 17*, 23–28.

Valliere, V. M. (1997). Relationships between alcohol use, alcohol expectancies, and sexual offenses in convicted offenders. In B. K. Schwartz & H. R. Cellini (Eds.), *The sex offender: New insights, treatment innovations, and legal developments*, Vol. 2 (pp. 3-1–3-14). Kingston, NJ: Civic Research Institute.

Vrij, A. (1993). Credibility judgments of detectives: The impact of nonverbal behavior, social skills, and physical characteristics on impression formation. *Journal of Social Psychology, 133*, 601–610.

Wall, A. M., & Schuller, R. A. (2000). Sexual assault and defendant/victim intoxication: Jurors' perceptions of guilt. *Journal of Applied Social Psychology, 30*, 253–274.

Ward, C. A. (1995). *Attitudes toward rape: Feminist and social psychological perspectives*. Thousand Oaks, CA: Sage.

Ward, C. A., Chapman, K., Cohn, E., White, S., & Williams, K. (1991). Acquaintance rape and the college coed scene. *Family Relations, 40*, 65–71.

Wechsler, H., & Isaac, N. (1992). Binge drinkers at Massachusetts colleges: Prevalence, drinking style, time trends, and associated problems. *Journal of the American Medical Association, 267*, 2929–2931.

Weinhardt, L. S., & Carey, M. P. (2000). Does alcohol lead to sexual risk behavior? Findings from event-level research. *Annual Review of Sex Research, 11*, 124–157.

Wertheimer, A. (2001). Intoxicated consent to sexual relations. *Law and Philosophy, 20*, 373–401.

Wild, T. C., Graham, K., & Rehm, J. (1998). Blame and punishment for intoxicated aggression: When is the perpetrator culpable? *Addiction, 93*, 677–687.

Wilsnack, S. C. (1984). Drinking, sexuality, and sexual dysfunction in women. In S. C. Wilsnack & L. J. Beckman (Eds.), *Alcohol problems in women* (pp. 189–227). New York: Guilford Press.

Wilsnack, S. C. (1991). Sexuality and women's drinking. *Alcohol, Health and Research World, 15*, 147–150.

Wilson, A. E., Calhoun, K. S., & McNair, L. D. (2002). Alcohol consumption and expectancies among sexually coercive college men. *Journal of Interpersonal Violence, 17*, 1145–1159.

Wilson, G. T., & Lawson, D. M. (1976a). Expectancies, alcohol, and sexual arousal in male social drinkers. *Journal of Abnormal Psychology, 85*, 587–594.

Wilson, G. T., & Lawson, D. M. (1976b). The effects of alcohol on sexual arousal in women. *Journal of Abnormal Psychology, 85*, 489–497.

Wilson, G. T., & Lawson, D. M. (1978). Expectancies, alcohol, and sexual arousal in women. *Journal of Abnormal Psychology, 87,* 358–367.

Wilson, G. T., & Niaura, R. (1984). Alcohol and the disinhibition of sexual responsiveness. *Journal of Studies on Alcohol, 45,* 219–224.

Winfield, I., George, L. K., Swartz, M., & Blazer, D. G. (1990). Sexual assault and psychiatric disorders among a community sample of women. *American Journal of Psychiatry, 147,* 335–341.

Workman, T. A. (2001). Finding the meanings of college drinking: An analysis of fraternity drinking stories. *Health Communication, 13,* 427–447.

Wyatt, G. E., Notgrass, C. M., & Newcomb, M. (1990). Internal and external mediators of women's rape experiences. *Psychology of Women Quarterly, 14,* 153–176.

Wydra, A., Marshall, W. L., Earls, C. M., & Barbaree, H. E. (1983). Identification of cues and control of sexual arousal by rapists. *Behavior Research and Therapy, 21,* 469–476.

Yegidis, B. L. (1986). Date rape and other forced sexual encounters among college students. *Journal of Sex Education and Therapy, 12,* 51–54.

Yuille, J. C., & Tollestrup, P. A. (1990). Some effects of alcohol on eyewitness memory. *Journal of Applied Psychology, 75,* 268–273.

Zorza, J. (2001). Drug facilitated rape. In A. J. Ottens & K. Hotelling (Eds.), *Sexual violence on campus* (pp. 53–75). New York: Springer.

INDEX

A
Abbott, Walter, 788
Abel Child Cognitions Scale, 452
Aberrant Behavior Checklist (ABC), 503
Absolute risk, 117
Abusive Behaviors Inventory (ABI), 724
Acculturation, 814–816
Acculturation Rating Scale for Mexican
    Americans (ARSMA), 815
Achenbach Child Behavior Checklist, 235, 241
Achievement tests, 238
Ackerman-Schoendorg Scales for Parent
    Evaluation of Custody (ASPECT), 239
Active elaborative processing, 944
Active processing mechanisms, 943–947
Activities of daily living (ADLs), 215
Actuarial assessment
    classification tree approach and, 109–110
    clinical assessment vs., 89–90
    recidivism predictions and, 414
    sexual offenders and, 454–456
    violence predictions and, 108–109
Actus reus determination, 87–88
Acute risk factors, 115
Adaptive Behavior Scales, 501
Addiction Severity Index (ASI), 329
Addington v. Texas (1979), 772–773
ADHD. *See* Attention Deficit Hyperactivity
    Disorder
Adjudicative competency, 175–205
    assessment of, 189–204
    competencies related to, 185–189
    contextual basis for, 202–203
    criticisms of tests for, 199–201
    developmental disabilities and, 499–503
    domains and subdomains of, 190
    forensic reports and, 65
    history of evaluations for, 175–176
    improving practices for assessing, 201–204
    interviews for evaluating, 192–196
    nomological aspects of, 176–178
    normed assessment tool for, 196–199
    procedural aspects of, 178–181

refusal of treatments for, 181–185
screening tests for determining, 191–192
specialized training for evaluating, 204
substantiating conclusions about, 203–204
treatments for restoring, 180–181
See also Mental competency
Administrative adherence, 248
Adolescents
    civil commitment of, 773
    criminal intent of, 873–874
    forensic evaluation of, 875–890
    psychopathy in, 399–400, 880–883
    violence risk assessment of, 879–880
    See also Children; Juvenile justice system
Adoption and Safe Families Act (1997), 686
Adultery, 430
Adult protective services (APS), 755
Adversarial system, 650
African Americans
    capital sentencing of, 812
    legal system bias and, 810–812
Ageism, 746
Aggressive behavior
    intermittent explosive disorder and, 478–479
    partner violence and, 713–735
    sexual assault and, 445–449
    See also Dangerousness; Violence
Aggressive Sexual Behavior Inventory (ASB),
    444
Aging process
    cognitive disorders associated with, 219–222
    elder abuse risk and, 747
    intellectual functioning and, 218
    memory changes and, 218–219
    partner violence and, 724
    physiological changes and, 217–218
    psychopathic criminals and, 415–416
    See also Elderly adults
Ailes, Roger, 933
Akin-Little, K. Angeleque, 369
Alcoholics Anonymous (AA), 333
Alcohol placebo effect, 1003
Alcohol Severity Index, 327

Alcohol use
  behavior under the influence of, 1021
  blood alcohol levels and, 323, 325
  criminal behavior and, 318
  DUI offenders and, 323
  legal issues and, 319–323
  partner violence and, 720, 725
  rape and, 998–1000, 1005–1006, 1009–1012, 1016–1020
  responsibility issues and, 320–321, 1016–1017, 1020–1022
  screening tools for, 327–328
  seductive coercion and, 1007
  sexual arousal and, 1000–1003, 1004
  treatments for, 332–335
  victim credibility and, 1017–1018
  voluntary sexual activity and, 1003–1009, 1014–1015
  women's sexual intentions and, 1012–1015, 1018–1019
  See also Intoxication; Substance abuse
Alcohol Use Disorders Identification Test (AUDIT), 327–328
Alpha strategies of persuasion, 920, 921–939
Alter Approach, 161
Alternative choice double bind, 923
Alternative questions, 911, 915–916, 923
Alzheimer's disease (AD), 219–220
American Association for Correctional Psychology, 864
American Association on Mental Retardation (AAMR), 490, 500, 501, 502
American Association of Police Polygraphists, 627
American Bar Association (ABA), 216
American Humane Society, 451
American Law Institute (ALI), 18, 88, 158
American Medical Association (AMA), 20, 275, 572, 573, 753
American Mutual Liability Insurance Co. v. King (1953), 10
American Polygraph Association, 627
American Psychiatric Association (APA), 7, 20, 337, 500, 813
American Psychological Association (APA)
  Code of Ethics, 45–46, 48, 51, 808, 820
  Guidelines for Child Custody Evaluations in Divorce Proceedings, 234–235
  Manual of Diagnosis and Professional Practice in Mental Retardation, 500
  Standards for Educational and Psychological Testing, 39, 40, 240, 627
  statement on sexual relations with clients, 19

American Society of Addiction Medicine (ASAM), 319, 335, 336
American Society of Trial Consultants, 783, 787
Americans with Disabilities Act (ADA), 491
AMNART Reading Test, 284
Amnesia, 562, 966
Amphetamines, 317–318
Analogous tactics, 954
Analogue studies
  of polygraph tests, 609–610, 612
  problems with, 612
Analytic Juror Rater, 788
Anger
  intermittent explosive disorder and, 478–479
  partner violence and, 725
Anger Index, 725
Antiandrogen interventions, 452, 453
Anticipatory counterarguments, 948
Antisocial behavior
  coercion model of, 374–375
  juvenile delinquency and, 880–883
Antisocial Personality Disorder (ASPD), 91, 378, 396, 397–398, 471, 671, 967
Antisocial Practices (ASP) content scale, 403
Antisocial scale (ANT), 405
Anxiety
  cognitive processing and, 957–958
  false confessions and, 966
  interrogation tactics and, 926–928
Anxiety disorders, 966
Anxiety Disorders Interview Schedule-Revised (ADIS-R), 354
Appellate process, 978–980
Applied behavior analysis, 504–505
Arizona v. Fulminante (1991), 969, 980
Aronson, Elliot, 949
Arrestees Drug Abuse Monitoring (ADAM) program, 319
Assessment
  ADHD, 384–385
  adjudicative competency, 189–204
  APA standards for, 40
  child sexual abuse, 258–262, 451–452
  clinical vs. actuarial, 89–90
  conduct disorder, 375–376
  criminal responsibility, 87–89, 157–174
  culturally competent, 813–821
  dangerousness, 85–101
  elder abuse, 755–759
  forensic reports and, 69–70
  inappropriate or inadequate, 138
  instruments used for, 162–163
  juvenile, 875–890

laboratory, 324–326
malingering, 286–289
mental competency, 222–225
mental disorders, 160–165, 281
parental fitness, 694–703
partner violence, 715–721, 723–728
psychological damages, 275–293
psychopathy, 400–408
PTSD, 351–361
sex offender, 453–456
substance abuse, 323–332, 335–337
violence, 103–127
See also Evaluation; Risk assessment
Association of Family and Conciliation Courts (AFCC), 234, 235
Association for Retarded Citizens (ARC), 491
Association for the Treatment of Sexual Abusers, 55
Ataque de nervios, 816, 817
Atkins v. Virginia (2002), 833
Atlantic Line Coast Railway v. Smith (1963), 10
Attention Deficit Hyperactivity Disorder (ADHD), 380–388
  assessment of, 384–385
  conduct disorder and, 372, 380, 387
  definition of, 380–382
  developmental progression of, 383–384
  diagnosis of, 380–382
  difficulties related to, 382–383
  false confessions and, 965
  forensic considerations for, 386–388
  impulsive behavior and, 472–473
  intervention/treatment for, 385–386
  medications for, 385–386
  parent training programs and, 386, 702
  prevalence of, 383
  risk factors for, 383
Attitudes
  commitment to, 941
  embeddedness of, 942–943
  intensity of, 941
  jury profiling and, 788
  partner violence and, 726
  personal importance of, 940–941
  resistance to changing, 939–943
Attitudes Toward Women Scale (ATW), 448
Attorneys
  attorney-client privilege and, 4
  jury selection by, 781–782
  overview of psychology for, 27–44
Attraction to Sexual Aggression Scale (ASA), 444, 661
Authoritarianism, 786

Authority, 934–935
Autonomy, 215
Availability heuristic error, 257, 722, 925
Avina, Claudia, 655
Azar, Sandra T., 685

B
Bacon, Francis, 947
Bahri, Ritu, 3
Base-rate errors, 256–257
Basis of Assessment section of forensic reports, 69–70
Batterer treatment programs, 729–732
Bazelon, David, 771
Beck Depression Inventory, Revised (BDI-II), 720, 725, 757
Beech Aircraft Corporation v. Rainey (1988), 11
Behavior
  analysis of, 504–505
  explanations for, 39
  predictions of, 41
Behavioral clues of lying, 637–644
  cautions about, 642
  feeling clues, 638–642
  implications of, 643–644
  legal process and, 646–649
  thinking clues, 638
Behavioral observations
  ADHD and, 385
  child custody evaluations and, 239
  conduct disorder and, 376
  forensic reports and, 72–73
  jury selection and, 796–797
  psychopathy and, 406–407
  substance abuse and, 324
Behavioral theory, 39
  exhibitionism and, 438
  frotteurism and, 441
  rape and, 446
  sexual sadism and, 443
Behavior disorders
  analyses of, 504–505
  See also Mental disorders
Behavior symptoms, 622–623
Behavior under the influence (BUI), 1021
Beitz, Kendra, 27
Beliefs
  resistance to changing, 939–943
  See also Attitudes
Belmont Report (NCPHS), 225
Belsher, Mary Lynn, 1021
Best Estimate procedures, 324
Best Interests of the Child (BIC) standard, 234

Between-evaluation inconsistencies, 307
Bias
    confirmation, 257, 571
    correspondence, 797–798, 970
    ethnic, 810–812
    evidence gathering and, 256–258, 259
    eyewitness reports and, 516, 525–526
    hindsight, 979
    interviewing techniques and, 670
    own-race, 525–526
    positive coercion, 977
    potential sources of, 259
    recap, 972
    truthfulness, 944–945
Biculturalism, 810
Bilingualism, 810
Biological factors
    ADHD and, 383
    conduct disorder and, 373
    developmental disabilities and, 493
    mental retardation and, 493, 494, 495–496
Biological theory, 39
    exhibitionism and, 438
    sexual sadism and, 443
    voyeurism and, 436
Biopsychosocial theory, 39
Bipolar Disorder, 472
Black's Law Dictionary, 268
Blood alcohol level (BAL), 323, 325
Bogus Pipeline procedure, 952–953
Boles, Richard, 245
Boomerang effect, 946
Borawick v. Shay (1995), 588
Borderline Personality Disorder, 471, 671, 858, 967
Borg maneuver, 904, 913, 949–953
Borum, Randy, 873
Bowers, Adrian H., 655
Boykin, Josh, 997–998, 1022
Boykin v. Alabama (1969), 185
Bradley, April R., 233
Brain injury, 221–222
Brehm, Jack, 927
Brief screening instruments, 327–328
Brief Symptom Inventory (BSI), 720
Broderick v. Ruder (1988), 658
Brogdon, M. Gino, Sr., 3
Brown v. State (1980), 10
Brunswig, Kirk A., 851
Buchanan, Jeffrey, 213, 743
Burden of proof, 668–672
Burkholder, Eric, 489
Burral v. State (1999), 582, 588
Burston, G. R., 743

Burt Rape Myth Acceptance Scale (RMAS), 448
Buss-Durkee Hostility Inventory (BDHI), 725
Butler, R. N., 743

C
CAGE test, 328
Cale, Ellison M., 395
California Psychological Inventory (CPI), 404
Campbell, Donald, 29
Caregivers
    elder abuse and, 745, 748–749
    financial difficulties of, 749–750
    living arrangements of, 750–751
    screening of, 754–755
    skills of, 748–749, 757, 760
    stress on, 745, 760
Carnegie, Dale, 933
Carter v. General Motors (1961), 270
Case histories, 563–565
Case law
    involuntary civil commitment and, 771–773
    psychological damage claims and, 269–271
    See also names of specific cases
Catherine the Great, 927
Causal risk factors, 115
Causal statements, 30
Center for Epidemiologic Studies Depression (CES-D) scale, 817
Center for Substance Abuse Treatment (CSAT), 321, 335, 336
Centers for Disease Control and Prevention(CDC), 233
Central route to persuasion, 921–932
Change of venue research, 784–785
Chapple v. Ganger (1994), 283
Child abuse and neglect, 685–703
    cultural differences and, 687–688
    developmental areas affected by, 700
    disparate definitions of, 686–688
    historical trends related to, 685–686
    investigations of, 689–690
    mandatory reporting of, 688–689
    parental fitness evaluation and, 694–703
    risk assessment for, 690–694
    special-needs children and, 701–703
    symptoms/needs indicative of, 700–701
    transgenerational violence and, 745
    types of, 687
    See also Child sexual abuse
Child Abuse Potential Inventory, 235, 692
Child custody evaluations, 233–241
    collateral information for, 239–240
    current statutes for, 234

INDEX　　1037

    direct observations for, 239
    ethical guidelines for, 234–235
    interpreting data for, 240
    potential problems with, 240–241
    procedures for, 235–239
    psychological tests for, 237–239
    tender years rationale in, 685
Child protective services (CPS), 688–689, 692
Children
    ADHD in, 380–388
    assessment issues with, 245–265
    civil commitment of, 773
    conduct disorder in, 370–380
    criminal intent of, 873–874
    effects of divorce on, 233
    eyewitness testimony of, 533–539
    forensic evaluation of, 875–890
    informed consent and, 68
    interviews with, 248–249, 260–262
    judicial testimony by, 246–249
    psychometric evaluation of, 247–248, 260
    psychopathy in, 399–400, 880–883
    research on event memory of, 249–256
    secondhand testimony of, 541–542
    suggestibility of, 534–535
    violence risk assessment of, 879
    See also Juvenile justice system
Child's Appercetion Test (CAT), 236
Child sexual abuse (CSA)
    assessment procedures for, 258–262
    biases in gathering evidence on, 256–258, 259, 570–571
    children's memory of, 254–256
    increasing reports of, 245–246
    legal definitions of, 687
    misdiagnosis of, 22–23
    recovered memories of, 555–574
    structured interview for, 261–262
    testimony by children on, 246–249
    validity of indicators of, 569–570
    See also Child abuse and neglect; Pedophilia
Child witnesses, 533–539
    exposure to misinformation by, 538–539
    interviews of, 535–538
    recent studies of, 534
    scripted protocols for, 536–538
    secondhand testimony of, 541–542
    suggestibility of, 534–535
Christy Brothers Circus v. Turnage (1928), 269–270
Churchill, Winston, 650
Citing information sources, 78–79
Civil commitment. *See* Involuntary civil commitment

Civil Rights Act (1964), 656
Civil trials, 136
Claar v. Burlington Railroad N.R.R. (1994), 12, 14
Clarke Sexual History Questionnaire (SHQ), 437, 438
Classical conditioning, 39
Classification tree method, 109–110
Classroom behavior modification, 386
Cleckley criteria, 396, 404
Cleckley, Hervey, 396
Clients
    sexual relationships with, 19–20
    therapeutic relationship with, 630, 863
Clinical assessment
    actuarial assessment vs., 89–90
    elder abuse and, 755–759
    juvenile justice system and, 875–883
    structured clinical judgment and, 113–114
    suicidal patients and, 149
    violence predictions and, 110–113
Clinical competence, 499
Clinical Findings section of forensic reports, 72
Clinical Impressions section of forensic reports, 73–76
Clinical interviews
    adjudicative competency assessment and, 192–196
    child custody evaluations and, 237
    PTSD assessment and, 353
    risk assessment and, 95–96
    substance abuse assessment and, 330–332
    See also Structured clinical interviews
Clinical jargon, 77–78
Clinical lie test, 614, 622–624
    description of, 622–623
    validity of, 623–624
Clinical practice parameters, 113
Clinician-Administered PTSD Scale (CAPS), 355
Closed-circuit television, 647
Cocaine, 317
Code of Ethics (APA), 45–46, 48, 51
Coerced-compliant confession, 901, 913, 949
Coerced-internalized confession, 901, 913, 950, 951
Coercion
    assessing, 971–972
    interrogation, 970–976
    perception of, 972–976
    polygrapher, 629
    sexual, 1007
    therapeutic, 52
Coercion model, 374
Coercive persuasion, 956

Coercive Sexual Fantasies Questionnaire, 444
Coexistence, 517
Cognitive ability
  age-related changes and, 217–219
  assessment of, 222–225, 758, 822–824
  distraction and, 959
  elder abuse and, 758
  ethical issues related to, 225–228
  informed consent and, 225–227
  interrogation tactics and, 955–960
  mental disorders and, 219–222
  physical exhaustion and, 956–957
  sleep deprivation and, 956–957
  social isolation and, 958–959
  time constraints and, 959–960
  See also Intellectual functioning; Mental competency
Cognitive-behavioral therapy
  ADHD and, 386
  elder abuse and, 760
  pedophilia and, 452–453
  sex-offender treatment and, 53, 54, 55–57, 58, 452–453, 677
  suicidal patients and, 143–144
Cognitive coping strategies, 700
Cognitive distortions, 440
Cognitive interview (CI), 532–533
Cognitive problem-solving skills training (PSST), 377
Cognitive theory, 39
Collateral information
  child custody evaluations and, 239–240
  cited in forensic reports, 70, 79
  substance abuse assessment and, 324
Collectivism, 818
Colorado v. Connelly (1986), 188, 214, 885
Coloured Progressive Matrices (CPM), 824
Commission errors, 137, 250
Commitment
  civil, 14–16, 767–779
  criminal, 17–19
  See also Involuntary civil commitment
Committee on Ethical Guidelines for Forensic Psychology, 273, 808
Commonwealth v. Crawford (1999), 956
Communication disorders, 965
Communication of risk, 116–119
Community
  conduct disorders and, 379
  therapeutic, 417
Community Competence Scale, 224
Community Reinforcement Approach (CRA), 333
Community supervision, 121

Community survey, 789–790
Competence to proceed, 887–889
Competency assessment, 222–225
  developmental disabilities and, 499–503
  ethnic issues and, 830–831
  juvenile justice system and, 885–889
  methods used for, 223–225
  questions related to, 222–223
Competency Screening Test (CST), 191–192
Competency to confess, 187–189
Competency to plead guilty, 185–187
Competency to proceed *pro se*, 185–187
Competency to stand trial, 17
  ethnicity and, 830–831
  forensic reports and, 65
  history of evaluations for, 175–176
  See also Adjudicative competency; Mental competency
Competency to Stand Trial Assessment Instrument (CAI), 193
Composition challenge, 785–786
Comprehensive Assessment and Referral Evaluation (CARE), 224
Comprehensive theories of rape, 446–447
Compulsive shopping, 481–482
Computerized Assessment and Response Bias (CARB), 287
Concealment lie, 636
Conditioning theory, 450–451
Conduct Disorder (CD), 370–380
  ADHD and, 372, 380, 387
  assessment of, 375–376
  definition of, 371
  developmental progression of, 374
  diagnosis of, 371–372
  forensic considerations for, 378–380
  impulsive behavior and, 473
  intervention/treatment for, 376–378
  prevalence of, 372
  risk factors for, 373
Confessions
  adjudicative competency and, 187–189
  classification of, 900–901
  coercive tactics and, 629, 970–976
  consequences of false, 967–980
  interrogation process and, 189, 899–900
  jury judgments of, 976–978
  mental disorders and, 963–967
  polygraph tests and, 629
  posttrial appeals and, 978–980
  pretrial consequences of, 967–968
  stress as impetus of, 917–920
  See also False confessions

INDEX 1039

Confidence/accuracy (CA) relation, 526–531
　recall and, 529–530
　recognition memory and, 527–529
Confidence of interrogators, 935
Confidentiality, 227–228
Confirmation bias, 257, 571
Conflict Tactics Scale (CTS), 717–718, 724
Conflict Tactics Scale-Revised (CTS2), 717–718, 721
Confrontation Clause, 647
Confusion, 954–955
Consequentialist theories, 47
Consuming resistance, 961
Contextual factors
　adjudicative competency and, 202–203
　elder abuse and, 749–751
Contrast effects, 923–925
Control questions, 603
Control question test (CQT), 614–618
　description of, 614–615
　directed lie test, 617
　positive control test, 617–618
　truth control test, 618
　validity studies of, 615–617
Conversion Disorder, 305
Cooper v. Oklahoma (1996), 178
Correctional facilities, 851–868
　behavior of psychopaths in, 412–413
　environmental aspects of, 852–853
　ethical issues in, 862–864
　malingerers in, 859–860
　psychologist roles in, 854–862
　research conducted in, 864–867
　risk assessments in, 856–857
　substance abuse treatment in, 335
　See also Prisons; Secure settings
Correctional psychologists, 852
Correspondence bias, 797–798, 970
Courage to Heal, The (Bass & Davis), 569
Court interventions, 321–322
Courtship disorder, 441
Covering law model, 29
Coy v. Iowa (1988), 647
Crack cocaine, 317
Credibility
　communicator, 934–935
　victim, 1017–1018
Crime victims
　eyewitness memories of, 521
　intoxication of, 1017–1018
　PTSD symptoms in, 350
　treatments for, 675–676, 733
　victim empathy training and, 440, 444–445

Criminal behavior
　ADHD and, 386–388
　conduct disorder and, 378–380
　mental disorders and, 90–91
　mental retardation and, 497
　psychopathy and, 91–92, 410–415
　recidivism and, 413–415
　sexual deviance and, 433–434, 456–458
　substance abuse and, 92, 316–319
Criminal commitment, 17–19
　competency to stand trial and, 17
　mental state of defendant and, 18–19
Criminal Interrogation and Confessions (Inbau, Reid, & Buckley), 905
Criminal Justice and Behavior (Brodsky), 861
Criminal justice system
　court interventions and, 321–322
　ethnic bias in, 810–812
　jury selection and, 781–801
　lie detection and, 645, 646–649
　mental retardation and, 496–498
　See also Juvenile justice system
Criminal responsibility
　assessment of, 87–89, 157–174, 831
　criticisms of evaluations for, 168–169
　elements of, 87–88
　ethnic issues and, 831
　legal standards for, 157–159
　mental disorders and, 160–165, 167–168
　specialized scales for evaluating, 89, 165–167
　substance abuse and, 320–321
　See also Insanity defense
Criminal trials
　civil trials vs., 136
　pretrial publicity in, 783–785
Crisis intervention, 860
Criterion-based content analysis (CBCA), 258
Criterion problem, 200
Critical events, 35
Cromartie v. State (1999), 13
Cross-examination of witnesses, 798
Cuban Americans, 815
　See also Hispanics
Cultural factors
　competency issues and, 830–831
　criminal responsibility and, 831
　employment litigation and, 834–835
　forensic assessment and, 813–821
　future research on, 838
　guidelines on accounting for, 808–810
　immigration cases and, 835–837
　language issues and, 819–821

legal system bias and, 810–812
psychological testing and, 821–829
psychopathy and, 399, 816–818
research and, 36–37
risk assessment and, 831–833
Cultural familial mental retardation, 493
Cultural heterogeneity, 814
Culturally competent assessment, 813–821
acculturation and, 814–816
cultural heterogeneity and, 814
language issues and, 819–821
personality tests and, 820–821
psychopathology and, 816–818
published resources on, 813
response styles and, 818–819
translator use and, 819–820
Culture-bound syndromes, 816–818
Custody evaluations. *See* Child custody evaluations
Cycle of violence, 745

D

Danger Assessment Scale (DAS), 727
Dangerousness, 85
conceptions of, 105–106
involuntary commitment and, 773–775
mental disorders and, 90–91
predictions of, 9, 87, 90, 93, 94–95
psychopathy and, 91–92
research on, 90–92, 97
substance abuse and, 92
Dangerousness assessment, 85–97
clinical vs. actuarial, 89–90
criminal responsibility and, 87–89
future directions in, 97
interview strategies for, 95–96
legal standards for, 86
methodological limitations of, 92–93
overview of, 86–87
research related to, 90–92, 97
static vs. dynamic risk factors in, 94–95
tools used for, 95
See also Violence risk assessment
Dangerous patient exception, 7
Daubert standard, 12–13, 69, 587–597, 821
Daubert v. Merrell Dow Pharmaceuticals (1993), 11–14, 69, 279, 580, 585–587, 649, 821
Davis, Deborah, 781, 897, 997
Davis, Kenny Bob, 1007
Death penalty
mental retardation and, 833–834
racial discrimination and, 812
Death qualification, 786

Deception
behavioral clues of, 637–644
detection of, 644–645, 648–649, 973–974
See also Lying
Deception guilt, 641
Decision making
biases in, 570–571
ethical issues and, 49
evidence-based, 150–151
fear and, 926
inferences in, 256
mental competency and, 214–215
violence risk assessment and, 107–116
Default assumptions, 945
Deflection strategy, 800–801
Delayed discovery doctrine, 557
Delirium disorders, 965
Delusions, 966
Dementia, 219, 965
Demographics
jury profiling and, 787–788
partner violence and, 724
Dempster, Rebecca, 103
Denial
motivated, 947
suspect, 908–909
Denney, Robert L., 267
Department of Defense Polygraph Institute (DODPI), 627
Dependence, 331
Deposition process, 135
Depression
child maltreatment and, 693–694
compulsive buying and, 482
elder abuse and, 757, 760
gambling problems and, 475
partner violence and, 720
DeRose v. Carswell (1987), 558, 559
Descartes, René, 897
Descriptive statements, 28, 29
Detailed Assessment of Post-traumatic Stress (DAPS), 282
Developmental disabilities (DD), 489–506
competence assessments and, 499–503
criminal justice system and, 496–498
diagnostic assessment of, 500–502
eyewitness testimony and, 539–541
federal laws related to, 491, 492
genetic factors and, 493
historical overview of, 490–492
nature of, 489–490
postnatal factors and, 494, 496
prenatal/perinatal factors and, 493–494

questions and answers about, 496–498
treatment assessment of, 504–505
See also Mental retardation
Developmental status issues, 875–877
Deviancy training, 375
Diagnostic Assessment for the Severely Handicapped (DASH), 503
Diagnostic interviews, 353–354
Diagnostic Interview Schedule (DIS), 330, 354, 814
Diagnostic profiling of jurors, 786–791, 795–797
asking diagnostic questions, 796
developing working hypotheses, 786–787
empirical development of profiles, 787–791
observing nonverbal responses, 796–797
Diagnostic and Statistical Manual of Mental Disorders (DSM-IV), 34
ADHD diagnosis, 380–382
conduct disorder diagnosis, 370, 371–372, 378
Glossary of Culture-Bound Syndromes, 816–817
impulse control disorders diagnosis, 471, 473
malingering description, 303, 408
mental disorders definition, 160, 964
Outline for Cultural Formulation, 813, 837
pedophilia diagnosis, 449
personality disorders descriptions, 671
psychopathy diagnosis, 396–397
PTSD diagnosis, 347, 348–349, 519
sexual deviance definition, 429, 430, 432
substance abuse diagnosis, 330, 331
Diagnostic and Treatment Guidelines on Elder Abuse and Neglect (AMA), 753, 755–756
Dialectical Behavior Therapy (DBT), 858
Dickerson v. United States (2000), 968
Digit Recognition Test (DRT), 309
Dillon v. Legg (1968), 270–271
Dimambro North End Association v. Williams (1983), 10
Diminished capacity, 18
Dimitrius, Jo-Ellan, 789
DIPP method for jury selection, 791–801
deflection process, 800–801
diagnosis in *voir dire*, 795–797
persuasion in *voir dire*, 797–799
pretrial diagnosis, 793–795
Direct confrontation, 906
Directed lie test (DLT), 614, 617
Direct examination of witnesses, 798
Direct experience, 940
Direct observation
of children's behavior, 376, 385
of parent-child interactions, 239

Discovery process, 134–136
Dispositional assessments, 890
Dissociative disorders, 161, 966
Distal risk factors, 723
Distortions, 636, 637
Diversionary tactics, 954
Diviero v. Uniroyal Tire Co. (1996), 14
Divorce
child custody evaluations and, 233–241
contemporary rate of, 233
Dix, Dorothea, 769
DNA evidence, 513–514, 522, 589, 898
Doe v. McKay (1988), 560
Domestic violence
child maltreatment and, 692
shelters for victims of, 732
See also Child abuse and neglect; Partner violence
Door-in-the-face technique, 924
Dorrance, Stanley, 1021
Double jeopardy, 777
Dream interpretation, 573
Driving under the influence (DUI), 323
Drope v. Missouri (1974), 17, 176, 177
Drug Abuse Screening Test (DAST), 720, 725
Drug diversion courts, 322, 334–335
Drug screens, 324–325
Drug use, 316–319
alcohol, 318
amphetamines, 317–318
cocaine, 317
heroin, 317
marijuana, 316–317
phencyclidine, 318
See also Substance abuse
Drunkenness. *See* Intoxication
DSM-IV. *See Diagnostic and Statistical Manual of Mental Disorders*
Due process, 787
DUI offenders, 323
Duping delight, 642
Durham standard, 18, 158
Durham v. United States (1954), 158
Dusky v. United States (1960), 17, 176, 177, 203, 214, 887
Duty of reasonable care, 8
Duty to protect, 774
Duty to warn, 7–9
Dynamic risk factors, 94–95, 114–116, 455

E
Early, Eleanor, 1004
Early Assessment Risk List (EARL), 879

Easterbrook hypothesis, 520
Eccleston, Lynne, 85
Ecological validity, 284–285
Edney v. Smith (1976), 274
Education for All Handicapped Children Act (1975), 491
Educational testing standards, 39, 40, 240, 627
Ego-depletion model, 961
Ekman, Paul, 635
Elaboration likelihood, 932
Elaborative processing, 921–932
   ability of, 946–947
   active, 944
   distraction and, 959
   motivation for, 945–946
   time constraints and, 959–960
Elder abuse, 743–762
   assessment of, 755–759
   barriers to identifying, 751
   caregivers and, 745, 748–749, 754–755, 760
   contextual risk factors for, 749–751
   definitions of, 743–744
   documentation of, 761–762
   family conflicts and, 750
   financial problems and, 749–750
   future directions in dealing with, 762
   interventions for, 759–761
   overcrowded living arrangements and, 750–751
   perpetrator risk factors for, 748–749
   prevalence of, 743
   screening process for, 752–755
   social support and, 750
   theoretical explanations for, 744–746
   treatment of, 751–752, 759–761
   victim risk factors for, 746–748
Elder Abuse Screening Test, 753
Elder Care: Family Training and Support (Barusch), 760
Elderly adults
   cognitive disorders associated with, 219–222
   intellectual functioning in, 218
   memory changes in, 218–219
   mental competency and, 213–228
   physiological changes in, 217–218
   See also Aging process
Ellis, Albert, 441
Embedded attitudes, 942–943
Emke-Francis, Paula, 175
Emotional abuse, 687
Emotional damages. *See* Psychological damages
Emotions
   cognitive processing and, 957–958
   facial expressions of, 639–640
   interrogator use of, 920, 926
   lying and, 638–642
   vocal reflection of, 640
Empathy training, 440, 444–445
Employee Polygraph Protection Act (EPPA), 602
Employees
   polygraph testing of, 602
   sexual harassment of, 655–679
   workers' compensation claims of, 834–835
Employment litigation, 834–835
Encoding of memories, 515–516
End-of-sentence assessment, 857
Episodic dyscontrol, 478
Epistemic errors, 30
Equal Employment Opportunity Commission (EEOC), 656, 665
Erickson, Milton, 954, 955
Erotic Preferences Examination Scheme (EPES), 436
Errors
   availability heuristic, 257
   base-rate, 256–257
   fundamental attribution, 797–798, 970, 974
   heuristic, 722
   investigative, 667–668, 670
   omission and commission, 137, 250
   polygraphy, 605–606, 608, 610
   recall, 591–592, 593–594
   scientific elimination of, 29–31
   Type I/Type II, 667–668, 670
Escala de Inteligenica Wechsler para Ninos (EIWN), 823
Escalating demands, 953
Estelle v. Smith (1981), 179
Ethical issues, 45–60
   APA Code of Ethics and, 45–46, 48, 51, 808, 820
   child custody evaluations and, 234–235
   confidentiality and, 227–228
   correctional settings and, 862–864
   decision-making process for, 49
   informed consent and, 225–227
   involuntary commitment and, 778–779
   mental competency and, 225–228
   moral philosophy and, 46–51
   polygraph tests and, 627–630
   psychological research and, 38
   risk management and, 144–148
   secure settings and, 862–864
   sex-offender treatment and, 51–60
   suicidal patients and, 147–148

Ethical Principles of Psychologists and Code of Conduct (APA), 808, 820
Ethics in Psychology (Koocher & Keith-Spiegel), 49
Ethnicity
    acculturation and, 814–816
    APA guidelines related to, 808–810
    competency issues and, 830–831
    criminal responsibility assessment and, 831
    culturally competent assessment and, 813–821
    employment litigation and, 834–835
    future research on, 838
    immigration cases and, 835–837
    intelligence tests and, 822–824
    language issues and, 819–821
    legal system bias and, 810–812
    mental retardation and, 833–834
    neuropsychological tests and, 824–825
    partner violence and, 724
    psychological tests and, 821–829
    psychopathy and, 399, 816–818
    risk assessment and, 831–833
Eugenics movement, 491
Evaluation
    child custody, 233–241
    juvenile, 875–890
    neuropsychological, 282–283
    parental fitness, 694–703
    psychological damages, 275–293
    retrospective, 157
    See also Assessment
Evaluation of Competency to Stand Trial (ECST), 196
Evasion strategies, 636
Evidence
    bias in gathering, 256–258
    decisions based on, 150–151
    exaggeration of, 950–952
    falsification of, 950–952
    probabilistic vs. particular, 943
    reliability of, 589
Excessive demands theory, 745
Exhausted caregiver theory, 745
Exhibitionism, 433, 435–440
    assessment of, 438–439
    course and epidemiology of, 438
    description of, 437–438
    etiology of, 438
    treatment of, 439–440
Expectancy-value approaches, 942
Expectations
    memory processes and, 516
    of social isolation, 958–959
Experiences
    attitudes based on, 940
    case-relevant, 788
Expert testimony, 9–14
    admissibility of, 10–13
    cultural issues and, 830–837
    false confessions and, 980–981
    recovered repressed memories and, 23
    rules for, 10, 11
    state courts and, 13–14
    suicide lawsuits and, 134–135
Explanatory statements, 29
External stress theory, 746
Eyewitness identification, 522–526
    lineup procedures and, 523–526
    other-race identifications and, 525–526
    relative judgments and, 524–525
Eyewitness testimony, 513–543
    child witnesses and, 533–539
    confidence/accuracy relation and, 526–531
    contemporary research on, 539–542
    developmental disabilities and, 539–541
    hypnotically refreshed, 531–532, 579–598
    identification procedures and, 522–526
    interviewing techniques for, 531–533, 535–538
    memory processes and, 514–519
    national guide on, 522–523
    secondhand witnesses and, 541–542
    stress and, 519–522

F
Fabrications, 636, 637
Face recognition, 527–529
Facial expressions, 639–640, 643
Factitious Disorder, 304
Fallibilism, 29
False allegations, 670–672
False confessions
    classification of, 900–901
    coercive tactics and, 629, 913, 970–976
    consequences of, 967–980
    expert witnesses and, 980–981
    interrogation process and, 189, 899–900, 902, 917–920, 967–980
    jury judgments of, 976–978
    mental disorders and, 963–967
    polygraph tests and, 629
    posttrial appeals and, 978–980
    prevalence of, 898
    stress as impetus of, 917–920
    See also Confessions
False evidence, 950–952
False interpretation, 670

False memories, 20–23
  emotional distress and, 21
  evidence on creation of, 566–567
  hypnosis and, 591–592
  malpractice actions and, 21–23
  sexual harassment and, 670
  See also Recovered memories
False negative/positive errors, 605–606, 608, 667
False statements, 29–30
Family counseling, 861–862
Family factors
  ADHD and, 386, 702
  child abuse risk and, 690–694
  conduct disorder and, 373, 379
  elder abuse and, 745, 750
  parental fitness and, 694–703
  partner violence and, 724
  special-needs children and, 701–703
Fanetti, Matthew, 245
Faretta v. California (1975), 186
Fare v. Michael C. (1976), 188, 885, 886
Fasulo v. Arafeh (1977), 772
Fear
  interrogation tactics and, 926–928
  lying and, 640–641
  scarcity effect and, 927–928
Federal Bureau of Prisons (FBP), 811
Federal Rules of Evidence, 5, 11, 13, 585
  Rule 104, 11
  Rule 702, 11, 12, 13, 585–586, 649
Feedback loops, 35
Feeling clues of lying, 638–642
Feminist theory, 446
Ferguson, Kyle E., 301
Field studies
  conducted in secure settings, 864–867
  of polygraph tests, 607–609
Financial abuse, 744
Fire setting, 477
Fisher, Jane E., 213
Fitness Interview Test (FIT), 195–196
Fit parenting, 695
Fitzgerald's Sexual Experiences Questionnaire, 659
Fixed markers, 115
Flashbulb memories, 519
Flattery, 962–963
Fledgling psychopathy, 881
Foa, Edna, 347
Follette, William C., 781
Foot-in-the-door technique, 953
Forced-choice tests, 309–310
Forensic psychology
  ethical issues in, 45–61
  juvenile evaluations in, 883–890
  report writing in, 63–81
  sexual deviance and, 434–435
  therapeutic relationship and, 863
Forensic reports, 63–80
  Basis of Assessment section, 69–70
  Behavioral Observations section, 72–73
  citing sources of information in, 78–79
  Clinical Findings section, 72
  Clinical Impressions section, 73–76
  collateral information in, 70, 79
  content and structure of, 66–76
  essential functions of, 63–64
  getting feedback about, 79–80
  guidelines for writing, 76–80
  Informed Consent section, 67–69
  Mental Status section, 72
  Psychological Testing section, 73
  Psychosocial History section, 70–72
  Recommendations section, 76
  referral questions and, 66–67
  risk assessment and, 75
  unique features of, 64–66
Forensic treatment
  institutional misbehavior and, 412–413
  partner violence and, 729–732
  risk management vs., 119–120
  sexual offenders and, 453–454, 456–458
  See also Treatments
Forgetting
  repression vs., 574
  See also Memory
Frank, Mark G., 635
Franklin v. Stevenson (1999), 559
Freud, Sigmund, 579
Frith's Case (1790), 176
Frotteurism, 431, 433, 441–442
  assessment of, 442
  course and epidemiology of, 442
  description of, 441
  etiology of, 441
  treatment of, 442
Fruzzetti, Alan E., 713
Frye test, 11, 13, 585, 586, 596, 649
Frye v. United States (1923), 11, 279, 581, 585
Functional abilities, 215–216
Functional family therapy (FFT), 377
Fundamental attribution error, 797–798, 970, 974

G

Galton, Sir Francis, 490
Galvanic skin response (GSR), 602
Gambling, pathological, 473–475

Gender differences
  elder abuse and, 746–747
  juvenile risk assessment and, 879
  partner violence and, 713–714
  psychopathy and, 398–399
  sexual harassment and, 655–679
  See also Men; Women
Gender politics, 670–671
General acceptance test, 11
General Electric Co. v. Joiner (1997), 12, 821
General intent, 998
Genetic factors
  ADHD and, 383
  developmental disabilities and, 493
  mental retardation and, 493, 494, 495–496
Gentry, Ruth A., 213
Gentry v. State (1994), 14
Georgia Court Competency Test (GCCT), 192
Georgia Supreme Court, 13–14
Geriatric Depression Scale, 757
Ghetti, Simona, 513
Ghezzi, Patrick M., 489
Gifford, Elizabeth V., 315
G.J.I. v. State of Oklahoma (1989), 888
Goals
  PTSD assessment, 350–351
  sex-offender treatment, 52
Godfrey v. State (1988), 14
Godinez v. Moran (1993), 178, 185, 187, 203
Golding, Stephen L., 175
Goode v. Florida (1978), 186
Goodman, Gail S., 513
Gordon, Nancy, 598
Grave disability, 775
Gross, Hans, 922
Group psychotherapy, 860–861
Guardianship, 216–217
Guided imagery, 573
Guided memory procedures, 519
Guidelines for Child Custody in Divorce Proceedings (APA), 808–809
Guidelines on Multicultural Education, Training, Research, Practice, and Organizational Change for Psychologists (APA), 809
Guidelines for Providers of Psychological Services to Ethnic, Linguistic, and Culturally Diverse Populations (APA), 809, 820
Guilt
  interrogation process and, 928–929
  polygraph tests and, 618–620
  reciprocity principle and, 929
Guilty But Mentally Ill (GBMI) verdict, 18–19, 159
Guilty knowledge test (GKT), 618–620
  description of, 618–619
  validity studies of, 619–620

H
Habeas corpus, 768
Hair plucking, 475–476
Hair tests, 326
Hallucinations, 966
Handbook of Cross-Cultural and Multicultural Personality Assessment (Dana), 813
Handbook of Jury Research (Abbott & Batt), 783
Handbook of Multicultural Assessment (Suzuki, Ponterotto, & Meller), 813
Handbook of Multicultural Mental Health (Cuellar & Paniagua), 813
Handbook of Psychophysiology (Greenfield & Sternbach), 628
Harassment, sexual. *See* Sexual harassment
Harding v. State of Maryland (1968), 532, 580–581
Hare, Robert, 400, 880
Harper standard, 13–14
Harper v. State (1982), 13–14
Harris, Dylan, 369, 388
Harris v. Forklift Systems, Inc. (1993), 657
Hawthorne, Nathaniel, 430
Health
  mental competency and, 217–222
  partner violence and, 720–721
Hearsay testimony, 541–542
Hecker, Jeffrey E., 63
Henderson, Deborah, 743
Hendricks, Leroy, 777
Hennis, Timothy, 902
Heroin, 317
Heuristic errors, 722
Heuristic processes, 932–939
High-end inducements, 914
Hindsight biases, 979
Hiscock Digit Memory Test, 287
Hispanics, 807–838
  acculturation of, 814–816
  APA guidelines related to, 808–810
  competency issues and, 830–831
  criminal responsibility assessment of, 831
  culturally competent assessment of, 813–821
  employment litigation and, 834–835
  future research related to, 838
  immigration cases and, 835–837
  intelligence testing of, 822–824
  language issues and, 819–821
  legal system bias and, 810–812

mentally retarded, 833–834
neuropsychological testing of, 824–825
population growth of, 807
psychological testing of, 821–829, 837–838
psychopathology and, 816–818
risk assessment of, 831–833
Histrionic personality disorder, 671, 967
Homosexuality
APA Code of Ethics and, 51
psychiatric categorization of, 430–431
Hostage negotiation, 860
Host Approach, 161
Hostile environment sexual harassment, 658, 665
Hostility Toward Women Scale (HTW), 448
Hot-cool systems hypothesis, 521
Hot spots, 648–649
How to Win Friends and Influence People (Carnegie), 933
Hucker, Stephen J., 471
Hui, Irene, 157
Hyles v. Cockrill (1983), 10
Hyperactivity, 381
Hypnosis
eyewitness testimony and, 531–532, 579–598
false memories and, 591–592
historical origins of, 579–580
repressed memories and, 572–573
television technique of, 595
Hypnotically refreshed testimony, 579–598
common-law approach to, 580–585
Daubert test and, 587–597
error rate of, 593–594
false memories and, 591–592
general guidelines for, 596
Hurd requirements for, 584
hypnotizability assessment and, 594–595
scientific reliability of, 585–587, 595–596
Hypomania (Ma) Scale, 403

I

Identification, eyewitness, 522–526
Identifying physical evidence, 247
Idiographic problem, 34
Idiosyncrasy error, 642
Illusory correlations, 570
Imagination
memory recovery and, 573–574
self-persuasion and, 931–932
Immigration cases, 835–837
Immigration and Nationality Act (1999), 836
Impact of Events Scale (IES), 282, 358–359, 719–720
Impact rule, 270

Impressionistic decision making, 110
Impression management
child custody evaluations and, 241
psychopathy and, 409–410
Impulse control disorders, 162, 370, 471–482
cerebral damage and, 472
childhood psychiatric disorders and, 472–473
classification of, 473, 480–481
compulsive shopping, 481–482
intermittent explosive disorder, 478–479
kleptomania, 479–480
major mental disorders and, 472
pathological gambling, 473–475
personality disorders and, 471–472
pyromania, 477
self-mutilation, 481
sexual behavior and, 480–481
substance abuse and, 472
trichotillomania, 475–476
Impulsivity
ADHD and, 381
definition of, 471
Inaccurate assessment, 138
Inattention, 380–381
Incapacitation, 121
Incarceration
of ethnic minorities, 811
of malingerers, 859–860
of mentally retarded individuals, 497
of partner batterers, 729
of sexual offenders, 456–457
See also Correctional facilities; Prisons
Incest. *See* Child sexual abuse
Incomplete assessment, 138
Index of Spouse Abuse Scale (ISAS), 724
Indicators of Abuse screen, 753
Individuals with Disabilities Education Act (IDEA), 491
Indoctrinating questions, 798–799
Inference in decision making, 256
Information control, 925
Informed consent
children and, 68
forensic reports and, 67–69
mental competency and, 225–227
polygraph tests and, 630
suicidal patients and, 149–150
Innocence Project, 189, 898, 972
In re Gault (1967), 773, 875
In re Winship (1970), 875
Insanity defense, 18
assessment scales for, 165–167
forensic reports and, 65

juvenile justice system and, 889–890
legal standards for, 157–159
mental disorders and, 88, 160–165, 167–168
risk assessment and, 86
substance abuse and, 320–321
See also Criminal responsibility
Insanity Defense Reform Act (IDRA), 158
Institute of Medicine (IOM), 337
Institutional misbehavior, 412–413
Instrumental activities of daily living (IADLs), 215
Insurance companies, 133–134
Intake assessment, 857–858
Intellectual functioning
age-associated changes in, 218
estimating premorbid level of, 283–284
tests for assessing, 822–824
See also Mental competency
Intelligence tests
child custody evaluations and, 238
ethnic issues and, 822–824
Intensity of attitudes, 941
Intentional infliction of emotional distress, 21
Intentionality
determination of, 88
psychological research on, 37
Interdisciplinary Fitness Interview (IFI), 194–195, 200
Intermittent explosive disorder, 478–479
International Classification of Diseases-10th edition (ICD-10), 328, 330, 370, 473
Internet addiction, 482
Internet psychotherapy, 23–24
Interrogation process, 897–981
accusatory phase of, 904–917
alpha strategies used in, 921–939
Borg maneuver in, 904, 913, 949–953
choosing suspects for, 901–902
communicator characteristics and, 932–935
confession as result of, 916, 917–920, 967–968
depersonalizing messages in, 955
disabling cognitive resources in, 955–960
disguising persuasive intent in, 948–949
diversionary tactics in, 954–955
elaborative processing and, 921–932, 944, 945–947
expert witnesses and, 980–981
false confessions and, 899–900, 902, 917–920, 967–980
false pretenses used in, 903–904
flattery used in, 962–963
gradual escalation of, 953
heuristic processes and, 932–939

judging coercion in, 970–976
mental disorders and, 963–967
omega strategies used in, 939–967
overcoming resistance in, 947–963
personality variables and, 963–967
persuasive influence and, 920–963
polygraph tests and, 629, 903–904
preinterrogation interview and, 905
recommended practices of, 905–912
Reid technique and, 904, 905–912
self-regulation and, 960–962
social proof and, 935–937
sources of resistance in, 939–947
stress and, 917–920
videotaping of, 972–976
Interrogatories, 134
Interrogators
authority of, 934–935
confidence of, 935
credibility of, 934–935
emotions used by, 920, 926
likability of, 932–934
Intertest inconsistency, 307
Interventions
ADHD, 385–386
conduct disorder, 376–378
elder abuse, 759–761
partner violence, 729–734
psychological, 41
substance abuse, 321–322, 334–335
See also Treatments
Interviews
adjudicative competency, 192–196
biases in conducting, 670
child sexual abuse, 248–249, 251–254, 260–262
child witness, 535–538
cognitive, 532–533
elder abuse, 754, 755, 756–759
eyewitness, 531–533, 535–538
hypnotic, 531–532
polygraph test, 603, 604
risk assessment, 95–96
scripted protocols for, 536–538
structured diagnostic, 353–354
Intoxication
diagnosis of, 331
involuntary, 321
laws related to, 1020–1021
rape by, 998–999, 1005–1006, 1010–1012, 1016–1017
responsibility issues and, 1016–1017
sexual arousal and, 1000–1008
victim credibility and, 1017–1018

voluntary sexual activity and, 1003–1009, 1014–1015
women's sexual intentions and, 1012–1015
See also Alcohol use
Intuition, 792
Investigations
  child maltreatment, 689–690
  errors in, 667–668, 670
  jury, 794–795
  psychologist assistance in, 856
  sexual harassment, 662–674
Involuntary civil commitment, 14–16, 767–779
  case law decisions on, 771–773
  criteria for, 773–776
  ethical issues and, 778–779
  history of, 768–770
  legal basis for, 770
  procedures for, 770–771
  rights of mental patients and, 15–16, 768
  sexual offenders and, 457–458, 776–778
  state's power of, 15, 767
Involuntary confessions, 901, 920
Involuntary intoxication, 321
Irresistible impulse test, 18
Isolation placement, 858–859

J

Jackson v. Indiana (1972), 180, 772
Jaffee v. Raymond (1996), 5–6, 7
James, William, 1008
Johnson, Bradley R., 767
Johnson v. Zerbst (1938), 185
Jones, Edward, 952
Jones v. State (1974), 10
Jordan v. Georgia Power Company (1995), 13
Judicial waiver, 884
Juries
  confession evidence and, 976–978, 979–980
  ethnic issues and, 812
  investigations of, 794–795
  lie detection by, 645
  mock, 568, 790–791, 975
Jury profiling questionnaire, 787–789
Jury selection, 781–801
  community surveys and, 789–790
  composition challenges and, 785–786
  deflection strategy in, 800–801
  diagnostic process in, 795–797
  DIPP method for, 791–801
  juror profiles for, 786–791
  overview of, 781–782
  persuasive questions in, 797–799
  pretrial diagnosis in, 793–795

pretrial publicity and, 783–785
scientific jury research and, 782–783
trial simulations and, 790–791
Juvenile delinquency
  ADHD and, 386–388
  antisocial behavior and, 880–883
  conduct disorder and, 378–380
  criminal intent and, 873–874
  statistics on, 369
  violent behavior and, 876
Juvenile justice system, 873–891
  clinical assessments and, 875–883
  competence evaluations and, 885–889
  developmental status and, 875–877
  dispositional evaluations and, 890
  history of, 873–875
  insanity defense and, 889–890
  mental state evaluations and, 889–890
  Miranda rights and, 885–886
  psychopathy evaluations and, 880–883
  transfer evaluations and, 883–885
  violence risk assessments and, 877–880
  See also Criminal justice system
Juveniles. *See* Children

K

Kansas v. Hendricks (1997), 458, 776–777
Karpman, Benjamin, 396
Kassin, Saul, 917, 936, 971, 972
Kaufman Brief Intelligence Test (K-BIT), 163
Keane PTSD (PK) scale, 361
Kennedy, John, 491
Kent v. United States (1966), 875, 876
Kevorkian, Jack, 144
Key Extended Entry Program (KEEP), 335
Kiechel, Katherine, 936
Klebold, Dylan, 369, 388
Kleptomania, 479–480
Knowledge claims, 30
Knowles, Eric, 920
Kohlenberg, Barbara S., 315
Kuhn, Thomas, 31
Kumho Tire Co., Ltd. v. Carmichael (1999), 12, 14, 580, 587, 597, 821

L

Laboratory assessments, 324–326
Laboratory studies
  of polygraph tests, 609–610, 612
  problems with, 612
Lake v. Cameron (1966), 771
Language issues, 819–821
  forensic evaluations and, 819

legal competency and, 830–831
    personality tests and, 820–821
    translator use and, 819–820
    See also Cultural factors
Lassiter, Daniel, 973, 975
Lavin, Michael, 45
Law enforcement personnel, 644–645
Leading questions, 572
Learning disabilities, 490
Legal authoritarianism, 787
Legal competency. *See* Adjudicative competency
Legal issues
    child custody statutes and, 234
    ethical issues and, 144–147
    ethnic bias and, 810–812
    psychology and, 3–24
    sexual deviance and, 433–434
    sexual harassment and, 657–658
    substance abuse and, 319–323, 334–335
Legislative exclusion, 884
Lego v. Twomy (1972), 969
LeRoux, Hillary, 213
Lessard v. Schmidt (1972), 771
Level of Service Inventory Revised, 95
Levensky, Eric R., 27, 713
Lewin, Kurt, 930
Lie detector tests. *See* Polygraph tests
Likability, 932–934
Likelihood to Sexually Harass (LSH) scale, 661, 662
Lilienfeld, Scott O., 395
Lindgren v. Moore (1995), 21
Lineup procedures, 523–526
Little, Steven G., 369
Loftus, Elizabeth F., 517, 555, 997
Loftus paradigm, 517
Longshore v. State (1978), 10
Lost enjoyment of life (LEL), 273
Low-end inducements, 914
Luck, 35–36
Lying, 635–650
    behavioral clues of, 637–644
    definition of, 636
    detection of, 601–631, 644–645, 648–649, 973–974
    emotional clues of, 638–642, 648–649
    facial expressions and, 639–640, 643
    feelings about, 640–642
    legal process and, 646–649
    methods of, 636–637
    polygraphy and, 601–631
    sexual harassment and, 670
    thinking clues of, 638

M
MacArthur Competence Assessment Tool for Treatment (MacCAT-T), 224
MacArthur Competency Assessment Tool-Criminal Adjudication (MacCAT-CA), 195–196, 197–199
Mahaffey, Martha B., 807
Male-to-female partner violence, 714–715
Malingering, 301–311
    clinical signs of, 859–860
    definition of, 303
    detection of, 286–289, 307–311
    differential diagnosis of, 304–305
    levels and patterns of, 305–307
    mental disorders assessment and, 164–165
    mild traumatic brain injury and, 302–303, 305–307
    psychological damages evaluation and, 285–286
    psychopathy and, 408–409
    secure settings and, 859–860
    tests of, 309–311
Malpractice, 137
Malpractice lawsuits
    false memories and, 21–23
    suicidal patients and, 132–144, 149–152
    See also Wrongful death lawsuits
Maltreatment of children. *See* Child abuse and neglect
Management
    impression, 241, 409–410
    risk, 119–123
Management consultant, 855
Mandated reporting
    child maltreatment and, 688–689
    sex-offender treatment and, 54–55
Manual of Diagnosis and Professional Practice in Mental Retardation (APA), 500
Marijuana, 316–317
Marital violence. *See* Partner violence
Marshall, Thurgood, 320
Martin, Earl F., 579
Mary D. v. John D. (1990), 558, 559
Maryland v. Craig (1990), 647
Mask of Sanity, The (Cleckley), 396
Mattox v. United States (1895), 647
Maturational status issues, 875–877
Maximization tactics, 924, 977
McCleskey v. Kemp (1987), 812
McCollum v. D'Arcey (1994), 559
McDonald, Wes, 997–998, 1022
McLearen, Alix M., 267
MCMI. *See* Millon Clinical Multiaxial Inventory
Measurement vs. prediction, 107–108

Medeiros, Jolene, 997–998, 1021
Medications
  ADHD and, 385–386
  adjudicative competency and, 181–184
  sexual deviance and, 440
  substance abuse treatment and, 334
Medina v. California (1992), 178
Meehl, Paul, 33
Megargee typology, 404
Meiers-Post v. Schafer (1988), 558
Memory
  age-associated changes in, 218–219
  alcohol intoxication and, 1019–1020
  children and, 249–256
  encoding process and, 515–516
  enhancement techniques, 20–23, 571–574
  eyewitness testimony and, 514, 515–519, 527–530
  false memory creation and, 20–23, 566–567, 591–592
  hypnosis research and, 591–592
  interrogation tactics and, 913, 958
  repressed/recovered memories and, 20–23, 555–574
  retention process and, 516–518
  retrieval process and, 518–519
  stress and, 519–522
  three stages of, 514, 515–519
Memory Distrust Syndrome, 913
Men
  intoxicated women and, 1006–1007
  psychopathy in, 398–399
  sexual harassment by, 655–679
  See also Gender differences
Mens rea determination, 87–88, 320, 998
Mental competency, 213–228
  age-associated changes and, 217–222
  assessment of, 222–225
  confidentiality and, 227–228
  decision-making ability and, 214–215
  definition of, 214, 501
  developmental disabilities and, 499–503
  disorders associated with, 219–222
  ethical issues related to, 225–228
  functional abilities and, 215–216
  guardianship and, 216–217
  informed consent and, 225–227
  physical health and, 217–222
  self-care and, 217
  See also Adjudicative competency
Mental disorders
  assessment of, 160–165, 281
  child maltreatment risk and, 693–694

  conduct disorders and, 379
  criminal responsibility and, 167–168
  culture-bound, 816–818
  dangerousness and, 90–91
  definition of, 964
  detecting malingering of, 164–165
  DSM-IV definition of, 432
  impulsivity and, 472
  interrogation process and, 963–967
  legal criteria for, 160–162
  link between crime and, 167–168
  partner violence and, 719–720
  sexual deviance and, 434
  See also Personality disorders
Mental health professionals, 3
Mental Health Systems Act (1980), 15
Mental Measurements Yearbook, The, 39, 279
Mental patients
  civil commitment of, 768–770
  rights of, 15–16, 768
Mental retardation (MR), 489–506
  child maltreatment risk and, 692–693
  competence assessments and, 499–503
  criminal justice system and, 496–498
  death penalty and, 833–834
  diagnostic assessment of, 500–502
  environmental causes of, 494
  eyewitness testimony and, 540–541
  false confessions and, 964
  federal laws related to, 491, 492
  genetic factors and, 493, 494, 495–496
  historical overview of, 490–492
  insanity defense and, 160
  levels of impairment in, 501–502
  nature of, 489–490
  postnatal factors and, 494, 496
  prenatal/perinatal factors and, 493–494
  psychopathology and, 502–503
  questions and answers about, 496–498
  treatment assessment of, 504–505
  See also Developmental disabilities
Mental State at the Time of the Offense Screening Evaluation (MSE), 89, 166–167
Mental state evaluations
  criminal responsibility and, 89, 166–167
  juvenile justice system and, 889–890
Mental Status section of forensic reports, 72
Mental suffering. *See* Psychological damages
Meritor Savings Bank v. Vinson (1986), 657, 658, 665
Mexican Americans, 815
  See also Hispanics
Michigan Alcoholism Screening Test (MAST), 328, 720, 725

Microexpressions, 640
Mild traumatic brain injury (MTBI)
    malingering and, 302–303, 305–311
    symptoms of, 301–302
    See also Traumatic brain injury
Miles v. Stainer (1997), 187
Miller Forensic Assessment of Symptoms Test, 289
Millon Clinical Multiaxial Inventory (MCMI/MCMI-II/MCMI-III), 163
    ethnic issues and, 827–828
    psychopathy measures, 404–405, 725
    Spanish translations of, 821
    substance use assessment and, 330
Mini-Mental Status Examination, 223, 758
Minimization tactics, 924, 977
Minnesota Multiphasic Personality Inventory (MMPI/MMPI-2), 162–163, 164, 165
    child custody evaluations and, 235, 236, 237–238
    child maltreatment risk predictions and, 692
    culturally competent assessment and, 818
    ethnic issues and, 825–827, 835
    malingering assessment and, 289
    psychopathy measures, 403–404
    PTSD scales, 361
    Spanish translations of, 821, 827
    substance use assessment and, 330
Minnesota Multiphasic Personality Inventory-A (MMPI-A), 163
Minnesota Sex Offender Screening Tool-Revised (MnSOST-R), 455
Miranda rights, 188, 189, 830–831, 885–886, 968–969
Miranda v. Arizona (1966), 188, 885, 968
Misinformation effect, 517–518, 566–567
Mississippi PTSD Scale (M-PTSD), 359–360
Mixed allegiance, 52, 54
MMPI. *See* Minnesota Multiphasic Personality Inventory
M'Naghten, Daniel, 88, 158
M'Naghten standard, 18, 88–89, 158, 165
Mobley v. State (1995), 14
Mock juries, 568, 790–791, 975
Mocniak, Uta H., 369
Model Penal Code test, 18
Moderator variables, 35
Molien v. Kaiser Foundation Hospitals (1980), 21, 271
Montoya v. Bebensee (1988), 21
Mood disorders, 966
Moral philosophy, 46–51
Moran v. Burbine (1986), 188

Morsbach, Sarah K., 555
Motivated denial, 947
Motivated social cognition, 926
Mrad, David, 293
Multidimensional Anger Inventory (MAI), 725
Multidimensional Assessment of Sex and Aggression (MASA), 444
Multidimensional Functional Assessment of Older Adults, 224
Multidisciplinary teams, 854–855
Multimethod forensic assessment, 69
Multiphasic Sex Inventory (MSI), 437, 438
Multiple Data Source Model (MDSM), 276–278
Multiple personality disorder, 161
Multisystemic therapy (MST), 377–378

N
Narcissistic personality disorder, 967
Narrative stories, 955
National Adult Reading Test (NART), 284
National Association for Court Management (NACM), 714
National Association for Retarded Citizens, 491
National Commission on Marijuana and Drug Abuse, 316
National Commission for the Protection of Human Participants (NCPHS), 225
National Criminal Justice Reference Service, 865
National Institute on Alcohol Abuse and Alcoholism (NIAAA), 318
National Institutes of Health (NIH), 334
National Institution of Justice, 729
National Jury Project, 793
National Victim Center, 451
National Weather Service (NWS), 117–118
Neglect
    elder abuse and, 744
    legal definition of, 687
    special-needs children and, 701
    See also Child abuse and neglect
Negligence lawsuits, 137
Negotiated consent, 227
Neil v. Biggers (1972), 527
Network analysis, 794–795
Neurological deficits, 441
Neuropsi test, 825
Neuropsychological evaluation, 282–283
    ecological validity of, 284–285
    ethnic issues and, 824–825
    malingering assessment and, 286–289, 302–303
    mild traumatic brain injury and, 302–303
    substance abuse and, 326

Neuropsychological Screening Battery for Hispanics (NeSBHIS), 824
Neuropsychology and the Hispanic Patient: A Clinical Handbook (Ponton & Leon-Carrion), 824
New York jogger case, 897–898
Nietzsche, Friedrich, 897
Nomothetic approach, 34
Nonconsequentialist theories, 47
Nondiagnostic criteria, 792
Nonverbal behavior, 796–797
Norfolk Southern Railway Company v. Baker (1999), 13
Norfolk and Western Railway Company v. Freeman Ayers et al. (2002), 271
Normative ethics, 227
Norms, 40
No self-harm contract, 774
Not guilty by reason of insanity (NGRI), 86, 161, 163, 164, 168
See also Insanity defense
Nuisance variables, 35
Numbing symptoms, 349
Nursing homes, 852

O

Oakes, Josiah, 768
OARS Multidimensional Functional Assessment Questionnaire (OMFAQ), 224
Objective Behavior Assessment (OBA), 504
Observer rating measures
  of parent-child interactions, 239
  of psychopathy, 406–407
Obsessive-compulsive disorder, 476
O'Connor v. Donaldson (1975), 16, 86, 772
Ocular analyses, 614
Odds ratios, 57
O'Donohue, William T., 27, 601, 655, 897
Office of Technology Assessment (OTA), 607
Oksol, Erin M., 601
Olsen, Nina, 685
Omega strategies of persuasion, 920, 939–963
Omission errors, 137, 250
Oniomania, 481–482
Ontic statements, 30
Open concepts, 37
Operant conditioning, 39
Oppositional Defiant Disorder (ODD), 372, 382, 965
Order of Railroad Telegraphers v. Railway Express Agency, Inc. (1944), 557
Oregon Social Learning Center (OSLC), 374
Oregon v. Miller (1985), 9

Orkin Exterminating Company, Inc. v. Carder et al. (1994), 13
Orne, Martin, 583
Orwell, George, 78
Othello error, 642
Otto, Randy, 873
Outline for Cultural Formulation (DSM-IV), 813, 837
Out-of-court settlements, 134
Outpatient commitment (OPC), 121–123
Overcrowded living arrangements, 750–751
Overwriting, 517
Owen v. Bair (1975), 10
Own-race bias, 525–526

P

Paced Auditory Serial Addition Test (PASAT), 307
Packard, E. P. W., 768
Page, Bradley, 975
Parameters, 53
Paraphilias, 435–453
  DSM-IV definitions of, 432–433
  exhibitionism, 433, 435–440
  forensic psychology and, 434–435
  frotteurism, 433, 441–442
  pedophilia, 433, 449–453
  rape, 445–449
  sexual sadism, 433, 442–445
  voyeurism, 433, 435–437
  See also Sexual deviance
Parens patriae, 15, 770, 776
Parent Attachment Structured Interview, 235
Parent-child observations, 239
Parent management training (PMT), 377, 386
Parents
  ADHD and, 386, 702
  conduct disorder and, 373, 377
  fitness evaluation of, 694–703
  mentally retarded, 692–693
  psychiatric disorders in, 693–694
  risk assessment of, 690–694
  skills required of, 698–699
  special-needs children and, 701–703
  terminating the rights of, 694–695, 701, 703
Parham, Robert W., 851
Parham v. J.R. (1979), 773
Parisi, Mark, 929
Parkinson's disease (PD), 221
Parole decisions, 857
Particular evidence, 943
Partner violence, 713–735
  arrests in cases of, 729
  assessment of, 715–721

INDEX

consequences of, 718–721
definition of, 714
legal goals for, 728
male-to-female, 714–715
nature, frequency, and severity of, 717–718
overview of, 713–714
perpetrator interventions and, 729–732
predicting future incidents of, 721–728
psychosocial treatments for, 729–732, 733
risk factors for, 722, 723–728
safety plans for, 733–734
shelters for victims of, 732
substance abuse and, 720, 725
victim interventions and, 732–734
Pate v. Robinson (1966), 178
Pathological gambling, 473–475
Pathological imprinting, 441
Peak-of-tension (POT) test, 622
Pedophilia, 433, 449–453
assessment of, 451–452
course and epidemiology of, 451
description of, 449–450
DSM-IV diagnosis of, 433, 449
etiology of, 450
theory of, 450–451
treatment of, 51–58, 452–453
See also Child sexual abuse
Peer relations
ADHD and, 382
conduct disorder and, 379
Peer review, 42, 150
Penile Plethysmography (PPG), 452
Penn Inventory for Post-traumatic Stress (Penn), 350–361
People v. Boykin (1999), 998
People v. Frazer (1999), 560
People v. Giardino (2000), 998, 1018, 1019
People v. Hughes (1983), 532
People v. Kelly, 321
People v. Lara (1967), 886
People v. Zayas (1989), 581, 589
Perceived Stress Scale, 758
Perceiver-induced constraint, 798
Peripheral details, 958
Perjury, 636
See also Lying
Perpetrator treatment
partner violence and, 729–732
sexual harassment and, 676–677
See also Treatments
Personality
conduct disorder and, 379
jury profiling and, 788–789

Personality Assessment Inventory (PAI), 163, 164, 404–405, 821, 828
Personality disorders
diagnosis of, 671, 882
DSM-IV descriptions of, 671
false allegations and, 671–672
false confessions and, 966–967
impulsivity and, 471–472
insanity defense and, 161
interrogation process and, 963–967
juveniles and, 882
See also Mental disorders
Perspective, 877
Persuasion, 920–963
alpha strategies of, 920, 921–939
Borg maneuver and, 949–953
central route to, 921–932
cognitive resources and, 955–960
disguising intent of, 948–949
diversionary tactics and, 954–955
flattery and, 962–963
gradual escalation and, 953
heuristic route to, 932–939
jury selection and, 797–799
lure strategy and, 797, 799
omega strategies of, 920, 939–963
overcoming resistance to, 947–963
self-persuasion and, 930–932
self-regulatory capacity and, 960–962
simple acknowledgment and, 962
sources of resistance to, 939–947
Pervasive developmental disorders, 965
Peterson v. Bruen (1990), 559
Phallometric testing, 439, 452
Phencyclidine (PCP), 318
Philosophy, moral, 46–51
Physical abuse, 687, 743
Physical exhaustion, 956–957
Piasecki, Melissa M., 315
Pietz, Christina A., 267
Pinel, Phillipe, 396
Pinocchio response, 642
Policy Guidance on Sexual Harassment (EEOC), 665
"Politics and the English Language" (Orwell), 78
Polk v. State (1981), 589
Polygenic heredity, 33–34
Polygraph tests, 601–631
accuracy of, 610–612
analogue studies of, 609–610, 612
choice points for, 625–627
clinical lie test, 614, 622–624

coercive tactics and, 629
control question test, 614–618
critics of, 606–607
errors on, 605–606, 608, 610
ethics of using, 627–630
false confessions and, 629
field studies of, 607–609
guilty knowledge test, 618–620
informed consent and, 630
interrogation process and, 629, 903–904
lack of standardization of, 624–625
lie detection and, 613–620
methodologies, 613–624
noise on, 626–627
overview of, 601–602
peak-of-tension test, 622
procedures, 602–604
psychological testing and, 627–629
psychopaths and, 410
relevant control test, 621–622
relevant/irrelevant test, 620–621
reliability of, 612–613
scoring of, 620, 625
sexual offenders and, 442, 601
therapeutic relationship and, 630
validity of, 604, 605–612, 626–627
voice stress analysis, 614, 624
Popper, Karl, 29
Portland Digit Recognition Test, 287
Positive coercion bias, 977
Positive control test (PCT), 614, 617–618
Positive impression management
child custody evaluations and, 241
psychopathy and, 409–410
Post-Concussion Syndrome, 292
Post-Traumatic Diagnostic Scale (PTDS), 357
Post-Traumatic Stress Disorder (PTSD), 347–362
acute vs. chronic, 348
assessment methods for, 351–361
clinical interviews about, 353
criminal responsibility and, 160–161
diagnosis of, 347–349
elder abuse and, 758
employment litigation and, 835
forensic evaluation of, 281–282
goals for assessing, 350–351
memories associated with, 519–520
partner violence and, 719–720
prevalence of, 349–350
self-monitoring of, 352
self-report instruments for, 356–361
sexual harassment and, 660–661, 675

standardized measures of, 353–361
symptoms of, 348–349
Posttrial appeals, 978–980
Powell v. Texas (1968), 320
Practical reasoning, 46
Predictions
actuarial, 108–109
clinical, 110–113
dangerousness, 9, 87, 90–95
false, 30
future behavior, 41
measurements vs., 107–108
risk assessment and, 106
suicide, 141–142
violence, 690
Predictive statements, 28–29
Preinterrogation interview, 905
Pressured-compliant confession, 901
Pressured-internalized confession, 901
Pretrial diagnosis, 793–795
Pretrial publicity, 783–785
Prevention
relapse, 334, 418, 452–453, 676–677, 861
suicide, 142–144, 151
Primacy effects, 257
Prima facie guilt, 88
Primary psychopaths, 396
Prisons
behavior of psychopaths in, 412–413
environment of, 852–853
ethical issues in, 862–864
ethnic minorities in, 811
forced treatment of inmates in, 776
malingerers in, 859–860
mentally retarded individuals in, 497
nursing homes compared to, 852
psychologist roles in, 854–862
research conducted in, 864–867
risk assessments in, 856–857
sexual offenders in, 456–457, 861
substance abuse treatment in, 335, 858
See also Correctional facilities
Pritchard, Shannon, 598
Probabilistic evidence, 943
Probabilistic laws, 29
Probably efficacious treatments, 41, 42, 43
Problem-focused coping, 703
Problem-solving skills training (PSST), 377
Proceeding *pro se*, 185–187
Products test, 18
Professional consultations, 150
Professional ethical claims, 30

Profiling selection, 787
Projective measures
    child custody evaluations and, 236, 238
    forensic evaluations and, 280–281
    psychopathy assessment and, 407–408
Project Match, 333–334
Prosecutorial election, 884
Prospective studies, 563
Protection Orders (POs), 728, 733
Protocol for Evaluating Forensic Interviews of Children (PEFIC), 261, 262
Proximal cause, 137
Proximal risk factors, 723
Proximate cause, 268
Proxy variables, 36
Psychiatric Research Interview for Substance and Mental Disorders (PRISM), 330
Psychoanalysis, 53, 54
Psychoanalytic theory
    exhibitionism and, 438
    frotteurism and, 441
    rape and, 446
    sexual sadism and, 443
    voyeurism and, 435–436
Psychogenic amnesia, 562
Psychological abuse, 744
Psychological assessment, 38–39, 40
    See also Assessment
Psychological damages, 267–293
    case law and, 269–271
    evaluation of, 275–293
    example of, 289–291
    future research on, 291–293
    injuries compensable as, 271–273
    intellectual functioning and, 283–284
    malingering and, 285–289
    MDSM model for evaluating, 276–278
    neuropsychological impairment and, 282–283
    professional issues related to, 273–275
    psychological testing for, 278–282
    sexual harassment and, 660–661
    tort law and, 267–269
Psychological disorders. *See* Mental disorders; Personality disorders
Psychological Inquiry (1999), 926
Psychological Maltreatment of Women Scale (PMWI), 724
Psychological problems
    elder abuse and, 747–748, 758
    partner violence and, 719–720
Psychological reactance, 927
Psychological reports. *See* Forensic reports
Psychological research
    conducted in secure settings, 864–867
    ethical constraints on, 38
    questions for evaluating, 42
    reasons for slow progress in, 31–38
    scientific method and, 29–31
Psychological Stress Evaluator (PSE), 624
Psychological testing
    APA standards for, 39, 40, 240, 627
    child custody evaluations and, 235–237
    ethnic issues and, 821–829, 837–838
    forensic reports and, 70, 73
    malingering and, 309–311
    polygraphy as type of, 627–629
    psychological injury evaluations and, 278–282
    translated tests and, 820–821
Psychological Testing of Hispanics (Geisinger), 813
Psychology
    assessment process in, 38–39, 40
    ethical issues in, 38, 45–61
    evaluation of research in, 42
    explanations for behavior in, 39
    legal issues and, 3–24
    predictions of future behavior in, 41
    reasons for slow progress in, 31–38
    scientific nature of, 28–31
    treatments and interventions in, 41, 42, 43
Psychology of inevitability, 949
Psychometric measures
    child sexual abuse and, 247–248, 260
    criminal responsibility and, 89
    parenting practices and, 697
    polygraph test and, 604–605
    PTSD assessment and, 353–361
    risk assessment and, 96
Psychopathic Deviate (Pd) Scale, 403
Psychopathic Personality Inventory (PPI), 405–406
Psychopathology Instrument for Mentally Retarded Adults (PIMRA), 503
Psychopathy, 395–420
    aging process and, 415–416
    Antisocial Personality Disorder and, 396, 397–398
    assessment of, 400–408, 880–883
    conceptualizations of, 396–397
    criminal behavior and, 410–415
    culture-bound, 816–818
    dangerousness and, 91–92
    elder abuse and, 748
    false allegations and, 671–672
    forensic populations and, 398–400

guidelines for working with, 418–420
institutional misbehavior and, 412–413
interrogation process and, 963–967
juveniles and, 399–400, 880–883
malingering and, 408–409
mental retardation and, 502–503
observer rating measures of, 406–407
partner violence and, 724–725
positive impression management and, 409–410
projective measures of, 407–408
recidivism and, 413–415
self-report measures of, 402–406
sexual crimes and, 411–412
treatment of, 416–418
violent crimes and, 410–411
Psychopathy Checklist (PCL), 400–402, 775, 880
Psychopathy Checklist-Revised (PCL-R), 95, 400–402, 448, 828–829, 831, 857
Psychopathy Checklist Screening Version (PCL:SV), 400, 829
Psychopathy Q-Sort (PQS), 406–407
Psychosocial History section of forensic reports, 70–72
Psychosocial maturity, 877
Psychotherapists
　dangerousness predictions by, 9
　duty of reasonable care for, 7–9
　legal liability of, 21–23
　psychotherapist-patient privilege and, 4–9
　recovered memories and, 21–23
　sex between clients and, 19–20
　therapeutic relationship and, 630, 863
　violence risk assessment and, 124
Psychotherapy
　Internet-based, 23–24
　secure settings and, 860–861
　substance abuse treatment and, 333–334
Psychotic disorders, 160, 966
Psychotropic medications, 181–184
PTSD. *See* Post-Traumatic Stress Disorder
PTSD-Interview (PTSD-I), 356
PTSD Symptom Scale–Interview (PSS-I), 355–356, 719
PTSD Symptom Scale–Self-Report (PSS-SR), 357–358, 719
Purdue PTSD Scale-Revised (PPTSD-R), 360
Pyromania, 477

Q
Qin, Jianjian, 513
Q-sort rating method, 406–407
Quantity/quality issues, 937–939

Questions
　alternative, 911, 915–916
　control, 603
　diagnostic, 796
　indoctrinating, 798–799
　leading, 572
　persuasive, 797–799
　referral, 66–67
　relevant, 603
Quid pro quo sexual harassment, 657, 665

R
Race
　legal system bias and, 810–812
　partner violence and, 724
　See also Ethnicity
Ramona, Holly, 560
Ramona v. Isabella (1995), 560
Rape, 445–449
　alcohol laws related to, 1021
　assessing perpetrators of, 447–448
　course and epidemiology of, 447
　description of, 445
　etiology of, 446–447
　eyewitness memories of, 521
　false claims of, 1019–1020
　intoxicated victims of, 998–1000, 1005–1006, 1010–1012, 1016–1020
　offender treatment for, 448–449
　psychopathy and, 411–412
　victim credibility and, 1017–1018
Rape Empathy Scale, 448
Rape Myth Acceptance Scale (RMAS), 448, 661
Rapid Risk Assessment for Sexual Offense Recidivism (RRASOR), 455
Reactance theory, 946
Readiness to change (RTC), 332
Reading skills, 819
Reasonable-person test, 268
Reasonable woman standard, 665–666
Reasoning ability, 223
Recall memory, 529–530
Recap bias, 972
Receiver Operator Characteristic (ROC) analyses, 112
Recidivism
　child maltreatment and, 689, 691
　domestic violence and, 692, 729
　predictors of, 90, 93, 120, 856–857
　psychopathy and, 413–415
　sexual crimes and, 414–415
Reciprocity principle, 929

Recognition memory, 527–529
Recovered memories, 20–23, 555–574
　admissibility of cases of, 557–561
　components of, 555
　decision-making biases and, 570–571
　delayed discovery doctrine and, 557
　expert testimony and, 23
　false memory creation and, 566–567
　future research on, 574
　juror attitudes toward, 568–569
　legal issues related to, 21–23, 556–561
　memory enhancement techniques and, 20–23, 571–574
　scientific studies of, 561–566
　sexual abuse indicators and, 569–570
　See also Repressed memories
Referral questions, 66–67
Regina v. M'Naghten (1843), 158
Regina v. Taylor (1992), 195
Reid technique, 904, 905–912
Reilly, Peter, 902, 951, 975
Reiss Screen for Maladaptive Behavior, 503
Relapse prevention
　psychopathy treatment and, 418
　sexual-offender treatment and, 452–453, 676–677, 861
　substance abuse treatment and, 334
Relational claims, 30
Relative judgments, 524–525
Relative risk, 117
Relative transparency, 52, 54–55
Relevant control test (RCT), 621–622
Relevant/irrelevant (R/I) test, 620–621
Relevant questions, 603
Reliability, 40, 247–248
　interview, 248
　polygraph, 612–613
Renfrow, Chris, 293
Rennie v. Klein (1981), 16
Reno, Janet, 245, 542
Repeated imagination paradigm, 566, 567
Repetitive self-mutilation, 481
Reporting requirements
　child maltreatment and, 688–689
　sex-offender treatment and, 54–55
Reports. *See* Forensic reports
Representativeness heuristic error, 722
Repressed memories, 20–23, 555–574
　admissibility of cases of, 557–561
　decision-making biases and, 570–571
　definition of, 555
　delayed discovery doctrine and, 557
　false memory creation and, 566–567

　future research on, 574
　juror attitudes toward, 568–569
　legal history of, 556–561
　memory enhancement techniques and, 20–23, 571–574
　normal forgetting vs., 574
　scientific studies of, 561–566
　sexual abuse indicators and, 569–570
　See also Recovered memories
Research coordinator, 862
Research in psychology. *See* Psychological research
Resistance to persuasion, 939–963
　attitudes/beliefs and, 939–943
　Borg maneuver and, 949–953
　diverting, 954–955
　minimizing, 953
　sources of, 939–947
　strategies for overcoming, 947–963
Response class problem, 33
Responsibility, 877
　See also Criminal responsibility
Retention of memories, 516–518
Retrieval of memories, 518–519
Retroactive interference, 516–517
Retrospective evaluation, 157
Retrospective studies, 562–563
Reverse diagnostic criteria, 792
Reverse psychology, 927
Rey 15-Item Visual Memory Test, 287, 310
Reyes, Matias, 898
Riggins v. Nevada (1992), 181–182, 183
Right to refuse treatment, 16
Right to treatment, 15–16
Right to waive counsel, 185–186
Right-wrong test, 18
Risk
　communication of, 116–119
　definitions of, 104–105
　management of, 119–123
Risk assessment
　child maltreatment, 690–694
　clinical vs. actuarial, 89–90
　communication of risk and, 116–119
　conduct disorder and, 379–380
　dangerousness and, 86–87, 90–92
　definitions of, 105–106
　ethnicity and, 831–833
　forensic reports and, 75
　future directions in, 97
　interview strategies for, 95–96
　juvenile offender, 877–880
　management of risk and, 119–123

methodological limitations of, 92–93
partner violence and, 723–728
secure settings and, 856–857
sex offenders and, 454–456
static vs. dynamic factors in, 94–95, 114–116
suicidal patients and, 141–142
tools used for, 95
violence, 103–127, 690, 877–880
Risk communication, 116–119
preliminary guidelines for, 119
requisite characteristics of, 116
Risk factors
ADHD, 383, 386–388
conduct disorder, 373, 379–380
elder abuse, 746–751
partner violence, 722, 723–728
sexual harassment, 678
Risk management, 119–123
ethics and, 144–148
forensic treatment vs., 119–120
overview of strategies for, 121–123
post-suicide, 152–154
Roark v. Commonwealth (2000), 581
Robinson v. California (1962), 320
Rock v. Arkansas (1987), 582
Roesch, Ronald, 157
Rogers Criminal Responsibility Assessment Scales (R-CRAS), 89, 165–166
Rolader v. State (1991), 14
Rorschach Inkblot Test, 236, 281, 407–408
Rouse v. Cameron (1967), 16
Royal Canadian Mounted Police (RCMP), 608
Ruth v. Dight (1969), 557

S

Safety plans, 733–734
Salience effect, 974
Saliva tests, 325
Sawyer, Thomas, 951
Sbraga, Tamara Penix, 429
Scalia, Antonin, 647
Scarcity effect, 927–928
Scarlet Letter, The (Hawthorne), 430
Schaaf, Jennifer M., 513
Scheck, Barry, 972
Schedule for Affective Disorders and Schizophrenia (SADS), 163, 164, 169
Schizophrenia, 160, 966
Schizoptypal personality disorder, 966–967
Schools
ADHD and, 382, 386
conduct disorder and, 373
shootings in, 369

Science
psychology as, 28–31
social vs. natural, 31
Scientific evidence, 10–13
Scientific jury research, 782–783
Scientific method, 29–31
Scoular, R. Jamie, 63
Screening tests
adjudicative competency, 191–192
elder abuse, 753
substance abuse, 327–330
Scripted interview protocols, 536–538
Secondary psychopaths, 396
Secondhand testimony, 541–542
Secure settings, 851–868
environmental aspects of, 852–853
ethical issues in, 862–864
malingerers in, 859–860
psychologist roles in, 854–862
research conducted in, 864–867
risk assessments in, 856–857
similarities between, 851–852
tasks of psychologists in, 852
See also Correctional facilities
Seduction, sexual, 1004, 1007
Selective attention, 943–944
Self-affirmation, 963
Self-care, 217, 775
Self-defeating behavior, 959
Self-esteem, 963
Self-Evaluation of Life Function Scale (SELF), 224
Self-monitoring, 352
Self-mutilation, 481
Self-persuasion, 930–932
Self-regulation, 960–962
Self-reports
of psychopathy, 402–406
of PTSD symptoms, 356–361
of substance abuse, 326–327
Sell v. United States (2002), 182–183
Sentences
ethnic disparity of, 811
substance abuse and, 322
Separation anxiety disorder, 965
Sequential lineup, 525
Settled insanity, 320
Sex differences. *See* Gender differences
Sex discrimination, 656, 657
Sex Offender Risk Assessment Guide (SORAG), 455, 831, 832, 856
Sex-offender treatment, 51–60, 453–454
assessment issues and, 453–454

civil commitment and, 457–458, 776–778
cognitive-behavioral therapy and, 53, 54, 55–57, 58
exhibitionism and, 439–440
frotteurism and, 442
moral issues related to, 58–60
pedophilia and, 51–58, 452–453
psychoanalysis and, 53, 54
rapists and, 448–449
relapse prevention and, 452–453, 861
reporting requirements and, 54–55
sexual harassment and, 676–677
sexual sadism and, 444–445
unique features of, 51–53
voyeurism and, 437
Sex Offender Treatment Evaluation Program (SOTEP), 56, 57, 58
Sexual abuse
 legal definitions of, 687
 recovered memories of, 555–574
 See also Child sexual abuse
Sexual Abuse (journal), 57
Sexual Abuse Structured Interview for Children (SASIC), 261–262
Sexual arousal
 alcohol use and, 1000–1008
 intoxicated rape victims and, 1005–1006
Sexual assault
 alcohol use and, 1009–1012, 1016–1020
 false claims of, 1019–1020
 prison assessment of, 859
 victim credibility and, 1017–1018
 See also Rape
Sexual behavior
 alcohol use and, 1007–1008
 consent issues and, 1015–1016, 1017, 1018–1019
 ethical issues and, 51–58
 impulse control disorders and, 480–481
 normative vs. deviant, 431
 therapeutic relationship and, 19–20
 voluntary vs. coercive, 1008–1009
Sexual crimes
 civil commitment and, 457–458
 ethnic issues and, 831–833
 incarceration and, 456–457
 legal categories of, 433–434
 psychopathy and, 411–412
 recidivism and, 414–415
 risk assessment for, 454–456, 831–833
Sexual deviance, 429–460
 assessment of, 453–456
 civil commitment and, 457–458
 DSM-IV definitions of, 429, 432–433

exhibitionism as, 437–440
forensic psychology and, 434–435
frotteurism as, 441–442
historical changes in defining, 430–431
incarceration and, 456–457
legal conceptualizations of, 433–434
mental illness and, 434
normative behavior and, 431
paraphilias and, 432–433, 435–456
pedophilia as, 449–453
psychological conceptualizations of, 432–433
rape as, 445–449
risk assessment of, 454–456
sexual sadism as, 442–445
treatment issues for, 453–454
trends in managing, 456–458
variability of, 431
voyeurism as, 435–437
Sexual Experiences Survey (SE), 448
Sexual Fantasy Questionnaire (SFQ), 437
Sexual harassment, 655–679
 burden of proof in, 668–672
 concept of, 664–665
 errors investigating, 667–668, 670
 false allegations of, 670–672
 four-factor model of, 660
 frequency of, 658–659
 future directions in managing, 677–679
 hostile environment, 658, 665
 investigation of, 662–674
 legal definition of, 656–657
 likelihood of, 661–662
 mediation and, 673, 674
 perpetrator treatment and, 676–677
 psychological effects of, 660–661
 quid pro quo, 657, 665
 reasonable woman standard and, 665–666
 retaliation in cases of, 674
 targets of, 659–660
 types of, 659, 666
 victim treatment and, 675–676
Sexual Harassment Investigation Protocol (SHIP), 664, 670
Sexual History Questionnaire (SHQ), 437, 438
Sexually anatomically detailed (SAD) dolls, 254–256
Sexually violent predator (SVP) statutes, 457–458, 776–777
Sexual orientation, 51
Sexual sadism, 433, 442–445
 assessment of, 444
 course and epidemiology of, 443–444
 description of, 442–443

etiology of, 443
treatment of, 444–445
Sexual Violence Risk-20 (SVR-20), 114, 116, 831–832
SF-36 Health Status Survey, 721
Shneckloth v. Bustamonte (1973), 968
Shoplifting, 479–480
Shopping, compulsive, 481–482
Short Acculturation Scale for Hispanics (SAS), 815
Shortcut evidence, 932
Short Portable Mental Status Questionnaire, 758
Sigall, Harold, 952
Simpatia, 818, 819
Single-culprit paradigm, 611–612
Situation-taxonomy problem, 33
Skeem, Jennifer, 175
Sleep deprivation, 956–957
Social-cognitive theory, 446
Social comparison, 935
Social consensus heuristic, 936
Social exchange theory, 745
Social impact, 937
Social isolation, 958–959
Socialization (So) Scale, 404
Social learning theory, 39, 436
Social proof, 935–937
Social skills deficits, 725
Social stressors, 379
Social support, 750
Social validation, 696
Sociobiological theory
  rape and, 446
  voyeurism and, 436
Socioeconomic status (SES)
  child maltreatment reports and, 689
  nuisance variables and, 35
  parenting practices and, 698, 702
  partner violence and, 723
Sociopathy, 396
Somatization, 304, 817–818, 835
Somatization Disorder, 304
Somatoform Disorders, 304
Source confusion, 932
Source monitoring, 518, 931–932
Special-needs children, 701–703
Specialty Guidelines for Forensic Psychologists, 273, 274, 808
Specific intent, 998
Spending, compulsive, 481–482
Spinoza, Benedict, 945
Spousal Assault Risk Assessment Guide (SARA), 113–114
Spousal privilege, 4

Stable risk factors, 115
Standard of care
  legal definition of, 140
  suicide lawsuits and, 135, 140–141
Standardized measures
  PTSD assessment and, 353–361
  See also Psychometric measures
Standard jury questionnaires, 793
Standard Progressive Matrices (SPM), 824
Stanford-Binet Intelligence Test, 491
Statements
  descriptive, 28
  explanatory, 29
  predictive, 28–29
Statement Validity Analysis (SVA), 258
State of New Jersey v. Michaels (1994), 539
State-Trait Anger Expression Inventory (STAXI), 448
State-Trait Anger Scale, 725
State-Trait Anxiety Scale, 757
State v. Brown (1983), 581
State v. Clemens (2001), 188
State v. Collins (1983), 588
State v. Hungerford (1997), 560
State v. Hurd (1981), 532, 582–584, 591, 594
State v. Tuttle (1989), 588, 589
State v. Weston (1984), 588
STATIC 99 scale, 455–456
Static risk factors, 94, 114–115, 455
Statistical Index of General Recidivism Scale (SIR), 414
Statistical Information on Recidivism (Cormier), 95
Statistics (Freedman, Pisani, & Purves), 57
Statute of limitations, 557
Stay'N Out program, 335
Stealing, compulsive, 479–480
Stepped-care treatment models, 336–337
Stereotypical expectations, 516
Stimulation tests, 603
Stogner v. California (2003), 560
Storytelling, 955
Strain Questionnaire, 757
Strategic misdirection, 792, 794, 797
Stress
  acculturation, 815–816
  cognitive processing and, 957–958
  confessions motivated by, 917–920
  elder abuse and, 746, 749, 757–758, 760
  eyewitness accuracy and, 519–522
  interrogation process and, 917–920
  partner violence and, 725
  special-needs children and, 702–703
  See also Post-Traumatic Stress Disorder

Strict psychological damages, 272
Strohmer-Prout Behavior Rating Scale (BRS), 503
Strosahl, Kirk, 129
Structured Anchored Clinical Judgment-Minimum (SACJ-Min), 455
Structured Assessment of Violence Risk in Youth (SAVRY), 879–880
Structured Clinical Interview for the DSM (SCID), 163, 330, 331, 354, 479
Structured clinical interviews
   child sexual abuse assessment and, 261–262
   elder abuse assessment and, 756–759
   PTSD assessment and, 354–356
   See also Clinical interviews
Structured clinical judgment, 113–114
Structured diagnostic interviews, 353–354
Structured Interview for PTSD (SI-PTSD), 356
Structured Interview of Reported Symptoms (SIRS), 164, 165, 289
Structured professional judgment (SPJ), 878–879
Subjective units of discomfort (SUDS) scale, 352
Substance abuse, 315–338
   assessment of, 323–332, 335–337, 858
   child maltreatment risk and, 693
   clinical interviews for, 330–332
   conduct disorder and, 379
   court interventions and, 321–322, 334–335
   criminal behavior and, 92, 316–319
   dangerousness and, 92
   elder abuse and, 747, 748
   false confessions and, 966
   impulsive behavior and, 472
   insanity defense and, 161
   laboratory tests for, 324–326
   legal issues and, 319–323
   neuropsychological testing for, 326
   partner violence and, 720, 725
   readiness to change and, 332
   screening instruments for, 327–330
   secure settings and, 858
   self-reports of, 326–327
   treatments for, 332–335, 336–337
   See also Alcohol use; Drug use
Substance Abuse Subtle Screening Inventory (SASSI), 328–329
Substance dependence, 331
Substance withdrawal symptoms, 331
Suggestibility of children, 534–535
Suicidal patients, 129–154
   agency policies and, 151–152
   assessment of, 138, 139–140, 858
   behavior of, 129–130, 150
   ethical issues in treating, 144–148
   hospitalization of, 138–139, 142–143
   involuntary commitment of, 773–774
   legal risks presented by, 130–131
   outpatient treatment of, 143–144
   post-suicide risk management guidelines, 152–154
   predicting suicide by, 141–142
   prevalence of, 129
   prevention strategies for, 142–144, 151
   protective measures for, 139–140
   reducing the legal risks of, 149–152
   secure settings and, 858
   standards of care for, 135, 140–141
   wrongful death lawsuits and, 132–141
Supplemental juror questionnaires, 793–794
Suspects, choice of, 901–902
Sutcliffe, Peter, 642
Sweat tests, 325–326
Symptom Checklist-90-Revised (SCL-90-R), 720
Systematic distortion hypothesis, 570
Systemic inducements, 914

T

Tarasoff v. Regents of the University of California (1976), 8, 86, 104, 560, 774
Television technique, 595
Telling the truth falsely, 636–637
Temperament, 373
Temperance, 877
Tender years, 685
Termination of parental rights (TPR), 694–695, 701, 703
Test of Memory Malingering (TOMM), 288, 309–310
Test of Nonverbal Intelligence, Third Edition (TONI-3), 824
Thematic Apperception Test (TAT), 236, 281, 408
Theme development, 903, 906–908, 914–915, 922, 955
Theoretical reasoning, 46
Therapeutic coercion, 52
Therapeutic Community (TC) treatment, 417
Therapeutic relationship
   forensic relationship vs., 863
   polygraph test and, 630
   sexual contact in, 19–20
Therapists. *See* Psychotherapists
Thinking clues of lying, 638
Thompson v. National Railroad Passenger Corp. (1980), 273
Thornton, David, 455
Thought reform, 956
Threat appraisal, 929

Threat assessment, 877–878
Three-strikes laws, 457
Tifton Brick and Block Co. v. Meadow (1955), 10
Time constraints, 959–960
Time-limited offer technique, 928
Time Line Follow Back (TLFB) procedure, 329–330
Title VII, Civil Rights Act (1964), 656, 657
Tort law, 267–269
"Totality-of-the-circumstances" test, 584, 594
Total percent agreement procedure, 613
Toxic psychosis, 317
Training assessments, 504
Trammel v. United States (1980), 4
Transfer evaluations, 883–885
Transgenerational violence, 745
Translators, 819–820
Trauma-relevant relapse prevention (TRRPT), 675
Trauma Screening Questionnaire (TSQ), 358
Trauma Symptom Checklist (TSC), 720
Trauma Symptom Inventory (TSI), 282
Traumatic brain injury (TBI)
  impulsive behavior and, 472
  mental competence and, 221–222
  prevalence of, 301
  See also Mild traumatic brain injury
Traumatic memories, 519–520
Treadwell, Kimberli, 347
Treating expert, 135
Treatments, 41
  competency restoration, 180–185
  conduct disorder, 376–378
  elder abuse, 751–762
  partner violence, 729–732
  probably efficacious, 41, 42, 43
  professional morality and, 58–60
  psychopathy, 416–418
  sex-offender, 51–58, 453–454
  sexual harassment, 675–677
  stepped-care models of, 336–337
  substance abuse, 332–335, 336–337
  well-established, 41, 42, 43
  See also Forensic treatment
Trial attorneys
  jury selection by, 781–782
  See also Attorneys
Trial simulations, 790–791
Trichotillomania, 475–476
Truth control test (TCT), 614, 618
Truth and Deception (Reid & Inbau), 629

Truth effect, 938
Truthfulness bias, 944–945
Truth-in-sentencing laws, 456
Tsai, Amy C., 555
Tuman v. Genesis (1997), 21
Tunnel memory, 958
Turing, Allen, 51
Twain, Mark, 154
Twelve-step programs, 333
Type I/Type II errors, 667–668, 670
Tyson, Nancy, 558
Tyson v. Tyson (1986), 556, 558

U
UCLA Loneliness Scale, 448
Undifferentiated Somatoform Disorder, 304–305
Uniform Crime Report (FBI), 369
Uniform Guardianship and Protective Proceeding Act (1997), 216
Uniform Health Care Decisions Act (1993), 217
Uniform Patient Placement Criteria (UPPC), 336
United States v. Alvarez (1975), 274
United States v. Bradshaw (1982), 178
United States v. Brawner (1972), 158
Universal laws, 28–29
Unstructured decision making, 110
Upjohn Co. v. United States (1981), 4
Urine tests, 326
U.S. Merit Systems Protection Board (USMSPB), 659

V
Validity, 40, 248
  ecological, 284–285
  polygraph, 604, 605–612
Validity Indicator Profile (VIP), 287
Varble, Duane, 743
Variable markers, 115
Variable risk factors, 115
Variables
  moderator, 35
  nuisance, 35
  number of, 36
  proxy, 36
Vascular dementia, 220–221
Vasomotor response (VMR), 602
Verbal abuse, 744
Victim empathy training, 440, 444–445
Victim treatment
  partner violence and, 733

sexual harassment and, 675–676
See also Treatments
Victoria Symptom Validity Test, 287
Videotaped interrogations, 972–976
Viljoen, Jodi L., 157
Vineland Adaptive Behavior Scales, 501
Violence
    eyewitness memories and, 520–521
    juvenile offenders and, 876, 877–880
    mental disorders and, 90–91
    partner, 713–735
    psychopathy and, 91–92, 410–411
    recidivism and, 414–415
    risk assessment for, 103–127, 690, 877–880
    substance abuse and, 92
    transgenerational, 745
    workplace, 855–856
    See also Aggressive behavior; Dangerousness
Violence Risk Appraisal Guide (VRAG), 95, 727–728, 775, 831, 832, 856
Violence risk assessment, 103–124
    accuracy of, 106–107
    actuarial prediction in, 108–109
    classification tree approach to, 109–110
    clinical prediction in, 110–113
    decision-making approaches and, 107–116
    definitions of, 104–106
    ethnicity and, 831–833
    multistage model of, 106
    overview of, 103–104
    prediction vs. measurement in, 107–108
    research on, 123–124
    risk communication and, 116–119
    risk management and, 119–123
    static vs. dynamic predictors in, 114–116
    structured clinical judgment in, 113–114
    See also Dangerousness assessment
Vocational Rehabilitation Act (1973), 491
Voice
    electronic analysis of, 614, 624
    emotions reflected in, 640
Voice stress analysis, 614, 624
Voir dire. *See* Jury selection
Voluntary confessions, 901, 920
Voyeurism, 433, 435–437
    assessment of, 436–437
    course and epidemiology of, 436
    description of, 435
    etiology of, 435–436
    treatment of, 437
Vygotskian theory, 697–698

W

Ward, Tony, 58, 85
Washington State Institute for Public Policy, 457
Washington v. Harper (1990), 181, 776
Ways of Coping Checklist, 758
Webber, Emily J., 315
Wechsler Adult Intelligence Scale–Third Edition (WAIS-III), 163, 164, 284, 305, 822
Wechsler Intelligence Scale for Children (WISC), 236, 822
Wechsler Memory Scale–Third Edition (WMS-III), 305
Wechsler Preschool and Primary School of Intelligence–Revised (WPPSI-R), 822
Wechsler Test of Adult Reading (WTAR), 284, 292
Welcomeness, legal concept of, 665
Well-established treatments, 41, 42, 43
White, Diarmuid, 918–919
Wide Range Achievement Test-Revised, 284
Wife battering. *See* Partner violence
Wiley, Diane, 793
Willful misconduct, 137
Williams, Diane, 656
Williams, W. Larry, 489
Williams v. Saxbe (1976), 656, 657
Wisconsin Card Sorting Test (WCST), 307
Withdrawal syndromes, 331
Women
    intoxication and sexual consent of, 1004–1006, 1012–1015, 1018–1019
    measuring attitudes toward, 448
    partner violence against, 714–715
    psychopathy in, 398–399
    sexual harassment of, 655–679
    See also Gender differences
Woodham, Luke, 369
Word Memory Test (WMT), 288, 310–311
Workability, 146
Workers' compensation, 834–835
Working hypotheses, 786–787
Workplace
    employment litigation and, 834–835
    polygraph testing in, 602
    sexual harassment in, 655–679
    violence in, 855–856
World Health Organization (WHO), 500, 824
Wrongful death lawsuits, 132–141
    characteristic claims in, 137–140

civil trial and, 136
discovery process and, 134–136
key tenets of, 136–137
malpractice claims and, 133–134
reducing the risk of, 149–152
standard of care and, 140–141
See also Malpractice lawsuits
Wyatt v. Stickney (1971), 16

Y
Yerkes-Dodson law, 520
Youtsey v. United States (1899), 176
Yury, Craig, 213

Z
Zone of danger, 270
Zone of proximal development, 697